CONTENTS

Eastern Europe

FINLAND ★Helsinki

Uppsala •

Stockholm ★

★Tallinn

ESTONIA

100 kilometers

100 miles

Moscow ★

SWEDEN

• Visby

LATVIA

★Riga

RUSSIA

Kalmar •
Växjö •   Öland •

LITHUANIA

Vilnius ★

Minsk •

• Malmö

RUSSIA

Gdańsk •   • Malbork

BELARUS

Kiev ★

Poznań •

• Toruń

Warsaw ★

G
E
R
M
A
N
Y

Berlin ★

POLAND

Oder River

UKRAINE

Elbe R.

• Dresden

Vistula R.

Auschwitz •   • Lviv

• Kraków

Danube R.

★Prague

CZECH REPUBLIC

Český
Krumlov   • Brno

TATRA MTNS.

Levoča •
SLOVAKIA

MOLDOVA

Chişinău •   Odessa •

• Melk   Bratislava ★   • Eger

Iaşi ★

BUCOVINA

• Salzburg

Vienna ★

MARAMUREŞ

• Cluj-Napoca

• Hallstatt

Győr •   ★Budapest

HUNGARY

Szeged •

• Sighişoara

AUSTRIA

Pécs •

ROMANIA

TRANSYLVANIA   • Braşov

Bled •   SLOVENIA

Ljubljana ★   ★Zagreb

CROATIA

Novi
Sad •   • Timişoara

Bucharest ★

• Venice

ISTRIA

Rovinj •   Plitvice
Lakes

BOS.-
HERZ.

Belgrade ★

Danube R.

Constanţa •

Pula •
Ravenna •   SAN
MARINO

SERBIA

Veliko
• Tarnovo

Varna •

Black
Sea

• Ancona

Split •   Sarajevo ★

BULGARIA

TUSCANY

DALMATIAN
COAST

Mostar •   Podgorica Priština

★   ★Sofia

Plovdiv •

• Assisi

UMBRIA

Dubrovnik •   • Kotor

MONT.   KOSOVO

★Skopje

• Rila

Istanbul •

Civita •

★Rome

Tiranë ★

MACEDONIA

• Thessaloniki

T
U
R
K
E
Y

VATICAN
CITY

ITALY   Naples •

Bari •

ALBANIA

• Pompeii

• Brindisi

Meteora •

Sorrento •

AMALFI
COAST

• Paestum

Corfu

GREECE

Aegean
Sea

Tyrrhenian
Sea

Ionian
Sea

Delphi •

Athens ★

Ephesus)

Sámos •

• Palermo

Cefalù •

Olympia •   • Nafplio

Bodrum •
Mykonos

• Sicily   • Taormina

PELOPONNESE

Paros   Naxos

Agrigento •

Kardamyli •

Santorini

MALTA

Gorge of
Samaria •

Crete

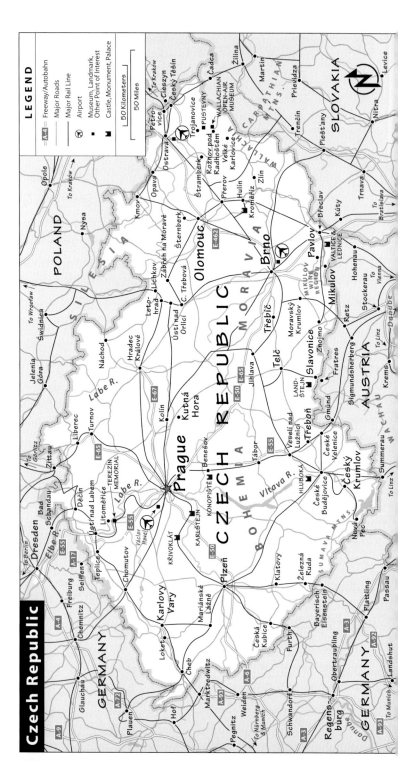

Czech Republic

LEGEND

- A-4 — Freeway/Autobahn
- Major Roads
- Major Rail Line
- ✈ Airport
- ■ Museum, Landmark, Other Point of Interest
- ▪ Castle, Monument, Palace

50 Kilometers
50 Miles

Hungary

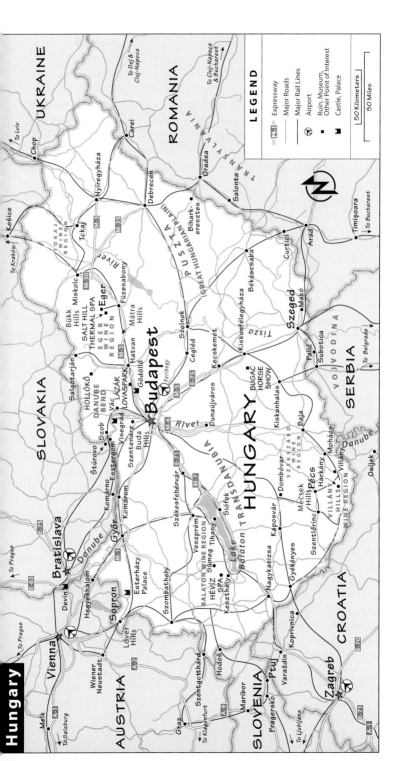

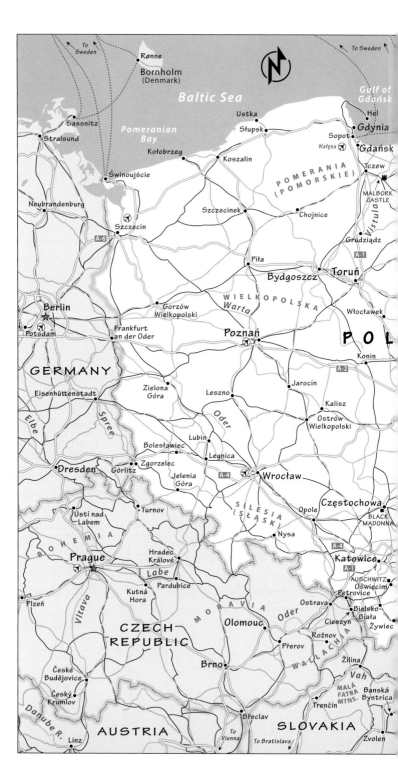

Prague

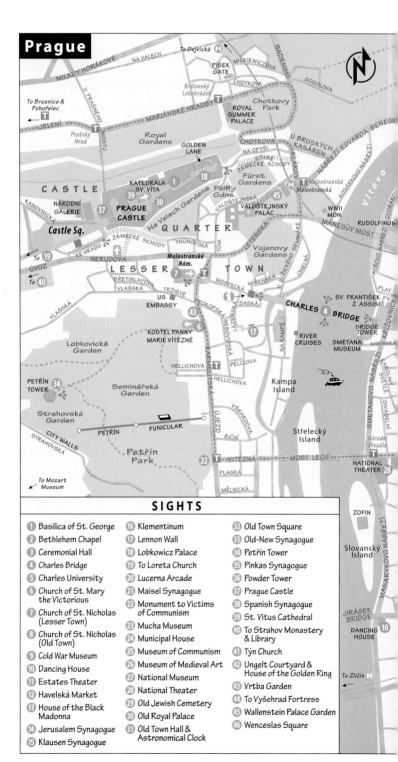

SIGHTS

1. Basilica of St. George
2. Bethlehem Chapel
3. Ceremonial Hall
4. Charles Bridge
5. Charles University
6. Church of St. Mary the Victorious
7. Church of St. Nicholas (Lesser Town)
8. Church of St. Nicholas (Old Town)
9. Cold War Museum
10. Dancing House
11. Estates Theater
12. Havelská Market
13. House of the Black Madonna
14. Jerusalem Synagogue
15. Klausen Synagogue
16. Klementinum
17. Lennon Wall
18. Lobkowicz Palace
19. To Loreta Church
20. Lucerna Arcade
21. Maisel Synagogue
22. Monument to Victims of Communism
23. Mucha Museum
24. Municipal House
25. Museum of Communism
26. Museum of Medieval Art
27. National Museum
28. National Theater
29. Old Jewish Cemetery
30. Old Royal Palace
31. Old Town Hall & Astronomical Clock
32. Old Town Square
33. Old-New Synagogue
34. Petřín Tower
35. Pinkas Synagogue
36. Powder Tower
37. Prague Castle
38. Spanish Synagogue
39. St. Vitus Cathedral
40. To Strahov Monastery & Library
41. Týn Church
42. Ungelt Courtyard & House of the Golden Ring
43. Vrtba Garden
44. To Vyšehrad Fortress
45. Wallenstein Palace Garden
46. Wenceslas Square

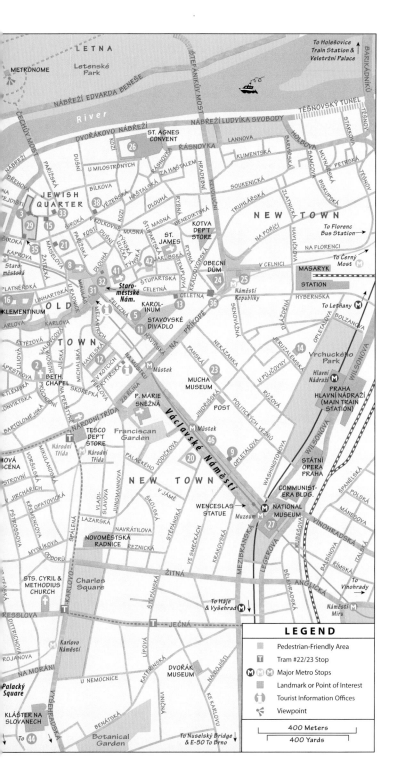

Budapest

LEGEND

- ■ Pedestrian-Friendly Area
- Ⓜ M1 Metró Stop
- Ⓜ M2 Metró Stop
- Ⓜ M3 Metró Stop
- Ⓜ M4 Metró Stop
- ■ Landmark or Point of Interest
- 🛈 Tourist Information Offices

BUDA SIGHTS

1. Budapest History Museum
2. Cave Church
3. Chain Bridge
4. Citadella Fortress & Liberation Monument
5. Fisherman's Bastion
6. Funicular to Castle Hill
7. Gellért Baths
8. Hospital in the Rock & Nuclear Bunker
9. Hungarian National Gallery
10. Labyrinth Entrance
11. Matthias Church
12. Museum of Military History
13. Royal Palace
14. Rudas Baths
15. St. Mary Magdalene Church Remains
16. Turul Bird Statue

200 Meters
200 Yards

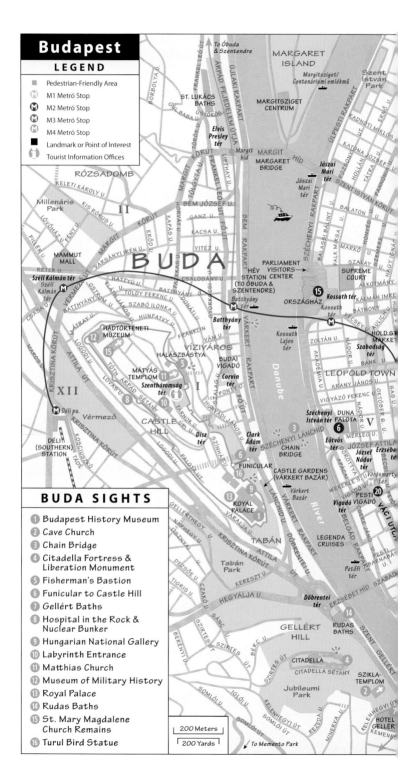

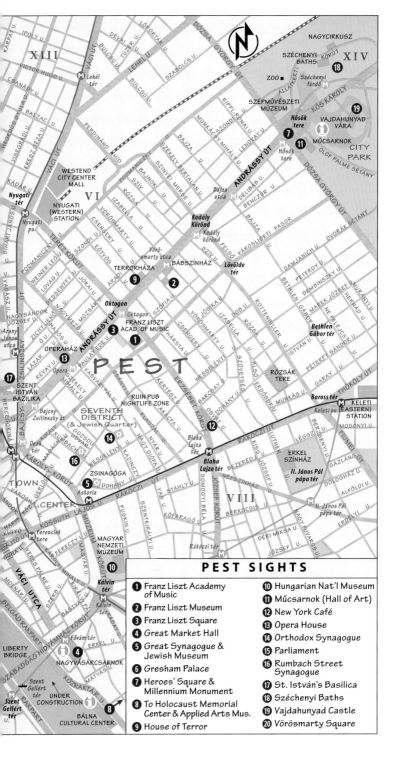

PEST SIGHTS

1 Franz Liszt Academy of Music
2 Franz Liszt Museum
3 Franz Liszt Square
4 Great Market Hall
5 Great Synagogue & Jewish Museum
6 Gresham Palace
7 Heroes' Square & Millennium Monument
8 To Holocaust Memorial Center & Applied Arts Mus.
9 House of Terror
10 Hungarian Nat'l Museum
11 Műcsarnok (Hall of Art)
12 New York Café
13 Opera House
14 Orthodox Synagogue
15 Parliament
16 Rumbach Street Synagogue
17 St. István's Basilica
18 Széchenyi Baths
19 Vajdahunyad Castle
20 Vörösmarty Square

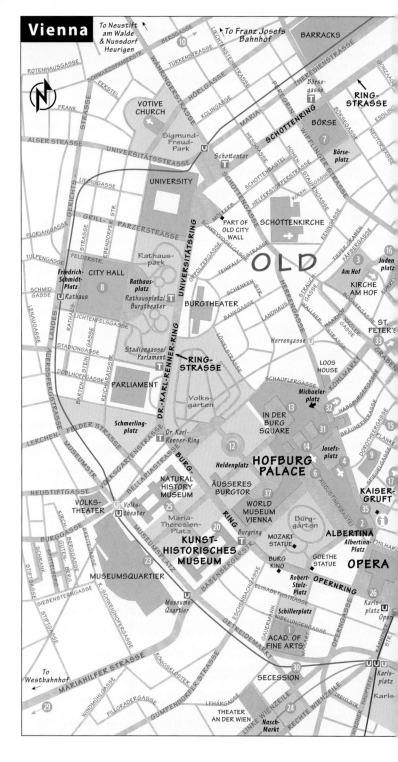

SIGHTS

1. Academy of Fine Arts (temp. closed)
2. Albertina Museum
3. Am Hof Square
4. Augustinian Church & State Hall
5. To Belvedere Palace & Mus. of Military History
6. Butterfly House
7. Börse (Stock Exchange)
8. City Hall
9. Dorotheum Auction House
10. To Freud Museum
11. Haus der Musik
12. Heldenplatz
13. Hofburg Imperial Apartments
14. Hofburg Treasury & Boys' Choir Chapel
15. Jewish Museum Dorotheergasse
16. Jewish Museum Judenplatz
17. Kaisergruft (Crypt)
18. To Karlskirche
19. To Kunst Haus Wien & Hundertwasserhaus
20. Kunsthistorisches Museum
21. Mozarthaus Vienna Museum
22. Museum of Applied Art (MAK)
23. MuseumsQuartier
24. Naschmarkt
25. Natural History Museum
26. Opera
27. Plague Column
28. To Prater Park
29. To Schönbrunn Palace & Imperial Furniture Collection
30. Secession Building
31. Spanish Riding School
32. St. Michael's Church Crypt
33. St. Peter's Church
34. St. Stephen's Cathedral
35. Theatermuseum (Acad. of Fine Arts)
36. Wien Ticket Pavilion
37. World Museum Vienna

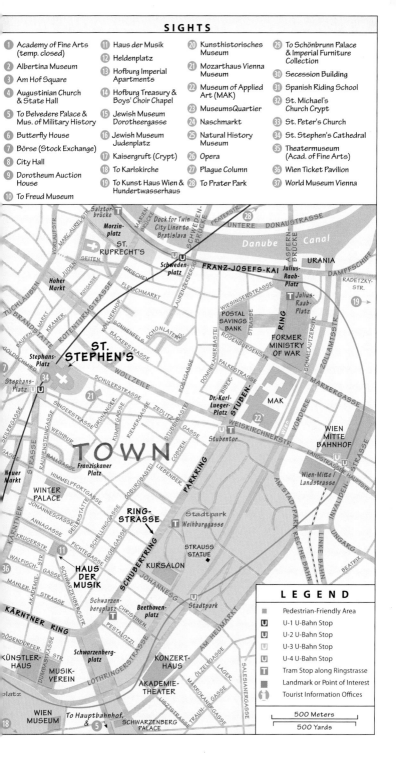

LEGEND

- Pedestrian-Friendly Area
- U U-1 U-Bahn Stop
- U U-2 U-Bahn Stop
- U U-3 U-Bahn Stop
- U U-4 U-Bahn Stop
- T Tram Stop along Ringstrasse
- Landmark or Point of Interest
- Tourist Information Offices

500 Meters
500 Yards

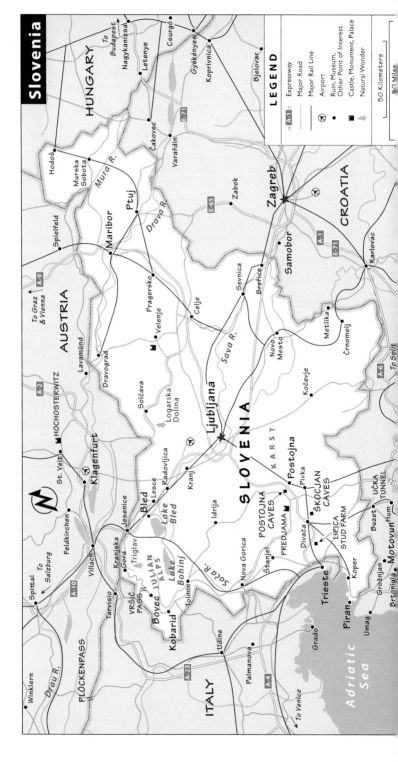

Rick Steves®

EASTERN
EUROPE

Welcome to Rick Steves' Europe

Travel is intensified living—maximum thrills per minute and one of the last great sources of legal adventure. Travel is freedom. It's recess, and we need it.

I discovered a passion for European travel as a teen and have been sharing it ever since—through my tours, public television and radio shows, and travel guidebooks. Over the years, I've taught thousands of travelers how to best enjoy Europe's blockbuster sights—and experience "Back Door" discoveries that most tourists miss.

Written with my talented co-author, Cameron Hewitt, this  book offers you a balanced mix of Eastern Europe's lively cities and cozy towns, from the Hungarian metropolis of Budapest to the quaint Czech village of Český Krumlov to the pristine Julian Alps of Slovenia. It's selective: Rather than listing dozens of Poland's medieval castles, we recommend only the best ones. And it's in-depth: Our self-guided museum tours and city walks provide insight into the region's vibrant history and today's living, breathing culture.

We advocate traveling simply and smartly. Take advantage of our money- and time-saving tips on sightseeing, transportation, and more. Try local, characteristic alternatives to expensive hotels and restaurants. In many ways, spending more money only builds a thicker wall between you and what you traveled so far to see.

We visit Eastern Europe to experience it—to become temporary locals. Thoughtful travel engages us with the world, as we learn to appreciate other cultures and new ways to measure quality of life.

Judging by the positive feedback we receive from our readers, this book will help you enjoy a fun, affordable, and rewarding vacation—whether it's your first trip or your tenth.

Thanks, and happy travels!

Rick Steves

INTRODUCTION

Until 1989, Eastern Europe was a foreboding place—a dark and gloomy corner of the "Evil Empire." But the dismal grays and preachy reds of communism live on only in history books, museums, and kitschy theme restaurants. Today's Eastern Europe is a traveler's delight, with friendly locals, lively squares, breathtaking sights, fascinating history, reasonable prices, and a sense of pioneer excitement.

Wander among Prague's dreamy, fairy-tale spires, bask in the energy of Kraków's Main Market Square, and soak with chess players in a Budapest bath. Ponder Europe's most moving Holocaust memorial at Auschwitz. Enjoy nature as you glide across Lake Bled to a church-topped island in the shadow of the Julian Alps. Taste a proud Hungarian vintner's wine and say, *"Egészségedre!"* (or stick with "Cheers!").

This book covers Eastern Europe's top big-city, small-town, and back-to-nature destinations—from the Hungarian metropolis of Budapest to the quaint Czech village of Český Krumlov to the pristine Julian Alps of Slovenia. It then gives you all the specifics and opinions necessary to wring the maximum value out of your limited time and money. If you're planning for a month or less in this region, this book is all you need.

Experiencing Europe's culture, people, and natural wonders economically and hassle-free has been my goal for several decades of traveling, tour guiding, and writing. With this book, I pass on to you all of the lessons I've learned.

Eastern Europe is a sprawling region; a comprehensive guidebook would span many volumes. To keep things simple and focused, this book covers the best of Eastern Europe in three sections. The **core countries** of the Czech Republic, Poland, Hungary,

Top Destinations of Eastern Europe

GDAŃSK AND THE TRI-CITY

POMERANIA

WARSAW

POLAND

AUSCHWITZ-BIRKENAU

KRAKÓW

PRAGUE

NEAR PRAGUE

ČESKÝ KRUMLOV

CZECH REPUBLIC

SLOVAKIA

VIENNA

BRATISLAVA

EGER

AUSTRIA

BUDAPEST

HUNGARY

ROMANIA

JULIAN ALPS

SLO-VENIA

LAKE BLED

LJUBLJANA

CROATIA

BOSNIA-HERZEGOVINA

TO BULGARIA

MONTE-NEGRO

200 Kilometers

200 Miles

"Eastern Europe" vs. "Central Europe"

"Eastern Europe" means different things to different people. To most Americans, it includes any place that was once behind the Iron Curtain—from Berlin to Moscow. But people who actually live in many of these countries proudly consider themselves "*Central* Europeans." In fact, some even get a bit offended by the "Eastern" label. (To them, "Eastern Europe" means Russia and its immediate satellites.) While I'm careful to describe this area as "Central Europe" when I'm actually traveling there, if I used that term back home, many Americans might wonder if I meant Switzerland or Italy.

And so, while I have deep respect for the people of this region, I'm calling this book "Eastern Europe" so as to best serve its target audience—North Americans. These travelers readily identify the countries I cover here—**Czech Republic, Poland, Hungary, Slovenia,** and highlights of **Austria** and **Slovakia**—as "Eastern Europe." For those venturing beyond that core zone, this book also includes tips to help you get started in a few additional countries that Americans also tend to label this way: **Croatia, Bosnia-Herzegovina, Montenegro, Bulgaria,** and **Romania.**

Taken together, this list represents a striking cultural diversity that scatters across a huge swath of Europe. But, while each country certainly has its own strong identity, they share a common legacy. All of them (except Austria) fell under communist control during the last half of the 20th century. And perhaps even more importantly, for centuries leading up to World War I, they were all part of the Austrian Habsburg Empire. Before the Habsburgs, the kings and emperors of these countries also frequently governed their neighbors. And all of these countries (except Hungary and Romania) are populated predominantly by people of Slavic heritage, who share common ancestors and speak closely related Slavic languages.

I hope that natives, sticklers, and historians will understand the liberties I've taken with the title of this book. After all, would you buy a book called *Rick Steves Former Habsburg Empire*?

and Slovenia—where most travelers focus their time—receive full coverage.

I've also included full coverage for two important **gateway cities:** Vienna, Austria, and Bratislava, Slovakia. While there's not room in this book to cover other destinations in Austria and Slovakia, you're likely to pass through these capital cities on your way between the major core destinations.

The **"More Eastern Europe"** section, near the back of this book, is a roundup of other countries in this area that may serve as logical add-ons. These include Croatia, Bosnia-Herzegovina, Montenegro, Bulgaria, and Romania.

Just thinking about the places featured in this book makes me want to polka.

Planning Your Trip

This section will help you get started on planning your trip—with advice on trip costs, when to go, and what you should know before you take off.

TRIP COSTS

The countries in this book are a relatively good value for travelers. Food and transportation are quite affordable, and accommodations are generally cheaper than in places like France or Germany.

Five components make up your trip costs: airfare to Europe, transportation in Europe, room and board, sightseeing and entertainment, and shopping and miscellany. The prices I've listed below are more or less average for all of the destinations in this book. Prices are generally lower in Poland and higher in Slovenia and Vienna; the Czech Republic and Hungary are in between. Of course, big cities (such as Prague and Budapest) are much more expensive than smaller towns (like Český Krumlov and Eger).

Airfare to Europe: A basic round-trip flight from the US to Prague can cost, on average, about $1,000-2,000 total, depending on where you fly from and when (cheaper in winter). Consider saving time and money in Europe by flying into one city and out of another; for instance, flying into Prague and out of Vienna. Overall, Kayak.com is the best place to start searching for flights on a combination of mainstream and budget carriers.

Transportation in Europe: For a three-week whirlwind trip of my recommended destinations by public transportation, allow $300 per person. If you plan to rent a car, allow $250 per week, not including tolls, gas, and supplemental insurance. A short flight can be cheaper than the train (check www.skyscanner.com for intra-European flights).

Room and Board: You can thrive in Eastern Europe on $100 a day per person for room and board (more in big cities). This allows $15 for lunch, $25 for dinner, and $60 for lodging (based on two people splitting the cost of a comfortable $120 double room that includes breakfast). Students and tightwads can enjoy Eastern Europe for as little as $60 a day ($30 per hostel bed, $30 for groceries and snacks).

Sightseeing and Entertainment: Figure $4-8 per major sight (with some more expensive sights, such as the Hungarian Parliament or Opera House in Budapest, at around $10-20), and $20-30 for

Not Your Father's Eastern Europe

Americans sometimes approach Eastern Europe expecting grouchy service, crumbling communist infrastructure, and grimy, depressing landscapes. But those who visit are pleasantly surprised at the area's beauty and diversity, as well as how safe and easy it is to travel here. Most natives speak excellent English, and many pride themselves on impressing their guests.

Service standards are occasionally a bit lower than in other parts of Europe. Museum ticket-takers and train conductors may be a bit grouchier and more monolingual than the norm. On the other hand, locals are generally less jaded and more excited to meet you than their counterparts in many big-name Western European destinations. For me, any rough edges add to the charm and carbonate the experience.

The East-West stuff still fascinates us, but to people here, the Soviet regime is old news, Cold War espionage is the stuff of movies, and oppressive monuments to Stalin and Lenin are a distant memory. Twentysomethings have no firsthand memories of communism at all. Nearly 30 years after the fall of the Iron Curtain, Eastern Europeans (or, as they prefer to be called, *Central* Europeans) think about communism only when tourists bring it up. Freedom is a more than a generation old, and—for better or for worse—McDonald's and mobile phones are every bit as entrenched here as anywhere else in Europe. All of the countries in this book (except Bosnia and Montenegro) belong to the European Union, and everyone seems to be looking forward to more progress in the future.

splurge experiences (e.g., going to concerts, taking a lake cruise, or soaking in a Budapest bath). You can hire your own private guide for four hours for about $100-150—a great value when divided among two or more people. An overall average of $30 a day works for most people. Don't skimp here. After all, this category is the driving force behind your trip—you came to sightsee, enjoy, and experience Eastern Europe.

Shopping and Miscellany: Figure $2 per postcard, coffee, beer, or ice-cream cone. Shopping can vary in cost from nearly nothing to a small fortune. Good budget travelers find that this category has little to do with assembling a trip full of lifelong memories.

SIGHTSEEING PRIORITIES

So much to see, so little time. How to choose? Depending on the length of your trip, assuming you are focusing on the core countries, and taking geographic proximity into account, here are my recommended priorities.

Eastern Europe at a Glance

This covers only the core destinations of Eastern Europe. For some add-on options, see page 987.

Czech Republic

▲▲▲**Prague** Romantic Czech capital with a remarkably well-preserved Old Town, sprawling hilltop castle, informative Jewish Quarter, and rollicking pubs.

▲**Near Prague** Kutná Hora's offbeat bone church and grand cathedral, Terezín's Nazi concentration camp memorial, and Franz Ferdinand's residence at Konopiště Castle.

▲▲**Český Krumlov** Picturesque town hugging a river bend under a castle.

Poland

▲▲▲**Kraków** Poland's cultural, intellectual, and historical capital, with a huge but cozy main square, easy-to-enjoy Old Town, thought-provoking Jewish quarter, and important castle.

▲▲▲**Auschwitz-Birkenau** The largest and most notorious Nazi concentration camp, now a compelling museum and memorial.

▲▲**Warsaw** Poland's modern capital, with an appealing urban tempo, a reconstructed Old Town, and good museums.

▲▲**Gdańsk and the Tri-City** Historic Hanseatic trading city, with a cancan of marvelous facades and the shipyard where the Solidarity trade union challenged the communists in 1980.

▲**Pomerania** The Teutonic Knights' gigantic, Gothic Malbork Castle and the red-brick, gingerbread-scented city of Toruń.

Hungary

▲▲▲**Budapest** Grand Danube-spanning cityscape peppered with opulent late-19th-century buildings, excellent restaurants, layers of epic history, and uniquely exhilarating thermal baths.

▲▲**Eger** Strollable town with a gaggle of gorgeous Baroque buildings and locally produced wines.

Slovenia

▲▲**Ljubljana** Slovenia's vibrant, relaxing capital, with fine architecture and an inviting riverside promenade and market.

▲▲▲**Lake Bled** Photogenic lake resort huddled in mountain foothills, with a church-topped island and cliff-hanging castle.

▲▲Julian Alps Cut-glass peaks easily conquered by a twisty mountain road over the Vršič Pass, ending in the tranquil Soča River Valley, with the fine WWI museum in Kobarid.

Gateway Cities

▲▲▲Vienna, Austria Glorious onetime Habsburg capital boasting stately palaces and world-class museums, convivial wine gardens, a rich musical heritage, and a genteel elegance that has long outlived the emperor's reign.

▲▲Bratislava, Slovakia The Slovak capital, with a rejuvenated Old Town and lots of new construction.

3 days:	Prague
5 days, add:	Budapest
7 days, add:	Český Krumlov, slow down
10 days, add:	Kraków, Auschwitz
14 days, add:	Ljubljana, Lake Bled
16 days, add:	Vienna
18 days, add:	Julian Alps, Bratislava
20 days, add:	Eger, slow down
25 days, add:	Gdańsk, Warsaw, Toruń (or save these for a Poland-focused trip)

This includes nearly everything on the map on page 11. If you don't have time to see it all, prioritize according to your interests. The "Eastern Europe a Glance" sidebar earlier in this chapter can help you decide where to go. The three-week itinerary (see sidebar) includes all of the stops in the first 20 days.

With more time—or for a different focus to your trip—consider some of the neighboring countries. See the "More Eastern Europe" section near the end of this book for ideas on how to splice in Croatia, Bosnia-Herzegovina, Montenegro, Bulgaria, and Romania.

WHEN TO GO

The "tourist season" runs roughly from May through September. Summer has its advantages: the best weather, very long days (light until after 21:00), and the busiest schedule of tourist fun.

In spring and fall—May, June, September, and early October—travelers enjoy fewer crowds and milder weather. This is my favorite time to travel here. Cities are great at this time of year, but some small towns get quieter and quieter the further off-season you get, and are downright deserted and disappointing in early May and late October.

Winter travelers find concert season in full swing, with absolutely no tourist crowds (except in always-packed Prague, or during Christmas markets in Kraków, Budapest, and other cities), but some accommodations and sights are either closed or run on a limited schedule. Confirm your sightseeing plans locally, especially when traveling off-season. The weather can be cold and dreary, and night will draw the shades on your sightseeing before dinnertime. (For more information, see the climate chart in the appendix.)

BEFORE YOU GO

You'll have a smoother trip if you tackle a few things ahead of time. For more information on these topics, see the Practicalities chapter (and www.ricksteves.com, which has helpful travel tips and talks).

Make sure your passport is valid. If it's due to expire within six months of your ticketed date of return, you need to renew it.

Allow up to six weeks to renew or get a passport (www.travel.state.gov).

Arrange your transportation. Book your international flights, and decide how you'll connect the dots in Europe. It's worth thinking about buying train tickets online in advance, getting a rail pass, renting a car, or booking cheap European flights. (You can wing it once you're there, but it may cost more.) Drivers: Consider bringing an International Driving Permit (sold at AAA offices in the US, www.aaa.com) along with your license.

Book rooms well in advance, especially if your trip falls during peak season or any major holidays or festivals.

Make reservations or buy tickets ahead for major sights. If you plan to visit the Auschwitz-Birkenau Concentration Camp Memorial, you're required to reserve ahead on their website (you'll want to do this as far ahead as you can set a date—ideally three months in advance). To visit the Schindler's Factory Museum in Kraków, it's smart to reserve ahead during busy times. To tour the Hungarian Parliament in Budapest, consider reserving online a few days ahead to ensure your choice of entrance time. Reservations are also recommended if you plan on visiting Vienna's Schönbrunn Palace in summer or on a weekend.

Hire local guides in advance. Popular guides can get booked up. If you want a specific guide, reserve ahead by email.

Consider travel insurance. Compare the cost of the insurance to the cost of your potential loss. Check whether your existing insurance (health, homeowners, or renters) covers you and your possessions overseas.

Call your bank. Alert your bank that you'll be using your debit and credit cards in Europe. Ask about transaction fees, and get the PIN number for your credit card. You don't need to bring the local currency for your trip; you can withdraw local currency from cash machines in Europe.

Use your smartphone smartly. Sign up for an international service plan to reduce your costs, or rely on Wi-Fi in Europe instead. Download any apps you'll want on the road, such as maps, translation, transit schedules, and Rick Steves Audio Europe (see sidebar).

Rip up this book! Turn chapters into mini guidebooks: Break the book's spine and use a utility knife to slice apart chapters, keeping gummy edges intact. Reinforce the chapter spines with clear wide tape; use a heavy-duty stapler; or make or buy a cheap cover (see the Travel Store at www.ricksteves.com), swapping out chapters as you travel.

Pack light. You'll walk with your luggage more than you think. Bring a single carry-on bag and a daypack. Use the packing checklist in the appendix as a guide.

Eastern Europe: Best Three-Week Trip by Public Transportation

Day	Plan	Sleep in
1	Fly into Kraków	Kraków
2	Kraków	Kraków
3	Side-trip to Auschwitz	Kraków
4	Travel to Prague (cheap flight, long train ride, or private driver)	Prague
5	Prague	Prague
6	Prague	Prague
7	Prague (side-trip to Kutná Hora)	Prague
8	Train to Český Krumlov (tour Konopiště Castle en route)	Český Krumlov
9	Český Krumlov	Český Krumlov
10	Shuttle bus to Vienna	Vienna
11	Vienna	Vienna
12	Vienna	Vienna
13	Train to Budapest (stop in Bratislava en route)	Budapest
14	Budapest	Budapest
15	Budapest	Budapest
16	Budapest (side-trip to Eger)	Budapest
17	Train or bus to Ljubljana	Ljubljana
18	Ljubljana	Ljubljana
19	Rent a car to explore Lake Bled	Lake Bled
20	Lake Bled and Julian Alps	Lake Bled
21	Fly home from Ljubljana	

This is an urban-focused itinerary—spending most nights in big cities (except for Český Krumlov and Lake Bled), and side-tripping to smaller towns. This itinerary assumes you're using public transportation (saves on some long drives and costly international car drop-off fees). Get creative. From Kraków to Prague, you could take a nine-hour night train or a complicated daytime connection—or you could shop around for a cheap flight. Better yet, splurge on a private driver based in Kraków or Prague (see those chapters) to take you there (5-hour drive), and fit in a stop at Auschwitz en route (about $400-500). Train connections between Český Krumlov and Vienna require multiple changes, but shuttle

Travel Smart

If you have a positive attitude, equip yourself with good information (this book), and expect to travel smart, you will.

Read—and reread—this book. To have an "A" trip, be an "A" student. Note opening hours of sights, closed days, crowd-beating tips, and whether reservations are required or advisable. For exam-

services do the trip affordably in under four hours. From Budapest to Ljubljana, consider the direct train (8.5 hours, leaves at 8:30) or a potentially faster bus (6 hours, www.flixbus.com). Also, it's very smart to strategically rent a car for a few days in places where it's warranted—for example, to explore the countryside between Prague and Český Krumlov, or between Ljubljana and Lake Bled; as long as you're dropping off the car in the same country, there are usually no (or minimal) extra charges.

Two-Week Variation: If you're tight on time, skip Slovenia and cut out some of the side-trips (Kutná Hora, Eger).

ple, most museums throughout Eastern Europe close on Mondays. Hotels in resort towns (such as those in the Julian Alps) are most crowded on Fridays and Saturdays, whereas weekdays are tight in convention cities (for instance, Budapest and Warsaw). Expect seasonal closures. Check the latest at www.ricksteves.com/update.

Be your own tour guide. As you travel, get up-to-date info on sights, reserve tickets and tours, reconfirm hotels and travel

INTRODUCTION

🎧 Stick This Guidebook in Your Ear!

My free Rick Steves Audio Europe app makes it easy to download my audio tours of many of Europe's top attractions and listen to them offline during your travels. In this book, these include my Prague City Walk, Vienna City Walk, St. Stephen's Cathedral Tour, and Ringstrasse Tram Tour. Sights covered by audio tours are marked in this book with this symbol: 🎧. The app also offers insightful travel interviews from my public radio show with experts from Eastern Europe and around the globe. It's all free! You can download the app via Apple's App Store, Google Play, or Amazon's Appstore. For more info, see www.ricksteves.com/audioeurope.

arrangements, and check transit connections. Visit local tourist information offices (TIs). Upon arrival in a new town, lay the groundwork for a smooth departure; confirm the train, bus, or road you'll take when you leave.

Outsmart thieves. Pickpockets abound in crowded places where tourists congregate. Treat commotions as smokescreens for theft. Keep your cash, credit cards, and passport secure in a money belt tucked under your clothes; carry only a day's spending money in your front pocket. Don't set valuable items down on counters or café tabletops, where they can be quickly stolen or easily forgotten.

Minimize potential loss. Keep expensive gear to a minimum. Bring photocopies or take photos of important documents (passport and cards) to aid in replacement if they're lost or stolen. Back up photos and files frequently.

Beat the summer heat. If you wilt easily, choose a hotel with air-conditioning, start your day early, take a midday siesta at your hotel, and resume your sightseeing later. Churches offer a cool haven (though dress modestly—some churches, particularly in Poland, discourage bare shoulders or short shorts).

Be flexible. Even if you have a well-planned itinerary, expect changes, strikes, closures, sore feet, bad weather, and so on. Your Plan B could turn out to be even better.

Attempt the language. Many Eastern Europeans—especially in the tourist trade and in cities—speak English, but if you learn some of the local lan-

guage, even just a few phrases, you'll get more smiles and make more friends. For more tips on hurdling the language barrier, see page 1106. Practice the survival phrases near the end of this book, and even better, bring a phrase book or use a translation app such as Google Translate.

Connect with the culture. Interacting with locals carbonates your experience. Enjoy the friendliness of the Eastern European people. Ask questions; most locals are happy to point you in their idea of the right direction. Set up your own quest for the best bit of communist kitsch, mug of Czech beer, bowl of borscht, or scenic mountain viewpoint. When an opportunity pops up, make it a habit to say "yes."

Eastern Europe...here you come!

CZECH REPUBLIC
Česká Republika

CZECH REPUBLIC

Česká Republika

The Czech Republic is geographically small. On a quick visit, you can enjoy a fine introduction while still packing in plenty of surprises. The country has a little of everything for the traveler. Quaint villages? Check. Beautiful landscapes? Check. World-class art? Czech, Czech, and Czech.

While the Czechs have long occupied the lands of the present-day Czech Republic, for most of their history they were treated as second-class citizens, under the thumb of foreign rulers (generally from Germany or Austria). That the Czech nation exists as an independent state today is practically a Cinderella story. So let's get to know the underdog Czechs.

In Czech towns and villages, you'll find a simple joy of life—a holdover from the days of the Renaissance. The deep spirituality of the Baroque era still shapes the national character. The magic of Prague, the beauty of Český Krumlov, and the lyrical quality of the countryside relieve the heaviness caused by the turmoil that passed through here. Get beyond Prague and explore the country's medieval towns. These rugged woods and hilltop castles will make you feel as if you're walking through the garden of your childhood dreams.

Given their imaginative, sometimes fanciful culture, it's no surprise that the Czechs have produced some famously clever writers—from Franz Kafka (who wrote about a man waking up as a giant cockroach) to Karel Čapek (who wrote about artificially created beings he dubbed "roboti," or robots). The unique entertainment form of Black Light Theater—a combination of illusion, pantomime, puppetry, and modern dance—exemplifies Czech creativity (see page 121). And beloved Czech characters—such as the smiling Good Soldier Švejk, who befuddles his Austro-Hungarian army officers by cleverly playing dumb, and the ubiquitous little cartoon mole called Krtek—will quickly become familiar, as you'll see them all over the streets of Prague.

Czechs refuse to dumb things down. Education and intellect are important, and academics are honored in Czech society. At the

end of communism, the parliament elected a poet, playwright, and philosopher, Václav Havel, to serve two terms as president.

Beyond his intellect, the masses that took to the streets in 1989 no doubt also appreciated Havel's independent thinking and bold actions (he had been imprisoned by communist authorities for his activities promoting human rights). Perhaps because they've seen their national affairs bungled by centuries of foreign overlords, many Czechs have a healthy suspicion of authority, and an admiration for those willing to flout it (including the current EU-bashing president). Other Czechs with a rebellious spirit are national hero Jan Hus (who refused to recant his condemnation of Church corruption, and was burned at the stake), contemporary artist David Černý (whose outrageous stunts are always a lightning rod for controversy), and, of course, the man voted by a wide margin to be the greatest Czech of all time, Jára Cimrman. A fictional character originally created in the 1960s by a pair of radio satirists, Cimrman has taken on a life of his own—and today is something of a nationwide practical joke. (For more on Cimrman, see the sidebar later in this chapter.)

The Czechs' well-studied, sometimes subversive, often world-weary outlook can be perceived by outsiders as cynicism. Czechs have a sharp, dry, often sarcastic sense of humor, and a keen sense of irony. They don't suffer fools lightly...and watching a united nations of clueless tourists trample their capital city for the past generation hasn't done wonders for their patience. Cut the Czechs some slack, and show them respect: Be one of the very few visitors who bothers to learn a few pleasantries—hello, please, thank you—in their language. (See "Czech Language," later.) You'll notice a difference in how you're treated.

Of the Czech Republic's three main regions—Bohemia, Mora-

CZECH REPUBLIC

Czech Republic Almanac

Official Name: As of 2016, the country's new official short name is Czechia. It's better known as the Česká Republika, born on January 1, 1993, along with Slovakia, when the nation of Czechoslovakia—formed after World War I and dominated by the USSR after World War II—split into two countries.

Population: 10.6 million people. About 64 percent are ethnic Czechs, who speak Czech, and another 5 percent are Moravian. Unlike some of their neighbors (including the very Catholic Poles and Slovaks), Czechs are inclined to be agnostic: One in 10 is Roman Catholic, but the majority (54 percent) list their religion as unaffiliated, and another 35 percent list none.

Latitude and Longitude: 50°N and 14°E (similar latitude to Vancouver, British Columbia).

Area: 30,450 square miles (slightly smaller than South Carolina).

Geography: The Czech Republic comprises three regions (called "lands" here)—Bohemia (Čechy), Moravia (Morava), and a small slice of Silesia (Slezsko).

Biggest Cities: Prague (the capital, 1.3 million), Brno (378,000), Ostrava (300,000), and Plzeň (169,000).

Economy: The gross domestic product equals about $372 billion (similar to Maryland). The GDP per capita is approximately $35,200 (compared to $59,500 for the average American). Major moneymakers for the country include machine parts, cars and trucks (VW subsidiary Škoda is a highly respected automaker), and beer (the leading brand is Pilsner Urquell). Industrial pro-

via, and small Silesia—the best-known is Bohemia, where Prague is. It has nothing to do with beatnik bohemians, but with the Celtic tribe that inhabited the land before the coming of the Germans and the Slavs. A longtime home of Czechs, Germans, and Jews, Bohemia is circled by a naturally fortifying ring of mountains and cut down the middle by the Vltava River. The winegrowing region of Moravia (to the east) is more Slavic and colorful, and more about the land.

Tourists often conjure up images of Bohemia when they think of the Czech Republic. But the country consists of more than rollicking beer halls and gently rolling landscapes. It's also about dreamy wine cellars and fertile Moravian plains, with the rugged Carpathian Mountains on the horizon. Politically and geologically, Bohemia and Moravia are two distinct regions. The soils and climates in which the hops and wine grapes grow are very different... and so are the two regions' mentalities. The boisterousness of the Czech polka contrasts with the melancholy of the Moravian ballad;

duction declined during the economic slowdown, but not beer consumption (the vast majority of Czech beer is consumed domestically). More than a third of trade is with next-door-neighbor Germany; as a result, Germany's economic health one year generally predicts the Czech Republic's fortunes the next.

Currency: 20 Czech crowns (*koruna,* Kč) = about $1.

Government: From 1948 to 1989, Czechoslovakia was a communist state under Soviet control. Today, the Czech Republic is a member of the European Union (since 2004) and a vibrant democracy, with about a 60 percent turnout for elections. Its parliament is made up of 200 members of the Chamber of Deputies elected every four years and 81 senators elected for six years. The president is selected every five years. No single political party dominates; the current leadership is a coalition of a populist centrist party led by a food- and fertilizer-industry tycoon, the Social Democrats (left), and the Communists. Ailing President Miloš Zeman, reelected in 2018 to his second and final term, is a controversial figure viewed as either the average man's champion or someone increasingly out of touch with reality—and bent on steering the country's foreign policy toward Russia.

Flag: The Czech flag is red (bottom), white (top), and blue (a triangle along the hoist side).

The Average Czech: The average Czech has 1.4 kids (slowly rising after the sharp decline that followed the end of communism), will live 79 years, and has one television in the house.

the political viewpoint of the Prague power broker is at odds with the spirituality of the Moravian bard.

Only a tiny bit of Silesia—around the town of Opava—is part of the Czech Republic today; the rest of the region is in Poland and Germany. People in Silesia speak a wide variety of dialects that mix Czech, German, and Polish.

Ninety percent of the tourists who visit the Czech Republic see only Prague. But if you venture outside the capital, you'll enjoy traditional towns and villages, great prices, a friendly and gentle countryside dotted by nettles and wild poppies, and almost no international tourists. Since the time of the Habsburgs, fruit trees have lined the country roads for everyone to share. Take your pick.

HELPFUL HINTS

Tolls: If you're driving on highways in the Czech Republic, you're required to buy a toll sticker *(dálniční známka)* at the border, a post office, or a gas station (310 Kč/10 days, 440 Kč/1 month).

Your rental car may already come with the necessary sticker—ask.

Rail Passes: The Czech Republic is covered by a Eurail Czech Republic pass, a Central Europe Triangle Pass (Vienna-Budapest-Prague or Vienna-Salzburg-Prague), a four-country European East pass (together with Austria, Hungary, and Slovakia), and the more expensive Eurail Global Pass. If your train travel will be limited to a handful of rides and/or short distances (for example, within the Czech Republic), you're probably better off without a pass—Czech tickets are cheap to buy as you go. But if you're combining Prague with international destinations, a rail pass could save you money.

For more detailed advice on figuring out the smartest rail pass options for your train trip, visit RickSteves.com/rail.

CZECH HISTORY

The Czechs have always been at a crossroads of Europe—between the Slavic and Germanic worlds, between Catholicism and Protestantism, and between Cold War East and West. As if having foreseen all of this, the mythical founder of Prague—the beautiful princess Libuše—named her city "Praha" (meaning "threshold" in Czech). Despite these strong external influences, the Czechs have retained their distinct culture...and a dark, ironic sense of humor to keep them laughing through it all.

Charles IV and the Middle Ages (500s-1300s)

The pagan, Slavic tribes that arrived in this part of Europe in the sixth century AD were first united by the Prague-based Přemysl dynasty. The main figure of this era was Duke Václav I (AD 907-935)—later immortalized in a Christmas carol as "Good King Wenceslas"—who converted the Czechs to Christianity and founded a cathedral at Prague Castle, on a bluff overlooking the Vltava River.

In 1004, Bohemia was incorporated into the Holy Roman Empire (an alliance of mostly German-speaking kingdoms and dukedoms). Within 200 years—thanks to its strategic location and privileged status within the empire—Prague had become one of Europe's largest and most highly cultured cities.

The 14th century was Prague's Golden Age, when Holy Roman Emperor Charles IV (1316-1378) ruled. Born to a Luxembourger nobleman and a Czech princess, Charles IV was an ambitious man on the cusp of the Renaissance. He lived and studied in several European lands, spoke five languages, and counted Petrarch as a friend—but always felt a deep connection to his mother's Czech roots.

Selecting Prague as his seat of power, Charles imported French architects to make the city a grand capital, founded the first university north of the Alps, and invigorated the Czech national spirit. (He popularized the legend of Wenceslas to give his people a near-mythical, King Arthur-type cultural standard-bearer.) Much of Prague's history and architecture—including the famous Charles Bridge, Charles University, St. Vitus Cathedral, and Karlštejn Castle—can be traced to this dynamic man's rule.

Under Charles IV, the Czech people gained esteem among Europeans. Charles was born under a lucky star: During his time, the dominance of divinely sanctioned monarchs peaked. A generation later, after a religious and social upheaval, his son faced much stronger opposition when trying to implement Charles-like absolute power.

Jan Hus and Religious Wars (1300s-1600s)

Jan Hus (c. 1369-1415) was a local preacher and professor who got in trouble with the Vatican a hundred years before Martin Luther. Like Luther, Hus preached in the people's language rather than in Latin. To add insult to injury, he spoke out against Church corruption. Tried for heresy and burned in 1415, Hus became both a religious martyr and a national hero. While each age has defined Hus to its liking, the way he challenged authority while staying true to his beliefs has long inspired and rallied the Czech people. (For more on Hus, see page 59.)

Inspired by Hus' reformist ideas, the Czechs rebelled against both the Roman Catholic Church and German political control. This burst of independent thought led to a period of religious wars. Protestant Czech patriots—like the rough-and-rugged war hero Jan Žižka (often depicted in patriotic art with his trademark eye patch)—fought to maintain Czech autonomy. But ultimately, these rebels were overwhelmed by their Catholic opponents. The result of these wars was the loss of autonomy to Vienna.

Ruled by the Habsburgs of Austria, Prague stagnated—except during the rule of King Rudolf II (1552-1612), a Holy Roman Emperor. With Rudolf living in Prague, the city again blossomed as a cultural and intellectual center. Astronomers Johannes Kepler and Tycho Brahe flourished, as did other scientists, and much of the inspiration for Prague's great art can be attributed to the king's patronage.

Not long after this period, Prague entered one of its darker spells. The Thirty Years' War (1618-1648) began in Prague when

Jára Cimrman: The Greatest Czech?

"I am such a complete atheist that I am afraid God will punish me." Such is the pithy wisdom of Jára Cimrman, the man overwhelmingly voted the "Greatest Czech of All Time" in a 2005 national poll. Who is Jára Cimrman? A philosopher? An explorer? An inventor? He is all these things, yes, and much more.

Born in the mid-19th century, Cimrman studied in Vienna before journeying the world. He traversed the Atlantic in a steamboat he designed himself, taught drama to peasants in Peru, and drifted across the Arctic Sea on an iceberg. He invented the lightbulb, but Edison beat him to the patent office by five minutes. It was he who suggested to the Americans the idea for a Panama Canal, though, as usual, he was never credited. Indeed, Cimrman surreptitiously advised many of the world's greats: Eiffel on his tower, Einstein on his theories of relativity, Chekhov on his plays. ("You can't just have *two* sisters," Cimrman told the playwright. "How about three?") Long before the world knew of Sartre or Camus, Cimrman was writing tracts such as *The Essence of the Existence*, which would become the foundation for his philosophy of "Cimrmanism," also known as "nonexistentialism." (Its central premise: "Existence cannot not exist.")

Despite Jára Cimrman's genius, the "Greatest Czech" poll's sponsors had a single objection to his candidacy: He's not real,

Czech Protestant nobles, wanting religious and political autonomy, tossed two Catholic Habsburg officials out the window of the castle. (This was one of Prague's many defenestrations—a uniquely Czech solution to political discord, in which offending politicians are literally thrown out the window.) The Czech Estates Uprising lasted two years, ending in a crushing defeat in the Battle of White Mountain (1620), which marked the end of Czech freedom. Twenty-seven leaders of the uprising were executed (today commemorated by crosses on Prague's Old Town Square), most of the old Czech nobility was dispossessed, and Protestants had to convert to Catholicism or leave the country.

Often called "the first world war" because it engulfed so many nations, the Thirty Years' War was particularly tough on Prague. During this period, its population dropped from 60,000 to 25,000. The result of this war was 300 years of Habsburg rule from afar, as Prague became a German-speaking backwater of Vienna. While the Austrian rule contributed to economic prosperity—and was fairly liberal compared to its Russian and Prussian neighbors—Czechs still tend to despise the Habsburgs. They see them as a pompous royal family that invented the concept of the modern zoo (at Vienna's Schönbrunn Palace) and then tried to impose it on the

but the brainchild of Czech humorists Zdeněk Svěrák and Jiří Šebánek, who brought this patriotic Renaissance Man to life in 1967 in a satirical radio play.

How should we interpret the fact that the Czechs chose a fictional character as their greatest countryman over any of their flesh-and-blood national heroes—say, Charles IV (the 14th-century Holy Roman Emperor who established Prague as the cultural and intellectual capital of Europe), or Martina Navrátilová (someone who plays a sport with bright green balls)?

I like to think that the vote for Cimrman says something about the country's enthusiasm for blowing raspberries in the face of authority. From the times of the Czech kings who used crafty diplomacy to keep the German menace at bay, to the days of Jan Hus and his criticism of the Catholic Church, to the flashes of anticommunist revolt that at last sparked the Velvet Revolution in 1989—the Czechs have maintained a healthy disrespect for those who would tell them how to live their lives. Their vote for a fictional personage, says Cimrman's co-creator Svěrák, shows two things about the Czech nation: "That it is skeptical about those who are major figures and those who are supposedly the 'Greatest.' And that the only certainty that has saved the nation many times throughout history is its humor."

people of their empire (before deciding it was better to turn them into cannon fodder).

Czech National Revival (1800s-1918)

The end of Prague as a German city came gradually. During the centuries that the Czech language and culture were suppressed, "Prag" and other cities were populated mainly by German-speaking urbanites, while "backwards" peasants kept the old Czech ways alive in the countryside. But as the Industrial Revolution attracted Czech farmers and country folk to the cities, the demographics of the Czech population centers began to shift. Between 1800 and 1900—though it remained part of the Habsburg Empire—Prague went from being an essentially German town to a predominantly Czech one.

As in the rest of Europe, the 19th century was a time of great nationalism, when the age of divine kings and ruling families came to a fitful end. The Czech spirit was first stirred by the work of historian František Palacký, who dug deep into the Czech archives to forge a national narrative. During this time, Czechs were inspired by the completion of Prague's St. Vitus Cathedral, the symphonies of Antonín Dvořák, and the operas of Bedřich Smetana, which were performed in the new National Theater.

Alfons Mucha, a prodigiously talented Czech artist who made a name for himself in the high society of turn-of-the-century Paris, embodied this wave of nationalism. When he could have lived out his days in the lap of luxury in Paris or New York City, Mucha chose instead to return to his homeland and spend decades painting a magnum opus celebrating the historical journey of the Czechs and all Slavs—the *Slav Epic*.

After the Habsburgs' Austro-Hungarian Empire suffered defeat in World War I, their vast holdings broke apart and became independent countries. Among these was a union of Bohemia, Moravia, and Slovakia, the brainchild of a clever politician named Tomáš Garrigue Masaryk (see sidebar on page 110). The new nation, Czechoslovakia, was proclaimed in 1918, with Prague as its capital.

Troubles of the 20th Century (1918-1989)

Independence lasted only 20 years. In the notorious Munich Agreement of September 1938—much to the dismay of the Czechs and Slovaks—Great Britain and France peacefully ceded to Hitler the so-called Sudetenland (a fringe around the edge of Bohemia, populated mainly by people of German descent; see sidebar on page 194). It wasn't long before Hitler seized the rest of Czechoslovakia...and the Holocaust began. Under the ruthless Nazi governor Reinhard Heydrich, tens of thousands of Jews were sent first to the concentration camp at Terezín, and later to Auschwitz and other death camps. After Heydrich was assassinated by a pair of Czech paratroopers, the campaign of genocide grew even worse. Out of the 55,000 Jews living in Prague before the war, more than 80 percent perished during the Holocaust; throughout Czechoslovakia, an estimated 260,000 Jews were murdered.

For centuries, Prague's cultural makeup had consisted of a rich mix of Czech, German, and Jewish people—historically, they were almost evenly divided. With the Jewish population decimated, part of that delicate tapestry was gone forever. And after World War II ended, more than two million people of Germanic descent who lived in Czechoslovakia were pushed into Germany. Their forced resettlement—which led to the deaths of untold numbers of Germans (what some today might call "ethnic cleansing")—was demanded by the public and carried out by Czechoslovak President Edvard Beneš, who had ruled from exile in London throughout the war. Today's Czech Republic is largely homogenous—about 95 percent Czechs.

Although Prague escaped the bombs of World War II, it went directly from the Nazi frying pan into the communist fire. A local uprising freed the city from the Nazis on May 8, 1945, but the Soviets "liberated" them on May 9.

The period of 1945 to 1948 is a perfect case study of how, in trying times, a country can lose its freedom through its own folly. The popular perception that Czechoslovakia simply fell into the Soviet sphere of influence is only partly true. While the Soviets had special interest in controlling Czechoslovakia (particularly because of its uranium deposits), Czechoslovakia was represented by an internationally recognized exile government during the war. This government was allowed to come back and rule until the 1946 election. And up until 1948, Czechoslovakia was still a sovereign state (though it was under Soviet pressure) whose elected leaders were responsible for shaping its eventual orientation.

The first mistake was that the government in exile (despite Churchill's warnings) signed a binding cooperation pact with the Soviet Union in 1943. Then the communists won the most seats in the 1946 election—garnering more than 40 percent of the vote in the Czech lands (in Slovakia, they came in second). In 1947, parliament voted against the Marshall Plan. When the country's leaders and electorate realized the communists weren't playing according to any rulebook, it was too late. By 1948, the communists controlled all the powerful ministries and suppressed student-led protests calling for democracy. For more than 40 years, they would not hold a free election.

The early communist era (1948-1968) was a mixture of misguided zeal, Stalinist repressions, and attempts to wed socialism with democracy. The "Prague Spring" period of reform—initiated by a young generation of progressive communists in 1968, led by the charismatic Slovak politician Alexander Dubček—came to an abrupt halt under the treads of Warsaw Pact tanks (for details, see page 81). Dubček was exiled (and made a backwoods forest ranger), and the years of "normalization" following the unsuccessful revolt were particularly disheartening. A wave of protests spread through the country in 1969, as furious young Czechs and Slovaks lit themselves on fire to decry communist oppression. But the status quo would hold strong for another 20 years.

The underground Metro system, begun in the mid-1970s, was not just for mass transit, but was also designed to be a giant fallout shelter for protection against capitalist bombs. In the mid-1980s, the communists began constructing Prague's huge Žižkov TV tower (now the city's tallest structure)—not only to broadcast Czech TV transmissions, but also to jam Western signals.

Every small town had its own set of loudspeakers for broadcasting propaganda. (You'll still see these if you look closely as you pass through the countryside.) Locals remember growing up with these mouthpieces of government boasting of successes ("This year, despite many efforts of sabotage on the part of certain individuals in service of imperialist goals, we have surpassed the planned output of steel by 195 percent"); calling people to action ("There will be no school tomorrow as all will join the farmers in the fields for an abundant harvest"); or quelling disturbances ("Some citizens may have heard about alien forces in our society taking advantage of this week's anniversary to spread unrest. This is to reassure you that the situation is firmly under control and nothing is happening in Olomouc or in Prague. Nevertheless, for their own safety, we suggest all citizens stay home.").

Eventually the Soviet empire crumbled, beginning with re-forms in Hungary in the summer of 1989 and culminating in the fall of the Berlin Wall that October. A few weeks later, Czecho-slovakia regained its freedom in the student- and artist-powered 1989 "Velvet Revolution," so-called because there were no casual-ties...or even broken windows (see page 83). Václav Havel, a poet, playwright, and philosopher who had been imprisoned by the communist regime, became Czechoslovakia's first postcommunist president.

"It's Not You, It's Me": The Peaceful Breakup (1989-1993)

In the postcommunist age of new possibility, the two peoples of Czechoslovakia began to wonder if, in fact, they belonged together.

Ever since they joined with the Czechs in 1918, the Slovaks felt overshadowed by Prague (unmistakably the political, econom-ic, and cultural center of the country). Slovakia, which in the pre-ceding 50 years had been stripped even of the right to run schools in its own language, stood no chance of true independence after World War I. And over the years, the Czechs resented the financial burden of carrying their poorer neighbors to the east. In this new world of flux and freedom, longstanding trends and tensions came to a head. (You could argue that Austro-Hungary's multiethnic successor states—such as Czechoslovakia and Yugoslavia—were miniature copies of the mother country. It was only a matter of time before those states, too, would subdivide into smaller national states.)

The dissolution of Czechoslovakia began over a hyphen, as the Slovaks wanted to rename the country Czecho-Slovakia. Ideally, this symbolic move would come with a redistribution of powers: two capitals and two UN reps, but one national bank and a single currency. This idea was rejected, and in June 1992, the Slovak na-tionalist candidate Vladimír Mečiar fared surprisingly well in the elections—suggesting that the Slovaks were serious about seces-sion. The politicians plowed ahead, getting serious about the split in September 1992. The transition took only three months from start to finish.

The split became official on January 1, 1993, and each country ended up with its own capital, currency, and head of state. For most, the breakup dissolved tensions, and a decade and a half later, Czechs and Slovaks still feel closer to each other than to any other nationality.

Since the split, the Czech Republic has had three significant turning points. In March 1999, it joined NATO. On May 1, 2004, the country joined the European Union. Three and a half years later, it entered the Schengen Agreement, effectively erasing its borders for the purposes of work and travel. The Czech Republic had become a fully integrated member of the European community.

The Czech Republic Today (2000 to Present)

After 14 years in office, a term-limited Václav Havel stepped down in 2003. He died in 2011. While he's fondly remembered by Czechs as a great thinker, writer, and fearless leader of the opposition movement during the communist days, many consider him to have been less successful as a president.

The next president, Václav Klaus, had been the pragmatic author of the economic reforms in the 1990s. Klaus' surprising win in the 2003 election symbolized a change from revolutionary times, when philosophers became kings, to modern humdrum politics, when offices are gained by bargaining with the opposition (Communist Party votes in parliament were the decisive factor in Klaus' election).

Behind-the-scenes deals in parliament allowed Klaus to be reelected, drawing public outrage and eventually a change in the country's constitution. This led, in January 2013, to the first election of a president directly by the people (rather than by parliament).

The winner was Miloš Zeman, the other political heavyweight of the 1990s. President Zeman—a tobacco, pork, and *Becherovka*-powered man of the people—represents the social-democratic ČSSD, one of two dominant parties in postcommunist politics.

President Zeman is a controversial figure with slippery politics. He began his career on the left, has since swung hard to the right, and fires up his base with populist rhetoric. (If you're thinking "the Czech Donald Trump," you're not far off. He even has an Ivanka-like daughter, Kateřina Zemanová, who plays a major role in his administration.)

However, the Czech president is largely a figurehead. The main power broker, the prime minister, is chosen in the parliamentary elections. And in 2017, the country faced a choice: settle for its imperfect traditional parties, or empower a recently emerged antiestablishment candidate—food industry mogul, world's second wealthiest Czech, and former secret police collaborator Andrej

Babiš, head of the Action of Dissatisfied Citizens party. The election resulted in a hung parliament, paving the way for Babiš to take office, leading a coalition of his own party and an assortment of smaller independent voting blocs (including communists).

The election of Babiš, however, was not a definitive sea change away from the traditional, dominant parties of the Czech system. In 2018, Miloš Zeman was reelected to a second presidential term, narrowly defeating an independent challenger. And the senate elections in the fall of 2018 went in favor of the *other* dominant party, ODS.

While it's fascinating to track the nuances of Czech politics, in general, the recent trajectory of Czech history is trending positive. Both in the capital and in rural villages, the country feels more affluent than ever before, all while celebrating its inherent Czechness. And Prague is, quite justifiably, one of the most popular tourist destinations in Europe.

CZECH CUISINE

The Czechs have one of Europe's most stick-to-your-ribs cuisines. Heavy on meat, potatoes, and cabbage, it's hearty and tasty—designed to keep peasants fueled through a day of hard work. Some people could eat this stuff forever, while others seek a frequent break in the form of ethnic restaurants (bigger towns such as Prague, Český Krumlov, and Kutná Hora have several options).

Soups

Polévka (soup) is the most essential part of a meal. The saying goes: "The soup fills you up, the dish plugs it up." *Pečivo* (bread) may be served with soup, or you may need to ask for it; it's always charged separately depending on how many *rohlíky* (rolls) or slices of *chleba* (yeast bread) you eat.

Some of the thick soups for a cold day are:

Zelná (or **zelňačka**): Cabbage

Čočková: Lentil

Fazolová: Bean

Dršťková: Tripe—delicious if fresh, chewy as gum if not

The lighter soups are:

Hovězí (or **slepičí vývar s nudlemi**): Beef or chicken broth with noodles

Pórková: Leek

Květáková: Cauliflower

Main Dishes

These can either be *hotová jídla* (quick, ready-to-serve standard dishes, in some places available only during lunch hours, generally

Czech Dumplings

Czech dumplings *(knedlíky)* resemble steamed white bread. They come in plain or potato *(bramborové)* varieties; are meant to be drowned in gravy (dumplings never accompany sauceless dishes); and are eaten with a knife and fork.

Sweet dumplings, listed in the dessert section on a menu, are a tempting option in summer, when they are loaded with fresh strawberries, blueberries, apricots, or plums, and garnished with custard and melted butter. Beware, though, that many restaurants cheat by filling the sticky dough with a smattering of jam or fruit preserve; before ordering, ask the waiter for details, or discreetly inspect that plate at your neighbor's table. Dumplings with frozen fruit lose some of the flavor, but are still worth trying.

11:00-14:30) or the more specialized *jídla na objednávku* or *minutky* (plates prepared when you order).

Below are some popular meat dishes. Note that the word *pečené* (roasted) shows up frequently on menus.

Guláš: Thick, meaty stew

Pečená kachna: Roasted duck

Pečené kuře: Roasted chicken

Smažený řízek: Fried pork fillet, like Wiener schnitzel

Svíčková na smetaně: Beef tenderloin in cream sauce

Vepřové koleno: Pork knuckle

Vepřová pečeně: Pork roast

If you're spending the night out with friends, have a beer and feast on the huge *vepřové koleno,* usually served with mustard *(hořčicí),* horseradish sauce *(křenem),* and yeast bread *(chleba).*

In this landlocked country, fish options are typically limited to *kapr* (carp) and *pstruh* (trout), prepared in a variety of ways and served with potatoes or fries—although Czech perch and Norwegian salmon have cropped up on many local menus.

Vegetarians can go for the delicious *smažený sýr s bramborem* (fried cheese with potatoes) or default to *čočka s vejci* (lentils with fried egg).

Salads and Sides

Starches and Garnishes: *Hotová jídla* come with set garnishes, but if ordering à la carte *(jídla na objednávku)*, you'll typically need to order your garnishes separately (otherwise you'll get only the main dish). In either case, the most common sides are *knedlíky* (bread dumplings), *zelím* (cabbage), and *bramborem* (potatoes).

Salad: *Šopský salát*, like a Greek salad, is usually the best salad option (a mix of tomatoes, cucumbers, peppers, onion, and feta cheese with vinegar and olive oil). The server will bring it with the main dish, unless you specify that you want it before.

Dessert

Consider the following for *moučník* (dessert):

Lívance: Small pancakes with jam and curd

Palačinka: Crêpes served with fruit or jam

Zmrzlinový pohár: Ice-cream sundae

Many restaurants will offer fruit-filled dumplings and different sorts of *koláče* (pastries) and *štrůdl* (apple strudel), but it's much better to get these from a bakery. A *větrník* is a super-decadent, glazed cream puff.

All over Prague's Old Town, you'll find kiosks selling a treat called *trdlo* or *trdelník*. This is a long ribbon of dough wrapped around a stick, slowly cooked on a rotisserie, then rolled in cinnamon, sugar, or other toppings. While these aren't "traditional Czech" (they were imported quite recently from Hungary), they do offer a fresh, sweet treat. Try to get one that's still warm, rather than one wrapped in plastic—it makes a big difference.

Beverages

Coffee: No Czech meal is complete without a cup of coffee. Espresso is popular, and locals drink it with added water and cream on the side. In most places, you'll find *turecká káva* (Turkish coffee—finely ground coffee that only partly dissolves, leaving "mud" on the bottom; drink it without milk). This is how Czechs traditionally brewed their coffee.

Water: Water comes bottled and often costs more than beer (tap water is generally not served). Czech mineral waters *(minerálka)* have a high mineral content. They're naturally carbonated because they come from the springs in the many Czech spas (Mattoni, the most common brand, is from Carlsbad). If you want still water, ask for *neperlivá*.

Beer, Wine, and Liqueurs: Bohemia is beer country, with Europe's best and cheapest brew. Moravians prefer wine and *slivovice*

Czech Beer

Czechs are among the world's most enthusiastic beer *(pivo)* drinkers—adults drink an average of 80 gallons a year. The pub is a place to have fun, complain, discuss art and politics, talk hockey, and chat with locals and visitors alike. *Na zdraví* means "to your health" in Czech. Whether you're in a *restaurace* (restaurant), *hostinec* (pub), or *hospoda* (bar), a beer will land on your table upon the slightest hint to the waiter, and a new pint will automatically appear when the old glass is almost empty (until you tell the waiter to stop). Order beer from the tap *(točené* means "draft," *sudové pivo* means "keg beer"). More and more pubs are upgrading to beer from the tank *(tankové)*. A *pivo* is large (0.5 liter—17 oz); a *malé pivo* is small (0.3 liter—10 oz).

The Czechs perfected the first Pilsner-style lager, introduced by a Bavarian in nearby Plzeň, and the result, Pilsner Urquell, is on tap in many local pubs. But the Czechs produce plenty of other good beers; most of the famous brands, including Krušovice, Gambrinus, Staropramen, and Kozel, are owned internationally. Budvar, from the town of Budějovice ("Budweis" in German), is the last state-owned brewery. For years, the Czech and the American breweries disputed the "Budweiser" brand name. The solution: Czech Budweiser is sold under its own name in Europe, China, and Africa, while in America it is marketed as Czechvar.

The big degree symbol on beer bottles doesn't indicate alcohol content. Instead, it is a measurement used by brewers to track the density of certain ingredients. As a rough guide, 10 degrees is

about 3.5 percent alcohol, 12 degrees is about 4.2 percent alcohol, and 11 and 15 degrees are dark beers. The most popular Czech beers are about as potent as German beers and only slightly stronger than typical American brews. Traditional establishments have beers from only one brewery on tap: one 10-degree, one 12-degree, one dark, and one nonalcoholic beer.

In recent years, Czechs have moved toward local microbrews. More restaurants are making their own beer or serving beer only from independent breweries. Modern beer bars *(pivní bar,* with a range of microbrews on tap) are popping up like crazy. The one word to characterize a successful Czech microbrew is *balance*. While Czechs do like to try new tastes, they are looking for a beer they can spend an evening with, drinking several pints throughout the night.

(SLEE-voh-veet-seh)—a plum brandy so highly valued that it's the de facto currency of the Carpathian Mountains (often used to barter with sheepherders and other mountain folk). *Medovina* ("honey wine") is mead.

In bars and restaurants, you can go wild with memorable liqueurs, most of which cost about a dollar a shot. Experiment. *Fernet,* a bitter drink made from many herbs, is the leading Czech aperitif. Absinthe, made from wormwood and herbs, is a watered-down version of the hallucinogenic drink that's illegal in much of Europe. It's famous as the muse of many artists (including Henri de Toulouse-Lautrec in Paris more than a century ago). *Becherovka,* made of 13 herbs and 38 percent alcohol, was used to settle upset aristocratic tummies and as an aphrodisiac. This velvety drink remains popular today. *Becherovka* and tonic mixed together is nicknamed *beton* ("concrete"). If you drink three, you'll find out why.

CZECH LANGUAGE

Czech is a Slavic language closely related to its Polish and Slovak neighbors. These days, English is widely spoken, and you'll find the language barrier minimal—unless you're dealing with a clerk or service person over age 50.

Czech pronunciation can be tricky. The language has a dizzying array of diacritical marks (little doo-hickeys over some letters that affect pronunciation). Most notably, some letters can be topped with *a háček (č, š, ž, ň, ě).* Here are some clues for Czech pronunciation:

j sounds like "y" as in "yarn"
c sounds like "ts" as in "cats"
č sounds like "ch" as in "chicken"
š sounds like "sh" as in "shrimp"
ž sounds like "zh" as in "leisure"
ň sounds like "ny" as in "canyon"
ě sounds like "yeh" as in "yet"
ď sounds like the "dj" sound in "ledge"

Prague is flooded with tourists, most of whom don't bother to learn a single word of the local language. Study the Czech survival phrases on the following pages and give it your best shot. The locals will appreciate your efforts.

When navigating town, these words might be helpful: *město* (MYEHS-toh, town), *náměstí* (NAH-myehs-tee, square), *ulica* (OO-leet-sah, street), *nábřeží* (NAH-bzheh-zhee, embankment road), and *most* (mohst, bridge).

Czech Survival Phrases

The emphasis in Czech words usually falls on the first syllable—though don't overdo it, as this stress is subtle. A vowel with an accent (á, é, í, ú, ý) is held longer. The combination ch sounds like the guttural "kh" sound in the Scottish word "loch." The uniquely Czech ř (as in Dvořák) sounds like a cross between a rolled "r" and "zh"; in the phonetics, it's "zh." Here are a few English words that all Czechs know: super, OK, pardon, stop, menu, problem, and no problem.

English	Czech	Pronunciation
Hello. (formal)	Dobrý den.	**doh**-bree dehn
Hi. / Bye. (informal)	Ahoj.	**ah**-hoy
Do you speak English?	Mluvíte anglicky?	**mloo**-vee-teh **ahn**-glits-kee
Yes. / No.	Ano. / Ne.	**ah**-noh / neh
I don't understand.	Nerozumím.	**neh**-roh-zoo-meem
Please. / You're welcome. / Can I help you?	Prosím.	**proh**-seem
Thank you.	Děkuji.	**dyeh**-kwee
Excuse me. / I'm sorry.	Promiňte.	**proh**-meen-teh
Good.	Dobře.	**dohb**-zheh
Goodbye.	Nashledanou.	**nah**-skleh-dah-noh
one / two / three	jeden / dva / tři	**yay**-dehn / dvah / tzhee
four / five / six	čtyři / pět / šest	**chtee**-zhee / pyeht / shehst
seven / eight	sedm / osm	**seh**-dum / **oh**-sum
nine / ten	devět / deset	**dehv**-yeht / **deh**-seht
hundred / thousand	sto / tisíc	stoh / **tee**-seets
How much?	Kolik?	**koh**-leek
local currency	koruna (Kč)	koh-**roo**-nah
Write it?	Napište to?	**nah**-pish-teh toh
Is it free?	Je to zadarmo?	yeh toh **zah**-dar-moh
Is it included?	Je to v ceně?	yeh tohf **tsay**-nyeh
Where can I find / buy...?	Kde mohu najít / koupit...?	guh-**deh** moh-hoo **nah**-yeet / **koh**-pit
I'd like... (said by a man)	Rád bych...	rahd bikh
I'd like... (said by a woman)	Ráda bych...	**rah**-dah bikh
We'd like...	Rádi bychom...	**rah**-dyee **bee**-khohm
...a room.	...pokoj.	**poh**-koy
...a ticket to ___. (destination)	...jízdenka do ___.	**yeez**-dehn-kah doh ___
Is it possible?	Je to možné?	yeh toh **mohzh**-neh
Where is...?	Kde je...?	guh-**deh** yeh
...the train station	...nádraží	**nah**-drah-zhee
...the bus station	...autobusové nádraží	**ow**-toh-boo-soh-veh **nah**-drah-zhee
...the tourist information office	...turistická informační kancelář	**too**-rih-stit-skah **een**-for-mahch-nee **kahn**-tseh-lahzh
...the toilet	...vécé	**veht**-seh
men / women	muži / ženy	**moo**-zhee / **zheh**-nee
left / right / straight	vlevo / vpravo / rovně	**vleh**-voh / **fprah**-voh / **rohv**-nyeh
At what time...?	V kolik...?	**fkoh**-leek
...does this open / close	...otevírají / zavírají	**oh**-teh-vee-rah-yee / **zah**-vee-rah-yee
Just a moment, please.	Moment, prosím.	**moh**-mehnt **proh**-seem
now / soon / later	teď / brzy / později	tedge / **bir**-zih / **pohz**-dyeh-yee
today / tomorrow	dnes / zítra	duh-**nehs** / **zee**-trah

In a Czech Restaurant

CZECH REPUBLIC

English	Czech	Pronunciation
I'd like to reserve... (said by a man)	Rád bych zarezervoval...	rahd bikh zah-reh-zehr-voh-vahl
I'd like to reserve... (said by a woman)	Ráda bych zarezervovala...	**rah**-dah bikh **zah**-reh-zehr-voh-vah-lah
...a table for one / two.	...stůl pro jednoho / dva.	stool proh **yehd**-noh-hoh / dvah
Nonsmoking.	Nekuřácký.	neh-kuhzh-aht-skee
Is this table free?	Je tento stůl volný?	yeh **tehn**-toh stool **vohl**-nee
Can I help you?	Mohu vám pomoci?	**moh**-hoo vahm poh-**moht**-see
The menu (in English), please.	Jídelní lístek (v angličtině), prosím.	**yee**-dehl-nee **lee**-stehk (**fahn**-gleech-tee-nyeh) **proh**-seem
Service is / isn't included.	Spropitné je / není zahrnuto.	**sproh**-pit-neh yeh / **neh**-nee **zah**-har-noo-toh
"to go"	s sebou	**seh**-boh
with / and / or	s / a / nebo	suh / ah / **neh**-boh
ready-to-eat meal	hotová jidla	**hoh**-toh-vah **yeed**-lah
meal on request	minutky	**mih**-noot-kee
appetizers	předkrm	**pzhehd**-krim
bread	chléb	khlehb
cheese	sýr	seer
sandwich	sendvič	**sehnd**-vich
soup / salad	polévka / salát	poh-**lehv**-kah / **sah**-laht
meat	maso	**mah**-soh
poultry	drůbež	**droo**-behzh
fish	ryby	**rih**-bih
fruit / vegetables	ovoce / zelenina	**oh**-voht-seh / **zeh**-leh-nyee-nah
dessert	dezert	**deh**-zehrt
(tap) water	voda (z kohoutku)	**voh**-dah (**skoh**-hoht-koo)
mineral water	minerální voda	**mih**-neh-rahl-nyee **voh**-dah
carbonated / not carbonated (spoken)	s bublinkami / bez bublinek	**sboob**-leen-kah-mee / behz **boo**-blee-nehk
carbonated / not carbonated (printed)	perlivá / neperlivá	**pehr**-lee-vah / **neh**-pehr-lee-vah
milk	mléko	**mleh**-koh
(orange) juice	(pomerančový) džus	(**poh**-mehr-ahn-choh-vee) "juice"
coffee / tea	káva / čaj	**kah**-vah / chai
wine	víno	**vee**-noh
red / white	červené / bílé	**chehr**-veh-neh / **bee**-leh
sweet / dry	sladké / suché	**slahd**-keh / **soo**-kheh
glass / bottle	sklenka / lahev	**sklehn**-kah / **lah**-hehv
beer	pivo	**pee**-voh
light / dark	světlé / tmavé	**svyeht**-leh / **tmah**-veh
Cheers!	Na zdraví!	nah zdrah-**vee**
Enjoy your meal.	Dobrou chuť.	**doh**-broh khoot
More. / Another.	Více. / Další.	**veet**-seh / **dahl**-shee
The same.	To samé.	toh **sah**-meh
The bill.	Účet.	**oo**-cheht
I'll pay.	Zaplatím.	**zah**-plah-teem
tip	spropitné	**sproh**-pit-neh
Delicious!	Výborné!	**vee**-bohr-neh

PRAGUE

Few cities can match Prague's over-the-top romance, evocative Old World charm...and tourist crowds. Prague is equal parts historic and fun. No other place in Europe has become popular so quickly. And for good reason: Prague—the only Central European capital to escape the bombing of the last century's wars—is one of Europe's best-preserved cities. It's filled with sumptuous Art Nouveau facades, offers tons of cheap Mozart and Vivaldi concerts, and brews some of the best beer in Europe.

Prague is a photographer's delight. You'll wind through walkable neighborhoods, past statues of bishops and pastel facades adorned with gables, balconies, lanterns, and countless little architectural details. Prague itself seems a work of art. Besides its medieval and Baroque look, it's a world of willowy Art Nouveau paintings and architecture. You'll also see rich remnants of its strong Jewish heritage and stark reminders of the communist era. And you'll meet an entrepreneurial mix of locals and expats, each with their own brilliant scheme of how to make money in the tourist trade.

Escape the crowds into the back lanes and pretend you're strolling through the 18th century. Duck into pubs to enjoy the hearty food and good pilsner beer, and tour museums packed with fine art. You'll leave Prague dreaming of coming back.

PLANNING YOUR TIME

A few days in Prague is plenty of time to get a solid feel for the city and enjoy some side-trips. If you're in a rush, you'll need a minimum of two full days (with three nights) for a good introduction to the city.

Keep in mind that Jewish Quarter sights close on Saturday and Jewish holidays. Some museums, mainly in the Old Town, are closed on Monday.

Prague in Two or More Days

Here's my suggested plan for experiencing Prague in two days. With more time, I've offered more suggestions.

Day 1

9:00	Orient yourself to the city's core with my Old Town and Charles Bridge Walk. Along the way, take time to enter some of the sights (such as the Municipal House) and climb the old tower at either end of the Charles Bridge to enjoy the view.
13:00	Have lunch in the Old Town or Lesser Town.
15:00	Explore the Jewish Quarter.
Evening:	Choose among a beer hall, live music, and Black Light Theater.

Day 2

8:00	Zip up to Prague Castle on the tram. Be at St. Vitus Cathedral when it opens at 9:00, then visit the rest of the castle sights.
11:00	As you leave the castle, tour the Lobkowicz Palace.
12:00	Have lunch on Castle Square, at the Strahov Monastery, or in the Lesser Town.
13:30	Explore the Castle Quarter and Lesser Town (options include Loreta Church, Strahov Monastery, Nerudova street, Lesser Town Square, Lennon Wall, or Kampa Island).
15:30	Metro to the Muzeum stop (at the National Museum) and visit Wenceslas Square.
16:30	Tour the Mucha Museum.
Tips:	You could tour the Cold War Museum (on Wenceslas Square) while there, but check tour times in advance and adjust your day plan as needed. If you'd rather sleep in today, flip this plan—visit Wenceslas Square and the Mucha Museum; then tram up to the castle in the early afternoon (after 14:00) as the crowds disperse.

Day 3 and Beyond

With more time, fit in additional museums that interest you. If you have four days or more, Prague has a variety of worthwhile day trips at its doorstep. I'd prioritize Kutná Hora (delightful small town with gorgeous cathedral and famous bone church), the Terezín Memorial (Holocaust history), and/or Konopiště Castle (with

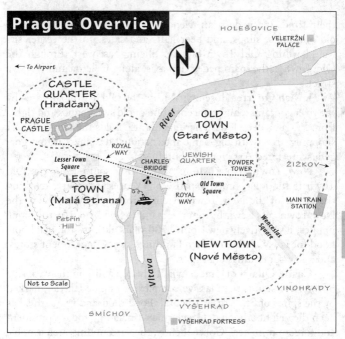

a lived-in Habsburg interior). Český Krumlov is another wonderful destination, but it's a bit far for a day trip—it's much better if you stay overnight.

Orientation to Prague

PRAGUE BY NEIGHBORHOOD

Residents call their town "Praha" (PRAH-hah). It's big, with about 1.3 million people. But during a quick visit, you'll focus on its relatively compact old center.

The Vltava River divides the city in two. East of the river are the Old Town and New Town (with its iconic Wenceslas Square), the main train station, and most of the recommended hotels. To the west of the river is Prague Castle, and below that, the sleepy Lesser Town. Connecting the two halves are several bridges, including the landmark Charles Bridge.

Think of Prague as a collection of neighborhoods. Until about 1800, Prague was four distinct towns with four town squares, all separated by fortified walls. Each town had a unique character, drawn from the personality of its first settlers. Today, much of Prague's charm survives in the distinct spirit of these towns.

Old Town (Staré Město): Nestled in the bend of the river, this is the historic core, almost traffic-free, where most tourists spend their time. It's pedestrian-friendly, with small winding streets, old buildings, shops, and beer halls and cafés. In the center sits the charming Old Town Square. Slicing east-west through the Old Town is the main pedestrian axis, along Celetná and Karlova streets.

Jewish Quarter (Josefov): Within the Old Town, this area by the river contains a high concentration of old synagogues and sights from Prague's deep Jewish heritage. It also holds the city's glitziest shopping area (with big-name international designers filling gorgeously restored Art Nouveau buildings).

New Town (Nové Město): Stretching south from the Old Town is the long, broad expanse of Wenceslas Square, marking the center of the New Town. Arcing around the Old Town, the New Town cuts a swath from riverbank to riverbank. As the name implies, it's relatively new ("only" 600 years old). It's the neighborhood for noisy traffic, modern buildings, fancy department stores, and a few communist-era sights.

Castle Quarter (Hradčany): High atop a hill on the west side of the river stands the massive complex of Prague Castle, marked by the spires of St. Vitus Cathedral. For a thousand years, this has been the neighborhood of Czech rulers (including today's president and foreign minister). Consequently, the surrounding area is noble and leafy, with high art and grand buildings, little commerce, and few pubs.

Lesser Town (Malá Strana): Nestled at the foot of Castle Hill is this pleasant former town of fine palaces and gardens (and a few minor sights). This is Prague's diplomatic neighborhood, made to feel elegant by stately embassies, but lacking some of the funky personality of the Old Town.

The Royal Way: Cutting through the towns—from the Powder Tower through the Old Town, crossing the Charles Bridge, and winding up to St. Vitus Cathedral—is the ancient path of coronation processions. Today, this city spine (the modern streets of Celetná, Karlova, and Nerudova) is marred by tacky trinket shops and jammed by tour groups—explore beyond it if you want to see the real Prague.

TOURIST INFORMATION

TIs are at several key locations, including on the **Old Town Square** (in the Old Town Hall, just to the left of the Astronomical Clock; Mon-Fri 9:00-19:00, Sat-Sun 9:00-18:00; Nov-Easter closes an hour earlier); on the castle side of **Charles Bridge** (daily 10:00-18:00, closed Nov-Easter); and in the Old Town, around the corner from **Havelská Market** (at Rytířská 31; Mon-Sat 9:00-19:00, closed Nov-March). For general tourist information in English, dial 221-714-444 (Mon-Fri 8:00-19:00), or check the useful TI website: www.prague.eu. Look for the helpful transit guide and information on guided walks and bus tours. TIs can also book local guides, concerts, and occasionally hotel rooms.

Monthly event guides include the *Prague Guide* (small fee), and the free *Prague This Month* and *Heart of Europe* (summer only).

Prague Card: This pricey sightseeing pass covers public transit (including the airport bus); admission or discounts to a number of sights; and a free bus tour and river cruise. For most travelers, it's not worth the steep cost (€48/2 days).

ARRIVAL IN PRAGUE

Most visitors arrive at Prague's main train station (Hlavní Nádraží), on the eastern edge of downtown—a 20-minute walk, short taxi ride, or bus ride to the Old Town Square and many of my recommended hotels. Prague's Václav Havel Airport—12 miles from downtown—is easily connected to the city center by public bus, airport bus, minibus shuttle, and taxis. For details on all of these options, see Prague Connections, at the end of this chapter.

HELPFUL HINTS

Rip-Offs: There's no particular risk of violent crime in Prague, but—as in any heavily touristed city—naive tourists can get taken by con artists. Most scams fall into the category of being charged a two-scoop price for one scoop of ice cream, having extra items appear on your restaurant bill, or not getting the correct change. Jaded salesclerks in the tourist zone know that the 20-to-1 exchange rate easily confuses foreigners. Any time you pay for something, make a mental note of how much it costs, how much you're handing over, and how much you expect back. Count your change. Don't be in a rush. Wait until you get all the money you're due.

Freestanding ATMs are notorious for bad rates. Use an ATM attached to an actual bank (look for names that include the word *banka* or *spořitelna,* and avoid Euronet machines).

Pickpockets: They're abundant in Prague. They can be little children or adults dressed as professionals—sometimes even as tourists with jackets draped over their arms to disguise busy fingers. Thieves work crowded and touristy places in teams—for example, they might create a commotion at the door to a Metro or tram car. Assume any big distraction is a smoke-screen for theft, keep things zipped up, and wear a money belt. All of this can sound intimidating, but Prague is safe. Simply stay alert.

Medical Help: A 24-hour **pharmacy** is at Palackého 5 (a block from Wenceslas Square, tel. 224-946-982). For above-standard assistance in English (including dental care), consider

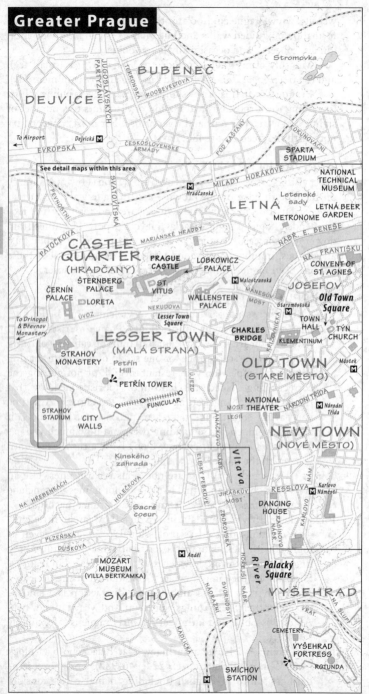

Greater Prague

PRAGUE

Stromovka

BUBENEČ

DEJVICE

JUGOSLÁVSKÝCH PARTYZÁNŮ
TERRONSKÁ
ROOSEVELTOVA

To Airport
Dejvická M

EVROPSKÁ
ČESKOSLOVENSKÉ ARMÁDY
POD KAŠTANY
KORUNOVAČNÍ

SPARTA STADIUM

See detail maps within this area

MILADY HORÁKOVÉ

Hradčanská M

NATIONAL TECHNICAL MUSEUM

LETNÁ
Letenské sady

METRONOME

LETNÁ BEER GARDEN

PEVNOSTNÍ
SVATOVÍTSKÁ
MARIÁNSKÉ HRADBY
PATOČKOVA

NA FRANTIŠKU
NÁBŘ. E. BENEŠE

CASTLE QUARTER
(HRADČANY)

PRAGUE CASTLE

LOBKOWICZ PALACE

CONVENT OF ST. AGNES

ČERNÍN PALACE

ŠTERNBERG PALACE

ST. VITUS

LORETA

M Malostranská
MANESŮV MOST

JOSEFOV

Old Town Square

ÚVOZ
NERUDOVA

WALLENSTEIN PALACE

Staroměstská M

TOWN HALL

TÝN CHURCH

To Drinopol & Břevnov Monastery

Lesser Town Square

CHARLES BRIDGE

KŘIŽOVNICKÁ

KLEMENTINUM

LESSER TOWN
(MALÁ STRANA)

Petřín Hill

OLD TOWN
(STARÉ MĚSTO)

Můstek M

STRAHOV MONASTERY

PETŘÍN TOWER

ÚJEZD

FUNICULAR

NATIONAL THEATER

NÁRODNÍ TŘÍDA

Národní Třída M

STRAHOV STADIUM

CITY WALLS

MOST LEGII

JANÁČKOVO NÁBŘ.

NEW TOWN
(NOVÉ MĚSTO)

Kinského zahrada

ELIŠKY PEŠKOVÉ

JIRÁSKŮV MOST

Vltava

RESSLOVA

Karlovo Náměstí

Karlovo Náměstí M

NA HŘEBENKÁCH

HOLEČKOVA

Sacré coeur

ZBOROVSKÁ

DANCING HOUSE

KARLOVO

RAŠÍNOVO NÁBŘ.

PLZEŇSKÁ

DUŠKOVA

M Anděl

River

Palacký Square

MOZART MUSEUM
(VILLA BERTRAMKA)

SMÍCHOV

NÁDRAŽNÍ

SVORNOSTI NÁBŘ.

HOŘEJŠÍ NÁBŘ.

VYŠEHRAD

NA SLUPI

RADLICKÁ

CEMETERY

VYŠEHRAD FORTRESS

SMÍCHOV STATION

M

ROTUNDA

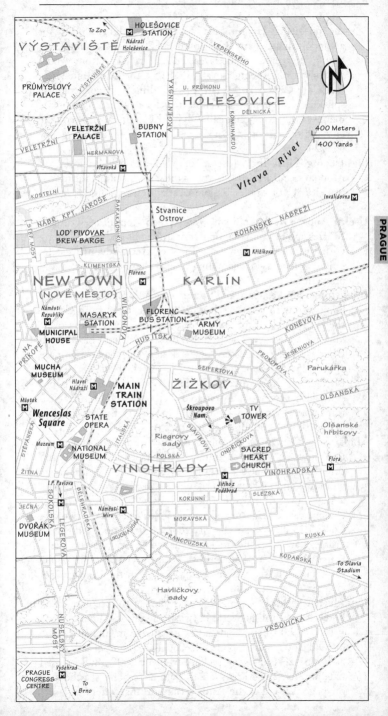

PRAGUE

the top-quality **Hospital Na Homolce** (less than 1,000 Kč for an appointment, daily 8:00-16:00 call 252-922-146, for after-hours emergencies call 257-211-111; bus #167 from Anděl Metro station, Roentgenova 2, Praha 5). The **Canadian Medical Care Center** is a small, private clinic with an English-speaking Czech staff at Veleslavínská 1 in Praha 6 (appointment—3,000 Kč, house call—4,500 Kč, halfway between the city and the airport, tel. 235-360-133, after-hours emergency tel. 724-300-301).

Sightseeing Tips: The Museum of Medieval Art is closed on Mondays, and Jewish Quarter sights are closed on Saturdays. St. Vitus Cathedral at Prague Castle is closed Sunday morning for Mass.

Useful Apps: Czech Tourism's free **Czech Republic—Land of Stories** app has info on popular destinations and events, along with historical background. The free **Beer Adventures** app guides you on a suds-sampling tour of Prague bars, pubs, and breweries.

Bookstores: Shakespeare and Sons is a friendly English-language bookstore with a wide selection of translations from Czech, the latest publications, and a reading space downstairs overlooking a river channel (daily 11:00-19:00, one block from Charles Bridge on Lesser Town side at U Lužického Semináře 10, tel. 257-531-894, www.shakes.cz). In the heart of the Jewish Quarter, the **Franz Kafka Society** has a fine little bookstore with a thoughtfully curated shelf of Czech lit in English translation—from Kafka to Švejk to tales of the Little Mole (daily 10:00-18:00, Široká 14, tel. 224-227-452).

Maps: A good map of Prague is essential. For ease of navigation, look for one with trams and Metro lines marked, and tiny sketches of the sights (30-70 Kč; sold at kiosks, exchange windows, and tobacco stands). The *Kartografie Praha* city map, which shows all the tram lines and major landmarks, also includes a castle diagram and a street index. It comes in two versions: 1:15,000 covers the city center (good enough for most visitors), and 1:25,000 includes the whole city (worthwhile if you're sleeping in the suburbs). If using your mobile phone for navigation, see the tips on page 1092 in the Practicalities chapter.

Laundry: A **full-service laundry** near most of the recommended hotels is at Karolíny Světlé 11 (wash and dry in 3 hours, Mon-Fri 7:30-19:00, closed Sat-Sun, 200 yards from Charles Bridge on Old Town side, mobile 721-030-446); another laundry is at Rybná 27 (same-day pickup, Mon-Fri 8:00-18:00, closed Sat-Sun, tel. 224-812-641; for locations of both, see the map on page 125). **Prague Andy's Laundromat** offers full ser-

Prague's Best Views

Enjoy the "Golden City of a Hundred Spires" during the early evening, when the light is warm and the colors are rich. Good viewpoints include the following:

PRAGUE

- The garden terrace in front of **Strahov Monastery,** above the castle (see page 111)
- The many balconies and spires at **Prague Castle**
- **Villa Richter** restaurants, overlooking the city from just below the castle past the Golden Lane
- The top of either tower on **Charles Bridge**
- **Old Town Square clock tower** (with a handy elevator)
- **Hotel u Prince's** rooftop dining terrace overlooking the Old Town Square (also with an elevator, free but for diners only)
- The steps of the **National Museum** overlooking Wenceslas Square
- The top of the **Žižkov TV tower,** offering spaceship views of the city, in the Žižkov/Vinohrady neighborhood east of the city center (150 Kč for elevator to observatory at 300 feet, free access to Oblaca restaurant at 200-foot level for customers)

vice (weekdays only) and self-service (daily 8:00-20:00, near Náměstí Míru Metro stop at Korunní 14, Praha 2, mobile 723-112-693, www.praguelaundromat.cz).

Bike Rental: Prague has improved its network of bike paths, making bicycles a feasible option for exploring the center of the town and beyond (see http://mapa.prahounakole.cz for a map). Two bike-rental shops are located near the Old Town Square: **Praha Bike** (daily 9:00-22:00, Dlouhá 24, mobile 732-388-880, www.prahabike.cz) and **City Bike** (daily 9:00-19:00, Králodvorská 5, mobile 776-180-284, www.citybike-prague.com). They rent bikes for about 300 Kč for two hours or 500 Kč a day (1,500-Kč deposit), and also organize guided bike tours. Another shop offers **electric bikes** (590 Kč/half-day, 890 Kč/day, April-Oct daily 9:00-19:00, tours available, just above American Embassy in Lesser Town at Vlašská 15, mobile 604-474-546, www.ilikeebike.com).

Car Rental: You won't want or need to drive within compact Prague, but a car can be handy for exploring the countryside. All the biggies have offices in Prague (check each company's website, or ask at the TI).

Travel Service and Tours: Magic Praha is a tiny travel service run by Lída Jánská. A Jill-of-all-trades, she can help with accommodations and transfers throughout the Czech Republic, as well as private tours and side-trips to historic towns (mobile 604-207-225, www.magicpraha.cz, magicpraha@magicpraha.cz).

GETTING AROUND PRAGUE

You can walk nearly everywhere. Brown street signs (in Czech, but with helpful little icons) direct you to tourist landmarks. For a sense of scale, the walk from the Old Town Square to the Charles Bridge takes less than 10 minutes (depending on crowds).

Prague's Pedestrian Freeways: Four pedestrian thoroughfares cut (like congested freeways in US cities) through the essentially traffic-free center of Prague. You'll find yourself swept along on an international river of touristic humanity on the following streets: **Na Příkopě** ("On the Moat";  from the bottom of Wenceslas Square to the Municipal House and Republic Square); **Celetná** (from Municipal House to the Old Town Square); **Karlova** (from the Old Town Square to the Charles Bridge); and **Melantrichova/Na Můstku** (from the bottom of Wenceslas Square to the Old Town Square). The shops along these tourist-clogged arteries are generally tourist traps. If you simply walk a block away, you'll find better values and more charming corners.

Commit to Public Transportation: It's worth figuring out the public transportation system, which helps you reach farther-flung sights (such as Prague Castle), and can save time and sweat jumping from spot to spot within the center. The Metro is slick, the trams fun, and Uber quick and easy. Prague's tram system is especially wonderful—trams rumble by frequently and take you just about anywhere. Be bold and you'll swing through Prague like Tarzan.

By Public Transportation

Excellent, affordable public transit (Metro, trams, and buses) is perhaps the best legacy of the communist era (locals with annual passes ride for 10 Kč a day).

Tickets: The Metro, trams, and buses all use the same tickets:
- 30-minute **short-trip ticket** *(krátkodobá)*, which allows as many transfers as you can make in a half-hour—24 Kč
- 90-minute **standard ticket** *(základní)*—32 Kč
- **24-hour pass** *(jízdenka na 24 hodin)*—110 Kč
- **3-day pass** *(jízdenka na 3 dny)*—310 Kč

Buy tickets from your hotel, at Metro stops, newsstand kiosks, or from machines. To avoid wasting time looking for a ticket-seller when your tram is approaching, stock up on tickets before you set out. Since Prague is a great walking town, most find that having a few individual tickets works better than a pass.

Be sure to validate your ticket as you board the tram or bus, or as you enter the Metro station, by sticking it in the machine, which stamps a time on it. Inspectors routinely ambush ticketless riders (including tourists) and fine them 700 Kč on the spot.

Schedules and Frequency: Trams run every few minutes in the daytime (a schedule is posted at each stop). The Metro closes at midnight, but nighttime tram routes (identified with white numbers on blue backgrounds at tram stops) run all night at 30-minute intervals. You can find more information and a complete route planner in English at www.dpp.cz. The official **Prague Trips by Public Transport app** provides details about routes, fares, and connections, and allows you to buy mobile tickets. You can also pick up a transit guide at the TI.

Trams: Navigate by signs that list the end stations. At the platform, a sign lists all the stops for each tram in order. Remember that trams going one direction leave from one platform, while the other direction might leave from a different platform nearby—maybe across the street or a half-block away. When the tram arrives, open the doors by pressing the green button. Once aboard, validate your ticket in the machine.

As you go, follow along carefully so you'll be ready when your stop comes up. Newer trams have electronic signs that show either the next stop *(příští)*, or a list of upcoming stops. Also, listen to the recorded announcements for the name of the stop you're currently at, followed by the name of the stop that's coming up next. (Confused tourists, thinking they've heard their stop, are

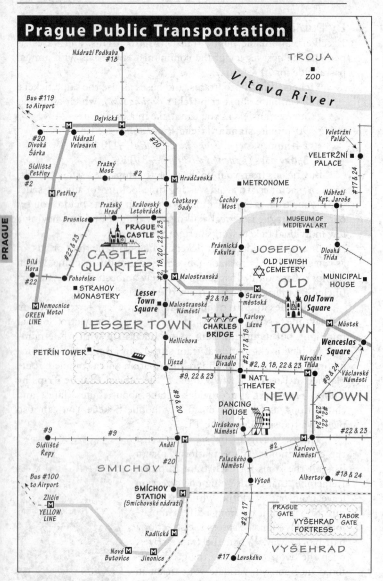

Prague Public Transportation

notorious for rushing off the tram one stop too soon.) It's best to sit on the right near the front, where it's easy to see the sign on the platform of each stop.

Tram #22 (or **#23,** the retro 1960s version) is practically made for sightseeing, connecting the New Town with the Castle Quarter (find the line marked on the Prague Metro map). The tram uses some of the same stops as the Metro (making it easy to get to—or travel on from—the tram route). Of the many stops this tram

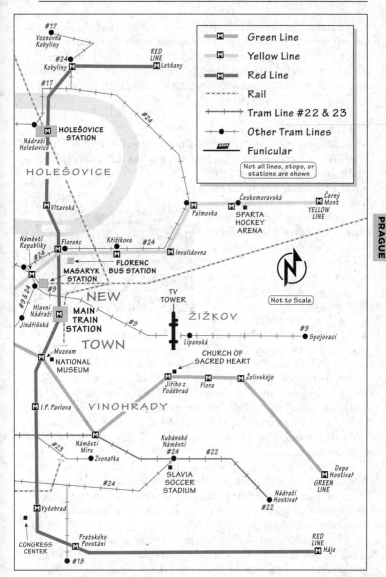

makes, the most convenient are two in the New Town (Národní Třída, between the bottom of Wenceslas Square and the river; and Národní Divadlo, at the National Theater), two in the Lesser Town (Malostranské Náměstí, on the Lesser Town Square; and Malostranská Metro stop, near the riverbank), and three above Prague Castle (Královský Letohrádek—for the Summer Palace and "back door" entry to Prague Castle; Pražský Hrad—for the main castle entry; and Pohořelec—for the Strahov Monastery).

Metro: The three-line Metro system is handy and simple, but doesn't always get you right to the tourist sights (landmarks such as the Old Town Square and Prague Castle are several blocks from the nearest Metro stops). Although it seems that all Metro doors lead to the neighborhood of Výstup, that's simply the Czech word for "exit."

By Uber and Taxi

While Prague is fraught with rip-off taxis, it's well-served by Uber. If you're comfortable with Uber at home, it works the same way here and you can generally get a ride within five minutes with no fuss and at about half the taxi fare. The great things about Uber are that your driver knows exactly where you want to go without you having to pronounce the Czech name, you know exactly what it will cost, and you don't deal with cash.

If you use taxis, here are a few tips to avoid being overcharged: Legitimate local rates are cheap: Drop charge starts at 40 Kč; per-kilometer charge is around 30 Kč; and waiting time per minute is about 6 Kč. These rates are clearly marked on the door, so be sure the cabbie honors them. Also insist that cabbies turn on the meter, and that it's set at the right tariff, or *"sazba"* (usually but not always tariff #1). Unlike in many cities, there's no extra charge for calling a cab—the meter starts only after you get in. Tip by rounding up; locals never tip more than 5 percent.

Have a ballpark idea of what your ride will cost. Figure about 150-200 Kč for a ride between landmarks within the city center (for example, from the main train station to the Old Town Square, or from the Charles Bridge to the castle). Even the longest ride in the center should cost under 300 Kč.

To improve your odds of getting a fair metered rate, call for a cab (or ask someone at your hotel or restaurant to call for you), rather than hailing one on the street. **AAA Taxi** (tel. 222-333-222) and **City Taxi** (tel. 257-257-257) are the most likely to have English-speaking staff and honest cabbies. Avoid cabs waiting at tourist attractions and train stations; these are far more likely to be crooked—waiting to prey on unwary tourists.

And what if the cabbie surprises you at the end with an astronomical fare? If you think you're being overcharged, challenge it. Point to the rates on the door. Get your hotel receptionist to back you up. Pull out your phone and threaten to call the police. (Be-

Prague Pronunciations

English	Czech
Main train station	*Hlavní Nádraží* (HLAV-nee NAH-drah-zhee)
Old Town	*Staré Město* (STAR-eh MYEHS-toh)
Old Town Square	*Staroměstské Náměstí* (STAR-oh-myehst-skeh NAH-myehs-tee)
New Town	*Nové Město* (NOH-vay MYEHS-toh)
Lesser Town	*Malá Strana* (MAH-lah STRAH-nah)
Jewish Quarter	*Josefov* (YOO-zehf-fohf)
Castle Quarter	*Hradčany* (HRAD-chah-nee)
Charles Bridge	*Karlův Most* (KAR-loov most)
Wenceslas Square	*Václavské Náměstí* (vaht-SLAHF-skeh NAH-myehs-tee)
Vltava River	*Vltava* (VUL-tah-vah)

PRAGUE

cause of legislation to curb dishonest cabbies, the police will stand up for you.) Or, simply pay what you think the ride should cost and walk away.

Tours in Prague

WALKING TOURS

A staggering number of small companies offer walking tours of the Old Town, the castle, and more (for the latest, pick up fliers at the TI). Since guiding is a routine side-job for university students, you'll generally get hardworking young guides with fine language skills at good prices. While I'd rather go with my own local guide (described later), public walking tours are cheaper (4 hours for about 450 Kč), cover themes you might not otherwise consider, connect you with other English-speaking travelers, and allow for spontaneity. The quality depends on the guide rather than the company. Your best bet is to show up at the Astronomical Clock a couple of minutes before 8:00, 10:00, or 11:00, then chat with a few of the umbrella-holding guides there. Choose the one you click with. Guides also have fliers advertising additional walks.

"Free" Tours: As is the case all over Europe, "free" walking tours are not really free—you're expected to tip your guide (with paper bills rather than coins) when finished. While these tours are fine for the backpacker and hostel crowd (for whom they're designed), the guides are usually expat students (generally from the US or Australia) who memorize a script and give an entertaining performance as you walk through the Old Town, with little respect

Prague at a Glance

Rather than a checklist of museums, Prague is a fine place to wander around and just take in the fun atmosphere.

In the Old Town

▲▲▲The Old Town Square Magical main square of Old World Prague, with dozens of colorful facades, the dramatic Jan Hus Memorial, looming Týn Church, and fanciful Astronomical Clock. **Hours:** Týn Church generally open to sightseers Tue-Fri 11:00-13:00 & 15:00-17:00, Sat 10:00-17:00, Sun 10:00-12:00, closed Mon; clock strikes on the hour daily 9:00-21:00, until 20:00 in winter; clock tower open Tue-Sun 9:00-21:00, Mon from 11:00. See page 54.

▲▲▲The Charles Bridge Atmospheric, statue-lined bridge that connects the Old Town to the Lesser Town and Prague Castle. See page 69.

▲▲▲Jewish Quarter Finest collection of Jewish sights in Europe, featuring various synagogues and an evocative cemetery. **Hours:** Museum sights open Sun-Fri 9:00-18:00, Nov-March until 16:30, closed Sat and on Jewish holidays; Old-New Synagogue open Sun-Thu 9:00-18:00, off-season until 17:00, Fri closes one hour before sunset, closed Sat and Jewish holidays. See page 70.

▲▲Museum of Medieval Art Best Gothic art in the country, at the former Convent of St. Agnes. **Hours:** Tue-Sun 10:00-18:00, closed Mon. See page 77.

▲Havelská Market Colorful open-air market that sells crafts and produce. **Hours:** Daily 9:00-18:00. See page 66.

In the New Town

▲▲▲Wenceslas Square Lively boulevard at the heart of modern Prague. See page 78.

▲▲Municipal House Pure Art Nouveau architecture, including Prague's largest concert hall and several eateries. **Hours:** Daily 10:00-18:00, but most of interior is viewable by tour only. See page 86.

for serious history. When it comes to guided tours, nothing is free (except for my self-guided audio tour; see page 12).

LOCAL GUIDES

In Prague, hiring a guide is particularly smart (and a ▲▲ experience). Because prices are usually per hour (not per person), small groups can hire an inexpensive guide for several days. Guides meet

▲**Cold War Museum** Re-creation of a nuclear fallout shelter, in the basement of a hotel. **Hours:** English tours depart daily at 14:30, 16:00, and 17:30; more in high season. See page 82.

▲**Mucha Museum** Easy-to-appreciate collection of Art Nouveau works by Czech artist Alfons Mucha. **Hours:** Daily 10:00-18:00. See page 85.

▲**Museum of Communism** The rise and fall of the regime, from start to Velvet finish. **Hours:** Daily 9:00-20:00. See page 86.

In the Lesser Town
▲**Petřín Hill** Lesser Town hill with public art, a funicular, and a replica of the Eiffel Tower. **Hours:** Funicular—daily 8:00-22:00; tower—daily 10:00-22:00, shorter hours off-season. See page 92.

In the Castle Quarter
▲▲▲**St. Vitus Cathedral** The Czech Republic's most important church, featuring a climbable tower and a striking stained-glass window by Art Nouveau artist Alfons Mucha. **Hours:** Daily 9:00-17:00, Nov-March until 16:00, closed Sunday mornings for Mass. See page 99.

▲▲**Prague Castle** Traditional seat of Czech rulers, with St. Vitus Cathedral, Old Royal Palace, Basilica of St. George, shop-lined Golden Lane, and lots of crowds. **Hours:** Castle sights—daily 9:00-17:00, Nov-March until 16:00; castle grounds—daily 5:00-24:00. See page 93.

▲▲**Lobkowicz Palace** Delightful private art collection of a Czech noble family. **Hours:** Daily 10:00-18:00. See page 108.

▲**Strahov Monastery and Library** Baroque center of learning, with ornate reading rooms and old-fashioned science exhibits. **Hours:** Daily 9:00-12:00 & 13:00-17:00. See page 111.

▲**Loreta Church** Beautiful Baroque church, a pilgrim magnet for centuries, containing what some believe to be part of Mary's house from Nazareth. **Hours:** Daily 9:00-17:00, Nov-March 9:30-16:00. See page 113.

PRAGUE

you wherever you like and tailor the tour to your interests. Visit their websites for details on various walks, airport transfers, countryside excursions, and other services offered, and then make arrangements by email.

Personal Prague Guide Service: Šárka Kačabová uses her teaching background to help you understand Czech culture, and has a team of personable and knowledgeable guides (RS% prices:

600 Kč/hour for 2-3 people, 800 Kč/hour for 4-8 people, fifth hour free, mobile 777-225-205, www.personalpragueguide.com, sarka@me.com).

PragueWalker: Katerina Svobodová, a hardworking historian-guide who knows her stuff, manages a team of enthusiastic and friendly guides (700 Kč/hour for groups up to 6 people; mobile 603-181-300, www.praguewalker.com, katerina@praguewalker.com).

Individual Guides: These generally young guides (which is good, because they learned their trade post-communism) typically charge about 2,000-2,500 Kč for a half-day tour.

Jana Hronková has a natural style—a welcome change from the more strict professionalism of some of the busier guides—and a penchant for the Jewish Quarter (mobile 732-185-180, www.experience-prague.info, janahronkova@hotmail.com). **Zuzana Tlášková** speaks English as well as Hebrew (mobile 774-131-335, tlaskovaz@seznam.cz). **Martin Bělohradský,** formerly an organic chemistry professor, is particularly enthusiastic about fine arts and architecture (mobile 723-414-565, martinb5666@gmail.com). **Jana Krátká** enjoys sharing Prague's tumultuous 20th-century history with visitors (mobile 776-571-538, janapragueguide@gmail.com). Friendly **Petra Vondroušová** designs tours to fit your interests (mobile 602-319-420, www.compactprague.com, petra.vondrous@seznam.cz). To add more nuance and context to this guidebook, consider a tour with its co-author, **Honza Vihan** (mobile 603-418-148, honzavihan@hotmail.com). **Kamil and Pavlína** run a family business specializing in tours of Prague and beyond. They also provide sightseeing and transport as far as Vienna and Berlin (mobile 605-701-861, www.prague-extra.com, info@prague-extra.com). **Running Tours Prague** are guided by Radim Prahl, a local with an appetite for ultra-marathons; he'll run you past monuments, through parks, and down back alleys at your own pace (1,500 Kč for two people; mobile 777-288-862, www.runningtoursprague.com).

JEWISH QUARTER TOURS

Jewish guides (of varying quality) meet small groups twice daily in season for three-hour tours in English of the Jewish Quarter. **Wittmann Tours** charges 1,100 Kč, which includes entry to the Old-New Synagogue and the six other major Jewish Quarter sights (Sun-Fri at 10:30, also at 14:00 in May-Oct, no tours Sat and Jan-mid-March, minimum three people). Tours meet in the little park (just beyond the café), directly in front of Hotel InterContinental at the end of Pařížská street. They also offer an all-day minibus tour to the Terezín Memorial (tel. 603-168-427 or 603-426-564, www.

wittmann-tours.com). In addition, several of the **private local guides** recommended earlier do good tours of the Jewish Quarter.

TOURS OUTSIDE OF PRAGUE

To get beyond the sights listed in most guidebooks, or for a deeply personal look at the usual destinations, call **Tom and Marie Zahn.** Tom is American, Marie is Czech, and together they organize and lead family-friendly day excursions (in Prague and through-out the country). Their tours are creative and affordable, and they teach travelers how to find off-the-beaten-track destinations on their own. Their specialty is Personal Ancestral Tours & History (P.A.T.H.)—with sufficient notice, they can help Czech descen-dants find their ancestral homes, perhaps even a long-lost relative. Tom and Marie can also help with other parts of your Eastern European travel by linking you with associates in other countries, especially Germany, Hungary, Poland, Romania, Slovakia, and Ukraine (US tel. 360-450-5959, Czech tel. 257-940-113, www.pathways.cz for tours, www.pathfinders.cz for genealogy research, info@pathfinders.cz).

Reverend Jan Dus, an enthusiastic pastor who lived in the US for several years, now serves a small congregation about 100 miles east of Prague. Jan can design itineraries, and likes to help travel-ers connect with locals in little towns, particularly in northeastern Bohemia and Moravia. He also has an outstanding track record in providing genealogical services (US tel. 800-807-1562, www.revjan.com, rev.jan.services@gmail.com).

Old Town and Charles Bridge Walk

Nestled in the bend of the river is Prague's compact, pedestrian-friendly Old Town. A boomtown since the 11th century, the Old Town has long been the busy commercial quarter, filled with mer-chants, guilds, students, and supporters of the Church and social reformer Jan Hus (who wanted a Czech-style Catholicism). Here Prague feels like the Gothic metropolis that it—at its heart—still is. It's also Prague's tourism ground zero, jammed with tasteful landmarks and tacky amusements alike.

This walk starts in the heart of the neighborhood, the **Old Town Square** (rated ▲▲▲). From here we'll snake through the surrounding neighborhood, get a glimpse of the New Town (at Wenceslas Square), and end on the Charles Bridge—one of the most atmospheric spots in all of Europe.

Length of This Walk: Allow three hours for this walk.

Crowd Warning: Much of this walk is extremely touristy and packed with sightseers all day long. A huge bottleneck occurs in front of the Astronomical Clock near the top of each hour.

PRAGUE

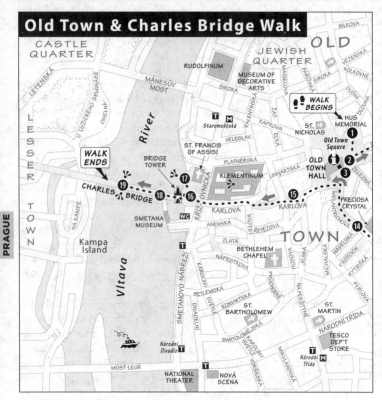

Old Town & Charles Bridge Walk

Tours: 🎧 My Prague City Walk audio tour covers sights in both the Old Town and New Town.

◐ SELF-GUIDED WALK

• *Begin with the Old Town Square's centerpiece, the...*

❶ Memorial to Jan Hus

This monument is an enduring icon of the long struggle for (Czech) freedom. In the center, Jan Hus—the reformer who became the

symbol of Czech nationalism—stands tall amid the rising flames. Hus, born in 1369, was a priest who challenged both the Church's and the secular rulers' claim to dominion. His defiant stance—as depicted so powerfully in this monument—galvanized the Czech people, who

rallied to fight not just for their religious beliefs but also for inde-

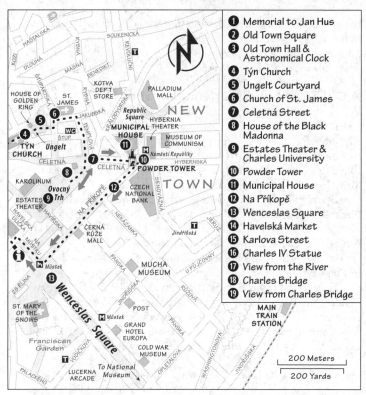

① Memorial to Jan Hus
② Old Town Square
③ Old Town Hall & Astronomical Clock
④ Týn Church
⑤ Ungelt Courtyard
⑥ Church of St. James
⑦ Celetná Street
⑧ House of the Black Madonna
⑨ Estates Theater & Charles University
⑩ Powder Tower
⑪ Municipal House
⑫ Na Příkopě
⑬ Wenceslas Square
⑭ Havelská Market
⑮ Karlova Street
⑯ Charles IV Statue
⑰ View from the River
⑱ Charles Bridge
⑲ View from Charles Bridge

PRAGUE

pendence from any man-made (rather than natural, or God-given) controls.

But Hus was centuries ahead of his time. He was arrested, charged with heresy, excommunicated, and, in 1415, burned at the stake. His followers, called Hussites, picked up the torch and fought on for two decades in the Hussite Wars, which killed tens of thousands and left Bohemia a virtual wasteland.

Surrounding Hus's statue are the Hussites who battled the entrenched powers of their time. Look into the faces of these medieval warriors of faith—it was a bitter fight. Two hundred years later, in 1620, a disorganized Czech rebellion was crushed by the united Habsburgs at White Mountain just outside Prague—effectively ending Czech independence and freedom of worship for three centuries.

Each subsequent age has interpreted Hus to its liking: For Protestants, Hus was the founder of the first Protestant church (though he was actually an ardent Catholic); for revolutionaries, this critic of the temporal powers was a proponent of social equality; for nationalists, this Czech preacher was the defender of the language; and for communists, this ideologue was first to preach the gospel of communal ownership (though he never spoke against individual property per se).

• *Stepping away from the Hus Memorial, stand in the center of the Old Town Square, and take a 360-degree...*

❷ Old Town Square Orientation Spin Tour

Whirl clockwise to get a look at Prague's diverse architectural styles: Gothic, Renaissance, Baroque, Rococo, and Art Nouveau. Remember, Prague was largely spared the devastating aerial bombardments of World War II that leveled so many European cities (like Berlin, Warsaw, and Budapest). Few places can match the Old Town Square for Old World charm.

Start with the green domes of the Baroque **Church of St. Nicholas.** Originally Catholic, now Hussite, this church is a popular venue for concerts. The Jewish Quarter is a few blocks behind the church, down the uniquely tree-lined "Paris Street" (Pařížská)—which also has the best lineup of Art Nouveau houses in Prague.

Spin to the right. Behind the Hus Memorial is a fine yellow building that introduces us to Prague's wonderful world of Art Nouveau: pastel colors, fanciful stonework, wrought-iron balconies, colorful murals—and what are those firemen statues on top doing? Prague's architecture is a wonderland of ornamental details.

Continue spinning a few doors to the right to the large, red-and-tan Rococo **Kinský Palace,** which displays the National Gallery's top-notch temporary exhibits (there's a handy WC in the courtyard).

Immediately to the right of the Rococo palace stands the tower-like **House by the Bell,** one of the finest examples of a 13th-century Gothic patrician house anywhere in Europe (also the oldest building on the square).

Farther to the right is the towering, Gothic **Týn Church** (pron. "teen"), with its fanciful twin spires. It's been the Old Town's leading church in every era. In medieval times, it was Catholic. When the Hussites came to dominate the city (c. 1420s), they made it the headquarters of their faith. After the Habsburg victory in 1620, it reverted to Catholicism. The symbolism tells the story: Between the church's two towers, find a golden medallion of the Virgin Mary. Beneath that is a niche with a golden chalice. In Hussite times, the chalice symbolized their cause—that all should be able to take Communion. When the

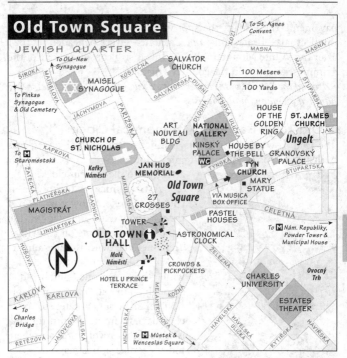

Catholics triumphed, they melted down the original chalice and made it into the golden image of Mary (above). In 2016, the chalice was returned to the niche.

The row of pastel houses in front of Týn Church has a mixture of Gothic, Renaissance, and Baroque facades and gables. If you like live music, the convenient **Via Musica box office** near the church's front door has all the concert options; we'll pass it later on this walk.

Spinning right, to the south side of the square, take in more **glorious facades,** each a different color with a different gable on top—step gables, triangular, bell-shaped. The tan 19th-century Neo-Gothic house at #16 has a steepled bay window and a mural of St. Wenceslas on horseback.

Finally, you reach the pointed 250-foot-tall spire marking the 14th-century **Old Town Hall.** In the 19th century, a building was constructed on the square's west side that once stretched from the Old Town to the Church of St. Nicholas. Then, in the last days of World War II, German tanks knocked it down...to the joy of many Prague citizens who considered it an ugly 19th-century stain on the medieval square.

Approach the Old Town Hall. At the base of the tower, near the corner of the tree-filled park, find **27 white crosses** inlaid in the pavement. These mark the spot where 27 nobles, merchants, and intellectuals—Protestants *and* Catholics—were beheaded in 1621 after the White Mountain defeat. This is still considered one of the grimmest chapters in the country's history.

• *Around the left side of the tower are two big, fancy, old clock faces, being admired by many, many tourists.*

❸ Old Town Hall and Astronomical Clock

The Old Town Hall, with its distinctive trapezoidal tower, was built in the 1350s, during Prague's Golden Age. First, turn your attention to the famous clock.

Astronomical Clock: See if you can figure out how it works. Of the two giant dials on the tower, the top one tells the time on two rings: The inner one, with Roman numerals, is similar to present-day clocks, while the outer one, numbered 1 through 24 in a strange but readable Bohemian script, rotates to reset each day at sunset. Within the dial is yet another revolving disc, where today's zodiac sign is marked.

If all this seems complex, it must have been a marvel in the early 1400s, when the clock was installed. Remember that back then, everything revolved around the Earth (the fixed middle background—with Prague marking the center, of course). The clock was heavily damaged during World War II, and much of what you see today is a reconstruction.

The second dial, below the clock, was added in the 19th century. It shows the signs of the zodiac, scenes from the seasons of a rural peasant's life, and a ring of saints' names. There's one for each day of the year, and a marker on top indicates today's special saint. In the center is a castle, symbolizing Prague.

Four statues flank the upper clock. These politically incorrect symbols evoke a 15th-century outlook: The figure staring into a

mirror stands for vanity, a Jewish moneylender holding a bag of coins is greed, and (on the right side) a Turk with a mandolin symbolizes hedonism. All these worldly goals are vain in the face of Death, whose hourglass reminds us that our time is unavoidably running out.

The clock strikes the top of

Jan Hus and the Early Reformers

Jan Hus (c. 1369-1415) lived and preached more than a century before Martin Luther (1483-1546), but they had many things in common. Both were college professors as well as priests. Both drew huge public crowds as they preached in their university chapels. Both condemned Church corruption, promoted local religious autonomy, and advocated for letting the common people participate more in worship rituals. Both established their national languages. (It's Hus who gave the Czech alphabet its unique accent marks so that the letters could fit the sounds.) And, by challenging established authority, both got in big trouble.

Hus was born in the small southern Bohemian town of Husinec, and moved to Prague to study at the university. He served as a rector at Charles University starting in 1402. Preaching from the pulpit in Bethlehem Chapel (still open to the public), Hus drew inspiration from the English philosopher John Wycliffe (c. 1320-1384), who was an early advocate of reforming the Catholic Church to strip the clergy of its power.

Hus' revolutionary sermons drew huge crowds of reverent but progressive-minded Czechs. He proposed that the congregation should be more involved in worship (for example, be allowed to drink the wine at Communion) and have services and scriptures written in the people's language, not in Latin. Even after he was excommunicated in 1410, Hus continued preaching his message.

In 1414, the Roman Catholic Church convened the Council of Constance to grapple with the controversies of the day. First they posthumously excommunicated Wycliffe, proclaiming him a heretic and exhuming his corpse to symbolically burn at the stake. Then they called Hus to Constance, where on July 6, 1415, they declared him a heretic. After refusing to recant his beliefs and praying that God would forgive his enemies, Hus was tied to a stake and burned alive. But by this time, Hus' challenging ideas had been embraced by many Czechs, and sparked the bloodiest civil war in the country's history.

The Council, this early Catholic precursor to the Counter-Reformation, kept things under control for three generations. But in the 16th century, a German monk named Martin Luther found a more progressive climate for these same revolutionary ideas. Thanks to the new printing press, and his more widely spoken German language, Luther was able to spread his message cheaply and effectively. While Hus loosened Rome's grip on Christianity, Luther orchestrated the Reformation that finally broke it. Today, both are honored as national heroes as well as religious reformers.

the hour and puts on a little **glockenspiel show** daily from 9:00 to 21:00 (until 20:00 in winter). As the hour approaches, keep your eye on Death. First, Death tips his hourglass and pulls the cord, ringing the bell, while the moneylender jingles his purse. Then the windows open and the 12 apostles shuffle past, acknowledging the gang of onlookers. Finally, the rooster at the very top crows and the hour is rung. The hour is often wrong because of Daylight Saving Time (completely senseless to 15th-century clockmakers).

Sights Inside the Old Town Hall: The ornately carved Gothic entrance door to the left of the clock leads to the TI, a pay WC, and the ticket desk for the clock tower elevator and Old Town Hall tours. Step into the **entry hall** (free). It's beautifully decorated with a 1904 Art Nouveau mosaic that celebrates Prague (Lady Prague on the throne is being honored by characters representing all the nationalities of the Habsburg Empire) and various Czech mythological scenes.

You can pay to see other sights inside. One ticket (250 Kč, sold on floors 1 and 3) covers the tour of the Old Town Hall—you'll see a few sterile rooms and the workings of the Astronomical Clock—as well as the trip up the tower by elevator (from floor 3) for the big view (Tue-Sun 9:00-21:00, Mon from 11:00; 4 tours/day in English—usually noon, 14:00, 16:00, and 18:00; 45 minutes).

• *Now head back across the square to tour the pointy Týn Church. Enter by making your way through the cluster of buildings in front of it. (If the church is not open, you can usually look in from the locked gate just inside the door.)*

❹ Týn Church

This is the Old Town's main church (worth ▲). While it has roots dating back to the 1100s, this structure dates from Prague's Golden Age. It was built around 1360 as the university church by the same architect who did St. Vitus Cathedral at Prague Castle.

Cost and Hours: 25 Kč requested donation; Tue-Fri 11:00-13:00 & 15:00-17:00, Sat 10:00-17:00, Sun 10:00-12:00, closed Mon.

Visiting the Church: The structure is full of light, with soaring Gothic arches. The ornamentation reflects the church's troubled history. Originally Catholic, it was taken over by the Hussites, who whitewashed it and stripped it of Catholic icons. When the Catholic Habsburgs retook the church, they redecorated with a vengeance—encrusting its once elegant and pure Gothic columns with ornate Baroque altars and statues of Mary and the saints.

At the front-right corner of the church (to the right of the pulpit), on the pillar is a brown stone slab showing a man in armor with a beard and ruff collar, his hand resting on a globe. This is

Tycho Brahe (1546-1601), the first modern astronomer—whom the Habsburgs brought with them while they ruled Prague.

Now circle around to face the stunning **main altar,** topped with a statue of the archangel Michael with a flaming sword. A painting (on the lower level) shows Mary ascending to heaven where (in the next painting up) she's to be crowned. To the right of the altar is a statue of one of Prague's patron saints—John of Nepomuk (always easy to identify thanks to his halo of stars).

You're surrounded by the **double-eagle symbol** of the Catholic Habsburgs: on the flag borne by a knight statue on the altar, atop the organ behind you (Prague's oldest), and above you on the ceiling.

Leaving the Church: After exiting the church, walk through the **Via Musica** ticket office (on your immediate right; a handy place to get tickets for live classical music tonight—see page 120). Leaving at the far end, turn right, where you'll walk by the northern (formerly main) entrance to the Týn Church with the most delicate pieces of Gothic stone masonry in town—all original 14th-century.

To the left across the street, look at the fine Renaissance building with graffiti and openings for muskets. In what was economically the most important place in the Old Town, this was a fortress within a fortified town. Notice the carved stone gate to a courtyard and also the house to the left.

Tucked immediately behind Týn Church is a welcome oasis of tranquility in the midst of the Old Town Square hubbub.

• *Through an imposing gate, enter the courtyard called the Ungelt, once the commercial nucleus of medieval Prague.*

❺ The Ungelt Courtyard

This pleasant, cobbled, quiet courtyard of upscale restaurants and shops is one of the Old Town's oldest places. During the Bohemian Golden Age (c. 1200-1400), the Ungelt was a multicultural hub of international trade. Prague—located at the geographical center of Europe—attracted Germans selling furs, Italians selling fine art, Frenchmen selling cloth, and Arabs selling spices. They converged on this courtyard, where they could store their goods and pay their customs (which is what *Ungelt* means, in German). In return, the king granted them protection, housing, and a stable for their horses. By day, they'd sell their wares on the Old Town Square. At night, they'd return here to drink and exchange news. After centuries of disuse, the Ungelt has been marvelously restored—a great place for dinner, and a reminder that Prague has been a cosmopolitan center for most of its history.

• *Exit the Ungelt at the far end. Just to your left, across the street, is the...*

❻ Church of St. James (Kostel Sv. Jakuba)

Perhaps the most beautiful church interior in the Old Town, the Church of St. James (worth ▲) has been the home of the Minorite

Order almost as long as merchants have occupied the Ungelt. A medieval city was a complex phenomenon: Commerce and a life of contemplation existed side by side.

Step inside or, if it's locked, peek through the glass door. Artistically, St. James is a stunning example of how simple medieval spaces could be rebuilt into sumptuous feasts of Baroque decoration. The original interior was destroyed by fire in 1689; what's here now is an early-18th-century remodel. The blue light in the altar highlights one of Prague's most venerated treasures—the bejeweled Madonna Pietatis. Above the pietà, as if held aloft by hummingbird-like angels, is a painting of the martyrdom of St. James.

Cost and Hours: Free, Tue-Sun 9:30-12:00 & 14:00-16:00, closed Mon.

• *Exiting the church, do a U-turn to the left (heading up Jakubská street, along the side of the church, past some rough-looking bars). After one block, turn right on Templová street. Head two blocks down the street (passing a nice view of the Týn Church's rear end, and some self-proclaimed "deluxe toilets") and go through the arcaded passageway, where you emerge onto* ❼ **Celetná Street** *(since the 10th century, this has been a corridor in the busy commercial quarter—filled with merchants and guilds).*

To your right is a striking, angular, cinnamon-colored building called the...

❽ House of the Black Madonna (Dům u Černé Matky Boží)

Back around the turn of the 20th century, Prague was a center of avant-garde art. Art Nouveau blossomed here (as we'll soon see), as did Cubism. The House of the Black Madonna's Cubist exterior is a marvel of rectangular windows and cornices— stand back and see how masterfully it makes its statement while mixing with its neighbors...then get up close and study the details. The interior houses a Cubist café (the recommended Grand Café Orient, one flight up the parabolic spiral staircase)—complete with cube-shaped chairs and square-shaped rolls. The Kubista gallery on the far corner shows more examples of this unique style.

• *The long skinny square that begins just to the left of the Cubist house is the former fruit market (Ovocný Trh). For a peek at the local university and a historic theater, side-trip to the end of this square, then return to this spot.*

❾ Estates Theater and Charles University

The **Estates Theater** (Stavovské Divadlo) is the fancy green-and-white Neoclassical building at the end of the square. Built in the 1780s in a deliberately Parisian style, it was the prime opera venue in Prague at a time when an Austrian prodigy was changing the course of music. Mozart premiered *Don Giovanni* in this building (with a bronze statue of Il Commendatore, a character from that opera, duly flanking the main entrance), and he directed many of his works here. Today, the Estates Theater continues to produce *The Marriage of Figaro, Don Giovanni,* and *The Magic Flute.*

The main building of Prague's **Charles University,** the Karolinum, is next door (on the right as you face the theater, tucked down a little courtyard). Prague in the late 1500s was one of the most enlightened places in Europe. Astronomers Tycho Brahe (who tracked the planets) and his assistant Johannes Kepler (who formulated the laws of motion) both worked here. Charles University has always been at the center of Czech political thinking and revolutions, from Jan Hus in the 15th century to the passionately patriotic Czech students who swept communists out of power in the Velvet Revolution. The ground-floor Gothic interior of the Karolinum can be visited for free—find the modern main entrance in the little fenced-off courtyard by the lions fountain (just turn left as you walk past the guard).

• *Return to the House of the Black Madonna, then turn right and head up busy Celetná street to the big, black...*

❿ Powder Tower

The 500-year-old Powder Tower was the main gate of the old town wall. It also housed the city's gunpowder—hence the name. This is the only surviving bit of the wall that was built to defend the city in

the 1400s. (Though you can go inside, it's not worth paying to tour the interior.)

• *Pass regally through the Powder Tower. In so doing, you're leaving the Old Town. You emerge into a big, busy intersection. To your left is the Municipal House, a cream-colored building topped with a green dome. Find a good spot where you can view the facade.*

⓫ Municipal House (Obecní Dům)

The Municipal House is the "pearl of Czech Art Nouveau." Art Nouveau flourished during the same period as the Eiffel Tower and Europe's great Industrial Age train stations.

The same engineering prowess and technological advances that went into making those huge erector-set rigid buildings were used by artistic architects to create quite the opposite effect: curvy, organically flowing lines, inspired by vines and curvaceous women. Art Nouveau was a reaction against the sterility of modern-age construction. Look at the elaborate wrought-iron balcony—flanked by bronze Atlases hefting their lanterns—and the lovely stained glass (like in the entrance arcade).

Mosaics and sculptural knickknacks (see the faces above the windows) made the building's facade colorful and joyous. Study the bright mosaic above the balcony, called *Homage to Prague.* A symbol of the city, the goddess Praha presides over a land of peace and high culture—an image that stoked cultural pride and nationalist sentiment. On the balcony is a medallion showing the three-tower castle that is the symbol of Prague.

The Municipal House was built in the early 1900s, when Czech nationalism was at a fever pitch. Having been ruled by the Austrian Habsburgs for the previous 300 years, the Czechs were demanding independence. This building was drenched in patriotic Czech themes. Within a few short years, in 1918, the nation of Czechoslovakia was formed—and the independence proclamation was announced to the people right here, from the balcony of the Municipal House.

The interior of the Municipal House has some of Europe's finest Art Nouveau decor and is worth ▲▲. It's free to enter and wander the public areas. While to really appreciate the building you must attend a concert here or take one of the excellent tours offered throughout the day, any visit here gets a sweet dose of Art

Prague: The Queen of Art Nouveau

Prague is Europe's best city for Art Nouveau. That's the style of art and architecture that flourished throughout Europe around 1900. It was called "nouveau"—or new—because it was associated with all things modern: technology, social progress, and enlightened thinking. Art Nouveau was neo-nothing, but instead a fresh answer to all the revival styles of the late-19th century, and an organic response to the Eiffel Tower art of the Industrial Age.

By taking advantage of recent advances in engineering, Art Nouveau liberated the artist in each architect. Notice the curves and motifs expressing originality—every facade is unique. Artists such as Alfons Mucha believed that the style should apply to all facets of daily life. They designed everything from buildings and furniture to typefaces and cigarette packs.

Though Art Nouveau was born in Paris, it's in Prague where you'll find some of its greatest hits: the Municipal House and nearby buildings, Grand Hotel Europa (on Wenceslas Square), the exuberant facades of the Jewish Quarter, the Jerusalem Synagogue, and—especially—the work of Alfons Mucha. You can see his stained-glass window in St. Vitus Cathedral (at Prague Castle) and his art at the excellent Mucha Museum (near Wenceslas Square). The fate of Mucha's final masterpiece, *The Slav Epic,* is still up in the air. Ask at the Mucha Museum ticket desk for the latest update.

PRAGUE

Nouveau. (For details on visiting the Municipal House interior, see page 86.)

• *Now head west down Na Příkopě (to the left as you face the Powder Tower).*

⓫ Na Příkopě, the Old City Wall

The street called Na Příkopě was where the old city wall once stood. More specifically, the name Na Příkopě means "On the Moat," and you're walking along what was once the moat outside the wall. To your right is the Old Town. To the left, the New. Look at your city map and conceptualize medieval Prague's smart design: The city was protected on two sides by its river, and on the other two sides by its walls (marked by the modern streets called Na Příkopě, Revoluční, and Národní Třída). The only river crossing back then was the fortified Charles Bridge.

• *Continue up Na Příkopě street to an intersection (and nearby Metro stop) called Můstek. To your left stretches the vast expanse of the wide boulevard called...*

⓭ Wenceslas Square

Wenceslas Square—with the National Museum and landmark statue of St. Wenceslas at the very top—is the centerpiece of Prague's New Town (rated ▲▲▲). This square was originally founded as a thriving horse market. Today it's a modern world of high-fashion stores, glitzy shopping malls, fine old facades (and some jarringly modern ones), fast-food restaurants, and sausage stands.

• *Let's plunge back into the Old Town and return to the Old Town Square. Turn around, and with your back to Wenceslas Square, head downhill on the street called Na Můstku—"along the bridge" that crossed the moat (příkopě) we've been following until now. After one touristy block, Na Můstku jogs slightly to the left and becomes Melantrichova. A block farther along, on the left, is the thriving...*

⓮ Havelská Market

This open-air market, offering crafts and produce, was first set up in the 13th century for the German trading community. Though heavy on souvenirs these days, the market (worth ▲) still feeds hungry locals and vagabonds. Lined with inviting benches, it's an ideal place to enjoy a healthy snack—and merchants are happy to sell a single vegetable or piece of fruit. The market is also a fun place to browse for crafts. It's a homegrown, homemade kind of place; you may be dealing with the actual artist or farmer. The cafés in the old arcades offer a relaxing vantage point from which to view the action.

• *Continue along Melantrichova street. Eventually—after passing increasingly tacky souvenir shops—Melantrichova curves right and spills out at the Old Town Square, right by the Astronomical Clock. At the clock, turn left down Karlova street. The rest of our walk follows Karlova to the Charles Bridge. Begin by heading along the top of the Small Market Square (Malé Náměstí, with lots of outdoor tables), then follow Karlova's twisting course—Karlova street signs keep you on track, and Karlův Most signs point to the bridge. Or just go generally downhill and follow the crowds.*

⓰ Karlova Street

Although traffic-free, Karlova street is utterly jammed with tourists as it winds toward the Charles Bridge. But the route has plenty of historic charm if you're able to ignore the contemporary tourism. As you walk, look up. Notice historic symbols and signs of shops, which advertised who lived there or what they sold. Cornerstones, designed to protect buildings from careening carriages, also date from centuries past.

The touristy feeding-frenzy of today's Prague is at its ugliest along this commercial gauntlet. Obviously, you'll find few good values on this drag.

The **Klementinum** (which once housed Charles University's library) is the large building that borders Karlova street on the right. Just past the intersection with Liliová, where the street opens into a little square, turn right through the archway (at #1) and into a tranquil courtyard that feels an eternity away from the touristy hubbub of Karlova. You can also visit the Klementinum's impressive ▲ Baroque interior on a guided tour.

• *Karlova street leads directly to a tall medieval tower that marks the start of Charles Bridge. But before entering the bridge, stop on this side of the river. To the right of the tower is a little park with a great view of both the bridge and the rest of Prague across the river.*

⓱ Charles IV Statue: The Bohemian Golden Age

Start with the statue of the bridge's namesake, Charles IV (1316-1378). Look familiar? He's the guy on the 100-koruna bill. Charles was the Holy Roman Emperor who ruled his vast empire from Prague in the 14th century—a high-water mark in the city's history. The statue shows one of Charles' many accomplishments: He holds a contract establishing Charles University, the first in central Europe. The women around the pedestal symbolize the school's four traditional subjects: theology, the arts, law, and medicine.

Charles was the preeminent figure in Europe in the Late Middle Ages, and the father of the Prague we enjoy today. His domain encompassed the modern Czech Republic, and parts of Germany, Austria, Italy, and the Low Countries.

Charles was cosmopolitan. Born in Prague, raised in Paris, crowned in Rome, and inspired by the luxury-loving pope in Avignon, Charles returned home bringing Europe's culture with him.

Besides founding Charles University, he built Charles Bridge, much of Prague Castle and St. Vitus Cathedral, and the New Town (modeled on Paris). His Golden Bull of 1356 served as Europe's constitution for centuries (and gave anti-Semite Charles first right to the property of Jews). Power-hungry, he expanded his empire through networking and shrewd marriages, not war. Charles traded ideas with the Italian poet Petrarch and imported artists from France, Italy, and Flanders (inspiring the art of the Museum of Medieval Art—described later, under "Sights in the Old Town"). Under Charles, Prague became the most cultured city in Europe. Seemingly the only thing Charles did not succeed in was renaming Prague: He wanted it to be called "New Jerusalem."

Now look up at the **bridge tower** (which you can climb for wonderful views, see next stop). Built by Charles, it's one of the finest Gothic gates anywhere. The statuary shows the 14th-century hierarchy of society: people at street level, above them kings, and bishops above the kings.

• *Stroll to the riverside, belly up to the banister, and take in the...*

❼ View from the River

Before you are the Vltava River and Charles Bridge. Across the river, atop the hill, is Prague Castle topped by the prickly spires of St. Vitus Cathedral. **Prague Castle** has been the seat of power in this region for over a thousand years, since the time of Wenceslas. By some measures, it's the biggest castle on earth.

The **Vltava River** (from Celtic "wild waters") is better known by the German mutation of the same name, Moldau. It bubbles up from the Šumava Hills in southern Bohemia and runs 270 miles through a diverse landscape, like a thread connecting the Czech people. As we've learned, the Czechs have struggled heroically to carve out their identity while surrounded by mightier neighbors— Austrians, Germans, and Russians. The Vltava is their shared artery.

The **view of Charles Bridge** from here is photogenic to the max. The historic stone bridge, commissioned in 1342, connects the Old Town with the district called the Lesser Town at the base of the castle across the river. The bridge is almost seven football fields long, lined with lanterns and 30 statues, and bookmarked at each end with medieval towers.

You can climb either of the bridge towers. The tower on the **Old Town side** of the river (Staroměstská Mostecká Věž) is the one above you. Climbing its 138 steps rewards you with some of Prague's best views: a stunning vista of the bridge, jammed with people heading for the castle; and 180 degrees away, a perfect panorama that reminds you why Prague is called the "Golden City of a Hundred Spires." On the **Lesser Town side** (Malostranská Mostecká Věž), you can huff up 146 steps for fine views of the bridge, the neighborhood rooftops, and the castle. If you're trying to decide which to climb, consider that for snapping photos, the light is better if you climb the Old Town tower early in the day, and the Lesser Town tower late in the day (90 Kč to climb each tower, daily 10:00-22:00, March and Oct until 20:00, Nov-Feb until 18:00).

• *Now wander onto the bridge. Make your way slowly across the bridge, checking out several of the statues, all on the right-hand side.*

⓲ Charles Bridge (Karlův Most)

Among Prague's defining landmarks, this much-loved ▲▲▲ bridge offers one of the most pleasant and entertaining strolls in

Europe. Musicians, artisans, and a constant parade of people make it a festival every day. You can return to this bridge throughout the day to enjoy its various charms. Early and late, it can be enchantingly lonely. It's a photographer's delight during that "magic hour," when the sun is low in the sky. The impressively expressive statues on either side of the bridge depict saints.

Partway along the bridge, on your right, find a small **brass relief** showing a cross with five stars embedded in the wall of the bridge (it's just below the little grate that sits on top of the stone bannister). The relief depicts a figure floating in the river, with a semicircle of stars above him. This marks the traditional spot where St. John of Nepomuk, the national saint of the Czech people, is believed to have been tossed off the bridge and into the river.

For the rest of that story, continue two more statue groups to the bronze Baroque statue of **St. John of Nepomuk,** with the five golden stars encircling his head. This statue always draws a crowd. John was a 14th-century priest to whom the queen confessed all her sins. According to a 17th-century legend, the king wanted to know his wife's secrets, but Father John dutifully refused to tell. The shiny plaque at the base of the statue shows what happened next: John was tortured and eventually killed by being thrown off the bridge. The plaque shows the heave-ho. When he hit the water, five stars appeared, signifying his purity. Notice the date on the inscription—1683. This oldest statue on the bridge was unveiled on the supposed 300th anniversary of the martyr's death. Traditionally, people believe that touching the St. John plaque will make a wish come true. But you get only one chance in life to make this wish, and you may never tell anyone what that wish is.

• *A good way to end this walk is to enjoy the* ⓳ *city and river view from near the center of the bridge. From here, you can continue across the bridge to the Lesser Town (Kampa Island, on your left as you cross the bridge, is a tranquil spot to explore; for more on sights in this area, see "Sights in the Lesser Town," later). You can also hike or take the tram up to the castle from here (a 10-minute walk to the right is the Malostranská stop for the Metro or for the handy tram #22 or #23). Or retrace your steps across the bridge to enjoy more time in the Old Town.*

Sights in the Old Town (Staré Město)

I've arranged Prague's sights by neighborhood for handy sightseeing. Remember that Prague started out as four towns—the Old Town and New Town on the east side of the river, and the Castle Quarter and Lesser Town on the west—and it's still helpful for sightseers to think of the city that way.

My Old Town and Charles Bridge Walk, earlier, covers the main sights in this area, including the **Old Town Square** and its many monuments—the **Týn Church** and the **Old Town Hall/ Astronomical Clock**—along with the **Church of St. James** and the **Charles Bridge.** It also points out key landmarks, including **the Ungelt** courtyard, **House of the Black Madonna,** and **Powder Tower.**

Here are some additional sights in the Old Town. Or consider following along with my ∩ Prague City Walk audio tour, which covers sights in both the Old Town and New Town (though not necessarily all sights listed here).

JEWISH QUARTER (JOSEFOV)

Prague's Jewish Quarter, worth ▲▲▲, is Europe's most accessible sight for learning about an important culture and faith that's interwoven with the fabric of Central and Eastern Europe. Within a three-block radius, several original synagogues, cemeteries, and other landmarks survive, today collected into one big, well-presented museum—the Jewish Museum in Prague. It can get crowded here, so time your visit carefully (early or late is best). For background on typical synagogue architecture, see the sidebar on page 291.

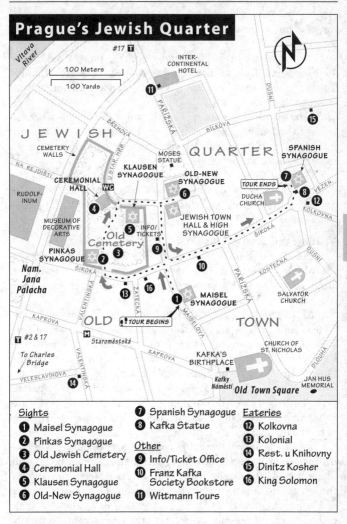

Prague's Jewish Quarter

Sights
1. Maisel Synagogue
2. Pinkas Synagogue
3. Old Jewish Cemetery
4. Ceremonial Hall
5. Klausen Synagogue
6. Old-New Synagogue
7. Spanish Synagogue
8. Kafka Statue

Other
9. Info/Ticket Office
10. Franz Kafka Society Bookstore
11. Wittmann Tours

Eateries
12. Kolkovna
13. Kolonial
14. Rest. u Knihovny
15. Dinitz Kosher
16. King Solomon

Jewish Museum in Prague (Židovské Muzeum v Praze)

The "museum" consists of four synagogues, a ceremonial hall, and a cemetery—each described below and covered by the same ticket.

Cost and Hours: 350 Kč, 530-Kč combo-ticket also includes Old-New Synagogue; Sun-Fri 9:00-18:00, Nov-March until 16:30, closed Sat—the Jewish Sabbath—and on Jewish holidays; their website lists all closures; 300-Kč audioguide is overkill, tel. 222-317-191, www.jewishmuseum.cz.

Buying Tickets and Avoiding Lines: Buy your ticket at the Maisel or Klausen synagogues or at the Information Center at Maiselova 15 (near the intersection with Siroka street). While you can also buy tickets at the Pinkas Synagogue, this tends to have long lines.

The Pinkas Synagogue can be packed, especially between 10:00 and 11:30, so be there right as it opens or later in the day. To save time in line, buy your ticket in advance at the other, less-crowded, locations.

Dress Code: Men are expected to cover their heads when entering an active synagogue or cemetery. While you'll see many visitors ignoring this custom, it's respectful to bring a cap or borrow a museum-issued yarmulke.

Getting There: The Jewish Quarter is an easy walk from Old Town Square, up delightful Pařížská street (next to the green-domed Church of St. Nicholas). The Staroměstská Metro stop is just a couple of blocks away.

Visiting the Jewish Museum

You can see the sights in any order. The tour listed here starts at the Maisel Synagogue. Alternatively, you could plan your time around the crowded Pinkas Synagogue. It's best to be there right as it opens to avoid the crowds.

Maisel Synagogue (Maiselova Synagóga): This pastel-colored Neo-Gothic synagogue, originally built as a private place of worship, now houses an interactive exhibit on Jewish history in the Czech lands up until 1800 and a few precious medieval objects. During the Nazi occupation, employees of the Jewish Museum used this building as a warehouse for a vast collection of Judaica gathered from vanished communities around the country. Rumor had it that Hitler planned to turn this collection into a "Museum of the Extinct Race."

Inside, the interactive exhibit retraces a thousand years of Jewish history in Bohemia and Moravia. Well explained in English, topics include the origin of the Star of David, Jewish mysticism, the Golem legend, the history of discrimination, and the creation of Prague's ghetto. Pre-WWII photographs of small-town synagogues from the region are projected on a large screen. Notice the eastern wall, with the holy ark containing a precious Torah mantel. Look for the banner of the Prague Jewish Butchers Guild, the emblem of the Cobblers Guild, a medieval seal ring, and the bema grillwork from Prague's demolished Zigeuner Synagogue.

Pinkas Synagogue (Pinkasova Synagóga): For many visitors, this house of worship—today used as a memorial to Holocaust victims—is the most powerful of the Jewish Quarter sights.

Enter and go down the steps leading to the **main hall** of this small late Gothic/early Renaissance synagogue. Notice the old stone-and-wrought-iron bema in the middle, the niche for the ark

Prague's Jewish Quarter

Jews first came to Prague in the 10th century. The least habitable, marshy area closest to the bend was allotted to the Jewish community. The Jewish Quarter's main intersection (Maiselova and Široká streets) was the meeting point of two medieval trade routes. For centuries, Jews coexisted—at times tensely—with their non-Jewish Czech neighbors.

During the Crusades in the 12th century, the pope declared that Jews and Christians should not live together. Jews had to wear yellow badges, and their quarter was walled in and became a ghetto (minority neighborhood) of wooden houses and narrow lanes. In the 16th and 17th centuries, Prague had one of the biggest ghettos in Europe, with 11,000 inhabitants. Within its six gates, Prague's Jewish Quarter was a gaggle of 200 wooden buildings.

Faced with institutionalized bigotry and harassment, Jews relied mainly on profits from moneylending (forbidden to Christians) and community solidarity to survive. While their money bought them protection (the kings taxed Jewish communities heavily), it was often also a curse. Throughout Europe, when times got tough and Christian debts to the Jewish community mounted, entire Jewish communities were evicted or killed. The worse pogroms were in 1096 and in 1389, when around 3,000 Jews were killed.

In 1781, Emperor Josef II, motivated more by economic concerns than by religious freedom, eased much of the discrimination against Jews. In 1848, the Jewish Quarter's walls were torn down, and the neighborhood—named Josefov in honor of the emperor who provided this small measure of tolerance—was incorporated as a district of the Old Town.

In 1897, ramshackle Josefov was razed and replaced by a new modern town—the original 31 streets and 220 buildings became 10 streets and 83 buildings. They leveled the medieval-era buildings (except the synagogues) and turned this into perhaps Europe's finest Art Nouveau neighborhood, boasting stately facades with gables, turrets, elegant balconies, mosaics, statues, and all manner of architectural marvels. By the 1930s, Prague's Jewish community was prospering.

But then World War II hit. Of the 55,000 Jews living in Prague in 1939, just 10,000 survived the Holocaust to see liberation in 1945. And in the communist era—when the atheistic regime was also anti-Semitic—recovery was slow.

Today there are only 3,000 "registered" Jews in the Czech Republic, and of these, only 1,700 are in Prague. Today, in spite of their tiny numbers, the legacy of Prague's Jewish community lives on. And while today's modern grid plan has replaced the higgledy-piggledy medieval streets of old, Široká ("Wide Street") remains the main street. A few Jewish-themed shops and restaurants in the area add extra ambience to this (otherwise modern) neighborhood.

PRAGUE

at the far end, the crisscross vaulting overhead, and the Art Nouveau stained glass filling the place with light.

But the focus of this synagogue is its walls, inscribed with the handwritten **names** of 77,297 Czech Jews sent to the gas chambers at Auschwitz and other camps. Czech Jews were especially hard hit by the Holocaust. More than 155,000 of them passed through the nearby Terezín camp alone. Most died with no grave marker, but they are remembered here.

The names are carefully organized: Family names are in red, followed in black by the individual's first name, birthday, and date of death (if known) or date of deportation. You can tell by the dates that families often perished together. The names are gathered in groups by hometowns (listed in gold, as well as on placards at the base of the wall). As you ponder this sad sight, you'll hear the somber reading of the names alternating with a cantor singing the Psalms.

On your way out, watch on the right for the easy-to-miss stairs up to the small **Terezín Children's Art Exhibit.** Well described in English, these drawings were made by Jewish children imprisoned at Terezín, 40 miles northwest of Prague (a worthy day trip from here). This is where the Nazis shipped Prague's Jews for processing before transporting them east to death camps. Thirty-five thousand Jews died at Terezín of disease and starvation, and many tens of thousands more died in other camps. Of the 8,000 children transported from Terezín, only 240 came back. The teacher who led the drawing lessons and hid these artworks believed children could use imagination to liberate their minds from the camp. Their art survives to defy fate.

Old Jewish Cemetery (Starý Židovský Hřbitov): Hiding behind a wall and sitting above the street level, this is where Prague's Jews buried their dead. A stroll through the crooked tombstones is a poignant experience.

Enter one of the most wistful scenes in Europe and meander along a path through 12,000 evocative tombstones. They're old, eroded, inscribed in Hebrew, and leaning this way and that. A few of the dead have larger ark-shaped tombs. Most have a simple epitaph with the name, date, and a few of the deceased's virtues.

From 1439 until 1787, this was the only burial ground allowed for the Jews of Prague. Over time, the graves had to be piled on top of each other—seven or eight deep—so there are actually closer to

85,000 dead here. Graves were never relocated because of the Jewish belief that, once buried, a body should not be moved. Layer by layer, the cemetery grew into a small plateau. Tune in to the noise of passing cars outside, and you realize that you're several feet above the modern street level—which is already high above the medieval level.

People place pebbles on honored tombstones. This custom, a sign of respect, shows that the dead have not been forgotten and recalls the old days, when rocks were placed upon a sandy gravesite to keep the body covered. Others leave scraps of paper that contain prayers and wishes.

Ceremonial Hall (Obřadní Síň): This rustic stone tower (1911), at the edge of the cemetery, was a mortuary house used to prepare the body and perform purification rituals before burial. The inside is painted in fanciful, flowery Neo-Romanesque style. It's filled with a worthwhile exhibition on Jewish medicine, death, and burial traditions.

Klausen Synagogue (Klauzová Synagóga): This 17th-century synagogue is devoted to Jewish religious practices. The ground-floor displays touch on Jewish holidays. Upstairs, exhibits illustrate the rituals of everyday Jewish life. It starts at birth. There are good-luck amulets to ensure a healthy baby, and a wooden cradle that announces, "This little one will become big." The baby is circumcised (see the knife) and grows to celebrate a coming-of-age Bar or Bat Mitzvah around age 12 or 13. Marriage takes place under a canopy, and the couple sets up their home—the exhibit ends with some typical furnishings.

Note that the Spanish Synagogue—described next—is a few blocks away from the core of the Jewish Quarter. Before heading over there, consider visiting the nearby **Old-New Synagogue** (described at the end of this section).

Spanish Synagogue (Španělská Synagóga): Called "Spanish" though its design is Moorish (which was all the rage when this was built in the 19th century), this has the most opulently decorated interior of all the synagogues. It marked a time of relative wealth and importance for Prague's Jews, who in this era were increasingly welcome in the greater community and (in many cases) chose to adopt a more reformed approach to worship. Exhibits explain the lives of Czech Jews in the 19th and early 20th centuries, when they were believed to be living their best days yet...unaware that the Holocaust was looming.

The decor is exotic and awe-inspiring. Intricate interweaving designs (of stars and vines) cover every inch of the red-gold and green walls and ceiling. A rose window with a stylized Star of David graces the ark.

The new synagogue housed a new movement within Judaism—a Reform congregation—that worshipped in a more modern way. The bema has been moved to the front of the synagogue, so the officiant faces the congregation. There's also a prominent organ (upper right) to accompany the singing.

Displays of Jewish history bring us through the 18th, 19th, and tumultuous 20th centuries to today. In the 1800s, Jews were increasingly accepted and successful in the greater society. But tolerance brought a dilemma—was it better to assimilate within the dominant culture or to join the growing Zionist homeland movement? To reform the religion or to remain orthodox?

Upstairs, the **balcony exhibits** focus on Czech Jews in the 1900s. Start in the area near the organ, which explains the modern era of Jewish Prague, including the late-19th-century development of Josefov. Then work your way around the balcony, with exhibits on Jewish writers (Franz Kafka), philosophers (Edmund Husserl), and other notables (Freud). This intellectual renaissance came to an abrupt halt with World War II and the mass deportations to Terezín (see more sad displays on life there, including more children's art and a box full of tefillin prayer cases). The final displays bring it home: After 2,000 years of living away from their Holy Land roots, the Jewish people had a homeland—the modern nation of Israel. Finish your visit across the landing in the **Winter Synagogue,** showing a trove of silver—Kiddush cups, Hanukkah lamps, Sabbath candlesticks, and Torah ornaments.

Next to the Spanish Synagogue is a bizarre statue commemorating the writer **Franz Kafka.** In a short story, Kafka describes a dream in which the protagonist is being carried through an unknown city on the shoulders of a headless giant.

Old-New Synagogue (Staronová Synagóga)

The oldest surviving and most important building in the Jewish Quarter, the Old-New Synagogue goes back at least seven centuries. While the exterior seems simple compared to ornate neighboring townhouses, the interior is atmospherically 13th-century.

Cost and Hours: 200 Kč, 530-Kč combo-ticket also includes Jewish Museum of Prague; Sun-Thu 9:00-18:00, off-season until 17:00, Fri closes one hour before sunset, closed Sat and on Jewish holidays; admission includes worthwhile 10-minute tour, tel. 222-317-191, www.synagogue.cz.

Visiting the Synagogue: Built in 1270, this is the oldest synagogue in Eastern Europe (and some say the oldest still-working synagogue in all of Europe). The name may come from the fact that it was "New" when built but became "Old" when other, newer synagogues came on the scene. The exterior is simple, with a unique sawtooth gable. Standing like a bomb-hardened bunker, it feels as though it has survived plenty of hard times.

As you enter, you descend a few steps below street level to 13th-century street level and the medieval world.

The **interior** is pure Gothic—thick pillars, soaring arches, and narrow lancet windows. If it looks like a church, well, the architects were Christians. The stonework is original, and the woodwork (the paneling and benches) is also old. This was one of the first Gothic buildings in Prague.

Seven centuries later, it's still a working synagogue. There's the stone bema in the middle where the Torah is read aloud, and the ark at the far end, where the sacred scrolls are kept. To the right of the ark, one chair is bigger, with a Star of David above it. This chair always remains empty out of respect for great rabbis of the past. Where's the women's gallery? Here, women worshipped in rooms that flanked the hall, watching the service through those horizontal windows in the walls.

Before leaving, check out the **lobby** (the long hall where you show your ticket). It has two fortified old lockers—in which the most heavily taxed community in medieval Prague stored its money in anticipation of the taxman's arrival.

NORTH OF THE OLD TOWN SQUARE, NEAR THE RIVER

Stray just a couple of blocks north of the Old Town Square and you'll find a surprisingly tourist-free world of shops and cafés, pastel buildings with decorative balconies and ornamental statues, winding lanes, cobblestone streets, and mosaic sidewalks. It's also home to this fine, underrated museum.

▲▲Museum of Medieval Art (Středověké umění v Čechách a Střední Evropě)

Prague flourished in the 14th century, and the city has amassed an impressive collection of altarpieces and paintings from that age. Today this art is housed in the tranquil former Convent of St. Agnes, which was founded in the 13th century by a Czech princess-turned-nun as the first hospital in Prague. A visit here is your best chance to see exquisite medieval art in Prague.

Cost and Hours: 220 Kč; Tue-Sun 10:00-18:00, closed Mon; two blocks northeast of the Spanish Synagogue, along the river at Anežská 12; tel. 224-810-628, www.ngprague.cz.

Sights in the New Town (Nové Město)

Enough of pretty, medieval Prague—let's leap into the modern era. The New Town, with Wenceslas Square as its focal point, is today's urban Prague. This part of the city offers bustling boulevards and interesting neighborhoods. Even today, the New Town is separated from the Old Town by a "moat" (the literal meaning of the street called Na Příkopě). As you cross bustling Na Příkopě, you leave the medieval cuteness and souvenir shops behind, and enter a town of malls and fancy shops that cater to locals and visitors alike. The New Town is one of the best places to view Prague's remarkable Art Nouveau art and architecture, and to learn more about its communist past.

Download my 🎧 Prague City Walk audio tour, which covers sights in both the Old Town and New Town.

WENCESLAS SQUARE AND NEARBY

These sights are on or within a few blocks of the elongated main square of the New Town.

▲▲▲Wenceslas Square Walk (Václavské Náměstí)

More a broad boulevard than a square, this city landmark is named for St. Wenceslas, whose equestrian statue overlooks the square's top end. Wenceslas Square

functions as a stage for modern Czech history: The creation of the Czechoslovak state was celebrated here in 1918; in 1968, the Soviets suppressed huge popular demonstrations (called the Prague Spring) at the square; and, in 1989, more than 300,000 Czechs and Slovaks converged here to demand their freedom (in the Velvet Revolution). Today it's a busy thoroughfare of commerce.

◑ Self-Guided Walk: For a taste of Prague's 20th-century history, take a stroll beginning at the top of the square. (To get here quickly, ride the Metro to the Muzeum stop.)

• *Begin at the big...*

Statue of Duke Wenceslas I: The "Good King" of Christmas-carol fame was actually a wise and benevolent 10th-century duke. Václav (as he's called by locals) united the Czech people, back when this land was known as Bohemia. A rare example of a well-educated and literate ruler, Wenceslas Christianized and lifted the culture. He astutely allied the powerless Czechs with the Holy

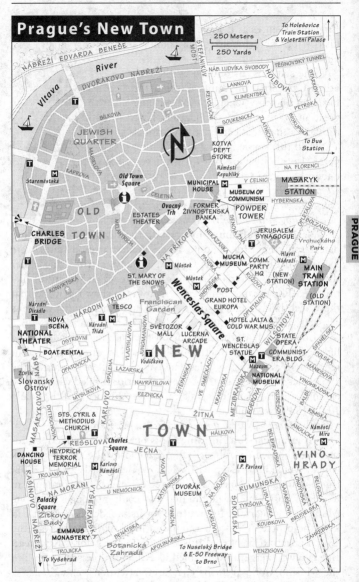

Prague's New Town

250 Meters

250 Yards

To Holešovice Train Station & Veletržní Palace

PRAGUE

Roman Empire of the German nation. And he began to fortify Prague's castle as a center of Czech government. After his murder in 929, Wenceslas was canonized as a saint. He became a symbol of Czech nationalism (and appears on the 20-Kč coin). Later kings knelt before his tomb to be crowned. And he remains an icon of Czech unity whenever the nation has to rally. Like King Arthur in

England, Wenceslas is more legend than history, but he symbolizes the country's birth.

The statue is surrounded by the four other Czech patron saints. Notice the focus on books. A small nation without great military power, the Czechs have thinkers as national heroes, not warriors.

And this statue is a popular meeting point. Locals like to say, "I'll meet you under the horse's tail."

• *Circle behind the statue and stand below that tail; turn your attention to the impressive building at the top of Wenceslas Square.*

National Museum: This grand, lavishly restored building dates from the 19th century, when modern nation-states were forming in Europe and the Czech people were still living under the auspices of Austria's Habsburg Empire. Bold structures like this Neo-Renaissance building were a way to show the world that the Czech lands had a distinct culture and a heritage of precious artifacts, and that Czechs deserved their own nation.

Look closely at the columns on the building's facade. Those light-colored patches (meticulously preserved during the recent renovation) are covering holes where Soviet bullets hit during the 1968 crackdown. The state-of-the-art interior is filled with diverse exhibits ranging from minerals to modern history (250 Kč, daily 10:00-18:00, www.nm.cz).

• *To the left of the National Museum (as you face it) is a...*

Communist-Era Building: This out-of-place modern structure once housed the rubber-stamp Czechoslovak Parliament back when it voted in lockstep with Moscow. Between 1994 and 2008, this building was home to Radio Free Europe. After communism fell, RFE lost some of its funding and could no longer afford its Munich headquarters. In gratitude for its broadcasts—which had kept the people of Eastern Europe in touch with real news—the Czech government offered this building to RFE for 1 Kč a year. But as RFE energetically beamed its American message deep into the Muslim world from here, it drew attention—and threats—from Al-Qaeda. In 2009, RFE moved to a new fortress-like headquarters literally across the cemetery wall from Franz Kafka's grave (an easier-to-defend locale). Now this is an annex of the National Museum.

• *Start walking down Wenceslas Square. Pause about 30 yards along, at the little patch of bushes. In the ground on the downhill side of those bushes is a...*

Memorial to the Victims of 1969: After the Russian crack-

The Prague Spring and Its Fall

In January 1968, Slovak politician Alexander Dubček replaced the aging apparatchiks at the helm of the Communist Party of Czechoslovakia. Handsome and relatively youthful, Dubček used the brand of a smiling playboy; he appeared on magazine covers in his Speedo, about to dive into a swimming pool. Young Czechs and Slovaks embraced Dubček as a potential hero of liberalization.

In April, Dubček introduced his "Action Program," designed to tiptoe away from strict and stifling Soviet communism and forge a more moderate Czechoslovak variation. Censorship eased, travel restrictions were relaxed, state companies began forming joint ventures with Western firms, money poured into the sciences, and a newspaper called "Tomorrow" (rather than "Today") became the most popular in the country. Plays put on at the Semafor Theater (in today's Světozor mall) lampooned Brezhnev and his ilk. During this so-called "Prague Spring," optimism soared.

But then, around midnight on August 20, 1968, the thundering sound of enormous airplanes ripped across the floodlit rooftops of Prague. The Soviets had dispatched over 200,000 Warsaw Pact troops to invade Czechoslovakia, airlifting tanks right into the capital city. Dubček and his team were arrested and taken to Moscow. Czechs and Slovaks took to the streets, boycotting and striking. Tanks rolled through Wenceslas Square, spraying protesters with bullets...some of which are still embedded in the National Museum's pillars. Over the course of the occupation, 72 Czechs and Slovaks were killed.

Dubček stepped down and went into internal exile, and his successor—the hardliner Gustáv Husák—immediately pursued a policy of "normalization." People who refused to sign a petition commending the "Russian Liberation" were fired from their jobs and forced to find worse ones. Some protesters—including Jan Palach—went to the extreme of setting themselves on fire to protest against the regime. Tens of thousands of Czechs and Slovaks reluctantly emigrated to the West, fearing what might come next.

While the ill-fated tale of the Prague Spring is pessimistic, it provides an insightful bookend to what happened 21 years later: The children of the generation that suffered Czechoslovakia's bitterest disappointment ushered in mass demonstrations that ended this dark era.

down of 1968, a young philosophy student named Jan Palach,
inspired by a video of monks
immolating themselves in protest in Vietnam, decided that
the best way to stoke the flame
of independence was to do the
same right here. On January
16, 1969, Palach stood on the
steps of the National Museum

and ignited his body. He died a few days later. A month later, another student did the same thing, followed by another. Czechs are
keen on anniversaries, and—20 years after Palach's defining act, in
1989—hundreds of Czechs gathered here again in protest. A sense
of new possibility swept through the city, and 10 months later, the
communists were history.

• *Farther down Wenceslas Square, locate the building on the right with
the beige travertine facade (and many balconies). This is the...*

Jalta Hotel and Cold War Museum: This building is most
representative of the 1950s Neoclassical, Socialist Realist style.
Designed at the height of the Cold War as a hotel for VIPs, it
came with an underground crisis fallout shelter that visiting Soviet
generals could use as a command center in case nuclear war broke
out. The bunkers were refurbished to their original state by a group
of Czechoslovak army fans and converted into the ▲ **Cold War
Museum,** with a command room, hospital room, spying room (for
listening in on phone calls), and an air-filtering facility (visits are
by tour only, 200 Kč for one-hour tour in English, depart daily
at 14:30, 16:00, and 17:30 from Jalta Hotel, www.en.muzeum-
studene-valky.cz).

• *Continue down Wenceslas Square.*

Architecture Along Wenceslas Square: As you walk, you'll
notice the architecture is unlike the historic Old Town—nearly everything here is from the past two centuries. Wenceslas Square is
a showcase of Prague's many architectural styles: You'll see Neo-
Gothic, Neo-Renaissance, and Neo-Baroque from the 19th century. There's curvaceous Art Nouveau from around 1900. And there's
the modernist response to Art Nouveau—Functionalism from the
mid-20th century, where the watchword was "form follows function" and beauty took a back seat to practicality. You'll see buildings from the 1950s communist era, forgettable glass-and-steel
buildings of the 1970s, modern stores from the 2000s, and new
construction.

The Velvet Revolution: Opposite Grand Hotel Europa (on
the left side of the square), find the Marks & Spencer building and
its **balcony** (partly obscured by tree branches).

The Velvet Revolution of 1989

On the afternoon of November 17, 1989, 30,000 students gathered in Prague's New Town to commemorate the 50th anniversary of the suppression of student protests by the Nazis, which had led to the closing of Czech universities through the end of World War II. Remember, this was just a few weeks after the fall of the Berlin Wall, and the Czechs were feeling the winds of change blowing across Central Europe. The 1989 demonstration—initially planned by the Communist Youth as a celebration of the communist victory over fascism—spontaneously turned into a protest *against* the communist regime. "You are just like the Nazis!" shouted the students. The demonstration was supposed to end in the National Cemetery at Vyšehrad (the hill just south of the New Town). But when the planned events concluded in Vyšehrad, the students decided to march on toward Wenceslas Square...and make some history.

As they worked their way north along the Vltava River toward the New Town's main square, the students were careful to keep their demonstration peaceful. Any hint of violence, the demonstrators knew, would incite brutal police retaliation. Instead, as the evening went on, the absence of police became conspicuous. (In the 1980s, the police never missed a chance to participate in any demonstration...preferably outnumbering the demonstrators.) At about 20:00, as the students marched down Národní Třída toward Wenceslas Square, three rows of police suddenly blocked the demonstration at the corner of Národní and Spálená streets. A few minutes later, military vehicles with fences on their bumpers (having crossed the bridge by the National Theater) appeared behind the marching students. This new set of cops compressed the demonstrators into the stretch of Národní Třída between Voršilská and Spálená. The end of Mikulandská street was also blocked, and police were hiding inside every house entry. The students were trapped.

At 21:30, the "Red Berets" (a special anti-riot commando force known for its brutality) arrived. The Red Berets lined up on both sides of this corridor. To get out, the trapped students had to run through the passageway as they were beaten from the left and right. Police trucks ferried captured students around the corner to the police headquarters (on Bartolomějská) for interrogation.

The next day, university students throughout Czechoslovakia decided to strike. Actors from theaters in Prague and Bratislava joined the student protest. Two days later, the students' parents—shocked by the attacks on their children—marched into Wenceslas Square. Sparked by the events of November 17, 1989, the wave of peaceful demonstrations ended later that year on December 29, with the election of Václav Havel as the president of a free Czechoslovakia.

PRAGUE

Picture the scene on this square on a cold November night in 1989. Czechoslovakia had been oppressed for the previous 40 years by communist Russia. But now the Soviet empire was beginning to crumble, jubilant Germans were dancing on top of the shattered Berlin Wall, and the Czechs were getting a whiff of freedom.

Czechoslovakia's revolution began with a bunch of teenagers, who—following a sanctioned gathering—decided to march on Wenceslas Square (see sidebar). After they were surrounded and beaten by the communist riot police, their enraged parents, friends, and other members of the community began to pour into this square to protest. Night after night, this huge square was filled with more than 300,000 ecstatic Czechs and Slovaks who believed freedom was at hand. Each night they would jingle their key chains in the air as if saying to their communist leaders, "It's time for you to go home now." Finally they gathered and found that their communist overlords had left—and freedom was theirs.

On that night, as thousands filled this square, a host of famous people appeared on that balcony to greet the crowd. There was a well-known priest and a rock star famous for his rebellion against authority. There was Alexander Dubček, the hero of the Prague Spring reforms of 1968. And there was Václav Havel, the charismatic playwright who had spent years in prison, becoming a symbol of resistance—a kind of Czech Nelson Mandela. Now he was free. Havel's voice boomed over the gathered masses. He proclaimed the resignation of the Politburo and the imminent freedom of the Republic of Czechoslovakia. He pulled out a ring of keys and jingled it. Thousands of keys jingled back in response.

In previous years, the communist authorities would have sent in tanks to crush the impudent masses. But by 1989, the Soviet empire was collapsing, and the Czech government was shaky. Locals think that Soviet head of state Mikhail Gorbachev (mindful of the Tiananmen Square massacre a few months before) might have made a phone call recommending a nonviolent response. Whatever happened, the communist regime was overthrown with hardly any blood being spilled. It was done through sheer people power—thanks to the masses of defiant Czechs who gathered here peacefully in Wenceslas Square, and Slovaks doing the same in Bratislava. A British journalist called it "The Velvet Revolution," and the name caught on in the West. Locals call it simply "The Revolution."

• *A block from the bottom of Wenceslas Square, look for the gate tucked behind the Jungmann statue on Jungmannovo Náměstí. Head through to find the...*

Franciscan Garden: Ahhh! This garden's white benches and spreading rosebushes are a universe away from the fast beat of the city, which throbs behind the buildings corralling this little oasis.

The peacefulness reflects the purpose of its Franciscan origin. St. Francis, the founder of the order, thought God's presence could be found in nature. In the 1600s, Prague became an important center for a group of Franciscans from Ireland. Enjoy the herb garden and children's playground. (And a WC is just out the far side of the garden.) The park is a popular place for a discreet rendezvous; it's famous among locals for kicking off romances.

• *Exit the garden at the opposite corner from where you entered (past the little yellow gardening pavilion—which now houses a design boutique—and the herb garden). Continue straight ahead to reach the Old Town or turn right along Na Příkopě street to visit the Mucha Museum, Municipal House, or Museum of Communism. For places farther afield, hop on the Metro at Můstek. The rest of Prague is yours to enjoy.*

▲▲Mucha Museum (Muchovo Museum)

This enjoyable little museum features a small selection of the insistently likeable art of Alfons Mucha (MOO-khah, 1860-1939), a founding father of the Art Nouveau movement (and creator of Prague's most famous artwork, the *Slav Epic*, a huge 20-canvas ode to his nation that had been on a world tour; for info on its current location, check with the Mucha Museum ticket desk). It's all crammed into a too-small space, some of the art is faded, and the admission price is steep—but there's no better place to gain an understanding of Mucha's talent, his career, and the influence he's had on the world art scene. And the museum, partly overseen by Mucha's grandson, gives you a peek at some of the posters that made Mucha famous. You'll learn how these popular patriotic banners, filled with Czech symbols and expressing his people's ideals and aspirations, aroused the national spirit. Enjoy decorative posters from his years in Paris, including his celebrated ads for the French actress Sarah Bernhardt. Check out the photographs of his models, which Mucha later re-created in pencil or paint, and be sure to see the 30-minute film on the artist's life.

Cost and Hours: 240 Kč, daily 10:00-18:00, good English descriptions, two blocks off Wenceslas Square at Panská 7, tel. 224-233-355, www.mucha.cz. Peruse the well-stocked gift shop.

NEAR NA PŘÍKOPĚ

At the bottom of Wenceslas Square, the street running to the right is called Na Příkopě. It is a showcase of Art Nouveau: Be sure to keep your eyes up as you stroll here. City tour buses leave from along this street, which also offers plenty of shopping temptations.

▲Museum of Communism (Muzeum Komunismu)

This small museum offers a fascinating look at the "dream, reality, and nightmare" of communism. You'll walk through the years (with good English descriptions) starting with the 1918 birth of Czechoslovakia through World War II, when the Soviets "liberated" Czechoslovakia from the Nazis. The communists quickly came to power, with statues of Stalin and propaganda permeating Czech society. Then the dark side: attempted escapes, police, interrogation, and torture as a video on the wall shows images that humanize the tragedy of this period. A section on the eventual fall of communism is inspiring.

Cost and Hours: 290 Kč, daily 9:00-20:00, a block off Republic Square at V Celnici 4, tel. 224-212-966, www.museumofcommunism.com.

▲▲Municipal House (Obecní Dům)

The cultural and artistic leaders who financed this Art Nouveau masterpiece (1905-1911) wanted a ceremonial palace to reinforce self-awareness of the Czech nation. While the exterior is impressive, the highlight is the interior—and at least part of it is free. To extend your Art Nouveau bliss, take a guided tour or attend a concert here.

Cost and Hours: The entrance halls and public spaces are free to explore, daily 10:00-18:00. For an in-depth look at all the sumptuous halls and banquet rooms, you'll have to join a one-hour **tour** (290 Kč, English tours—usually 3/day departing between 11:00 and 17:00; limited to 35 people—buy your ticket online or from the ground-floor shop where tours depart; Náměstí Republiky 5, tel. 222-002-101, www.obecnidum.cz).

Concerts: Performances are held regularly in the lavish Smetana Hall (schedule on website). Note that many concerts brag they are held in the Municipal House, but are performed in a smaller, less impressive hall in the same building.

Visiting the House: Don't be timid about poking around the interior, which is open to the public. Having lunch or a drink in one of the eateries is a great way to experience the decor, but you can also just glimpse them from the doorway (as you "check out the menu").

Enter under the green, wrought-iron arcade. In the **rotunda,** admire the mosaic floor, stained glass, the woodwork doorway and the lighting fixtures. To the left is the **café** *(kavárna)*—a harmony of woodwork, marble, metal, and glittering chandeliers. Opposite the café is the equally stunning **restaurant** (both described on page 137).

From the rotunda, step into the **lobby,** where you can look up the staircase that leads up to the main concert hall (no tourist access upstairs). Also in the lobby is the box office, selling concert tickets and guided English tours of the building.

Facing the staircase, go right and head **downstairs**—yes, tourists are welcome there. Admire the colorful tiles in the stairwell, and more colorful tiles in the downstairs main room. Look for the plaster model of this building and the adjacent Powder Tower, which shows how the angled facade conceals a surprisingly large performance space. Also check out the **American Bar** (salute the US flags above the bar) and the **Plzeňská Restaurant** (with its dark-wood booths and colorful tile scenes of happy peasants).

Finish your tour by going back upstairs to find the **Modernista shop** (tucked to the left as you face the main staircase)—full of fancy teacups and jewelry.

Also upstairs, you may find **temporary exhibits** (usually around 150 Kč), typically about Art Nouveau. This style was heavy on the applied arts (as opposed to fine arts like painting), so you'll see elegant lamps, chairs, prints, and clothes. To reach this space, you're allowed to ascend the main staircase, pass by the guard, and glimpse into the stylish Smetana Hall along the way.

Sights in the Lesser Town (Malá Strana)

Huddled under the castle on the west bank of the river, and just over the Charles Bridge, the Lesser Town is a Baroque time capsule. It's the oldest of the four towns that make up Prague, dating to the early 10th century. It's also the best-preserved part of the city, with only a few buildings here dating from after 1800. Though underappreciated, there is nothing "lesser" about this part of town. If you like hidden, quiet alleyways rather than busy commercial bustle, you'll want to take time to explore the neighborhood.

LESSER TOWN SQUARE AND NEARBY

From the end of the Charles Bridge (with TI in tower), Mostecká street leads two blocks up to the Lesser Town Square and the huge Church of St. Nicholas. This square (Malostranské Náměstí) is split into an upper and lower part by the domineering Church of St. Nicholas. A Baroque plague column oversees the upper square.

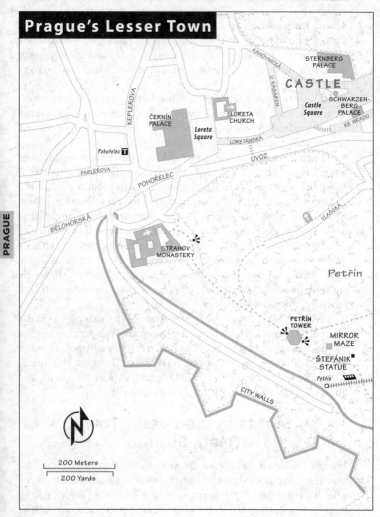

Prague's Lesser Town

(Note that there's a handy Via Musica ticket office on the uphill side.)

Church of St. Nicholas (Kostel Sv. Mikuláše)

When the Jesuits came to Prague, they found the perfect piece of real estate for their church and its associated school—right on the Lesser Town Square. The church (built 1703-1760) is the best example of High Baroque in town.

Cost and Hours: Church—70 Kč, daily 9:00-17:00, Nov-Feb until 16:00; tower climb—90 Kč, daily 10:00-22:00, shorter hours in winter, tower entrance is outside the right transept.

Visiting the Church: The church's interior is giddy with

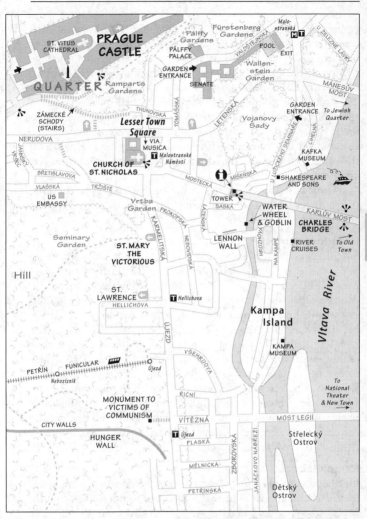

curves and illusions. This is "dynamic Baroque," with circles intersecting circles creating an illusion of movement. Stand directly under the tallest dome and look up. Spin slowly around, greeting four giant statues—the fathers of the Eastern Church. Look up and see the earthly world merging with heaven above.

The **altar** features a lavish gold-plated Nicholas, flanked by the two top Jesuits: the founder, St. Ignatius Loyola, and his missionary follower, St. Francis Xavier—one killing evil, the other spreading the Gospel.

Climb the staircase in the left transept up to the **gallery** for a close-up look at a collection of large canvases and illusionary frescoes by Karel Škréta, who is considered the greatest Czech Baroque painter. At first glance, the canvases are utterly dark, but as sunbeams shine through the window, various parts of the paintings brighten. The church walls seem to nearly fuse with the sky, suggesting that happenings on earth are closely connected to heaven.

Tower Climb: For a good look at the city and the church's 250-foot dome, climb the 215 steps up the bell tower. Closed to the public during the communist period, the deck was used by the secret police to spy on activities at the nearby embassies of the US, Britain, and West Germany. There is a good exhibit in English on this aspect, as well as on the May 5, 1945, uprising against the Nazi occupiers.

Concerts: The church hosts evening classical music concerts; tickets are usually on sale at the church ticket desk (500 Kč, generally nightly at 18:00 except Tue, www.stnicholas.cz).

Nerudova Street

This steep, cobbled street, connecting the Lesser Town Square up to the castle, is named for Jan Neruda, a gifted 19th-century journalist. It's lined with old buildings still sporting the characteristic doorway signs (such as two golden suns, a red lion, a green lobster, or three violins) that once served as street addresses. The surviving signs have been carefully restored and protected by law. They represent the family name, the occupation, or the various passions of the people who once inhabited the houses. In the 1770s, in order to run her empire (and collect taxes) more effectively, Habsburg Empress Maria Theresa decreed that house numbers were to be used instead of these quaint names. The neighborhood is filled with noble palaces, now generally used as foreign embassies (the American embassy is a couple of blocks to the left as you hike uphill) and as offices of the Czech Parliament.

Kampa Island

One hundred yards from the castle end of the Charles Bridge, stairs on the left lead down to the main square of Kampa Island (mostly

created from the rubble of the Lesser Town, after it was devastated in a 1540 fire). The island features relaxing pubs, a breezy park, hippies, lovers, a fine contemporary art gallery, and river access. At the far end of Kampa Square is the park entrance. Midway through the park (on the left) is the former mill building, Sovovy Mlýny. In it is the **Museum Kampa,** home to the Jan and Meda Mládek Collection that features works once prohibited by the former communist regime and other modern artworks (80 Kč for permanent exhibit, 250 Kč covers all exhibits, daily 10:00-18:00, www.museumkampa.cz).

Returning to Kampa Square, as you leave the park take the first lane on the left, which winds around to a little bridge. The high-water mark at the end of the bridge dates from 1890. The **old water wheel** is the last survivor of many mills that once lined the canal here, powering industry before the arrival of steam power. Each mill had its own protective water spirit or goblin *(vodník)*. Note the one sitting on a tree stump by the wheel.

Lennon Wall (Lennonova Zeď)

Near the old water wheel described above and just across the padlock-bedecked bridge, beneath the trees on the right, is the colorful Lennon Wall. While V. I.

Lenin's ideas hung like a water-soaked trench coat upon the Czech people, singer John Lennon's ideas gave many locals hope and a vision. When Lennon was killed in 1980, this large wall was spontaneously covered with memorial graffiti. Night after night, the police would paint over the "All You Need Is Love" and "Imagine" graffiti. And day after day, it would reappear. Until independence came in 1989, travelers, freedom lovers, and local hippies gathered here. Even today, people come here to imagine. *"John žije"* is Czech for "John lives."

SOUTH OF LESSER TOWN SQUARE
Church of St. Mary the Victorious
(Kostel Panny Marie Vítězné)

This otherwise ordinary Carmelite church displays Prague's most worshipped treasure, the Infant of Prague (Pražské Jezulátko). Kneel at the banister in front of the tiny lost-in-gilded-Baroque altar, and find the prayer in your language (of the 13 in the folder). Brought to Czech lands during the Habsburg era by a Spanish noblewoman who came to marry a Czech nobleman, the Infant has become a focus of worship and miracle tales in Prague and Spanish-speaking countries. South Americans come on pilgrimage to Prague just to see this one statue. An exhibit upstairs shows tiny embroidered robes given to the Infant, including ones from Habsburg Empress Maria Theresa of Austria (1754) and Vietnam

(1958), as well as a video showing a nun lovingly dressing the doll-like sculpture.

Cost and Hours: Free, Mon-Sat 9:30-17:30, Sun 13:00-18:00, English-language Mass Sun at 12:00 and Thu at 17:00, Karmelitská 9, www.pragjesu.cz.

▲Petřín Hill (Petřínské Sady)

This hill, topped by a replica of the Eiffel Tower, features several unusual sights.

Monument to Victims of Communism (Pomník Obětem Komunismu): The sculptural figures of this poignant memorial, representing victims of the totalitarian regime, gradually atrophy as they range up the hillside steps. They do not die but slowly disappear, one limb at a time. The statistics inscribed on the steps say it all: From 1948 until 1989, in Czechoslovakia alone, 205,486 people were imprisoned, 248 were executed, 4,500 died in prison, 327 were shot attempting to cross the border, and 170,938 left the country.

Hunger Wall (Hladová Zed'): To the left of the Victims of Communism monument is this medieval defense wall, which was Charles IV's 14th-century equivalent of FDR's work-for-food projects. The poorest of the poor helped build this structure just to eke out a bit of income.

To the right (about 50 yards away) is the base of a handy **funicular** you can ride up the hill to the Petřín Tower (uses tram/Metro ticket, runs daily every 10-15 minutes 8:00-22:00).

Petřín Hill Summit and Tower: The top of Petřín Hill is considered the best place in Prague to take your date for a romantic city view. Built for an exhibition

in 1891, the 200-foot-tall Petřín Tower—an elegant pure Art Nouveau steel-and-wood structure—is one-fifth the height of its Parisian big brother, which was built two years earlier. But, thanks to this hill, the top of the tower sits at the same elevation as the real Eiffel Tower. Before you climb up, appreciate the tower's sinuous curves. Climbing the 400 steps rewards you with amazing views of the city (105 Kč, daily 10:00-22:00, shorter hours off-season). A **mirror maze** next door to the tower is fun for a quick wander if you're already here (75 Kč, same hours as tower). Next to the maze, in front of the cupola-topped observatory, notice the statue of **Milan Rastislav Štefánik**

(1880-1919), the charismatic Slovak astronomer and patriot who brought home tens of thousands of Czech and Slovak freedom fighters left stranded in Siberia by the Bolshevik Revolution.

Sights in the Castle Quarter (Hradčany)

Looming above Prague, dominating its skyline, is the Castle Quarter. Prague Castle and its surrounding sights are packed with Czech history, as well as with tourists. In addition to the castle, I enjoy visiting the nearby Strahov Monastery (a 10-minute hike above it), which has a fascinating old library and beautiful views over all of Prague.

PRAGUE CASTLE (PRAŽSKÝ HRAD)

This vast and sprawling complex has been the seat of Czech power for centuries. It collects a wide range of sights, including the country's top church, its former royal palace, and an assortment of history and art museums (together rated ▲▲). The castle is Prague's most crowded sight and can be a bit intimidating to sightseers, but the casual visitor will find that a quick and targeted visit is ideal.

Getting There

By Tram: Trams #22 and #23 take you up to the castle. Catch it at one of these three convenient stops: the Národní Třída stop (between Wenceslas Square and the National Theater in the New Town); in front of the National Theater (Národní Divadlo, on the riverbank in the New Town); and at Malostranská (the Metro stop in the Lesser Town). If you plan to take the tram back to town after your castle visit, bring an extra ticket with you, as there's no handy place to buy one at the castle—and inspectors can be ruthless about checking tourists. After rattling up the hill, the tram makes three stops near the castle.

Královský Letohrádek (Royal Summer Palace) allows a scenic but slow approach through the Royal Gardens to the bridge near the castle's northern entrance, and lets you avoid the worst crowds at peak times.

Pražský Hrad (Prague Castle) offers the quickest commute to the castle—from the tram stop, simply walk along U Prašného Mostu and over the bridge, past the stonefaced-but-photo-op-friendly guards at the northern entrance, and into the castle's Second Courtyard.

Pohořelec is best if you'd like to start with the Strahov Monastery, then hike 10 minutes down to the castle (by way of Loreta Church).

By Taxi or Uber: Ask your driver to drop you at either

Prague Castle Overview

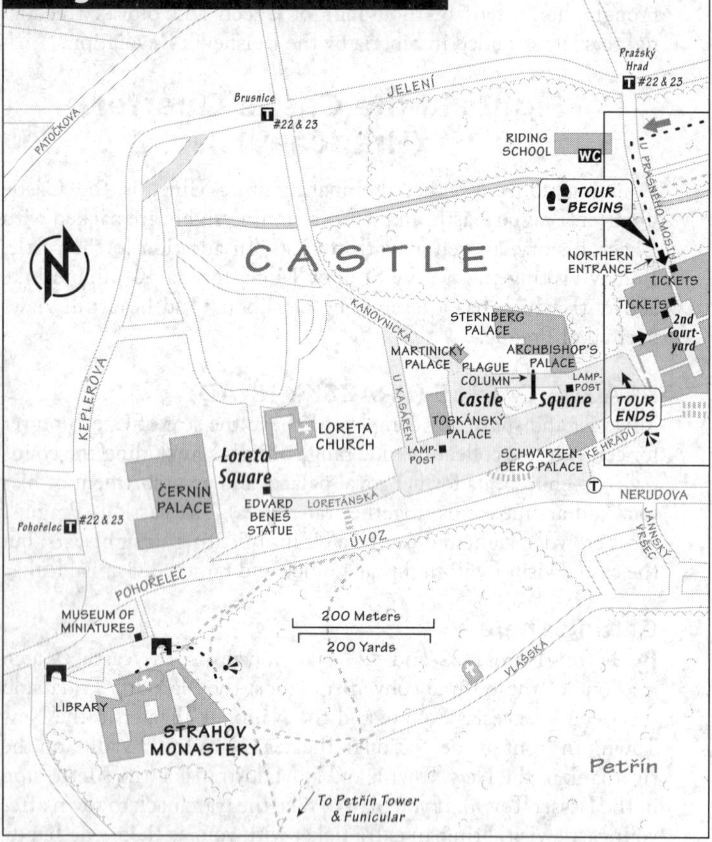
Pražský Hrad
#22 & 23
JELENÍ
Brusnice
#22 & 23
PATOČKOVA
RIDING SCHOOL
WC
TOUR BEGINS
U PRAŠNÉHO MOSTU
CASTLE
NORTHERN ENTRANCE
TICKETS
TICKETS
2nd Court-yard
KANOVNICKÁ
STERNBERG PALACE
MARTINICKÝ PALACE
ARCHBISHOP'S PALACE
PLAGUE COLUMN
LAMP-POST
Castle Square
TOUR ENDS
KEPLEROVA
U KASÁREN
TOSKÁNSKÝ PALACE
LORETA CHURCH
Loreta Square
LAMP-POST
SCHWARZEN-BERG PALACE
KE HRADU
NERUDOVA
ČERNÍN PALACE
EDVARD BENEŠ STATUE
LORETÁNSKÁ
Pohořelec
#22 & 23
ÚVOZ
JÁNSKÝ VRŠEK
POHOŘELEC
MUSEUM OF MINIATURES
200 Meters
200 Yards
VLAŠSKÁ
LIBRARY
STRAHOV MONASTERY
Petřín
To Petřín Tower & Funicular

Královský Letohrádek or Pražský Hrad (see earlier). Another option is to have them drop you off just under the castle at the top of Nerudova street (at the little square under the staircase) and climb 200 yards up the pedestrian-only cobblestone street from there.

By Foot: The fairly steep, three-quarter-mile uphill walk takes about 20 minutes from the river. From the Charles Bridge, follow the main cobbled road (Mostecká) to Lesser Town Square, marked by the huge, green-domed Church of St. Nicholas. From there, hike uphill along Nerudova street. After about 10 minutes, a steep lane on the right leads to Castle Square.

Planning Your Time

Prague Castle is the city's most crowded sight. The grounds become a sea of tourists during peak times (worst 9:30-14:00 in high season). The most cramped area is the free-to-enter vestibule inside

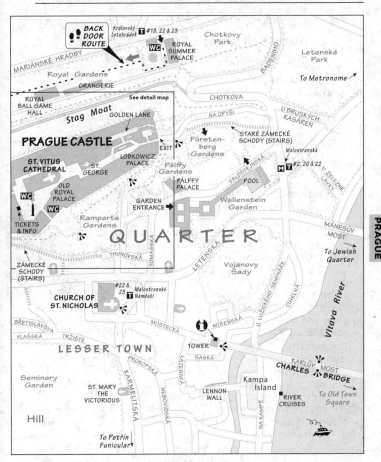

PRAGUE

St. Vitus Cathedral; any sight that you pay to enter—including other parts of the cathedral—will be less jammed.

Minimize the effect of crowds and maximize your enjoyment by following one of these plans.

Early-Bird Visit: Leave your hotel no later than 8:00 (earlier is even better). Ride the tram to the Pražský Hrad stop and buy your tickets in the Second Courtyard. Look around **Castle Square,** and most important, be sure that you're standing at the front door of **St. Vitus Cathedral** when it opens at the stroke of 9:00. For 10 minutes, you'll have the sacred space to yourself...then, on your way out, you'll pass a noisy human traffic jam of multinational tour groups clogging the entrance. Visit the rest of the castle sights at your leisure: the Old Royal Palace, the Basilica of St. George, and Lobkowicz Palace.

Sneaking in Through the Back Door at Peak Times: If you're arriving in the middle of the sightseeing day, a smart and enjoyable

Sneaking into Prague Castle Through the Back Door

If you anticipate crowds at Prague Castle, here's a delightful way to sneak in through the back door—likely avoiding a long security line at Castle Square and enjoying an elegant, untouristed dimension of the castle while you're at it. Ride tram #22 or #23 (or Uber) to the Královský Letohrádek tram stop. Ideally, arrive here at 10:00, when the grounds open (closed Nov-March).

The **Royal Summer Palace** is directly across the street from the tram stop. The palace is the purest Renaissance building in town. You can't go inside, but the building's detailed reliefs are worth a close look.

The Summer Palace is, from an architectural history point of view, one of the most groundbreaking in Prague. After four centuries of medieval Gothic, it announced (in the 1520s, quite late) the arrival of the Italian Renaissance and of a distinctly different attitude to life: "The Dark Ages are over, enjoy and play." Commissioned by Ferdinand, the first in a series of Habsburg rulers, it broke, literally, out of the fortress mentality. The gardens required the construction of a security-compromising bridge across the deep moat that separates them from the castle fortress.

Study the delicate works of **stucco.** In good Renaissance style, they're based on classical, rather than Christian, stories. The one depicted here is Virgil's *Aeneid*. Survey the characteristic green copper roof, visible from all over town—built to resemble the overturned keel of a seafaring ship. Ferdinand's three kingdoms of Austria, Bohemia, and Hungary were all landlocked, but he was born in Spain—shortly after Columbus discovered America—and his brother, another Habsburg, ruled Spain at the time. The roof is effectively an homage to the vessels that spread Habsburg pan-European dominance across the globe.

The Renaissance **fountain** in front of the palace is cast from a special type of resonant "bell bronze." To appreciate this feature, kneel down under the fountain and listen to how the dropping water makes the fountain hum. The audio rainbow you hear is the reason it's called the Singing Fountain. (Many Czechs think

way to avoid the long security lines is to ride the tram to Královský Letohrádek (the Royal Summer Palace) and approach the castle via the Royal Gardens. The garden security check generally has no lines. For a detailed description of this plan, see the sidebar, above.

Afternoon Visit/Adding on Strahov Monastery and Loreta Church: If you're heading to Prague Castle after lunch and want

the tune you hear predicts the future. While I hear a trip to Tibet, hopeful would-be brides swear they hear Mendelssohn's "Wedding March.")

Walk to the end of the palace, to the Modernist **sculpture** of a nude boy with a laurel leaf (*Victory* by Jan Štursa). From here appreciate the no-nonsense fortress-like appearance of the castle complex across the deep natural moat (including three medieval fortified towers)—quite a contrast to the palatial appearance projected to town from the other side.

From here, set your sights on the cathedral's lacy, black spires marking the castle's entrance. As you walk through the gardens (following the path generally to the right along the wall of the castle to the complex entrance), you'll enjoy fine views of the cathedral.

Take a moment to appreciate the **Royal Gardens** (Královská Zahrada)—the first "exotic" garden in town. Tree varieties, newly discovered by those seafaring ships, were imported from across the world. The first tulips in Europe were grown in this garden in the 1530s (and then imported by the Dutch, which changed Holland's history).

On the left, pass the white, Renaissance **Ball Game Hall.** Study the Greek mythology-inspired decor. The allegorical figures at the top depict (from left to right) the four elements, the seven virtues, and the seven sciences.

Continue along. On the right, notice the small, ostensibly empty **house,** with a pseudo-Baroque entry adjoining two side wings. Since the 1950s this had been the residence of communist "people's" presidents (who, in a royal gesture, used the adjacent garden only for themselves).

In the late 1980s, this was where the estranged and aging last communist president Gustáv Husák lived and eventually (so hated by his countrymen) went insane. His successor, Václav Havel, refused to reside in the house his former jailer had used, and opened the garden to the public. To many Czechs, enjoying the formerly off-limits garden of kings and presidents still is a celebration of freedom and democracy.

As you leave the garden, you'll come to the Powder Bridge, which leads to the castle complex. You're now ready to join the self-guided castle tour.

to add on an efficient visit to the sights above the castle, ride the tram to the Pohořelec stop. Tour the Strahov Monastery, then drop by Loreta Church on your way (downhill) to Castle Square. By the time you hit the Castle Square sights, the crowds should be thinning out (if St. Vitus is jammed, circle back later). The only risk is running out of time to enter all the sights by closing time.

PRAGUE

Note that if you do this plan too early (starting with Strahov and Loreta), you'll wind up at the busiest entrance (Castle Square) at the busiest time...no fun. Instead, save these sights for after your castle visit.

Nighttime Visit: The castle is least crowded at night. True, the sights are closed, but the castle grounds are free, safe, peaceful, floodlit, and open late. The tiny, normally jammed Golden Lane (medieval merchant street) is empty and romantic at night—and no ticket is required.

Orientation to Prague Castle

Cost: Admission to the castle grounds is free, but you need a ticket to enter the sights. Most visitors choose "Circuit B"—think "B" for "basic" (250 Kč)—which covers the highlights: St. Vitus Cathedral, the Old Royal Palace, the Basilica of St. George, and the Golden Lane. The more comprehensive "Circuit A" (350 Kč) adds a few sights, most notably The Story of Prague Castle exhibit, which interests those with a healthy appetite for history. Tickets are good for two days.

Hours: Castle sights—daily 9:00-17:00, Nov-March until 16:00; castle grounds—daily 5:00-24:00; castle gardens—daily 10:00-18:00 in summer, closed Nov-March. On Sunday, St. Vitus Cathedral is closed until noon for Mass. The cathedral can close unexpectedly for special services (check the event calendar at www.katedralasvatehovita.cz or call 724-933-441 to confirm).

Information: Tel. 224-371-111, www.hrad.cz.

More Sights at the Castle: Additional sights within the complex are covered by separate tickets and have their own hours: the **St. Vitus Treasury in the Chapel of the Holy Cross** (300 Kč, daily 10:00-18:00, last entry one hour before closing), climbing the **Great South Tower of St. Vitus Cathedral** (150 Kč, daily 10:00-18:00, until 16:00 in winter), and **Lobkowicz Palace** (275 Kč, daily 10:00-18:00, tel. 233-312-925, www.lobkowicz.cz).

Tours: An **audioguide** is available from the ticket offices (350 Kč plus 500-Kč deposit). I'd skip it in favor of this book's self-guided tour.

◎ Self-Guided Tour

• *Begin your visit to the castle complex at the northern entrance, which leads from the Royal Gardens to the castle. If approaching from Castle Square, you can join this tour at stop #2, the Second Courtyard.*

❶ Powder Bridge (Prašný most)

Before you cross the bridge, survey the scene ahead of you. To your left is the most impressive view of the prickly steeples and flying buttresses of the majestic St. Vitus Cathedral, which stands in the middle of the medieval iceberg called Prague Castle. It's a 1,900-foot-long series of courtyards, churches, and palaces, covering 750,000 square feet—by some measures, the largest castle on earth. Crossing the bridge (actually a landfill), look down into the abysmal Stag Moat (Jelení příkop) that naturally protects the fortress from the north.

The stoic **guards** at this northern entrance make a great photo-op, as does the changing of the guard (on the hour). In fact, there's a guard-changing ceremony at every gate. The biggest, but most crowded, ceremony occurs at noon, at the top gate by Castle Square.

• *Before you enter, buy your castle ticket in the tiny (and least crowded) office on the left. Walk through the double gate and emerge into the...*

❷ Second Courtyard

During the 18th century, Empress Maria Theresa commissioned her favorite Italian architect to connect the disparate buildings in the castle grounds into a unified Neoclassical whole. While Maria Theresa never resided here, the imposing—and to this day largely empty—complex was meant to project the aura of undisputed Habsburg power. This included painting the whole thing in the Habsburgs' favorite shade of yellow. Locals still feel uncomfortable in these "Viennese" surroundings and rush through the courtyard to take cover in one of the blessedly medieval interiors.

Before you do the same, note the fountain and Renaissance well in the middle of the square. Just to the left of the well, the modern green awning (with the golden-winged, cat-like griffin) marks the entrance to the **offices of the Czech president.** If the president is in town, his flag flies over the roof at the opposite end of the square.

• *Now walk through the passageway (to the left of the president's office) that leads into the Third Courtyard. When you emerge, you'll see the impressive facade of St. Vitus Cathedral. Even without a ticket, tourists can step into the church entryway for a nice (if very crowded) view of the nave (and a bit of the Mucha stained glass)—but it's worth paying to see the whole church.*

❸ St. Vitus Cathedral (Katedrála Sv. Víta)

This Roman Catholic cathedral, worth ▲▲▲, is the Czech national church—it's where kings were crowned, royalty have their tombs, the relics of saints are venerated, and the crown jewels are kept. Since AD 920, a church has stood on this spot, marking the very origins of the Czech nation.

PRAGUE

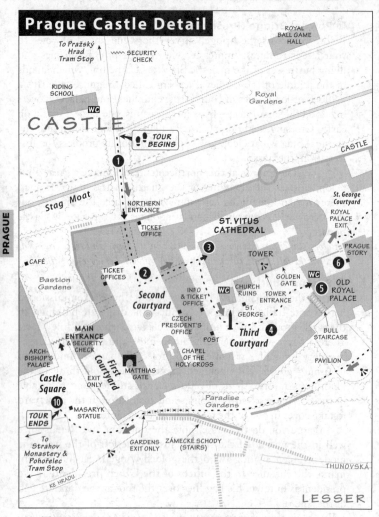

Prague Castle Detail

To Pražský Hrad Tram Stop

⋘ SECURITY CHECK

ROYAL BALL GAME HALL

RIDING SCHOOL

WC

CASTLE

Royal Gardens

👣 TOUR BEGINS

CASTLE

❶

Stag Moat

NORTHERN ENTRANCE

TICKET OFFICE

St. George Courtyard

ROYAL PALACE EXIT

ST. VITUS CATHEDRAL

PRAGUE STORY

❸

TOWER

❻

CAFÉ

TICKET OFFICES

❷

GOLDEN GATE

WC

Bastion Gardens

Second Courtyard

INFO & TICKET OFFICE

WC

CHURCH RUINS

TOWER ENTRANCE

❺

OLD ROYAL PALACE

ST. GEORGE

CZECH PRESIDENT'S OFFICE

❹

MAIN ENTRANCE & SECURITY CHECK

POST

Third Courtyard

BULL STAIRCASE

ARCH- BISHOP'S PALACE

First Courtyard

EXIT ONLY

CHAPEL OF THE HOLY CROSS

PAVILION

Castle Square

MATTHIAS GATE

Paradise Gardens

TOUR ENDS

❿

MASARYK STATUE

To Strahov Monastery & Pohořelec Tram Stop

GARDENS EXIT ONLY

ZÁMECKÉ SCHODY (STAIRS)

THUNOVSKÁ

KE HRADU

LESSER

The letters below correspond to the cathedral map.

Ⓐ Entrance Facade: The two soaring towers of this Gothic wonder rise up 270 feet. The ornate facade features pointed arches, elaborate tracery, Flamboyant pinnacles, a rose window, a dozen statues of saints, and gargoyles sticking out their tongues.

So what's up with the four guys in modern suits carved into the stone, as if supporting the

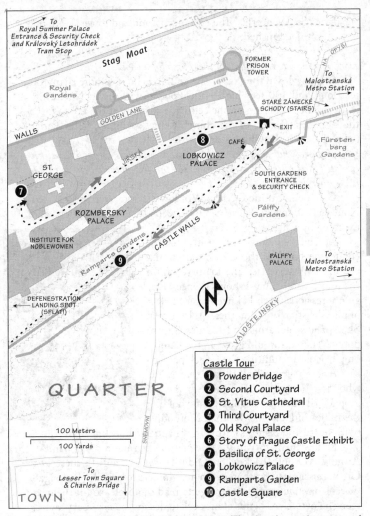

To
Royal Summer Palace
Entrance & Security Check
and Královský Letohrádek
Tram Stop

Stag Moat

Royal
Gardens

WALLS

GOLDEN LANE

FORMER
PRISON
TOWER

To
Malostranská
Metro Station

STARÉ ZÁMECKÉ
SCHODY (STAIRS)

EXIT

Fürsten-
berg
Gardens

JIŘSKÁ

ST.
GEORGE

7

8

CAFÉ

LOBKOWICZ
PALACE

SOUTH GARDENS
ENTRANCE
& SECURITY CHECK

Pálffy
Gardens

ROZMBERSKY
PALACE

INSTITUTE FOR
NOBLEWOMEN

Ramparts Gardens

CASTLE WALLS

9

PÁLFFY
PALACE

To
Malostranská
Metro Station

DEFENESTRATION
LANDING SPOT
(SPLAT!)

VALDŠTEJNSKÝ

QUARTER

100 Meters

100 Yards

To
Lesser Town Square
& Charles Bridge

TOWN

SNĚMOVNÍ

Castle Tour
1. Powder Bridge
2. Second Courtyard
3. St. Vitus Cathedral
4. Third Courtyard
5. Old Royal Palace
6. Story of Prague Castle Exhibit
7. Basilica of St. George
8. Lobkowicz Palace
9. Ramparts Garden
10. Castle Square

PRAGUE

big round window on their shoulders? They're the architects and builders who finished the church six centuries after it was started.

Even though church construction got under way in 1344, wars, plagues, and the reforms of Jan Hus conspired to stall its completion. Finally, fueled by a burst of Czech nationalism, Prague's top church was finished in 1929 for the 1,000th Jubilee anni-

versary of St. Wenceslas. The entrance facade and towers were the last parts to be finished.

• *Enter the cathedral. If it's not too crowded in the free entrance area, work your way to the middle of the church for a good...*

❶ **View down the Nave:** The church is huge—more than 400 feet long and 100 feet high—and flooded with light. Notice the intricate "net" vaulting on the ceiling, especially at the far end. It's the signature feature of the church's chief architect, Peter Parler (who also built the Charles Bridge).

• *Now make your way through the crowds and pass through the ticket turnstile (left of the roped-off area). The third window on the left wall is worth a close look.*

❷ **Mucha Stained-Glass Window:** This masterful 1931 Art Nouveau window was designed by Czech artist Alfons Mucha and executed by a stained-glass craftsman.

Mucha's window was created to celebrate the birth of the Czech nation and the life of Wenceslas. The main scene (in the four central panels) shows Wenceslas as an impressionable child kneeling at the feet of his Christian grandmother, St. Ludmila. She spreads her arms and teaches him to pray. Wenceslas would grow up to champion Christianity, uniting the Czech people.

Above Wenceslas are the two saints who first brought Christianity to the region: Cyril (the monk in black hood holding the Bible) and his older brother, Methodius (with beard and bishop's garb). They baptize a kneeling convert.

Follow their story in the side panels, starting in the upper left. Around AD 860 (back when Ludmila was just a girl), these two Greek missionary brothers arrive in Moravia to preach. The pagan Czechs have no written language to read the Bible, so (in the next scene below), Cyril bends at his desk to design the necessary alphabet (Glagolitic, which later developed into Cyrillic), while Methodius meditates. In the next three scenes, they travel to Rome and present their newly translated Bible to the pope. But Cyril falls ill, and Methodius watches his kid brother die.

Methodius carries on (in the upper right), becoming bishop of the Czech lands. Next, he's arrested for heresy for violating the pure Latin Bible. He's sent to a lonely prison. When he's finally set free, he retires to a monastery, where he dies mourned by the faithful.

At the bottom center are two beautiful (classic Mucha) maidens, representing the bright future of the Czech and Slovak peoples.

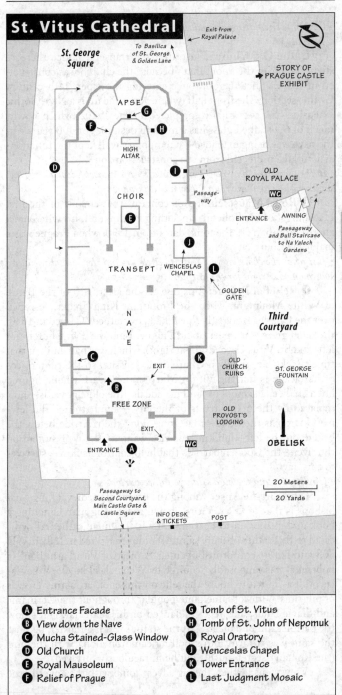

St. Vitus Cathedral

St. George Square

Exit from Royal Palace

To Basilica of St. George & Golden Lane

STORY OF PRAGUE CASTLE EXHIBIT

APSE

HIGH ALTAR

CHOIR

OLD ROYAL PALACE

WC

ENTRANCE · AWNING

Passageway

Passageway and Bull Staircase to Na Valech Gardens

TRANSEPT

WENCESLAS CHAPEL

GOLDEN GATE

N A V E

Third Courtyard

FREE ZONE

EXIT

OLD CHURCH RUINS

ST. GEORGE FOUNTAIN

OLD PROVOST'S LODGING

EXIT

WC

OBELISK

ENTRANCE

PRAGUE

20 Meters
20 Yards

Passageway to Second Courtyard, Main Castle Gate & Castle Square

INFO DESK & TICKETS

POST

A Entrance Facade
B View down the Nave
C Mucha Stained-Glass Window
D Old Church
E Royal Mausoleum
F Relief of Prague

G Tomb of St. Vitus
H Tomb of St. John of Nepomuk
I Royal Oratory
J Wenceslas Chapel
K Tower Entrance
L Last Judgment Mosaic

• *Continue circulating around the church, following the one-way, clockwise route.*

❶ The Old Church: Just after the transept, notice there's a slight incline in the floor. That's because the church was constructed in two distinct stages. You're entering the older, 14th-century Gothic section. The front half (where you came in) is a Neo-Gothic extension that was finally completed in the 1920s (which is why much of the stained glass has a modern design). For 400 years—as the nave was being extended—a temporary wall kept the functional altar area protected from the construction zone.

• *In the choir area (on your right), soon after the transept, look for the big, white marble tomb surrounded by a black iron fence.*

❷ Royal Mausoleum: This contains the remains of the first Habsburgs to rule Bohemia, including Ferdinand I, his wife Anne, and Maximilian II. The tomb dates from 1590, when Prague was a major Habsburg city.

• *Just after the choir, as you begin to circle around the back of the altar, watch on your right for the fascinating, carved-wood...*

❸ Relief of Prague: This depicts the aftermath of the Battle of White Mountain, when the Protestant King Frederic escaped over the Charles Bridge (before it had any statues). Carved in 1630, the relief gives you a peek at old Prague. Find the Týn Church (far left) and St. Vitus Cathedral (far right), which was half-built at that time. Back then the Týn Church was Hussite, so the centerpiece of its facade is not the Virgin Mary (more of a Catholic figure), but a chalice, a symbol of Jan Hus' ideals. The old city walls—now replaced by the main streets of the city—stand strong. The Jewish Quarter is the flood-prone zone along the riverside below the bridge on the left—land no one else wanted. The weir system on the river—the wooden barriers that help control its flow—survives to this day.

• *Circling around the high altar, you'll see various...*

Tombs in the Apse: Among the graves of medieval kings and bishops is that of **❹ St. Vitus,** shown as a young man clutching a book and gazing up to heaven. Why is this huge cathedral dedicated to this rather obscure saint, who was martyred in Italy in AD 303 and never set foot in Bohemia? A piece of Vitus' arm bone (a holy relic) was supposedly acquired by Wenceslas I in 925. Wenceslas built a church to house the relic on this spot, attracting crowds of pilgrims. Vitus became quite popular throughout the Germanic and Slavic lands, and revelers danced on his feast day. (He's now the patron saint of dancers.) At the statue's feet is a rooster, because the saint was thrown into a boiling cauldron along with the bird (the Romans' secret sauce)...but he miraculously survived.

A few steps farther, the big silvery tomb with the angel-borne

canopy honors ❽ **St. John of Nepomuk.** Locals claim it has more than a ton of silver.

Just past the tomb, on the wall of the choir (on the right), is another finely carved, circa-1630 **wood relief** depicting an event that took place right here in St. Vitus: Protestant nobles trash the cathedral's Catholic icons after their (short-lived) victory.

Ahead on the left, look up at the ❾ **royal oratory,** a box supported by busy late-Gothic, vine-like ribs. This private box, connected to the king's apartment by an outside corridor, let the king attend Mass in his jammies. The underside of the balcony is morbidly decorated with dead vines and tree branches, suggesting the pessimism common in the late Gothic period, when religious wars and Ottoman invasions threatened the Czech lands.

• *From here, walk 25 paces and look left through the crowds and door to see the richly decorated chapel containing the tomb of St. Wenceslas. Two roped-off doorways give visitors a look inside. The best view is from the second one, around the corner and to the left, in the transept.*

❿ **Wenceslas Chapel:** This fancy chapel is the historic heart of the church. It contains the tomb of St. Wenceslas, patron saint of

the Czech nation; it's where Bohemia's kings were crowned; and it houses (but rarely displays) the Bohemian crown jewels. The chapel walls are paneled with big slabs of precious and semiprecious stones. The jewel-toned stained-glass windows (from the 1950s) admit a soft light. The chandelier is exceptional. The place feels medieval.

The tomb of St. Wenceslas is a colored-stone coffin topped with an ark. Above the chapel's altar is a statue of Wenceslas, bearing a lance and a double-eagle shield. He's flanked by (painted) angels and the four patron saints of the Czech people. Above Wenceslas are portraits of Charles IV (who built the current church) and his beautiful wife. On the wall to the left of the altar, frescoes depict the saint's life, including the episode where angels arrive with crosses to arm the holy warrior. For centuries, Czech kings were crowned right here in front of Wenceslas' red-draped coffin.

• *Leave the cathedral, turn left (past the public WC), and survey the…*

PRAGUE

PRAGUE

❹ Third Courtyard

The **obelisk** was erected in 1928—a single piece of granite celebrating the 10th anniversary of the establishment of Czechoslovakia and commemorating the soldiers who fought for its independence. It was originally much taller, but broke in transit—an inauspicious start for a nation destined to last only 70 years.

From here, you get a great look at the sheer size of St. Vitus Cathedral and its fat green **tower** (325 feet tall). Up there is the Czech Republic's biggest **bell** (16.5 tons, from 1549), nicknamed "Zikmund." You can view the bell as you climb up the 287 steps of the tower to the observation deck at the top (❻ **tower tickets and entry** near sculpture of St. George—a 1960s replica of the 13th-century original).

It's easy to find the church's **Golden Gate** (for centuries the cathedral's main entry)—look for the glittering ❼ **14th-century mosaic of the Last Judgment.** The modern, cosmopolitan, and ahead-of-his-time Charles IV commissioned this monumental decoration in 1370 in the Italian style. Jesus oversees the action, as some go to heaven and some go to hell. The Czech king and queen kneel directly beneath Jesus and six patron saints. On coronation day, royalty would walk under this arch, a reminder to them (and their subjects) that even those holding great power are not above God's judgment.

Across from the Golden Gate, in the corner, notice the copper, scroll-like **awning** supported by bulls. This leads to a fine garden just below the castle. The stairway, garden, and other features around the castle were designed in the 1920s by the Slovene architect Jože Plečnik (see page 755). Around the turn of the 20th century, Prague was considered the cultural standard-bearer of the entire Slavic world—making this a particularly prestigious assignment.

• *In the corner of the Third Courtyard, near the copper awning, is the entrance to the...*

❺ Old Royal Palace (Starý Královský Palác)

The highlight of the palace building (dating from the 12th century), and worth ▲▲, is the large **Vladislav Hall**—200 feet long, with an impressive vaulted ceiling of vine-shaped (late-Gothic) tracery. It could be filled with market stalls, letting aristocrats shop without actually going into town. It was big enough for jousts—even the staircase (which you'll use as you exit) was designed to let a mounted soldier gallop in. Beginning in the 1500s, nobles met here to elect the king. The tradition survived into modern times. As recently as the 1990s, the Czech parliament crowded into this room to elect their president.

On your immediate right, enter the two small Renaissance rooms known as the **"Czech Office."** From these rooms, two governors used to oversee the Czech lands for the Habsburgs in Vienna. Head for the far room, wrapped in windows. In 1618, angry Czech Protestant nobles poured into these rooms and threw the two Catholic governors out the window. An old law actually permits this act—called defenestration—which usually targets bad politicians.

As you re-enter the main hall, go to the far end and out on the **balcony** for a sweeping view of Prague.

• *The next sight requires the "Circuit A" ticket; if you don't have one, skip down to the following stop.*

Otherwise, as you exit the Royal Palace, hook left around the side of the building and backtrack a few steps uphill to find stairs leading down to...

❻ The Story of Prague Castle Exhibit (Příběh Pražského Hradu)

This museum of old artifacts (with good English descriptions) is your best look at castle history and its kings, all housed in the cool Gothic cellars of the Old Royal Palace. Throughout the exhibit, models of the castle show how it grew over the centuries.

• *Directly across the courtyard from the rear buttresses of St. Vitus is a very old church with a pretty red facade. This is the...*

❼ Basilica of St. George (Bazilika Sv. Jiří)

Step into one of the oldest structures (worth ▲) at Prague Castle to see this re-created Romanesque church (a product of a 19th-century "purification" that removed the successive layers of Baroque) and the burial place of Czech royalty. The church was founded by Wenceslas' dad before 920, and the present structure dates from the 12th century. (Its Baroque facade and side chapel that survived the purification came later.) Inside, the place is beautiful in its simplicity. Notice the characteristic thick walls and rounded arches. In those early years, building techniques were not yet advanced enough to use those arches for the ceiling—it's made of wood instead.

This was the royal burial place before St. Vitus was built, so the

PRAGUE

tombs here contain the remains of the earliest Czech kings. Climb the stairs that frame either side of the altar to study the area around the apse. St. Wenceslas' grandmother, Ludmila, was reburied here in 925. Her stone tomb is in the added Gothic chapel just to the right of the altar. Inside the archway leading to her tomb, look for her portrait.

• *Exit the church and continue walking downhill. Notice the basilica's gorgeous Renaissance side entrance, with St. George fighting the dragon in the tympanum. You'll next see the basilica's Romanesque nave and towers—a strong contrast to the lavish painted Baroque facade. Farther down, to the left, were the residences of soldiers and craftsmen (now making up the touristy Golden Lane), and to the right, tucked together, were the palaces of Catholic nobility who wanted both to be close to power and able to band together should the Protestants grab the upper hand. Your next stop is at the far end of the street, on the right.*

❽ Lobkowicz Palace (Lobkowiczký Palác)

This palace, rated ▲▲, displays the private collection of a prominent Czech noble family, including paintings, ceramics, and musical scores. The Lobkowiczes' property was confiscated twice in the 20th century: first by the Nazis at the beginning of World War II, and then by the communists in 1948. In 1990, William Lobkowicz, then a Boston investment banker, returned to Czechoslovakia to fight a legal battle to reclaim his family's property and, eventually, to restore the castles and palaces to their former state. The obvious care that went into creating this museum, the collection's variety, and the personal insight that it opens into the past and present of Czech nobility make the Lobkowicz worth an hour of your time. Your conscientious host is William Lobkowicz, who narrates the delightful, included audioguide. Use the map that comes with your ticket to home in on the highlights:

• *Once you're done touring the palace, you have several choices, including visiting the ▲ Golden Lane—a medieval merchant street with shops (included in your basic ticket but very touristy and skippable).*

*Otherwise, you can **exit the castle complex** by squirting slowly through a fortified door at the bottom end of the castle with all the other tourists. A scenic rampart just below the lower gate offers a commanding view of the city. From there, you can either head to the Malostran-*

ská tram/Metro station and riverbank, or loop around to Castle Square *(where this tour continues) and/or to Strahov Monastery.*

To reach Malostranská station, follow the crowds down the 700-some steps of a steep lane called Staré Zámecké Schody ("Old Castle Stairs"). To continue this tour (or to reach Strahov Monastery), take a hard right as you leave the castle gate, and stroll through the long, delightful...

❾ Ramparts Garden (Zahrada Na Valech)

These gardens come with commanding views of the city below (free, daily 10:00-18:00 or later, closed Nov-March). Along the way, notice the Modernist layout of the gardens, designed by Jože Plečnik of Slovenia. Halfway through the long park is a circular viewpoint. At roughly the same distance under the brick wall of the Royal Palace, find a Baroque column commemorating the miraculous survival of the defenestrated overlords. As you exit the garden at the far end through a narrow gate on top of a wide, monumental staircase, notice the cool wolf snout design of the adjacent door knob, another Plečnik trademark.

• *Make your way into...*

❿ Castle Square (Hradčanské Náměstí)

Castle Square was the focal point of pre-modern power. The **Fighting Titans** sculpture, depicting two triumphant gladiators, marks the main entry into the residence of Czech kings. The archbishop lived (and still lives) in the **Archbishop's Palace**—the ornate, white-and-yellow Rococo building with the oversized facade. Above the doorway is the family coat of arms of the archbishop that built this palace: three white goose necks in a red field. The portal on the left leads to the **Sternberg Palace** art museum, with European paintings.

Closer to you, near the overlook, the statue of a man in a business suit (marked *TGM*) honors the father of modern Czechoslovakia: **Tomáš Garrigue Masaryk.** At the end of World War I, Masaryk—a university professor and pal of Woodrow Wilson—united the Czechs and the Slovaks into one nation and became its first president.

Entertaining bands play regularly by the Masaryk statue. (If the Prague Castle Orchestra is playing, say hello to friendly, mustachioed Josef, and consider buying the group's CD—it's terrific.)

On the left side of the

Tomáš Garrigue Masaryk (1850-1937)

Tomáš Masaryk founded the first democracy in Eastern Europe at the end of World War I, uniting the Czechs and the Slovaks to create Czechoslovakia. Like Václav Havel 70 years later, Masaryk was a politician whose vision extended far beyond the mountains enclosing the Bohemian basin.

Masaryk, from a poor servant family in southern Moravia, earned his Ph.D. in sociology in Vienna, studied in Leipzig, then became a professor at Charles University of Prague. By then, he was married to American Charlotta Garrigue, a social revolutionary from a unitarian New York family. Through Charlotta, Masaryk was introduced to America's high society, which proved crucial in 1918 when he successfully campaigned here for the recognition of his new country.

Masaryk was greatly impressed with America, and his admiration for its democratic system (and his wife) became the core of his evolving political creed. He traveled the world and served in the Vienna parliament. At the outbreak of World War I, while most other Czech politicians stayed in Prague and supported the Habsburg Empire, 64-year-old Masaryk went abroad in protest and formed a highly original plan: to create an independent, democratic republic of Czechs and Slovaks. Masaryk and his supporters recruited an army of 100,000 soldiers who were willing to fight with the Allies against the Habsburgs, establishing a strong case to put on official desks in Paris, London, and Washington.

On the morning of October 28, 1918, news of the unofficial capitulation of the Habsburgs reached Prague. Supporters of Masaryk's plan quickly took control of the city and proclaimed the free republic. As the people of Prague tore down double-headed eagles (a symbol of the Habsburgs), the country of Czechoslovakia was born.

On December 21, 1918, four years after he had left the country as a political unknown, Masaryk arrived in Prague as the greatest Czech hero since the revolutionary priest Jan Hus. He told the jubilant crowd, "Now go home—the work has only started." Throughout the 1920s and 1930s, Masaryk was a vocal defender of democratic ideals in Europe against the rising tide of totalitarian ideologies.

Today Masaryk is one of only a few foreign leaders to be honored with a statue in Washington, DC.

square, behind the statue, the building with a step-gable roofline is **Schwarzenberg Palace,** where the aristocrats from Český Krumlov stayed when they were visiting from their country estates. Notice the envelope-shaped patterns stamped on the exterior. These Renaissance-era adornments etched into wet stucco—called sgraffito—decorate buildings throughout the castle, and all over Prague and the Czech Republic. Today Schwarzenberg Palace is an art museum with a collection of Baroque-era Czech paintings and sculpture.

The dark gray Baroque sculpture in the middle of the square is a **plague column.** Erected as a token of gratitude to Mary and the saints for saving the population from epidemic disease, these columns are an integral part of the main squares of many Habsburg towns.

Two more palaces are worth looking at. At the far-right corner of the square, past the plague column, is the delightful **Martinický Palace,** with delicate Renaissance portals and detailed figural sgraffito depicting the feats of biblical Joseph and mythic Hercules. The pastel **Toskánský Palace** at the western end of the square is a beautifully balanced example of Baroque palatial architecture.

• *At the top corner of Toskánský Palace, you have the option of either continuing up along Loretánská street to the Loreta Church and Strahov Monastery, described later, or taking the scenic staircase on the left down to the top of Nerudova street in the Lesser Town.*

SIGHTS ABOVE THE CASTLE

The Strahov Monastery, with its twin Baroque domes, and the pretty Loreta Church sit above the castle and are easy to combine with your castle visit. Visiting the monastery first allows you to walk downhill to the castle (with fine views and passing Loreta Church on the way), but it also means you'll wind up at the busiest entrance to the castle. If you anticipate crowds, see the castle sights first, then walk back up to Loreta and Strahov.

Getting There: If coming from central Prague, take tram #22 or #23 to the Pohořelec stop. Follow the tracks for 50 yards, take the pedestrian lane that rises up beside the tram tracks, and enter the fancy gate on the left near the tall red-brick wall. You'll see the twin spires of the monastery; the library entrance is on the little square with the monastery church. If coming from the castle, exit Castle Square past the Toskánský Palace and walk up along the Loretánská street to the church and monastery.

▲Strahov Monastery and Library (Strahovský Klášter a Knihovna)

This fine old monastery has perched on the hill just above Prague Castle since the 12th century. Medieval monasteries were a mix of

industry, agriculture, and education, as well as worship and
theology. In its heyday, Strahov
Monastery had a booming economy of its own, with vineyards,
a brewery, and a sizable beer
hall—all now open once again.
You can explore the monastery
complex, check out the beautiful old library, and even enjoy a

brew (no longer monk-made, but still refreshing).

Cost and Hours: Grounds—free and always open; library—120 Kč, daily 9:00-12:00 & 13:00-17:00, tel. 233-107-718,
www.strahovskyklaster.cz. A pay WC is just to the right of the
monastery entrance.

Visiting the Monastery and Library: The monastery's **main
church,** dedicated to the Assumption of St. Mary, is an originally

Romanesque structure decorated
by the monks in textbook Baroque (usually closed, but look
through the gate inside the front
door to see its interior). Notice
the grand effect of the Baroque
architecture—both rhythmic and
theatric. Go ahead, inhale. That's
the scent of Baroque.

Buy your ticket in the adjacent building, and head up the
stairs to the **library,** offering a peek at how enlightened thinkers
in the 18th century influenced learning. The **display cases** in the
library gift shop show off illuminated manuscripts, described in
English. Some are in old Czech, but because the Enlightenment
promoted the universality of knowledge (and Latin was the universal language of Europe's educated elite), there was little place
for regional dialects—therefore, few books here are in the Czech
language.

Two rooms (seen only from the doors) are filled with 10th-
to 17th-century books, shelved under elaborately painted ceilings.
The theme of the first and bigger hall is **philosophy,** with the history of Western man's pursuit of knowledge painted on the ceiling.
The second hall—down a hallway lined with antique furniture—
focuses on **theology.** As the Age of Enlightenment began to take
hold in Europe at the end of the 18th century, monasteries still
controlled the books. Notice the gilded, locked case containing the
libri prohibiti (prohibited books) at the end of the room, above the
mirror. Only the abbot had the key, and you had to have his bless-

ing to read these books—by writers such as Nicolas Copernicus, Jan Hus, Jean-Jacques Rousseau, and even including the French encyclopedia.

The **hallway** connecting the two library rooms was filled with cases illustrating the new practical approach to natural sciences. In the crowded area near the philosophy hall, find the dried-up elephant trunks (flanking the narwhal or unicorn horn) and one of the earliest models of an electricity generator.

Nearby: That hoppy smell you're enjoying in front of the monastery is the recommended **Klášterní Pivovar,** where they brew beer just as monks have for centuries (in the little courtyard directly across from the library entrance; described on page 141).

Tucked in another courtyard across from the Strahov Monastery, the **Museum of Miniatures** (Muzeum Miniatur) displays 40 teeny exhibits—each under a microscope—crafted by an artist from a remote corner of Siberia (100 Kč, kids—50 Kč, daily 9:00-17:00, Strahovské Nádvoří 11, tel. 233-352-371).

Downhill from the Museum of Miniatures and through the gate, just after the Bellavista Restaurant, find the ▲ **monastery garden view terrace** to the right. From the public perch beneath the restaurant tables, you'll have exquisite views over the domes and spires of Prague.

Loreta Square (Loretánské Náměstí)

On the way to Castle Square (from Strahov Monastery, or directly from the tram stop) is Loreta Square, dominated by the beautiful Baroque **Loreta Church** (described below).

Černín Palace, on the uphill (left) side of the square, was once the unfortunate site of a modern-day defenestration. On March 10, 1948, soon after the communists took over, popular Czechoslovak politician Jan Masaryk (son of Tomáš Garrigue Masaryk, Czechoslovakia's first president) was found dead in this building's courtyard, below a palace bathroom window. While authorities at the time ruled it a suicide, an independent forensic examination in the 1990s confirmed foul play. The most likely theory is that Masaryk was killed by the Soviet secret police, who had learned of Masaryk's plans to leave the country and represent it while in exile.

In 2005, a controversial memorial to Czechoslovakia's second president, **Edvard Beneš,** was unveiled in front of the Černín Palace. Beneš cozied up with Stalin during World War II, and after the war he masterminded the eviction of more than two million Germans from Czechoslovakia (see sidebar on page 194). Notice the slumping posture and look of worry on his face.

▲Loreta Church

This church has been a hit with pilgrims for centuries, thanks to its dazzling bell tower, peaceful yet plush cloister, sparkling trea-

PRAGUE

sury, and much-venerated Holy House. In the middle of the cloister courtyard, you'll find what's considered by some pilgrims to
be part of Mary's actual home in Nazareth. You'll also see one of
Prague's most beautiful Baroque churches, a fine treasury collection (upstairs), and—in a tiny chapel in one corner—"St. Bearded
Woman," the patron saint of unhappy marriages.

Cost and Hours: 150 Kč; daily 9:00-17:00, Nov-March 9:30-
16:00; audioguide-150 Kč, tel. 220-516-740, www.loreta.cz.

Shopping in Prague

Most shops are open on weekdays 9:00-17:00 or 18:00—and often
longer, especially for tourist-oriented shops. Some close on Saturday afternoons and/or all day Sunday.

SHOPPING STREETS IN THE CENTER

For easy shopping in the tourist zone, consider the following streets.

The Ungelt, the courtyard tucked behind the Týn Church just
off of the Old Town Square, is packed with touristy but decent-
quality shops. Material has a fine selection of contemporary-style
bead jewelry, and Botanicus is an excellent herbal cosmetics shop.
Fajans Majolica has traditional blue-and-white Czech pottery
(www.fajans.cz), and V Ungeltu and Hračky, Loutky sell marionettes.

Michalská, a semihidden lane right in the thick of the tourist
zone, has a variety of shops (from the Small Market Square/Malé
Náměstí near the Astronomical Clock, go through the big stone
gateway marked *459*).

On **Havelská** street, you can browse the open-air Havelská
Market, a touristy but enjoyable place to shop for inexpensive
handicrafts and fresh produce (daily 9:00-18:00, two long blocks
south of the Old Town Square).

Celetná, exiting the Old Town Square to the right of Týn
Church, is lined with big stores selling all the traditional Czech
goodies. Tourists wander endlessly here, mesmerized by the window displays.

Na Příkopě, the mostly pedestrianized street following the
former moat between the Old Town and the New Town, has the
city center's handiest lineup of modern shopping malls. The best is
Slovanský Dům ("Slavic House," at #22), where you'll wander past
a 10-screen multiplex deep into a world of classy restaurants and
designer shops surrounding a peaceful, parklike inner courtyard.
Černá Růže ("Black Rose," at #12) has a great Japanese restaurant around a small garden; Moser's flagship crystal showroom is
also here. The Galerie Myslbek, directly across the street, has fancy
stores in a space built to Prague's scale. Na Příkopě street opens

up into Republic Square (Náměstí Republiky)—boasting Prague's biggest mall, Palladium, hidden behind a pink Neo-Romanesque facade. Across the square is the communist-era brown steel-and-glass 1980s department store Kotva ("Anchor"), an obsolete beast on the verge of extinction.

Národní Třída (National Street), which continues past Na Příkopě in the opposite direction (toward the river), is less touristy and lined with some inviting stores.

Karlova, the tourist-clogged drag connecting the Old Town Square to the Charles Bridge, should be avoided entirely. Shops along here sell made-in-China trinkets at too-high prices to lazy and gullible tourists.

SOUVENIR IDEAS

Consider shopping for these Czech specialties.

Puppets: It takes a rare artist to turn pieces of wood into nimble puppets, and prices for the real deal can reach into the thousands of dollars. But given that puppets have a glorious past and vibrant present in the Czech Republic, even a simple jester, witch, or Pinocchio can make a thoughtful memento of your Czech adventure. You'll see cheap trinket puppets at souvenir stands across town. Buying a higher-quality keepsake is more expensive (starting in the $100 range). Here are a few better options to consider:

Marionety Truhlář, near the Lesser Town end of Charles Bridge (U Lužického Semináře 5); **Galerie Michael,** just a few doors down at U Lužického Semináře 7, (www.marionettesmichael.cz); the no-name **Loutky** ("Puppets") shop at the top of Nerudova (at #51, www.loutky.cz); and, in the Ungelt courtyard, **Hračky, Loutky** ("Toys, Puppets").

Glass and Crystal: Legally, to be called "crystal" (or "lead crystal"), it must contain at least 24 percent lead oxide, which lends the glass that special, prismatic sparkle. The lead also adds weight, makes the glass easier to cut, and produces a harmonious ringing when flicked. ("Crystal glass" has a smaller percentage of lead.)

Well-respected sources for Czech glass and crystal include **Moser,** the most famous Czech brand—and one of the most expensive (flagship store at the Černá Růže shopping mall at Na

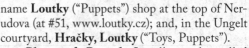

PRAGUE

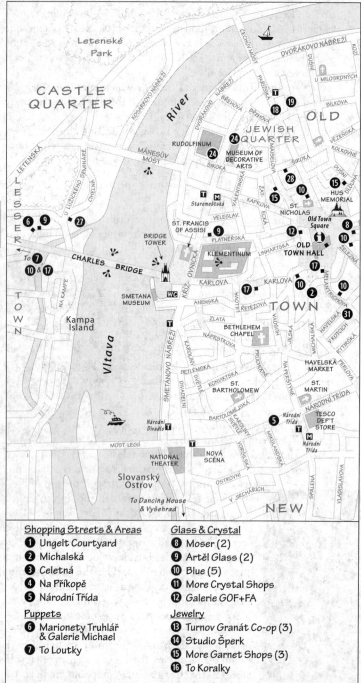

Shopping Streets & Areas
1 Ungelt Courtyard
2 Michalská
3 Celetná
4 Na Příkopě
5 Národní Třída

Puppets
6 Marionety Truhlář & Galerie Michael
7 To Loutky

Glass & Crystal
8 Moser (2)
9 Artěl Glass (2)
10 Blue (5)
11 More Crystal Shops
12 Galerie GOF+FA

Jewelry
13 Turnov Granát Co-op (3)
14 Studio Šperk
15 More Garnet Shops (3)
16 To Koralky

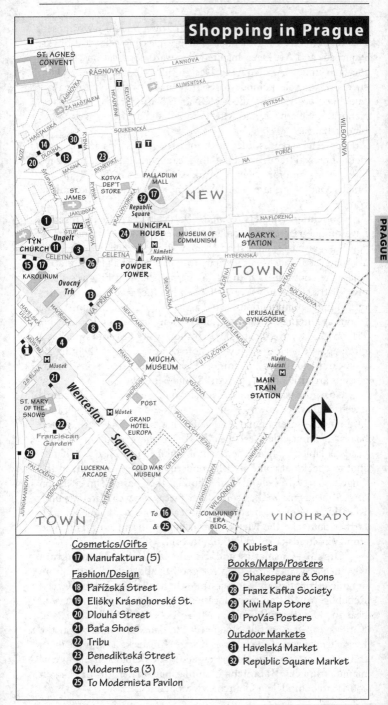

Shopping in Prague

PRAGUE

Cosmetics/Gifts
⑰ Manufaktura (5)

Fashion/Design
⑱ Pařížská Street
⑲ Elišky Krásnohorské St.
⑳ Dlouhá Street
㉑ Baťa Shoes
㉒ Tribu
㉓ Benediktská Street
㉔ Modernista (3)
㉕ To Modernista Pavilon

㉖ Kubista

Books/Maps/Posters
㉗ Shakespeare & Sons
㉘ Franz Kafka Society
㉙ Kiwi Map Store
㉚ ProVás Posters

Outdoor Markets
㉛ Havelská Market
㉜ Republic Square Market

Příkopě 12, plus a branch on the Old Town Square www.moser-glass.com); **Artěl,** with a small but eye-pleasing selection of Art Nouveau- and Art Deco-inspired glassware (for locations, see listing later under "Art Nouveau Design Shops"); and **Blue,** a chain specializing in sleek, modern designs—many of them in the namesake hue (locations include Malé Náměstí 13, Pařížská 3, Melantrichova 6, Celetná 2, and Mostecká 24, and at the airport; www.bluepraha.cz).

Celetná street is lined with touristy glass shops selling a variety of crystal items. But for a unique, experiential take on Czech glass, visit Antonin Manto-Mrnka's **Galerie GOF+FA** (on the Small Market Square at Malé Náměstí 6, www.mantogallery.com).

Bohemian Garnets *(Granát):* These blood-colored gemstones have unique refractive—some claim even curative—properties. If you buy garnet jewelry, shop around, use a reputable dealer, and ask for a certificate of authenticity to avoid buying a glass imitation (these are common). Of the many garnet shops in Prague's shopping districts, **Turnov Granát Co-op** has the largest selection. It's refreshingly unpretentious, with a vaguely retro-communist vibe (shops at Dlouhá 28, Panská 1, and inside the Pánská Pasáž at Na Příkopě 23; www.granat.eu). **J. Drahoňovský's Studio Šperk** is a more upscale-feeling shop with more creative designs (Dlouhá 19, www.drahonovsky.cz). Additional shops specializing in Turnov garnets are at Dlouhá 1, Celetná 8, and Maiselova 3.

Costume Jewelry and Beads: You'll see *bižutérie* (costume jewelry) all over town. Round, glass beads—sometimes called Druk beads—are popular, and can range from large marble-sized beads to minuscule "seed beads." The biggest producer of glass beads is Jablonex, from the town of Jablonec nad Nisou. A handy spot to check out some stylish, modern pieces is **Material,** in the Ungelt courtyard behind Týn Church. They have a fun selection of seed beads, as well as some finer pieces (www.i-material.com). **Koralky,** one of the best-supplied bead shops in Prague, is a bit farther out; take the Metro's green line to the Jiřího z Poděbrad stop (Vinohradská 76, www.koralky.cz).

Organic Cosmetics and Handmade Gifts: Manufaktura is your classy, one-stop shop for good-quality Czech gifts, from organic cosmetics to handicrafts—all handmade in the Czech Republic. You'll find many locations in Prague, including several near the Old Town Square (at Melantrichova 17, Celetná 12, and Karlova 26); at Republic Square (in the Palladium mall); near the Lesser Town end of the Charles Bridge (Mostecká 17); in the main train station; and even along Prague Castle's Golden Lane (www.manufaktura.cz). **Botanicus** is similar but smaller (in the Ungelt courtyard behind Týn Church, www.botanicus.cz).

Fashion and Design: Czechs have a unique sense of fashion. One popular trend is garments that are adorned with embroidery, leather, beads, hand-painted designs, or other flourishes—all handmade and therefore unique. Shops selling these come and go, and in many cases several small designers work together and share a boutique—look for an "atelier." Vintage clothes are also as popular among young Czech hipsters as they are with their American counterparts.

The Jewish Quarter's **Pařížská street** has the highest concentration of big-name international designers, but for something more local, focus on some of the side streets that run parallel to Pařížská. One block over, **Elišky Krásnohorské street** features boutiques selling local designs. A block farther east, more boutiques line **Dušní street.** A short walk away, **Dlouhá street**—which exits the Old Town Square near the Jan Hus statue—offers more Czech designers.

On and Near Wenceslas Square: Fashionistas are sometimes surprised to learn that the famous and well-respected **Baťa** shoe brand is not Italian, but Czech; their seven-story flagship store, on Wenceslas Square (at #6), is nirvana for shoe lovers. Nearby, one of the pavilions inside the Franciscan Garden (hiding just off of Wenceslas Square) houses **Tribu,** a fun and youthful boutique with clothes, jewelry, and other unique pieces (www.tribu.cz).

Funky Hipster Design: Benediktská, a tiny street tucked in a quiet corner of the Old Town, has a little cluster of creative boutiques.

Art Nouveau Design Shops: Prague is Europe's best Art Nouveau city—and several shops give you a chance to take home some of that eye-pleasing style, in the form of glassware, home decor, linens, posters, and other items. **Artěl**—a chain owned by an American (Karen Feldman) who fell in love with Prague and its unique sense of style—is thoughtfully curated (locations at Old Town side of Charles Bridge—Platnéřská 7, and Lesser Town end of Charles Bridge—U Lužického Semináře 7; www.artelglass.com). **Modernista** (downstairs inside the Municipal House) has a fine selection of Art Nouveau and Art Deco jewelry, glassware, wooden toys, books, and so on. Their flagship store is in the **Modernista Pavilon,** a sleek, gorgeously restored former train station that's also home to a variety of trendy fashion and home-decor shops, out in the Vinohrady neighborhood (Vinohradská 50, www.modernista.cz). **Kubista,** in the House of the Black Madonna, has a fun-to-peruse selection of Czech Cubist dishes, jewelry, furniture, books, and more (Ovocný Trh 19, www.kubista.cz).

Books, Maps, Posters, and Music: Try **Shakespeare and Sons** (with a big selection in the Lesser Town) or **Franz Kafka Society** (with a smaller selection in the Jewish Quarter), both open daily and described on page 42. **Kiwi Map Store,** near Wenceslas Square, is Prague's best source for maps and travel guides (Jungmannova 23).

ProVás is a poster shop stocking a wide array of unique posters—originals, reprints, and lots of vintage ads from the 1920s (closed Sat-Sun, Rybná 21).

What Not to Buy: Many Prague souvenir shops sell very non-Czech (especially Russian) items to tourists who don't know better. Amber may be pretty, but—considering it's found along the Baltic Sea coast—obviously doesn't originate from this landlocked country. Stacking dolls, fur hats, and vodka flasks also fall into this category.

Entertainment in Prague

Prague booms with live and inexpensive theater, classical music, jazz, and pop entertainment. Everything is listed in several monthly cultural events programs (free at TIs).

Buying Tickets: Don't bother gathering fliers as you wander through town. To really understand all your options (the street Mozarts are pushing only their own concerts), drop by a **Via Musica** box office. There are two: One is next to Týn Church on the Old Town Square (daily 10:30-19:30, tel. 224-826-969), and the other is in the Lesser Town Square across from the Church of St. Nicholas (daily 10:00-20:00, tel. 257-535-568, www.viamusica.cz). If you don't see a posted list of today's events, just ask for it.

Tips: Locals dress up for the more serious concerts, opera, and ballet, but many tourists wear casual clothes—as long as you don't show up in shorts, sneakers, or flip-flops, you'll be fine. For church concerts, ticket prices at the door are often soft and negotiable.

THEATER AND CONCERTS
Black Light Theater
A kind of mime/modern dance variety show, Black Light Theater has no language barrier and is, for some, more entertaining than a classical concert. Unique to Prague, Black Light Theater originated in the 1960s as a playful and mystifying theater of the absurd. These days aficionados and critical visitors lament that it's either becoming a cheesy variety show or that its rudimentary special effects cannot compare with today's technical possibilities. Shows

last about an hour and a half. Arrive a few minutes early to avoid sitting in the first two rows, which are too close and can ruin the illusion. Each of the following theaters has its own spin on what Black Light is supposed to be. (The other Black Light theaters advertised around town aren't as good.)

Black Light Theatre Srnec: Founded and still run by Jiří Srnec, a visual artist and music composer who invented the Black Light Theater concept in 1961, this is the most "back-to-basics" option. With simple narratives, it revels in the childlike, goofy wonder of the effects. The intimate size of the theater also allows for mimes to spontaneously engage with the audience. Their primary show, *Anthology,* traces the development of the art over the past 60 years; the opening "Laundry Girl" skit is the first-ever performed by Black Light (450 Kč, generally weekly at 20:00, on the right in the second courtyard of the Savarin Palace at Na Příkopě 10, mobile 774-574-475, www.srnectheatre.com).

Image Theater: This show has more mime and elements of the absurd and tries to incorporate more dance along with the illusions. They offer the most diverse lineup of programs, including a "best of" and several short-term, themed shows—recent topics have been African safari and outer space. Some find Image's shows to be a bit too slapsticky (480 Kč, nightly at 20:00, off Národní Třída 25 in the Metro passageway, tel. 222-314-448, www.imagetheatre.cz).

Ta Fantastika: With haunting puppetry and a little artistic nudity, this show tries to be poetic, but it's less "fun" than some of the others. It takes itself perhaps the most seriously of the three (680 Kč, nightly at 18:00 and 21:30, reserved seating, near east end of Charles Bridge at Karlova 8, tel. 222-221-366, www.tafantastika.cz).

Classical Concerts

Each day, six to eight classical concerts designed for tourists fill delightful Old World halls and churches with music of the crowd-pleasing sort: Vivaldi, Best of Mozart, Most Famous Arias, and works by the famous Czech composer Antonín Dvořák. Concerts typically cost 400-1,000 Kč, start anywhere from 13:00 to 21:00, and last about an hour. Typical venues include two buildings on the Lesser Town Square (the Church of St. Nicholas and the Prague Academy of Music in Liechtenstein Palace), the Klementinum's Chapel of Mirrors, the Old Town Square (in a different Church of St. Nicholas), and the stunning Smetana Hall in the Municipal House. Musicians vary from excellent to amateurish.

To ensure a memorable venue and top-notch musicians, choose a concert in one of three places—Smetana Hall, the Rudolfinum, or the National Theater—featuring Prague's finest ensembles (such as the Prague Symphony Orchestra or Czech Philharmonic).

The **Prague Symphony Orchestra** plays mainly in the gorgeous Art Nouveau Smetana Hall of the Municipal House. Their ticket office is inside the building, just to the left past the main glass door entrance (Mon-Fri 10:00-18:00, tel. 222-002-336, www.fok.cz).

The **Czech Philharmonic** performs in the classical Neo-Renaissance Rudolfinum across the street from the Pinkas Synagogue. Their ticket office is on the right side of the Rudolfinum building, under the stairs (250-1,000 Kč, open Mon-Fri 10:00-18:00, and until just before the show starts on concert days, on Palachovo Náměstí on the Old Town side of Mánes Bridge, tel. 227-059-352, www.ceskafilharmonie.cz).

Both orchestras perform in their home venues about five nights a month from September through June. Most other nights these spaces are rented to agencies that organize tourist concerts of varying quality. Check first whether your visit coincides with either ensemble's performance before settling for any of these substitutes.

You'll find tickets for tourist concerts advertised and sold on the street in front of these buildings. Although the music may not be the finest, these concerts do allow you to experience music in one of Prague's best venues on the night of your choice. This is especially worth considering if you want to enjoy classical music in the Municipal House when the Symphony Orchestra isn't in town (but make sure your concert takes place in Smetana Hall rather than in the smaller and far less spectacular Grégr Hall).

Opera and Ballet

A handy ticket office for the three following theaters (all part of the National Theater group) is directly across the street from the main entrance to the Estates Theater on Železná street.

The **National Theater** (Národní Divadlo), on the New Town side of Legií Bridge, has a stunning Neo-Renaissance interior to match its status as the top venue in the country (300-1,000 Kč, shows from 19:00, weekend matinees also at 14:00, tel. 224-912-673, www.narodni-divadlo.cz).

The **Estates Theater** (Stavovské Divadlo) is where Mozart premiered and personally directed many of his most beloved works (see page 63). *Don Giovanni, The Marriage of Figaro,* and *The Magic Flute* are on the program a couple of times each month (800-1,400 Kč, shows from 20:00, between the Old Town Square and the New Town on a square called Ovocný Trh, tel. 224-214-339, www.narodni-divadlo.cz).

The **State Opera** (Státní Opera), formerly the German Theater, is simpler in style even though it is from the same period as the National Theater. Ballets and operas by non-Czech composers are typically performed here (400-1,200 Kč, at 19:00

or 20:00, 101 Wilsonova, on the busy street between the main train station and Wenceslas Square, see map on page 79, tel. 224-227-693, www.narodni-divadlo.cz).

MUSIC CLUBS

Young locals keep Prague's many music clubs in business. Most clubs—from rock to folk to jazz—are neighborhood institutions with decades of tradition, generally holding only 100-200 people. Most have a cover charge.

The Old Town

Roxy, a few blocks from the Old Town Square, features live bands from outside the country twice a week—anything from Irish punk to Balkan brass—and experimental DJs on other nights (Dlouhá 33, www.roxy.cz).

    Agharta Jazz Club, which showcases some of the best Czech and Eastern European jazz, is just steps off the Old Town Square in a cool Gothic cellar (Železná 16, www.agharta.cz).

The New Town

Lucerna Music Bar is popular for its '80s and '90s video parties on Friday and Saturday nights. The scene is young and trendy (in the basement of Lucerna Arcade, Vodičkova 36, www.musicbar.cz).

    Reduta Jazz Club launches you straight into the 1960s-era classic jazz scene (when jazz provided an escape for trapped freedom lovers in communist times). The top Czech jazzmen—Stivín and Koubková—regularly perform. President Bill Clinton once played the sax here (on Národní Třída next to Café Louvre, www.redutajazzclub.cz).

The Lesser Town

Malostranská Beseda, with its tight, steamy, standing-room-only space, is the only club in the center with daily live performances. The crowd tends to be a bit older (Malostranské Náměstí 21, www.malostranska-beseda.cz).

Sleeping in Prague

Peak months for hotels in Prague are May, June, and September. Easter and New Year's are the most crowded times, when prices are jacked up a bit. Book any accommodations well in advance, especially if you'll be traveling during peak season or if your trip coincides with a major holiday (see the appendix). For more information and tips on hotel rates and deals, making reservations, and finding a short-term rental, see the "Sleeping" section in the Practicalities chapter.

Sleep Code

Hotels in this book are categorized according to the average price of a standard double room with breakfast in high season. I've given *very* rough conversions to dollars using 20 Kč = $1.

$$$$	**Splurge:** Most rooms over 3,400 Kč (roughly $170)
$$$	**Pricier:** 2,600-3,400 Kč ($130-170)
$$	**Moderate:** 1,800-2,600 Kč ($90-130)
$	**Budget:** 1,000-1,800 Kč ($50-90)
¢	**Backpacker:** Under 1,000 Kč ($50)
RS%	**Rick Steves discount**

Unless otherwise noted, credit cards are accepted, hotel staff speak basic English, and free Wi-Fi is available. Comparison-shop by checking prices at several hotels (on each hotel's own website, on a booking site, or by email). For the best deal, *book directly with the hotel.* Ask for a discount if paying in cash; if the listing includes **RS%,** request a Rick Steves discount.

OLD TOWN HOTELS AND PENSIONS

You'll pay higher prices to stay in the Old Town, but for many travelers, the convenience is worth the expense. These places are all within a 10-minute walk of the Old Town Square.

$$$$ Hotel Metamorphis is a splurge, with solidly renovated rooms in Prague's former caravanserai (hostel for foreign merchants in the 12th century). Its breakfast room is in a spacious medieval cellar with modern artwork. Some of the street-facing rooms, located above two popular bars, are noisy at night (Malá Štupartská 5, tel. 221-771-011, www.hotelmetamorphis.cz, hotel@metamorphis.cz).

$$$$ Hotel Maximilian is a sleek, mod, 71-room place with Art Deco black design; big, plush living rooms; and all the business services and comforts you'd expect in a four-star hotel. It faces a church on a perfect little square just a short walk from the action (Haštalská 14, tel. 225-303-111, www.maximilianhotel.com, reservation@maximilianhotel.com).

$$$$ Design Hotel Jewel Prague (U Klenotníka), with 11 modern, comfortable rooms in a plain building, is three blocks off the Old Town Square (RS%, no elevator, Rytířská 3, tel. 224-211-699, www.hoteljewelprague.com, info@jewelhotel.cz).

$$$ Brewery Hotel u Medvídků ("By the Bear Cubs") has 43 comfortable rooms in a big, rustic, medieval shell with dark wood furniture. Upstairs, you'll find lots of beams—or, if you're not careful, they'll find you (RS%, "historical" rooms cost slightly more, apartment available, Na Perštýně 7, tel. 224-211-916, www.umedvidku.cz, info@umedvidku.cz, manager Vladimír). The pension runs a popular beer-hall restaurant with live music most Fri-

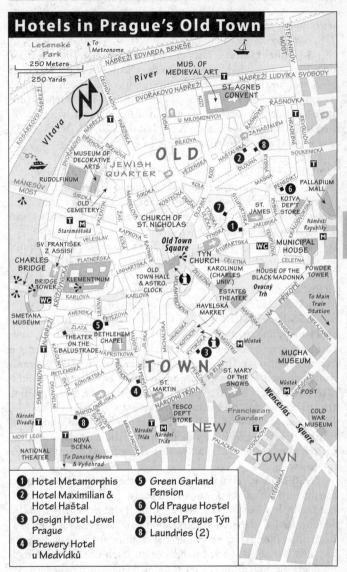

Hotels in Prague's Old Town

Letenské Park
To Metronome
250 Meters
250 Yards

Vltava

River

NÁBŘEŽÍ EDVARDA BENEŠE

MUS. OF MEDIEVAL ART

NÁBŘEŽÍ LUDVÍKA SVOBODY

ST. AGNES CONVENT

DVOŘÁKOVO NÁBŘEŽÍ

KOŽ

RÁSNOVKA

U MILOSRDNÝCH

DUŠNÍ

BÍLKOVA

O L D

ZAHÁSTALEM

HRADEBNÍ

REVOLUČNÍ

SOUKENICKÁ

PALLADIUM MALL

MUSEUM OF DECORATIVE ARTS

JEWISH QUARTER

RUDOLFINUM

MÁNESŮV MOST

ŠIROKÁ

OLD CEMETERY

SV. FRANTIŠEK Z ASSISI

CHARLES BRIDGE

BRIDGE TOWER

KLEMENTINUM

SMETANA MUSEUM

THEATER ON THE BALUSTRADE

BETHLEHEM CHAPEL

NÁRODNÍ DIVADLO

MOST LEGIÍ

NATIONAL THEATER

NOVÁ SCÉNA

To Dancing House & Vyšehrad

ŠIROKÁ

KOSTEČNÁ

CHURCH OF ST. NICHOLAS

Old Town Square

TÝN CHURCH

OLD TOWN HALL & ASTRO. CLOCK

KAROLINUM (CHARLES UNIV.)

ESTATES THEATER

HAVELSKÁ MARKET

ST. JAMES

KOTVA DEP'T STORE

Náměstí Republiky

MUNICIPAL HOUSE

HOUSE OF THE BLACK MADONNA

POWDER TOWER

To Main Train Station

Ovocný Trh

CELETNÁ

ST. MARTIN

NÁRODNÍ TŘÍDA

TESCO DEP'T STORE

Franciscan Garden

ST. MARY OF THE SNOWS

MUCHA MUSEUM

Můstek

POST

COLD WAR MUSEUM

Wenceslas Square

N E W

T O W N

① Hotel Metamorphis
② Hotel Maximilian & Hotel Haštal
③ Design Hotel Jewel Prague
④ Brewery Hotel u Medvídků
⑤ Green Garland Pension
⑥ Old Prague Hostel
⑦ Hostel Prague Týn
⑧ Laundries (2)

days and Saturdays until 23:00—request an inside room for maximum peace.

$$ Green Garland Pension (U Zeleného Věnce), on a central cobbled lane, has a small-place feel rare for the Old Town. Located in a thick 14th-century building with open beams, it has a blond-hardwood charm decorated with a warm and personal touch. The nine clean and simply furnished rooms are two and three floors up, with no elevator (RS%, family room, Řetězová 10, tel. 222-220-178, www.uzv.cz, pension@uzv.cz).

$$ Hotel Haštal is next to Hotel Maximilian (listed earlier) on the same quiet, hidden square in the Old Town. A popular hotel even back in the 1920s, this family-run place has been renovated to complement the neighborhood's vibrant circa-1900 architecture. Its 31 rooms are comfortable and insulated against noise (RS%; free tea, coffee, and wine; air-con, Haštalská 16, tel. 222-314-335, www.hastal.com, info@hastal.com).

UNDER THE CASTLE, IN THE LESSER TOWN

Several of these listings are buried on quiet lanes deep in the Lesser Town, among cobbles, quaint restaurants, rummaging tourists, and embassy flags. For locations, see the "Restaurants & Hotels in the Lesser Town & Castle Quarter" map, later.

$$$$ Vintage Design Hotel Sax's 22 rooms are decorated in a retro, meet-the-Jetsons fashion. With a fruity atrium and a distinctly modern, stark feel, this is a stylish, no-nonsense place (RS%, air-con, elevator, free tea and pastries daily at 17:00, Jánský Vršek 3, tel. 257-531-268, www.sax.cz, hotel@sax.cz).

$$$ Hotel Julián is an oasis of professional, predictable decency in an untouristy neighborhood. Its 33 spacious, fresh, well-furnished rooms and big, homey public spaces hide behind a noble Neoclassical facade. The staff is friendly and helpful (RS%, family rooms, air-con, elevator, plush and inviting lobby, summer roof terrace, parking lot; Metro: Anděl, then take tram #9, #12, or #20 to the left as you leave Metro station for two stops; Elišky Peškové 11, Praha 5, reservation tel. 257-311-150, www.hoteljulian.com, info@julian.cz). Free lockers and a shower are available for those needing a place to stay after checkout (while waiting for an overnight train, for example).

$$$ Dům u Velké Boty ("House at the Big Boot"), on a quiet square in front of the German Embassy, is the rare quintessential family hotel in Prague: homey, comfy, and extremely friendly. Mellow Kuba, the second generation in charge and a film producer in winter, treats every guest as a (thirsty) friend and always has a supply of good advice and stories. Each of the 12 rooms is uniquely decorated, most in a tasteful, 19th-century Biedermeier style (RS%, cheaper rooms with shared bath, family rooms, cash only, children up to age 10 sleep free—toys provided, Vlašská 30, tel. 257-532-088, www.dumuvelkeboty.cz, info@dumuvelkeboty.cz). There's no hotel sign on the house—look for the splendid geraniums in the windows.

$$$ Mooo Apartments, in a meticulously restored 500-year-old house built around a secluded balconied courtyard, offers 13 spacious apartments with kitchenettes (RS%, no breakfast, some rooms without air-con, down the staircase from Nerudova at Jánský vršek 8, tel. 277-016-830, www.mooo-apartments.com, castle@mooo-apartments.com). For supplies, use the Žabka convenience store diagonally across the way. Mooo has an additional, larger location in a hip part of New Town.

$$ Residence Thunovská, just below the Italian embassy on a relatively quiet staircase leading up to the castle, rents six rooms in a house that once belonged to the Mannerist artist Bartholomeus Sprangler. The all-renovated rooms are historic and equipped with kitchenettes and Italian furniture. The original chimney that runs through the house is inscribed with the date 1577, and the rest of the house is not much younger. The manager, Dean, a soft-spoken American who married into Prague, treats his guests as trusted friends (RS%, breakfast extra—served in the next-door café, Thunovská 19, look for the Consulate of San Marino sign, reception open 9:00-19:00, otherwise on-call, tel. 257-531-189, mobile 721-855-880, www.thunovska19.cz).

PRAGUE

HOSTELS IN THE CENTER

It's tough to find a double for less than 2,500 Kč in the old center. But Prague has an abundance of hostels—each with a distinct personality, and each excellent in its own way for anyone wanting a cheap dorm bed or an extremely simple twin-bedded room for a reasonable price. For travelers seeking low-priced options, keep in mind that hostels are no longer the exclusive domain of backpackers. For locations of these hostels, see the "Hotels in Prague's Old Town" map, earlier.

¢ Old Prague Hostel is a small, well-worn place on the second and third floors of an apartment building on a back alley near the Powder Tower. The spacious rooms were once apartment bedrooms, so it feels less institutional than most hostels, but the staff can be indifferent and older travelers might feel a bit out of place. The TV lounge/breakfast room is a good hangout (private rooms available, in summer reserve two weeks ahead for doubles, a few days ahead for bunks; Benediktská 2, tel. 224-829-058, www.oldpraguehostel.com, info@oldpraguehostel.com).

¢ Hostel Prague Týn—quiet, mature, and sterile—is hidden in a silent courtyard two blocks from the Old Town Square. The management is very aware of its valuable location, so they don't have to bother being friendly (private rooms available, reserve one week ahead, Týnská 19, tel. 224-808-301, www.hostelpraguetyn.com, info@hostelpraguetyn.com).

Eating in Prague

A big part of Prague's charm is found in wandering aimlessly through the city's winding old quarters, marveling at the architecture, watching the people, and sniffing out fun restaurants. In addition to meat-and-potatoes Czech cuisine, you'll find trendy, student-oriented bars and some fine ethnic eateries (in general, Indian and Italian food tends to be very good, Thai and Vietnamese mediocre, Chinese drowned in soy sauce). For ambience, the options include traditional, dark Czech beer halls; elegant Art Nouveau dining rooms; and modern cafés.

Generally, if you walk just a few minutes away from the tourist flow, you'll find better value, atmosphere, and service. The more touristy a place is, the more likely you'll pay too much—either in inflated prices or because waiters pad the bill.

I've listed eating and drinking establishments by neighborhood. Most of the options—and highest prices—are in the Old Town. For a light meal, consider one of Prague's many cafés.

Several areas are pretty and well situated for sightseeing, but lined only with touristy restaurants. While these places are not necessarily bad values, I've listed only a few of your many options—just survey the scene in these spots and choose whatever looks best. **Kampa Square,** just off the Charles Bridge, feels like a quiet, small-town square. **Havelská Market** is surrounded by a mix of fancy restaurants and cheap little eateries. The massive **Old Town Square** is the place to nurse a drink or enjoy a meal while watching the tide of people, both tourists and locals, sweep back and forth. **Bethlehem Square,** still part of the Old Town but away from the main tourist flow, is my choice for an atmospheric outdoor evening meal.

EATING TIPS

I rank restaurants from $ budget to $$$$ splurge. For general advice on eating, see the "Eating" section in the Practicalities chapter.

Paying and Tipping: Look at your bill carefully to make sure it's correct (especially in touristy spots). Restaurants with sit-down service include a service charge on the bill. On top of that, locals tip by rounding up (usually up to 10 percent for good service—but not more). While many places accept credit cards, I pay for meals in cash—it makes your server happier.

Smoking in Restaurants: Like most European countries, the Czech Republic does not permit smoking inside restaurants and cafés. It is generally OK, however, to smoke in outdoor seating areas, which nonsmokers may occasionally find unpleasant.

Dining with a View: For great views, consider these options, all described in detail later: **Villa Richter** (next to Prague Castle,

Restaurant Price Code

Eateries in this book are categorized according to the average cost of a typical main course. Drinks, desserts, and splurge items can raise the price considerably.

$$$$ Splurge: Most main courses over 500 Kč (roughly $25)
 $$$ Pricier: 250-500 Kč ($12-25)
  $$ Moderate: 120-250 Kč ($6-12)
   $ Budget: Under 120 Kč ($6)

In the Czech Republic, a pub, basic sit-down eatery, and less-touristy café or teahouse is **$**; a typical restaurant—or a fancy café with coffee over 50 Kč and tea over 100 Kč—is **$$**; an upscale restaurant is **$$$**; and a swanky splurge is **$$$$**.

above Malostranská Metro stop); **Bellavista Restaurant** at the Strahov Monastery; **Petřínské Terasy** and **Nebozízek** (next to the funicular stop halfway up Petřín Hill); and **Čertovka** in the Lesser Town (superb views of the Charles Bridge).

Traditional Czech Places: While many Czechs have gradually come to prefer the cosmopolitan taste of the world to the mundane taste of pork and sauerkraut, they still like to revisit traditional institutions once in a while to reconnect with the childhood flavors of tripe soup or goulash. So while "authentic" Czech restaurants in the center have become touristy, they're still great fun, a good value, and enjoyed by locals as well. Expect unadorned spaces, curt service, and reasonably good, inexpensive food.

Cheap-and-Cheery Sandwich Shops: All around town you'll find modern little sandwich shops (like the Panería chain) offering inexpensive fresh-made sandwiches (grilled if you like), pastries, salads, and drinks. You can get the food to go, or eat inside at simple tables.

Groceries and Farmers Markets: Ask your hotelier for the location of the nearest grocery store. An even cheaper chain of small grocery stores, with several locations in the Old Town, is Žabka (look for a colored shopping basket sign outside).

Farmers markets crop up around the city and tantalize picnickers. Apart from vegetables, you'll find quality cheeses, juices, cakes, coffee, and more (www.farmarsketrziste.cz). The most central is on **Republic Square** (Náměstí Republiky), just across the street from the Municipal House and the Powder Tower (Tue-Fri, www.farmarsketrhyprahy1.cz). The most scenic is the **Náplavka** ("River Landing") market on the Vltava embankment, just south of the Palacký Bridge (Sat 8:00-14:00).

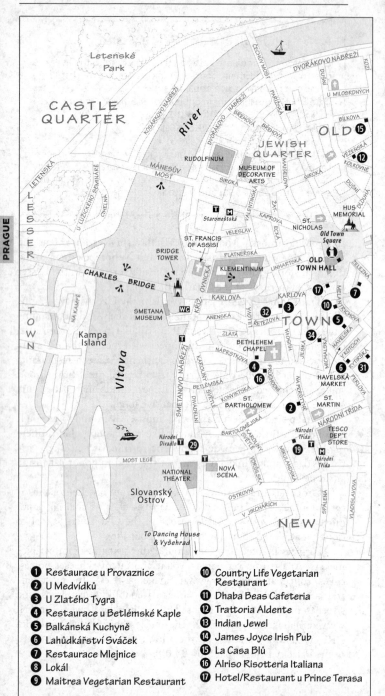

PRAGUE

1 Restaurace u Provaznice
2 U Medvídků
3 U Zlatého Tygra
4 Restaurace u Betlémské Kaple
5 Balkánská Kuchyně
6 Lahůdkářství Sváček
7 Restaurace Mlejnice
8 Lokál
9 Maitrea Vegetarian Restaurant

10 Country Life Vegetarian Restaurant
11 Dhaba Beas Cafeteria
12 Trattoria Aldente
13 Indian Jewel
14 James Joyce Irish Pub
15 La Casa Blů
16 Alriso Risotteria Italiana
17 Hotel/Restaurant u Prince Terasa

Prague Restaurants in Old & New Towns

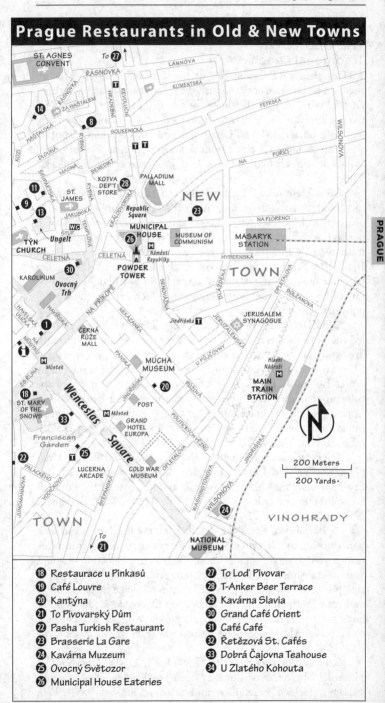

18 Restaurace u Pinkasů
19 Café Louvre
20 Kantýna
21 To Pivovarský Dům
22 Pasha Turkish Restaurant
23 Brasserie La Gare
24 Kavárna Muzeum
25 Ovocný Světozor
26 Municipal House Eateries

27 To Loď Pivovar
28 T-Anker Beer Terrace
29 Kavárna Slavia
30 Grand Café Orient
31 Café Café
32 Řetězová St. Cafés
33 Dobrá Čajovna Teahouse
34 U Zlatého Kohouta

THE OLD TOWN
Traditional Czech

$$ Restaurace u Provaznice ("By the Ropemaker's Wife") has all the Czech classics, peppered with the story of a once-upon-a-time-faithful wife. (Check the menu for details of the gory story.) Natives congregate under bawdy frescoes for the famously good "pig leg" with horseradish and Czech mustard. This is a handy spot on a peaceful lane just a block from the commotion at the bottom of Wenceslas Square (daily 11:00-24:00, Provaznická 3, tel. 224-232-528).

$$ U Medvídků ("By the Bear Cubs") started out as a brewery in 1466 (they still offer a range of their own microbrews, including one of the oldest-ever wheat beers) and is now a flagship beer hall of the Czech Budweiser. The one large room is bright, noisy, and touristy (daily 11:30-23:00, a block toward Wenceslas Square from Bethlehem Square at Na Perštýně 7, tel. 224-211-916). The smaller beer bar next to the restaurant (daily 16:00 until late) is used by university students during emergencies—such as after most other pubs have closed.

$ U Zlatého Tygra ("By the Golden Tiger") has long embodied the proverbial Czech pub, where beer turns strangers into kindred spirits as they share their life stories with one another. Today, "The Tiger" is a buzzing shrine to one of its longtime regulars, the writer Bohumil Hrabal, whose fictions immortalize many of the colorful characters that once warmed the wooden benches here. Locals line up for good authentic Czech pub grub and a great (noisy) atmosphere (tight seating, daily 15:00-23:00, just a block off Karlova at Husova 17, tel. 222-221-111).

$ Restaurace u Betlémské Kaple, behind Bethlehem Chapel, is not "ye olde" Czech. It's peaceful, woody, and spacious. Locals appreciate the cheap lunch deals and fish specialties. Portions are splittable and prices are good (daily 11:00-23:00, Betlémské Náměstí 2, tel. 222-221-639).

$ Balkánská Kuchyně ("Balkan Home Kitchen"), run by a hardworking couple who escaped to Prague in the 1990s from war-torn Sarajevo, serves a mouthwatering, rotating selection of soups and main dishes (such as moussaka, minced meat-stuffed peppers, rice pilaf, or chicken biryani). Make your choice at the counter and your "Serbian mom" will heat it up (Mon-Sat 11:00-14:30 or until meals sell out, closed Sun; only basic English spoken, next to Havelská Market, inside a passageway at Havelská 9, tel. 776-840-384).

$ Lahůdkářství Sváček ("The Deli"), at the other end of Havelská Market, serves quality open-faced sandwiches, cheeses, sausages, pickled vegetables, and salads (Mon-Sat 9:00-19:30, closed Sun, turn left at the end of the stands, the deli is on the second corner at Rytířská 1).

$$ Restaurace Mlejnice ("The Mill") is a fun little pub strewn with farm implements and happy eaters, located just out of the tourist crush two blocks from the Old Town Square. They serve traditional specials, hearty salads, and modern Czech plates. Reservations are smart for dinner (daily 11:00-23:00, between Melantrichova and Železná at Kožná 14, tel. 224-228-635, www. restaurace-mlejnice.cz).

$$ Lokál is a hit for its good-quality Czech classics. Filling a long, arched space, the restaurant plays on nostalgia: The stark interior is a deliberate 1980s retro design, and it celebrates the hungry and thirsty working class. The name roughly means "the neighborhood dive"—a reference to the basic canteens of that age. Reservations are smart (daily 11:00 until late, Dlouhá 33, tel. 222-316-265, http://lokal-dlouha.ambi.cz).

Vegetarian and Modern

$$ Maitrea Vegetarian Restaurant is a favorite Old Town vegetarian place, where a spirit of wellness and feng shui prevails. The ground floor is fresh and modern. Downstairs is a world of fountains, pillows, and Buddhas. The creative and extensive international menu will stoke your appetite (vegan-friendly, daily 11:30-22:00, cheap lunch specials Mon-Fri, half a block downhill from the Týn Church north door at Týnská 6, tel. 221-711-631).

$$ Country Life Vegetarian Restaurant is a cafeteria with a well-displayed buffet of salads and hot veggie dishes. It's midway between the Old Town Square and the bottom of Wenceslas Square. They're serious about their vegetarianism, serving only plant-based, unprocessed, and unrefined food (pay by weight, Sun-Thu 9:00-20:30, Fri until 17:00, closed Sat, through courtyard at Melantrichova 15/Michalská 18, tel. 224-213-366).

$$ Dhaba Beas Cafeteria is run by a Punjabi chef. Diners grab a steel tray and scoop up whatever looks good—typically various choices of *dal* (lentils) and *sabji* (vegetables) with rice or *chapati* (pancakes). The food is sold by weight—you'll likely spend 130 Kč for lunch. Tucked away in a courtyard behind the Týn Church, this place is popular with university students and young professionals (Mon-Fri 11:00-20:00, Sat from 12:00, Sun 12:00-18:00, Týnská 19, mobile 608-035-727).

Ethnic Eateries and Bars

Dlouhá, the wide street leading away from the Old Town Square behind the Jan Hus Memorial, takes you into a neighborhood west of the Jewish Quarter where you can eat your way around the world. Here are a few favorites from this United Nations of eateries:

PRAGUE

Italian: $$ Trattoria Aldente prides itself on its multiple varieties of fresh homemade pasta cooked perfectly "to the bite" (daily 11:30-23:30, Vězeňská 4, tel. 222-313-185).

Indian: Located in the Ungelt courtyard behind the Týn Church, **$$$ Indian Jewel** was among the first in a recent wave of authentic Indian restaurants to arrive in Prague. It sits in a pleasant, artfully restored courtyard, and is my choice for outdoor dining. They offer Indian classics, vegetarian options, and good-value lunch specials on weekdays. The hardworking owner, Sanjeev, is proud of his rare-in-Prague tandoor oven—ideal for baking authentic breads (daily specials, daily 11:00-22:30, Týn 6, tel. 222-310-156).

Irish: $ James Joyce Irish Pub may seem like a strange recommendation in Prague—home of some of the world's best beer—but it has the kind of ambience that locals (and few tourists) seek out. They serve basic pub grub, fish and chips, and curries. Expats have favored this pub for Guinness ever since the Velvet Revolution enabled the Celts to return to one of their original homelands. Worn wooden floors, dingy walls, and the Irish manager transport you right into the heart of blue-collar Dublin (daily 11:00 until late, U Obecního Dvora 4, tel. 224-818-851). Sunday evening comes with live folk music.

Mexican: One of the last student bastions in the Old Town, **$$ La Casa Blů,** with cheap lunch specials, Mexican plates, Staropramen beer, and greenish mojitos, is your own little pueblo in Prague. Painted in warm oranges and reds, energized by upbeat music, and guarded by creatures from Mayan mythology, La Casa Blů attracts a fiesta of happy eaters and drinkers (daily 11:00-23:00, Sun from 14:00, on the corner of Kozí and Bílkova, tel. 224-818-270).

Italian near Bethlehem Square: Located on a quiet square near Bethlehem Chapel, **$$$ Alriso Risotteria Italiana** offers creative gluten-free dishes in a classy setting with seating both inside and out. Locals come here for the moist and flavorful rice bread (daily 11:00-23:00, Betlémské Náměstí 11, tel. 222-233-341).

Jewish Quarter

These eateries are well placed to break up a demanding tour of the Jewish Quarter—all within two blocks of each other on or near Široká (see map on page 71). Also consider the ethnic eateries listed above.

$$$ Kolkovna, the flagship restaurant of a chain allied with Pilsner Urquell, is big and woody yet modern, serving a fun mix of Czech and international cuisine—ribs, salads, cheese plates, and beer. It feels a tad formulaic...but not in a bad way (a bit overpriced, daily 11:00-24:00, across from Spanish Synagogue at V Kolkovně 8, tel. 224-819-701).

$$ Kolonial ("Bicycle Place"), across the street from the Pinkas Synagogue, has a modern interior playing on the bicycle theme, six beers on tap, and an imaginative menu drawing from Czech, French, Italian, and Spanish cuisine (daily specials, daily 9:00-24:00, Široká 6, tel. 224-818-322).

$ Restaurace u Knihovny ("By the Library"), situated steps away from the City and National libraries as well as the Pinkas Synagogue, is a favorite lunch spot for locals who work nearby. The cheap daily lunch specials consist of seven variations on traditional Czech themes. The service is friendly, and the stylish red-brick interior is warm (daily 11:00-23:00, on the corner of Veleslavínova and Valentinská, mobile 732-835-876).

$$$ Dinitz Kosher Restaurant, around the corner from the Spanish Synagogue, is the most low-key and reasonably priced of the kosher restaurants in the Jewish Quarter (Shabbat meals by prepaid reservation only, Sun-Thu 11:30-22:30, Fri until 14:30, Bílkova 12, tel. 222-244-000, www.dinitz.cz). For Shabbat meals, the fancier **$$$ King Solomon Restaurant** is a better value (Široká 8, tel. 224-818-752, www.kosher.cz).

Dining with an Old Town Square View
$$$$ Hotel u Prince Terasa, atop the five-star hotel facing the Astronomical Clock, is designed for foreign tourists. A sleek elevator inside the hotel takes you to the rooftop terrace, packed with tables and an open-air grill. The view is arguably the best in town—especially at sunset. The menu is fun but overpriced, with photos that make ordering easy. Servers can be rude, dishonest, and aggressive. Confirm exact prices before ordering. This place is also great for a drink at sunset or late at night (daily until 24:00, outdoor heaters, Staroměstské Náměstí 29, tel. 737-261-842).

THE NEW TOWN
Traditional Czech
$$ Restaurace u Pinkasů, founded in 1843, is known among locals as the first place in Prague to serve Pilsner beer. It's popular for solid, basic Czech pub grub. You can sit in its traditional interior, in front to watch the street action, or out back in a delightful garden shaded by the Gothic buttresses of the neighborhood church (daily 9:00-24:00, near the bottom of Wenceslas Square, between the Old Town and New Town, Jungmannovo Náměstí 16, tel. 221-111-150).

$$ Café Louvre is an elegant favorite from long ago (it opened in 1902 and maintains its classic atmosphere). It features simple tables, paper tablecloths, and an army of young waiters serving up decent food (Czech classics, vegetarian dishes, lunch specials) at good prices (two-course lunch offered 11:00-15:00, open daily 8:00-23:30, Národní 22, tel. 224-930-949). For more on the café-and-billiards dimension of Café Louvre, see the "Cafés" section, later.

$$ Kantýna serves "meat from the bone" (a.k.a., very fresh). A cross between a traditional butcher's shop and a modern pick-from-the-counter canteen, this place offers the best quality fast food for carnivores. They also serve a wide selection of freshly made soups, salads, and traditional desserts (daily 11:30-23:00, a block off the middle of Wenceslas Square, just down the street from the Mucha Museum at Politických Vězňů 5, no reservations).

$$ Pivovarský Dům ("The Brewhouse"), on the corner of Ječná and Lípová, is popular with locals for its rare variety of fresh beers (yeast, wheat, and fruit-flavored), fine classic Czech dishes, and an inviting interior that mixes traditional and modern (daily 11:00-23:00, reservations recommended in the evenings, walk up Štěpánská street from Wenceslas Square for 10 minutes, or take tram #22 for two stops from Národní to Štěpánská; Lípová 15, tel. 296-216-666, www.pivovarskydum.com).

Other New Town Eateries

$$ Pasha Turkish Restaurant, near the bottom of Wenceslas Square, has a nice ambience, quality ingredients, and wonderful, authentic, ready-to-eat Turkish dishes—lots of grills, salads, and vegetables (daily 11:00-23:00, a block from Můstek Metro stop, just beyond Franciscan garden at Jungmannova 27, tel. 224-948-481).

$$ Brasserie La Gare, just off Republic Square (Náměstí Republiky), opened with the mission to prove to Czechs that French food can be simple and inexpensive. The menu includes such classics as *escargots de Bourgogne* and coq au vin. The red-hued, modern interior also contains a French bakery and a deli (lunch specials, daily 11:00-24:00, V Celnici 3, tel. 222-313-712).

$ Kavárna Muzeum, in the former communist parliament building (now part of the National Museum) at Wenceslas Square, offers daily menus, freshly roasted coffee, soups, and sandwiches in a pleasant, kid-friendly setting (daily 10:00-19:00, Vinohradská 1, tel. 224-284-511).

$ Ovocný Světozor ("World of Fruit") is a colorful joint that's popular for its ice cream, but they also sell really cheap (and good) Czech-style open-face sandwiches—plus cakes and other desserts. Ask for an English menu (Mon-Fri 8:00-20:30; Sat from 9:00, Sun from 10:00, in the Světozor Mall off Wenceslas Square at Vodičkova 39).

Art Nouveau Splendor in the Municipal House

$$$ Kavárna Obecní Dům, a dressy café, is drenched in chandeliered, Art Nouveau elegance and offers the best value and experience here. Light, pricey meals and drinks come with great atmosphere and bad service (daily 7:30-23:00, live piano or jazz trio 16:00-20:00, tel. 222-002-763).

$$$$ The French restaurant in the next wing is fine and formal, oozing Mucha elegance and slinky romance. While quite expensive for dinner, they have a reasonably priced three-course lunch special (daily 12:00-16:00 & 18:00-23:00, tel. 222-002-777).

$$$ The beer cellar is overpriced and generally filled with tour groups (daily 11:30-23:00).

THE LESSER TOWN

These characteristic eateries are handy for a bite before or after your Prague Castle visit.

$$ Malostranská Beseda, in the impeccably restored former Town Hall, weaves together an imaginative menu of traditional Czech dishes (both classic and little known), vegetarian fare, and fresh fish. It feels a bit sterile and formulaic, but you can choose among three settings: the ground-floor restaurant on the left; the café on the right (serves meals, but it's OK to have only coffee or cake); or the packed beer hall downstairs, where Pilsner Urquell is served (daily 11:00-23:00, Malostranské Náměstí 21, tel. 257-409-112). The restaurant has a recommended music club upstairs.

$$ Lokál u Bílé Kuželky ("By the White Bowling Pin"), a branch of the Old Town's recommended Lokál restaurant, is the best bet for quick, cheap, well-executed Czech classics on this side of the river (Mon-Fri 11:30-24:00, Sat-Sun 12:00-22:00, Míšeňská 12; from the Charles Bridge, turn right around the U Tří Pštrosů Hotel just before the Lesser Town gate; tel. 257-212-014).

$$ U Magistra Kelly is the quintessential neighborhood pub/restaurant serving inexpensive dishes, a variety of beers, and a selection of wines from two family-owned Moravian wineries (daily 12:00-22:00, tucked away from the Nerudova tourist bustle down a staircase and inside a traditional balconied courtyard at Šporkova 5, tel. 257-217-770).

$$ Lo Veg Restaurant, on the top two floors and a tiny terrace of a narrow medieval house, serves vegan variations on Czech classics as well as Asian fare. The setting is a tasteful mix of Renais-

PRAGUE

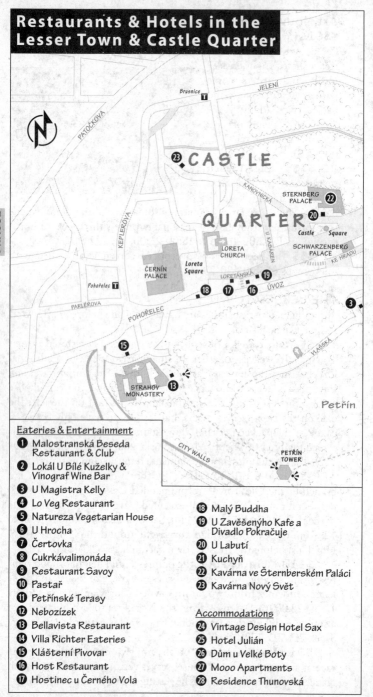

Restaurants & Hotels in the Lesser Town & Castle Quarter

Eateries & Entertainment

1. Malostranská Beseda Restaurant & Club
2. Lokál U Bílé Kuželky & Vinograf Wine Bar
3. U Magistra Kelly
4. Lo Veg Restaurant
5. Natureza Vegetarian House
6. U Hrocha
7. Čertovka
8. Cukrkávalimonáda
9. Restaurant Savoy
10. Pastař
11. Petřínské Terasy
12. Nebozízek
13. Bellavista Restaurant
14. Villa Richter Eateries
15. Klášterní Pivovar
16. Host Restaurant
17. Hostinec u Černého Vola
18. Malý Buddha
19. U Zavěšenýho Kafe a Divadlo Pokračuje
20. U Labutí
21. Kuchyň
22. Kavárna ve Šternberském Paláci
23. Kavárna Nový Svět

Accommodations

24. Vintage Design Hotel Sax
25. Hotel Julián
26. Dům u Velké Boty
27. Mooo Apartments
28. Residence Thunovská

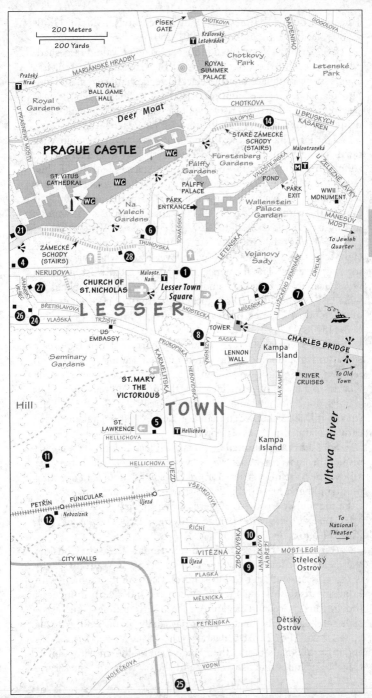

PRAGUE

sance roof beams, Balinese art, and gorgeous vistas (daily 11:30-22:00, Nerudova 36, mobile 702-901-060).

$$ Natureza Vegetarian House, on a quiet walnut tree-shaded patio next to the Gothic walls of St. Lawrence Church, is a snug, family-run place offering eclectic vegetarian, vegan, and gluten-free food. Choose from soups, salads, veggie burgers, Asian-inspired dishes, burritos, risottos, desserts, and fancy nonalcoholic drinks (daily 9:00-20:00, Hellichova 14, tel. 721-678-883).

$ U Hrocha ("By the Hippo"), a small authentic pub with tar dripping from its walls, is packed with beer drinkers. Expect simple, traditional meals—basically meat starters with bread. Just below the castle near Lesser Town Square (Malostranské Náměstí), it's actually the haunt of many members of parliament, which is around the corner (daily 12:00-23:00, chalkboard lists daily meals in English, Thunovská 10, tel. 257-533-389).

$$ Vinograf Wine Bar is a small, intimate place with just eight tables. It's run by Czech wine lover Karel, who enjoys helping visitors appreciate his wines. He prepares a daily list of Czech wines available by the glass and serves meat-and-cheese plates for wine tasters who'd like a light meal (daily 16:00-24:00, a few steps off the end of Charles Bridge at Míšeňská 8, next to Lokál, tel. 603-116-085).

$$$$ Čertovka, down an alley so narrow that it requires a signal to regulate foot traffic, offers outdoor seating on two small terraces right on the water, with some of the best views of the Charles Bridge. Given the location, the prices are reasonable, but waiters don't bother being nice (daily 11:30-23:30, off the little square at U Lužického Semináře 24, no reservations taken, arrive early to claim a spot, tel. 257-534-524).

$$ Cukrkávalimonáda ("Sugar, Coffee, Lemonade") is part restaurant and part patisserie, serving big salads, made-to-order sandwiches, artful pastries, and freshly squeezed juice in a setting mixing old and new decor. The bistro—an oasis just a block away from the tourist crush—is 50 yards down the first street to the left after you exit the Charles Bridge (daily 9:00-19:00, Lázeňská 7, tel. 257-225-396).

Across the Bridge from the National Theater: Consider these elegant choices near the riverfront. **$$$ Restaurant Savoy** is the closest you'll get to Parisian food culture in Prague—with exquisite dishes mixing French, Viennese, and Czech influences; thoughtful service; and elegant Art Deco surroundings (lunch specials weekdays only, breakfast all day, daily 9:00-22:30, Vítězná 5, tel. 257-311-562). **$$$ Pastař** ("The Pasta Maker") is serious about freshly made pasta. Their small menu—Italian with a bit of Czech—includes fine fish and meat dishes as well, and the service is attentive and friendly (daily 11:30-22:30, Malostranské Nábřeží 558, mobile 777-009-108).

Near the Funicular, on Petřín Hill: These two places are near the funicular stop halfway up Petřín Hill and offer great views over the city. **$$$ Petřínské Terasy** has woody seating indoors, or outside on the terrace (daily 12:00-23:00; Petřín 393, tel. 257-320-688), while **$$$$ Nebozízek** is more modern, with glassed-in seating (cash only, daily 11:00-23:00, Petřín 411, tel. 257-315-329).

THE CASTLE QUARTER

$$$ Bellavista Restaurant is in the garden of the Strahov Monastery, where the abbot himself would come to meditate in a peaceful garden setting. You'll pay for the amazing city views, but if the weather's nice, this is a good value, with traditional grilled meats, pasta, and salads (daily 11:00-24:00, tel. 220-517-274).

Villa Richter, at the end of the castle promontory (closest to the river) and surrounded by vineyards, consists of three classy restaurants, each with killer Prague views (all open daily 10:00-23:00, tel. 257-219-079). At **$$$ Panorama Pergola,** a string of outdoor tables lines a vineyard terrace overlooking the city (wine, sandwiches, cold plates, and hot views). **$$$$ Piano Nobile** is more pretentious, with Italian and French dishes and romantic white-linen tables indoors and out—it's the perfect place to propose (three-course meals). **$$$ Piano Terra** serves more affordable Czech dishes. To reach these places, walk 40 yards below the lower castle gate to a gate leading to a vineyard, then stroll downhill through the vineyard.

$$ Klášterní Pivovar ("Monastery Brewery"), founded by an abbot in 1628 and reopened in 2004, has two large rooms and a pleasant courtyard. This is the place, though touristy, to taste a range of unpasteurized beers brewed on the premises, including amber, wheat, and IPA. To accompany the beer, try the strong beer-flavored cheese served on toasted black-yeast bread (daily 10:00-22:00, Strahovské Nádvoří 301, tel. 233-353-155). It's directly across from the entrance to the Strahov Library (don't confuse it with the enormous, tour group-oriented Klášterní Restaurace next door, to the right).

$$$ Host Restaurant is hidden in the middle of a staircase that connects Loretánská and Úvoz streets. This spot, which boasts super views of the Lesser Town and Petřín Hill, has a modern black-and-white design and an imaginative menu. For a good deal, try asking for the "business lunch" *menu* that's advertised only in Czech (daily 11:30-22:00, as you go up Loretánská, watch for stairs leading down to the left at #15—just before the arcaded passageway, mobile 728-695-793).

$ Hostinec u Černého Vola ("By the Black Ox") is a dingy old-time pub—its survival in the midst of all the castle splendor and tourism is a marvel. It feels like a kegger on the banks of the river Styx, with classic bartenders serving up Kozel beer (traditional "Goat" brand with excellent darks) and beer-friendly gut-bomb snacks (fried cheese, local hot dogs). The pub is located on Loretánská (50 yards from Loreta Church, no sign outside, look for the only house on the block without an arcade, daily 10:00-22:00, English menu on request, tel. 220-513-481).

$$ Malý Buddha ("Little Buddha") serves delightful food—especially vegetarian—and takes its theme seriously. You'll step into a mellow, low-lit escape of bamboo and peace, where you'll be served by people with perfect complexions and almost no pulse to the no-rhythm of meditative music. Eating in their little back room is like dining in a temple (Tue-Sun 12:00-22:30, closed Mon, between the castle and Strahov Monastery at Úvoz 46, tel. 220-513-894).

$ U Zavěšenýho Kafe a Divadlo Pokračuje ("By the Hanging Coffee" and "The Show Goes On"), just below Loreta Square on the way to the castle, is a creative little pub/restaurant that has attracted a cult following among Prague's literati. You can "hang" a coffee here for a local vagabond by paying for an extra coffee on your way out (daily 11:00-24:00, Loretánská 13, mobile 605-294-595).

$$ U Labutí ("By the Swans") offers Czech food for a good price in a tranquil courtyard, just across from the Plague Column on Castle Square (daily 10:00-22:00, Hradčanské Náměstí 11, tel. 220-511-191).

$$ Kuchyň ("Kitchen"), just behind the Tomáš Masaryk statue on Castle Square, has a terrace with great city views. After bringing your drink, rather than showing you the menu your server will take you into the kitchen, where the chef will raise the lids and let your nose and taste buds choose your meal from the pots steaming with Czech classics (daily 10:00-23:30, Hradčanské Náměstí 1, mobile 736-152-891).

$ Kavárna ve Šternberském Paláci is the locals' getaway from the tourist scene on Castle Square. It's tucked behind the Archbishop's Palace. They serve soup or goulash with bread and drinks in a quiet courtyard at unbeatable prices. Check out the garden with stunning sculptures that's through the door on the left corner of the courtyard (Tue-Sun 10:00-18:00, closed Mon, Hradčanské Náměstí 15, mobile 721-138-290).

$ Kavárna Nový Svět ("New World Café"), on a quiet lane down from the Loreta Church, offers a tasty break from the tourist crowds for cake and coffee (Thu-Tue 11:00-20:00, closed Wed, Nový Svět 2).

MICROBREWERIES AND BEER BARS

These places give you a good sense of the popular craft beer scene.

$$ Loď Pivovar ("The Brewery Barge") brews three staple beers and a range of specials on the premises. The upper deck is effectively an open-air beer garden, the middle deck doubles up as a restaurant with traditional Czech dishes, while the eye-at-water-level bottom deck is a pub that pairs beer with traditional Czech tapas (daily 11:30-23:00, at Dvořákovo nábřeží just under the Štefánik Bridge, near the St. Agnes Convent, tel. 773-778-788).

$$ T-Anker is a beer terrace sitting on top of the 1970s Kotva department store just off Republic Square. While their *Tanker* beer is specially made for this location, they do a good a job of rotating beers from around Prague and the country on their nine taps. The view of the Old Town towers is unbeatable (daily 11:00-23:00; either enter through the main doors of Kotva and take the elevator to the fourth floor and then the escalator up one more floor, or take the side entrance from Králodvorská street and then the elevator to the fifth floor; tel. 722-445-474).

CAFÉS

The Prague coffeehouse scene is alive and kicking. While some cafés are dripping with history, new ones are popping up almost daily. Cafés in the Old Town and New Town are as much about the ambience as they are about the coffee. For locations, see the "Prague Restaurants in Old & New Towns" map, earlier.

$$ Kavárna Slavia, across from the National Theater (facing the Legií Bridge on Národní street), is a fixture in Prague, famous as a hangout for its literary elite. Today, it's clearly past its prime, with an Art Deco interior, tired piano entertainment, and celebrity photos on the wall. But its iconic status makes it a fun stop for a coffee (daily 8:00-23:00, sit as near the river as possible, Smetanovo Nábřeží 2, tel. 224-218-493). Notice the *Drinker of Absinthe* painting on the wall (and on the menu)—with the iconic Czech writer struggling with reality.

$$ Grand Café Orient is only one flight up off busy Celetná street, yet a world away from the crush of tourism below. Located in the Cubist House of the Black Madonna, the café is upstairs and fittingly decorated with a Cubist flair. With its stylish, circa-1910 decor toned to dark green, this space is full of air and light—and a good value as well. The café takes its Cubism seriously: Traditionally round desserts are served square (sandwiches, salads, vanilla squares and other desserts, great balcony seating, Mon-Fri 9:00-22:00, Sat-Sun from 10:00, Ovocný Trh 19, at the corner of Celetná near the Powder Tower, tel. 224-224-240).

$$ Café, just off to the right from the main drag connecting the Old Town and Wenceslas Square, serves salads, sandwiches, and cakes in a fancy setting (daily 9:00-23:00, Rytířská 10, tel. 224-210-597).

$$ Café Louvre, listed earlier under the New Town eateries, has a rich history of illustrious visitors (it is purportedly where Franz Kafka, in jest, first read his stories to friends). While it's busy with diners during mealtimes, it relaxes into a café ambience at other times. The back room has long been the place for billiards (100 Kč/hour).

$$ Cafés on Řetězová Street: A little away from the tourist crush of Karlova is a quiet street with three peaceful and inviting cafés (all open daily, generally 9:00-22:00): **Café Ebel** (at #3) offers connoisseurs coffee brews from around the world, fresh muffins, and an inviting place to relax; **Café Montmartre** (#7, no food) still feels like a meeting place for dissident poets from the 1950s; and **Literary Café Řetězová** (#10, light bites) serves coffee, tea, beer, and booze in what feels like an old living room.

TEAHOUSES

In the 1990s, after the borders opened, many young Czechs ventured beyond Western Europe to places like Southeast Asia, Africa, or Peru. When they returned, many gravitated toward Eastern-style teahouses, where the civilization-weary spirit was soothed by the strong taste of yogi chai and the scent of incense. While the teahouse boom has passed, two fine examples still survive in handy Old Town and New Town locales.

$ Dobrá Čajovna ("Good Teahouse"), only a few steps off the bustle of Wenceslas Square, takes you into a peaceful, bamboo-shaded world that elevates tea to a religious ritual. You'll be given an English menu—which lovingly describes each tea—and a bell. The menu lists a world of tea (very fresh, prices by the small pot), "accompaniments" (such as Exotic Miscellany), and light meals "for hungry tea drinkers." When you're ready to order, ring your bell to beckon a tea monk (Mon-Fri 10:00-21:30, Sat-Sun from 14:00, through a short passageway near the base of Wenceslas Square, opposite McDonald's, at Václavské Náměstí 14, tel. 224-231-480).

$ U Zlatého Kohouta ("By the Golden Rooster"), nestled in the corner of a picturesque (and well-hidden) Old Town courtyard, feels even more intimate and less formulaic than Dobrá Čajovna. Japanese woodblock prints and old Chinese maps adorn the walls, and the menu ranges from Taiwanese oolongs to Himalayan yogi teas to a Czech grandma's dried-fruit potions. Sit in one of three tiny vaulted rooms or outside in the circa-1800 workaday courtyard with Tibetan prayer flags flapping above (Mon-Fri 12:00-21:30, Sat-Sun from 14:00; from the end of the Havelská Market farthest from the church, take a sharp right and head down a narrow street, then look for a small courtyard entry in the corner on the left at Michalská 3, tel. 705-223-526).

Prague Connections

BY TRAIN

Prague's **main train station** (Hlavní Nádraží; "Praha hl. n." on schedules) serves all international trains; most trains within the Czech Republic, including high-speed SC Pendolino trains; and buses to and from Nürnberg and Munich. Trains serving Berlin also stop at the secondary **Holešovice station** (Nádraží Holešovice, located north of the river). Both stations have ATMs (best rates) and exchange bureaus (rotten rates). You'll find handy Czech train and bus schedules at www.idos.cz.

To get a better geographical picture, remember that the Czech Republic is a country of landlocked, would-be sailors (recall the greeting *"ahoj"*). Accordingly, the four main international rail lines connect Prague to the closest ports on the four seas: the **North Sea Line** to Hamburg (7 hours) via Dresden and Berlin; the **Baltic Line** to Gdańsk (11 hours, one change) via Warsaw; the **Black Sea Line** to Varna (40 hours, one change) via Budapest and Belgrade; and the **Adriatic Line** to Split (20 hours, two changes) via Vienna and Zagreb.

Main Train Station (Hlavní Nádraží)

The station is a busy hive of shops and services; posted maps help you find your way. Three parallel tunnels connect the tracks to the arrival hall. Taking any of these, you'll first reach a low-ceilinged corridor with several services: To the right are Spořitelna ATMs (best rates), a variety of handy picnic-supply shops, and the "official" taxi stands (avoid these rip-off cabbies—explained later).

Continuing straight down past this corridor, you'll reach the waste-of-space main hall, where you'll find four Metro entrances in the center (two for each direction; see "Getting from the Main Station to Your Hotel," later). Another good ATM (Unicredit) is under the stairs across from the main ticket office. **Lockers** are in the corner under the stairs on the right, and a **Billa supermarket** is in the corner under the stairs to the left.

The **Touristpoint** office—at the left end of the main hall (as you face the tracks)—can call you a taxi to avoid the "official" cabs out front: The driver will meet you at the desk. The office also offers a last-minute room-finding service, books car rentals, and sells maps, international phone cards, sightseeing tours, and adrenaline experiences (daily 8:00-22:00, tel. 224-946-010, www.touristpoint. cz, info@touristpoint.cz).

Buying Tickets: For most trains, head for the **Czech Rail-**

ways (**České Dráhy**) **ticket office**—marked *ČD Centrum*—in the middle of the main hall under the stairs. The regular ticket desks are faster if you already know your schedule and destination, but not all attendants speak good English. For more in-depth questions, look for the tiny **ČD Travel** office, on the left as you enter the main office, which sells both domestic and international tickets, and is more likely to provide help in English (Mon-Fri 9:00-18:00, Sat until 14:00, closed Sun, shorter hours in winter, tel. 972-241-861, www.cd.cz).

The **RegioJet travel office,** with desks at both sides of the main ticket office, sells international train tickets from the DB (Deutsche Bahn—German railways) system and offers various DB deals and discounts. RegioJet also runs its own trains to Olomouc and Košice, Slovakia, and sells a variety of domestic (e.g., to Český Krumlov) and international (Vienna) bus tickets without a commission (daily until 19:45, tel. 539-000-511, www.regiojet.cz). Despite its name, RegioJet does not sell plane tickets.

The **Leo Express ticket office,** across the hall from the ČD Centrum, sells tickets for its trains to Olomouc and Košice (www.le.cz).

Bus Stops: To reach the bus stops for the AE bus to the airport and the DB buses to Nürnberg and Munich, head upstairs to the Art Nouveau hall (explained later) and head outside.

Deciphering Schedules: Platforms are listed by number and—confusingly—sometimes also by letter. *S (sever)* means "south"—the corridor to the left as you face the tracks; *J (jih)* means "north"—the corridor to the right. But in practice, you can take any corridor and walk along the platform to your train. *B1* means the bus platform (upstairs and out front), while *1B*—used by Leo Express trains—is the shorter track at the far-right end of platform 1.

A Bit of History: If you have time to kill waiting for a train, go exploring. First named for Emperor Franz Josef, the station was later renamed for President Woodrow Wilson (see the commemorative **plaque** in the main exit hall leading away from the tracks, and the large bronze **statue** in the park in front of the station). The Czechs appreciate Wilson's promotion of self-determination after World War I, which led to the creation of

the free state of Czechoslovakia in 1918. Under the communists (who weren't big fans of Wilson), it was bluntly renamed Hlavní Nádraží—"Main Station." They enlarged the once-classy Art Nouveau station and painted it the compulsory dreary gray with reddish trim.

For a glimpse at the station's genteel pre-communist times, find your way up into its original **Art Nouveau Hall** (from the main concourse, look for up escalators with *Historical Building of the Station* signs). You'll emerge to stand under a grandly restored dome with elaborate decorations, providing an almost shocking contrast to the businesslike aura of the rest of the station.

Getting from the Main Station to Your Hotel

Even though the main train station is basically downtown, getting to your hotel can be a little tricky.

On Foot: Most hotels I list in the Old Town are within a 20-minute walk of the train station. Exit the station into a small park, walk through the park, and then cross the street on the other side. Head down Jeruzalémská street to the Jindřišská Tower and tram stop, walk under a small arch, then continue slightly to the right down Senovážná street. At the end of the street, you'll see the Powder Tower—the grand entry into the Old Town—to the left. Alternatively, Wenceslas Square in the New Town is a 10-minute walk—exit the station, cross the park, and walk to the left along Opletalova street.

By Metro: The Metro is easy. The entrance is right inside the station's main hall—look for the red *M* with two directions: *Háje* or *Letňany*. To purchase tickets from the machine by the Metro entrance, you'll need Czech coins (get change at the change machine in the corner near the luggage lockers, or break a bill at a newsstand or grocery). Validate your ticket in the yellow machines *before* you go down the stairs to the tracks.

To get to hotels in the Old Town, take the Letňany-bound red line from the train station to Florenc, then transfer to the yellow line (direction: Zličín) and get off at either Náměstí Republiky, Můstek, or Národní Třída; these stops straddle the Old Town.

Or, you can catch the Háje-bound red line to the Muzeum stop, then transfer to the green line (direction: Nemocnice Motol) and get off at either Můstek or Staroměstská. The next stop, Malostranská, is a 15-minute walk from my recommended hotels in the Lesser Town.

For details on Prague's public transit, see page 45.

By Taxi or Uber: The fair metered rate into the Old Town is about 200 Kč; if your hotel is farther out or across the river, it should be no more than 300 Kč. Avoid the "official" taxi stand that's marked inside the station: These thugs routinely overcharge arriving tourists (and refuse to take locals, who know the going rate and can't be fooled). Instead, to get an **honest cabbie,** exit the station's main hall through the big glass doors, then cross 50 yards

PRAGUE

through a park to Opletalova street. A few taxis are usually waiting there in front of Hotel Chopin, on the corner of Jeruzalémská street. Alternatively, the Touristpoint office, described earlier, can call a taxi for you (AAA Taxi—tel. 222-333-222; City Taxi—tel. 257-257-257). Before getting into a taxi, always confirm the maximum price to your destination, and make sure the driver turns on the meter. For more pointers on taking taxis, see page 48.

Uber works the same way it does at home and costs nearly half as much as a taxi. Drivers pick up from the small parking lot next to platform 1B.

By Tram: The nearest tram stop is to the right as you exit the station (about 200 yards away). Tram #9 (headed away from railway tracks) takes you to the neighborhood near the National Theater and the Lesser Town, but isn't useful for most Old Town hotels.

Holešovice Train Station (Nádraží Holešovice)

This station, slightly farther from the center, is suburban mellow. The main hall has the same services as the main train station, in a more compact area. On the left are international and local ticket windows (open 24 hours) and an information office. On the right is an uncrowded café (daily 8:00-19:30). Two ATMs are just outside the first glass doors, and the Metro is 50 yards to the right (follow signs toward *Vstup*, which means "entrance"; it's three stops to Hlavní Nádraží—the main station—or four stops to the city-center Muzeum stop). Taxis and trams are outside to the right (allow 300 Kč for a cab to the center).

Train Connections

All international trains pass through the main station (Hlavní Nádraží); some also stop at Holešovice (Nádraží Holešovice). Direct overnight trains connect Prague to Budapest, Kraków, Warsaw, and Zurich. For tips on rail travel, see the "Transportation" section of the Practicalities chapter.

From Prague's Main Station to Domestic Destinations: **Konopiště Castle** (train to **Benešov**, 2/hour, 1 hour, then 1.5-mile walk to castle), **Kutná Hora** (hourly, 1 hour, more with change in Kolín; to reach Kutná Hora's town center or bone church, you'll need to change to a local train), **Český Krumlov** (8/day, 1/day direct, 3.5 hours—bus is faster and cheaper, but may be booked up), **České Budějovice** (almost hourly, 2.5 hours), **Olomouc** (at least

PRAGUE

hourly, 2.5 hours), **Brno** (every 2 hours direct, 2.5 hours, more with changes).

From Prague's Main Station to International Destinations: **Berlin** (6/day direct, 4 hours), **Dresden** (every 2 hours, 2 hours), **Nürnberg** (1/day, change in Cheb, 5 hours, bus is better), **Munich** (7/day direct, 6 hours; bus is faster), **Frankfurt** (2/day early morning, 8 hours, 2 changes, more options with bus to Nürnberg), **Vienna**—Vídeň in Czech (7/day direct, 4 hours, more with change), **Budapest** (5/day direct, 6.5 hours; 1 night train, 8.5 hours), **Kraków** (1/day direct, 7 hours; 2/day with change in Katowice, 8 hours; 1 direct night train, 8 hours), **Warsaw** (2/day direct, 8 hours; more with change in Ostrava, 8 hours; 1 night train, 11 hours), **Zurich** (1 night train, 14 hours).

BY BUS

Prague's main bus station is at Florenc, east of the Old Town (Metro: Florenc). But some connections use other stations, including Roztyly (Metro: Roztyly), Na Knížecí (Metro: Anděl), Holešovice (Metro: Nádraží Holešovice), Hradčanská (Metro: Hradčanská), or the main train station (Metro: Hlavní Nádraží). Be sure to confirm which station your bus uses.

From Prague by Bus to: Terezín (hourly, 1 hour, departs from Holešovice), **Český Krumlov** (hourly, 3.5 hours, some from Florenc, others leave from Na Knížecí or Roztyly), **Brno** (2/hour from Florenc, 2.5 hours), **Nürnberg,** Germany (6/day via IC Bus, 4 hours, covered by rail passes, departs in front of main train station), **Munich,** Germany (4/day via ExpressBus, 5 hours, covered by rail passes, departs from main train station), **Budapest** (1-4/day via Orange Ways, not covered by rail passes, 7 hours).

BY PLANE
Václav Havel Airport

Prague's modern, tidy, user-friendly Václav Havel Airport (formerly Ruzyně Airport) is located 12 miles (about 30 minutes) west of the city center. Terminal 2 serves destinations within the EU except for Great Britain (no passport controls); Terminal 1 serves Great Britain and everywhere else. The airport has ATMs (avoid the change desks), transportation services (such as city transit and shuttle buses), kiosks selling city maps and phone cards, and a TI (airport code: PRG, airport tel. 220-113-314, operator tel. 220-111-111, www.prg.aero).

Getting from the Airport to Your Hotel

Getting between the airport and downtown is easy. Leaving either airport terminal, you have several options, listed from cheapest to priciest:

Dirt Cheap: Take bus #119 to the Nádraží Veleslavín stop (15 minutes), then take the Metro into the center (another 10 minutes, 32 Kč, buy tickets at info desk in airport arrival hall). This is also fastest as it avoids traffic jams.

Budget: Take the airport express (AE) bus to the main train station, or to the Masarykovo Nádraží Station near Republic Square—Náměstí Republiky (50 Kč, runs every half-hour daily about 6:00-21:00, 40 minutes, look for the *AE* sign in front of the terminal and pay the driver, www.cd.cz). From either station, you can take the Metro, hire a taxi, or walk to your hotel. The Masarykovo Nádraží stop is slightly closer to downtown.

Moderate: Prague Airport Transfers offers 24-hour shuttle and taxi service (shuttle bus—140 Kč/person to city center, shared taxi—290 Kč/person; tel. 222-554-211 from Czech Republic or 516/340-3070 from US, www.prague-airport-transfers.co.uk, info@prague-airport-transfers.co.uk).

Uber is another affordable option, usually costing about half the price of a taxi. Use the airport Wi-Fi to summon a car; your driver picks up in the parking lot facing Terminal 1 (the app should direct you to the designated pickup location).

Expensive: Catch a taxi. Cabbies wait at the curb directly in front of the arrival hall. Or book a yellow AAA taxi through their office in the airport hall—you'll get a 50 percent discount coupon for the trip back. AAA taxis wait in front of exit D at Terminal 1 and exit E at Terminal 2 (metered rate, generally 600 Kč to downtown).

BY PRIVATE CAR SERVICE

Mike's Chauffeur Service is a reliable, family-run company with fair and fixed rates around town and beyond. Friendly Mike's motto is, "We go the extra mile for you." If Mike is busy, he'll send one of his colleagues—all of whom speak English (round-trip fares, with waiting time included, prices valid through 2020 with this book: Český Krumlov—3,800 Kč, Terezín—1,900 Kč, 4 percent surcharge for credit-card payment; these prices for up to 4 people, minibus for up to 8 also available; tel. 241-768-231, mobile 602-224-893, www.mike-chauffeur.cz, mike.chauffeur@cmail.cz). On the way to Český Krumlov, Mike will stop at no extra charge at Hluboká Castle and/or České Budějovice, where the original Bud beer is made. Mike can also arrange a local guide for your time in many of these places. And for day trips from Prague, Mike can bring bicycles along and will pedal with you.

Mike also offers "Panoramic Transfers" to **Vienna** (7,000 Kč, depart Prague at 8:00, arrive Český Krumlov at 10:00, stay up to 5 hours, 1-hour scenic Czech riverside-and-village drive, then a 2-hour autobahn ride to your Vienna hotel, maximum 4 people);

Budapest (9,500 Kč via Bratislava or Český Krumlov, 6 hours); and **Kraków** (9,300 Kč direct, or 9,800 Kč with a stop at Auschwitz; these prices include all road taxes). Mike can also pick you up in any of these cities and bring you to Prague. Check Mike's website for special deals on last-minute transfers, including super-cheap "deadhead" rides when you travel in the opposite direction of a full-fare client.

NEAR PRAGUE

Kutná Hora • Terezín Memorial • Konopiště Castle

Prague has plenty to keep a traveler busy, but don't overlook the interesting day trips in the nearby Bohemian countryside. Within a short bus or train ride of Prague (in different directions), you'll find a variety of worthwhile stopovers.

Kutná Hora

Kutná Hora (KOOT-nah HO-rah) is a refreshingly authentic, yet unmistakably gorgeous town that sits on top of what was once Europe's largest silver mine. In its heyday, the mine was so productive that Kutná Hora was Bohemia's "second city" after Prague. Much of Europe's standard coinage was minted here, and the king got a 12 percent cut of every penny. In addition to financing much of Prague's grand architecture, these precious deposits also paid for Kutná Hora's particularly fine cathedral. But by about 1700, the mining and minting petered out, and the city slumbered.

Once rich, then ignored, Kutná Hora is now appreciated by tourists looking for a handy side trip from Prague. While most visitors come here primarily for the famous, offbeat Sedlec Bone Church, the delightful town itself trumps it—with one of the finest Czech churches outside of Prague (St. Barbara's Cathedral), a breathtaking prom-

Day Trips

E-40 · Bautzen   Görlitz   E-40
Zgorzelec
GERMANY   POLAND
To
Berlin
● Dresden
Elbe
Bad
Schandau
170
Zinnwald   Děčín
E-55   50 Kilometers
Cínovec
8   50 Miles
Teplice   Ústí nad Labem
Litoměřice
Terezín
Bohušovice   CONCENTRATION CAMP
MEMORIAL
C Z E C H   R E P U B L I C
Mělník
Křivoklát   Slaný   E-55   9
To Karlovy   Park   E-6
Vary   Lidice   VÁCLAV   Labe   River   To Hradec
HAVEL   Králové
Rakovník   Lány   AIRPORT   ★ Prague   E-67
KŘIVOKLÁT   Nižbor   12
Kolín
Berounka   603   2
River   Beroun   KARLŠTEJN   Kutná Hora
Karlštejn   Řevnice
Village   Srbsko   To Brno
E-50
KONOPIŠTĚ   Benešov
4
To Plzeň   Vltava River   E-50
To Tábor & Český   3   To Brno
Krumlov

NEAR PRAGUE

enade overlooking the valley, a fascinating silver mine, and a cute, cobbled town center with pretty pastel houses.

All in all, underrated Kutná Hora makes a strong case for the title of "best Czech stop outside of Prague." Unlike dolled-up Český Krumlov, Kutná Hora is a typical Czech town. The shops on the main square cater to locals, and the factory between the Sedlec Bone Church and the train station—since the 1930s, the biggest tobacco processor in the country—is now Philip Morris' headquarters for Central Europe. Kutná Hora is about as close to quintessential Czech life as you can get.

GETTING TO KUTNÁ HORA

The town is 45 miles east of Prague. Direct trains from Prague stop at Kutná Hora's main train station, two miles from the town center (hourly, 1 hour; other trains are slower and require transfer in Kolín). From the main station, a local train shuttles visitors in just a few minutes to Sedlec station (near the Sedlec Bone Church), then to the central Město station (near the rest of the sights). After getting off at the main station, follow the passage beneath the tracks to the cute little yellow local train. For train schedules, see www.jizdnirady.idnes.cz.

In Prague, make sure to buy a ticket to "Kutná Hora Město" rather than "Kutná Hora hl. n." (the main station)—the price is nearly the same, and this gives you the flexibility to get off and on at any of the three Kutná Hora stations.

PLANNING YOUR TIME

For the most efficient visit, head to the Sedlec Bone Church first, then explore the town center of Kutná Hora. Kutná Hora is quiet on Sundays, when most shops are closed.

Here's my suggested plan: At Kutná Hora's main train station, transfer to the local train. Get off at its first stop (Kutná Hora Sedlec), and walk five minutes to the Bone Church, stopping at St. Mary's Basilica along the way. After your visit, head to St. Barbara's Cathedral in the town center via public bus, taxi, or train. After touring the cathedral, follow my self-guided walk to the Czech Museum of Silver and take an English-language mine tour (book ahead online or by phone, or simply drop by in advance to sign up). At the end of the day, walk to Město station (about 15 minutes) to catch the train back to Kutná Hora's main train station, where you'll transfer to a train back to Prague.

Orientation to Kutná Hora

For a relatively small town (about 20,000 people), Kutná Hora is tricky to navigate: It's long and skinny, with a spaghetti of lanes spilling across the summit of a promontory that stretches from the main train station, past the Bone Church, to the historical center.

TOURIST INFORMATION

The main TI is on **Palacký Square** (Palackého Náměstí), housed in the same building as the Alchemy Museum (daily 9:00-18:00; Oct-March Mon-Fri until 17:00, Sat-Sun until 16:00; tel. 327-512-378, www.kutnahora.cz). It also rents bicycles (220 Kč/day, mobile 605-802-874).

Smaller TIs are located across from the **Bone Church** (mobile 731-402-307), and in front of the **cathedral** (handy WCs). You can hire a local guide at the cathedral TI (500 Kč/hour Tue-Sun, no tours Mon, smart to reserve ahead, tel. 327-516-710, mobile 736-485-408, infocentrum@kh.cz).

ARRIVAL IN KUTNÁ HORA

The main train station, **Kutná Hora Sedlec,** is a short walk from the Bone Church. From the station, head one block down the street perpendicular to the tracks, stopping at the large St. Mary's Basilica on your right. Cross the main street and find the small Bone Church in the middle of the cemetery directly ahead.

If you're skipping the Bone Church (or not visiting it first), stay on the train to the **Kutná Hora Město station** in the valley. From there, hike up to St. Barbara's Cathedral (about 20 minutes) to find the start of my self-guided Kutná Hora walk.

Kutná Hora Walk

Kutná Hora's most famous sight—the Bone Church—is on the outskirts of town, and listed later. This self-guided walk connects the rest of the sights you'll want to see in a near-loop of the historical center. Before you get too far into the walk, call or drop by the Czech Museum of Silver to book a spot on the mine tour. No stop on this walk is more than 10 minutes from the museum, so you can bail out and head for your tour at any point and easily resume the walk later.

• *Begin in the inviting park surrounding the cathedral.*

St. Barbara's Cathedral and Park: Rising like three pointy tents from a forest of buttresses, St. Barbara's strikes an exquisite Gothic profile. This culmination of Czech Gothic architecture was funded with a "spare no expense" attitude by a town riding the crest of a wave of mining wealth. Be sure to tour the **cathedral's interior** (see listing, later)—but also take the time to do a slow lap around the pristine park that surrounds it.

Behind the church's apse, belly up to the **viewpoint** for an orientation to the city. From left to right, visually trace the historical center that perches along the promontory's crest: The long former Jesuit College now houses a modern art museum. The big, gray building that plunges down the cliff is the town's "little castle" *(Hrádek),* with the Czech Museum of Silver. And the spire to the right of that bookends this walk. Surveying this scene, think about the history of a town made very, very rich by the glittering deposits it sits upon. Wealthy as it was, this was still an industrial town: The river below was so polluted they called it "Stink" in Czech. Notice the vineyards draping the hill. Kutná Hora is closer to Moravia (the

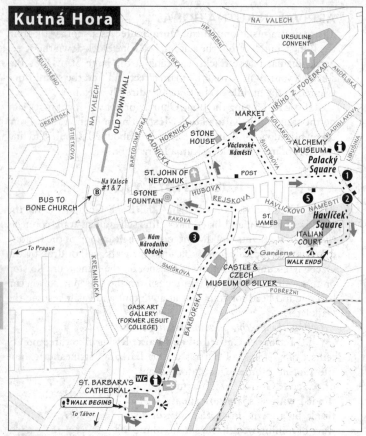

Kutná Hora

eastern Czech Republic) than it is to Prague—here, you're beginning to see the transition from beer country in Bohemia to the wine country of Moravia.

• *After circling the church, walk along the grand...*

Terrace: Just before you head along the panoramic promenade, notice the handy TI in the little house on the left. Then stroll regally along the stately white building, which now houses GASK, the contemporary Art Gallery of the Central Bohemian Region (single exhibit—80 Kč, open Tue-Sun 10:00-18:00, closed Mon year-round and Jan-Feb).

Near the end of the terrace, continue following the broad cobbled footpath downhill...and keep an eye out for an army of white-jacketed, white-helmeted miners trudging up the hill for their daily shift. Or maybe they're tourists, about to explore the former silver mine at the **Czech Museum of Silver,** which occupies the big building on your right (see listing, later).

• *At the little park in front of the museum, take the left (level) fork, fol-*

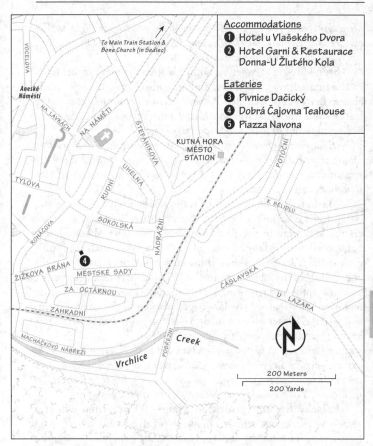

Accommodations
1 Hotel u Vlašského Dvora
2 Hotel Garni & Restaurace Donna-U Žlutého Kola

Eateries
3 Pivnice Dačický
4 Dobrá Čajovna Teahouse
5 Piazza Navona

NEAR PRAGUE

lowing Stone Fountain *signs. When you hit the bigger street (with lots of parked cars), turn left (uphill, on Rejskova), and bear left around the big drab building. You'll emerge into a little square (Rejskovo Náměstí), with a big and impressive...*

Stone Fountain (Kamenná Kašna): The intensive mining under Kutná Hora released arsenic and other toxins, poisoning the water supply. The city struggled with obtaining clean drinking water, which had to be brought to town by a sophisticated system of pipes, then stored in large tanks. At the end of the 15th century, the architect Rejsek built a 12-sided, richly decorated Gothic structure over one of these tanks. Although no longer functioning, the fountain survives unchanged—the only structure like it in Bohemia.

• *Facing the fountain, hook right around the corner and head down Husova street. On the left, you'll pass the stately town library (Městská Knihovna), then the gorgeous late-Baroque/Rococo Church of St. John of Nepomuk (named for the Czech patron saint). Turn left up the street*

after this church (Lierova). At the top of the street, turn right on Vá-
clavské Náměstí (Kutná Hora's own Wenceslas Square). On your left,
you'll spot the frilly decorations on the...

Stone House (Kamenný Dům): Notice the meticulous detail
in the grape leaves, branches, and animals on this house's facade
and up in its gable. Talented Polish craftsmen delicately carved the
brittle stone into what was considered a marvel of its time. Skip the
boring museum of local arts and crafts inside.

• *Continue past the house as the street opens up into a leafy and inviting*
square. For a slice of authentic Czech life, continue straight when the
street narrows again; a half-block down on your right, under the tržnice
sign, is the town's humble...

Market: This double row of stalls selling knockoff Nikes and
cheap jeans is as much a part of Czech urban life today as farmers markets were in the past (Mon-Fri 7:30-16:45, shorter hours
Sat, closed Sun). Many of the stalls are run by Vietnamese immigrants, the Czech Republic's third-largest minority (after Slovaks
and Poles). Many came here in the 1970s as part of a communist
solidarity program that sent Vietnamese workers to Czech textile
factories. They learned the language, adapted to the environment,
and, after 1989, set off on a road to entrepreneurial success that allowed them to bring over friends and relatives.

• *Backtrack a few steps uphill, then turn left to walk down through the*
postcard-perfect Šultysova street, with a towering plague column at its
center. Turn left at the street past the column, enjoying the pretty, color-
ful arcades. You'll emerge into the lively main square.

Palacký Square (Palackého Náměstí): Beautiful but still
somehow local, this square enjoys colorful facades, tempting al
fresco restaurant tables, and generous public benches. Across the
square on the left, notice the TI; inside the same building is the
Alchemy Museum, featuring an alchemist's study complete with
ancient books (60 Kč, daily 9:00-18:00, Oct-March until 17:00).

• *Exit the square at the far-right corner, following the traffic-free street*
(in the gap between buildings, toward the green house). You'll enter...

Havlíček Square (Havlíčkovo Náměstí): The monuments on
this leafy, parklike square are a Who's Who of important Czech
patriots.

Straight ahead, the stone
statue with his arm outstretched
is **Karel Havlíček** (1821-1856),
the founder of Czech political journalism (and the square's
namesake). From Kutná Hora,
Havlíček ran an influential
magazine highly critical of the
Habsburg government. In 1851,

he was forced into exile and detained for five years in the Tirolean Alps under police surveillance. His integrity is reflected by the quote inscribed on the statue: "You can try to bribe me with favors, you can threaten me, you can torture me, yet I will never turn a traitor." His motto became an inspiration for generations of Czech intellectuals, most of whom faced a similar combination of threats and temptations. Havlíček (whose name means "little Havel") was much revered in the 1970s and 1980s, when the *other* Havel (Václav) was similarly imprisoned for his dissent.

Below and to the right, the bronze, walrus-mustachioed statue in front of the big building honors the founder of Czechoslovakia, **Tomáš Garrigue Masaryk** (1850-1937; see sidebar on page 110). Circle around behind the pedestal to see the brief inscription tracing the statue's up-and-down history, which parallels the country's troubled 20th-century history: erected by Kutná Hora townspeople on October 27, 1938 (the eve of Czechoslovakia's 20th birthday); torn down in 1942 (by occupying Nazis, who disliked Masaryk as a symbol of Czech independence); erected again on October 27, 1948 (by freedom-loving locals, a few months after the communist coup); torn down again in 1957 (by the communists, who considered Masaryk an enemy of the working class); and erected once again on October 27, 1991. Notice that the Czechs, ever practical, have left a blank space below the last entry.

Masaryk stands in front of the **Italian Court** (Vlašský Dvůr). Step inside its fine courtyard. This palace, located on the site where Czech currency was once made, became Europe's most important mint and the main residence of Czech kings in the 1400s. It's named for the Italian minters who came to Kutná Hora to teach the locals their trade. Most of the present-day building is a 19th-century reconstruction. Today, it hosts a moderately interesting museum on minting and local history. While the main Gothic hall (now a wedding chamber) and the Art Nouveau-decorated St. Wenceslas Chapel are interesting, you can visit them only with a 40-minute guided tour (rarely in English; Czech tour comes with English handout; daily 9:00-18:00, shorter hours Oct-March).

Exiting the courtyard of the Italian Court, turn right and watch on the wall to your right for a small bronze tablet showing a hand flashing a peace sign, covered with barbed wire. This is an unassuming little **memorial** to the victims of the communist regime's misrule and torture.

Continue straight down the steps into a little park, and then turn right to reach a great **viewpoint.** It overlooks the distinctive roof of the cathedral and the scenic valley below.

• *Your walk is finished. If you're headed for your tour at the **Czech Museum of Silver**, take this scenic route: Walk back up to Havlíček Square, circle around the Italian Court, curl along the downhill side of St. James'*

Church, and enjoy the views. Eventually the view terrace dead-ends at a little lane that bends right and uphill, depositing you at the museum.

*If you're headed back to Prague, it takes about 15 minutes to walk to the **Kutná Hora Město train station** from Havlíček Square. Head downhill past the park, which funnels you between two buildings. Take the first left on Roháčova, then the first right on Sokolská. When you reach the wide cross-street (Nádražní), turn left and follow the train tracks to the little pink station.*

Sights in Kutná Hora

ON THE OUTSKIRTS
▲▲Sedlec Bone Church (Kostnice v Sedlci)

Located about 1.5 miles from the town's historical center, the Sedlec Bone Church sits in a serene graveyard and looks unassuming from the outside. But inside, it's filled with the bones of 40,000 people—stacked into neat, 20-foot-tall pyramids decorating the walls and ceilings. The 14th-century plagues and 15th-century wars provided all the raw material necessary for the monks who made these designs.

Cost and Hours: 90 Kč, 120 Kč combo-ticket with St. Mary's, daily April-Sept 8:00-18:00, March and Oct 9:00-17:00, Nov-Feb 9:00-16:00, good 40-Kč audioguide adds 15 minutes of commentary to make it more meaningful, tel. 327-561-143, www.kostnice.cz.

Visiting the Church: Stand outside the church. This is a place of reflection. The cemetery here was "seeded" with holy earth brought from Jerusalem, which made this sacred ground. Demand was high, and corpses that could no longer pay the rent (i.e., those who lacked surviving relatives with enough disposable income for postmortem real estate) were "evicted." What to do with the bones? Recycle them as church decorations with a message.

The monks, who first placed these bones 400 years ago, were guided by the belief that in order to live well, one must constantly remember death (*memento mori*—"what we are now, someday you shall be"). They also wanted to remind viewers that the earthly church was a community of both the living and the dead, a countless multitude that would one day stand before God. Later bone stackers were more interested in design than theology...as evidenced by the many show-off flourishes you'll see around the church.

Approach the church. Ignore the dull upper chapel, and head down below (look for the *kostinec* sign). Flanking the stairwell are two giant chalices made of bones (a symbol of Jan Hus' egalitarian approach to worship).

Downstairs, on either side are giant stacks of bones, reaching up to the top of the Gothic vaults (there are six such bone-pyramids in this small chapel). The skulls are neatly arranged on top, in the belief that this closeness to God would serve them well when Jesus returns to judge the living and the dead. Straight ahead dangles a chandelier, which supposedly includes at least one of every bone in the human body. In the glass case on the right (by the pillar), see the skulls with gnarly holes and other wounds. These belonged to soldiers who died fighting in the Hussite Wars—a boom time for this cemetery.

Finally, head into the left wing of the church, where you'll find a giant coat of arms of the aristocratic Schwarzenberg family—decorated with the skull of an Ottoman invader (a fearsome foe of the time), whose "eye" is being pecked out by a raven made of human bones.

Your visit is over. Head into town, thankful all of your limbs are intact.

Nearby: You'll pass the magnificent Sedlec **St. Mary's Basilica** as you walk from the train station to the Bone Church. Predating both the silver mine and the town of Kutna Hora, St. Mary's is worth a peek (50 Kč, 120 Kč combo-ticket with Bone Church, Mon-Sat 9:00-18:00, Sun from 11:00, shorter hours off-season, tel. 326-551-049, www.sedlec.info/en/cathedral).

Getting from the Bone Church to Town: A helpful TI on the left of the church can direct you to the public bus or call you a taxi (about 140 Kč to St. Barbara's Cathedral—the start of my self-guided walk). The public bus runs from the Bone Church to the Na Valech stop (#1 runs Mon-Fri 2/hour; #7 runs hourly Sat-Sun; 15 minutes). From the stop, walk straight along the main street (Kremnická) for 400 yards; St. Barbara's will be on your left.

IN THE CENTER
▲▲St. Barbara's Cathedral (Chrám Sv. Barbory)
The cathedral was founded in 1388 by miners, who dedicated it to their patron saint. The dazzling interior celebrates the town's sources of wealth, with frescoes featuring mining and minting. This church was a stunning feat of architecture by two Gothic geniuses of Prague, Matyáš Rejsek and Benedict Ried. And, like Prague's cathedral, it sat unfinished and sealed off for centuries, until it was finally completed in the early 20th century.

Cost and Hours: 60 Kč, daily 9:00-18:00, shorter hours Nov-March, audioguide-40 Kč, tel. 327-515-796, www.khfarnost.cz.

Visiting the Cathedral: While this tour covers the highlights, you can ask to borrow slightly more detailed info sheets at the ticket desk or rent the more in-depth audioguide.

Head inside, walk to the middle of the main nave, and just take it all in. Intricate, lacy vaulting decorates an impossibly high ceiling that's also decorated with the coats of arms of local miners. This is the epitome of Gothic: a mind-bogglingly tall nave supported by flying buttresses that create space for not one, but two levels of big windows; pointed arches where the columns converge; and an overall sense of verticality and light.

Take in the gorgeous **high altar**—a Last Supper scene of carved and painted wood. Then circle clockwise around the apse, past Baroque altars. Tune into the fine **stained-glass windows** (throughout the church) by František Urban, a somewhat less talented contemporary of Alfons Mucha, who nevertheless employs a similarly eye-pleasing Art Nouveau flair to illustrate scenes from church history. (A tiny version of this church's distinctive triple-pointed roofline appears in the background of several windows.)

Continue around the apse. The second-to-last chapel, called the **Smíšek Chapel,** is an artistic highlight. The late-Gothic frescoes—*The Arrival of the Queen of Sheba, The Trial of Trajan,* and especially the fresco under the chapel's window depicting two men with candles—are the only remaining works of a Dutch-trained master in Gothic Bohemia. The final chapel, called the **St. Wenceslas Chapel,** has frescoes under the windows showing miners going about their daily labor.

Continue up the side nave. Midway along, look for the **miner statue** on a pillar on your right. He's wearing a typical white miner's coat. White fabric was the cheapest option (as it required no dyes), and was easier to see in the dark. The leather mat wrapped around his waist made it easier for him to slide down chutes inside the mine. Most miners were healthy, unattached men in their 20s. An average of five miners died each day—from cave-ins, collapsing scaffolding, built-up poisonous gases, fires, and so on. At the back wall of the long chapel on your left, notice the precious frescoes from 1463 showing two people minting coins.

Loop around the back of the church, coming back up the left nave. You'll pass finely carved wooden **choir benches** that blend, in perfect Gothic harmony, with the church's architecture.

▲Hrádek Castle and the Czech Museum of Silver (České Muzeum Stříbra)

Located in Kutná Hora's 15th-century Hrádek ("little castle"), the Czech Museum of Silver offers a fascinating look at the primary source of local wealth and pride. Over the centuries, this mine produced some 2,500 tons of silver, copper, and zinc. Today you can visit the facility only with a 1.5-hour tour, which lets you spelunk in the former miners' passages that run beneath the entire town center. Note that the tour involves some tight squeezes and may be uncomfortable if you're claustrophobic. Bring warm clothing—mines are cold.

Cost and Tours: The English tour of the mine (Route II) costs 120 Kč; Route I, which includes only the aboveground museum, is pointless. You can book tours online only two or more days in advance. It's better to call ahead (the day before or the morning of your visit) to ask when English tours are scheduled—wait through the Czech recording and ask to speak to someone in English. Without advance reservations, drop by the museum soon after you arrive in Kutná Hora to reserve.

Hours: Tue-Sun 10:00-18:00, April and Oct until 17:00, Nov until 16:00, closed Mon year-round and Dec-March.

Information: Tel. 327-512-159, www.cms-kh.cz.

Visiting the Museum and Mine: First, your guide takes you to see an intriguing horse-powered winch that once hoisted 2,000 pounds of rock at a time out of the mine. You'll learn the two methods miners used to extract the precious ore: either by hammering with a chisel or pick, or by setting a fire next to a rock—heating it until it naturally cracked.

Then you'll don a miner's coat and helmet, grab a bulky communist-era flashlight, and walk like the Seven Dwarves through the town center to a secret doorway. It's time to climb deep into the mine for a wet, dark, and claustrophobic tour of the medieval shafts that honeycomb the rock beneath the town—walking down 167 steps, traversing 900 feet of underground passages (but it feels even longer), then walking back up 35 steps.

Along the way, you'll see white limestone deposits in the form of mini-stalagmites and stalactites, and peer down into a 26-foot-deep pool of crystal-clear water. Squeezing through very tight passages, you'll feel like (fill in your own childbirth joke here). The mine holds a steady, year-round temperature of 54 degrees Fahrenheit while fat drops of condensation fall continually from the ceiling thanks to the nearly 100 percent humidity. Prepare for the moment when all the lights go out, plunging you into a darkness as total as you'll ever experience. You'll understand why miners relied on their other senses. For instance, when silver was struck, it made a telltale sound and smelled faintly like garlic.

Finally, ascending to ground level, your guide will explain safety mechanisms at the surface, and walk you through the smelting and minting processes that turned those raw deposits into coins for an entire continent.

Sleeping and Eating in Kutná Hora

Sleeping: Although one day is enough for Kutná Hora, staying overnight saves you money (hotels are much cheaper here than in Prague) and allows you to better savor the atmosphere of a small Czech town.

$ Hotel u Vlašského Dvora and **Hotel Garni** are two renovated townhouses run by the same management. Furnished in a mix of 1930s and modern style, the hotels come with access to a fitness center and sauna. Hotel Garni is slightly nicer (a few steps off main square at Havlíčkovo Náměstí 513, tel. 327-515-773, www.vlasskydvur.cz).

Eating: $$ Pivnice Dačický has made a theme of its namesake, a popular 17th-century author who once lived here. Solid wooden tables rest under perky illustrations of medieval town life, and a once-local brew, also named after Dačický, flows from the tap. They serve standard Czech fare, as well as excellent game and fish. While its regulars still come here for the cheap lunch specials, during tourist season the crowd is mostly international. Service can be slow when a group arrives (daily 11:00-23:00, Rakova 8, tel. 327-512-248, mobile 603-434-367).

$$ Dobrá Čajovna Teahouse also offers the chance to escape—not to medieval times, but to a Thai paradise. Filled with tea cases, water pipes, and character, this place is an ideal spot to dawdle away the time that this ageless town has reclaimed for you. On weekdays, they serve vegetarian lunch specials (Mon-Fri 11:00-22:00, Sat-Sun from 14:00, Havlíčkovo Náměstí 84, mobile 777-028-481).

$ Restaurace Donna-U Žlutého Kola ("Yellow Wheels") serves the fastest, tastiest Czech dishes in town, attracting a local crowd. There's a long menu in English, but the lunch specials are only listed on a separate sheet in Czech. When the weather's nice, sit in the shady courtyard behind the restaurant (daily, lunch specials until 15:00, on Havlíčkovo Náměstí, right above Hotel Garni, tel. 327-512-749).

$$ Piazza Navona features irritating English-language advertising ("the only true Italian restaurant in town"), but it still draws loyal customers thanks to its decent food and superb location on the main square (daily, Palackého Náměstí 90, tel. 327-512-588).

Kutná Hora Connections

To return to Prague, hop on a local train from Kutná Hora Město station, near the historical center (or Kutná Hora Sedlec station if you end your day at the Bone Church), and take it to the Kutná Hora main station for your train transfer to Prague. Note that the best Prague connection runs only about every two hours, so check schedules carefully; other options require an additional change and take much longer.

Terezín Memorial

Terezín (TEH-reh-zeen), an hour by bus from Prague, was originally a fortified town named after Habsburg Empress Maria Theresa (it's called "Theresienstadt" in German). It was built in the 1780s with state-of-the-art, star-shaped walls designed to keep out the Prussians. In 1941, the Nazis removed the town's 7,000 inhabitants and brought in 58,000 Jews, creating a

horribly overcrowded ghetto. Ironically, the town's medieval walls, originally meant to keep Germans out, were later used by Germans to keep the Jews in. As the Nazis' model "Jewish town" for deceiving Red Cross inspectors, Terezín fostered the illusion that its Jewish inmates lived relatively normal lives—making the sinister truth all the more cruel.

Compared to other such sights in Eastern and Central Europe (such as Auschwitz or Mauthausen), Terezín (worth ▲▲) feels different: First, it focuses less on the Nazis' ruthless and calculated methods, and instead celebrates the arts and culture that thrived here despite the conditions—imbuing the place with a tragic humanity. Second, the various museums, memorials, and points of interest are spread over a large area in two distinct parts: a drab grid of a town and the original fortress (across the river, a short walk away). This means you're largely on your own to connect the dots and flesh out the story (use my self-guided tour to help).

GETTING THERE

The camp is about 40 miles northwest of Prague. It's most convenient to visit Terezín by **bus** (described next) or **tour bus** (various tour companies in Prague offer full-day tours to Terezín, including Wittman Tours, www.wittmann-tours.com).

NEAR PRAGUE

Buses to Terezín leave about hourly from Prague's Holešovice train station (Nádraží Holešovice, on Metro line C). When you get off the Metro (coming from the city center), head toward the front of the train, go upstairs, turn right, and walk to the end of the corridor. You'll see bus stands directly ahead, outside the station. The Terezín bus departs from platform 7 (direction: Litoměřice, pay driver). You'll arrive in Terezín an hour later at the public bus stop on the main square, across from the TI and around the corner from the Museum of the Ghetto. Some buses also stop earlier, by the Small Fortress. The driver and fellow passengers may tell you to get off there, but my self-guided tour works best if you begin at the stop in town (after the bus passes a field of crosses on your right and travels across the river).

Two different companies (Busline and Kavka) run this route; for schedules that include both companies, see www.jizdnirady. idnes.cz—you want "Terezín LT." Be sure to check the return schedule, too—the bus for Prague leaves from Terezín's main square hourly and takes about an hour (pay driver).

PLANNING YOUR TIME

Because the sights are scattered, plan on lots of walking, and give yourself plenty of time: Three hours is barely enough for a minimal visit (and requires skipping some sights); allow at least four hours to quickly see everything, and more like six to really delve in. Your understanding of Terezín becomes immeasurably deeper with the help of a local guide (for a list of Prague-based guides, see page 50).

ORIENTATION TO TEREZÍN

Cost: The 210-Kč combo-ticket includes all parts of the camp.

Hours: Most sights, including the Museum of the Ghetto, Magdeburg Barracks, and Hidden Synagogue, are open daily 9:00-18:00, Nov-March until 17:30. The Columbarium and Crematorium are closed Sat. The Crematorium is open Sun-Fri 10:00-18:00, Nov-March until 16:00; the Small Fortress is open daily 8:00-18:00, Nov-March until 16:30.

Information: Tel. 416-782-225, mobile 606-632-914, www. pamatnik-terezin.cz.

Visitor Information: In Terezín town, the **TI** is located in the corner of the Town Hall facing the Prague bus stop. It has handy information (such as the Prague bus schedule and directions to town landmarks) and helpful staff who speak English (Sun 9:00-15:00, Mon-Thu 8:00-17:00, Fri 8:00-13:30, closed Sat, Náměstí ČSA 179, tel. 416-782-616, www.terezin.cz).

Tours: Guided tours in English are offered if enough people request them; call ahead to reserve a spot (included in entry).

Eating: Avoid the stale sandwiches in the **Museum of the**

Ghetto's dingy basement cafeteria. The **Small Fortress** has a
$ cafeteria.

In Terezín town, **$$ Pizzeria Na Obzoru** ("On the Ho-
rizon") serves pasta, steaks, and creamy risottos on its pastel-
colored, sailor-themed ground floor or in a brick-and-stone
vaulted cellar (daily 11:00-22:00, one block up the street from
the hidden synagogue at Dlouhá 24, mobile 731-771-841).
$ Atypic Restaurant offers Czech canteen classics popular
with students and museum employees, served on an airy ter-
race or in the cramped interior with a peek into the kitchen
(daily 9:30-21:00, Máchova 91, tel. 416-782-780).

BACKGROUND

Terezín was the Nazis' model "Jewish town," a concentration
camp dolled up for propaganda purposes. Here, in a supposedly
"self-governed Jewish resettlement area," Jewish culture seemed to
thrive, as "citizens" put on plays and concerts, published a maga-
zine, and raised their families. But it was all a carefully planned
deception, intended to convince Red Cross inspectors that Jews
were being treated well. The Nazis even coached prisoners on how
to answer the inspectors' anticipated questions.

The Nazi authorities also used Terezín as a place to relocate
elderly and disabled Jews from throughout the Third Reich—so the
ghetto was filled with prisoners not only from the Czech lands, but
from all over Europe.

In the fall of 1944, the Nazis began transporting Jews from
Terezín to even more severe death camps (especially Auschwitz) in
large numbers. Virtually all Terezín's Jews (155,000 over the course
of the war) ultimately ended up dying—either here (35,000) or in
extermination camps farther east.

One of the notable individuals held at Terezín was Viennese
artist Friedl Dicker-Brandeis. This daring woman, a leader in the
Bauhaus art movement, found her life's calling in teaching chil-
dren freedom of expression. She taught the kids in the camp to
distinguish between the central things—trees, flowers, lines—and
peripheral things, such as the conditions of the camp. In 1944,
Dicker-Brandeis volunteered to be sent to Auschwitz after her hus-
band was transported there; she was killed a month later.

Of the 15,000 children who passed through Terezín from
1942 to 1944, fewer than 100 survived. The artwork they created at
Terezín is a striking testimony to the cruel horror of the Holocaust.
In 1994, Hana Volavková, a Terezín survivor and the director of
the Jewish Museum in Prague, collected the children's artwork and
poems in the book *I Never Saw Another Butterfly*.

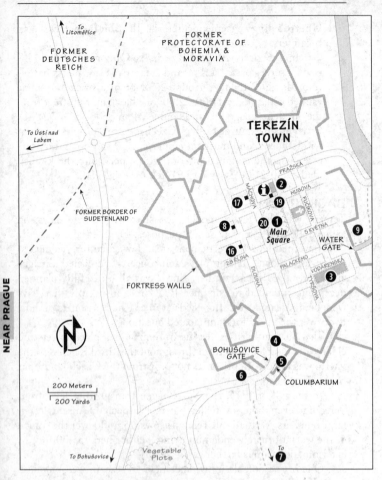

⊙ SELF-GUIDED TOUR

The Terezín experience consists of two parts: the walled town of Terezín, which became a Jewish ghetto under Hitler; and (a half-mile walk east, across the river) the Small Fortress, which was a Gestapo prison camp for mostly political prisoners of all stripes (including non-Jewish Czechs). The complete tour involves about four miles of walking (including the walk from the town to the Small Fortress, then back again to catch your return bus to Prague). Pace yourself. If you want to cut it short, I've suggested sections that you could skip.

Terezín Town

• *The bus from Prague drops you off at Terezín town's spacious...*

❶ Main Square (Náměstí Československé Armády): Today

Terezín

FORTRESS WALLS

SMALL FORTRESS

⑮

⑪ ⑫ ⑭

⑱ ⑬

NATIONAL CEMETERY

⑩ ✝ ✡

To Prague

New Ohře River

NEAR PRAGUE

<u>Self-Guided Tour</u>
❶ Main Square
❷ Museum of the Ghetto
❸ Magdeburg Barracks
❹ Railway Tracks
❺ Columbarium
❻ Memorial Halls
❼ To Crematorium, Cemeteries & Memorial to Soviet Soldiers
❽ Hidden Synagogue
❾ Dry Moat
❿ National Cemetery
⓫ Gatehouse
⓬ Model Prison Cells, Washroom & Gavrilo Princip's Cell
⓭ History & Art Museum
⓮ Fourth Courtyard
⓯ Execution Ground & Mass Grave

<u>Eateries & Transit</u>
⓰ Pizzeria Na Obzoru
⓱ Atypic Restaurant
⓲ Cafeteria
⓳ Bus to/from Prague
⓴ Bus to/from Litoměřice

Terezín feels like a workaday, if unusually tidy, Czech town, with a tight grid plan hemmed in by its stout walls. And for much of its history, that's exactly what it was. But when Hitler annexed Czechoslovakia, he evicted the residents to create a ghetto for Jews forcibly transplanted here from Prague and elsewhere. Be-

cause it started out as a pretty town, rather than a gloomy prison or custom-built concentration camp, the Nazi authorities cultivated Terezín as a "model" to illustrate to the outside world how good the Jews had it here.

Petr Ginz, Young Artist and Writer

Born in 1928 to a Jewish father and non-Jewish mother, Prague teenager Petr Ginz was a talented artist and writer who penned numerous articles, short stories, and even a science-fiction novel. Petr was sent to the concentration camp at Terezín in 1942, where he edited the secret boys' publication *Vedem (We Are Ahead),* writing poetry and drawing illustrations, and paying contributors with food rations he received from home.

Some of Petr's artwork and writings were preserved by Terezín survivors and archived by the Jewish Museum in Prague. In 2003, Ilan Ramon, the first Israeli astronaut and the son of a Holocaust survivor, took one of Petr's drawings—titled *Moon Country*—into space aboard the final, doomed mission of the space shuttle Columbia.

The publicity over the Columbia's explosion and Petr's drawing spurred a Prague resident to come forward with a diary he'd found in his attic. It was Petr's diary from 1941 to 1942, hidden decades earlier by Petr's parents and chronicling the year before the teen's deportation to Terezín. *The Diary of Petr Ginz* has since been published in more than 10 languages.

In the diary, Petr matter-of-factly documented the increasing restrictions on Jewish life in occupied Prague, interspersing the terse account with dry humor. In the entry for September 19, 1941, Petr wrote, "They just introduced a special sign for Jews" alongside a drawing of the Star of David. He continued, "On the way to school I counted 69 'sheriffs,'" referring to people wearing the star.

Petr spent two years at Terezín before being sent to Auschwitz, where he died in a gas chamber at age 16.

Begin your tour by mentally filling the (now mostly empty) square with thousands of Jewish inmates, all wearing their yellow *Juden* Star of David patches. Picture the giant circus tent and barbed-wire fence that stood on this square for two years during the war. Inside, Jewish workers boxed special motors for German vehicles being used on the frigid Soviet front. As part of year-long preparations for the famous Red Cross visit (which lasted all of six hours on June 23, 1944), the tent and fence were replaced by flower beds (which you still see on the square today) and a pavilion for outdoor music performances.

• *The helpful little TI is across the street from the bus stop. Just around the corner—in the yellow former schoolhouse that faces the adjacent square—is the...*

❷ **Museum of the Ghetto:** This modern, concise, well-presented museum, with artifacts and insightful English descriptions, sets the stage for your Terezín visit. You can buy the Terezín combo-ticket here (and ask about the day's film schedule—explained below). You'll find two floors of **exhibits** about the development of the Nazis' "Final Solution." The ground floor includes some evocative memorials (such as a stack of seized suitcases and a list of Terezín's victims). The exhibit upstairs illuminates life in the ghetto with historical documents (including underground publications and letters—inmates were allowed to mail one per month), items belonging to inmates, and video footage of survivors' testimonies. In the stairwell are large illustrations of ghetto life, drawn by people who lived here.

In the basement is a theater showing four excellent **films.** One film documents the history of the ghetto (31 minutes), offering a helpful, if dry, overview of the sights you'll see. Two others (14 and 20 minutes) focus on children's art in the camp, and the last is a 10-minute montage of clips from *Der Führer schenkt den Juden eine Stadt (The Führer Gives a City to the Jews)*, by Kurt Gerron. Gerron, a Berlin Jew, was a 1920s movie star who appeared with Marlene Dietrich in *Blue Angel*. Deported to Terezín, Gerron in 1944 was asked by the Nazis to produce a propaganda film. The resulting film depicts healthy (i.e., recently arrived) "Jewish settlers" in Terezín happily viewing concerts, playing soccer, and sewing in their rooms—yet an unmistakable, deadly desperation radiates from their pallid faces. The only moment of genuine emotion comes toward the end, when a packed room of children applauds the final lines of the popular anti-Nazi opera *Brundibár:* "We did not let ourselves down, we chased the nasty Brundibár away. With a happy song, we won it all." Even the Nazis were not fooled: Gerron and his wife were shipped to Auschwitz, and the film was never shown in public.

• *To learn more about living conditions in the camp, return to the main square and continue straight past it, along Tyršova street. A few blocks down, just before the wall, on the left you'll find the...*

➌ **Magdeburg Barracks:** Peek inside the large courtyard, then continue upstairs and follow the one-way, counterclockwise loop. First you'll see a meticulously restored dormitory, complete with three-tiered beds, suitcases, eyeglasses, dolls, chessboards, sewing kits...and utterly no privacy. After Terezín's residents were evicted and Jews were imported in huge numbers,  every available space was converted from single-family apartments to outrageously cramped slumber mills like this. Jaunty music lures

NEAR PRAGUE

you around the corner to the first of several rooms celebrating the arts here at Terezín. You'll see exhibits on composers, artists, and writers, who expressed their creativity even in these horrifying conditions. These include profiles of individuals (such as young Petr Ginz—see sidebar) and a wide variety of stirring illustrations of life in the ghetto. Near the end is a room reproducing the camp cabaret stage, where inmates entertained each other.

• *With limited time or energy, consider skipping the next several stops, which take a long, if poignant, detour outside the walls. Jump ahead to the moat (see "Dry Moat," later) by leaving the barracks, turning right, and walking 100 yards to a brick gate. (If you do decide to skip the following stops, you can easily fit in the Hidden Synagogue at the end, before hopping on your bus back to Prague, as it's one block from the main square.)*

 To continue the full tour, exit the barracks, turn left, and walk until you dead-end at the city wall. Turn right and walk along the inside of the stout wall to the far corner. Slicing through the hole in the wall are the remnants of...

❹ **Railway Tracks:** In the early years of the camp, Jews arrived at the train station in the nearby town of Bohušovice and then had

to walk the remaining 1.5 miles to Terezín. This was too public a display for the Nazis, who didn't want townspeople to observe the transports and become suspicious (or to try to interact with the inmates in any way). So the prisoners were forced to construct a railway line that led right to Terezín...and then back out again to Auschwitz.

• *Follow the tracks outside the wall.*

❺ **Columbarium and** ❻ **Memorial Halls:** Exiting the wall, on the left is a Columbarium, where the Nazis deposited cardboard boxes containing the ashes of dead prisoners. The Germans originally promised that the remains would be properly buried after the war, but in 1945, to erase evidence, the ashes of Terezín victims were dumped into the Ohře River. Farther along, past the little pension/café and across the bridge, on the right you will find Jewish and Christian ceremonial halls and the main morgue.

• *When the main road swings right, take the left turn (marked* Krematorium*) and walk past bucolic vegetable plots and fruit gardens, and along a driveway lined with pointy poplar trees, to reach the...*

❼ **Crematorium and Cemeteries:** The low-lying yellow building (to the left of the monumental menorah) is the **crematorium,** where Nazis burned the bodies of those who died here.

Step inside to see a small exhibit on death and burial in the ghetto (explaining that, over time, single graves in coffins gave way to mass graves, then to simply burning bodies en masse and dumping the ashes in the river). Then  head into the chilling main chamber, where four ovens were kept busy cremating bodies.

Outside, surrounding the crematorium is a **Jewish cemetery** with the bodies of those who died before cremation became the norm. Farther to the right (as you face the crematorium) is a **Russian cemetery** and a **Memorial to Soviet Soldiers.** The Soviets liberated Terezín without a fight as the Nazis retreated, on May 8, 1945. But just days before, an epidemic of typhus had spread through the camp. In the weeks after the war ended, scores of Soviet soldiers and medical workers who tried to contain the epidemic died, along with hundreds of former prisoners.

• *Retrace your steps back through the wall, and continue straight ahead past the train tracks, up Dlouhá street. After three blocks, watch on the left for the low-profile green house at #17. Ring the bell to be admitted to the fascinating...*

❽ **Hidden Synagogue:** Inside you'll find a courtyard; the bakery that used to be here hid the synagogue behind it. This is the only one of the camp's eight hidden synagogues that survived. The atmospheric space is still inscribed with two Hebrew captions, which are translated as "May my eyes behold, how You in compassion return to Sinai," and "If I forget Jerusalem, may my tongue rot and my right arm fall off." These words indicate that the prayer room belonged to a congregation of Zionists (advocates of a Jewish state), who, one would expect, were specifically targeted by the Nazis.

Upstairs, a few prisoners lived in a tight attic space. Even though the cramped rooms (reconstructed with period items) seem impossibly small, they were a far better accommodation than the mass housing in which most prisoners were interned. It's thought that a group of craftsmen who labored in a nearby workshop were "lucky" enough to live here.

• *Leaving the synagogue house, turn right, and at the corner, turn left to pop out at the main square. To proceed to the Small Fortress, head down Tyršova as if you're going to the Magdeburg Barracks. Before you get there, turn left along the park, then continue one block up Palackého to the brick gate. You'll cross a bridge over a...*

❾ **Dry Moat:** Imagine this moat filled with plots of vegetables, grown by starving Jews for well-fed SS officers. Turn left and walk along the moat. The top of the fortification walls on the other side were once equipped with benches and pathways.

• *When you reach the main road, turn right across the New Ohře River (the original course of the river was diverted here when Terezín was built). After about five minutes, you'll come to a blocked-off, tree-lined driveway and the prison camp.*

Terezín Prison Camp

• *On the right side of the driveway is the wedge-shaped…*

❿ **National Cemetery:** The remains of about 10,000 victims of Terezín (including 2,386 individual graves; the rest were moved here from mass graves elsewhere) fill this cemetery, which was created after the war's end. The sea of headstones powerfully illustrates the scope of the crime that took place here. Notice that, in addition to the giant Star of David (closer to the fortress), a cross towers over the cemetery. This is a reminder that we've left the Jewish ghetto and are about to enter a very different part of the Terezín complex. From 1940 to 1945, this fortress functioned as a Gestapo prison, through which 32,000 inmates passed (of whom nearly 10 percent died here)—chiefly members of the Czech resistance and communists. While the majority of the camp's victims weren't Jewish, the 1,500 Jews interned here were treated with particular severity.

• *Now head under the black-and-white-striped gate.*

⓫ **Gatehouse:** Inside the gate, on the left, is a modest museum about the pre-WWII history of this fortress. If you need a break before continuing, you could pause at the handy cafeteria. The wood-and-metal chandeliers inside were produced by Jewish workers for the SS officers who once dined in these two rooms.

• *Continuing into the central part of the fortress, watch on the left for a turnstile into a long, skinny side courtyard. Go in and head to the end of the courtyard, under the notorious* Arbeit Macht Frei *sign painted above an arched gate (a postwar replica of the viciously sarcastic* "Work will set you free" *sign that was displayed at all camps). Go under this gate to reach a courtyard ringed with…*

⓬ **Model Prison Cells:** Step into some of the barracks on the right side of the courtyard to see tight, triple-decker bunks where prisoners were essentially stacked at bedtime. Halfway down the courtyard, under the *Block-A* sign, peek into the medical cell.

At the far end, the **washroom** in the right-hand corner (by #15) was built solely for the purpose of fooling Red Cross inspec-

tors. Go ahead, turn the
faucets: No pipes were ever
installed to bring in water.

The shower room
two doors to the left, on
the other hand, was used
to fool the Jews. Here
they got used to the idea
of communal bathing, so
they wouldn't be suspi-
cious when they were later
taken to similar-looking installations at Auschwitz. (There were no
gas chambers at Terezín—most of the deaths here were caused by
malnutrition, disease, and, to a lesser extent, execution.)

Before the Nazis, the Austrian monarchy used the Small Fortress as a prison. In the little side courtyard next to the shower
room, look for a ghostly doorway with a plaque that recalls the
most famous prisoner from that time, Bosnian Serb **Gavrilo Princip,** whose assassination of Archduke Franz Ferdinand and his
wife Žofie in 1914 sparked World War I (see sidebar, later). Princip
died here in 1918 of tuberculosis; of the six Sarajevo conspirators
imprisoned here, only two survived.

• *Return through the Arbeit Macht Frei gate, then back out into the
fortress' central yard. Turn left and continue deeper into the complex. The
large building on your right is marked by* Muzeum *signs.*

⓫ **History and Art Museum:** The ground floor of this building features an exhibit about the Nazi-era history of the Small
Fortress. Photographs and brief descriptions identify many of the
individuals who were imprisoned—and in many cases, executed.
Upstairs is a gallery of paintings by prominent Czech artists, mostly focusing on themes of camp life (and a few about the Spanish
Civil War).

• *Back out in the main yard, continue straight ahead, through two gateways in a row. You'll emerge into the wide, eerie...*

⓮ **Fourth Courtyard:** Here you'll have more opportunities
to step into former prison cells that flank the yard; some of these
house temporary exhibits. At the far end, you'll find a plaque in the
ground listing the 17 countries whose citizens perished at Terezín.

• *Returning to the fortress' main yard once more, turn right and follow
the long buildings. Turn right to find the...*

⓯ **Execution Ground and Mass Grave:** This is where firing
squads executed somewhere between 200 and 300 of Hitler's enemies. Many of Terezín's victims were buried in mass graves along
the fortress ramparts. After the war, these remains were moved to
the National Cemetery we saw on the way into the fortress.

• *Our tour ends here. As you ponder Terezín, remember the message of all such memorials: Never again.*

Konopiště Castle

Konopiště (KOH-noh-peesh-tyeh) was the Neo-Gothic residence of the Archduke Franz Ferdinand d'Este—the heir to the Austro-Hungarian Empire, whose assassination sparked World War I. Located 30 miles south of Prague, it's workable either as a day trip or on the way to Český Krumlov. While it's the least visually arresting of the castles near Prague, its interior has some captivating stories to tell about its former inhabitants.

Enjoyable for anyone, Konopiště is worth ▲ for most. But it's a must for Habsburg aficionados—historians find it worth ▲▲▲.

Construction of the castle began in the 14th century, but today's exterior and furnishings date from about 1900, when Franz Ferdinand renovated his new home. As one of the first castles in Europe to have an elevator, a WC, and running water, Konopiště shows "modern" living at the turn of the 20th century.

Those who lived at Konopiště played a role in one of the most important moments in European history: Franz Ferdinand's assassination in Sarajevo (chillingly illustrated by items displayed inside the castle). The shooting eventually meant the end of the age of hereditary, divine-right, multiethnic empires—and the dawn of a Europe of small, nationalistic, democratic nation-states. Historians get goose bumps at Konopiště, where if you listen closely, you can almost hear the last gasp of Europe's absolute monarchs.

The castle interior is only viewable via a guided tour. There are several tour options, but the best is Route 3 (limited space, so call ahead to reserve; explained later, under "Orientation to Konopiště").

GETTING THERE

By Train: Trains from Prague's main station drop you in Benešov (2/hour, 1 hour, www.idos.cz); a well-marked trail goes from the station to the castle (1.5 miles). To walk to the castle, as you exit the Benešov train station, turn left and walk along the street parallel to the railroad tracks. Turn left at the first bridge you see crossing over the tracks. Along the way you'll see trail markers on trees, walls, and lampposts—one yellow stripe between two white stripes. Follow these markers. As you leave town, watch for a marker with an arrow pointing to a path in the woods. Take this path to bypass the castle's enormous parking lot, which is clogged with souvenir shops and bus fumes.

By Car: Konopiště is about a 45-minute drive from Prague and a two-minute detour off of the main route to Český Krumlov (head east toward Brno on the D-1 expressway; take exit #21 toward *Benešov/České Budějovice/Linz;* after about 9 miles (15 kilometers), watch for the Konopiště turnoff on the right). Bypass the first, giant parking lot (ringed by restaurants); a bit farther along, on the left near the lake, is a smaller lot that's closer to the castle. From either lot, hike uphill about 10-15 minutes to Konopiště.

ORIENTATION TO KONOPIŠTĚ

Cost and Tours: The recommended Route 3 is 320 Kč (described later, under "Visiting the Castle"); Routes 1 and 2 are 220 Kč apiece; all three cost 690 Kč. Space on Route 3 is limited to eight people per hour: It's best to reserve a spot in advance by calling one day ahead or on the morning of your visit (worth the 20-Kč extra charge). All tickets are 30 percent cheaper if you join a Czech-speaking tour (but renting the English audioguide costs 50 Kč—effectively negating most of your savings).

Hours: May-Aug Tue-Sun 9:00-12:30 & 13:00-17:00; Sept Tue-Fri 9:00-16:00, Sat-Sun until 17:00; April and Oct Tue-Fri until 15:00, Sat-Sun until 16:00; closed Mon year-round and Nov-March.

Information: Tel. 317-721-366, www.zamek-konopiste.cz.

VISITING THE CASTLE

While there are three tour options, **Route 3** is the most intimate and interesting. It takes you through the rooms where Franz Ferdinand, his Czech bride Žofie, and their three kids lived while waiting for Uncle Franz Josef to expire. When the communists took over, they simply threw drop cloths over the furniture and let the place sit, untouched, for decades. Now every-

thing has been meticulously restored (with the help of 1907 photographs)—launching you right into a turn-of-the-20th-century time capsule.

The tour takes you through halls upon halls of hunting trophies (each one marked with the place and date of the kill), paint-

Archduke Franz Ferdinand (1863-1914)

Archduke Franz Ferdinand was born to the brother of the Habsburg emperor (Franz Josef) and a Neapolitan princess. After his cousin died under "mysterious circumstances," Franz Ferdinand was thrust into the role of heir apparent to the throne of the Austro-Hungarian Empire—one of the biggest realms Europe has ever seen. But he had to be patient: His Uncle Franz Josef took the throne in 1848 and would hold onto it for nearly 70 years. In fact, he outlived his nephew.

While he waited, Franz Ferdinand kept himself busy by spending time at his bachelor pad in Konopiště. At a ball in Vienna, he met a gorgeous but low-ranking Czech countess, Žofie Chotková. The couple danced all night. After long years of secret courtship, Franz Ferdinand announced his intentions to marry Žofie. His uncle was displeased—Žofie was "only" aristocratic, and the expected path for the heir apparent would be to wed a Western European princess. He insisted on a morganatic marriage so that Žofie could never be an empress and none of the children could inherit the throne. These family squabbles cemented Franz Ferdinand and Žofie's preference for living at Konopiště.

While waiting for a succession that would never arrive, Franz Ferdinand threw himself into his hobbies with zeal. He traveled around the world twice—partly for diplomatic reasons, but largely to pursue his passion for exotic hunting. Shooting anything in sight—deer, bears, tigers, elephants, and crocodiles—he killed about 300,000 animals, a few thousand of which stare morbidly at you from the walls at Konopiště. Franz Ferdinand and Žofie were also devoted parents, raising three children: Žofie, Max, and Ernesto.

In the Kaiser's Pavilion on the grounds of Konopiště, Franz Ferdinand met with German Kaiser Wilhelm and tried to talk him out of plotting a war against Russia. Wilhelm argued that a war would benefit both Germany and Austria: Germans wanted colonies, and the Austro-Hungarian Empire could use a war to divert attention from its domestic problems. But Franz Ferdinand foresaw war as suicidal for Austria's overstretched monarchy.

Soon after, Franz Ferdinand and Žofie went to Sarajevo, in the Habsburg-annexed territories of Bosnia and Herzegovina. There Gavrilo Princip, a Bosnian Serb separatist, shot the Habsburg archduke who so loved shooting, and Žofie. Franz Ferdinand's assassination ironically gave the Germans (and their allies in the Austro-Hungarian administration) the pretext to go to war against Serbia and its ally, Russia. World War I soon broke out. The event Franz Ferdinand had tried to prevent was, in fact, sparked by his death.

ings of royal relatives (including an entire wall of Italian kings—relations of Franz Ferdinand's Neapolitan mother), and photographs
of the many places they traveled and the three kids as they grew up.
The tour includes Franz Ferdinand's dressing room (with his actual
uniform and his travel case all packed up and ready to go); his private study (which feels like he just stepped away from his desk for
a cup of coffee); the living room (with 1,180 pairs of antlers on the
walls); the private dining room (with the table set for an intimate
family dinner for five); the master bedroom (with its huge bed);
the children's bedrooms, playrooms, and classroom (with their toys
and books still on the shelves); three bathrooms with running water
and flushing toilets; and—in the final room—a glass display case
containing the dress Žofie was wearing that fateful day in Sarajevo
(including her still-blood-stained corset). Down the hall are the
royal couple's death masks, Franz Ferdinand's bloody suspenders,
and the actual bullet that ended Žofie's life.

Route 2—which covers the oldest wing of the castle—is also
worth considering, and provides the most comprehensive look into
the castle, its history, and celebrated collections. You'll see the
oversized elevator (with a couch to make the family comfortable on
the 45-second ride upstairs), the library, and the staggeringly large
armory collection. Route 1, covering some other rooms, the hunting hall, and the balcony, is the least interesting.

Other Sights at the Castle: Your tour ticket includes two
quirky additional sights that are worth poking into. Franz Ferdinand's Shooting Range, just off of the castle courtyard, offers a
quick glimpse at the emperor-in-waiting's elaborate system of moving targets; a video demonstrates how the various targets would
move around to keep his skills sharp. The Museum of St. George,
tucked beneath the long terrace (around the side of the palace),
displays Franz Ferdinand's collection of hundreds of sculptures and
paintings of St. George slaying the dragon...taking a theme to an
extreme.

While the stretch between the parking lot and the castle entrance is overrun by tour groups, the gardens and the park are
surprisingly empty. In the summer, the flowers and goldfish in the
rose garden are a big hit with visitors. The peaceful 30-minute walk
through the woods around the lake (wooden bridge at the far end)
offers fine castle views.

Tucked away in the bushes behind the pond is a pavilion
coated with tree bark, a perfect picnic spot. This simple structure,
nicknamed the Kaiser's Pavilion, was the site of a fateful meeting between the German Kaiser Wilhelm and the Archduke Franz
Ferdinand.

Eating at Konopiště Castle: Three touristy restaurants sit
under the castle, and a café and restaurant are in the castle court-

yard, but I'd rather bring picnic supplies from Prague (or buy them at the grocery store by the Benešov train station). While the crowds wait to pay too much for lousy food in the restaurants, you'll enjoy the peace and thought-provoking ambience of a **picnic** in the shaded Kaiser's Pavilion. Or eat cheaply on Benešov's main square (try **$ U Zlaté Hvĕzdy**—"The Golden Star").

ČESKÝ KRUMLOV

Krumau

Surrounded by mountains, lassoed by its river, and dominated by its castle, this enchanted town mesmerizes visitors. When you see its awe-inspiring castle, delightful Old Town of cobbled lanes and shops, and easy canoeing options, you'll understand why having fun is a slam-dunk here. Romantics are floored by Český Krumlov's spectacular setting; you could spend all your time doing aimless laps from one end of town to the other.

The sharp bends in the Vltava provide natural moats, so it's no wonder Český Krumlov has been a choice spot for eons. Celtic tribes settled here a century before Christ. Then came Germanic tribes. The Slavic tribes arrived in the ninth century. The Rožmberks (Rosenbergs)—Bohemia's top noble family—ran the city from 1302 to 1602. You'll spot their rose symbol all over town.

The 16th century was the town's Golden Age, when Český Krumlov hosted artists, scientists, and alchemists from across Europe. In 1588, the town became home to an important Jesuit college. In 1602, the Rožmberks ran out of money to fund their lavish lifestyles, so they sold their territory to the Habsburgs—who ushered in a more Germanic period. After that, as many as 75 percent of the town's people were German—until 1945, when most Germans were expelled (for more on this era and its repercussions, see the sidebar later in this chapter).

Český Krumlov's rich mix of Gothic, Renaissance, and Baroque buildings is easy to miss. As you wander, be sure to look up...notice the surviving details in the fine stonework and pretty gables. Step into shops. Snoop into back lanes and tiny squares. Gothic buildings curve with the winding streets. Many precious Gothic and Renaissance frescoes were whitewashed in Baroque times (when the colorful trimmings of earlier periods were way out of style). Today, these frescoes are being rediscovered and restored.

Český Krumlov is a huge tourist magnet, which makes things colorful and easy for travelers. It can feel like a medieval theme park—but fortunately there are still a few hidden nooks and sleepy back alleys to savor. And a half-day float on the river can help you relax into the local pace.

PLANNING YOUR TIME

It's easy to enjoy Český Krumlov without ever paying to enter a sight (morning and evening are best for strolling without crowds). But a tour of the Baroque Theater at the castle is worth considering. If you want to join an English tour, reserve first thing in the morning (call ahead or visit in person), then build your day around your visit time. While you're at it, consider booking an English tour of the castle interior. Those who hate planning ahead can join a Czech tour of the theater or castle anytime (English info sheets provided). Visits to the synagogue and Seidel Photo Studio Museum bring more recent history alive.

If the outdoors is your thing, a paddle down the river is a highlight (options range from 30 minutes to all day), and a 30-minute walk up to the Křížový Vrch (Hill of the Cross) rewards you with a fine view of the town and its unforgettable riverside setting.

Many sights are closed on Monday, though the major attraction—the town itself—is always open. Evenings are for atmospheric dining and drinking.

Orientation to Český Krumlov

Český Krumlov (CHESS-key KROOM-loff) means, roughly, "Czech Bend in the River." Calling it "Český" for short sounds silly to Czech speakers (since dozens of Czech town names begin with "Český")—rather, they call it "Krumlov."

The city is extremely easy to navigate. The twisty Vltava River, which makes a perfect S through the town, ropes the Old Town into a tight peninsula. Above the Old Town is the Castle Town. Český Krumlov's one main street starts at the isthmus and winds through the peninsula, crossing a bridge before snaking through the Castle Town, the castle complex (a long series of courtyards), and the castle gardens high above. I've narrated this route on my self-guided walk. The main square, Náměstí Svor-

A Town Transformed by Tourism

A visit to Český Krumlov can actually be fascinating for *not* seeing any semblance of local life (the town's original residents more or less cleared out in 1945), and instead for seeing how tourism has transformed this living piece of history. Today, Czechs are about as entitled to claim Český Krumlov as their own as are the throngs of mesmerized visitors. To put things in perspective: The town center has fewer than 20 permanent residents…and receives two million visitors a year.

To highlight this demographic trend, an artist in 2018 hired families to live in four Old Town apartments (the job description included sipping coffee outside, hanging laundry out the windows, and encouraging their kids to play in the street). Locals (who say they rarely go into the Old Town as there is "no one to meet there anymore") shook their heads, and a Prague-based newspaper reported (with perhaps a dose of Schadenfreude) that only one particularly resilient family lasted a whole month on the job.

nosti—with the TI, ATMs, and taxis—dominates the Old Town and marks the center of the peninsula. All of my recommended restaurants, hotels, and sights are within a 5- to 10-minute walk of this square.

TOURIST INFORMATION

The helpful TI is on the **main square** (daily 9:00-18:00, June-Aug until 19:00, shorter hours in winter, tel. 380-704-622, www. ckrumlov.info). The 129-Kč *City Guide* book includes a fine town and castle map. The TI has a baggage-storage desk and can check train and bus schedules. Ask about concerts, city walking tours in English, and canoe trips on the river. They rent an audioguide featuring a one-hour town walk. A second, less-crowded TI—actually a private business—is in the lowest courtyard of the **castle** (daily 9:00-18:00, tel. 380-725-110).

Český Krumlov Card: This 200-Kč card, sold at the TI and participating sights, covers entry to the Round Tower, Castle Museum (but not castle tours), Museum of Regional History, and Seidel Photo Studio Museum. Do the math to decide if it makes sense for you.

ARRIVAL IN ČESKÝ KRUMLOV

By Train: The train station is a 20-minute walk from town (turn right out of the station, then walk downhill onto a steep cobbled path leading to an overpass into the town center). Taxis are stand-

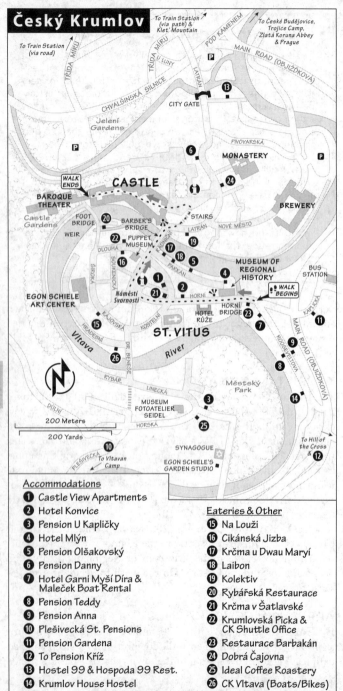

Český Krumlov

ČESKÝ KRUMLOV

Accommodations
1. Castle View Apartments
2. Hotel Konvice
3. Pension U Kapličky
4. Hotel Mlýn
5. Pension Olšakovský
6. Pension Danny
7. Hotel Garni Myší Díra & Maleček Boat Rental
8. Pension Teddy
9. Pension Anna
10. Plešivecká St. Pensions
11. Pension Gardena
12. To Pension Kříž
13. Hostel 99 & Hospoda 99 Rest.
14. Krumlov House Hostel

Eateries & Other
15. Na Louži
16. Cikánská Jizba
17. Krčma u Dwau Maryí
18. Laibon
19. Kolektiv
20. Rybářská Restaurace
21. Krčma v Šatlavské
22. Krumlovská Picka & CK Shuttle Office
23. Restaurace Barbakán
24. Dobrá Čajovna
25. Ideal Coffee Roastery
26. CK Vltava (Boats/Bikes)

ing by to zip you to your hotel (about 100 Kč), or call 602-113-113 to summon one.

By Bus: The bus station is just three blocks away from the Old Town. Follow signs for *Centrum*. Figure on 60 Kč for a taxi from the station to your hotel.

By Car: Parking lots ring the town center, each one marked by a blue *P* sign. If your hotel is in the mostly traffic-free center, you'll be allowed to drive in (gingerly passing hordes of tourists) and park on the main square just long enough to drop off your bags and get directions to one of the outer lots. The flow of traffic is one-way: Enter at the east end of town, on Horní street, then exit across two bridges at the south end of town, on Linecká street (get details from your hotel before you arrive).

HELPFUL HINTS

Festivals: Locals and visitors alike drink oceans of beer and celebrate the town's medieval roots at big events such as the Celebration of the Rose (Slavnosti Růže), where blacksmiths mint ancient coins, jugglers swallow fire, mead flows generously, and pigs are roasted on open fires (late June, www.ckrumlov. info). The summer also brings a top-notch international music festival, with performances in pubs, cafés, and the castle gardens (mid-July–mid-Aug, www.festivalkrumlov.cz). During St. Wenceslas celebrations, the square becomes a medieval market and the streets come alive with theater and music (late Sept).

Bike Rental: You can rent bikes at the **train station** (150 Kč/day with train ticket, slightly higher otherwise, tel. 380-715-000), **CK Vltava** (see listing under "Canoeing and Rafting the Vltava," later), and the recommended **Hostel 99.**

Tours in Český Krumlov

Walking Tours

Since the town itself, rather than its sights, is what it's all about here, taking a guided walk is the key to a meaningful visit. The TI offers several different guided walks. No reservations are necessary—just meet in front of the TI on the main square and pay the guide. Confirm times when you visit, as schedules can change. The **Old Town Tour** offers the best general town introduction (300 Kč, daily at 12:30, 1.5 hours); in peak season, this tour extends to include the castle exteriors (490 Kč, April-Oct daily at 14:30). There's also a nighttime version (departing between 19:30 and 20:30, depending on the season). For a self-guided town walk, consider the TI's audioguide (see "Tourist Information," earlier).

Local Guides

Oldřiška Baloušková studied in California before starting a family back in her hometown, which she knows through and through (500 Kč/hour, mobile 737-920-901, oldriskab@gmail.com). **Jiří (George) Václavíček,** a gentle and caring man who perfectly fits mellow Český Krumlov, is a joy to share this town with (500 Kč/hour, mobile 603-927-995, www.krumlovguide.com, jiri. vaclavicek@gmail.com). **Karolína Kortušová** is an enthusiastic, experienced guide. Her company, Krumlov Tours, can set you up with a good local tour guide, palace and theater admissions, river trips, and more (guides—500 Kč/hour, mobile 723-069-561, http://krumlovtours.com, info@krumlovtours.com).

Český Krumlov Walk

The town's best sight is its cobbled cityscape, surrounded by a babbling river and capped by a dramatic castle. Most of Český

Krumlov's modest sights are laced together in this charming self-guided walk from the top of the Old Town, down its spine, across the river, and up to the castle. The walk begins at a fine viewpoint...and ends at an even better one. I've divided it into two parts: downhill, through the Old Town to the river; then uphill, ascending through the castle complex on the other side. You can also do the two parts on different days. The second half of the walk makes a useful spine for organizing a visit to the castle quarter. To trace the route of this walk, see the "Český Krumlov" map.

THE OLD TOWN

• *Start at the bridge over the isthmus, which was once the fortified grand entry gate to the town. For the best view, step down to the little terrace in front of the restaurant gate.*

Horní Bridge: From this "Upper Bridge," note the natural fortification provided by the tight bend in the river. Trace the river to your right, where it curves around the last building in town, with a smokestack. This is the Eggenberg Brewery, makers of Český Krumlov's very own hometown brew (with daily tours—see listing under "Sights in Český Krumlov," later). Behind that, on the horizon, is a pile of white apartment high-rises—built in the last decade of the communist era to solve a housing shortage (many homes were demolished after their German owners were forced out at the end of World War II). To the left of the brewery stands a huge monastery (with the pointy red steeple; not generally open to the public). Behind that, on Kleť Mountain—the highest hilltop—stands a TV tower and a world-class astronomical observatory and research center.

Head back up to the middle of the bridge. Look down and left, then down and right. Notice how the Vltava wraps entirely around the town center. Rafters take about a half-hour to circle around the Old Town peninsula, beginning and ending under this bridge.

• *Head into town on...*

Horní Street: As you step off the bridge, Český Krumlov's aptly named "Upper Street" passes the **Museum of Regional History** on the right (see "Sights in Český Krumlov," later). Just past the museum, a little garden overlook affords a fine castle view.

Immediately across the street (on the left), notice the Renaissance facade of **Hotel Růže:** This former Jesuit college hides a beautiful courtyard, now filled with artistic vendor stands. Pop inside to shop or just admire its decoration of faux sgraffito "bricks," made by scratching into an outer layer of one color of plaster to reveal a different color beneath. This style was all the rage during the town's boom time, and we'll be seeing several more examples on this walk.

• *Walk another block down the main drag, until you reach steps on the left leading to the...*

Church of St. Vitus: Český Krumlov's main church was built as a bastion of Catholicism in the 15th century, when the Roman Catholic Church was fighting the Hussites. The 17th-century Baroque high altar shows a totem of religious figures: the Virgin Mary (crowned in heaven); St. Vitus (above Mary); and, way up on top, St. Wenceslas, the patron saint of the Czech people—long considered their ambassador in heaven. The canopy in the back, though empty today, once supported a grand statue of a Rožmberk atop a horse. The statue originally stood at the high altar. (Too egotistical for Jesuits, it was later moved to the rear of the nave, and then

lost for good.) While the 1906 Neo-Gothic main organ has been renovated, it's the cute little circa-1716 Baroque beauty that gets more attention—deservedly so (generally open daily 8:30-16:30, Sunday Mass at 9:30, daily Mass at 17:00 in the winter chapel; tel. 724-937-121).

• *Continuing on Horní street, you'll come to the...*

Main Square (Náměstí Svornosti): Lined with a mix of Renaissance and Baroque homes of burghers (all built on 12th-century Gothic foundations), the main square has a grand charm. The Town Hall (the crenellated white building, on the right) flies both the Czech flag and the town flag, which shows the rose symbol of the Rožmberk family, who ruled the town for 300 years.

Imagine the history that this square has seen: In the 1620s, the town was held by the (very Catholic) Habsburgs, just as Lutheran Protestantism was rising to threaten Catholic Europe. Krumlov was a seat of Jesuit power and learning, and the intellectuals of the Roman church allegedly burned books on this square. Later, when there was a bad harvest, locals blamed witches—and burned them, too. Every so often, terrible plagues rolled through the countryside. In a nearby village, all but two residents were killed by a plague.

But the plague stopped before devastating the people of Český Krumlov, and in 1715—as thanks to God—they built the plague monument that stands on the square today (on the left). Much later, in 1938, Hitler stood right here before a backdrop of long Nazi banners to celebrate the annexation of the Sudetenland. And in 1968, Russian tanks spun their angry treads on the roads to this square to intimidate locals who were demanding freedom.

• *From the main square, walk down Radniční street (on the right, just past the Town Hall) and cross the...*

Barber's Bridge (Lazebnický Most): This wooden bridge, decorated with two 19th-century statues, connects the Old Town and the Castle Town. On the right side stands a statue of St. John of Nepomuk, who's also depicted by a prominent statue on Prague's Charles Bridge. Among other responsibilities, he's the protector against floods. In the great floods in August 2002, the angry river submerged the bridge (but removable banisters minimized the damage). Stains just above the windows of the adjacent building show how high the water rose.

• *The second part of the walk involves lots of uphill hiking—but it's worth it to see the castle courtyards and dramatic views.*

KRUMLOV CASTLE

Big and imposing, the town castle boasts several fine courtyards, spectacular viewpoints, and gorgeous gardens—all of which are open to the public, free to enter, and fun to roam (though some areas may be closed on Mon). This part of the walk focuses on those public spaces, leading you from Barber's Bridge, through the heart of the castle, and up to a picturesque viewpoint just before the gardens. The castle also has several individual sights (Round Tower, Castle Museum, Upper Castle, Baroque Theater) that can be laced into this walk but require paid admission and/or a reserved tour (for details, see listings under "Sights in Český Krumlov," later).

• *Cross the bridge and head up shop-lined Latrán street, which bends to the right. Just after that bend, look for the stairs on your left (in front of the gray-and-white building). Head up, passing under a stone arch with the wood-carved rose symbol of the Rožmberk family. You'll emerge into the castle's...*

First (Lower) Courtyard: This is just the first of many courtyards that bunny-hop up through the castle complex. This was the site for workers and industry (stables, smithy, brewery, pharmacy, and so on)—convenient for aristocratic needs, but far enough away to keep noises and smells at bay.

Looking up, you can't miss the strikingly colorful **Round Tower** that marks the location of the first castle, built here to guard the medieval river crossing. With its 16th-century Renaissance paint job colorfully restored, it looks exotic, featuring fancy astrological decor, terra-cotta symbols of the zodiac, and a fine arcade.

• *Head up to the former drawbridge. Look over the sides of the bridge. Spot any bears?*

Bear Pits (Medvědí Příkop): These hold a family of European brown bears, as they have since the Rožmberks added bears to their coat of arms in the 16th century to demonstrate their (fake) blood relation to the distinguished Italian Orsini family (whose name means "bear-like"). Featured on countless coats of arms, bears have long been totemic animals for Europeans. Pronouncing the animal's real name was taboo in many cultures, and Czechs still refer to bears only indirectly. For example, in most Germanic languages the word "bear" is derived from "brown," while the Slavic *medvěd* literally means "honey eater."

Near the top of the bridge, notice the gently worded sign suggesting that—rather than toss down your junk-food leftovers—you add a few coins in the collection slot to finance "more varied meals and delicacies" for the bears.

• *Continue through the gateway into the...*

Second Courtyard: Here you'll spot more of the sgraffito (Renaissance faux features scraped into wet plaster) that decorates much of the castle. To your left, at the bottom of the courtyard, is the entrance to the **tower climb**

and the **Castle Museum.** Farther up on the left is the **ticket office** for castle tours, including the Baroque Theater—stop in now (if you haven't already) to see about a tour.

• *From here, things get steep as we enter the...*

Heart of the Castle Complex: Head up the bridge, noticing the little view terrace on the left—the first of several along here. You'll emerge into the **Third Courtyard,** then (after a corridor) the **Fourth Courtyard.** Nicely preserved paintings enliven their blocky facades. Wrapped around these courtyards is the castle proper, a mighty Renaissance building sometimes called the Upper Castle (interiors open to visitors—notice the meeting points for various tour options). Continuing straight out through the end of the Fourth Courtyard, you'll cross the breathtaking **Cloak Bridge**—a triple-decker, statue-lined, covered bridge spanning a vast gorge and connecting the castle firmly with the gardens that sprawl behind it. Enjoy the views—but believe it or not, even better ones are coming up.

Notice the **Baroque Theater,** at the far end of the bridge, which still uses traditional methods for moving scenery and producing sound effects. Aspects of this back-in-the-day stagecraft still survive on Broadway today. This is one of only two such original theaters in Europe.

• *After the bridge, continue uphill through the...*

Fifth Courtyard: Really more of a pathway, this connects the castle to its gardens. Walk along the white wall—with peekaboo windows—until you are almost at the gate up top. High on the wall to the right, notice the **sundial.** Check the time: It's dead-on... except for Daylight Saving Time, which was unknown to medieval timekeepers. Notice that the sundial cuts into one of the faux windows, painted on the lower level of the building to create Renaissance symmetry.

Now step through the low-profile door directly across from the sundial. You'll emerge at a spectacular **viewpoint** that takes in the entire town, its curving river, and even the colorful tower and most of the castle complex you just came through. Jockey your way through the selfie-snapping crowd and drink it in. (Or literally drink, at the little adjacent bar.)

• *Our walk is finished. But if you still have stamina, you can consider exploring the* **castle gardens**—*they're just uphill, through the gate from the Fifth Courtyard.*

ČESKÝ KRUMLOV

Sights in Český Krumlov

KRUMLOV CASTLE COMPLEX (KRUMLOVSKÝ ZÁMEK)

No Czech town is complete without a castle—and now that the nobles are gone, their mansions are open to us common folk. Český Krumlov is no different.

Its immense Krumlov Castle complex, one of the largest in Central Europe, perches on a rock promontory overlooking the Vltava River and the town. The original Gothic castle took shape here in the 13th century, and eventually the Rožmberk, Eggenberg, and Schwarzenberg families each inherited it in turn. In successive waves of additions and renovations, they built it into the splendid Renaissance/Baroque property you see today.

The following sights are listed in the order you'll reach them as you climb up through the complex (ideally following my self-guided walk, earlier). The Round Tower and Castle Museum can be visited at your leisure, while other castle interiors—including the excellent Baroque Theater—can only be seen with a guided tour (see next). On a quick visit, the only sight I'd bother paying admission for is the theater.

Reservations for Baroque Theater and Upper Castle: It's worth the 10 Kč reservation fee to hold a slot on an English tour of the Upper Castle interior or the Baroque Theater (the theater is the castle attraction most likely to sell out). To book ahead, stop by the ticket office in person, or call 380-704-721 to check English tour times and reserve a space. No other castle sights require (or accept) reservations.

Information: Tel. 380-704-711, www.castle.ckrumlov.cz.

▲Round Tower (Zâmecká Věž) and Castle Museum (Hradní Muzeum)

These two sights share a ticket office at the bottom of the castle's middle courtyard. While neither is a must, both are worth considering if you want a peek inside the castle without committing to a guided tour. These are also the only castle sights open on Mondays (in peak season).

Colorfully impressive from the outside, the **tower** is also fun to climb. Twist up the 163 well-worn wood and stone steps to the top, where you'll be rewarded with grand, 360-degree views over the

town, the rest of the castle complex, and
happy boaters floating on the river.

The exhibits at the **Castle Museum** focus on key moments in the lives
of the town's various ruling families:
Rožmberks, Eggenbergs, and Schwarzenbergs. Be sure to pick up the good, included audioguide as you enter. You'll see
a hall of aristocratic portraits; the offices,
bedrooms, and dining rooms of the various inhabitants; and a modest religious
treasury, armory, and musical instruments
collection. At the end you can sit in old-
timey cinema seats and watch archival
footage of the castle's residents from the 1920s and 1930s.

Cost and Hours: Tower—50 Kč, museum—100 Kč, combo-
ticket for both—130 Kč; both open daily 9:00-17:00, June-Aug
until 18:00, closed Mon Nov-March; last entry one hour before
closing.

▲Upper Castle (Horní Hrad)

While the Upper Castle grounds are free to explore, you'll need to
take a tour to access the interiors. Two different tour routes give you

a glimpse of the places where the
Rožmberks, Eggenbergs, and
Schwarzenbergs dined, studied,
worked, prayed, entertained,
and slept. (By European standards, the castle's not much, and
the tours move slowly.) Imagine
being an aristocratic guest here,
riding the dukes' assembly line
of fine living: You'd promenade
through a long series of elegant spaces and dine in the sumptuous
dining hall before enjoying a concert in the Hall of Mirrors, which
leads directly to the Baroque Theater (described next). After the
play, you'd go out into the château garden for a fireworks finale.

Cost and Hours: Choose from Tour I (Gothic and Renaissance rooms, of the most general interest) or Tour II (19th-century
castle life). Tours run June-Aug Tue-Sun 9:00-12:00 & 13:00-
18:00, spring and fall until 17:00, closed Mon and Nov-March.
Tours in Czech cost 150 Kč, leave regularly, and include an ad-
equate flier in English that contains about half the information
imparted by the guide. English tours are preferable, but cost more
(250 Kč), run less frequently, and are often booked solid. Pay to
reserve a slot in advance; see "Reservations for Baroque Theater and

Upper Castle," earlier, for details. You'll be issued a ticket with your tour time printed on it. Be in the correct courtyard at that time, or you'll be locked out.

▲▲Baroque Theater (Zámecké Divadlo)

Europe once had several hundred Baroque theaters. Using candles for light and fireworks for special effects, most burned down. Today, only two survive in good shape and are open to tourists: one at Stockholm's Drottningholm Palace; and one here, at Krumlov Castle. During the 45-minute tour, you'll sit on benches in the theater and then go under the stage to see the wood-and-rope contraptions that enabled scenes to be scooted in and out within seconds (while fireworks and smoke blinded the audience). It's a lovely little theater with an impressive 3-D effect that makes the stage look deeper than it really is, but don't bother with the tour unless you can snare a spot on an English one. The theater is used only once a year for an actual performance, attended by Baroque theater enthusiasts.

Cost and Hours: 300 Kč for English tour, 250 Kč for Czech tour, tours Tue-Sun May-Oct, no tours Mon and Nov-April; English departures at 10:00, 11:00, 13:00, 14:00, and 15:00. Due to the theater's fragility, groups are limited to 20 people, and English tours generally sell out. Reserve ahead—see "Reservations for Baroque Theater and Upper Castle," earlier.

Castle Gardens (Zámecká Zahrada)

This lovely, 2,300-foot-long garden crowns the castle complex. It was laid out in the 17th century, when the noble family would have it lit with 22,000 oil lamps, torches, and candles for special occasions. The lower part is geometrical and symmetrical—French garden-style. The upper part is wilder—English garden-style. Both are delightful.

Cost and Hours: Free, open May-Sept Tue-Sun 8:00-19:00, April and Oct until 17:00, closed Mon and Nov-March.

OTHER SIGHTS IN TOWN

▲Seidel Photo Studio Museum (Museum Fotoateliér Seidel)

This fully preserved, meticulously renovated 1905 Art Nouveau villa featuring original furnishings, a garden, and 100-year-old photo equipment offers a welcome respite from the crowds and the ubiquitous Middle Ages. The museum, set in the home and studio of Josef Seidel (1859-1935) and his son František (1908-1997), features more than 100,000 of their original photographs of life in this mountainous region—Šumava, or Bőhmerwald (Bohemian Forest)—between 1880 and 1950.

Josef Seidel was unique among his contemporaries in focusing

The Expulsion of Ethnic Germans from Czechoslovakia

For seven centuries, Czech- and German-speaking people jointly inhabited and cultivated the lands of Bohemia, Moravia, and Silesia. Then, during the 19th century, the growing importance of ethnic identity resulted in tensions between these communities and fierce competition between their institutions. This charged situation was made worse by the German- and Hungarian-dominated Habsburg monarchy, which treated local Slavs as second-class citizens.

The end of World War I handed the Slavs an unprecedented opportunity to claim the land for themselves. The principle that gave countries such as Poland, Czechoslovakia, and Yugoslavia independence was called "self-determination": Each nation had the right to its own state within the area in which its people formed the majority. But the peoples of Eastern Europe had mixed over the centuries, making it impossible to create functioning states based purely on ethnicity. In the case of Bohemia—which became Czechoslovakia—the borders were drawn along historical boundaries. While the country was predominantly Slavic, areas with overwhelming German majorities remained.

Amid an economic downturn that was particularly harsh for their communities, ethnic Germans were swayed by Nazi propaganda. In 1935, 63 percent of Germans in Czechoslovakia voted for the Sudeten Nazi Party, enabling Hitler to appeal to international powers on their behalf, using the principle of self-determination. The 1938 Munich Agreement ceded the German-speaking areas of Czechoslovakia to the Third Reich, and ethnic Czechs were forced to leave.

Over the course of World War II, many Czechs came to believe that peaceful coexistence with Germans in a single state was impossible. As the war wound down, Czechoslovakia's exiled president Edvard Beneš traveled to Washington and Moscow, securing backing for a state-organized expulsion of more than 2.2 million ethnic Germans still living in Czechoslovakia. From 1945 to 1946, Czechoslovak soldiers carried out the "transfer" orders: They typically entered a German-speaking town or village, took a

on just one region, and was the first in the country to use autochrome. Allowed to remain in Český Krumlov during and after World War II at a time when many Germans in the country were expelled, František continued his father's photography business, remaining here until his death in 1997. After his wife died in 2003, the town bought the house and converted it into a delightful museum and a cultural center for cross-cultural understanding. Restored, functional equipment offers hands-on experience with the

few prisoners, and threatened to execute the hostages unless everyone of German descent left. The expulsions sometimes turned violent: In June 1945, some 2,000 ethnic German civilians, including children, were executed near the town of Saatz.

While Beneš and most Czechs considered the expulsion of ethnic Germans as revenge for the war and historical injustices, the communists saw a future opportunity: The emptied region was to become a revolutionary laboratory. Ironically, the Czechs regained "their" land, but eroded their freedom; meanwhile the Germans lost the land in which their ancestors lay buried, but gained a chance to build a prosperous democracy.

For the next 40 years, the "transfer" of ethnic Germans was a taboo subject, as the communist anti-Nazi propaganda machine continued to roll on as if the war never ended. After 1989, the issue was reluctantly broached by politicians on both sides of the border, as it threatened to derail otherwise strong relations between the Czech and German governments. Toward 2004, tensions again rose, as Czech politicians resisted demands for reparations from Sudeten Germans in Berlin and Brussels, who thought repayment should be a precondition to Czech entry into the European Union.

Over the last decade, the subject finally became depoliticized. Former German residents have begun visiting their old homes, sharing stories of their trauma with young Czechs, who—having grown confident in their freedom—are able to take a more nuanced view of their country's history. In 2015, the Sudeten German Association stepped back from its support for repatriates' legal claims. A year later, the Czech Minister of Culture Daniel Herman delivered a speech at the annual Sudeten German convention in Nürnberg, addressing the audience as "dear compatriots" and expressing regret over the events of 1945-46. An act that would have amounted to political suicide just 10 years earlier was positively received by the Czech public. Seventy years after a traumatic divorce, a door to reconciliation finally opened.

ČESKÝ KRUMLOV

process of photography during the late 19th and early 20th centuries. You can literally smell the history.

Cost and Hours: 130 Kč, includes English audioguide; daily May-Sept 9:00-18:00, shorter hours off-season; Linecká 272, across the river south of Old Town, mobile 736-503-871, www. seidel.cz.

Synagogue

Completed in 1910 in a mixture of architectural styles, this synagogue served the small Jewish community of Český Krumlov and neighboring villages. In 1938, there were 200 congregants here, but only two members of the area's Jewish community survived after World War II. Terribly run-down for decades after the war, the synagogue was restored to its former glory in 2015 by the Prague Jewish community, with funding from the European Union and German and Austrian sponsors. It contains an exhibit on its history, and hosts concerts and contemporary art exhibits.

Cost and Hours: 50 Kč, daily 10:00-18:00, Za Soudem 282, across the river south of Old Town, mobile 601-590-213, www.synagoga-krumlov.cz.

Eating: The **$ Café Synagoga,** with an assortment of cakes, occupies the former basement residence of the rabbi's family and an adjacent peaceful garden.

Museum of Regional History
(Regionální Muzeum v Českém Krumlově)

This small museum gives you a quick look at regional costumes, tools, and traditions. When you pay, pick up the English translation of the displays (it also includes a lengthy history of Krumlov). Start on the top floor, where you'll see a Bronze Age exhibit, old paintings, a glimpse of noble life, and a look at how the locals rafted lumber from the Bőhmerwald mountains all the way to Vienna (partly by canal). Don't miss the fun-to-study ceramic model of Český Krumlov in 1800 (note the extravagant gardens high above the town). The lower floor comes with fine folk costumes and domestic art.

Cost and Hours: 50 Kč, Tue-Sun 9:00-12:00 & 12:30-17:00, July-Aug until 18:00, closed Mon, Horní 152, tel. 380-711-674, www.muzeumck.cz.

▲Eggenberg Brewery Tour

This may be one of the most intimate and accessible brewery tours in this land that so loves its beer. Tucked into a river bend on the edge of town, Eggenberg's spunky little brewery has an authenticity that can't be matched by the big, soulless corporate breweries (such as Pilsner Urquell, in Plzeň, or the Czech Budweiser, in nearby České Budějovice). This is your chance to learn about the beer-making process at a facility where they're still using the same giant copper vats  from 1915. While some of the facility has recently been modernized (and ongoing works may reroute the tour a bit), you'll still see lots of vintage equipment, including the original brew house (still in service), the fermentation vats, the cellars used for aging, and the bottling plant. Your tour ends with a visit to the pub, where you can sample some brews, including a "smoky" dark beer (Nakouřený Švihák), made with malt that tastes like salami, then aged for 100 days.

Cost and Hours: 100 Kč for the tour only, 130 Kč for tour and two tastes in the pub, 170 Kč for tour and four-pack of your choice of bottled beers to take away, 200 Kč includes everything; one-hour English tours daily at 11:00 year-round, also at 14:00 May-Oct, tel. 380-711-426, www.eggenberg.cz.

Getting There: It's just a short stroll up Nové Město street from the main drag below the castle. During ongoing reconstruction, you may instead have to loop around town to the back entrance on Pivovarska—about a 10-minute walk.

Křížový Vrch (Hill of the Cross)

For an easy 30-minute hike up to the hill with commanding views, walk to the end of Rooseveltova street, cross at the traffic light, then head straight for the first (empty) chapel-like Station of the Cross. Turning right, it's easy to navigate along successive Stations of the Cross until you reach the white church on the hill (closed to the public), set in the middle of wild meadows. Looking down into the valley at the medieval city nestled within the S-shaped river, framed by the rising hills, it's hard to imagine any town with a more powerful *genius loci* (spirit of the place). The view is best at sunset.

▲▲▲Canoeing and Rafting the Vltava

For a quintessentially Czech experience, join the locals for a paddle down the Vltava River, the country's most popular place for boating. Novices and hearty paddlers alike can spend as little as 30 minutes to a full day easing into a mellow, drifting mindset—stopping for a snack or a *pivo* at one of the many pubs and cafés along the way.

Rental companies all over town offer the same basic fleet: two- or three-person fiberglass canoes, and rubber rafts for 2-6 people. While the canoes are faster and more agile, they require some experience to navigate a few whitewater areas. The rafts, meanwhile, are slow and easy to navigate even for newcomers. A map, waterproof bag, and all the necessary gear is included, as is pickup from anywhere in town

ČESKÝ KRUMLOV

(arrange in advance). With limited time, you can start from town and paddle as far as you like, then head back; more serious paddlers can start at Rožmberk Castle for an all-day journey back into town (see below for details on both options).

Rental Companies: Ingetour launches in each of the five most useful locations (Rožmberk, Krumlov Vltavan, Krumlov Trojice, Zlatá Koruna, Boršov) and runs a regular bus connecting them (Rožmberk, Zlatá Koruna, and Boršov are also connected by bus and train). You can end your paddle at any of their locations without committing from the start. While it's best to reserve ahead, you can often just show up (raft rental—550 Kč/day, bus ticket—50 Kč extra, tel. 775-748-800, www.ingetour.cz, info@ingetour. cz). Ingetour, like many other companies, also offers guided day-trips (500-900 Kč/person depending on trip length). You can also try **Maleček** (Rooseveltova 28, tel. 380-712-508, www.malecek. cz, lode@malecek.cz) or **CK Vltava** (Hradební 60, tel. 380-711-988, www.ckvltava.cz). CK Vltava offers a boat-and-bike option, boating down to Zlatá Koruna Abbey and cycling back via Dívčí Skála castle (Maiden's Rock).

Downstream from Český Krumlov (1-7 hours): This plan allows you to paddle for as long as you want. Start at the Vltavan campsite above Český Krumlov, where most rental companies are based (it's easiest to arrange a ride there with your rental company). From here, it's about an hour (with some challenging sections) to the Trojice campsite at the other end of Český Krumlov (you can bail out here if you've had enough). Two hours more brings you to **Zlatá Koruna Abbey,** a beautifully set Gothic monastery (see listing under "Near Český Krumlov," later). While many end their trip at the abbey (bus and train stations are close by), those who venture farther into the nature reserve that follows are rewarded with spectacular scenery and minimal river traffic (though this section gets a bit more treacherous). It can take close to four hours before you reach the next stop in **Boršov.** To return to Český Krumlov from Boršov, you can take the Ingetour bus (last departure at 16:30) or the train (5-minute walk from dock; trains at 16:22, 18:22, and 20:22; 30 minutes).

Upstream from Rožmberk to Český Krumlov (6 hours): The advantages of this plan are: another majestic castle (Rožmberk, www.hrad-rozmberk.cz), plenty of drinking/eating options along the way (this is the busiest stretch of the river), pristine areas for swimming, and potentially—if you time it right—a sunset float through Český Krumlov at the end. You'll start your journey in the middle of the Rožmberk village (ask at the TI for bus or train info, or arrange transportation with your rental company) and finish back in Český Krumlov proper.

Roma in Eastern Europe

Numbering 12 million, the Roma people constitute a bigger European nation than the Czechs, Hungarians, or the Dutch. (The term "Gypsies," previously the common name for this group, is now considered derogatory and inaccurate.)

Descended from several low north-Indian castes, the Roma began to migrate through Persia and Armenia into the Ottoman Empire a thousand years ago. Known for their itinerant lifestyle, expertise in horse trading, skilled artisanship, and flexibility regarding private property, the Roma were both sought out and suspected in medieval Europe.

The Industrial Revolution threatened the Roma's traditional livelihoods, making their wandering lifestyle difficult to sustain. In the 1940s, Hitler sent hundreds of thousands of Roma to the gas chambers. In the occupied Protectorate of Bohemia and Moravia (Czechoslovakia minus the Sudetenland that had been annexed to Germany), Hitler had the help of Czech policemen who ran the two Roma "transfer" camps in Lety and Hodonín, where hundreds died even before being transported to Auschwitz. Only 10 percent of the protectorate's 5,000-strong pre-war Roma population survived.

After the war, tens of thousands of Roma from eastern Slovakia were relocated into the Sudetenland. At this time, the communist governments in Eastern Europe required Roma to speak the country's major language, settle in towns, and work in new industrial jobs. Rather than producing well-adjusted citizens, the result was an erosion of time-honored Roma values, as the policy shattered traditionally cohesive communities. It left the new Roma generation prone to sexual, alcohol, and drug abuse, and filled state-run orphanages with deprived Roma toddlers.

When the obligation and right to work disappeared with the communist regimes in 1989, rampant unemployment and dependence on welfare joined the list of Roma afflictions. As people all over Eastern Europe found it difficult to adjust to the new economic realities, they again turned on the Roma as scapegoats. Many Roma now live in segregated ghettos. Those who make it against the odds and succeed in mainstream society typically do so by turning their backs on their Roma heritage.

In this context, the Roma in Český Krumlov are a surprising success story. The well-integrated, proud Roma community here (numbering 1,000, or 5 percent of the town's population) is considered a curious anomaly even by experts. Their success could be due to a number of factors: the legacy of the multicultural Rožmberks, the fact that almost everyone in Český Krumlov is a relative newcomer, or maybe it's how local youngsters, regardless of skin color, tend to resolve their differences over a beer in the local "Gypsy Pub" (Cikánská Jizba), with a trendy Roma band setting the tune.

ČESKÝ KRUMLOV

NEAR ČESKÝ KRUMLOV
Zlatá Koruna Abbey (Klášter Zlatá Koruna)

This Cistercian abbey was founded in the 13th century by a Bohemian king to counter the growing influence of the Vítek family, the ancestors of the mighty Rožmberks. As you enter the grounds, notice the magnificent central linden tree, with its strange, cape-like leaves; it's said to have been used by the anti-Catholic Hussites when they hanged the monks. The one-hour tour takes you through the rare two-storied Gothic Chapel of the Guardian Angel, the main church, and the cloister, while a 10-minute tour takes you to the abbot's chapel with the original Gothic Zlatá Koruna Madonna, the most treasured painting in the region. After the order was dissolved in 1785, the abbey functioned briefly as a village school, before being turned into a factory during the Industrial Revolution. Damage from this period is visible on the cloister's crumbling arches. The Gothic interiors adjacent to the ticket office serve as exhibition space for Český Krumlov's school of the arts, displaying the imaginative creations of the school's 6- to 18-year-old students (free).

Cost and Hours: 100 Kč for one-hour tour in Czech, generally runs every half-hour, pick up English leaflet; 20 Kč for the 10-minute Madonna tour; April-Oct Tue-Sun 9:00-16:00, June-Aug until 17:00, closed Mon and Nov-March, call 380-743-126 to arrange English tour, www.klaster-zlatakoruna.eu.

Getting There: Drivers can reach the abbey in about 10 minutes from Český Krumlov (head north out of town and follow route #39). But it's more fun to get there by raft or canoe—the abbey is directly above the river at the end of a three-hour float (see "Canoeing and Rafting the Vltava," earlier).

Sleeping in Český Krumlov

Český Krumlov is filled with small pensions and hostels. Summer is busy all around. While you can generally find a room in a modern pension in the not-so-scenic outskirts upon arrival, plan to book months ahead to stay near the center, and at least a year ahead for places in the heart of town. Though I usually recommend booking directly with hotels, many of these small pensions are easier to book through Booking.com. My favorite neighborhood—also necessary to reserve well in advance—is called Plešivecká; it's in the historic part of town, just a five-minute walk from the center, yet somehow away from all the tourist commotion, with plenty of local shops and residents around.

IN AND NEAR THE OLD TOWN

$$$ Castle View Apartments rents seven diverse apartments. These are the best-equipped rooms I've found in town—the bathroom floors are heated, all come with kitchenettes, and everything's done just right. Their website describes each stylish apartment; the "view" ones really do come with eye-popping vistas (RS%, apartment sleeps up to 6, breakfast at a nearby hotel, Šatlavská 140, mobile 731-108-677, www.castleview.cz, info@castleview.cz).

$$ Hotel Konvice is run by a German couple—and their three children—with a personal touch. Each room is uniquely decorated (a block above the main square at Horní 144, tel. 380-711-611, www.boehmerwaldhotels.de, info@stadthotel-krummau.de).

$ Pension U Kapličky, on a quiet street adjacent to a chapel and a city park, consists of two artistically designed apartments in an unusually shaped medieval house. Jitka, a teacher of stone carving at the local arts academy and one of the last old-timers still calling central Český Krumlov home, lives downstairs and bakes pastries for breakfast (reserve months ahead, Linecká 60, mobile 606-434-090, www.ckrumlov.cz/ck/ukaplicky, ukaplicky@ckrumlov.cz).

BELOW THE MAIN SQUARE

Secluded Parkán street, which runs along the river below the square, has a hotel and a row of small pensions. These places have a family feel and views of the looming castle above.

$$$ Hotel Mlýn, at the end of Parkán, is a tastefully furnished hotel with more than 30 rooms and all the amenities (elevator, pay parking, Parkán 120, tel. 380-731-133, www.hotelmlyn.eu, info@hotelmlyn.eu).

$ Pension Olšakovský, which has a delightful breakfast area on a terrace next to the river, treats visitors as family guests (free parking, Parkán 114, mobile 604-430-181, www.olsakovsky.cz, info@olsakovsky.cz).

AT THE BASE OF THE CASTLE

A quiet, cobbled pedestrian street (Latrán) runs below the castle just over the bridge from the Old Town. Lined with cute shops, it's a 10-minute walk downhill from the train station.

$ Pension Danny is a little funky place, with homey rooms and a tangled floor plan above a restaurant (in-room breakfast, Latrán 72, tel. 603-210-572, www.pensiondanny.cz, recepce@pensiondanny.cz).

ČESKÝ KRUMLOV

BETWEEN THE BUS STATION AND THE OLD TOWN

Rooseveltova street, midway between the bus station and the Old Town (a four-minute walk from either), is lined with several fine little places. The key here is tranquility—the noisy bars of the town center are out of earshot.

$$ Hotel Garni Myší Díra ("Mouse Hole") hides 11 bright and woody Bohemian contemporary rooms overlooking the Vltava River just outside the Old Town (includes transfer to/from bus or train station, free parking, Rooseveltova 28, tel. 380-712-853, www.hotelmysidira.com). The no-nonsense reception, which closes at 20:00, runs the recommended boat rental company (Maleček, at the same address), along with a similar pension with comparable prices, **Villa Margarita,** farther along Rooseveltova.

$ Pension Teddy offers three deluxe rooms that share a balcony overlooking the river and have original 18th-century furniture. Or stay in one of four modern-style rooms, some of which also face the river (cash only, staff may be unhelpful, pay parking, Rooseveltova 38, tel. 777-713-277, mobile 724-003-981, www.pensionteddy.cz, info@pensionteddy.cz).

$ Pension Anna is well-run, with two doubles, six apartments, and a restful little garden. Its apartments are spacious suites, with a living room and stairs leading to the double-bedded loft. The upstairs rooms can get stuffy during the summer (pay parking, Rooseveltova 41, tel. 380-711-692, www.pensionanna-ck.cz, pension.anna@quick.cz). If you book a standard double and they bump you up to an apartment, don't pay more than the double rate.

IN THE PLEŠIVECKÁ NEIGHBORHOOD

To reach this historical part of town—one of the last genuine-feeling neighborhoods in Český Krumlov—cross the Dr. Beneše Bridge, then take the staircase up directly ahead of you. It leads into a small, quiet square, with a couple of hotels and cafés. Take the street diagonally to the left (Plešivecká), which descends back toward the river where you'll find more local life. You'll need to book up to a year in advance to stay in this neighborhood. There's a handy COOP supermarket at the end of Plešivecká street.

With rooms between **$** and **$$**, Pensions **Athanor** (Plešivecké Náměstí 271, tel. 720-611-712, www.apartmanyathanor.cz, info@apartmanyathanor.cz), **Antoni** (Plešivecká 100, tel. 602-421-124, http://pension-antoni.cz, info@pension-antoni.cz), and **Weber** (Plešivecká 129, tel. 605-162-478, www.penzionweber.cz, weber.f@seznam.cz) are perfectly located along Plešivecká street.

ČESKÝ KRUMLOV

OUTSIDE THE CITY CENTER

$ Pension Gardena has 16 spacious, airy rooms in two adjacent, tactfully renovated historical buildings. A family business with a garden, it's on the way into town from the bus station just a hundred yards above Horní Bridge (Kaplická 21, tel. 380-711-028, mobile 607-873-974, www.pensiongardena.com, gardena@seznam.cz).

$ Pension Kříž, with five rooms in a new house, is tucked away in a quiet, modern villa district under the Křížový Vrch (Hill of the Cross), just a five-minute walk from Horní Bridge (Křížová 71, mobile 775-421-012, www.penzion-kriz.cz, ubytovani@penzion-kriz.cz).

HOSTELS

Of the hostels in town, Hostel 99 (closest to the train station) is clearly the high-energy, youthful party place. Krumlov House (closer to the bus station) is more mellow. Both are well-managed, and each is a five-minute walk from the main square.

¢ Hostel 99's picnic-table terrace looks out on the Old Town. While the gentle sound of the river gurgles outside your window late at night, you're more likely to hear a youthful international crowd having a great time. The hostel caters to its fun-loving young guests, offering a day-long river rafting and pub crawl, with a free keg of beer each Wednesday (private rooms available, laundry, no curfew or lockout, recommended Hospoda 99 restaurant, 10-minute downhill walk from train station or two bus stops to Spicak; Vezni 99, tel. 380-712-812, www.hostel99.cz, hostel99@hotmail.com).

¢ Krumlov House Hostel is take-your-shoes-off-at-the-door, shiny, hardwood-with-throw-rugs mellow. Efficiently run by a Canadian/American couple, it has a hip and trusting vibe and feels welcoming to travelers of any age (private rooms and apartments available, breakfast available July-Aug only, well-stocked guest kitchen, laundry, Rooseveltova 68, tel. 380-711-935, www.krumlovhostel.com, info@krumlovhostel.com). The hostel sponsors "WriteAway," a literary retreat for traveling writers (http://writeaway.literarybohemian.com).

Eating in Český Krumlov

With a huge variety of creative little restaurants, Český Krumlov is a fun place to eat. In peak season the good places fill up fast, so make reservations or eat early.

IN AND NEAR THE OLD TOWN

$$ Na Louži seems to be everyone's favorite Czech bistro, with 40 seats (many at shared tables) in one 1930s-style room decorated

ČESKÝ KRUMLOV

with funky old advertisements. They serve good, inexpensive, un-pretentious local cuisine and hometown Eggenberg beer on tap (daily 10:00-23:00, near the Egon Schiele Art Center at Kájovská 66, tel. 380-711-280, www.nalouzi.com).

$$ Cikánská Jizba ("Gypsy Pub") is a Roma tavern filling one den-like, barrel-vaulted room. The Roma staff serves Slovak-style food (most of the Czech Republic's Roma population came from Slovakia). While this rustic little restaurant—which packs its 10 tables under a mystic-feeling Gothic vault—won't win any culinary awards, you never know what festive and musical activities will erupt, particularly on Friday nights, when the band Cindži Renta ("Wet Rag") performs here (daily 13:00-24:00; off-season Mon-Sat 17:00-24:00, closed Sun; 2 blocks toward castle from main square at Dlouhá 31, tel. 380-717-585).

$$ Krčma u Dwau Maryí ("Tavern of the Two Marys") is a characteristic old place with idyllic riverside picnic tables, serving ye olde Czech cuisine and drinks. The fascinating menu explains the history of the house and makes a good case that the food of the poor medieval Bohemians was tasty and varied. Buck up for buckwheat, millet, greasy meat, or the poor-man's porridge (daily 11:00-23:00, Parkán 104, tel. 380-717-228).

$$ Laibon, while still a top choice for a filling vegetarian meal, has a chef who is evidently not inclined to calibrate her spices or rely exclusively on fresh ingredients (beware of canned pea soup). Settle down in the meditative inside or head out onto the castle-view river terrace and observe the raft-and-canoe action while you eat (daily 11:00-23:00, Parkán 105).

$$ Kolektiv tries to inject some modern sophistication into this old town. It has a stark minimalist interior, a chalkboard menu, well-executed light café fare with some international flavors, a good cocktail selection, and stylish—if stuffy—service (daily 8:00-20:00, Fri-Sat until 21:00, Latrán 13, across from the castle stairs, tel. 776-626-644).

$$ Rybářská Restaurace ("Fisherman's Restaurant") doesn't look particularly inviting from the outside, but this is *the* place in town to taste fresh carp and trout. Choose between indoor tables under fishnets or riverside picnic benches outside, and ask about their cheap daily specials that feed the floating Czech crowds (daily 11:00-22:00, on the island by the millwheel, mobile 723-829-089).

$$$ Krčma v Šatlavské is an old prison gone cozy, with an open fire, big wooden tables under a rustic old medieval

vault, and tables outdoors on the pedestrian lane. It's great for a late drink or roasted game (cooked on an open spit). *Medovina* is hot honey wine (daily 12:00-24:00, on Šatlavská, follow lane leading to the side from TI on main square, mobile 608-973-797).

$ Krumlovská Picka, a tiny, atmospheric place on the island by the millwheel, offers takeout pizza and freshly baked-and-filled baguettes. Cuddle near the oven inside or picnic on the outside terrace (daily 12:00-23:00, Dlouhá 97).

$$$ Restaurace Barbakán is built into the town fortifications, with a terrace hanging high over the river. It's a good spot for old-fashioned Czech cooking and beer at reasonable prices, at the top of town and near the recommended Rooseveltova street accommodations (open long hours daily, Horní 26, tel. 380-712-679).

OUTSIDE THE CITY CENTER

$$ Hospoda 99 Restaurace serves good, cheap soups, salads, and meals. It's the choice of hostelers and locals alike for its hamburgers, vegetarian food, Czech dishes, and cheap booze (meals served 10:00-22:00, bar open until 24:00, at Hostel 99, Vezni 99, tel. 380-712-812). This place is booming until late, when everything else is hibernating.

$ Dobrá Čajovna, at the base of the castle, is a typical example of the quiet, exotic-feeling teahouses that flooded Czech towns in the 1990s as alternatives to smoky, raucous pubs. Though directly across from the castle entrance, it's a world away from the tourist hubbub. With its meditative karma inside and a peaceful terrace facing the monastery out back, it provides a relaxing break (daily 13:00-22:00, Latrán 54).

IN THE PLEŠIVECKÁ NEIGHBORHOOD

Good, traditional eateries with outdoor seating line the Vltava in the Plešivecká neighborhood; just cross the Dr. Beneše Bridge and head right along the river.

$ Ideal Coffee Roastery, on the corner of Linecká just past the Seidel Photo Studio Museum, is a tiny local place far away from the crowds and dead serious about the quality of its cakes and fairtrade brews (daily 10:00-19:00, Horská 70).

Český Krumlov Connections

BY PUBLIC TRANSPORTATION

Almost all trains to and from Český Krumlov require a transfer in the city of **České Budějovice,** a transit hub just to the north. Buses, on the other hand, are direct. Bus and train timetables are available at www.idos.cz.

If you have time in České Budějovice between connections,

consider a visit to the town's gigantic medieval main square, Náměstí Přemysla Otakara II (about a six-block walk from the station). Store your bags in lockers at the train station, then exit the station to the right, cross the street at the crosswalk, and head straight down Lannova třida (which becomes Kanovnická street) to the square.

By Train
From Český Krumlov by Train to: České Budějovice (6/day, 45 minutes), **Prague** (8/day, 1/day direct, 3.5 hours; bus is faster and cheaper, but often books up and doesn't allow a stopover in Budějovice), **Vienna** (5/day with changes in Budějovice and Linz, 5 hours), **Budapest** (6/day with changes in Budějovice and Linz, 7 hours).

By Bus
The town has finally invested its tourist-generated millions in a bus station. A five-minute walk above town, you can judge for yourself whether the state-of-the-art station was truly worth the money (bus info tel. 380-711-190). Student Agency (www.studentagency.cz), Flixbus (www.flixbus.cz), and Leo Express (www.leoexpress.com) have online reservation systems, the newest buses, and a free drink for passengers.

From Český Krumlov by Bus to: Prague (10/day, 3.5 hours; tickets can be bought at the Český Krumlov TI), **České Budějovice** (transit hub for other destinations such as Třeboň, Telč, and Třebíč; hourly, 40 minutes).

BY SHUTTLE SERVICE
From Český Krumlov to Austria and Beyond: Several companies offer handy shuttle service. The best of the bunch is CK Shuttle, with free Wi-Fi on board and affordable fares: 800 Kč per person one-way to **Vienna** (4/day, 3.5 hours), **Salzburg** (4/day, 3 hours), **Hallstatt** (3/day, 3 hours), or **Prague** (3/day, 2.5 hours). They can also take you to Linz (where you can hop on the speedy east-west main rail line through Austria), Budapest, Munich, and other places. They offer door-to-door service to and from your hotel (office at Dlouhá 95, www.ckshuttle.cz). Another reliable option is Sebastian Tours (higher prices, mobile 607-100-234 or 608-357-581, www.sebastianck-tours.com, sebastiantours@hotmail.com).

POLAND

Polska

POLAND

Polska

Poland is a land of surprises. Some travelers imagine Poland as a backwards, impoverished land of rusting factories, smoggy cities, and gloomy citizens—only to be left speechless when they step into Kraków's vibrant main square, Gdańsk's colorful Royal Way, or Warsaw's trendy hipster zones. Today's Poland has a vibrant urbanity, an enticing food and design culture, dynamic history, and kindhearted natives.

The Poles are a proud people—as moved by their spectacular failures as by their successes. Their quiet elegance has been tempered by generations of abuse by foreign powers. In a way, there are two Polands: lively, cosmopolitan urban centers, and countless tiny farm villages in the countryside. A societal tension exists between city-dwelling progressives and what they call the "simple people" of Poland: hardworking small-town Poles descended from generations of farmers, who still live an uncomplicated, agrarian lifestyle. There's a large contingent of these salt-of-the-earth folks, who tend to be politically conservative and staunchly Euroskeptic.

Poland is arguably Europe's most devoutly Catholic country. Their profound faith has united the Poles through many tough times.

Squeezed between Protestant Germany (originally Prussia) and Eastern Orthodox Russia, Poland wasn't even a country for generations (1795-1918)—but its Catholicism helped keep its spirit alive. Under communism, Poles found their religion a source of strength as well as rebellion—they could express dissent against the atheistic re-

gime by going to church. Be sure to step into some serene church interiors. These aren't museums—you'll almost certainly see locals engrossed in prayer. (Visit with respect: Maintain silence, and if you want to take pictures, do so discreetly.)

Much of Poland's story is a Jewish story. Before World War

II, 80 percent of Europe's Jews lived in Poland. Warsaw was the world's second-largest Jewish city (after New York), with 380,000 Jews (out of a total population of 1.2 million). Poland was a magnet for Jewish refugees because of its relatively welcoming policies. Still, Jews were forbidden from owning land; that's why they settled mostly in cities.

But the Holocaust (and a later Soviet policy of sending "troublemaking" Jews to Israel) decimated the Jewish population. This tragic chapter, combined with postwar border shifts and population movements, made Poland one of Europe's most ethnically homogeneous countries. Today, virtually everyone in the country is an ethnic Pole, and only a few thousand Polish Jews remain.

Poland has long been staunchly pro-America. Of course, their big neighbors (Russia and Germany) have been their historic enemies. And when Hitler invaded in 1939, the Poles felt let down by their supposed European friends (France and Britain), who declared war on Germany but provided virtually no military support to the Polish resistance. America, meanwhile, is seen as the big ally from across the ocean—and the home of the largest population of Poles outside of Poland.

On my first visit to Poland, I had a poor impression of Poles, who seemed brusque and often elbowed ahead of me in line. I've since learned that all it takes is a smile and a cheerful greeting—preferably in Polish—to break through the thick skin that helped these kind people survive the difficult communist times. With a friendly *Dzień dobry!*, you'll turn any grouch into an ally.

It may help to know that, because of the distinct cadence of Polish, Poles speaking English sometimes sound more impatient, gruff, or irritated than they actually are. Part of the Poles' charm

Poland Almanac

Official Name: Rzeczpospolita Polska (Republic of Poland), or Polska for short.

Snapshot History: This thousand-year-old country has been dominated by foreign powers for much of the past two centuries, finally achieving true independence (from the Soviet Union) in 1989.

Population: 38.5 million people, slightly less than California. About 97 percent are ethnic Poles who speak Polish (though English is also widely spoken). Four out of every five Poles are practicing Catholics. The population is relatively young compared to most European countries, with an average age of 41 (Germany's is 47).

Latitude and Longitude: 52°N and 20°E (similar latitude to Berlin, London, and Edmonton, Alberta).

Area: 121,000 square miles, the same as New Mexico (or Illinois and Iowa put together).

Geography: Because of its overall flatness, Poland has been a corridor for invading armies since its infancy. The Vistula River (650 miles) runs south-to-north up the middle of the country, passing through Kraków and Warsaw, and emptying into the Baltic Sea at Gdańsk. Poland's climate is generally cool and rainy—40,000 storks love it.

Biggest Cities: Warsaw (the capital, 1.7 million), Kraków (767,000), and Łódź (747,000).

Economy: The Gross Domestic Product is $1.1 trillion, with a GDP per capita of $29,500. The 1990s saw an aggressive and successful transition from state-run socialism to privately owned capitalism. Only five percent of Poles are unemployed, but one in five lives below the poverty line (mostly low-income farmers).

POLAND

is that they're not as slick and self-assured as many Europeans: They're kind, soft-spoken, and quite shy. On a recent train trip in Poland, I offered my Polish seatmate a snack—and spent the rest of trip enjoying a delightful conversation with a new friend.

HELPFUL HINTS

Restroom Signage: To confuse tourists, the Poles have devised a secret way of marking their WCs. You'll see doors marked with *męska* (men) and *damska* (women)—but even more often, you'll simply see a triangle (for men) or a circle (for women).

Train Station Lingo: "PKP" is the abbreviation for Polish National Railways ("PKS" is for buses). In larger towns with several train stations, you'll normally use the one called Główny (meaning "Main"—except in Warsaw, where it's Centralna).

Currency: 1 złoty (zł, or PLN) = 100 groszy (gr) = about 25 cents; 4 zł = about $1.

Government: Poland's mostly figurehead president selects the prime minister and cabinet, with legislators' approval. They govern along with a two-house legislature (Sejm and Senat) of 560 seats. Prime Minister Mateusz Morawiecki represents the majority political party, the right-wing Law and Justice (Prawo i Sprawiedliwość, or PiS for short). President Andrzej Duda, formerly of the Law and Justice party (but currently a conservative-leaning independent), began his five-year term in 2015.

Flag: The upper half is white, and the lower half is red—the traditional colors of Poland. Poetic Poles claim the white represents honor, and the red represents the blood spilled by the Poles to protect that honor. The flag sometimes includes a coat of arms with a crowned eagle (representing Polish sovereignty). Under Soviet rule, the crown was removed from the emblem, and the eagle's talons were trimmed. On regaining its independence, Poland coronated its eagle once more.

Not-so-Average Poles: Poland's three big airports offer a rundown of just a few of the country's biggest names: St. John Paul II (in Kraków), Fryderyk Chopin (in Warsaw), and Lech Wałęsa (in Gdańsk). And, despite the many "Polack jokes" you've heard, you're already familiar with many other famous Polish intellectuals—you just don't realize they're Polish. The "Dumb Polack" Hall of Fame includes Mikołaj Kopernik **(Nicolas Copernicus),** scientist **Marie Curie** (née Skłodowska), writer Teodor Józef Korzeniowski (better known as **Joseph Conrad,** author of *Heart of Darkness*), architect **Daniel Libeskind** (known for redeveloping One World Trade Center in New York City)...and one of this book's co-authors.

POLAND

Dworzec główny means "main train station." Most stations have several platforms *(peron),* each of which has two tracks *(tor).* Departures are generally listed by the *peron,* so keep your eye on both tracks for your train. Arrivals are *przyjazdy,* and departures are *odjazdy.* Left-luggage counters or lockers are marked *przechowalnia bagażu. Kasy* are ticket windows. These can be marked (sometimes only in Polish) for specific needs—domestic tickets, international tickets, and so on; ask fellow travelers to be sure you select the right line. The line you choose will invariably be the slowest one—leave plenty of time to buy your ticket. On arriving at a station, to get into town, follow signs for *wyjście* (sometimes followed by *do centrum* or *do miasta*).

Top 10 Dates that Changed Poland

AD 966: The Polish king, Mieszko I, is baptized a Christian, symbolically uniting the Polish people and founding the nation.

1385: The Polish queen (called a "king" by sexist aristocrats of the time) marries a Lithuanian duke, starting the two-century reign of the Jagiełło family.

1410: Poland defeats the Teutonic Knights at the Battle of Grunwald, part of a Golden Age of territorial expansion and cultural achievement.

1572: The last Jagiellonian king dies, soon replaced by bickering nobles and foreign kings. Poland declines.

1795: In the last of three Partitions, the country is divvied up by its more-powerful neighbors: Russia, Prussia, and Austria.

1918: Following World War I, Poland finally reclaims its land and sovereignty.

1939: The Free City of Danzig (today's Gdańsk) is invaded by Nazi Germany, starting World War II. At war's end, the country is "liberated" (i.e., occupied) by the Soviet Union.

1980: Lech Wałęsa leads a successful strike, demanding more freedom from the communist regime.

1989: Poland gains independence under its first president—Lech Wałęsa. Fifteen years later, Poland joins the European Union.

2010: President Lech Kaczyński and 95 other high-level government officials are killed in a plane crash in Russia.

Transit Route Planner: For a good public transit route planner for most Polish cities, try www.jakdojade.pl.

Busy May: May 1 is May Day and May 3 is Constitution Day, when the entire country closes up for several days. Later in the month, younger kids get out of school, so families go on vacation (and Kraków is one of the most popular domestic destinations).

Telephones: Remember these Polish prefixes: 800 is toll-free, and 70 is expensive (like phone sex). Many Poles use mobile phones (which come with the prefix 50, 51, 53, 60, 66, 69, 72, 78, 79, or 88). For tips on dialing to, from, and within Slovenia, see the Practicalities chapter.

POLISH HISTORY

Poland is flat. Take a look at a topographical map of Europe, and it's easy to see the Poles' historical dilemma: The path of least resistance from northern Europe to Russia leads right through Poland. Over the years, many invaders—from Genghis Khan to Napoleon to Hitler—have taken advantage of this fact. The country has been called "God's playground" for the many wars that have rumbled through its territory. Poland has been invaded by Soviets, Nazis, French, Austrians, Russians, Prussians, Swedes, Teutonic Knights, Tatars, Bohemians, Magyars—and, about 1,300 years ago, Poles.

Medieval Greatness

The first Poles were the Polonians ("people of the plains"), a Slavic band that arrived here in the eighth century. In 966, Mieszko I, duke of the Polonian tribe, adopted Christianity and founded the Piast dynasty, which would last for more than 400 years. Centuries before Germany, Italy, or Spain first united, Poland was born.

Poland struggled against two different invaders in the 13th century: the Tatars (Mongols who ravaged the south) and the Teutonic Knights (Germans who conquered the north). But despite these challenges, Poland persevered. The last king of the Piast dynasty was also the greatest: Kazimierz the Great, who famously "found a Poland made of wood and left one made of brick and stone," and helped bring Poland (and its then-capital, Kraków) to international prominence. The progressive Kazimierz also invited Europe's much-persecuted Jews to settle here, establishing Poland as a haven for the Jewish people, which it would remain until the Nazis arrived.

Kazimierz the Great died at the end of the 14th century without a male heir. His grand-niece, Princess Jadwiga, became "king" (the Poles weren't ready for a "queen") and married Lithuanian Prince Władysław Jagiełło, uniting their countries against a common enemy, the Teutonic Knights. Their marriage marked the beginning of the Jagiellonian dynasty and set the stage for Poland's Golden Age.

During this time, Poland expanded its territory, the Polish nobility began to acquire more political influence, Italy's Renaissance (and its architectural styles) became popular, and the Toruń-born astronomer Nicholas Copernicus shook up the scientific world with his bold new heliocentric theory. Up on the Baltic coast, the port city of Danzig (today's Gdańsk) took advantage of its Hanseatic League trading partnership to become one of Europe's most prosperous cities.

POLAND

Foreign Kings and Partitions

When the Jagiellonians died out in 1572, political power shifted to the nobility. Poland became a republic of nobles governed by its wealthiest 10 percent—the *szlachta*, who elected a series of foreign kings. In the 16th and 17th centuries—with its territory spanning from the Baltic Sea to the Black Sea—the Polish-Lithuanian Commonwealth was the largest state in Europe.

But over time, many of the elected kings made poor diplomatic decisions and squandered the country's resources. To make matters worse, the nobles' parliament (Sejm) introduced the concept of *liberum veto* (literally "I freely forbid"), whereby any measure could be vetoed by a single member. This policy, which effectively demanded unanimous approval for any law to be passed, paralyzed the Sejm's already-waning power.

Sensing the Commonwealth's weakness, in the mid-17th century forces from Sweden rampaged through Polish and Lithuanian lands in the devastating "Swedish Deluge." While Poland eventually reclaimed its territory, a third of its population was dead. The Commonwealth continued to import self-serving foreign kings, including Saxony's Augustus the Strong and his son, who drained Polish wealth to finance vanity projects in their hometown of Dresden.

By the late 18th century, the Commonwealth was floundering...and surrounded by three land-hungry empires (Russia, Prussia, and Austria). The Poles were unaware that these neighbors had entered into an agreement now dubbed the "Alliance of the Three Black Eagles" (all three of those countries, coincidentally, had that same symbol); like vultures, they began to circle Poland's white eagle. Stanisław August Poniatowski, elected king with Russian support in 1764, would be Poland's last.

Over the course of less than 25 years, Russia, Prussia, and Austria divided Polish territory among themselves in a series of three Partitions. In 1772 and again in 1790, Poland was forced into ceding large chunks of land to its neighbors. Desperate to reform their government, Poles enacted Europe's first democratic constitution (and the world's second, after the US Constitution) on May 3, 1791—still celebrated as a national holiday. This visionary document protected the peasants, dispensed with both *liberum veto* and the election of the king, and set up something resembling a modern nation. But the constitution alarmed Poland's neighbors, who swept in soon after with the third and final Partition in 1795. "Poland" disappeared from Europe's maps, not to return until 1918.

Even though Poland was gone, the Poles wouldn't go quietly. As the Partitions were taking place, Polish soldier Tadeusz Kościuszko (also a hero of the American Revolution) returned home to lead an unsuccessful military resistance against the Russians in 1794.

Napoleon offered a brief glimmer of hope to the Poles in the early 19th century, when he marched eastward through Europe and set up the semi-independent "Duchy of Warsaw" in Polish lands. But that fleeting taste of freedom lasted only eight years; with Napoleon's defeat, Polish hopes were dashed. The Congress of Vienna, which again redistributed Polish territory to Prussia, Russia, and Austria, is sometimes called (by Poles) the "Fourth Partition." In a classic case of "my enemy's enemy is my friend," the Poles still have great affection for Napoleon for how fiercely he fought against their mutual foes.

The Napoleonic connection also established France as a safe haven for refugee Poles. After another failed uprising against Russia in 1830, many of Poland's top artists and writers fled to Paris—including pianist Fryderyk Chopin and Romantic poet Adam Mickiewicz (whose statue adorns Kraków's main square and Warsaw's Royal Way). These Polish artists tried to preserve the nation's spirit with music and words; those who remained in Poland continued to fight with swords and fists. By the end of the 19th century, the image of the Pole as a tireless, idealistic insurgent emerged. During this time, some Romantics—with typically melodramatic flair—dubbed Poland "the Christ of nations" for the way it was misunderstood and persecuted by the world, despite its nobility.

Poles didn't just flock to France during the Partitions. Untold numbers of Polish people uprooted their lives to pursue a better future in the New World. About 10 million Americans have Polish ancestry, and most of them came stateside from the mid-19th to early 20th century. Because the sophisticated and educated tended to remain in Poland, these new arrivals were mostly poor farmers who were (at first) unschooled and didn't speak English, placing them on a bottom rung of American society. It was during this time that the tradition of insulting "Polack jokes" emerged. Some claim these originated in Chicago, which was both a national trendsetter in humor and a magnet for Polish immigrants. Others suggest that German immigrants to America imported insulting stereotypes of their Polish neighbors from the Old World. Either way, the jokes became more vicious through the 20th century, until the Polish government actually lobbied the US State Department to put a stop to them.

As the map of Europe was redrawn following World War I, Poland emerged as a reborn nation, under the war hero-turned-head of state, Marshal Józef Piłsudski. The newly reformed "Second Polish Republic," which patched together the bits and pieces of territory that had been under foreign rule for decades, enjoyed a diverse ethnic mix—including Germans, Russians, Ukrainians,

Lithuanians, and an enormous Jewish minority. A third of Poland spoke no Polish.

This interwar period was particularly good to the Jewish people. Jews were, for the first time, legally protected citizens of Poland, with full voting rights. Cities like Warsaw, Kraków, and Wilno (today's Vilnius, Lithuania)—where Jews made up a quarter to a third of the population—saw the blossoming of a rich Jewish culture.

Meanwhile, the historic Baltic port city of Gdańsk—which was bicultural (German and Polish)—was granted the special "Free City of Danzig" status to avoid dealing with the prickly issue of whether to assign it to Germany or Poland. But the peace was not to last.

World War II

On September 1, 1939, Adolf Hitler began World War II by attacking Danzig to bring it into the German fold. Before the month was out, Hitler's forces had overrun Poland, and the Soviets had taken over a swath of eastern Poland (today part of Ukraine, Belarus, and Lithuania).

The Nazis considered the Poles *slawische Untermenschen,* "Slavic sub-humans" who were useful only for manual labor. And Poland was also home to a huge population of Jewish people. Nazi Germany annexed Polish regions that it claimed historic ties to, while the rest (including "Warschau" and "Krakau") became a puppet state ruled by the *Generalgouvernement* and Hitler's handpicked governor, Hans Frank. The Nazis considered this area *Lebensraum*— "living space" that wasn't nice enough to actually incorporate into Germany, but served perfectly as extra territory for building things that Germans didn't want in their backyards...such as the notorious death camp, Auschwitz-Birkenau.

The Poles anxiously awaited the promised military aid of France and Britain; when help failed to arrive, they took matters into their own hands, forming a ragtag "Polish Home Army" and staging incredibly courageous but lopsided battles against their powerful German overlords (such as the Warsaw Uprising). Throughout the spring of 1945, as the Nazis retreated from their failed invasion of the Soviet Union, the Red Army gradually "liberated" the rubble of Poland from Nazi oppression—guaranteeing it another four decades of oppression under another regime.

During World War II, occupied Poland had the strictest laws in the Nazi realm: This was the only place where, if you were caught trying to help Jews escape, your entire family could be executed. And yet, many Poles risked their lives to help escapees.

With six million deaths over six years—including both Polish Jews and ethnic Poles—Poland suffered the worst per-capita

POLAND

WWII losses of any nation. By the war's end, one out of every five Polish citizens was dead—and 90 percent of those killed were civilians. While the human and infrastructure loss of World War II was incalculable, that war's cultural losses were also devastating—for example, some 60,000 paintings were lost.

At the war's end, the victorious Allies shifted Poland's borders significantly westward—folding historically German areas into Polish territory and appropriating previously Polish areas for the USSR. This prompted a massive movement of populations—which today we'd decry as "ethnic cleansing"—as Germans were forcibly removed from western Poland, and Poles from newly Soviet territory were transplanted to Poland proper. Entire cities were repopulated (such as the formerly German metropolis of Breslau, which was renamed Wrocław and filled with refugee Poles from Lwów, now Lviv, in Ukraine). After millions died in the war, millions more were displaced from their ancestral homes. When the dust settled, Poland was almost exclusively populated by Poles.

Saddle on a Cow: Poland Under Communism

Poland suffered horribly under the communists. A postwar intimidation regime was designed to frighten people "on board" and coincided with government seizure of private property, rationing, and food shortages. The country enjoyed a relatively open society under Premier Władysław Gomułka in the 1960s, but the impractical, centrally planned economy began to unravel in the 1970s. Stores were marked by long lines stretching around the block.

The little absurdities of communist life—which today seem almost comical—made every day a struggle. For years, every elderly woman in Poland had hair the same strange magenta color. There was only one color of dye available, so if you had dyed hair, the choice was simple: Let your hair grow out (and look clownishly half red and half white), or line up and go red.

During these difficult times, the Poles often rose up—staging major protests in 1956, 1968, 1970, and 1976. Stalin famously noted that introducing communism to the Poles was like putting a saddle on a cow.

When an anticommunist Polish cardinal named Karol Wojtyła (later known as St. John Paul II) was elected pope in 1978, then visited his homeland in 1979, it was a sign to his countrymen that change was in the air. In 1980, Lech Wałęsa, an electrician at the shipyards in Gdańsk, became the leader of the Solidarity movement, the first workers' union in communist Eastern Europe. After an initial 18-day strike at the Gdańsk shipyards, the communist regime gave in, legalizing Solidarity.

But the union grew too powerful, and the communists felt their control slipping away. On Sunday, December 13, 1981, Po-

The Heritage of Communism

While communism is an ugly memory for most Poles, those who were teenagers when it ended—with only gauzy memories of communist times, and no experience grappling with its adult realities—have some nostalgia. A friend who was 13 in 1989 recalled those days this way:

"My childhood is filled with happy memories. Under communism, life was family-oriented. Careers didn't matter. There was no way to get rich, no reason to rush, so we had time. People always had time.

"But there were also shortages. We stood in line not knowing what would be for sale. We'd buy whatever shoes were available and then trade for the right size. At grocery stores, vinegar and mustard were always on the shelf, along with plastic cheese to make it seem less empty. We had to carry ration coupons, which we'd present when buying a staple that was in short supply. We didn't necessarily buy  what we needed—just anything that could be bartered on the black market. I remember my mother and father had to 'organize' for special events...somehow find a good sausage and some Coca-Cola.

"Instead of a tidy roll of toilet paper, bathrooms came with a wad of old newspapers. Sometimes my uncle would bring us several toilet paper rolls, held together with a string— the best gift anyone could give.

"Boys in my neighborhood collected pop cans. Cans from other countries represented a world of opportunities beyond our borders. Parents could buy these cans on the black market, and the few families who were allowed to travel returned home with a treasure trove of cans. One boy up the street from me went to Italy, and proudly brought home a Pepsi can. Everyone wanted to see this huge status symbol. But a month later, communism ended, you could buy whatever you wanted, and everyone's can collections were worthless.

"We had real chocolate only for Christmas. The rest of the year, we got something called 'chocolate-like product,' which was sweet, dark, and smelled vaguely of chocolate. And we had oranges from Cuba for Christmas, too. Everybody was excited when the newspapers announced, 'The boat with the oranges from Cuba is just five days away.' The smell of Christmas was so special: chocolate and oranges. Now we have that smell every day. Still, my happiest Christmases were under communism."

land's head of state, General Wojciech Jaruzelski, declared martial law in order to "forestall Soviet intervention." (Whether the Soviets actually would have invaded remains a hotly debated issue.) Tanks ominously rolled through the streets of Poland on that snowy December morning, and the Poles were terrified.

Martial law lasted until 1983. Each Pole has chilling memories of this frightening time. During riots, the people would flock into churches—the only place they could be safe from the ZOMO (riot police). People would go for their evening walks during the 19:30 government-sanctioned national news as a sign of protest. But Solidarity struggled on, going underground and becoming a united movement of all demographics, 10 million members strong (more than a quarter of the population).

In July 1989, the ruling Communist Party agreed to hold open elections (reserving 65 percent of representatives for themselves). Their goal was to appease Solidarity, but the plan backfired: Communists didn't win a single contested seat. These elections helped spark the chain reaction across Eastern Europe that eventually tore down the Iron Curtain. Lech Wałęsa became Poland's first postcommunist president.

Poland in the 21st Century

When 10 new countries joined the European Union in May 2004, Poland was the most ambivalent of the bunch. After centuries of being under other empires' authority, the Poles were hardly eager to relinquish some of their hard-fought autonomy to Brussels. Many Poles thought that EU membership would make things worse (higher prices, a loss of traditional lifestyles) before they got better. But most people agreed that their country had to join to survive in today's Europe.

The most obvious initial impact of EU membership was the droves of job-seeking young Poles who migrated to other EU countries (mostly Britain, Ireland, and Sweden, which were the first to waive visa requirements for Eastern European workers). Many found employment at hotels and restaurants. In the mid-aughts, visitors to London and Dublin noticed a surprising language barrier at hotel front desks, and Polish-language expat newspapers joined British gossip rags on newsstands. Those who remained in Poland were concerned about the "brain drain" of bright young people flocking out of their country. But with the economic crisis, quite a few Polish expats returned home. And as Britain moves to leave the EU (Brexit), Poland will likely see another wave of returnees.

Poland is by far the most populous of the Eastern European EU members, with nearly 39 million people (about the same as Spain, or about half the size of Germany). This makes Poland the

Polish Jokes

Through the dreary communist times, the Poles managed to keep their sense of humor. A popular target of jokes was the riot police, called the ZOMO. Here are just a few of the things Poles said about these unpopular cops:

- ZOMO police are hired based on the 90-90 principle: They have to weigh at least 90 kilograms (200 pounds), and their I.Q. must be less than 90.
- ZOMO are dispatched in teams of three: one who can read, one who can write, and a third to protect those other two smart guys.
- A ZOMO policeman was sitting on the curb, crying. Someone came up to him and asked what was wrong. "I lost my dog!" he said. "No matter," the person replied. "He's a smart police dog. I'm sure he can find his way back to the station." "Yes," the ZOMO said. "But without him, I can't!"

The communists gave their people no options at elections: If you voted, you voted for the regime. Poles liked to joke that in some ways, this made communists like God—who created Eve, then said to Adam, "Now choose a wife." It was said that communists could run a pig as a candidate, and it would still win; a popular symbol of dissent became a pig painted with the words "Vote Red."

There were even jokes about jokes. Under communism, Poles noted that there was a government-sponsored prize for the funniest political joke: 15 years in prison.

sixth largest of the 26 EU member states—giving it serious political clout, which it has already asserted...sometimes to the dismay of the EU's more established powers.

On the American political spectrum, Poland may be the most conservative country in Europe. Poles are phobic when it comes to "big government"—likely because they've been subjugated and manipulated by so many foreign oppressors over the centuries. For most of the 2000s, the country's right wing was represented by a pair of twin brothers, Lech and Jarosław Kaczyński. (The Kaczyński brothers were child actors who appeared in several popular movies together.) Their conservative Law and Justice Party (PiS for short) is pro-tax cuts, fiercely Euroskeptic (anti-EU), and very Catholic. In the 2005 presidential election, Lech Kaczyński emerged as the victor; several months later, he took the controversial step of appointing his identical twin brother Jarosław as Poland's prime minister.

The political pendulum swung back toward the center in October 2007, when the Kaczyński brothers' main political rival, the pro-EU Donald Tusk, led his Civic Platform Party to victory in the parliamentary elections. The name Kaczyński loosely means "duck"—so the Poles quipped that they were led by "Donald and the Ducks."

Tragically, the levity wasn't to last. On April 10, 2010, a plane carrying President Lech Kaczyński crashed in a thick fog near the city of Smolensk, Russia. All 96 people on board—including top government, military, and business officials, high-ranking clergy, and others—were killed, plunging the nation into a period of stunned mourning. Poles wondered why, yet again, an unprecedented tragedy had befallen their nation. (Ironically, the group's trip was intended to put a painful chapter of Poland's history to rest: a commemoration of the Polish officers and enlisted men killed in the Soviet massacre at Katyń.)

Meanwhile, Poland's economy kept chugging along, even as the rest of Europe and much of the world were bogged down by the economic crisis. More than a quarter of Poland's trade is with neighboring Germany—another of Europe's healthiest economies—and Poland was the only European Union country that didn't have a recession in 2009. Why? Poland is a big, self-sustaining, insular economy. (Although in recent years, Poland's relatively weak currency—"cheaper" than the euro, yet also shielded from euro volatility—and robust economy have lured foreign investment, paradoxically threatening that autonomy.)

Over the last decade, the political pendulum has just kept on swinging, as key governmental posts have gone back and forth between the two dominant parties—the Civic Platform (which controlled parliament 2007-2015) and Law and Justice (2015-present).

Since taking power, Law and Justice—chaired by Jarosław Kaczyński—has come under fire for policies that many observers have termed "nationalistic" and borderline-authoritarian (in the vein of Viktor Orbán's Fidesz in Hungary, or Donald Trump in the US). They've packed the ostensibly autonomous Constitutional Tribunal with party loyalists, purged opposition civil servants and military leaders, levied fines against critical news coverage in a manner that threatens freedom of the press, and removed the director of the brand-new Museum of the Second World War in Gdańsk—deeming the exhibit "not Polish enough" and installing a new director who altered many of the exhibits. Because of these and other concerns, in late 2017, the EU initiated Article 7 of the EU Treaty for the first time—stripping Poland of some of its voting rights within the EU. (Hungary has sided with Poland in the dispute, triggering the invocation of Article 7 against itself as well.)

In a high-profile act that drew vocal international criticism, in summer 2018, Law and Order removed 27 long-serving judges (approximately one-third of the top judiciary) from Poland's Supreme Court. While the party insisted they were simply rooting out corruption (claiming those judges were holdovers of the communist

Bar Mleczny (Milk Bar)

When you see a "bar" in Poland, it doesn't mean alcohol—it means cheap grub. Eating at a *bar mleczny* (bar MLECH-neh) is an essential Polish sightseeing experience. These cafete-
rias, which you'll see all over
the country, are an incredibly
cheap way to get a good
meal...and, with the right attitude, a fun cultural experience.

In the communist era,
the government subsidized
the food at milk bars, allowing workers to enjoy a meal
out. The name comes from
the cheese cutlets that were
sold here, back in a time when
good meat was rare. The tradition continues today, as milk-
bar prices remain astoundingly low: about $5 for a filling meal.
And, while communist-era fare was gross, today's milk-bar
cuisine is usually quite tasty.

Milk bars usually offer many of the traditional tastes listed
in the "Polish food" section. Common items are soups (such as
żurek and *barszcz*), a variety of cabbage-based salads, *kotlet*
(fried pork chops), pierogi (similar to ravioli, with various fillings), and *naleśniki* (pancakes). You'll see glasses of juice and
(of course) milk, but most milk bars also stock bottles of water
and Coke.

There are two types of milk bars: updated, modern cafeterias that cater to tourists (English menus), add some modern
twists to their traditional fare, and charge about 50 percent
more; and time-machine dives that haven't changed for decades. At truly traditional milk bars, the service is aimed at
locals, which means no English menu and a confusing ordering
system.

Every milk bar is a little different, but here's the general
procedure: Head to the counter, wait to be acknowledged,
and point to what you want. Handy vocabulary: *to* (sounds like
"toe") means "this"; *i* (pronounced "ee") means "and."

If the milk-bar lady asks you any questions, you have
three options: Nod stupidly until she just gives you something;
repeat one of the things she just said (assuming she's asked
you to choose between two options, like meat or cheese in
your pierogi); or hope that a kindly English-speaking Pole in
line will leap to your rescue. If nothing else, ordering at a milk
bar is an adventure in gestures. Smiling seems to slightly extend the patience of milk-bar staffers.

Once your tray is all loaded up, pay the cashier, do a double-take when you realize how cheap your bill is, then find a
table. After the meal, bus your own dishes to the little window.

system), tens of thousands of Poles filled the streets of cities and towns in protest. All of this has raised troubling questions about the long-term viability of Polish democracy, and about Poland's role within the EU.

And yet, at the same time, Donald Tusk—Poland's former prime minister and most high-profile left-leaning politician—has become a major player in the EU government; in 2017, he was re-elected to his second term as the president of the European Council. It remains to be seen where the Polish political pendulum swings next. But one thing is clear: The Poles—although a bit late to the party—are making their presence felt in European politics.

POLISH FOOD

Polish food is hearty and tasty. Because Poland is north of the Carpathian Mountains, its weather tends to be chilly, limiting the kinds of fruits and veg-etables that flourish here.

As in other northern European countries (such as Russia or Scandinavia), dominant staples include potatoes, dill, berries, beets, and rye. Much of what you might think of as "Jewish cuisine" turns up on Polish menus (gefilte fish, potato pancakes, chicken soup, and so forth)—which makes sense, given that Poles and Jews lived in the same area for centuries.

Polish soups are a highlight. The most typical are *żurek* and *barszcz*. *Żurek* (often translated as "sour soup" on menus) is a thick-ened, light-colored soup made from a sourdough base, usually con-taining a hard-boiled egg and pieces of *kiełbasa* (sausage). *Barszcz*, better known to Americans as borscht, is a savory beet soup that you'll see in several varieties: *Barszcz czerwony* (red borscht) is a thin, flavorful broth with a deep red color, sometimes containing dump-lings or a hard-boiled egg. *Barszcz ukraiński* (Ukrainian borscht) is thicker, with cream and vegetables (usually cabbage, beans, and carrots). In summer, try the "Polish gazpacho"—*chłodnik,* a savory cream soup with beets, onions, and radishes that's served cold. I never met a Polish soup I didn't like...until I was introduced to *flaki* (sometimes *flaczki*)—tripe soup.

Another familiar Polish dish is pierogi. These ravioli-like dumplings come with various fillings. The most traditional are minced meat, sauerkraut, mushroom, cheese, and blueberry; many restaurants also experiment with more exotic fillings. Pierogi are often served with specks of fatty bacon to add flavor. Pierogi are a budget traveler's dream: Restaurants serving them are everywhere, and they're generally cheap, tasty, and very filling.

Bigos is a rich and delicious sauerkraut stew cooked with meat, mushrooms, and whatever's in the pantry. It's sort of the Polish version of chili—it's a beloved comfort food, especially in the cold of winter, and everyone has their own recipe. *Gołąbki* is a dish of cabbage leaves stuffed with minced meat and rice in a tomato or mushroom sauce. *Kotlet schabowy* (fried pork chop)—once painfully scarce in communist Poland—remains a local favorite to this day.

Kaczka (duck) is popular, as is freshwater fish: Look for *pstrąg* (trout), *karp* (carp, beware of bones), and *węgorz* (eel). On the Baltic Coast (such as in Gdańsk), you'll also see *łosoś* (salmon), *śledź* (herring), and *dorsz* (cod). Poles eat lots of potatoes, which are served with nearly every meal. Look for *placki ziemniaczane*—potato pancakes.

Some dreary old foods are newly hip in today's Poland. Herring-and-vodka bars are trendy, many following the "4/8 model"—4 zł for a shot of vodka, 8 zł for a herring snack. The Polish street food *zapiekanka*—a toasted baguette with melted cheese, rubbery mushrooms from a can, and a drizzle of ersatz ketchup—began life as a "hardship food" under communism, as a pale imitation of pizza. These days it has been reborn as a street-food staple; *zapiekanka* vendors top them with a world of creative flavors. The bagel-like rings you'll see sold on the street, *obwarzanki* (singular *obwarzanek*), are also cheap, and usually fresh and tasty. And, as throughout Europe, gourmet hamburgers are in—including a trend for vegan burgers.

Poland has good pastries—look for a *cukiernia* (pastry shop). The classic Polish treat is *pączki*, glazed jelly doughnuts. They can have different fillings, but most typical is a wild-rose jam. *Szarlotka* is apple cake—sometimes made with chunks of apples (especially in season), sometimes with apple filling. *Sernik* is cheesecake, and *makowiec* is poppy-seed cake. *Winebreda* is an especially gooey Danish. *Babeczka* is like a cupcake filled with pudding. And *Napoleonka* is a French-style treat with layers of crispy wafers and custard.

Lody (ice cream) is popular. The tall, skinny cones of soft-serve ice cream are called *świderki*, sometimes translated as "American ice cream." The most beloved traditional candy is *ptasie mleczko* (birds' milk), which is semisour marshmallow covered with chocolate. E. Wedel is the country's top brand of chocolate, with outlets in all the big cities.

Thirsty? *Woda* is water, *woda mineralna* is bottled water (*gazowana* is with gas, *niegazowana* is without), *kawa* is coffee, *herbata* is tea, *sok* is juice, and *mleko* is milk. Żywiec, Okocim, and Lech are the best-known brands of *piwo* (beer).

Wódka (vodka) is a Polish staple—the word means, rough-ly, "precious little water." Żubrówka, the most famous brand of vodka, comes with a blade of grass from the bison reserves in eastern Poland (look for the bison on the label). The bison "fla-vor" the grass...then the grass flavors the vodka. Poles often mix Żubrówka with apple juice, and call this cocktail *szarlotka* ("apple cake"). For "Cheers!" say, *"Na zdrowie!"* (nah ZDROH-vyeh).

Unusual drinks to try if you have the chance are *kwas* (a cold, fizzy, Ukrainian-style nonalcoholic beverage made from day-old rye bread) and *kompot* (a hot drink made from stewed berries). Poles are unusually fond of carrot juice (often cut with fruit juice); Kubuś is the most popular brand.

"Bon appétit" is *"Smacznego"* (smatch-NEH-goh). To pay, ask for the *rachunek* (rah-KHOO-nehk).

POLISH LANGUAGE

Polish is closely related to its neighboring Slavic languages (Slo-vak and Czech), with the biggest difference being that Polish has lots of fricatives (hissing sounds—"sh" and "ch"—often in close proximity).

Polish intimidates Americans with long, difficult-to-pro-nounce words. But if you take your time and sound things out, you'll quickly develop an ear for it. One rule of thumb to help you out: The stress is generally on the next-to-last syllable.

Polish has some letters that don't appear in English, and some letters and combinations are pronounced differently than in English:

ć, ci, and **cz** all sound like "ch" as in "church"
ś, si, and **sz** all sound like "sh" as in "short"
ż, ź, zi, and **rz** all sound like "zh" as in "leisure"
dż and **dź** both sound like the "dj" sound in "jeans"
ń and **ni** sound like "ny" as in "canyon"
ę and **ą** are pronounced nasally, as in French: "e*n*" and "a*n*"
c sounds like "ts" as in "cats"
ch sounds like "kh" as in the Scottish "loch"
j sounds like "y" as in "yellow"
w sounds like "v" as in "Victor"
ł sounds like "w" as in "with"

So to Poles, "Lech Wałęsa" isn't pronounced "lehk wah-LEH-sah," as Americans tend to say—but "lehkh vah-WEHN-sah."

The Polish people you meet will be impressed and flattered if you take the time to learn a little of their language. To get started, check out the selection of Polish survival phrases on the following pages.

As you're tracking down addresses, these words will help: *miasto* (mee-AH-stoh, town), *plac* (plahts, square), *rynek* (REE-nehk, big market square), *ulica* (OO-leet-sah, road), *aleja* (ah-LAY-yah, avenue), and *most* (mohst, bridge). And that long word you see everywhere—*zapraszamy*—means "welcome."

Polish Survival Phrases

Keep in mind a few Polish pronunciation tips: **w** sounds like "v," **ł** sounds like "w," **ch** is a back-of-your-throat "kh" sound (as in the Scottish "loch"), and **rz** sounds like the "zh" sound in "pleasure." The vowels with a tail (**ą** and **ę**) have a slight nasal "n" sound at the end, similar to French.

English	Polish	Pronunciation
Hello. (formal)	*Dzień dobry.*	jehn **doh**-brih
Hi. / Bye. (informal)	*Cześć.*	cheshch
Do you speak English? (asked of a man)	*Czy Pan mówi po angielsku?*	chih pahn **moo**-vee poh ahn-**gyehl**-skoo
Do you speak English? (asked of a woman)	*Czy Pani mówi po angielsku?*	chih **pah**-nee **moo**-vee poh ahn-**gyehl**-skoo
Yes. / No.	*Tak. / Nie.*	tahk / nyeh
I (don't) understand.	*(Nie) rozumiem.*	(nyeh) roh-**zoo**-myehm
Please. / You're welcome. / Can I help you?	*Proszę.*	**proh**-sheh
Thank you (very much).	*Dziękuję (bardzo).*	jehn-**koo**-yeh (**bard**-zoh)
Excuse me. / I'm sorry.	*Przepraszam.*	psheh-**prah**-shahm
(No) problem.	*(Żaden) problem.*	(**zhah**-dehn) **proh**-blehm
Good.	*Dobrze.*	**dohb**-zheh
Goodbye.	*Do widzenia.*	doh veed-**zay**-nyah
one / two / three	*jeden / dwa / trzy*	**yeh**-dehn / dvah / tzhih
four / five / six	*cztery / pięć / sześć*	**chteh**-rih / pyench / sheshch
seven / eight	*siedem / osiem*	**shyeh**-dehm / **oh**-shehm
nine / ten	*dziewięć / dziesięć*	**jeh**-vyench / **jeh**-shench
hundred / thousand	*sto / tysiąc*	stoh / **tih**-shants
How much?	*Ile?*	**ee**-leh
local currency	*złoty (zł)*	**zwoh**-tih
Write it.	*Napisz to.*	**nah**-peesh toh
Is it free?	*Czy to jest za darmo?*	chih toh yehst zah **dar**-moh
Is it included?	*Czy jest to wliczone?*	chih yehst toh vlee-**choh**-neh
Where can I find / buy...?	*Gdzie mogę dostać / kupić...?*	guh-**dyeh** moh-geh **doh**-statch / **koo**-peech
I'd like... (said by a man)	*Chciałbym...*	**khchaw**-beem
I'd like... (said by a woman)	*Chciałabym...*	**khchah**-wah-beem
We'd like...	*Chcielibyśmy...*	**khchehl**-ee-bish-mih
...a room.	*...pokój.*	**poh**-kooey
...a ticket to ___.	*...bilet do ___.*	**bee**-leht doh ___
Is it possible?	*Czy jest to możliwe?*	chih yehst toh mohzh-**lee**-veh
Where is...?	*Gdzie jest...?*	guh-**dyeh** yehst
...the train station	*...dworzec kolejowy*	**dvoh**-zhehts koh-leh-**yoh**-vih
...the bus station	*...dworzec autobusowy*	**dvoh**-zhehts ow-toh-boos-**oh**-vih
...the tourist information office	*...informacja turystyczna*	een-for-**maht**-syah too-ris-**titch**-nah
...the toilet	*...toaleta*	toh-ah-**leh**-tah
men / women	*męska / damska*	**mehn**-skah / **dahm**-skah
left / right / straight	*lewo / prawo / prosto*	**leh**-voh / **prah**-roh / **proh**-stoh
At what time...?	*O której godzinie...?*	oh kuh-**too**-ray gohd-**zhee**-nyeh
...does this open / close	*...będzie otwarte / zamknięte*	**bend**-zheh oht-**vahr**-teh / zahm-**knyehn**-teh
Just a moment.	*Chwileczkę.*	khvee-**letch**-keh
now / soon / later	*eraz / niedługo / później*	**teh**-rahz / nyed-**woo**-goh / **poozh**-nyey
today / tomorrow	*dzisiaj / jutro*	**jee**-shigh / **yoo**-troh

In a Polish Restaurant

English	Polish	Pronunciation
I'd like to reserve... (said by a man)	Chciałbym zarezerwować...	**khchaw**-beem zah-reh-zehr-**voh**-vahch
I'd like to reserve... (said by a woman)	Chciałabym zarezerwować...	**khchah**-wah-beem zah-reh-zehr-**voh**-vahch
We'd like to reserve...	Chcielibyśmy zarezerwować...	**khchehl**-ee-bish-mih zah-reh-zehr-**voh**-vahch
...a table for one person / two people.	...stolik na jedną osobę / dwie osoby.	**stoh**-leek nah **yehd**-now oh-**soh**-beh / dvyeh oh-**soh**-bih
Is this table free?	Czy ten stolik jest wolny?	chih tehn **stoh**-leek yehst **vohl**-nih
Can I help you?	W czym mogę pomóc?	vchim **moh**-geh **poh**-moots
The menu (in English), please.	Menu (po angielsku), proszę.	**meh**-noo (poh ahn-**gyehl**-skoo) **proh**-sheh
service (not) included	usługa (nie) wliczona	oos-**woo**-gah (nyeh) **vlee**-choh-nah
cover charge	wstęp	vstenp
"to go"	na wynos	nah **vih**-nohs
with / without	z / bez	z / behz
and / or	i / lub	ee / loob
milk bar (cheap cafeteria)	bar mleczny	bar **mletch**-nih
fixed-price meal (of the day)	zestaw (dnia)	**zehs**-tahv (dih-**nyah**)
specialty of the house	specjalność zakładu	speht-**syahl**-nohshch zah-**kwah**-doo
half portion	pół porcji	poow **ports**-yee
daily special	danie dnia	**dah**-nyeh dih-**nyah**
appetizers	przystawki	pshih-**stahv**-kee
bread	chleb	khlehb
cheese	ser	sehr
sandwich	kanapka	kah-**nahp**-kah
soup	zupa	**zoo**-pah
salad	sałatka	sah-**waht**-kah
meat / poultry	mięso / drób	**myehn**-soh / droob
fish / seafood	ryba / owoce morza	**rih**-bah / oh-**voht**-seh **moh**-zhah
fruit / vegetables	owoce / warzywa	oh-**voht**-seh / vah-**zhih**-vah
dessert	deser	**deh**-sehr
(tap) water	woda (z kranu)	**voh**-dah (**skrah**-noo)
mineral water	woda mineralna	**voh**-dah mee-neh-**rahl**-nah
carbonated / not carbonated	gazowana / niegazowana	gah-zoh-**vah**-nah / **nyeh**-gah-zoh-vah-nah
milk	mleko	**mleh**-koh
(orange) juice	sok (pomarańczowy)	sohk (poh-mah-rayn-**choh**-vih)
coffee / tea	kawa / herbata	**kah**-vah / hehr-**bah**-tah
wine	wino	**vee**-noh
red / white	czerwone / białe	chehr-**voh**-neh / bee-**ah**-weh
sweet / dry / semi-dry	słodkie / wytrawne / półwytrawne	**swoht**-kyeh / vih-**trahv**-neh / poow-vih-**trahv**-neh
glass / bottle	szklanka / butelka	**shklahn**-kah / boo-**tehl**-kah
beer	piwo	**pee**-voh
vodka	wódka	**vood**-kah
Cheers!	Na zdrowie!	nah **zdroh**-vyeh
Enjoy your meal.	Smacznego.	smatch-**neh**-goh
More. / Another.	Więcej. / Inny.	**vyehnt**-say / **ee**-nih-nih
The same.	Taki sam.	**tah**-kee sahm
the bill	rachunek	rah-**khoo**-nehk
I'll pay.	Ja płacę.	yah **pwaht**-seh
tip	napiwek	nah-**pee**-vehk
Delicious!	Pyszne!	**pish**-neh

KRAKÓW

Kraków is easily Poland's best destination: a beautiful, old-fashioned city buzzing with history, enjoyable sights, tourists, and college students. Even though the country's capital moved from here to Warsaw 400 years ago, Kraków remains Poland's cultural and intellectual center. Increasingly (and justifiably) popular, Kraków is giving Prague a run for its money on the "must visit" tourist route.

What's so special about it? First off, Kraków is simply charming; more than any town in Europe, it seems made for aimless strolling. And its historic walls and former moat corral an unusually full range of activities and interests: bustling university life; thought-provoking museums; breathtaking churches that evoke a powerful faith (and include many sights relating to Poland's favorite son, St. John Paul II); sprawling parks that invite you to just relax; vivid Jewish heritage sights; a burgeoning foodie and nightlife scene; and compelling side trips to the most notorious Holocaust site anywhere (Auschwitz-Birkenau), a communist-planned workers town, and a mine filled with salty statues. With so many opportunities to learn, to have fun, or to do both at once, it's no surprise that Kraków has become a world-class destination.

PLANNING YOUR TIME

Don't skimp on your time in Kraków. It takes a minimum of two days to experience the city, and a third (or even a fourth) day lets you dig in and consider a world of fascinating side trips.

Almost everyone coming to Kraków also visits the Auschwitz-Birkenau Concentration Camp Memorial—and should. As it's about an hour and a half away, this demands the better part of a day to fully appreciate (either as a round-trip from Kraków, or en route to or from another destination). Visiting Auschwitz requires a reservation, which should be arranged long in advance.

If you have only two full days (the "express plan"), start off with my self-guided walk through the Old Town and a quick stroll up to Wawel Castle, then head over to the Schindler's Factory Museum and wind down your day in Kazimierz. Your second day is for a side trip to Auschwitz. This plan gives you a once-over-lightly look at Kraków, but leaves almost no time for entering the sights.

More time buys you the chance to relax, enjoy, and linger: Tackle the Old Town and Wawel Castle on the first day, Kazimierz and museums of your choice on the second day, and Auschwitz (and other side trips) with additional days. If you have a special interest, you could side-trip to the St. John Paul II pilgrimage sites on the outskirts of town, or to the communist architecture of the Nowa Huta suburb. Wieliczka Salt Mine is another crowd-pleasing, half-day option.

Regardless of how long you stay, your evening choices are many and varied: Savor the Main Market Square over dinner or a drink, take in a jazz show, do a pub crawl through the city's many youthful bars and clubs (best in Kazimierz), or enjoy traditional Jewish music and cuisine (also in Kazimierz).

Orientation to Kraków

Kraków (Poles say KROCK-oof, but you can say KRACK-cow; it's sometimes spelled "Cracow" in English) is mercifully compact, flat, and easy to navigate. While the urban sprawl is big (with 767,000 people), the tourist's Kraków feels small—from the main square, you can walk to just about everything of interest in less than 15 minutes. Just to the south is Poland's main river, the Vistula (Wisła, VEES-wah).

Most sights—and almost all recommended hotels and restaurants—are in the **Old Town** (Stare Miasto, STAH-reh mee-AH-stoh), which is surrounded by a greenbelt called the Planty (PLAHN-tee). In the center of the Old Town lies the Main Market Square (Rynek Główny, REE-nehk GWOHV-nee)—it's such an important landmark, I call it simply "the Square." At the Old Town's northeast corner, just outside the ring road, is the main train station. And at the southern end of the Old Town, on the riverbank, is the hill called **Wawel** (VAH-vehl)—with a historic castle, museums, and Poland's national church.

About a 20-minute walk (or quick tram/taxi ride) southeast of the Square is the neighborhood called **Kazimierz** (kah-ZHEE-mehzh)—with Jewish landmarks and Holocaust sites (including the Schindler's Factory Museum) and the city's best foodie and nightlife area.

A few more attractions are just beyond the core, including the St. John Paul II pilgrimage sites (in the Łagiewniki neighborhood), the communist-planned town of Nowa Huta, Wieliczka Salt Mine, and the Kościuszko Mound.

TOURIST INFORMATION

Kraków has many helpful TIs, called InfoKraków (*www.infokrakow.pl*). Five branches are in or near the Old Town (all open daily May-Sept 9:00-19:00, Oct-April until 17:00, unless otherwise noted):

• In the **Planty** park, between the main train station and Main Market Square (in round kiosk at ulica Szpitalna 25, tel. 12-354-2720)

• On **ulica Św. Jana,** just north of the Main Market Square (specializes in concert tickets, daily year-round 9:00-19:00, at #2, tel. 12-354-2725)

• In the **Cloth Hall** right on the Main Market Square (tel. 12-354-2716)

• In the **Wyspiański Pavilion,** just south of the Square on ulica Grodzka (daily 9:00-17:00, plac Wszystkich Świętych 3, not at the window but inside the building, tel. 12-354-2723)

• Just west of **Wawel Hill** (also covers the entire region, Powiśle 11, tel. 12-354-2710)

Other TI branches are in **Kazimierz** (daily 9:00-17:00, ulica Józefa 7, tel. 12-354-2728) and the **airport** (daily 9:00-19:00, tel. 12-285-5341).

Note that the TIs sell tickets for *only* one tour company, See Kraków; for additional options, see "Tours in Kraków," later, and look around online.

Sightseeing Pass: The TI's **Kraków Tourist Card** includes admission to 40 city museums (basically everything except the Wawel Hill sights and Wieliczka Salt Mine)—but admissions are so cheap, it's unlikely you'd save money with the card. Given how walkable Kraków is, the version that does not include public transit is a better value than the one that does.

Warning: Many private travel agencies, room-booking services, and tour operators masquerade as TIs, with deceptive blue-and-white *i* signs. If I haven't listed them in this section, they're not a real TI.

Kraków City History Museum's Visitors Center: Tucked in the Cloth Hall (on the quiet western side) is a little information office operated by the Kraków City History Museum, where you can book tickets, without a line, for the popular Schindler's Factory Museum and Rynek Underground Museum. If you anticipate

KRAKÓW

Kraków's Old Town

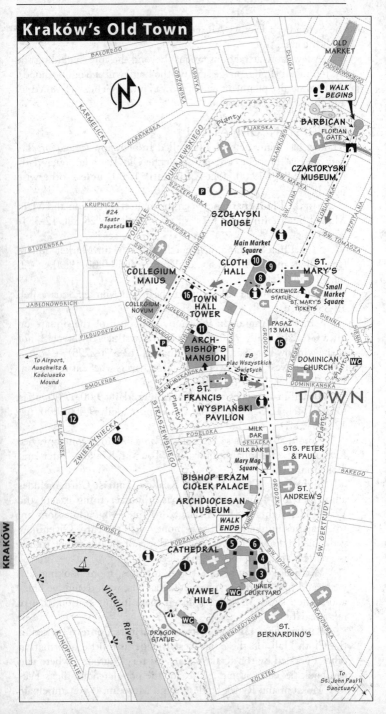

BAŁOREGO

ŁOBZOWSKA

ASNYKA

DŁUGA

PADEREWSKIEGO

OLD MARKET

WALK BEGINS

KARMELICKA

GARBARSKA

DUNAJEWSKIEGO

Planty

PIJARSKA

SŁAWKOWSKA

BARBICAN

FLORIAN GATE

CZARTORYSKI MUSEUM

SW. MARKA

SW. JANA

FLORIAŃSKA

SZPITALNA

SW. TOMASZA

KRUPNICZA

#24 Teatr Bagatela

PODWALE

SZCZEPAŃSKA

OLD

SZOŁAYSKI HOUSE

ŚW. ANNY

SZEWSKA

JAGIELLOŃSKA

SW. MARII

Main Market Square

CLOTH HALL

10 9 8

ST. MARY'S

STUDENSKA

COLLEGIUM MAIUS

16

TOWN HALL TOWER

MICKIEWICZ STATUE

Small Market Square

ST. MARY'S TICKETS

JABŁONOWSKICH

COLLEGIUM NOVUM

GOŁEBIA

BRACKA

PASAŻ 13 MALL

SIENNA

PIŁSUDSKIEGO

OLSZEWSKIEGO

11

ARCH-BISHOP'S MANSION

#8 plac Wszystkich Świętych

15

GRODZKA

STOLARSKA

Planty

DOMINICAN CHURCH

WC

SMOLEŃSK

FRANCISZKAŃSKA

Planty

ST. FRANCIS

WYSPIAŃSKI PAVILION

DOMINIKAŃSKA

TOWN

12

ZWIERZYNIECKA

14

STRASZEWSKIEGO

POSELSKA

MILK BAR

SENACKA

MILK BAR

Mary Mag. Square

STS. PETER & PAUL

SAREGO

FELICIANEK

BISHOP ERAZM CIOŁEK PALACE

ARCHDIOCESAN MUSEUM

WALK ENDS

KANONICZA

GRODZKA

ST. ANDREW'S

ŚW. IDZIEGO

POWIŚLE

PODZAMCZE

CATHEDRAL

5 6

1 4

3

2

WC

WAWEL HILL

7

INNER COURTYARD

WC

ŚW. GERTRUDY

STRADOMSKA

ST. BERNARDINO'S

DRAGON STATUE

Vistula River

BERNARDYŃSKA

KONOPNICKIEJ

KOLETEK

To Airport, Auschwitz & Kościuszko Mound

To St. John Paul II Sanctuary

KRAKÓW

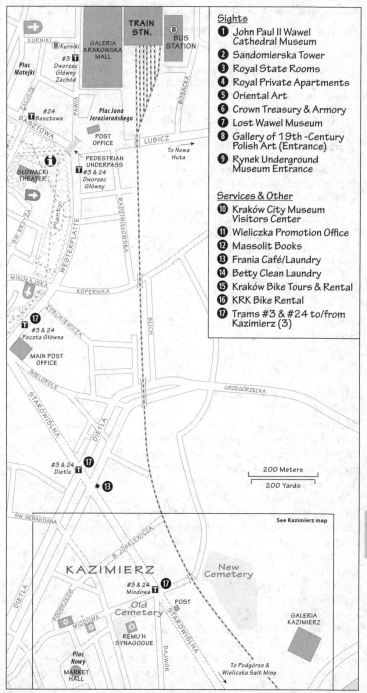

Sights

1. John Paul II Wawel Cathedral Museum
2. Sandomierska Tower
3. Royal State Rooms
4. Royal Private Apartments
5. Oriental Art
6. Crown Treasury & Armory
7. Lost Wawel Museum
8. Gallery of 19th-Century Polish Art (Entrance)
9. Rynek Underground Museum Entrance

Services & Other

10. Kraków City Museum Visitors Center
11. Wieliczka Promotion Office
12. Massolit Books
13. Frania Café/Laundry
14. Betty Clean Laundry
15. Kraków Bike Tours & Rental
16. KRK Bike Rental
17. Trams #3 & #24 to/from Kazimierz (3)

KRAKÓW

Don't Miss Out!
Book Key Sights in Advance

A few popular Kraków attractions can fill up at busy times, and it pays to reserve ahead. If you're going to **Auschwitz,** book as far in advance as possible—ideally three months ahead (details in the next chapter). In Kraków, during very busy times you'll want to reserve several days ahead for **Schindler's Factory Museum,** the **Wieliczka Salt Mine,** and the **Rynek Underground Museum** (in roughly that order of popularity). You can only book up to three days in advance online—but in person, you can prebook even the same day for Schindler and Rynek, at the ticket office in the Cloth Hall—see "Tourist Information," earlier.

What constitutes **"busy times"?** Summers and weekends are the most crowded, reaching a peak during Poland's many long summer holiday weekends (Labor Day and Constitution Day, May 1-3; Corpus Christi, usually in late May or early June; and Assumption, Aug 15). If coming at these times, anticipate crowds and book well ahead.

---

crowds at either museum—particularly likely on the free day for each one (Mon and Tue, respectively), or on summer weekends—drop by this office to book an entry time (daily 10:00-19:00, until 20:00 in summer, at #1).

ARRIVAL IN KRAKÓW
By Train

Kraków's main train station (called "Kraków Główny," KROCK-oof GWOHV-nee) sits just northeast of the Old Town, adjoining the sprawling Galeria Krakowska shopping mall. The station and the mall face a broad plaza (plac Dworcowy) across the ring road from the Planty park and Old Town. My recommended Old Town hotels are within about a 15- to 20-minute walk, or a quick tram or taxi ride. (If you're staying in the Old Town, the tram doesn't save you much time; for those staying in Kazimierz—a 30-minute walk away—the tram is definitely worthwhile.)

The main concourse has all of the amenities: ATMs, lockers (under the big schedule board between the ticket windows), WCs, takeaway coffee, and a handy Biedronka minisupermarket. From this area, five numbered escalators lead up to the corresponding train platforms. If you need to buy tickets, tucked under the escalators is a long row of numbered ticket windows (some for domestic tickets only, others for domestic and international—check signs before you line up; a few are marked with UK flags to denote English-speaking staff). In the middle of the ticket windows (between #11 and #12) is the PKP Passenger Service Center, which may have a longer wait but is more likely to have staff who speak English (no extra fee). Remember, you can also buy most tickets online (*www.rozklad-pkp.pl*)—saving you a trip to the station or a long wait in line.

Getting Between the Station and Downtown: The easiest option is to take a **taxi** (they wait in the parking lot on the station's rooftop—go up the stairs or elevator from your platform). The usual metered rate to downtown is a reasonable 10-15 zł; only take a taxi marked with a company name and telephone number. You can also order an **Uber,** which is often cheaper (see "Getting Around Kraków," later).

If you prefer to walk or take a tram, you first must navigate the Galeria Krakowska shopping mall. Begin by following *Exit to the City* signs. Once inside the mall, continue straight ahead. To **walk,** follow *Old Town* signs, which eventually route you to the left. You'll pop out at a big plaza where you'll continue straight, taking the broad ramp down into a pedestrian underpass beneath the ring road. Emerging at the other side, bear right up the ramp into the Planty. The Main Market Square is straight ahead (you'll see the twin spires of St. Mary's Church).

If you'd rather take a **tram,** continue straight ahead through the mall, following signs to *Pawia street*. Emerging here, you'll see the Dworzec Główny Zachód tram stop. Buy a ticket from the machine and hop on tram #3 in the direction of Nowy Bieżanów. This tram stops at the eastern edge of the Old Town (Poczta Główna stop) before continuing to Kazimierz (Miodowa stop). (Note: Avoid the tram stop you'll see signposted inside the station—it's served by trams that don't go anywhere near the Old Town or Kazimierz.)

There is a **shortcut** to avoid going through the sprawling and sometimes congested mall: The modern train station is attached to the old station (the yellow building facing the big plaza, now hosting art exhibitions) by a sidewalk under a green canopy. This can save you a little walking (and a lot of shopping temptations). It's tricky to find from inside the station: Go behind the Biedronka supermarket, near track 1, and exit toward Lubicz street. Walk up the ramp and follow the green canopy to the plaza.

To get **from town to the station** (or to the bus station behind it), head to the northeast corner of the Planty, take the underpass beneath the ring road, walk across the plaza and into the Galeria Krakowska mall, and once inside, follow signs to *Railway Station* and *Station Hall*.

By Bus

The bus station is directly behind the main train station. When arriving by bus, it's easiest to get into town by first heading into the

Kraków: A Snapshot History

Kraków grew wealthy from trade in the late 10th and early 11th centuries. Traders who passed through were required to stop here for a few days and sell their wares at a reduced cost. Local merchants turned around and sold those goods with big price hikes...and Kraków thrived. In 1038, it became Poland's capital.

Tatars invaded in 1241, leaving the city in ruins. Krakovians took this opportunity to rebuild their streets in a near-perfect grid, a striking contrast to the narrow, mazelike lanes of most medieval towns. The destruction also paved the way for the spectacular Main Market Square—still Kraków's best feature.

King Kazimierz the Great sparked Kraków's Golden Age in the 14th century (see the "Kazimierz the Great" sidebar, later). In 1364, he established the university that still defines the city (and counts Copernicus and St. John Paul II among its alumni).

But Kraków's power waned as Poland's political center shifted to Warsaw. In 1596, the capital officially moved north. And with the three Partitions of the late 18th century, Poland disappeared from the map and Kraków became a poor provincial backwater of Vienna.

After Napoleon briefly reshuffled Europe in the early 19th century, Kraków was granted the status of a relatively independent city-state for about 30 years. The Free City of Kraków, a tiny sliver wedged between three of Europe's mightiest empires, enjoyed an economic boom that saw the creation of the Planty park, the arrival of gas lighting and trams, and the construction of upscale suburbs outside the Old Town. Only after the unsuccessful Kraków Uprising of 1846 was the city forcefully brought back into the Austrian fold. But despite Kraków's reduced prominence, Austria's comparatively liberal climate allowed the city to become a haven for intellectuals and progressives (including a young revolutionary thinker from Russia named Vladimir Lenin).

The Nazis overran Poland in September of 1939, installing

train station, then continuing through it, following the directions on the previous page.

To get *to* the bus station from the Old Town (for example, if you need to catch a bus to Auschwitz), follow the directions above, then walk all the way through to the far end of the train station area (past platform 5, exit marked for *bus station*). Exiting the train station, escalate up to the bus terminal (marked *MDA Dworzec Autobusowy*). Inside are the standard amenities (lockers and WCs), domestic and international ticket windows, and an electronic board showing the next several departures. Some bus departures, marked on the board with a *G*, leave from the upper *(gorna)* stalls, which you can see out the window. Other bus departures, marked with a *D*, leave from the lower *(dolna)* stalls in the garage beneath your

a ruling body called the *Generalgouvernement,* headed by Hans Frank. Germany wanted to quickly develop "Krakau" (as they called it) into the German capital of the nation. They renamed the Main Market Square "Adolf-Hitler-Platz," tore down statues of Polish figures (including the Adam Mickiewicz statue that dominates the Main Market Square today), and invested heavily in construction and industrialization (opening the door for Oskar Schindler to come and take over a factory from its Jewish owners). The German overlords imposed a "New Order" that included seizing businesses, rationing, and a strict curfew for Poles and Jews alike. A special set of "Jewish laws" targeted, then decimated, Poland's huge Jewish population.

Kraków's cityscape—if not its people—emerged from World War II virtually unscathed. But when the communists took over, they decided to give intellectual (and potentially dissident) Kraków an injection of good Soviet values—in the form of heavy industry. They built Nowa Huta, an enormous steelworks and planned town for workers, on Kraków's outskirts, dooming the city to decades of smog.

St. John Paul II was born (as Karol Wojtyła) in nearby Wadowice and served as archbishop of Kraków before being called to Rome. Today, the hometown boy-turned-saint draws lots of pilgrims and is, for many, a big part of the city's attraction. Saintly ties aside, Kraków might be the most Catholic town in Europe's most Catholic country; be sure to visit a few of its many churches.

The story of Kraków continues to play out. In recent years, its Kazimierz district has come back to life—both with Jewish-themed cultural sights and with some of Eastern Europe's best bars, food trucks, and restaurants. This mingling of the historic with the contemporary typifies a city that always has been, and continues to be, Poland's heartbeat.

feet; to find these, use the stairs or the elevator right in the middle of the bus terminal. Note that some minibuses, such as those to Auschwitz, also leave from, or near, this station (though the buses and minibuses that go to the Wieliczka Salt Mine leave from nearby streets—see page 312). Because the bus station area can be challenging to navigate, leave yourself plenty of time before departure.

By Car

Centrum signs lead you into the Old Town—you'll know you're there when you hit the ring road that surrounds the Planty park. Parking garages surround the Old Town. Your hotelier can advise you on directions and parking.

KRAKÓW

By Plane

The modern **John Paul II Kraków-Balice Airport** is about 10 miles west of the center (airport code: KRK, airport info: tel. 12-295-5800, www.krakowairport.pl). The easiest way downtown is to hop on the slick and speedy **train** (follow signs up the ramp, then across the sky bridge to the parking garage; 9 zł, buy ticket from machine or from conductor on board, 2/hour, 18 minutes to Kraków's main train station—see arrival instructions earlier, under "By Train"). Alternatively, you can take **public bus** #208 or (at night) #902—follow signs to the right end of the building to find the stop (4 zł, goes to main bus station—see arrival instructions earlier, under "By Bus," 50-minute trip depending on traffic). There's also a **taxi** stand in front of the terminal (ask about the fare up front—rates vary, but official cabs should not exceed 90 zł, more expensive at night, about 30 minutes). You can also order an Uber (typically cheaper than a taxi), or arrange a taxi transfer in advance (such as with recommended driver Andrew Durman, listed later, under "Tours in Kraków").

Many budget flights—including those on Wizz Air and Ryanair—use the **International Airport Katowice in Pyrzowice** (Międzynarodowy Port Lotniczy Katowice w Pyrzowicach, airport code: KTW, www.katowice-airport.com). This airport is about 18 miles from the city of Katowice, which is about 50 miles west of Kraków. Direct buses run sporadically between Katowice Airport and Kraków's main train station area (50 zł, trip takes 1.75 hours, generally scheduled to meet incoming flights). You can also take the bus from Katowice Airport to Katowice's train station (hourly, 50 minutes), then take the train to Kraków (hourly, 1.5 hours). Wizz Air's website is useful for figuring out your connection: www.wizzair.com.

HELPFUL HINTS

Exchange Rate: 1 złoty (zł, or PLN) = about 25 cents; 4 zł = about $1.

Sightseeing Tips: Some sights are closed on Monday (including the Gallery of 19th-Century Polish Art, Szołayski House, and a few museums in Kazimierz), but many sights are open (including the churches and Jagiellonian University Museum, and in Kazimierz, all of the Jewish-themed sights). On Saturday, most of Kazimierz's Jewish-themed sights are closed. Before heading out, check the "Kraków at a Glance" sidebar on page 242. Also be aware of days that certain sights are free: On Sunday, the National Museum branches (including the Gallery of 19th-Century Polish Art in the Cloth Hall) are free, but some are open limited hours. On Monday, Schindler's Factory Museum is free (and especially crowded), as are two sights at Wawel Castle (open only mornings April-Oct). And on Tuesday, the Rynek Underground Museum is free (and crowded).

Remember: You may want to book ahead for the popular Schindler's Factory Museum, Wieliczka Salt Mine, and Rynek Underground Museum (see details in each listing)—and you definitely need to book well ahead for a visit to Auschwitz (see next chapter).

Bookstore: For an impressive selection of new and used English books, try **Massolit Books,** just west of the Old Town. They also have a café with drinks and light snacks, and a good children's section (daily 10:00-20:00, ulica Felicjanek 4, tel. 12-432-4150, www.massolit.com).

Laundry: Frania Café, halfway between the Old Town and Kazimierz, is an inviting café/pub with ample washers and dryers, relaxing ambience, free Wi-Fi, a full bar serving espresso drinks and laundry-themed hard drinks, long hours, and a friendly staff (you can pay extra for them to do it for you in 2-3 hours—consider dropping it off on your way to Kazimierz and picking it up on the way back, daily 7:30-24:00, ulica Starowiślna 26, mobile 783-945-021).

Betty Clean is a full-service laundry that's slightly closer to the Old Town, but pricey (15 zł/shirt, 27 zł/pants, takes 24 hours, 50 percent more for express 3-hour service, Mon-Fri 7:30-19:30, Sat 8:00-15:30, closed Sun, just outside the Planty park at ulica Zwierzyniecka 6, tel. 12-423-0848).

GETTING AROUND KRAKÓW

Kraków's top sights and best hotels are easily accessible by foot. You'll need wheels only if you're going to outlying areas (Kazimierz, Nowa Huta, John Paul II pilgrimage sites, and so on).

By Public Transit

Trams and buses zip around Kraków's urban sprawl. The same tickets work system-wide and can be purchased at most kiosks, or at the machines you'll see at most stops (these accept coins and small bills). You can also buy tickets on board—most trams have machines (coins only); otherwise, buy your ticket from the driver for a bit more. If your coin won't work in the machine, do as the locals do and rub it against the metal, then try inserting it again. For a good route planner, see www.jakdojade.pl.

A *bilet jednoprzejazdowy,* which covers any single journey (including transfers), costs 3.80 zł. However, many journeys you're likely to take—such as between the Old Town and Kazimierz—are likely to be brief, so you'll save by buying a 20-minute ticket *(20-minutowy)* for 2.80 zł. You can also get longer-term tickets for

KRAKÓW

24 hours (15 zł), 48 hours (24 zł), and 72 hours (36 zł). These prices are for a "one-zone" ticket, which covers almost everything of interest in Kraków (including Nowa Huta, the St. John Paul II pilgrimage sites, and the Kościuszko Mound)—unless you're headed for the airport or Wieliczka Salt Mine, which are beyond the city limits and require a slightly more expensive *aglomeracyjny* ticket (4 zł for a single journey). Always validate your ticket when you board the bus or tram (24-, 48-, and 72-hour tickets must be validated only the first time you use them).

Tram #3 is particularly handy. It goes from the side of the train station (Dworzec Główny Zachód) to the ring road in front of the station (Dworzec Główny), then stops at the eastern edge of the Old Town (Poczta Główna, at the main post office) before continuing to Kazimierz (Miodowa is at the north end, near ulica Szeroka; Św. Wawrzyńca is at the south end, near the old tram depot) and Podgórze, near Schindler's Factory Museum (plac Bohaterow Getta). Tram #24 is also useful: It stops at the western edge of the Old Town (Teatr Bagatela), then loops around the northern edge to stop near the Barbican (Stary Kleparz) before meeting up with tram #3 in front of the train station (Dworzec Główny) and continuing on to Kazimierz and Podgórze (same stops as listed above).

By Taxi or Uber

Only take cabs that are clearly marked with a company logo and telephone number. Legitimate Kraków taxis start at 7 zł and charge about 3 zł per kilometer (while unofficial taxis charge whatever they like). Rides generally cost less than 20 zł, but can take longer than you'd expect: Due to the Old Town's many traffic restrictions and pedestrian zones, a "short ride across town" may require looping all the way around the ring road. You're more likely to get the fair metered rate by calling or hailing a cab, rather than taking one waiting at tourist spots. To call a cab, try **Radio Taxi** (tel. 19191).

Uber is typically cheaper than Kraków's official taxis (though prices can spike during busy "surge" periods). In my experience, Polish Uber drivers (and their cars) are a bit less polished and professional than those back home—but they're cheap, usually friendly, and handy.

By Bike

The riverfront bike path is enticing on a nice day; the Planty park, while inviting, can be a bit crowded for biking. **Kraków Bike Tours** rents a wide variety of new, good-quality bikes (10 zł/first hour, cheaper per hour for longer rentals, 50 zł/day, 60 zł/24 hours; they also have electric bikes for about double these prices; daily 9:30-19:00, until 15:00 off-season, just off the Square at Grodzka 2; see listing later, under "Tours in Kraków"). Nearby, **KRK Bike Rental** rents basic, cheaper bikes (9 zł/hour, 50 zł/24 hours, daily 9:00-21:00, less in bad weather, closed Nov-March, ulica Św. Anny 4, mobile 509-267-733, www.krkbikerental.pl).

Tours in Kraków

Local Guides

Hiring a guide in Kraków is fun and affordable, and makes a huge difference in your experience. I've enjoyed working with three in particular, any of whom can show you the sights in Kraków and also have cars for day-tripping into the countryside: **Tomasz Klimek** (400 zł/half-day, 800 zł/day, slightly more with a car, mobile 605-231-923, tomasz.klimek@interia.pl); **Anna Bakowska** (400 zł/4 hours, 600 zł/day, mobile 604-151-293, www.leadertour.eu, leadertour@wp.pl); and **Marta Chmielowska** (350 zł/4 hours, 600 zł/day, same prices by foot or car, can be more for larger groups and for long-distance trips, mobile 603-668-008, martachm7@gmail.com). I wouldn't bother hiring a guide for the trip to Auschwitz (which generally costs 600-700 zł)—only official Auschwitz guides can legally give tours onsite, so you'll wind up joining one of the tours once there; instead, it's a better value to hire a driver (like Andrew, listed next).

Drivers

Since Kraków is such a useful home base for day trips, it can be handy to splurge on a private driver for door-to-door service. **Andrew (Andrzej) Durman,** a Pole who lived in Chicago and speaks fluent English, is a gregarious driver, translator, miracle worker, and all-around great guy. While not a licensed tour guide, Andrew is an eager conversationalist and loves to provide lively commentary while you roll. Although you can hire Andrew for a simple airport transfer or an Auschwitz day trip, he also enjoys tackling more ambitious itineraries, from helping you track down your Polish roots to taking you on multiple-day journeys around Poland and beyond. These prices are transportation only for up to 4 people: 400 zł to Auschwitz, 250 zł to Wieliczka Salt Mine, 80 zł for transfer from Kraków-Balice Airport, 500 zł for transfer from Katowice Airport, or 600 zł for an all-day trip into the countryside—such as into the High Tatras or to track down your Polish roots near Kraków (more to cover gas costs for trips longer than 100 km one-way; long-distance transfers for up to 4 people to Prague, Budapest, Vienna, or Berlin for 1,800 zł—or 200 zł extra if he picks you up there; also available for multiday trips—price negotiable, all prices higher for bigger van, tel. 12-411-5630, mobile 602-243-306, www.tour-service.pl, andrew@tour-service.pl). If he's busy, Andrew may send you with one of his English-speaking colleagues, such as Lucas or Matthew.

KRAKÓW

Kraków at a Glance

▲▲▲**Main Market Square** Stunning heart of Kraków and a people magnet any time of day. See page 253.

▲▲▲**Schindler's Factory Museum** Building where Oskar Schindler saved over 1,000 Jewish workers, now an engaging exhibit about Kraków's WWII experience. **Hours:** April-Oct Mon 10:00-16:00 (closes at 14:00 first Mon of month), Tue-Sun 9:00-20:00; Nov-March Mon 10:00-14:00, Tue-Sun 10:00-18:00. See page 302.

▲▲**Planty** Once a moat, now a scenic park encircling the city. See page 246.

▲▲**St. Mary's Church** Landmark church with extraordinary wood-carved Gothic altarpiece. **Hours:** Mon-Sat 11:30-18:00, Sun from 14:00. See page 249.

▲▲**Cloth Hall** Fourteenth-century market hall with souvenirs. **Hours:** Summer Mon-Fri 9:00-18:00, Sat-Sun until 15:00 or later; winter Mon-Fri 9:00-16:00, Sat-Sun until 15:00. See page 254.

▲▲**St. Francis Basilica** Lovely Gothic church with some of Poland's best Art Nouveau. **Hours:** Mon-Sat 10:00-16:00, Sun 13:00-15:30; open longer hours for services and prayer. See page 257.

▲▲**Wawel Cathedral** Poland's national church, with tons of tombs, a crypt, and a climbable tower. **Hours:** Mon-Sat 9:00-17:00, Sun from 12:30; Oct-March daily until 16:00. See page 264.

▲▲**Wawel Castle Grounds** Historic hilltop with views, castle, cathedral, courtyard with chakras, and a passel of museums. **Hours:** Grounds open daily 6:00 until dusk, but many of the museums closed Mon, and Sun in winter. See page 269.

▲▲**Gallery of 19th-Century Polish Art** Worthwhile collection of paintings by should-be-famous artists, upstairs in the Cloth Hall. **Hours:** Tue-Fri 9:00-17:00, Sat 10:00-18:00, Sun 10:00-16:00, closed Mon. See page 275.

KRAKÓW

Local guide Marta Chmielowska's husband, **Czesław** (a.k.a. Chester), can also drive you to nearby locations (350 zł for all-day trip to Auschwitz for 1-3 people, 450 zł for 4-8 people; 250 zł to Wieliczka Salt Mine, including waiting time, or a very long day combining Wieliczka and Auschwitz for 600 zł; 1,700 zł for a transfer to Prague; to book, see Marta's contact information, earlier).

▲▲**Rynek Underground Museum** Exhibit on medieval Kraków filling excavated cellars beneath the Main Market Square. **Hours:** Mon 10:00-20:00 (closed second Mon of each month), Tue until 16:00, Wed-Sun until 22:00, shorter hours in winter. See page 282.

▲▲**Old Jewish Cemetery** Poignant burial site in Kazimierz, with graves from 1552 to 1800. **Hours:** Sun-Fri 9:00-16:00, sometimes until 18:00 May-Sept, closes earlier in winter and by sundown on Fri, closed Sat. See page 289.

▲**Czartoryski Museum** Varied collection, with European paintings and Polish armor, handicrafts, and decorative arts. **Hours:** Likely closed for restoration. See page 280.

▲**Jagiellonian University Museum Collegium Maius** Proud collection of historic university, surrounding a tranquil courtyard where medieval professors lived. **Hours:** Entry with 30-minute guided tour Mon-Fri 10:00-14:20, Tue and Thu until 17:20 in April-Oct, no tours Sat-Sun; one-hour version in English usually Mon-Fri at 13:00, no tours Sat-Sun; free entry without tour Sat 10:00-13:30. See page 284.

▲**New Jewish Cemetery** Graveyard with tombs from after 1800, partly restored after Nazi desecration. **Hours:** Sun-Fri 8:00-16:00, closed Sat. See page 297.

▲**Ethnographic Museum** Traditional rural Polish life on display. **Hours:** Tue-Sun 10:00-19:00, closed Mon. See page 295.

▲**Pharmacy Under the Eagle** Small exhibit about the Holocaust in Kraków, including three evocative films. **Hours:** Mon 10:00-14:00, Tue-Sun 9:00-17:00; closed second Tue of each month. See page 299.

▲**Museum of Contemporary Art in Kraków** Today's thought-provoking art, displayed in renovated old warehouses behind Schindler's Factory Museum. **Hours:** Tue-Sun 11:00-19:00, closed Mon. See page 305.

KRAKÓW

Walking Tours

Various companies run daily city walking tours in English in summer. Most do a three-hour tour of the Old Town as well as a three-hour tour of Kazimierz, the Jewish district (most charge about 50 zł per tour, depending on company). Three people can hire their own great private local guide for about the same amount of money they'd spend on a group walking tour.

Because the scene is continually evolving, it's best to pick up local fliers (the TI works exclusively with one company, See Kraków, but hotel reception desks generally have more options), then choose the one that fits your interests and schedule. You'll also see ads for "free" tours—which are, of course, not really free (the guide gets paid only if you tip generously).

Food Tours

In this stealth-foodie city, you have multiple good options. **Eat Polska**—which does a marvelous job of connecting food to culture and history, making the experience equal parts informative and delicious—does top-notch, insightful food tours (at 13:00, 290 zł, 4 hours) and vodka tours with food pairings (at 17:00, 290 zł, 3.5 hours; for details on either, and other culinary experiences, see www.eatpolska.com). **Urban Adventures,** more casual and locally based, does evening food walks that basically assemble a full meal with a little sightseeing thrown in (at 18:00, 310 zł, RS%—email to ask for discount code, 3 hours, www.urbanadventures.com, info@urbanadventures.com).

Crazy Guides

This irreverent company offers tours to the communist suburb of Nowa Huta and other outlying sights. For details, see page 315.

Bike Tours

Kraków Bike Tours is a well-established operation that runs daily four-hour bike tours in English, with 25 stops in the Old Town, Kazimierz, and Podgórze (90 zł, May-Sept daily at 10:00 and 15:00, spring and fall only 1/day at 12:00, confirm schedule and meet tour at their office down the passage at Grodzka 2—right at the bottom of the Square, mobile 510-394-657, www.krakowbiketour.com).

Bus Tours to Auschwitz or Wieliczka

As Kraków is so easily enjoyed on foot, taking a bus tour doesn't make much sense in town. But they can be handy for reaching outlying sights. Various tour companies run big-bus itineraries to Auschwitz (6 hours), Wieliczka Salt Mine (4 hours), and other regional side trips (each itinerary around 150-180 zł).

Given the difficulty of reserving your own appointment at Auschwitz (explained in the next chapter), one of these bus tours—which include a guided tour of the camp—may be your most convenient option. **See Kraków** (which has a monopoly at the TI, www.seekrakow.com) and **Discover Cracow** (www.discovercracow.com) both use smaller 19-seat minibuses. They sometimes offer hotel pickup, which seems convenient, but you'll waste a lot of time driving around the city to other hotels. **Cracow City Tours** (www.cracowcitytours.com) uses larger 50-seat buses with a central pickup point (on plac Matejki, across the ring road from the Barbican, at the north end of the Old Town).

At any company, the on-bus guiding is hit-or-miss but largely irrelevant—since you'll be handed off to an official Auschwitz guide once at the camp. Note that the many tour offices and faux-TIs you'll see around town simply sell tickets for these companies. If you waited too long to reserve at Auschwitz and are desperate to get in at short notice, try dropping in to various agencies around town to see if anyone has space.

Buggy Tours

You'll see (and hear) horse-drawn buggies that trot around Kraków from the Main Market Square. The going rate is a hefty 200 zł for a 30-minute tour to the castle and back. After dark, they're lit up like fanciful Cinderella coaches—a memorable scene, all lined up in front of St. Mary's Church.

Golf-Cart Tours

Several outfits around town (including on the Square) offer tours on a golf cart with recorded commentary. Given the limits on car traffic in the old center, this can be a handy way to connect the sights for those with limited mobility. Generally you'll pay about 180 zł for a 30-minute tour around the Old Town; to extend the trip to Kazimierz, it's 360 zł; and adding the Podgórze former Jewish ghetto and Schindler's Factory Museum costs a total of 540 zł (these prices are for the entire golf cart, up to 5 people).

Kraków's Royal Way Walk

This self-guided walk is designed to link up most of Kraków's major sights. Most of the walk follows a route called the "Royal Way," because the king used to follow this same path when he returned to Kraków after a journey. After the capital moved to Warsaw, most kings still used Wawel Cathedral for important events. In fact, from 1320 to 1795, nearly every Polish king traversed Kraków's Royal Way at least twice: on the day he was crowned and on the day he was buried. You could sprint through this walk in about an hour and a half (less than a mile altogether), but it's much more fun if you take it like the kings did...slowly.

• *Begin just outside the main gate (the Florian Gate) at the north end of the Old Town. Face the tall, rectangular tower.*

▲Barbican (Barbakan) and City Walls

Tatars—those mysterious and terrifying invaders from Central Asia—destroyed Kraków in 1241. To better defend their rebuilt city, Krakovians built this wall. The original rampart had 47 watch-

towers and eight gates. (You can
see a bronze model of the wall
just to the right of the tower.)

Now turn around. The big,
round defensive fort standing
outside the wall is the **Barbican,**
built to provide extra fortification to weak sections—namely,
the gates. Imagine how it looked
in 1500, when the Barbican
stood outside the town moat with a long bridge leading to the Florian Gate—the city's main entryway. Today you can pay to scramble along the passages and fortifications of the Barbican, though
there's little to see inside, other than a small but good exhibit giving you a sense of how the walls were designed (9 zł, April-Oct
daily 10:30-18:00, closed Nov-March). The same ticket also lets
you climb up onto the surviving stretch of Old Town walls flanking
the Florian Gate (entry from inside walls).

• *The greenbelt within which the Barbican sits is called the...*

▲▲Planty

By the 19th century, Kraków's no-longer-necessary city wall had
fallen into disrepair. As the Austrian authorities were doing all
over their empire, they decided
to tear down what remained,
fill in the moat, and plant trees.
(The name comes not from the
English "plant" but from the
Polish *plantovac,* or "flat"—because they flattened out this area
to create it.) Today, the Planty
is a beautiful park that stretches
2.5 miles around the entire pe-

rimeter of Kraków's Old Town. To give your Kraków visit an extra
dimension, consider a quick bike ride around the Planty (best early
in the morning, when it's less crowded) with a side trip along the
parklike riverbank near Wawel Castle; you'll see bike-rental places
around the Old Town, including the two mentioned on page 240.

Circle around the left side of the Barbican. On your left, keep
an eye out for a unique monument depicting an elderly, bearded
man in the corner of a huge frame. This honors **Jan Matejko,** arguably Poland's most beloved painter, who specialized in giant-scale
epic historical scenes several times larger than this frame. We'll
hear Matejko's name many more times on this walk.

As you continue around the Barbican, look down to see the

much lower ground level around its base—making it easy to imagine that the Planty was once anything but flat.

• *Across the busy street from the Barbican, standing in the middle of the long park, is the...*

Grunwald Monument

This memorial honors one of the most important battles in the history of a nation that has seen more than its share: the Battle of Grunwald on July 15, 1410, when Polish and Lithuanian forces banded together to finally defeat the Teutonic Knights, who had been running roughshod over the lands along the Baltic. (For more on the battle and the knights, see page 507.) Lying dramatically slain at the base of this monument, like a toppled Goliath, is the defeated Grand Master of the Teutonic Knights—German crusaders who had originally been brought to Poland as mercenaries. It's easy to see this vanquished statue as a thinly veiled metaphor for one of Poland's powerful, often domineering neighbors. When the Nazis took power here, this statue was one of the first things they tore down. When they left, it was one of the first things the Poles put back up.

• *If you'd like to see a slice of Krakovian life, side-trip one block to the left of the monument, to the local farmers market.*

The Old Market (Stary Kleparz)

The colorful Old Market offers a refreshing dash of Kraków that has nothing to do with history or tourism. It's just lots of hard-scrabble people selling what they grow or knit, and lots of others buying. Wander around as if on a cultural scavenger hunt. Find the freshest doughnuts *(pączki)*, the most popular bakery, the villager selling slippers she knitted, the smelliest smoked-fish stand, and the old man with the smoked cheese (Mon-Sat 7:00-18:00—but busiest and most interesting in the morning, closed Sun).

• *Now retrace your steps to the Barbican, and enter the Old Town by walking through the...*

Florian Gate (Brama Floriańska)

As you approach the gate, look up at the **crowned white eagle**—representing courage and freedom—the historic symbol of the Polish people.

Inside the gate, notice the little chapel on the right with a replica of the famous **Black Madonna of Częstochowa**, the most important religious symbol among Polish Catholics. The original, located in Częstochowa (70 miles north of Kraków), is an Eastern Orthodox-style icon of mysterious origin with several mystical legends attached to it. After the icon's believed role in protecting a monastery from Swedish invaders in the mid-17th century, it was named "Queen and Protector of Poland."

Once through the gate, look back at it. High above is **St. Florian,** patron of the fire brigade. As fire was a big concern for a wooden city of the 15th century, Florian gets a place of honor.

You'll often see traditionally clad **musicians** near the gate, performing their lilting folk melodies for tips.

• *You're standing at the head of Kraków's historic (and now touristic) gamut...*

▲Floriańska Street (Ulica Floriańska)

Hanging on the inside of the city wall in both directions is a makeshift **art gallery,** where—traditionally—starving students hawk the works they've painted at the Academy of Fine Arts (across the busy street from the Barbican). These days, the art is so kitschy, this stretch of the town's fortification is nicknamed "The Wailing Wall." The entrance to get on top of the wall—covered by the Barbican ticket—is at the left end of this starving artists' gallery. If you detoured even farther along the wall, soon you'd reach the Czartoryski Museum, an eclectic collection of artifacts that's due to reopen any year now (see page 280).

Now begin strolling down **Floriańska street** (floh-ree-AHN-skah). Notice that all over town, storefronts advertising themselves as "tourist information" offices are actually tourist sales agencies (legitimate TIs are listed on page 231). Along with the fast-food joints, also notice some uniquely Polish snacks: The various pizza and kebab windows also sell *zapiekanka*—a toasted baguette with toppings, similar to a French bread pizza. Or, for an even quicker bite, buy an *obwarzanek* (ring-shaped, bagel-like roll, typically fresh) from a street vendor; many still use their old-fashioned blue carts.

About halfway down the first block, on the left (at #45, round green sign), look for **Jama Michalika** ("Michael's Cave"). Around the turn of the 20th century, this dark, atmospheric café was a hangout of the *Młoda Polska* (Young Poland) movement—the Polish answer to Art Nouveau (explained on page 253). The walls are papered with sketches from poor artists—local bohemians who couldn't pay their tabs. Today it hosts a folk troupe that performs traditional music and dance with dinner many evenings (see listing under "Entertainment in Kraków," page 324). Poke around inside this circa-1900 time warp and appreciate this unique art gallery.

About a block farther down, at #20 (on the right), **Staropolskie Trunki** ("Old Polish Drinks") offers an education in vodka, with a long bar and countless local vodkas and liquors—all open and ready to be tasted (four tastes for 10 zł with an explanation from the bartender, daily 10:00-late).

• *Continue into the Main Market Square, where you'll run into...*

▲▲St. Mary's Church (Kościół Mariacki)

A church has stood on this spot for 800 years. The original church was destroyed by the first Tatar invasion in 1241, but all subsequent versions—including the current one—have been built on the same foundation. You can look down the sides to see how the Main Market Square has risen about seven feet over the centuries.

How many church towers does St. Mary's have? Technically, the answer is one. The shorter tower belongs to the church; the taller one is a municipal watchtower, from which you'll hear a bugler playing the hourly *hejnał* song. According to Kraków's favorite legend, during that first Tatar invasion, a town watchman saw the enemy approaching and sounded the alarm. Before he could finish the tune, an arrow pierced his throat—which is why, even today, the *hejnał* stops suddenly partway through. Today's buglers—12 in all—are firemen first, musicians second. Each one works a 24-hour shift up there, playing the *hejnał* four times on the hour—with one bugle call for each direction. (It's even broadcast on national Polish radio at noon.) While you're in Kraków, you'll certainly hear one of these tiny, hourly, broken performances.

KRAKÓW

To see one of the most finely crafted Gothic altarpieces anywhere, it's worth paying admission to enter the church. The front door is open 14 hours a day and is free to those who come to pray, but tourists use the door around the right side (buy your ticket across the little square from this door).

Cost and Hours: 10 zł, Mon-Sat 11:30-18:00, Sun from 14:00.

Visiting the Church: Inside, you're struck by the lavish decor. This was the church of the everyday townspeople, built out of a spirit of competition with the royal high church at Wawel Castle.

At the altar is one of the best medieval woodcarvings in existence—the exquisite, three-part altarpiece by German Veit Stoss (Wit Stwosz in Polish). Carved in 12 years and completed in 1489, it's packed with emotion rare in Gothic art. Get as close as you can and study the remarkable details. Stoss used oak for the structural parts and linden trunks for the figures. The open altar depicts the Dormition (death—or, if splitting theological hairs, heavenly sleep) of the Virgin. The artist catches the apostles around Mary, reacting in the seconds after she collapses. Mary is depicted in three stages: life leaving her earthly body, being escorted to heaven by Jesus, and (at the very top) being crowned in heaven. The six scenes on the sides are the Annunciation, birth of Jesus, visit by the Three Magi, Jesus' Resurrection, his Ascension, and Mary becoming the mother of the apostles at Pentecost.

There's more to St. Mary's than the altar. While you're admiring this church's art, notice the flowery Neo-Gothic painting covering the choir walls. Stare up into the starry, starry blue ceiling. As you wander around, consider that the church was renovated a century ago by three Polish geniuses from two very different artistic generations: the venerable positivist Jan Matejko and his Art Nouveau students, Stanisław Wyspiański and Józef Mehoffer (we'll learn more about these two later on our walk). The huge silver bird under the organ loft in back is that symbol of Poland, the crowned white eagle.

Tower Climb: You may be able to climb up the 271 stairs to the top of the taller tower to visit the *hejnał* fireman. While it's a huff—with some claustrophobic stone stairs, followed by some steep, acrophobic wooden ones—the view up top is the best you'll find of the Square (15 zł, pay at the ticket office for the church, departs at :10 and :40 past each hour, Tue-Sat 9:10-11:40 & 13:10-17:40, Sun 13:10-17:40 only, closed Mon; March and Nov-Dec open only good-weather Thu-Sat; closed Jan-Feb).

• *Leaving the church, notice the neck clamps dangling from the exterior walls near the side door. If you were leaving Mass in centuries past,*

Kazimierz the Great (1333-1370)

Out of the many centuries of Polish kings, only one earned the nickname "great," and he's the only one worth remembering: Kazimierz the Great.

K. the G., who ruled Poland from Kraków in the 14th century, was one of those larger-than-life medieval kings who left his mark on all fronts—from war to diplomacy, art patronage to womanizing. His scribes bragged that Kazimierz "found a Poland made of wood, and left one made of brick and stone." He put Kraków on the map as a major European capital. He founded many villages (some of which still bear his name—including one that's an important neighborhood of Kraków) and replaced wooden structures with stone ones (such as Kraków's Cloth Hall). Kazimierz also established the Kraków Academy (today's Jagiellonian University), the second-oldest university in Central Europe. And to protect all of these new building projects, he heavily fortified Poland by building a series of imposing forts and walls around its perimeter. If you have a 50-zł note, take a look at it: That's Kazimierz the Great on the front, and on the back you'll see his capital, Cracovia, and the most important town he founded, Casmirus.

Most of all, Kazimierz is remembered as a progressive, tolerant king. In the 14th century, other nations were deporting—or even interning—their Jewish subjects, who were commonly scapegoated for anything that went wrong. But the enlightened Kazimierz created policies that granted Jews more opportunities (often related to banking and trade) and allowed them a chance for higher social standing—establishing the country as a safe haven for Jews in Europe.

Kazimierz the Great was the last of Poland's long-lived Piast dynasty. Although he left no male heir—at least, no legitimate one—Kazimierz's advances set the stage for Poland's Golden Age (14th-16th century). After his death, Poland united with Lithuania (against the common threat of the Teutonic Knights), the Jagiellonian dynasty was born, and Poland became one of Europe's mightiest medieval powers.

KRAKÓW

there would be criminals chained here for public humiliation. You'd spit on them before turning right and stepping into one of the biggest market squares anywhere.

▲▲▲Main Market Square (Rynek Główny), a.k.a. "The Square"

Kraków's marvelous Square, one of Europe's most gasp-worthy public spaces, bustles with street musicians, colorful flower stalls, cotton-candy vendors, loitering teenagers, the local breakdancing troupe, businesspeople commuting by foot, gawking tourists, soap-balloon-blowers, and the lusty coos of pigeons. The Square is where

Kraków lives. It's often filled with various special events, markets, and festivals. The biggest are the seasonal markets before Easter and Christmas, but you're likely to stumble on something special going on just about any time of year (especially June through Aug).

The Square was established in the 13th century, when the city had to be rebuilt after being flattened by the Tatars. At the time, it was the biggest square in medieval Europe. It was illegal to sell anything on the street, so everything had to be sold here on the Main Market Square. It was divided into smaller markets, such as the butcher stalls, the ironworkers' tents, and the still-standing Cloth Hall (described later).

Notice the modern **fountain** with the glass pyramid at this end of the Square. A major excavation of the surrounding area created a museum of Kraków's medieval history that literally sprawls beneath the Square (for more on the recommended **Rynek Underground Museum,** see page 282).

The statue in the middle of the Square is a traditional meeting place for Krakovians. It depicts Romantic poet **Adam Mickiewicz** (1789-1855), who's considered the "Polish Shakespeare." His epic masterpiece, *Pan Tadeusz,* is still regarded as one of the greatest works in Polish literature. A wistful, nostalgic tale of Polish-Lithuanian nobility, *Pan Tadeusz* stirred patriotism in a Poland that had been dismantled by surrounding empires through a series of three Partitions.

If you survey the Square from here, you'll notice that the Old Town was spared the bombs of World War II. The Nazis considered Kraków a city with Germanic roots and wanted it saved. But they were quick to destroy any symbols of Polish culture or pride. The statue of Adam Mickiewicz, for example, was pulled down immediately after occupation.

Near the end of the Square, you'll see the tiny, cubical, copper-domed **Church of St. Adalbert,** one of the oldest churches in Kraków (10th century). This Romanesque structure predates the Square. Like St. Mary's (described earlier), it seems to be at an angle because it's aligned east-west, as was the custom when it was built. (In other words, the churches aren't crooked—the Square is. Any other "crooked" building you see around town predates the 13th-century grid created during the rebuilding of Kraków.)

Drinks are reasonably priced at cafés on the Square (most around 10-15 zł). Find a spot where you like the view and the

The Młoda Polska (Young Poland) Art Movement

Polish art in the late 19th century was ruled by positivism, a school with a very literal, straightforward focus on Polish his-

tory (Jan Matejko led the charge; see page 399). But when the new generation of Kraków's artists came into their own in the early 1900s, they decided that the old school was exactly that. Though moved by the same spirit and goals as the previous generation—evoking Polish patriotism at a time when their country was being occupied—these new artists used very different methods. They were inspired by a renewed appreciation of folklore and peasant life. Rather than being earnest and literal (an 18th-century Polish war hero on horseback), the new art was playful and highly symbolic (the artist frolicking in a magical garden in the idyllic Polish countryside). This movement became known as Młoda Polska (Young Poland)—Art Nouveau with a Polish accent.

Stanisław Wyspiański (vees-PAYN-skee, 1869-1907) was the leader of Młoda Polska. He produced beautiful artwork, from simple drawings to the stirring stained-glass images in Kraków's St. Francis Basilica. Wyspiański was an expert at capturing human faces with realistic detail, emotion, and personality. The versatile Wyspiański was also an accomplished stage designer and writer. His patriotic play *The Wedding*—about the nuptials of a big-city artist and a peasant girl—is regarded as one of Poland's finest dramas. You'll find excellent examples of Wyspiański's art in Kraków's St. Francis Basilica and Szołayski House, and in Warsaw's National Museum.

Józef Mehoffer (may-HOH-fehr), Wyspiański's good friend and rival, was another great Młoda Polska artist. Mehoffer's style is more expressionistic and abstract than Wyspiański's, often creating an otherworldly effect. See Mehoffer's work in Kraków's St. Francis Basilica and at the artist's former residence (see the Józef Mehoffer House); and in Warsaw, at the National Museum.

Other names to look for include **Jacek Malczewski** (mahl-CHEHV-skee), who specialized in self-portraits, and **Olga Boznańska** (bohz-NAHN-skah), the movement's only prominent female artist. Both are featured in Warsaw's National Museum; Malczewski's works also appear in Kraków's Gallery of 19th-Century Polish Art.

KRAKÓW

chairs, then sit and sip. Order a coffee, Polish *piwo* (beer, such as Żywiec, Okocim, or Lech), or a shot of *wódka* (Żubrówka is a quality brand; for more on Polish drinks, see page 224). For a higher vantage point, the Cloth Hall's **Café Szał terrace**—overlooking the Square and St. Mary's Church—offers one of the best views in town (open daily until 24:00, affordable drinks, some light meals, slow service, enter through Gallery of 19th-Century Polish Art entrance).

As the Square buzzes around you, imagine this place before 1989. There were no outdoor cafés, no touristy souvenir stands, and no salespeople hawking cotton candy or neon-lit whirligigs. The communist government shut down all but a handful of the businesses. They didn't want people to congregate here—they should be at home, because "a rested worker is a productive worker." The buildings were covered with soot from the nearby Lenin Steelworks in Nowa Huta. The communists denied the pollution, and when the student "Green Brigades" staged a demonstration in this Square to raise awareness in the 1970s, they were immediately arrested. How things have changed.

• *The huge, yellow building right in the middle of the Square is the...*

▲▲Cloth Hall (Sukiennice)

In the Middle Ages, this was the place where cloth sellers had their market stalls. Kazimierz the Great turned the Cloth Hall into a permanent structure in the 14th century. In 1555, it burned down and was replaced by the current building. The crowned letter *S* (at the top of the gable above the entryway) stands for King Sigismund the Old, who commissioned this version of the hall. As Sigismund fancied all things Italian (including women—he married an Italian princess), this

structure is in the Italianate Renaissance style. Sigismund kicked off a nationwide trend, and you'll still see Renaissance-style buildings like this one all over the country, making the style typically Polish. We'll see more works by Sigismund's imported Italian architects at Wawel Castle.

The Cloth Hall is still a functioning market—selling mostly souvenirs, including wood carvings, chess sets, jewelry (especially amber), painted boxes, and trinkets (see hours under "Shopping in Kraków," page 318). Cloth Hall prices are slightly inflated, but still cheap by American standards. You're paying a little extra for

the convenience and the atmosphere, but you'll see locals buying gifts here, too.

Pay WCs are at each end of the Cloth Hall. The upstairs of the Cloth Hall is home to the excellent **Gallery of 19th-Century Polish Art** (enter behind the statue of Adam; for a self-guided tour, see page 275).

• *Browse through the Cloth Hall passageway. As you emerge into the sleepier half of the Square, the big tower on your left is the...*

Town Hall Tower

This is all that remains of a town hall building from the 14th century—when Kraków was the powerful capital of Poland. After the 18th-century Partitions of Poland, Kraków's prominence took a nosedive. As the town's importance crumbled, so did its town hall. It was cheaper to tear down the building than to repair it, and all that was left standing was this nearly 200-foot-tall tower. In summer, you can climb the tower, stopping along the way to poke around an exhibit on Kraków history, but the views from up top are disappointing (9 zł, free on Mon, open March-Oct daily 10:30-18:00—except closed first Tue of each month, Nov-Dec 11:00-17:00, closed Jan-Feb).

Nearby: The **gigantic head** at the base of the Town Hall Tower is a sculpture by contemporary artist Igor Mitoraj, who studied here in Kraków.

Typical of Mitoraj's works, the head is an empty shell that appears to be wrapped in cloth. While some locals enjoy having a work by their fellow Krakovian in such a prominent place, others disapprove of its sharp contrast with the Square's genteel Old World ambience. Tourists enjoy playing peek-a-boo with the head's eyes.

• *When you're finished on the Square, we'll head toward Wawel Hill. The official Royal Way makes a beeline for the castle, but we'll take a scenic detour to see some less touristy back streets, visit Kraków's historic university and one of its best churches, and go for a quick walk through the Planty park.*

Exit the square at the corner nearest the Town Hall Tower, down ulica Św. Anny. After one block, turn left onto Jagiellońska street. Enter the courtyard of the big, red-brick building on your right.

Jagiellonian University and the Collegium Maius

Kraków had the second university in Central Europe (founded in 1364, after Prague's). Over the centuries, Jagiellonian U. has boasted such illustrious grads as Copernicus and St. John Paul II.

And today, the city's character is still defined largely by its huge student population (numbering around 150,000). Many of the university buildings fill the area to the west of the Old Town, so you'll see more students (and fewer tourist traps) in this part of town than elsewhere.

This building—called the Collegium Maius—is the historic heart of Kraków's university culture. It dates from the 15th century. In the Middle Ages, professors were completely devoted to their scholarly pursuits. They were unmarried and lived, ate, and slept here in an almost monastic environment. They taught downstairs and lived upstairs. In many ways, this building feels more like a monastery than a university. While this courtyard is the most interesting part, you can also tour the interior (for details, see page 284). The courtyard also hosts free temporary exhibits; look for posters.

The university also comes with some chilling history. On November 6, 1939, the occupying Nazis called all professors together for a meeting. With 183 gathered unknowingly in a hall, they were unceremoniously loaded into trucks and sent to their deaths in concentration camps. Hitler knew: If you want to decapitate a culture, you kill its intelligentsia.

Before you leave, if you're a fan of rich, thick hot chocolate, enjoy a cup at **Kawiarnia U Pęcherza** (down the stairs near the entrance)—widely regarded as the best in town.

Head down the *sgraffito*-lined passage on the side of the courtyard (it's the first door on your left as you entered the courtyard—just past the little security office). You'll emerge into the **Professors' Garden,** a tranquil space filled with red brick, ivy, stony statues, and inviting benches (open daily 9:00-18:30 or until dusk, closed in winter).

• *Exit the garden through the fancy gate and turn right on Jagiellońska. Spot any students? You'll follow this for two more blocks, passing the much larger and newer, but still red-brick,* **Collegium Novum** *build-*

ing—the modern administrative headquarters of Jag U., built in the late 19th century to commemorate the 500th anniversary of the building we just left.

Jagiellońska dead-ends at a dynamic statue on a pillar. Turn left into the inviting **Planty**—*the ring park we saw at the start of this walk. You'll stroll about five minutes through the Planty—dodging bikes and hearing the rattle of trams through the trees—with the Old Town buildings on your left and the ring road through the park on your right. When you reach a street with tram tracks, cross it and turn left. Pause in the park just before the church, and take note of the light-yellow building on the left (across the street), with a picture of St. John Paul II smiling down from above the stone doorway.*

Archbishop's Palace

This building was St. John Paul II's residence when he was the archbishop of Kraków. And even after he became pope, it remained his home-away-from-Rome for visits to his hometown. After a long day of saying formal Mass during his visits to Kraków, he'd wind up here. Weary as he was, before going to bed he'd stand in the window above the entrance for hours, chatting casually with the people assembled below— about religion, but also about sports, current events, and whatever was on their minds.

In 2005, when the pope's health deteriorated, this street filled with his supporters, even though he was in Rome. For days, somber locals focused their vigil on this same window, their eyes fixed on a black crucifix that had been placed here. At 21:37 on the night of April 2, 2005, the pope passed away in Rome. Ten thousand Krakovians were on this street, under this window, listening to a Mass broadcast on loudspeakers from the church. When the priest announced the pope's death, every single person simultaneously fell to their knees in silence. For the next several days, thousands of the faithful continued to stand on this street, staring intently at the window where they last saw the man they considered to be the greatest Pole.

• *Now go through the back door of one of Kraków's finest churches...*

▲▲St. Francis Basilica (Bazylika Św. Franciszka)

This beautiful Gothic church, which was St. John Paul II's home church while he was archbishop of Kraków, features some of Poland's best Art Nouveau in situ (in the setting for which it was

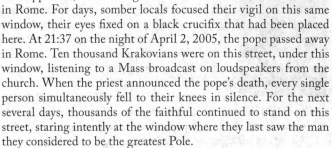

intended). After an 1850 fire, it was redecorated by the two leading members of the Młoda Polska (Young Poland) movement: Stanisław Wyspiański and Józef Mehoffer. The glorious decorations inside this church are the result of their great rivalry run amok.

Cost and Hours: Free; open for visitors Mon-Sat 10:00-16:00, Sun 13:00-15:30; longer hours for services and prayer.

Visiting the Basilica: Step through the door and let your eyes adjust to the low light. Take a few steps up the nave, pausing at the third pew on the left. On the back of this pew, notice the **silver plate** labeled "Jan Paweł II"—marking JPII's favorite place to pray when he lived in the Archbishop's Palace across the street.

Now walk another 20 feet down the nave, and notice the painting on the right, with an orange-and-blue background. This depicts **St. Maksymilian Kolbe,** the Catholic priest who sacrificed his own life to save a fellow inmate at Auschwitz in 1941 (notice the *16670*—his concentration camp number—etched into the background; read his story on page 356). Kolbe is particularly beloved here, as he actually served at this church.

Now turn around and look up above the door you entered. There, in all its glory, is the stained-glass window titled *God the Father Let It Be,* created by the great Art Nouveau artist Stanisław Wyspiański—and regarded by some as his finest masterpiece. (For more on Wyspiański, see page 253.) The colors beneath the Creator change from yellows and oranges (fire) to soothing blues (water), depending on the light. Wyspiański was supposedly inspired by Michelangelo's vision of God in the Sistine Chapel, though he used a street beggar to model God's specific features. Wyspiański also painted the delightful floral stained-glass windows that line the nave, high up—fitting for a church dedicated to a saint so famous for his spiritual connection to nature.

Now turn back around to face the main altar, and head into the **chapel** on the left (marked *Całun Turyński*). This important chapel houses a replica of the Shroud of Turin—which, since it touched the original shroud, is also considered a holy relic (displayed along the side of the chapel). At the main altar in this chapel, notice the plaques honoring Michał Tomaszek and Zbigniew Strzałkowski. These two Polish priests traveled to Peru as missionaries. There,

KRAKÓW

they (along with an Italian priest) were murdered by communist guerrillas calling themselves the Shining Path. Today they are considered martyrs.

Before leaving this chapel, look high on the walls at the glorious Stations of the Cross. These are painted by **Józef Mehoffer**—a friend and rival of Wyspiański—as a response to Wyspiański's work.

Now head back into the nave, turn left, and walk toward the main altar. (If a service is going on, you may not be able to get very far—just look from here.) On the walls, notice Wyspiański's gorgeous Art Nouveau floral patterns.

Up in the apse, take a moment to appreciate the Wyspiański-designed **stained-glass windows** flanking the high altar. On the right is St. Francis, the church's namesake. On the left is the Blessed Salomea—a medieval Polish woman who became queen of Hungary but later returned to Poland and entered a convent after her husband's death. Notice she's dropping a crown—repudiating the earthly world and giving herself over to the simple, stop-and-smell-God's-roses lifestyle of St. Francis. Salomea (who's buried in a side chapel) founded this church. Notice also the Mucha-like paintings by Wyspiański on the pilasters between the windows...yet one more sumptuous Art Nouveau detail in this church that's so rich with them.

• *Head back outside. If no services are going on, you can slip out the side door, to the left of the altar. Otherwise, head back out the way you came and hook right. Either way, you're heading to the right along Franciszkańska street. After passing a few monuments and a tram stop, turn right down busy...*

Grodzka Street

Now you're back on the Royal Way proper. At the corner of Grodzka street stands the modern, copper-colored **Wyspiański Pavilion.** Step inside (daily 9:00-17:00), past the little TI, to see three recent stained-glass windows based on designs Wyspiański once submitted for a contest to redecorate Wawel Cathedral. Although these designs were rejected back then, they were finally realized on the hundredth anniversary of his death (in 2007). Visible from inside the building during the day, and gloriously illuminated to be seen outside the building at night, they represent three Polish historical figures: the gaunt St. Stanisław (Poland's first saint), the skel-

Karol Wojtyła (1920-2005):
The Greatest Pole

The man who became St. John Paul II began his life as Karol Wojtyła, born to a humble family in the town of Wadowice near Kraków on May 18, 1920. Karol's mother died when he was a young boy. When he was a teenager, he moved with his father to Kraków to study philosophy and drama at Jagiellonian University. Young Karol was gregarious and athletic—an avid skier, hiker, swimmer, and soccer goalie. During the Nazi occupation in World War II, he was forced to work in a quarry. In defiance of the Nazis, he secretly studied theology and appeared in illegal underground theatrical productions. When the war ended, he resumed his studies, now at the theology faculty.

After graduating in 1947, Wojtyła swiftly rose through the ranks of the Catholic Church hierarchy. By 1964, he was archbishop of Kraków, and just three years later, he became the youngest cardinal ever. Throughout the 1960s, he fought an ongoing battle with the regime when they refused to allow the construction of a church in the Kraków suburb of Nowa Huta. After years of saying Mass for huge crowds in open fields, Wojtyła finally convinced the communists to allow the construction of the Lord's Ark Church in 1977. A year later, Karol Wojtyła was called to the papacy—the first non-Italian pope in more than four centuries. In 1979, he paid a visit to his native Poland. In a series of cautiously provocative speeches, he demonstrated to his countrymen the potential for mass opposition to communism.

Imagine you're Polish in the 1970s. Your country was devastated by World War II and has struggled under an oppressive regime ever since. Food shortages are epidemic. Lines stretch around the block even to buy a measly scrap of bread. Life is bleak, oppressive, and hopeless. Then someone who speaks your language—someone you've admired your entire life, and one of the only people you've seen successfully stand up to the regime—becomes one of the world's most influential people. A Pole like you is the leader of a billion Catholics. He makes you believe that

etal Kazimierz the Great (in the middle), and the swooning King Henry the Pious.

If you're not churched out, you can dip into the **Dominican Church**—just a block away, to your left (described on page 284).

Now continue down Grodzka street. This lively thoroughfare, connecting the Square with Wawel, is teeming with shops—and some of Kraków's best restaurants (see "Eating in Kraków," later). Survey your options now, and choose (and maybe reserve) your favorite for dinner tonight. This street is also characterized by its fine arcades over the sidewalks. While this might seem like a charming Renaissance feature, the arcades were actually added by the Nazis

the impossible can happen. He says to you again and again: *"Nie lękajcie się"*—"Have no fear." And you begin to believe it.

From his bully pulpit, the pope had a knack for cleverly challenging the communists—just firmly enough to get his point across, but stopping short of jeopardizing the stature of the Church in Poland. Gentle but pointed wordplay was his specialty. The inspirational role he played in the lives of Lech Wałęsa and the other leaders of Solidarity emboldened them to rise up; it's no coincidence that the first successful trade union strikes in the Soviet Bloc took place shortly after John Paul II became pope. Many people (including Mikhail Gorbachev) credit John Paul II for the collapse of Eastern European communism.

Even as John Paul II's easy charisma attracted new worshippers to the Church (especially young people), his conservatism on issues such as birth control, homosexuality, and female priests pushed away many Catholics. Under his watch, the Church struggled with pedophilia scandals. Many still fault him for turning a blind eye and not putting a stop to these abuses much earlier. By the end of his papacy, John Paul II's failing health and conservatism had caused him to lose stature in worldwide public opinion.

And yet, approval of the pope never waned in Poland. His compatriots—even the relatively few atheists and agnostics— saw John Paul II both as the greatest hero of their people...and as a member of the family, like a kindly grandfather. When Pope John Paul II died on April 2, 2005, the mourning in his homeland was particularly deep and sustained. Musical performances of all kinds were canceled, and the irreverent MTV-style music channel simply went off the air out of respect.

A speedy nine years after his death, Karol Wojtyła became St. John Paul II in April of 2014. Out of 265 popes, only two have been given the title "great." There's already talk in Rome of increasing that number to three. Someday soon we may speak of this man as "St. John Paul the Great." His fellow Poles already do.

after they invaded in 1939; they wanted to convert Kraków into a city befitting its status as the capital of their Polish puppet state.

This is also a good street to find some of Kraków's **milk bars** (two are listed on page 339). The most traditional one is about two blocks down, on the right (at #45), with a simple *Bar Mleczny* sign. These government-subsidized cafeterias are the locals' choice for a quick, cheap, filling, lowbrow lunch. Prices are deliriously cheap (soup costs about a dollar), and the food isn't bad. For more on milk bars, see page 222.

• *One more block ahead, the small square on your right is...*

Mary Magdalene Square
(Plac Św. Marii Magdaleny)

This square offers a great visual example of Kraków's deeply religious character. In the Middle Ages, Kraków was known as "Small Rome" for its many churches. Today, there are 142 churches and monasteries within the city limits (32 in the Old Town alone)—more per square mile than anywhere outside of Rome. You can see several of them from this spot: The nearest, with the picturesque white facade and row of saints out front, is the **Church of Saints Peter and Paul** (Poland's first Baroque church, and a popular tourist concert venue). The statues lining this church's facade are the 11 apostles (minus Judas), plus Mary Magdalene, the square's namesake. The next church to the right, with the twin towers, is the Romanesque **St. Andrew's** (now with a Baroque interior). Dating from the rough-and-tumble 11th century, it was designed to double as a place of last refuge—notice the arrow slits around the impassable lower floor. According to legend, a spring inside this church provided water to citizens who holed up here during the Tatar invasions. The church was spared, but that didn't save the rest of Kraków from being overrun by marauding armies. Imagine this stone fortress of God being the only building standing amid a smoldering and flattened Kraków after the 13th-century destruction.

If you look farther down the street, you can see three more churches. And even the square next to you used to be a church, too—it burned in 1855, and only its footprint survives.

• *Go through the square and turn left down...*

Kanonicza Street (Ulica Kanonicza)

With so many churches around here, the clergy had to live somewhere. Many lived on this well-preserved street—supposedly the oldest street in Kraków. As you walk, look for the cardinal hats over three different doorways. The **Hotel Copernicus,** on the left at #16, is named for a famous guest who stayed here five centuries ago. Directly across the street at #17, the **Bishop Erazm Ciołek Palace** hosts a good exhibit of medieval art and Orthodox icons. Next door, the yellow house at #19 is where Karol Wojtyła lived for 10 years after World War II—long before he became St. John Paul II. Today this building houses the **Archdiocesan Museum,** which is the top spot in the Old Town to learn about Kraków's favorite son. Both of these sights are described later, under "Sights in Kraków."

• *This marks the end of Kanonicza street—and the end of our self-guided walk. But there's still much more to see. Across the busy street, a ramp leads up to the most important piece of ground in all of Poland: Wawel (described next).*

KRAKÓW

Sights in the Old Town

WAWEL HILL

Wawel (VAH-vehl), a symbol of Polish royalty and independence, is sacred territory to every Polish person. A castle has stood here since the beginning of

Poland's recorded history. Today, Wawel—awash in tourists—is the most visited sight in the country. Crowds and an overly complex admissions system for the hill's many historic sights can be exasperating. Thankfully, a stroll through the cathedral and around the castle grounds requires no tickets, and— with the help of the following commentary—is enough. I've described these sights in the order of a handy self-guided walk. The many museums on Wawel (all described in this section) are mildly interesting but can be skipped (grounds open daily from 6:00 until dusk, inner courtyard closes 30 minutes earlier). In May and June, it's mobbed with students, as it's a required field trip for Polish schoolkids.

Wawel Sights: The sights you'll enter at Wawel are divided into two institutions: church and castle, each with separate tickets. Tickets for the castle sights are sold at two points (at the long line at the top of the ramp, or with no line at the top of the hill, across the central square). The most important church sight—the cathedral— is mostly free, but to enter the paid sights inside (or the museum), get a ticket at the office across from the cathedral entrance.

• *From Kanonicza street—where my self-guided walk ends—head up the long ramp to the castle entry.*

Entry Ramp

Huffing up this ramp, it's easy to imagine how this location—rising above the otherwise flat plains around Kraków—was both strategic and easy to defend. When Kraków was part of the Habsburg Empire in the 19th century, the Austrians turned this castle complex into a fortress, destroying much of its delicate beauty. When Poland regained its independence after World War I, the castle was returned to its former glory. The bricks you see on your left as you climb the ramp bear the names of Poles from around the world who donated to the cause.

The jaunty equestrian statue ahead is **Tadeusz Kościuszko**

KRAKÓW

(1746-1817). If that name seems familiar, it's because Kościuszko was a hero of the American Revolution and helped design West Point. When he returned to his native Poland, he fought bravely but unsuccessfully against the Russians (during the Partitions that would divide Poland's territory among three neighboring powers). Kościuszko also gave his name to several American towns, a county in Indiana, a brand of mustard from Illinois, and the tallest mountain in Australia.

• *Hiking through the Heraldic Gate next to Kościuszko, you pass the ticket office (if you'll be going into the museums, use the other ticket office, with shorter lines, on the top of the hill—see "Tickets and Reservations," later). As you crest the hill and pass through the stone gate, on your left is...*

▲▲Wawel Cathedral

Poland's national church is its Westminster Abbey. While the history buried here is pretty murky to most Americans, to Poles, this

church is the national mausoleum. It holds the tombs of nearly all of Poland's most important rulers and greatest historical figures.

Cost and Hours: It's usually free to walk around the main part of the church. You must buy a 12-zł ticket to climb up the tallest tower; visit the crypt, the royal tombs, and some of the lesser chapels; and tour the John Paul II Wawel Cathedral Museum. Buy this ticket at the house across from the cathedral entry—marked *KASA*—where you can also rent an audioguide (7 zł). The cathedral is open Mon-Sat 9:00-17:00, Sun from 12:30, Oct-March daily until 16:00 (tel. 12-429-9516, www.katedra-wawelska.pl). Note that the cathedral's museum (described later) is closed on Sunday.

Cathedral Exterior

Before entering, go around to the far side of the cathedral to take in its profile. This uniquely eclectic church is the product of centuries of haphazard additions...yet somehow, it works. It began as a simple, stripped-down Romanesque church in the 12th century. (The white base of the nearest tower is original. Anything at Wawel that's made of white limestone like this was probably part of the earliest Romanesque structures.) Kazimierz the Great and his predecessors gradually surrounded the cathedral with some 20 chapels, which were further modified over the centuries, making this beautiful church a happy hodgepodge of styles. To give you a sense of the historical sweep, scan the chapels from left to right: 14th-century Gothic, 12th-century Romanesque (the base of the tower), 17th-century Baroque (the inside is Baroque, though the exterior is a copy of its Renaissance neighbor), 16th-century Renaissance, and 18th- and 19th-century Neoclassical. (This variety in styles is even more evident in the chapels' interiors, which we'll see soon.)

Pay attention to the two particularly interesting domed chapels to the right of the tall tower. The gold one is the Sigismund Chapel, housing memorials to the Jagiellonian kings—including Sigismund the Old, who was responsible for Kraków's Renaissance renovation in the 16th century. The Jagiellonian Dynasty was a high point in Polish history. During that golden 16th century, Poland was triple the size it is today, stretching all the way to the Ottoman Empire and the Black Sea. Poles consider the Sigismund Chapel, made with 80 pounds of gold, to be the finest Renaissance chapel north of the Alps. The copper-domed chapel next to it, home to the Swedish Vasa dynasty, resembles its neighbor (but it's a copy built 150 years later, and without all that gold).

Go back around and face the church's **front entry** for more architectonic extravagance. The tallest tower, called the Sigismund Tower, has a clock with only an hour hand. Climbing a few steps into the entry, you see Gothic chapels (with pointy windows) flanking the door, a Renaissance ceiling, lavish Baroque decoration over the door, and some big bones (a simple whale rib and two vertebrae). In the Middle Ages, these were thought to have been the bones of the mythic Wawel dragon and put here as an oddity to be viewed by the public. (Back then, there were no museums, so unusual items like these were used to lure people to the church.) The door is the original from the 14th century, with fine wrought-iron work. The K with the crown stands for Kazimierz the Great. The black marble frame is made of Kraków stone from nearby quarries.

Cathedral Interior

The cathedral interior is slathered in Baroque memorials and tombs, decorated with tapestries, and soaked in Polish history. The ensemble was designed to help keep Polish identity strong through the ages. It has...and it still does.

After you step inside, you'll follow the one-way, clockwise route that leads you through the choir, then around the back of the apse, then back to the entry.

At the entry, look straight ahead to see the silver tomb under a **canopy,** inspired by the one in St. Peter's Basilica at the Vatican. It contains the remains of the first Polish saint, Stanisław (from the 11th century). In front of the canopy, look for a metallic reliquary that's shaped like a book with its pages being ruffled by the wind (labeled, in Latin, *Sanctus Johannes Paulus II*). The glass capsule in the reliquary holds a drop of St. John Paul II's blood. It takes this shape because of what believers consider a highly significant moment during his memorial service: Before a crowd of thousands on St. Peter's Square in Rome, a book was placed on John Paul II's simple wooden coffin. As the service processed, its pages were

ruffled back and forth by the wind, until they were finally slammed shut...as if the Holy Spirit were "closing the book" on his life.

Go behind this canopy into the ornately carved **choir** area. For 200 years, the colorful chair to the right of the high altar has been the seat of Kraków's archbishops, including Karol Wojtyła, who served here for 14 years before becoming pope. It's here that Polish royal coronations took place.

Now you'll continue into the left aisle. From here, if you have a ticket, you can enter two of the optional attractions: Seventy claustrophobic wooden stairs lead up to the 11-ton **Sigismund Bell** and pleasant views of the steeples and spires of Kraków. Then, to the left (closer to where you entered), descend into the little **crypt** (with a rare purely Romanesque interior), which houses the remains of Adam Mickiewicz, the Romantic poet whose statue dominates the Main Market Square, and another beloved Romantic poet and playwright, Juliusz Słowacki. You'll also find a white marble monument to Fryderyk Chopin (who's buried in Paris), put here on the 200th anniversary of his birth in 2010.

Now continue around the apse (behind the main altar). After curving around to the right, look for the red-marble tomb (on the right) of The Great One—**Kazimierz,** of course. Look for *Kazimierz Wielki*—at his feet you can see a little beaver. This is an allusion to a famous saying about Kazimierz, the nation-builder: He found a Poland made of wood, and left one made of brick and stone.

You may notice that there's one VIP (Very Important Pole) who's missing...Karol Wojtyła, a.k.a. John Paul II. Even so, a few more steps toward the entrance, on the left, is the **Chapel of St.**

John Paul II. The late pontiff left no specific requests for his body, and the Vatican controversially (to Poles, at least) chose to entomb him in Vatican City, instead of sending him back home to Wawel. While Karol Wojtyła's remains are in St. Peter's Basilica, this chapel was recently converted to honor him—with a plaque in the floor and an altar with his picture. Someday, Poles hope, he may be moved here (but, the Vatican says, don't hold your breath).

Directly opposite the chapel, you'll see the rusty funeral regalia (orb and scepter) of **St. Jadwiga;** ten steps farther is her white

sarcophagus (with a dog at her feet). This 14th-century "king" of Poland advanced the fortunes of her realm by partnering with the king of Lithuania. The resulting Jagiellonian dynasty fought off the Teutonic Knights, helped Christianize Lithuania, and oversaw a high-water mark in Polish history. (Despite the queen's many contributions, the sexism of the age meant that she was considered a "king" rather than a "queen.") She was sainted by Pope John Paul II in 1997.

Across from Jadwiga, peek into the gorgeous 16th-century **Sigismund Chapel,** with its silver altar (this is the gold-roofed chapel you just saw from outside). Locals consider this the "Pearl of the Polish Renaissance" and the finest Renaissance building outside Italy.

Just beyond is a door leading back outside. If you don't have a ticket, your tour is finished—head out here. But those with a ticket can keep circling around.

Next, look into the **Vasa Chapel:** Remember that its exterior matches the restrained, Renaissance style of the Sigismund Chapel, but the interior is clearly Baroque, slathered with gold and silver—quite a contrast.

To the left of the main door, take a look at the Gothic **Holy Cross Chapel,** with its seemingly Orthodox-style 14th-century frescoes.

In the back corner of the church—on the other side of the main door—is the entrance to the **royal tombs.** (You'll exit outside the church, so be sure you're done in here first.) Once downstairs, the first big room, an original Romanesque space called St. Leonard's Crypt, houses Poland's greatest war heroes: Kościuszko (of American Revolution fame), Jan III Sobieski (who successfully defended Vienna from the Ottomans; he's in the simple black coffin with the gold inscription *J III S*), Sikorski, Poniatowski, and so on.

Poles consider this room highly significant as the place where St. John Paul II celebrated his first Mass after becoming a priest (in November of 1946). Then you'll wander through several rooms of second-tier Polish kings, queens, and their kids. Head down more stairs to find the plaque honoring the Polish victims of the Katyń massacre in the USSR during World War II. Stepping into the next room, you'll see the cathedral's newest tomb: President Lech Kaczyński and his wife Helena, who were among the 96 Polish politicians killed in a tragic 2010 plane crash—which was delivering those diplomats to a ceremony memorializing the Katyń massacre. Up a few stairs is the final grave, belonging to Marshal Józef Piłsudski, the WWI hero who later seized power and was the de facto ruler of Poland from 1926 to 1935. His tomb was moved here so the rowdy soldiers who came to pay their respects wouldn't disturb the others.

• *Nearby (and covered by the same ticket as the tower and crypt) is the cathedral's museum.*

John Paul II Wawel Cathedral Museum

This small museum, up the little staircase across from the cathedral entry, was recently spiffed up and rededicated to Kraków's favorite archbishop. It fills four rooms with artifacts relating to both the cathedral and St. John Paul II.

Downstairs is the Royal Room, with vestments, swords, regalia, coronation robes, and items that were once buried with the kings, as well as early treasury items (from the 11th through 16th century). Upstairs is the "Papal Room" with items from St. John Paul II's life: his armchair, vestments, caps, shoes, and miter (pointy pope hat), plus souvenirs from his travels. (If you're into papal memorabilia, the collection at the nearby Archdiocesan Museum—described later—is better.) The adjoining room holds a later treasury collection (17th through 20th century).

Cost and Hours: Admission to this museum is included with your ticket to the cathedral's special options (Sigismund Bell tower, plus crypt and royal tombs); open Mon-Sat 9:00-17:00, Oct-March until 16:00, closed Sun year-round; tel. 12-429-3321.

• *When you're finished with the cathedral sights, stroll around the...*

▲▲Wawel Castle Grounds

In the rest of the castle, you'll uncover more fragments of Kraków's history and have the opportunity to visit several museums. I con-

sider the museums skippable, but if you want to visit them, buy tickets before you enter the inner courtyard. Read the descriptions on page 272 to decide which museums appeal to you.

➲ Self-Guided Tour: This guided stroll, which doesn't enter any of the admission-charging attractions, is plenty for most visitors.

• *For a historical orientation, stand with the cathedral to your back, and survey the empty field between here and the castle walls.*

Gothic Church Ruins: This hilltop has seen lots of changes over the years. Kazimierz the Great turned a small fortress into a mighty Gothic castle in the 14th century. But that original fortress burned to the ground in 1499, and ever since, Wawel has been in flux. For example, in the grassy field, notice the foundations of two Gothic churches that were destroyed when the Austrians took over Wawel in the 19th century and needed a parade ground for their troops. (They built the red-brick hospital building beyond the field, now used by the Wawel administration.)

• *Facing the cathedral, look right to find a grand green-and-pink entryway. Go through here and into the palace's dramatically Renaissance-style...*

Inner Courtyard: If this space seems to have echoes of Florence, that's because it was designed and built by young Florentines after Kazimierz's original castle burned down. Notice the three distinct levels: The ground floor housed the private apartments of the higher nobility (governors and castle administrators); the middle level held the private apartments of the king; and the top floor—much taller, to allow more light to fill its large spaces—were the public state rooms of the king. The ivy-covered wing to the right of where you entered is Fascist in style, built as the headquarters of the notorious Nazi governor of German-occupied Poland, Hans

KRAKÓW

Frank. (He was tried and executed in Nürnberg after the war.) At the far end of the courtyard is a false wall, designed to create a pleasant Renaissance symmetry, and also to give the illusion that the castle is bigger than it is. Looking through the windows, notice that there's nothing but air on the other side. When foreign dignitaries visited, these windows could be covered to complete the illusion. The entrances to most Wawel museums are around this courtyard, and some believe that you'll find something even more special: chakra.

Adherents to the Hindu concept of **chakra** believe that a powerful energy field connects all living things. Some believe that, mirroring the seven chakra points on the body (from head to groin), there are seven points on the surface of the earth where this energy is most concentrated: Delhi, Delphi, Jerusalem, Mecca, Rome, Velehrad...and Wawel Hill—specifically over there in the corner (immediately to your left as you enter the courtyard—the stretches of wall flanking the door to the baggage-check room). Look for peaceful people (here or elsewhere on the castle grounds) with their eyes closed. One thing's for sure: They're not thinking of Kazimierz the Great. The smudge marks on the wall are from people pressing up against this corner, trying to absorb some good vibes from this chakra spot.

The Wawel administration seems creeped out by all this. They've done what they can to discourage this ritual (such as putting up information boards right where the power is supposedly most focused), but believers still gravitate from far and wide to hug the wall. Give it a try...and let the chakra be with you. (Just for fun, ask a Wawel tour guide about the chakra, and watch her squirm—they're forbidden to talk about it.)

• *If you want to visit some of the **castle museums** (you can enter four of the five from this courtyard), you'll first need to buy tickets elsewhere. Stick with me for a little longer to finish our tour of the grounds, and we'll wind up near a ticket office.*

Head downhill through the square, across to the gap in the buildings beyond the field, to the...

Viewpoint over the Vistula: Belly up to the wall and enjoy the panorama over the **Vistula River** and Kraków's outskirts. The "Polish Mississippi"—which runs its entire course in Polish lands—is the nation's artery for trade and cultural connection. It stretches 650 miles from the foothills of the Tatra Mountains in southern Poland, through most of the country's major cities (Kraków, Warsaw, Toruń), before emptying into the Baltic Sea in Gdańsk.

From this viewpoint, you can see some unusual landmarks, including the odd wavy-roofed building just across the river (which houses the Manggha Japanese art gallery) and the biggest conference center in Poland (opened in 2015, to the left of the wavy building). A bit farther to the left is an eyesore of a communist concrete hotel, now used as a billboard. In the summer, you'll see a popular and very cool "beach bar" filling the field in front of the building (the Forum Przestrzenie, described later). To the right, the suspiciously symmetrical little bulge that tops the highest hill on the horizon is the artificial Kościuszko Mound (described later). And on a particularly crisp day, far in the distance (beyond the wavy building), you can see the Tatra Mountains marking the border of Slovakia.

Now look directly below you, along the riverbank (to the left), to find a fire-belching monument to the **dragon** that was instrumental in the founding of Kraków. Once upon a time, a prince named Krak founded a town on Wawel Hill. It was the perfect location—except for the fire-breathing dragon that lived in the caves under the hill and terrorized the town. Prince Krak had to feed the dragon all of the town's livestock to keep the monster from going after the townspeople. But Krak, with the help of a clever shoemaker, came up with a plan. They stuffed a sheep's skin with sulfur and left it outside the dragon's cave. The dragon swallowed it and, before long, developed a terrible case of heartburn. To put the fire out, the dragon started drinking water from the Vistula. He kept drinking and drinking until he finally exploded. The town was saved, and Kraków thrived. Today visitors enjoy watching the dragon blow fire into the air (about every four minutes, but can vary from a big plume to a tiny puff).

If you'd like a higher viewpoint on the riverfront, you can pay 4 zł to climb 137 stairs to the top of **Sandomierska Tower** (at the far end of the hill, past the visitors center, no elevator). But I'd skip it—the view from up top is only through small windows (May-June daily 10:00-18:00, June-Aug until 19:00, Sept-Oct until 17:00, closed Nov-April).

• *Our Wawel tour is finished. If you'd like to explore some of the museums, you can buy your tickets in the nearby visitors center (head back into the main Wawel complex—with the empty field—and turn right); here you'll also find WCs, a café, a gift shop, and other amenities. Or go down to the riverfront park: Walk downhill (through the Dragon's Den, or use the main ramp and circle around the base of the hill) to reach the park—one of the most delightful places in Kraków to simply relax, with beautiful views back on the castle complex.*

KRAKOW

Wawel Castle Museums

There are five museums and exhibits in Wawel Castle (not including the cathedral and Cathedral Museum, the Dragon's Den, or Sandomierska Tower—all described earlier).

While the following sights are fascinating to Poles, casual visitors often find that the best visit is simply to enjoy the cathedral and the castle grounds (following my self-guided tour, earlier). Each sight has its own admission and slightly different hours. English descriptions are posted, and you can rent an audioguide for 20 zł that covers some of the sights. If you do visit all of the sights, start with the Royal State Rooms and/or Royal Private Apartments (which share an entrance), then—on your way back down—see the Oriental Art exhibit, then the Crown Treasury and Armory. Finally, head back to the outer courtyard for the Lost Wawel exhibit.

Tickets and Reservations: Each sight has separate tickets (prices listed later), which you'll buy at one of two ticket windows. Most people line up at the top of the entry ramp, but it's faster to buy tickets at the visitors center at the far corner of the castle grounds (across the field from the cathedral, near the café). You generally can't buy tickets at the door of each sight, so decide in advance which ones you want to see and buy all your tickets at the start of your visit. A limited number of tickets are sold for each sight; boards show the number of available tickets. Tickets come with an assigned entry time (though you can usually sneak in before your scheduled appointment). In summer, ticket lines can be long, and sights can sell out by midmorning. You can make a reservation for some sights (tel. 12-422-1697, extra fee), but frankly, if they're sold out, you're not missing much.

Hours: Unless otherwise noted, the museums are open April-Oct Tue-Fri 9:30-17:00, Sat-Sun from 10:00, closed Mon; Nov-March Tue-Sat 9:30-16:00, closed Sun-Mon. The last ticket is sold 1.25 hours before closing, and the last entry is one hour before closing.

Exceptions: In summer (April-Oct), Lost Wawel and the Crown Treasury and Armory are free and open on Mondays (9:30-13:00). Off-season (Nov-March), everything is closed on Monday and most are closed on Sunday except Lost Wawel and the Royal State Rooms (Jan-March only).

Information: Tel. 12-422-5155 ext. 219, www.wawel.krakow.pl.

Eating: Various light eateries circle the castle courtyard, but if you just want a drink, it's hard to beat the affordable self-service café next to the Lost Wawel entrance, with fine views across to the cathedral.

▲Royal State Rooms (Komnaty Królewskie)

While precious to Poles, these rooms are mediocre by European standards. Still, this is the best of the Wawel museums. First, climb up to the top floor and wander through some ho-hum halls with antique furniture to reach the Throne Room, with 30 carved heads in the ceiling. According to legend, one of these heads got mouthy when the king was trying to pass judgment—so its

mouth has been covered to keep it quiet. Continue into some of the palace's finest rooms, with 16th-century Brussels tapestries (140 of the original series of 300 survive), remarkably decorated wooden ceilings, and gorgeous leather-tooled walls. Wandering these halls (with their period furnishings), you get a feeling for the 16th- and 17th-century glory days of Poland, when it was a leading power in Eastern Europe. The Senate Room, with its throne and elaborate tapestries, is the climax. On your way back down to the courtyard, you'll walk right past the Oriental Art exhibit.

Cost and Hours: 20 zł, see hours listed earlier, Nov-March also open—and free—Sun 10:00-16:00, enter through courtyard.

Royal Private Apartments (Prywatne Apartamenty Królewskie)

The rooms, which look similar to the State Rooms, can only be visited with a guided (and included) 45-minute tour. As spaces are strictly limited, these tend to sell out the fastest (on busy days, they may book up by around 10:00).

Cost and Hours: 25 zł, request English tour when buying your ticket—they depart 3/hour, see hours listed earlier, enter through courtyard.

Oriental Art (Sztuka Wschodu)

Though small, this exhibit displays swords, carpets, banners, vases, and other items dating from the 1683 Battle of Vienna, in which the Ottoman army attempted to capture the Austrian capital. A painting in the entrance room sets the stage. These are trophies of Jan III Sobieski, the Polish king who led a pan-European army to victory in that battle.

Cost and Hours: 8 zł, see hours listed earlier, enter through courtyard; don't miss entry on your way back downstairs from Royal State Rooms.

KRAKÓW

Crown Treasury and Armory (Skarbiec i Zbrojownia)
This is a decent collection of swords, saddles, and shields; ornately decorated muskets, crossbows, and axes; and cannons in the basement. In the room with the suits of armor, look on the right wall for the winged armor of the Hussars—Polish warriors who made a terrifying noise when riding at top speed on horseback. Back upstairs is the smaller treasury section. From the central room of precious tankards and platters, smaller adjoining rooms hold the most precious items. Up two stairs, look for the regalia given to Jan III Sobieski as thanks for his defeat of the Ottoman invaders in the Battle of Vienna: giant swords consecrated by the pope and the mantle (robe) of the Order of the Holy Ghost from France's King Louis XIV. Nearby is the 13th-century coronation sword of the Polish kings.

Cost and Hours: 20 zł, see hours listed earlier, April-Oct also open—and free—Mon 9:30-13:00, enter through courtyard.

Lost Wawel (Wawel Zaginiony)
This exhibit traces the history of the hill and its various churches and castles. On your way in, view the model of the entire castle complex in the 18th century (pre-Austrian razing). From here, the one-way route leads through scarcely explained excavations of a 10th-century church. On the way, you'll see models of the cathedral at various historical stages (originally Romanesque—much simpler, before all the colorful, bulbous domes, chapels, and towers were added—then Gothic, and so on). Then you'll loop through a collection of architectural decorations, ending with a display of tiles from 16th-century stoves that once heated the place.

Cost and Hours: 10 zł, see hours listed earlier; April-Oct also open—and free—Mon 9:30-13:00; Nov-March also open—and free—Sun 9:30-13:00; enter near snack bar across from side of cathedral.

NATIONAL MUSEUM BRANCHES
Kraków's National Museum (Muzeum Narodowe) is made up of a series of small but interesting collections scattered throughout the city (www.mnk.pl). I've listed the best of the National Museum's branches below, and you can find details on current exhibitions at the National Museum website. A 50-zł **combo-ticket** covers the permanent collections in all of these museums (good for your entire stay)—worth considering if you'll be visiting more than three of them. National Museum branches are free to enter on Sunday (but some have reduced hours).

▲▲Gallery of 19th-Century Polish Art
(Galeria Sztuki Polskiej XIX Wieku)

This small and surprisingly enjoyable collection of works by obscure Polish artists fills the upper level of the Cloth Hall. While you probably won't recognize any of the Polish names in here—and this collection isn't quite as impressive as Warsaw's National Gallery—many of these paintings are just plain delightful. It's worth a visit to see some Polish canvases in their native land, and to enjoy views over the Square from the hall's upper terraces.

Cost and Hours: 20 zł, free on Sun; open Tue-Fri 9:00-17:00, Sat 10:00-18:00, Sun 10:00-16:00, closed Mon; dry 7-zł audioguide, entrance on side of Cloth Hall facing Adam Mickiewicz statue, tel. 12-424-4600.

Background: During the 19th century—when every piece of art in this museum was created—there was no "Poland." The country had been split up among its powerful neighbors in a series of three Partitions and would not appear again on the map of Europe until after World War I. Meanwhile, the 19th century was a period of national revival throughout Europe, when various previously marginalized ethnic groups began to take pride in what made them different from their neighbors. So the artists you see represented here were grappling with trying to forge a national identity at a time when they didn't even have a nation. You'll sense a pessimism that comes from a country that feels abused by foreign powers, mingled with a resolute spirit of national pride.

➲ Self-Guided Tour: The collection fills just four rooms: Two small rooms in the center and two big halls on either side. On a quick visit, focus on the highlights in the big halls I mention here.

Entering the Cloth Hall, buy your ticket and head up the stairs—pausing on the first floor to peek out onto the inviting **café terrace** for a fine view of the Square and St. Mary's. Then continue up to the main exhibit, on the second floor.

The first two small rooms don't feature much of interest. You enter **Room I** (Bacciarelli Room), with works from the Enlightenment; straight ahead is **Room II** (Michałowski Room), featuring Romantic works from 1822 to 1863. The larger, twin halls on either side merit a linger.

Siemiradzki Room (Room III, on the right): This features art of the Academy—that is, "conformist" art embraced by the art critics of the day. Entering the room, turn right and survey the canvases counterclockwise. The space is dominated by the works of Jan

KRAKÓW

Matejko, a remarkably productive painter who specialized in epic historical scenes that also commented on his own era (for more on Matejko, see page 399).

• *Circling the room, look for these paintings.*

Jan Matejko, *Wenyhora:* The first big canvas is Matejko's depiction of Wenyhora, a late-18th-century Ukrainian soothsayer who, according to legend, foretold Poland's hardships—the three Partitions, Poland's pact with Napoleon, and its difficulties regaining nationhood. Like many Poles of the era, Matejko was preoccupied with Poland's tragic fate, imbuing this scene with an air of inevitable tragedy.

Jacek Malczewski, *Death of Ellenai:* A similar gloominess is reflected in this canvas. The main characters in a Polish Romantic poem, Ellenai and Anhelli, have been exiled to a remote cabin in Siberia (in Russia, one of the great powers occupying Poland). Just when they think things can't get worse...Ellenai dies. Anhelli sits immobilized by grief.

• *A few canvases down, dominating the right side of the hall, is...*

Jan Matejko, *Tadeusz Kościuszko at Racławice:* One of the heroes of the American Revolution, now back in his native Poland

fighting the Russians, doffs his hat after his unlikely victory at the Battle at Racławice. In this battle (which ultimately had little bearing on Russia's drive to overtake Poland), a ragtag army of Polish peasants defeated the Russian forces. Kościuszko is clad in an American uniform, symbolizing Matejko's respect for the American ideals of democracy and self-determination.

• *Dominating the far wall is...*

Henryk Siemiradzki, *Nero's Torches:* On the left, Roman citizens eagerly gather to watch Christians being burned at the stake (on

the right). The symbolism is clear: The meek and downtrodden (whether Christians in the time of Rome, or Poles in the heyday of Russia and Austria) may be persecuted now, but we have faith that their noble ideals will ultimately prevail.

• *On the next wall, find...*

Pantaleon Szyndler, *Bathing Girl:* This piece evokes the orientalism popular in 19th-century Europe, when romanticized European notions of the Orient (such as harem slave girls) were popular artistic themes. Already voyeuristic, the painting was originally downright lewd until Szyndler painted over a man leering at the woman from the left side of the canvas.

• *The huge canvas on this wall is...*

Jan Matejko, *The Prussian Homage:* The last Grand Master of the fearsome Teutonic Knights swears allegiance to the Polish king in 1525. This historic ceremony took place in the Main Market Square in Kraków, the capital at the time. Notice the Cloth Hall balustrade and the spires of St. Mary's Church in the background. Matejko has painted his own face on one of his favorite historical figures, the jester Stańczyk at the foot of the throne (for more on Stańczyk, see page 399).

• *Continue the rest of the way around the room. Keep an eye out for Tadeusz Ajdukiewicz's portrait of Helena Modrzejewska, a popular actress of the time, attending a party in this very building. Finally, backtrack through Room I and continue into the...*

Chełmoński Room (Room IV): Featuring works of the late 19th century, this section includes Realism and the first inklings of Symbolism and Impressionism. Just as elsewhere in Europe (including Paris, where many of these artists trained), artists were beginning to throw off the conventions of the Academy and embrace their own muse.

• *As you turn right and proceed counterclockwise through the room, the first stretch of canvases features landscapes and genre paintings. Among these, a particularly fine canvas is...*

Władysław Malecki, *A Gathering of Storks:* The majestic birds stand under big willows in front of the setting sun. Even seemingly innocent wildlife paintings have a political message: Storks are particularly numerous in Poland, making them a subtle patriotic symbol.

• *A few canvases down, find...*

Józef Brandt, *A Meeting on a Bridge:* This dramatic painting shows soldiers and aristocrats pushing a farmer into a ditch—a comment on the state of the Polish people at that time. Just to the right, see Brandt's Fight for a Turkish Standard. This artist specialized in battle scenes, frequently involving a foe from the East—as was often the reality here along Europe's buffer zone with Asia.

• *Just to the left of Brandt's works is...*

Samuel Hirszenberg, *School of Talmudists:* Young Jewish students pore over the Talmud. One of them, deeply lost in thought, may be pondering more than ancient Jewish law. This canvas suggests the inclusion of Jews in Poland's cultural tapestry during this age. While still subject to pervasive bigotry here, many Jewish refugees found Poland to be a relatively welcoming, tolerant place to settle on a typically hostile continent.

• *Dominating the end of the room is...*

KRAKÓW

Józef Chełmoński, Four-in-Hand: In this intersection of worlds, a Ukrainian horseman gives a lift to a pipe-smoking nobleman. Feel the thrilling energy as the horses charge directly at you through splashing puddles.

• *Heading back toward the entrance, on the right wall, watch for...*

Witold Pruszkowski, *Water Nymphs:* Based on Slavic legends (and wearing traditional Ukrainian costumes), these mischievous, siren-like beings have just taken one victim (see his hand in the foreground) and are about to descend on another (seen faintly in the upper-right corner). Beyond this painting are some travel pictures from Italy and France (including some that are very Impressionistic, suggesting a Parisian influence).

• *Flanking the entrance/exit door are two of this room's best works. First, on the right, is...*

Władysław Podkowiński, *Frenzy:* This gripping painting's title (Szał), tellingly, has been translated as either Ecstasy or Insanity. A pale, sensuous woman—possibly based on a socialite for whom the artist fostered a desperate but unrequited love—clutches an all-fired-up black stallion that's frothing at the mouth. This sexually charged painting caused a frenzy indeed at its 1894 unveiling, leading the unbalanced artist to attack his own creation with a knife (you can still see the slash marks in the canvas).

• *And finally, on the other side of the door is...*

Jacek Malczewski, *Introduction:* A young painter's apprentice on a bench contemplates his future. Surrounded by nature and with his painter's tools beside him, it's easy to imagine this as a self-portrait of the artist as a young man...wondering if he's choosing the correct path. Malczewski was an extremely talented Młoda Polska artist who tends to be overshadowed by his contemporary, Wyspiański. Viewing this canvas—and others by him—makes me feel grateful that he decided to stick with painting.

Szołayski House (Kamienica Szołayskich)

This restored mansion, just one block from the Main Market Square, features high-quality temporary exhibits, most often with artists from the early 20th century. Recent exhibits have featured "Kraków in 1900" and French sculptor Auguste Rodin; many have showcased Art Nouveau works by the Młoda Polska movement (for more on this movement and its members, see the sidebar earlier in this chapter). In the past, the museum featured that movement's prodigiously talented headliner, Stanisław Wyspiański—and in the future, he may be back here. But in the meantime, find out what's on, and if the artist or theme interests you, check it out.

Cost and Hours: 20 zł—but varies with exhibits, Tue-Fri 9:00-17:00, Sat 10:00-18:00, Sun 10:00-16:00, closed Mon, one block northwest of the Square at plac Szczepański 9, tel. 12-433-5450.

Nearby: The charming and stately square that Szołayski House faces, **plac Szczepański,** is a hub for youthful, cutting-edge, artistic types. Tucked in a corner of the Old Town, just away from the Square, it's a strange and wonderful little oasis of urban sophistication holding out against the rising tide of tacky tourism. In addition to Szołayski House itself, the square has several bohemian cafés (including the recommended Charlotte). If you follow Szczepańska street one more block out to the Planty, then turn left, you'll find **Bunkier Sztuki,** an art gallery that fills an unfortunate communist-era building that really does feel like a bunker. But this conformist architecture is filled with quite the opposite: changing exhibitions of contemporary art (12 zł, free on Tue, open Tue-Sun 11:00-19:00, closed Mon, http://bunkier.art.pl). The gallery's fine café, under a delightfully airy canopy facing the Planty, has a Parisian ambience—a great place to escape the crowds and/or rain (see "Eating in Kraków," later).

Bishop Erazm Ciołek Palace
(Pałac Biskupa Erazma Ciołka)

This branch of the National Museum features two separate art collections. Upstairs, the extensive "Art of Old Poland" section shows off works from the 12th through the 18th century, with room after room of altarpieces, sculptures, paintings, and more. The "Orthodox Art of the Old Polish Republic" section on the ground floor offers a taste of the remote Eastern reaches of Poland, with icons and other ecclesiastical art from the Orthodox faith. You'll see a sizeable section of the iconostasis (wall of icons) from the town of Lipovec. Both collections are covered by the same ticket and are very well presented in a modern facility. Items are labeled in English, but there's not much description beyond the 7-zł audioguide.

Cost and Hours: 10 zł, free on Sun; open Tue-Fri 9:00-16:00, Sat 10:00-18:00, Sun 10:00-16:00, closed Mon; Kanonicza 17, tel. 12-424-9371.

Kraków's Homeless Masterpieces

Kraków is home to a few priceless paintings—and one in particular, an exquisite Leonardo da Vinci—that officially belong to the Czartoryski Museum. However, that museum has been closed for renovation for several years, and there's no confident ETA for its reopening. In the meantime, these magnificent paintings have been shuffled around the city, displayed here and there, making them tricky to track down. Art lovers will want to get the latest on where to see these masterpieces. At last sighting, the Leonardo was being displayed at the Main Branch of the National Museum, while the Rembrandt was at the National Museum's Europeum gallery (for details on both, see "More National Museum Branches," later).

When you find them, here are the details:

Leonardo da Vinci's *Lady with an Ermine*

This small (21 x 16 inches) but magnificently executed portrait of a teenage girl is a rare surviving work by one of history's greatest minds. Spend some time lingering over the canvas (dating from 1489 or 1490). The girl is likely Cecilia Gallerani, the young mistress of Ludovico Sforza, the duke of Milan and Leonardo's employer. The ermine (white during winter) suggests chastity (thus bolstering Cecilia's questioned virtue) but is also a naughty reference to the duke's nickname, Ermellino—notice that his mistress is sensually, um, "stroking the ermine."

Painted before the *Mona Lisa*, the portrait was immediately recognized as revolutionary. Cecilia turns to look at someone, her gaze directed to the side. Leonardo catches this unguarded, informal moment, an unheard-of gesture in the days of the posed, front-facing formal portrait. Her simple body language and faraway gaze speak volumes about her inner thoughts and personality. Leonardo tweaks the generic Renaissance "pyramid" composition, turning it to a three-quarters angle, and softens it with curved lines that trace from Cecilia's eyes and down her cheek and slop-

KRAKÓW

Czartoryski Museum (Muzeum Czartoryskich)

This eclectic collection, displaying armor, handicrafts, decorative arts, and paintings, has been closed for a years-long renovation, and its reopening date is unclear. When it does open, it should once again display priceless paintings by Leonardo da Vinci and Rembrandt (see sidebar).

Beyond the famous paintings, the rest of the collection in-

ing shoulders before doubling back across her folded arms. The background—once gray and blue—was painted black in the 19th century.

In a recent high-tech analysis using special lights and cameras, conservators were able to virtually peel back layers of paint to see earlier "drafts" of the painting (Leonardo was known to tinker with his works over time). They've revealed that the ermine was likely not included in the original version. Perhaps Leonardo added it later as a nod to the duke.

Lady with an Ermine is a rare surviving portrait in oil by Leonardo. It's better preserved than her famous cousin in Paris (*Mona Lisa*), and—many think—simply more beautiful. Can we be sure it's really by the enigmatic Leonardo? Yep—the master's fingerprints were found literally pressed into the paint (he was known to work areas of paint directly with his fingertips).

Other Masterpieces

Rembrandt van Rijn's *Landscape with the Good Samaritan* (1638) is a small, detailed painting depicting the popular parable. It is one of only a few known landscapes by Rembrandt. On the right, the samaritan helps the wounded man onto his horse (as a little boy watches). To the left, much farther down the road (just beyond the waterfall), find the two tiny figures walking—the priest and the Levite who passed the injured man by.

The museum technically owns a third masterpiece, **Raphael's** *Portrait of a Young Man,* but its whereabouts are unknown. Arguably one of the most famous and most valuable stolen paintings of all time, it's quite likely a self-portrait (but possibly a portrait of Raphael by another artist), depicting a Renaissance dandy, clad in a fur coat, with a self-satisfied smirk. Painted (perhaps) by the Renaissance master in 1513 or 1514, and purchased by a Czartoryski prince around the turn of the 19th century, the work was seized by the occupying Nazis during World War II. Along with the paintings by Leonardo and Rembrandt, this Raphael decorated the Wawel Castle residence of Nazi governor Hans Frank. But when Frank and the Nazis fled the invading Red Army at the end of the war, many of their pilfered artworks were lost—including the Raphael.

KRAKÓW

cludes ornate armor (including a ceremonial Turkish tent from the 1683 siege of Vienna, plus feathered Hussar armor), tapestries, treasury items, majolica pottery, Meissen porcelain figures, an impressive painting gallery (including Italian, French, and Dutch High Renaissance and Baroque, as well as Czartoryski family portraits), and ancient art (mostly sculptures and vases).

The museum's collection came about, in part, thanks to Poland's 1791 constitution (Europe's first), which inspired Princess Izabela Czarto-ryska to begin gathering bits of Polish history and culture. She fled with the collection to Paris after the 1830 insurrection, and 45 years later, her grandson returned it to its present Kraków location. When he ran out of space, he bought part of the monastery across the street, joining the buildings with a fancy passageway. Dur-

ing World War II, the Nazis hauled the collection to Germany; although most of it has been returned, some pieces are still missing.

Cost and Hours: Get the latest from the TI about when the museum will reopen, or check www.mnk.pl/branch. It's 2 blocks north of the Main Market Square and a short walk from the Florian Gate at ulica Św. Jana 19.

More National Museum Branches

While less interesting than the branches listed earlier, the National Museum's **Main Branch** (Gmach Główny) is worth a visit for museum completists. It features 20th-century Polish art and temporary exhibits (10 zł, more for special exhibits, a few blocks west of the Main Market Square at aleja 3 Maja 1). It regularly hosts compelling special exhibits, and until the Czartoryski Museum (described earlier) reopens, this is where you'll most likely find Leonardo da Vinci's *Lady with an Ermine*. The **Europeum** collection, housed in a restored granary, features works by European masters, including Breughel and Veneziano, along with a range of lesser-known artists; until the Czartoryski Museum reopens, it's the most likely place you'll find Rembrandt's *Landscape with the Good Samaritan* (just west of the Old Town at plac Sikorskiego 6). For more branches, and to confirm the location of these masterpieces, see www.mnk.pl.

OTHER OLD TOWN ATTRACTIONS
▲▲Rynek Underground Museum (Podziemia Rynku)

Recent work to renovate the Square's pavement unearthed a wealth of remains from previous structures. Now you can do some urban spelunking with a visit to this high-tech medieval-history museum, which is literally underground—beneath all the photo-snapping tourists on the Square above.

Cost and Hours: 21 zł, free on Tue; open Mon 10:00-20:00 (but closed second Mon of each month), Tue until 16:00, Wed-Sun until 22:00, shorter hours Nov-March; last entry 1.25 hours before closing, enter at north end of Cloth Hall, Rynek Główny

1, tel. 12-426-5060, www.
podziemiarynku.com.

Crowd-Beating Tips:
This museum can sell out on
very busy days (especially on
Tuesdays—when it's free—
and on summer weekends).
It's possible to book ahead
online up to three days in
advance; alternatively, you
can buy advance tickets in
person around the opposite
side of the Cloth Hall, at the
Kraków City History Mu-

seum's visitors center (see "Tourist Information," earlier). If you've
reserved a ticket, just go straight to the museum's main entrance.
To try visiting spontaneously, show up at the entrance; if immediate tickets are available, they'll send you down to buy them. If not,
you can circle around to the visitors center to buy a ticket for later
during your visit.

Visiting the Museum: You'll enter through a door near the
north end of the Cloth Hall (close to the fountain, facing St.
Mary's). Climb down a flight of stairs and follow the numbered
panels—1 to 70—through the exhibit (all in English). Cutting-
edge museum technology illuminates life and times in medieval
Kraków: Touchscreens let you delve into topics that intrigue you,
3-D virtual holograms resurrect old buildings, and video clips illustrate everyday life on unexpected surfaces (such as a curtain of
fog).

All of this is wrapped around large chunks of early structures that still survive beneath the Square; several "witness columns" of rock and dirt are accompanied by diagrams helping you
trace the layers of history. Interactive maps emphasize Kraków's
Europe-wide importance as an intersection of major trade routes,
and several models, maps, and digital reconstructions give you a
good look at Kraków during the Middle Ages—when the Old
Town looked barely different from today. You'll see a replica of
a blacksmith's shop and learn how "vampire prevention burials"
were used to ensure that the suspected undead wouldn't return
from the grave. In the middle of the complex, look up through
the glass of the Square's fountain to see the towers of St. Mary's
above. Under the skylight is a model of medieval Kraków. While it
looks much the same as today, notice a few key changes: the moat
ringing the Old Town, where the Planty is today; and the several
smaller market halls out on the Square.

Deeper in the exhibit, explore the long corridors of ruined

KRAKÓW

buildings that once ran alongside the length of the Cloth Hall. There are many intriguing cases showing artifacts that shops would have sold (jewelry, tools, amber figurines, and so on). Also in this area, you'll find a corridor with images of the Square all torn up for the recent renovation, plus a series of five modern brick rooms, each showing a brief, excellent film outlining a different period of Kraków's history. These "Kraków Chronicles" provide a big-picture context to what otherwise seems like a loose collection of cool museum gizmos, and also help you better appreciate what you'll see outside the museum's doors.

▲Jagiellonian University Museum: Collegium Maius

Kraków's historic university building can be toured with a student guide. While the courtyard itself (described earlier in "Kraków's Royal Way Walk") is the best part, the musty interior is mildly interesting. You'll choose between two different guided tours: 30 minutes (very popular) or one hour. It's smart to call ahead to find out when the shorter tour is scheduled in English, and to reserve for either tour (tel. 12-663-1307 for advance reservations, or tel. 12-663-1521 for same day, www.maius.uj.edu.pl). The building is two short blocks west of the Main Market Square, at ulica Jagiellońska 15.

The **30-minute tour** covers the "main exhibition" route: the library, refectory (with a gorgeously carved Baroque staircase), treasury (including Polish filmmaker Andrzej Wajda's honorary Oscar), assembly hall, and some old scientific instruments (12 zł, a few tours per day in English, 20 people maximum, leaves every 20 minutes Mon-Fri 10:00-14:20, Tue and Thu until 17:20 in April-Oct, these are the last tour times, no tours Sun). On Saturday mornings, you can see the route on your own, for free (10:00-13:30).

The **one-hour tour** adds some more interiors, room after room of more old scientific instruments, medieval art (mostly church sculptures), a Rubens, a small landscape from the shop of Rembrandt, and Chopin's piano (16 zł, usually in English Mon-Fri at 13:00, no tours Sat-Sun).

Dominican Church, a.k.a. Holy Trinity Church (Bazylika Trójcy Świętej)

In most towns, this church would be something special. In church-crazy Kraków, it's an also-ran. Still, it's easy to see (just a couple of blocks south of the Square) and worth a peek.

Cost and Hours: Free but donation requested, daily 6:30-13:00 & 16:00-20:00, facing plac Dominikański at Stolarska 12.

Visiting the Church: Inside, you'll find a Neo-Gothic space that was rebuilt after a devastating 1850 fire. You may be approached and offered an audioguide to tour the church, in exchange for a donation; it's a good little tour and worth doing, if you have the time.

Or, for a quick visit, tune in to just a few details: The unique metal chandeliers are one of many modern flourishes added during the late-19th-century restoration of the church. Climb the staircase in the left aisle to reach the chapel of St. Hyacinth. Locally known as St. Jacek, this early Dominican leader—called the "Apostle of the North"—is also the patron saint of pierogi (stuffed dumplings, similar to ravioli). During a famine, St. Jacek supposedly invented pierogi and—in a loaves-and-fishes-type miracle—produced plateful after plateful, feeding the desperate locals. His image adorns Kraków's annual Pierogi Cup contest, and to this day, when old-fashioned Poles are surprised, they might exclaim, *"Święty Jacek z pierogami!"* ("St. Hyacinth and his pierogi!"). Back down in the main part of the church, stroll slowly past the gorgeously carved wooden seats of the choir area (behind the altar); then, at the main altar, identify the three parts of the Trinity: Jesus (short beard), God (long beard), and Holy Spirit (beardless dove).

Archdiocesan Museum (Muzeum Archidiecezjalne)

This museum, in a building where St. John Paul II lived both as a priest and as a bishop, is the best place in town to learn more about Kraków's favorite son (without making the long trip to the St. John Paul II Sanctuary on the outskirts—described later). The exhibition includes John Paul II's personal effects, including clothes, handwritten notes, travel gear, bike, kayak, and skis—reminding visitors that he was one sporty pope. Then you'll tour the lavish private apartments where he lived from 1958 until 1967, as archbishop of Kraków. Throughout the collection are many portraits and photographs of the late pontiff—making his cult of personality almost palpable.

Cost and Hours: 5 zł, Tue-Sun 10:00-17:00, closed Mon, Kanonicza 19-21, tel. 12-421-8963, www.muzeumkra.diecezja.pl.

KRAKÓW

Sights in Kazimierz

The neighborhood of Kazimierz (kah-ZHEE-mehzh), 20 minutes by foot southeast of Kraków's Old Town, is the historic heart of Kraków's once-thriving Jewish community. After years of neglect, the district began a re-
juvenation in the early 2000s. Today, while not quite as slick and polished as Prague's Jewish Quarter, Kazimierz's assortment of synagogues, cemeteries, and museums helps visitors appreciate the neighborhood's rich Jew-
ish history. At the same time, Kazimierz also happens to be the city's edgy, hipster culture

center—jammed with colorful bars, creative eateries, and designer boutiques. This unlikely combination—where somber synagogues coexist with funky food trucks—makes Kazimierz a big draw for travelers both young and old.

Planning Your Visit: Try to visit any day except Saturday, when most Jewish-themed sights are closed (except the Old Syna-
gogue, High Synagogue, and Galicia Jewish Museum). Monday comes with a few closures of non-Jewish sights: the Ethnographic Museum, Museum of Contemporary Art in Kraków, and Museum of Municipal Engineering. On Monday, the Schindler's Factory Museum is free, but it's open shorter hours and is more crowded than usual. It's always smart to book ahead for the Schindler's Factory Museum, which can sell out. For more suggestions on what to do in Kazimierz, see the Shopping, Entertainment, Sleeping, and Eating sections.

Etiquette: To show respect, men cover their heads while visiting a Jewish cemetery or synagogue. Most sights offer loaner yarmulkes, or you can wear your own hat.

Getting to Kazimierz: From Kraków's Old Town, it's about a 20-minute **walk.** From the Main Market Square, head down ulica Sienna (near St. Mary's Church) and through the Planty park. When you hit the busy ring road, bear right and continue down Starowiślna for 15 more minutes. The **tram** shaves off a few minutes: Find the stop along the ring road, on the left-hand side of ulica Sienna (across the street from the Poczta Główna, or main post office). Catch tram #3 or #24, and ride two stops to Miodowa. Walking or by tram, at the intersection of Starowiślna and Miodowa, you'll see a tiny park with food trucks across the street and to the right. To reach the heart of Kazimierz—ulica Sze-

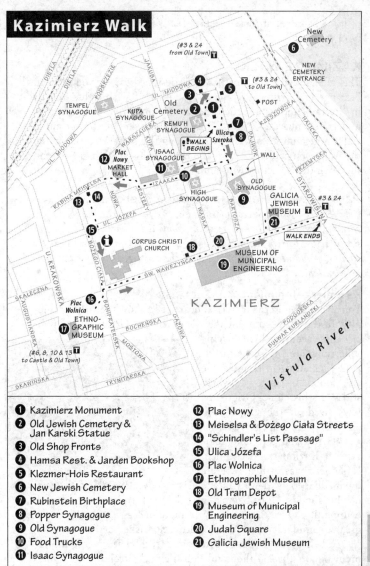

Kazimierz Walk

1. Kazimierz Monument
2. Old Jewish Cemetery & Jan Karski Statue
3. Old Shop Fronts
4. Hamsa Rest. & Jarden Bookshop
5. Klezmer-Hois Restaurant
6. New Jewish Cemetery
7. Rubinstein Birthplace
8. Popper Synagogue
9. Old Synagogue
10. Food Trucks
11. Isaac Synagogue
12. Plac Nowy
13. Meiselsa & Bożego Ciała Streets
14. "Schindler's List Passage"
15. Ulica Józefa
16. Plac Wolnica
17. Ethnographic Museum
18. Old Tram Depot
19. Museum of Municipal Engineering
20. Judah Square
21. Galicia Jewish Museum

roka—cut through this park. The same trams continue to the sights in Podgórze (including the Schindler's Factory Museum).

To return to the Old Town, catch tram #3 or #24 from the intersection of Starowiślna and Miodowa (kitty-corner from where you got off the tram).

Information: An official **TI** is just a few blocks off the bottom of ulica Szeroka, at ulica Józefa 7 (daily 9:00-17:00, tel. 12-422-0471).

KAZIMIERZ WALK

This self-guided walk, worth ▲▲, is designed to help you get your bearings in Kazimierz, connecting both its Jewish sights (mostly in "Part 1") and its eclectic other attractions, from trendy bars to underrated museums ("Part 2"). Allow about an hour for the entire walk, not counting museum visits along the way. From the end of the walk, you can easily cross the river to this area's biggest sight, the Schindler's Factory Museum.

Part 1: Jewish Heritage on Ulica Szeroka

• *We'll start on ulica Szeroka ("Broad Street")—the center of the neighborhood, which feels like more of an elongated square than a "street." Begin at the bottom (southern) edge of the small, grassy park, near the strip of restaurants. In the park with the tall trees, look for the low-profile, stone...*

Kazimierz Monument

You're standing in the historical heart of Kraków's Jewish community. In the 14th century, King Kazimierz the Great enacted policies that encouraged Jews fleeing other kingdoms to settle in Poland—including in Kraków. He also founded this town, which still bears his name. Originally, Jews lived in the Old Town, but they were scapegoated after a 1495 fire and forced to relocate to Kazimierz. Back then, Kazimierz was still a separate  town, divided by a wall into Christian (west) and Jewish (east) neighborhoods. Ulica Szeroka was the main square of the Jewish community. Over time, Jews were more or less accepted into the greater community, and Jewish culture flourished here.

All that would change in the mid-20th century. The **monument** honors the "65 thousand Polish citizens of Jewish nationality from Kraków and its environs"—more than a quarter of the city's pre-WWII population—who were murdered by the Nazis during the Holocaust. When the Nazis arrived, they immediately sent most of Kraków's Jews to the ghetto in the eastern Polish city of Lublin. Soon after, they forced Kraków's remaining 15,000 Jews into a walled ghetto at Podgórze, across the river. The Jews' cemeteries were defiled, and their buildings were ransacked and destroyed. In 1942, the Nazis began transporting Kraków's Jews to death camps (including Płaszów, just on Kraków's outskirts, and Auschwitz).

Only a few thousand Kraków Jews survived the war. During the communist era, this waning population was ignored or mistreated. After 1989, interest in Kazimierz's unique Jewish history was faintly rekindled. But it was only when Steven Spielberg chose to film *Schindler's List* here in 1993 that the world took renewed interest in Kazimierz. (A local once winked to me, "They ought to build a statue to Spielberg on that square.") Although the current Jewish population in Kraków numbers only 200, Kazimierz has become an internationally known destination for those with an interest in Jewish heritage.

• *Facing the park, look to the left. The arch with the Hebrew characters marks the entrance to the...*

▲▲Old Jewish Cemetery (Stary Cmentarz)

This small cemetery was used to bury members of the Jewish community from 1552 to 1800. With more than a hundred of the top

Jewish intellectuals of that age buried here, this is considered one of the most important Jewish cemeteries in Europe.

Cost and Hours: 10 zł includes cemetery and attached Remu'h Synagogue; hours vary with demand—especially outside peak season—but generally open Sun-Fri 9:00-16:00, can be open until 18:00 May-Sept, closes earlier off-season and by sundown on Fri, closed Sat yearround, ulica Szeroka 40.

Visiting the Cemetery: Walk under the arch, pay the admission fee, step into the cemetery, and survey the tidy rows of headstones. This early Jewish resting place (later replaced by the New Cemetery, described later) was desecrated by the Nazis during the Holocaust. In the 1950s, it was discovered, excavated, and put back together as you see here. Shattered gravestones form a mosaic **wall** around the perimeter.

Notice that many graves have a curved top or are engraved with an archlike pattern—suggesting passage into another realm. As in all Jewish cemeteries

and memorials, you'll see many small stones stacked on the graves. The tradition comes from placing stones—representing prayers—over desert graves to cover the body and prevent animals from disturbing it.

Behind the little synagogue to the left, in the elevated, fenced area near the tree, the tallest **tombstone** belonged to Moses Isserles (a.k.a. Remu'h), an important 16th-century rabbi. He is believed to have been a miracle worker, and his grave was one of the only ones that remained standing after World War II. Notice the written prayers crammed into the cracks and crevices of the tombstone.

Near the gate to the cemetery, step into the tiny **Remu'h Synagogue** (c. 1553, covered by cemetery ticket). Tight and cozy, this has been carefully renovated and is fully active. Notice the original 16th-century frescoed walls and ceilings, and the historic donation box at the door. For more on typical synagogue architecture, see the sidebar.

• *Back outside, turn left and continue up to the top of...*

Ulica Szeroka

Just above the cemetery gate, notice a bronze statue of a gentleman seated on a bench. This is a tribute to **Jan Karski** (1914-2000), a Catholic Pole and resistance fighter who published his eyewitness account *The Story of a Secret State* about the Holocaust in 1944. Karski—the ultimate whistleblower—was one of the first people who spoke out about Nazi atrocities, at a time when even many world leaders had only an inkling about what was happening in Hitler's realm. Karski's revelations, so shocking as to be literally unbelievable to many, went ignored by some key leaders—arguably extending the horrors of the Holocaust.

Just above that, at the top corner of the square, notice the side street with a row of rustic old Jewish **shop fronts,** which evoke the bustle of prewar Kazimierz. The Jewish names—Rattner, Weinberg, Nowak, Holcer—stand testament to the lively soul of this neighborhood in its heyday. This lane leads to Miodowa street, which you can follow left to reach two of Kazimierz's lesser-known synagogues (Tempel and Kupa, both described later).

The building at the top of the square houses the recommended **Hamsa** restaurant (with modern Israeli food) and **Jarden Bookshop,** which serves as an unofficial information point for the neighborhood and sells a wide variety of fairly priced books on Kazimierz and Jewish culture in the region (Mon-Fri 9:00-18:00, Sat-Sun from 10:00, ulica Szeroka 2).

Kitty-corner from the bookshop, notice **Klezmer-Hois**—one of many restaurants offering live traditional Jewish klezmer music nightly in summer (for more on klezmer music, and details on your options, see the sidebar on page 327).

The Synagogue

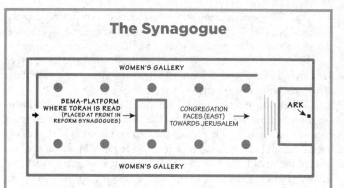

A synagogue is a place of public worship, where Jews gather to pray, sing, and read from the Torah. Most synagogues have similar features, though they vary depending on the congregation.

The synagogue generally faces toward Jerusalem (so in Kraków, worshippers face east). At the east end is an alcove called the **ark,** which holds the Torah. These scriptures (the first five books of the Christian Old Testament) are written in Hebrew on scrolls wrapped in luxuriant cloth. The other main element of the synagogue is the **bema,** an elevated platform from which the Torah is read aloud (the equivalent of a pulpit in a Christian church). In traditional Orthodox synagogues, the bema is near the center of the hall, and the reader stands facing the same direction as the congregation. In other branches of Judaism, the bema is at the front, and the reader faces the worshippers. Orthodox synagogues have separate worship areas for men and women, usually with women in the balcony.

The synagogue walls might be decorated with elaborate patterns of vines or geometric designs, but never statues of people, which could be considered idol worship. A lamp above the ark is always kept lit, as it was in the ancient temple of Jerusalem, and candelabras called menorahs also recall the temple. Other common symbols are the two tablets of the Ten Commandments given to Moses, or a Star of David, representing the Jewish king's shield.

At a typical service, the congregation arrives at the start of Sabbath (Friday evening). As a sign of respect toward God, men don yarmulkes (small round caps). As the cantor leads songs and prayers, worshippers follow along in a book of weekly readings. At the heart of the service, everyone stands as the Torah is ceremoniously paraded, unwrapped, and placed on the bema. Someone—the rabbi, the cantor, or a congregant—reads the words aloud. The rabbi ("teacher") might give a commentary on the Torah passage.

The **New Jewish Cemetery**—less touristed and a striking contrast to the Old Jewish Cemetery we just saw—is a worthwhile detour, about a five-minute walk away (and described earlier in this section). To get there, cut through the grassy little lot between Jarden Bookshop and Klezmer-Hois, turn right, cross the busy street, then go through the railway underpass.

When you're ready to move on, do a 180 and head back downhill on ulica Szeroka. You'll pass the little park again, then come to a row of lively, mostly Jewish-themed **restaurants** with outdoor tables. Several places along here (especially Ester Hotel, at the bottom of the row) feature outdoor klezmer music in good weather—allowing you to get a taste of this unique musical form before committing to a full meal.

Halfway down this side of the square, the green house at #14 is where **Helena Rubinstein** was born in 1870. At age 31, she emigrated to Australia, where she parlayed her grandmother's traditional formula for hand cream into a cosmetics empire. Many cosmetics still used by people worldwide today were invented by Rubinstein, who died at age 92 in New York City as one of the most successful businesswomen of all time—just one of many illustrious Jewish residents of Kazimierz.

Two doors past the Rubinstein house, notice the round arch marking the courtyard of the **Popper Synagogue,** which is now home to an extensive bookstore that's worth a peek.

Continue past the restaurants to the very bottom of ulica Szeroka, and pause at the steps before heading down into the sunken area around the Old Synagogue. To the synagogue's left, notice a short, reconstructed stretch of Kazimierz's 14th-century **town wall.** This is a reminder that medieval Kazimierz was a separate city from Kraków. It's easy to read some history into a map of Kazimierz (you'll find one on the big panel in front of the Old Synagogue, down the stairs): Today's Starowiślna and Dietla streets—which frame off Kazimierz in a triangle of land hemmed in by the riverbank—were once canals (Kazimierz was built on an island). When King Kazimierz the Great—who reportedly didn't care much for Krakovians—founded this district in 1335, he envisioned it as a separate town to rival Kraków. It wasn't until around 1800 that the two towns merged.

• *The building at the bottom of the square is the...*

Old Synagogue (Stara Synagoga)

The oldest surviving Jewish building in Poland (15th century) sits eight steps below street level. Jewish structures weren't allowed to be taller than Christian ones—and so, in order to have the proper proportions, the synagogue's "ground floor" had to be underground. Today the synagogue houses a good three-room museum on local

Jewish culture, with informative English descriptions and a well-preserved main prayer hall (11 zł, free on Mon; Mon 10:00-14:00, Tue-Sun 9:00-17:00; shorter hours off-season; good 50-stop audioguide-10 zł; ulica Szeroka 24, tel. 12-422-0962).

• *A few more Jewish sights can be found in the surrounding streets; I'll point these out in "Part 2," though the rest of this walk focuses on a more recent chapter of the neighborhood.*

Part 2: Contemporary Kazimierz

• *Stand with your back to the Old Synagogue, at the top of the stairs, and turn left, heading up the little alley next to Szeroka 28—called Lewkowa.*

Hipster Kazimierz

Follow Lewkowa between some old buildings. When you pop out into an open area, angle right, then continue straight along ulica Ciemna. Soon you'll hit an inviting little **pod of food trucks** (described on page 341). Pause here—perhaps while nursing an açaí smoothie, a Thai-style rolled ice cream, or a taco—and ponder the explosion of youthful culture that's taken place in Kazimierz over the last generation.

At the end of World War II, Kazimierz was badly damaged and depopulated. And so it remained for generations, as the communist authorities brushed Jewish heritage under the rug. By the early 2000s, Kazimierz's artistically dilapidated buildings, low rents, and easy proximity to the Old Town became enticing to creative young people. A variety of artsy entrepreneurs took root here, beginning with a cluster of ramshackle, rustic bars (inspired partly by Budapest's "ruin pub" scene). Today the district has the city's (and probably Poland's) highest concentration of trendy food trucks, cafés, bars, restaurants, and design shops—several of which we'll see as we continue.

• *From the food trucks, continue straight ahead (on Izaaka street). This leads you along the left side of...*

Isaac Synagogue (Synagoga Izaaka)

One of Kraków's biggest synagogues, this was built in the 17th century. Inside, the walls in the prayer hall are decorated with giant paintings of prayers for worshippers who couldn't afford to buy books (with translations posted below). The synagogue also serves as the local center for the Hasidic Jewish group Chabad, with a ko-

KRAKÓW

sher restaurant and a library (10 zł; Sun-Thu 8:30-20:00, Fri 8:30-14:30, closed Sat year-round, shorter hours off-season; ulica Kupa 18, tel. 12-430-2222). In addition to its Sabbath services, this is Kraków's only synagogue with daily prayers (at 8:30). They also host klezmer music concerts many evenings at 18:00 (60 zł).

• *Just past Isaac Synagogue is the heart of Kazimierz's nightlife zone (also bustling by day). Dive in, passing some characteristic cafés (on your left) and the chic Taawa nightclub (on your right). Then jog right at the glitzy Plac Nowy 1 beer hall to reach...*

Plac Nowy

Kazimierz's endearing "new" market square, plac Nowy (plats NOH-vee), retains much of the gritty flavor of the district before tourism and gentrification. The circular brick building in the center is a slaughterhouse where Jewish butchers would properly kill livestock, kosher-style. Today its windows are filled with little stand-up eateries ranging from burgers and ice cream to the traditional local pizza-like *zapiekanki*. Circle the market hall and browse for a snack (for more on the plac Nowy scene, see "Eating in Kraków," later). Good Lood has Kraków's best artisanal ice cream—if you don't mind the line. This square is also ringed by several fun and funky bars—enjoyable by day, but hopping at night (see page 326).

• *Leave plac Nowy along Meiselsa street (to the left from where you entered, past the yellow Jewish Cultural Center). After one block, pause at the intersection of...*

Meiselsa and Bożego Ciała Streets

The Holocaust was a dark chapter that dominates Kazimierz's history. But this intersection is a reminder that, up until the Nazis arrived, Kazimierz was a place where Jews and Christians lived side by side, in relative harmony.

Notice the street names, which mix Jewish and Catholic namesakes: ulica Meiselsa ("Meisels Street"—honoring a deeply respected 19th-century rabbi) and ulica Bożego Ciała ("Corpus Christi Street"—named for the towering brick church you can see just ahead). As if to celebrate the ecumenism of this intersec-

tion, a street artist has painted a graffiti Gene Kelly on the wall... very "happy again" indeed that Kazimierz is blossoming and full of life.

• *Backtrack a few steps up Meiselsa and duck into the courtyard on the right, under the dilapidated arch.*

Schindler's List Passage

This courtyard is a popular tourist spot thanks to its brush with fame, as a location for some key scenes in *Schindler's List* (find the black-and-white stills from the movie—and actual historic photos—partway down on the right, just before the arch). Spielberg connection aside, this is a particularly evocative setting to nurse a relaxing drink at the atmospheric café.

• *Carry on all the way through the passage. You'll pop out at...*

Ulica Józefa: Design Street

This street has Kazimierz's highest concentration of funky, one-off boutiques: jewelry, fashion, housewares, and more. For a rundown of the best options along here, see the "Shopping in Kraków" section, later. There's also a TI just across the street.

• *When you're ready to move along, take ulica Józefa right a few steps to the intersection with ulica Bożego Ciała, turn left, and follow it a long block. You'll pass Corpus Christi Church on your left, then arrive at...*

Plac Wolnica

Remember that Kazimierz was originally a separate town from Kraków. This was its main market square, designed to one-up its crosstown rival—right down to the dramatic, red-brick Catholic church on the corner (Corpus Christi). If you're still hungry, this square also has good craft beer, good ice cream, and good vegan burgers (see page 343).

The former Kazimierz Town Hall at the far end of the square houses an unusually good **Ethnographic Museum** (Muzeum Etnograficzne)—worth ▲. If you're interested in Polish folk culture, it's worth a visit (13 zł, free on Sun, open Tue-Sun 10:00-19:00, closed Mon, ulica Krakowska 46, tel. 12-430-6023, www.etnomuzeum.eu). On the ground floor, you'll find models of traditional rural Polish homes, as well as musty replicas of the interiors (like an open-air folk museum moved inside). The exhibit continues upstairs, where each in a long lineup of traditional Polish folk costumes is identified by specific region. Follow the one-way route through exhibits on village lifestyles, rustic tools, and musical instruments (including a Polish bagpipe). A highlight is the explanation of traditional holiday celebrations—from elaborate crèche scenes at Christmas, to a wall of remarkably painted Easter eggs. Some items are labeled in English, but it's mostly in Polish. The top floor features temporary exhibits.

KRAKÓW

• *There's more to see in Kazimierz. But if you're pooped, you could catch tram #6, #8, #10, or #13 back to Wawel Castle, then on to the plac Wszystkich Świętych stop in the heart of the Old Town (catch tram from along Krakowska street, behind the Ethnographic Museum).*

To continue the walk from plac Wolnica, head up ulica Św. Wawrzyńca (at the corner where you entered the square, with the Corpus Christi Church on your left).

Ulica Św. Wawrzyńca: Industrial Kazimierz

By the late 19th century, Kazimierz was not just a Jewish cultural hotspot but also a center of local industry. (It's no coincidence that Oskar Schindler had his factory near here.) After the church, on your left, look for the glass-and-steel arched roof of the Industrial Age **old tram depot,** which now houses a recommended brewpub. In sunny summer weather, the pebbly courtyard is filled with happy drinkers.

Across the street, notice the many tram tracks leading into a courtyard with several more storage sheds for local trams. This gorgeously restored complex now houses the **Museum of Municipal Engineering** (Muzeum Inżynierii Miejskiej). Exhibits include a history of the town's public transit system (including several antique trams), old Polish-made cars and motorcycles (among them the tiny commie-era Polski Fiat), typography and historical printing presses, and a hands-on area for kids (15 zł, family ticket—40 zł, free on Tue; open Tue 10:00-16:00, Wed-Fri 9:00-20:00, Sat-Sun 10:00-20:00, closed Mon; Św. Wawrzyńca 15, tel. 12-421-1242, www.mim.krakow.pl).

Continue along ulica Św. Wawrzyńca a few more steps. At the intersection with Wąska, **Judah Square** (Skwer Judah) is a vacant lot with a gaggle of enticing food carts watched over by a giant mural. Commissioned for Kraków's Jewish Cultural Festival in 2013, the illustration was painted by Israeli street artist Pilpeled. It shows a young boy who feels small and scared, but lionhearted nevertheless—a poignant symbol for the Holo-

caust survivors of Kazimierz. If you're ready for a meal or snack, you'll find several good options here.

• *A half-block farther down ulica Św. Wawrzyńca is another place for refreshment, the recommended Craftownia (Polish microbrews on tap, on the left at #22). Next you'll reach the intersection with Dajwór street. Turn left here and walk a few steps up the street; on the right, you'll find the...*

Galicia Jewish Museum (Galicja Muzeum)

This museum, worth ▲ and housed in a restored Jewish furniture factory, focuses on the present rather than the past. The permanent "Traces of Memory" photographic exhibit shows today's remnants of yesterday's Judaism in the area around Kraków (a region known as "Galicia"). From abandoned synagogues to old Jewish grave-stones flipped over and used as doorsteps, these giant postcards of Jewish artifacts (with good English descriptions) ensure that an important part of this region's heritage won't be forgotten. Good temporary exhibits complement this permanent collection (16 zł, daily 10:00-18:00, one block east of ulica Szeroka at ulica Dajwór 18, tel. 12-421-6842, www.galiciajewishmuseum.org). The museum also serves as a sort of cultural center, with a good bookstore and café.

• *Notice yet another cluster of food trucks across the street from the museum.*

Our Kazimierz orientation walk is finished. From here, you have several options. To **return to ulica Szeroka,** where we began, walk up Dajwór street past the museum, then angle left through the park at the reconstructed chunk of town wall—you'll wind up at the Old Synagogue.

For the next two options, you'll first head back down to ulica Św. Wawrzyńca, turn left, and walk one more block to the inter-section with Starowiślna street. Just to the left on Starowiślna, look for the tram stops. The tram stop on the far side of the street takes you **back to the Old Town** (tram #3 or #24). From the tram stop on the near side of the street, tram #3 or #24 zips you to the **sights in Podgórze**—including Ghetto Heroes' Square and the Schindler's Factory Museum (both described later). You can also reach the Podgórze sights on foot by turning right on Starowiślna and cross-ing the bridge (about a 10-minute walk).

MORE JEWISH SIGHTS IN KAZIMIERZ

In addition to the sights connected by the walk above, here's an-other cemetery and a few more synagogues to round out your Jew-ish Kazimierz experience.

▲New Jewish Cemetery (Nowy Cmentarz)

This burial place—much larger than the Old Jewish Cemetery—has graves of those who died after 1800. It was vandalized by the Nazis, who sold many of its gravestones to stonecutters and used others as pavement in their concentration camps. Many have since been cemented back in their original positions, while others—which could not be replaced—have been used to create the moving mosaic wall and Holocaust monument (on the right as you enter). Most gravestones are in one of four languages: Hebrew (generally

KRAKÓW

the oldest, especially if there's no
other language, though some are
newer "retro" tombstones); Yiddish (sounds like a mix of German and Hebrew and uses the
Hebrew alphabet); Polish (Jews
who assimilated into the Polish
community); and German (Jews
who assimilated into the German community). The earliest
graves are simple stones, while

later ones imitate graves in Polish Catholic cemeteries—larger,
more elaborate, and with a long stone jutting out to cover the body.
Notice that some new-looking graves have old dates. These were
most likely put here well after the Holocaust (or even after the
communist era) by relatives of the dead.

Cost and Hours: Free, Sun-Fri 8:00-16:00, closed Sat. It's
tricky to find: Go under the railway tunnel at the east end of ulica
Miodowa, and jog left as you emerge. The cemetery is to your right
(enter through gate with small *cmentarz żydowski* sign).

Synagogues

In addition to the three synagogues mentioned on the Kazimierz
Walk (Old Synagogue, Isaac, and Remu'h), others also welcome
visitors. Each of these charges a small admission fee and is closed
Saturdays (unless noted). The **High Synagogue**—so called because
its prayer room is upstairs—displays changing exhibits, most of
which focus on the people who lived here before the Holocaust
(daily, ulica Józefa 38). **Tempel Synagogue** (Synagoga Templu)
has the grandest interior—big and dark, with elaborately decorated, gilded ceilings and balconies (corner of ulica Miodowa and
ulica Podbrzezie). The **Jewish Community Centre** next door offers activities both for members of the local Jewish community and
for tourists (lectures, genealogical research, Friday-night Shabbat
meals, Hebrew and Yiddish classes, and so on; www.jcckrakow.
org). Nearly across the street, the smaller **Kupa Synagogue** (Synagoga Kupa)—clean and brightly decorated—sometimes hosts temporary exhibits (Miodowa 27).

NEAR KAZIMIERZ: PODGÓRZE

The neighborhood called Podgórze (POD-goo-zheh), directly
across the Vistula from Kazimierz, has one of Kraków's most famous sights: Schindler's Factory Museum. I've listed these sights
in the order you'll reach them as you come from Kazimierz or the
Old Town.

Background: This is the neighborhood where the Nazis

forced Kraków's Jews into a ghetto in early 1941. (Schindler's List and the films in the Pharmacy Under the Eagle museum depict the sad scene of the Jews loading their belongings onto carts and trudging over the bridge into Podgórze.) Non-Jews who had lived here were displaced to make way for the new arrivals. The ghetto was surrounded by a wall with a fringe along the top that resembled Jewish gravestones—a chilling premonition. A short section of this wall still stands along Lwowska street. The tram continued to run through the middle of Podgórze, without stopping—giving Krakovians a chilling glimpse at the horrifying conditions inside the ghetto.

Getting There: To go directly to Ghetto Heroes' Square, continue through Kazimierz on tram #3 or #24 (described earlier, under "Getting to Kazimierz") to the stop called plac Bohaterow Getta. Or you can ride the tram or walk 10 minutes across the bridge from the end of my Kazimierz Walk.

Ghetto Heroes' Square (Plac Bohaterow Getta)

This unassuming square is the focal point of the visitor's Podgórze. Today the square is filled with a monument consisting of 68 empty

metal chairs—representing the 68,000 people deported from here. This is intended to remind viewers that the Jews of Kazimierz were forced to carry all of their belongings—including furniture—to the ghetto on this side of the river. It was also here that many Jews waited to be sent to extermination camps. The small, gray building at the river end of Ghetto Heroes' Square feels like a train car inside, evocative of the wagons that carried people from here to certain death.

▲Pharmacy Under the Eagle (Apteka pod Orłem)

This small but good museum, on Ghetto Heroes' Square, tells the story of Tadeusz Pankiewicz, a Polish Catholic pharmacist who chose to remain in Podgórze when it became a Jewish ghetto. During this time, the pharmacy was an important meeting point for the ghetto residents, and Pankiewicz and his staff heroically aided and hid Jewish victims of the Nazis. (Pankiewicz survived the war and was later acknowledged by Israel as one of the "Righteous Among the Nations"—non-Jews who risked their lives to help the Nazis' victims during World War II. You'll see his medal on display in the white memorial room at the end of the museum.) Today the pharmacy hosts an exhibit about the Jewish ghetto. You'll enter into the re-created pharmacy, where the "windows" are actually screens that show footage from the era. Push buttons, pull out drawers, answer the phone—it's full of interactive opportunities to better understand what ghetto life was like. You'll learn about people who worked in the pharmacy (including riveting interviews with eye-witnesses—some in English, others subtitled) and hear Pankiewicz telling stories about that tense time. You'll also learn a bit about the pharmacy business from that period.

Cost and Hours: 11 zł; if you're also going to the Schindler's Factory Museum, buy the 32-zł combo-ticket; free on Mon; open Mon 10:00-14:00, Tue-Sun 9:00-17:00, closed the second Tue of each month; plac Bohaterow Getta 18, tel. 12-656-5625, www.mhk.pl/branches/eagle-pharmacy.

▲▲▲Schindler's Factory Museum (Fabryka Emalia Oskara Schindlera)

One of Europe's best museums about the Nazi occupation fills some of the factory buildings where Oskar Schindler and his Jew-ish employees worked. The mu-seum tells the story of Schindler and his workers and also broad-ens its perspective to take in the full experience of all of Kraków during the painful era of Nazi rule. It's loaded with in-depth information (all in English), and touchscreens invite you to learn more and watch eyewitness in-terviews.  Scattered randomly between the exhibits are replicas of everyday places from the age—a photographer's shop, a tram car, a hairdresser's salon—designed to give you a taste of 1940s Kraków. Throughout the museum are calendar pages outlining wartime events and giving a sense of chronology. Note that you'll see noth-ing of the actual factory or equipment, as the threat of the advanc-ing Red Army forced Schindler to move his operation lock, stock, and barrel to Nazi-occupied Czechoslovakia in 1944.

Cost and Hours: 24 zł, 29-zł combo-ticket with next-door Museum of Contemporary Art, 32-zł "Memory Trail" combo-ticket with Pharmacy Under the Eagle; free on Mon; open April-Oct Mon 10:00-16:00 (except closes at 14:00 first Mon of month), Tue-Sun 9:00-20:00; Nov-March Mon 10:00-14:00, Tue-Sun 10:00-18:00; last entry 1.5 hours before closing, tel. 12-257-1017, www.mhk.pl/branches/oskar-schindlers-factory.

Advance Reservations: Crowds can be a real problem at this popular sight—especially on Mondays (when it's free, and many other museums are closed), during the summer holidays (June-

Aug), and midday (usually worst 11:00-16:00). At busy times, you may have to wait in a long line—an hour or more—just to buy a ticket. And then, once inside, congestion can make it challenging to fully appreciate the place. If you anticipate crowds, you can book tickets for no extra fee up to three days before your visit (www.bilety.mhk.pl); or you can buy tickets anytime (even for later the same day) at the Kraków City Museum visitors center in the Cloth Hall on the Main Market Square (see "Tourist Information" near the beginning of this chapter).

Crowd-Beating Tips: Even if you avoid the ticket line, the museum can still be jammed inside. The best strategy is to arrive early (9:00 or soon after on most days) or late (in summer, arriving by 18:00 gives you two hours to tour the exhibits)—but be warned that if you're arriving late without a reservation, it's possible on very busy days that all tickets could be sold out.

Getting There: It's in a gloomy industrial area a five-minute walk from Ghetto Heroes' Square (plac Bohaterow Getta): Go up Kącik street (to the left of the big, glass skyscraper), go under the railroad underpass, and continue two blocks, past MOCAK (the Museum of Contemporary Art in Kraków, described later) to the second big building on the left (ulica Lipowa 4). Look for signs to *Emalia*.

Visiting the Museum: You'll begin on the ground floor, where you'll buy your ticket and have the chance to tour the special exhibits. There's also a "film café" (interesting for fans of the movie) with refreshments. Then head upstairs to the first floor.

First Floor: The 35-minute **film**, called *Lipowa 4* (this building's address), sets the stage with interviews of both Jews and non-Jews describing their wartime experience (find it just off the museum's first, circular room; subtitled in English, it runs continuously). From here, the one-way route winds through the permanent exhibit, called **"Kraków Under Nazi Occupation 1939-1945."** First, while idyllic music plays, "stereoscopic" (primitive 3-D)

photos of prewar Kraków capture an idyllic age when culture flourished and the city's Jews (more than one-quarter of the population) blended more or less smoothly with their Catholic-Pole neighbors. But then, a video explains the Nazi invasion of Poland in early September of 1939: It took them only a few weeks to overrun the coun-

Oskar Schindler (1908-1974) and His List

Steven Spielberg's instant-classic, Oscar-winning 1993 film, *Schindler's List,* brought the world's attention to the inspiring story of Oskar Schindler, the compassionate German business-man who did his creative best to save the lives of the Jewish work-ers at his factory in Kraków. Spielberg chose to film the story right here in Kazimierz, where the events actually unfolded.

Oskar Schindler was born in 1908 in the Sudetenland (cur-rently part of the Czech Republic, then predominantly German). Early on, he displayed an idiosyncratic interpretation of ethics that earned him both wealth and enemies. As Nazi aggressions escalated, Schindler (who was very much a Nazi) carried out es-pionage against Poland; when Germany invaded the country in 1939, Schindler smelled a business opportunity. Early in the Nazi occupation of Poland, Schindler came to Kraków and lived in an apartment at ulica Straszewskiego 7 (a block from Wawel Castle). He took over the formerly Jewish-owned Emalia factory at ulica Lipowa 4, which produced metal pots and pans that were dipped into protective enamel; later the factory also began producing ar-maments for the Nazi war effort. The factory was staffed by about 1,000 Jews from the nearby Płaszów Concentration Camp, which was managed by the ruthless SS officer Amon Göth (depicted in *Schindler's List*—based on real events—shooting at camp inmates for sport from his balcony).

At a certain point, Schindler began to sympathize with his Jewish workers, and he increasingly did what he could to protect them and offer them better lives. Schindler fed them far better than most concentration-camp inmates and allowed them to sell some of the pots and pans they made on the black market to make money. After he saw many of his employees and friends murdered during an SS raid in 1943, he ramped up these efforts. He would come up with bogus paperwork to classify those threat-

try (which desperately awaited the promised help of their British and French allies, who never arrived).

Through the next several rooms, watch the film clip of SS soldiers marching through the Main Market Square—renamed "Adolf-Hitler-Platz"—and read stories about how the Nazis' *Gen-eralgouvernement* attempted to reshape the life of its new capital, "Krakau." (Near the tram car, look for the decapitated head of the Grunwald monument—described on page 247—which had been a powerful symbol of a Polish military victory over German forces.) You'll see the story of a newly German-owned shop selling Nazi propaganda and learn how professors at Kraków's Jagiellonian University were arrested to prevent them from fomenting rebel-lion among their students. During this time, even Polish secondary schools were closed—effectively prohibiting learning among Poles,

ened with deportation as "essential" to the workings of the factory—even if they were unskilled. He sought and was granted permission to build a "concentration camp" barracks for his workers on the factory grounds, where they lived in far better conditions than those at Płaszów. These lucky few became known as *Schindlerjuden*—"Schindler's Jews."

As the Soviet army encroached on Kraków in October of 1944, word came that the factory would need to be relocated west, farther from the front line. While Schindler could easily have simply turned his workers over to the concentration camp system and certain death—as most other industrialists did—he decided to bring them with him to his new factory at Brünnlitz (Brněnec, in today's Czech Republic). He assembled a list of 700 men and 300 women who worked with him, along with 200 other Jewish inmates, and at great personal expense, moved them to Brünnlitz. At the new factory, Schindler and the 1,200 people he had saved produced grenades and rocket parts—virtually all of them, the workers later claimed, mysteriously defective.

After the war, Schindler—who had spent much of his fortune protecting his Jewish workers—hopped around Germany and Argentina, repeatedly attempting but failing to break back into business (often with funding from Jewish donors). He died in poverty in 1974. In accordance with his final wishes, he was buried in Jerusalem, and today his grave is piled high with small stones left there by appreciative Jewish visitors. He has since been named one of the "Righteous Among the Nations" for his efforts to save Jews from the Holocaust. Thomas Keneally's 1982 book *Schindler's Ark* brought the industrialist's tale to a wide audience that included Steven Spielberg, who vaulted Schindler to the ranks of a pop-culture icon.

whom the Nazis considered inferior. But Polish students continued to meet clandestinely with their teachers. You'll also see images of Hans Frank—the hated puppet ruler of Poland—moving into the country's most important symbol of sovereignty, Wawel Castle.

The exhibit also details how early Nazi policies targeted Jews with roundups, torture, and execution. (Down the staircase is an eerie simulation of a cellar prison.) As the Nazis ratcheted up their genocidal activities, troops swept through Kraków on March 3, 1941, forcing all the remaining Jews in town to squeeze into the newly created Podgórze ghetto. At the bottom of the stairs, look for the huge pile of plunder—Jewish wealth stolen by the Nazis.

Second Floor: Climb upstairs using the long **staircase,** which was immortalized in a powerful scene in *Schindler's List*. At the top of the stairs on the right is a small room that served as "Schindler's office" for the film; more recently, it's been determined that his actual office was elsewhere (we'll see it soon).

You'll walk through a corridor lined by a replica of the wall that enclosed the **Podgórze ghetto** and see poignant exhibits about the horrific conditions there (including a replica of the cramped living quarters). The Nazis claimed that Jews had to be segregated here, away from the general population, because they "carried diseases."

Continue into the office of Schindler's secretary, with exhibits about Schindler's life and video touchscreens that play testimonial footage of Schindler's grateful

employees. Then proceed into the actual **Schindler's office.** The big map (with German names for cities) was uncovered only in recent years when the factory was being restored. Because Schindler's short tenure here was the only time in the factory's history that these Polish place names would appear in German, it's believed that this map was hung over his desk. Facing the map is a giant monument of enamel pots and pans, like those that were made in this factory. There are 1,200 pots—one for each Jewish worker that Schindler saved. Inside the monument, the walls are lined with the names on Schindler's famous list. The creaky floorboards are intentional: a reminder that the Nazis knew every step you took.

Proceeding through the exhibit, you'll learn more about everyday life—both for ghetto dwellers and for everyday non-Jewish Krakovians,

including the Polish resistance (see the Home Army's underground print shop). More eyewitness accounts relate the terrifying days of March 13 and 14, 1943, when the Podgórze ghetto was liquidated, sending survivors to the nearby Płaszów Concentration Camp. The replica of the Płaszów quarry,

where inmates were forced to work in unimaginably difficult conditions, provides a poignant memorial for those who weren't fortunate enough to wind up on Schindler's list.

Now head all the way back down to the ground floor.

Ground Floor: Exhibits here capture the uncertain days near the end of the war in the summer of 1944, when Nazis arrested between 6,000 and 8,000 suspected saboteurs after the Warsaw Uprising and sent them to Płaszów (see the replica of a basement hideout for 10 Jews who had escaped the ghetto); and later, when many Nazis had fled Kraków, leaving residents to await the Soviet Union's Red Army (see the replica air-raid shelters). The Red Army arrived here on January 18, 1945—at long last, the five years, four months, and twelve days of Nazi rule were over. The Soviets caused their own share of damage to the city before beginning a whole new occupation that would last for generations...but that's a different museum.

Finally, walk along the squishy floor—evoking how life for anyone was unstable and unpredictable during the Nazi occupation—into the **Hall of Choices.** The six rotating pillars tell the stories of people who chose to act—or not to act—when they witnessed atrocities. Think about the ramifications of the choices they made...and what you would have done in their shoes. The final room holds two books: a white book listing those who tried to help, and a black book listing Nazi collaborators. Exiting the museum, notice the portraits of Oscar Schindler's workers who lived long and happy lives after the war.

Nearby: Before heading back to downtown Kraków, consider paying a visit to the superb—and very different—**art museum** that fills the buildings on the factory grounds, behind this main building (described next). Or, for a glass of wine, head just a few doors down from the museum to find the delightful **Krakó Slow Wines** (marked *Lipowa 6F*). This mellow, inviting wine bar and shop is well stocked with wines mostly from Central and Eastern Europe (daily 10:00-22:00, mobile 669-225-222, www.krakoslowwines.pl).

▲Museum of Contemporary Art in Kraków (Muzeum Sztuki Współczesnej w Krakowie)

Called "MOCAK" for short, this museum exhibits a changing array of innovative and thought-provoking works by contemporary artists, often with heavy themes tied to the surrounding Holocaust sites. With the slogan Kunst macht frei ("Art will set you free"—a pointed spin on the Nazis' Arbeit macht frei concentration camp motto), the museum occupies warehouse buildings once filled by Schindler's workers.

Now converted to wide-open, bright-white halls, the buildings house many temporary exhibits as well as two permanent ones (the MOCAK Collection in the basement, and the library in the smaller side building). Pick up the floor plan as you enter. It's all well described in English and engaging even for those who don't usually like modern art.

Cost and Hours: 14 zł, 29-zł combo-ticket with next-door Schindler's Factory Museum, free on Tue; open Tue-Sun 11:00-19:00, closed Mon, last entry one hour before closing; Lipowa 4, tel. 12-263-4001, www.mocak.pl.

John Paul II Pilgrimage Sights

Catholics coming to Kraków eager to walk in the footsteps of St. John Paul II appreciate the city's dazzling churches and its Archdiocesan Museum. And for most, that's enough. But true pilgrims head for worthwhile sights outside the city center: two sanctuaries related to John Paul II on the outskirts of Kraków; and the John Paul II Family Home Museum in the town of Wadowice, an hour's drive away (and covered later).

Sanctuaries in Kraków

The two biggest, most impressive JPII destinations are about four miles south of Kraków's Old Town, in the Łagiewniki neighborhood. While the main attraction here for pilgrims is the John Paul II Sanctuary, historically and geographically you'll come first to the Divine Mercy Sanctuary—so I've covered that first. The sights aren't worth the trek for the merely curious, but they offer a glimpse of the deep faith that characterizes the Polish people.

Getting There: A **taxi** or **Uber** from downtown costs around 30-40 zł one-way and takes 20-30 minutes. Public transit connections to this area are still in flux, so ask for advice from the TI. But most likely, the best plan is to take **tram #8** (which loops around the Old Town, including stops next to St. Francis Basilica at plac Wszystkich Świętych, near Wawel Castle, and at plac Wolnica in Kazimierz) to the Divine Mercy Sanctuary (Sanktuarium Bożego Miłosierdzia stop)—about 30 minutes. From the tram stop, take the pedestrian underpass, turn right, cross the train tracks, and huff a few minutes uphill along the wall to find the entrance to the complex. (You can see the glass steeple of the church from the tram stop—a handy visual landmark.)

After touring the Divine Mercy sights, you'll head to the St. John Paul II Sanctuary—a long walk (20-25 minutes) or a short, inexpensive taxi trip (10-15 zł).

KRAKÓW

Divine Mercy Sanctuary
(Sanktuarium Bożego Miłosierdzia)

This complex, built around a humble red-brick convent, honors the early-20th-century St. Faustina, who saw a miraculous vision of Jesus that became a powerful religious symbol for many Catholics. Today, pilgrims from around the world come here to revere the relics both of Faustina and of John Paul II (who advocated for her sainthood), and to learn more about her story from the convent's present-day sisters—many of whom speak English.

Background: One cold and blustery evening in 1931, Sister Faustina Kowalska (1905-1938) answered the convent doorbell to find a beggar asking for some food. Faustina brought some soup to the man, who revealed his true nature: a figure of Jesus Christ clad in a white robe, with one hand raised in blessing and the other touching his chest. Emanating from his chest were twin beams of light: red (representing blood, the life of souls) and white (water, which through baptism washes souls righteously clean). Transformed by her experience, Faustina worked with an artist to create a painted version of the image—called the Divine Mercy—which has been embraced by Polish Catholics as one of the most important symbols of their faith.

Always frail in health, Faustina died at 33—the same age as Jesus. The story of Faustina deeply moved a young Karol Wojtyła. When he became pope, he dedicated the first Sunday after Easter as the day of Divine Mercy worldwide. In 2000, he made his fellow Krakovian the first Catholic saint of the third millennium. To properly revere the newly important St. Faustina, a bold, futuristic church and visitors center was built alongside her original convent.

Cost and Hours: All three parts of the complex—the smaller original chapel, a replica of Faustina's cell, and the huge, modern church, with its soaring bell tower—are free to enter, but donations are happily accepted. Each part has slightly different hours (listed later; www.faustyna.pl). Note that the daily 15:00 "Hour of Mercy" service—in both the chapel and the modern church—is worth planning around.

Visiting the Complex: Entering the complex through the side gate, look uphill to find a **walkway** with flags from around the world and plaques translating the Divine Mercy's message—"Jesus, I trust in you"—in dozens of languages.

Just before entering the **original chapel,** look up and to the

KRAKÓW

right—the window with the flowers marks the cell where Faustina died. Inside the chapel (daily 6:00-21:15), the altar to the left of the main altar displays an early copy of Faustina's Divine Mercy painting. Her relics are in the white case just below; in the white kneeler just in front of the chapel, notice the little reliquary holding one of her bones (which worshippers can embrace as they pray).

Leaving the chapel, turn left and go to the far end of the accommodations building. Enter the door on the right to find the **replica of Faustina's cell.** While this is a newer building, here they've created Faustina's convent cell, including many of her personal effects. Drop a coin in the slot for an evocative headphone description of these items, and of the vision of Jesus that put her convent on the map (usually open daily 8:30-18:00).

From here, head downhill and circle around the large brick building—passing (on the right) an area for outdoor Mass.

Dominating the campus is the futuristic, glass-and-steel **main church.** Consecrated by Pope John Paul II on his final visit to Poland in 2002, this build-ing has several elements (daily 7:00-20:00). The lower level has a variety of small chapels, each one donated by Catholic worshippers in a different country (Germany, Hungary, Slovakia, and so on)—and each with a dramatically different style. The central chapel on this level has a modern altar and another bone of St. Faustina. Upstairs, the main sanctuary is a sleek cylindrical space with wooden sunbeams sharply radiating from the altar area. That altar—framed by the gnarled limbs of windblown trees, representing the suffering of human existence—contains a replica of the Divine Mercy painting, flanked by the woman who saw the vision (Faustina, on the right) and the Polish pope who made it a worldwide phenomenon (John Paul II, on the left).

Head back out to the terrace surrounding the church. The bold **tower**—as tall as St. Mary's on Main Market Square, and with a statue of John Paul II at the bottom—has an elevator that you can ride up to a glassed-in viewpoint offering panoramas over the Divine Mercy campus, the adjacent John Paul II Sanctuary complex, and—on the distant horizon—the spires of Wawel Cathedral and Kraków's Old Town (daily 8:00-19:00). Near the base of the tower is a **canopy** where Mass is said on Divine Mercy Sunday each year, before a crowd of 100,000 who fill the fields below.

Connecting to the St. John Paul II Sanctuary: You can see the rectangular, brick tower of the JPII Sanctuary from the Divine

Mercy Sanctuary. However, an expressway is being built between the two churches, so access can be tricky (but will improve once the project is complete). Plan on a 20- to 25-minute walk. Better yet, go to the Divine Mercy Sanctuary's hotel (the boxy, white building just uphill from the main church). If no taxis are waiting in the parking lot out front, order an Uber or ask the reception desk to call a taxi for you; the ride should cost only 10-15 zł.

St. John Paul II Sanctuary
(Sanktuarium Św. Jana Pawła II)

This new complex, funded entirely by private donors, celebrates the life and sainthood of Kraków's favorite son. Construction is ongoing, but for now there are at least two sections of the complex worth visiting: the sanctuary and museum.

Cost and Hours: Sanctuary—free, daily 7:30-19:00, until 18:00 in winter, www.sanktuariumjp2.pl; museum—10 zł, daily 9:00-17:00.

Sanctuary of St. John Paul II: This hypermodern church is big and splendid. In the **downstairs** area, the central chapel features paintings of JPII's papal visits to various pilgrimage sites, both in Poland (Częstochowa) and abroad (Fátima, Lourdes). Ringing that central area is a variety of interesting smaller chapels.

On the outer wall, look for three in particular: The Kaplica Kapłańska is a replica of the St. Leonard's Crypt under Wawel Cathedral—where a young priest named Karol Wojtyła celebrated his first Mass. In this chapel, you'll see JPII's empty papal tomb from the crypt beneath St. Peter's Basilica at the Vatican. (When he became a saint, his remains—which, controversially, are kept in Rome rather than his homeland—were moved up into the main part of the church, and this simple grave marker was donated to this church.) You'll also see a reliquary in the shape of a book with fluttering pages, holding a small amount of John Paul II's blood (for the story of the book, see page 266). This blood was kept in secret by JPII's personal secretary, only revealed after his death, when it was divvied up among a select few churches. Nearby, another chapel holds the tombs of a few recent cardinals; as they're running out of space below Wawel Cathedral, this chapel is poised to han-

dle the overflow. And the Kaplica Św. Kingi features finely executed reliefs in rock salt, in the style of Wieliczka Salt Mine.

Head upstairs to the sleek, modern **main sanctuary.** The concrete structure supports large walls, providing a canvas for dynamic mosaics of Bible stories. Above the main altar, in the middle, you'll see the Three Kings delivering their gifts to the Baby Jesus and the Virgin Mary—with St. John Paul II serenely overlooking the scene. Other scenes include Adam and Eve, Jesus calming the storm, the wedding feast at Cana, and the Last Supper. In the back-left corner, a smaller chapel has a display case with the blood-spattered vestments that St. John Paul II was wearing on May 13, 1981, when he was shot by a would-be assassin.

The sanctuary anchors a sprawling complex of conference facilities and other attractions for pilgrims. Poke around. The museum, described next (and on the right as you exit the sanctuary's main door), is the sight most worth visiting.

St. John Paul II Museum: This collects the many gifts bestowed on the beloved pope (African carved masks and ivory tusks; Latin American tapestries; the key to the city of Long Branch, New Jersey; a pair of glass doves of peace given to him—perhaps with a touch of irony—by US vice president Dick Cheney); ornate worship aids (chalices, crosses, and so on); and modern art that celebrates the modern pope and his life's work. There are also personal items, from his papal ski and hiking gear to the place settings from his Vatican dinner table to his stylish red leather shoes. You'll also see the throne from his last visit to Poland in 2002, and a replica of the humble room across the street from St. Francis Basilica where he stayed on visits back to his homeland.

Returning to Kraków: Taxis may be waiting at the sanctuary; otherwise, you can ask the museum desk to call one for you (or order an Uber). By public transportation, you can walk about 10 minutes downhill (crossing the white bridge over the railway tracks) to busy Zakopiańska street; near the Cinema City, you'll find a stop for tram #8 back to the Old Town.

John Paul II Sights in Wadowice

Karol Wojtyła was born and lived up until age 18 in Wadowice (VAH-doh-veet-seh), about 30 miles (a one-hour drive) southwest of Kraków. As it's roughly in the same direction as Auschwitz, a local guide or driver can help you connect both places for one busy day of contrasts. Visiting by public bus or minibus is possible (about 1.25 hours one-way); ask the TI for details.

The lovely town of Wadowice (about 20,000 people) has a quaint and beautifully restored main square with a pretty Baroque steeple. John Paul II pilgrims find it worth a visit to see the **John Paul II Family Home Museum,** which fills four floors of the tenement building where his family lived through his adolescence. You'll explore a multimedia overview of the life and times of one of the newest Catholic saints, including rooms of the family home, a collection of clothing and other articles that belonged to JPII, photographs and video clips of his life and of the tumultuous period in which he lived, and plenty of interactive displays to bring the entire story to life. Admission is limited, and you'll be accompanied the entire time. Ideally, time your visit to go with an English guide (typically 2/day, likely at 11:00 and 14:00—confirm in advance); otherwise, you'll join the Polish tour. Either way, the tour can be a bit rushed, with less time to linger over the exhibits than you might like (20 zł with a Polish guide, 30 zł with English guide, free and crowded on Tue—book 2 weeks ahead; open daily May-Sept 9:00-19:00, April and Oct until 18:00, Nov-March until 16:00, closed last Tue of each month; last entry 1.5 hours before closing, across the street from the town church at ulica Kościelna 7, tel. 33-823-2662, www.homejp2.com).

Sights Outside Kraków

These interesting sights—an impressive salt mine, a purpose-built communist town, and an unusual earthwork—require a bus, tram, or train ride to reach.

▲▲Wieliczka Salt Mine (Kopalnia Soli Wieliczka)

Wieliczka (veel-EECH-kah), a salt mine southeast of Kraków, is beloved by Poles. Hundreds of feet beneath the ground, the mine is filled with sculptures that miners have lovingly carved out of the salt. You'll explore this unique gallery—learning both about the art and about medieval mining techniques—on a required tour. Though the sight is a bit overrated, it's unique and practically obligatory if you're in Kraków for a few days. In my experience, about half of those who visit love Wieliczka, while half feel it's a waste of time—but it can be hard to predict which half you're in. Read this description before you decide. And expect a lot of walking.

Cost and Hours: The standard "tourist route" costs 89 zł and is by guided tour only. English-language tours leave April-Oct 8:00-19:00 and Nov-March 9:00-17:00 (these are first and last tour times). Other routes are more in-depth (such as the interactive "Miner's Route," where visitors wear coveralls and helmets and operate some of the old equipment); for details see the website.

KRAKÓW

Information: The mine is in the town of Wieliczka at ulica Daniłowicza 10 (tel. 12-278-7302, www.kopalnia.pl).

Crowd-Beating Tips: This popular sight can be plagued by crowds, and there's a strict limit on how many people can be in the mine at once (due to the ventilation system). It's busiest between 10:00 and 16:00—try to arrive before or after those times (the ticket office opens at 7:30; since the last English tour leaves at 19:00 in summer, arriving in the afternoon can be a good way to stretch your sightseeing day). It's most crowded on weekends and in the summer, and overrun on long holiday weekends.

If you're coming on a summer weekend, any day during peak hours, or anytime you anticipate crowds, it's smart to book ahead online (no extra charge). You can also buy your tickets—and get an appointed entry time—at the **Wieliczka Promotion Office,** in Kraków's Old Town (Mon-Fri 9:00-18:00, closed Sat-Sun, Wiślna 12a). However, reservations are only possible up until three days before; after that, you'll have to show up and take your chances. At any time, it's possible to call ahead to the mine to ask about how busy it is, and to get advice about the best time to show up.

Getting There: The salt mine is 10 miles from Kraków. By far the easiest option is to hop on the **train** at Kraków's main train station (2/hour, 4 zł, 20 minutes, get off at Wieliczka Rynek-Kopalnia; from there, walk up through the parking lot and follow signs to the Daniłowicza shaft and entrance, about 5 minutes). In a pinch, you can take **bus #304** (at Kurniki stop, across from church near Galeria Krakowska mall) or a **minibus,** but these take longer (40 minutes)—get details at the TI, or review your options at the www.jakdojade.pl/krakow route finder. **Private drivers** also make this trip (see page 241).

Getting In: You'll begin at the bustling area around the Daniłowicz shaft. If you reserved a ticket online, follow signs to online tickets pickup point. If you need to buy a ticket on the spot, find the ticket sales line. Once you have a ticket, line up at the English tour area. This waiting area is outdoors, with flimsy canopies to protect from the elements (if it's wet, bring rain gear); they're hoping to build a new indoor waiting area soon.

Visitor Information: You'll pay an extra 10 zł to use your camera—but be warned that flash photos often don't turn out, thanks to the irregular reflection of the salt crystals. Dress warmly—the mine is a constant 57 degrees Fahrenheit. Before entering, you'll have to check large bags.

Eating: There's a good little **$ cafeteria** deep down in the mine, at the end of the tour route. Up at the surface is a wide range of eateries, from snack stands to sit-down restaurants.

Background: Going all the way back to Neolithic times, prehistoric tribes gathered salt from springs in this area. In the 1280s,

Wieliczka Salt Mine began producing salt in earnest. Under Kazimierz the Great, one-third of Poland's income came from these precious deposits—back in an age when salt was called "white gold" and was extremely valuable for its ability to preserve foods. (The Romans even paid workers in salt—*salarium*, the origin of our word "salary.") The mines were so valuable that Kazimierz the Great enacted laws protecting the miners—the first known instance of worker-protection laws in Europe. Wieliczka was controlled by the Polish crown and, after the Partitions, by the Austro-Hungarian Empire (which outfitted miners with military-style uniforms). During this time, around the Industrial Revolution (and under efficient Austrian management), the mine hit peak productivity.

Wieliczka miners spent much of their lives underground, leaving for work before daybreak and returning after sundown, rarely emerging into daylight. To pass the time, beginning in the 17th century, miners carved figures, chandeliers, and even entire underground chapels out of the salt. For many modern visitors, these carvings are the most memorable part of Wieliczka.

Until just a few years ago, the mine still produced salt. Today's miners—about 400 of them—primarily work on maintaining the 200 miles of chambers. This entire network is supported by pine beams—over time, the salt strengthens the wood (some you'll see are more than 200 years old), whereas metal would rust. Per tradition, the wood beams are painted white, to reflect the dim light of the miners' oil lamps. Today visitors see only about 1.5 percent of the sprawling mines. (You would not want to visit the original medieval mines, which have tunnels only about three feet tall.)

Visiting the Mine: From the lobby, your guide leads you 380 steps down a winding staircase. If you've always wanted to feel true vertigo, peer between the banisters on your way down. Once at level 1, you begin a 1.5-mile stroll, generally downhill (more than 800 steps down altogether), past 20 of the mine's 2,000 chambers (with signs explaining when they were dug), finishing 443 feet below the surface (at level 3). When you're done, an elevator beams you back up.

As you spelunk, your guide offers a canned commentary about the history of the mines. You'll learn how the miners lived and worked, using horses who spent their entire adult lives without ever seeing the light of day. You'll see the gigantic horse-pulled wheels used to operate lifts

KRAKÓW

within the mines, and find out why igniting pockets of methane gas near the ceiling was the most dangerous part of the job (the mortality rate for miners was about 1 in 10). All along the way, you'll walk through tunnels caved out of the rock salt; although it can be dark in color (mixed with other minerals such as sandstone and gypsum), it's about 90 percent pure salt. To transport the salt out of the mine, the miners would either carve it into big blocks or crush it and pour it into barrels.

The tour takes you through vast underground caverns, past subterranean lakes (32 percent salt—like the Black Sea, the maximum allowed by nature), and introduces you to some of the mine's many sculptures. You'll see Copernicus (who actually visited here in the 15th century), an army of salt elves, the Polish military hero Józef Piłsudski, and this region's favorite son, St. John Paul II.

Your jaw will drop as you enter the enormous **Chapel of St. Kinga,** carved over three decades in the early 20th century. Look for the salt-relief carving of the Last Supper (its 3-D details are astonishing, considering it's just six inches deep). The chapel is still used for services every Sunday morning at 7:30.

From there, you'll see a few more chambers, including one with a big lake and a brief sound-and-light show. Your tour finishes in a deep-down shopping zone about 1.5 hours after you started. From here you can decide to return to the surface, or add on the Mine Museum.

Returning to the Surface: You'll loop around through a handy cafeteria, then present yourself at the exit, where there are three lines. When you're ready to head up, get in the *exit for individual tourists* line, and the attendant will decide which of two elevators you'll use for the ride up: the old-school Daniłowicz shaft, back up to where you began; or the slick, modern Regis shaft, which pops you out closer to the town center of Wieliczka. From there, it's a pleasant 10-minute walk past the town church and castle, and through a park, back to where you started—a guide will take you the whole way, or you can peel off to explore the town (the main square is just uphill from the shaft). Note that you have zero say over which exit you use—it depends entirely on crowds. The line can seem long, but it moves fast—you'll rarely wait more than 10-15 minutes.

Optional Add-On—Mine Museum: If you're not pooped, you can tack on a visit to the museum (included in your ticket)—which adds about an hour and a mile more walking. While overkill for most, the museum is worthwhile for those who enjoyed exploring the mine and would appreciate a little more historical context. Just get in the *museum* line instead of the *exit* line. A guide will take you through the exhibits, showing you the fancy Habsburg-era miner uniforms; historic maps and etchings of the networks of mines, and cutaway scenes of life below the surface; tools and mining equipment (including a variety of Aladdin-style oil lamps, and huge slings used to lower horses into the mines); a photo gallery of famous visitors, including kings, queens, popes, presidents, and Lech Wałęsa; and a remarkably detailed model of the town of Wieliczka circa 1645. Afterwards, you'll head up to the surface on one of the two elevators.

In the winter only, you can pay an extra 8 zł near the entrance to the museum for a little **underground train ride,** about 2.5 km to a station and back again (not possible in high season).

Nearby: Near the parking lot, you'll see the **"Graduation Tower,"** a modern fort-like structure with a wooden walkway up top. The tower is designed to evaporate and then condense the supposedly very healthy brine from deep underground. The resulting moist, salty air is used to treat patients with lung problems. While locals are prescribed visits here, for most tourists it's not worth the extra money.

▲Nowa Huta

Nowa Huta (NOH-vah HOO-tah, "New Steel Works"), an enormous planned workers' town, offers a glimpse into the stark, grand-scale aesthetics of the communists. Because it's five miles east of central Kraków and a little tricky to see on your own, skip it unless you're determined—it can be tricky to appreciate. But architects and communist sympathizers may want to make a pilgrimage here.

Getting There: Tram #4 goes from near Kraków's Old Town (catch the tram on the ring road near Kraków's main train station, at the Dworzec Główny stop) along John Paul II Avenue (aleja Jana Pawła II) to Nowa Huta's main square, plac Centralny (about 30 minutes total), then continues a few minutes farther to the main gate of the Tadeusz Sendzimir Steelworks—the end of the line. From there it returns to plac Centralny and back to Kraków.

Tours: True to its name, Mike Ostrowski's **Crazy Guides** is a loosely run operation that takes tourists to Nowa Huta in genuine communist-era vehicles (mostly Trabants and Polski Fiats). If you've got an interest in the history—and would enjoy spending the day careening around the streets of Kraków in a car that feels like a cardboard box with a lawnmower engine—hire one of their laid-back hipster guides (159 zł/person for 2.5-hour "communism tour" of Nowa Huta; 199 zł/person for 4-hour "communism deluxe" tour that also includes lunch at a milk bar and a visit to their period-decorated communist apartment; other options available—described on website, mobile 500-091-200, www.crazyguides.com, info@crazyguides.com). If you're already hiring a **local guide** in Kraków, consider paying a little extra to add a couple of hours for a short side trip by car to Nowa Huta.

KRAKÓW

Background: Nowa Huta was the communists' idea of paradise. It's one of only three towns outside the Soviet Union that
were custom-built to showcase socialist ideals. (The others are Du-
naújváros—once called Sztálinváros—south of Budapest, Hungary; and Eisenhüttenstadt—once called
Stalinstadt—near Brandenburg, Germany.) Completed in just 10 years (1949-
1959), Nowa Huta was built primarily because the Soviets felt that smart and sassy
Kraków needed a taste of heavy industry.
Farmers and villagers were imported to
live and work in Nowa Huta. Many of the
new residents, who weren't accustomed to
city living, brought along their livestock
(which grazed in the fields around unfinished buildings). For commies, it was
downright idyllic: Dad would cheerily
ride the tram into the steel factory, mom

would dutifully keep house, and the kids could splash around at
the man-made beach and learn how to cut perfect red stars out
of construction paper. But Krakovians had the last laugh: Nowa
Huta, along with Lech Wałęsa's shipyard in Gdańsk, was one of
the home bases of the Solidarity strikes that eventually brought
down the regime. Now, with the communists long gone, Nowa
Huta remains a major suburb of Poland's cultural capital, with a
whopping 200,000 residents.

Touring Nowa Huta: Nowa Huta's focal point used to be
known simply as **Central Square** (plac Centralny), but in a fit of
poetic justice, it was recently renamed for the anticommunist Ronald Reagan. A map of Nowa Huta looks like a clamshell: a semi-
circular design radiating from Central/Reagan Square. Numbered
streets fan out like spokes on a wheel, and trolleys zip workers directly to the immense factory.

Believe it or not, the inspiration for Nowa Huta was the Renaissance (which, thanks to the textbook Renaissance design of
the Cloth Hall and other landmarks, Soviet architects considered
typically Polish). Notice the elegantly predictable arches and galleries that would make Michelangelo proud. The settlement was
loosely planned on the gardens of Versailles (comparing aerial
views of those two very different sites—both with axes radiating
from a central hub—this becomes clear). When first built (before
it was layered with grime), Nowa Huta was delightfully orderly,
primly painted, impeccably maintained, and downright beautiful...
if a little boring. It was practical, too: Each of the huge apartment
blocks is a self-contained unit, with its own grassy inner courtyard,

school, and shops. Driveways (which appear to dead-end at underground garage doors) lead to vast fallout shelters.

Today's Nowa Huta—while gentrifying—is a far cry from its glory days. Wander around. Poke into the courtyards. Reflect on what it would be like to live here. It may not be as bad as you imagine. Ugly as they may seem from the outside, these buildings are packed with happy little apartments filled with color, light, and warmth.

The wide boulevard running northeast of Central/Reagan Square, now called Solidarity Avenue (aleja Solidarności, lined with tracks for tram #4), leads to the **Tadeusz Sendzimir Steelworks.** Originally named for Lenin, this factory was supposedly built using plans stolen from a Pittsburgh plant. It was designed to be a cog in the communist machine—reliant on iron ore from Ukraine and therefore worthless unless Poland remained in the Soviet Bloc. Down from as many as 40,000 workers at its peak, the steelworks now employs only about 10,000. Today there's little to see other than the big sign, stern administration buildings, and smokestacks in the distance. Examine the twin offices flanking the sign—topped with turrets and a decorative frieze inspired by Italian palazzos, these continue the Renaissance theme of the housing districts.

Another worthwhile sight in Nowa Huta is the **Lord's Ark Church** (Arka Pana, several blocks northwest of Central/Reagan Square on ulica Obrońców Krzyża). Back when he was archbishop of Kraków, Karol Wojtyła fought for years to build a church in this most communist of communist towns. When the regime refused, he insisted on conducting open-air Masses before crowds in fields—until the

communists finally capitulated. Consecrated on May 15, 1977, the Lord's Ark Church has a Le Corbusier–esque design that looks like a fat, exhausted Noah's Ark resting on Mount Ararat—encouraging Poles to persevere through the floods of communism. While architecturally interesting, the church is mostly significant as a symbol of an early victory of Catholicism over communism.

Kościuszko Mound (Kopiec Kościuszki)

On a sunny day, the parklands west of the Old Town are a fine place to get out of the city and commune with Krakovians at play. On the outskirts of town is the Kościuszko Mound, a nearly perfectly conical hill erected in 1823 to honor Polish and American military hero Tadeusz Kościuszko. The mound incorporates soil that was brought here from battlefields where the famous general fought, both in Poland and in the American Revolution. Later, under Habsburg rule, a citadel with a chapel was built around the mound, which provided a fine lookout over this otherwise flat terrain. And more recently, the hill was reinforced with steel and cement to prevent it from eroding away. You'll pay to enter the walls and walk to the top—up a curlicue path that makes the mound resemble a giant soft-serve cone—and inside you'll find a modest Kościuszko museum. While not too exciting, this is a pleasant place for an excursion on a nice day.

Cost and Hours: 14 zł, includes museum, mound open daily 9:00-dusk, museum open daily 9:30-19:00—shorter hours off-season, café, tel. 12-425-1116, www.kopieckosciuszki.pl.

Getting There: Ride tram #1 or #6 (from in front of the Wyspiański Pavilion or the main post office) to the end of the line, called Salvator. From here, you can either follow the well-marked path uphill for 20 minutes, or hop on bus #100 to the top (runs at :10 past each hour).

Shopping in Kraków

Two of the most popular Polish souvenirs—amber and pottery—come from areas far from Kraków. You won't find any great bargains on those items here, but several shops specializing in them are listed next. Somewhat more local are the many wood carvings you'll see.

The **Cloth Hall,** smack-dab in the center of the Main Market Square, is the most convenient place to pick up any Polish souvenirs. It has a great selection at respectable prices (summer Mon-Fri 9:00-18:00, Sat-Sun until 15:00—but many stalls remain open later; winter Mon-Fri 9:00-16:00, Sat-Sun until 15:00).

Here are some other souvenir ideas, and neighborhoods or streets that are particularly enjoyable for browsing.

Jewelry

The popular **amber** *(bursztyn)* you'll see sold around town is found on northern Baltic shores; if you're also heading to Gdańsk, wait until you get there (for more on amber, see page 456). One unique alternative that's a bit more local is **"striped flint"** *(krzemień pasiasty),* a stratified stone that's polished to a high shine. It's mined in a very specific subregion near Kraków, and has become popular among Hollywood celebrities. Each piece has its own unique wavy, sandy patterns.

Jewelry shops abound in the Old Town. For a good selection

of striped flint, amber, and other jewelry, try the no-name shop on **plac Mariacki,** the little square facing the side entrance of St. Mary's Church; they also have a selection of Polish folk costumes in the basement (at #9). A few more jewelry and design shops cluster along Sławkowska street, which runs north from the Main Market Square.

Polish Pottery

"Polish pottery," with distinctive blue-and-white designs, is made in the region of Silesia, west of Kraków (in and around the town of Bolesławiec). But, assuming you won't be going there, you can browse one of the shops in Kraków. **Ceramika Bolesławiecka,** on a busy urban street between the Old Town and Kazimierz, has a tasteful, affordable selection of pottery that's oriented more for locals than tourists (closed Sun, Starowiślna 37). In the Old Town—and with inflated prices to match—two places face each other across Sławkowska street, just a block north of the Square: **Dekor Art** at #11 and **Mila** at #14.

Foods, Drinks, and Cosmetics

Krakowski Kredens is a handy, well-curated shop for overpriced but good-quality traditional foods from Kraków and the surrounding region, Galicia. While the deli case in the back is a pricey place to shop for a picnic (head for a supermarket instead), this is a good chance to stock up on souvenir-quality Polish foods for the folks back home. They have several locations around Kraków—and elsewhere in Poland—but one handy branch is just in front of the Florian Gate at Floriańska 42 (www.krakowskikredens.pl).

Szambelan, a block south of the Main Market Square, is a fun concept for vodka lovers: Peruse the giant casks of three dozen different flavored vodkas, buy an empty bottle, and they'll fill and seal it to take home (Gołębia 2 at the corner with Bracka).

Mydlarnia u Franciszka, with a few locations around Kraków (including a handy one just south of the Main Market Square at Gołębia 2), sells a variety of fragrant soaps, lotions, shampoos, and other cosmetics, some produced locally.

T-Shirts

Two creative shops in the Old Town sell souvenir T-shirts that are a step up in quality (and price) from the generic shops on the square. **Chrum** specializes in locally themed ironic T-shirts (closed Sun, across the street from the Barbican at plac Matejki 3, www. chrum.com), while **Red is Bad** sticks with tasteful, classic Polish eagles and flags on quality materials (closed Sun, just west of the Square at Szewska 25, www.redisbad.pl).

KRAKÓW

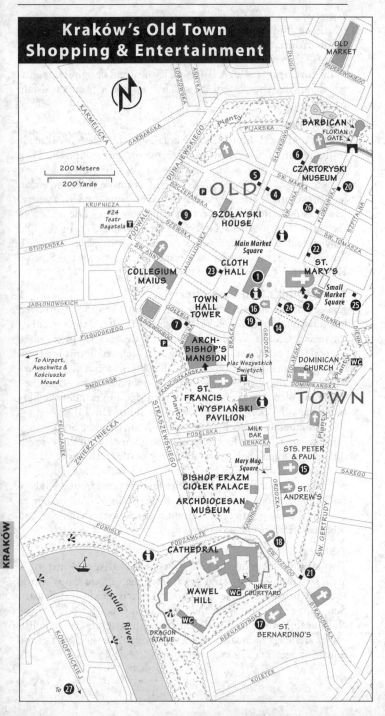

Kraków's Old Town Shopping & Entertainment

Shopping
1. Cloth Hall
2. Plac Mariacki Jewelry
3. Ceramika Bolesławiecka
4. Dekor Art
5. Mila & Chopin Gallery/Royal Chamber Orchestra Hall
6. Krakowski Kredens
7. Szambelan & Mydlarnia u Franciszka
8. Chrum
9. Red is Bad
10. To Ulica Józefa Shops
11. Kacper Global Shoes
12. Galeria Krakowska
13. Galeria Kazimierz
14. Pasaż 13 Mall

Entertainment
15. Sts. Peter and Paul Church
16. St. Adalbert Church
17. St. Bernadino's/Bernardynów
18. St. Idziego/Giles Church
19. Polonia House/Dom Polonii
20. Jama Michalika
21. Hotel Royal (bus to Skansen Smaków)
22. Jazz Club u Muniaka
23. Harris Piano Jazz Bar
24. Buddha Nightclub
25. Vodka Café Bar
26. Staropolskie Trunki (Vodka Tasting)
27. To Forum Przestrzenie

KRAKÓW

Designer Shops along Ulica Józefa, in Kazimierz

As the epicenter of Kraków's hipster scene, Kazimierz is the best place in town to browse one-off boutiques (both design and fashion). Several good options line up along ulica Józefa, mostly concentrated along a two-block stretch. Head just one block south from plac Nowy on Estery street, turn right, and keep an eye out for these shops (mostly on the left side of the street): **Blazko,** at #11, has some modern, colorful jewelry, handmade right on the premises. A few doors down **Galerie d'Art Naïf** features fascinating works by untrained artists, and (next door) **Deccoria Galeria** feels like a junk shop, cluttered with handmade jewelry, art, accessories, and vintage clothes. Next are **Paon Nonchalant,** with Polish fashion, and a vintage shop. **Art Factory,** at #9, is worth a browse for colorful jewelry, accessories, and housewares by local designers. **Pracownia** ("Lab"), farther down and also at #9, sells handmade art, jewelry, and clothes. And more clothes by Polish designers are across the street at **Nuumi Boutique** (#14).

A couple of blocks away, just off plac Wolnica, is another great spot for local design, housewares, jewelry, and casual fashion (i.e., creative T-shirts): **Idea Fix** and **The Hive Store,** which share a storefront at Bocheńska 7 (daily).

Up closer to Kazimierz's main drag, ulica Szeroka, **Kacper Global** has a large outlet selling made-in-Poland shoes in styles from athletic to casual to stylish (Miodowa 33).

Shopping Malls

Two enormous shopping malls lie just beyond the tourist zone. The gigantic **Galeria Krakowska,** with nearly 300 shops, shares a square with the train station (Mon-Sat 9:00-22:00, Sun 10:00-21:00, has a kids' play area upstairs from the main entry). Only slightly smaller is **Galeria Kazimierz** (daily 10:00-21:00, just a few blocks east of the Kazimierz sights, along the river at Podgórska 24). A small but swanky mall called **Pasaż 13** is a few steps off the southeast corner of the Main Market Square, where Grodzka street enters the Square. Enter the mall under the balcony marked Pasaż 13. You'll find a cool brick-industrial interior, with upscale international chains...and not much that's Polish (Mon-Sat 11:00-21:00, Sun until 17:00).

Entertainment in Kraków

As a town full of both students and tourists, Kraków has plenty of fun options, especially at night.

IN THE OLD TOWN

For locations of the following places, see the map on page 320.

Main Market Square

Intoxicating as the Square is by day, it's even better at night...pure enchantment. Have a meal or sip a drink at an outdoor café, or just grab a bench and enjoy the scene. There's often live al fresco music coming from somewhere (either at restaurants, at a temporary stage set up near the Town Hall Tower, or from talented buskers). You could spend hours doing slow laps around the Square after dark, and never run out of diversions. For a great view over the Square at twilight, nurse a drink at **Café Szał**—on the Cloth Hall's upper terrace (long hours, enter through Gallery of 19th-Century Polish Art).

Concerts

You'll find a wide range of musical events, from tourist-oriented Chopin concerts and classical "greatest hits" selections in quaint old ballrooms and churches, to folk-dancing shows, to serious philharmonic performances. Several companies offer competing concerts; some of the best established include www.cracowconcerts.com, www.newculture.pl, and www.facebook.com/orkiestrasm. The free, monthly *Karnet* cultural-events book lists everything (also online at www.karnet.krakow.pl). Because the offerings change from week to week, inquire locally about what's on during your visit. Hotel lobbies are stocked with fliers, but to get all of your options, visit the TI north of the Square on ulica Św. Jana, which specializes in cultural events (they can book tickets for most concerts with no extra fee and can tell you how to get tickets for the others).

Popular Classical Concerts: The three main choices are organ concerts in churches (usually at 17:00); orchestral or chamber music; or Chopin (either can happen anytime between 18:00 and 20:00). The going rate for most concerts is around 65 zł. Many are held in churches (such as **Sts. Peter and Paul** on ulica Grodzka, **St. Adalbert** on the Square, **St. Bernadino's/Bernardynów** near Wawel Castle, or **St. Idziego/Giles** near Wawel Castle). You'll also find concerts in fancy mansions on or near the Main Market Square (including the **Polonia House/Dom Polonii** upstairs from Wierzynek restaurant at #14, near ulica Grodzka; and the **Chopin Gallery**—also billed as the **Royal Chamber Orchestra Hall**—just up Sławkowska street from the Square at #14). Occasionally in summer, they're also held in various gardens around town (July-Aug only, as part of a festival).

Folk Music: Various venues present dinner shows in the old center. At any of these, a small, hardworking ensemble of colorfully costumed Krakovian singers, dancers, and musicians put on a fun little folk show. While the food, the space, and the clientele are all quite tired, it's a nice taste of Polish folk traditions—and the

KRAKÓW

performers try hard to involve members of the audience in the pol-
kas and circle dances. Options include the historic **Jama Michalika,** with its dusty old Art Nouveau interior right along Floriańska
street (120 zł includes dinner; Wed and Sat at 19:00; Floriańska
45, tel. 12-422-1561, www.cracowconcerts.com); or two restaurants right on the Square: **Pod Złotym Karpiem** (at #10; 120 zł
for dinner and show, Thu-Fri and Sun at 18:00, tel. 604-093-570,
www.cracowconcerts.com) or **Tradycyja Restaurant** (at #15; 60 zł
for just the show, 120 zł to add dinner; Sat at 19:00; mobile 602-
850-900, www.newculture.pl).

For a more serious folk music performance—and to really
make an evening of it—consider a show in a more rustic setting
just outside of town. The restaurant **Skansen Smaków,** filling a log
cabin-like building, has shows each Thursday night. You'll meet
the bus at the Hotel Royal near Wawel Castle at 18:30, ride to the
restaurant, have a traditional Polish feast during the show, then be
brought back home to the Old Town by 22:00 (150 zł, book ahead,
tel. 12-357-1006, www.skansensmakow.pl).

Jazz

Kraków has a surprisingly thriving jazz scene. Several popular
clubs hide on the streets surrounding the Main Market Square
(open nightly, most shows start around 21:30, sometimes free or
a cover of 15-30 zł for better shows). **Jazz Club u Muniaka** is the
most famous and best for all-around jazz in a sophisticated cellar
environment (ulica Floriańska 3, tel. 12-423-1205). **Harris Piano
Jazz Bar,** right on the Square (at #28), is more casual and offers a
mix of traditional and updated "fusion" jazz, plus blues (tel. 12-
421-5741, www.harris.krakow.pl).

Nightlife in the Old Town

The entire Old Town is crammed with nightclubs and discos pump-
ing loud music on weekends. On a Saturday, the pedestrian streets
can be more crowded at midnight than at noon. However, with the
exception of the jazz clubs mentioned earlier, most of the nightspots in the Old Town are garden-variety dance clubs, completely
lacking the personality and creativity of the Kazimierz nightspots
described next. Worse, to save money, young locals stand out in
front of nightclubs to drink their own booze (BYOB) rather than
pay high prices for the drinks inside—making the streets that
much more crowded and noisy. For low-key hanging out, people
choose a café on the Square; otherwise, they head for Kazimierz.

In addition to the Harris Piano Jazz Bar (listed earlier), two
places on the Square worth checking out are near the southeast
corner. At #6, head into the passage to find the **Buddha** nightclub, with comfy lounge sofas under awnings in an immaculate-
ly restored old courtyard. For something funkier and even more

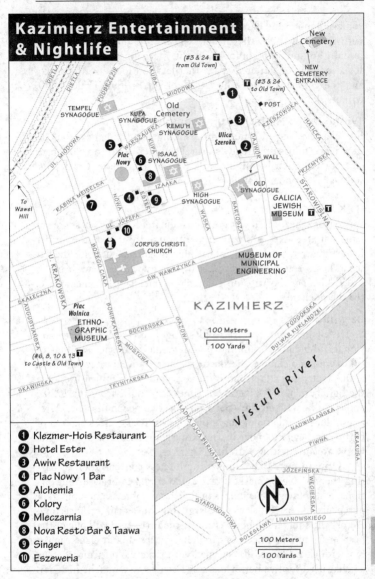

Kazimierz Entertainment & Nightlife

1. Klezmer-Hois Restaurant
2. Hotel Ester
3. Awiw Restaurant
4. Plac Nowy 1 Bar
5. Alchemia
6. Kolory
7. Mleczarnia
8. Nova Resto Bar & Taawa
9. Singer
10. Eszeweria

local, go down the passage at #19, which runs a surprisingly long distance through the block. Soon you'll start to see tables for the **Herring Embassy;** you'll eventually emerge at **Stolarska street,** a still-enjoyable but far less touristy scene (for more on the Herring Embassy and Stolarska, see page 337).

If you have (or would like to cultivate) an appreciation for vodka, stop by the **Vodka Café Bar,** serving more than 100 types of vodkas, liquors, and hard drinks. You can buy a tasting flight board with six small shots; they'll help you narrow down your options (usually around 33-50 zł for the flight, more for top-shelf vodkas). It's a mellow, uncluttered space that lets you focus on the vodka and the company (Mon-Thu 14:00-24:00, Fri-Sun 13:00-24:00, Mikołajska 5).

Tytano Dolne Młyny Cultural Complex

For lively evening and late-night drinking and dining near the Old Town, don't miss this trendy cultural complex, filling an old tobacco factory about a 10-minute walk west of the Square. For details, see page 340 under "Eating in Kraków."

IN KAZIMIERZ

Aside from the Old Town's gorgeous Square, Kraków's best area to hang out after dark is Kazimierz. Although this is also the former Jewish quarter, the Jewish Sabbath has nothing to do with the bar scene here. You can, however, still hear traditional Jewish music called klezmer. For tips on enjoying a concert of klezmer music, see the sidebar.

Bars and Clubs

Squeezed between centuries-old synagogues and cemeteries are wonderful hangouts running the full gamut from sober and tasteful to wild and clubby. The classic recipe for a Kazimierz bar: Find a dilapidated old storefront, fill it with ramshackle furniture, turn the lights down low, pipe in old-timey jazz music from the 1920s, and sprinkle with alcohol. Serves one to two dozen hipsters. After a few clubs of this type caught on, a more diverse cross-section of nightspots began to move in, including some loud dance clubs. The whole area is bursting with life.

On and near Plac Nowy: The highest concentration of bars ring the plac Nowy market square. Do a loop to browse your options. **Plac Nowy 1** specializes in Polish microbrews and upmarket pub grub in a bright, sleek (and arguably "un-Kazimierz") setting. Across the square, **Alchemia,** one of the first—and still one of the best—bars in Kazimierz, is candlelit, cluttered, and claustrophobic, with cave-like rooms crowded with rickety old furniture, plus a cellar used for live performances (Estery 5, www.alchemia.com.pl). Between these two is **Kolory,** with a pleasant Parisian brasserie ambience (Estery 10). Late at night, the little windows in the plac Nowy **market hall** do a big business selling zapiekanki (baguette with toppings) to hungry bar-hoppers.

On Rabina Meiselsa street, just a half-block off plac Nowy, under the arch to a characteristic courtyard is **Mleczarnia,** a topnotch beer garden with rickety tables squeezed under the trees and its cozy old-fashioned pub across the street (at #20).

Klezmer Music in Kazimierz

On a balmy summer night, Kazimierz's main square, ulica Szeroka, is filled with the haunting strains of klezmer—traditional Jewish music from 19th-century Poland, generally with violin, string bass, clarinet, and accordion. Skilled klezmer musicians can make their instruments weep or laugh like human voices. There are two main ways to enjoy some klezmer music: at a restaurant or at a concert.

Restaurants: Several eateries on ulica Szeroka offer klezmer music, typically starting between 19:00 and 20:00. The musicians move from room to room, and the menus tend to be a mix of traditional Jewish and Polish cuisine (which are quite similar). But don't come here just for the food—it's an afterthought to the music. While most places claim to do concerts "nightly year-round," they can be canceled anytime it's slow (especially off-season)—confirm ahead.

Some old-school restaurants offer reasonably priced food but charge 30 zł per person for the music. Probably your best choice is the well-established **$$$ Klezmer-Hois,** filling a venerable former Jewish ritual bathhouse and making you feel like you're dining in a rich grandparent's home (daily 8:00-22:00, at #6, tel. 12-411-1245, www.klezmer.pl).

A newer trend is for restaurants with outdoor seating on ulica Szeroka to offer "free" al fresco klezmer music for customers (though the food tends to be that much more expensive). Because the music is free, anybody (at neighboring restaurants, or simply strolling past) can enjoy a taste of klezmer. Just show up, comparison-shop music and menus, and—if you like what you hear—pick a place for dinner or a drink. Eateries offering this option include **$$ Hotel Ester** (at #20, with relatively reasonable prices and live music that begins in the early afternoon rather than evening) and **$$$ Awiw** (at #13, overpriced food).

Concerts: To really focus on klezmer as an art form, pay a bit more to attend a concert. Popular options include the **Jascha Lieberman Trio** (schedule at www.jaschalieberman. com); or a performance in arguably the most powerful space, the giant old prayer hall of **Isaac Synagogue** (60 zł, Sun-Mon and Wed-Thu at 18:00, Kupa 18, www.sibelia.pl). There are also concerts in season in Kraków's Old Town, near the Main Market Square (most afternoons at 17:30, Sławkowska 14, www. cracowconcerts.com). For the latest lineup, check for fliers around town, or ask at any TI.

Don't worry too much about seeking out a particular musician—they are equally good, and each brings a unique style to the music. Many venues share musicians, so on any given night it's hard to predict who's performing where. Bottom line: If you're interested in klezmer music, you can't go wrong in Kazimierz.

KRAKÓW

Near Isaac Synagogue: A block east of plac Nowy, a few more places cluster on the wide street in front of Isaac Synagogue. The huge **Nova Resto Bar** dominates the scene with a long covered terrace, a vast interior, and seating in their courtyard—all with a cool color scheme Las Vegas polka-dot style. This feels upscale and a bit pretentious compared to many of the others, but it's the place to be seen (25-40-zł meals, Estery 18). Upstairs is the similarly trendy music club **Taawa** (http://taawa.pl). Facing this double-decker wall of style are some smaller, more accessible options: **Singer** is classy and mellow, with most of its tables made of old namesake sewing machines (Estery 20), while **Warsztat** has an exploding-instruments-factory ambience (Izaaka 3; also recommended later, under "Eating in Kraków").

On Józefa Street: More good bars are just a short block south. Along Józefa, you'll find a pair of classic Kazimierz joints: **Eszeweria,** which wins the "best atmosphere" award, feels like a Polish speakeasy that's been in mothballs for the last 90 years—a low-key, unpretentious, and inviting hangout (Józefa 9). A block up, look for **Kolanko No. 6,** with a cozy bar up front, a pleasant beer garden in the inner courtyard, and a fun events hall in back (Józefa 17, www.kolanko.net; also recommended later, under "Eating in Kraków").

Beach Bar on the Riverbank

South of the river, roughly between Kazimierz and Wawel Castle, **Forum Przestrzenie** fills a dilapidated concrete hotel—a mostly abandoned dinosaur from communist times, today used primarily as an extra-large billboard. But in recent years, the ground floor has been taken over by a lively hipster bar—especially appealing in the balmy summer months, when comfy low-slung chairs sprawl across a tidy lawn and a pebbly "beach"

with views across the Vistula to Wawel Castle. They serve coffee, wine, beer, summery cocktails, and cheap bar snacks. A few artists and designers also have boutiques here (open daily in good weather 10:00-late, skip the trip if it's not nice out, ulica Marii Konopnickiej 28, mobile 515-424-724, www.forumprzestrzenie.com).

Sleeping in Kraków

Kraków is popular, with lots of accommodations options. Healthy competition keeps Kraków's prices reasonable and makes choosing a hotel fun rather than frustrating. Rates are soft; hoteliers don't need much of an excuse to offer discounts, especially on weekends or off-season. I've focused my accommodations in two areas: in and near the Old Town; and in Kazimierz, a hipper, more affordable neighborhood that is home to both the old Jewish quarter and a thriving dining and nightlife zone.

Both zones can suffer from discos that thump loud music on weekend nights to attract roving gangs of rowdy drinkers. The "quiet after 22:00" law is flagrantly ignored. I've tried to avoid the areas most plagued by noise, but my accommodations do come with some risk of noise; to help your odds, ask for a quiet room when you reserve...and bring earplugs.

IN AND NEAR THE OLD TOWN

Most of my listings are inside (or within a block or two of) the Planty park that rings the Old Town. Sleeping inside the Old Town comes with pros (maximum atmosphere; handy location for sightseeing and dining) and cons (high prices; the potential for noise—especially on weekends—as noted earlier). Places just outside the Old Town are still handy, but quieter and cheaper. If you need a room in a pinch, several slick, international chains (Ibis, Mercure, Puro) have branches near the train station.

Guesthouses

These good-value pensions come with lots of stairs (no elevators) and are located in the heart of the Old Town along busy pedestrian streets. Many lack air-conditioning, so they can be noisy with the windows open in the summer, especially on weekends. Don't expect a 24-hour reception desk; it's always smart to tell them your arrival time, especially if it's late in the day.

$$ Tango House, run by dance instructor Marcin Miszczak, is in a well-located building with an ancient-feeling stairwell decorated with faded Art Nouveau paintings. Its eight long, skinny, retro-stylish rooms have parquet floors (ask for quieter courtyard room to avoid weekend noise, ulica Szpitalna 4, tel. 12-429-3114, www.tangohouse.pl, tangohouse@gmail.com).

$$ Globtroter Guest House offers 17 basic, somewhat stuffy, rustic-feeling rooms with high ceilings and big beams around a serene garden courtyard. Jacek (Jack), who really understands and respects travelers, conscientiously focuses on value—keeping prices reasonable by not offering needless extras (RS%, 2 people can cram into a single to save money, family rooms, breakfast at nearby café extra, pay laundry service, fun 700-year-old brick cellar lounge down below, go down passageway at #7 at the square called plac Szczepański, tel. 12-422-4123, www.globtroter-krakow.com, globtroter@globtroter-krakow.com).

$$ La Fontaine B&B, run by a French-Polish family, offers

KRAKÓW

Sleep Code

Hotels are classified based on the average price of a standard
double room with breakfast in high season.

$$$$	**Splurge:** Most rooms over 550 zł
$$$	**Pricier:** 400-550 zł
$$	**Moderate:** 250-400 zł
$	**Budget:** 100-250 zł
¢	**Backpacker:** Under 100 zł
RS%	**Rick Steves discount**

Unless otherwise noted, credit cards are accepted, hotel staff
speak basic English, and free Wi-Fi is available. Comparison-
shop by checking prices at several hotels (on each hotel's own
website, on a booking site, or by email). For the best deal, *book
directly with the hotel.* Ask for a discount if paying in cash; if
the listing includes **RS%,** request a Rick Steves discount.

---

26 rooms and apartments just off the Main Market Square. Tastefully decorated with French flair, it's cute as a poodle. Most of the
rooms have a little lounge with a microwave and fridge—many in
the hall, some inside the room. If you don't mind huffing up lots of
stairs, this is a fine value (air-con in some rooms, low slanted ceilings in some rooms, ulica Sławkowska 1, tel. 12-422-6564, www.
bblafontaine.com, biuro@bblafontaine.com).

    Outside the Old Town: $$ Cracowdays is the farthest of my
listings from the center of town, about a 15-minute walk away (a
tram can cut a few minutes off the trek). But it's also a notch more
refined than the guesthouses listed previously. It sits in a pleasant
residential neighborhood west of the Main Market Square, with
eight beautifully decorated and thoughtfully tended rooms, all
sharing a central kitchen (two stand-alone studio apartments in
another building, air-con, Grabowskiego 7, mobile 604-460-860,
www.cracowdays.com, reservation@cracowdays.com).

Hotels

$$$$ Donimirski Boutique Hotels, with three locations in or
near Kraków's Old Town, set the bar for splurge hotels in Kraków
(www.donimirski.com). All Donimirski hotels come with friendly
staff, discounts for my readers, and classy little extras that add up
to a memorable hotel experience. **Hotel Polski Pod Białym Orłem**
has 60 classic rooms conveniently located near the Florian Gate
just inside the Old Town walls (RS%, apartments available, air-
con, elevator, ulica Pijarska 17, tel. 12-422-1144, hotel.polski@
donimirski.com). **Hotel Gródek** offers 23 rooms a three-minute
walk behind St. Mary's Church, on a quiet dead-end street overlooking the Planty park (RS%, pay parking, Na Gródku 4, tel.

12-431-9030, grodek@donimirski.com). And **Hotel Pugetów,** with six small but plush rooms, is in the workaday neighborhood between the Main Market Square and Kazimierz (RS%, air-con, pay parking, ulica Starowiślna 15A, tel. 12-432-4950, pugetow@ donimirski.com).

$$$$ Hotel Senacki is a business-class place renting 20 comfortable rooms between Wawel Castle and the Main Market Square. The staff is warm, professional, and conscientious, and the location is perfect, making this an ideal splurge in the center. Top-floor "attic" rooms have low beams, skylight windows, and a flight of stairs after the elevator (air-con, elevator—but doesn't go to "attic" rooms, ask about nearby pay parking, ulica Grodzka 51, tel. 12-422-7686, www.hotelsenacki.pl, senacki@hotelsenacki.pl).

$$$$ Hotel Wawel has 39 rooms on a well-located street that's quieter than the Old Town norm. It's colorful and serene; above the swanky marble lobby are hallways creatively painted with the history of the building and images from around Kraków. Out back, a fountain gurgles in a cute little courtyard (air-con, elevator—but doesn't go to top floor, steam room and whirlpool bath extra, ulica Poselska 22, tel. 12-424-1300, www.hotelwawel.pl, hotel@hotelwawel.pl).

$$$ Bracka 6, wonderfully located just one short block off the Main Market Square, is a sort of a hybrid between a hotel and an apartment house. The 16 stylish rooms—with sleek lines, lots of glass, and exposed brick—each have a kitchen, so breakfast is extra. It's on the second and third floors with no elevator, and the reception is open limited hours (daily 8:00-22:00 or so)—but the lack of full hotel amenities keeps the prices affordable for this level of modern elegance (air-con, Bracka 6, tel. 12-341-4011, www. bracka6.pl, info@bracka6.pl).

$$$ Hotel Wielopole sits a block outside the Planty, on the way to the lively Kazimierz district. Its 35 tight rooms are tucked down a side street just past the main post office, facing a big Holiday Inn. The staff are proud of their attentive service, and they circulate a informative little newsletter daily (air-con, elevator, vegetarian restaurant in cellar, Wielopole 3, tel. 12-422-1475, www. wielopole.pl, office@wielopole.pl).

$$$ Hotel Amber sits on a dreary urban street just outside the Planty park, but still less than a 10-minute walk from the Square. Run by the same company as Hotel Wielopole (described above), it has an equally pleasant emphasis on welcoming service. The hotel has two parts: 18 perfectly fine, if smallish, rooms in the original building; and 20 slightly more upscale rooms in the newer "design" section. Both parts share a small gym, sauna, and garden in back (air-con, elevator, Garbarska 8-10, tel. 12-421-0606, www.hotel-amber.pl, office@hotel-amber.pl).

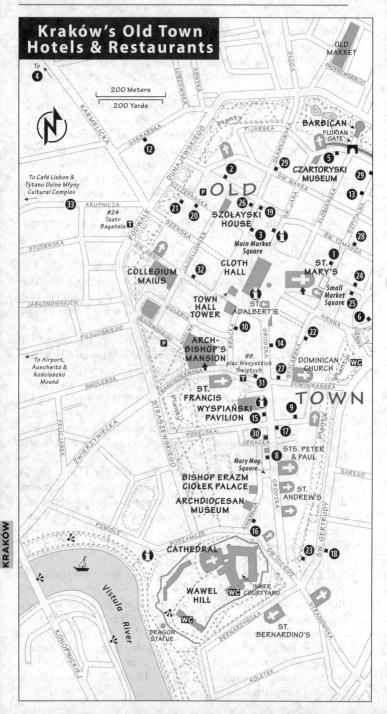

Kraków's Old Town Hotels & Restaurants

200 Meters
200 Yards

To Café Lisbon &
Tytano Dolne Młyny
Cultural Complex

To Airport,
Auschwitz &
Kościuszko
Mound

OLD MARKET

BARBICAN
FLORIAN GATE

CZARTORYSKI MUSEUM

OLD

SZOŁAYSKI HOUSE

Main Market Square

CLOTH HALL

ST. MARY'S

Small Market Square

COLLEGIUM MAIUS

TOWN HALL TOWER

ST. ADALBERT'S

ARCH-BISHOP'S MANSION

#8 plac Wszystkich Świętych

DOMINICAN CHURCH

WC

ST. FRANCIS

WYSPIAŃSKI PAVILION

TOWN

STS. PETER & PAUL

Mary Mag. Square

BISHOP ERAZM CIOŁEK PALACE

ARCHDIOCESAN MUSEUM

ST. ANDREW'S

CATHEDRAL

WAWEL HILL

WC

INNER COURTYARD

WC

DRAGON STATUE

ST. BERNARDINO'S

Vistula River

KRAKÓW

Accommodations

1. Tango House
2. Globtroter Guest House
3. La Fontaine B&B
4. To Cracowdays
5. Hotel Polski Pod Białym Orłem
6. Hotel Gródek
7. Hotel Pugetów
8. Hotel Senacki & Bar Grodzki
9. Hotel Wawel
10. Bracka 6
11. Hotel Wielopole
12. Hotel Amber
13. Kraków City Apartments
14. Kraków for You Apartments

Eateries

15. Restauracja pod Aniołami
16. Pod Nosem
17. Miód Malina
18. Pod Baranem
19. Ed Red
20. Charlotte
21. Café Bunkier
22. Ambasada Śledzia
23. Pod Wawelem Beer Hall
24. Cyklop Pizza & Jadłodajnia "U Stasi"
25. Moa Burger
26. Krowarzywa
27. Lajkonik Sandwiches
28. Milkbar Tomasza
29. U Babci Maliny (2)
30. Bar Mleczny pod Temidą
31. Restauracja Samoobsługowa Polakowski
32. Chimera Cafeteria
33. Krupnicza Street Eateries

KRAKÓW

Apartments

Apartments aren't just for long stays—these places welcome even one-nighters. As reception times are limited, be sure to clearly communicate your arrival time. A wide variety of apartments is easy to find at online booking sites, but both of these places have a reception desk that manages several units, making them a bit more hotelesque than the norm. Still, you're on your own for breakfast, and don't expect your room to be cleaned during your stay.

$$ Kraków City Apartments has six straightforward, modern studio apartments tucked away in a quiet courtyard at the corner of the Old Town (self check-in—arrange details in advance, ulica Szpitalna 34, mobile 507-203-050, www.krakowapartments. info, info@krakowapartments.info, Andrzej and Katarzyna).

$$ Kraków for You Apartments offers 12 modern, well-decorated studios and one- and two-bedroom units with kitchenettes around a courtyard along one of Kraków's most happening streets, just a few steps off the Main Market Square (reception open daily 10:00-20:00, request quieter courtyard room, lots of stairs with no elevator, go down the passage at Grodzka 4, tel. 12-421-4835, mobile 660-541-085, www.krakowforyou.com, info@krakowforyou. com, Mikołaj).

IN KAZIMIERZ

Kazimierz is both Kraków's Jewish heart and soul, and its trendiest eating and nightlife zone. Sleeping here puts you in close proximity to synagogues and klezmer concerts, as well as to food trucks and hip nightclubs (expect some noise, especially on weekends). Keep in mind that, while pleasant in its own right, Kazimierz is a 20-minute walk or a 5-minute tram ride from Kraków's atmospheric old center (for details on getting to Kazimierz from the Old Town, see page 286). For locations, see the map on page 287.

$$$$ Metropolitan Boutique Hotel is an upscale refuge, just a block before the heart of Kazimierz (just off the busy road on the way to Kraków's Old Town). Its 59 rooms—with exposed brick and slick modern style—sit along a somewhat dreary but conveniently located side street (air-con, elevator, gym, Joselewicza 19, tel. 12-442-7500, www.hotelmetropolitan.pl).

$$$ Rubinstein Residence sits right in the middle of ulica Szeroka—surrounded by klezmer restaurants and synagogues, in the heart of the neighborhood. It fills a painstakingly restored old townhouse (parts of it dating to the 15th century) with heavy wood beams and 30 swanky rooms—some of them palatial suites that incorporate old features like frescoes and pillars. The rooftop terrace—with views over Kazimierz and to the Old Town—sets this place above, and is open to the public after 17:00 (air-con, elevator, Szeroka 12, tel. 12-384-0000, www.rubinstein.pl, recepcja@rubinstein.pl).

$$ Karmel Hotel, with 11 rooms above an Italian restaurant, sits on a pleasant side street near the heart of Kazimierz. It offers elegance at a reasonable price (some rooms have air-con, upstairs with no elevator, some night noise on weekends, ulica Kupa 15, tel. 12-430-6697, www.karmel.com.pl, hotel@karmel.com.pl).

$ Residence Tournet, well run by friendly Piotr and Sylwia Działowy, is your cheap-and-cheery option, offering 18 colorful, overly perfumed rooms near the edge of Kazimierz toward Wawel Castle (elevator plus a few stairs, reception open 7:00-22:00, ulica Miodowa 7, tel. 12-292-0088, www.accommodation.krakow.pl, tournet@nocleg.krakow.pl).

Eating in Kraków

Kraków has a wide array of great restaurants—for each one I've listed, there are two or three nearly as good. As the restaurant scene changes constantly, I've chosen established places that have a proven track record for reliably good food. In my listings, you'll find a mix of old-school Polish eateries and modern foodie alternatives (which are still rooted in the local tradition). You could also consider a food tour (see "Tours in Krakow" near the beginning of this chapter).

IN THE OLD TOWN

Kraków's Old Town is loaded with dining options. Prices are often reasonable even on the Main Market Square. And a half-block away, they get even better. All of these eateries (except the milk bars) are likely to be booked up on weekends—always reserve ahead. You'll find plenty of expensive, tourist-oriented restaurants on the Main Market Square, though I haven't recommended any here—while they vary in quality, all are overpriced. To enjoy the same experience more affordably, have just a drink on the Square and dine elsewhere.

$$$ Restauracja pod Aniołami ("Under Angels") offers a dressy, candlelit atmosphere on a wonderful covered patio or in a deep, steep, romantic cellar with rough wood and medieval vaults. Peruse the elaborately described menu of medieval noblemen's dishes. The cuisine is traditional Polish, with an emphasis on grilled meats and trout (on a wood-fired grill). Every meal begins with smalec (spread made with lard, fried onion, bacon, and apple). Don't go here if you're in a hurry—only if you want to really slow down and enjoy your dinner. Reservations are smart (daily 13:00-24:00, ulica Grodzka 35, tel. 12-421-3999, www.podaniolami.pl).

$$$$ Pod Nosem ("Under the Nose") is a smart choice for

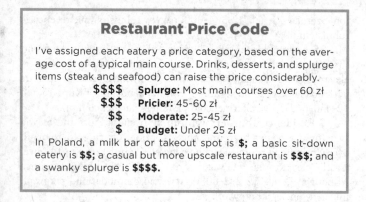

Restaurant Price Code

I've assigned each eatery a price category, based on the average cost of a typical main course. Drinks, desserts, and splurge items (steak and seafood) can raise the price considerably.

$$$$ **Splurge:** Most main courses over 60 zł
$$$ **Pricier:** 45-60 zł
$$ **Moderate:** 25-45 zł
$ **Budget:** Under 25 zł

In Poland, a milk bar or takeout spot is **$**; a basic sit-down eatery is **$$**; a casual but more upscale restaurant is **$$$**; and a swanky splurge is **$$$$**.

refined, updated Polish cuisine in a sophisticated, less touristy atmosphere. It's tucked at the far end of sleepy Kanonicza lane, just beyond the tourists and before Wawel Castle. In a tight dining room that skips the kitsch, they offer an extensive wine list and a short menu of artfully executed Polish dishes (daily 12:00-22:00, Kanonicza 22, tel. 12-376-0014, www.kanonicza22.com).

$$$ Miód Malina ("Honey Raspberry") is a delightful, acceptably kitschy Polish-Italian fusion restaurant filled with the comforting aroma of its wood-fired oven. The menu is mostly Polish, with a few Italian dishes thrown in. Sit in the cozy, warmly painted interior or out in the courtyard (reservations smart, daily 12:00-23:00, ulica Grodzka 40, tel. 12-430-0411, www.miodmalina.pl).

$$ Pod Baranem ("Under the Ram") is a solid midrange bet for well-executed, traditional Polish food. Respected by locals, it sits just outside the tourist chaos, quietly facing the Planty near Wawel Castle. Several cozy rooms—tasteful but not stuffy—sprawl through a homey old building (daily 12:00-22:00, lighter meals before 19:00, Św. Gertrudy 21, tel. 12-429-4022, www.podbaranem.com).

Steak House: $$$$ Ed Red, by acclaimed local chef Adam Chrząstowski, serves up the best steaks in Kraków. He carefully sources his beef from Poland and dry-ages it himself (21 or 45 days). A short walk from the Main Market Square, the space is classy but not stuffy, with exposed brick, leather benches, and a busy open kitchen. They have a long list of top-quality, dry-aged steaks, as well as a short menu of affordably priced alternatives. Reservations are smart (daily 12:00-23:00, Sławkowska 3, mobile 690-900-555, www.edred.pl).

Youthful Style at Plac Szczepański: While seemingly every corner of the Old Town is jammed with tourists, the pleasant square called plac Szczepański feels more like the terrain of university students—a carefully protected bastion of the local upscale art culture. While just two blocks from the Square, this small array of cafés and galleries has a vibe that's more Warsaw-urbane than ye olde Kraków.

$ Charlotte is a winner—it's a classy, French-feeling bakery/café/wine bar. They make their own breads and pastries in the basement (with lots of seating—you can watch the bakers work if you come early enough in the morning), cultivate a stay-awhile coffeehouse ambience upstairs, and throw in a few square-facing sidewalk tables to boot. And it's affordable, serving up sandwiches, pastries, and salads. While the food is light café fare rather than a filling dinner, after 18:00 they redecorate to give it a more sophisticated flair (Mon-Fri 7:00-24:00, Sat from 9:00, Sun 9:00-22:00, plac Szczepański 2, tel. 12-431-5610).

Just around the corner, facing the Planty park, is the delightful **$$ Café Bunkier.** It belongs to the hulking Bunker Sztuki contemporary art gallery, but—in contrast to that building's concrete vibe—the café sits under a glass canopy that faces the lush greenbelt, with well-worn wooden tables and an almost Parisian ambience. While it's not the place for a filling meal, it's worth coming here for some light food and drinks while enjoying Kraków's greenery. It's especially cozy on a rainy day. And when it's nice out, they open up the walls and put you right in the heart of the park (daily 9:00-24:00, food from 12:00, plac Szczepański 3a, tel. 12-431-0585).

On Stolarska Street: Stolarska street, a neatly pedestrianized, oddly untrammeled "embassy row" just a block away from the Main Market Square, is worth exploring for a meal or a drink. Stolarska has a fun variety of more locals-oriented bars and cafés. Begin at the Small Market Square (Maly Rynek) behind St. Mary's Church and head south. On the left, look for the ridiculously long sign that perfectly identifies the business: Pierwszy Lokal Na Stolarskiej Po Lewej Stronie Idąc Od Małego Rynku ("The first pub on the left side of Stolarska coming from the Small Market Square"). Notice that this once-sleepy street is lined with embassies and consulates—it's easy to spot the flags of Germany, the US, and France.

On the left, in the stretch of cafés under canopies, you'll see the **$ Ambasada Śledzia** ("Herring Embassy"), with a divey, youthful atmosphere and a "Polish tapas" approach: A dozen different types of herring and other light meals, plus a variety of vodka to wash it down, are posted on the menu. You'll order at the bar, then find a table or take it to go (open long hours daily, Stolarska 8). Across the street and 50 paces back up, the Pasaż Bielaka (look for the low-profile stone doorway at #5) runs through the middle of the block all the way out to the Main Market Square (emerging at Rynek Główny #19); partway along is another sprawling branch of the Herring Embassy.

Beer Hall: $$ Pod Wawelem ("Under Wawel") is a rollicking Czech-style beer hall right on the Planty park near Wawel Castle. It's packed with locals seeking big, sloppy, greasy portions of meaty fare, with giant mugs of various beers on tap (including Polish and Bavarian). Choose between the bustling interior and the outdoor terrace right on the Planty. Locals come here not for a romantic dinner but for a rowdy evening out with friends (different specials every day—such as giant schnitzel, pork ribs, or roasted chicken; daily 12:00-24:00, ulica Św. Gertrudy 26-29, tel. 12-421-2336).

Pizza: $ Cyklop, with 10 tables wrapped around the cook and his busy oven, has good wood-fired pizzas and a cozy, charming ambience (daily 11:00-23:00, near St. Mary's Church at Mikołajska 16, tel. 12-421-6603).

Burgers (and Vegan Burgers): Gourmet hamburgers are all the rage in Poland. One of the best options in the center is **$ Moa Burger,** with a dozen different types of big, sloppy, "New Zealand-style" hamburgers. Order at the counter, then find a seat at a shared table (daily 11:00-23:00, Mikołajska 3, tel. 12-421-2144). Another fad is vegan "burgers"; a handy place in the center is **$ Krowarzywa** (a pun roughly meaning both "Cow Alive" and "Cow Vegetable")—with a hip atmosphere and an enticing menu of meatless options (daily 12:00-23:00, Sławkowska 8, mobile 531-777-136).

Quick Sandwich: If you need a break from milk bars (described next) but want to grab a sandwich on the go, stop by **$ Lajkonik,** a modern bakery/coffee shop (piekarnia i kawiarnia) that sells fresh takeout sandwiches (Mon-Fri 7:00-21:00, Sat from 8:00, Sun 8:00-22:00, handy location right in front of the Dominican Church at Dominikański 2, others are just outside the Old Town).

Milk Bars and Other Quick, Cheap, Traditional Eats

Kraków is a good place to try the cheap cafeterias called "milk bars." For pointers on eating at a milk bar, review the sidebar on page 222.

$ Milkbar Tomasza is an upgraded milk bar popular with local students. Modern and relatively untouristy, it serves big, split-table portions of high-quality food—a mix of Polish and international—plus breakfast dishes all day (cheap soup and salad deals, great big salads, Tue-Sun 8:00-20:00, closed Mon, ulica Tomasza 24, tel. 12-422-1706).

$ U Babci Maliny ("Granny Raspberry"), with a grinning Granny on the sign, is well established and much appreciated for its big portions of flavorful traditional food. One location, frequented almost entirely by Krakovians, is designed for university students and staff and is tucked into an inner courtyard of the Science Academy. Find the door at Sławkowska 17, then make your way into the inner courtyard, with an entrance to a rustic cellar where it looks like a kitschy cottage bomb went off (Mon-Fri 11:00-22:30, Sat-Sun from 12:00). Another location is across the street from the National Theater building at Szpitalna 38. The main floor, also done up in a kitschy cottage style, is self-service and budget priced, while the cellar—with a drawing-room vibe—has table service and is about 20 percent more expensive (daily 11:00-23:00). Both locations have walls of photos of the owner posing with bodybuilders and ultimate fighters...not quite in keeping with the country theme.

$ **Jadłodajnia "U Stasi"** is a throwback that makes you feel like you're in on Kraków's best-kept secret. Its hidden location—tucked at the far end of the passage with the recommended Cyklop pizzeria—attracts a wide range of loyal local clientele, from hardscrabble seniors to politicians, artists, and actors. They're all here for well-executed, unpretentious, home-style Polish lunch grub. There can be a bit of a language barrier, so go with the flow: Pick up the English menu as you enter, find a table, wait for them to take your order, enjoy your meal, then pay as you leave. This is an excellent value and a real, untouristy Polish experience. The short menu changes every day—and when they're out, they're out (Mon-Fri 12:00-17:00, closed Sat-Sun, Mikołajskiej 16).

Throwback Milk Bars on Grodzka Street: Just a couple of blocks south of the Main Market Square, on busy ulica Grodzka, two classic milk bars somehow survive the onslaught of the modern world. First, at the corner with Senacka, is the remarkably basic and traditional milk bar, $ **Bar Mleczny pod Temidą.** The next best thing to a time machine to the communist era, this place has grumpy monolingual service, a mostly

KRAKÓW

local clientele, and cheap but good food (daily 9:00-20:00). A few more steps down, also on the right (just before the two churches), $ **Bar Grodzki** is a single tight little room with shared tables. They specialize in tasty potato pancake dishes (placki ziemniaczane). Order high on the menu and try the rich and hearty "Hunter's Delight"—potato pancake with sausage, beef, melted cheese, and spicy sauce. The English menu posted by the counter makes ordering easy. Order, sit, and wait to be called to fetch your food (daily 9:00-19:00).

$ Restauracja Samoobsługowa Polakowski is a glorified milk bar with country-kitchen decor and cheap, tasty Polish fare. The tongue-twisting samoobsługowa simply means "self-service"—as at other milk bars, you'll order at the counter and bus your dishes when done. Curt service...cute hats (daily 11:00-21:00, facing St. Francis Basilica and the Wyspiański Pavilion at plac Wszystkich Świętych 10).

$ Chimera Cafeteria, just off the Main Market Square, is a handy spot for a quick lunch in the center. It serves fast traditional meals to a steady stream of students. You'll order at the counter—choose a big plate (6 items) or medium plate (4 items), and select from an array of salads and main dishes by pointing to what looks good. Then eat outside on their quiet garden courtyard (good for vegetarians, daily 9:00-22:00, near university at ulica Św. Anny 3). I'd skip their expensive full-service restaurant (in the basement), which shares an entryway.

Lively Student Zone Just West of the Old Town

A few minutes' walk west of the Old Town is a trendy, energetic neighborhood with more students than tourists. If ye olde Kraków is getting a little olde, this area is a closer, easier escape than Kazimierz.

Krupnicza Street: This street, which begins just across the ring road from the Planty, is a handy strip to browse for affordable eateries, as it's lined with student-oriented places with more interesting food than in the Old Town. To get here, head out Szewska street from the middle of the Square (to the west), cross the busy ring road, and bear left at the Teatr Bagatela. Several eateries along here are worth considering: **$$ Sisi** is a cellar café with international and Austrian fare (think Wiener schnitzel, at #3 on the right); **$$ Pod Norenami** has a pan-Asian menu that includes sushi, ramen, curries, gyoza, and wok dishes (at #6 on the left); **$$ Dynia** features a hip brick interior and an inviting garden courtyard (at #20 on the left); and **$$ Meho Café,** with a short menu of international-Polish fusion dishes, is the eatery attached to the Józef Mehoffer House Museum. In summer, the interior garden courtyard is a delightful escape from the city bustle (at #26 on the left). At the end of the street, hook right to find the best place in the area for a sweet treat: **$ Café Lisboa,** which serves great coffee and excellent *pastéis de nata*, the national dessert of Portugal—made by a Pole who went to Belém to learn how to make it just right (Dolnych Młynów 3).

Just a block beyond Café Lisboa is...

Tytano Dolne Młyny Cultural Complex: This former tobacco factory has recently been developed into a cultural complex—a fun-to-explore collection of bars and restaurants. Still run-down and

funky, but bursting with
creative energy, it's the
youthful yin to Kraków's
venerable yang. While
sleepy during the day, the
Tytano complex is well
worth walking through in
the evening, especially on
weekends—and it really
gets rolling late at night.

Enter the complex through the gate at Dolnych Młynów 10, near
$$ Veganic—a restaurant with beautifully presented, mostly vegan
fare in a casual yet sophisticated setting. You'll pass a few cafés and
bars as you angle ahead to the right, then around the biggest build-
ing, to the heart of the complex just behind. You'll pass **$$ Tao,**
with pan-Asian food and themed cocktails; and the cozy **$ Bon-
jour Çava,** a coffee-and-cakes eatery with outdoor tables in a low-
key garden setting, and some light meals. Anchoring the center of
the complex is the industrial-sized **$$ Międzymiastowa** ("Long
Distance") restaurant—the most yuppie-feeling choice here, with a
big, inviting terrace, an extensive list of gin drinks, and a menu of
serviceable international dishes. Nearby is a lane leading to a trio
of popular bars: **Strefa,** a tight cocktail bar with a good wine list
and interesting bites; **Weźże Krafta,** a taproom with 25 different
microbrews on tap and outdoor wood-pallet benches; and—at the
lane's dead end—Hala Główna, a student dive bar with ramshackle
tables spilling out under twinkle lights, a dozen craft beers on tap,
hard drinks, and pizza. Around the corner, a parallel alley is home
to **Zet Pe Te,** with lots of outdoor white-wooden-pallet benches
under twinkle lights; their vast, industrial interior often hosts DJs
or live music. And tucked down a little courtyard nearby is **$ Grill
Garaż,** a casual eatery with meat sizzling on the open hood com-
partment of a vintage VW Beetle.

IN KAZIMIERZ

The entire district is bursting with lively cafés and bars—it's a hap-
pening night scene. And, beyond the Jewish-themed places along
ulica Szeroka (see the sidebar on page 327), Kazimierz's restaurants
are less touristy and more diverse than the Old Town's. For loca-
tions, see the map on page 342.

Fast and Cheap

Kazimierz has some great takeout and street food—handy for a
lunch break from daytime sightseeing here, or for an affordable
dinner break from bar-hopping.

$ Food Trucks: Kazimierz has three vacant lots filled with

Kazimierz Hotels & Restaurants

Accommodations

1. To Metropolitan Boutique Hotel
2. Rubinstein Residence
3. Karmel Hotel
4. Residence Tournet

Eateries

5. Judah Square Food Trucks
6. Isaac Synagogue Food Trucks
7. Dajwór 21 Food Trucks
8. Plac Nowy Eateries
9. Nova Krova
10. Good Lood
11. Pod Ursa Maior
12. Bagelmama
13. Hummus Amamamusi
14. Stara Zajezdnia
15. Craftownia
16. Bottiglieria 1881
17. Hamsa Restaurant
18. Alchemia & Alchemia od Kuchni
19. Kolanko No. 6
20. Warsztat (3)
21. Lody Tradycyjna Receptura

fun-to-browse food trucks—most open daily for lunch and dinner. Each one comes with about a half-dozen entirely different options. The first and best is at **Judah Square.** Named for its big graffiti mural (by an Israeli street artist), it's tucked at the southern fringe of the tourists' Kazimierz, near the old tram depot (corner of Św. Wawrzyńca and Wąska). Mainstays here include Andrus (super-decadent and gooey roasted pork sandwiches); Boogie Truck burgers; Yatai sushi; Belgian-style fries; Pan Kumpir baked potatoes; and the beloved Chimney Cake Bakery, which rotisserie-roasts dough and sugar into a sweet and crunchy cake, then fills it with ice cream and other toppings.

Right in the heart of the tourist zone, another food truck pod fills a vacant lot **behind Isaac Synagogue,** just steps from ulica Szeroka. Here you'll find painted-wooden-pallet furniture, hammocks, twinkle lights, and a mellow vibe. Likely options here include hot dogs, Mexican tacos, açaí smoothies, burgers, veggie wraps, Thai ice cream, and—of course—more chimney cakes. Another pod of food trucks—called **Truckarnia**—is at Dajwór 21, across the street from the Galicia Jewish Museum. Trucks here include updated Polish dishes, burgers, tacos, and paella. Note that any and all of these could reshuffle their carts—or be gone entirely, replaced by a ritzy new building—at any moment. But it's clear that, in general, Kazimierz's food-truck scene is here to stay.

Polish Fast Food on Plac Nowy: The centerpiece of the plac Nowy market is a circular brick slaughterhouse, which has recently been taken over by Kazimierz foodies. Each of the shop windows—which once housed butchers and basic Polish grub—is now operated by a different pop-up eatery, from burgers to kebabs to Belgian fries. But the real specialty here is the Poles' beloved zapiekanek—a toasted baguette with cheese, ketchup, and a bewildering array of other toppings. You can take a spin around the building to survey your options—noting where the lines are longest (locals know which zapiekanek is best). For dessert, line up at Good Lood, top-quality ice cream that's made fresh each morning and available until it's sold out (this is an outpost of the main branch a few blocks away on plac Wolnica—see next).

Foodie Favorites on Plac Wolnica: The big main square of Kazimierz (a couple of blocks south of plac Nowy) has a few locally beloved eateries. **$ Nova Krova** ("New Cow") sells entirely vegan and organic "burgers" and other sandwiches in a hip, woody atmosphere (Mon-Sat 12:00-21:00, Sun from 10:00, at #12). And just kitty-corner, on hot days you'll see a long line at **Good Lood** (a pun on lody—ice cream), with scoops of fresh and flavorful homemade ice cream (daily 11:00-22:00 or until the flavors run out—since it's made fresh daily, at #11). **Pod Ursa Maior**—highly respected by local beer lovers—is a microbrew pub serving the six types of beer they brew in the mountains southeast of Kraków. Each beer comes with a complex backstory, and some of the profits go to wildlife causes—like nursing injured bears and wolves back to health (long hours daily, at #10).

Creative Bagels: $$ Bagelmama, run by an American named Nava (who has worked as a private chef for tennis star John McEnroe), is a casual bagel shop that's popular with expats and locals. The bagels come dressed with a wide variety of spreads, and they also sell sandwiches, soups, salads, desserts, and fresh juices. You can eat in or get it to go (daily 9:00-17:00, ulica Dajwór 10, tel. 12-346-1646).

Hummus Bar: Hole-in-the-wall **$ Hummus Amamamusi** is a bar selling creamy, top-quality homemade hummus with various toppings, bread, and veggies. They also make homemade soft drinks and great coffee (Mon-Fri 9:00-20:00, Sat-Sun from 10:00, Meiselsa 4, tel. 533-306-288).

Beer: Beer lovers find two different experiences along Św. Wawrzyńca. **$$ Stara Zajezdnia** ("Old Tram Depot") fills exactly that—a cavernous old industrial hall—with tables and happy drinkers, draining huge mugs of the five different types of beer brewed on the premises. (You can also order a sampler.) In good weather, the vast courtyard out front becomes an idyllic, self-service beer garden filled with relaxing lounge chairs (Św. Wawrzyńca 12, mobile 664-323-988). For craft beer aficionados, **Craftownia** has 18 Polish microbrews on tap (and many more by the bottle) in a nondescript setting (Mon-Thu 14:00-late, Fri-Sun from 12:00, Św. Wawrzyńca 22, mobile 515-010-565). And to complete your beer crawl, don't miss **Pod Ursa Maior,** nearby on plac Wolnica and described earlier.

Ice Cream: Lody Tradycyjna Receptura has, true to its name, some of the best "ice cream from a traditional recipe" in Kraków—if not in Poland. The straightforward, seasonal flavors—just a few varieties—are made fresh each morning and sold until they run out. Locals line up here—and if you have a sweet tooth, you should, too (daily 9:00-19:00, Starowiślna 83). **Good Lood,** a newer version offering essentially the same concept, has an equally loyal following at its two locations—one on plac Wolnica, and the other in the plac Nowy market hall (both described earlier).

Dining in Kazimierz

For a good-quality sit-down meal, consider these options.

$$$$ Bottiglieria 1881 is a chic, sophisticated wine bar tucked unassumingly just off plac Wolnica. The cellar is stocked with wines from all over the world (with an emphasis on Italian), all complemented by the short, seasonal, thoughtfully designed menu with modern Polish and international dishes. Come for a glass or for a full meal (Tue-Sat 12:00-23:00, closed Sun-Mon, Bochenska 5, mobile 660-661-756).

$$$ Hamsa, with a prime location at the top of ulica Szeroka, offers "hummus and happiness," with an updated take on Israeli food (that's Middle Eastern, not traditional Jewish fare). Don't come here for matzo balls and klezmer music, but for an enticing menu of mezes (small plates, like hummus and various dips) and grilled meat dishes in a modern, hip atmosphere (daily 9:00-24:00, ulica Szeorka 2, mobile 515-150-145).

Kazimierz Bars and Cafés with Food

Some of my favorite atmospheric Kazimierz bars also serve food. It's not high cuisine—the food is an afterthought to the busy bar.

$$ Alchemia od Kuchni is an inviting little subway-tiled street-food restaurant—a sleek space around the corner from the ramshackle main branch. You can order at the counter for a bite to go, or opt for table service (daily 8:00-23:00, Estery 5).

$$ Kolanko No. 6 is a great spot for classic Kazimierz atmosphere. The bar up front is filled with old secondhand furniture. Walking toward the back, you discover an inviting garden with tables and, beyond that, a hall where they host events. They serve light meals, specializing in crêpes, toasted sandwiches, salads, and international dishes (daily 10:00-24:00, Józefa 17, tel. 12-292-0320).

$$ Warsztat ("Workshop") is littered with musical instruments: The bar is a piano, and the tight interior is crammed with other instruments and rakishly crooked lampshades. The menu is an odd hybrid of Italian, Middle Eastern, and Polish cuisine, and the portions are big (salads, pizzas, pastas, and meats; daily 9:00-24:00, Izaaka 3, tel. 12-430-1451). They also have two other locations: a small one (focusing on Polish dishes) by the front door of the Tempel Synagogue, and a bigger one on Bożego Ciała street.

Kraków Connections

For getting between Kraków and **Auschwitz,** see page 364 in the next chapter. To confirm rail journeys, check specific times online (www.rozklad-pkp.pl) or at the main train station. You can also buy tickets on this website; you'll be sent a PDF, which you can show the conductor onboard the train.

From Kraków by Train to: Warsaw (hourly, about 2.5 hours, slick EIC express train, requires seat reservation), **Gdańsk** (6/day direct, 5.5 hours on EIC express, plus night train, 8.5 hours), **Toruń** (7/day, 5.5 hours, most transfer at Warsaw's Zachodnia station), **Prague** (1/day direct, 7.5 hours, plus 1 night train, 10 hours; additional connections may be possible with change in Katowice and other points), **Berlin** (2-3/day, 9-10 hours with change at Warsaw's Zachodnia station, more options with multiple changes; plus 1 direct and handy Deutsche Bahn IC bus, 7.5 hours, www.bahn.com), **Budapest** (1/day, 9 hours, change in Katowice, longer connections with more changes; night train connection requires change in Vienna, 1/night, 11.5 hours; also consider long-distance bus—7 hours, www.flixbus.com), **Vienna** (2/day, 8-9 hours, 1-2 changes;

KRAKÓW

plus direct night train, 8.5 hours). In addition to traditional trains (run by the Polish Railways or the main rail operators in neighboring countries), the private Czech rail company Leo Express may be running some trains between Kraków and the Czech Republic (see www.leoexpress.com).

By Bus: For certain long-distance trips, you can save time and money by taking a bus instead of a train. The dominant company is Flixbus (www.flixbus.pl), but others have come and gone in recent years.

AUSCHWITZ-BIRKENAU

The unassuming regional capital of Oświęcim (ohsh-VEENCH-im) was the site of one of humanity's greatest crimes: the systematic murder of at least 1.1 million innocent people. From 1941 until 1945, Oświęcim was the home of Auschwitz, the biggest, most notorious concentration camp in the Nazi system. Today, Auschwitz is the most poignant memorial anywhere to the victims of the Holocaust.

"Auschwitz" (OWSH-vits) actually refers to a series of several camps in Poland—most importantly Auschwitz I, in the village of Oświęcim (50 miles west of Kraków), and Auschwitz II, a.k.a. Birkenau (about 1.5 miles west of Oświęcim). Auschwitz visitors generally start with Auschwitz I, then ride a shuttle bus to Birkenau. **Auschwitz I,** where public transportation from Kraków arrives, has the main museum building, the *Arbeit Macht Frei* gate, and indoor museum exhibits in former prison buildings. **Birkenau** (BEER-keh-now), on a much bigger scale and mostly outdoors, has the infamous guard tower, a vast field with ruins of barracks, a few tourable rough barracks, the notorious "dividing platform," a giant monument flanked by remains of destroyed crematoria, and a prisoner processing facility called "the Sauna."

A visit here is obligatory for Polish 14-year-olds; students usually come again during their last year of school. And it's an important pilgrimage for school groups from other countries. Many visitors leave flowers and messages; one message—from a German visitor—reads, "Nations who forget their own history are sentenced to live it again."

GETTING THERE

To reach Auschwitz from Kraków, it's easiest to join a package tour or hire a private guide or driver (75-minute drive each way). But the trip is also doable by public transportation (1.75-2.5 hours). For details, see "Auschwitz Connections," at the end of this chapter.

Orientation to Auschwitz

Cost: Free to enter grounds during nonpeak times (donations accepted); 50 zł to join a tour at Auschwitz I—required April-Oct 10:00-16:00 and off-season 10:00-13:00. (Alternatively, you could join a "study tour," or hire your own guide—see the "Guided Tours at Auschwitz" sidebar.) At other times, you're allowed to visit Auschwitz I on your own—though the tour is still well worth considering. Any time of year, Birkenau grounds can be toured without a guide, though you'll likely need a guide to climb the guard tower.

Hours: The museum opens daily at 7:30. Closing times change with the season: June-Aug at 19:00, April-May and Sept at 18:00, March and Oct at 17:00, Feb at 16:00, Jan and Nov at 15:00, and Dec at 14:00. These are "last entry" times; the grounds at Auschwitz I stay open 1.5 hours later (though many buildings—including the national memorials—close promptly at these times). The grounds at Birkenau, where many groups end their visits, may stay open even later.

Information: Tel. 33-844-8100, www.auschwitz.org.

Mandatory Reservations: With more than 2 million visitors each year, Auschwitz struggles with crowds. Reservations are free

Why Visit Auschwitz?

Why visit a notorious concentration camp on your vacation? Auschwitz-Birkenau is one of the most moving sights in Europe, and certainly the most important of all the Holocaust memorials. Seeing the camp can be difficult: Many visitors are overwhelmed by sadness and anger, as well as inspiration at the remarkable stories of survival. Auschwitz survivors and victims' families want tourists to come here and experience the scale and the monstrosity of the place. In their minds, a steady flow of visitors will ensure that the Holocaust is always remembered—so nothing like it will ever happen again.

Auschwitz isn't for everyone. But I've never met anyone who toured Auschwitz and regretted it. For many, it's a profoundly life-altering experience—at the very least, it will forever affect the way you think about the Holocaust.

and required—whether visiting on your own or with a tour. Book as soon as your dates are set—ideally weeks or even months in advance—at http://visit.auschwitz.org.

Entrance slots for individuals typically become available three months before the date of visit, at noon Poland time (and can fill quickly, especially for May and June, when school groups flood the site). Online reservations are no longer available five days before the visit. These details can change—confirm on the website.

If an English tour isn't available for your preferred date, consider booking one in a foreign language (once inside, you can split off and use this chapter's self-guided tour).

After you've booked your reservation online, print out or save your **eticket barcode** to your phone or tablet. To get in, you'll need both the bar code and ID for each person in your group.

Without Reservations: If you arrive without an advance ticket, there are a couple of last-minute options: You can book a **day tour** through a private company in Kraków, which includes both transportation and a tour of the camp (see the "Guided Tours at Auschwitz" sidebar). Or take your chances and **just show up**—a few tickets are reserved for same-day visitors. A white booth in front of the main building (facing the parking lot, opens at 7:30) lists available spaces on upcoming tours (typically, the later you arrive, the longer the wait). You can pass any wait time by first going to Birkenau, which has less strict timing requirements.

Getting from Auschwitz I to Birkenau: Buses shuttle visitors two miles between the camps (free, every 10 minutes; Nov-March 2/hour, schedule posted at bus stops outside the main building of each site, timed to correspond with tours). Taxis are also standing by (about 15 zł). Or you can walk the 30 minutes between the camps, which gives you a chance for reflection. Along the way, you'll pass the Judenrampe, an old train car like the ones used to transport prisoners.

Services: Auschwitz I's main building has a helpful information desk, bookshops, exchange offices, baggage storage (large bags must be checked), and WCs. You'll also find the theater and posted maps of the camp. The guard tower at Birkenau has another bookshop and more WCs.

Film: The 17-minute movie (too graphic for children) was shot by Ukrainian troops days after the Red Army liberated the camp (included in tours, otherwise 4 zł, ask for the schedule for showings in English when you arrive).

Eating: A café and decent cafeteria are at the main Auschwitz building. More options are in the commercial complex across the street.

Expect Changes: The Auschwitz museum is continually maintained and updated. Some things may be different than described here, but everything is well-signposted.

Etiquette: The camp encourages visitors to remember that Auschwitz is the place where more than a million people lost their lives. Behave and dress here as you would at a cemetery.

Auschwitz Tour

AUSCHWITZ I

• *From the entrance building, step out and look over the grassy field to get oriented.*

Before World War II, this camp was a base for the Polish army. When Hitler occupied Poland, he took over these barracks and turned it into a concentration camp for his Polish political enemies. The location was ideal, with a nearby rail junction and rivers providing natural protective boundaries. An average of

Guided Tours at Auschwitz

Visiting Auschwitz on your own works well, given the abundance of English descriptions (and this chapter's self-guided tour). However, due to crowds, to enter Auschwitz I during peak times (April-October 10:00-16:00; off-season 10:00-13:00), you must either join one of the museum's organized tours or reserve a private guide. Even during these busy times, you can enter Birkenau without a guide.

Organized Museum Tours: The Auschwitz Museum's excellent guides are serious and frank historians, who feel a strong sense of responsibility about sharing the story of the camp. The regularly scheduled 3.5-hour English tour covers Auschwitz, Birkenau, and the film (50 zł; 90 zł for 6-hour "study tour"). These tours must be prebooked at http://visit.auschwitz.org. Arrive for your scheduled tour 30 minutes early.

Private Official Museum Guides: If you have a special interest or a small group, it's affordable and worthwhile to hire one of the museum's guides for a private tour. Choose between the basic 3.5-hour tour (430 zł) or a longer "study tour" (610 zł/6 hours, 700 zł/8 hours—possible all in one day, or spread over two days; rates are higher for more than 10 people). Because English-speaking guides are limited, reserve as far ahead as possible (ideally up to 6 months) at http://visit.auschwitz.org.

Day Tours from Kraków: Various Kraków-based companies sell round-trip tours from Kraków to Auschwitz, which include a guided tour of the camp (typically around 160-180 zł). I can't vouch for their quality, but the main outfits are **See Kraków** (www.seekrakow.com), **Discover Cracow** (www.discovercracow.com), and **Cracow City Tours** (www.cracowcitytours.com)—for details, see page 244.

Local Guides and Drivers from Kraków: For easy transportation to the camp and help with booking an organized English tour, hire a Kraków-based guide or driver. These aren't officially registered museum guides, so aren't allowed to show you around the site, but it can be worth the splurge to have someone else deal with the logistics. They can usually make a reservation for you—but the reservation still needs to be booked well ahead of time. I've listed my favorite guides and drivers on page 241.

14,000 prisoners were kept at this camp at one time. (Birkenau could hold up to 100,000.) In 1942, Auschwitz became a death camp for the extermination of European Jews and others whom Hitler considered "undesirable." By the time the camp was liberated in 1945, at least 1.1 million people had been murdered here—approximately 960,000 of them Jewish.

• *Go closer to the camp entrance, approaching the notorious...*

AUSCHWITZ-BIRKENAU

"Arbeit Macht Frei" Gate

Although this gate imparts the message "Work Sets You Free," it's cruelly ironic. The only way out of the camp for the prisoners was through the crematorium chimneys. Note that the "B" was welded on upside down by belligerent inmates, who were forced to make this sign (and much of the camp). This is actually a replica; the original was stolen one night in December 2009, then recovered two days later, cut up into several pieces. The original is now safely in the museum's possession, but no longer displayed.

Just inside the gate and to the right, the camp orchestra (made up of prisoners) used to play marches; having the prisoners march made them easier to count.

• *From the gate, proceed straight up the "main street" of the camp.*

You'll pass two rows of barracks. The first one holds a variety of national memorials. We'll circle back here later, if you'd like to enter some of them. The second row of barracks holds the main museum exhibitions. Blocks 4 and 5 focus on how Auschwitz prisoners were killed. Blocks 6, 7, and 11 explore the conditions for prisoners who survived here a little longer than most. In each block, arrows guide you on a one-way route through the numbered rooms; in many cases, exhibits are both downstairs and upstairs—don't miss these.

• *Start with...*

Block 4: Extermination

In Room 1, a map identifies the countries from which Auschwitz prisoners were brought—as far away as Norwegian fjords and Greek isles. In an alcove along the side of the room is an urn filled with ashes, a symbolic memorial to all the camp's victims.

Room 2 shows photographs of Jewish ghettos from all over Europe being "liquidated"—that is, its residents assembled and deported to various concentration camps. Thanks to its massive occupancy, Auschwitz was a destination for many.

Room 3 displays rare photos of scenes inside the camp. To prevent a riot, the Nazis claimed at first that this was only a transition camp for resettlement in Eastern Europe. At the far end of Room 3, a helpful orientation map for visitors shows the town of Oświęcim, Auschwitz I, Auschwitz II (Birkenau), and other parts of the camp network.

Upstairs in Room 4 is a model of a Birkenau crematorium. People entered on the left, then undressed in the underground

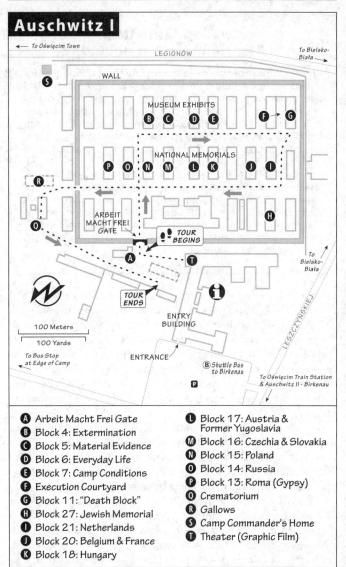

Auschwitz I

← *To Oświęcim Town*

LEGIONÓW

To Bielsko-Biała →

WALL

S

MUSEUM EXHIBITS

B **C** **D** **E** **F** **G**

NATIONAL MEMORIALS

P **O** **N** **M** **L** **K** **J** **I**

R

Q

ARBEIT MACHT FREI GATE

👣 *TOUR BEGINS*

H

A

T

To Bielsko-Biała

TOUR ENDS

🧭

100 Meters

100 Yards

To Bus Stop at Edge of Camp

ENTRY BUILDING

ENTRANCE

🛈

B *Shuttle Bus to Birkenau*

P

To Oświęcim Train Station & Auschwitz II - Birkenau

LESZCZYŃSKIEJ

A Arbeit Macht Frei Gate
B Block 4: Extermination
C Block 5: Material Evidence
D Block 6: Everyday Life
E Block 7: Camp Conditions
F Execution Courtyard
G Block 11: "Death Block"
H Block 27: Jewish Memorial
I Block 21: Netherlands
J Block 20: Belgium & France
K Block 18: Hungary

L Block 17: Austria & Former Yugoslavia
M Block 16: Czechia & Slovakia
N Block 15: Poland
O Block 14: Russia
P Block 13: Roma (Gypsy)
Q Crematorium
R Gallows
S Camp Commander's Home
T Theater (Graphic Film)

AUSCHWITZ-BIRKENAU

---

rooms (hanging their belongings on numbered hooks and encouraged to remember their numbers to retrieve their clothes later). They then moved into the "showers" and were killed by Zyklon-B gas (hydrogen cyanide), a German-produced cleaning agent that is lethal in high doses. This efficient factory of murder took about 20 minutes to kill 8,000 people in four gas chambers. Elevators brought the bodies up to the crematorium. Members of

Chilling Statistics:
The Holocaust in Poland

The majority of people murdered by the Nazis during the Holocaust were killed right here in Poland. For centuries, Poland was known for its relative tolerance of Jews, and right up until the beginning of World War II, Poland had Europe's largest concentration of Jews: 3,500,000. Throughout the Holocaust, the Nazis murdered 4,500,000 Jews in Poland (many of them brought in from other countries) at camps, including Auschwitz, and in ghettos such as Warsaw's.

By the end of the war, only 300,000 Polish Jews had survived—less than 10 percent of the original population. Many of these survivors were granted "one-way passports" (read: deported) to Israel, Western Europe, and the US by the communist government in 1968 (following a big student demonstration with a strong Jewish presence). Today, only about 10,000 Jews live in all of Poland.

the *Sonderkommand*—Jewish inmates who were kept isolated and forced by the Nazis to work here—removed the corpses' gold teeth and shaved off their hair (to be sold) before putting the bodies in the ovens. It wasn't unusual for a *Sonderkommand* worker to discover a wife, child, or parent among the dead. A few of these workers committed suicide by throwing themselves at electric fences; those who didn't were systematically executed by the Nazis after a two-month shift. Across from the model of the crematorium are canisters of Zyklon-B.

Across the hall in the dimly lit Room 5 is one of the camp's most powerful exhibits: a wall of actual victims' hair—4,400 pounds of it. Also displayed is cloth made of the hair, used to make Nazi uniforms. The Nazis were nothing if not efficient...nothing, not even human body parts, could be wasted.

Back downstairs in Room 6 is an exhibit on the plunder of victims' personal belongings. People being transported here were encouraged to bring luggage—and some victims had even paid in advance for houses in their new homeland. After they were killed, everything of value was sorted and stored in warehouses that prisoners named "Canada" (after a country they associated with great wealth). Although the Canada warehouses were destroyed, you can see a few of these items in the next building.
• *Head next door.*

Block 5: Material Evidence of the Nazis' Crimes
The exhibits in this block consist mostly of piles of the victims' goods, a tiny fraction of everything the Nazis stole. As you wander

through the rooms, you'll see eyeglasses; fine Jewish prayer shawls; crutches and prosthetic limbs (the first people the Nazis exterminated were mentally and physically ill German citizens); and a pile of pots and pans. Then, upstairs, you'll witness a seemingly endless mountain of shoes; children's clothing; and suitcases with names of victims—many marked *Kind,* or "child." Visitors often wonder if the suitcase with the name "Frank" belonged to Anne, one of the Holocaust's most famous victims. After being discovered in Amsterdam by the Nazis, the Frank family was transported here to Auschwitz, where they were split up. Still, it's unlikely this suitcase was theirs. Anne Frank and her sister Margot were sent to the Bergen-Belsen camp in northern Germany, where they died of typhus shortly before the war ended. Their father, Otto Frank, survived Auschwitz and was found barely alive by the Russians, who liberated the camp in January 1945.

• *Proceed to the next block.*

Block 6: Everyday Life

Although the purpose of Auschwitz was to murder its inmates, not all were killed immediately. After an initial evaluation, some prisoners were registered and forced to work. (This did not mean they were chosen to live—just to die later.) This block shows various aspects of daily existence at the camp.

14172
DABROWSKI JAN
ur. 8.2 1920 r., robotnik
przybył 30.7.1941, zginął: wrzesień 1942.

The halls are lined with photographs of victims, each identified with a name, birthdate, occupation, date of arrival at Auschwitz, date of death, and camp registration number. The dates reveal that these people survived here an average of two to three months. (Flowers are poignant reminders that these victims are survived by loved ones.) Similar photographs hang in several other museum buildings, as well; as with the plundered items in the last block, keep in mind that these represent only a tiny fraction of the masses of people murdered at Auschwitz.

Room 1 (on the left as you enter the front door) displays drawings of the arrival process. After the initial selection, those chosen to work were showered, shaved, and photographed. After a while, photographing each prisoner got to be too expensive, so prisoners were tattooed instead (see photographs): on the chest, on the arm, or—for children—on the leg. A display shows the symbols that prisoners had to wear to show their reason for internment—Jew,

St. Maksymilian Kolbe (1894-1941)

Among the many inspirational stories of Auschwitz is that of a Polish priest named Maksymilian Kolbe. Before the war, Kolbe traveled as a missionary to Japan, then worked in Poland for a Catholic newspaper. While he was highly regarded for his devotion to the Church, some of his writings had an unsettling anti-Semitic sentiment. But during the Nazi occupation, Kolbe briefly ran an institution that cared for refugees—including Jews.

In 1941, Kolbe was arrested and interned at Auschwitz. When a prisoner from Kolbe's block escaped in July of that year, the Nazis punished the remaining inmates by selecting 10 of them to be put in the Starvation Cell until they died—based on the Nazi "doctrine of collective responsibility." After the selection had been made, Kolbe offered to replace a man who expressed concern about who would care for his family. The Nazis agreed. (The man Kolbe saved is said to have survived the Holocaust.)

All 10 of the men—including Kolbe—were put into Starvation Cell 18. Two weeks later, when the door was opened, only Kolbe had survived. The story spread throughout the camp, and Kolbe became an inspiration to the inmates. To squelch the hope he had given the others, Kolbe was executed by lethal injection.

In 1982, Kolbe was canonized by the Catholic Church. Some critics—mindful of his earlier anti-Semitic rhetoric—still consider Kolbe's sainthood controversial. But most Poles feel he redeemed himself for his earlier missteps through this noble act at the end of his life.

Roma (Gypsy), homosexual, political prisoner, and so on. At the end of the room, a display case holds actual camp uniforms.

Across the hall, Room 4 shows the starvation that took place here. The 7,500 survivors that the Red Army found when the camp was liberated were essentially living skeletons (the "healthier" inmates had been forced to march to Germany). Of those liberated, one-fifth died soon after of disease and starvation.

In Room 5, you can see scenes from the prisoner's workday (sketched by survivors after liberation). Prisoners worked as long as the sun shone—8 hours in winter, up to 12 hours in summer—mostly on farms or in factories.

Room 6 is about Auschwitz's child inmates, 20 percent of the camp's victims. Blond, blue-eyed children were either "Germanized" in special schools or, if younger, adopted by German families. Dr. Josef Mengele conducted gruesome experiments here on children, especially twins and triplets, ostensibly to find ways to increase fertility for German mothers. Also in this room, look for a display of the prisoners' daily ration (in the glass case): a pan of tea or coffee in the morning; thin vegetable soup in the afternoon; and a piece of bread (often made with sawdust or chestnuts) for dinner. This makes it clear that Auschwitz was never intended to be a "work camp," where people were kept alive, healthy, and efficient to do work. Rather, people were meant to die here—if not in the gas chambers, then through malnutrition and overwork.

• *Block 7 shows living and sanitary conditions at the camp, which you'll see in more detail later at Birkenau. Blocks 8-10 are vacant (medical experiments were carried out in Block 10). And Block 11 was the most notorious of all.*

Block 11: The Death Block

Step into the walled-in **courtyard** between Blocks 10 and 11. The wall at the far end is where the Nazis shot several thousand po-

litical prisoners, leaders of camp resistance, and religious leaders. Notice that the windows are covered, so that nobody could witness the executions. Also take a close look at the memorial—the back of it is made of a material designed by Nazis to catch the bullets without a ricochet. Inmates were shot at short range—about three feet. The pebbles represent prayers from Jewish visitors.

Now head into the **"Death Block"** (#11), from which nobody ever left alive. Death here required a "trial"—but it was never a fair trial. Room 2 (on the left as you enter) is where these sham trials were held, lasting about two minutes each. In Room 5, you can see how prisoners lived in these barracks—three-level bunks, with three prisoners sleeping in each bed (they had to sleep on their sides so they could fit). In Room 6, people undressed before they were executed.

In the **basement,** you'll see several types of cells. The Starvation Cell (#18) held prisoners selected to starve to death when a fellow prisoner escaped; Maksymilian Kolbe spent two weeks here to save another man's life (see sidebar on Kolbe). In the Dark Cell (#20), which held up to 30, people had only a small window for ventilation—and if it became covered with snow, the prisoners suffocated. In the Standing Cells (#22), four people would be forced to stand together for hours at a time (the bricks went all the way to the ceiling then).

Upstairs, you'll find gallows and a bench used for administering lashes. Filling this floor are exhibits on various forms of punishment, mostly focusing on resistance within the camp, escapees, and local Poles who were executed—either for trying to assist the prisoners, or for fighting with Nazi officers.

• *Leaving Block 11, proceed straight ahead, between the buildings, to the other row of barracks. Several of these blocks house...*

National Memorials

These exhibits were created not by museum authorities, but by representatives of the home countries of the camps' victims. As these memorials overlap with the general exhibits, and are designed for Europeans to learn more about the victims from their own home countries, most visitors skip this part of the site. On the other hand, while the main museum exhibits await renovation and modernization, the displays in these national memorials tend to be slicker and better-presented than the ones we just saw. (Some of these may be works in progress, as old exhibits are routinely upgraded.) As you walk along this street toward our next stop (the crematorium), consider stepping into the ones that interest you.

The first one you see is the memorial to **Jewish** victims (Block 27). It's compelling and thoughtfully presented, relying heavily on video clips, evocative music, and sound effects.

Most of the other national memorials are on the right side of the street. Across from the Jewish memorial, Block 21 honors **Dutch Jews;** including perhaps the most famous Dutch victim of the concentration camp, Anne Frank.

Block 20, a former hospital block, is shared by **Belgium** and **France.** A room near the entrance explains how some prisoners were killed by lethal injection, with portraits and biographical sketches of victims. Upstairs is the powerful Belgium exhibit, with a room featuring victims' portraits. Block 18 holds a very modern, conceptual exhibit about **Hungary**'s victims, with an eerie heartbeat sound pervading the space. Block 17, which is likely a work in progress, is intended to memorialize victims from **Austria** and the **former Yugoslavia.** Across from this block, notice the long gallows used for mass hangings. Block 16 contains a new and well-presented exhibit about **Czech** and **Slovak** victims.

Block 15 honors victims from **Poland,** focusing on the 1939 Nazi invasion of the country, which resulted in the immediate internment of Polish political prisoners. Exhibits explain the process of "Germanization"—such as renaming Polish streets with German names—and (upstairs) the underground resistance that fought to get back some control over Poland.

Block 14 is the **Russian** national memorial. However, this one's a bit controversial: While Russia claims to have lost "Russian" Jews to the Holocaust, virtually all of them were technically Polish

Jews who had been living within Russia. (They spoke Polish, not Russian.) To sidestep the hot topic of how to identify these victims, this memorial focuses not on victims, but on the Russian liberation of the camp.

Block 13 houses the **Roma (Gypsy)** exhibit. You'll learn that the Roma, along with the Jews, were considered no better than "rats, bedbugs, and fleas," and explore elements of the so-called *Zigeunerfrage*—the "Gypsy question" about what to do with this "troublesome" population.

• *At the end of this row of barracks, you reach a guard tower and a barbed-wire fence. Jog a few steps to the right, through the hole in the fence, then angle left toward the earthen mound with the giant, ominous brick chimney. The entrance is at the far end of the building.*

Crematorium

Up to 700 people at a time could be gassed here. People undressed outside, or just inside the door. As you enter, bear right and find your way into the big "shower room." Look for the vents in the ceiling—this is where the SS men dropped the Zyklon-B. In the adjacent room is a replica of the furnace. This facility could burn 340 bodies a day—so it took two days to burn all of the bodies from one round of executions. (The Nazis didn't like this inefficiency, so they built four more huge crematoria at Birkenau.)

• *Turning left as you exit the crematorium takes you back to the entrance building. But first, circle around to the opposite side of the crematorium for the closest thing this story has to a happy ending.*

Shortly after the war, camp commander Rudolf Höss was tried, convicted, and sentenced to death. Survivors requested that he be executed at Auschwitz, and in 1947, he was hanged here. The **gallows** are preserved behind the crematorium (about a hundred yards from his home where his wife—who is said to have loved her years here—raised their children in a villa maintained by slaves and furnished with possessions of the dead).

• *Take your time with Auschwitz I. When you're ready, continue to the second stage of the camp—Birkenau.*

AUSCHWITZ II—BIRKENAU

In 1941, realizing that the original Auschwitz camp was too small to meet their needs, the Nazis began a second camp in some nearby farm fields. The original plan was for a camp that could hold 200,000 people, but at its

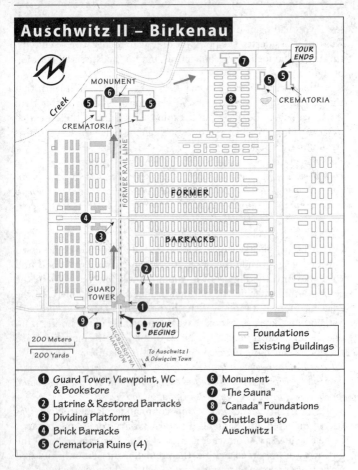

Auschwitz II – Birkenau

MONUMENT

Creek

CREMATORIA

CREMATORIA

FORMER RAIL LINE

FORMER

BARRACKS

GUARD TOWER

TOUR ENDS

"The Sauna"

CREMATORIA

TOUR BEGINS

200 Meters
200 Yards

MĘCZENSTWA NARODÓW

To Auschwitz I & Oświęcim Town

Foundations
Existing Buildings

❶ Guard Tower, Viewpoint, WC & Bookstore
❷ Latrine & Restored Barracks
❸ Dividing Platform
❹ Brick Barracks
❺ Crematoria Ruins (4)
❻ Monument
❼ "The Sauna"
❽ "Canada" Foundations
❾ Shuttle Bus to Auschwitz I

peak, Birkenau (Brzezinka) held only about 100,000. They were still adding onto it when the camp was liberated in 1945.

• *Train tracks lead past the main building and into the camp. The first sight that greeted prisoners was the...*

Guard Tower

If you've seen *Schindler's List*, the sight of this icon of the Holocaust—shown in stirring scenes from the movie—may make you queasy.

Climb to the top of the entry building (also houses WCs and bookstore) for an overview of the massive camp. As you look over the camp, you'll see a vast field of chimneys and a few intact wooden and brick barracks. Some of the barracks were destroyed by Germans. Most were dismantled to be used for fuel and building materials shortly after the war. But the first row has been reconstructed (using components from the original structures). The train tracks lead straight back to the dividing platform, and then dead-end at the ruins of the crematorium and camp monument at the far side.

• *Descend the tower, enter the camp, turn right, and walk through the barbed-wire fence to reach the...*

Wooden Barracks

The first of these barrack buildings was the **latrine:** The front half of the building contained washrooms, and the back was a row of toilets. There was no running water, and prisoners were in charge of keeping the latrine clean. Because of the resulting un-sanitary conditions and risk of dis-ease, the Nazis were afraid to come in here—so the latrine became the heart of the black market and the inmates' resistance movement.

The third barrack was a **bunk-house.** Each inmate had a personal number, a barrack number, and a bed number. Inside, you can see the beds (angled so that more could fit). An average of 400 prisoners—but up to 1,000—would be housed in each of these buildings. These wooden structures, designed as stables by a German com-

pany (look for the horse-tying rings on the wall), came in pre-fab pieces that made them cheap and convenient. Two chimneys connected by a brick duct provided a little heat. The bricks were smoothed by inmates who sat here to catch a bit of warmth.

• *Return to the train tracks, and follow them toward the monument about a half-mile away, at the back end of Birkenau. At the intersection of these tracks and the perpendicular gravel road (halfway to the monument)—now marked by a lonely train car—was the gravel pitch known as the...*

Dividing Platform

A Nazi doctor would stand facing the guard tower and evaluate each prisoner. If he pointed to the right, the prisoner was sentenced to death, and trudged—unknowingly—to the gas chamber. If he pointed to the left, the person would be registered and live a little longer. It was here that families from all over Europe were torn apart forever.

• *Photographs near the wooden building—on the left-hand side as you face the back of the camp complex—show the sad scene. Just beyond that building is a field with some...*

Brick Barracks

Enter one of these buildings. The supervisors lived in the two smaller rooms near the door. Farther in, most barracks still have the wooden bunks that held about 700 people per building. Four or five people slept on each bunk, including the floor—reserved for new arrivals. There were chamber pots at either end of the building. After a Nazi doctor died of typhus, sanitation improved, and these barracks got running water.

Now head back to the train tracks. As you walk along the camp's only road, which leads along the tracks to the crematorium, imagine the horror of this place—no grass, only mud, and all the barracks packed with people, with smoke blowing in from the busy crematoria. This was an even worse place to die than Auschwitz I.

• *The train tracks lead to the camp memorial and crematorium. At the end of the tracks, go 50 yards to the left and climb the three concrete steps to view the ruin of the...*

Crematorium

This is one of four crematoria here at Birkenau, each with a capacity to cremate more than 4,400 people per day. At the far-right end of the ruins, see the stairs where people entered the rooms to undress. They were given numbered lockers, conning them into thinking they were coming back. (The Nazis didn't want a panic.) Then they piled into the "shower room"—the underground passage branching away from the memorial—and were killed. Their bodies were burned in the crematorium (on the left), giving off a scent of sweet almonds (from the Zyklon-B). Beyond the remains of the crematorium is a hole—once a gray lake where tons of ashes were dumped. This efficient factory of death was destroyed by the Nazis as the Red Army approached, leaving the haunting ruins you see today.

When the Soviets arrived on January 27, 1945, the nightmare of Auschwitz-Birkenau was over. The Polish parliament voted to turn these grounds into a museum, so that the world would understand, and never forget, the horror of what happened here.

• *At the back of the camp stands the...*

Monument

Built in 1967 by the communist government in its heavy "Socialist Realist" style, this monument represents gravestones and the chimney of a crematorium. The plaques, written in each of the languages

spoken by camp victims (including English, far right), explain that the memorial is "a cry of despair and a warning to humanity."
• *With more time, you could continue deeper into...*

The Rest of the Camp
There's much more to see for those who are interested—Birkenau sprawls for a frightening distance. One worthwhile extension is the

reception and disinfection building that prisoners called **"the Sauna"** (the long building with four tall chimneys). It was here that prisoners would be forced to strip and be deloused; their belongings were seized and taken to the "Canada" warehouses (described earlier) to be sorted. Walking through here (on glass floors designed to protect the original structure below), you'll see artifacts of the grim efficiency with which prisoners were "processed"—their heads were shaved, they were tattooed with a serial number, and they were assigned uniforms and wooden clogs to wear. Portraits at the end of the building humanize those who passed through here. Look for the cart, which was used to dispose of ashes.

In front of the Sauna is a field of foundations of the **"Canada" warehouses.** Nearby are the other two destroyed **crematoria.**

Auschwitz Connections

The Auschwitz Museum is in the town of Oświęcim, about 50 miles west of Kraków. By bus or minibus, the journey takes 1.75 hours each way (longer by train); driving shaves off about 10-20 minutes.

FROM KRAKÓW TO AUSCHWITZ
The easiest way to reach Auschwitz is with a **package tour** (about 160-180 zł/person) or **private guide or driver** (around 400 zł/carload); both of these options are described on page 241. While the package tours are more convenient than going on your own, three people can hire their own driver for less and have a more intimate experience.

If you're using public transportation, here are your choices (each one of these costs around 10-15 zł):

The most comfortable public-transit option is to take one of the frequent **buses,** mostly run by PKS Oświęcim (at least hourly, 1.75 hours, get schedule at any Kraków TI, buses depart from Kraków's main bus station behind the train station). Buy a one-way ticket from the bus-station ticket office or from the driver to leave your options open for getting home. Look for buses to "Oświęcim" (not necessarily "Auschwitz"). Note that these buses can be full, and there's no way to reserve a seat—line up early (generally about 15 minutes ahead). If you don't get on a bus, you'll have to wait for the next one (or, if there's a minibus leaving sooner, you can take one of those instead—described next). Once in the town of Oświęcim, buses from Kraków stop first at the train station, then continue on to one of two stops near the museum: About half of the buses go directly into the parking lot at the museum itself (this stop may be called *Auschwitz Museum/ul. Leszczyńskiej*), while the rest use a low-profile bus stop on the edge of the Auschwitz camp grounds (you'll see a small *Muzeum Auschwitz* sign on the right just before the stop, and a blue *Oświęcim Muzeum PKS* sign at the stop itself). From this bus stop, follow the sign down the road and into the parking lot; the main museum building is across the lot on your left. Note that since some buses don't actually go into the museum's parking lot, the Auschwitz stop can be easy to miss—don't be shy about letting your driver know where you want to go: *"Muzeum?"*

Several **minibuses** from Kraków head for Auschwitz (sporadic departures—generally 1-2/hour, 1.75 hours). Like the larger buses, some go directly to the museum, while others use the bus stop at the edge of camp. These generally depart from the lower platform of the main bus station (but confirm the departure point at the TI). While intended for local commuters, these can be crammed with tourists, but they work fine in a pinch.

You could ride the **train** to Oświęcim, but it's less convenient than the bus because it leaves you at the train station, farther from the museum (nearly hourly, fewer Sat-Sun, 2-2.5 hours). If you do wind up at the Oświęcim train station, it's about a 20-minute walk to the camp (turn right out of station, go straight, then turn left at roundabout, camp is several blocks ahead on left). Or you can take a taxi (around 15 zł).

RETURNING FROM AUSCHWITZ TO KRAKÓW

Upon arrival at Auschwitz I, plan your departure by visiting the information window at the main building. They can give you a schedule of departures and explain where the bus or minibus leaves from. (If you intend to stay late into the afternoon, make a point of figuring out the last possible bus or train back to Kraków, and plan accordingly.) Remember to allow enough time to make it from Birkenau back to Auschwitz I to catch your bus.

Although most minibuses and a few buses back to Kraków leave from the camp parking lot itself, if you're taking the bus,

On the Way to Auschwitz:
The Polish Countryside

You'll spend about an hour gazing out the window as you drive or ride to Auschwitz. This may be your only real look at the Polish countryside. Ponder these thoughts about what you're passing...

The small houses you see are traditionally inhabited by three generations at the same time. Nineteenth-century houses (the few that survive) often sport blue stripes, which in those days announced that a daughter was eligible for marriage. Once they saw these blue lines, local boys were welcome to come a-courtin'.

Big churches mark small villages. Like in the US, tiny roadside memorials and crosses indicate places where fatal accidents have occurred.

Polish farmers traditionally had small lots that were notorious for not being very productive. These farmers somewhat miraculously survived the communist era without having to merge their farms. For years, they were Poland's sacred cows: producing little, paying almost no tax, and draining government resources. But since Poland joined the European Union in 2004, they're being forced to get up to snuff...and, in many cases, collectivize their farms after all.

Since most people don't own cars, bikes are common and public transit is excellent. There are lots of bus stops, as well as minibuses that you can flag down anywhere for a 2-zł ride. The bad roads are a legacy of communist construction, exacerbated by heavy truck use and brutal winters.

Poland has more than 2,000 counties, or districts, each with its own coat of arms; you'll pass several along the way. The forests are state-owned, and locals enjoy the right to pick berries in the summer and mushrooms in the autumn (you may see people—often young kids—selling their day's harvest by the side of the road). The mushrooms are dried and then boiled to make tasty soups in the winter.

you'll most likely catch it from the stop on the edge of the Auschwitz I grounds. To reach this bus stop, leave the Auschwitz I building through the main entry and walk straight along the parking lot, then turn right on the road near the end of the lot. At the T-intersection, cross the street to the little bus stop with the blue *Oświęcim Muzeum PKS* sign. Don't be distracted by the ads for a nearby travel agency—you can buy tickets on board.

There's no public transportation back to Kraków from Birkenau, where most people end their tours; you'll have to take the shuttle bus back to Auschwitz I first.

WARSAW

Warszawa

Warsaw (Warszawa, vah-SHAH-vah in Polish) is Poland's capital and biggest city. It's huge, famous, and important...but not particularly romantic. If you're looking for Old World quaintness, head for Kraków. If you're tickled by spires and domes, get to Prague. But if you want to experience a truly 21st-century city, Warsaw's your place.

A decade ago, the city was dreary and uninviting. But things have changed here dramatically. The Varsovians (as locals are called) are chic and sophisticated. Young professionals dress and dine as well as the Parisians and Milanese, and they've mastered the art of navigating an urban jungle in heels or a man bun. Today's Warsaw has gleaming new office towers, glitzy shopping malls, swarms of international businesspeople, inviting parks and pedestrian zones, hipster culture to rival Brooklyn or Portland, and a gourmet coffee shop or designer pastry store on every corner.

Stroll down revitalized boulevards that evoke the city's glory days, pausing at an outdoor café to sip coffee and nibble at a *pączek* (the classic Polish jelly doughnut). Drop by a leafy park for an al fresco Chopin concert, packed with patriotic Poles. Commune with the soul of Poland at the city's many state-of-the-art museums—take your pick: Poland's artists (National Museum), its favorite composer (Chopin Museum), its dramatic history (Museum of Warsaw and Warsaw Uprising Museum), its dedication

Warsaw History: Ebbs and Flows

Warsaw has good reason to be a city of the future: The past hasn't been very kind. Historically, Warsaw has seen wave after wave of foreign rulers and invasions—especially during the last hundred years. But in this horrific crucible, the enduring spirit of the Polish people was forged. As one proud Varsovian told me, "Warsaw is ugly because its history is so beautiful."

Founded around 1300, Warsaw gradually gained importance through the late Middle Ages. In the mid-16th century, it became the seat of the Sejm (parliament of nobles), and it took over as seat of the royal court (and therefore Poland's capital) in 1596.

The city's Golden Age was between the World Wars, when Poland—newly reconstituted after a century and a half of foreign rule under the Partitions—was proudly independent. Interwar Warsaw saw a flourishing of commerce, construction, and the arts almost unmatched in Europe at that time, when it was also the largest and most culturally rich Jewish city in Europe.

Sadly, this age of optimism was cut brutally short by the city's darkest days, as the Nazis occupied the city (and all of Poland) at the outbreak of World War II. First, its Jewish residents were forced into a tiny ghetto. They rose up...and were slaughtered (the Ghetto Uprising—see page 408). Then, in the war's waning days, its surviving residents rose up...and were slaughtered (the Warsaw Uprising—see page 415). Fed up with the troublesome Varsovians, Hitler sent word to systematically demolish the entire city, block by block. At the war's end, Warsaw was virtually gone. An estimated 800,000 residents were dead—nearly two out of every three.

The Poles almost gave up on what was then a pile of rubble, planning to build a brand-new capital city elsewhere. But ultimately they decided to rebuild, creating a city of contrasts: painstakingly restored medieval lanes and retrofitted communist apartment blocks (*bloki* in Polish). And its evolution continues. Since the end of communism, Warsaw has become a hub of international trade and diplomacy—adding sleek skyscrapers to its skyline. It's clear that Warsaw is currently living one of its finest moments.

to the sciences (Copernicus Science Center), and its Jewish story (Museum of the History of Polish Jews). You can also dig into one of Europe's most interesting foodie scenes, where a world of wildly creative chefs open new restaurants all the time—at budget prices. If you picture a dreary metropolis, think again. Warsaw is full of surprises.

PLANNING YOUR TIME

One day is the absolute minimum to get a quick taste of Warsaw—but you'll have to sightsee very selectively. The city can easily fill two or three days, and even then you'll need to pick and choose. Review your museum-going options to decide how much time you need.

No matter how long you stay, get your bearings by taking a stroll through Polish history, following my Royal Way Walk from Palm Tree Circle to the Old Town. With more time, extend your stroll on my Old Town Walk for a sampling of Warsaw's historic core. Then visit other sights according to your interests and time: Jewish history, the Warsaw Uprising, Polish artists, royalty, hands-on science gizmos, hipster hangouts, or Chopin. To slow down and take a break from the city, relax in Łazienki Park.

For dinner, buck the tourist trend by leaving the overpriced Old Town and riding a tram, the Metro, a taxi, or Uber to the hip Śródmieście district, which has the highest concentration of quality eateries.

Orientation to Warsaw

Warsaw sprawls with 1.7 million residents. Everything is on a big scale—it seems to take forever to walk just a few "short" blocks.

Get comfortable with public transportation (or taxis or Uber), and plan your sightseeing to avoid backtracking.

The tourist's Warsaw blankets a mild hill on the west bank of the Vistula River (in Polish: Wisła, VEES-wah). To break things into manageable chunks, I think of the city as three major zones (from north to south):

The **Old Town and Royal Way,** at Warsaw's northern edge, is the most touristy area. Here you'll find the Old Town (Stare Miasto, STAH-reh mee-AH-stoh), the adjacent and nearly-as-old New Town (Nowe Miasto, NOH-vay mee-AH-stoh), the Royal Castle on Castle Square (Plac Zamkowy, plahts zahm-KOH-vee), and the historical artery called the Royal Way (Szlak Królewski, shwock kroh-LEHV-skee). This bustling strip has strollable boulevards, genteel cafés, expansive squares and parks, and stately landmarks both historic and faux-historic (much of this area was rebuilt after World War II).

"Palm Tree Circle" is my nickname for the center of the city, near the traffic circle with a fake palm tree—where busy Jerusa-

WARSAW

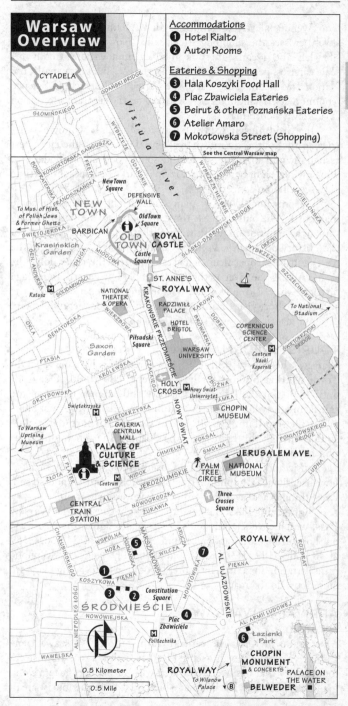

Warsaw Overview

See the Central Warsaw map

CYTADELA

Vistula River

SŁOMIŃSKIEGO

GDANSKI BRIDGE

WYBRZEŻE GDAŃSKIE

WYBRZEŻE HELSKIE

PONIATERSKA

KONWIKTORSKA SANGUSZKI

FRANCISZKAŃSKA

FRETA

New Town Square

NEW TOWN

DEFENSIVE WALL

JAGIELLOŃSKA

To Mus. of Hist. of Polish Jews & Former Ghetto

ŚWIĘTOJERSKA

BARBICAN

Old Town Square

OLD TOWN

ROYAL CASTLE

ŚLĄSKO-DĄBROWSKI BRIDGE

WYBRZEŻE OKRZEI

SZCZECIŃSKIE

Krasińskich Garden

GEN. ANDERSA

DŁUGA

MIODOWA

Castle Square

Square

ST. ANNE'S

ROYAL WAY

KAROWA

DOBRA

To National Stadium

M Ratusz

SOLIDARNOŚCI

NATIONAL THEATER & OPERA

WIERZBOWA

KRAKOWSKIE PRZEDMIEŚCIE

RADZIWIŁŁ PALACE

BROWARNA

COPERNICUS SCIENCE CENTER

OKÓŁ

SENATORSKA

Piłsudski Square

HOTEL BRISTOL

ŚWIĘTOKRZYSKI BRIDGE

M Centrum Nauki Kopernik

PTASIA

Saxon Garden

WARSAW UNIVERSITY

KRÓLEWSKA

CZACKIEGO

OKÓŁ

GRZYBOWSKA

HOLY CROSS

M Nowy Świat Uniwersytet

TAMKA

To Warsaw Uprising Museum

Świętokrzyska M

ŚWIĘTOKRZYSKA M

NOWY ŚWIAT

CHOPIN MUSEUM

PONIATOWSKIEGO BRIDGE

GALERIA CENTRUM MALL

FOKSAL

PALACE OF CULTURE & SCIENCE

CHMIELNA

SMOLNA

JERUSALEM AVE.

E. PLATER

M Centrum

WIDOK

JEROZOLIMSKIE

PALM TREE CIRCLE

NATIONAL MUSEUM

LUPNA

ZŁOTA

AL. JEROZOLIMSKIE

NOWOGRODZKA

Three Crosses Square

CENTRAL TRAIN STATION

ŻURAWIA

WSPÓLNA

MARSZAŁKOWSKA

WILCZA

KRUCZA

ROYAL WAY

CHAŁUBIŃSKIEGO

HOŻA

5

7

AL. PIĘKNA

ROZBRAT

1 KOSZYKOWA

PIĘKNA

MOKOTOWSKA

AL. UJAZDOWSKIE

3

2 Constitution Square

ŚRÓDMIEŚCIE

NOWOWIEJSKA

Plac Zbawiciela

4

AL. ARMII LUDOWEJ

6 Łazienki Park

N

M Politechnika

CHOPIN MONUMENT & CONCERTS

WAWELSKA

AL. NIEPODLEGŁOŚCI

0.5 Kilometer

ROYAL WAY

To Wilanów Palace (B)

PALACE ON THE WATER

BELWEDER

0.5 Mile

lem Avenue (aleja Jerozolimskie, ah-LAY-uh yeh-ro-zoh-LIM-skyeh) crosses the shopping street called Nowy Świat (NOH-vee SHVEE-aht). Nearby are some good accommodations, trendy upscale eateries, pedestrianized shopping streets and glitzy malls, the National Museum (Polish art), the Palace of Culture and Science (communist-era landmark skyscraper), and the central train station (Warszawa Centralna).

The **Śródmieście** (SHROD-myesh-cheh, "Downtown") district, to the south, is a mostly residential zone with the city's best restaurant and nightlife scene and some good accommodations. The only real sight here is lush Łazienki Park, with its summertime al fresco Chopin concerts.

In sprawling Warsaw, many more sights—including some major ones—lie outside these three areas, but all are within a long walk or a short ride on public transit. These include the Museum of the History of Polish Jews and Warsaw Uprising Museum (to the west) and the Copernicus Science Center (to the east, along the river). Across the river is the hardscrabble but gentrifying Praga district; while a trendy scene is emerging there, it's beyond the scope of a short visit (Śródmieście is similar, more accessible, and easier to reach).

TOURIST INFORMATION

Warsaw's helpful, youthful TI has three branches: on the **Old Town Market Square** (daily May-Sept 9:00-20:00, Oct-April until 18:00), at the **Palace of Culture and Science** (enter on the side facing the train station, on Emilii Plater; daily May-Sept 8:00-19:00, Oct-April until 18:00), and at **Chopin Airport** (daily 9:00-19:00—though this branch may be closing). The general information number for all TIs is 22-19115. All branches offer advice on live music and have piles of free, useful brochures ("city breaks," Jewish heritage, Chopin, mermaids, St. John Paul II, and so on). Everything is also available online (www.warsawtour.pl).

Sightseeing Pass: Busy sightseers might consider the **Warsaw Pass,** which covers admission to most major sights, the best hop-on, hop-off bus tour, and a Chopin concert (119 zł/24 hours, 159 zł/48 hours, 189 zł/72 hours, sold at the TI); you can add public transportation for a little bit more. If your museum-going plans are ambitious, do the math.

ARRIVAL IN WARSAW
By Train

Most trains arrive at the **central train station** (Warszawa Centralna, vah-SHAH-vah tsehn-TRAHL-nah), a communist-era monstrosity that has been renovated with surprising grace. (Don't get off at Warszawa Zachodnia, which is far from the tourist area.)

Warszawa Centralna can be tricky to navigate: Three parallel concourses run across the tracks, accessed by three different sets of escalators from each platform, creating a subterranean maze (with well-signed lockers, ticket windows, and lots of shops

and eateries). Be patient: To get your bearings, ride up on your platform's middle escalator, then look for signs to the wide-open **main hall** (follow signs for *main hall/hala główna*). Here you'll find a row of ticket windows, a railroad service center, a supermarket, eateries, waiting areas (upstairs), and (from outside, near the taxi stand) views of the adjacent Palace of Culture and Science and Złota 44 skyscrapers. If you have a little time to kill, walk across the street to the super-modern Złote Tarasy Shopping Mall (described on page 405).

Getting into Town: To reach the tourist zone and most of my recommended hotels, a taxi/Uber is the easiest choice, while the bus is more economical (but more challenging to find).

Taxis wait outside the main hall. Many are dishonest—look for one with a company logo and telephone number, and ask for an estimate up front (the fare should be no more than about 20-30 zł for most of my recommended hotels). You can also order an **Uber.**

From the station, **bus #175** or **#128** takes you to the Royal Way and Old Town in about 10 minutes (see "Getting Around Warsaw," later). You can catch either bus in front of the skyscraper with the Hotel Marriott, across busy Jerusalem Avenue from the station. Because it's hard to find this stop from the station's mazelike corridors, it's probably simplest to ascend to street level (on the aleja Jerozolimskie side) and cross surface streets to reach the well-marked Marriott tower. Both buses terminate just off Piłsudski Square, a five-minute walk from the Old Town. **Bus #160** also goes to the Old Town (though not via the Royal Way), but it departs from the opposite side of the station: To find its stop from the main hall, go out the side door toward *ul. Emilii Plater.* Before boarding any bus, buy a ticket from the machine near the stop—or get one within the station's underground zone, at any kiosk marked *RUCH.*

Buying Train Tickets: Lining one wall of the main arrival hall *(hala główna)* are 16 **ticket windows.** A more user-friendly **passenger service center** is in the opposite corner (daily 9:10-20:30). While it can be slower to buy tickets or make reservations in the office (take a number as you enter), staff members are more likely to speak English and have patience for clueless tourists. Additional ticket windows are in the maze of corridors under the station. (You can also book most train tickets online at www.rozklad-pkp.pl.) If buying tickets in person, allow yourself plenty of time to wait in line. Remember: Even if you have a rail pass, a reservation is still required on many express trains (including EIC trains to Kraków or Gdańsk). If you're not sure, ask. To get to your train, first find your way to the right platform (*peron,* as noted on schedules), then keep an eye on both tracks *(tor)* for your train. Train info: Tel. 19436 (22-19436 from outside Warsaw), www.rozklad-pkp.pl.

By Plane
Fryderyk Chopin International Airport

Warsaw's Fryderyk Chopin International Airport (Port Lotniczy im. Fryderyk Chopina, airport code: WAW, tel. 22-650-4220, www.lotnisko-chopina.pl) is about six miles southwest of the center. It's relatively small and manageable; outside the arrivals area, you'll find a TI, ATMs, car-rental offices, and exchange desks *(kantor).*

To get into town, you can take the train or bus (similar prices, around 5 zł). The train is faster, but the bus makes more stops in the city center and may get you closer to your hotel. From the arrivals area, just follow signs to either option.

The **train** departs about every 15 minutes and takes 20-30 minutes. To find it, turn right in the arrivals area and follow the green line on the floor. Exiting the airport, you'll head downstairs (under the big *Stacja Kolejawa* sign) to find the tracks. The line into town is operated by two different companies (SKM and KM)— take whichever one departs first. Be ready for your stop: Half the trains make fewer stops and take you to Centralna station; others make a few more stops and use the Warszawa Śródmieście station—which feeds into the same underground passages as Centralna (these trains also continue one more stop to the Warszawa Powiśle station, which is a bit closer to Nowy Świat and can be more convenient to some hotels). Whether arriving at Centralna station or Warszawa Śródmieście, see the "By Train" arrival instructions, earlier.

Bus #175 departs from the curb in front of arrivals every 15-20 minutes and runs into the city center (Centralna station, the Royal Way, and Piłsudski Square near the Old Town, 30-45 minutes depending on traffic; buy ticket from machine before you board).

For a **taxi,** head to the official taxi stand. Taxis have a fixed rate of about 45 zł to most downtown hotels (trip takes 30 minutes depending on traffic). It's generally cheaper to order an **Uber** (except at very busy times).

Modlin Airport

Modlin Airport (airport code: WMI), about 21 miles northwest of the city center, primarily serves budget airlines (especially Ryanair). The most direct option for getting to downtown Warsaw is by shuttle bus—**ModlinBus** and **OKbus** both connect the airport to downtown (33 zł, 2/hour, one-hour trip, cheaper if you book ahead online—www.modlinbus.com or www.okbus.pl). An alternative is the well-coordinated **bus-plus-train connection:** Take a shuttle bus to Modlin's main train station, then hop on a train to Warszawa Centralna station (19 zł, hourly, 1-1.5 hours total, www.mazowieckie.com.pl). If you want to ride a **taxi** all the way into Warsaw, the maximum legitimate fare is 200 zł (or 250 zł at night). Airport info: www.modlinairport.pl.

GETTING AROUND WARSAW

Sprawling Warsaw can be exhausting to get around. Get comfortable with public transportation and taxis/Uber.

By Public Transit: Warsaw's efficient, affordable public transportation network includes buses, trams, and the two-line Metro (transit info: www.ztm.waw.pl). Everything is covered by the same tickets. Most rides within the tourist zone take less than 20 minutes, so the default is the 3.40-zł "20-minute city travelcard" *(bilet 20-minutowy)*. For longer journeys, a single ticket *(bilet jednorazowy)* covers any trip up to 75 minutes for 4.40 zł. A 24-hour travelcard *(bilet dobowy)*—which pays for itself if you take at least five trips—costs 15 zł. Ticket machines, which are at most major stops, are easy to use; they have English instructions and take both coins and credit cards. Or you can buy tickets at any kiosk with a *RUCH* sign. While you may find ticket machines on board some buses and trams, it's safest to buy your ticket before boarding. Be sure to validate your ticket as you board by inserting it in the little yellow box.

Most of the city's major attractions line up on a single axis, the Royal Way, which is served by several different buses (but no trams). **Bus #175**—particularly useful on arrival—links Chopin Airport, the central train station, the Royal Way, and Old Town (it terminates at Piłsudski Square, about a five-minute walk from Castle Square). Once you're in town, the designed-for-tourists **bus #180** conveniently connects virtually all the significant sights and neighborhoods: the former Jewish Ghetto and Museum of the History of Polish Jews, Castle Square/Old Town, the Royal Way, Łazienki Park, and Wilanów Palace (south of the center). This particularly user-friendly bus lists sights in English on the posted schedule inside (other buses don't).

Bus routes beginning with "E" (marked in red on schedules) are express, so they go long distances without stopping (these don't run July-Aug). Note that on Saturdays and Sundays in summer

Central Warsaw

Rondo Babka

PARKING LOT WITH FORMER GHETTO WALL

UMSCHLAGPLATZ MONUMENT

STAWKI

MURANÓW
(Former Jewish Ghetto)

FORMER SS HQ

BUNKER

MUSEUM OF THE HISTORY OF POLISH JEWS

GHETTO HEROES SQUARE

Muranów

Plac Krasinskich

Krasińskich Garden

Nalewki

Ratusz

Plac Bankowy

SOLIDARNOŚCI

ELEKTORALNA

PL. MIROWSKI

PTASIA

GRZYBOWSKA

Plac Grzybowski

Plac Bankowy

TWARDA

ŚWIETOKRZYSKA

GRZYBOWSKA

Muzeum Powstania Warszawskiego

ŁUCKA

PROSTA

WARSAW UPRISING MUSEUM

Rondo Daszynskiego

Rondo Daszyńskiego

PANSKA

SIENNA

ZŁOTE TARASY MALL

Dworzec Centralny Bus #160

CENTRAL TRAIN STATION

ZŁOTA

PROSTA

CHMIELNA

Dw. Centralny

Dworzec Centralny Bus #175

Accommodations

1. Hotel Indigo
2. Between Us B&B
3. Chopin Boutique B&B
4. Zgoda by DeSilva
5. Apple Inn
6. Oki Doki City Hostel
7. Hotel Bristol
8. Hotel Le Régina
9. Castle Inn
10. Duval Apartments

Eateries

11. Kamanda Lwowska
12. Bibenda
13. Butchery & Wine
14. A. Blikle
15. E. Wedel Pijalnia Czekolady
16. Odette
17. Warszawa Powiśle
18. Kawiarnia Kafka
19. Restauracja pod Samsonem
20. Freta 33
21. Zapiecek (5)

400 Meters

400 Yards

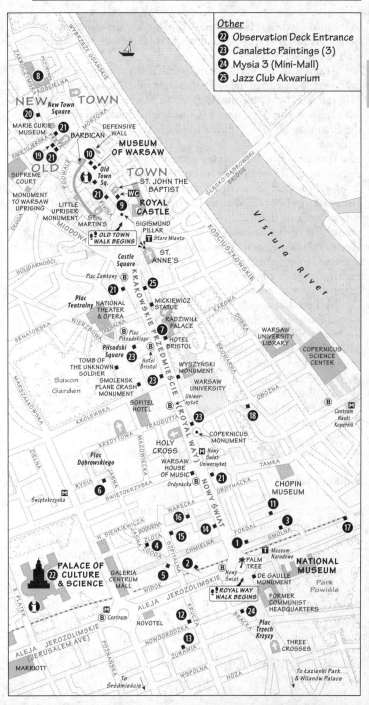

Other
22 Observation Deck Entrance
23 Canaletto Paintings (3)
24 Mysia 3 (Mini-Mall)
25 Jazz Club Akwarium

(May-mid-Oct), the Nowy Świat-Krakowskie Przedmieście section of the Royal Way is closed to traffic, so the above routes detour along a parallel street.

Trams can be particularly useful for reaching the trendy Śródmieście district in the south. Several trams (including #4, #15, #18, and #35) run along the north-south Marszałkowska corridor, with stops at plac Konstytucji (Constitution Square, the heart of the Śródmieście) and at plac Zbawiciela (with a cluster of great eateries).

Warsaw's two-line **Metro** system, designed for commuters, can be useful for hops between certain sights—especially line 2, which runs east to west; its most convenient stops are Rondo Daszyńskiego (near the Warsaw Uprising Museum), Świętokrzyska (where you can transfer to line 1), Nowy Świat-Uniwersytet (in the middle of the Royal Way, near the Copernicus Monument), Centrum Nauki Kopernik (on the riverbank, near the Copernicus Science Center), and Stadion Narodowy (National Stadium, across the river). The north-south line 1, which stops at the train station (Centrum), is less useful for visitors.

By Taxi: Use only cabs that are clearly marked with a company logo and telephone number; official cabs have a mermaid decal on the front door (or call your own: Locals like City Taxi, tel. 19459; MPT Radio Taxi, tel. 19191; or Ele taxi, tel. 22-811-1111). All official taxis have similar rates: 8 zł to start, then 3 zł per kilometer (4.50 zł after 22:00 or in the suburbs). **Uber** also works well in Warsaw, just like back home; it's typically cheaper than a taxi and can be useful in situations where you're not near a taxi stand or a convenient public-transit stop.

Tours in Warsaw

Walking Tours

Each year, new companies crop up offering walking tours in Warsaw. These tend to have one of two approaches: A "free" tour of the main sights (with generous tipping expected); or communism-themed tours, often with a ride to a gloomy apartment-block area for a taste of the Red old days. The TI and most hotels have brochures. Survey the latest offerings, do some homework (check online reviews), and pick a tour that suits your interests.

Private Guides

Having a talented local historian as your guide in this city, with such a complex and powerful story to tell, greatly enhances your experience. I've worked with two excellent young guides: smart and charming **Monika Oleśko** (350 zł/3 hours, 550 zł/5.5 hours; more for larger groups, by bike, or by car; mobile 535-770-843, warsawteller.wordpress.com, olesko.monika@gmail.com) and professorial **Hubert Pawlik** (520 zł/5-hour city walking tour, 650 zł with his car, other tours—including options by car—are explained on his website, mobile 502-298-105, www.warsaw-citytours.com, guide@warsaw-citytours.com). Both Monika and Hubert offer theme tours and can tailor the time to your interests.

Food Tours

Eat Polska does excellent food and vodka tours around this fast-emerging foodie mecca. A top-quality guide will take your small group to a variety of restaurants and bars around the city, with tasting samples at each one. The guides do an exceptional job of providing insightful context about what you're tasting, making this educational about both Polish cuisine and Polish culture in general. If you have a serious interest in food, this is the most worthwhile tour in town (food tours typically daily at 13:00, 290 zł, 4 hours; vodka tours with food pairings daily at 17:00, 290 zł, 3.5 hours; www.eatpolska.com).

Bus Tours

Warsaw's spread-out landscape makes it a natural for a hop-on, hop-off bus—although heavy traffic may make you wish you'd taken a tram or the Metro instead. The best choice is CitySightseeing, with red buses (60 zł/24 hours, 80 zł/48 hours, two routes). Skip City-Tour (yellow buses), which is more expensive and less frequent.

Walks in Warsaw

I've outlined two self-guided walks in Warsaw. The "Royal Way Walk" covers the most interesting one-mile section of the Royal Way—in the heart of the city, from Palm Tree Circle to Castle Square. It's followed by the "Old Town Walk," which starts in Castle Square and explores Warsaw's Old Town. Allow about 1.75 hours to do both walks back-to-back.

ROYAL WAY WALK

The Royal Way (Szłak Królewski) is the six-mile route that the kings of Poland used to travel from their main residence (at Castle Square in the Old Town) to their summer home (Wilanów Palace, south of the center and not worth visiting). This busy boulevard changes names from Nowy Świat to Krakowskie Przedmieście as it stretches from south to north. Not counting sightseeing stops, figure about 30 minutes to walk along Nowy Świat ("Part 1"), then another 45 minutes along Krakowskie Przedmieście to the Old Town ("Part 2").

Warsaw at a Glance

▲▲▲Museum of the History of Polish Jews Exceptional, expansive exhibit on the full Jewish experience through Polish history. **Hours:** Mon and Thu-Fri 10:00-18:00, Wed and Sat-Sun 10:00-20:00, closed Tue. See page 407.

▲▲Royal Castle Warsaw's best palace, rebuilt after World War II, but retaining its former opulence and many original furnishings. **Hours:** May-Sept Mon-Sat 10:00-18:00, Fri until 20:00, Sun 11:00-18:00; Oct-April Tue-Sat 10:00-16:00, Sun 11:00-16:00, closed Mon. See page 393.

▲▲Old Town Market Square Re-creation of Warsaw's glory days, with lots of colorful architecture. See page 390.

▲▲National Museum Collection of mostly Polish art, with unknown but worth-discovering works by Jan Matejko and the Młoda Polska (Art Nouveau) crew. **Hours:** Tue-Sun 10:00-18:00, Fri until 21:00, closed Mon. See page 397.

▲▲Warsaw Uprising Museum State-of-the-art space tracing the history of the Uprising and celebrating its heroes. **Hours:** Mon and Wed-Fri 8:00-18:00, Thu until 20:00, Sat-Sun 10:00-18:00, closed Tue. See page 413.

▲▲Copernicus Science Center Spiffy new science museum with well-explained, hands-on exhibits in English; Warsaw's best family activity. **Hours:** Tue-Fri 9:00-18:00, Sat-Sun 10:00-19:00, closed Mon. See page 403.

▲Castle Square Colorful spot with whiffs of old Warsaw—Royal Castle, monuments, and a chunk of the city wall—and cafés just off the square. See page 388.

▲Łazienki Park Lovely, sprawling green space with Chopin statue, peacocks, and Neoclassical buildings. **Hours:** Always open; wonderful outdoor Chopin concerts mid-May-late Sept generally Sun at 12:00 and 16:00. See page 417.

▲Museum of Warsaw In-depth treatment of the history of Warsaw, with excellent movie in English. **Hours:** Tue-Sun 10:00-19:00, closed Mon. See page 396.

Palace of Culture and Science Huge "Stalin Gothic" skyscraper with a more impressive exterior than interior, housing theaters, multiplex cinema, observation deck, and more. **Hours:** Observation deck—daily 10:00-20:00, may be open later in summer. See page 404.

Part 1: Palm Tree Circle and Nowy Świat

• *Start this walk at the traffic circle officially named for Charles de Gaulle, but colloquially known as...*

Palm Tree Circle

This is one of the city's main intersections, marked by the iconic palm tree. Stand near the communist-era monument under the spruce trees (on the curb, kitty-corner from the biggest building) and get oriented.

You're standing at the intersection of two major boulevards: **Nowy Świat** (where we're heading next) and **Jerusalem Avenue** (aleja Jerozolimskie, which heads from Warszawa Centralna station across the river). This street once led to a Jewish settlement called New Jerusalem. Like so much else in Warsaw, it's changed names many times. Between the World Wars, it became "May 3rd Avenue," celebrating Poland's 1791 constitution (Europe's first). But this was too nationalistic for the occupying Nazis, who called it simply Bahnhofstrasse ("Train Station Street"). Then the communists switched it back to "Jerusalem," strangely disregarding the religious connotations of that name. (Come on, guys—what about a good, old-fashioned "Stalin Avenue"?) The strikingly wide boulevards were part of the city's post-WWII Soviet rebuilding. Communist urban planners felt that eight- to twelve-lane roads were ideal for worker pageantry like big May Day parades...and, when the workers aren't happy, for Soviet tanks to thunder around, maintaining order.

You can't miss the giant **palm tree** in the middle of Jerusalem Avenue. When a local artist went to the real Jerusalem, she was struck by the many palm trees—and wanted to erect one along Warsaw's own little stretch of "Jerusalem." This artificial palm tree went up in 2002 as a temporary installation. It was highly controversial, dividing the neighborhood. One snowy winter day, the pro-palm tree faction—who appreciated the way the tree spiced up this otherwise dreary metropolis—camped out here in bikinis and beachwear to show their support. They prevailed, and the tree is now a permanent fixture.

The big, blocky building across the street (on the left side of the intersection) was the **headquarters of the Communist Party,** built in 1948. *Nowy Świat* translates as "New World," inspiring a popular communist-era joke: What do you see when you turn your back on the Communist Party? A "New World." Ironically, when the economy was privatized in 1991, this building became home to Poland's stock exchange. And then the country's only dealership for Ferraris—certainly not an automobile for the proletariat—moved in downstairs.

On the corner in front of the former Communist Party HQ, a statue of **Charles de Gaulle** strides confidently up the street. A gift from the government of France, this celebrates the military tactician who came to Warsaw's rescue when the Red Army invaded from the USSR after World War I.

To the left of the Communist Party building is the vast **National Museum**—a good place for a fascinating lesson in Polish art (see the self-guided tour later, under "Sights in Warsaw").

Before walking down Nowy Świat, notice the small but powerful **monument** near you. In 1956, this was dedicated to the "Poles who fought for People's Poland"—with a strong communist connotation. In a classic example of Socialist Realism, the communists appropriated a religious theme that Poles were inclined to embrace (this pietà composition)...and politicized it. But in 2014, the statue was rededicated to the "*partyzantom* who fought for free Poland in World War II." "Partisan" was a bad word in the 1950s, when it was used to describe the soldiers of the Polish Home Army—which fought against both the Nazis and the Soviets.

• *From here, turn your back to the Communist Party building and head into a new world—down Nowy Świat—to the first intersection. As you stroll, notice how massive, intense Warsaw suddenly becomes more intimate and accessible.*

Nowy Świat

This charming shopping boulevard, lined with boutiques, cafés, and restaurants, feels upscale and elegant. Before World War II, Nowy Świat was Warsaw's most popular neighborhood. And today, once again, rents are higher here than anywhere else in town. While most tourists flock into the Old Town, Varsovians and visiting businesspeople prefer this zone and farther south. The city has worked hard to revitalize this strip with broad

sidewalks, flower boxes, old-time lampposts, and strict restrictions on traffic (only buses and taxis—and on summer weekends, it's entirely traffic-free).

Look down the street and notice the harmonious architecture. In the 1920s, this street was anything but cohesive: an eclectic and decadent strip of Art Deco facades, full of individualism. Rather than rebuild in that "trouble-causing" style, the communists used an idealized, more conservative, Neoclassical style, which feels more like the 1820s than the 1920s.

Ulica Chmielna, the first street to the left, is an appealing pedestrian boutique street leading to Emil Wedel's chocolate heaven (a five-minute walk away; described later, under "Eating in Warsaw"). Between here and the Palace of Culture and Science stretches one of Warsaw's top shopping neighborhoods (culminating at the Galleria Centrum mall, just across from the Palace).

Across the street from Chmielna (on the right) is the restaurant street called **Foksal.** On a balmy summer evening, this street is filled with chatty al fresco diners.

A few steps farther down Nowy Świat, on the left, don't miss the recommended **A. Blikle** pastry shop and café—a venerable spot for Polish sweets, especially *pączki* (rose-flavored jelly doughnuts). Step inside for a dose of the 1920s: good-life Art Deco decor and historical photos. Or, if you're homesick for Starbucks, drop in to one of the second-wave coffee shops that line this stretch of Nowy Świat—many with American-style lattes "to go" (one of many American customs that the Poles have embraced).

A half-block down the street (on the left, at #39) is a rare surviving bit of preglitz Nowy Świat: Bar Mleczny Familijny, a classic **milk bar**—a government-subsidized cafeteria filled with locals seeking a cheap meal (an interesting cultural artifact, but not recommended for a meal; for more about milk bars, see the sidebar on page 222). But don't be surprised if it's gone by the time you visit; in this high-rent district, it's unlikely that these few remaining holdovers from the old days will survive for much longer.

Eat and shop your way along Nowy Świat. About one more block down, **Ordynacka street** (on the right) leads downhill to the Chopin Museum, worth considering for musical pilgrims.

At the end of the block on the left (at #63), the **Warsaw House of Music** hosts live concerts of various kinds, and sells tickets for nightly Chopin concerts back near Palm Tree Circle (for details, see "Entertainment in Warsaw," later).

• *Continuing along Nowy Świat through a duller stretch, you'll walk alongside a hulking, gloomy building before popping out in a pleasant square with a big statue of Copernicus.*

Part 2: Krakowskie Przedmieście
• *The street name changes to Krakowskie Przedmieście (meaning, roughly, "suburb in the direction of Kraków") at the big...*

Copernicus Statue
This statue, by the great Danish sculptor Bertel Thorvaldsen, stands in front of the Polish Academy of Science. **Mikołaj Kopernik** (1473-1543) was born in Toruń and went to college in Kraków. The

WARSAW

Nazis stole his statue and took it to Germany (which, like Poland, claims Copernicus as its own). Now it's back where it belongs. The concentric circles radiating from the front of the statue represent the course of the planets' orbits, from Mercury to Saturn.

Just to Copernicus' left is a low-profile, black-marble **Chopin bench**—one of many scattered around the center. These benches mark points related to his life (in this case, his sister lived across the street). Each of these benches plays Chopin's music with the push of a button (though because of passing traffic, this one is tough to hear).

Directly in front of the statue, in the glass case, find a replica of a **Canaletto painting** of this same street scene in 1778, and compare it to today's reality. As the national archives were destroyed, city builders referred to historic paintings like these for guidance after WWII. You'll see other Canaletto replicas like this one scattered around the city.

• *Across from Copernicus, the Church of the Holy Cross is worth a look.*

Church of the Holy Cross (Kościół Św. Krzyża)

We'll pass many churches along this route, but the Church of the Holy Cross is unique (and free to enter). Composer **Fryderyk Cho-**

pin's heart is inside one of the pillars of the nave (first big pillar on the left, look for the marker). After two decades of exile in France, Chopin's final wish was to have his heart brought back to his native Poland after his death. During World War II, the heart was hidden away in the countryside for safety.

Check out the bright gold chapel, located on the left as you face the altar, near the front of the church. It's dedicated to a saint whom Polish Catholics believe helps them with **"desperate and hopeless causes."** People praying here are likely dealing with some tough issues. The beads draped from the altarpieces help power their prayers, and the many little brass plaques are messages of thanks for prayers answered.

In the back-left corner (as you face the altar) is a chapel dedicated to Poland's favorite son, **St. John Paul II.** His ghostly image appears out of the wall; beneath him is a rock inscribed with the words *Tu es Petrus* (Latin for "You are Peter"—what Jesus said when he made St. Peter the first-ever pope), embedded with a capsule containing JPII's actual blood.

Just opposite, in the back-right corner, behind the giant barbed wire, is a memorial to the 22,000 Polish POWs—mostly officers and prominent civilians—massacred by Soviet soldiers in 1940 near **Katyń,** a village in today's Russia. Stalin was determined to decapitate Poland's military intelligentsia in a ruthless mass killing, which Poles have never forgotten.

Leaving the church, notice the 19th-century, bronze-and-granite **statue of Christ bearing the cross** along the balustrade. In front, a placard reads, "Lift up your hearts." Even as Warsaw bore the burden of Russian occupation, this statue inspired them to be strong and not lose hope. It was one of many crosses they bore: a Catholic nation pinched between Orthodox Russians and Protestant Germans.

• *Cross the street (appreciating how pedestrian-friendly it is—crossing here used to be a real-life game of Frogger), and continue left.*

Warsaw University

A long block up the street on the right, you'll see the gates (marked *Uniwersytet*) to the main campus of **Warsaw University,** founded in 1816. This lively student district has plenty of bookstores and cafeterias.

Keep strolling, appreciating the fine facades. The 18th century was a time of great political decline for Poland, as a series of incompetent foreign kings mishandled crises and squandered funds. But ironically, it was also Warsaw's biggest economic boom time. Along this boulevard, aristocratic families of the period built **mansions**—most of them destroyed in World War II and rebuilt since. Some have curious flourishes (just past the university on the right, look for the doorway supported by four bearded brutes admiring their overly defined abs...it's supposed to be a six-pack, but I count ten). Over time, many of these families donated their mansions to the university.

• *The bright-yellow church a block up from the university, on the right, is the...*

Church of the Nuns of the Visitation (Kościół Sióstr Wizytek)

This Rococo confection from 1761 is the only church on this walk that survived World War II, and is notable because Chopin was briefly the organist here.

The monument in front of the church commemorates **Cardinal Stefan Wyszyński,** who was the head of the Polish Catholic Church from 1948 to 1981. He took this post soon after the arrival of the communists, who opposed the Church, but also realized it would be risky for them to shut down the churches in such an ardently religious country. The Communist Party and the Catholic Church coexisted tensely in Poland, and when Wyszyński protested a Stalinist crackdown in 1953, he was arrested and imprisoned. Three years later, in a major victory for the Church, Wyszyński was released. He continued to fight the communists, becoming a great hero of the Polish people in their struggle against the regime.

Across the street is another then-and-now Canaletto illustration.

• *Farther up (on the right, past the park) is the elegant, venerable...*

Hotel Bristol

A striking building with a round turret on its corner, the Hotel Bristol was used by the Nazis as a VIP hotel and bordello, and survived World War II. If you wan-

der through any fancy Warsaw lobby...make it this one. Step in like you're staying here and explore its fine public spaces, with fresh Art Deco and Art Nouveau flourishes. The café in front retains its Viennese atmosphere, but the *pièce de résistance* is the stunning Column Bar deeper in, past the dramatically chandeliered lounge.

• *Leave the Royal Way briefly here for a worthwhile detour. With the corner turret of Hotel Bristol at your back, cross the street and bear left between the buildings. You'll pop out at a vast expanse called...*

Piłsudski Square (plac Marszałka Józefa Piłsudskiego)

The vast, empty-feeling Piłsudski Square (pew-SOOD-skee) has been important Warsaw real estate for centuries, constantly changing with the times. In the 1890s, the Russians who controlled this part of Poland began construction of a huge and magnificent Orthodox cathedral on this spot. But soon after it was completed, Poland regained its independence, and anti-Russian sentiments ran hot. So in the 1920s, just over a decade after the cathedral went up, it was torn down. During the Nazi occupation, this square took the name "Adolf-Hitler-Platz." Under the communists, it was Zwycięstwa, meaning "Victory" (of the Soviets over Hitler's fascism).

When the regime imposed martial law in 1981, the people of Warsaw silently protested by filling the square with a giant cross made of flowers. The huge **plaque** in the ground near the road commemorates two monumental communist-era Catholic events on this square: John Paul II's first visit as pope to his homeland on June 2, 1979; and the May 31, 1981 funeral of Cardinal Stefan Wyszyński, whom we met across the street. The cross nearby also honors the 1979 papal visit, with one of his most famous and inspiring quotes to his countrymen: "Let thy spirit descend, let thy spirit descend, and renew the face of the earth—of *this* earth" (meaning Poland, in a just-barely-subtle-enough dig against the communist regime that was tolerating his visit).

Stand in the center, near the giant flagpole, with the Royal Way at your back, for this quick, spin tour orientation: Ahead are the Tomb of the Unknown Soldier and Saxon Garden; 90 degrees to the right is the old National Theater, eclipsed by a modern business center/parking garage; another 90 degrees to the right is a statue of Piłsudski (which you passed to get here); and 90 more degrees to the right is the Sofitel—formerly the Victoria Hotel, the ultimate plush, top-of-the top hotel where all communist-era VIPs stayed.

In front of the hotel, the monument that resembles a giant black staircase commemorates a recent tragedy: The 2010 crash of a plane carrying 96 top government officials, including President Lech Kaczyński. There were no survivors. (A week later, the funeral for Kaczyński on this square drew more than 100,000 mourners.)

To the right of the hotel, on the horizon, you can see Warsaw's newly emerging skyline. The imposing Palace of Culture and Science, which once stood alone over the city, is now joined by a cluster of brand-new skyscrapers, giving Warsaw a Berlin-esque vibe befitting its important role as a business center of Eastern Europe.

Walk to the fragment of colonnade by the park that marks the **Tomb of the Unknown Soldier** (Grób Nieznanego Żołnierza). The colonnade was once part of a much larger palace built by the Saxon prince electors (Dresden's Augustus the Strong and his son), who became kings of Poland in the 18th century. After the palace was destroyed in World War II, this fragment was kept to memorialize Polish soldiers. The names of key battles over 1,000 years are etched into the columns, the urns contain dirt from major Polish battlefields, and the two soldiers are pretty stiff. Every hour on the hour, they do a crisp Changing of the Guard—which, poignantly, honors those who have perished in this country, so shaped by wars against foreign invaders.

Just behind the tomb is the stately **Saxon Garden** (Ogród Saski), inhabited by genteel statues, gorgeous flowers, and a spurting fountain. This park was also built by the Saxon kings of Poland.

Like most foreign kings, Augustus the Strong and his son cared little for their Polish territory, building gardens like these for themselves instead of investing in more pressing needs. Poles say that foreign kings such as Augustus did nothing but "eat, drink, and loosen their belts" (it rhymes in Polish). According to Poles, these selfish absentee kings were the culprits in Poland's eventual decline. But they do appreciate having such a fine venue for a Sunday stroll.

Walk back out toward the Royal Way, stopping at the statue you passed earlier. In 1995, the square was again renamed—this

time for **Józef Piłsudski** (1867-1935), the guy with the big walrus moustache. With the help of a French captain named Charles de Gaulle (whom we met earlier), Piłsudski forced the Russian Bolsheviks out of Poland in 1920 in the so-called Miracle on the Vistula. Piłsudski is credited with creating a once-again-independent Poland after more than a century of foreign oppression, and he essentially ran Poland as a virtual dictator after World War I. Of course, under the communists, Piłsudski was swept under the rug. But since 1989, he has enjoyed a renaissance as many Poles' favorite prototype anticommunist hero. His name adorns streets, squares, and bushy-mustachioed monuments all over the country.

• *Return to Hotel Bristol, turn left, and continue your Royal Way walk.*

Radziwiłł Palace

Next door to the hotel, you'll see the huge Radziwiłł Palace. The Warsaw Pact was signed here in 1955, officially uniting the Soviet satellite states in a military alliance against NATO. This building has also, from time to time, served as the Polish "White House." Along the

street in front of the palace is another monument to that horrifying 2010 plane crash, which effectively decapitated Poland's leadership.

• *Beyond Radziwiłł Palace, on the right, you'll reach a park with a...*

Statue of Adam Mickiewicz

Poland's national poet, Adam Mickiewicz spearheaded Poland's cultural survival during more than a century when the country disappeared from maps—absorbed by Austria, Prussia, and Russia. This was an age when underdog nations (and peoples without nations) all over Europe had their own national revival movements. The statue was erected in 1898 with permission from the Russian czar, as long as the people paid for it themselves. It's still an important part of community life: Polish high school students have a big formal ball (like a prom) 100 days before graduation. After the ball, if students come here and hop around the statue on one leg, it's supposed to bring them good luck on their finals. Mickiewicz, for his part, looks like he's suffering from a heart attack—perhaps in response to the impressively ugly National Theater and Opera a block in front of him.

• *Continue to the end of the Royal Way, marked by the big pink palace. Just before the castle, on your right, is...*

St. Anne's Church

This Rococo church has playful capitals inside and out and a fine pulpit shaped like the prow of a ship—complete with a big anchor.

The richly ornamented apse, behind the altar, survived World War II. This church offers organ concerts nearly daily in summer (see "Entertainment in Warsaw," later).

For a scenic finale to your Royal Way stroll, climb the 150 steps of the **view tower** by the church (6 zł, generally open daily 10:00-18:00, later in summer, closed in bad winter weather). You'll be rewarded with excellent views—particularly of Castle Square and the Old Town. From up top, visually retrace your steps along the Royal Way, and notice the emerging skyline surrounding the Palace of Culture and Science. The tower also affords a good look at the Praga district across the river, where the Red Army waited for the Nazis to level Warsaw during the uprising. Help was so close at hand...but stayed right where it was.

• *Just across from the view tower entrance, look for another Chopin bench (in front of #79). From St. Anne's Church, it's just another block to Castle Square, the TI, and the start of my "Old Town Walk."*

OLD TOWN WALK

In 1945, not a building remained standing in Warsaw's "Old" Town (Stare Miasto). Everything you see here is rebuilt, mostly finished by 1956. Some think the Old Town seems artificial, in a Disney World kind of way. For others, the painstaking postwar

WARSAW

reconstruction feels just right, with Old World squares and lanes charming enough to give Kraków a run for its money. Before 1989, stifled by communist repression and choking on smog, the Old Town was an empty husk of its historic self. But now, the outdoor restaurants and market stalls have returned, and tourists (and a few Varsovians) are out strolling.

This concise walk, which can be done in about 30 minutes (and is a natural continuation of the Royal Way Walk outlined earlier), offers a quick overview of Warsaw's rebuilt historic core—starting at Castle Square and ending at the Barbican and New Town, with an optional return through the back streets.

• *Begin by standing on the gateway square to the Old Town, at the base of the tall pillar.*

Castle Square (Plac Zamkowy)

This square (rated ▲) is packed with Polish history. Get comfy for a quick overview:

Historically, the Polish kings called Kraków home. But things began to change in 1572, with the expiration of the second great Polish dynasty—the Jagiellonians. Rather than elevate another Polish aristocratic family to the throne, the Polish nobility decided to keep power in their own hands. From that point on, Poland was ruled by the Sejm, or Republic of Nobles—consisting of the kingdom's wealthiest 10 percent. The Sejm elected various foreign kings for limited stints on their throne. While this system kept Poland under its own control (to a degree), it wound up being unworkable: Poor choices of sovereigns, coupled with infighting among the nobles, paralyzed Poland and ultimately led to it being wiped from the map of Europe for a century and a half.

The guy on the 72-foot-tall **pillar** is Sigismund III, the first Polish king from the Swedish Vasa dynasty (or Waza in Polish). In 1596, it was Sigismund who relocated his royal seat from Kraków to Warsaw: Warsaw was the meeting point of the Sejm, and it was closer to the center of 16th-century Poland (which had expanded to the east).

Turn your attention to the big, pink **Royal Castle.** A castle has stood here since Warsaw was founded around 1300, but it grew much more important after Warsaw became the capital: It was both the meeting place of the Sejm and the residence of the king...sort of like Buckingham Palace and the Houses of Parliament rolled into one. The palace reached its peak under Stanisław

August Poniatowski—the final Polish king—who imported artists and architects to spiff up the interior.

During World War II, Luftwaffe bombs all but obliterated the palace—only one wall remained standing. Reconstruction stalled because Stalin considered it a palace for the high-class elites. It was finally rebuilt in the more moderate 1970s, funded by local donations. The castle's opulent interior—one of the finest in Eastern Europe—is well worth touring, and described on page 393. (I'll wait while you tour the castle...then let's meet out here to resume the walk.)

Along the right side of the castle, notice the **two previous pillars** lying on a lawn. The first one, from 1644, was falling apart and had to be replaced in 1887 by a new one made of granite. In 1944, a Nazi tank broke this second pillar—a symbolic piece of Polish heritage—into the four pieces (still pockmarked with bullet holes) that you see here today. As Poland rebuilt, its citizens put Sigismund III back on his pillar. Past the pillars are views of Warsaw's red-and-white National Stadium across the river—built for the Euro Cup soccer tournament in 2012.

Across the square from the castle, you'll see the partially reconstructed **defensive wall.** This rampart once enclosed the entire Old Town. Like all of Poland, Warsaw has seen invasion from all sides.

Explore the café-lined lanes that branch off Castle Square. Street signs indicate the year that each lane was originally built.

The first street is **ulica Piwna** ("Beer Street"). If you take a little detour up this street, you'll find **St. Martin's Church** (Kościół Św. Martina, on the left). Run by Franciscan nuns, this church has a simple, modern interior. Walk up the aisle and find the second pillar on the right. Notice the partly destroyed crucifix—it's the only church artifact that survived World War II. Across the street and closer to Castle Square, admire the carefully carved doorway of the house called *pod Gołębiami* ("Under Doves")—dedicated to the memory of an old woman who fed birds amidst the Old Town rubble after World War II.

Back on Castle Square, find the white **plaque** on the wall (at plac Zamkowy 15). It explains that 50 Poles were executed by Nazis on this spot on September 2, 1944. You'll see plaques like this all over the Old Town, each one commemorating victims or opponents of the Nazis. The brick planter under the plaque is often filled with fresh flowers to honor the victims.

• *Leave the square at the far end, on* **St. John's Street** *(Świętojańska). On the plaque under the street name sign, you can guess what the dates mean, even if you don't know Polish: This building was constructed from 1433 to 1478, destroyed in 1944, and rebuilt from 1950 to 1953.*

Partway down the street on the right, you'll come to the big brick...

Cathedral of St. John the Baptist (Katedra Św. Jana Chrzciciela)

This cathedral-basilica is the oldest (1370) and most important church in Warsaw. Superficially unimpressive, the church's own archbishop admitted that it was "modest and poor"—but "the historical events that took place here make it magnificent" (much like Warsaw itself). Poland's constitution was consecrated here on May 3, 1791. Much later, this church became the final battle-ground of the 1944 Warsaw Uprising—when a Nazi "tracked mine" (a huge bomb on tank tracks—this one appropriately named *Goliath*) drove into the church and exploded, massacring the rebels. You can still see part of that tank's tread hanging on the outside wall of the church (through the passage on the right side, between the buttresses near the end of the church).

Cost and Hours: Cathedral—free, crypt—5 zł, both open to tourists Mon-Sat 10:00-17:00, Sun from 15:00, closed during services and summertime organ concerts (see "Entertainment in Warsaw," later).

Visiting the Cathedral: Head inside. Typical of brick church-es, it has a "hall church" design, with three naves of equal height. In the back-left corner, find the chapel with the tomb of Cardinal Stefan Wyszyński—the great Polish leader who, as Warsaw's arch-bishop, morally steered the country through much of the Cold War. (Notice the request to pray for his beatification, as Poles would love to see him become a saint.) Nearby, the crypt holds graves of sev-eral important Poles, including Stanisław August Poniatowski (the last Polish king) and Nobel Prize-winning author Henryk Sienkie-wicz. Then head up the nave to the main altar, which holds a copy of the Black Madonna—proclaimed "everlasting queen of Poland" after a victory over the Swedes in the 17th century. The original Black Madonna is in Częstochowa (125 miles south of Warsaw)— a mecca for Slavic Catholics, who visit in droves in hopes of a miracle. In the chapel left of the high altar, look for the crucifix ornamented with real human hair.

• *Continue up the street and enter Warsaw's grand...*

Old Town Market Square (Rynek Starego Miasta)

For two centuries, this was a gritty market square. Sixty-five years ago, it was a pile of bombed-out rubble. And today, like a phoenix from the ashes, it's risen to remind residents and tourists alike of the prewar glory of the Polish capital (which is why it's rated ▲▲).

Head to the **mermaid fountain** in the middle of the square. The mermaid is an important symbol in Warsaw—you'll see her everywhere. Legend has it that a mermaid *(syrenka)* lived in the Vistula River and protected the townspeople. While this siren supposedly serenaded the town, she's most appreciated for her strength (hence the sword). This square seems to declare that life goes on in Warsaw, as it always has. Children frolic here, oblivious to the turmoil their forebears withstood.

When the fountain gurgles, the kids giggle. People enjoy cranking the old well until it spurts.

Each of the square's four sides is named for a prominent 18th-century Varsovian: Kołłątaj, Dekert, Barss, and Zakrzewski. These men served as "Presidents" of Warsaw (mayors, more or less), and Kołłątaj was also a framer of Poland's 1791 constitution. Take some time to explore the square. Enjoy the colorful architecture. Notice that many of the buildings were intentionally built to lean out into the square—to approximate the higgledy-piggledy wear and tear of the original buildings.

If you'd like to learn more about Warsaw's history, visit the Museum of Warsaw on the Dekert (north) side of the square (described later, under "Sights in Warsaw").

• *Exit the square on Nowomiejska (at the mermaid's 2 o'clock, next to the Museum of Warsaw, under the second-story niche sculpture of St. Anne). After a block, you'll reach the* **barbican** *(barbakan). This defensive gate of the Old Town, similar to Kraków's, protected the medieval city from invaders. Once you've crossed through the barbican, you're officially in Warsaw's...*

New Town (Nowe Miasto)

This 15th-century neighborhood is "new" in name only: It was the first part of Warsaw to spring up outside the city walls (and is therefore slightly newer than the Old Town). The New Town is a fun place to wander: only a little less charming than the Old Town, but with a more real-life feel—people live and work here. You can walk two blocks to reach its centerpiece—the **New Town Square** (Rynek Nowego

Miasta)—watched over by the distinctive green dome of St. Kazimierz Church.

Scientists might want to pay homage at the museum (and
birthplace) of Warsaw native **Marie Skłodowska-Curie,** a.k.a.
Madame Curie (1867-1934); it's along the street between the New
Town Square and the barbican. This Nobel Prize winner was the
world's first radiologist—discovering both radium and polonium
(named for her native land) with her husband, Pierre Curie. Since
she lived at a time when Warsaw was controlled by oppressive Russia, she conducted her studies in France. The museum—with photos, furniture, artifacts, and a paucity of English information—is
a bit of a snoozer, best left to true fans (11 zł, Tue-Sun 9:00-16:30,
closed Mon, ulica Freta 16, tel. 22-831-8092, www.muzeum-msc.
pl).

• *Our walk is finished. You can head back the way you came to reach the
Old Town Square to snap some photos or nurse an overpriced drink. Or,
to see a side of the Old Town that many tourists miss, consider this scenic
detour back to Castle Square.*

From the Barbican to Castle Square

Go back through the barbican and over the little bridge, turn right,
and walk along the houses that line the inside of the wall. You'll
pass a leafy garden courtyard on the left—a reminder that people
actually live in the tourist zone within the Old Town walls. Just beyond the garden on the right, look for the carpet-beating rack, used
to clean rugs (these are common fixtures in people's backyards).
Go left into the square called Szeroki Dunaj ("Wide Danube") and
look for another mermaid (over the Thai restaurant). Continue through the square and turn right at Wąski Dunaj ("Narrow
Danube"). After about 100 yards, you'll pass the city wall. Just to
the right (outside the wall), you'll see the monument to the **Little
Upriser** of 1944, a child wearing a grown-up's helmet and too-big
boots, and carrying a machine gun. Children—especially Scouts
(Harcerze)—played a key role in the resistance against the Nazis.
Their job was mainly carrying messages and propaganda.

Now continue around the wall (the upper, inner part is more
pleasant). Admire more public art as you head back to Castle
Square.

Sights in Warsaw

THE OLD TOWN

These sights are linked by my "Old Town Walk," earlier.

WARSAW

▲▲Royal Castle (Zamek Królewski)

Warsaw's Royal Castle, dominating Castle Square at the entrance to the Old Town, has the most opulent interior in Poland. Many of its furnishings are original (hidden away when it became clear the

city would be demolished in World War II). A visit to the castle is like perusing a great Polish history textbook. In fact, you'll likely see grade-school classes sitting cross-legged on the floors. Watching the teachers quizzing eager young history buffs, try to imagine what it's

like to be a young Pole growing up in a country with such a tumultuous history. Wednesday is a good day to visit—it's free, and although some royal rooms are closed, enough are open to make a visit worthwhile.

Cost and Hours: 30 zł, free on Wed (when some royal rooms are closed); open May-Sept Mon-Sat 10:00-18:00, Fri until 20:00, Sun 11:00-18:00; Oct-April Tue-Sat 10:00-16:00, Sun 11:00-16:00, closed Mon; last entry one hour before closing; plac Zamkowy 4, tel. 22-355-5170, www.zamek-krolewski.pl.

Tours: The castle has a well-produced audioguide (17 zł, worth the extra cost) and good English information posted throughout. For the basics, use my commentary to follow the one-way route through the castle.

Services: A public WC is on the courtyard just around the corner of the castle, with more inside and downstairs.

Visiting the Castle: Because the castle visitor route often changes, it's possible you won't see the rooms in this exact order; match the labels in each room to the corresponding text below.

Entering the courtyard, go to the right to buy tickets, then cross to the opposite side to enter. In the lobby, turn left, pass the audioguide-rental room, then follow *Castle Route* signs upstairs.

The first big room is the **Council Chamber,** where a "Permanent Council" consisting of the king, 18 senators, and 18 representatives met to chart Poland's course. Next is the **Great Assembly Hall,** heavy with marble and chandeliers. The statues of Apollo and Minerva flanking the main door are modeled after King

Stanisław August Poniatowski and Catherine the Great of Russia, respectively. (The king enjoyed a youthful romantic dalliance with Catherine on a trip to Russia, and never quite seemed to get over her...much to his wife's consternation, I'm sure.)

From here, you'll pass through the Great Antechamber and do a little loop through some opulent apartments with silk wallpaper and fine paintings. The highlight is three giant canvases by historical painter **Jan Matejko,** each showing a different chapter in Polish history (for more on Matejko, see page 399). First is *Stefan Batory at Pskov,* in which the Polish king negotiates with Ivan the Terrible's envoys to break their siege of a Russian town. Notice the hussars—fearsome Polish soldiers wearing winged armor.

Then, in one big room at the end of this wing, two more Matejko canvases show a high point and a low point in Poland's story: On the left wall, the *Constitution of 3 May 1791* shows the giddy procession (with this castle in the background) heading up the street to the Cathedral of St. John the Baptist to consecrate the first constitution in Europe. But from there, Poland's fortunes tumbled dramatically. On the wall near where you entered, *Rejtan—The Fall of Poland* shows the nobleman Tadeusz Rejtan (on the right) lying in front of a door and pulling his shirt open in violent protest against his colleagues in the Sejm debating the First Partition in 1773, which ceded some Polish territory to neighboring Russia, Prussia, and Austria. Two Partitions later, Poland was erased from the map of Europe for a century and a half.

You'll loop back, passing through a long corridor with royal portraits and busts, then cut through the Great Antechamber again. You'll wind up in the **Marble Room,** with more portraits of Polish greats ringing the top of the room. Above the fireplace is a portrait of Stanisław August Poniatowski (the last Polish king).

From here, step into the **Knights' Hall,** with yet more busts and portraits of VIPs—Very Important Poles. The statue of Chronos—God of time, with the globe on his shoulders—is actually a functioning clock, though now it's stopped at 11:15 to commemorate the exact time in 1944 when the Nazis bombed this palace to bits.

Next, step into the **Throne Room.** Notice the crowned white eagles, the symbol of Poland, decorating the banner behind the throne. The Soviets didn't allow anything royal or aristocratic, so postwar restorations came with crownless eagles. Only after 1989 were these eagles crowned again. Peek into the **Conference**

Room, with portraits of Russia's Catherine the Great, England's George III, and France's Louis XVI—in whose esteemed royal league Stanisław August Poniatowski liked to consider himself.

After four more grand rooms (including the King's Bedroom, with a gorgeous silk canopy over the bed), you'll enter the **Canaletto Room,** filled with canvases of late-18th-century Warsaw painted in exquisite detail by this talented artist. (This Canaletto, also known for his panoramas of Dresden, was the nephew of another more famous artist with the same nickname, known for painting Venice's canals.) Paintings like these helped post-WWII restorers resurrect the city from its rubble. To the left, on the lower wall, the biggest canvas features the view of Warsaw from the Praga district across the river; pick out the few landmarks that are still standing (or, more precisely, have been resurrected). The castle you're in dominates the center of the painting, overlooking the river. Notice the artist's self-portrait in the lower left. Opposite, on the right side of the room, is Canaletto's depiction of the election of Stanisław August Poniatowski as king, in a field outside Warsaw (notice the empty throne in the middle of the group). Among the assembled crowd, each flag represents a different Polish province.

From here, head left of the big "view of Warsaw" painting into the **side chapel,** reserved for the king. In the box to the left of the altar is the heart of Tadeusz Kościuszko, a hero of both the American Revolution and the Polish struggle against the Partitions (for more about the Partitions, see page 214).

As you cross over to the other part of the castle, you'll pass through the **Four Seasons Gallery** (with some fine but faded Gobelin tapestries) before entering a few rooms occupied by the houses of parliament—a reminder that this "castle" wasn't just the king's house, but also the meeting place of the legislature. In the **New Deputies' Chambers,** notice the maps showing Poland's constantly in-flux borders—a handy visual aid for the many school groups that visit here.

After several rooms, you'll reach the grand **Senators' Chamber,** with the king's throne, surrounded by different coats of arms. Each one represents a region that was part of Poland during its Golden Age, back when it was united with Lithuania and its territory stretched from the Baltic to the Black Sea (see the map on the wall). In this room, Poland adopted its 1791 constitution (notice the replica in the display case to the left of the throne).

It was the first in Europe, written soon after America's and just months before France's. And, like the Constitution of the United States, it was very progressive, based on the ideals of the Enlightenment. But when the final Partitions followed in 1793 and 1795, Poland was divided between neighboring powers and ceased to exist as a country until 1918—so the constitution was never fully put into action.

On your way back downstairs, you'll likely be routed through the ground-floor **Gallery of Paintings, Sculpture, and Decorative Arts,** which includes a fine cabinet of silver and crystal, and the 36 paintings of the Lanckroński Collection. It's fine to zip through here quickly, but be sure to slow down in the final room to appreciate two canvases by Rembrandt (both from 1641). *Girl in a Picture Frame* is exactly that—except that she's "breaking the frame" by resting her hands on a faux frame that Rembrandt has painted inside the real one...shattering the fourth wall in a way that was unusual for the time. The other, *A Scholar at His Writing Table,* shows the hirsute academic glancing up from his notes. Circle around behind the canvases to see X-rays of the paintings, which have helped experts better understand the master's techniques.

Other Castle Sights: Consider a detour to the **Kubicki Arcades** (Arkady Kubiciego), the impressively excavated arcades deep beneath the castle. From the entrance lobby, head downstairs to the area with the cloakroom, bathrooms, and bookshop, then find the long escalator that takes you down to the arcades. It's free to wander the long, cavernous, and newly  clean and gleaming space, made elegant by grand drapes.

The **"Tin-Roofed Palace"** (Pałac pod Blachą) features an extensive oriental carpet collection and seven unimpressive apartments of Prince Józef Poniatowski, the king's brother; it's not worth the 15 zł extra.

▲Museum of Warsaw (Muzeum Warszawy)

Four adjoining townhouses on the north side of the Old Town Square have been connected and turned into this in-depth museum that tells the story of Warsaw. While there's too much detail for a casual visitor's attention span, it's well presented and offers some interesting insight into this great city.

Cost and Hours: 20 zł, includes audioguide, free on Tue, open Tue-Sun 10:00-19:00, closed Mon, Rynek Starego Miasta 28–42, tel. 22-277-4300, www.muzeumwarszawy.pl.

Visiting the Museum: The permanent collection, called "Warsaw in 23 Rooms," offers exactly that. Pick up the detailed map and the dense-but-informative audioguide, and head down into the cellars for an orientation to the city's history—with a timeline, lots of graphs, maps, and helpful models of key landmarks. Then head upstairs and weave your way through the labyrinthine collection; your geo-tagged audioguide knows (roughly) where you are and offers commentary.

Back up on the ground floor, in the courtyard, you'll find architectural decorations from city buildings, as well as the original mermaid statue from the square. Then work your way up through four floors: Floor 1 has a photography gallery, paintings of Warsaw, and a model of the Old Town in the late 18th century. Floor 2 features bronzes, silverwork, portraits of important Varsovians, and clothing. Floor 3 has a moving collection of "relics" from the difficult WWII days and a more lighthearted exhibit on "Warsaw packaging"—with nostalgic vintage advertising. Floor 4 features antique clocks and the "Schiele Room"—named not for the artist, but for the local merchant family whose furnishings and personal objects you can see here. You can continue all the way up into the attic ("viewing platform") to look down over the square, and to see panoramas of the Old Town's rooftops.

The museum sporadically presents a poignant 20-minute film (in English) tracing the tragic WWII experience of this city—from a thriving interwar metropolis, to a bombed-out wasteland, to the focus of a massive rebuilding effort. Ask at the entrance if an English showing of this film is scheduled during your visit.

NEAR PALM TREE CIRCLE

These sights are in the city center, near Palm Tree Circle—where Jerusalem Avenue crosses Nowy Świat.

East of the Royal Way (Toward the River)
▲▲National Museum (Muzeum Narodowe)

A celebration of underrated Polish artists, this museum offers a surprisingly engaging and—if you follow my tour—concise overview of this country's impressive painters (many of whom are unknown outside their home country). A modern, state-of-the-art exhibition space allows these unsung canvases to really belt it out. Polish and other European artists are displayed side by side, as if to assert Poland's worthiness on the world artistic stage. After seeing a few of the masterpieces here, you won't disagree.

Cost and Hours: 20 zł, more for temporary exhibits, permanent collection free on Tue; Tue-Sun 10:00-18:00, Fri until 21:00, closed Mon, last entry 45 minutes before closing; audioguide-10 zł;

one block east of Nowy Świat at aleja Jerozolimskie 3, tel. 22-629-3093, www.mnw.art.pl.

⊘ Self-Guided Tour: The collection fills several separate galleries. The museum's strongest point—and the bulk of this tour—is its 19th-century Polish art. But before diving in, consider some of the other collections.

Overview: To get your bearings, pick up a floor plan as you enter. On the ground floor are Ancient Art (from Greek pieces to artifacts left by early Polish tribes); Gallery Faras (highlighting the museum's fine collection of archaeological findings from that ancient Egyptian city); and a good collection of Medieval Art, which gathers altarpieces from churches around Poland—organized both chronologically and geographically—and displays some of the most graphic crucifixes and pietàs I've seen.

Upstairs is the excellent Gallery of 19th-Century Art (described next), which flows into the Old Polish and European Portrait Gallery. Nearby, through the gift shop, is the worthwhile 20th- and 21st-Century Art collection, with an impressive array of Modern and Postmodern Polish artists, including photographers and filmmakers. The underwhelming Old European Painting collection (pre-19th-century) is split up among all three floors.

To cut to the chase, focus on the **Gallery of 19th-Century Art.** We'll start with the granddaddy of Polish art, Jan Matejko.

• *From the entrance lobby, head up the left staircase, then turn left across the mezzanine and enter the collection. Matejko is hiding at the far end of this wing: Entering the collection, angle right, then straight, heading all the way to the room at the far end, which is dominated by a gigantic battlefield canvas. (If you get lost, ask the attendants, "mah-TAY-koh?")*

Jan Matejko: While not the most talented of artists—he's a fairly conventional painter, lacking a distinctive, recognizable style—Matejko more than made up for it with vision and productivity. His typically super-sized paintings are steeped in proud Polish history. Matejko's biggest work here—in fact, the biggest canvas in the whole building—is the enormous ***Battle of Grunwald.*** This epic painting commemorates one of Poland's high-water marks: the dramatic victory of a Polish-Lithuanian army over the Teutonic Knights, who had been terrorizing northern Poland for decades (for more on the Teutonic Knights, see page 507). On July 15, 1410, some 40,000 Poles and Lithuanians (led by the sword-waving Lithuanian in red, Grand Duke Vytautas) faced off against 27,000 Teutonic Knights (under their Grand Master, in white) in one of the medieval world's bloodiest battles. Matejko plops us right in the thick of the battle's climax, painting life-size figures and framing off a 32-foot-long slice of the two-mile battle line.

In the center of the painting, the Teutonic Grand Master is about to become a shish kebab. Duke Vytautas leads the final

Jan Matejko (1838-1893)

Jan Matejko (yawn mah-TAY-koh) is Poland's most important painter, period. In the mid- to late-19th century, the nation of Poland had been dissolved by foreign powers, and Polish artists struggled to make sense of their people's place in the world. Rabble-rousing Romanticism seemed to have failed (inspiring many brutally suppressed uprisings), so Polish artists and writers turned their attention to educating the people about their history, with the goal of keeping their traditions alive.

Matejko was at the forefront of this so-called positivist movement. He saw what the tides of history had done to Poland and was determined to make sure his countrymen learned from it. He painted two types of works: huge, grand-scale epics depicting monumental events in Polish history; and small, intimate portraits of prominent Poles. Polish schoolchildren study history from books with paintings of virtually every single Polish king—all painted by the incredibly prolific Matejko.

Matejko is admired not for his technical mastery (he's an unexceptional painter) or for the literal truth of his works—he was notorious for fudging historical details to give his canvases a bit more propagandistic punch. But he is revered for the emotion behind—and inspired by—his works. His paintings are utilitarian, straightforward, and dramatic enough to stir the patriot in any Pole. The intense focus on history by Matejko and other positivists is one big reason why today's Poles are still so in touch with their heritage.

You'll see Matejko's works in Warsaw's National Museum and Royal Castle, as well as in Kraków's Gallery of 19th-Century Polish Art (above the Cloth Hall). You can also visit his former residence in Kraków.

charge. And waaaay up on a hill (in the upper-right corner, on horseback, wearing a silver knight's suit) is Władysław Jagiełło, the first king of the Jagiellonian dynasty...ensuring his bloodline will survive another 150 years.

Matejko spent three years covering this 450-square-foot canvas in paint. The canvas was specially made in a single seamless piece. This was such a popular work that almost as many fans turned out for its unveiling as there are figures in the painting. On the TV nearby, you can see how the vast painting was recently restored.

From Poland's high point in the *Battle of Grunwald*, look on the right wall for another, much smaller Matejko canvas, *Stańczyk*, to see how Poland's fortunes shifted drastically a century later. This more intimate portrait depicts a popular Polish figure: the court jester Stańczyk, who's smarter than the king, but not allowed to say so. This complex character, representing the national conscience, is a favorite symbol of Matejko's. Stańczyk slumps in gloom. He's just read the news (on the table beside him) that the city of Smolensk has fallen to the Russians after a three-year siege (1512-1514). The jester had tried to warn the king to send more troops, but the king was too busy partying (behind the curtain). The painter Matejko—who may have used his own features for Stańczyk's face—also blamed the nobles of his own day for fiddling while Poland was partitioned.

More Matejkos fill this room. Just to the right of *Stańczyk* is a self-portrait of the gray-bearded artist (compare their features), then a painting of the hoisting of the Sigismund Bell to the cathedral tower in Kraków (it's still there). Farther right, you'll see Matejko's portraits of his children and his wife.

On the final wall is a smaller but very dramatic scene, *The Sermon of Piotr Skarga.* In the upper-right corner, this charismatic, early-17th-century Jesuit priest waves his arms to punctuate his message: Poland's political system is broken. Skarga is addressing fat-cat nobles and the portly King Sigismund II Vasa (seated and wearing a ruffled collar), who were acting in their own self-interests instead of prioritizing what was best for Poland. Notice that Skarga's audience isn't hearing his ravings—they seem bored, bugged, or both. The king is even taking a nap. They should have listened: Poland's eventual decline is often considered the fault of its unworkable political system. After the Partitions, the ahead-of-his-time Skarga was rehabilitated as a visionary who should have been heeded. Notice that, like Stańczyk, Skarga is a self-portrait of Matejko.

• *Leaving Matejko, we'll pass through several more rooms of lesser-known Polish painters to the opposite wing, where we'll meet several of Matejko's students—each of whom developed his own style and left his mark on the Polish art world. On the way, I'll point out a few canvases worth a pause.*

Other Polish Painters: First, head back down the long corridor the way you came (passing some Matejko copycats), cutting through a corner of the Portrait Gallery. When you reach the door you came in, bear right to stay inside the gallery. At the end of that first, large room, you'll find some battle scenes by **Józef Brandt**—the only painter who rivaled Matejko in capturing epic warfare on canvas. Many of Brandt's scenes focus on confronting an enemy from the east, which was Poland's lot for much of its history. His biggest work here, *Rescue of Tatar Captives,* is typical of his scenes.

Continue straight into the next room, with some fine landscape scenes. This room (the partition in the middle) also has works by the talented **Józef Chełmoński**: *Indian Summer* and (around back) *Storks*—a young boy and his grandfather look to the sky, as a formation of storks flies overhead.

Turn right and go through one more long room, watching for **Aleksander Gierymski**'s small, evocative, personality-filled *Jewish Woman Selling Oranges* (on the left wall).

• *You'll emerge into a big room that kicks off the collection of...*

Młoda Polska: Matejko's pupils took what he taught them and incorporated the Art Nouveau styles that were emerging around Europe to create a new movement called "Young Poland" (see page 253). This room features works by two of the movement's big names.

On the left wall are paintings by **Jacek Malczewski,** some of them depicting the goateed, close-cropped artist in a semisurrealistic, Polish countryside context. Malczewski painted more or less realistically, but enjoyed incorporating one or two subtle, symbolic elements evocative of Polish folkloric tradition—magical realism on canvas. *The Death of Ellenai* (1907) shows the pivotal scene in Juliusz Słowacki's epic 1838 poem, *Anhelli,* in which a young nobleman exiled from Poland during the Partitions is forced to make his way through the wastelands of Siberia. When his young and idealistic travel companion, Ellenai, perishes, Anhelli kisses her feet and abandons all hope.

Most of the works on the opposite wall are by **Józef Mehoffer,** who paints with brighter colors in a more stylized form, with more abstraction. Mehoffer's hypnotic *Strange Garden* is a bucolic vision of blue-clad Mary Poppinses, nude cherubs, lots of flowers... and a gigantic, hovering, golden dragonfly that places the otherwise plausible scene in the realm of pure fantasy. In the middle of the room, the small version of Auguste Rodin's *The Kiss* reminds us how this emotion-conveying style, called Symbolism, was also finding expression elsewhere in Europe.

The next room, at the end of the hall, features some lesser-known painters from the age. Among these, **Olga Boznańska**'s works are worth lingering over: gauzy, almost Impressionistic portraits that skillfully capture the humanity of each subject.

Head back into the Malczewski/Mehoffer room and find the small, darkened adjoining rooms. The first one features additional Malczewski paintings; the second is a treasure trove of works by the founder and biggest talent of Młoda Polska, **Stanisław Wyspiański.** The specific items in this room are subject to change—as Kraków, which owns the best collection of hometown boy Wyspiański, shuffle his works in and out of special exhibitions—but you'll likely see both paintings and pastel works by this Art Nouveau juggernaut. Wyspiański also designed stage sets and redecorated some important churches; some of the large pastel-on-paper works you may see here were used as studies for those projects. And you'll likely see some self-portraits and portraits of his wife and children.

Pondering the works here—and throughout the museum—think about how such a talented artist from a small country can be left out of textbooks across the ocean.

Chopin Museum (Muzeum Fryderyka Chopina)

The reconstructed Ostrogski Castle houses this slick museum honoring Poland's most famous composer, with manuscripts, letters, and original handwritten compositions by the composer. Unfortunately, the museum's high-tech gadgetry does more to distract from this rich collection of historic artifacts than to bring it to life. While Chopin devotees may find it riveting, those with only a passing familiarity with the composer may leave feeling like they still don't know much about this Polish cultural giant.

Cost and Hours: 22 zł, free (and crowded) on Sun, open Tue-Sun 11:00-20:00, closed Mon, last entry 45 minutes before closing, 3 blocks east of Nowy Świat at ulica Okólnik 1, tel. 22-441-6251, www.chopin. museum.

Visiting the Museum: You'll be given an electronic card; tap it against glowing red dots to access additional information. You'll proceed more or less chronologically through the composer's life, with various opportunities to hear his compositions. Beginning in the cellars, you'll learn about Chopin's early life in Żelazowa Wola and Warsaw, and find listening stations where you can nurture your appreciation of Chopin by listening to his music.

Then you'll head upstairs into the mansion, with a replica of Chopin's drawing room in Paris, and his last piano, which he used for composing during the final two years of his life (1848-1849). Exhibits here trace themes of the composer's life, such as the women he knew (including his older sister Ludwika, his mother, and George Sand—the French author who took a male pseudonym in order to be published, and who was romantically linked with Chopin). The second floor recounts Chopin's travels around Europe.

Concerts: Under the palace is a **concert hall,** which hosts performances by students (call museum to reserve a space—only 70 seats available; usually Oct-July Thu at 18:00, and typically free).

Nearby: The park next to the museum surrounds the Chopin

University of Music; hanging out here, you'll often hear students rehearsing inside.

Other Chopin Sight: The composer's tourable **birth house** is in a park in Żelazowa Wola, 34 miles from Warsaw. While interesting to Chopin devotees, it's not worth the trek for most. On summer weekends, the Chopin Museum sometimes runs a handy bus to the house—ask at the museum (departs from Marszałkowska street, 30 minutes each way; 9 zł for the bus, 23 zł for the park and birth house; birth house open Tue-Sun 9:00-19:00, Oct-March until 17:00, closed Mon year-round, tel. 46-863-3300).

▲▲Copernicus Science Center (Centrum Nauki Kopernik)

This facility, a wonderland of completely hands-on scientific doodads that thrill kids and kids-at-heart, is a futuristic romper room. Filling two floors of an industrial-mod, purpose-built space, this is Warsaw's best family activity. Exhibits are described in both Polish and English, and there are frequent demonstrations and special events—ask when you buy your ticket or check their website.

Cost and Hours: 31 zł, 21 zł for kids 19 and under, slightly more on weekends, open Tue-Fri 9:00-18:00, Sat-Sun 10:00-19:00, closed Mon, typically opens one hour earlier April-June and closes one hour later July-Aug, last entry one hour before closing, Wybrzeże Kościuszkowskie 20, tel. 22-596-4100, www.kopernik.org.pl.

Crowd-Beating Tips: This popular attraction can be busy on weekends and school holidays. If you anticipate crowds, book ahead on their website to secure your preferred entry time. On weekdays, it's generally no problem to walk right in.

Getting There: It's an easy downhill walk from Warsaw's Royal Way, but the hike back up is fairly steep. Near the modern bridge—about a five-minute walk from the museum—are a Metro stop and a bus stop (both called Centrum Nauki Kopernik). From here, bus #102 goes to Nowy Świat, then up the Royal Way (Uniwersytet and Zachęta stops) before heading west to the Warsaw Uprising Museum. Metro line 2 connects the science center to the National Stadium, the Royal Way (near the Copernicus statue), and the Warsaw Uprising Museum.

Visiting the Center: The science center is a sprawling, two-floor playhouse of hands-on, interactive exhibits. The specifics are always in flux, so pick up a map as you enter and just enjoy exploring. Kids love trying out the

WARSAW

various tools and machines, playing with the air cannons, looking at themselves in the funhouse mirrors, and running a slinky down an inclined treadmill. On the main floor there's a special area for kids under 5 (called "Buzzz!"). There's also a section for teens called "RE: Generation," which uses touchscreens to investigate the biological underpinnings of emotion—from what makes you laugh to what grosses you out—and examines how cultures around the world are both similar and different.

Attached to the center is the **"Heavens of Copernicus" planetarium.** Inside is an exhibit that's covered by your entry ticket, but you'll pay extra for a show (3-D shows—27 zł for adults, 21 zł for kids 19 and under; cheaper for 2-D shows, in Polish with English headset, show starts at the top of each hour—ask for schedule at ticket desk).

Nearby: The riverside embankment near the center has a few areas that are fun to stroll; it was created when the busy riverfront highway was rerouted into an underground tunnel. From here you have good views of the modern Holy Cross Bridge (Most Świętokrzyski) and the National Stadium, proudly wrapped in the patriotic red and white of the Polish flag. These riverbanks are a popular hangout by day and after dark; in the summer, a stroll along here reveals a world of picnics, family outings, and impromptu parties.

West of the Royal Way (near Centralna Station)
Palace of Culture and Science
(Pałac Kultury i Nauki, or PKiN)

This massive skyscraper, dating from the early 1950s, is the tallest building between Frankfurt and St. Petersburg (760 feet with the spire, though several new buildings are threatening to eclipse that peak). While you can ride the lift to its top for a commanding view, the highlight is simply viewing it up close from ground level.

Viewing the Skyscraper: This building was a "gift" from Stalin that the people of Warsaw couldn't refuse. Varsovians call it "Stalin's Penis"...using cruder terminology than that. (There are seven such "Stalin Gothic" erections in Moscow.) If it feels like an Art Deco Chicago skyscraper, that's because the architect was inspired by the years he spent studying and working in Chicago in the 1930s. Because it was to be "Soviet in substance, Polish in style," Soviet architects toured Poland to absorb

local culture before starting the project. Notice the frilly decorative friezes that top each level—evocative of Poland's many Renaissance buildings (such as Kraków's Cloth Hall). The clock was added in 1999 as part of the millennium celebrations. Since the end of communism, the younger generation doesn't mind the structure so much—and some even admit to liking it for the way it enlivens the predictable glass-and-steel skyline springing up around it.

Everything about the Pałac is big. Approach it from the east side (facing the busy Marszałkowska street and the slick Galeria Centrum shopping mall). Stand in front of the granite tribune where communist VIPs surveyed massive May Day parades and pageantry on the once-imposing square, which today holds a sloppy parking lot. From there, size up the skyscraper—its grand entry flanked by massive statues of Copernicus on the right (science) and the great poet Mickiewicz on the left (culture). It's designed to show off the strong, grand-scale Soviet aesthetic and architectural skill. The Pałac contains various theaters (the culture), museums of evolution and technology (the science), a congress hall, a multiplex (showing current movies), an observation deck, and lots of office space. With all this Culture and Science under one Roof, it's a shame that only the ground-floor lobby (which feels like stepping into 1950s Moscow and is free to enter) and the 30th-floor observatory deck are open to the public.

Observation Deck: You can zip up to the "XXX Floor" in 20 seconds on the retrofitted Soviet elevators—but the trip is overpriced and the view's a letdown (20 zł, daily 10:00-20:00, may be open later in summer, enter through main door on east side of Pałac—opposite from Centralna station, tel. 22-656-7600, www.pkin.pl).

Złote Tarasy Shopping Mall

Tucked behind Centralna station, "Golden Terraces" is a supermodern shopping mall with a funky, undulating glass-and-steel roof. No, you didn't come all the way to Poland to visit a shopping mall. But if you're at the station, crossing the street to peek in here offers a taste of Poland's race into the future.

Hours: Mon-Sat 9:00-22:00, Sun 9:00-21:00, lots of designer shops, food court on top level, www.zlotetarasy.pl.

Złota 44

This skyscraper, with its dramatic swooping lines rising high from the Złote Tarasy shopping mall, was designed by world-renowned architect Daniel Libeskind (who also redeveloped the 9/11 site in New York City). Born in Poland, at a very young age Libeskind emigrated with his family to the US, returning only recently to embark on this project. Its shape evokes an eagle (a symbol for Poland) just beginning to take flight. Of all the shiny new towers popping up in Warsaw's skyline, this is the most architecturally interesting—and offers a striking counterpoint to the Stalinist Palace of Culture and Science nearby. (For more on the building, visit www. zlota44.com/en.)

JEWISH WARSAW

In the early 1600s, an estimated 80 percent of all Jews lived in Poland—then the largest country in Europe. But after centuries of dwelling in relative peace in tolerant and pragmatic Poland, Warsaw's Jews suffered terribly at the hands of the Nazis. Several sights in Warsaw commemorate those who were murdered, and those who fought back. Because the Nazis leveled the ghetto, there is literally nothing left except the street plan, some monuments, and the heroic spirit of its former residents. However, the top-notch Museum of the History of Polish Jews—which opened in 2014—has rejuvenated the area, making it a magnet for those interested in this chapter of Polish history.

Getting There: To reach Ghetto Heroes Square and the museum from the Old Town, you can hop a taxi or Uber (10 zł) or take a bus (to the Nalewki-Muzeum stop; bus #180 is particularly useful; bus #111 reaches this stop from farther south—Piłsudski Square, the university, and the National Museum). You can also walk there in about 15 minutes: Go through the barbican gate two blocks into the New Town, turn left on Świętojerska, and walk straight 10 minutes—passing the green-glass Supreme Court building. En route, at the corner of Świętojerska and Nowiniarska, watch for the pattern of bricks in the sidewalk, marking *Ghetto Wall 1940-1943*.

▲Ghetto Heroes Square (Plac Bohaterow Getta)

The square is in the heart of what was the Jewish ghetto—now surrounded by bland Soviet-style apartment blocks. After the uprising, the entire ghetto was reduced to dust by the Nazis, leaving the communists to rebuild to their own specifications. Today the district is called Muranów ("Rebuilt").

The **monument** in the middle of the square commemorates those who fought and died "for the dignity and freedom of the Jewish Nation, for a free Poland, and for the liberation of humankind." The statue features heroic Jewish men who knew that an inglorious death at the hands of the Nazis awaited them. Flames in the background show Nazis burning the ghetto. The opposite side features a sad procession of Jews trudging to concentration camps, with subtle Nazi bayonets and helmets moving things along.

As you face the monument, look through the trees to the right to see a seated statue. **Jan Karski** (1914-2000) was a Catholic Pole and resistance fighter who traveled extensively through Poland during the Nazi occupation, collected evidence, and then reported on the Warsaw Ghetto and the Holocaust to the leaders of the Western Allies (including a personal meeting with FDR). In 1944, while the Holocaust was still going on, Karski published his eyewitness account, *The Story of a Secret State* (which you can see on this statue's armrest). After the war he became a US citizen, and in 2012 President Barack Obama awarded him a posthumous Presidential Medal of Freedom.

• *The huge, glassy building facing the monument from across the square is the...*

▲▲▲Museum of the History of Polish Jews (Muzeum Historii Żydów Polskich, a.k.a. POLIN)

This world-class attraction thoughtfully traces the epic, millennium-long story of Jews in Poland. This is not a "Holocaust museum;" rather, it provides stirring, comprehensive documentation of the very rich Polish Jewish experience across the centuries. In-depth, engaging, vividly illustrated, and eloquently presented, the exhibits present a powerful context for the many Jewish cultural sites around Poland—offering insights both for people familiar with the story and for beginners. The museum is at once expansive and intimate, with ample descriptions, videos, and touchscreens; you could spend all day here, but two hours is the minimum. It wins my vote for the best museum in Poland, and it's easily Europe's best Jewish museum—and a strong contender for the best European historical museum, period. The building also hosts cultural events and temporary exhibits.

Cost and Hours: Core exhibition—25 zł, more for temporary exhibits, Mon and Thu-Fri 10:00-18:00, Wed and Sat-Sun 10:00-20:00, closed Tue, last entry 2 hours before closing, essential audioguide-10 zł, cafeteria, Anielewicza 6, tel. 22-471-0300, www.polin.pl.

Visiting the Museum: Before entering, view the building's striking **exterior** (designed by Finnish architect Rainer Mahlamä-

Warsaw's Jews and the Ghetto Uprising

From the Middle Ages until World War II, Poland was a relatively safe haven for Europe's Jews. While other kings were imprisoning and deporting Jews in the 14th century, the progressive king Kazimierz the Great welcomed Jews into Poland, even granting them special privileges (see page 251).

By the 1930s, there were more than 380,000 Jews in Warsaw—nearly a third of the population (and the largest concentration of Jews in any European city). The Nazis arrived in 1939. Within a year, they had pushed all of Warsaw's Jews into one neighborhood and surrounded it with a wall, creating a miserably overcrowded ghetto (crammed with an estimated 460,000 people, including many from nearby towns). There were nearly 600 such ghettos in cities and towns all over Poland.

By the summer of 1942, more than a quarter of the Jews in the ghetto had either died of disease, committed suicide, or been murdered. The Nazis started moving Warsaw's Jews (at the rate of 5,000 a day) into what they claimed were "resettlement camps." Most of these people—300,000 in all—were actually murdered at Treblinka or Auschwitz. Finally, the waning population—now about 60,000—began to get word from concentration camp escapees about what was actually going on there. Spurred by this knowledge, Warsaw's surviving Jews staged a dramatic uprising.

On April 19, 1943, the Jews attacked Nazi strongholds. The overwhelming Nazi war machine—which had rolled over much of Europe—imagined they'd be able to put down the rebellion easily. Instead, they struggled for a month to finally crush the Ghetto Uprising. The ghetto's residents and structures were "liquidated." About 300 of Warsaw's Jews survived, thanks in part to a sort of "underground railroad" of courageous Varsovians.

Warsaw's Jewish sights are emotionally moving, but even more so if you know some of their stories. You may have heard of **Władysław Szpilman,** a Jewish concert pianist who survived the war with the help of Jews, Poles, and even a Nazi officer. Szpilman's life story was turned into the highly acclaimed, Oscar-winning film *The Pianist,* which powerfully depicts events in Warsaw during World War II.

Less familiar to non-Poles—but equally affecting—is the story of Henryk Goldszmit, better known by his pen name, **Janusz Korczak.** Korczak wrote imaginative children's books that are still enormously popular among Poles. He worked at an orphanage in the Warsaw ghetto. When his orphans were sent off to concentration camps, the Nazis offered the famous author a chance at freedom. Korczak turned them down, choosing to die at Treblinka with his children.

ki). You'll enter (and go through a security checkpoint) at the large, asymmetrical hole in the side of the building. Once you're inside, the symbolism becomes clear: This represents Moses parting the Red Sea. (While the main exhibit covers the thousand years of Jews in Poland, this sets the stage by going back even further—to the Jewish origin story.)

Buy your tickets for the core exhibition and rent the invaluable 60-stop audioguide, which helps provide a concise structure for your exploration of the sprawling exhibitions. Then head downstairs and follow the one-way route. In this high-tech, interactive space, exhibits in eight galleries mingle with actual artifacts to bring history to life.

You'll begin by passing through a simulated forest—evocative of legends about the Jews' arrival in Poland—to reach the **First Encounters** exhibit. Here you'll learn how Jewish merchants made their way to Poland in the 10th century (with maps of their trade routes and samples of what they sold). The story is told partly from the perspective of Ibrahim ibn Yakub, a Sephardic Jew who penned early travelogues about Europe. Look for the display case that holds a coin from the ninth century, with Hebrew characters, that was minted in Poland. In 1264, Duke Bolesław the Pious—the first of many tolerant Polish rulers—extended rights and protections to his Jewish subjects, allowing them to thrive. In the next room, on the left wall are illustrations of the leading Polish cities of the time, and on the right wall are Polish medieval monarchs, with in-depth explanations of each one's policies toward their Jewish subjects.

Next, the **Paradisus Iudaeorum** explains how, as Jews became more established in Polish society in the 15th and 16th centuries, they enjoyed better and better living conditions. (Meanwhile, anti-Semites bitterly complained that Poland was becoming a "Jewish Paradise"—the name of this exhibit.) The centerpiece here is a gigantic, interactive model of Kraków and its Jewish  quarter, Kazimierz. In the library section, you can flip through virtual pages of books from the era—representing the flourishing of education during this time.

Continuing into the next area, you'll enter a dark hallway that explains the Khmelnytsky Uprising—a mid-17th-century Cossack rebellion against the Polish lords and the Jews who served them. This brought a new wave of pogroms and 10,000 Jewish deaths.

After the uprising, Polish lords invited Jews to privately owned market towns—called *shtetls*—to help re-establish the economy. **The Jewish Town** offers a fascinating look at different walks of life in a typical Jewish community: the market, where Jews and Christians could mingle at the tavern; the home, where a family would live, work, eat, and sleep in a single room; the cemetery (touchscreens invite you to learn about the symbolism of Jewish tombstones); and the synagogue, with a gloriously colorful replica of a ceiling and bema (prayer platform) from a wooden syna-

gogue from the village of Gwoździec—dripping with symbolism that's explained on nearby touchscreens. An exhibit also traces the mid-18th-century rise of Hasidism—a mystical branch of Judaism—in the eastern Polish lands (today's Ukraine).

With the Partitions of the late 18th century (when Polish territory was divided among neighboring powers), Polish Jews found themselves split among three different empires—symbolized by a room with giant portraits of the rulers of Prussia, Russia, and Austria, all facing the Polish throne. **Encounters with Modernity** examines how Jews in different parts of the Polish lands had very different experiences. You'll see a replica salon of a wealthy Jewish family who mingled with elites, and learn about the debate at that time of what the role of Jews in society should be (illustrated by a fine collection of items from Jewish ceremonies commemorating rites of passage). You'll also learn about the competing movements within Judaism that emerged during this era: Hasidism, led by charismatic Tzadiks who promised a closer spiritual connection to God, and the more reform-minded Haskalah, an intellectual approach inspired by the Enlightenment.

A mesmerizing, painterly film follows a day in the life of a young student at a *yeshiva* (school). A railway station represents the Industrial Revolution, when the world got smaller and brought a new world of opportunities...and of threats. You'll learn how some Jews worked hard to integrate with their dominant cultures (such as the painter Maurycy Gottlieb). This period also saw the emergence of modern anti-Semitism, including a brutal pogrom in Warsaw in 1881. As Jews sought to define a modern Jewish identity in the late 19th century, many emigrated—some to North or South America, and still others to the Holy Land (the beginnings of Zionism).

All of this sets the stage for World War I, when Jews were drafted into various armies—and often forced to fight one another. But at war's end, Poland was reconstituted as an independent nation. You'll step out onto **The Jewish Street,** which re-creates an interwar shopping street from a Jewish community. ("The Jewish Street" was also slang for the Jewish world in general.) It was between the world wars—when a newly independent Poland extended full citizenship and voting rights to its Jewish citizens—that Jewish cultural life flourished as never before. One-third of Poland's population was Jewish—that's three million people. You'll see re-created Warsaw sites relating to newspapers, cinema, writers, and artists; and you'll learn about Jewish tourism of the era (when middle-class Jews would travel around Poland and Europe to visit Jewish cultural sites). Don't miss the mezzanine area upstairs, with exhibits about education and reform—including bilingual schooling (Yiddish and Polish), the beloved educator and author Janusz Korczak, and the debate over "ghetto benches" (segregated seating areas in schools).

However, this was also a time of rising anti-Semitism, segregation, boycotts, and anti-Jewish quotas; during this period, some 140,000 Jews emigrated to the Holy Land. After one more nostalgic stroll down "The Jewish Street," you come to September 1, 1939, when the Nazis invaded Poland. They stripped Jews of their rights and possessions; humiliated, labeled, tortured, and executed them; and eventually implemented the **Holocaust.** The exhibit traces, step by step, the escalation of the Nazis' "Final Solution," with a focus on events here in Warsaw: Forcing Jews into a ghetto (you'll walk across a platform representing the bridge that connected the two parts of the ghetto, offering Jewish people fleeting glimpses of "normal" life going on outside their walls); the liquidation of the ghetto and the movement of Warsaw's Jews to the death camp at Treblinka; and the Ghetto Uprising, a desperate last stand in which the dwindling number or Warsaw's Jews put up a valiant, but ultimately doomed, fight. Making these stories personal are contemporaneous diaries, documents, and photographs.

The exhibit poses difficult questions about how non-Jewish Poles helped—or did not help—the Jews who were gradually disappearing from their cities. And it explains how a sort of "underground railroad" worked at great peril to save as many Jews as possible—as depicted in the movie *The Pianist.* (Look for the chess set carved by a Jew in hiding.) All told, 9 out of every 10 Polish Jews were murdered in the Holocaust. Only about 300,000 survived.

Finally, **The Postwar Years** follows Holocaust survivors in the years just after the war, when, astonishingly, they were scapegoated for war crimes. About 150,000 more (half the total survivors) fled to the newly created state of Israel, and those who remained had to navigate an unfriendly, anti-Semitic communist regime. In 1968, the communists launched an "anti-Zionist" campaign; eventually around 15,000 Polish Jews lost their citizenship and left for Israel, Western Europe, and the US. Not until the fall of communism could the rest finally enter a world of new possibilities. The final room poses a powerful question: Given this rich yet traumatic history, what is the future for Jews in Poland?

The creation of this museum—the first time that the full story of the Jews of Poland has ever been told in such a mainstream way, and in all its epic scope—represents a critical milestone in celebrating a culture that has survived a harrowing history.

Ghetto Walking Tour

For a poignant stroll through what was the ghetto, with faint echoes of a tragic history, take this brief, lightly guided walk for a few blocks. The neighborhood itself is drab and boxy, though increasingly gentrified. It was rebuilt in characterless communist style after it was leveled during the Holocaust. You'll have to work hard to resurrect the memory of what went on here.

Stand along the street facing the monument, with the museum behind it. Turn right and walk along Zamenhofa—which, like many streets in this neighborhood, is named for a hero of the Ghetto Uprising. From here, you'll follow a series of three-foot-tall, black stone memorials to uprising heroes—the **Path of Remembrance.** Like stations of the cross, each recounts an event of the uprising. Every April 19th (the day the uprising began), huge crowds follow this path.

In a block and a half, just beyond the corner of Miła (on the left, partly obscured by some bushes), you'll find a **bunker** where about 100 organizers of the uprising hid (and where they committed suicide when the Nazis discovered them on May 8, 1943).

Continue following the black stone monuments up Zamenhofa (which becomes Dubois), then turn left at the corner, onto broad and busy Stawki. The ugly gray building on your left (a half-block down at #5, near the tram stop) was the **headquarters of the SS** within the ghetto. This is where the transportation of Warsaw's Jews to concentration camps was organized.

Using the crosswalk at the tram stop, cross Stawki and proceed straight ahead into the gap between the two buildings. At the back of this parking lot is a surviving part of the red-brick **ghetto wall,** with a few remaining scraps of 1940s barbed wire.

Farther up Stawki street, on the right, is the finale of this walk: the **Umschlagplatz** monument. That's German for "transfer place," and it marks the spot where the Nazis brought Jewish families to prepare them to be loaded onto trains bound for Treblinka or Auschwitz. This was the actual site of the touching scene in the film *The Pianist* where the grandfather shares bits of chocolate with his family before being forever separated. In the walls of the monument are inscribed the first names of some of the victims.

WARSAW UPRISING SIGHTS

While the 1944 Warsaw Uprising is a recurring theme in virtually all Warsaw sightseeing, two sights in particular—one a monument, the other a museum—are worth a visit for anyone with a special interest. Neither is right along the main tourist trail; the monument is closer to the sightseeing action, while the museum is a subway, tram, or taxi ride away.

Warsaw Uprising Monument

The most central sight related to the Warsaw Uprising is the monument at plac Krasińskich (intersection of ulica Długa and Miodowa,

one long block and about a five-minute walk northwest of the New Town). Larger-than-life soldiers and civilians race for the sewers in a desperate attempt to flee the Nazis. Just behind the monument is the oxidized-copper facade of Poland's Supreme Court.

▲▲Warsaw Uprising Museum (Muzeum Powstania Warszawskiego)

Thorough, modern, and packed with Polish field-trip groups, this museum celebrates the heroes of the uprising. It's a bit cramped, and finding your way through the exhibits can be confusing, but it works hard to illuminate this complicated chapter of Warsaw's history. The location is inconvenient (a taxi/Uber, Metro, tram, or bus ride west of Centralna station) and, because it takes some time to visit, may not be worth the trek for those with a casual interest. But history buffs find it worthwhile.

Cost and Hours: 25 zł, free on Sun; open Mon and Wed-Fri 8:00-18:00, Thu until 20:00, Sat-Sun 10:00-18:00, closed Tue; tel. 22-539-7947, www.1944.pl.

Audioguide: The informative, two-hour audioguide is ideal if you really want to delve into the whole story (10 zł, rent it in the gift shop). But the museum is so well described, you can just wander aimlessly and be immersed in the hellish events.

Eating: The museum's **$ café** is oddly pleasant, serving drinks and light snacks amidst genteel ambience from interwar Warsaw. In summer you can dine on a peaceful terrace. You'll also find a few business lunch-type places in the surrounding office zone.

Getting There: The museum is on the western edge of downtown—a long, dull walk through urban gloom—at ulica Przyokopowa 28. The newly opened Rondo Daszyńskiego Metro stop has been a shot in the arm to this area, which has sprouted a sleek, supermodern zone of office blocks. While it's easiest to reach by taxi or Uber (figure about 10 minutes and 20 zł from the Royal Way), you can get close on public transit. Ride the Metro to Rondo Daszyńskiego, exit toward *Muzeum Powstania Warszawskiego,* walk one block (with the huge traffic circle at your back), turn right on Przyokopowa, and walk another long block to the brick wall surrounding the museum (entrance at far end). You can also reach Rondo Daszyńskiego on bus #178 from Castle Square, bus #105 from the Royal Way (Uniwersytet stop), or bus #109 from Centralna station. There's a slightly closer tram stop, called Muzeum Powstania Warszawskiego, which you can reach on tram #22 or #24 from Centralna station or the street in front of the National Museum.

Visiting the Museum: Buy your ticket at the little house at the far end of the entrance courtyard (marked *kasa*), then head into the main hall. The high-tech main exhibit sprawls across three floors. It tells the story of the uprising chronologically, with a keen focus on military history. The exhibit covers several topics, but doesn't provide a big-picture narrative; to fully understand the context of what you're seeing, read the sidebar before your visit.

As you enter, the **Room of the Little Insurgent** on the right is a children's area, reminding visitors young and old that Varsovian kids played a role in the Warsaw Uprising, too.

The **ground floor** sets the stage with Germany's invasion and occupation of Poland. The Generalgouvernement (Nazi puppet government of occupied Poland, ruled by Hans Frank in Kraków) wasted no time in asserting its control over the Poles; you'll learn how they imprisoned and executed priests, professors, and students. You'll also hear the story of the earlier, smaller uprisings that preceded the Warsaw Uprising, including the Poland-wide Operation Tempest (Burza) in 1943. During those earliest rebellions, Warsaw was intentionally left out of the fray...but only for the time being. The print shop shows how propaganda was spread during the occupation, despite the watchful eye of the Nazis.

To keep with the chronological flow, skip the middle floor for now, and ride the elevator to the **top floor** (#2), which covers the main part of the uprising. You'll meet some of the uprising's heroes and learn about their uniforms, weapons, and methods. The room in the middle, with felt drapes, tells the story of the Wola Massacre, in which some 40,000 residents of that Warsaw neighborhood were executed in just three days. Beyond that, the "Kino Palladium" movie screen shows fascinating Home Army newsreel footage from the period (with English subtitles). To the right of the screen, you'll walk through a simulated sewer, reminiscent of the one that many Home Army soldiers and civilians used to evade the Germans. Imagine terrified troops quietly traversing a sewer

The Warsaw Uprising

By the summer of 1944, it was becoming clear that the Nazis' days in Warsaw were numbered. The Red Army drew near, and by late July, Soviet tanks were within 25 miles of downtown Warsaw.

The Varsovians could simply have waited for the Soviets to cross the river and force the Nazis out. But they knew that Soviet "liberation" would also mean an end to Polish independence. The Polish Home Army numbered 400,000—30,000 of them in Warsaw alone—and was the biggest underground army in military history. The uprisers wanted Poland to control its own fate, and they took matters into their own hands. The symbol of the resistance was an anchor made up of a *P* atop a *W* (which stands for *Polska Walcząca*, or "Poland Fighting"—you'll see this icon all around town). Over time, the Home Army had established an extensive network of underground tunnels and sewers, which allowed them to deliver messages and move around the city without drawing the Nazis' attention. These tunnels gave the Home Army the element of surprise.

On August 1, 30,000 Polish resistance fighters launched an attack on their Nazi oppressors. They poured out of the sewers and caught the Nazis off guard. The ferocity of the Polish fighters stunned the Nazis. But the Nazis regrouped, and within a few days, they had retaken several areas of the city—murdering tens of thousands of innocent civilians as they went. In one notorious incident, some 5,500 Polish soldiers and 6,000 civilians who were surrounded by Nazis in the Old Town were forced to flee through the sewers; many drowned or were shot. (This scene is depicted in the Warsaw Uprising Monument on plac Krasińskich.)

Two months after it had started, the Warsaw Uprising was over. The Home Army called a cease-fire. About 18,000 Polish uprisers had been killed, along with nearly 200,000 innocent civilians. An infuriated Hitler ordered that the city be destroyed—which it was, systematically, block by block, until virtually nothing remained.

Through all this, the Soviets stood still, watched, and waited. When the smoke cleared and the Nazis left, the Red Army marched in and claimed the wasteland that was once called Warsaw. After the war, General Dwight D. Eisenhower said that the scale of destruction here was the worst he'd ever seen. The communists later tracked down the surviving Home Army leaders, killing or imprisoning them.

Depending on whom you talk to, the desperate uprising of Warsaw was incredibly brave, stupid, or a little of both. As for the Poles, they remain fiercely proud of their struggle for freedom. In 2004, 60 years after the uprising, the Warsaw Uprising Museum opened to document and commemorate this tragedy.

line like this one more than a mile long (but with lower ceilings)—and doing it while knee-deep in liquid sewage. At the end of the "sewer," stairs lead down to the middle floor.

The **middle floor** focuses on the grueling aftermath of the uprising. The later days of the uprising are outlined, battle by battle. A chilling section describes how Warsaw became a "city of graves," with burial mounds and makeshift crosses scattered everywhere. One room honors the Field Postal Service, which, at great personal risk, continued mail delivery of both military communiqués and civilian correspondences. Many of these brave "mailmen" were actually Scouts who were too young to fight. Nearby, another room re-creates a clandestine radio broadcast station set up in a living room.

If you need a break, look for the red corridor leading through the USSR section to the **café** and WC.

End your visit by walking down the stairs into the **main hall,** which is dominated by two large-scale exhibits: a replica of an RAF Liberator B-24 J, used for airborne surveillance of wartime Warsaw; and a giant movie

screen showing more newsreels assembled by the Home Army's own propaganda unit during the uprising. Under the screen, behind the black curtains, an exhibit tells the story of Germans in Warsaw, along with another, more claustrophobic walk-through sewer.

Also in the main hall, look for the entrance to the seven-minute 3-D film *City of Ruins (Miasto Ruin),* with virtual aerial footage of the postwar devastation. This gives you a look at the reality of the thousand people (nicknamed "Robinson Crusoes") who lived in bombed-out Warsaw immediately after the war. It's worth waiting in line to see this powerful film.

The **park** surrounding the building features several thought-provoking sights. A Chevy truck armored by the Home Army is both a people's tank and an example of how outgunned they were. Along the back is the Wall of Memory, a Vietnam War Memorial-type monument to soldiers of the Polish Home Army who were killed in action. You'll see their rank and name, followed by their code name, in quotes. The Home Army observed a strict policy of anonymity, forbidding members from calling each other by anything but their code names. The bell in the middle is dedicated to the commander of the uprising, Antoni Chruściel (code name "Monter").

WARSAW

SOUTH OF THE CENTER
▲Łazienki Park (Park Łazienkowski)

The huge, idyllic Łazienki Park (wah-ZHYEN-kee) is where Varsovians go to play. The park is sprinkled with fun Neoclassical buildings, strutting peacocks, and young Poles in love. It was built by Poland's very last king (before the final Partition), Stanisław August Poniatowski, to serve as his summer residence and provide a place for his citizens to relax.

On the edge of the park (along Belwederska) is a **monument to Fryderyk Chopin.** The monument, in a rose garden, is flanked

by platforms, where free summer piano **concerts** of Chopin's music are given weekly (mid-May–late Sept only, generally Sun at 12:00 and 16:00—confirm at TI). The statue shows Chopin sitting under a wind-blown willow tree. Although he spent his last 20 years and wrote most of his best-known music in France, his inspiration came from wind blowing through the willow trees of his native land, Poland. The Nazis were quick to destroy this statue, which symbolizes Polish culture. They melted the original (from 1926) down for its metal. Today's copy was recast after World War II. Savor this spot; it's great in summer, with roses wildly in bloom, and in autumn, when the trees provide a golden backdrop for the black, romantic statue.

Venture down into the ravine and to the center of the park, where (after a 10-minute hike) you'll find King Poniatowski's strik-

ing **Palace on the Water** (Pałac na Wodzie)—literally built in the middle of a river. Nearby, you'll spot a clever amphitheater with seating on the riverbank and the stage on an island. The king was a real man of the Enlightenment, host-ing weekly Thursday dinners here for artists and intellectuals. But Poland's kings are long gone, and proud peacocks now rule this roost.

Łazienki Park is also slated to be the future home of the state-of-the-art **Museum of Polish History,** which is being built along the Łazienkowska highway (near Ujazdów Castle, at the northeastern edge of the park). When it opens—likely 2021 or later—this museum will be yet another big draw for visitors (to check on the progress, see www.en.muzhp.pl).

Getting There: The park is just south of the city center on the Royal Way. Buses #116 and #180 run from Castle Square in the Old Town along the Royal Way directly to the park (get off at the stop called Łazienki Królewskie, by Belweder Palace— you'll see Chopin squinting through the trees on your left). Maps at park entrances locate the Chopin monument, Palace on the Water, and other park attractions.

Shopping in Warsaw

You'll notice that many Varsovians are chic, sophisticated, and very well-dressed. To see where they outfit themselves, go window-shopping. **Mysia 3** is a super-hip mini mall with three concise floors dedicated to mostly Polish fashion designers, but also has cutting-edge housewares and decor (Mon-Sat 10:00-20:00, Sun 12:00-18:00, across Jerusalem Avenue from Nowy Świat, inside the former communist propaganda office at Mysia 3, www.mysia3.pl). Warsaw's main "fashion row" is a bit farther south, in the Śródmieście district. **Mokotowska street,** which angles northeast from trendy plac Zbawiciela, is lined with dozens of chichi boutiques, jewelry shops, shoe stores, designer pastry shops, hair salons, and hipster barbers. The highest concentration is a few short blocks north of plac Zbawiciela, north of Piękna. If you enjoy this zone, the area immediately to the west—along Wilcza and Poznańska streets—has more of the same.

Entertainment in Warsaw

Warsaw fills the summer with live music options. In addition to more serious options (opera, symphony, etc.), consider these crowd-pleasing choices.

CHOPIN

My favorite Warsaw music option is to enjoy a Chopin performance. There's nothing like hearing Chopin's compositions passionately played by a teary-eyed Pole who really feels the music. The best option is the outdoor concert in front of the big Chopin statue in **Łazienki Park,** but it is held only one day a week in summer (free, mid-May-late-Sept generally Sun at 12:00 and 16:00, www.lazienki-krolewskie.pl; for more on this option, see the Łazienki Park listing on page 417).

If you're not in town on a Sunday, the next best thing is the **Chopin Salon.** Jarek Chołodecki, who runs the recommended

Chopin Boutique B&B, hosts an intimate piano concert in his delightful salon nightly at 19:30. The performance can cover a range of musical styles and composers—but generally there are piano pieces featuring Chopin. The concert lasts around 45 minutes and is followed by wine, homemade cakes, and social time. A small group of locals and travelers gathers around Jarek's big shiny Steinway grand to hear great music by talented young artists in a great city (50 zł, ulica Smolna 14, reservations required, tel. 22-829-4801, www.bedandbreakfast.pl).

The **Chopin Museum** has a concert series where music academy students recommended by their professors perform an hour-long concert. These are free and typically take place October through July each Thursday at 18:00 (call ahead to reserve a seat, tel. 22-441-6100, www.en.chopin.nifc.pl).

Additionally, various **touristy Chopin concerts** are popping up all over the city; figure 60 zł for a piano performance set in a drawing room or small theater. Ask your hotel or the TI for the latest fliers.

OTHER MUSIC

Warsaw House of Music, in a refurbished town house along the Royal Way, hosts an even wider range of musical events. The lineup does include some Chopin, but goes beyond touristy cliches to delve into other historical musical forms from Warsaw, including Jewish klezmer music, interwar Polish cabaret songs, Slavic folk songs, and traditional and contemporary jazz (50 zł, daily at 17:00, Nowy Świat 63, tel. 22-692-4824).

Two big, historic churches in and near the Old Town put on 30-minute **organ concerts** most days through the summer. Choose between the Cathedral of St. John the Baptist, with an austere brick interior, right in the heart of the Old Town (15 zł, May-Sept Mon-Sat at 14:00, no concerts Sun); or the frilly, Rococo St. Anne's Church, with a more sumptuous interior, just outside the Old Town (15 zł, May-early Oct Mon-Sat at 12:00, no concerts Sun). Both are run by the same company (mobile 501-158-477, www.kapitula.org).

Free outdoor **jazz concerts** take place each Saturday in summer right on the Old Town Square (July-Aug at 19:00). You'll also spot the outdoor **Jazz Club Akwarium** along the Royal Way, in the park next to the Adam Mickiewicz statue; at this casual venue, music lovers relax in slingback chairs, while serious concerts fill the cellar (music most Thu-Sun nights starting sometime between 19:00 and 21:00, Krakowskie Przedmieście 60A, mobile 664-063-050).

LIVELY HANGOUT ZONES

The Old Town and New Town are totally for tourists. To find some more interesting areas to explore and hang out after dark, your first stop should be **plac Zbawiciela** in the Śródmieście and the surrounding streets (see page 427). Locals also enjoy spending a balmy afternoon or evening on the **Vistula riverbanks.** Long ignored by Varsovians, the left (west) bank has undergone a dramatic renovation, with beautiful parklike embankments ideal for strolling. Meanwhile, the right (east) bank is still rugged and undeveloped, with forests and natural beaches—the biggest being around the eastern base of the Poniatowski Bridge (where Jerusalem Avenue crosses the river).

Sleeping in Warsaw

Because Warsaw is a major business destination, its hotel rates fluctuate from day to day. I've categorized hotels based on estimated prices during busy times, but you may find prices much higher or much lower depending on what's happening in town. Regardless, you'll find Warsaw affordable for a European capital—for what you'd spend on a basic room in Rome or Amsterdam, you can get a palatial room in a top-end hotel here. That said, two of my Warsaw favorites—Chopin Boutique B&B and Duval Apartments— are both affordable and characteristic, making them excellent all-around choices.

I've arranged my listings by neighborhood. For locations, see the map on page 374. Keep in mind that in the Old Town, you'll rarely see a local, while in Śródmieście, you'll rarely see a tourist. Choose your Warsaw experience.

NEAR PALM TREE CIRCLE (NOWY ŚWIAT AND JERUSALEM AVENUE)

Considering how spread out Warsaw is, this is a convenient location for reaching various sights around the city. While comfortable inside, these hotels are in big buildings on uninspiring urban streets.

$$$ Hotel Indigo, part of a high-end chain, surrounds a glassy atrium with 60 posh rooms at reasonable prices. This is a great value for elegance in a central location (breakfast extra, aircon, elevator, Smolna 40, tel. 22-418-8900, www.indigowarsaw. com, reservation@indigowarsaw.com).

$$$ Between Us B&B is an inviting home-away-from-home for hipsters in Warsaw. Beata rents three trendy rooms above a youthful café centrally located in downtown Warsaw, near the bottom end of this price range. As this place books up early, reserve far ahead (on second floor, no elevator, check in at Między Nami café downstairs, Bracka 20, tel. 22-828-5417, mobile 603-096-701, www.between-us.eu, info@between-us.eu).

$$ Chopin Boutique B&B offers comfort, class, personality, hospitality, and value in an ideal location. Jarek Chołodecki, who lived near Chicago for many years, returned to Warsaw and converted this beautifully renovated apartment building into a bed-and-breakfast with 30 endearingly creaky, creatively decorated, antique-furnished rooms. Quirky, charming Jarek is a good host (you'll feel like you're

staying with your Warsaw sophisticate cousin), and his well-trained staff provide a warm professionalism that's rare at this price range. You'll enjoy breakfast (with locally sourced foods) at big communal tables in the cellar restaurant, escape from the city in the garden courtyard, and have the opportunity to take in a nightly Chopin concert in the ground-floor salon—see "Entertainment in Warsaw," earlier (RS%, elevator, bike rental, ulica Smolna 14, tel. 22-829-4801, www.bedandbreakfast.pl, office@bedandbreakfast.pl).

$$ Zgoda by DeSilva, an impersonal but comfortable apartment hotel, has 51 efficient units designed for business travelers on a tight budget (breakfast extra or use the kitchenette, air-con, elevator, Zgoda 6, tel. 22-553-6200, www.desilva.pl, zgoda@desilva.pl).

$$ Apple Inn, with 10 tight, modern rooms in the attic of a hulking building, is your cheap-and-cheery option in the center (breakfast extra, shared kitchen and library, sometimes unstaffed—clearly communicate your arrival time, Chmielna 21, unit 22B—ride elevator to fourth floor, mobile 601-746-006, www.appleinn.pl, Marta).

¢ **Oki Doki City Hostel,** on a pleasant square a few blocks in front of the Palace of Culture and Science, is colorful, creative, and easygoing. Each of its 37 rooms was designed by a different artist with a special theme—such as Van Gogh, Celtic spirals, heads of state, or Lenin. It's run by Ernest—a Pole whose parents loved Hemingway—and his wife Łucja, with help from their sometimes-jaded staff (private rooms available, plac Dąbrowskiego 3, tel. 22-828-0122, www.okidoki.pl, okidoki@okidoki.pl).

IN ŚRÓDMIEŚCIE ("DOWNTOWN")

Foodies, people who hate tourists, and travelers who really want to disappear into Warsaw choose to sleep in Śródmieście. A 10- to 15-minute walk (or quick tram ride) south of Jerusalem Avenue, it feels urban-residential and very local. And if trendy restaurants are on your agenda, sleeping near the culinary hotspots in Śródmieście is an efficient strategy. Compared to most of my other Warsaw listings, these feel a bit chic and trendy...just right for the neighborhood.

$$$$ Hotel Rialto is a professional-feeling boutique hotel with Art Deco flair—both inside (in the lobby, respected restaurant, and 44 rooms) and out. It's a splurge that feels sophisticated, but without pretense. They plan to add another 100 rooms in the adjacent building (air-con, elevator, Wilcza 73, nearest tram/bus stop at Koszykowa, tel. 22-584-8700, www.rialto.pl, info@rialto.pl).

$$$ Autor Rooms is classy and intimate—a third-floor apartment with four rooms (each one different) and a shared breakfast table. It's off a busy street in an urban jungle just off Constitution Square, but once you're settled in, it's a handy home base (elevator, Lwowska 17, nearest tram/bus stop at plac Konstytucji, mobile 797-992-737, www.autorrooms.pl, hello@autorrooms.pl).

IN OR NEAR THE OLD TOWN

The Old Town area has some fine splurges and easy access to the romantic, rebuilt historic core. But it's less handy to Warsaw's trendier side.

$$$$ Hotel Bristol is Warsaw's top splurge—as much a landmark as a hotel (see description on page 384), this classic address on the Royal Way is where you're likely to spot visiting dignitaries and celebrities. (Just inside the round entrance on the corner, find the wall of brass knobs identifying past VIP guests—from

Pablo Picasso to Ed Sheeran.) The public spaces are palatial, with sumptuous Art Deco lounges, bars, and coffee shops that make you want to dress up just to hang out. And the 206 rooms are fresh, elegant, and well-equipped. If you like a posh home base, check the rates here first—you may be surprised at how affordable opulence can be (air-con, classy old vintage elevator, gym, swimming pool, sauna, Krakowskie Przedmieście 42, tel. 22-551-1000, www. hotelbristolwarsaw.pl, bristol@luxurycollection.com).

$$$ Hotel Le Régina is another tempting splurge, buried in the quiet and charming New Town (just beyond the Old Town). From its elegant public spaces to its 61 top-notch rooms, everything here is done with class (pricey breakfast extra, elevator, exercise room, pool, Kościelna 12, tel. 22-531-6000, www.leregina. com, reception.leregina@mamaison.com).

$$$ Castle Inn, sitting on Castle Square at the entrance to the Old Town, is the next rung up the ladder for youth hostelers who've outgrown the grungy backpacker scene. Run by the owners of Oki Doki Hostel (described earlier), it has 22 creative and colorful rooms, each with different decor (breakfast extra, lots of stairs and no elevator, can be noisy—request quiet room, Świętojańska 2, tel. 22-425-0100, www.castleinn.pl, castleinn@castleinn.pl).

$$ Duval Apartments, named for a French woman who supposedly had an affair with the Polish king in this building, offers four beautifully appointed rooms above a restaurant and teahouse (called Same Fusy) a few steps off the square in the Old Town. Each spacious room has a different theme: traditional Polish, Japanese, glass, or retro. Offering B&B comfort with hotel anonymity, this is an excellent value and one of my Warsaw favorites (lots of stairs with no elevator, breakfast extra, some restaurant noise— light sleepers should request a quiet room, Nowomiejska 10, mobile 608-679-346, www.duval.net.pl, duval@duval.net.pl). Arrange a meeting time with Agnieszka or Marcin when you reserve.

Eating in Warsaw

Warsaw is, quite unexpectedly, one of Eastern Europe's best foodie cities...not that the tourists who stick to the kitschy, conventional, Old Town eateries would know. While there are some fine places in the historic center to sample traditional Polish food, that's better done in Old World Kraków; in Warsaw, don't be shy about exploring some local neighborhoods to find a more eclectic, modern, cosmopolitan food scene. Prices are low, so even a "splurge" restaurant lets you experience high-end experimental cuisine for a fraction of the cost of a similar place in a Western European capital.

But be warned: The food scene here changes at a bewildering pace. What's hot and new one year is shuttered the next. Don't be surprised if some places I list here are closed when you visit. On the upside, that means there's always something new to check out. Ask around, do some online research (try checking www.warsawfoodie.pl), and find out what's trending right now.

Wherever you dine, most restaurants are open until the "last guest," which usually means about 23:00 (sometimes later in summer)—but can be earlier than expected on slow nights. If dining late, call ahead. For locations, see the map on page 374.

NEAR PALM TREE CIRCLE (NOWY ŚWIAT AND JERUSALEM AVENUE)

These practical options are right in the middle of your sightseeing plans—handy for lunch on the go, or worth going out of your way for to enjoy a memorable dinner. The clientele is a mix of local yuppies, savvy business travelers, and casual tourists smart enough to steer clear of Old Town restaurants.

$$$ Kamanda Lwowska is the best spot in central Warsaw for traditional Polish cooking. It's named for the former Polish city that's now in Ukraine (Lwow, a.k.a. Lviv). It has a few outdoor seats in a parklike setting and a charming, cluttered old cellar with just a touch of kitsch. The friendly and fun staff serves up well-executed Polish classics (daily 10:00-24:00, Foksal 10, tel. 22-828-1031). The street between here and Nowy Świat, called Foksal, is lined with an ever-changing lineup of lively, contemporary eateries where diners cram the al fresco tables.

$$ Bibenda is a rustic-trendy bar with cocktails and an enticing seasonal menu of Polish fusion dishes. The creative chefs use Polish classics as a starting point, then jazz them up with elements borrowed from corresponding dishes in other cultures. For example, you might see fried chicken (a Polish staple), marinated in buttermilk (from the American south), with a raspberry/chipotle glaze (from Mexico). Or perhaps a *gołąbki* (Polish cabbage roll) done in the style of a Turkish *dolma* (stuffed grape leaves). It's creative, delicious, and surprisingly affordable; reservations are wise at dinnertime (Tue-Sun 12:00-late, closed Mon, Nowogrodzka 10, mobile 502-770-303, www.bibenda.pl). The street Bibenda is on—Nowogrodzka—is lined with other, nearly-as-appealing bars and casual eateries to suit every taste (craft beer, whisky, wine bar, and so on).

$$$$ Butchery & Wine, in an unassuming location on

Restaurant Price Code

I've assigned each eatery a price category, based on the average cost of a typical main course. Drinks, desserts, and splurge items (steak and seafood) can raise the price considerably.

$$$$	**Splurge:** Most main courses over 60 zł
$$$	**Pricier:** 45-60 zł
$$	**Moderate:** 25-45 zł
$	**Budget:** Under 25 zł

In Poland, a milk bar or takeout spot is **$**; a basic sit-down eatery is **$$**; a casual but more upscale restaurant is **$$$**; and a swanky splurge is **$$$$**.

---

a drab urban street, serves upscale comfort food, specializing in steaks. The main location is a small, lively room of business travelers; across the alley is a more casual bar-like annex with a similar menu. The wine list is extensive, and reservations are smart (Mon-Sat 12:00-22:00, Sun until 20:00, Żurawia 22 and 20, tel. 22-502-3118, www.butcheryandwine.pl).

Polish Treats—Old and New

These places are on or close to the busy Nowy Świat boulevard.

A. Blikle, Poland's most famous pastry shop, serves a wide variety of delicious treats. This is where locals shop for cakes when they're having someone special over for coffee. The specialty is *pączki* (PONCH-kee), the quintessential Polish doughnut, filled with rose-flavored jam. You can get your goodies "to go" in the shop, or pay double to enjoy them with coffee in the swanky, classic café with indoor or outdoor seating (daily 9:00-21:00, Nowy Świat 35, tel. 22-828-6601). They also have a sit-down restaurant, but I come here only for the *pączki*. You'll see many other A. Blikle branches around town, but this is the original.

E. Wedel Pijalnia Czekolady thrills chocoholics. Emil Wedel made Poland's favorite chocolate, and today, his former residence houses this chocolate shop and genteel café. This is the spot for delicious pastries and a *real* hot chocolate—*czekolada do picia* ("drinking chocolate"), a cup of melted chocolate, not just hot chocolate milk. Or, if you fancy chocolate mousse, try *pokusa*. Wedel's was *the* Christmas treat for locals under communism. Cadbury bought the company when Poland privatized, but they kept the E. Wedel name, which is close to all Poles' hearts...and taste buds (Mon-Fri 8:00-22:00, Sat from 9:00, Sun 9:00-21:00, Szpitalna 8, tel. 22-827-2916, www.wedelpijalnie.pl/en).

Odette, tucked in a sleek, new, mixed-use complex hiding a block behind Nowy Świat, is a good choice for updated treats: pris-

WARSAW

tinely executed designer cakes at reasonable prices. Look through the glass door to the kitchen (Tue-Sun 10:00-20:00, Mon from 13:00, Wojciecha Górskiego 6, unit 7, mobile 604-745-444). These upscale dessert shops are all the rage—keep an eye out for them all over the city.

In Powiśle, near the Riverbank

The low-lying Powiśle neighborhood—squeezed in the little canyon between the Royal Way and the river—is newly trendy, thanks partly to its proximity to the inviting riverbank parks. My recommendations are simply fun hangout cafés, good for a drink or a light meal if you're in the area.

$ Warszawa Powiśle is a café/bar occupying the old, communist-style ticket office for the suburban train station of the same name. Tucked along a picturesque bike lane beneath the towering legs of a bridge, its sidewalk is jammed with cool Varsovians and in-the-know visitors. I'd skip the basic food (light sandwiches, dumplings) and instead just enjoy the vibe with a drink (daily 9:00 until late, Kruczkowskiego 3B, tel. 22-474-4084).

$ Kawiarnia Kafka combines a used bookstore (with books sold by weight) with a hip, creative café. Inside you'll find comfy chairs, stay-awhile tables, and checkerboard tiles; outside, on the lawn across from the café, guests lounge in slingback chairs (Mon-Fri 9:00-22:00, Sat-Sun 10:00-22:00, Oboźna 3, tel. 22-826-0822).

IN ŚRÓDMIEŚCIE ("DOWNTOWN")

Warsaw's Śródmieście district is the epicenter of Polish hipster/foodie culture—where you'll find young Varsovian foodies digging into affordable dishes at the trendiest new places. This area is a 15-minute walk south of Jerusalem Avenue, and also well-served by public transportation (for example, trams #4, #15, #18, and #35 run frequently along the main north-south Marszałkowska corridor to plac Zbawiciela; of these, tram #4 stops in the middle of the road below Castle Square, where the Royal Way meets the Old Town); the Politechnika Metro stop is also nearby. Listed next are a few different restaurant-hunting zones, with a handful of specific recommendations. For locations, see the map on page 369.

Hala Koszyki

This trendy food hall, which opened in 2016 in a renovated brick market hall from 1906, is your handiest one-stop shop for sampling Warsaw's current dining scene. Outside—sandwiched between the two brick entrances—is a sprawling zone of al fresco tables amidst lush trees strewn with twinkle lights. Inside you'll find more than a dozen entirely different eateries, cover-

ing all of the culinary bases: Spanish tapas, sushi, Indian, Latin American, Italian, Thai, hummus bar, beer hall, tea salon, gourmet chocolates, *gelateria*, and more (most are **$$-$$$**). It's anchored by the big bar in the middle, surrounded by communal seating. Nearby, look for the Bazar Koszyki—a tight row of nine different international street food stalls (udon, hot dogs, *Flammkuchen*, pierogi, pho). The upper level, ringed by design studios, has quieter seating and views over the action. The complex also has some serious sit-down eateries, including **$$$ Ćma** ("Moth"), with updated Polish fare and occasional live DJs. The complex, and most of its eateries, is open daily (Mon-Sat 8:00-22:00, Sun 9:00-20:00, Koszykowa 63, www.koszyki.com). They also have live performances (concerts for kids on Sun afternoons, Polish stand-up comedy on Wed nights, and so on)—check the website for details.

On Plac Zbawiciela

Named "Holiest Savior Square" for the looming church, this is a dizzying six-way intersection with a big traffic circle ringed by hulking old colonnades. To get a quick taste of the Śródmieście scene, come here first and just do a slow loop around the circle, surveying your options. Starting to the right of the steeple and moving clockwise, here are a few options you'll see: **$$ Izumi Sushi, $ Karma** coffee shop, and **$$ Tuk Tuk** Thai street food are all popular, with great seating out on the square. Continuing two crosswalks around the circle, you'll cross Mokotowska; looking left here, you may spot a line of people at **Sucré**—an unpretentious hole-in-the-wall serving all-natural,

homemade ice cream. The next section (after Mokotowska) has **Pałaszowanie,** serving cheap but creative *zapiekanki* (French bread pizza), followed by the trendy **$$ Charlotte** designer bakery and wine bar, with homemade treats and tables spilling out all over the square. Up above, **Plan B** is a hipster dive bar with drinks, snacks, and views down over the square; this is where revelers head at 2 in the morning, after the restaurants are closed (find the graffiti-slathered staircase up, just past Charlotte).

On and near Poznańska Street

A few short blocks west of plac Zbawiciela, this street is also lined with trendy and youthful eateries (especially around the intersection with Wilcza street; the nearest tram/bus stop is Hoża, and it's also not far from plac Konstytucji). Strolling this strip, you'll find several enticing options. **$$ Beirut,** a rustic and casual bar serving up excellent Middle Eastern food, is the culinary anchor of this neighborhood—always packed and lively. The hummus bar, on the left, has a wide variety of *mezes* (small plates) and grilled meats, while the "Kraken Rum Bar" on the right has fish dishes (portions are modest—plan to share a few, order at the counter then find a table, daily, Poznańska 12). **$$ Tel Aviv,** with gluten-free and vegan Middle Eastern food across the street, is the upscale answer to Beirut...and enjoys handling its overflow (daily, Poznańska 11). A few steps away, two more options are at the intersection with Wilcza: **$$$$ Nolita** is one of Warsaw's splurges—top-end, white-tablecloth fine dining, but still affordable on a European scale (closed Sat lunch and all day Sun, Wilcza 46, www.nolita.pl). **$$$ Wilcza 50** is a big, glitzy, crank-'em-out place offering international fare in a modern and spacious setting (daily, Wilcza 50).

Fine Dining near Łazienki Park

$$$$ Atelier Amaro, which has two Michelin stars, is a worthwhile splurge for foodies. If you're going to spend $100 on dinner anywhere in Poland...do it here. Filling an otherwise unexceptional brick building at the corner of Łazienki Park, the restaurant comes with high-end service and top-quality cuisine. Influenced by the New Nordic school, chef Wojciech Modest Amaro (who hosts the Polish versions of *Top Chef* and *Hell's Kitchen*) sources his ingredients as locally as possible, and creates a multicourse meal that feels like a journey through the forests and farms of Poland—with abundant earthy, savory, smoky flavors. You'll pay around 300 zł per person, depending on how many "moments" (courses) you choose, plus wine and vodka, but it's worthwhile for foodies who want to experience how a talented chef interprets the Polish culinary tradition at a very high level. Reservations are essential (Wed-Fri 12:00-

15:00 & 18:00-24:30, Tue and Sat 18:00-24:30 only, closed Sun-Mon, Agrykola 1, tel. 22-628-5747, www.atelieramaro.pl).

IN OR NEAR THE OLD TOWN

The restaurants in the Old Town and surrounding streets are 100 percent for tourists. Dining right on the Old Town Market Square is exorbitantly expensive, but could be worth it for those who treasure a romantic memory. Still, I'd rather walk a block or two to one of these options, which are as good as it gets in this area. For locations, see the map on page 374.

$$ Restauracja pod Samsonem ("Under Samson") is a quirky throwback and a sentimental favorite. The menu is affordable, well-executed, unfussy Jewish and Polish comfort food. The outdoor seating, on the New Town's main drag just outside the barbican, is enjoyable in good weather. And the staff is old-school: gruff, playfully opinionated, and stingy (you'll have to pay to check your coat or use the bathroom—yes, even if you're dining here). But nostalgic locals appreciate this as a stubborn remnant of the old days—a time before service with a smile, fine dining for business travelers, and hipster fusion restaurants (daily 10:00-23:00, Freta 3, tel. 22-831-1788).

$$ Freta 33—a block farther into the New Town, facing the serene New Town Square—has decent international fare (such as pastas), fine outdoor seating, and a contemporary subway-tile interior (daily 12:00-23:00, Freta 33, tel. 22-635-0931).

$$ Zapiecek, with a half-dozen locations in and near the Old Town, is a kitschy chain serving up cheap and cheery traditional Polish dishes. Yes, it's something of a tourist trap. But the prices are reasonable, and the food is better and more authentic than it has any right to be. They proudly make their prizewinning pierogi by hand every morning. If you need a quick, traditional meal anywhere near the Old Town...you could do much worse (handiest location faces the Cathedral of St. John the Baptist at Świętojańska 13, others are on the main drag through the New Town at Freta 1 and Freta 18, two more on the Royal Way at Nowy Świat 64 and Krakowskie Przedmieście 55, all open long hours daily).

Warsaw Connections

Almost all trains into and out of Warsaw go through hulking Warszawa Centralna station (described earlier, under "Arrival in Warsaw," including ticket-buying tips). If you're heading to Gdańsk, note that the red-brick Gothic city of Toruń and the impressive Malbork Castle are both on the way, but are on separate train lines—making it difficult to do both en route (see the Gdańsk and Pomerania chapters). Also be aware that EIC and IC express trains to many destinations—including Kraków and Gdańsk—require seat reservations, even if you have a rail pass.

You can buy most tickets online (www.rozklad-pkp.pl)—saving you a trip to Centralna station. To confirm rail journeys, check specific times online or at the station.

From Warszawa Centralna Station by Train to: Kraków (hourly, about 2.5 hours), **Gdańsk** (hourly, 3 hours), **Malbork** (hourly, 2.5 hours), **Toruń** (every 2 hours direct, 3 hours on express IC train, more with changes), **Prague** (2/day direct, including 1 night train, more with change in Ostrava, 8 hours), **Berlin** (4/day direct, 6.5 hours, no direct night train), **Budapest** (1/day direct, 10 hours; 1/day overnight, 13 hours; also 2/day with change in Břeclav, Czech Republic, 10 hours), **Vienna** (2/day direct, 7 hours; plus 1 night train, 10 hours).

By Bus: Flixbus—described on page 346—runs bus routes throughout Poland and to international destinations (www.flixbus.pl).

GDAŃSK & THE TRI-CITY

Gdańsk (guh-DAYNSK) is a true find on the Baltic Coast of Poland. Some travelers may associate Gdańsk with dreary images of striking dockworkers from the nightly news in the 1980s. But there's more to this city than shipyards, Solidarity, and smog. Gdańsk may be *the* great undiscovered Eastern European destination—rich with history and culture, slathered with gorgeous architecture old and new, loaded with world-class museums and great restaurants, and just plain fun.

Exploring Gdańsk is a delight. The historical center is a gem, with block after block of red-brick churches and narrow, colorful, ornately decorated Hanseatic burghers' mansions. The riverfront embankment, with its trademark medieval crane, oozes salty maritime charm. Gdańsk's history is also fascinating—from its 17th-century Golden Age to the headlines of the late 20th century, big things happen here. You might even see ol' Lech Wałęsa still wandering the streets. And yet Gdańsk is also unmistakably a city of the future, with state-of-the-art construction projects popping up all over. In many areas, it feels more Scandinavian than Polish.

Gdańsk and two nearby towns (Sopot and Gdynia) together form an area known as the "Tri-City," offering several day-trip opportunities north along the coast (see page 489). The belle-époque seaside resort of Sopot beckons to tourists, while the modern burg of Gdynia sets the pace for today's Poland. Beyond the Tri-City, the sandy Hel Peninsula is a popular spot for summer sunbathing, and Malbork Castle (covered in the next chapter) is an easy half-hour train ride away.

PLANNING YOUR TIME

Gdańsk, with more than its share of great sights (and tempting side-trips), demands two full days—which also makes the long trip up here more worthwhile. If you're in a rush, those with a limited appetite for sightseeing could squeeze it into one day. If you have more time, Gdańsk will fill it.

Gdańsk sightseeing has three major components: the Royal Way (historic main drag with good museums); the river embankment, leading to the WWII history museum; and the modern shipyard where Solidarity was born (with a fascinating museum). If you have just one (very busy) day, follow my self-guided walk through the Main Town and then out to the Solidarity sights, followed by a spin through the WWII museum (closed Mon) and a stroll along the riverfront back into town.

With two days, I'd devote one day to the Main Town, riverbank, and WWII museum, and a second day to the Solidarity sights, rounding out your time with other attractions: Art lovers enjoy the National Museum (with a stunning altar painting by Hans Memling), history buffs make the pilgrimage to Westerplatte (where World War II began), castle fans side-trip to Malbork, and church and pipe-organ fans might visit Oliwa Cathedral in Gdańsk's northern suburbs (on the way to Sopot).

If you have more time, consider the wide variety of side-trips. The most popular option is the half-day round-trip to Malbork Castle (30-45 minutes each way by train, plus two or three hours to tour the castle—see next chapter). It only takes a quick visit to enjoy the resort town of Sopot (25 minutes each way by train), but on a sunny day, the town's beaches may tempt you to laze around longer. Gdynia is skippable, but it does have one great sight (the Emigration Museum) and rounds out your take on the Tri-City. And if you have a full day and great weather, and you don't mind fighting the crowds for a patch of sandy beach, go to Hel.

Gdańsk gets busy in late June, when school holidays begin, and it's crowded with (mostly German, Norwegian, and Swedish) tourists from July to mid-September—especially during St. Dominic's Fair (Jarmark Św. Dominika, three weeks from late July to mid-Aug), with market stalls, concerts, and other celebrations.

Several Gdańsk museums are closed Monday—especially outside summer. Monday is a good day to visit churches or the European Solidarity Center, or to take a side-trip to Sopot (but not to Malbork Castle or Gdynia's Emigration Museum, which are also closed Monday).

Orientation to Gdańsk

With 460,000 residents, Gdańsk is part of the larger urban area known as the Tri-City (Trójmiasto, total population of 1 million).

But the tourist's Gdańsk is compact, welcoming, and walkable—virtually anything you'll want to see is within a 20-minute stroll of everything else.

Focus on the Main Town (Główne Miasto), home to most of the sights described, including the spectacular Royal Way main drag, ulica Długa. The Old Town (Stare Miasto) has a handful of old brick buildings and faded, tall, skinny houses—but the area is mostly drab and residential, and not worth much time. Just beyond the northern end of the Old Town (about a 20-minute walk from the heart of the Main Town) is the entrance to the Gdańsk Shipyard, with the excellent European Solidarity Center and its top-notch museum. From here, shipyards sprawl for miles.

The second language in this part of Poland is German, not English. As this was a predominantly German city until the end of World War II, German tourists flock here in droves. But you'll win no Polish friends if you call the city by its more familiar German name, Danzig. You'll also find that Gdańsk is becoming an increasingly popular cruise destination, with about 100 ships calling here each year (most dock at the nearby city of Gdynia, and passengers take a bus or train in). During summer daytime hours, the town is filled with little excursion groups.

TOURIST INFORMATION

Gdańsk has two different TI organizations. Most helpful is the **regional TI,** which occupies the Upland Gate, at the start of my self-guided walk (Mon-Fri 9:00-20:00, Sat-Sun until 18:00; Oct-mid-May daily 9:00-18:00; tel. 58-732-7041, www.pomorskie.travel). The **city TI** has three branches—one conveniently located at the bottom end of the main drag, at Długi Targ 28 (just to the left as you face the river gate; daily 9:00-19:00, Sept-April until 17:00; tel. 58-301-4355, www.visitgdansk.com), with satellite TIs at the Madison shopping center (across from the train station) and at the airport.

Sightseeing Pass: Busy sightseers should consider the **Tourist Card,** which includes entry to several sights in Gdańsk, Gdynia, and Sopot, and discounts at others (such as 20 percent off the European Solidarity Center). Check the list of what's covered, and do the arithmetic (50 zł/24 hours, 65 zł/48 hours, 80 zł/72 hours, pay more to add local transit, sold only at TIs).

ARRIVAL IN GDAŃSK

By Train at Gdańsk's Main Train Station (Gdańsk Główny): If you're on a PKP train, get off at the Gdańsk Główny stop. This station is a pretty brick palace on the western edge of the old center. (To save money, architects in Colmar, France copied this exact design to build their city's station.) Trains to other parts of Poland (marked *PKP*) typically use platforms 1 or 2; regional trains with connections to the Tri-City (marked *SKM*) use the shorter platform 3.

Inside the terminal building, you'll find lockers, ATMs, ticket windows, and ticket machines. Outside, the pedestrian underpass by the McDonald's leads you beneath the busy road—a TI is in the Madison shopping center just beyond.

The easiest choice for reaching your hotel is to hop in a **taxi** or request an **Uber** (about 15 zł to any of my recommended hotels). Or it's a 15-minute walk to the heart of the Main Town and many recommended hotels: Go through the underpass, exit to the right, circle around the right side of Cinema City, and follow the busy road until you see the brick towers on your left.

By Train at Gdańsk Śródmieście: If you're arriving in Gdańsk on a commuter SKM train, consider staying on one more stop to the Gdańsk Śródmieście station, which is a slightly shorter walk to the start of my Gdańsk Walk. From Gdańsk Śródmieście, use the underpass to reach the gigantic Forum shopping mall. Walk straight through the mall to the far end; after exiting, if you look to the right, you'll see a pedestrian underpass leading to the Upland Gate and the start of my walk.

By Plane: Gdańsk's architecturally impressive, user-friendly airport, named for Lech Wałęsa, is about five miles west of the city center (airport code: GDN, tel. 58-348-1163, www.airport.gdansk. pl). The 25-minute **taxi** ride into town should cost no more than 60 zł; an **Uber** costs about half that much (except during peak times). Public **bus** #210 heads into the center and stops near the main train station and at Brama Wyżynna, near the heart of the Main Town (3.20 zł, buy ticket at machine at stop or on board for a bit more; 2/hour Mon-Fri, hourly Sat-Sun, 40 minutes).

Gdańsk at a Glance

▲▲▲Gdańsk Walk Stroll down the city's colorful showpiece main drag, ending at the famous shipyards and the European Solidarity Center. See page 436.

▲▲▲Solidarity Sights and Gdańsk Shipyard Home to the beginning of the end of Eastern European communism, with a towering monument and excellent museum. **Hours:** Memorial and shipyard gate—always open. European Solidarity Center exhibit—May-Sept Mon-Fri 10:00-19:00, Sat-Sun until 20:00; Oct-April Mon and Wed-Fri 10:00-17:00, Sat-Sun until 18:00, closed Tue. See page 461.

▲▲Main Town Hall Ornate meeting rooms, town artifacts, and tower with sweeping views. **Hours:** Mon 10:00-13:00, Tue-Sat until 18:00, Sun 11:00-18:00; Oct-April Tue until 13:00, Wed and Fri-Sun until 16:00, Thu until 18:00, closed Mon. See page 457.

▲▲Artus Court Grand meeting hall for guilds of Golden Age Gdańsk, boasting an over-the-top tiled stove. **Hours:** Same as Main Town Hall. See page 458.

▲▲St. Mary's Church Giant red-brick church crammed full of Gdańsk history. **Hours:** Mon-Sat 9:00-17:30, Sun from 13:00, tower open until 20:00 or 21:00 in summer but closed in winter. See page 448.

▲▲Museum of the Second World War Poland's definitive museum on the most devastating conflict in human history. **Hours:** June-Sept Tue 10:00-19:00, Wed-Sun 10:00-20:00; Oct-May Tue-Fri until 19:00, Sat-Sun until 20:00; closed Mon year-round. See page 472.

▲Amber Museum High-tech exhibit of valuable golden globs of petrified tree sap. **Hours:** Same as Main Town Hall, above. See page 455.

▲Uphagen House Tourable 18th-century interior, typical of the pretty houses that line ulica Długa. **Hours:** Same as Main Town Hall. See page 456.

▲National Maritime Museum Sprawling exhibit on all aspects of the nautical life, housed in several venues connected by a ferry boat. **Hours:** July-Aug daily 10:00-18:00; Sept-Oct and March-June Tue-Sun until 16:00, closed Mon; Nov-Feb Tue-Sun until 15:00, closed Mon. See page 460.

GDAŃSK & THE TRI-CITY

GETTING AROUND GDAŃSK

Nearly everything is within easy walking distance of my recommended hotels, but public transportation can be useful for reaching outlying sights such as Oliwa Cathedral, Westerplatte, Sopot, Gdynia, and Hel (specific transportation options for these places are described in each listing).

By Public Transportation: Gdańsk's trams and buses work on the same tickets: single-ride ticket—3.20 zł, one-hour ticket—3.80 zł, 24-hour ticket—13 zł. Major stops have user-friendly ticket machines, which take credit cards. Otherwise, buy tickets *(bilety)* at kiosks marked *RUCH*, or buy one on board from the driver (single-ride not available—you have to buy the one-hour ticket). In the city center, the stops worth knowing about are Plac Solidarności (near the European Solidarity Center), Gdańsk Główny (in front of the main train station), and Brama Wyżynna (near the Upland Gate and the Gdańsk Śródmieście commuter train station).

By Taxi or Uber: Taxis cost about 8 zł to start, then 2-3 zł per kilometer (a bit more at night). However, taxis waiting at stands often have inflated rates; it's safer to call a cab (try Neptun, tel. 19686 or 585-111-555; EcoCar, tel. 123-456-789; or Dajan, tel. 58-19628). Uber works well in Gdańsk and is typically cheaper than a taxi.

Tours in Gdańsk

Private Guides

Hiring a local guide is an exceptional value. **Agnieszka Syroka**—personable and knowledgeable—is a wonderful guide (450 zł/up to 4 hours, more for all day, mobile 502-554-584, www.tourguidegdansk.com, syroka.agnieszka@gmail.com). **Jacek "Jake" Podhorski,** who teaches economics at the local university, guides in the summer and enjoys sharing fascinating memories of the communist days (400 zł/3 hours, 100 zł extra with his car, mobile 603-170-761, ekojpp@ug.edu.pl).

Gdańsk Walk

In the 16th and 17th centuries, Gdańsk was Poland's wealthiest city, with gorgeous architecture (much of it in the Flemish Mannerist style) rivaling that in the two historic capitals, Kraków and Warsaw. During this Golden Age, Polish kings would visit this city of well-to-do Hanseatic

League merchants and gawk along the same route trod by tourists today.

The following self-guided walk—rated ▲▲▲—introduces you to the best of Gdańsk. It bridges the two historic centers (the Main Town and the Old Town), dips into St. Mary's Church (the city's most important church), and ends at the famous shipyards and Solidarity Square (where Poland began what ultimately brought down the USSR). I've divided the walk into two parts (making it easier to split up, if you like): The first half focuses on a loop through the Main Town (with most of the high-profile sights), while the second part carries on northward, through the less-touristy Old Town to the shipyards.

PART 1: THE MAIN TOWN

• *Begin at the west end of the Main Town, just beyond the last gate at the edge of the busy road.*

❶ Upland Gate (Brama Wyżynna)

The Main Town's fortifications were expanded with a Renaissance wall bound by the Upland Gate (built in 1588). "Upland" refers to the hills you see beyond—considered high country in this flat region. Standing with your back to the busy arterial (which traces the old moat), study the gate. Find its three coats of arms (the black eagle for Royal Prussia, the crowned white eagle for Poland, and the two crosses for Gdańsk). Recall that this city has, for almost the entirety of its history before the mid-20th century, been bicultural: German and Polish, coexisting more or less peacefully. Also notice the little wheels that once hoisted a drawbridge.

Now look across the busy street, to the supermodern **Forum shopping center.** While controversial for its over-the-top design (and for covering over a historic canal), this replaced a ragtag old flea market area—so, like many things in Gdańsk, it's a melding of new and old. A lion—symbol of Gdańsk—perches high on the corner of the rust-colored main building. I'm not in the habit of telling travelers to visit shopping malls...but this one really is worth a look.

• *It's a straight line from here to the river. Walk through the arch (which houses a TI) to the next arch, just a few steps ahead.*

❷ Torture Chamber (Katownia) and Prison Tower (Wieża Więzienna)

The tall, Gothic brick gate before you was part of an earlier protective wall made useless after the Renaissance walls were built in 1588. While today these structures house the Amber Museum (described later), it's free to walk through the evocative passage. Inside, find gargoyles (on the left, a town specialty) and the shackles from which prisoners were hung (on the right). Look up at the

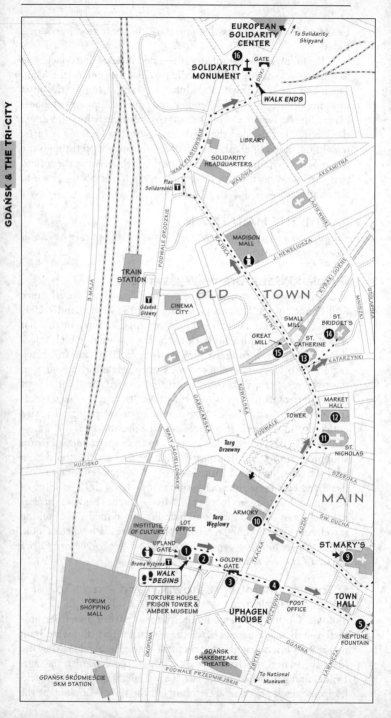

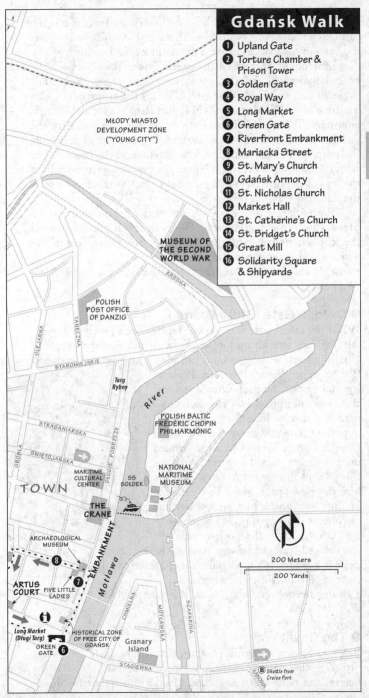

Gdańsk Walk

1. Upland Gate
2. Torture Chamber & Prison Tower
3. Golden Gate
4. Royal Way
5. Long Market
6. Green Gate
7. Riverfront Embankment
8. Mariacka Street
9. St. Mary's Church
10. Gdańsk Armory
11. St. Nicholas Church
12. Market Hall
13. St. Catherine's Church
14. St. Bridget's Church
15. Great Mill
16. Solidarity Square & Shipyards

GDAŃSK & THE TRI-CITY

MŁODY MIASTO DEVELOPMENT ZONE ("YOUNG CITY")

MUSEUM OF THE SECOND WORLD WAR

KROSNA

POLISH POST OFFICE OF DANZIG

OLEJARNA

TANECZNA

STAROMIEJSKIE

Targ Rybny

River

POLISH BALTIC FRÉDÉRIC CHOPIN PHILHARMONIC

STRAGANIARSKA

GROBA

ŚWIĘTOJAŃSKA

DŁUGIE POBRZEŻE

MARITIME CULTURAL CENTER

SS SOŁDEK

NATIONAL MARITIME MUSEUM

TOWN

THE CRANE

ARCHAEOLOGICAL MUSEUM

EMBANKMENT

Motława

ARTUS COURT

FIVE LITTLE LADIES

8

7

Long Market (Długi Targ)

HISTORICAL ZONE OF FREE CITY OF GDAŃSK

GREEN GATE

6

CHMIELNA

MOTŁAWSKA

Granary Island

STĄGIEWNA

SZAFARNIA

200 Meters

200 Yards

ŁĄKOWA

B Shuttle from Cruise Port

inside of the high gable to the headless man, identifying this as the torture chamber. This old jail—with its 15-foot-thick walls—was used as a prison even in modern times, under Nazi occupation.

Leaving the Torture Chamber and Prison Tower through the far end, look to your left (100 yards away) to see a long, brick building with four fancy, uniform gables. This is the **armory** *(zbrojownia),* one of the finest examples of Dutch Renaissance architecture anywhere. Though this part of the building appears to have the facades of four separate houses, it's an urban camouflage to hide its real purpose from potential attackers. But there's at least one clue to what the building is really for: Notice the exploding cannonballs at the tops of the turrets. (We'll get a better look at the armory from the other side, later in this walk.)

The round, pointy-topped tower next to the armory is the **Straw Tower** (Baszta Słomiana). Gunpowder was stored here, and the roof was straw—so if it exploded, it could easily blow its top without destroying the walls.

• *Straight ahead, the final and fanciest gate between you and the Main Town is the...*

❸ Golden Gate (Złota Brama)

While the other gates were defensive, this one's purely ornamental. The four women up top represent virtues that the people of Gdańsk should exhibit toward outsiders (left to right): Peace, Freedom, Prosperity, and Fame. The gold-lettered inscription, a psalm in medieval German, compares Gdańsk to Jerusalem: famous and important. Directly above the arch is the Gdańsk coat of arms: two white crosses under a crown on a red shield. We'll see this symbol all over town. Photographers love the view of the Main Town framed in this arch. Inside the arch, study the old photos showing the 1945 bomb damage. On the left is the glorious view you just enjoyed...ravaged by war. And on the  right is a heartbreaking aerial view of the city in 1945, when 80 percent of its buildings were in ruins.

• *Passing through the Golden Gate, you reach the Main Town's main drag.*

❹ The Royal Way

Before you stretches ulica Długa (cleverly called the "Long Street")—the main promenade of what, 600 years ago, was the biggest and richest city in Poland, thanks to its profitable ties to the Hanseatic League of merchant cities. This promenade is nicknamed the "Royal Way" because (just as in Warsaw and Kraków) the king would follow this route when visiting town.

Walk half a block, and then look back at the Golden Gate. The women on top of this side represent virtues the people of Gdańsk should cultivate in themselves (left to right): Wisdom, Piety, Justice, and Concord (if an arrow's broken, let's take it out of the quiver and fix it). The inscription—sharing a bit of wisdom as apropos today as it was in 1612—reads, "Concord makes small countries develop, and discord makes big countries fall." Gdańsk was cosmopolitan and exceptionally tolerant in the Middle Ages, attracting a wide range of people, including many who were persecuted elsewhere: Jews, Scots, Dutch, Flemish, Italians, Germans, and more. Members of each group brought with them strands of their culture, which they wove into the tapestry of this city—demonstrated by the eclectic homes along this street. Each facade and each gable was different, as nobles and aristocrats wanted to display their wealth. On my last visit, a traveler seeing this street for the first time gasped to me, "It's like stepping into a Fabergé egg."

During Gdańsk's Golden Age, these houses were taxed based on frontage (like the homes lining Amsterdam's canals)—so they were built skinny and deep. The widest houses belonged to the super-elite. Different as they are from the outside, every house had the same general plan inside. Each had three parts, starting with the front and moving back: First was a fancy drawing room, to show off for visitors. Then came a narrow corridor to the back rooms—often along the side of an inner courtyard. Because the houses had only a few windows facing the outer street, this courtyard provided much-needed sunlight to the rest of the house. The residential quarters were in the back, where the family actually lived: bedroom, kitchen, office. To see the interior of one of these homes, pay a visit to the interesting **Uphagen House** (at #12, on the right, a block and a half in front of the Golden Gate; described later).

This lovely street wasn't always so lively and carefree. At the end of World War II, the Royal Way was in ruins. That epic war actually began here, in what was then the "Free City of Danzig." Following World War I, nobody could decide what to do with this influential and multiethnic city. So, rather than assign it to Germany or Poland, it was set apart as its own little autonomous statelet. In 1939, Danzig was 80 percent German-speaking—enough for Hitler to consider it his. And so, on September 1 of that year, the Nazis seized it in one day with relatively minor damage (though the attack on the Polish military garrison on the city's Westerplatte peninsula lasted a week).

But six years later, when the Soviets arrived (March 30, 1945), the city was devastated. This was the first traditionally German city that the Red Army took on their march toward Berlin. And, while it was easy for the Soviets to seize the almost empty city, the commander then insisted that it be leveled, building by building—in retaliation for all the pain the Nazis had caused in Russia. (Soviets didn't destroy nearby Gdynia, which they considered Polish rather than German.) Soviet officers turned a blind eye as their soldiers raped and brutalized residents. An entire order of horrified nuns committed suicide by throwing themselves into the river.

It was only thanks to detailed drawings and photographs that these buildings could be so carefully reconstructed. Notice the cheap plaster facades done in the 1950s—rough times under communism, in the decade after World War II. (Most of the town's medieval brick was shipped to Warsaw for a communist-sponsored "rebuild the capital first" campaign.) While the fine facades were restored, the buildings behind the facades were completely rebuilt to modern standards.

Just beyond Uphagen House, **Cukiernia Sowa** ("The Owl," on the right at #13) is *the* place for cakes and coffee. Directly across the street, **Grycan** (at #73) has been a favorite for ice cream here for generations.

Just a few doors down, on the left, are some of the most striking **facades** along the Royal Way. The blue-and-white house with

the three giant heads is from the 19th century, when the hot style was eclecticism—borrowing bits and pieces from various architectural eras. This was one of the few houses on the street that survived World War II.

At the next corner on the right is the huge, blocky, red **post office,** which doesn't quite fit with the skinny facades lining

the rest of the street. Step inside. With doves fluttering under an airy glass atrium, the interior's a class act. Directly across the street, the candy shop **(Ciuciu Cukier Artist)** is often filled with children clamoring to see lollipop-making demos. Step in and inhale a universal whiff of childhood.

A few doors farther down, on the left at #62, pop into the **Millennium Gallery** amber shop (which would love to give you an educational amber polishing demo) to see the fascinating collection of old-timey photos, letting you directly compare Gdańsk's cityscape before and after the WWII destruction.

Above the next door, notice the colorful **scenes.** These are slices of life from 17th-century Gdańsk: drinking, talking, shopping, playing music. The ship is a *koga*, a typical symbol of Hanseatic ports like Gdańsk.

Across the street and a few steps down are the fancy facades of three houses belonging to the very influential medieval **Ferber family,** which produced many burghers, mayors, and even a bishop. On the house with the little dog over the door (#29), look for the heads in the circular medallions. These are Caesars of Rome. At the top of the building is Mr. Ferber's answer to the constant question, "Why build such an elaborate house?"—*PRO INVIDIA*, "For the sake of envy."

A few doors down, on the right, is Gdańsk's most scenically situated milk bar, the recommended **Bar Mleczny Neptun.** Back in communist times, these humble cafeterias were subsidized to give workers an affordable place to eat out. To this day, they offer simple and very cheap grub.

Next door (at #35) is the **Russian Culture Center,** with Russian movies and art exhibits. Poland has no love lost for Russia, but in this multicultural city, this just fits.

Before you stands the **Main Town Hall** (Ratusz Głównego Miasta) with its mighty brick clock tower. Consider climbing its observation tower and visiting its superb interior, which features ornately decorated meeting rooms for the city council (described later).

• *Just beyond the Main Town Hall, ulica Długa widens and becomes...*

❺ Long Market (Długi Targ)

Step from the Long Street into the Long Market, and do a slow, 360-degree spin to appreciate the amazing array of proud architecture here in a city center that rivals the magnificent Grand Place in Brussels. The centerpiece of this square is one of Gdańsk's most important landmarks, the statue of **Neptune**—God of the sea. He's a fitting symbol for a city that dominates the maritime life of Poland. Behind him is another worthwhile museum, the **Artus Court.** Step up to the magnificent door on the right side and study the golden relief just above, celebrating the Vistula River (in so many ways the lifeblood of the Polish nation): Lady Vistula is exhausted after her heroic journey, and is finally carried by Neptune to her ultimate destination, the Baltic Sea. (This is just a preview of the ornate art that fills the interior of this fine building—described later.)

Midway down the Long Market (on the right, across from the Hard Rock Café) is a glass case with the **thermometer and barometer of Daniel Fahrenheit.** Although that scientist was born here, he did his groundbreaking work in Amsterdam.

• *At the end of the Long Market is the...*

Gdańsk History

Visitors to Gdańsk are surprised at how "un-Polish" the city's history is. In this cultural melting pot of German, Dutch, and Flemish merchants (with a smattering of Italians and Scots), Poles were only a small part of the picture until the city became exclusively Polish after World War II. However, in Gdańsk, cultural backgrounds traditionally took a back seat to the bottom line. Wealthy Gdańsk was always known for its economic pragmatism—no matter who was in charge, merchants here made money.

Gdańsk is Poland's gateway to the waters of Europe, where its main river (the Vistula) meets the Baltic Sea. The town was first mentioned in the 10th century, and was seized in 1308 by the Teutonic Knights (who called it "Danzig"; for more on the Teutonic Knights, see page 507). The Knights encouraged other Germans to settle on the Baltic coast, and gradually turned Gdańsk into a wealthy city. In 1361, Gdańsk joined the Hanseatic League, a trade federation of mostly Germanic merchant towns that provided mutual security. By the 15th century, Gdańsk was a leading member of this mighty network, which virtually dominated trade in northern Europe (and also included Toruń, Kraków, Lübeck, Hamburg, Bremen, Bruges, Bergen, Tallinn, Novgorod, and nearly a hundred other cities).

In 1454, the people of Gdańsk rose up against the Teutonic Knights, burning down their castle and forcing them out of the city. Three years later, the Polish king borrowed money from wealthy Gdańsk families to hire Czech mercenaries to take the Teutonic Knights' main castle, Malbork (described in the next chapter). In exchange, the Gdańsk merchants were granted special privileges, including exclusive export rights. Gdańsk now acted as a middleman for much of the trade passing through Polish lands, and paid only a modest annual tribute to the Polish king.

The 16th and 17th centuries were Gdańsk's Golden Age. Now a part of the Polish kingdom, the city had access to an enormous hinterland of natural resources to export—yet it maintained a privileged, semi-independent status. Like Amsterdam, Gdańsk became a progressive and booming merchant city. Its mostly Germanic and Dutch burghers imported Dutch, Flemish, and Italian architects to give their homes an appropriately Hanseatic flourish. At a time of religious upheaval in the rest of Europe, Gdańsk became known for its tolerance—a place that opened its doors to all visitors (many Mennonites and Scottish religious refugees emigrated here). It was also a haven for great thinkers, including philosopher Arthur Schopenhauer and scientist Daniel Fahrenheit (who invented the mercury thermometer).

Along with the rest of Poland, Gdańsk declined in the late 18th century and became part of Prussia (today's northern Germany) during the Partitions. But the people of Gdańsk—even those of German heritage—had taken pride in their independence and weren't enthusiastic about being ruled from Berlin. After World War I, in a unique compromise to appease its complex ethnic makeup, Gdańsk did not fall under German or Polish control, but once again became an independent city-state: the Free City of Danzig (about 750 square miles, populated by 400,000 ethnic Germans and 15,000 Poles). The city, along with the so-called Polish Corridor connecting it to Polish lands, effectively cut off Germany from its northeastern territory. On September 1, 1939, Adolf Hitler started World War II when he invaded Gdańsk in order to bring it back into the German fold. Later, nearly 80 percent of the city was destroyed when the Soviets "liberated" it from Nazi control.

After World War II, Gdańsk officially became part of Poland, and was painstakingly reconstructed (mostly replicating the buildings of its Golden Age). In 1970, and again in 1980, the shipyard of Gdańsk witnessed strikes and demonstrations that would lead to the fall of European communism. Poland's great anticommunist hero and first postcommunist president, Lech Wałęsa, is Gdańsk's most famous resident, and still lives here. When he flies around the world to give talks, he leaves from Gdańsk's "Lech Wałęsa Airport."

A city with a recent past that's both tragic and uplifting, Gdańsk celebrated its 1,000th birthday in 1997. Very roughly, the city has spent about 700 years as an independent entity, and about 300 years under Germanic overlords (the Teutonic Knights, Prussia, and the Nazis). But today, Gdańsk is decidedly its own city. And, as if eager  to prove it, Gdańsk is making big improvements at a stunning pace: new museums (the European Solidarity Center and WWII museum), cultural facilities (the Shakespeare Theater), sports venues (a stadium that resembles a blob of amber, built for the 2012 Euro Cup tournament), and an ongoing surge of renovation and refurbishment that has the gables of the atmospheric Hanseatic quarter gleaming once again.

❻ Green Gate (Zielona Brama)

This huge gate (named for the Green Bridge just beyond) was built as a residence for visiting kings...who usually preferred to stay back by Neptune instead (maybe because the river, just on the other side of this gate, stank). It might not have been good enough for kings and queens, but it's plenty fine for a former president: Lech Wałęsa's office is upstairs. A few steps down the skinny lane to the left is the endearing little **Historical Zone of the Free City of Gdańsk** museum, which explains the interwar period when "Danzig" was an independent and bicultural city-state (described later).

• *Now go through the gate, walk out onto the Green Bridge, anchor yourself in a niche on the left, and look downstream.*

❼ Riverfront Embankment

The Motława River—a side channel of the mighty Vistula—flows into the nearby Baltic Sea. This port was the source of Gdańsk's phenomenal Golden Age wealth. This embankment was jam-packed in its heyday, the 14th and 15th centuries. It was so crowded with boats that you would hardly have been able to see the water, and boats had to pay a time-based moorage fee for tying up to a post.

Look back at the Green Gate and notice that these bricks are much smaller than the locally made ones we saw earlier on this walk. These bricks are Dutch: Boats from Holland would come here empty of cargo, but with a load of bricks for ballast. Traders filled their ships with goods for the return trip, leaving the bricks behind.

The old-fashioned **galleons** and other tour boats moored nearby depart hourly for a fun cruise to Westerplatte (where on September 1, 1939, Germans fired the first shots of World War II) and back. Though kitschy, the galleons are a fun way to get out on the water (details under "Gdansk Connections—By Boat" on page 488).

Across the river is **Granary Island** (Wyspa Spichrzów), where grain was stored until it could be taken away by ships. Before World War II, there were some 400 granaries here; almost all were destroyed...and this island remained rubble until just a few years ago, when developers began erecting a passel of modern new buildings (evoking the old Gdańsk gables) and wrapped the island in a scenic boardwalk—a wonderful place for a stroll. The three older-looking granaries downstream, in the distance on the next island, house exhibits for the National Maritime Museum (described later).

From your perch on the bridge, look down the embankment (about 500 yards, on the left) and find the huge wooden **crane**

(żuraw) bulging over the water. This monstrous 15th-century crane—a rare example of medieval port technology—was once used for loading and repairing ships...beginning a shipbuilding tradition that continued to the days of Lech Wałęsa. The crane mechanism was operated by several workers scrambling around in giant hamster wheels. Treading away to engage the gears and pulleys, they could lift 4 tons up 30 feet, or 2 tons up 90 feet.

• *Walk along the embankment about halfway to the crane, passing the lower embankment, with excursion boats heading to the Westerplatte monument. Pause when you reach the big brick building with green window frames and a tower. This red-brick fort houses the **Archaeological Museum** (described later). Its collection includes the five ancient stones in a small garden just outside its door (on the left). These are the **Prussian Hags**—mysterious sculptures from the second century AD (a.k.a. "Five Little Ladies," each described in posted plaques).*

Turn left through the gate in the middle of the brick building. You'll find yourself on the most charming lane in town...

❽ Mariacka Street

The calm, atmospheric "Mary's Street" leads from the embankment to St. Mary's Church. Stroll the length of it, enjoying the most romantic lane in Gdańsk. (If you need a coffee break, the recommended Drukarnia—on the right—is tops.) The **porches** extending out into the street, with access to cellars underneath, were a common feature in Gdańsk's Golden Age. For practical reasons, after the war, these were restored only on this street. Notice how the porches are bordered with fine stone relief panels and gargoyles attached to storm drains. If you get stuck there in a hard rainstorm, you'll understand why in Polish these are called "pukers." Enjoy a little amber comparison-shopping. As you stroll up to the towering brick St. Mary's Church, imagine the entire city like this cobbled lane of proud merchants' homes, with street music, delightful facades, and brick church towers high above.

Look up at the church tower viewpoint—filled with people who hiked 409 steps for the view. Our next stop is the church, which you'll enter on the far side under the tower. Walk around the left side of the church, appreciating the handmade 14th-century bricks on the right and the plain post-WWII facades on the left. (Reconstructing the Royal Way was better funded. Here, the priority was simply getting people housed again.) In the distance is the fancy facade of the armory (where you'll head after visiting the church).

• *But first, go inside...*

❾ St. Mary's Church (Kościół Mariacki)

Of Gdańsk's 13 medieval red-brick churches, St. Mary's (rated ▲▲) is the one you must visit. It's the largest brick church in the world—with a footprint bigger than a football field (350 feet long and 210 feet wide), it can accommodate 20,000 standing worshippers.

Cost and Hours: 4 zł, 10 zł with tower climb, Mon-Sat 9:00-17:30, Sun from 13:00, tower open until 20:00 or 21:00 in summer but closed in winter.

➲ **Self-Guided Tour:** Inside, sit directly under the fine carved and painted 17th-century Protestant pulpit, two-thirds of the way down the nave (on the left side), to get oriented.

Overview: Built from 1343 to 1502 by the Teutonic Knights (who wanted a suitable centerpiece for their newly captured main city), St. Mary's remains an important symbol of Gdańsk. The church started out Catholic, became Lutheran in the mid-1500s, and then became Catholic again after World War II. (Remember, Gdańsk was a Germanic city before World War II and part of the big postwar demographic shove, when Germans were sent west, and Poles from the east relocated here. Desperate, cold, and homeless, the new Polish residents moved into what was left of the German homes.) While the church was originally frescoed

from top to bottom, the Lutherans whitewashed the entire place. Today, some of the 16th-century whitewash has been peeled back (behind the high altar—we'll see this area soon), revealing a bit of the original frescoes. The floor is paved with 500 gravestones of merchant families. Many of these were cracked when bombing sent the brick roof crashing down in 1945.

Most Gothic churches are built of stone in the basilica style—with a high nave in the middle, shorter aisles on the side, and flying buttresses to support the weight. (Think of Paris' Notre-Dame.) But with no handy source of stone available locally, northern Polish churches are built of brick, which won't work with the basilica design. So, like all Gdańsk churches, St. Mary's is a "hall church"—with three naves the same height and no exterior buttresses.

Also like other Gdańsk churches, St. Mary's gave refuge to the Polish people after the communist government declared martial law in 1981. When a riot broke out and violence seemed imminent, people flooded into churches, knowing that the ZOMO riot police wouldn't dare follow them inside.

Most of the church decorations are original. A few days before the Soviets arrived to "liberate" the city in 1945, locals—knowing what was in store—hid precious items in the countryside. Take some time now to see a few of the highlights.

• *From this spot, you can see most of what we'll visit in the church: As you face the altar, the astronomical clock is at 10 o'clock, the Ferber family medallion is at 1 o'clock, the Priests' Chapel is at 3 o'clock (under a tall, colorful window), and the magnificent 17th-century organ is directly behind you (it's played at each Mass and during free concerts on Fri in summer).*

Pulpit: For Protestants, the pulpit is important. Designed as an impressive place from which to share the Word of God in the people's language, it's located midnave, so all can hear.

• *Opposite the pulpit is the moving...*

Priests' Chapel: The 1965 statue of Christ weeping commemorates 2,779 Polish chaplains executed by the Nazis. See the grainy black-and-white photo of one about to be shot, above on the right.

• *Head up the nave to the...*

High Altar: The main altar, beautifully carved in 1517, is a triptych showing the coronation of Mary. She is surrounded by the Trinity: flanked by God and Jesus, with the dove representing the Holy Spirit overhead. The church's medieval stained glass was destroyed in 1945. Poland's biggest stained-glass window, behind the altar, is from 1980.

• *Start circling around the right side of the altar. Look right to find (high on a pillar) the big, opulent family marker.*

Ferber Family Medallion: The falling baby (under the crown) is Constantine Ferber. As a precocious child, li'l Constantine leaned out his window on the Royal Way to see the king's processional come through town. He slipped and fell, but landed in a salesman's barrel of fish. Constantine grew up to become the mayor of Gdańsk.

• *As you continue around behind the altar, search high above you, on the walls to your right, to spot those restored pre-Reformation frescoes. Behind the altar, look for an...*

Empty Glass Case: This case was designed to hold Hans Memling's *Last Judgment* painting, which used to be in this church, but is currently being held hostage by the National Museum (described later, under "Sights in Gdansk"). To counter the museum's claim that the church wasn't a good environment for such a precious work, the priest had this display case built—but that still wasn't enough to convince the museum to give the painting back. (You'll see a smaller replica of the painting soon.) Because of a recent church renovation, this case may be missing when you visit.

• *Now circle back the way you came to the area in front of the main altar, and proceed straight ahead into the transept. High on the wall to your right, look for the...*

Astronomical Clock: This 42-foot-tall clock is supposedly the biggest wooden clock in the world. Below it is an elaborate circular calendar that, like a medieval computer, calculates on which day each saint's festival day falls in different years (see the little guy on the left, with the pointer). Above are zodiac signs and the time (back then, the big hand was all you needed). Way up on top, Adam and Eve are naked and ready to ring the bell. Adam's been swinging his clapper at the top of the hour since 1473...but sadly, the clock is broken.

• *A few steps in front of the clock is a modern chapel with the...*

Memorial to the Polish Victims of the 2010 Plane Crash: The gold-shrouded Black Madonna honors the 96 victims of an air disaster that killed much of Poland's government—including the president and first lady—during a terrible storm over Russia. The main tomb is for Maciej Płażyński, from Gdańsk, who was leader of the parliament. On the left, the jagged statue has bits of the wreckage and lists each victim by name.

• *Head a few steps back toward the entrance, then look back at one of the nearby pillars to find a large painting (facing the back of the church).*

Replica of *Last Judgment* Altarpiece: This is a smaller, mustier replica of the exquisite, priceless altarpiece housed in the National Museum. If you're not planning to go see it at the National Museum, you could read the description on page 477 now.

• *Near where you entered are stairs leading to the...*

Church Tower: You can climb 409 steps to burn off some pierogi and earn a grand city view. It's a long hike (and you'll know it—every 10th step is numbered). But because the viewpoint is surrounded by a roof, the views are distant and may not be worth the effort. The first third is up a tight, medieval spiral staircase. Then you'll walk through the eerie, cavernous area between the roof and the ceiling, before huffing up steep concrete steps that surround the square tower (as you spiral up, up, up around the bells). Finally you'll climb a little metal ladder and pop out at the viewpoint.

• *Leaving the church, angle left and continue straight up atmospheric ulica Piwna ("Beer Street") toward the sprightly facade of the armory.*

⑩ The Gdańsk Armory (Zbrojownia)

The 1605 armory, which we saw from a distance at the start of this walk, is one of the best examples of Dutch Renaissance architecture in Europe. Athena, the goddess of war and wisdom, stands in the center, amid motifs of war and ornamental pukers.

• *If you want to make your walk a loop, you're just a block away from where we started (to the left). Or, to continue through the Old Town to the European Solidarity Center's fine museum, follow the second part of this walk, next.*

PART 2: THROUGH THE OLD TOWN TO THE SHIPYARDS

The second part of this walk works its way out of the Main Town and heads into the Old Town, toward Solidarity Square and the shipyards. We'll walk along this street (which changes names a couple of times) nearly all the way. The walk ends at the European Solidarity Center's fine museum. You'll want plenty of time to tour the museum and linger over its exhibits, so if you're already pooped or it's getting late in the day, consider finishing this walk another time.

• *Facing the armory, turn right and head up Kołodziejska, which quickly becomes Węglarska. After two blocks (that is, one block before the big market hall), detour to the right down Świętojańska and use the side door to enter the brick church.*

⓫ St. Nicholas Church (Kościół Św. Mikołaja)

Near the end of World War II, when the Soviet army reached Gdańsk on its march westward, they were given the order to burn all the churches. Only this one survived—because it happened to be dedicated to Russia's patron saint. As the best-preserved church in town, it has a more impressive interior than the others, with lavish black-and-gold Baroque altars.

• *Backtrack out to the main street and continue along it, passing a row of seniors selling their grown and foraged edibles. Immediately after the church is Gdańsk's...*

⓬ Market Hall

Built in 1896 and renovated in 2005, Gdańsk's market hall is fun to explore. Appreciate the delicate steel-and-glass canopy overhead. This is a totally untouristy scene: You'll see everything from skintight *Polska* T-shirts, to wedding gowns, to maternity wear. The meat is downstairs, and the veggies are outside on the adjacent square. As this was once the center of a monastic community, the basement has the graves of medieval Dominican monks, which were exposed when the building was refurbished: Peer over the glass railing, and you'll see some of those scant remains.

Across the street from the Market Hall, a round, red-brick

tower, part of the city's protective wall back in 1400, marks the end of the Main Town and the beginning of the Old Town.

• *Carry on. For an ice cream break, watch on the right (after crossing the street) for the recommended Paolo Gelateria. Another block up the street, on the right, is the huge...*

⓭ St. Catherine's Church (Kościół Św. Katarzyny)

"Katy," as locals call it, is the oldest church in Gdańsk. In May of 2006, a carelessly discarded cigarette caused the church roof to burst into flames. Local people ran into the church and pulled everything outside, so nothing valuable was damaged; even the carillon bells were saved. However, the roof and wooden frame were totally destroyed. The people of Gdańsk were determined to rebuild this important symbol of the city. Within days of the fire, fundraising concerts were held to scrape together most of the money needed to raise the roof once more. Step inside. On the left side of the gate leading to the nave, photos show bomb damage. Farther in, on the left, are vivid photos of the more recent conflagration. The interior is evocative, with still-bare-brick walls that almost seem intentional—as if they're trying for an industrial-mod look.

• *The church hiding a block behind Katy—named for Catherine's daughter Bridget—has important ties to Solidarity and is worth a visit. Go around the right side of Katy and skirt the parking lot to find the entrance, on the side of the church, near the far end.*

⓮ St. Bridget's Church (Kościół Św. Brygidy)

This was the home church of Lech Wałęsa during the tense days of the 1980s. The church and its priest, Henryk Jankowski, were particularly aggressive in supporting the ideals of Solidarity. Jankowski became a mouthpiece for the movement. In gratitude for the church's support, Wałęsa named his youngest daughter Brygida.

Cost and Hours: 4 zł, daily 10:00-18:00.

Visiting the Church: Head inside. For your visit, start at the high altar, then circle clockwise back to the entry.

The enormous, unfinished **high altar** is made entirely of amber—more than a thousand square feet of it. Features that are already in place include the Black Madonna of Częstochowa, a royal Polish eagle, and the Solidarity symbol (tucked below the Black Madonna). The structure, like a scaffold, holds pieces as they are completed and added to the ensemble. The video you may see playing overhead gives you a close-up look at the amber elements.

The wrought-iron gate of the adjacent **Chapel of Fatima** (right of main altar) recalls great battles and events in Polish history from 966 to 1939, with important dates boldly sparkling in gold. Some say the Polish Church is too political. But it was only through a politically engaged Church that this culture survived the Partitions of Poland over a century and a half, plus the brutal antireligious policies of the communist period. The national soul of the Polish people—whether religious or not—is tied up in the Catholic faith.

Henryk Jankowski's tomb—a white marble box with dark-red trim—is along the same wall, but closer to the back of the church. Jankowski was a key figure during Solidarity times; the tomb proclaims him *Kapelan Solidarności* ("Solidarity Chaplain"). But his public standing took a nosedive near the end of his life—thanks to ego-driven projects like his amber altar, as well as accusations of anti-Semitism and corruption. Forced to retire in 2007, Jankowski died in 2010.

In the rear corner, where a figure lies lifeless on the floor under a wall full of wooden crosses, is the tomb of Solidarity martyr **Jerzy Popiełuszko.** A courageous and famously outspoken Warsaw priest, in 1984 Popiełuszko was kidnapped, beaten, and murdered by the communist secret police. Notice that the figure's hands and feet are bound—as his body was found. The crosses on the wall above are historic—each one was carried at various strikes against the communist regime. The communists believed they could break the spirit of the Poles with brutality—like the murder of Popiełuszko. But it only made the rebels stronger and more resolved to ultimately win their freedom.

Under the choir loft, step into the evocative chapel with **memorials** to other 20th-century Polish martyrs.

Near the exit, on a monitor, a fascinating 12-minute **video** shows great moments of this church, with commentary by Lech Wałęsa himself.

• *Return to the main street, turn right, and continue on. The big brick building ahead on the left, with the many windows in its roof, is the Great Mill. Walk past that and look down at the canal that once powered it.*

ⓑ The Great Mill

This huge brick building dates from the 14th century. Look at the waterfalls and imagine standing here in 1400—with the mill's 18 wheels spinning 24/7, powering grindstones that produced 20 tons of flour a day. Like so much else here, the mill survived until 1945. Until recently it housed a shopping mall; now it's slated to be the new home of the Amber Museum (described later).

The **park** just beyond the mill is worth a look. In the distance is the Old City Town Hall (Dutch Renaissance style, from 1595). The monument in the middle honors the 17th-century astronomer Jan Haweliusz. He's looking up at a giant, rust-colored wall with a map of the heavens. Haweliusz built the biggest telescopes of his era to better appreciate and understand the cosmos. Behind the mill stands the miller's home—its opulence indicates that, back in the Middle Ages, there was a lot of money in grinding. Just steps into the family-friendly park is a fountain that brings shrieks of joy to children on hot summer days.

• *To get to the **shipyards**, keep heading straight up Rajska. You'll pass the modern Madison shopping mall. After another long block, jog right, passing to the right of the big, ugly, and green 1970s-era skyscraper. On your right, marked by the famous red logo on the roof, is today's **Solidarity headquarters** (which remains the strongest trade union in Poland, with 700,000 members, and is also active in many other countries). On the corner in front of the Solidarity building, you may see two big chunks of **wall**: a piece of the Berlin Wall and a stretch of the shipyard wall that Lech Wałęsa scaled to get inside and lead the strike. The message: What happened behind one wall eventually led to the fall of the other Wall.*

From here, hike on (about 200 yards) toward the huge, rust-colored building in the distance, angling left to reach the trio of tall, skinny crosses in front of it.

⑩ Solidarity Square and the Shipyards

Three tall crosses mark Solidarity Square and the rust-colored European Solidarity Center (with an excellent museum). For the exciting story of how Polish shipbuilders set in motion events that led to the end of the USSR, turn to page 461.

Sights in Gdańsk

MAIN TOWN (GŁÓWNE MIASTO)

The following sights are all in the Main Town, listed roughly in the order you'll see them on the self-guided walk of the Royal Way.

Museum of Gdańsk

The Museum of Gdańsk has four excellent branches—the Amber Museum, Uphagen House, Main Town Hall, and Artus Court—and a few lesser ones. Along with St. Mary's Church (described earlier), these are the four most important interiors in the Main Town. All have the same hours, but you must buy a separate ticket for each.

Cost and Hours: 12 zł for Amber Museum and Main Town Hall, 10 zł for Uphagen House and Artus Court, likely free Mon in summer and Tue off-season; hours are notoriously changeable, but here's my best guess: May-Sept Mon 10:00-13:00, Tue-Sat until 18:00, Sun 11:00-18:00; Oct-April Tue until 13:00, Wed and Fri-Sun until 16:00, Thu until 18:00, closed Mon.

Information: The museums share a phone number and website (central tel. 58-767-9100, www.muzeumgdansk.pl).

▲Amber Museum (Muzeum Bursztynu)

Housed in a pair of connected brick towers (the former Prison Tower and Torture Chamber) just outside the Main Town's Golden Gate, this museum has two oddly contradictory parts. One shows off Gdańsk's favorite local resource, amber, while the other focuses on implements of torture. You'll follow the one-way route through four exhibits on amber (with lots of stairs), and then walk the rampart to the other tower for a little torture. Note: The amber collection will likely be moved to the Great Mill, perhaps in 2020. For a primer before you visit, read the "All About Amber" sidebar.

Visiting the Museum: The exhibit has four parts: First, head up to the **second floor** for a look at amber in nature. View inclusions (organic items trapped in resin) through a magnifying glass and microscope, and see dozens of samples showing the full rainbow of amber shades. Interactive video screens explain the creation of amber. The **third-floor** exhibit explains amber in culture: the "Amber Route" (the ancient Celtic trade road connecting Gdańsk to Italy) and its medicinal uses. This floor also displays a wide range of functional items made from amber: clocks, pipe stems, candlesticks, chandeliers, jewelry boxes, and much more. Take a whiff—what's that smell? It's a cathedral. Amber is an ingredient in incense. The **fourth floor** shows off more artistic items made of amber: sculptures, candelabras, beer steins, chessboards, and a model ship with delicately carved sails. At the **top floor,** you'll find a modern gallery showing more recent amber craftsmanship and displays about amber's role in fashion today, particularly in jewelry.

Then, walking along the upper rampart level of the courtyard, you'll enter an exhibit about the building itself and the town's fortifications. This leads to the **Prison Tower** and the torture exhib-

All About Amber

Poland's Baltic seaside is known as the Amber Coast. You can see amber *(bursztyn)* in Gdańsk's Amber Museum, in the collection at Malbork Castle (see the Pomerania chapter), and in shop windows everywhere. This fossilized tree resin originated here on the north coast of Poland 40 million years ago. It comes in as many different colors as Eskimos have words for snow: 300 distinct shades, from yellowish white to yellowish black, from opaque to transparent. (I didn't believe it either, until I toured Gdańsk's museum.) Darker-colored amber is generally mixed with ash and sand—making it more fragile, and generally less desirable. Lighter amber is mixed with gasses and air bubbles.

Amber has been popular since long before there were souvenir stands. Archaeologists have found Roman citizens (and their coins) buried with crosses made of amber. Almost 75 percent of the world's amber is mined in northern Poland, and it often simply washes up on the beaches after a winter storm. Some of the elaborate amber sculptures displayed at the museum are joined with "amber glue"—melted-down amber mixed with an adhesive agent. More recently, amber craftsmen are combining amber with silver to create artwork—a method dubbed the "Polish School."

Some Poles believe that, in addition to being good for the economy, amber is good for their health. A traditional cure for arthritis pain is to pour strong vodka over amber, let it set, and then rub it on sore joints. Other remedies call for mixing amber dust with honey or rose oil. It sounds superstitious, but users claim that it works.

it—with sound effects, scant artifacts, and mannequins helpfully demonstrating the grisly equipment.

▲Uphagen House (Dom Uphagena)

This interesting place, at ulica Długa 12, is your chance to glimpse what's behind the colorful facades lining this street. It's the only grand Gdańsk mansion rebuilt as it was before 1945, and it has the typical configuration of three parts: dolled-up visitors' rooms in front, a corridor along the courtyard, and private rooms in the back. The finely decorated salon was used to show off for guests. You'll see several examples of **"Gdańsk-style furniture,"** characterized by three big, round feet along the front, lots of ornamentation, and usually a virtually impossible-to-find lock (sometimes hidden behind a movable decoration). Passing into the dining room, note the knee-high paintings of hunting and celebrations. Along the passage to the back, each room has a theme: butterflies in the smoking room, flowers in the next room, birds in the music room. In the private rooms at the back, the decor is simpler.

Back downstairs, you'll see the rustic working rooms: a humble bedroom, the kitchen, and the pantry. Step out into the courtyard to appreciate how it carves a little fresh air and sunshine out of a densely packed city. Back inside, look for the cross-section model showing the three parts of the house you just walked through. You'll exit through a room with photos of the house before the war, which were used to reconstruct what you see today.

▲▲Main Town Hall (Ratusz Głównego Miasta)

This landmark building contains remarkable decorations from Gdańsk's Golden Age. You can also climb 293 concrete steps to the top of the **tower** for commanding views (5 zł extra, mid-June-mid-Sept only).

Visiting the Main Town Hall: After buying your ticket, walk through the courtyard, then up the stairs to the first historic room. Ogle the finely crafted spiral staircase. The ornately-carved wooden **door,** which we'll pass through in a minute, is all-original, from the 1600s. Above the door are two crosses under a crown. This seal of Gdańsk is being held—as it's often depicted—by a pair of lions. The felines are stubborn and independent, just like the citizens of Gdańsk. The surface of the door is carved with images of crops. Around the frame of the door are mermen, reminding us that this agricultural bounty, like so many of Poland's resources, is transported on the Vistula and out through Gdańsk.

Step into the **Great Weta Hall,** a meeting room with big portraits and big windows. Then go back through the first room and through the ornate door into the **Red Hall,** where the Gdańsk city council met in the summertime. (The lavish fireplace, with another pair of lions holding the coat of arms of Gdańsk, was just for show. There's no chimney.) City council members would sit in the seats around the room, debating city policy. Marvel at the 17th-century inlaid wood panels (just overhead) showing slices of local life. Paintings on the wall above represent the seven virtues that the burghers meeting in this room should possess.

The exquisite ceiling—with 25 paintings in total—is all about theology. Including both Christian and pagan themes, the ceiling was meant to inspire the decision makers in this room to make good choices. Study the oval painting in the middle (from 1607)—

the museum's highlight. It shows the special place Gdańsk occupies between God, Poland, and the rest of the world. In the foreground, the citizens of Gdańsk go about their daily lives. Above them, high atop the arch, God's hand reaches down (from within clouds of Hebrew characters) and grasps the Main Town Hall's steeple. The rainbow arching above also symbolizes God's connection to Gdańsk. Mirroring that is the Vistula River, which begins in the mountains of southern Poland (on the right), runs through the country, and exits at the sea in Gdańsk (on the left, where the rainbow ends).

Continue into the less-impressive **Winter Hall,** with another fireplace (this one actually hooked up to a chimney) and another coat of arms held by lions. Keep going through a few more rooms with historical artifacts. Then head upstairs, past a floor with temporary exhibits. Higher up is a fascinating exhibit about Gdańsk's time as a **"free city"** between the World Wars—when, because of its delicate ethnic mix of Poles and Germans, it was too precarious to assign it to either country. You'll see border checkpoints, uniforms, signs in German (the predominant language of "Danzig"), and reconstructed rooms (homes and shops) from the era. Near the end of this room, you have the option to climb up to the top of the tower. Otherwise, you'll head back out the way you came.

▲▲Artus Court (Dwór Artusa)
In the Middle Ages, Gdańsk was home to many brotherhoods and guilds (like businessmen's clubs). For their meetings, the city provided this elaborately decorated hall, named for King Arthur—a medieval symbol for prestige and power. Just as in King Arthur's Court, this was a place where powerful and important people came together. Of many such halls in Baltic Europe, this is the only original one that survives (in tall, white, triple-

arched building behind Neptune statue at Długi Targ 43). Note: On days when it's free (Mon in summer, Tue in winter), you have to enter at the top and bottom of each hour.

Visiting the Artus Court: In the grand hall, various **cupboards** line the walls. Each organization that met here had a place to keep its important documents and office supplies. Suspended from the ceiling are seven giant **model ships** that depict Baltic vessels, symbolic of the city's connection to the sea.

In the far-back corner is the museum's highlight: a gigantic **stove** decorated with 520 colorful tiles featuring the faces of kings, queens, nobles, mayors, and burghers—a mix of Protestants and Catholics, as a reminder of Gdańsk's religious tolerance. Almost all the tiles are original, having survived WWII bombs.

Notice the huge **paintings** on the walls above, with 3-D animals emerging from flat frames. Hunting is a popular theme in local artwork. Like minting coins, hunting was a privilege usually reserved for royalty, but it was extended in special circumstances to the burghers of special towns...like Gdańsk. These "paintings" are new, digitally generated reproductions of the originals, which were damaged in World War II.

The next room—actually in the next building—is a typical **front room** of the burghers' homes lining ulica Długa. Ogle the gorgeously carved wooden staircase and the Gdańsk-style cupboards.

Other Museums in the Main Town
Historical Zone of the Free City of Gdańsk (Strefa Historyczna Wolne Miasto Gdańsk)

In a city so obsessed with its Golden Age and Solidarity history, this charming little collection illuminates a unique but often-over-looked chapter in the story of Gdańsk: The years between World Wars I and II, when—in an effort to find a workable compromise in this ethnically mixed city—Gdańsk was not part of Germany or Poland, but a self-governing "free city" *(wolne miasto)*. Like a holdover from medieval fiefdoms in modern times, the city-state of Gdańsk even issued its own currency and stamps. This modest museum, up a tight spiral staircase, earnestly shows off artifacts from the time—photos, stamps, currency (the Gulden), maps, flags, promotional tourist leaflets, and other items from the free city, all marked with the Gdańsk symbol of two white crosses under a crown on a red shield. The brochure explains that four out of five people living in the free city identified themselves not as Germans or Poles, but as "Danzigers." While some might find the subject obscure, this endearing collection is a treat for WWII history buffs. Be sure to borrow the English translations at the entrance.

Cost and Hours: 8 zł, Tue-Sun 12:00-18:00, Sept-April until 17:00, closed Mon year-round, down the little alley just in front of the Green Gate at Warzywnicza 10A, tel. 58-320-2828, www.strefahistorycznawmg.pl.

Archaeological Museum (Muzeum Archeologiczne)

This museum is worth a quick peek for those interested in archaeology. Highlights include distinctive urns with cute faces (which date from the Hallstatt Period and were discovered in slate graves around Gdańsk); Bronze and Iron Age tools; before-and-after photos of WWII Gdańsk; and a reconstructed 12th-century Viking-

GDAŃSK & THE TRI-CITY

like Slavonic longboat. You can also climb the building's tower, with good views up Mariacka street toward St. Mary's Church.

Cost and Hours: Museum—8 zł (free on Sat), tower—5 zł; July-Aug Tue-Fri 9:00-17:00, Sat-Sun 10:00-17:00; Sept-June Tue and Thu-Fri 8:00-16:00, Wed 9:00-17:00, Sat-Sun 10:00-16:00; closed Mon year-round; ulica Mariacka 25, tel. 58-322-2100, www.archeologia.pl.

▲National Maritime Museum (Narodowe Muzeum Morskie)

Gdańsk's history and livelihood are tied to the sea. This collection, spread among several buildings on either side of the river, examines all aspects of this connection. Nautical types may get a thrill out of the creaky, sprawling museum, but most visitors find it little more than a convenient way to pass some time and enjoy a cruise across the river. The museum's lack of English information is frustrating; fortunately, some exhibits have descriptions you can borrow.

Cost and Hours: Each part of the museum has its own admission (6-8 zł; ask about combo-tickets). The Maritime Cultural Center is worth neither the time nor the money for grown-ups. The hours fluctuate, but it's usually open July-Aug daily 10:00-18:00; Sept-Oct and March-June Tue-Sun until 16:00, closed Mon; Nov-Feb Tue-Sun until 15:00, closed Mon; ulica Ołowianka 9, tel. 58-301-8611, www.nmm.pl.

Visiting the Museum: The exhibit has four parts. The first two parts—the crane and the Maritime Cultural Center—are on the Main Town side of the river. The landmark medieval **crane** (żuraw), Gdańsk's most important symbol, houses a humble exhibit on living in the city during its Golden Age (16th-17th centuries). For more on the crane itself, see page 447.

The **Maritime Cultural Center,** a modern exhibit right next door to the crane, is not worth the exercise unless you are leading a school group. For adults, the most interesting part is "Working Boats," on the second floor.

The rest of the museum—the Old Granaries and the *Sołdek* steamship—is across the river on Ołowianka Island, which you can reach via the little **ferry** (named the *Motława*, like the river; 1.50 zł one-way). The ferry runs about every 15 minutes in peak season (during museum hours only), less frequently in shoulder season, and not at all in the winter.

Once on the island, visit the three rebuilt **Old Granaries** (Spichlerze). These make up the heart of the exhibit, tracing the history of Gdańsk—particularly as it relates to the sea—from pre-

historic days to the present. Models of the town and region help put things in perspective. Other exhibits cover underwater exploration, navigational aids, artifacts of the Polish seafaring tradition, peeka-boo cross-sections of multilevel ships, and models of the modern-day shipyard where Solidarity was born. This place is home to more miniature ships than you ever thought you'd see, and the Nautical Gallery upstairs features endless rooms with paintings of boats.

Finally, crawl through the holds and scramble across the deck of a decommissioned steamship called the *Sołdek*, docked per-manently across from the crane (ship generally closed in winter). This was the first postwar vessel built at the Gdańsk shipyard. Below decks, you can see where the crew shoveled the coal; wander through a maze of pipes, gears, valves, gauges, and ladders; and visit the rooms where the sailors lived, slept, and ate. You can even play captain on the bridge.

SOLIDARITY AND THE GDAŃSK SHIPYARD

Gdańsk's single most memorable experience is exploring the ship-yard (Stocznia Gdańska) that witnessed the beginning of the end of communism's stranglehold on Eastern Europe. Taken together, the sights in this area are worth ▲▲▲. Here in the former industrial wasteland that Lech Wałęsa called the "cradle of freedom," this evocative site tells the story of the brave Polish shipyard workers who took on—and ultimately defeated—an Evil Empire. A visit to the Solidarity (Solidarność) sights has two main parts: Solidarity Square (with the memorial and gate in front of the shipyard), and the outstanding museum inside the European Solidarity Center.

Getting to the Shipyard: These sights cluster around Solidar-ity Square (Plac Solidarności), at the north end of the Old Town, about a 20-minute walk from the Royal Way. For the most interest-ing approach, follow Part 2 of my self-guided walk (earlier), which ends here. Or take tram #7 or #8 from the Brama Wyżynna stop (near the Upland Gate) or the train station to the Plac Solidarnośći stop.

Background: After the communists took over Eastern Eu-rope at the end of World War II, oppressed peoples throughout the Soviet Bloc rose up in different ways. The most dramatic upris-ings—Hungary's 1956 Uprising (see page 582) and Czechoslova-kia's 1968 "Prague Spring" (see page 81)—were brutally crushed under the treads of Soviet tanks. The formula for freedom that fi-nally succeeded was a patient, nearly decade-long series of strikes and protests spearheaded by Lech Wałęsa and his trade union, called Solidarność—"Solidarity." (The movement also benefited from good timing, as it coincided with the *perestroika* and *glasnost* policies of Soviet premier Mikhail Gorbachev.) While politicians tussled from their plush offices, imagine the courage it took for

Wałęsa and his fellow workers to fight communism on the front lines—armed with nothing more than guts.

Solidarity Square (Plac Solidarności) and the Monument of the Fallen Shipyard Workers

The seeds of August 1980 were sown a decade before. Since becoming part of the Soviet Bloc, the Poles staged frequent strikes, protests, and uprisings to secure their rights, all of which were put down by the regime. But the bloodiest of these took place in December of 1970—a tragic event memorialized by the **three-crosses monument** that towers over what's now called Solidarity Square.

The 1970 strike was prompted by price hikes. The communist government set the prices for all products. As Poland endured drastic food shortages in the 1960s and 1970s, the regime frequently announced what it called "regulation of prices." Invariably, this meant an increase in the cost of essential foodstuffs. (To be able to claim "regulation" rather than "increase," the regime would symbolically lower prices for a few select items—but these were always nonessential luxuries, such as elevators and TV sets, which nobody could afford anyway.) The regime was usually smart enough to raise prices on January 1, when the people were fat and happy after Christmas, and too hungover to complain. But on December 12, 1970, bolstered by an ego-stoking visit by West German Chancellor Willy Brandt, Polish premier Władysław Gomułka increased prices. The people of Poland—who cared more about the price of Christmas dinner than relations with Germany—struck back.

A wave of strikes and sit-ins spread along the heavily industrialized north coast of Poland, most notably in Gdańsk, Gdynia, and Szczecin. Thousands of angry demonstrators poured through the gate of this shipyard, marched into town, and set fire to the Communist Party Committee building. In an attempt to quell the riots, the government-run radio implored the people to go back to work. On the morning of December 17, workers showed up at shipyard gates across northern Poland, and were greeted by the army and police. Without provocation, the Polish army opened fire on the workers. While the official death toll for the massacre stands at 44, others say the true number is much higher. The monument, with a trio of 140-foot-tall crosses, honors those lost to the regime that December.

Go to the middle of the **wall** behind the crosses, to the monument of the worker wearing a flimsy plastic work helmet, attempting to shield himself from bullets. Behind him is a list—pock-marked with symbolic bullet holes—of workers murdered on that day. *Lat* means "years old"—many teenagers were among the dead. The quote at the top of the wall is from St. John Paul II, who was elected pope eight years after this tragedy. The pope was known for his clever way with words, and this very carefully phrased quote—which served as an inspiration to the Poles during their darkest hours—skewers the regime in a way subtle enough to still be tolerated: "Let thy spirit descend, and renew the face of the earth—of *this* earth" (that is, Poland).

Stretching to the left of this center wall are plaques representing labor unions from around Poland—and around the world (look for the Chinese characters)—expressing solidarity with these workers. To the right is an enormous Bible verse: "May the Lord give strength to his people. May the Lord bless his people with the gift of peace" (Psalms 29:11).

Inspired by the brave sacrifice of their true comrades, shipyard workers rose up here in August of 1980, formulating the **"21 Points"** of a new union called Solidarity. Their demands included the right to strike and form unions, the freeing of political prisoners, and an increase in wages. The 21 Points are listed in Polish on the panel at the far end of the right wall, marked *21 X TAK* ("21 times yes"). An unwritten precondition to any agreement was the right for the workers of 1980 to build a memorial to their comrades slain in 1970. The government agreed, marking the first time a communist regime ever allowed a monument to be built to honor its own victims. Wałęsa called it a harpoon in the heart of the communists. The towering monument, with three crucified anchors on top, was designed, engineered, and built by shipyard workers. The monument was finished just four months after the historic agreement was signed.

• *Now continue to the gate and peer through into the birthplace of Eastern European freedom.*

Gdańsk Shipyard (Stocznia Gdańska) Gate #2

When a Pole named Karol Wojtyła was elected pope in 1978—and visited his homeland in 1979—he inspired his 40 million countrymen to believe that im-possible dreams can come true. Prices continued to go up, and the workers continued to rise up. By the summer of 1980, it was clear that the dam was about to break.

In August, Anna

Lech Wałęsa

In 1980, the world was turned on its ear by a walrus-mustachioed shipyard electrician. Within three years, this seemingly run-of-the-mill Pole had precipitated the collapse of communism, led a massive 10-million-member trade union with enormous political impact, been named *Time* magazine's Man of the Year, and won a Nobel Peace Prize.

Lech Wałęsa was born in Popowo, Poland in 1943. After working as a car mechanic and serving two years in the army, he became an electrician at the Gdańsk Shipyard in 1967. Like many Poles, Wałęsa felt stifled by the communist government, and was infuriated that a system that was supposed to be for the workers clearly wasn't serving them.

When the shipyard massacre took place in December of 1970 (see page 462), Wałęsa was at the forefront of the protests. He was marked as a dissident, and in 1976, he was fired. Wałęsa hopped from job to job and was occasionally unemployed—under communism, a rock-bottom status reserved for only the most despicable derelicts. But he soldiered on, fighting for the creation of a trade union and building up quite a file with the secret police.

In August 1980, Wałęsa heard news of the beginnings of the Gdańsk strike and raced to the shipyard. In an act that has since become the stuff of legend, Wałęsa scaled the shipyard wall to get inside.

Before long, Wałęsa's dynamic personality won him the unofficial role of the workers' leader and spokesman. He negotiated with the regime to hash out the August Agreements, becoming a rock star-type hero during the so-called 16 Months of Hope... until martial law came crashing down in December 1981. Wałęsa was arrested and interned for 11 months in a country house. After

Walentynowicz—a Gdańsk crane operator and known dissident—was fired unceremoniously just short of her retirement. This sparked a strike in the Gdańsk Shipyard (then called the Lenin Shipyard) on August 14, 1980. An electrician named Lech Wałęsa had been fired as an agitator years before. But on hearing news of the strike, Wałęsa went to the shipyard and climbed over the wall to get inside. The strike now had a leader.

These were not soldiers, nor were they idealistic flower children. The strike participants were gritty, salt-of-the-earth manual laborers: forklift operators, welders, electricians, machinists. Imagine being one of the 16,000 workers who stayed here for 18 days

being released, he continued to struggle underground, becoming a symbol of anticommunist sentiment.

Finally, the dedication of Wałęsa and Solidarity paid off, and Polish communism dissolved—with Wałęsa rising from the ashes as the country's first postcommunist president. But the skills that made Wałęsa a rousing success at leading an uprising didn't translate well to the president's office. Wałęsa proved to be a stubborn, headstrong politician, frequently clashing with the parliament. He squabbled with his own party, declaring a "war at the top" of Solidarity and rotating higher-ups to prevent corruption and keep the party fresh. He also didn't choose his advisors well, enlisting old friends as staffers who wound up immersed in scandal. His overconfidence was his Achilles' heel, and his governing style verged on authoritarian.

Unrefined and none too interested in scripted speeches, Wałęsa was a simple man who preferred playing ping-pong with his buddies to attending formal state functions. Though lacking a formal education, Wałęsa had unsurpassed drive and charisma... but that's not enough to lead a country—especially during an impossibly complicated, fast-changing time.

Wałęsa was defeated at the polls, by the Poles, in 1995, and when he ran again in 2000, he received a humiliating one percent of the vote. Since leaving office, Wałęsa has kept a lower profile, but still delivers speeches worldwide. Many poor Poles grumble that Lech, who started life simple like them, has forgotten the little people. But his fans point out that he gives much of his income to charity. And on his lapel, he still always wears a pin featuring the Black Madonna of Częstochowa—the most important symbol of Polish Catholicism.

Poles say there are at least two Lech Wałęsas: the young, bombastic, working-class idealist Lech, at the forefront of the Solidarity strikes, who will always have a special place in their hearts; and the failed President Wałęsa, who got in over his head and tarnished his legacy.

during the strike—hungry, cold, sleeping on sheets of Styrofoam, inspired by the new Polish pope, excited about finally standing up to the regime...and terrified that at any moment you might be gunned down, like your friends had been a decade before.

Workers, afraid to leave the shipyard, communicated with the outside world through this gate—wives and brothers showed up here and asked for a loved one, and those inside spread the word until the striker came forward. Occasionally, a truck pulled up inside the gate, with Lech Wałęsa standing atop its cab with a megaphone. Facing the thousands of people assembled outside the gate, Wałęsa gave progress reports on the negotiations and pleaded for supplies. The people of Gdańsk responded, bringing armfuls of bread and other food to keep the workers going. Solidarity.

During the strike, two items hung on the fence. One of them (which still hangs there today) was a picture of Pope John Paul II—a reminder to believe in your dreams and have faith in God (for more on the Pope and his role in Solidarity, see page 260). The other item was a makeshift list of the strikers' 21 Points—demands scrawled in red paint and black pencil on pieces of plywood.

• *Walk through the passage at the right end of the gate and enter the former shipyard.*

There's not much to see today, but during its peak from 1948 to 1990, the **shipyard** churned out over a thousand ships and employed 16,000 workers. About 60 percent of these ships were exported to the USSR—and so, when the Soviet Bloc broke apart in the 1990s, they lost a huge market. Today the facilities employ closer to 1,200 workers...who now make windmills.

Before entering the museum, take a look around. This part of the shipyard, long abandoned, is slated for redevelopment into a **"Young City"** (Młode Miasto)—envisioned as a new city center for Gdańsk, with shopping, restaurants, offices, and homes. Rusting shipbuilding equipment is being torn down, and old brick buildings are being converted into gentrified flats. The nearby boulevard called Nowa Wałowa will be the spine connecting this area to the rest of the city. Farther east, plans call for the harborfront to be rejuvenated, creating a glitzy marina and extending the city's delightful waterfront people zone to the north (see www.ycgdansk.com). Fortunately, the shipyard gate, monument, and other important sites from the Solidarity strikes—now considered historical monuments—will remain.

• *The massive, rust-colored European Solidarity Center, which faces Solidarity Square, houses the museum where we'll learn the rest of the story.*

▲▲▲European Solidarity Center (Europejskie Centrum Solidarności)

Europe's single best sight about the end of communism is made even more powerful by its location: in the very heart of the place where those events occurred. Filling just one small corner of a huge, purpose-built educational facility, the permanent exhibition uses larger-than-life photographs, archival footage, actual artifacts, interactive touchscreens, and a state-of-the-art audioguide to eloquently tell the story of the end of Eastern European communism.

Cost and Hours: 20 zł, includes audioguide; May-Sept Mon–Fri 10:00–19:00, Sat–Sun until 20:00; Oct–April Mon and Wed–Fri 10:00–17:00, Sat–Sun until 18:00, closed Tue; last entry one hour before closing, Plac Solidarności 1, tel. 58-772-4000, www.ecs.gda.pl.

◆ Self-Guided Tour: First, appreciate the architecture of the **building** itself. From the outside, it's designed to resemble the rusted hull of a giant ship—seemingly gloomy and depressing. But step inside to find an interior flooded with light, which cultivates a surprising variety of life—in the form of lush gardens that make the place feel like a very expensive greenhouse. You can interpret this symbolism a number of ways: Something that seems dull and dreary from the outside (the Soviet Bloc, the shipyards themselves, what have you) can be full of brightness, life, and optimism inside.

In the lobby, buy your ticket and pick up the essential, included audioguide. The exhibit has much to see, and some of it is arranged in a conceptual way that can be tricky to understand without a full grasp of the history. I've outlined the basics in this self-guided tour, but the audioguide can illuminate more details—including translations of films and eyewitness testimony from participants in the history.

• *The permanent exhibit fills seven lettered rooms—each with its own theme—on two floors. From the lush lobby, head up the escalator and into...*

The Birth of Solidarity (Room A): This room picks up right in the middle of the dynamic story we just learned out on the square. It's August of 1980, and the shipyard workers are rising up. You step straight into a busy shipyard: punch clocks, workers' lockers, and—up on the ceiling—hundreds of plastic helmets. A big **map** in the middle of the room shows the extent of the shipyard in 1980. Nearby stands a **truck;** Lech Wałęsa would stand on top of the cab of a truck like this one to address the nervous locals who had amassed outside the shipyard gate, awaiting further news.

In the middle of the room, carefully protected under glass, are those original **plywood panels** onto which the strikers scrawled their 21 demands, then lashed to the gate. Just beyond that, a giant video screen and a map illustrate how the strikes that began here spread like a virus across Poland. At the far end of the room, behind the partition, stand **two tables** that were used during the talks to end the strikes (each one with several actual items from that era, under glass).

After 18 days of protests, the communist authorities finally agreed to negotiate. On the afternoon of August 31, 1980, the Governmental Commission and the Inter-Factory Strike Committee (MKS) came together and signed the August Agreements, which legalized Solidarity—the first time any communist government permitted a workers' union. As Lech Wałęsa sat at a big table and signed the agreement, other union reps tape-recorded the proceedings and played them later at their own factories to prove that the unthinkable had happened. Take a moment to linger over the rousing **film** that plays on the far wall, which begins with the strike, carries through with the tense negotiations that a brash young Lech Wałęsa held with the authorities, and ends with the triumphant acceptance of the strikers' demands. Lech Wałęsa rides on the shoulders of well-wishers out to the gate to spread the good news. The gate opens, the strikers file out, and the crowd cheers: "Leszek! Leszek!" (Lech-y! Lech-y!)

• *Back by the original 21 demands, enter the next exhibit...*

The Power of the Powerless (Room B): This section traces the roots of the 1980 strikes, which were preceded by several far less successful protests. It all begins with a kiss: a giant photograph of Russian premier Leonid Brezhnev mouth-kissing the Polish premier Edward Gierek, with the caption **"Brotherly Friendship."** Soviet premiers and their satellite leaders really did greet each other "in the French manner," as a symbolic gesture of their communist brotherhood.

Working your way through the exhibit, you'll see the door to a **prison cell**—a reminder of the intimidation tactics used by the Soviets in the 1940s and 1950s to deal with their opponents as they exerted their rule over the lands they had liberated from the Nazis.

The typical **communist-era apartment** is painfully humble. After the war, much of Poland had been destroyed, and population shifts led to housing shortages. People had to make do with tiny spaces and ramshackle furnishings. Communist propaganda blares from both the radio and the TV.

A map shows **"red Europe"** (the USSR plus the satellites of Poland, Czechoslovakia, Hungary, and East Germany), and a **timeline** traces some of the smaller Soviet Bloc protests that led up to Solidarity: in East Germany in 1953, in Budapest and Poznań in 1956, the "Prague Spring" of 1968, and other 1968 protests in Poland.

In the wake of these uprisings, the communist authorities cracked down even harder. Peek into the **interrogation room,** with a wall of file cabinets and a lowly stool illuminated by a bright spotlight. (Notice that the white Polish eagle on the seal above the desk is missing its golden crown—during communism, the Poles were allowed to keep the eagle, but its crown was removed.)

The next exhibit presents a day-by-day rundown of the **1970 strikes,** from December 14 to 22, which resulted in the massacre of the workers who are honored by the monument in front of this building. In the glass case, the leather jacket with bullet holes was worn by a 20-year-old worker who was killed that day. A wall of mug shots gives way to exhibits chronicling the steady rise of dissent groups through the 1970s, culminating in the June 1976 protests in the city of Radom (prompted, like so many other uprisings, by unilateral price hikes). On your way out of this section, you pass through a mock-up of a grocery store from the period...with empty shelves.

• *Loop back through Room A, and proceed straight ahead into...*

Solidarity and Hope (Room C): While the government didn't take the August Agreements very seriously, the Poles did...and before long, 10 million of them—one out of every four, or effectively half the nation's workforce—joined Solidarity. So began what's often called the **"16 Months of Hope."** Newly legal, Solidarity continued to stage strikes and make its opposition known. Slick Solidarity posters and children's art convey the childlike enthusiasm with which the Poles seized their hard-won kernels of freedom. The communist authorities' hold on the Polish people began to slip. Support and aid from the outside world poured in, but the rest of the Soviet Bloc looked on nervously, and the Warsaw Pact army assembled at the Polish border and glared at the uprisers. The threat of invasion hung heavy in the air.

• *Exiting this room, head up the staircase and into...*

At War with Society (Room D): In this black room, you're greeted by a wall of TV screens delivering a stern message. On Sunday morning, December 13, 1981, the Polish head of state, **General Wojciech Jaruzelski**—wearing his trademark dark glasses—appeared on national TV and announced the introduction of **martial law.** Solidarity was outlawed, and its leaders were arrested. Frightened Poles heard the announcement and looked out their windows to see Polish Army tanks rumbling through the snowy streets. (On the opposite wall, see footage of tanks and heavily armed soldiers intimidating their countrymen into compliance.) Jaruzelski claimed that he imposed martial law to prevent the Soviets from invading. Today, many historians question whether martial law was really necessary, though Jaruzelski remained unremorseful through his death in 2014.

Continuing deeper into the exhibit, you come to a **prisoner transport.** Climb up inside to watch chilling scenes of riots, demonstrations, and crackdowns by the ZOMO riot police. In one gruesome scene, a demonstrator is quite intentionally run over by a truck. From here, pass through a gauntlet of *milicja* riot-gear shields to see the truck crashing through a gate. Overhead are the uniforms of miners from the **Wujek mine** who were massacred on December 16, 1981 (their names are projected on the pile of coal below).

Martial law was a tragic, terrifying, and bleak time for the Polish people. It didn't, however, kill the Solidarity movement, which continued its fight after going underground. Passing prison cells, you'll see a wall plastered with handmade, underground posters and graffiti. Notice how in this era, **Solidarity propaganda** is much more primitive; circle around the other side of the wall to see several presses that were actually used in clandestine Solidarity print shops during this time. The outside world sent messages of support as well as supplies—represented by the big wall of cardboard boxes. This approval also came in the form of a Nobel Peace Prize for Lech Wałęsa in 1983; you'll see video clips of his wife accepting the award on his behalf (Wałęsa feared that if he traveled abroad to claim it, he would not be allowed back into the country). On the other side of the room is an exhibit about Pope John Paul II's visit in the very tense days of 1983.

• *But even in these darkest days, there were glimmers of hope. Enter...*

The Road to Democracy (Room E): By the time the Pope visited his homeland again in 1987, martial law had finally been lifted, and Solidarity—still technically illegal—was gaining momentum, gradually pecking away at the communists. Step into the small inner room with footage of the **Pope's third pilgrimage** to his homeland in 1987, by which time (thanks in no small part to his inspirational role in the ongoing revolution) the tide was turning.

Step into the room with the big, white **roundtable.** With the moral support of the pope and the entire Western world, the brave Poles were the first European country to throw off the shackles of communism when, in the spring of 1989, the "Roundtable Talks" led to the opening up of elections. The government arrogantly called for parliamentary elections, reserving 65 percent of seats for themselves.

In the next room, you can see Solidarity's strategy in those **elections:** On the right wall are posters showing Lech Wałęsa with each candidate. Another popular "get out the vote" measure was the huge poster of Gary Cooper—an icon of America, which the Poles deeply respect and viewed as their friendly cousin across the Atlantic—except that, instead of a pistol, he's packing a ballot. Rousing reminders like this inspired huge voter turnout. The communists' plan backfired, as virtually every open seat went to Solidarity. It was the first time ever that opposition candidates had taken office in the Soviet Bloc. On the wall straight ahead, flashing a V-for-*wiktoria* sign, is a huge photo of Tadeusz Mazowiecki—an early leader of Solidarity, who became prime minister on June 4, 1989.

• *For the glorious aftermath, head into the final room.*

The Triumph of Freedom (Room F): This room is dominated by a gigantic **map of Eastern Europe.** A countdown clock on the right ticks off the departure of each country from communist clutches, as the Soviet Bloc "decomposes." You'll see how the success of Solidarity in Poland—and the ragtag determination of a scruffy band of shipyard workers right here in Gdańsk—inspired people all over Eastern Europe. By the winter of 1989, the Hungarians had opened their borders, the Berlin Wall had crumbled, and the Czechs and Slovaks had staged their Velvet Revolution. (Small viewing stations that circle the room reveal the detailed story for each country's own road to freedom.) Lech Wałęsa—the shipyard electrician who started it all by jumping over a wall—became the first president of postcommunist Poland. And a year later, in Poland's first true elections since World War II, 29 different parties won seats in the parliament. It was a free-election free-for-all.

In the middle of the room stands a white wall with **inspirational quotes** from St. John Paul II and Václav Havel—the Czech poet-turned-protester-turned-prisoner-turned-president—which are repeated in several languages. On the huge wall, the **Solidarity "graffiti"** is actually made up of thousands of little notes left behind by visitors to the museum. Feel free to grab a piece of paper and a pen and record your own reflections.

• *Finally, head downstairs into a peaceful space.*

Culture of Peaceful Change (Room G): Many visitors find that touring this museum—with vivid reminders of a dramatic and pivotal moment in history that took place in their own lifetimes and was brought about not by armies or presidents, but by everyday people—puts them in an emotional state of mind. Designed for silent reflection, this room overlooks the monument to those workers who were gunned down in 1970. It shows footage of Pope John Paul II, Lech Wałęsa, Martin Luther King Jr., and others who dedicated their lives to peaceful change.

• *For an epilogue, continue deeper into the former shipyard to see one more important landmark from 1980. Exit the building the way you came in, and turn left. The path leads to a low-profile, red-brick building about 80 yards ahead, the...*

▲Sala BHP

This is the building where the communists sat down across the table from Lech Wałęsa and his team and worked out a compromise (as seen in the videos inside the European Solidarity Center). Entering, turn left into the Small Hall to view a series of photos that illustrate Solidarity history; these are all the more poignant because they lack the bombastic presentation of the glitzy museum. The images speak for themselves. The other side of the building (right from the entrance) is the actual hall where those fateful meetings took place, with a long table set up on the stage. You'll see a model of the shipyard, circa 1980, and models of the various ships that were built here.

GDAŃSK & THE TRI-CITY

Cost and Hours: Free, daily 10:00-18:00, Oct-April until 16:00, www.salabhp.pl.

NORTH OF THE MAIN TOWN
▲▲Museum of the Second World War (Muzeum II Wojny Światowej)

In 2017, Poland's definitive WWII museum opened in a state-of-the-art, purpose-build facility a 10-minute walk north of Gdańsk's Main Town. It uses artifacts, creative design, insightful storytelling, and ample archival footage to tell the story of the war that began right at Gdańsk's doorstep—focusing on the Polish experience, but also expanding its focus to other aspects of the conflict. At more than 50,000 square feet, it's one of the biggest historical exhibits in the world. (Pace yourself.) While those with a limited appetite for history may find it overwhelming, even those with a casual interest will be glad they invested two or three hours touring its exhibits.

As impressive as the museum is, it could have been that much better. The original design presented an ambitiously global, yet personal, perspective on the war—carefully calibrated to be even-handed and international in its outlook. But as it neared completion, ruling politicians from the nationalistic Law and Justice Party deemed it too pacifistic and "not Polish enough." They replaced the museum director and his staff, and hired a

new director who changed several exhibits to be more singularly patriotic—playing up the "martyrdom" aspect of Poland's role in the war. In the end, it's sad to think that this museum could have been Europe's best WWII museum—if only trained historians had been allowed to control it, rather than politicians. For that reason, I rate it ▲▲ rather than ▲▲▲.

Cost and Hours: 23 zł, essential audioguide-5 zł; June-Sept Tue 10:00-19:00, Wed-Sun 10:00-20:00; Oct-May Tue-Fri until 19:00, Sat-Sun until 20:00; closed Mon year-round; Plac Władysława Bartoszewskiego 1, tel. 58-760-0960, www.muzeum1939.pl.

Getting There: It's a short walk north of the historical center. The most appealing approach is to walk north along the riverfront promenade all the way to its end; you'll see the giant, rust-red, glassy tower on your left.

Visiting the Museum: As you approach, appreciate the symbolic architecture of the site. The ground level—nicely landscaped, with inviting slingback chairs in the summer—represents the present. The museum's exhibit space is entirely underground—representing the past. And the tower rising above represents the future. All of the buildings are clad in rusted steel—the material of choice in this shipbuilding city.

Head down the stairs at the base of the tower, go inside, and take the elevator down to level -3. This area has ticket desks, a cloakroom, WCs, a **$** bistro, a shop, a cinema, temporary exhibits, and the entrance to the permanent exhibition. When you buy your ticket, spring for the audioguide, which helpfully navigates the highlights of the sprawling exhibits and translates some of the films. It's geo-tagged, so it knows where you are and informs you accordingly.

Head through the turnstile. A long **corridor** stretches to your right; 18 clearly numbered exhibition halls weave in and out of this corridor, chronologically telling the story. As you crisscross through the corridor, take a moment to ponder its exhibits about everyday life in wartime, covering such topics as food and cooking, fashion and style, the black market, travel, and music.

Before heading into the main exhibition, consider turning left, into the **Time Travel** exhibit. Designed for Polish kids, it follows two children and their everyday life, before, during, and after the war—with the same apartment re-created for each time period.

The first part of the exhibit is straight ahead from the entrance turnstile: A movie that sets the stage by recapping the events of World War I and the interwar period.

Now proceed down the corridor and work your way chronologically through the numbered exhibits. Section **01** traces the rise of communism in the Soviet Union (the quern stone was used for grinding grain by ethnic Poles in Ukraine, many of whom perished under Stalin's policies); Fascism in Italy (the Fiat embodies the populism—a car in every driveway—that drove Mussolini's propaganda); and Nazism in Germany (with a bust and posters of Hitler, some hateful anti-Semitic propaganda, and a clip from Leni Riefenstahl's *Triumph of the Will*).

Section **02** is a reconstructed Polish street from the interwar period. (Remember this—you'll see it again later.) The nearby hallway outlines the rise of imperialism in Japan, Franco's ascent in Spain, and Germany's dismantling of the Versailles system that ended the conflict of World War I. Gdańsk—then called Danzig—held a unique position: It was a

free city, with Germany on one side and Poland on the other. As Hitler rose, Western Europeans already knew that Danzig would be a bulwark against his aggression—giving rise to the slogan "Die for Danzig." You'll see a replica of the secret Molotov-Ribbentrop Pact between the USSR and Nazi Germany, agreeing to divide Poland down the middle—and clearing the way for invasion.

In section **03,** you'll learn how that invasion took place on September 1, 1939, when Hitler invaded Poland (en route to Danzig) and quickly overran the country—the first use of his relentless Blitzkrieg ("Lightning War") strategy. One exhibit explains the first volley of that war, in which 200 Poles defended the military transit depot Westerplatte against 3,000 Nazi troops for seven days. You'll learn about the brutal Nazi atrocities from that first invasion, including photos of bombed-out cities. One of the museum's highlights is the film *Siege,* shot and narrated by American correspondent Julien Bryan, who was in Warsaw during the invasion and witnessed the Nazis bombarding a church during Mass, the bombing of a maternity ward, and a village of peasants machine-gunned from the air while digging up potatoes. You'll learn how soon, the Soviet Union also invaded (per their secret agreement)—meeting the Nazis in the middle and splitting Poland in half.

Across the main corridor, section **04** outlines Soviet conquests in other parts of Europe (Finland, the Baltic states, Romania). Section **05** (with a JU-87 dive bomber suspended from the wall) explains how this was a new kind of war, relying heavily on air warfare (Hitler's Luftwaffe).

Back across the corridor, section **06** documents the ruthlessness of the Nazis, including their starvation of Soviet POWs (the "Hunger Plan" that killed more than three million captured troops); the 871-day Siege of Leningrad (today's St. Petersburg, where one million civilians starved to death); and air raids that killed another one million civilians.

Across the corridor, section **07** considers how totalitarian regimes recruited collaborators in the countries they occupied—employing methods from propaganda to intimidation. You'll see a replica of a "Red Corner"—a workers' meeting hall, draped in communist propaganda, that you'd find in any workplace or institution. A film on Soviet propaganda methods explains Stalin's philosophy of "national in form, Soviet in content"—appropriating locally beloved symbols, but infusing them with a communist agenda.

At section **08,** giant letters spell out TERROR. This ex-

hibit explains how totalitarian regimes rounded up and executed elites (such as the USSR's Katyń Massacre of Polish intelligentsia, close to the heart of every Pole). The room with a vast map on the floor illustrates forced resettlement; the doors lining the walls have exhibits explaining specific examples. You'll learn how heavily the occupying forces relied on forced labor—essentially exploiting 20 million slaves—including workers here in Gdańsk (the metal plates on the walls were used to keep track of workers). This section also has a powerful exhibit on daily life in Nazi concentration camps, with many powerful objects: striped uniforms and wooden clogs; a homemade nativity scene and tiny figures carved from a toothbrush by prisoners; a violin; and a baby's christening gown. You'll also see a wheelchair from a psychiatric hospital near Gdańsk. All of its inmates were executed.

Section **09** explores the methodical implementation of the Holocaust, including a train car used to transport prisoners. A

wall of suitcases is a re-minder of how prisoners were stripped of belong-ings on arrival. You'll walk through a room displaying photographs of hundreds of Holocaust victims. Sec-tion **10** considers other in-stances of ethnic cleansing during World War II, in-cluding Serbs killed in the Nazi puppet state of Croatia, and Poles killed in Ukraine.

Section **11**—with the giant letters *OPÓR* ("Resistance")—explains the various ways that occupied peoples rose up. Poland maintained a government in exile, and a military that participated in Allied offensives (Poles were the first to reach the top of Monte Cassino in Italy)—essentially a continuation of prewar statehood, despite occupation. You'll learn both about civilian resistance movements, and partisan fighting forces on the battlefields (such as Tito's Partisans in Yugoslavia). This section also honors various uprisings against totalitarian regimes.

Section **12** features the clandestine front—spies, espionage, and the battle over secrets. In a room with an actual Enigma ma-chine, you'll learn how it was Polish mathematicians who first broke the Nazis' secret code...then furnished that breakthrough to the British. Today, Alan Turing and the other codebreakers at Britain's Bletchley Park get virtually all of the credit for the tens of thousands of lives that were saved. (Many Poles believe that the breaking of the Enigma code was Poland's single most important contribution to winning the war.)

Section **13** considers the ways that countries mobilize—economically and societally—in times of war. Wartime brought about such innovations as the jet engine, the computer, and the nuclear bomb. While the Nazis relied on slave labor to build armaments, the Allies mobilized female citizens...and outproduced their enemies three-to-one. In this section, you'll see a Sherman Firefly tank (built in the UK).

Section **14** explains how the tide of war turned toward the Allies, while section **15** considers the postwar reality—which was cooked up even before Hitler was dead, when Churchill, FDR, and Stalin met in Yalta, agreeing to divvy up Europe after their victory. (Many Poles still consider this a betrayal: After their suffering and valiant contributions, they were effectively left to the whim of the USSR after the war.) The postwar period was bittersweet: victory parades celebrating the defeat of evil, but also a Poland left in ruins, the rise of a ruthless Soviet empire in Eastern Europe, and a series of forced population resettlements (to match the new borders) that uprooted millions.

Section **16** shows the same city street we saw earlier—but now in ruins, presided over by a Soviet tank. A mockup of a courtroom considers both the triumphs and the failings of the postwar justice system: Yes, high-profile war criminals were prosecuted. But the overflowing file cabinet on the dark side of the room is a reminder of the many lower-level war criminals who were never brought to justice.

Cross the destroyed street to section **17,** with photos of cities that were left in ruins at war's end, and section **18,** divided by a symbolic "Iron Curtain"—a reminder that World War II was only the beginning of a painful chapter for Poland and all of Eastern Europe.

Just before you exit, playing overhead is a cheaply produced, rabble-rousing, nakedly patriotic **movie**...a sad reminder of the way a wonderful museum was mucked up by politics. (Before the right-wing government fired the museum director, this film was very different—ending the exhibit on a pensive note rather than a nationalistic one.)

Despite its shortcomings, the Museum of the Second World War is a powerful and comprehensive look at the most devastating conflict in human history, from the perspective of the country that was perhaps the most devastated by it.

Nearby: A short walk over a canal (across the Więcierze Bridge) from the museum is the **Polish Post Office of Danzig**

(on plac Obrońców Poczty Polskiej). History buffs recognize this landmark as part of the initial Nazi attacks on September 1, 1939, which began World War II. The post office—which was a nerve center for local Polish intelligence officers—was attacked by Nazi forces and defended by Polish officers. After 15 hours of fighting, everyone inside was dead or had fled; those who escaped were later executed. Immortalized in the 1959 Günter Grass historical novel *The Tin Drum*, today this building is a museum suitable only for real history buffs.

SOUTH OF THE MAIN TOWN

A 10- to 15-minute walk south of the Main Town, these sights round out the Gdańsk experience for those with a special interest in art or theater.

National Museum in Gdańsk (Muzeum Narodowe w Gdańsku)

This art collection, housed in what was a 15th-century Franciscan monastery, is worth ▲▲ to art lovers for one reason: Hans Memling's glorious *Last Judgment* triptych altarpiece, one of the two most important pieces of art to be seen in Poland (the other is Leonardo da Vinci's *Lady with an Ermine*, usually in Kraków's Czartoryski Museum). If you're not a purist, you can settle for seeing the much smaller replica in St. Mary's Church. But if medieval art is your bag, make the 10-minute walk here from the Main Town.

Cost and Hours: 10 zł, May-Sept Tue-Sun 10:00-17:00, Oct-April Tue-Sun 9:00-16:00, closed Mon year-round, last entry 45 minutes before closing; walk 10 minutes due south from ulica Długa's Golden Gate, after passing the Shakespeare Theater take the pedestrian underpass beneath the big cross street, then continue down the busy street until you see signs for the museum; ulica Toruńska 1, tel. 58-301-6804, www.mng.gda.pl.

Visiting the Museum: From the entry, the **altarpiece by Hans Memling** (c. 1440-1494) is at the top of the stairs and to the right. The history of the painting is as interesting as the work itself. It was commissioned in the mid-15th century by the Medicis' banker in Florence, Angelo di Jacopo Tani. The ship delivering the painting from Belgium to Florence was hijacked by a Gdańsk pirate, who brought the altarpiece to his hometown to be displayed in St. Mary's Church. For centuries, kings, emperors, and czars admired it from afar, until Napoleon seized it in the early 19th century and took it to Paris to hang in the Louvre. Gdańsk finally got the painting back, only to have it exiled again—this time into St. Petersburg's Hermitage Museum—after World War II. On its return to Gdańsk in 1956, this museum claimed it—though St. Mary's wants it back.

Have a close look at Memling's well-traveled work. It's the end of the world, and Christ rides in on a rainbow to judge humankind. Angels blow reveille, waking the dead, who rise from their graves. The winged archangel Michael—dressed for battle and wielding the cross like a weapon—weighs the grace in each person, sending them either to the fires of hell (right panel) or up the sparkling-crystal stairway to heaven (left).

It takes all 70 square feet of paneling to contain this awesome scene. Jam-packed with dozens of bodies and a Bible's worth of symbolism, and executed with astonishing detail, the painting can keep even a non-art lover occupied. Notice the serene, happy expressions of the righteous, as they're greeted by St. Peter (with his giant key) and clothed by angels. And pity the condemned, their faces filled with terror and sorrow as they're tortured by grotesque devils more horrifying than anything Hollywood could devise.

Tune in to the exquisite details: the angels' robes, the devils' genetic-mutant features, the portrait of the man in the scale (a Medici banker), Michael's peacock wings. Get as close as you can to the globe at Christ's feet and Michael's shining breastplate: You can just make out the whole scene in mirror reflection. Then back up and take it all in—three panels connected by a necklace of bodies that curves downward through hell, crosses the earth, then rises up to the towers of the New Jerusalem. On the back side of the triptych are reverent portraits of the painting's patron, Angelo Tani, and his new bride, Catarina.

Beyond the Memling, the remainder of the collection isn't too thrilling. The rest of the upstairs has more Flemish and Dutch art, as well as paintings from Gdańsk's Golden Age and various works by Polish artists. The ground floor features a cavernous, all-white cloister filled with Gothic altarpiece sculptures, gold and silver wares, and Gdańsk-style furniture.

Gdańsk Shakespeare Theater (Teatr Szekspirowski)

Gdańsk has a long and proud tradition of staging plays by Shakespeare. As early as the 17th century, theater troupes from England would come to this cosmopolitan trading city to perform. In 1993, local actors revived the tradition with an annual Gdańsk Shakespeare Festival. And in 2014, the city built the state-of-the-art Gdańsk Shakespeare Theater to honor its connection to the Bard.

The building's minimalist, black-brick, blocky architecture—with a few symbolic faux-buttresses to echo the gables of the surrounding buildings—was criticized for not blending in very well with its surroundings. But the celebration of theater that takes place inside is welcomed by all. The main theater can be modified to create three different types of performance spaces (proscenium, thrust stage, and theater in the round)—and even has a retractable roof to wash the actors with direct sunlight.

If you want to take a peek, just follow Pcztowa street south from the middle of ulica Długa; the box office is at Bogusławskiego 1.

Tours and Performances: Theater lovers can take a one-hour guided tour of the building for 18 zł (usually daily at 15:00). Call or check their website for details on the tour and upcoming performances (tel. 58-351-0101, www.teatrszekspirowski.pl).

Shakespeare contributes only a tiny piece of the theater's full lineup—it plays host to a wide variety of performances and festivals throughout the year. You're most likely to find Shakespeare performed in English during the annual Shakespeare Festival, which is typically in the summer (details on theater website).

OUTER GDAŃSK

These two sights—worthwhile only to those with a particular interest in them—are each within the city limits of Gdańsk, but they take some serious time to see round-trip.

Oliwa Cathedral (Katedra Oliwska)

The suburb of Oliwa, at the northern edge of Gdańsk, is home to this visually striking church. The quirky, elongated facade hides a surprisingly long and skinny nave. The ornately decorated 18th-century organ over the main entrance features angels and stars that move around when the organ is played. While locals are proud of this place, it's hard to justify the effort it takes to get out here. Skip it unless you just love Polish churches or you're going to a concert.

Concerts: The animated organ performs its 20-minute show frequently, especially in summer (in high season, concerts at the top of most hours—confirm schedule online or at Gdańsk TI before making the trip, www.archikatedraoliwa.pl). Note that on Sundays and holidays, there are no concerts before 15:00.

Getting There: Oliwa is about six miles northwest of central Gdańsk, on the way to Sopot and Gdynia. To reach Oliwa from Gdańsk's main train station, you have two options: Ride **tram #6** or **#12**, get off at the Oliwa stop and walk a few minutes through the park to the church (about 30 minutes total); or take an **SKM commuter train** to the Gdańsk Oliwa stop (15 minutes), then walk 15 minutes (or take a 10-zł taxi ride) to Oliwski Park and the cathedral.

Westerplatte

World War II began on September 1, 1939, when Adolf Hitler sent the warship *Schleswig-Holstein* to attack this Polish munitions depot, which was guarding Gdańsk's harbor. Though it may give serious WWII history buffs goosebumps, most visitors will find little to see here aside from a modest museum, a towering monument, and some old bunkers.

Getting There: The most enjoyable approach is on a cruise—either on a modern boat, or on a fun old-fashioned galleon (45 minutes each way; see page 488). You can also take **bus** #106, #138, or (in summer) #606 from the main train station (about 30 minutes).

Shopping in Gdańsk

The big story in Gdańsk is amber *(bursztyn)*, a fossil resin available in all shades, shapes, and sizes (see the "All About Amber" sidebar, earlier). The best place to browse and buy amber is along the atmospheric ulica Mariacka (between the Motława River and St. Mary's Church). This pretty street, with old-fashioned balconies and dozens of display cases, is fun to wander even if you're not a shopper. Other good places to buy amber are along the riverfront embankment and on ulica Długa.

To avoid rip-offs—such as amber that's been melted and reshaped—always buy it from a shop, not from someone standing on the street. (But note that most shops also have a display case and salesperson out front, which are perfectly legit.) Prices everywhere are about the same, so instead of seeking out a specific place, just window shop until you see what you want. Styles range from gaudy necklaces with huge globs of amber, to tasteful smaller pendants in silver settings, to cheap trinkets. All shades of amber—from near-white to dark brown—cost about the same, but you'll pay more for inclusions (bugs or other objects stuck in the amber).

Gdańsk also has several modern shopping malls, most of them in the Old Town or near the main train station. The most impressive is the Forum, across the street from the Upland Gate; the Madison shopping center is between the Main Town and the Solidarity shipyard.

Sleeping in Gdańsk

The high season is generally May through September; at all of these places, you'll pay a bit less in the off-season. Many hotels are booked up (mostly with German and Scandinavian tourists) in peak season—reserve ahead.

IN THE MAIN TOWN

The Main Town is convenient for sightseeing, but can come with nighttime noise—particularly in summer, when loud bars and discos keep things lively. Request a quiet room...and pack earplugs.

$$$ Hotel Wolne Miasto ("Free City") offers lush, wood-carved public spaces with photos of old Gdańsk and 68 richly

> # Sleep Code
>
> Hotels are classified based on the average price of a standard double room with breakfast in high season.
>
> | | |
> |---|---|
> | $$$$ | **Splurge:** Most rooms over 550 zł |
> | $$$ | **Pricier:** 400-550 zł |
> | $$ | **Moderate:** 250-400 zł |
> | $ | **Budget:** 100-250 zł |
> | ¢ | **Backpacker:** Under 100 zł |
> | RS% | **Rick Steves discount** |
>
> Unless otherwise noted, credit cards are accepted, hotel staff speak basic English, and free Wi-Fi is available. Comparison-shop by checking prices at several hotels (on each hotel's own website, on a booking site, or by email). For the best deal, *book directly with the hotel.* Ask for a discount if paying in cash; if the listing includes **RS%,** request a Rick Steves discount.

decorated rooms on the edge of the Main Town, just two blocks from the main drag. It's above a popular disco that gets noisy on weekends (Thu-Sat nights), so it's especially important to request a quieter room when you reserve (elevator, ulica Świętego Ducha 2, tel. 58-322-2442, www.hotelwm.pl, rezerwacja@hotelwm.pl).

$$$ **Hotel Admirał** is simply practical: a big, solidly built, business-class place with 44 comfortable rooms tucked in a quiet residential alley at the north end of the embankment, just a few steps off the old fish market. Their rates are soft, so the hotel is especially worth considering if you can get a deal (air-con, elevator, Tobiasza 9, tel. 58-320-0320, www.admiralhotel.pl, recepcja@admiralhotel.pl).

$$ **Gotyk House,** a good value, is run with warmth and pride by Andrzej, an energetic armchair historian who works hard to make his little hotel comfortable while still respecting the sanctity of Gdańsk's oldest house (and supposedly the residence of Copernicus' longtime lover). The chimes from St. Mary's Church, next door, provide a pleasant soundtrack. The original, historic building has five rooms; a modern annex out back holds six additional rooms with air-conditioning and more refined touches. Neither building has an elevator, so be ready for stairs (ulica Mariacka 1, tel. 58-301-8567, www.gotykhouse.eu, reservation@gotykhouse.eu).

$$ **Aparthotel Neptun** lacks personality, but owns a great location—on a slightly dreary side street between delightful Mariacka and the bustling Royal Way. While it's just a few steps to most of the town's big sights, it's just far enough away to avoid crowds and weekend noise. The 39 rooms and apartments are modern, efficient, well-equipped, and forgettable...but well-priced for the

GDAŃSK & THE TRI-CITY

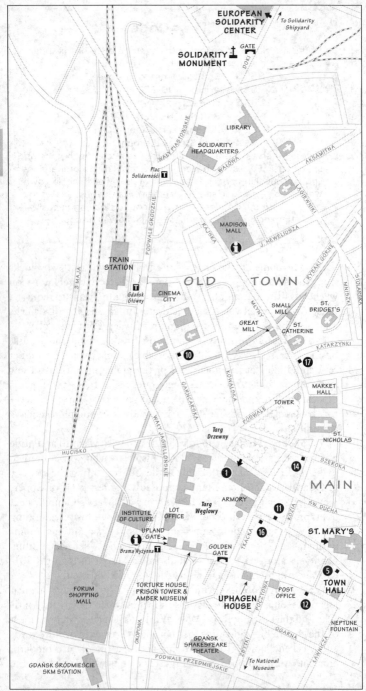

EUROPEAN
SOLIDARITY
CENTER

To Solidarity
Shipyard

GATE

SOLIDARITY
MONUMENT

DOK

WAŁY PIASTOWSKIE

LIBRARY

SOLIDARITY
HEADQUARTERS

WAŁOWA

AKSAMITNA

Plac
Solidarności

JAGIEŁKI

J. HEWELIUSZA

KASKA

PODWALE GRODZKIE

MADISON
MALL

RYBAKI GÓRNE

SZOLARSKA

TRAIN
STATION

OLD   TOWN

MNISZKI

Gdańsk
Główny

CINEMA
CITY

MŁYNY

SMALL
MILL

ST.
BRIDGET'S

GREAT
MILL

ST.
CATHERINE

10

KATARZYNKI

17

GARNCARSKA

KOWALSKA

PODWALE

MARKET
HALL

TOWER

ST.
NICHOLAS

WAŁY JAGIELLOŃSKIE

HUCISKO

Targ
Drzewny

SZEROKA

14

MAIN

1

ARMORY

INSTITUTE
OF CULTURE

LOT
OFFICE

Targ
Węglowy

11

KOZIA

ŚW. DUCHA

16

ST. MARY'S

UPLAND
GATE

TKACKA

Brama Wyżynna

GOLDEN
GATE

5

TOWN
HALL

FORUM
SHOPPING
MALL

TORTURE HOUSE,
PRISON TOWER &
AMBER MUSEUM

UPHAGEN
HOUSE

POCZTOWA

POST
OFFICE

12

NEPTUNE
FOUNTAIN

OGARNA

GDAŃSK
SHAKESPEARE
THEATER

To National
Museum

ZBYTKI

ŁAWNICZA

OKOPOWA

PODWALE PRZEDMIEJSKIE

GDAŃSK ŚRÓDMIEŚCIE
SKM STATION

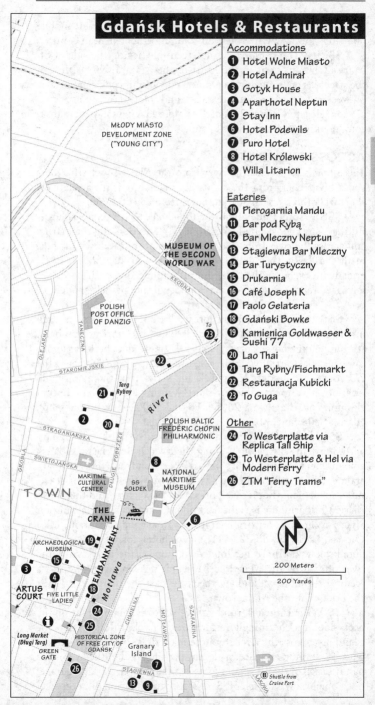

Gdańsk Hotels & Restaurants

Accommodations

1 Hotel Wolne Miasto
2 Hotel Admirał
3 Gotyk House
4 Aparthotel Neptun
5 Stay Inn
6 Hotel Podewils
7 Puro Hotel
8 Hotel Królewski
9 Willa Litarion

Eateries

10 Pierogarnia Mandu
11 Bar pod Rybą
12 Bar Mleczny Neptun
13 Stągiewna Bar Mleczny
14 Bar Turystyczny
15 Drukarnia
16 Café Joseph K
17 Paolo Gelateria
18 Gdański Bowke
19 Kamienica Goldwasser & Sushi 77
20 Lao Thai
21 Targ Rybny/Fischmarkt
22 Restauracja Kubicki
23 To Guga

Other

24 To Westerplatte via Replica Tall Ship
25 To Westerplatte & Hel via Modern Ferry
26 ZTM "Ferry Trams"

MŁODY MIASTO
DEVELOPMENT ZONE
("YOUNG CITY")

MUSEUM OF
THE SECOND
WORLD WAR

KROSNA

POLISH
POST OFFICE
OF DANZIG

To
23

STAROMIEJSKIE

OLEJARNA

TANECZNA

Targ
Rybny

River

POLISH BALTIC
FRÉDÉRIC CHOPIN
PHILHARMONIC

STRAGANIARSKA

GROBLA

SWIETOJANSKA

DLUGIE POBRZEZE

MARITIME
CULTURAL
CENTER

SS
SOLDEK

NATIONAL
MARITIME
MUSEUM

TOWN

THE
CRANE

ARCHAEOLOGICAL
MUSEUM

EMBANKMENT

Motlawa

ARTUS
COURT

FIVE LITTLE
LADIES

GRIMIELNA

MOTLAWSKA

SZAFARINA

200 Meters

200 Yards

Long Market
(Długi Targ)

HISTORICAL ZONE
OF FREE CITY OF
GDAŃSK

Granary
Island

GREEN
GATE

STAGIEWNA

ŁAKONA

B Shuttle from
Cruise Port

central location (breakfast extra, elevator, spa, Grzaska 1, mobile 604-466-466, www.apartneptun.com, info@apartneptun.com).

$$ Stay Inn couldn't be more central—facing the side of St. Mary's Church, right in the heart of the Main Town. Although the street it's on is quieter than most, a downstairs pub can be noisy on weekends. Its 42 rooms are stylish and colorful (breakfast extra, air-con, elevator, Piwna 28, tel. 58-354-1543, www.stayinngdansk.com, booking@stayinngdansk.com).

ACROSS THE RIVER

These hotels are across the river from the Main Town. That puts you a bit farther from the sightseeing action, but it's a relatively short walk (no more than 10 minutes from any of these).

$$$$ Hotel Podewils is the top choice for a friendly splurge. Filling a storybook-cute house from 1728, overlooking the marina and across the river from a fine panorama of the Gdańsk embankment, it's classy. The public spaces and 10 rooms have all the modern amenities, but with plush, almost Baroque, decor (air-con, Szafarnia 2, tel. 58-300-9560, www.podewils.pl, gdansk@podewils.pl).

$$$ Puro Hotel, just a short walk from Gdańsk's main drag in the middle of Granary Island, is part of a Norwegian chain. It's big (eight floors), splashy, and fills brand-new buildings with towering glass atriums, a big restaurant, and a top-floor bar. The 211 rooms are modern, practical, and stylish; for the quality and location, it's a great value for those wanting a big hotel (air-con, elevator, spa, Stągiewna 26, tel. 58-563-5000, www.purohotel.pl, gdansk@purohotel.pl).

$$ Hotel Królewski fills a renovated red-brick granary with 30 rooms sitting right along the river, facing classic Gdańsk embankment views. As it's across the river from the landmark crane—a long walk from the heart of town—the location isn't entirely convenient. But it's well priced for the quality, and the Polish Baltic Philharmonic is right next door (apartments, try asking for a view room for no extra charge, elevator, good restaurant, ulica Ołowianka 1, tel. 58-326-1111, www.hotelkrolewski.pl, office@hotelkrolewski.pl). To get into town, hop on the ferry across the river offered by the Maritime Museum; if it's not running, it's a scenic 15-minute walk along the river, past the marina, and over the bridge into the Main Town.

$$ Willa Litarion, run by the Owsikowski family, sits on the back side of a charmingly restored row of colorful houses on the island just across the river from the main drag. It's tall and skinny, with no elevator, and faces a gloomy parking lot, but the location is handy. Each of the 13 small rooms is different (pay parking garage, ulica Spichrzowa 18, tel. 58-320-2553, www.litarion.pl, recepcja@

> ## Restaurant Price Code
>
> I've assigned each eatery a price category, based on the average cost of a typical main course. Drinks, desserts, and splurge items (steak and seafood) can raise the price considerably.
>
> $$$$ **Splurge:** Most main courses over 60 zł
> $$$ **Pricier:** 45-60 zł
> $$ **Moderate:** 25-45 zł
> $ **Budget:** Under 25 zł
>
> In Poland, a milk bar or takeout spot is **$**; a basic sit-down eatery is **$$**; a casual but more upscale restaurant is **$$$**; and a swanky splurge is **$$$$**.

litarion.pl). Several other, similar (but less appealing) "villas" line this same street—if you're in a pinch for a room, this is a handy place to go ringing doorbells.

Eating in Gdańsk

In addition to traditional Polish fare, Gdańsk has some excellent Baltic seafood. Herring *(śledź)* is popular here, as is cod *(dorsz)*. Natives brag that their salmon *(łosoś)* is better than Norway's. For a stiff drink, sample *Goldwasser* (similar to Goldschlager). This sweet and strong liqueur, flecked with actual gold, was supposedly invented here in Gdańsk. The following options are all in the Main Town, within three blocks of the Royal Way.

AFFORDABLE RESTAURANTS IN THE CITY CENTER

These places are well priced, tasty, quick, and wonderfully convenient—on or very near the Royal Way (ulica Długa). They're worth considering even if you're not on a tight budget.

$$ Pierogarnia Mandu, serving a wide variety of pierogi—all handmade (see them working through the window), with modern flourish—is *the* foodie hotspot in Gdańsk. Hiding in a nondescript residential zone between the train station and the main tourist area, it's worth seeking out for pierogi, plus a variety of other international dumplings. As it's popular, be prepared to wait for a table; it can take 30-45 minutes for your dumplings to be made fresh (daily 11:00-22:00, Elżbietańska 4, tel. 58-300-0000).

$$ Bar pod Rybą ("Under the Fish") is nirvana for fans of baked potatoes *(pieczony ziemniak)*. They offer more than 20 varieties, piled high with a wide variety of toppings and sauces, from Mexican beef to herring to Polish cheeses. They also serve fish dishes with salad and potatoes, making this a cheap place to sample local seafood. The interior has big, comfy couches, and the outdoor seating fills a big stone balcony on atmospheric Piwna street (daily 10:00-22:00, Piwna 61, tel. 58-305-1307). Piwna street is lined with other tempting options—it's a fun street to browse for a meal.

$ Bar Mleczny Neptun is your handiest milk-bar option in the Main Town. A hearty meal, including a drink, runs about $5. This popular place has outdoor seating along the most scenic stretch of the main drag, and an upstairs dining room overlooking it all. The items on the counter are for display—point to what you want, and they'll dish it up fresh (Mon-Fri 7:30-20:00, Sat-Sun 10:00-20:00, may have shorter hours off-season, ulica Długa 33, tel. 58-301-4988). For more on milk bars, see page 222.

$ Stągiewna Bar Mleczny, in the middle of Granary Island just beyond the Royal Way, is a classy, updated, modern milk bar with appealing outdoor seating—good for lunch or an early dinner (daily 9:00-18:00, Stągiewna 15, mobile 570-112-222).

$ Bar Turystyczny is misnamed—not just for tourists, it has become beloved by locals as the central area's favorite milk bar. Easy to miss on the way between the Main Town and the Solidarity sights, it's always jammed (daily 8:00-18:00, Szeroka 8, tel. 58-301-6013).

Coffee: Drukarnia ("Printer") is the best spot in town for gourmet coffee in a modern, trendy setting that still melds well with the tradition all around it. The interior is industrial-mod, and the outdoor seating fills two levels of a stone balcony on Gdańsk's loveliest street, Mariacka. In addition to coffee and creative tea drinks, they have craft beers, breakfast, and other light bites—sandwiches and cakes (daily 10:00-22:00, Mariacka 36, mobile 510-087-064).

Hipster Bar/Café: Café Joseph K, on charming Piwna street, is a popular hangout for coffee, craft beer, and creative cocktails. Similar to Drukarnia (but edgier and less coffee-focused), they have a modern interior and stay-awhile outdoor tables (daily 10:00-24:00, Piwna 1, mobile 572-161-510).

Ice Cream: The people of Gdańsk—and its many visitors—seem obsessed with ice cream *(lody)*. For high quality, creative flavors and generous portions, stop by **Paolo Gelateria,** on the way between the Main Town and the Solidarity sights (Mon-Fri 10:00-20:00, Sat-Sun until 21:00, across from the Great Mill at Podwale Staromiejskie 96, mobile 504-222-651).

ON THE RIVERFRONT EMBANKMENT

Perhaps the most appealing dining zone in Gdańsk stretches along the riverfront embankment near the landmark medieval crane. On a balmy summer evening, the outdoor tables here are enticing. This area is popular—consider scouting a table during your sightseeing, and reserve your choice for dinner later that night. While these places are mostly interchangeable, I've listed a few to consider, in the order you'll reach them as you walk north along the embankment. These places are more expensive than other options in town, but the views are worth it.

$$$ Gdański Bowke is kitschy, but fun and lively. The menu of classic local dishes looks like a big, vintage newspaper. They brew their own beer, and often have live music out on the embankment (daily 10:00-23:00, Długie Pobrzeże 11, tel. 58-380-1111).

$$$$ Kamienica Goldwasser is a classy choice, offering high-quality Polish and international cuisine. Choose between cozy, romantic indoor seating on several levels, or scenic outdoor seating (daily 10:00-24:00, occasional live music, Długie Pobrzeże 22, tel. 58-301-8878).

Just beyond Goldwasser, **$$$ Sushi 77** (Długie Pobrzeże 30, tel. 58-682-1823) and **$$$ Lao Thai** (ulica Targ Rybny 11, www.laothai.pl) are good-quality Asian eateries and also have riverfront seating. Or carry on farther for more Asian cuisine at Guga, described later.

$$$$ Targ Rybny/Fischmarkt ("The Fish Market") has less appealing outdoor seating that overlooks a park (the onetime fish market that it's named for) and parking lot. But the warm, mellow-yellow nautical ambience inside is pleasant, making this a good option in bad weather. It features classy but not stuffy service, and the expected emphasis on fish (daily 10:00-23:00, ulica Targ Rybny 6C, tel. 58-320-9011).

$$$ Restauracja Kubicki, along the water just past the Hilton, has a long history (since 1918), but a recent remodel has kept the atmosphere—and its food—feeling fresh. This is a good choice for high-quality Polish and international cuisine in a fun, sophisticated interior that's a clever mix of old and new (daily 12:00-23:00, Wartka 5, tel. 58-301-0050).

$$ Guga, all the way at the end of the embankment (past the drawbridge, near the WWII museum), has a modern ambience and a short menu of Asian fusion dishes. There are two parts: "Salty" for a snack or meal, or "Sweet" for dessert (Mon-Thu 9:00-20:00, Fri-Sun until 22:00, Stara Stocznia 2, mobile 533-272-642).

Gdańsk Connections

BY TRAIN

Gdańsk is well-connected to the Tri-City via commuter SKM trains (explained later, under "Getting Around the Tri-City"). It's also connected to Warsaw and Kraków by the high-speed EIC line (which requires reservations). Given the distance between Gdańsk and other Polish destinations, also consider domestic flights: LOT has easy flights between Gdańsk and Kraków for not much more than a train ticket.

From Gdańsk by Train to: **Hel** (town on Hel Peninsula, 3/day direct July-Aug only, 2 hours; otherwise about hourly with change in Gdynia), **Malbork** (2/hour, about half are express EIC trains that take 30 minutes, the rest are slower regional trains that take around 45 minutes), **Toruń** (4/day direct, 2.5 hours; more with a change in Bydgoszcz or Iława, 3 hours), **Warsaw** (hourly, 3 hours on express EIC train), **Kraków** (6/day direct, 5.5 hours, 1 more with change in Warsaw; plus 8.5-hour night train), **Berlin** (1/day direct, 6 hours; 3/day, 7.5 hours, change in Poznań).

BY BOAT

Boats depart from Gdańsk's embankment to nearby destinations, including **Westerplatte** (the monument marking where World War II started) and **Hel** (the beachy peninsula, described later). As schedules change often, confirm your plans carefully at the TI. All boat trips are weather permitting, especially faster hydrofoils. In shoulder season (April-June and Sept-Oct), most boats stop running from Gdańsk, but several routes still run between Sopot, Gdynia, and Hel. Boats generally don't run in winter (Nov-March).

To Westerplatte: To travel by boat to the monument at Westerplatte, you have three options. Most enjoyable is to ride a replica **17th-century galleon,** either the *Galeon Lew* ("Lion Galleon") or the *Czarna Perła* ("Black Pearl"). These over-the-top, touristy boats depart hourly from the embankment just outside the Green Gate for a lazy 1.5-hour round-trip cruise to Westerplatte and back. (You can choose to get off at Westerplatte and take a later boat back.)

You'll see more industry than scenery, but it's a fun excuse to set sail, even if you don't care about Westerplatte (45 zł round-trip, 30 zł one-way, the two boats take turns departing at the top of each hour 10:00-19:00 in July-Aug, fewer departures May-June and Sept, from the embankment near the landmark crane, mobile 601-629-191, www.galeony.pl). Two other, duller alternatives leave from right nearby: big, modern **Żegluga Gdańska** boats (www.zegluga.pl); or cheaper but less frequent city-run **ZTM "ferry trams"** *(tramwaj wodny)*, which depart from the embankment on the south side of the bridge (3-4/day).

To Hel: Various boats zip out to Hel in two hours during the summer. This route is most likely run by Żegluga Gdańska (May and Sept weekends only, June-Aug 3/day, 35 zł one-way, www.zegluga.pl).

BY CRUISE SHIP

A few cruise ships (under 800 passengers) dock in **Gdańsk,** near the Westerplatte monument (described earlier; connected to the center by 45-minute pleasure-boat trip or 30-minute ride on bus #106, #138, and—in summer—#606). But most cruises advertising a stop in Gdańsk actually dock in the nearby town of **Gdynia.** For details on this town, see page 493.

The Tri-City (Trójmiasto)

Gdańsk is the anchor of the three-part metropolitan region known as the Tri-City (Trójmiasto). The other two parts are as different as night and day: Sopot, a swanky resort town, and Gdynia, a practical, nose-to-the-grindstone business center. The Tri-City as a whole is home to bustling industry and a sprawling university, with several campuses and plenty of well-dressed, English-speaking students. Beyond the Tri-City, the long, skinny Hel Peninsula—a sparsely populated strip of fishing villages and fun-loving beaches—arches dramatically into the Baltic Sea.

Sopot—boasting sandy beaches, tons of tourists, and a certain elegance—is clearly the most appealing day-trip option. Gdynia is less romantic, but comes with an excellent Emigration Museum and offers a glimpse into workaday Poland. Hel, which requires the better part of a day to visit, is worthwhile only if you've got perfect summer weather and a desire to lie on the beach.

GETTING AROUND THE TRI-CITY

Gdańsk, Sopot, and Gdynia are connected by two different types of trains: regional commuter trains (*kolejka,* operated by SKM) use track 3 at Gdańsk's main train station, while trains operated by Poland's national railway (PKP) use tracks 1 and 2. The SKM trains are cheaper, a bit slower, and more frequent than long-distance PKP trains—they go in each direction about every 10-15 minutes

GDAŃSK & THE TRI-CITY

Gdańsk Day Trips

To Karlskrona, Sweden

Władysławowo

Jastarnia

To Szczecin & Berlin · Jurata · Hel Peninsula

Hel

Baltijsk · RUSSIA (Kaliningrad)

20 Kilometers
20 Miles

Baltic Sea

Gdynia

Sopot · Oliwa

WESTERPLATTE

TRI-CITY

Gdańsk

Wiślany Lagoon

A-194

To Kaliningrad & Vilnius, Lithuania

Motława River

Braniewo

Pruszcz Gdański

E-75

Vistula River

E-77

P O L A N D

Tczew

Elbląg

Orneta

Malbork

Pasłęk

To Poznań & Berlin

Starogard Gdański

To Toruń & Warsaw

E-77

To Warsaw

(less frequently after 19:30 and Sun). Trains to Hel are always operated by PKP.

Buying Tickets: Confusingly, SKM trains and PKP trains are covered by different tickets, and the fastest PKP trains (marked *IC, EIC,* or *TLK*) require reservations—effectively a third type of ticket. Prices are comparable between systems, typically around 4-6 zł one-way between Gdańsk and Gdynia (though trains requiring reservations can be much more).

It can be challenging to figure out which train is leaving next, and to buy a ticket for the right train. First, check posted schedules (or look online) to establish which train you want. For an SKM train, you can buy tickets at machines labeled *SKM Bilety* (English instructions), or at the SKM ticket office (outside the station, facing the SKM tracks). SKM tickets purchased at a machine come already validated, but if you buy one at the office, you'll need to stamp your ticket in the easy-to-miss yellow slots at the platform.

For a PKP train, you can stand in line at the ticket windows; however, English-speaking staff can be limited.

Another option is to look for the general ticket machines inside the station, which typically inform you about all upcoming trains and sell you tickets for any type (English instructions, take Polish cash; American credit cards may not work).

Using the Right Stop: Each city has multiple stops. Remember, in Gdańsk, use either Gdańsk Główny (the main station for SKM and PKP) or Gdańsk Śródmieście (SKM only). For Sopot, use the stop called simply Sopot. For Gdynia, it's Gdynia Główna (the main station).

Boat Alternative: For a more romantic—and much slower— approach, consider a boat (see "Gdańsk Connections," earlier).

Sopot

Sopot (SOH-poht), dubbed the "Nice of the North," was a celebrated haunt of beautiful people during the 1920s and 1930s, and it remains a popular beach getaway to this day.

Sopot was created in the early 19th century by Napoleon's doctor, Jean Georges Haffner, who believed Baltic Sea water to be therapeutic. By the 1890s, it had become a fashionable seaside resort. This gambling center boasted enough high-roller casinos to garner comparisons to Monte Carlo.

The casinos are gone, but the health resorts remain, and you'll still see more well-dressed people here per capita than just about anywhere else in the country. While it's not quite Cannes, Sopot feels relatively high class, which is unusual in otherwise unpretentious Poland. But even so, a childlike spirit of summer-vacation fun pervades this St-Tropez-on-the-Baltic, making it an all-around enjoyable place.

You can get the gist of Sopot in just a couple of hours. Zip in on the train, follow the main drag to the sea, wander the pier, get your feet wet at the beach, then head back to Gdańsk. Why not come here in the late afternoon, enjoy those last few rays of sunshine, stay for dinner, then take a twilight stroll on the pier?

Orientation to Sopot

The main pedestrian drag, Monte Cassino Heroes street (ulica Bohaterów Monte Cassino), leads to the Molo, the longest pleasure pier in Europe. From the Molo, a broad, sandy beach stretches in each direction. Running parallel to the surf is a tree-lined, people-filled path made for strolling.

Tourist Information: The TI is near the base of the Molo at

Plac Zdrojowy 2 (daily 10:00-18:00, mobile 790-280-884, www. sopot.pl).

Arrival in Sopot: From the SKM station, exit to the left and walk down the street. After a block, you'll see the PKP train station on your left. Continue on to the can't-miss-it main drag, ulica Bohaterów Monte Cassino (marked by the big red-brick church steeple). Follow it to the right, down to the seaside.

Sights in Sopot

▲Monte Cassino Heroes Street
(Ulica Bohaterów Monte Cassino)

Nicknamed "Monciak" (MOHN-chak) by locals, this in-love-with-life promenade may well be Poland's most manicured street (and is named in honor of the Polish soldiers who helped the Allies pry Italy's Monte Cassino monastery from Nazi forces during World War II). Especially after all the suburban and industrial dreck you passed through to get here, it's easy to be charmed by this pretty drag. The street is lined with happy tourists, trendy cafés, al fresco restaurants, movie theaters, and late-19th-century facades (known for their wooden balconies).

The most popular building along here (on the left, about half-way down) is the so-called **Crooked House** (Krzywy Domek), a trippy, Gaudí-inspired building that looks like it's melting. Hard-partying Poles prefer to call it the "Drunken House," and say that when it looks straight, it's time to stop drinking.

Molo (Pier)

At more than 1,600 feet long, this is Europe's longest wooden entertainment pier. While you won't find any amusement-park rides, you will be surrounded by vendors, artists, and Poles having the time of their lives. Buy a *gofry* (Belgian waffle topped with whipped cream and fruit) or an oversized cloud of *wata cukrowa* (cotton candy), grab your partner's hand, and stroll with gusto (8 zł, free Oct-April, open long hours daily, www.molo.sopot.pl).

Climb to the top of the Art Nouveau lighthouse for a waterfront panorama. Scan the horizon for sailboats and tankers. Any pirate ships? For a jarring reality check, look over to Gdańsk. Barely visible from the Molo are two of the most important sites in 20th-century history: the towering monument at Westerplatte, where World War II started, and the cranes rising up from the Gdańsk Shipyard, where Solidarity was born and European communism began its long goodbye.

In spring and fall, the Molo is a favorite venue for pole vaulting—or is that Pole vaulting?

The Beach

Yes, Poland has beaches. Nice ones. When I heard Sopot compared to places like Nice, I'll admit that I scoffed. But when I saw those stretches of inviting sand as far as the eye can see, I wished I'd packed my swim trunks. (You could walk from Gdańsk all the way to Gdynia on beaches like this.) The sand is finer than anything I've seen in Croatia...though the water's not exactly crystal-clear. Most of the beach is public, except for a small private stretch in front of the Grand Hotel Sopot. Year-round, it's crammed with locals. At these northern latitudes, the season for bathing is brief and crowded.

Overlooking the beach next to the Molo is the **Grand Hotel Sopot**. It was renovated to top-class status just recently, but its history goes way back. They could charge admission for a multiroom suite that has hosted the likes of Adolf Hitler, Marlene Dietrich, and Fidel Castro (but not all at the same time). With all the trappings of Sopot's belle époque—dark wood, plush upholstery, antique furniture—this room had me imagining Hitler sitting at the desk, looking out to sea, and plotting the course of World War II.

Gdynia

Compared to its flashier sister cities, straightforward Gdynia (guh-DIN-yah) is all business. Gdynia is less historic than Gdańsk or Sopot, as it was built almost entirely in the 1920s to be Poland's main harbor after "Danzig" became a free city. Called "The Gateway to Poland," the waterfront is built on large concrete piers (a communist-style fountain in the middle of the park marks the original coastline). Although nowhere near as attractive as Gdańsk or Sopot, Gdynia has an upscale, modern feel and a lovely waterfront promenade (www.gdynia.pl).

Gdynia is a major business center, and—thanks to its youthful, progressive city government—has edged ahead of the rest of Poland economically. It enjoys one of the highest income levels in the country. The fine Modernist architecture of the downtown has been renovated, and Gdynia is becoming known for its top-tier shopping—all the big designers have boutiques here. If a local has been shopping on Świętojańska street in Gdynia, it means that he or she has some serious zloty.

Because Gdańsk's port is relatively shallow, the biggest cruise ships must put in at Gdynia...leaving confused tourists to poke around town looking for some medieval quaintness, before coming to their senses and heading for Gdańsk. Gdynia is also home to a major military harbor and an important NATO base.

To get a taste of Gdynia, take the train to the Gdynia Główna station, follow signs to *wyjście do miasta*, cross the busy street, and walk 15 minutes down Starowiejska. When you come to the intersection with the broad Świętojańska street, turn right (in the direction the big statue is looking) and walk two blocks to the tree-lined park on the left. Head through the park to the Southern Pier (Molo Południowe). This concrete slab—not nearly as charming as Sopot's wooden-boardwalk version—features a modern shopping mall and a smattering of sights, including an aquarium and a pair of permanently moored museum boats.

The big sightseeing draw in Gdynia is at the fairly distant Nabrzeże Francuskie (French Quay, where cruise ships arrive—handy for cruisers but a taxi ride away for tourists coming on the train). Here you'll find the excellent Emigration Museum, telling the story of Poles who left through Gdynia to find a better life in the New World (described next).

Sights in Gdynia

▲▲Emigration Museum (Muzeum Emigracji)

This museum, right next to Gdynia's cruise terminal, fills the former Marine Station building at the address Polska 1. This building opened in 1933, becoming the main port of departure for Polish American Lines passenger steamers to New York City and Quebec. For a time, vast numbers of Poles emigrated to the New World through right here. (Before that time, they mostly went through Hamburg or Bremen.) After World War II, the

Iron Curtain slammed shut, the line was severed, and the Marine Station remained bombed-out for decades. Now it has been renovated and hosts a high-tech, engaging museum that tells the story of the 3.5 million Poles who left their homeland in search of a better life between the mid-19th century and World War II. Concise yet informative, engaging, and all in English, the exhibit is a delight for anyone, and worth ▲▲▲ for patriotic Polish-Americans.

Cost and Hours: 10 zł, free on Wed, open Tue 12:00-20:00, Wed-Sun 10:00-18:00, closed Mon, good 5-zł audioguide, www.polska1.pl.

Getting There: It's a 25-minute, dreary walk from Gdynia's main train station. A taxi makes things easier. Unfortunately, the ones out front charge about 25 zł, but if you call a legitimate taxi or order an Uber, the fair rate is closer to 10-15 zł (try Hallo Express, tel. 19190). Or you can take a bus: #119, #133, #137, or #147 go from along Władysława IV avenue (between the train station and the waterfront) to the Dworzec Morski/Muzeum Emigracji stop.

Visiting the Museum: Buy your ticket on the main floor, where you'll also find WCs, a café, and a museum shop. Then head upstairs, through the middle of the cavernous building, to find the exhibit entrance. Inside, the permanent exhibition tells the story of Polish emigration. You'll see photos of famous Poles who left (from Kościuszko to Chopin), and learn about the various waves of emigration throughout Polish history, and what sparked each one: the Partitions in the late 18th century; failed uprisings in 1830 and 1864; and the potato famine (Poland suffered like Ireland did—the wall of potatoes symbolizes how important this staple was to peasant life). The Industrial Revolution sparked a different kind of (internal) emigration, as rural farming families moved into the cities for work.

The exhibit introduces the Sikora family, and follows their emigration from Chmielnik to Chicago, by way of the port of Bremen. You'll learn how the "emigration industry" operated: Steamer lines conducted a medical examination of each passenger before they left Europe—because if they were rejected upon examination once they arrived in the New World, the company had to pay to ship them back. Exhibits include a mock-up of a train station, the deck of an Atlantic steamship, a cross-section of life below decks, and a peek into a tight sleeping quarters, crammed with bunks where the poorest passengers would spend 10 days on turbulent seas. Finally you arrive in New York City. Imagine seeing a wall of skyscrapers after a long journey from a thatched village. The train car is a reminder that from New York, new arrivals spread out across North America. Chicago is famous for its huge Polish émigré population, but you'll learn that many Poles also went to Brazil ("Brazilian Fever").

You'll learn about the history of Gdynia (a purpose-built port, created entirely after World War I) and see a giant replica of the MS *Stefan Bathory*—a passenger steamer that was built here. (Sadly, when transatlantic travel ended after World War II, ships like this one were scrapped.) In the World War II section, trees cut down to their stumps represent the forced displacement of

populations during and after the war. You'll learn about the "Polish diaspora" around the world (Chicago, Rio, Britain, Australia). At the end of World War II, Polish officers who had fought alongside the Western Allies were warned not to return to Poland—where they'd be executed as potential rabble-rousers against the Soviet regime. So they stayed where they were, creating a new wave of "emigration." The exhibit ends with a kitschy look at Poland under communism (and Solidarity).

Exiting the exhibit, step out onto the long terrace that looks out over the cruise port. While it serves tourists today, this port evokes the millions of brave Poles who left behind everything they knew, set sail across a dangerous ocean, and had the courage to seek a new life in a New World.

ARRIVING BY CRUISE IN GDYNIA

Many Northern European cruises include a stop at "Gdańsk"; most of these actually put in at Gdynia's sprawling port. And, while Gydnia's town center is relatively manicured and pleasant, its port area is the opposite—like a Soviet Bloc bodybuilder, it's muscular and hairy. Cruise ships are shuffled among hardworking industrial piers with few amenities.

Each of the port's many piers is named for a country or region. Most cruise ships use **French Quay** (Nabrzeże Francuskie), which is surrounded by heavy industry. Smaller ships can use the convenient **Pomeranian Quay** (Nabrzeże Pomorskie, part of the Southern Pier), which is an easy walk from the center). Port information: www.port.gdynia.pl.

The French Quay is home to Gdynia's best sight, the **Emigration Museum.** It deserves at least an hour of your time—or more, if you have Polish ancestry. This is a good place to spend any remaining time before "all aboard."

To get from your cruise ship to Gdańsk, the best option is a **shuttle bus-plus-train connection.** The shuttle drops you off at Skwer Kociuski, in downtown Gdynia (5-10 minute trip). From here, it's about a 15-minute walk to the train station (Dworzec Główna). From here you can ride the train into Gdańsk, which takes 30-40 minutes (for details on your various train options, see "Getting Around the Tri-City," earlier). Returning to Gdynia on the train, you want the Gdynia Główna stop.

Taxi drivers line up to meet arriving cruise ships. Cabbies here are usually unofficial (and therefore can set their own, inflated rates). It's worth ordering an Uber or calling for a taxi to get legitimate rates: 10-15 zł to Gdynia's train station (*Dworzec*, DVOH-zhets); 125 zł to Gdańsk's Main Town; and 60-80 zł to Sopot (typically cheaper by Uber). Taxi drivers generally take euros, though their off-the-cuff exchange rate may not be favorable.

For more details on Gdynia's port—and several others on the Baltic, North Sea, and beyond—pick up the *Rick Steves Scandinavian and Northern European Cruise Ports* guidebook.

Hel Peninsula (Mierzeja Helska)

Out on the edge of things, this slender peninsula juts 20 miles into the ocean, providing a sunny retreat from the big cities—even as it shelters them from Baltic winds. Trees line the peninsula, and the northern edge is one long, sandy, ever-shifting beach.

On hot summer days, Hel is a great place to frolic in the sun with Poles. Sunbathing and windsurfing are practically religions here. Small resort villages line Hel Peninsula: Władysławowo (at the base), Chałupy, Kuźnica, Jastarnia, Jurata, and—at the tip—a town also called Hel. Beaches right near the towns can be crowded in peak season, but you're never more than a short walk away from your own stretch of sand. There are few permanent residents, and the waterfront is shared by budget campgrounds, hotels hosting middle-class families, and mansions of Poland's rich and famous (former president Aleksander Kwaśniewski has a summer home here).

The easiest way to go to Hel—aside from coveting thy neighbor's wife—is by boat (see "Gdańsk Connections," earlier). Trains from Gdańsk also reach Hel (summer only), and from Gdynia, you can take a train, bus, or minibus. But overland transit is crowded and slow—especially in summer, when Hel is notorious for its hellish traffic jams.

POMERANIA

Malbork Castle • Toruń

The northwestern part of Poland—known as Pomerania (Pomorze)—has nothing to do with excitable little dogs, but it does offer two attractions worth singling out. Malbork, the biggest Gothic castle in Europe, is one of the best castles in Eastern Europe. Farther south, the Gothic town of Toruń—the birthplace of Copernicus, and a favorite spot of every proud Pole—holds hundreds of red-brick buildings...and, it seems, even more varieties of tasty gingerbread. The story of this region—which was part of the German world for much of its history—is tied inexorably to the Teutonic Knights, who ruled over this northern swath of present-day Poland (see the sidebar later in this chapter) and fortified their holdings with elegant red brick...still the hallmark of Pomerania.

Be prepared for a higher language barrier here; unlike Kraków and Warsaw, English is not the default.

PLANNING YOUR TIME

Malbork works well as a side trip from Gdańsk (frequent trains, 30-45 minutes each way), and it's also on the main train line from Gdańsk to Warsaw. While Toruń doesn't merit a long detour, it's worth a stroll or an overnight if you want to sample a smaller Polish city. Unfortunately, Toruń is on a different train line than Malbork—if you visit both in one day, it'll be a very long one. Ideally, if traveling round-trip from Warsaw, see one of these destinations coming to Gdańsk, and visit the other on the way back. Or do Malbork as a side trip from Gdańsk, then visit Toruń on the way to or from Warsaw. Malbork isn't worth an overnight (since it's so close to Gdańsk), but Toruń can be a delightful place to settle in for the night.

Malbork Castle

Malbork Castle is soaked in history. The biggest brick castle in the world, the largest castle of the Gothic period, and one of Europe's most imposing fortresses, it sprawls on a marshy plain at the edge of the town of Malbork, 35 miles southeast of Gdańsk. This was the headquarters of the Teutonic Knights, the Germanic band of ex-Crusaders who dominated northern Poland in the Middle Ages.

Touring the massive castle, you'll see good exhibits on amber and armor; walk though vast halls with graceful Gothic arches and fan vaulting; learn a bit about the Teutonic Knights; and see enough red brick to last a lifetime. Visiting the whole place is a bit exhausting, but this chapter's self-guided tour helps you focuses on the highlights.

GETTING THERE

Malbork is conveniently located right on the express train line between Gdańsk and Warsaw. Coming by train from Gdańsk, you'll enjoy views of the castle on your right as you cross the Nogat River. Store your luggage at the station's lockers (next to the exit doors) and head into town.

To get from the station to the castle, it's an easy, 10-minute, mostly downhill **walk:** Leave the station to the right, walk straight past the bus stops, and go through the pedestrian underpass beneath the busy road (by the red staircase). Ascending the stairs on the other side, turn right and follow the busy road (noticing peek-a-boo views on your right of the castle's main tower). Take the first right and head down Kościuszki, the main shopping street (partway down on the right, a fancy peach-colored building houses the TI). Near the bottom of Kościuszki, at the fountain and the McDonald's, jog right, then—at the roundabout—turn left to cross the moat. The castle ticket office will be on your right.

The fair metered price for a **taxi** to the castle is no more than 12 zł, but the cabbies waiting at the station charge 20 zł.

To return to the station, just reverse the walking directions. To avoid the uphill walk, ask the info desk clerk in the castle ticket office to call a (fairly priced) taxi for you.

POMERANIA

ORIENTATION TO MALBORK CASTLE

Cost and Hours: Mid-April-Sept—40 zł, open Tue-Sun 9:00-19:00; Oct-mid-April—30 zł, open Tue-Sun 10:00-15:00; closed Mon year-round; grounds stay open an hour later than the castle.

Information: Tel. 55-647-0978, www.zamek.malbork.pl.

Crowd-Beating Tips: The castle is busiest at midday, when there can be a line for tickets. If so, you can buy a ticket on their website with your phone.

Tours: Your ticket includes a good **audioguide,** but supply is limited—they may run out during peak times (11:00-14:00). While informative, the system's location-detection doesn't always work well. This chapter's self-guided tour is more concise and lets you go at your own pace.

If they're out of audioguides, you may be required to enter the castle with a guided tour in Polish—but you can split off on your own as soon as you're inside. In summer, there's usually an **English tour** (included in ticket price) at 10:30. Any time of year, you can pay 240 zł for a private English tour (ideally book ahead, tel. 55-647-0902, kasa@zamek.malbork.pl). If you show up and there's no scheduled English tour, ask whether an English-speaking guide is available. If so, take the initiative to play "tour organizer" and gather a group of English speakers to split the cost of a private tour.

Services and Eating: WCs are downstairs from the ticket office and scattered within the castle complex. Several cheap **$ food stands** cluster outside the castle (by the river). For a good meal inside the castle complex, the **$$$ Gothic Café,** in a cellar under the stairs to the armory in the Middle Castle, is a serious restaurant with surprisingly high-quality food by a renowned chef. Dishing up traditional Polish fare inspired by historic dishes, it's handy for its 50-zł lunch deal that includes a main dish and soup (tel. 55-647-0889, www.gothic.com.pl). Immediately across the courtyard, **$$ Restauracja Piwniczka** is cheaper and simpler, with stick-to-your-ribs beer-hall fare served in atmospheric cellars or at outdoor tables.

Best Views: The views of massive Malbork are stunning—especially at sunset, when its red brick glows. Be sure to walk out across the footbridge over the Nogat River. The most scenic part of the castle is the twin-turreted, riverside Bridge

Gate, which used to be connected by a bridge to the opposite bank.

BACKGROUND

When the Teutonic Knights were invited to Polish lands in the 13th century to convert neighboring pagans, they found the perfect site for their new capital here, on the bank of the Nogat River. Construction began in 1274. After the Teutonic Knights conquered Gdańsk in 1308, the order moved its official headquarters from Venice to northern Poland, where they remained for nearly 150 years. They called their main castle Marienburg, the "Castle of Mary," in honor of the order's patron saint. Poles call it "Malbork."

At its peak in the early 1400s, Malbork was both the imposing home of a seemingly unstoppable army and Europe's final bastion of chivalric ideals. Surrounded by swamplands, with only one gate in need of defense, it was a tough nut to crack. Malbork Castle was never taken by force in the Middle Ages, though it had to withstand various sieges by the Poles during the Thirteen Years' War (1454-1466)—including a campaign that lasted more than three years. Finally, in 1457, the Polish king gained control of Malbork by buying off Czech mercenaries guarding the castle. Malbork became a Polish royal residence for 300 years. But when Poland was partitioned in the late 18th century, this region went back into German hands. The castle became a barracks, windows were sealed up, delicate vaulting was damaged, bricks were quarried for new buildings, and Malbork deteriorated.

In the late 19th century, Romantic German artists and poets rediscovered the place. An architect named Konrad Steinbrecht devoted 40 years of his life to Malbork, painstakingly resurrecting the palace's medieval splendor. A half-century later, the Nazis used the castle to house POWs. Hitler—who, like many Germans, had a soft spot for Malbork's history—gave the order to defend it to the last man. About half of the castle was destroyed by the Soviet army, who saw it as a symbol of long-standing German domination. But it was restored once again, and today Malbork has been returned to its Teutonic glory.

⊘ SELF-GUIDED TOUR

The official tour of Malbork lasts about three hours; my tour of the highlights takes about half that long, unless you linger. Use the map in this section to navigate. The castle complex is a bit of a maze, with multiple entrances and exits for each room, often behind closed (but unlocked) doors. Don't be shy about grabbing a medieval doorknob and letting yourself in.

POMERANIA

Malbork Castle

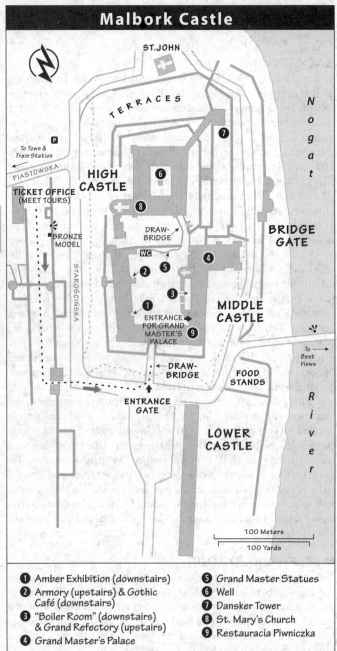

1 Amber Exhibition (downstairs)
2 Armory (upstairs) & Gothic Café (downstairs)
3 "Boiler Room" (downstairs) & Grand Refectory (upstairs)
4 Grand Master's Palace
5 Grand Master Statues
6 Well
7 Dansker Tower
8 St. Mary's Church
9 Restauracia Piwniczka

Entering the Castle Complex

From the ticket office, exit straight ahead and belly up to the brick wall by the bronze model for a panoramic view of the giant complex. Slowly pan across one of Europe's most intimidating fortresses—home to the Grand Master, monks, and knights of the Teutonic Order. The High Castle (where the monks lived) is on the left, marked by the 30-foot-tall statue of Mary at the end of St. Mary's Church. To the right is the Middle Castle, where the knights lived. We'll loop around the right end (Middle Castle), working our way inside, and ending at the High Castle.

The bronze **model** shows the realm of the Teutonic Knights at their peak—stretching from Gdańsk in the north to Toruń to the south, and, waaaay up on the northeast, the city of Kłajpeda, today part of Lithuania. For more than a century (1308-1410), the Teutonic Knights were a formidable presence. For more on this history, see the sidebar later in this chapter.

• *Now turn right and cross the drawbridge under the brick tower. Keep going alongside the moat, turning left to cross another drawbridge into the castle ward. Ahead and to the right, the long, low-lying building was the Lower Castle, where servants and support staff lived. Just before that, on the left, is yet another drawbridge. Show your ticket here and cross partway over the bridge—pausing just outside the brick gate.*

Entrance Gate

Above the door to the brick gate is a sculpture of the Virgin Mary with Baby Jesus, next to a shield and helmet. The message is two-fold: This castle is protected by Mary, and the Teutonic Knights are here to convert pagans—by force, if necessary.

From the drawbridge, look right to observe the formidable fortifications. The Teutonic Knights connected nearby lakes to create a system of canals, forming a moat around the castle that could be crossed only by drawbridge. The rooster-capped corner tower (which contains a toilet) is connected by a sky bridge to the fancy Gothic 14th-century facade of the brick infirmary—kept at a distance for disease control.

Continue farther, until you're inside the gate structure itself. Imagine the gate behind you slamming shut. Look up to see wooden chutes where archers are preparing to rain arrows down on you. Your last thought: Maybe we should have left the Teutonic Knights alone after all.

Before you're pierced by arrows, read the castle's history in its walls: The foundation is made of huge stones—rare in these marshy lands—brought from Sweden. But most of the castle, like so many other buildings in northern Poland, was built with handmade red brick. Throughout the castle, the darker-colored, rougher brick is original, and the lighter-colored, smoother brick was used during later restorations (in the 19th century, and again after World War II). Marvel at the ironclad doors and the heavy portcullis.

Venture through two more enclosed spaces, watching for the holes in the wall (for more guards and soldiers). Ponder the fact that you must pass through five separate, well-defended gates to reach the...

Middle Castle (Zamek Średni)

This part of Malbork, built at an uphill incline to make it even more imposing, was designed to impress. Knights and monks lived here.

Let's get oriented: To your left is the east wing, where visiting monks would sleep. Today this houses the Amber Exhibition (ground floor) and the armory (upstairs). To the right (west) as you enter the main courtyard is the Grand Refectory (closer to the entrance) and the Grand Master's Palace (the taller, squarer building at the far end).

• *Enter the ground floor of the building on the left (go through the small door, and take a few steps down). Here you'll tour the...*

Amber Exhibition

Amber, precious petrified tree sap, is found here in Poland; for a primer, read the "All About Amber" sidebar on page 456. You'll start 42 million years ago and follow the story of amber, then walk down the dimly lit corridor, checking out huge chunks of raw amber and illuminated displays of inclusions (bugs and other organic objects stuck in the amber, à la *Jurassic Park*). Some of the ancient amber artifacts displayed here are up to 3,000 years old, found in graves.

At the end of the corridor, U-turn and work your way back up a parallel hall, lined with all manner of exquisite amber creations: boxes, brooches, necklaces, chess sets, pipes, miniature ships, wine glasses, and belts for skinny-waisted, fashion-conscious women. Many of the finely decorated jewelry boxes and chests have ivory, silver, or shell inlays—better for contrast than gold. The portable religious shrines and altars allowed travelers to remain reverent on the road and still pack light. Notice the wide range of amber colors—from opaque white to transparent yellow to virtually black.

• *Exit at the far end, passing the recommended Gothic Café on your way back outside. As you emerge into the Middle Castle courtyard, go up the*

POMERANIA

wooden staircase on your right, go inside, turn left and walk to the end of the long hall, and go up the stairs. Here you'll find the...

Armory

This enjoyable, well-displayed collection includes an impressive array of swords, armor, and other armaments. Look for the 600-year-old

"hand-and-a-half" swords—too big to be held in one hand. Tucked behind the cannons is a giant shield. A row of these shields could be lined up to form a portable wall—called a phalanx—to protect the knights. In the big room with the decoratively hilted swords, look for the terrifying "flame-bladed sword." You'll also see pikes, maces, crossbows, rifles, and horse armor. And in the room with the body armor, the centerpiece is a suit of armor from the Hussars—Polish horseback knights. Equipped with wings, it created a terrifying sound when the horses were galloping.

• *At the end of the armory, head down the modern stairs and back outside (noticing the handy WC straight ahead). Cross the main courtyard, angling downhill, and enter the smaller courtyard through the passage next to the stubby, dark-wood-topped tower. Find the (unlabeled and sometimes closed) door to a dark, steep flight of stairs that leads down into the...*

"Boiler Room"

The Teutonic Knights had a surprisingly sophisticated method for heating this huge complex. You see a furnace down below and a holding area for hot rocks above. The radiant heat given off by the rocks spread through the vents without also filling them with smoke (illustrated by a chart on the wall). This is one of 11 such "boiler rooms" in the castle complex. As you tour the rest of the castle, keep an eye out for saucer-sized heating vents in the floor.

• *Climb back up the stairs, take an immediate left through a tiny arch, and then go left again, up through the second door (not down through the first door, which takes you out of the castle). This leads into the...*

Grand Master's Palace

This was one of the grandest royal residences in medieval Europe, used in later times by Polish kings and German kaisers. (Today it's sometimes used for special exhibitions.)

• *From the kitchen—with its huge chimney (wow!)—turn left into the big and bright...*

Grand Refectory: With remarkable palm vaulting and grand

POMERANIA

frescoes, this dining hall hosted feasts for up to 400 people to celebrate a military victory or to impress visiting dignitaries. In the floor, notice the 36 heating vents—which are directly above the boiler room you just visited—designed to keep the VIPs warm.

• *At the far end of the refectory, climb the stairs into the...*

Private Rooms of the Grand Master: Though the Teutonic Order dictated that the monks sleep in dormitories, the Grand Master made an exception for himself—with this suite of private rooms. This area is a bit of a maze, so stick with me (or just wander around looking for each of these rooms): From the hall where you enter, turn left into another hall, with show-off decor—including some 15th-century original frescoes of wine leaves and grapes. The door on your left leads to the Grand Master's private **chapel,** dedicated to St. Catherine. Head back into the ivy-draped hall, and go through the door on the left, where a narrow hallway leads past the Grand Master's **private bedroom,** decorated with (now very faint) frescoes of four virgins—female martyrs. Continue past the bedroom to the end of this passage, angle left past the columns and a coin collection (on your right—the knights minted their own coins), then go through the door on the right, into the green-walled **private study** of the Grand Master.

Continue through the study, and you'll step into the Top Knight's private dining room, the **Winter Refectory,** with fewer windows (better insulation) and more of the little heating vents in the floor. The walls are draped with tapestries, which also helped warm things up a bit.

For a dramatic contrast, continue into the next room—the **Summer Refectory.** With big stained-glass windows and delicate vaulting supported by a single central pillar, this room was clearly not designed with defense in mind. In fact, medieval Polish armies focused their attacks on this room. On one legendary occasion, the attackers—tipped off by a spy—knew that an important meeting was going on here and fired a cannonball into the room. It just missed the pillar. (You can see where the cannonball hit the wall, just above the fireplace.) The ceiling eventually did collapse during World War II.

Continue through the

The Teutonic Knights

The Order of the Teutonic Knights began in the Holy Land in 1191, during the Third Crusade. These militarized German monks built hospitals and cared for injured knights. When the Crusades ended in the 12th century, the knights returned to Europe and reorganized as a chivalric order of Christian mercenaries—pagan-killers for hire.

In 1226, a northern Polish duke called in the Teutonic Knights to subdue a tribe of pagans who had been attacking

his lands. Clad in their white cloaks with skinny black crosses, the Teutonic Knights spent 60 years "saving" the pagans by turning them into serfs or massacring them.

Job done, the Teutonic Knights decided to stick around. With the support of the pope and the Holy Roman Emperor (who were swayed by the knights' religious zeal), the knights built one of Europe's

biggest and most imposing fortresses: Malbork. In 1308, they seized large parts of northern Poland (including Gdańsk), cutting off Polish access to the Baltic Sea. The knights grew rich from Hanseatic trade, specializing in amber, grain, and timber. By the late 14th century, the Teutonic Knights had grown to become Europe's largest-ever monastic state and were threatening to overtake Lithuania.

Inspired by a mutual desire to oust the Teutonic Knights, the Poles and the Lithuanians teamed up. In 1386, Polish Princess Jadwiga married Lithuanian Prince Władysław Jagiełło, kick-starting a grand new dynasty: the Jagiellonians.

Every Pole knows the date July 15, 1410: the Battle of Grunwald. King Władysław Jagiełło and Lithuanian Grand Duke Vytautas the Great led a ragtag army of some 40,000 soldiers—Lithuanians, Poles, other Slavs, and even speedy Tatar horsemen—against 27,000 Teutonic Knights. At the end of the day, some 18,000 Poles and Lithuanians were dead—but so were half of the Teutonic Knights, and the other half had been captured. Poland and Lithuania were victorious.

The Battle of Grunwald marked the beginning of the end for the Teutonic Knights, who were conclusively defeated during the Thirteen Years' War (1454-1466). The order officially dissolved in 1575, when they converted to Protestantism and much of their land was folded into Prussia. Later, 19th-century Polish Romantics reimagined the Teutonic Knights as an early symbol of Germanic oppression—poignant among Poles, who suffered through a new round of German abuse in World War II. Some conspiracy theorists believe the Teutonic Knights are still very much active...but that's another story.

POMERANIA

Summer Refectory, stepping out into a hallway. Turn right, notic-ing the washbasin and trough along the corridor. Anyone wanting an audience with the Grand Master had to wash both his hands and his feet. Farther along, find the stairs down (on your left).

• *Take those stairs back out in the courtyard. On your right are four...*

Grand Master Statues

Though this was a religious order, these powerful guys look more like kings than monks. From left to right, shake hands with Hermann von Salza (who was Grand Master when the Teutonic Knights came to Poland); Siegfried von Feuchtwangen (who ac-tually moved the T. K. capital from Venice to Malbork, and who conquered Gdańsk for the knights—oops, can't shake his hand, which was supposedly chopped off by Soviet troops); Winrich von Kniprode (who oversaw Malbork's Golden Age and turned it into a castle fit for a king); and Markgraf Albrecht von Hohenzollern (the last Grand Master before the order dissolved and converted to Protestantism).

• *We're heading into the final section of the castle. Before we do, it's a good time for a break—WCs and eateries are on this courtyard. When you're ready, continue into the High Castle. To the right of the Grand Masters, cross over the...*

Drawbridge

As you cross, notice the extensive system of fortifications and moats protecting the innermost part of the castle just ahead. Once inside the gate, on your left is a door leading to a green zone that runs around the High Castle. Here you'll see a collection of stone cata-pult balls that were actually fired at this castle when it was under siege. (Look high above to see the dents such stones can make.) This is a fun area to explore on your way back out of the castle...if you're not castled out by that point.

Continue straight ahead from the drawbridge, into a passage that's lined with holes to the sides (for surveillance) and with chutes up above (to pour scalding water or pitch on unwanted visitors). It's not quite straight—so a cannon fired here would hit the side wall of the passage, rather than enter the High Castle and its central courtyard. Which is what you're about to do now.

High Castle (Zamek Wysoki)

This is the heart of the castle, and its oldest section. From this spot, the Teutonic Knights governed their vast realm—the largest monk-ruled territory in European history. As much a monastery as a fortress, the High Castle was off-limits to all but 60 monks of the Teutonic Order and their servants. (The knights stayed in the Middle Castle.) Here you'll find the monks' dormitories, chapels, church, and refectory. As this was the nerve center of the Teutonic

Knights, it was also their last line of defense. They stored enormous amounts of food here in case of a siege.

In the middle of the High Castle courtyard is a **well**—an essential part of any inner castle, especially one as prone to sieges as Malbork. At the top is a sculpture of a pelican. Because this noble bird was believed to kill itself to feed its young (notice that it's piercing its own chest with its beak), it was often used in the Middle Ages as a symbol for the self-sacrifice of Jesus.

POMERANIA

• *Take some time to explore the...*

Ground Floor

Immediately to your left is a door leading to the **prison,** with small "solitary confinement" cells near the entrance. Diagonally across the courtyard, hiding in the far corner, is an exhibit on **stained-glass windows** from the castle church.

Back near where you entered the courtyard, step into the **kitchen.** This exhibit—with a long table piled with typical ingredients from that time—gives you a feel for medieval monastery life. The monks who lived here ate three meals a day, along with lots of beer (made here) and wine (imported from France, Italy, and Hungary). A cellar under the kitchen was used as a simple refrigerator—big chunks of ice were cut from the frozen river in winter, stored in the basement, and used to keep food cool in summer. Behind the long table, see the big dumbwaiter (with shelves for hot dishes), which connects this kitchen with the refectory upstairs. Step into the giant stove and peer up into the biggest chimney in the castle.

• *Now go back out into the courtyard and climb up the stairs near where you first entered.*

Middle Floor

• *From the top of the stairs, the first door on the left (with the colorfully painted arch) leads to the most important room of the High Castle, the...*

Chapter Room: Monks gathered here after Mass, and it was also the site for meetings of Teutonic Knights from throughout the realm. If a Grand Master was killed in battle, the new one would be elected here. Carvings above each chair indicated the status of the man who sat there. The big chair belonged to the Grand Master. Notice the little windows high on the wall above his chair, connecting this room to the church next door. Ecclesiastical music would filter in through these windows; imagine the voices of 60 monks bouncing around with these acoustics.

While monks are usually thought to pursue simple lives, the elegant vaulting in this room is anything but plain. The 14th-century frescoes (restored in the 19th century) depict Grand Masters. In the floor are more vents for the central heating.

• *Leave the Chapter Room and walk straight ahead, imagining the monk-filled corridors of Teutonic times. The first door on the right is the...*

Treasury: As you explore the five rooms of the tax collector and the house administrator, notice the wide variety of safes and other lock boxes. Documents, amber, and coins were kept behind heavily armored and well-locked doors.

• *Continue around the cloister. At the end of the corridor, spot the little devil at the bottom of the vaulting (on the right, just above your head). He's pulling his beard and crossing his legs—pointing you down the long corridor leading about 100 yards away from the cloister to the...*

Dansker Tower: From the devil's grimace, you might have guessed that this tower houses the latrine. Four wooden toilet stalls filled this big room. Where one is missing, you can look down to see how the "toilets" simply dropped the waste into the moat. For obvious sanitary (and olfactory) reasons, this potty tower is set apart from the main part of the castle. The bins above the toilets were filled with cabbage leaves, to be used by the T. K. as TP (and as an organic form of Preparation H). This tower could also serve as a final measure of defense—it's easier to defend than the entire castle. Food was stored above, just in case. More info on this grand castle WC is on the wall.

• *Return down the long corridor. Before the end, on the right-hand side of the long passage, a door leads into the...*

Church Exhibition: Once dormitories for the monks, these three rooms now display a wide range of relics from the church. In the last room, on the far wall, is the artistic highlight of the castle: a finely carved and gilded three-panel altarpiece from 1504 featuring the coronation of Mary. Mary's face is mesmerizing. Characteristic of the late Gothic period, the robes seem to fly unrealistically (as if they were bent metal).

• *Back out in the main cloister, turn right, and continue to the end, arriving at the...*

Golden Gate: This elaborate doorway—covered in protective glass—marks the entrance to St. Mary's Church. Before entering, examine this rare original **door.** Ringed with detailed carvings from the New Testament, and symbolic messages about how monks of the Teutonic Order should live their lives, it's a marvelous example of late-13th-century

art. At the bottom-left end of the arch, find the five wise virgins who, having filled their lamps with oil and conserved it wisely, are headed to heaven. On the right, the five foolish virgins who overslept and used up all their oil are damned, much to their dismay.

Step inside **St. Mary's Church** to appreciate a glorious Gothic interior—recently reopened after a lengthy restoration. Straight

ahead from where you entered, look for the 14th-century cross, which was partly burned when the castle was destroyed. Throughout the space, notice how the restorers intentionally used different materials to distinguish repairs from different eras: the brighter plaster dates from the recent work, while the darker plaster (closer to the area where you entered) is from the 19th century.

• *Back outside, go through the narrow door next to the Golden Gate and hike up the tight spiral staircase to the final set of exhibits.*

Top Floor

Walk through a space with temporary exhibits. At the end, descend into the **monks' common room** (left, at the bottom of the stairs). Over the fireplace is a relief depicting the Teutonic Knights fighting the pagans. To the left and above (see the stone windows) is a balcony where musicians entertained the monks after a meal.

The next, very long room, with seven pillars, is the **refectory,** where the monks ate in silence. Along the right-hand wall are lockable storage boxes for tableware. At the end of this room, just beyond another ornate fireplace, notice the grated hole in the wall. This is where the dumb-

POMERANIA

waiter comes up from the kitchen (which we saw below). Beyond this room is an exhibit about the architectural renovation of the castle.

• *Your Malbork tour ends here. You leave the way you came. En route, you can walk around terraces lining the inner moat, between the castle walls (stairs lead down off the drawbridge, by the catapult balls). It's hardly a must-see, but it's pleasant enough, with the Grand Master's garden, a cemetery for monks, and the remains of the small St. Anne's Chapel (with Grand Master tombs).*

MALBORK CONNECTIONS

From Malbork by Train to: Gdańsk (2/hour, 30 minutes on express EIC train, 45 minutes on slower regional train), **Toruń** (about every 2 hours, 2.5 hours, change in Iława), **Warsaw** (hourly, 2.5 hours on express EIC train).

Toruń

Toruń (TOH-roon) is a pretty, lazy Gothic town conveniently located about halfway between Warsaw and Gdańsk. It's worth a few hours to stroll the lively streets, ogle the huge red-brick buildings, and savor the flavor of perhaps Poland's most livable city.

With about 210,000 residents and 30,000 students (at Copernicus University), Toruń is a thriving burg. Like Kraków (and unlike most other Polish cities), Toruń escaped destruction during World War II and remains well-preserved today. Locals brag that their city is a "mini Kraków." But that sells both cities short. Toruń lacks Kraków's over-the-top romanticism, and its sights are quickly exhausted. On the other hand, Toruń may well be Poland's most user-friendly city: tidy streets with a sensible grid plan, wide pedestrian boulevards crammed with locals who greet each other like they're long-lost friends, and an easygoing ambience that seems to say, "Hey—relax." And, while the city has its share of tourists, almost none are Americans.

Toruń clings fiercely to its two claims to fame: It's the proud birthplace of the astronomer Copernicus (Mikołaj Kopernik), and home to a dizzying variety of gingerbread treats (*piernika*; pyer-NEE-kah).

Orientation to Toruń

Everything in Toruń worth seeing is in the walled Old Town, climbing up a gentle hill from the Vistula River. The broad, traffic-free main drag, ulica Szeroka (called Różana at the entrance of town), bisects the Old Town, running parallel to the river. You can walk from one end of the town center to the other in about 15 minutes. The helpful **TI** is on the main square, behind the Old Town Hall (Mon-Fri 9:00-18:00, Sat-Sun from 10:00, shorter hours and closed Sun Oct-April, Rynek Staromiejski 25, tel. 56-621-0930, www.visittorun.com).

ARRIVAL IN TORUŃ

Toruń's main train station (Toruń Główny) is across the river from the Old Town, about a mile away. The main hall has ticket windows, ATMs, and lockers (near the bistro).

To reach the Old Town, you can take a **taxi**—they wait out the door from the main hall (15 zł or less to Plac Rapackiego, the start of my Toruń Walk). To go by **bus,** first buy a ticket from the Relay kiosk inside the station, then take the pedestrian underpass outside (look for *ul. Kjawska* sign and bus icon, past platform 4). Surfacing, find the bus stop for bus #22 or #27. Take the bus to Plac Rapackiego, the first stop after the long bridge. To return to the station, catch the bus across the busy road from where you got off. You can return on bus #22 or #27, or on bus #11, #14, or #36, which go to the opposite side of the station. Note: Public transit is free for anyone over age 65 (just show your passport).

Alternate Train Station: Some (but not all) trains also stop at **Toruń Miasto** station, which is a bit closer to the Old Town (about a 15-minute walk along the river). Check schedules carefully to see if your train stops here; those overnighting in town may find it more convenient.

Toruń Walk

This brief self-guided walk takes you through the heart of Toruń—showing you pretty much everything you'd want to see on a brief visit. With no stops, you could do it in 30 minutes.

• *The bus stop is at...*

Plac Rapackiego: The park that rings Toruń—once the site of the medieval city wall—is an inviting people zone. From the bus stop, walk straight ahead through the park, toward town. You'll pass a self-service bike repair station *(stacja naprawy rowerów)* and a futuristic sculpture (labeled *Solimnia Regit*) honoring hometown boy Copernicus' heliocentric theory...more on him later. The big, historic, ornately gabled building on your left is the Collegium

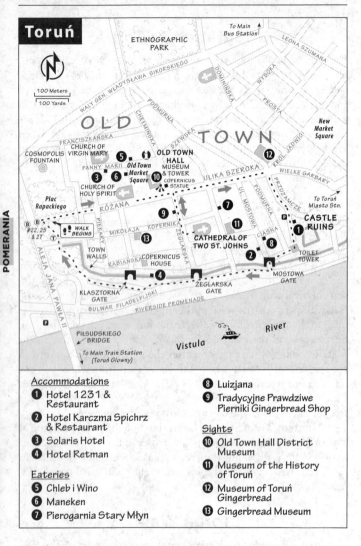

Toruń

Accommodations
1. Hotel 1231 & Restaurant
2. Hotel Karczma Spichrz & Restaurant
3. Solaris Hotel
4. Hotel Retman

Eateries
5. Chleb i Wino
6. Maneken
7. Pierogarnia Stary Młyn

8. Luizjana
9. Tradycyjne Prawdziwe Pierniki Gingerbread Shop

Sights
10. Old Town Hall District Museum
11. Museum of the History of Toruń
12. Museum of Toruń Gingerbread
13. Gingerbread Museum

Maximum, the historic headquarters of Toruń's prestigious university.

Carry on straight ahead, going below the narrow house marked *1930* and the adjoining local Solidarity headquarters. You'll pop out on the town's main drag.

• *Continue one block straight along the main street to reach the bustling…*

Old Town Market Square (Rynek Staromiejski): This square is surrounded by huge brick buildings and outdoor restaurants buzzing with lively locals (for tips, see "Eating in Toruń," later).

The **Old Town Hall** (Ratusz Staromiejski) fills the middle of the square. Like the similar Cloth Hall in Kraków, this building began life as a general market. Toruń is, at its heart, a trading city, and benefitted tremendously from its membership in the Hanseatic League—a trade union of Northern European maritime cities. Toruń's prime position on the Vistula River, navigable by oceangoing vessels, put it on the map and allowed it to prosper. The Old Town Hall contains a fine, if dated, museum, and you can pay to climb its tower for a town view (described later, under "Sights in Toruń").

The building with the pointy spires on the right (across from the Old Town Hall) is the **Artus Court,** where the medieval town council and merchants' guilds met. While the town was founded in 1231, the current building is Neo-Gothic, dating from 1891.

The guy playing his violin in front of the Old Town Hall is a **rafter**—one of the medieval lumberjacks who lashed tree trunks together and floated them down the Vistula to Gdańsk. This particular rafter came to Toruń when the town was infested with frogs. He wooed them with his violin and marched them out of town. (Hmm...sounds like a certain pied piper...)

Walk in front of the Old Town Hall (passing the ticket desk for the museum and tower climb). At the far end, the bigger statue depicts **Mikołaj Kopernik,** known internationally as Nicolaus Copernicus (1473-1543). This Toruń-born son of aristocrats turned the world on its ear when he suggested that the sun, not the earth, is the center of the universe (the "heliocentric theory"). Toruń is seriously proud of this local boy done good—he's the town mascot, as well as the namesake of the local university. Among its fields of study, Copernicus U. has a healthy astronomy program. There's a planetarium in the Old Town (just past the far corner of the square) and a giant radio telescope on the outskirts. Despite all the local fuss over Copernicus, there's some dispute about his "nationality": He was born in Toruń, but at a time when it was the predominantly German town of "Thorn." So is he Polish...or German? (For more on Copernicus, you can visit his birth house—now a museum—just two blocks away and described later, under "Sights in Toruń.")

Copernicus faces a shiny **donkey** at the corner of Szeroka and Żeglarska streets. Notice the sharp ridge on the donkey's back, which recalls a humiliating punishment. Centuries ago, delinquents and petty criminals needing to be set straight would be forced to straddle this donkey—after townspeople had tied heavy stones to their feet, weighing them down painfully.

• But you're on vacation—and, rather than humiliation, you get gingerbread. Follow your nose to the right, down Żeglarska street, which is lined with...

Gingerbread Shops: For Poles, Toruń is synonymous with gingerbread (piernika)—you'll smell its heavenly scent all over

town. When Chopin visited, most of his impressions of Toruń revolved around gingerbread. Today, this Toruń treat can be topped
with different kinds of jams or glazes, and/or dipped in chocolate.
But historically, gingerbread was more straightforward—and a
valuable commodity. The honey used in its dough and for glazing
acted as a preservative, allowing gingerbread to be traded far and
wide. And its spices aid digestion, so it served a medicinal purpose
as well. Thanks to Hanseatic League connections, Toruń's bakers
had access to exotic, imported spices such as white ginger, cinnamon, clove, anise, citrus skins, cardamom, and peppercorns (for
which *piernika* is named). Traditionally, gingerbread dough was
pressed into wooden molds, giving each cookie a distinctive shape.

While you'll spot a half-dozen options for buying gingerbread within a few steps of here, I like the one marked **Tradycyjne
Prawdziwe Pierniki** (on the right, at #25). This shop has a fun
system: All the varieties cost the same, so you can assemble just the
mix you like by pointing. *Róża* is rose, *malina* is raspberry, *czarna
porzeczka* is black currant, *morela* is apricot, and—of course—*cze-
kolada* is chocolate.

• *A few steps down and across the street is the...*

Cathedral of Two Saint Johns (Katedra Św. Jana Chrzciciela i
Jana Ewangelisty): Dedicated in the 12th century to both John the
Baptist and John the Evange-
list, this is the parish church of
the Old Town. Its massive bulk
dominates the view of Toruń
from across the river. From
here at street level, appreciate
the architectural heaviness: The
marshy land lacked big stones,
so instead of flying buttresses,
medieval engineers designed an
overbuilt brick structure so they could go big.

Stepping inside, you find graceful Gothic austerity—with delicate ribs and whitewashed walls. The gravestones of big shots pave
the floor. Each trade guild had its own chapel, with its own fancy
altar. On the wall to the left of the main altar, notice the finely
restored 13th-century *Last Judgment* fresco. As you leave, head to
the back-right corner (opposite where you came in) and find the
colorful baptismal font where, in 1473, Copernicus was baptized
(free entry, tower climb extra, open Mon-Sat 9:00-17:30, Sun from
14:30).

• *Having satisfied your ginger tooth and seen the town's most important
church, head back to the square and that painful donkey, turn right, and
join the human stream down the appropriately named...*

Ulica Szeroka ("Wide Street"): This enjoyable pedestrian promenade leads through the heart of town. Embedded in the paving bricks are the coats of arms of Toruń's medieval trading partners. And on each side of the street is an eclectic commotion of fun facades.

About 30 yards before the road forks at the stately, white Empik building, look down narrow Przedzamcze street to the right to see fragments of the town wall. This marks the border between the Old Town and the New Town (chartered only about 30 years later—both in the 13th century). While these areas are collectively known today as the unified "Old Town," they were quite different in the Middle Ages—each with its own market square, and separated by a wall. Because the New Town lacked the easy access to the river, most of its residents were craftspeople who supplied the traders in the Old Town. (If you're curious to see the New Town Square and Town Hall, take the left fork at the Empik building and walk two blocks up ulica Królowej Jadwigi.)

• *One of the city's two gingerbread museums is just ahead on the left (described later, under "Sights in Toruń").*

But for now, turn right down Przedzamcze, bear left at the parking lot, and continue under the stubby, standalone brick gate. Emerging on the other side, you'll see an old mill straight ahead, and a crenellated brick tower on your right. You're standing in the middle of what's left of...

Toruń Castle: This castle, built by the Teutonic Knights who were so influential in northern Poland in the Middle Ages (see page 507), was destroyed in the 15th century by the locals—who, aside from a heap of bricks, left only the tower that housed the Teutonic toilets. The ruins nearby—basically just foundations—have nothing much to offer. But what survives is one of the better toilet towers in Europe—which was connected to the castle by an elevated walkway and located far enough away to keep things hygienic. The old mill next to the toilet is now a recommended hotel and restaurant named 1231, for the date the Teutonic Order arrived here.

• *Our walk is over. You can backtrack the way you came and explore more of the city (including the sights listed next). Or you can take a quick riverside stroll: Go under the toilet tower and down to the Vistula River, turn right, and stroll along the castle and 14th-century city walls back to your starting point (and the bus stop back to the station). The road is called Bulwar Filadelfijski—for Toruń's sister city in Pennsylvania.*

Sights in Toruń

Toruń is more about strolling than it is about sightseeing—the town's museums are underwhelming. Aside from its half-dozen red-brick churches (any of which are worth dropping into), the following attractions are worth considering on a rainy day.

Hours: Almost all of these sights—everything except the second Gingerbread Museum—are operated by the city and have the same hours: Tue-Sun 10:00-18:00, Oct-April until 16:00, closed Mon year-round (www.muzeum.torun.pl).

City History Museums

Toruń operates two different history museums. Both show off intimate bits and pieces of history—from pewter tankards to old gingerbread molds—that show the richness of this traders' city. They're essentially redundant—pick one.

The **Old Town Hall District Museum,** inside the centerpiece building on the main square, has more impressive spaces—including Gothic corridors and royal meeting rooms upstairs. But the collection is dusty and challenging to appreciate. The highlight is the Gothic Gallery on the main floor—featuring medieval church art saved from the region's churches, with lots of Marys (the patron of the Teutonic Order), and a close-up look at some 14th-century stained glass (13 zł, Rynek Staromiejski 1). You can also pay (separately) 13 zł to climb the 176 narrow wooden steps to the top of the **tower,** for great views over the city center.

A few blocks away, the **Museum of the History of Toruń** fills an old red-brick granary with four floors of well-explained artifacts, colorful exhibits, and English translations. While the space is less impressive, it's a more meaningful experience (10 zł, Łazienna 16). You can pay extra to watch an informative, 13-minute 3-D movie (with English subtitles) about the town's history on the top floor.

Gingerbread Museums

Toruń also has two competing museums about gingerbread. Neither is essential—the main Toruń gingerbread experience is simply dropping into a shop and buying some to snack on—but they both, in different ways, teach about this important local product. Unlike cookies, you should choose just one of these museums.

The **Museum of Toruń Gingerbread,** just off the main drag at the far end of town, is more of a traditional museum. It fills the historic red-brick Weese family gingerbread factory, established in 1885. (The company still makes gingerbread, in a modern plant on the outskirts.) After watching a brief film, you'll walk through three floors of quaint, modern exhibits that trace the history of gingerbread: historic artifacts (molds, ovens) in the cellar; a re-created late-19th-century street on the upper floor; and an interesting overview of the gingerbread-making process on the main floor (10 zł, Strumykowa 4). While they also offer hands-on gingerbread demonstrations, they're not reliably in English (though you can book one for 70 zł extra, details on website).

The similarly named **Gingerbread Museum** (Muzeum Piernika), between the main square and the river, is for those wanting an English demonstration rather than a traditional museum. Costumed medieval bakers spend about an hour walking you through the traditional process of rolling, cutting out, baking, and tasting your own batch of gingerbread cookies. After aging for 12 weeks to achieve the proper consistency, the dough bakes for only 12 minutes—or, according to the medieval bakers, about 50 Hail Marys. At the end, they spend another 20 minutes demonstrating how the process changed in the early 20th century, with the advent of modern equipment (17 zł, daily 10:00-18:00, Polish tours start at the top of each hour, English tours run 2/day—usually at 13:00 and 16:00, in peak times it's smart to reserve online in advance, Rabiańska 9, tel. 56-663-6617, www.muzeumpiernika.pl).

Copernicus House (Dom Kopernika)

Filling a pair of gabled brick buildings between the main square and the river, this museum celebrates the hero of Toruń. As much about medieval Toruń as about the famous astronomer, and sprawling over several floors, the exhibits loosely explain Nicolaus Copernicus' life and achievements, with several re-created Gothic rooms. However, it's not engaging and fails to do justice to this very important native son; it's skippable for casual visitors (13 zł, Kopernika 15, tel. 566-605-613). If you visit, skip the "4-D cinema" (which costs extra)—while it provides a weighty introduction to astronomy and astrophysics, from the Big Bang to the plight of Pluto, it barely mentions Copernicus.

Other Toruń Museums

Toruń is a popular destination for Polish families, and the TI loves to suggest attractions for those with more time. The **"Mill of Knowledge"** is a hands-on science museum designed for kids, with six floors of interactive exhibits. The **Travelers Museum** focuses on Toruń native Tony Halik, who hosted a travelogue TV show that was many Poles' gateway to the world. The city has two **open-air folk museums:** one just north of the Old Town, and a better one, called Olender, across the river. And in the park ringing the Old Town, just a two-minute walk from the bus stop, is the **Fontanna Cosmopolis,** a dancing fountain that thrills kids with a little music-and-lights show each evening.

POMERANIA

Sleeping in Toruń

$$ Hotel 1231, filling a restored 13th-century mill at the bottom of town, has 22 modern rooms near the top of this price range, and a good restaurant (Przedzamcze 6, tel. 607-553-812, www.hotel1231.pl).

$$ Hotel Karczma Spichrz ("Granary") has 24 rooms in a renovated old granary, and 20 more in a newer annex. Rustic and creaky, it has huge wooden beams around every corner (low ceilings, thin floors and walls can be noisy, elevator, a block off the main drag toward the river at ulica Mostowa 1, tel. 56-657-1140, www.spichrz.pl).

$ Solaris Hotel, just off the main square, has 23 stylish rooms tucked into a historic town house (Panny Marii 9, tel. 56-471-3042, www.hotel-solaris.pl).

$ Hotel Retman ("Rafter") has 29 older but nicely appointed rooms over a restaurant just down the street from the Gingerbread Museum (ulica Rabiańska 15, tel. 56-657-4460, www.hotel-retman.pl).

Eating in Toruń

On the Old Town Market Square: The square surrounding the Old Town Hall is ringed with stay-awhile al fresco tables, any of which is a good choice for a scenic meal; most are open long hours daily. Favorites include **$$ Chleb i Wino** ("Bread and Wine"), which feels a bit more upscale, with Polish and Mediterranean dishes; and **$ Maneken,** the original outpost of a popular chain, which serves crêpes.

Traditional Restaurants in Hotels: The recommended **$$ Spichrz** and **$$$ 1231** hotels both have traditional restaurants in historic spaces, with tempting menus of stick-to-your-ribs traditional fare. Spichrz is a bit ye olde and more casual; 1231 feels more upscale (see contact information earlier).

Hearty Pierogi: Pierogarnia Stary Młyn ("Old Mill"), on a side street near the history museum, has an over-the-top-rustic interior (and some outdoor tables) and a long menu of pierogi—boiled, baked, pan-fried—with various fillings (daily, Łazienna 28, tel. 566-210-309).

Cajun: Luizjana, named for the US state, offers Cajun cooking that's better than it has any right to be (daily for dinner, Mon-Fri also for lunch, ulica Mostowa 10).

POMERANIA

Toruń Connections

Toruń is a natural stopover on the way between Warsaw and Gdańsk. The connection to Warsaw or Gdańsk is quick and easy; to reach Malbork, you'll usually need to change.

From Toruń by Train to: Warsaw (every 2 hours direct, 3 hours on express IC train), **Gdańsk** (4/day direct, 2.5 hours; additional options with a change in Bydgoszcz or Iława, 3 hours), **Malbork** (about every 2 hours, 2.5 hours, change in Iława), **Kraków** (1/day direct, 6.5 hours; more options with a change at Warsaw's Zachodnia station: 7/day, 6 hours), **Berlin** (4/day, 6 hours, change in Poznań).

By Bus: If heading to **Gdańsk,** consider buses operated by Arriva, which are cheaper and faster than the train (about 2 hours; www.arrivabus.pl).

POMERANIA

HUNGARY

Magyarország

HUNGARY

Magyarország

Hungary is an island of Asian-descended Magyars in a sea of Slavs. Even though the Hungarians have thoroughly integrated with their Slavic and German neighbors in the millennium-plus since they arrived, there's still something about the place that's distinctly Magyar (MUD-jar). Here in quirky, idiosyncratic Hungary, everything's a little different from the rest of Europe in terms of history, language, culture, customs, and cuisine—but it's hard to put your finger on exactly how.

Just a century ago, this country controlled half of one of Europe's grandest realms: the Austro-Hungarian Empire. Today, perhaps clinging to their former greatness, many Hungarians remain old-fashioned and nostalgic. With their dusty museums and bushy moustaches, they love to remember the good old days. Buildings all over the country are marked with plaques boasting *MŰEMLÉK* ("historical monument").

Thanks to this focus on tradition, the Hungarians you'll encounter are generally polite, formal, and professional. Hungarians have class. Everything here is done with a proud flourish. When a waiter comes to your table in a restaurant, he'll say, *"Tessék parancsolni"*—literally, "Please command, sir." The standard greeting, *"Jó napot kívánok,"* means, "I wish you a good day." Women sometimes hear the even more formal greeting, *"Kezét csókolom"*—"I kiss your hand." And when your train or bus makes a stop, you won't be alerted by a mindless, blaring beep—but instead, by peppy music. (You'll be humming these contagious little ditties all day.)

Hungarians are also orderly and tidy...in their own sometimes unexpected ways. Yes, Hungary has its share of litter, graffiti, and crumbling buildings, but you'll find great reason within the chaos. The Hungarian railroad has a long list of discounted fares—for seniors, kids, dogs...and monkeys. (It could happen.) My favorite town name in Hungary: Hatvan. This means "Sixty" in Hungarian...and it's exactly 60 kilometers from Budapest. You can't argue with that logic.

This tradition of left-brained thinking hasn't produced many great Hungarian painters or poets who are known outside their

homeland. But the Hungarians, renowned for their ingenuity, have made tremendous contributions to science, technology, business, and industry. Hungarians of note include Edward Teller (instrumental in creating the H-bomb), John von Neumann (a pioneer of computer science), András Gróf (who, as Andy Grove, emigrated to the US and became the CEO of Intel), George Soros (the billionaire investor famous—or notorious—for supporting left-wing causes), and László József Bíró (inventor of the ballpoint pen). A popular local joke claims that Hungarians are so clever that they can enter a revolving door behind you and exit in front of you.

Perhaps the most famous Hungarian "scientist" invented something you probably have in a box in your basement: Ernő Rubik, creator of the famous cube. Hungarians' enjoyment of a good mind-bending puzzle is also evident in their fascination with chess, which you'll see played in cafés, parks, and baths.

Like their Viennese neighbors, Hungarians know how to enjoy the good life. Favorite activities include splashing and soaking in their many thermal baths. Taking the waters Hungarian-style deserves to be your top priority while you're here. Though public baths can sound intimidating, they're a delight. In the following chapters I recommend my three favorite baths in Budapest, a fine bath in Eger, and a couple more just outside of Eger. For each, I've included instructions to help you enjoy the warm-water fun like a pro. (To allay your first fear: Yes, you can wear your swimsuit.)

Hungarians have also revived an elegant, Vienna-style café culture that was dismantled by the communists. Whiling away the afternoon at a genteel coffeehouse as you nurse a drink or a delicate

Hungary Almanac

Official Name: Magyarország (Hungary).

Population: Hungary's 10 million people are 85 percent ethnic Hungarians. One in 50 is Roma (Gypsy). About 40 percent of the populace is Catholic, and nearly 15 percent is Protestant. Of the world's approximately 12 million ethnic Hungarians, one in six lives outside Hungary (mostly in areas of Romania, Slovakia, Serbia, and Croatia that were once part of Hungary).

Latitude and Longitude: 47°N and 20°E; similar latitude to Seattle, Paris, and Vienna.

Area: 36,000 square miles, similar to Indiana or Maine.

Geography: Hungary sits in the Carpathian Basin, bound by the Carpathian Mountains (in the north) and the Dinaric Mountains (in the south). Though it's surrounded by mountains, Hungary itself is relatively flat, with some gently rolling hills. The Great Hungarian Plain—beginning on the east bank of the Danube in Budapest—stretches all the way to Asia. Hungary's two main rivers—the Danube and Tisza—run north-south through the country, neatly dividing it into three regions.

Biggest Cities: Budapest (the capital, nearly 2 million), Debrecen (in the east, 205,000), and Miskolc (in the north, 165,000).

Economy: The Gross Domestic Product is $290 billion, with a per capita GDP of nearly $30,000. Thanks to its progressive "goulash communism," Hungary had a head start on many other former Soviet Bloc countries and is now thriving, privatized...and largely foreign-owned. In the 1990s, many communist-era workers (especially women) lost their jobs. Today, the workforce is small (only 60 percent employment) but highly educated and skilled. Grains, metals, machinery, and automobiles are major exports, and about one-quarter of trade is with Germany.

Currency: 275 forints (Ft, or HUF) = about $1.

Government: The single-house National Assembly (199 seats) is the only ruling branch directly elected by popular vote. The legislators in turn select the figurehead president (currently János Áder) and the ruling prime minister (Viktor Orbán); both belong to the far right, nativist Fidesz party.

Flag: Three horizontal bands, top to bottom: red (representing strength), white (faithfulness), and green (hope). It often includes the Hungarian coat of arms: horizontal red-and-white stripes (on the left); the patriarchal, or double-barred, cross (on the right); and the Hungarian crown (on top).

The Average János: The typical Hungarian eats a pound of lard a week (they cook with it). The average family has three members and spends almost three-fourths of its income on housing. According to a condom-company survey, the average Hungarian has sex 131 times a year (behind only France and Greece), making them Europe's third-greatest liars.

dessert is a favorite pastime. (For the best options in Budapest, see "Budapest's Café Culture" on page 669.)

Classical music is revered in Hungary, perhaps as nowhere else outside Austria. Aside from scientists and businessmen, the best-known Hungarians are composers: Béla Bartók, Zoltán Kodály, and Franz Liszt.

While one in five Hungarians lives in Budapest, the countryside plays an important role in the country's economy—this has always been a highly agricultural region. The sprawling Great Hungarian Plain (Puszta) that makes up a vast swath of Hungary is the country's breadbasket. You'll pass through fields of wheat and corn, but the grains are secondary to Hungarians' (and tourists') true love: wine. Hungarian winemaking standards plummeted under the communists, but many vintner families have reclaimed their land, resumed their traditional methods, and are making wines worthy of pride once more. (For details, see the "Hungarian Wines" sidebar, later.)

Somehow Hungary, at the crossroads of Europe, has managed to become cosmopolitan while remaining perfectly Hungarian. The Hungarians—like Hungary itself—are a cross-section of Central European cultures: Magyars, Germans, Czechs, Slovaks, Poles, Serbs, Jews, Ottomans, Romanians, Roma (Gypsies), and many others. Still, no matter how many generations removed they are from Magyar stock, there's something different about Hungarians. It's a unique European culture that's a pure joy to discover.

HELPFUL HINTS

First Name Last: Hungarians list a person's family name first, and the given name is last—just as in many other Eastern cultures (think of Kim Jong-un). So the composer known as "Franz Liszt" in German is "Liszt Ferenc" in his homeland.

Hello Goodbye: Hungarians have a charming habit of using the English word "hello" for both "hi" and "bye," just like the Italians use "ciao." You might overhear a Hungarian end a telephone conversation with a cheery "Hello!"

Telephones: When it comes to dialing, Hungary is unique in two ways: First, to dial domestic long-distance from a landline, you have to dial 06, then the area code and number. And second, it can be tricky to call a Hungarian mobile number (generally beginning with +3620, +3630, +3631, or +3670). In this book, I have listed these numbers as you'll dial them from any international line or any mobile phone (including a Hungarian one), starting with +36. (You can also replace the "+" with 00 if calling from Europe, or 011 if calling from the US.) However, if you are dialing these numbers from a landline within Hungary, you'll need to replace the "+36" with "06." So, to call a local guide with the number +3620-926-0557, you'd dial exactly that if calling from your American phone or from a Hungarian mobile phone. But if calling from your Budapest hotel room, dial 0620-926-0557. For more tips on calling, see page 1110.

Toll Sticker: Driving on Hungarian expressways requires a toll sticker (*autópálya matrica*, also called a "vignette," 2,975 Ft/week, 4,780 Ft/month, www.motorway.hu). Ask about this when you rent your car (if it's not already included, you'll have to buy one).

HUNGARIAN HISTORY

The Hungarian story—essentially the tale of a people finding their home—is as epic as any in Europe. Over the course of a millennium, a troublesome nomadic tribe that was the scourge of Europe gradually assimilated with its neighbors and—through a combination of tenacity and diplomacy—found itself controlling a vast swath of Central and Eastern Europe. Locals toss around the names of great historical figures such as Kossuth, Széchenyi, and Nagy as if they're talking about old friends. Take this crash course so you can keep up.

The story begins long, long ago and far, far away...

Welcome to Europe

The land we call Hungary has long been considered the place—culturally and geographically—where the West (Europe) meets the East (Asia). The Roman province of Pannonia once extended to the final foothills of the Alps that constitute the Buda Hills, on the west side of the Danube. Across the river, Rome ended and the barbarian wilds began. From here, the Great Hungarian Plain stretches in a long, flat expanse all the way to Asia—hemmed in to the north by the Carpathian Mountains. (Geologists consider this prairie-like plain to be the westernmost steppe in Europe—resembling the terrain that covers much of Central Asia.) After Rome collapsed and Europe fell into the Dark Ages, Hungary became the territory of Celts, Vandals, Huns, and Avars...until some out-of-towners moved into the neighborhood.

The seven nomadic Magyar tribes, led by the mighty Árpád (and, according to legend, guided by the mythical Turul bird), thundered into the Carpathian Basin in AD 896. But after their long and winding westward odyssey, the Great Hungarian Plain felt comfortingly like

home to the Magyars—reminiscent of the Asian steppes of their ancestors.

The Magyars would camp out in today's Hungary in the winters, and in the summers, they'd go on raids throughout Europe. They were notorious as incredibly swift horsemen, whose use of stirrups (an eastern innovation largely unknown in Europe at the time) allowed them to easily outmaneuver foes and victims. From Italy, France, Germany's Rhine, the Spanish Pyrenees, all the way to Constantinople (modern-day Istanbul)—the Magyars had the run of the Continent.

For half a century, the Magyars ranked with the Vikings as the most feared people in Europe. To Europeans, this must have struck a chord of queasy familiarity: a mysterious and dangerous eastern tribe running roughshod over Europe, speaking a gibberish language, and employing strange, terrifying, relentless battle techniques. No wonder they called the new arrivals "Hungarians."

Planted in the center of Europe, the Magyars effectively drove a wedge in the middle of the sprawling Slavic populations of the Great Moravian Kingdom (basically today's "Eastern Europe"). The Slavs were split into north and south—a division that persists today: Czechs, Slovaks, and Poles to the north; and Croats, Slovenes, Serbs, Bosniaks, and Bulgarians to the south. (You can still hear the division caused by the Magyars in the language: While Czechs and Russians call a castle *hrad,* Croats and Serbs call it *grad.*)

After decades of terrorizing Europe, the Magyars were finally defeated by a German and Czech army at the Battle of Augsburg in 955. Géza, Grand Prince of the Hungarians—realizing that if they were to survive, his people had to put down roots and get along with their neighbors—made a fateful decision that would forever shape Hungary's future: He adopted Christianity; baptized his son, Vajk; and married him to a Bavarian princess at a young age.

On Christmas Day in the year 1000, Vajk changed his name to István (Stephen) and was symbolically crowned by the pope (for more on István, see page 620). At István's request, a Venetian missionary, Gerardo di Sagredo, came to Buda to help convert the Hungarians. But he was martyred for his efforts, becoming known to Hungarians as St. Gellért. The domestication of the nomadic Magyars was difficult—due largely to the resistance of István's uncles—but was ultimately successful. Hungary became a legitimate Christian kingdom, welcomed by its neighbors. Under kings such as László I, Kálmán "the Book Lover," and András II, Hungary entered a period of prosperity. Medieval Hungary ruled a vast empire—including large parts of today's Slovakia, Romania (Transylvania), Serbia (Vojvodina), and Croatia.

The Tatars, the Ottomans, and Other Outsiders (AD 1000-1686)

One of Hungary's earliest challenges came at the hands of fellow invaders from Central Asia. Through the first half of the 13th century, the Tatars—initially led by Genghis Khan—swept into Eastern Europe from Mongolia. In the summer of 1241, Genghis Khan's son and successor, Ögedei Khan, broke into Hungarian territory. The Tatars sacked and plundered Hungarian towns, laying waste to the kingdom. It was only Ögedei Khan's death in early 1242—and the ensuing dispute about succession—that saved the Hungarians, as Tatar armies rushed home and the Mongolian Empire contracted. The Hungarian king, Béla IV, was left to rebuild his ruined kingdom—creating some of the first stout hilltop castles that still line the Danube.

Each of Béla's successors left his own mark on Hungary, as the Magyar kingdom flourished. When the original Árpád dynasty died out in 1301, they imported French kings (from the Naples-based Anjou, or Angevin, dynasty) to continue building their young realm. King Károly Róbert (Charles Robert) won over the Magyars, and his son Nagy Lajos (Louis the Great) expanded Hungarian holdings.

This was a period of flux for all of Central and Eastern Europe, as the nearby Czech and Polish kingdoms also saw their longstanding dynasties expire. For a time, royal intermarriages juggled the crowns of the region between various ruling families. Most notably, for 50 years (1387-1437) Hungary was ruled by Holy Roman Emperor Sigismund of Luxembourg, whose holdings also included the Czech lands, parts of Italy, much of Croatia, and more.

For more than 150 years, Hungary did not have a Hungarian-blooded king. This changed in the late 15th century, when a shortage of foreign kings led the enlightened King Mátyás (Matthias) Corvinus to ascend to the throne. The son of popular military hero János Hunyadi, King Matthias fostered the arts, sparked a mini-Renaissance, and successfully balanced foreign threats to Hungarian sov-

ereignty (the Habsburgs to the north and west, and the Ottomans to the south and east). Under Matthias, Hungarian culture and political power reached a peak. (For more on this great Hungarian king, see page 615.)

But even before the reign of "good king Mátyás," the Ottomans (from today's Turkey) had already begun slicing their way through the Balkan Peninsula toward Central Europe. In 1526, the Ottomans entered Hungary when Sultan Süleyman the Magnificent killed Hungary's King Lajos II at the Battle of Mohács. By 1541, they took Buda. The Ottomans would dominate Hungarian life (and history) until the 1680s—nearly a century and a half.

The Ottoman invasion divided Hungary into thirds: Ottoman-occupied "Lower Hungary" (more or less today's Hungary); rump "Upper Hungary" (basically today's Slovakia), with its capital at Bratislava (which they called "Pozsony"); and the loosely independent territories of Transylvania, ruled by Hungarian dukes. During this era, the Ottomans built some of the thermal baths that you'll still find throughout Hungary.

Ottoman-occupied Hungary became severely depopulated, and many of its towns and cities fell into ruins. While it was advantageous for a Hungarian subject to adopt Islam (for lower taxes and other privileges), the Ottomans rarely forced conversions—unlike the arguably more oppressive Catholics who controlled other parts of Europe at the time. Ottoman rule meant that Hungary took a different course than other parts of Europe during this time. The nation fully enjoyed the Renaissance, but missed out on other major European historical events—both good (the Age of Discovery and Age of Reason) and bad (the devastating Catholic-versus-Protestant wars that plagued much of the rest of Europe).

Crippled by the Ottomans and lacking power and options, desperate Hungarian nobles offered their crown to the Austrian Habsburg Empire, in exchange for salvation from the invasion. The Habsburgs instead used Hungary as a kind of "buffer zone" between the Ottoman advance and Vienna. And that was only the beginning of a very troubled relationship between the Hungarians and the Austrians.

Habsburg Rule, Hungarian National Revival, and Revolution (1686-1867)

In the late 17th century, the Habsburg army, starting from Vienna, began a sustained campaign to push the Ottomans out of Hungary in about 15 years. They finally wrested Buda and Pest from the Ottomans in 1686. The Habsburgs repopulated Buda and Pest with Germans, while Magyars reclaimed the countryside.

The Habsburgs governed the country as an outpost of Austria. The Hungarians—who'd had enough of foreign rule—fought them tooth and nail. Countless streets, squares, and buildings throughout the country are named for the "big three" Hungarian patriots who resisted the Habsburgs during this time: Ferenc Rákóczi (who led the unsuccessful War of Independence in 1703-1711), István Széchenyi (a wealthy count who funded grand structures to give his Magyar countrymen something to take pride in), and Lajos Kossuth (who led the Revolution of 1848).

The early 19th century saw a thawing of Habsburg oppression. Here as throughout Europe, "backward" country traditions began to trickle into the cities, gaining more respect and prominence. It was during this time of reforms that Hungarian (rather than German) became the official language. It also coincided with a Romantic Age of poets and writers (such as Mihály Vörösmarty and Sándor Petőfi) who began using Hungarian to create literature for the first time. By around 1825, the Hungarian National Revival was underway, as the people began to embrace the culture and traditions of their Magyar ancestors. Like people across Europe—from Ireland to Italy, and from Prague to Scandinavia—the Hungarians were rediscovering what made them a unique people.

In March of 1848, a wave of Enlightenment-fueled nationalism that began in Paris ignited a revolutionary spirit in cities such as Vienna, Milan...and Budapest. On March 15, the Revolution of 1848 began with Petőfi reading a rabble-rousing poem on the steps of the National Museum in Pest.

In the spring of 1849, the Hungarians mounted a bloody but successful offensive to take over a wide swath of territory, including Buda and Pest. But in June, Franz Josef enlisted the aid of his fellow divine monarch, the Russian czar, who did not want the Magyars to provide an example for his own independence-minded subjects. Some 200,000 Russian reinforcements flooded into Hungary, crushing the revolution by August. After the final battle, the Habsburgs executed 13 Hungarian generals, then celebrated by clinking mugs of beer. To this very day, clinking beer mugs is, for many traditional Hungarians, just bad style.

For a while, the Habsburgs cracked down on their unruly Hungarian subjects. After an important military loss to Bismarck's Prussia in 1866, Austria understood that it couldn't control its rebellious Slavic holdings all by itself. And so, just 18 years after crushing the Hungarians in a war, the Habsburgs handed them the reins. With the Compromise *(Ausgleich)* of 1867, Austria granted

Budapest the authority over the eastern half of their lands, creating the so-called Dual Monarchy of the Austro-Hungarian Empire. Hungary was granted their much-prized "home rule," where most matters (except finance, foreign policy, and the military) were administered from Budapest rather than Vienna. The Habsburg emperor, Franz Josef, agreed to a unique "king and emperor" *(König und Kaiser)* arrangement, where he was emperor of Austria, but only king of Hungary. In 1867, he was crowned Hungarian king in both Buda (at Matthias Church) and Pest (on today's March 15 Square). The insignia "K+K" *(König und Kaiser)*—which you'll still see everywhere—evokes these grand days.

Budapest's Golden Age (1867-1918)

The *Ausgleich* marked a precipitous turning point for the Hungarians, who once again governed their traditional holdings: large parts of today's Slovakia, Serbia, and Transylvania, and smaller parts of today's Croatia, Slovenia, Ukraine, and Austria. To better govern their sprawling realm, in 1873, the cities of Buda, Pest, and Óbuda merged into one mega-metropolis: Budapest.

Serendipitously, Budapest's new prominence coincided with the 1,000th anniversary of the Hungarians' ancestors, the Magyars, arriving in Europe...one more excuse to dress things up. Budapest's long-standing rivalry with Vienna only spurred them to build bigger and better. The year 1896 saw an over-the-top millennial celebration, for which many of today's greatest structures were created (see page 563).

No European city grew faster in the second half of the 19th century than Budapest; in the last quarter of the 19th century alone, Budapest doubled in size, building on the foundation laid by Széchenyi and other patriots. By 1900, the city was larger than Rome, Madrid, or Amsterdam. But before long, the Hungarians began to make the same mistakes the Habsburgs had—trampling on the rights of their minorities, and enforcing a policy of "Magyarization" that compelled subjects from all ethnic backgrounds to adopt the Hungarian language and culture. Soon the Golden Age came crashing to an end, and Hungary plunged into its darkest period.

The Crisis of Trianon (1918-1939)

World War I marked the end of the age of divine monarchs, as the Romanovs of Russia, the Ottomans of Asia Minor, and, yes, the Habsburgs of Austria-Hungary saw their empires break apart. Hungary, which had been riding the Habsburgs' coattails for the past half-century, now paid the price. As retribution for their role on the losing side of World War I, the 1920 Treaty of Trianon (named for the palace on the grounds of Versailles where it was

Pre-Trianon Hungary

After Trianon, the newly shrunken Kingdom of Hungary had
to reinvent itself. The Hungarian crown sat unworn in the Royal

signed) reassigned two-thirds of Hungary's former territory and
half of its population to Romania, Ukraine, Czechoslovakia, and
Yugoslavia.

It is impossible to overstate the impact of the Treaty of Trianon on the Hungarian psyche—and on Hungarian history. Not
unlike the overnight construction of the Berlin Wall, towns along
the new Hungarian borders were suddenly divided down the middle. Many Hungarians found themselves unable to visit relatives or
commute to jobs that were in the same country the day before. This
sent hundreds of thousands of Hungarian refugees—now "foreigners" in their own towns—into Budapest, sparking a bittersweet
boom in the capital.

To this day, the Treaty of Trianon is regarded as one of the
greatest tragedies of Hungarian history. Like the Basques and the
Serbs, the Hungarians feel separated from each other by circumstances outside their control. Today, more than two million ethnic
Hungarians live outside Hungary (mostly in Romania)—and many
Hungarians claim that these lands still belong to the Magyars. The
sizeable Magyar minorities in neighboring countries have often
been mistreated—particularly in Romania (under Ceauşescu), Yugoslavia (under Milošević), and Slovakia (under Mečiar). You'll see
maps, posters, and bumper stickers with the distinctive shape of a
much larger, pre-WWI Hungary...patriotically displayed by Magyars who feel as strongly about Trianon as if it happened yesterday.
Some Hungarians see the enlargement of the European Union as
a happy ending in the big-picture sense: They have finally been
reunited with Slovakia, Romania, and Croatia.

After Trianon, the newly shrunken Kingdom of Hungary had
to reinvent itself. The Hungarian crown sat unworn in the Royal

Palace, as if waiting for someone worthy to claim it. The WWI hero Admiral Miklós Horthy had won many battles with the Austro-Hungarian navy. Though the new Hungary had no sea and no navy, Horthy retained his rank and ruled the country as a regent. A popular joke points out that during this time, Hungary was a "kingdom without a king" and a landlocked country ruled by a sea admiral. This sense of compounded deficiency pretty much sums up the morose attitude Hungarians have about those gloomy post-Trianon days.

A mounting financial crisis, and lingering resentment about the strict post-WWI reparations, made Hungary fertile ground for some bold new fascist ideas.

World War II and the Arrow Cross (1939-1945)

As Adolf Hitler rose to power in Germany, some other countries that had felt mistreated in the aftermath of World War I—including Hungary—saw Nazi Germany as a vehicle to greater independence. Admiral Horthy joined forces with the Nazis with the hope that they might help Hungary regain the crippling territorial losses of Trianon. In 1941, Hungary (somewhat reluctantly) declared war on the Soviet Union in June—and against the US and Britain in December.

Being an ally to the Nazis, rather than an occupied state, also allowed Hungary a certain degree of self-determination through the war. And, although Hungary had its own set of anti-Semitic laws and was complicit in the mass murder of Jews lacking citizenship and living within their borders, the vast majority of its sizeable Jewish population was spared from immediate deportation to Nazi concentration camps. Winning back chunks of Slovakia, Transylvania, and Croatia in the early days of World War II also bolstered the Nazis' acceptance in Hungary.

As Nazism took hold in Germany, the Hungarian fascist movement—spearheaded by the Arrow Cross Party (Nyilaskeresztes Párt)—gained popularity within Hungary. As Germany increased its demands for Hungarian soldiers and food, Admiral Horthy resisted...until Hitler's patience wore thin. In March of 1944, the Nazis invaded and installed the Arrow Cross in power. The Arrow Cross made up for lost time, immediately beginning a savage campaign to execute Hungary's Jews—not only sending them to death camps, but also butchering them in the streets. As the end of the war neared, Hungarian Nazi collaborators resorted to desperate measures, such as lining up Jews along the Danube and shooting them into the river. To save bullets, they'd sometimes tie several victims together, shoot one, and throw him into the freezing Danube—dragging the others in with him. Hungary lost nearly 600,000 Jews to the Holocaust.

The Soviet Army eventually "liberated" Hungary, but at the expense of Budapest: A months-long siege, from Christmas of 1944 to mid-February of 1945, reduced the proud city to rubble. One out of every ten Hungarian citizens perished in the war.

Communism...with a Pinch of Paprika (1945-1989)

After World War II, Hungary was gradually compelled to adopt Moscow's system of government. The Soviet-puppet hardliner premier, Mátyás Rákosi, ruled Hungary with an iron fist. Everyday people were terrorized by the KGB-style secret police (called the ÁVO, later ÁVH) and intimidated into accepting the new regime. Non-Hungarians were deported, potential and actual dissidents disappeared into the horrifying gulag system of Siberia (and similar forced-work camps in Hungary), food shortages were epidemic, people were compelled to spy on their friends and families, and countless lives were ruined. Coming on the heels of Trianon and two devastating world wars, communist rule was a blow that Hungary is still recovering from.

Beginning on October 23, 1956, the Hungarians courageously staged a monumental uprising, led by Communist Party reformer Imre Nagy. Initially, it appeared that one of the cells on the Soviet Bloc might win itself the right to semiautonomy. But Moscow couldn't let that happen. In a Tiananmen Square-style crackdown, the Soviets sent in tanks to brutally put down the uprising and occupy the city. When the dust settled, 2,500 Hungarians were dead, and 200,000 fled to the West. (If you know any Hungarian Americans, their families more than likely fled in 1956.) Nagy was arrested, given a sham trial, and executed in 1958. For more on these events, see the "1956" sidebar on page 582.

The Hungarians were devastated. They were frustrated that the Suez Canal crisis distracted the world from their uprising. Many felt betrayed that the US—which spoke so boldly against the Soviet Union—did not offer them military support (contrary to the promises of the American-operated Radio Free Europe). While the US and its Western allies understandably did not want to turn the Cold War hot, the Hungarians (also understandably) felt abandoned.

Weeks after the uprising came the now-legendary "Blood in the Water" match at the Melbourne Olympics. Soviet satellite states were often ordered to "throw" matches to allow the USSR's athletes to prevail. On December 6, 1956, Moscow issued such a decree to the Hungarian men's water polo team in their semifinal against the Soviet Union. The Hungarians refused and played their hearts out, much to the delight of their fans (and the rest of the world). The game turned violent, and in one indelible image, a Hungarian athlete emerged from the pool with blood pouring from a gash above his right eye. The Hungarians won, 4-0, and went on to take the gold.

After the uprising, the USSR installed János Kádár—a colleague of Nagy's who was loyal to Moscow—to lead Hungary. For a few years, things were bleak, as the secret police ratcheted up their efforts against potential dissidents. But in the 1960s, Kádár's reformist tendencies began to cautiously emerge. Seeking to gain the support of his subjects (and avoid further uprisings), Kádár adopted the optimistic motto, "If you are not against us, you are with us." While still mostly cooperating with Moscow, Kádár gradually allowed the people of Hungary more freedom than citizens of neighboring countries had—a system dubbed "goulash communism." The "New Economic Mechanism" of 1968 partly opened Hungary to foreign trade. People from other Warsaw Pact countries—Czechs, Slovaks, and Poles—flocked to Budapest's Váci utca to experience "Western evils" unavailable to them back home, such as Adidas sneakers and Big Macs. People half-joked that Hungary was the happiest barrack in the communist camp.

In the late 1980s, the Eastern Bloc began to thaw. And Hungary—which was always skeptical of the Soviets (or any foreign rule)—was one of the first satellite states that implemented real change. In February of 1989, the Hungarian communist parliament, with little fanfare, essentially voted to put an expiration date on their own regime. There were three benchmarks in that fateful year: May 2, when Hungary was the first Soviet Bloc country to effectively open its borders to the West (by removing its border fence with Austria); June 16, when communist reformer Imre Nagy and his comrades were given a proper, ceremonial reburial on Heroes' Square; and August 19, when, in the first tentative steps toward the reunification of Europe, Hungarians and Austrians came together in a field near the town of Sopron for the so-called "Pan-European Picnic." (Some 900 East Germans seized this opportunity to make a run for the border...and slipped into the West when Hungarian border guards refused orders to shoot defectors.) On October 23—the anniversary of the 1956 Uprising—the truly democratic Republic of Hungary triumphantly replaced the People's Republic of Hungary.

Hungary Today: Capitalism, Gyurcsány, and Orbán (1989-Present)

The transition from communism to capitalism was not easy. While many Hungarians were eager for the freedom to travel and pursue the interests that democracy allowed them, many others struggled to cope with the sudden reduction of government-provided services.

In 2004, Hungary joined the European Union. And in recent years, Hungary has often been in the international news, as its fitful transition to democracy has taken some attention-grabbing turns.

The Hungarian Socialist Party (MSzP), which took control of parliament in 2002, stubbornly maintained and even extended some social programs, despite worries that mounting public debt would bankrupt the country.

As a result, rampant inflation continued to wrack the country. In late 2008, with Prime Minister Ferenc Gyurcsány warning of "state bankruptcy" and a currency collapse, Hungary received a $25 billion bailout package from the EU, International Monetary Fund, and World Bank. Gyurcsány finally resigned in early 2009, acknowledging that he was getting in the way of Hungary's economic recovery.

Viktor Orbán, of the nationalistic, right-wing Fidesz Party, became prime minister in a landslide in May of 2010. Fidesz—a strange hybrid of populist and authoritarian—stands for traditional Christian and Hungarian values, economic interventionism, and severe skepticism about immigration and European Union membership.

Orbán seized on his two-thirds coalition majority to adopt a new, Fidesz-favorable constitution that stripped away checks and balances and entrenched party leaders in institutions that had previously been considered apolitical. Almost immediately, international observers—including the EU and US—grew concerned.

In early 2011, Orbán's party created a new FCC-like media authority with broad latitude for suppressing material that it considers inappropriate. Fidesz also extended Hungarian citizenship to people of Hungarian descent living in neighboring countries. This stoked century-old Hungarian resentment about the territorial losses from the Treaty of Trianon. Orbán also insists on flying the flag of Transylvania (a part of Hungary that was lost in Trianon)—rather than the EU flag—from the Hungarian Parliament.

Fidesz has a penchant for reinterpreting Hungarian history—rehabilitating some figures (such as Miklós Horthy, who forged an alliance with Hitler's Nazi Germany), while brushing other, less Fidesz-friendly figures under the rug. The party went on a renaming binge—rechristening more than two dozen streets, squares, and other features of Budapest—and has been aggressive about tearing down old monuments and erecting new ones.

On a positive note, Fidesz has also been proactive about funneling European Union funds into public-works projects, and Budapest has made stunning progress in renovating formerly dreary streets and squares. But this always seems to come with a Fidesz-approved aesthetic that evokes the party's values. Some critics have described these new spaces—vast and bombastic, as if designed to trumpet historical greatness and host military parades—as "fascistic."

Other Orbán and Fidesz policies have also been controversial—from nationalizing the school system (the same Fidesz-approved textbooks are now used in every school in Hungary) to proposing a per-use internet tax. (That last one resulted in enormous public protests in the fall of 2014, and Orbán quickly backpedaled.)

Outrageous as Fidesz seems to younger, EU-supporting, highly educated Hungarians, the party pleased its base enough to easily retain its power in the 2014 parliamentary elections. (Fidesz's control of the media didn't hurt its chances either.) Many international observers worry that Fidesz's success could be the death knell for true democracy in Hungary.

In the fall of 2015, Fidesz was in the international news once more, as Orbán took a particularly hard line against Syrian immigrants flooding through Eastern Europe on their way to a better life in wealthy Western European nations. The government erected barbed wire fences and dispatched an intimidating border defense squad to make it clear that refugees weren't welcome. While humanitarians condemned Orbán's actions—which violated the European Union's open-borders agreements, and left many desperate people with nowhere to go—his supporters touted his success in preventing unwanted refugees from flooding the country.

In the 2018 elections, Fidesz retained control of parliament, keeping Orbán firmly in position as prime minister. But in the months following that, it appeared that Hungarians had finally reached a breaking point. In December 2018, Fidesz announced a new law to roll back overtime protections for workers. (Because of their restrictive immigration stance, and because young Hungarian workers have left the country in droves to escape restrictive Fidesz policies, Hungary suffers from a labor shortage.) The policy—nicknamed the "Slave Law"—spurred widespread protests against Fidesz. Even many Fidesz supporters criticized the irony of a party ostensibly dedicated to "family values" essentially requiring people to work longer hours. It could be that the "Slave Law" represents a sea change that will eventually sweep Fidesz from power.

With the rise of Donald Trump in the United States, Orbán is seen as a harbinger of sorts for a new, pan-national movement of traditionalism and nativism. While most Americans have never heard of Orbán, they're very familiar with his political playbook.

HUNGARIAN CUISINE

Hungarian cuisine is the undisputed best in Central Europe. It delicately blends Magyar peasant cooking (with rich spices), refined by the elegance of French preparation, with a delightful smattering of flavors from the vast, multiethnic Austro-Hungarian Empire (including Germanic, Balkan, Jewish, and Carpathian). Everything is heavily seasoned: with paprika, tomatoes, and peppers of every shape, color, size, and flavor.

An *étterem* ("eatery") is a nice sit-down restaurant, while a *vendéglő* is usually more casual (similar to a tavern or an inn), and a *bisztró* is a trendy eatery with a concise but well-executed menu. A *söröző* ("beer place") is a pub that sells beer and pub grub. A *kávéház* ("coffeehouse"), or café, is where Hungarians gather to meet friends, get a caffeine fix...and sometimes to have a great meal. Other cafés serve only light food, or sometimes only desserts. But if you want a wide choice of cakes, look for a *cukrászda* (pastry shop—*cukr* means "sugar").

When foreigners think of Hungarian cuisine, what comes to mind is goulash. But tourists are often disappointed when "real Hungarian goulash" isn't the thick stew that they were expecting. The word "goulash" comes from the Hungarian *gulyás leves*, or "shepherd's soup"—a tasty, rustic, nourishing dish originally eaten by cowboys and shepherds on the Great Hungarian Plain. Here in its homeland, it's a clear, spicy broth with chunks of meat, potatoes, and other vegetables. Elsewhere (such as in neighboring Germanic and Slavic countries), the word "goulash" does describe a thick stew. The hearty Hungarian stew called *pörkölt* is probably closer to what most people think of as goulash.

Aside from the obligatory *gulyás*, make a point of trying another unusual Hungarian specialty: cold fruit soup *(hideg gyümölcs leves)*. This sweet, cream-based treat—generally eaten before the meal, even though it tastes more like a dessert—is usually made with *meggy* (sour cherries), but you'll also see versions with *alma* (apples), *körte* (pears), and other fruits. Other Hungarian soups *(levesek)* include *bableves* (bean soup), *zöldségleves* (vegetable soup), *gombaleves* (mushroom soup), *halászlé* (fish broth with paprika), and *húsleves* (meat or chicken soup).

Hungarians adore all kinds of meat. *Hús* or *marhahús* is beef,

csirke is chicken, *borjú* is veal, *kacsa* is duck, *liba* is goose, *sertés* is pork, *sonka* is ham, *kolbász* is sausage, *szelet* is schnitzel (*Bécsi szelet* means Wiener schnitzel)—and the list goes on. One trendy ingredient you'll see on menus is *mangalica*. This uniquely Hungarian, free-range woolly pig (basically a domesticated boar) is high in unsaturated fat—which fits perfectly with the current foodie culture that elevates the mighty pig. *Libamáj* is goose liver, which shows up everywhere (anything prepared "Budapest style" is topped with goose liver). Lard is used extensively in cooking, making Hungarian cuisine very rich and filling.

Meat is often covered with delicious sauces or garnishes, from rich cream sauces to spicy pastes to fruit jam. For classic Hungarian flavors, you can't beat chicken or veal *paprikás* (described in the "Paprika Primer" sidebar).

Vegetarians have a tricky time in traditional Hungarian restaurants, many of which offer only a plate of deep-fried vegetables. A traditional Hungarian "salad" is composed mostly or entirely of pickled vegetables (cucumbers, cabbage, peppers, and others); even many modern restaurants haven't quite figured out how to do a good, healthy, leafy salad. Fortunately, the more modern, trendy eateries in the capital often offer excellent vegetarian options.

Starches *(köretek)* can include *nokedli* (small, boiled "drop noodles," a.k.a. *Spätzle*), *galuska* (noodles), *burgonya* (potatoes), *sült krumpli* (French fries), *krokett* (croquettes), or *rizs* (rice). *Kenyér* (bread) often comes with the meal. A popular snack—especially to accompany a wine tasting—is a *pogácsa*, a little ball of cheesy fried dough (like a savory doughnut).

Sometimes your main dish will come with steamed, grilled, or deep-fried vegetables. A common side dish is *káposzta* (cabbage, often prepared like sauerkraut). You may also see *töltött káposzta* (cabbage stuffed with meat) or *töltött paprika* (stuffed peppers). *Lecsó* (LEH-chew) is the Hungarian answer to ratatouille: a richly flavorful stew of tomatoes, peppers, and other vegetables.

Thin, crêpe-like pancakes *(palacsinta)* are usually a starter, but sometimes served as a main dish. A delicious traditional Hungarian dish is *Hortobágyi palacsinta* (Hortobágy pancakes, named for the Great Hungarian Plain where the dish originates). This is a savory crêpe wrapped around a tasty meat filling and drenched with creamy paprika sauce.

Pancakes also appear as desserts, stuffed and/or covered with

Paprika Primer

The quintessential ingredient in Hungarian cuisine is paprika. In Hungarian, the word *paprika* can mean both peppers (red or green) and the spice that's made from them. Peppers can be stewed, stuffed, sautéed, baked, grilled, or pickled. For seasoning, red shakers of dried paprika join the salt and pepper on tables.

Locals say paprika is best from the sunny south of Hungary. There are more than 40 varieties of paprika spice, with two main types: hot (*csípős* or *erős*) and sweet (*édesnemes* or simply *édes,* often comes in a white can; sometimes also called *csemege*—"delicate"). Hungarians typically cook with sweet paprika to add flavor and color. Then, at the table, they put out hot paprika so each diner can adjust the heat to his or her preferred taste. A can or bag of paprika is a handy and tasty souvenir of your trip.

On menus, anything cooked *paprikás* (PAW-pree-kash) comes smothered in a spicy red paprika gravy, thickened with sour cream. Most often you'll see this option with *csirke* (chicken) or *borjú* (veal), and it's generally served with dumpling-like boiled egg noodles called *nokedli* (similar to German *Spätzle*). This dish is *the* Hungarian staple—if you sample just one dish in Hungary, make it chicken or veal *paprikás.*

To add even more kick to your food, ask for a jar of the bright-red, sambal-like paste called *Erős Pista* (EH-rewsh PEESH-taw). Literally "Spicy Steve," this Hungarian answer to Tabasco is best used sparingly. Or try *Édes Anna* (AY-desh AW-naw, "Sweet Anna"), a variation that's more sweet than spicy. You'll also see tubes of *Gulyáskrém* (a bright-orange, sweet-but-not-hot paste for jazzing up soups) and *Piros Arany* ("Red Gold," a deep-red, intensely flavorful, spicy paste).

fruit, jam, chocolate sauce, walnuts, poppy seeds, or whipped cream. Most famous is the *Gundel palacsinta,* named for *the* top-of-the-line Budapest restaurant—stuffed with walnuts and raisins in a rum sauce, topped with chocolate sauce, and flambéed.

Pastries are a big deal in Hungary. In the late 19th century, pastry-making caught on here in an attempt to keep up with the renowned desserts of rival Vienna. Today, Hungary's streets are still lined with *cukrászda* (pastry shops) where you can simply point to whichever treat you'd like. Try the *Dobos torta* (a many-layered chocolate-and-vanilla cream cake), *flódni* (layer cake of Jewish origin, with apples, walnuts, and poppy seeds), *Rákóczi turós* (sweet cheese curd cake with jam), *somlói galuska* (rum-soaked sponge cake), *krémes* (delicate custard wafer cake), anything with *gesztenye* (chestnuts), and *rétes* (strudel with various fillings, including *túrós*, curds). And many *cukrászda* also serve *fagylalt* (ice cream, *fagyi* for short), sold by the *gomboc* (ball).

When the server comes to take your order, he might say *"Tessék"* (TEHSH-shayk), or maybe the more formal *"Tessék parancsolni"* (TEHSH-shayk PAW-rawn-chohl-nee)—"Please command, sir." When they bring the food, they will probably say, *"Jó étvágyat!"* (yoh AYT-vah-yawt)—"Bon appétit." When you're ready for the bill, you can simply say, *"Fizetek"* (FEE-zeh-tehk)—"I'll pay."

Drinks

Kávé (KAH-vay) and *tea* (TEH-aw) are coffee and tea. (Confusingly, *tej* is not tea—it's milk.) As for water (*víz*, pronounced "veez"), it comes as *szódavíz* (soda water, sometimes just carbonated tap water) or *ásványvíz* (spring water, more expensive).

Hungary is first and foremost a wine country. For the complete rundown on Hungarian wines, see the sidebar.

Hungary isn't particularly well-known for its beer (*sör*, pronounced "shewr"), but Dreher and Borsodi are two of the better brands. *Világos* is lager; if you prefer something darker, look for *barna* (brown). And, like everywhere, craft breweries are opening up all over the country. I've recommended some places to try Hungarian microbrews in Budapest (see the Entertainment in Budapest chapter) and in Eger.

Hungary is almost as proud of its spirits as its wines. The local firewater, *pálinka*, is a powerful schnapps made from various fruits (most often plum, *szilva;* or apricots, *barack*). Also look for the pear-flavored Vilmos brandy.

Unicum is a unique and beloved Hungarian bitter liquor made of 40 different herbs and aged in oak casks. Look for the round bottle with the red cross on the label. The flavor is powerfully unforgettable—like Jägermeister, but harsher. Unicum started out as a medicine and remains a popular digestif for easing an upset stomach (especially if you've eaten too much rich food—not an uncommon problem in Hungary). Purists claim it's better to drink it at room temperature (so you can fully appreciate its bouquet), but novices find it easier to slug back when chilled. If the original Uni-

Hungarian Wines

Wine (*bor*) is an essential part of Hungarian cuisine. Whites (*fehér*) can be sweet (*édes*), half-dry (*félszáraz*), or dry (*száraz*).

Whites include the standards (riesling, chardonnay), as well as some wines made from more typically Hungarian grapes: *leányka* ("little girl"), a half-dry, fairly heavy, white table wine; *cserszegi fűszeres,* a spicy, light white that can be fruity; the half-dry, full-bodied *hárslevelű* ("linden leaf"); and the dry *furmint* and *kéknyelű* ("blue stalk").

Reds (*vörös*) include the familiar varieties (cabernet sauvignon, cabernet franc, merlot, pinot noir), and some that are less familiar. *Kekporto* is better known as *blauer Portugieser* in German-speaking countries. In Eger, don't miss **Bull's Blood,** a.k.a. Egri Bikavér, a distinctive blend of reds that comes with a fun local legend (described on page 699). The spicy, medium-body *kékfrankos* ("blue Frank-ish") supposedly got its name because when Napoleonic soldiers were here, they could pay either with valuable blue-colored bank notes or unstable white ones...and local vintners wanted the blue francs. (Like most wine origin legends, this story is untrue—*kékfrankos* wasn't cultivated here until after Napoleon's time.)

The most famous Hungarian wine is **Tokaji Aszú,** a sweet, late-harvest, honey-colored dessert wine made primarily from *furmint* grapes. Known as the "wine of kings, and the king of

cum overwhelms your palate, try one of the newer variations: Unicum Next, with more of a citrus flavor, and Unicum Szilva (with a golden plum on the label), which is aged in plums that cut some of the bitterness with a rich sweetness (www.zwack.hu).

If you're drinking with some new Magyar friends, impress them with the standard toast: *Egészségedre* (EH-gehs-shay-geh-dreh; "to your health").

HUNGARIAN LANGUAGE

Even though Hungary is surrounded by Slavs, Hungarian is not at all related to Slavic languages (such as Polish, Czech, or Croatian). In fact, Hungarian isn't related to *any* European language, except for very distant relatives Finnish and Estonian. It isn't even an Indo-European language—meaning that English is more closely related to Hindi, Russian, and French than it is to Hungarian.

Hungarian is agglutinative: To create meaning, you start with

wines," Tokaji Aszú is a D.O.C. product, meaning that to have that name, it must be grown in a particular region. Tokaj is a town in northeastern Hungary, while *aszú* is a "noble rot" grape. The wine's unique, concentrated flavor is made possible by a fungus (*Botrytis cinerea*) that thrives on the grapes in the late fall. The grapes are left on the vine, where they burst and wither like raisins before they are harvested in late October and November. This sucks the water out of the grape, leaving behind very high sugar

content and a deep golden color. Tokaji Aszú wines are numbered, from three to six, indicating how many eight-gallon tubs (*puttony*) of these "noble rot" grapes were added to the base wine—the higher the number, the sweeter the wine. Other variations on Tokaji can be less sweet. (This might sound like another bizarre Hungarian custom, but the French Sauterne and German Beerenauslese wines are also made from "noble rot" grapes. The similarly named French Tokay wine—which derives from the same word—is a different story altogether.)

Finally, note that, except for Bull's Blood and Tokaji Aszú, Hungarian wines are not widely available in the US. A bottle or two (transported in your checked luggage) is a unique souvenir.

a root word and then tack on suffixes—sometimes resulting in a pileup of extra sounds. The emphasis always goes on the first syllable, and the following syllables are droned in a kind of a monotone—giving the language a distinctive cadence that Hungary's neighbors love to tease.

While the language can be overwhelming for tourists, one easy word is *"Szia"* (SEE-yaw), which means both hello and goodbye (like "ciao" or "aloha"). Sometimes Hungarians simply say the English word "hello" to mean either "hi" or "bye." Another handy word that Hungarians (and people throughout Central Europe) will understand is *Servus* (SEHR-voos, spelled *Szervusz* in Hungarian)—the old-fashioned greeting from the days of the Austro-Hungarian Empire. If you draw a blank on how to say hello, just offer a cheery, *"Servus!"*

Hungarian pronunciation is straightforward, once you remember a few key rules. The trickiest: *s* alone is pronounced "sh," while *sz* is pronounced "s." This explains why you'll hear in-the-know travelers pronouncing Budapest as "BOO-daw-pesht." You might catch the *busz* up to Castle Hill—pronounced "boose." And "Franz Liszt" is easier to pronounce than it looks: It sounds just like "list." To review:

s sounds like "sh" as in "shirt"

sz sounds like "s" as in "saint"

Hungarian has a set of unusual palatal sounds that don't quite have a counterpart in English. To make these sounds, gently press the thick part of your tongue to the roof of your mouth (instead of using the tip of your tongue behind your teeth, as we do in English):

gy sounds like "dg" as in "hedge"

ny sounds like "ny" as in "canyon" (not "nee")

ty sounds like "tch" as in "itch"

cs sounds like "ch" as in "church"

As for vowels: The letter *a* almost sounds like o (aw, as in "hot"); but with an accent *(á)*, it brightens up to the more standard "ah." Likewise, while *e* sounds like "eh," *é* sounds like "ay." An accent *(á, é, í, ó, ú)* indicates that you linger on that vowel, but not necessarily that you stress that syllable. Like German, Hungarian has umlauts *(ö, ü)*, meaning you purse your lips when you say that vowel: roughly, *ö* sounds like "ur" and *ü* sounds like "ew." A long umlaut *(ő, ű)* is the same sound, but you hold it a little longer. Words ending in *k* are often plural.

Here are a few other letters that sound different in Hungarian than in English:

c and **cz** both sound like "ts" as in "cats"

zs sounds like "zh" as in "leisure"

j and **ly** both sound like "y" as in "yellow"

OK, maybe it's not *so* simple. But you'll get the hang of it...and Hungarians will appreciate your efforts.

For a complete list of Hungarian survival phrases, see the following pages. As you navigate, remember these key Hungarian terms: *tér* (pronounced "tehr," square), *utca* (OOT-zaw, street), *út* (oot, boulevard), *körút* (KUR-root, ring road), *híd* (heed, bridge), and *város* (VAH-rohsh, town). To better match what you'll see locally, in the following chapters I've mostly used these Hungarian terms (instead of the English equivalents).

Hungarian Survival Phrases

Remember, the letter *a* is pronounced "aw," while *á* is a brighter "ah." In the phonetics, *dj* is pronounced like the *j* in "jeans."

English	Hungarian	Pronunciation
Hello. (formal)	Jó napot kívánok.	yoh **nah**-poht **kee**-vah-nohk
Hi. / Bye. (informal)	Szia. / Hello.	**see**-yaw / "Hello"
Do you speak English?	Beszél angolul?	beh-sayl **awn**-goh-lool
Yes. / No.	Igen. / Nem.	**ee**-gehn / nehm
I (don't) understand.	(Nem) értem.	(nehm) **ayr**-tehm
Please.	Kérem.	**kay**-rehm
You're welcome.	Szívesen.	**see**-veh-shehn
Thank you (very much).	Köszönöm (szépen).	**kur**-sur-nurm (**say**-pehn)
Excuse me. / I'm sorry.	Bocsánat.	**boh**-chah-nawt
No problem.	Semmi gond.	**sheh**-mee gohnd
Good.	Jól.	yohl
Goodbye.	Viszontlátásra.	**vee**-sohnt-lah-tahsh-raw
one / two / three	egy / kettő / három	edj / **keh**-tur / **hah**-rohm
four / five / six / seven	négy / öt / hat / hét	naydj / urt / hawt / hayt
eight / nine / ten	nyolc / kilenc / tíz	nyolts / **kee**-lehnts / teez
hundred / thousand	száz / ezer	sahz / **eh**-zehr
How much?	Mennyi?	**mehn**-yee
forint (local currency)	forint (Ft)	**foh**-reent
Where is it?	Hol van?	hohl vawn
Is it free (no charge)?	Ingyen van?	een-**jehn** vawn
Where can I find / buy...?	Hol találok / vehetek...?	hohl **taw**-lah-lohk / **veh**-heh-tehk
I'd like / We'd like...	Kérnék / Kérnénk...	**kayr**-nayk / **kayr**-naynk
...a room.	...egy szobát.	edj **soh**-baht
...a ticket (to ___).	...egy jegyet (___-ig).	edj **yehdj**-eht (___-ig)
Is it possible?	Lehet?	leh-**heht**
Where is the ___?	Hol van a ___?	hohl vawn aw ___
big train station (in Budapest)	pályaudvar	**pah**-yood-vawr
small train station (elsewhere)	vasútállomás	**vaw**-shoot-ah-loh-mahsh
bus station	buszpályaudvar	**boos**-pah-yood-vawr
tourist information office	turista információ	**too**-reesh-taw **een**-for-maht-see-yoh
toilet	toalet / WC	**toh**-aw-leht / **vayt**-say
men / women	férfi / női	**fayr**-fee / **nur**-ee
left / right	bal / jobb	bawl / yohb
straight	egyenesen	**edj**-eh-neh-shehn
At what time...?	Mikor...?	**mee**-kor
...does this open / close	...nyit / zár	nyit / zahr
Just a moment.	Egy pillanat.	edj **pee**-law-nawt
now / soon / later	most / hamarosan / később	mohsht / **haw**-maw-roh-shawn / **kay**-shurb
today / tomorrow	ma / holnap	maw / **hohl**-nawp

HUNGARY

In a Hungarian Restaurant

English	Hungarian	Pronunciation
I'd like to reserve a table for one / two people.	*Szeretnék foglalni egy asztalt egy / két fő részére.*	**seh**-reht-nayk **fog**-lawl-nee edj **aws**-tawlt edj / kayt few **ray**-say-reh
Is this table free?	*Ez az asztal szabad?*	ehz oz **aws**-tawl saw-**bawd**
Can I help you?	*Tessék?*	**tehsh**-shayk
The menu (in English), please.	*Kérem az (angol), étlapot.*	**kay**-rehm oz (**awn**-gohl) **ayt**-law-poht
service (not) included	*a számla a felszolgálási díjat (nem) tartalmazza*	aw **sahm**-law aw **fehl**-sohl-gah-lah-shee **dee**-yawt (nehm) **tawr**-tawl-maw-zaw
"to go"	*elvitelre*	**ehl**-vee-tehl-reh
with / without	___*-val / nélkül*	___*-vawl / **nayl**-kewl
and / or	*és / vagy*	aysh / vawdj
fixed-price meal (of the day)	*(napi) menü*	(**naw**-pee) **meh**-new
daily special	*napi ajánlat*	**naw**-pee **aw**-yahn-lawt
main courses	*főételek*	**fur**-ay-teh-lehk
appetizers	*előételek*	**eh**-lur-ay-teh-lehk
bread / cheese	*kenyér / sajt*	**kehn**-yayr / shayt
sandwich	*szendvics*	**send**-veech
soup / salad	*leves / saláta*	**leh**-vehsh / **shaw**-lah-taw
meat / poultry	*hús / szárnyasok*	hoosh / **sahr**-nyaw-shohk
fish	*halak*	**haw**-lawk
seafood	*tengeri halak*	**tehn**-geh-ree **haw**-lawk
fruit / vegetables	*gyümölcs / zöldség*	**jewm**-urlch / **zulrd**-shayg
dessert	*desszert*	**deh**-sehrt
vegetarian	*vegetáriánus*	**veh**-geh-tah-ree-ah-noosh
(tap) water	*(csap) víz*	(chawp) veez
mineral water	*ásványvíz*	**ash**-vawn-veez
milk / (orange) juice	*tej / (narancs) lé*	**tay**ee / (**naw**-rawnch) lay
coffee / tea	*kávé / tea*	**kah**-vay / **teh**-aw
beer / wine	*sör / bor*	shohr / bohr
red / white	*vörös / fehér*	**vur**-rursh / **feh**-hayr
sweet / dry / semi-dry	*édes / száraz / félszáraz*	**ay**-dehsh / **sah**-rawz / **fayl**-sah-rawz
glass / bottle	*pohár / üveg*	**poh**-hahr / **ew**-vehg
Cheers!	*Egészségedre!*	**eh**-gehs-sheh-geh-dreh
More. / Another.	*Még. / Máskikat.*	mayg / **mah**-shee-kawt
The same.	*Ugyanazt.*	**oodj**-aw-nawst
Bill, please. (literally, "I'll pay.")	*Fizetek.*	**fee**-zeh-tehk
tip	*borravaló*	**boh**-raw-vaw-loh
Bon appétit!	*Jó étvágyat!*	yoh **ayt**-vah-yawt
Delicious!	*Finom!*	**fee**-nohm

BUDAPEST

Budapest is a unique metropolis at the heart of a unique nation. Here you'll find experiences like nothing else in Europe: Feel your stress ebb away as you soak in hundred-degree water, surrounded by opulent Baroque domes...and by Speedo- and bikini-clad Hungarians. Ogle some of Europe's most richly decorated interiors, which echo a proud little nation's bygone glory days. Perk up your ears with a first-rate performance at one of the world's top opera houses—at bargain prices. Ponder the region's bleak communist era as you stroll amid giant Soviet-style statues designed to evoke fear and obedience. Try to wrap your head around Hungary's colorful history...and your tongue around its notoriously difficult language. Dive into a bowl of goulash, the famous paprika-flavored peasant soup with a kick. Go for an after-dinner stroll along the Danube, immersed in a grand city that's bathed in floodlights.

Europe's most underrated big city, Budapest can be as challenging as it is enchanting. The sprawling Hungarian capital is a city of nuance and paradox—cosmopolitan, complicated, and tricky for the first-timer to get a handle on. Think of Budapest as that favorite Hungarian pastime, chess: It's simple to learn...but takes a lifetime to master. This chapter is your first lesson. Then it's your move.

PLANNING YOUR TIME

Budapest demands at least two full days—and that assumes you'll be selective and move fast. To slow down and really dig into the city, give it a third or fourth day. Adding more time allows for various day trips.

Budapest is quite decentralized: Strategize your sightseeing to minimize backtracking. Just about everything is walkable, but distances are far, and public transit saves valuable time.

When divvying your time between Buda and Pest, keep in mind that (aside from the Gellért and Rudas Baths) Buda's sightseeing is mostly concentrated on Castle Hill, and can easily be done in less than a day, while Pest deserves as much time as you're willing to give it. Save relatively laid-back Buda for when you need a break from the big city.

Below are some possible plans, depending on the length of your trip. Note that these very ambitious itineraries assume you want to sightsee at a speedy pace. In the **evening,** you have a wide range of options (detailed under "Entertainment in Budapest" and "Nightlife in Budapest," later): enjoying good restaurants, taking in an opera or concert, snuggling on a romantic floodlit river cruise, relaxing in a thermal bath, exploring the city's unique ruin pubs and other nightlife venues, or simply strolling the Danube embankments and bridges.

Budapest in Two Days

Day 1: Spend it in Pest. Begin at the Parliament and stroll through Leopold Town, then walk through Pest town center to the Great Market Hall. Then circle around the Small Boulevard to Deák tér; if you're not wiped out yet, walk up Andrássy út to Heroes' Square and City Park. Or, if you're exhausted already, just take the M1/yellow Metró line to Hősök tere, ogle the Heroes' Square statues and Vajdahunyad Castle, and reward yourself with a soak at Széchenyi Baths. Note that this schedule leaves virtually no time for entering museums, though you might be able to fit in one or two big sights; the most worthwhile are the Parliament (book tickets ahead online), the Opera House, and the House of Terror.

Day 2: In the morning, tackle any Pest sights you didn't have time for yesterday (or take the bus out to Memento Park). After lunch, ride bus #16 from Deák tér to Buda's Castle Hill. Finally, head back to Pest for some final sightseeing and dinner.

Budapest in Three or More Days

Day 1: Get your bearings in Pest. Begin by strolling through Leopold Town (including a tour of the Parliament—book tickets ahead online). Next, follow my Andrássy út Walk (including touring the Opera House and the House of Terror) to Heroes' Square and City Park Walk. End your day with a soak at the Széchenyi Baths.

Day 2: Delve deeper into Pest, starting with a stroll through the town center. After visiting the Great Market Hall, you can cross the river to Buda for a soak at the Gellért or Rudas Baths, or circle around the Small Boulevard to see the National Museum and/or Great Synagogue and Jewish Quarter.

Day 3: Use the morning to see any remaining Pest sights, then ride from Deák tér out to Memento Park on the park's 11:00 direct bus. On returning, grab a quick lunch and take bus #16 from Deák tér to Castle Hill.

With More Time: If you have a fourth day, spread the Day 1 activities over more time, and circle back to any sights you've missed.

Orientation to Budapest

Budapest is huge, with nearly two million people. Like Vienna, the city was built as the head of a much larger empire than it currently governs. But Budapest is surprisingly easy to manage once you get the lay of the land and learn the excellent public transportation network. Those who are comfortable with the Metró, trams, and buses have the city by the tail (see "Getting Around Budapest," later).

The city is split down the center by the Danube River. On the east side of the Danube is flat **Pest** (pronounced "pesht"), and on the west is hilly **Buda.** A third part of the city, **Óbuda,** sits to the north of Buda.

Buda: Buda is dominated by Castle Hill (packed with tourists by day, dead at night). The pleasant Víziváros ("Water Town"; VEE-zee-vah-rohsh) neighborhood is between the castle and the river; nearby is the square called Batthyány tér (a handy hub for the Metró—M2/red line—plus tram lines and the HÉV suburban railway). To the south is the taller, wooded Gellért Hill, capped by the Liberation Monument, with a pair of thermal baths at its base—Gellért and Rudas.

Pest: Just across the river from Castle Hill, "Downtown" Pest is divided into two sections. The more polished northern half, called Leopold Town (Lipótváros), surrounds the giant Parliament building. This is the governmental, business, and banking district (sleepy after hours). The southern half, the grittier and more urban-

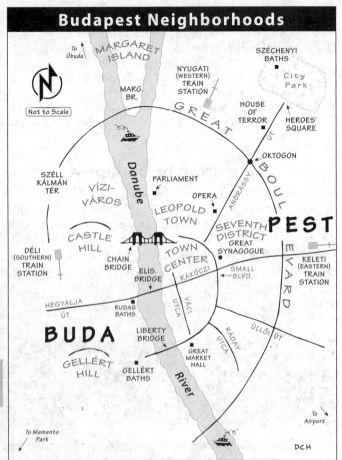

Budapest Neighborhoods

To Óbuda

MARGARET ISLAND

N
Not to Scale

MARG. BR.

NYUGATI (WESTERN) TRAIN STATION

SZÉCHENYI BATHS

City Park

GREAT

HOUSE OF TERROR

HEROES' SQUARE

OKTOGON

SZÉLL KÁLMÁN TÉR

Danube

VÍZI-VÁROS

PARLIAMENT

OPERA

ANDRÁSSY ÚT

BOULEVARD

LEOPOLD TOWN

PEST

CASTLE HILL

CHAIN BRIDGE

SEVENTH DISTRICT

GREAT SYNAGOGUE

DÉLI (SOUTHERN) TRAIN STATION

ELIS. BRIDGE

TOWN CENTER

RÁKÓCZI

SMALL BLVD.

KELETI (EASTERN) TRAIN STATION

HEGYALJA ÚT

RUDAS BATHS

VÁCI UTCA

BUDA

LIBERTY BRIDGE

RÁDAY UTCA

ÜLLŐI ÚT

GELLÉRT HILL

GELLÉRT BATHS

GREAT MARKET HALL

River

To Memento Park

To Airport

DCH

feeling Town Center (Belváros, literally "Inner Town"), is a thriving shopping, dining, nightlife, and residential zone that bustles day and night. Major landmarks here include the vast Great Market Hall and the famous (and overrated) Váci utca shopping street.

Additional key sights lie along the Small Boulevard ring road (connected by trams #47 and #49), including—from north to south—the Great Synagogue (marking the start of the Jewish Quarter, which feels a bit rundown but features several Jewish sights, as well as the Seventh District, a hopping nightlife zone with cool ruin pubs), the National Museum, and the Great Market Hall. Even more points of interest are spread far and wide along the Great Boulevard ring road (circled by trams #4 and #6), including Margaret Island (the city's playground, in the middle of the Danube), the Nyugati/Western train station, the prominent Oktogon intersection (where it crosses Andrássy út), the opulent New York Café (with the Keleti/Eastern train station just up the street), and the intersection with Üllői út, near the Holocaust Memorial Center and Applied Arts Museum.

Roads: The Town Center is hemmed in by the first of Pest's four concentric ring roads (körút). The innermost ring is called the Kiskörút, or "Small Boulevard." The next ring, several blocks farther out, is called the Nagykörút, or "Great Boulevard." These ring roads change names every few blocks, but they are always called körút. Arterial boulevards, called út, stretch from central Pest into the suburbs like spokes on a wheel. One of these boulevards, Andrássy út, begins near Deák tér in central Pest and heads out to Heroes' Square and City Park; along the way it passes some of the city's best eateries, hotels, and sights (Opera House, House of Terror).

Bridges: Buda and Pest are connected by a series of characteristic bridges. From north to south, there's the low-profile **Margaret** Bridge (Margit híd, crosses Margaret Island), the famous **Chain** Bridge (Széchenyi Lánchíd), the white and modern **Elisabeth** Bridge (Erzsébet híd), and the green **Liberty** Bridge (Szabadság híd). Four more bridges lie beyond the tourist zone: the Petőfi and Rákóczi bridges to the south, and Árpád and Megyeri bridges to the north.

Districts: Budapest uses a district system (like Paris and Vienna). There are 23 districts *(kerület)*, identified by Roman numerals. For example, Castle Hill is in district I, central Pest is district V, and City Park is in district XIV. Addresses often start with the district number (as a Roman numeral).

TOURIST INFORMATION

The city of Budapest runs several official TIs (tel. 1/438-8080, www.budapestinfo.hu). These are primarily interested in selling tickets for tour operators and concert companies that they partner with, but they do hand out good information and can answer some questions. The main branch is at **Deák tér,** a few steps from the M2 and M3 Metró station (daily 8:00-20:00, Sütő utca 2, near the McDonald's, district V). Other locations include **Heroes' Square** (in the ice rink building facing Vajdahunyad Castle, daily 9:00-19:00), in the middle of Castle Hill at **Szentháromság tér** (daily 10:00-18:00, Tárnok utca 15), in the **Bálna** building behind the Great Market Hall (daily 10:00-18:00), and in both terminals at the **airport** (daily until 22:00). Also look for TI "mobile info points" set up in highly trafficked areas (look for the teal-and-white umbrellas).

The helpfulness of Budapest's TIs can vary, but all sell the Budapest Card and offer free, useful publications, including the *Budapest Guide* booklet. Be aware that many for-profit agencies

Snapshot History of Budapest

Budapest is a rich cultural stew made up of Hungarians, Germans, Slavs, and Jews, with a dash of Turkish paprika, all simmered for centuries in a thermal bath. Each group has left its mark, but through it all, something has remained that is distinctly...Budapest.

Budapest sits on a thin layer of earth covering thermal springs. Those waters attracted the ancient Romans, who, 2,000 years ago, established Aquincum just north of today's city center.

In AD 896, a nomadic group from Central Asia called the Magyars took over the Carpathian Basin (roughly today's Hungary). After running roughshod over Europe, the Magyars—the ancestors of today's Hungarians—settled down, adopted Christianity, and became fully European. The twin towns of Buda and Pest emerged as the leading cities of Hungary. Gradually Buda and Pest became both a de facto capital and a melting pot for the peoples of Central and Eastern Europe.

In the 16th century, the Ottomans invaded. (Castle restorers have even found the remains of Ottoman camels in the area.) They occupied Budapest (and much of Hungary) for nearly a century and a half, introducing their way of life and practices—such as soaking in thermal baths. Finally, the Habsburg monarchs from neighboring Austria liberated Hungary—and kept it for themselves.

After many decades of Hungarian uprisings, the Compromise of 1867 created the Austro-Hungarian Empire; six years later, the cities of Buda, Pest, and Óbuda merged to become Budapest, which governed a sizeable chunk of Eastern Europe. For the next few decades, Budapest boomed, and Hungarian culture blossomed. A flurry of construction surrounded the year 1896—Hungary's 1,000th birthday.

But with World War I, Budapest's fortunes reversed: Hungary lost the war, and two-thirds of its land. Hungary again backed a loser in World War II; the ruins of Budapest were claimed by the Soviets, who introduced communism to Hungary. Although a bold uprising in 1956 was brutally put down, a milder "goulash communism" eventually emerged here. Budapest became a place where other Eastern Bloc residents could experiment with "Western evils," from Big Macs to Nikes.

By the end of communism in 1989, the city's rich architectural heritage was in shambles. Forever torn between a nostalgic instinct to cling to past glory days, and a modern drive to innovate, Budapest has reinvented its cityscape with a mix of old and new. The latest chapter in Budapest's history has been written by Prime Minister Viktor Orbán, who has overseen an unprecedented burst of urban renewal, but also a rise in authoritarianism and emotionally charged nationalism.

Budapest's uniquely epic history—still a work in progress—has shaped a glorious metropolis that fascinates both Hungarians and tourists alike.

masquerade as "TIs" or "info points" (such as in the train stations); these are unofficial, but some can be helpful in a pinch.

Sightseeing Passes: The **Budapest Card** includes all public transportation, walking tours of Buda and Pest, admission to a handful of sights (including the National Museum, National Gallery, and Memento Park), access to a shuttle bus up to the castle area, and 10-50 percent discounts on many other major museums and attractions (€22/24 hours, €33/48 hours, €43/72 hours, www.budapest-card.com). If you take advantage of the included walking tours, the Budapest Card can be a good value for a very busy sightseer—do the arithmetic.

Absolute Tour Center: This office, conveniently located near Andrássy út (behind the Opera House at Lázár utca 16), can also be helpful in answering questions. They also have bike rentals and secondhand books upstairs, and are the hub for walking, bike, and Segway tours—all described later, under "Tours in Budapest" (sporadic hours, usually open daily 9:00-20:00, Nov-March until 18:00, tel. 1/269-3843, mobile +3620-929-7506, www.absolutetours.com).

ARRIVAL IN BUDAPEST
By Train

Budapest has three major train stations (*pályaudvar*, abbreviated *pu.*): Keleti ("Eastern") station, Nyugati ("Western") station, and Déli ("Southern") station; a fourth, suburban station—Kelenföld—is a common transfer point for destinations to the south (including Pécs). Before departing from Budapest, it's essential to confirm which station your train leaves from.

The Keleti/Eastern and Nyugati/Western train stations, in Pest, are both cavernous, slightly run-down, late-19th-century masterpieces. The Déli/Southern train station—behind Castle Hill in Buda—mingles its dinginess with modern, concrete flair. All three stations are seedy and overdue for renovation. But once you get your bearings, they're easy to navigate. At all stations, access to the tracks is monitored: You might have to show your ticket to reach the platforms (though this is loosely enforced).

The taxi stands in front of each train station are notorious for ripping off tourists; it's better to stick to public transit. But if you must take a taxi, it's far more reliable to phone for one (call 211-1111 or 266-6666 and tell the English-speaking dispatcher where you are). For tips on this—and on using the Metró system to connect into downtown Budapest—see "Getting Around Budapest," later.

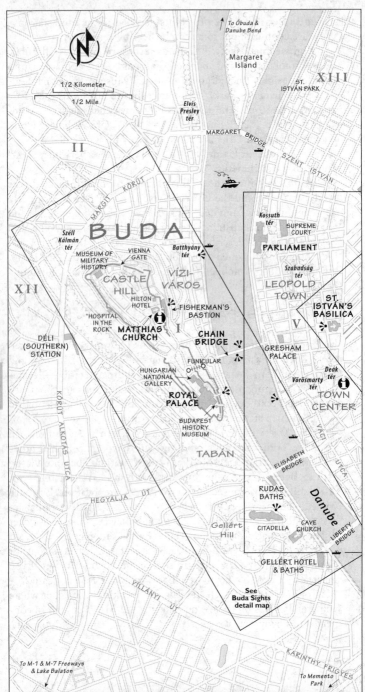

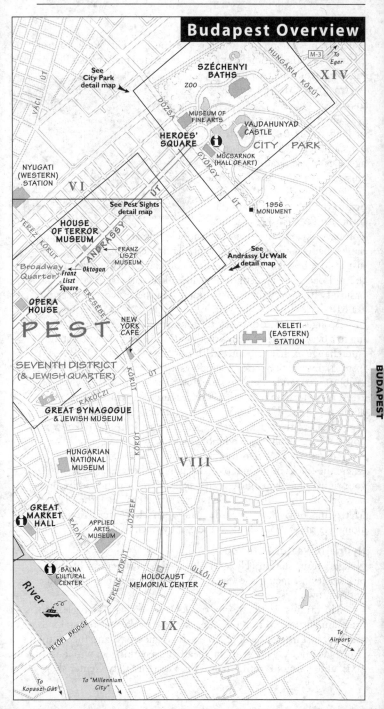

Budapest Overview

To Eger
M-3

HUNGÁRIA KÖRÚT

XIV

See City Park detail map ▶

SZÉCHENYI BATHS

ZOO

VÁCI ÚT

DÓZSA

MUSEUM OF FINE ARTS

HEROES' SQUARE

VAJDAHUNYAD CASTLE

CITY PARK

MŰCSARNOK (HALL OF ART)

GYÖRGY

NYUGATI (WESTERN) STATION

VI

ANDRÁSSY ÚT

See Pest Sights detail map

1956 MONUMENT

TERÉZ KÖRÚT

HOUSE OF TERROR MUSEUM

FRANZ LISZT MUSEUM

See Andrássy Út Walk detail map

"Broadway Quarter"

Oktogon

Franz Liszt Square

ERZSÉBET

OPERA HOUSE

PEST

NEW YORK CAFE

KELETI (EASTERN) STATION

SEVENTH DISTRICT (& JEWISH QUARTER)

KÖRÚT ÚT

RÁKÓCZI

GREAT SYNAGOGUE & JEWISH MUSEUM

HUNGARIAN NATIONAL MUSEUM

VIII

KÖRÚT

JÓZSEF

GREAT MARKET HALL

RÁDAY

APPLIED ARTS MUSEUM

BÁLNA CULTURAL CENTER

FERENC KÖRÚT

HOLOCAUST MEMORIAL CENTER

ÜLLŐI ÚT

River

PETŐFI BRIDGE

IX

To Airport

To Kopaszi-Gát

To "Millennium City"

BUDAPEST

Keleti/Eastern Station

Keleti train station (Keleti pu.) is just south of City Park, east of central Pest. The station faces a newly renovated plaza called Baross tér, with stops for two different Metró lines (M2/red and M4/green).

On arrival, go to the front of long tracks 6-9 to reach the exits and services. Several travel agencies masquerading as TIs cluster near the head of the tracks. A handy OTP **ATM** is just to the left of the main door (other ATMs inside the station have rip-off rates—but two more legitimate ATMs are inside banks that face the square out front). Train ticket machines are also just inside the main door. There's no official TI at the station, but the railroad runs a customer service office with train advice and basic city info (near the front of track 9, in the left corner, near the ATM).

Along **track 6,** from back to front, you'll see a side door (leading to a beautifully restored arrivals hall and an exit to a taxi stand), Interchange exchange booth (with bad rates—use the OTP ATM instead), international ticket windows *(nemzetközi jegypénztár),* and grubby gyro stands. Pay WCs are down the hall past the gyro places. Across the main hall, more services run along **track 9,** including domestic ("inland") ticket windows and lockers. The big staircase at the head of the tracks leads down to more domestic ticket windows, WCs, telephones, and more lockers.

To take the **Metró** into town, head down the main stairs where the tracks dead-end, pass through a ticket area, and then (on your right) a handy public transit ticket and information office. Just beyond that, the underpass opens up: Turn left to reach the M2/red Metró line, or right to reach the M4/green Metró line. **Taxis** wait alongside the station (through the exit by track 6).

Nyugati/Western Station

Nyugati train station (Nyugati pu.) is the most central of Budapest's stations, facing the Great Boulevard on the northeast edge of downtown Pest.

Most trains use the shorter **tracks 1-9,** which are set back from the main entrance. From the head of these tracks, use the stairs or escalator just inside the doors to reach an underpass and the Metró (M3/blue line). Or exit straight ahead into a parking lot with buses, taxis, and—around to the right—the WestEnd City Center shop-

ping mall. (The useful trams around the Great Boulevard are outside the main door, at the head of the longer tracks 10-13.)

The longer **tracks 10-13** extend all the way to the main entrance. Ticket machines line the tracks; ticket windows are through
an easy-to-miss door by
platform 13 (marked *je-
gypénztár* and *információ*).
This area is being reno-
vated, so you may have
to hunt around for inter-
national ticket windows
(nemzetközi jegypénztár)
and for lockers. An **ATM**
is just inside the main

door, on the right (use the one marked with the OTP logo).

From the head of tracks 10-13, exit straight ahead out the
main entrance and you'll be on Teréz körút, the very busy Great
Boulevard ring road. In front of the building is the stop for the
handy trams #4 and #6 (which zip around the Great Boulevard); to
the right are stairs leading to an underpass (use it to avoid crossing
this busy intersection, or to reach the Metró's M3/blue line); and
to the left is the classiest Art Nouveau McDonald's on the planet,
filling the station's former waiting room. (Seriously. Take a look
inside.)

Trains to the **airport** generally depart from the longer tracks
on the far side (tracks 14 and higher).

Déli/Southern Station

In the late 19th century, local newlyweds caught the train at Déli
train station (Déli pu.) for their honeymoon in Venice. Renovated
by the heavy-handed communists, today the station—tucked behind Castle Hill on the Buda side—is dreary. From the tracks, go
straight ahead into the vast main hall, with well-marked domestic
and international ticket windows at opposite ends. A left-luggage
desk is outside beyond track 1. Downstairs, you'll find several shops
and eateries, and access to the very convenient M2/red Metró line,
which takes you to several key points in town: Batthyány tér (on
the Buda embankment, at the north end of the Víziváros neighborhood), Deák tér (the heart of Pest, with connections to two other
Metró lines), and Keleti train station (where you can transfer to the
M4/green Metró line).

By Plane

Budapest's **Liszt Ferenc Airport** is 10 miles southeast of the center (code: BUD, tel. 1/296-7000, www.bud.hu). Many Hungarians
still call the airport by its former name, "Ferihegy." The airport's

lone passenger terminal is called "Terminal 2" ("Terminal 1" closed years ago). The terminal has two adjacent parts, which you can walk between in just a few minutes: the smaller Terminal 2A is for flights from EU/Schengen countries (no passport control required), while Terminal 2B is for flights from other countries. Both sections have ATMs and TI desks (open daily 8:00-23:00 in 2A, and daily 10:00-22:00 in 2B). Car rental desks are in the arrivals area for 2B.

Getting Between the Airport and Downtown Budapest: Public bus #100E is the most cost-effective option, conveniently connecting the airport to downtown before making just three stops near key Metró stations: Astoria, Kálvin tér, and Deák tér. You can buy the 900-Ft ticket at the machine before you board, or—with exact change only—from the driver (2/hour, 40-60 minutes depending on traffic).

The fastest door-to-door option is to take a **taxi.** Fötaxi has a monopoly at the taxi stand out front; figure about 7,500 Ft to downtown, depending on traffic.

The **airport shuttle** minibus is a decent value for solo travelers, but two people will pay just a few dollars more to share a taxi (4,900 Ft/1 person, 6,000 Ft/2 people; minibus ride to any hotel in the city center takes about 30-60 minutes depending on hotel location, plus waiting time; tel. 1/550-0000, www.minibud.hu; if arranging a minibus transfer *to* the airport, call at least 24 hours in advance). Because they prefer to take several people at once, you may have to wait awhile at the airport for a quorum to show up.

By Car

Avoid driving in Budapest if you can—roads are narrow, and fellow drivers, bikes, and pedestrians make the roads feel like an obstacle course. Especially during rush hour (7:00-9:00 and 16:00-18:00), congestion is maddening, and since there's no complete expressway bypass, much of the traffic going through the city has to go *through* the city. Don't drive down roads marked with a red circle, or in lanes marked for buses; these can be monitored by automatic traffic cameras, and you could be mailed a ticket.

There are three concentric ring roads, all of them slow: the Small Boulevard (Kiskörút), Great Boulevard (Nagykörút), and outermost Hungária körút, from which highways and expressways spin off to other destinations. Farther out, the M-0 expressway makes a not-quite-complete circle around the city center, helping to divert some traffic.

Parking: While in Budapest, unless you're heading to an out-of-town sight (such as Memento Park), park the car at or near your hotel and take public transportation. Public street parking costs 175-525 Ft per hour (pay in advance at machine and put ticket on dashboard). Within the Great Boulevard, it's generally free to park from 20:00 until 8:00 the next morning (farther out, it's free after 18:00). But in some heavily touristed areas, you may have to pay around the clock. Always check signs carefully, and confirm with a local (such as your hotelier) that you've parked appropriately. Also, be sure to park within the lines—otherwise, your car is likely to get "booted" (I've seen more than one confused tourist puzzling over the giant red brace on his tire). A guarded parking lot is safer, but more expensive (figure 3,000-4,000 Ft/day, ask your hotel or look for the blue *P*s on maps). As rental-car theft can be a problem, ask at your hotel for advice.

HELPFUL HINTS

Rip-Offs: Budapest is quite safe, especially for a city of its size. Occasionally tourists run into con artists or pickpockets; as in any big city, wear a money belt and secure your valuables in touristy places and on public transportation.

Restaurants on the Váci utca shopping street are notorious for overcharging tourists. Anywhere in Budapest, avoid restaurants that don't list prices on the menu. Check your bill carefully. Most restaurants add a 10-12 percent service charge; if you don't notice this, you might accidentally double-tip (for more on tipping, see page 1105). Also, at Váci utca and at train stations, avoid using the rip-off currency exchange booths (such as Interchange or Checkpoint). You'll do much better simply getting cash from an ATM associated with a major bank (including OTP, MKB, K&H, and various big international banks).

Budapest's biggest crooks? Unscrupulous cabbies. For tips on outsmarting them, see "Getting Around Budapest—By Taxi," later. Bottom line: Locals *always* call for an official, regulated cab, rather than hail one on the street or at a taxi stand. Ask your hotel or restaurant to call one for you.

Medical Help: Near Buda's Széll Kálmán tér, **FirstMed Centers** is a private, pricey, English-speaking clinic (by appointment or urgent care, call first, Hattyú utca 14, 5th floor, district I, M2: Széll Kálmán tér, tel. 1/224-9090, www.firstmedcenters. com). Hospitals *(kórház)* are scattered around the city.

Monday Closures: Most of Budapest's museums are closed on Mondays. But you can still take advantage of plenty of other sights and activities: all three major baths, Memento Park, Great Synagogue and Jewish Quarter, Matthias Church on Castle Hill, St. István's Basilica, Parliament tour, Great Market Hall and Bálna Budapest, Opera House tour, City Park (and Zoo), Danube cruises, concerts, and bus, walking, and bike tours.

English Bookstore: There's a fine selection of new books, mostly in

BUDAPEST

English, at **Bestsellers;** it's near St. István's Basilica (Mon-Fri 9:00-18:30, Sat 11:00-18:00, Sun 12:00-18:00, Október 6 utca 11—see map on page 655, tel. 1/312-1295).

Pharmacies: The helpful **BENU Gyógyszertár** pharmacy is dead-center in Pest, between Vörösmarty and Széchenyi squares. Because they cater to clientele from nearby international hotels, they have a useful directory that lists the Hungarian equivalent of US prescription medicines (Mon-Fri 8:00-20:00, closed Sat-Sun, Dorottya utca 13, district V, M1: Vörösmarty tér, for location see map on page 653, tel. 1/317-2374). Each district has one 24-hour pharmacy (these should be noted outside the entrance to any pharmacy).

Laundry: The self-service launderette chain **Bubbles** is open 24/7, unstaffed, automated, and takes credit cards. The most convenient location is near the Small Boulevard, at the inner edge of the Seventh District, at Paulay Ede 3, M1: Bajcsy-Zsilinszky út; check their website for others (www.bubbles.hu). Two additional, cheap self-service launderettes are also in the Seventh District: **Laundry Budapest** has lots of machines (daily 9:00-24:00, last wash at 22:00, Dohány utca 37, near M2: Blaha Lujza tér, tel. 1/781-0098, www.laundrybudapest.hu), and **Bazar Hostel** has a few (daily 24 hours, closer to the Great Synagogue, at Dohány utca 22). For locations, see the map on page 659.

For full service, **Broadway Hostel & Apartments** is just behind the Opera House (walk straight behind the Opera House and turn right on Ó utca, then look left for signs at #24—you'll go up the main stairs and turn left to find the laundry office in the arcade; if nobody is at the laundry office, ask at the apartment house reception nearby; district VI, M1: Opera, tel. +3670-771-9164). **Vajnóczki Tisztítószalon,** a block from the Oktogon, is a dry cleaner (next-day service, Mon-Fri 8:00-18:00, Sat until 13:00, closed Sun, Szófia utca 8, tel. 1/342-3796). For both locations, see the map on page 649.

Bike Rental: Budapest—with lots of traffic congestion—isn't the easiest place for cyclists. But as the city adds more bike lanes and traffic-free zones, those comfortable with urban cycling may be tempted. You can rent a bike at **Yellow Zebra** (3,500 Ft/all day, 4,500 Ft/24 hours; electric bikes-15,000 Ft/all day, 18,000 Ft/24 hours; see "Absolute Tour Center" listing, earlier under "Tourist Information").

Budapest also has a subsidized public bike network called **Bubi** (for "**Bu**dapest **Bi**kes"). Bike stations are scattered throughout the Town Center and adjoining areas; you can pick a bike up at any station and drop it off at any other. First, you

Tonight We're Gonna Party Like It's 1896

Visitors to Budapest need only remember one date: 1896. For the millennial celebration of their ancestors' arrival in Europe,  Hungarians threw a blowout party. In the thousand years between 896 and 1896, the Magyars had gone from being a nomadic Central Asian tribe that terrorized the Continent to sharing the throne of one of the most successful empires Europe had ever seen.

Budapest used its millennial celebration as an excuse to build monuments and buildings appropriate for the co-capital of a huge empire, including these landmarks:

- **Heroes' Square** and **Millennium Monument**
- **Vajdahunyad Castle** (in City Park)
- **Parliament** building (96 meters tall, 96 front steps)
- **St. István's Basilica** (also 96 meters tall)
- M1/yellow Metró line, a.k.a. *Földalatti* ("Underground")
- **Great Market Hall** (and four other market halls)
- **Andrássy út** and most of the fine buildings lining it
- **Opera House**
- A complete rebuilding of **Matthias Church** (on Castle Hill)
- **Fisherman's Bastion** (by Matthias Church)
- Green **Liberty Bridge** (then called Franz Josef Bridge)

The key number in Hungary is 96—even the national anthem (when sung at the proper tempo) takes 96 seconds. But after all this fuss, it's too bad that the date was wrong: A commission—convened to establish the exact year of the Magyars' debut—determined it happened in 895. But city leaders knew they'd never make an 1895 deadline, and requested the finding be changed to 896.

buy a "ticket" at http://molbubi.bkk.hu or at a docking station (500 Ft/24 hours, 1,000 Ft/72 hours, 2,000 Ft/week, plus a 25,000-Ft deposit on your credit card for the duration of the ticket). Once you have a ticket, it's free to use a bike for 30 minutes or less, then costs 500 Ft for each additional 30 minutes. Ask at the TI if you need help figuring out the system.

Drivers: Friendly, English-speaking **Gábor Balázs** can drive you around the city or into the surrounding countryside (5,000 Ft/hour, 3-hour minimum in city, 4-hour minimum in countryside—good for a Danube Bend excursion, mobile +3620-936-4317, bgabor.e@gmail.com). **Zsolt Gál** is also available for transfers, side-trips, and longer trips to Prague or Vienna, and specializes in helping people track down Jewish sites in the surrounding areas (mobile +3670-452-4900, forma111562@gmail.com). Note that these are drivers, not tour guides. For a licensed tour guide who also does countryside driving trips, see "Tours in Budapest," later.

Best Views: Budapest is a city of marvelous vistas. Some of the best are from the Citadella fortress (high on Gellért Hill), the promenade in front of the Royal Palace and the Fisherman's Bastion on top of Castle Hill, and the embankments or many bridges spanning the Danube (especially the Chain Bridge). Don't forget the view from the tour boats on the Danube—particularly lovely at night.

GETTING AROUND BUDAPEST

Budapest sprawls. Connecting your sightseeing just on foot is tedious and unnecessary. It's crucial to get comfortable with the well-coordinated public transportation system: Metró lines, trams, buses, trolley buses, and boats. Budapest's transit system website is www.bkk.hu.

Tickets

The same tickets work for the entire system. Buy them at kiosks, Metró ticket windows, or machines (with English instructions, credit cards accepted). As prices are affordable and it can be frustrating to find a ticket machine (especially when you see your tram or bus approaching), I generally invest in a multiday ticket to have the freedom of hopping on at will.

Your options are as follows:

• **Single ticket** (*vonaljegy*, for a ride of up to an hour on any means of transit; transfers allowed only within the Metró system)—350 Ft (or 450 Ft if bought from the driver)

• **Short single Metró ride** (*Metrószakaszjegy*, 3 stops or fewer on the Metró)—300 Ft

• **Transfer ticket** (*átszállójegy*—allowing up to 90 minutes, including one transfer between Metró and bus)—530 Ft

• **Pack of 10 single tickets** *(10 darabos gyűjtőjegy)*, which can be shared—3,000 Ft (that's 300 Ft per ticket, saving you 50 Ft per ticket; note that these must stay together as a single pack—they can't be sold separately)

• Unlimited multiday travel cards for Metró, bus, and tram, including a **24-hour travelcard** (*24 órás jegy*, 1,650 Ft/24 hours),

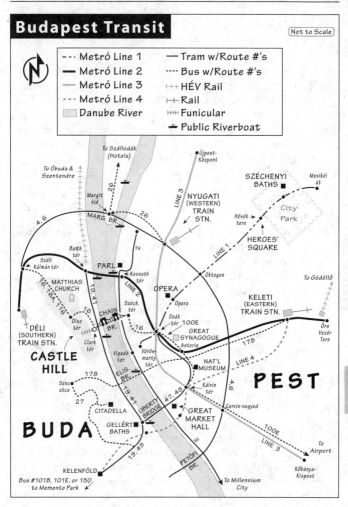

Budapest Transit

Not to Scale

- - - Metró Line 1
— Metró Line 2
Metró Line 3
- - - Metró Line 4
Danube River

— Tram w/Route #'s
- - - Bus w/Route #'s
HÉV Rail
Rail
Funicular
Public Riverboat

72-hour travelcard (*72 órás jegy,* 4,150 Ft/72 hours), and **seven-day travelcard** (*hetijegy,* 4,950 Ft/7 days)

• **24-hour group travel card** (*csoportos 24 órás jegy,* 3,300 Ft), covering up to five adults—a great deal for groups of three to five people

• **Budapest Card,** which combines a multiday ticket with sightseeing discounts (see "Tourist Information," earlier)

Always validate single-ride tickets as you enter the bus, tram, or Metró station (stick it in the elbow-high box). On older buses and trams that have little red validation boxes, stick your ticket in the black slot, then pull the slot toward you to punch holes in your ticket. Multiday tickets need be validated only once. The stern-looking people with green armbands waiting as you enter or exit the Metró want to see your validated ticket. Cheaters are fined 8,000 Ft on the spot, and you'll be surprised how often you're checked. All public transit runs from 4:30 in the morning until 23:50; a few designated night buses and trams operate overnight.

New Transit Cards: Budapest plans to phase out paper tickets in favor of electronic pay-as-you-go cards (similar to London's Oyster card or New York's Metrocard). Ask around, or see www.bkk.hu for the latest.

Handy Terms: *Á ___ félé* means "in the direction of ___." *Megálló* means "stop" or "station," and *Végállomás* means "end of the line."

By Metró

Riding Budapest's efficient Metró, you really feel like you're down in the guts of the city. There are four working lines:

• **M1/yellow**—The first subway line on the Continent, this line runs just 20 steps below street level under Andrássy út from the center to City Park. Dating from 1896, "the Underground" (Földalatti) is so shallow that you must follow the signs on the street (listing end points— Mexikói út felé takes you toward City Park) to gauge the right direction, because there's no un-

derpass for switching platforms. Though recently renovated, the M1 line retains its old-time atmosphere.

• **M2/red**—Built during the communist days, it's 115 feet deep and designed to double as a bomb shelter. Going under the Danube to Buda, the M2 connects the Déli/Southern train station, Széll Kálmán tér (where you catch bus #16, #16A, or #116 to the top of Castle Hill), Batthyány tér (Víziváros and the HÉV suburban railway), Kossuth tér (behind the Parliament), Astoria (near the Great Synagogue on the Small Boulevard), and the Keleti/Eastern train station (where it crosses the M4/green line).

• **M3/blue**—This line makes a broad, boomerang-shaped swoop north to south on the Pest side. Key stops include the Nyugati/Western train station, Ferenciek tere (in the heart of Pest's Town Center), Kálvin tér (near the Great Market Hall and many recommended hotels; this is also where it crosses the M4/green line), and Corvin-negyed (near the Holocaust Memorial Center).

• **M4/green**—This line runs from southern Buda to the Gellért Baths, under the Danube to Fővám tér (behind the Great Market Hall) and Kálvin tér (where it crosses the M3/blue line), then up to

Rákóczi tér (on the Grand Boulevard) and the Keleti/Eastern train station (where it crosses the M2/red line). The M4 is the city's newest line (from 2014), and many of its stations boast boldly modern, waste-of-space concrete architecture that's eye-opening to simply stroll through; the one at Gellért tér has a thermal spring-fed waterfall coursing past the main staircase.

The three original lines—M1, M2, and M3—cross only once: at the **Deák tér** stop (often signed as *Deák Ferenc tér*) in the heart of Pest, near where Andrássy út begins.

Aside from the historic M1 line, most Metró stations are at intersections of ring roads and other major thoroughfares. You'll usually exit the Metró into a confusing underpass packed with kiosks, fast-food stands, and makeshift markets. Directional signs (listing which streets, addresses, and tram or bus stops are near each exit) help you find the right exit. Or do the prairie-dog routine: Surface to get your bearings, then head back underground to find the correct stairs up to your destination.

By HÉV

Budapest's suburban rail system, or HÉV (pronounced "hayv," stands for Helyiérdekű Vasút, "Railway of Local Interest"), branches off to the outskirts and beyond. On a short visit, it's unlikely that you'll need to use it, unless you're heading to the Óbuda neighborhood (for its museums), the charming Danube Bend town of Szentendre, or the royal palace at Gödöllő.

The HÉV line that begins at Batthyány tér in Buda's Víziváros neighborhood heads through Óbuda to Szentendre; from the station at Örs vezér tere, a different line runs east to Gödöllő.

The HÉV is covered by standard transit tickets and passes for rides within the city of Budapest (such as to Óbuda). But if going beyond—such as to Szentendre or Gödöllő—you'll have to pay more. Tell the ticket-seller (or punch into the machine) where you're going, and you'll be issued the proper ticket.

By Tram

Budapest's trams are handy and frequent, taking you virtually anywhere the Metró doesn't. Here are some trams you might use (note that all of these run in both directions):

Tram #2: Follows Pest's Danube embankment, parallel to Váci utca. From north to south, it begins at the Great Boulevard (Jászai Mari tér, near Margaret Bridge) and stops on either side of the Parliament (north side near the visitors center/Országház stop, as well as south side near the Kossuth tér Metró stop), Széchenyi István tér and the Chain Bridge, Vigadó tér, and the Great Market Hall (Fővám tér stop).

Trams #19 and #41: Run along Buda's Danube embankment

Budapest at a Glance

Pest

▲▲▲**Széchenyi Baths** Budapest's steamy soaking scene in City Park—the city's single best attraction. **Hours:** Daily 6:00-22:00. See page 609.

▲▲**Hungarian Parliament** Vast riverside government center with remarkable interior. **Hours:** English tours run daily 8:00-18:00; fewer on Mon and off-season. See page 575.

▲▲**Great Market Hall** Colorful Old World mall with produce, eateries, souvenirs, and great people-watching. **Hours:** Mon 6:00-17:00, Tue-Fri until 18:00, Sat until 15:00, closed Sun. See page 592.

▲▲**Great Synagogue** The world's second-largest, with fancy interior, good museum, and memorial garden. **Hours:** Sun-Thu 10:00-18:00 (May-Sept until 20:00), Fri 10:00-16:00; shorter hours off-season; always closed Sat and Jewish holidays. See page 595.

▲▲**Hungarian State Opera House** Neo-Renaissance splendor and affordable opera. **Hours:** Lobby/box office open Mon-Sat from 11:00 until show time—generally 19:00; Sun open 3 hours before performance—generally 16:00-19:00, or 10:00-13:00 if there's a matinee; English tours nearly daily at 14:00, 15:00, and 16:00. See page 600.

▲▲**House of Terror** Harrowing remembrance of Nazis and communist secret police in former headquarters/torture site. **Hours:** Tue-Sun 10:00-18:00, closed Mon. See page 602.

▲▲**Heroes' Square** Mammoth tribute to Hungary's historic figures, fronted by art museums. See page 606.

▲▲**City Park** Budapest's backyard, with Art Nouveau zoo, Transylvanian Vajdahunyad Castle replica, amusement park, and Széchenyi Baths. See page 608.

▲▲**Vajdahunyad Castle** Epcot-like replica of a Transylvanian castle and other historical buildings. See page 608.

from Batthyány tér (with an M2/red Metró station, and HÉV trains to Óbuda and Szentendre). From Batthyány tér, these trams run (north to south) through Víziváros, with several helpful stops: Clark Ádám tér (the bottom of the Castle Hill funicular, near the stop for bus #16 up to Castle Hill), Várkert Bazár (Castle Park with escalators and elevators up to the Royal Palace); Rudas Gyógyfürdő

▲▲**Holocaust Memorial Center** Excellent memorial and museum honoring Hungarian victims of the Holocaust. **Hours:** Tue-Sun 10:00-18:00, closed Mon. See page 609.

▲**St. István's Basilica** Budapest's largest church, with a saint's withered fist and great city views. **Hours:** Mon-Sat 9:00-17:00, Sun from 13:00; panorama terrace daily 10:00-17:30, summer until 18:30, off-season until 16:30. See page 587.

▲**Hungarian National Museum** Expansive collection of fragments from Hungary's history. **Hours:** Tue-Sun 10:00-18:00, closed Mon. See page 594.

▲**Margaret Island** Budapest's traffic-free urban playground, with spas, ruins, gardens, a game farm, and fountains, set in the middle of the Danube. See page 589.

Buda

▲▲**Matthias Church** Landmark Neo-Gothic church with gilded history-book interior and revered 16th-century statue of Mary and Jesus. **Hours:** Mon-Sat 9:00-17:00, Sun from 13:00. See page 617.

▲▲**Gellért Baths** Touristy baths in historic Buda hotel. **Hours:** Daily 6:00-20:00. See page 630.

▲▲**Rudas Baths** Half-millennium-old Turkish dome over a series of hot-water pools. **Hours:** Daily 6:00-20:00. See page 632.

▲**Hungarian National Gallery** Top works by Hungarian artists, housed in the Royal Palace. **Hours:** Tue-Sun 10:00-18:00, closed Mon. See page 614.

▲**Hospital in the Rock** Fascinating underground network of hospital and bomb-shelter corridors from World War II and the Cold War. **Hours:** Daily 10:00-20:00. See page 621.

Day Trips from Budapest

▲▲**Memento Park** Larger-than-life communist statues collected in one park, on the outskirts of town. **Hours:** Daily 10:00-sunset. See page 674.

BUDAPEST

(Rudas Baths); then around the base of Gellért Hill to Szent Gellért tér (Gellért Baths and M4/green Metró station).

Trams #4 and #6: Zip around Pest's Great Boulevard ring road (Nagykörút), connecting Nyugati/Western train station and the Oktogon with the southern tip of Margaret Island and Buda's Széll Kálmán tér (with M2/red Metró station, and buses up to the castle). At night, this route is replaced by bus #6.

Trams #47 and #49: Connect the Gellért Baths in Buda with Pest's Small Boulevard ring road (Kiskörút), with stops at the Great Market Hall (Fővám tér stop), the National Museum (Kálvin tér stop), the Great Synagogue (Astoria stop), and Deák tér (end of the line).

By Bus and Trolley Bus

I use the Metró and trams for most of my Budapest commuting. But some buses are useful for shortcuts within the city, or for reaching outlying sights. Note that the transit company draws a distinction between gas-powered "buses" and electric "trolley buses" (which are powered by overhead cables). Unless otherwise noted, you can assume the following are standard buses:

Buses #16, #16A, and #116: All head up to the top of Castle Hill (get off at Dísz tér, in the middle of the hill—the closest stop to the Royal Palace). You can catch any of these three at Széll Kálmán tér (M2/red Metró line). When coming from the other direction, bus #16 makes several handy stops in Pest (Deák tér, Széchenyi István tér), then crosses the Chain Bridge for more stops in Buda (including Clark Ádám tér, at Buda end of Chain Bridge on its way up to the castle).

Trolley buses #70 and #78: These zip from near the Opera House (intersection of Andrássy út and Nagymező utca) to the Parliament (Kossuth tér).

Bus #178: Goes from Keleti/Eastern train station to central Pest (Astoria and Ferenciek tere Metró stops), then over the Elisabeth Bridge to Buda.

Bus #26: Begins at Nyugati/Western train station and heads around the Great Boulevard to Margaret Island, making several stops along the island.

Bus #27: Runs from either side of Gellért Hill to just below the Citadella fortress at the hill's peak (Búsuló Juhász stop).

Bus #100E: This handy, speedy express bus connects Liszt Ferenc Airport to Deák tér, with only two other stops en route (Astoria and Kálvin tér Metró stops).

Buses #101B, #101E, and #150: These run from Kelenföld (the end of the line for the M4/green Metró line, with some trains to Pécs) to Memento Park.

By Boat

Budapest's public transit authority operates a system of Danube riverboats (*hajójárat*, marked with a stylish *D* logo) that connect strategic locations throughout the city. The riverboat system has drawbacks: Frequency is sparse (weekdays only, 1-2/hour, may run on weekends in summer), and it's typically slower than hopping on the Metró or a tram. But it's also a romantic, cheap alternative to pricey riverboat cruises, and can be a handy way to connect some sightseeing points. A 750-Ft ticket covers any trip; it's also covered by 24-hour, 72-hour, or seven-day travelcards (but not by the Budapest Card; if it's running on weekends, you have to buy a ticket regardless of your pass).

Lines #D11 and #D12 run in both directions through the city, including these stops within downtown Budapest: **Népfürdő utca (Árpád híd),** at the northern end of Margaret Island (the weekend boat also makes several additional stops on the island); **Jászai Mari tér,** at the Pest end of Margaret Bridge; **Batthyány tér,** on the Buda embankment in Víziváros; **Kossuth Lajos tér,** near the Parliament on the Pest side; **Várkert Bazár,** at the base of the grand entrance staircase to Buda Castle; **Petőfi tér,** on the Pest embankment next to the Legenda Cruises riverboats (dock 8); and **Szent Gellért tér,** at the Buda end of Liberty Bridge, next to the Gellért Baths. Some stops may be closed if the river level gets very low.

By Taxi

Budapest strictly regulates its official taxis, which must be painted yellow and have yellow license plates. These taxis are required to charge identical rates, regardless of company: a drop rate of 700 Ft, and then 300 Ft/kilometer, plus 75 Ft/minute for wait time. A 10 percent tip is expected. A typical ride within central Budapest shouldn't run more than 2,500 Ft.

If you take an unofficial taxi, there's a very high probability you'll get ripped off with much higher rates. Unfortunately, these cabbie crooks hang out at places frequented by tourists (such as at train stations). If you wave down a cab on the street, be sure it has a yellow license plate; otherwise, it's not official, and you might wind up paying double or triple. Better yet, do as the locals do and call a cab from a reputable company: **City Taxi** (tel. 1/211-1111), **Taxi 6x6** (tel. 1/266-6666), or **Főtaxi** (tel. 1/222-2222). Most dispatchers speak English, but if you're uncomfortable calling, you can ask your hotel or restaurant to call for you.

Uber currently does not operate in Hungary.

Tours in Budapest

BY FOOT
Local Guides

Budapest has an abundance of enthusiastic, hardworking guides who speak perfect English and enjoy showing off their city. A guide is particularly worthwhile if you have an appetite for Hungary's rich but complex history, or want to learn more about life under communism. While guides might be available last-minute, it's better to reserve in advance. **Péter Pölczman** is an exceptional guide who really puts you in touch with the Budapest you came to see (€110/half-day,

€190/full day, mobile +3620-926-0557, www.budapestyourself. com, peter.polczman@gmail.com). **Andrea Makkay** has professional polish and a smart understanding of what visitors really want to experience (€110/half-day, €190/full day, mobile +3620-962-9363, www.privateguidebudapest.com, andrea.makkay@gmail. com—arrange details by email; if Andrea is busy, she can send you with another guide). **George Farkas** is well-attuned to the stylish side of this fast-changing metropolis (€120/half-day, €240/full day, mobile +3670-335-8030, www.mybudapesttours.hu, georgefarkas@ gmail.hu). And **Eszter Bokros** brings enthusiasm to sharing her city (€110/half-day, €190/full day, mobile +3670-625-6655, eszterbokros1@gmail.com).

Elemér Boreczky, a semi-retired university professor, leads walking tours with a soft-spoken, scholarly approach, emphasizing Budapest's rich tapestry of architecture as "frozen music." Elemér is ideal if you want a walking graduate-level seminar about the easy-to-miss nuances of this grand city (€30/hour, mobile +3630-491-1389, http://culturaltours.mlap.hu, boreczky.elemer@gmail.com).

Péter, Andrea, George, Eszter, and Elemér have all been indispensable help to me in writing and updating this book.

Walking Tours

Budapest's best-established walking-tour company is **Absolute Tours,** run by Oregonian Ben Frieday. Travelers with this book get a discount on almost all the tours they offer (15 percent if you book online—enter coupon code "RICK"—or 10 percent for tours booked in person). Their options include the 3.5-hour All in One walking tour, offering a good overview of Budapest; the Hammer & Sickle Tour, with visits to a mini museum of communist artifacts and sites related to the 1956 Uprising; two different food tours (one focusing on street food and craft beer, the other on traditional foods in the Great Market Hall and wine tasting); and Enchanted Budapest, an evening walk that includes a one-hour cruise on the Danube. For prices and schedules, see www.absolutetours.com or contact the office (tel. 1/269-3843, mobile +3620-929-7506).

You'll also see various companies advertising **"free" walking tours.** While there is no set fee to take these tours, guides are paid only if you tip (they're hoping for at least 2,000 Ft/person). They offer a basic 2.5-hour introduction to the city, as well as itineraries focusing on the communist era and the Jewish Quarter. Because they're working for tips, the guides are highly motivated to impress their customers. But because the "free" tag attracts very large groups, these tours tend to be less intimate than paid tours, and (especially the introductory tours) take a once-over-lightly "infotainment" approach. As this scene is continually evolving, look for local fliers to learn about the options and meeting points.

BY BOAT
▲▲Danube Boat Tours
Cruising the Danube, while touristy, is a fun and convenient way to get a feel for the city's grand layout. The most established company, Legenda Cruises, is a class act that runs well-maintained, glassed-in panoramic boats day and night. All of their cruises include a free drink and romantic headphone commentary. By night, TV monitors show the interiors of the great buildings as you float by.

I've negotiated a special discount with Legenda for my readers—but you must book directly and ask for the Rick Steves price. By **day,** the 75-minute Duna Bella cruise costs 3,800 Ft for Rick Steves readers; if you want, you can hop off at Margaret Island to explore on your own, then return after 45 minutes on a later cruise (about hourly, in winter runs 1-2/day with no Margaret Island stop). By **night,** the one-hour "Danube Legend" cruise (with no Margaret Island visit) costs 4,800 Ft for Rick Steves readers (4/day, 2/day in winter). On weekends, it's smart to call ahead and reserve a spot for the evening cruises. Note: These special prices are for 2019, and may be slightly higher in 2020 and beyond.

The Legenda dock is in front of the Marriott on the Pest embankment (find pedestrian access under tram tracks at downriver

BUDAPEST

end of Vigadó tér, district V, M1: Vörösmarty tér, tel. 1/317-2203, www.legenda.hu). Competing river-cruise companies are nearby, but given the quality and the discount, Legenda offers the best value.

ON WHEELS
Bike and Segway Tours
The best option for tours by bike and Segway (a stand-up electric scooter) is **Yellow Zebra,** a sister company of Absolute Tours (bike tours—9,000 Ft, 16,000 Ft by electronic bike, 4 hours, winter tours possible Fri-Sun if weather allows; Segway tours—21,000 Ft, 2.5 hours, begins with 30-minute training). My readers get a 15 percent discount when booking online (www.yellowzebratours.com, enter coupon code "RICK"), or 10 percent off if booking in person. These tours meet at the Absolute Tour Center behind the Opera House (see "Tourist Information," earlier).

Bus Tours
Various companies run hop-on, hop-off bus tours, which make 12 to 16 stops as they cruise around town on a two-hour loop with headphone commentary (generally around 8,000 Ft/24 hours). Most companies also offer a wide variety of other tours, including dinner boat cruises and trips to the Danube Bend. Pick up fliers about all of these tours at the TI or in your hotel lobby.

RiverRide
This company offers a bus tour with a twist: Its amphibious bus can float on the Danube River, effectively making this a combination bus-and-boat tour. The live guide imparts dry English commentary as you roll (and float). While it's a fun gimmick, the entry ramp into the river (facing the north end of Margaret Island) is far from the most scenic stretch, and the river portion is slow-paced—showing you the same Margaret Island scenery twice, plus a circle in front of the Parliament. The Legenda Cruises boat tours, described earlier, give you more scenic bang for your buck (9,000 Ft, 2 hours, 3-4/day, departs from Széchenyi tér near Gresham Palace, tel. 1/332-2555, www.riverride.com).

PRIVATE TOURS INTO THE HUNGARIAN COUNTRYSIDE
The Hungarian countryside is well worth exploring. If you'd like a taste without driving yourself, hire **Ádám Kiss,** a licensed guide who lives in the folk-museum village of Hollókő. Ádám can pick you up in Budapest (at your hotel or the airport) and drive you to your choice of countryside destinations ($150 all day, plus travel costs; for example, for an all-day visit to Hollókő and Eger for two people, you'd pay about $300 total for round-trip transportation,

guiding, admissions, and lunch). Ádám also enjoys helping people track down their roots in the Hungarian countryside. Contact him for pricing (mobile +3620-379-6132, adamtheguide@gmail.com).

Sights in Pest

Most of Pest's top sights cluster in five neighborhoods: **Leopold Town** and the **Town Center** (together forming the city's "downtown"); the **Jewish Quarter,** just outside the inner ring road; along the grand boulevard **Andrássy út;** and at that boulevard's end, near **Heroes' Square and City Park.** Several other excellent sights are not contained in these areas: along the **Small Boulevard** (Kiskörút); along the **Great Boulevard** (Nagykörút); and along the boulevard called **Üllői út.**

Sightseeing Tips: Budapest boomed in the late 19th century, after it became the co-capital of the vast Austro-Hungarian Empire. Most of its finest buildings (and top sights) date from this age. To appreciate an opulent interior—a Budapest experience worth ▲▲▲—prioritize touring either the Parliament or the Opera House, depending on your interests. The Opera tour is more crowd-pleasing, while the Parliament tour is grander and a bit drier (with a focus on history and parliamentary process). Seeing both is also a fine option. "Honorable mentions" go to the interiors of St. István's Basilica, the Great Synagogue, New York Café, and both the Széchenyi and the Gellért Baths.

The 21st century is also a boom time in Budapest. The city is busy creating an ambitious Museum Quarter in City Park. They're erecting new, purpose-built homes for the National Gallery; Museum of Science, Technology, and Transport; and new House of Hungarian Music. Progress is ongoing, with the various buildings slated to open gradually over the next few years. In the meantime, you'll likely see construction underway. For details, see www.ligetbudapest.org.

LEOPOLD TOWN (LIPÓTVÁROS)

The Parliament building, which dominates Pest's skyline, is the centerpiece of the city's banking and business district. Called Lipótváros ("Leopold Town"), this snazzy "uptown" quarter features some of the best of Budapest's many monuments. Below, I've linked up the top sights in Leopold Town as a self-guided walk, starting at the grandiose Parliament building and ending at the Chain Bridge.

▲▲Hungarian Parliament (Országház)

With an impressive facade and an even more extravagant interior, the oversized Hungarian Parliament dominates the Danube river-

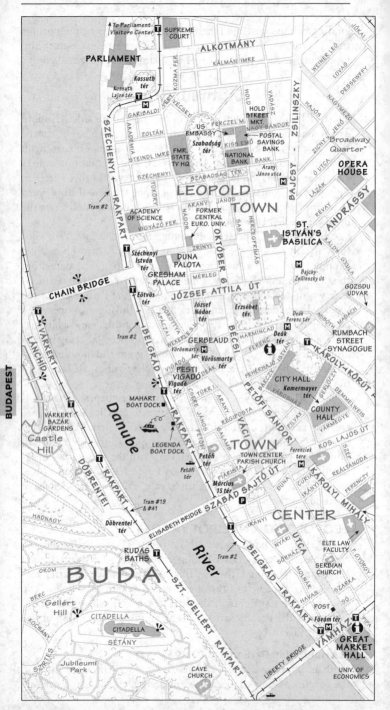

To Parliament Visitors Center
SUPREME COURT
ALKOTMÁNY
KÁLMÁN IMRE
JÓKAI
WEINER LEÓ
LOVAG
DESSEWFFY
NAGYMEZŐ
JENŐ
ZICHY "Broadway Quarter"
Ó UTCA
OPERA HOUSE

PARLIAMENT
Kossuth tér
Kossuth Lajos tér
GARIBALDI
ZOLTÁN
AKADÉMIA
STEINDL IMRE
SZÉCHENYI
VÉCSEY
KOZMA FER.
FŐT.
GARIBALDI
PERCZEL M.
HOLD STREET MKT.
HOLD
VADÁSZ
HAJÓS
NAGY SÁNDOR
BAJCSY - ZSILINSZKY
ZSILINSZKY

US EMBASSY
Szabadság tér
FMR. STATE TV HQ
NATIONAL BANK
POSTAL SAVINGS BANK
Bank
Arany János utca
LÁZÁR
RÉVAY
ANDRÁSSY

SZÉCHENYI RAKPART
Tram #2

LEOPOLD TOWN
SZABADSÁG TÉR
ARANY JÁNOS
FORMER CENTRAL EURO. UNIV.
HERCEGPRÍMÁS
KÁLDY GYULA
ST. ISTVÁN'S BASILICA

ACADEMY OF SCIENCE
VIGYÁZÓ FER.
NÁDOR
OKTÓBER 6
SAS
ZRÍNYI
M Bajcsy-Zsilinszky út
GOZSDU UDVAR

Széchenyi István tér
DUNA PALOTA
GRESHAM PALACE
MÉRLEG

CHAIN BRIDGE
Eötvös tér
JÓZSEF ATTILA ÚT
Deák Ferenc tér
ÁGBÓTH
MADÁCH
RUMBACH STREET SYNAGOGUE

Danube
VÁRKERT LÁNCHÍD
VÁRKERT BAZÁR GARDENS
Castle Hill
DÖBRENTEI RAKPART

BELGRÁD RAKPART
Tram #2
DOROTTYA
APÁCZAI
WEKERLE S.U.
József Nádor tér
Erzsébet tér
HARMINCAD
Deák tér
M
GERBEAUD
Vörösmarty M
Vörösmarty tér
BÉCSI
FERENC
FEHÉRHAJÓ ISTVÁN
CITY HALL
Kamermayer tér
Városház
VÁROSHÁZ
GERLÓCZY
SEMMELWEIS
COUNTY HALL
VÁRMEGYE

PESTI VIGADÓ
Vigadó tér
VIGADÓ
DEÁK
ARANY
CSERE TÜRR I.
VÁCI
PETŐFI SÁNDOR
PILVAX
KOS. LAJOS ÚT

MAHART BOAT DOCK
LEGENDA BOAT DOCK
RAKPART
PETŐFI
JÁNOS
GALAMB
RÉGIPOSTA
DUNA
CURIA
VÁCI
TOWN CENTER PARISH CHURCH
Ferenciek tere
IRÁNYI
KÁROLYI MIHÁLY
FERENCZY
REÁLTANODA

Petőfi tér
Petőfi tér
PIARISTA
Március 15 tér
SZABAD SAJTÓ ÚT
P
IRÁNYI
CENTER
NYÁRI UTCA
ELTE LAW FACULTY
F. GYÖRGY

ELISABETH BRIDGE
Döbrentei tér
Tram #19 & #41
HADNAGY
SZT. GELLÉRT RAKPART
River
Tram #2
SÖRHÁZ
MOLNÁR
HAVAS
SZERB
BELGRÁD RAKPART
SERBIAN CHURCH
SZARKA
POST
Fővám tér
M M
VÁMHÁZ
PIPA

RUDAS BATHS
BUDA
BERC
Gellért Hill
CITADELLA
CITADELLA
SÉTÁNY
ÖRÖM
KOCSÁNY
SZIRTES
Jubileumi Park
CAVE CHURCH
LIBERTY BRIDGE
GREAT MARKET HALL
UNIV. OF ECONOMICS

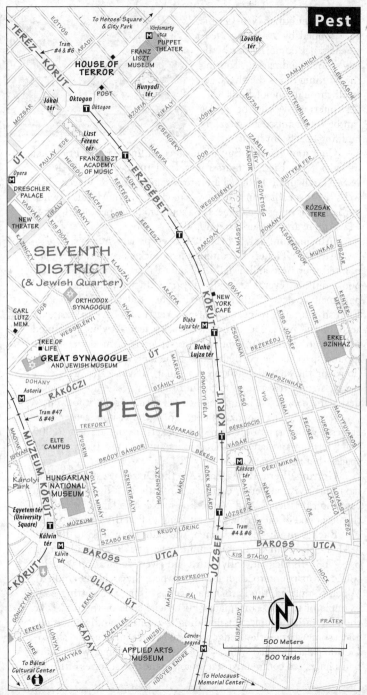

Pest

BUDAPEST

bank. A hulking Neo-Gothic base topped by a soaring Neo-Renaissance dome, it's one of the city's top landmarks. Touring the building offers the chance to stroll through one of Budapest's best interiors. While the guides can be hit-or-miss, the dazzling building speaks for itself.

Cost and Hours: Buy in advance online—5,800 Ft, ticket includes tour; English tours run several times daily 8:00-18:00, Nov-March until 16:00 (these are last tour times). Check their website for specifics on the day you're visiting. On Mondays when parliament is in session (generally about two times per month Sept-May), there are no tours after 10:00.

Information: Tel. 1/441-4904, www.parlament.hu.

Advance Tickets Recommended: Tickets come with an appointed tour time and usually sell out. To ensure getting a space, book online several days in advance at www.jegymester.hu/parlament. Select "Parliament Visit," then a date and time of an English tour, and print out your e-ticket (you'll have to create an account and pay a 250-Ft online booking fee). At your appointed time, head to the Parliament visitors center—a modern, underground space at the northern end of the long Parliament building (look for the statue of a lion on a pillar). If you can't print your ticket, arrive early and go to the information desk—not the ticket desk, which can have long lines—to ask them to print it for you.

If you didn't prebook a ticket, go to the visitors center ticket desk, which sells only same-day tickets, if any are left (6,000 Ft). Morning and late-afternoon tours are the most likely to have space—but no guarantees.

Getting There: Ride tram #2 to the Országház stop, which is next to the visitors center entrance (Kossuth tér 1, district V). You can also ride the M2/red Metró line to Kossuth tér, then walk to the other end of the Parliament building to find the visitors center.

Background: The Parliament was built from 1885 to 1902 to celebrate the Hungarian millennium year of 1896 (see sidebar on page 563). Its elegant, frilly spires and riverside location were inspired by its counterpart in London (where the architect studied). When completed, the Parliament was a striking and cutting-edge example of the mix-and-match Historicist style of the day. Like the Hungarian people, this building is at once grandly ambitious and a somewhat motley hodgepodge of various influences—a Neo-Gothic palace topped with a Neo-Renaissance dome, which once had a huge, red communist star on top of the tallest spire. Fittingly, it's the city's top icon. The best views of the Parliament are from across the Danube—especially in the late-afternoon sunlight.

Visiting the Parliament: The visitors center has WCs, a café, a gift shop, and the Museum of the History of the Hungarian National Assembly. With your ticket in hand, be at the airport-type security checkpoint inside the visitors center at least five minutes before your tour departure time.

On the 45-minute tour, your guide will explain the history and symbolism of the building's intricate decorations and offer a lesson in the Hungarian parliamentary system. You'll see dozens of bushy-mustachioed statues illustrating the occupations of workaday Hungarians through history, and find out why a really good speech was nicknamed a "Havana" by cigar-aficionado parliamentarians.

To begin the tour, you'll climb a 133-step staircase (with an elevator for those who need it) to see the building's monumental entryway and 96-step grand staircase—slathered in gold foil and frescoes, and bathed in shimmering stained-glass light. Then you'll gape up under the ornate gilded dome for a peek at the heavily guarded Hungarian crown, which is overlooked by statues of 16 great Hungarian monarchs, from St. István to Habsburg Empress Maria Theresa. Finally, you'll walk through a cushy lounge—across one of Europe's largest carpets—to see the legislative chamber.

• *The vast square behind the Parliament is studded with attractions. Stay where you are for a quick...*

Kossuth Tér Spin Tour

This square is sprinkled with interesting monuments and packed with Hungarian history. But it's gone through a lot of changes in the last few years, at the hands of architects and urban planners working under the steady guidance of the ruling Fidesz party, led by Viktor Orbán. A highly nationalistic, right-wing party, which swept to power after Hungarians grew weary of the bumblings of the poorly organized, shortsighted left-wing opposition party, Fidesz has exerted its influence over every walk of Hungarian life... beginning with the look of this building and square, and the monuments around it. The square itself used to be a more higgledy-piggledy mix of ragged asphalt, parks, monuments, and trees. But Fidesz wanted the mighty Parliament building to stand bold and unobstructed. Several older monuments (including, ironically, an "eternal" flame honoring victims of the communists) were swept away. Trees were cut down overnight, before would-be protesters could make a peep. And today the square has a scrubbed-clean look that some critics consider fascist.

Look to the right end of the Parliament. Poking up is a pillar topped by a lion being strangled and bitten by a giant snake (a typically heavy-handed Fidesz monument). This pillar marks the entrance to the Parliament visitors center; if you want to check on the availability of tours today, now's a good time.

Looking a bit farther to the right, at the end of the park you'll see another stony tribute, this one to the square's namesake, **Lajos Kossuth,** who led the 1848 Revolution against the Habsburgs.

The street that leaves this square behind Kossuth's left shoulder is Falk Miksa utca, Budapest's **"antique row"**—a great place to browse for nostalgic souvenirs.

Panning right from the Kossuth statue, across the tram tracks you'll see a stately palace. The design was the first runner-up for the Parliament building, so they built it here, to house the **Supreme Court.**

To the right, the **Ministry of Agriculture** was the second runner-up for the Parliament. Today it features a very low-profile, but poignant, monument to the victims of the 1956 Uprising against Soviet rule: At the right end of the protruding arcade, notice that the walls are pockmarked with little metal dollops (you may have to walk closer to see these clearly). Two days into the uprising, on October 25, the ÁVH (communist police) and Soviet troops on the rooftop above opened fire on demonstrators gathered in this square—massacring many and leaving no doubt that Moscow would not tolerate dissent. In the monument, each of the little metal knobs represents a bullet.

In the foreground, between you and the two big palaces, is a long, rectangular **reflecting pond**—a memorial to the people killed by government troops when they revolted here in 1956.

Spin farther to the right, where a dramatic equestrian statue of **Ferenc Rákóczi** stands in the park. Rákóczi valiantly—but unsuccessfully—led the Hungarians in their War of Independence (1703-1711) against the Habsburgs. Although they lived more than a century apart, Rákóczi and Kossuth—who now face each other across this square—were aligned in their rebellion against the Habsburgs.

Complete your 360 and face the Parliament again. Every so often, costumed soldiers appear on the front steps for a brief **"changing of the guard"** ceremony set to recorded music...another patriotic custom, compliments of Fidesz.

Now walk toward the far-left side of the Parliament (toward the river). Just before reaching the corner of the building, find the underground memorial marked *1956* (free, daily 10:00-18:00). Head down the stairs to find a poignant memorial to the **1956 Uprising** that began on this very square. Follow the red line on the floor—first right, and then left. You'll see photos of the events, good English descriptions, and video interviews of eyewitnesses to the massacre on this square on October 25, 1956 (as well as other government mass shootings around Hungary that fall). At the end of the hall is a memorial tomb to those killed by Hungarian secret police, and the symbol of the uprising: a tattered Hungarian flag with a hole cut out of the center.

• *Now let's take a quick...*

Monuments Stroll

Budapest is a city of great monuments, and some of the most vivid are on or near this square.

• *Circle around the left side of the giant Parliament building, passing another statue on a pillar, and walk all the way to the banister overlooking a spectacular view of Buda. Walk along the banister to the left until you come upon a statue of a young man, lost deep in thought, gazing into the Danube.*

Attila József (1905-1937): This beloved modern poet lived a tumultuous, productive, and short life before he killed himself by jumping in front of a train at age 32. József's poems of life, love, and death—mostly written in the 1920s and 1930s—are considered the high point of Hungarian literature. His birthday (April 11) is celebrated as National Hungarian Poetry Day.

Here József reenacts a scene from one of his best poems, "At the Danube." It's a hot day—his jacket lies in a heap next to him, his shirtsleeves are rolled up, and he cradles his hat loosely in his left hand. "As I sat on the bank of the Danube, I watched a watermelon float by," he begins. "As if flowing out of my heart, murky, wise, and great was the Danube." In the poem, József uses the Danube as a metaphor for life—for the way it has interconnected cities and also times—as he reflects that his ancestors likely pondered the Danube from this same spot. Looking into his profound eyes, you sense the depth of this artist's tortured inner life.

• *Stand along the railing in front of József, just above the busy road. If you visually trace the Pest riverbank to the left about 100 yards, just before the tree-filled riverfront park, you can barely see several low-profile dots lining the embankment. This is a...*

Holocaust Monument: Consisting of 50 pairs of bronze shoes, this monument commemorates the Jews who were killed when the Nazis' puppet government, the Arrow Cross, came to power in Hungary in 1944. While many Jews were sent to concentration camps, the Arrow Cross massacred some of them right here, shooting them and letting their bodies fall into the Danube.

• *If you'd like a closer look at the shoes, use the crosswalk (50 yards to your right) to cross the busy embankment road and follow the waterline. I'll wait right here.*

When you're ready to move on, turn your back to the Danube and walk directly inland, following the tram tracks past an entrance to the

BUDAPEST

1956

The year 1956 is etched into the Hungarian psyche. In that year, the people of Budapest staged the first major uprising against the communist regime. It also marked the first time that the Soviets implicitly acknowledged, in brutally putting down the uprising, that the people of Eastern Europe were not "communist by choice."

The seeds of revolution were sown with the death of a tyrant: Josef Stalin passed away on March 5, 1953. Suddenly the choke hold that Moscow had on its satellite states loosened. During this time of "de-Stalinization," Hungarian premier Imre Nagy presided over two years of mild reform, before his political opponents (and Moscow) became nervous and demoted him. (You can read more about Nagy later in this chapter.)

In 1955, Austria declared its neutrality in the Cold War. This thrust Hungary to the front line of the Iron Curtain and raised the stakes both for Hungarians who wanted freedom and for Soviets who wanted to preserve their buffer zone. When Stalin's successor, Nikita Khrushchev, condemned Stalin's crimes in a "secret speech" to communist leaders in February of 1956, it emboldened the Soviet Bloc's dissidents. A workers' strike in Poznań, Poland, in October inspired Hungarians to follow their example.

On October 23, 1956, the Hungarian uprising began. A student union group gathered in Budapest at 15:00 to articulate a list of 16 demands against the communist regime. Then they marched toward Parliament, their numbers gradually swelling. One protester defiantly cut the Soviet-style insignia out of the center of the Hungarian flag, which would become the uprising's symbol.

By nightfall, some 200,000 protesters filled Kossuth tér behind Parliament, calling for Imre Nagy, the one communist leader they believed could bring change. Nagy finally appeared around 21:00. Ever the pragmatic politician, he implored patience. Following the speech, a large band of protesters took matters into their own hands, marched to City Park, and tore down the hated Stalin statue that stood there (see page 608).

Another group went to the National Radio building to read their demands on the air. The ÁVH (communist police) refused to let them do it and eventually opened fire on the protesters. The peaceful protests evolved into an armed insurrection, as frightened civilians gathered weapons and supplies.

Overnight, Moscow decided to intervene. Budapesters awoke on October 24 to find Red Army troops occupying their city. That morning, Imre Nagy—who had just been promoted again to prime minister—promised reforms and tried to keep a lid on the simmering discontent.

The next day, October 25, a huge crowd gathered on Kossuth tér behind the Parliament to hear from Nagy. In the hubbub, shots rang out as Hungarian and Soviet soldiers opened fire on the (mostly unarmed) crowd. Of the victims, 72 deaths are known by name, but likely hundreds more were injured or perished.

The Hungarians fought back with an improvised guerilla resistance. They made use of any guns they could get their hands on, as well as Molotov cocktails, to strike against the Soviet occupiers. Many adolescents (the celebrated "Pest Youth") participated. The fighting tore apart the city, and some of the fallen were buried in impromptu graves in city parks.

Political infighting in Moscow paralyzed the Soviet response, and an uneasy cease-fire fell over Budapest. For 10 tense days, it appeared that the Soviets might allow Nagy to push through some reforms. Nagy, a firmly entrenched communist, had always envisioned a less repressive regime...but within limits. While he was at first reluctant to take on the mantle of the uprising's leadership, he gradually began to echo what he was hearing on the streets. He called for free elections, the abolishment of the ÁVH, the withdrawal of Soviet troops, and Hungary's secession from the Warsaw Pact.

But when the uprisers attacked and killed ÁVH officers and communist leaders in Budapest, it bolstered the case of the Moscow hardliners. On November 4, the Red Army launched a brutal counterattack in Budapest that left the rebels reeling. At 5:20 that morning, Imre Nagy's voice came over the radio to beg the world for assistance. Later that morning, he sought asylum at the Yugoslav Embassy across the street from City Park. He was never seen alive in public again.

János Kádár—an ally of Nagy's who was palatable to the uprisers, yet firmly loyal to Moscow—was installed as prime minister. The fighting dragged on for about another week, but the uprising was eventually crushed. By the end, 2,500 Hungarians and more than 700 Soviets were dead, and 20,000 Hungarians were injured. Communist authorities arrested more than 15,000 people, of whom at least 200 were executed (including Imre Nagy). Anyone who had participated in the uprising was blacklisted; fearing this and other forms of retribution, some 200,000 Hungarians fled to the West.

Though the 1956 Uprising met a tragic end, within a few years Kádár did succeed in softening the regime, and the milder, so-called "goulash communism" emerged. And today, even though the communists are long gone, the legacy of 1956 pervades the Hungarian consciousness. Some Budapest buildings are still pockmarked with bullet holes from '56, and many Hungarians who fled the country in that year still have not returned. October 23 remains Hungary's most cherished holiday.

Metró. From the back corner of Kossuth tér, veer right, to a little tree-filled park...

Vértanúk Tere and the Missing Imre Nagy Monument:
This small square was once the site of a stirring monument to the
1956 hero Imre Nagy, who stood on a bridge
facing the Parliament (see photo). Hungarians loved the symbolism: Nagy was literally
keeping a watchful eye on the government.
Unfortunately, late one night a few days after
Christmas of 2018, Fidesz authorities removed
the statue with little warning and no fanfare.
While Nagy has long been lionized as a Hungarian patriot, Viktor Orbán and Fidesz grew
uncomfortable about the role he played within
the communist system (see the sidebar on next
page). The removal of the statue is seen by historians as Fidesz taking yet one more step away
from grappling with a nuanced, complicated

past in a meaningful way, and instead marching in lockstep toward
a whitewashed, authoritarian future. You may see a different statue
in this space instead: Fidesz plans to reinstate a dull (and less open-
to-interpretation) monument that previously stood on Vértanúk
tere, honoring the "victims of communism" from 1918 to 1919. (If
you'd like to pay your respects to Nagy, his statue may eventually be
reinstated on Jászai Mari tér, near Margaret Bridge.)
• *Go up the short, diagonal street beyond Vértanúk tere, called Vécsey
utca. After just one block, you emerge into...*

▲Szabadság Tér ("Liberty Square")

One of Budapest's most genteel squares, this space is marked by a
controversial monument to the Soviet soldiers who liberated Hungary at the end of World War
II, and ringed by both fancy
old apartment blocks and important buildings (such as the
former Hungarian State Television headquarters, the US Embassy, and the National Bank
of Hungary). A fine café, fun-
filled playgrounds, statues of
prominent Americans (Ronald

Reagan and Harry Hill Bandholtz), and yet another provocative
monument (to the Hungarian victims of the Nazis) round out the
square's landmarks. Take a moment to tune into two of the more
recent (and more divisive) monuments on the square.
• *The first person you'll see as you enter the square, striding confidently*

Imre Nagy (1896-1958)

The Hungarian politician Imre Nagy (IHM-reh nodge), now thought of as an anticommunist hero, was actually a lifelong communist. In the 1930s, he allegedly worked for the Soviet secret police. In the late 1940s, he quickly moved up the hierarchy of Hungary's communist government, becoming prime minister during a period of reform in 1953. But when his proposed changes alarmed Moscow, Nagy was quickly demoted.

When the 1956 Uprising broke out, Nagy was drafted (reluctantly, some say) to become the head of the movement to soften the severity of the communist regime. Because he was an insider, it briefly seemed that Nagy might hold the key to finding a middle path between the suffocating totalitarian model of Moscow and the freedom of the West. Some suspect that Nagy himself didn't fully grasp the dramatic sea change represented by the uprising. When he appeared at the Parliament building on the night of October 23 to speak to the reform-craving crowds for the first time, he began by addressing his compatriots—as communist politicians always did—with, "Dear comrades..." When the audience booed, he amended it: "Dear friends..." The crowd went wild.

But the optimism was short-lived. The Soviets violently put down the uprising, arrested and sham-tried Nagy, executed him, and buried him disgracefully, face-down in an unmarked grave. The regime forced Hungary to forget about Nagy.

Later, when communism was in its death throes in 1989, the Hungarian people rediscovered Nagy as a hero. His body was located, exhumed, and given a ceremonial funeral at Heroes' Square. (It was also something of a coming-out party for Viktor Orbán—today the prime minister—who, as a twenty-something rebel, delivered an impassioned speech at the ceremony.) This event is considered a pivotal benchmark in that year of tremendous change. By the year's end, the Berlin Wall would fall, and the Czechs and Slovaks would stage their Velvet Revolution. But Nagy's reburial was the first in that series of toppling dominoes.

The next chapter in Nagy's legacy has been written by Fidesz, who have recently reversed the rehabilitation of Nagy's image. Because Nagy's ties to communism place him firmly on the left, Fidesz views him as an ideological enemy. (Critics note the hypocrisy of Orbán, who made his name lauding Nagy, now sweeping him into the dustbin of history.) The 2018 removal of the Nagy statue facing the Parliament is just the latest in a long, sad history of this great reformer being exploited as a political pawn. Hungarian patriots wonder: Will Nagy ever be allowed to rest?

BUDAPEST

away from the Parliament, is an actor-turned-politician you may recognize...

Ronald Reagan: When Fidesz took power in 2010, they quickly began rolling back previous democratic reforms and imposing alarming constraints on the media. Many international observers—including the US government—spoke out against what they considered an infringement on freedom of the press. In an effort to appease American concerns, Prime Minister Viktor Orbán erected this statue on one of his capital's main squares—and then, perhaps not quite grasping the subtleties of American politics, invited Secretary of State Hillary Clinton to the unveiling. It's fun to watch the steady stream of passersby (both Hungarians and tourists) do a double-take, chuckle, then snap a photo with The Gipper.

• *Now enjoy a slow stroll to the opposite end of the square, where you'll find the...*

Monument to the Hungarian Victims of the Nazis: This recent addition to the square—another heavy-handed Fidesz production—commemorates the German invasion of Hungary on March 19, 1944. Standing in the middle of a broken colonnade, an immaculate angel holds an orb with a double cross (part of the crown jewels and a symbol of Hungarian sovereignty). Overhead, a mechanical-looking black eagle (symbolizing Germany) screeches in, its talons poised to strike.

Although offensive enough for its lack of artistry, this monument was instantly controversial for the way it whitewashes Hungarian history. Viewing this, you might imagine that Hungary was a peaceful land that was unwittingly caught up in the Nazi war machine. In fact, the Hungarian government was an ally of Nazi Germany for more than three years before this invasion. And there's no question that, after the invasion, many Hungarians enthusiastically collaborated with their new Nazi overlords.

Mindful of the old adage about people who forget their own history, locals have created a **makeshift counter-memorial** to the victims of the World War II-era Hungarians (not just Germans) in front of this official monument.

On a lighter note, the **fountain** that faces the monument is particularly entertaining. Sensors can tell when you're about to walk through the wall of water...and the curtain of water automatically parts just long enough for you to pass. Go ahead...play Moses.

• *From the monument, continue two blocks straight ahead, up Herceg-primás utca. You'll emerge into a broad plaza in front of...*

▲St. István's Basilica (Szent István Bazilika)

Budapest's biggest church is one of its top landmarks. The grand interior celebrates St. István, Hungary's first Christian king. You can see his withered, blackened, millennium-old fist in a gilded reliquary. Or you can zip up on an elevator (or climb up stairs partway) to a panorama terrace with views over the rooftops of Pest. The skippable treasury has ecclesiastical items, historical exhibits, and artwork (reached by elevator, to the right as you face the church). The church also hosts regular organ concerts (advertised near the entry).

Cost and Hours: Interior—free but 200-Ft donation strongly suggested, open to tourists Mon-Sat 9:00-17:00, Sun from 13:00, open slightly later for worshippers; panorama terrace—600 Ft, daily 10:00-17:30, summer until 18:30, off-season until 16:30; treasury—400 Ft, same hours as terrace; music concerts Mon, Tue, and Thu—see page 638; Szent István tér, district V, M1: Bajcsy-Zsilinszky út or M3: Arany János utca.

Visiting the Church: Though it looks grand and old, this church only dates back about 130 years—like so many Budapest landmarks, it was built around the millennial celebrations of 1896.

Head up the grand stairs to get oriented. To the right is the ticket desk, the elevator to the treasury, and the entrance to the church. To the left is the elevator to the panoramic tower.

The church's **interior** is dimly lit but gorgeously restored; all the gilded decorations glitter in the low light. You'll see not Jesus but St. István (Stephen), Hungary's first Christian king, glowing above the high altar.

Stand in the back and enjoy the glittering entirety of the interior. The church's main claim to fame is the **"holy right hand" of St. István,** which you'll find along the right aisle, in front of a painting of István offering the Hungarian crown to the Virgin Mary. The sacred fist—a somewhat grotesque, 1,000-year-old withered stump—is inside a jeweled box. Pop in a 200-Ft coin for two minutes of light.

On your way out, in the exit foyer (back-left corner), you'll find a small exhibit about the building's history.

• *From here, you're very close to the boulevard called Andrássy út, which leads to the Opera House, House of Terror, and City Park (all described starting on page 600). To get there, walk around the right side of the ba-*

silica, and turn right on busy Bajcsy-Zsilinszky út; Andrássy út begins across the street, on your left.

But for now, we'll head to the Danube for a good look at the mighty Chain Bridge. Walk straight ahead from St. István's main staircase down Zrínyi Utca. This recently pedestrianized people zone passes (on the right) the former headquarters of Central European University, a graduate school largely funded by Hungarian-American George Soros. In 2018, CEU relocated to Vienna, after the Fidesz-controlled government refused to allow it to operate legally within Hungary. Later, after crossing Nádor utca, on the left you'll see Duna Palota, a venue and ticket office for Hungária Koncert's popular tourist shows (described later, under "Entertainment in Budapest").

*Zrínyi utca dead-ends at the big traffic circle called **Roosevelt tér**. Turn left and walk a half-block to the entrance (on the left) of the...*

Gresham Palace

This was Budapest's first building in the popular Historicist style— but it also incorporates elements of Art Nouveau. Budapest boomed in an era when architectural eclecticism—mashing together bits and pieces of different styles—was in vogue. But because much of the city's construction was compressed into a short window of time,

even these disparate styles enjoy an unusual harmony. Damaged in World War II, the building was an eyesore for decades. (Reportedly, an aging local actress refused to move out, so developers had to wait for her to, ahem, vacate before they could reclaim the building.) In 1999, the Gresham Palace was meticulously restored to its former glory and converted to a luxury hotel. Even if you can't afford to stay here (see "Sleeping in Budapest," later), saunter into the lobby and absorb the gorgeous details (Széchenyi tér 5, district V, M1: Vörösmarty tér or M2: Kossuth tér).

• *Grandly spanning the Danube from this spot is Budapest's best bridge...*

▲Chain Bridge (Széchenyi Lánchíd)

One of the world's great bridges connects Pest's Széchenyi tér and Buda's Clark Ádám tér. This historic, iconic bridge, guarded by lions (symbolizing power), is Budapest's most enjoyable and convenient bridge to cross on foot.

Until the mid-19th century, only pontoon barges spanned the Danube between Buda and Pest. In the winter, the pontoons had to be pulled in, leaving locals to rely on ferries (in good weather) or a frozen river. People often walked across the frozen Danube, only

to get stuck on the other side during a thaw, with nothing to do but
wait for another cold snap.

Count István Széchenyi was
stranded for a week trying to get to
his father's funeral. After missing
it, Széchenyi commissioned Budapest's first permanent bridge—
which was also a major symbolic
step toward another of Széchenyi's
pet causes, the unification of Buda
and Pest. The Chain Bridge was
built by Scotsman Adam Clark
between 1842 and 1849, and it im-
mediately became an important symbol of Budapest. The biggest
and longest span of its day, the Chain Bridge was a model for famous suspension bridges that followed, including the Golden Gate
in San Francisco and the Verrazano-Narrows in New York.

Széchenyi—a man of the Enlightenment—charged both
commoners and nobles a toll for crossing his bridge, making it
an emblem of equality in those tense times. Like all of the city's
bridges, the Chain Bridge was destroyed by the Nazis at the end of
World War II, but it was quickly rebuilt.

• *As you look out to the Danube from here, to the right you can see the
tip of...*

▲Margaret Island (Margitsziget)

In the Middle Ages, this island in the Danube (just north of the
Parliament) was known as the "Isle of Hares." In the 13th century, a desperate King Béla IV swore that if God were to deliver
Hungary from the invading Tatars, he would dedicate his youngest
daughter Margaret to the Church. When the Tatars left, Margaret
was shipped to a nunnery here. Margaret embraced her new life
as a castaway nun, and later refused her father's efforts to force her
into a politically expedient marriage with a Bohemian king. As a
reward for her faith, she became St. Margaret of Hungary.

Today, while the island officially has no permanent residents,
urbanites flock here to relax in a huge, leafy park in the midst of the
busy city...yet so far away. No cars are allowed on the island—just
public buses. The island rivals City Park as the best spot in town
for strolling, jogging, biking (you can rent a bike at Bringóhintó,
with branches at both ends of the island), and people-watching.
Rounding out the island's attractions are an iconic old water tower,
the remains of Margaret's convent, a rose garden, a game farm, and
a "musical fountain" that performs to the strains of Hungarian folk
tunes.

BUDAPEST

Getting There: Bus #26 begins at Nyugati/Western train station, crosses the Margaret Bridge, then drives up through the middle of the island—allowing visitors to easily get from one end to the other (3-6/hour). **Trams** #4 and #6, which circulate around the Great Boulevard, cross the Margaret Bridge and stop at the southern tip of the island, a short walk from some of the attractions. You can also reach the island by **public riverboat**—weekday boats reach the two ends of the island, and weekend ones make several stops along the way. It's also a long but scenic **walk** between Margaret Island and other points in the city.

• *If you'd like to head for the heart of Pest, Vörösmarty tér (and the sights listed next), it's just two long blocks away: Turn left out of the Gresham Palace, and walk straight on Dorottya utca.*

PEST TOWN CENTER (BELVÁROS)

Pest's Belváros ("Inner Town") is its gritty urban heart—simultaneously its most beautiful and ugliest district. You'll see fancy facades, some of Pest's best views from the Danube embankment, richly decorated old coffeehouses that offer a whiff of the city's Golden Age, and a cavernous, colorful market hall filled with Hungarian goodies. But you'll also experience crowds, grime, and pungent smells like nowhere else in Budapest. Atmospherically shot through with the crumbling elegance of former greatness, Budapest is a place where creaky old buildings and sleek modern ones feel equally at home. Remember: This is a city in transition. Enjoy the rough edges while you can. They're being sanded off at a remarkable pace—and soon, tourists like you will be nostalgic for the "authentic" old days.

Below, I've linked the main landmarks in the Town Center with a self-guided walk, starting at the square called Vörösmarty tér and ending at the Great Market Hall.

▲Vörösmarty Tér

The central square of the Town Center, dominated by the venerable Gerbeaud coffee shop and a giant statue of the revered Romantic poet Mihály Vörösmarty, is the hub of Pest sightseeing.

At the north end of the square is the landmark Gerbeaud café and pastry shop. Between the world wars, the well-to-do ladies of Budapest would meet here after shopping their way up Váci utca. Today it's still the meeting point in Budapest... for tourists, at least. Consider stepping inside to appreciate the elegant old decor, or for a cup of coffee and a slice of cake (but meals here are overpriced). Better yet, hold off for now—even more appealing cafés are nearby (and listed under "Budapest's Café Culture," on page 669).

The yellow **M1 Metró stop** in front of Gerbeaud is the entrance to the shallow *Földalatti*, or "underground"—the first subway on the Continent (built for the Hungarian millennial celebration in 1896). Today, it still carries passengers to Andrássy út sights, running under that boulevard all the way to City Park.

Walk to the far end of the square, and look up the street that's to your left. This traffic-free street (Deák utca)—also known as **"Fashion Street,"** with top-end shops—is the easiest and most pleasant way to walk to Deák tér and, beyond it, through Erzsébet tér to Andrássy út.

• *Extending straight ahead from Vörösmarty tér is a broad, bustling, pedestrianized shopping street.*

Váci Utca

Dating from 1810-1850, **Váci utca** (VAHT-see OOT-zaw) is one of the oldest streets of Pest. *Váci utca* means "street to Vác"—a town 25 miles to the north. This has long been the street where the elite of Pest would go shopping, then strut their stuff for their neighbors on an evening promenade. Today, the tourists do the strutting here—and the Hungarians go to American-style shopping malls.

This boulevard—Budapest's tourism artery—was a dreamland for Eastern Bloc residents back in the 1980s. It was here that they fantasized about what it might be like to be free, while drooling over Nikes, Adidas, and Big Macs before any of these "Western evils" were introduced elsewhere in the Warsaw Pact region. In fact, partway down the street (on the right, at Régi Posta utca) is the first McDonald's behind the Iron Curtain, where people from all over the Eastern Bloc flocked to dine. Since you had to wait in a long line—stretching around the block—to get a burger, it wasn't "fast food"...but at least it was "West food."

Ironically, this street—once prized by Hungarians and other Eastern Europeans because it felt so Western—is what many Western tourists today mistakenly think is the "real Budapest." Visitors mesmerized by this stretch of souvenir stands, tourist-gouging eateries, and upscale boutiques are likely to miss some more interesting and authentic areas just a block or two away. Don't fall for this trap. You can have a fun and fulfilling trip to this city without ever setting foot on Váci utca.

• *For a more appealing people zone than Váci utca, detour from Vörösmarty tér a block toward the river, to the inviting...*

Danube Promenade (Dunakorzó)

Some of the best views in Budapest are from this walkway facing Castle Hill—especially this stretch, between the white Elisabeth Bridge (left) and the iconic Chain Bridge (right). This is a favorite place to promenade *(korzó)*, strolling aimlessly and greeting friends.

Dominating this part of the promenade is the Neo-Romantic-style **Pesti Vigadó**—built in the 1880s and recently restored. Charmingly, the word *vigadó*—used to describe a concert hall—literally means "joyous place." In front, the playful statue of **the girl with her dog** captures the fun-loving spirit along this drag.

At the gap in the railing, notice the platform to catch **tram #2**, which goes frequently in each direction along the promenade—a handy way to connect riverside sights in Pest. It's also incredibly scenic—I consider this Europe's most beautiful tram ride. Take it once between the Great Market Hall (to the left) and the Parliament (to the right) just for fun.

About 30 more yards toward the Chain Bridge, find the little statue wearing a jester's hat. She's playing on the railing, with the castle behind her. The ***Little Princess*** is one of Budapest's symbols and a favorite photo-op for tourists. While many of the city's monuments have interesting backstories, more recent statues (like this one) are simply whimsical and fun.

• *Now walk along the promenade to the left (toward the white bridge). Directly in front of the corner Starbucks in the Marriott Hotel, watch for the easy-to-miss stairs leading down under the tram tracks, to a crosswalk that leads safely across the busy road to the riverbank. From the top of these stairs, look along the river.*

Lining the **embankment** are several long boats: Some are excursion boats for sightseeing trips up and down the Danube (especially pleasant at night), while others are overpriced (but scenic) restaurants. Kiosks along here dispense info and sell tickets for the various boat companies—look for Legenda Cruises (their dock is just downstream from here—go down the stairs, cross the road, then walk 100 yards left).

• *From here, both the promenade and Váci utca cut south through the Town Center. At the end of this zone is one of Budapest's top attractions.*

▲▲Great Market Hall (Nagyvásárcsarnok)

"Great" indeed is this gigantic marketplace. The Great Market Hall still keeps local shoppers happy, even as it has evolved into

one of the city's top tourist attractions. Goose liver,
embroidered tablecloths,
golden Tokaji Aszú wine,
pickled peppers, commu-
nist-kitsch T-shirts, sa-
vory *lángos* pastries, patriotic green-white-and-red
flags, and paprika of every

degree of spiciness...if it's Hungarian, you'll find it here. Come to
shop for souvenirs, to buy a picnic, or just to rattle around inside
this vast, picturesque, Industrial Age hall (Mon 6:00-17:00, Tue-
Fri until 18:00, Sat until 15:00, closed Sun, Fővám körút 1, district
IX, M4: Fővám tér or M3: Kálvin tér).

Visiting the Market Hall: Step inside the market and get your
bearings: The cavernous interior features three levels. The ground
floor has produce stands, bakeries, butcher stalls, heaps of paprika,
goose liver, and salamis. Upstairs are stand-up eateries and souvenirs. And in the basement are a supermarket, a fish market, and
piles of pickles.

Stroll along the market's "main drag" (straight ahead from
the entry), enjoying the commotion of produce stands and vendors
selling authentic Hungarian products. About halfway along, you'll
see **paprika** on both sides. Additional (and less touristy) stalls are
down the little alley on the left. As you browse, remember that
there are two types of paprika: sweet (*édes*, used for flavor) and hot
(*csípős*, used sparingly to add some kick). While you're at it, pick
up some spicy pastes (which hold their flavor better than the fast-
degrading powders): the spicy *Erős Pista*, the sweet *Édes Anna*, the
soup-enhancing *Gulyáskrém*, and the intensely spicy condiment
called, simply, "Red Gold" *(Piros Arany)*.

After you've worked your way to the far end of the hall, take
the escalator to the upper level. This is a convenient place to look for
souvenirs—with a great selection of both traditional (embroidery)
and not-so-traditional (commie-kitsch T-shirts). While there are
no real bargains here, the prices are a bit better than out along Váci
utca. For tips, see "Shopping in Budapest," later. The left wall (as
you face the front) is lined with fun, cheap, stand-up, Hungarian-
style fast-food joints and six-stool pubs. However, 90 percent of the
clientele is tourists—so the prices are high, and I don't recommend
this area for a meal.

Walk along here to get a glimpse of traditional foods. You'll
see many stands selling the deep-fried snack called *lángos* (LAHN-
gohsh)—similar to elephant ears, but savory rather than sweet. The
most typical version is *sajtos tejfölös*—with sour cream and cheese.
You can also add garlic *(fokhagyma)*. At the far end of the upper

BUDAPEST

gallery, the **Fakanál Étterem** cafeteria above the main entrance is handy but pricey.

For a less glamorous look at the market, head down the escalators near the front of the market (below the restaurant) to the basement. Stop at one of the fragrant **pickle stands** and take a look. Hungarians pickle just about everything: peppers and cukes, of course, but also cauliflower, cabbage, beets, tomatoes, garlic, and so on.

Nearby: The **Bálna Budapest** shopping mall and cultural center stands along the riverbank behind the Great Market Hall. Completed in 2013, the complex was created by bridging a pair of circa-1881 brick warehouses with a swooping glass canopy that earns its name, "The Whale" *(bálna)*. It's got a mix of shops, offices, eateries, conference rooms, and a branch of the TI—open until 18:00 (Sun-Thu 10:00-20:00, Fri-Sat until 22:00, www.balnabudapest.hu).

ALONG THE SMALL BOULEVARD (KISKÖRÚT)

The Hungarian National Museum and Great Synagogue, described below, are along the Small Boulevard, between the Liberty Bridge/Great Market Hall and Deák tér. The former Jewish Quarter, which sprawls behind the Great Synagogue, is also known as the Seventh District, one of Budapest's most happening nightlife zones, with a fun selection of ruin pubs (for details, see "Nightlife in Budapest," later).

▲Hungarian National Museum (Magyar Nemzeti Múzeum)

One of Budapest's biggest museums features all manner of Hungarian historic bric-a-brac, from the Paleolithic age to a more recent infestation of dinosaurs (the communists). Artifacts are explained by good, if dry, English descriptions. The museum adds substance to your understanding of Hungary's story—but it helps to have a pretty firm foundation first (read "Hungarian History" on page 528). The most engaging part is Room 20, which dis-

plays items from the communist period—including both pro- and (illegal) anti-Party propaganda. The exhibit ends with video footage of the 1989 end of communism—demonstrations, monumental parliament votes, and a final farewell to the last Soviet troops leaving Hungarian soil. The impressive Neoclassical building itself

is historic: The 1848 Revolution against Habsburg rule was proclaimed from the front steps.

Cost and Hours: 1,600 Ft—but can change depending on
temporary exhibits; Tue-Sun 10:00-18:00, closed Mon; audioguide available, near Great Market Hall at Múzeum körút 14, district VIII, M3: Kálvin tér, tel. 1/327-7773, www.hnm.hu.

▲▲Great Synagogue (Nagy Zsinagóga)

Also called the Dohány Street Synagogue, Budapest's gorgeous
synagogue is the biggest in Europe and the second biggest in the
world (after the Temple Emanu-El of
New York). A visit here has three parts:
touring its ornately decorated interior;
exploring the attached museum, which
offers a concise lesson in the Jewish
faith; and lingering in the evocative
memorial garden, with its weeping-
willow *Tree of Life* sculpture and other
poignant monuments.

Cost and Hours: 4,500 Ft for
Great Synagogue, museum, and garden, includes free tour; Sun-Thu
10:00-18:00 (May-Sept until 20:00),
Fri 10:00-16:00; Nov-Feb Sun-Thu
10:00-16:00, Fri until 14:00; closed Sat year-round and Jewish holidays; Dohány utca 2, district VII, near M2: Astoria or
the Astoria stop on trams #47 and #49, tel. 1/343-0420, www.
dohany-zsinagoga.hu.

BUDAPEST

❍ **Self-Guided Tour:** The synagogue's striking **exterior** captures the rich history of the building and the people it represents:
The synagogue was built in 1859 just outside what was then the city
limits. Although Budapest's Jews held fast to their own faith, they
also wished to demonstrate their worth and how well-integrated
they were with the greater community.

The two tall towers are not typical of traditional synagogues.
The Moorish-flavored architecture is a sign of the Historicism of
the time, which borrowed eclectic elements from past styles. Specifically, it evokes the Sephardic Jewish culture that flourished in
Iberia; many Hungarian Jews are descended from that group, who
fled here after being expelled from Spain in 1492. To some, the
towers evoke Moorish minarets. Others note how these towers—
along with the rosette (rose window)—helped the synagogue resemble Christian churches of the time. In fact, when it was built,
the synagogue was dubbed by one cynic as "the most beautiful
Catholic synagogue in the world."

Now step **inside.** Notice that the synagogue interior feels like a church with the symbols switched—with a basilica floor plan, three naves, two pulpits, and even a pipe organ. The organ—which Franz Liszt played for the building's inauguration—is a clue that this synagogue belonged to the most progressive of the three branches of Judaism here at the time. (Orthodox Jews would never be permitted to do the "work" of playing an organ on the Sabbath.)

In the ark, at the front of the main aisle, 25 surviving Torah scrolls are kept. Catholic priests hid these scrolls during World War II (burying them temporarily in a cemetery). The two-tiered balconies on the sides of the nave were originally for women, who worshipped separately from the men.

Ponder this building's recent history: Although it survived World War II, the Great Synagogue sat neglected for 40 years. But in 1990, it was painstakingly rebuilt, largely with financial support from the Hungarian-American cosmetics magnate Estée Lauder. Theodor Herzl, a pioneer of Zionism, was born in a house next door to the Great Synagogue (now gone). As you tour the place, think of all the other famous and influential people of Hungarian-Jewish descent from every walk of life: Harry Houdini (born Erich Weisz), Elie Wiesel, Joseph Pulitzer, Tony Curtis (and his daughter Jamie Lee), George Cukor, Goldie Hawn, George Soros, Peter Lorre, and Eva and Zsa Zsa Gabor. A visit to the Great Synagogue and surrounding Jewish Quarter offers insight into this vital facet of Hungarian history and contemporary life.

• *When you're finished inside, exit through the main doors, turn right, and go to the opposite end of the front courtyard. Enter the building, then head upstairs (by stairs or elevator) to the...*

Hungarian Jewish Museum (Magyar Zsidó Múzeum): This small but informative museum illuminates the Jewish faith, displaying a wide range of artifacts and succinct but engaging English explanations. The collection is always somewhat in flux, but typically you'll see objects representing the stages of Jewish life: a day, a week, a year, a lifetime. Everyday items reveal how Judaism was interwoven with all aspects of life. It also explains the major holidays of the Jewish calendar—from Rosh Hashanah and Yom Kippur to Purim and Hanukkah. One of the museum's prized pieces—typically displayed on the top floor—is a third-century tombstone from the Roman province of Pannonia (today's Hungary), roughly etched with a menorah.

• *Exiting back into the front courtyard, go down the passageway be-*

tween the synagogue and the museum (straight ahead from the security checkpoint) to reach the garden.

Tree of Life and Memorial Garden: During the Soviet siege that ended the Nazi occupation of Budapest in the winter of 1944-1945, many Jews in the ghetto here died of exposure, starvation, and disease. Soon after the Soviets liberated the city, an estimated 2,281 Jews were buried here—considered Hungary's largest mass grave from the Holocaust. The trees and headstones (donated by survivors) were added later. The pillars you'll pass have historical photos of the synagogue and Jewish Quarter.

In the garden behind the synagogue is the *Tree of Life,* created by renowned artist Imre Varga. This weeping willow, cast in steel, was erected in 1990, soon after the fall of communism made it possible to acknowledge the Holocaust. The willow makes an upside-down menorah, and each of the 4,000 metal leaves is etched with the name of a Holocaust victim. New leaves are added all the time, donated by families of the victims.

In the center of the garden is a symbolic grave for the many diplomats from other nations who saved Hungarian Jews. The most famous of these—and the biggest name on the monument—is **Raoul Wallenberg** (1912-1947). An improbable hero, this ne'er-do-well Swedish playboy from a prominent family was sent as a diplomat to Hungary because nobody else wanted the post. He was empowered by the Swedish government to do whatever he could— bribe, threaten, lie, or blackmail—to save as many Jews as possible from the Nazis. He surpassed everyone's low expectations by dedicating (and ultimately sacrificing) his life to the cause. By giving Swedish passports to Jews and admitting them to safe houses, he succeeded in rescuing tens of thousands of people from certain death. Shortly after the Soviets arrived, Wallenberg was arrested, accused of being a US spy, sent to a gulag...and never seen alive again. (Later, Russian authorities acknowledged he was executed in 1947, in Moscow's Lubyanka prison.)

The grave is also etched with the names of other "Righteous Among the Nations" who went above and beyond to save Jews. According to the Talmud, "Whoever saves one life, saves the world entire."

Other Jewish Quarter Sights

While this area was shrouded in soot and gloom during the communist period, today Budapest's Jewish Quarter is coming back to life. You'll find monuments and artifacts of Jewish history in these streets—but you sometimes have to hunt for them a bit.

Orthodox Synagogue: This synagogue is located on a nondescript urban street two blocks from the Great Synagogue. Built in the Vienna-inspired Secession style in 1912, this temple stood damaged and deserted for decades after World War II until being renovated in 2006. Today it invites visitors to see its colorful, sumptuously decorated interior (1,000 Ft; Sun-Thu 10:00-17:30, Fri until 16:00; Oct-April Sun-Thu 10:00-16:00, Fri until 13:30; closed Sat year-round; enter down little alley, Kazinczy utca 27, district VII, M2: Astoria).

Gozsdu Udvar: This long series of courtyards burrows through the middle of a city block, between Dob utca 16 and Király utca 13. When this neighbor-hood hosted a fast-growing Jewish population and space was at a premium, courtyards like this one were filled with community life: restaurants, shops, and other businesses. (Gozsdu Udvar—the best surviving example of this—was built by and named for a prominent 19th-century Jewish attorney from Transylvania, today part of Romania, who established a foundation to fund Transylvanians who wanted to study here.) After decades of neglect, this passage was spruced up and opened to the public. This genteel space—which evokes the Golden Age of Jewish life in Budapest—is once again filled with cafés and bars, and after hours it's a bustling nightlife hub.

Synagogue at Rumbach Street: This synagogue's colorful Moorish-style interior survives from the Golden Age of Jewish culture in Budapest. The late-19th-century building was designed by the great Viennese architect Otto Wagner. It was abandoned for years, but today it's wrapping up a lengthy, desperately needed renovation—and if it's open, it's well worth a look. You'll wander through the relatively small but very tall space, appreciating its lavish decorations (if open, likely Sun-Thu 10:00-18:00, Fri until 16:00—earlier off-season, closed Sat; from the *Tree of Life* monument, it's two blocks down Rumbach utca toward Andrássy út).

ANDRÁSSY ÚT

Connecting downtown Pest to City Park, Andrássy út is Budapest's main boulevard, lined with plane trees, shops, theaters, cafés, and locals living very well. Budapesters like to think of Andrássy út as the Champs-Elysées and Broadway rolled into one. While that's a stretch, it is a good place to stroll, get a feel for today's urban Pest, and visit a few top attractions (most notably the Opera House and the House of Terror) on the way to Heroes' Square and City Park.

I've arranged these sights in the order you'll reach them if you walk up the boulevard from where it begins, near Deák tér. The handy M1/yellow Metró line runs every couple of minutes just

BUDAPEST

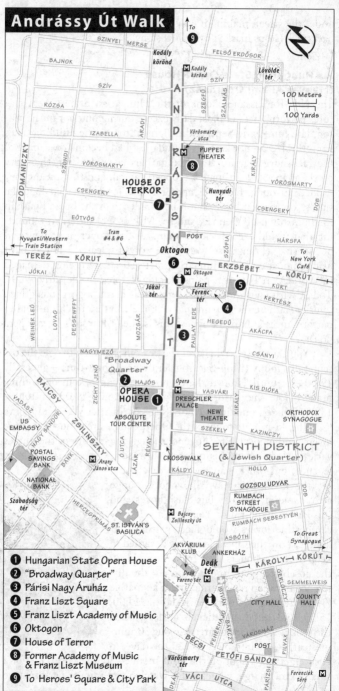

Andrássy Út Walk

SZINYEI MERSE

BAJNOK

SZÍV

Kodály körönd

FELSŐ ERDŐSOR

M Kodály körönd

SZÍV

Lövölde tér

RÓZSA

SZEGEDŐ

SZALMÁS

100 Meters
100 Yards

IZABELLA

ARADI

Vörösmarty utca

M PUPPET THEATER

❽

KIRÁLY

VÖRÖSMARTY

SZONDI

HOUSE OF TEROR

Hunyadi tér

CSENGERY

DOB

VÖRÖSMARTY

CSENGERY

PODMANICZKY

❼

EÖTVÖS

HÁRSFA

To Nyugati/Western Train Station

Tram #4 & #6

POST

SZÓFIA

Oktogon

To New York Café

TERÉZ — KÖRÚT

❻

ERZSÉBET — KÖRÚT

JÓKAI

i M Oktogon

KÜRT

WEINER LEÓ

LOVAG

DESSEWFFY

MOZSÁR

Jókai tér

Liszt Ferenc tér

❺

KERTÉSZ

❹

Á

PAULAY EDE

HEGEDŰ

AKÁCFA

❸

T

NAGYMEZŐ

CSÁNYI

ZICHY JENŐ

"Broadway Quarter"

❷

HAJÓS

Opera M

KIS DIÓFA

BAJCSY - ZSILINSZKY

VADÁSZ

NAGY SÁNDOR

OPERA HOUSE ❶

DRESCHLER PALACE

VASVÁRI

ORTHODOX SYNAGOGUE

US EMBASSY

ABSOLUTE TOUR CENTER

NEW THEATER

KIRÁLY

KAZINCZY

POSTAL SAVINGS BANK

Ó UTCA

LÁZÁR

RÉVAY

SZÉKELY

SEVENTH DISTRICT
(& Jewish Quarter)

M Arany János utca

CROSSWALK

KÁLDY

GYULA

HOLLÓ

DOB

NATIONAL BANK

Szabadság tér

HERCEGPRÍMÁS

ST. ISTVÁN'S BASILICA

M Bajcsy-Zsilinszky út

GOZSDU UDVAR

RUMBACH STREET SYNAGOGUE

RUMBACH SEBESTYÉN

ASBÓTH

To Great Synagogue

AKVÁRIUM KLUB

ANKERHÁZ

Deák Ferenc tér M

T KÁROLY — KÖRÚT

SEMMELWEIS

❶ Hungarian State Opera House
❷ "Broadway Quarter"
❸ Párisi Nagy Áruház
❹ Franz Liszt Square
❺ Franz Liszt Academy of Music
❻ Oktogon
❼ House of Terror
❽ Former Academy of Music & Franz Liszt Museum
❾ To Heroes' Square & City Park

FEHÉRHAJÓ NYÁRI

VÁROSHÁZ

GERLÓCZY

CITY HALL

COUNTY HALL

Vörösmarty tér

BÉCSI

PETŐFI SÁNDOR

POST

PILVAX

DEÁK

VÁCI UTCA

PARISI

Ferenciek tére M

To ❾

A N D R Á S S Y — Ú T

BUDAPEST

under the street, making it easy to skip several blocks ahead, or to backtrack (stops marked by yellow signs).

• *Three blocks up Andrássy út on the left is the...*

▲▲Hungarian State Opera House
(Magyar Állami Operaház)

The Neo-Renaissance home of the Hungarian State Opera features performances (almost daily except during outdoor music season, late June-early Sept) and delightful tours. The building dates from the 1890s, not long after Budapest had become co-capital of the Habsburg Empire. The Hungarians wanted to put their city on the map as a legitimate European capital, and that meant they needed an opera house. Emperor Franz Josef provided half the funds...on the condition that it be smaller than the opera house in his hometown of Vienna. And so, Miklós Ybl designed a building that would exceed Vienna's famous Staatsoper in opulence, if not in size. (Franz Josef was reportedly displeased.) It was built using almost entirely Hungarian materials. After being damaged in World War II, it was painstakingly restored in the early 1980s. Today, with lavish marble-and-gold-leaf decor, a gorgeous gilded interior slathered with paintings of Greek myths, and high-quality performances at bargain prices, this is one of Europe's finest opera houses.

You can drop in whenever the box office is open to ogle the ostentatious **lobby** (Mon-Sat from 11:00 until show time—generally 19:00—or until 17:00 if there's no performance; Sun open three hours before the performance—generally 16:00-19:00, or 10:00-13:00 if there's a matinee; Andrássy út 22, district VI, M1: Opera).

The 45-minute **tours** of the Opera House are a must for music lovers, and enjoyable for anyone, though the quality of the guides varies: Most spout plenty of fun, if silly, legends, but others can be quite dry. You'll see the main entryway, the snooty lounge area, some of the cozy but plush boxes, and the lavish auditorium. You'll find out why clandestine lovers would meet in the cigar lounge, how the Opera House is designed to keep the big spenders away from the rabble in the nosebleed seats, and how to tell the difference between real marble and fake marble (3,000 Ft; English tours nearly daily at 14:00, 15:00, and 16:00; buy tickets at desk inside the lobby; it's smart to arrive about 30 minutes early—or drop by earlier in the day—to

ensure getting a spot on the tour; mobile +3630-279-5677). For a small extra charge, you can also watch a five-minute performance of two arias after the tour...or you can hear the music just fine for free from the lobby.

To experience the Opera House in action, take in an excellent and affordable performance (see "Entertainment in Budapest," later).

• *The Opera House marks the beginning of an emerging dining-and-nightlife neighborhood dubbed the...*

"Broadway Quarter"

The major cross street, **Nagymező utca,** features a chic cluster of restaurants, bars, and theaters (especially on the left side of Andrássy). This is an enjoyable place to stroll on a summer evening. Many of my recommended restaurants described under "Eating in Budapest," later, are in this neighborhood.

A half-block down Andrássy út on the right (at #39) is a grand old early-20th-century building marked **Párisi Nagy Áruház** (Paris Department Store). One of the city's first department stores, this was a popular shopping stop for years, even through communism. It has since been renovated, but has repeatedly changed hands in recent years. Inside and upstairs is a gorgeous old frescoed ballroom, called Lotz Hall, that's home to the Café Párisi, a coffeehouse in a grand setting. If you need a coffee break, this is a fine place to do it.

• *Just after the end of the block is a popular outdoor dining area.*

Franz Liszt Square (Liszt Ferenc Tér)

This leafy square is surrounded by hip, expensive cafés and restaurants. (The best is the recommended restaurant **Menza.**)

Strangely, neither the statue on this square nor the one facing it, across Andrássy út, is of Franz Liszt. But deeper in the park, you'll find a modern statue of Liszt energetically playing an imaginary piano. And at the far end of the square, fronting a gorgeous piazza, is the **Franz Liszt Academy of Music,** founded by and named for this half-Hungarian, half-Austrian composer who had a Hungarian name and passport. Liszt loved his family's Magyar heritage (though he didn't speak Hungarian) and spent his last six years in Budapest. His Academy of Music has been stunningly restored inside and out—step into the magnificent lobby. This space, though smaller, gives the Opera House a run for its money...and speaking of money, the concerts here are even cheaper than at the already reasonably priced Opera (for details on performances, and for more on Liszt, see "Entertainment in Budapest," later).

• *One block up from Franz Liszt Square is the gigantic crossroads known as the...*

BUDAPEST

Oktogon

This vast intersection with its corners snipped off—where Andrássy út meets the Great Boulevard ring road (Nagykörút)—was called Mussolini tér during World War II, then November 7 tér in honor of the Bolshevik Revolution. Today kids have nicknamed it American tér for the fast-food joints littering the square and streets nearby.

From here, if you have time to delve into workaday Budapest, hop on tram #4 or #6, which trundle in both directions around the ring road. If you have time for a short detour to the most opulent coffee break of your life, head for the recommended **New York Café** (described later, under "Eating in Budapest"). Just get on a tram to the right (tram #6 toward Móricz Zsigmond körtér or tram #4 toward Fehérvári út), and get off at the Wesselényi utca stop.

• *There's one more major sight between here and Heroes' Square. Walk two more blocks up Andrássy út to reach the...*

▲▲House of Terror (Terror Háza)

The building at Andrássy út 60 was home to the vilest parts of two destructive regimes: first the Arrow Cross (the Gestapo-like

enforcers of Nazi-occupied Hungary), then the ÁVO and ÁVH secret police (the insidious KGB-type wing of the Soviet satellite government). Now re-envisioned as the "House of Terror," this building uses highly conceptual, bombastic exhibits to document (if not proselytize about) the ugliest moments in

Hungary's difficult 20th century. Enlightening and well-presented, it rivals Memento Park as Budapest's best attraction about the communist age.

Cost and Hours: 3,000 Ft, Tue-Sun 10:00-18:00, closed Mon, audioguide-1,500 Ft, Andrássy út 60, district VI, M1: Vörösmarty utca—*not* the Vörösmarty tér stop, tel. 1/374-2600, www.terrorhaza.hu.

Tours: The 1,500-Ft English audioguide is good but plodding and almost too thorough, and can be difficult to hear over the din of Hungarian soundtracks in each room.

Background: In the lead-up to World War II, Hungary initially allied with Hitler—both to retain a degree of self-determination and to try to regain its huge territorial losses after World War I's devastating Treaty of Trianon (see page 533). But in March of 1944, the Nazi-affiliated Arrow Cross Party was forcibly installed as Hungary's new government. The Nazi surrogates deported nearly 440,000 Jewish people to Auschwitz, murdered thousands more on the streets of Budapest, and executed hundreds in the basement of this building.

When the communists moved into Hungary after the war, they took over the same building as headquarters for their secret police (the ÁVO, later renamed ÁVH). To keep dissent to a minimum, the secret police terrorized, tried, deported, or executed anyone suspected of being an enemy of the state.

Visiting the Museum: The **atrium** features a Soviet T-54 tank, and a vast wall covered with 3,200 portraits of people who were murdered by the Nazis or the communists in this very building. The one-way exhibit begins two floors up, then spirals down to the cellar—just follow signs for Kiállítás/Exhibition. To begin, you can either take the elevator (to floor 2), or walk up the red stairwell nearby, decorated with old Socialist Realist sculptures from the communist days

Upstairs, the first room gives an overview of the **Double Occupation.** The video by the entrance sets the stage for Hungary's 20th century: its territorial losses after World War I; its alliance with, then invasion by, the Nazis; and its "liberation," then occupation, by the USSR.

After passing through a room displaying uniforms and other gear belonging to Hungarian Nazis, you'll reach the room devoted to the Gulag. The word "gulag" refers to a network of secret Soviet prison camps, mostly in Siberia. These were hard-labor camps where potential and actual dissidents were sent in order to punish them, remove their dangerous influence from society, and make an example of those who would dare to defy the regime. On the carpet, a giant map of the USSR shows the locations of some of these camps, where an estimated 600,000 to 700,000 Hungarian civilians and prisoners of war were sent...about half of whom never returned.

The **Changing Clothes** room—with rotating figures dressed alternately in Arrow Cross and communist uniforms—satirizes the readiness of many Hungarians to align themselves with whomever was in power.

The room on **The Fifties** examines the gradual insinuation of the communist regime into the fabric of Hungary. Their methods ranged from already-marked ballots to glossy propaganda—such as the paintings celebrating the peasants of the "people's revolution" and romanticized depictions of communist leaders (look for Lenin as the brave sailor). Behind the distorted stage is the dark underbelly of the regime: the constant surveillance that bred paranoia among the people. The **Resistance** room—empty aside from three very different kitchen tables—symbolizes the way that resistance to the regime emerged in every walk of life.

BUDAPEST

The exhibit continues downstairs, where the **Resettlement and Deportation** section explains the ethnic cleansing—or, in the more pleasant parlance of the time, "mutual population exchange"—that took place throughout Central and Eastern Europe in the years following World War II. In Hungary alone, 230,000 Germans were uprooted and deported. Meanwhile, Hungarians who had become ethnically "stranded" in other nations after the Treaty of Trianon were sent to Hungary (100,000 from Slovakia, 140,000 from Romania, and 70,000 from Yugoslavia). Most have still not returned to their ancestral homes.

In **Surrender of Property and Land,** we learn that under communism, the Hungarian people had to survive on increasingly sparse rations. Enter the labyrinth of pork-fat bricks, which remind old-timers of the harsh conditions of the 1950s. These one-kilo bricks of lard were actually a staple in the local diet: So often, dinner was simply lard on bread. Look for the ration coupons, which people had to present before being allowed to buy even these measly staples.

The next room examines the **ÁVO,** the communist secret police who intimidated the common people of Hungary—equivalent to the KGB in the Soviet Union. Before they were finished, the ÁVO/ÁVH imprisoned, abused, or murdered one person from every third Hungarian family. Their power came from enlisting untold numbers of civilians as informants.

After passing through the office of Gábor Péter (the first director of the ÁVO), you'll reach the **"Justice"** exhibit, which explores "show trials"—high-profile, loudly publicized, and completely choreographed trials of people who had supposedly subverted the regime. The burden of proof was on the accused, not on the accuser, and coerced confessions were fair game. From 1945 until the 1956 Uprising, more than 71,000 Hungarians were accused of political crimes, and 485 were executed.

Next you'll encounter another more upbeat method for controlling the people: bright, cheery communist **Propaganda.** The poster about the Amerikai Bogár warns of the threat of the "American Beetle" (from Kolorádó), which threatened Hungarian crops. When the communists collectivized traditional family farm plots, they tore down the trees and hedgerows that separated them—thereby removing birds that had kept pest populations in check. When a potato beetle epidemic hit, rather than acknowledging their own fault, the communists blamed an American conspiracy.

Rounding out this floor are sections on **"Hungarian Silver"** (actually aluminum—lampooning the lowbrow aesthetic of that era) and **Religion** (those who were publicly faithful were discriminated against, closely supervised by the secret police, and often arrested). Then you'll board an elevator that gradually lowers into the cellar. As it descends, you'll watch a three-minute video of a guard explaining the grotesque execution process. When the door opens, you're in the **Prison Cellar.** Wander through **former cells** used for different purposes. In the large room after the cells, you'll see a stool with a lamp; nearby are the **torture** devices: hot pads and electrical appliances. The bucket and hose were used to revive torture victims who had blacked out. After the torture room, a small room on the right contains a **gallows** that was used for executions (described earlier on your journey, in the elevator video). The room commemorating the **1956 Uprising** features a symbol of that uprising—a Hungarian flag with a hole cut out of the middle (a hastily removed Soviet emblem) and the slogan *Ruszkik Haza!* ("Russkies go home!"). For more on '56, see the sidebar on page 582.

After a sobering room that displays six symbolic gallows, the **Emigration** room features a wall of postcards. More than 200,000 Hungarians simply fled the country after the uprising. The **Hall of Tears** memorial commemorates all the victims of the communists from 1945 to 1967 (when the final prisoners were released from this building). The **Room of Farewell** shows several color video clips that provide a (relatively) happy ending: the festive and exhilarating days in 1991 when the Soviets departed, making way for freedom; the reburial of the Hungarian hero, Imre Nagy, at Heroes' Square; and the dedication of this museum.

The chilling finale: walls of photographs of the **"Victimizers"**—members and supporters of the Arrow Cross and ÁVO, many of whom are still living and who were never brought to justice. The Hungarians have a long way to go to reconcile everything they lived through in the 20th century. For many of them, this museum is an important first step.

• *Across the street and a few steps up Andrássy út is the...*

Franz Liszt Museum

In this surprisingly modest apartment where the composer once resided, you'll find a humble but appealing collection of artifacts. A pilgrimage site for Liszt fans, it's housed in the former Academy of Music, which also hosts Saturday-morning concerts (see "Entertainment in Budapest," later).

Cost and Hours: 2,000 Ft; Mon-Fri 10:00-18:00, Sat 9:00-17:00, closed Sun; dry English audioguide with a few snippets of music-700 Ft, otherwise scarce English information—borrow the information sheet as you enter; Vörösmarty utca 35, district VI, M1: Vörösmarty utca—*not* Vörösmarty tér stop, tel. 1/322-9804, www.lisztmuseum.hu.

• *While you can walk from here to Heroes' Square (visible in the distance, about a 15-minute walk), there's less to see along the rest of Andrássy út. If you prefer, hop on the Metró here and ride it three stops to Hősök tere.*

HEROES' SQUARE AND CITY PARK

The grand finale of Andrássy út, at the edge of the city center, is also one of Budapest's most entertaining quarters. Here you'll find the grand Heroes' Square, dripping with history (both monumental and recent); the vast tree-filled expanse of City Park, dressed up with fanciful buildings that include an Art Nouveau zoo and a replica of a Transylvanian castle; and, tucked in the middle of it all, Budapest's finest thermal spa and single best experience, the Széchenyi Baths. Over time, the vision is to relocate many of Budapest's leading museums to this park—creating a kind of museum quarter. If the sightseeing grind gets you down, take a mini vacation from your busy vacation and relax the way Budapesters do: Escape to City Park.

▲▲Heroes' Square (Hősök Tere)

Built in 1896 to celebrate the 1,000th anniversary of the Magyars' arrival in Hungary, this vast square culminates at a bold **Millennium Monument.** Standing stoically in its colonnades are 14 Hungarian leaders who represent the whole span of this nation's colorful and illustrious history. In front, at the base of a high pillar, are the seven original Magyar chieftains, the Hungarian War Memorial, and young Hungarian skateboarders of the 21st century. Look for

names you may recognize: István, Béla IV, Mátyás Corvinus. The sculptures on the top corners of the two colonnades represent, from left to right: Work and Welfare, War, Peace, and the Importance of Packing Light. The square is also flanked by a pair of museums.

Museums on Heroes' Square: The **Museum of Fine Arts** (Szépművészeti Múzeum) is Budapest's best chance to appreciate some European masters. You'll see mostly Germanic, Dutch, Belgian, and Spanish, rather than Hungarian, art, plus lesser works by the likes of Dürer, the Bruegels, Murillo, Velázquez, El Greco, Goya, and more (1,400 Ft; Tue-Sun 10:00-18:00, closed Mon, last entry one hour before closing; Dózsa György út 41, tel. 1/469-

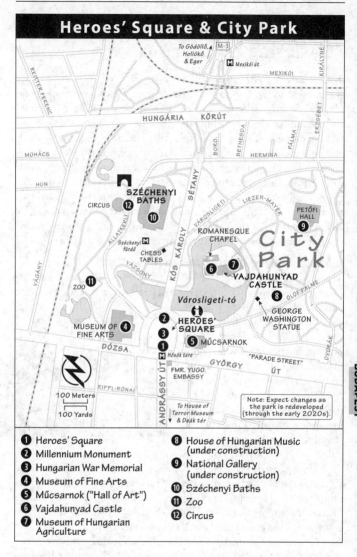

Heroes' Square & City Park

To Gödöllő,
Hollókő
& Eger

M-3

M Mexikói út

MEXIKÓI

KIRÁLYHÉ

REITTER FERENC

HUNGÁRIA   KÖRÚT

BORÓ

BETHESDA

PÁLMA

ERZSÉBET

MOHÁCS

HERMINA

HUN

SÉTÁNY

LIEZEN-MAYER

SZÉCHENYI
BATHS

CIRCUS   ⑫

⑩

PETŐFI
HALL
⑨

City
Park

ALLATKERTI

Széchenyi
fürdő

M

CHESS
TABLES

ROMANESQUE
CHAPEL

⑥ ⑦

VAJDAHUNYAD
CASTLE

VÁGÁNY

VÁZSONY

⑪

ZOO

Városligeti-tó

⑧

OLOF PALME

GEORGE
WASHINGTON
STATUE

KÖS KÁROLY

MUSEUM OF
FINE ARTS

④

②

③

⑤

HEROES'
SQUARE

MŰCSARNOK

DÓZSA

ANDRÁSSY ÚT

① Hősök tere

GYÖRGY

"PARADE STREET"

ÚT

DVÖAK

RIPPL-RÓNAI

FMR. YUGO.
EMBASSY

100 Meters

100 Yards

To House of
Terror Museum
& Deák tér

Note: Expect changes as
the park is redeveloped
(through the early 2020s).

BUDAPEST

❶ Heroes' Square
❷ Millennium Monument
❸ Hungarian War Memorial
❹ Museum of Fine Arts
❺ Műcsarnok ("Hall of Art")
❻ Vajdahunyad Castle
❼ Museum of Hungarian
   Agriculture

❽ House of Hungarian Music
   (under construction)
❾ National Gallery
   (under construction)
❿ Széchenyi Baths
⓫ Zoo
⓬ Circus

7100, www.szepmuveszeti.hu). Facing the Museum of Fine Arts from across Heroes' Square, the **Műcsarnok** ("Hall of Art") shows temporary exhibits by contemporary artists—of interest only to art lovers (price varies depending on the exhibits; Tue-Sun 10:00-18:00 except Thu 12:00-20:00, closed Mon; Dózsa György út 37, tel. 1/460-7000, www.mucsarnok.hu).

• *Now head for the park. From the Műcsarnok, use the crosswalk to circle around across the street from the Millennium Monument to reach the bridge directly behind it. (There's no crosswalk from the monument to the bridge.)*

Begin walking over the bridge into...

▲▲City Park (Városliget)

Budapest's not-so-central "Central Park," which sprawls beyond Heroes' Square, was the site of the overblown 1896 Millennial Exhibition, celebrating Hungary's 1,000th birthday. Explore the fantasy castle of Vajdahunyad (described below). Visit the animals and ogle the playful Art Nouveau buildings inside the city's zoo, or enjoy a circus under the big top. Go for a stroll, rent a rowboat, eat some cotton candy, or challenge a local Bobby Fischer to a game of chess. Or, best of all, take a dip in Budapest's ultimate thermal spa, the Széchenyi Baths. This is a fine place to just be on vacation. Be aware that parts of the park may be torn up, as the city is rejuvenating the area as a new Museum Quarter.

▲▲Vajdahunyad Castle (Vajdahunyad Vára)

Many of the buildings for Hungary's Millennial National Exhibition were erected with temporary materials, to be torn down at the end of the festival—as was the case for most world fairs at the time. But locals so loved Vajdahunyad Castle that it was rebuilt in brick and stone. The complex actually has four parts, each representing a high point in Hungarian architectural style: Romanesque chapel, Gothic gate, Renaissance castle, and Baroque palace (free and always open to walk around the grounds).

From this direction, the **Renaissance castle** dominates the view. It's a replica of a famous castle in Transylvania that once belonged to the Hunyadi family (János and Mátyás Corvinus—both of whom are represented on Heroes' Square). Notice its distinctive trapezoidal tower—typical of castles in Transylvania.

Cross over the bridge and through the **Gothic gateway.** Once inside the complex, on the left is a replica of a 13th-century Romanesque **Benedictine chapel.** Consecrated as an actual church, this is Budapest's most popular spot for weddings on summer weekends.

Farther ahead on the right is a big Baroque mansion housing the **Museum of Hungarian Agriculture** (Magyar Mezőgazdasági Múzeum, www.mezogazdasagimuzeum.hu). It brags that it's Europe's biggest agriculture museum, but most visitors find the lavish interior more interesting than the exhibits.

Facing the museum entry is a monument to **Anonymous**—

specifically, the Anonymous from the court of King Béla IV who penned the first Hungarian history in the Middle Ages.

• *The park's highlight is the big yellow building across the street from Vajdahunyad Castle...*

▲▲▲Széchenyi Baths (Széchenyi Fürdő)

Visiting the Széchenyi Baths is my favorite activity in Budapest. It's the ideal way to reward yourself for the hard work of sightseeing while enjoying a culturally enlightening experience.

Soak in hundred-degree water, surrounded by portly Hungarians squeezed into tiny swimsuits, while jets and cascades pound away your tension. Go for a vigorous swim in the lap pool, giggle and bump your way around the whirlpool, submerge yourself to the nostrils in water green with minerals, feel the bubbles from an underwater jet gradually caress their way up your leg, or challenge the locals to a game of Speedo-clad chess. And it's all surrounded by an opulent yellow palace with shiny copper domes. The bright blue-and-white of the sky, the yellow of the buildings, the pale pink of the skin, the turquoise of the water...Budapest simply doesn't get any better (for all the details, see "Experiences in Budapest," later).

NEAR ÜLLŐI ÚT

The following museum is near the city center, on the boulevard called Üllői út. You could stroll there in about 10 minutes from the Small Boulevard ring road (walking the length of the Ráday utca café street gets you very close), or hop on the M3/blue Metró line to Corvin-negyed (just one stop beyond Kálvin tér).

▲▲Holocaust Memorial Center (Holokauszt Emlékközpont)

This sight honors the nearly 600,000 Hungarian victims of the Nazis...one out of every 10 Holocaust victims. The impressive modern complex (with a beautifully restored 1920s synagogue as its centerpiece) is a museum of the Hungarian Holocaust, a monument to its victims, a space for temporary exhibits, and a research and documentation center of Nazi atrocities. Interesting to anybody, but essential to those interested in the Holocaust, this is Budapest's best sight about that dark time—and one of Europe's best, as well.

Cost and Hours: 1,400 Ft; Tue-Sun 10:00-18:00, closed Mon, last entry one hour before closing; Páva utca 39, district IX, M3: Corvin-negyed, tel. 1/455-3333, www.hdke.hu.

Getting There: From the Corvin-negyed Metró stop, use the exit marked *Holokauszt Emlékközpont* and take the left fork at the exit. Walk straight ahead two long blocks, then turn right down Páva utca.

Visiting the Center: You'll pass through a security checkpoint to reach the courtyard. Once inside, a black marble wall is etched with the names of victims. Head downstairs to buy your ticket.

The excellent permanent exhibit, called "From Deprivation of Rights to Genocide," traces (in English) the gradual process of disenfranchisement, marginalization, exploitation, dehumanization, and eventually extermination that befell Hungary's Jews as World War II wore on. The finale is the interior of the **synagogue,** now a touching memorial filled with glass seats, each one etched with the image of a Jewish worshipper who once filled it. Up above, on the mezzanine level, you'll find temporary exhibits and an information center that helps teary-eyed descendants of Hungarian Jews track down the fate of their relatives.

Nearby: A few blocks away (at Üllői út 33) is the fanciful, late-19th-century Applied Arts Museum—a green-roofed castle that's worth a quick look (from the outside, at least) for architecture fans (museum closed for renovation, likely at least through 2020).

Sights in Buda

Nearly all of Buda's top sights are concentrated on or near its two riverside hills: Castle Hill and Gellért Hill.

Two other major attractions—the part of town called Óbuda ("Old Buda") and Memento Park (filled with communist-era monuments)—are on the Buda side of the river but away from the center. These sights, along with several others, are described under "Day Trips from Budapest," at the end of the chapter.

CASTLE HILL (VÁRHEGY)

Once the seat of Hungarian royalty, and now the city's highest-profile tourist zone, Castle Hill is a historic spit of land looming above the Buda bank of the Danube. Scenic from afar, but (frankly) a bit soulless from up close, it's best seen quickly. I've listed these sights in order from south to north, and linked them together with a self-guided walk.

When to Visit: Castle Hill is jammed with tour groups in the

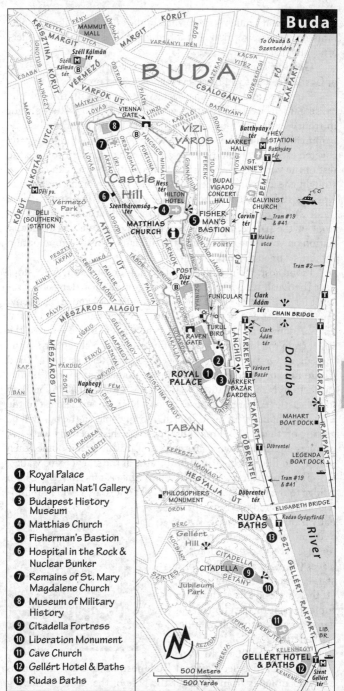

Buda

BUDAPEST

1 Royal Palace
2 Hungarian Nat'l Gallery
3 Budapest History Museum
4 Matthias Church
5 Fisherman's Bastion
6 Hospital in the Rock & Nuclear Bunker
7 Remains of St. Mary Magdalene Church
8 Museum of Military History
9 Citadella Fortress
10 Liberation Monument
11 Cave Church
12 Gellért Hotel & Baths
13 Rudas Baths

500 Meters
500 Yards

morning, but it's much less crowded in the afternoon. Since restaurants up here are touristy and a bad value, Castle Hill is an ideal after-lunch activity.

Getting There: The Metró and trams won't take you to the top of Castle Hill, but you have several other good options.

For a free and scenic approach, you can **walk** up through the castle gardens called Várkert Bazár (trams #19 and #41 stop right in front). From the monumental gateway facing the Danube embankment, head up the stairs into the park, then look right for the covered escalator. From its top, you can either turn left to hike the rest of the way up (on the switchbacked path), or you can carry on straight ahead to find an elevator (under a rust-colored canopy) that zips you right up to the view terrace in front of the Royal Palace (floor 2). From here, you can begin the walk at the viewpoint in front of the palace, then see the Turul bird statue and funicular station on your way back across the hill later. This is a good option if there's a line for the funicular.

From Pest, it's usually fastest to hop on **bus #16,** with stops near the Deák tér Metró hub (on Harmincad utca alongside Erzsébet tér; use exit "E" from the station underpass) and at Széchenyi tér, at the Pest end of the Chain Bridge. (You can also catch it at Clark Ádám tér at the Buda end of the Chain Bridge—across the street from the lower funicular station, and much cheaper than the funicular.) Or you can go via Széll Kálmán tér (on the M2/red Metró line, or by taking tram #4 or #6 around Pest's Great Boulevard); from here, bus #16, as well as buses **#16A** and **#116,** head up to the castle. All of these buses stop at Dísz tér, at the crest of the hill, about halfway along its length (most people on the bus will be getting off there, too). From Dísz tér, cross the street and walk five minutes along the row of flagpoles toward the green dome, then bear left to find the big Turul bird statue at the start of this walk.

The **funicular** (*sikló*, SHEE-kloh) lifts visitors from the Chain Bridge to the top of Castle Hill (1,200 Ft one-way, 1,800 Ft round-trip, not covered by transit pass, daily 7:30-22:00, departs every 5-10 minutes, closed for maintenance every other Mon). It leaves you right at the Turul bird statue, where this walk begins. (If there's a long line at the lower funicular station, just hop on bus #16 across the roundabout—described earlier.)

Finally, you'll see an oversized golf cart labeled **"official Budapest castle bus."** This runs every 15 minutes from points at the base of the castle (including near the bottom station of the funicular, and in front of the Várkert Bazár) up to essentially the same stops the public bus uses at the top of the castle. While handy, this is a pricey little tourist trip (2,100 Ft round-trip, runs daily 9:00-17:00) compared to simply taking a public bus; the only reason I'd take this is if I had a Budapest Card, which covers it.

To **leave the hilltop,** most visitors find it easiest just to walk down after their visit (see the end of this tour). But if you'll be taking the public bus down, it's smart to buy tickets for the return trip before you ascend Castle Hill—the only place to buy them up top is at the post office near Dísz tér (Mon-Fri 8:00-16:00, closed Sat-Sun).

• *Begin the walk at the big statue of the...*

Turul Bird

This mythical bird of Magyar folktales supposedly led the Hungarian migrations from the steppes of Central Asia in the ninth cen-

tury. He dropped his sword in the Carpathian Basin, indicating that this was to be the permanent home of the Magyar people. While the Hungarians have long since integrated into Europe, the Turul remains a symbol of Magyar pride. During a surge of nationalism in the 1920s, a movement named after this bird helped revive traditional Hungarian culture. And today, the bird is invoked by right-wing nationalist politicians—something of a dog whistle for rallying their base (similar to how the Confederate flag might be used in certain circles in the United States).

• *We'll return this way later. But for now, go through the monumental gateway by the Turul and climb down the stairs, then walk along the broad terrace in front of the...*

Royal Palace (Királyi Palota)

The imposing palace on Castle Hill barely hints at the colorful story of this hill since the day that the legendary Turul dropped his

sword. It was once the top Renaissance palace in Europe...but that was several centuries and several versions ago. In the early 15th century, the Renaissance King Mátyás (Matthias) Corvinus—who we'll learn

more about soon—converted a humble medieval palace on this site into one of Europe's most extravagant residences, putting Buda and

Hungary on the map. Just a few decades later, invading Ottomans occupied Buda and turned the palace into a military garrison. When the Habsburgs laid siege to the hill for 77 days in 1686, gunpowder stored in the cellar exploded, destroying the palace. The Habsburgs took the hill, but Buda was deserted and in ruins. The palace was rebuilt, then damaged again during the 1848 Revolution, then repaired again. As World War II drew to a close, Budapest became the front line between the Nazis and the approaching Soviets. The Red Army laid siege to the hill for 100 days. They eventually succeeded in taking Budapest...but the city—and the hill—were devastated.

The current palace—a historically inaccurate, post-WWII reconstruction—is a loose rebuilding of previous versions. It's big but soulless. The most prominent feature of today's palace—the green dome—didn't even exist in earlier versions. Fortunately, the palace does house some worthwhile museums (described later), and boasts the fine terrace you're strolling on, with some of Budapest's best views.

• *Behind the big equestrian statue is the main entrance to the...*

▲Hungarian National Gallery
(Magyar Nemzeti Galéria)

While not quite a must-see, this museum is the best place in Hungary to appreciate the works of homegrown artists, and to get a peek into the often-morose Hungarian worldview. The collection—which is eventually scheduled to move to a new home in City Park—includes a remarkable group of 15th-century, wood-carved altars from Slovakia (then "Upper Hungary"); piles of gloomy canvases dating from the dark days after the failed 1848 Revolution; several works by two great Hungarian Realist painters, Mihály Munkácsy and László Paál; and paintings by the troubled, enigmatic, and recently in-vogue Post-Impressionist Tivadar Csontváry Kosztka. The collection's highlights can be viewed quickly.

Cost and Hours: 1,800 Ft, Tue-Sun 10:00-18:00, closed Mon, audioguide-800 Ft, required bag check for large bags, café, in the Royal Palace—enter from terrace by Eugene of Savoy statue, district I, mobile +3620-439-7325, www.mng.hu.

• *Head back outside and face the palace. Go through the passage to the right of the National Gallery entrance (next to the café). You'll emerge into a courtyard decorated with a gorgeous fountain dedicated to King Matthias Corvinus (see the sidebar). Go around the right side of the fountain and through the passage, into the palace courtyard. At the far end of this too-big space is the entrance to the...*

Mátyás (Matthias) Corvinus: The Last Hungarian King

The Árpád dynasty—descendants of the original Magyar tribes—died out in 1301. For more than 600 years, Hungary would be ruled by elected foreign rulers...with one exception.

In the mid-15th century, the Hungarian military general János Hunyadi enjoyed great success on the battlefield against the Ottomans (including a pivotal victory in 1456's Battle of Belgrade). Meanwhile, Hungary's imported kings kept dying unexpectedly. Finally, the Hungarian nobility took a chance on a Hungarian-born ruler and offered the throne to Hunyadi's son, Mátyás (or Matthias in English). According to legend, they sent a raven with a ring in its mouth to notify Matthias, who was away in Prague. He returned to Buda, and took the raven both as his symbol and as his royal nickname: Corvinus (Latin for "raven").

Matthias Corvinus (r. 1458-1490) became the first Hungarian-descended king in more than 150 years. Progressive and well educated in the Humanist tradition, Matthias Corvinus was the quintessential Renaissance king. A lover of the Italian Renaissance, he patronized the arts and built palaces legendary for their beauty. As a benefactor of the poor, he dressed as a commoner and ventured into the streets to see firsthand how the nobles of his realm treated his people.

A strong, savvy leader, Matthias created Central Europe's first standing army—30,000 mercenaries known as the Black Army. No longer reliant on the nobility for military support, Good King Matthias was able to drain power from the nobles— earning him the nickname the "people's king."

Matthias was also a shrewd military tactician. Realizing that skirmishing with the Ottomans would squander his resources, he made peace with the sultan to stabilize Hungary's southern border. Then he swept north, invading Moravia, Bohemia, and even Austria. By 1485, Matthias moved into his new palace in Vienna, and Hungary was enjoying a Golden Age.

But just five years later, Matthias died mysteriously at the age of 47, and his empire disintegrated. Before long the Ottomans flooded back into Hungary, and the country entered a dark period. It is said that when Matthias died, justice died with him. To this day, Hungarians rank him the greatest of all kings, and they sing of his siege of Vienna in their national anthem. They're proud that for a few decades they had a truly Hungarian king—and a great one at that.

BUDAPEST

Budapest History Museum
(Budapesti Történeti Múzeum)

This earnest but dusty collection strains to bring the history of this city to life. If Budapest really intrigues you, this is a fine place to explore its history. Otherwise, skip it. The dimly lit fragments of 14th-century sculptures, depicting early Magyars, allow you to see how Asian those original Hungarians truly looked. The "Light and Shadow" exhibit deliberately but effectively traces the union between Buda and Pest. Rounding out the collection are exhibits on prehistoric residents and a sprawling cellar that unveils fragments from the oh-so-many buildings that have perched on this hill over the centuries.

Cost and Hours: 2,000 Ft; Tue-Sun 10:00-18:00, Nov-Feb until 16:00, closed Mon year-round; audioguide-1,200 Ft, some good English descriptions posted; district I, tel. 1/487-8800, www.btm.hu.

• *From the palace courtyard, it's time to...*

Walk to Matthias Church

Leaving the palace courtyard, walk straight up the slight incline (with the rebuilt Hungarian Royal Guard building on your left).

Then you'll pass under a gate with a raven holding a ring in its mouth (a symbol of King Matthias).

As you continue along the line of flagpoles, the big white building on your right (near the funicular station) is the **Sándor Palace,** the Hungarian

president's office. This is where you can see the relatively low-key changing of the guard each hour on the hour, with a special show at noon. After Sándor Palace is the yellow former **Court Theater** (Várszínház), which has seen many great performances over the centuries—including a visit from Beethoven in 1800. A few years back, Prime Minister Viktor Orbán (not known for humble gestures) grew jealous of the president's swanky digs, kicked out the dancers, and renovated this building as the prime minister's residence.

In the field in the middle of this terrace, you'll notice the **ruins** of a medieval monastery and church. Along the left side (past the flagpoles) is the ongoing excavation of the medieval Jewish quarter—more reminders that most of what you see on today's Castle Hill has been destroyed and rebuilt many times over.

At the end of the field, passing the hulking former **Ministry of War** building, you'll reach **Dísz tér** (Parade Square). Here you'll see convenient bus stops for connecting to other parts of Budapest (bus #16, #16A, or #116 to Széll Kálmán tér; or—departing from the stop directly in front of the post office on the left—bus #16 to the Pest side of the Chain Bridge; bus tickets sold at post office Mon-Fri 8:00-16:00, closed Sat-Sun). On the right, behind the low wall, is a courtyard with an open-air Hungarian **folk-art market.** While it's fun to browse, prices here are high (haggle away). The Great Market Hall (described earlier, under "Sights in Pest") has a better selection and generally lower prices.

Continue straight uphill on **Tárnok utca,** bearing right at the park; soon after, on the left, is the recommended Vár Bistro (a handy if uninspired lunch cafeteria). This area often disappoints visitors. After being destroyed by Ottomans, it was rebuilt in sensible Baroque, lacking the romantic time-capsule charm of a medieval old town. But if you poke your head into some courtyards, you'll almost always see some original Gothic arches and other medieval features.

As you continue along, ponder the fact that miles of **caves** were burrowed under Castle Hill—carved out by water, expanded by the Ottomans, and used by locals during the siege of Buda at the end of World War II. If you'd like to spelunk under Castle Hill, and learn about how the caves were used during the 20th century, it's worth going on the lengthy Hospital in the Rock tour (described later). A block to your left is the entrance to the less interesting and skippable Labyrinth of Buda Castle.

On the left, the **Prima grocery store** sells reasonably priced cold drinks, and has a coffee shop upstairs. A good spot for dessert is just up the little lane in front of the grocery store, under the passage: **Rétesbár,** selling strudel *(rétes)* with various fillings (daily 8:00-20:00, Balta köz).

The white, circular building in the park across from the grocery store is a **TI** that can answer questions and has a handy pictorial map of the castle area (daily 10:00-18:00).

Just beyond the grocery store, a warty plague column from 1713 marks **Szentháromság tér** (Holy Trinity Square), the main square of old Buda.
• *Dominating the square is...*

▲▲Matthias Church (Mátyás-Templom)

Arguably Budapest's finest church inside and out, this historic house of worship—with a frilly Neo-Gothic spire and gilded Hungarian historical motifs slathered on every interior wall—is Castle Hill's best sight. From the humble Loreto Chapel (with a tranquil statue of the Virgin that helped defeat the Ottomans), to altars devoted to top Hungarian kings, to a replica of the crown of Hungary, every inch of the church oozes history.

Cost and Hours: 1,800 Ft; Mon-Sat 9:00-17:00 (may close Sat afternoons in summer for weddings), Sun from 13:00; Szentháromság tér 2, district I, tel. 1/488-7716, www.matyas-templom.hu.

Background: Budapest's best church has been destroyed and rebuilt several times in the 800 years since it was founded by King Béla IV. Today's version—renovated at great expense in the late 19th century and restored after World War II—is an ornately decorated lesson in Hungarian history. The church's unofficial namesake isn't a saint, so it can't be formally named

for him. Its official name is the Church of Our Lady or the Coronation Church, but everyone calls it the Matthias Church, for Matthias Corvinus, the popular Renaissance king who got married here—twice.

◐ Self-Guided Tour: Examine the **exterior.** While the nucleus of the church is Gothic, most of what you see outside—including the frilly, flamboyant steeple—was added for the 1896 millennial celebrations. At the top of the stone corner tower facing the river, notice the raven—the ever-present symbol of King Matthias Corvinus.

Buy your ticket across the square from the church's side door, at the ticket windows embedded in the wall. Then enter the church. The good English descriptions posted throughout will supplement this tour.

The sumptuous **interior** is wallpapered with gilded pages from a Hungarian history textbook. Different eras are represented by symbolic motifs. Entering the side door, turn left and go to the back end of the church. The wall on the left represents the Renaissance, with a giant coat of arms of beloved King Matthias Corvinus. (The tough guys in armor on either side are members of his mercenary Black Army, the source of his power.) Notice another raven, with a ring in its beak.

Work your way clockwise around the church. The first chapel (in the back corner, to the left as you face the closed main doors)—the **Loreto Chapel**—holds the church's prize possession: a 1515 statue of Mary and Jesus. Anticipating Ottoman plundering, locals walled over its niche. The occupying

Ottomans used the church as their primary mosque—oblivious to the precious statue hidden behind the plaster. Then, a century and a half later, during the siege of Buda in 1686, gunpowder stored in the castle up the street detonated, and the wall crumbled. Mary's triumphant face showed through, terrifying the Ottomans. Supposedly this was the only part of town taken from the Ottomans without a fight.

Facing the doors, look about four paces to the right. At about eye-level, at the top of the stout pillar, a **carved capital** shows two men gesturing excitedly at a book. Dating from 1260, these carvings are some of the earliest surviving features in this church, which has changed much over the centuries.

As you look down the **nave,** notice the banners. They've hung here since the Mass that celebrated Habsburg monarch Franz Jo-

sef's coronation at this church on June 8, 1867. In a sly political compromise to curry favor in the Hungarian part of his territory, Franz Josef was "emperor" *(Kaiser)* of Austria, but only "king" *(König)* of Hungary. (If you see the old German phrase "K+K"—still used today as a boast of royal quality— it refers to this *"König und Kaiser"* arrangement.) So, after F. J. was crowned emperor in Vienna, he came down the Danube and said to the Hungarians, "King me."

Now stand at the modern altar in the middle of the church, and look down the nave to the **main altar.** Mary floats above it all, and hovering over her is a full-scale replica of the Hungarian crown, which was blessed by Pope John Paul II. More than a millennium after István, Mary still officially wears this nation's crown.

Left of the altar is the **László Chapel,** venerating a great Christian knight who fought pagans in the 11th century.

Climb the circular staircase (in the front-left corner) up to the **gallery.** Walk along the royal oratory to a small mezzanine that overlooks the altar area—giving you a better look at the altar's details. Then head back along the gallery. In the room with a small organ is a modest exhibit about Sisi—Empress Elisabeth—who has an almost cult following among Hungarians. From here, huff up even more steps to a few more modest exhibits, including a replica of the Hungarian crown, orb, and scepter.

Back down at ground level, you exit the church under a replica of a fine Gothic **tympanum.** The weathered original is on display below, offering an unusual close-up look. The carved scene celebrates the centrality of the book in spreading the word of God.

• *Back outside, at the end of the square next to Matthias Church, is the...*

Fisherman's Bastion (Halászbástya)

Seven pointy domes and a double-decker rampart run along the cliff in front of Matthias Church. Evoking the original seven Magyar tribes, and built for the millennial celebration of their arrival, the Fisherman's Bastion is one of Budapest's top landmarks. This fanciful structure adorns Castle Hill like a decorative frieze or wedding-cake flowers. While some suckers pay for the views from here, you can enjoy virtually the same view through the windows next to the bastion café for free.

Cost and Hours: 1,000 Ft, buy ticket at ticket office along the park wall across the square from Matthias Church, daily 9:00-20:00; after closing time and off-season, no tickets are sold, but bastion is open and free to enter; Szentháromság tér 5, district I.

• *Between the bastion and the church stands a...*

St. István Statue

Hungary's first Christian king (c. 967-1038) tamed the nomadic, pagan Magyars and established strict laws and the concept of private property. In the late 900s, Géza, Grand Prince of the Hungarians, lost a major battle against the forces of Christian Europe—and realized that he must raise his son Vajk (c. 967-1038) as a Catholic and convert his people, or they would be forcefully driven out of Europe. Vajk took the Christian name István (EESHT-vahn, "Stephen") and was baptized in the year 1000. The reliefs on this statue show the commissioners of the pope crowning St. István, bringing Hungary into the fold of Christendom. This pragmatic move put Hungary on the map as a fully European kingdom, forging alliances that would endure for centuries. Without this pivotal event, Hungarians believe that the Magyar nation would have been lost.

• *Head down the charming little street (named Szentháromság utca) that leads away from Matthias Church. Halfway down this street on the right, look for the venerable, recommended Ruszwurm café—the oldest in Budapest. Then continue out to the terrace and appreciate views of the Buda Hills—the "Beverly Hills" of Budapest, draped with orchards, vineyards, and the homes of the wealthiest Budapesters.*

If you go down the stairs here, then turn right up the street, you'll reach the entrance of the...

▲Hospital in the Rock and Nuclear Bunker (Sziklakórház és Atombunker)

Sprawling beneath Castle Hill is a 25,000-square-foot labyrinthine network of hospital and fallout-shelter corridors built during the mid-20th century. While pricey, this visit is a must for doctors, nurses, and World War II buffs. I enjoy this as a lively interactive experience to balance out an otherwise sedate Castle Hill visit.

Cost and Hours: 4,000 Ft for required one-hour tour, 10 percent discount if you have a Matthias Church ticket (but not vice-versa), daily 10:00-20:00, English tours run 1-2/hour, last tour departs at 19:00, gift shop like an army-surplus store, Lovas utca 4C, district I, mobile +3670-701-0101, www.sziklakorhaz.eu.

Getting There: To find the hospital, stand with your back to Matthias Church and the Fisherman's Bastion. Walk straight past the plague column and down the little street (Szentháromság utca), then go down the covered steps at the wall (or ride the elevator). At the bottom, turn right on Lovas utca, and walk 50 yards to the well-marked bunker entrance.

Visiting the Hospital and Bunker: First you'll watch a 10-minute movie (with English subtitles) about the history of the place. Then, on the tour, your guide leads you through the tunnels to see room after room of perfectly preserved WWII and 1960s-era medical supplies and equipment, most still in working order. More than 200 wax figures engagingly bring the various hospital rooms to life: giant sick ward, operating room, and so on. On your way to the fallout shelter, you'll pass the decontamination showers, and see primitive radiation detectors and communist propaganda directing comrades how to save themselves in case of capitalist bombs or gas attacks. In the bunker, you'll also tour the various mechanical rooms that provided water and ventilation to this sprawling underground city, and you'll learn about the atom bomb explosions in Hiroshima and Nagasaki.

• *Our Castle Hill walk is finished. If you're ready to head back down to the river (and the Víziváros neighborhood), you can make a graceful exit down the big staircase below the Fisherman's Bastion.*

If you'd like to spend more time exploring Castle Hill, poke around the northern part of the hill, where you'll find several interesting sights. Next door to Matthias Church, the modern **Hilton Hotel** *is built around the fragments of a 13th-century Dominican church (to see them, go inside the lobby café-bar, and look out the back windows). A few blocks farther north stand the remains of* **St. Mary Magdalene Church,** *destroyed during the Ottoman occupation but whose bell tower has been rebuilt. Around the corner is the dusty* **Museum of Military History.** *And along the tree-shaded terrace at the northern tip of the hilltop, look for the* **Turkish grave** *of a pasha (Ottoman ruler).*

From the northern end of the hill, you can head out through the

BUDAPEST

Vienna Gate and follow the road downhill to bustling Széll Kálmán tér and its handy Metró stop (M2/red line).

GELLÉRT HILL (GELLÉRTHEGY) AND NEARBY

Gellért Hill rises from the Danube just downriver from the castle. When King István converted Hungary to Christianity in the year 1000, he brought in Bishop Gellért, a monk from Venice, to tutor his son. But some rebellious Magyars put the bishop in a barrel, drove long nails in from the outside, and rolled him down this hill...tenderizing him to death. Gellért became the patron saint of Budapest and gave his name to the hill that killed

him. Today the hill is a fine place to commune with nature on a hike or jog, followed by a restorative splash in either the elegant Gellért Baths (in the Gellért Hotel) or the Turkish-style Rudas Baths (both worth ▲▲ and described later, under "Experiences in Budapest").

Citadella

This strategic, hill-capping fortress was built by the Habsburgs after the 1848 Revolution to keep an eye on their Hungarian subjects. There's not much to do up here (no museum or exhibits), but it's a good destination for an uphill hike, and provides the best panoramic view over all of Budapest.

The hill is crowned by the **Liberation Monument,** featuring a woman holding aloft a palm branch. Locals call it "the lady with the big fish" or "the great bottle opener." A heroic Soviet soldier, who once inspired the workers with a huge red star from the base of the monument, is now in Memento Park (see Memento Park listing later, under "Day Trips from Budapest").

Getting There: It's a steep hike up from the river to the Citadella. Bus #27 cuts some time off the trip, taking you up to the Búsuló Juhász stop (from which it's still an uphill hike to the fortress). You can catch bus #27 from either side of Gellért Hill. From the southern edge of the hill, catch this bus at the Móricz Zsigmond körtér stop (easy to reach: ride trams #19 or #41 south from anywhere along Buda's Danube embankment, or trams #47 or #49 from Pest's Small Boulevard ring road; you can also catch any of these trams at Gellért tér, in front of the Gellért Hotel).

Cave Church (Sziklatemplom)

Hidden in the hillside on the south end of the hill (across the street from Gellért Hotel) is Budapest's atmospheric cave church—burrowed right into the rock face. The communists bricked up this church when they came to power, but today it's open for visitors (600 Ft, unpredictable hours, closed to sightseers during frequent services).

Experiences in Budapest

THERMAL BATHS (FÜRDŐ)

Splashing and relaxing in Budapest's thermal baths is the city's top attraction. Though it might sound daunting, bathing with the Magyars is far more accessible than you'd think. The thermal baths I've described are basically like your hometown swimming pool—except the water is 100 degrees, there are plenty of jets and bubbles to massage away your stress, and you're surrounded by potbellied, scantily clad Hungarians. (For those seeking a more traditional, in-the-nude experience, Rudas Baths has that as well.)

All this fun goes way back. Hungary's Carpathian Basin is essentially a thin crust covering a vast reservoir of hot water. The word "Pest" comes from a Slavic word for "oven." The Romans named their settlement near present-day Budapest Aquincum—"abundant waters"—and took advantage of those waters by building many baths. Centuries later, the occupying Ottomans revived the custom. And today, thermal baths are as Hungarian as can be.

Locals brag that if you poke a hole in the ground anywhere in Hungary, you'll find a hot-water spring. Judging from Budapest, they could be right: The city has 123 natural springs and some two dozen thermal baths *(fürdő)*. The baths, which are all operated by the same government agency, are actually a part of the health-care system. Doctors prescribe treatments that include massage, soaking in baths of various heat and mineral compositions, and swimming laps. For these patients, a visit to the bath is subsidized.

But increasingly, there's a new angle on Hungary's hot water: entertainment. Adventure water parks are springing up all over the country, and even the staid old baths have been renovated, adding enjoyable jets and currents. Overcome your jitters, follow my instructions, and dive in...or miss out on *the* quintessential Budapest experience.

BUDAPEST

Baths Orientation

Some tourists may feel trepidation at the thought of bathing along-side locals. Relax! My readers overwhelmingly report that the thermal baths were their top Hungarian experience. If you go into it with an easygoing attitude, I promise you'll have a blast. The system has been modernized, and most bath attendants speak enough English to help you find your way.

Dress Code: While Budapest has several mostly nude, gen-der-segregated Turkish baths, my favorites—Széchenyi and Gel-lért—are less intimidating: Men and women are usually together, and you can keep your swimsuit on the entire time. (At the more traditional, gender-segregated baths—like the thermal section of Rudas on certain days—locals may be nude or wearing a *kötény*—a loose-fitting loincloth.)

What to Bring: If you have them, bring a swimsuit, towel, flip-flops, bottle of water, soap and shampoo, comb or brush, swim cap if you want to do laps, plastic bag for your wet swimsuit, and maybe sunscreen and leisure reading. Hotels sometimes frown on guests taking their room towels to the baths; try asking nicely if they have some loaner towels just for this purpose. A swim cap is required in lap pools; you can rent or buy a flimsy one there, but if you know you'll be swimming laps, see if you can grab a shower cap from your hotel.

Rental Towels and Swimsuits: At Budapest's baths, you can usually rent a towel or swimsuit (for men, Speedos are always available, trunks sometimes). These are generally available at a separate desk inside the complex. Rent your towel before you change, as you'll need cash (generally about 1,000 Ft rental fee, 2,000-Ft deposit per item). At the end, you'll return your towel to get your deposit back; you may also be asked for your paper receipt, so don't lose it.

Entry Procedure: Credit cards are accepted (but you'll need cash to rent towels). Don't bother with the "prepaid" tickets for the baths that are advertised in hotel lobbies around town; it's the same price to buy your tickets directly, and there's rarely a line.

All of Budapest's baths use the same easy system: When you pay, you'll be given a waterproof wristband. Put it on and keep it on. Touch it to the panel on the turnstile to enter, then again to be assigned a changing cabin, then again to unlock your cabin. At most baths (except Rudas), the door of your cabin should lock auto-matically when you close it (but test it to be sure). If you paid for a locker, just choose any empty one and touch it with your wristband in order to lock it; from then on, it can only be locked and unlocked with the same wristband. You can use your wristband to reopen your cabin or locker as often as you like. If you forget the number

Useful Bath Words

English	Hungarian
Bath	*Fürdő* (FEWR-dur)
Men	*Férfi* (FAYR-fee)
Women	*Női* (NUR-ee)
Changing cabin	*Kabin* (KAW-been)
Locker	*Szekrény* (SEHK-rayn)
Ticket office	*Pénztár* (PAYNZ-tar)
Thermal bath	*Gyógyfürdő* (JOHDGE-fewr-dur) or *Gőz* (gurz)

of your cabin or locker, just touch your wristband to the panel, and it'll remind you.

Lockers and Cabins: The main choice when buying your ticket is locker or cabin. The locker price is slightly cheaper and gives you access to a gender-segregated, gymnasium-type locker room (which often has communal cabins where modest bathers can change). A cabin is all yours, offering more privacy for changing. I've found both cabins and lockers to be safe, but storing valuables here is at your own risk (if you're nervous, you can pay a few hundred forints to rent a safe).

Main Pools: Each bath complex has multiple pools, used for different purposes. Big pools with cooler water are for serious swimming, while the smaller, hotter thermal baths (*gyógyfürdő*, or simply *gőz*) are for relaxing, enjoying the jets and current pools, and playing chess. The water bubbles up from hot springs at 77° Celsius (170° Fahrenheit), then is mixed with cooler water to achieve the desired temperatures. Most pools are marked with the water temperature in Celsius (cooler pools are about 30°C/86°F; warmer pools are closer to 36°C/97°F or 38°C/100°F, about like the hot tub back home; and the hottest are 42°C/108°F...yowtch!). Locals hit the cooler pools first, then work their way up to the top temps.

Other Bath Features: Most thermal baths also have a dry sauna, a wet steam room, a cold plunge pool (for a pleasurable jolt when you're feeling overheated), and sunbathing areas (which may be gender segregated and clothing optional). Some baths have fun flourishes: bubbles, whirlpools, massage jets, waterfalls, wave pools, and so on.

Sanitary Concerns: While the lap pools are chlorinated, most of the thermal baths are only lightly chlorinated or not at all. Unlike swimming pools in the US—where the water is recycled back into the pool—water here is slowly drained out and replaced with fresh water from the hot springs. Locals figure this continuous natural flushing makes chemicals unnecessary. Still, germophobes may not be entirely comfortable at the baths; either convince yourself to go with the flow, or skip the trip.

Massages: Don't expect a relaxing, pampering experience; the baths are operated by the Hungarian government as a wing of their national health system, so these are more medicinal. There are two basic choices. A **"relax massage"** or **"aroma massage"** is a restful rubdown, typically using oil (often scented). This is what's sometimes called a Swedish-style massage. The other option is a **"scrub massage"** or **"skin-firming massage."** Similar to a Turkish-style massage, this is (for some) less restful, as it's intended to exfoliate your skin and involves some very hard scrubbing. Remember that the spas are medical facilities, so the massage may be more functional and less serene than what you're used to back home. In the lobby of each bath, you'll find a long menu of massage options. It's affordable—figure around 6,000 Ft (basic 20-minute massage) to around 12,000 Ft (45 minutes); more elaborate "VIP" treatments cost more. Pay and arrange a time when you're buying your ticket. On busy days (especially Mon, Fri, and Sat), you may have to wait an hour or two; at other times, you may be able to get your massage immediately (or whenever you want).

Yet another choice is a **Thai massage.** You'll lie on a mat as the masseuse uses her feet, knees, and elbows.

The Baths

Of Budapest's two-dozen thermal baths, the three listed here are the best known, most representative, and most convenient for first-timers: The Széchenyi Baths are more casual and popular with locals; the Gellért Baths are touristy, famous, and genteel; and the Rudas Baths offer an appealing combination of a modern "wellness" section and a historic, 500-year-old, Turkish-feeling thermal section. To me, Széchenyi is second to none, but some travelers prefer the Gellért

or Rudas experience. As they're all quite different, doing more than one is an excellent option. For more information on all of Budapest's baths, see www.spasbudapest.com.

Széchenyi Baths (Széchenyi Fürdő)

The big, yellow, copper-domed building in the middle of City Park, Széchenyi (SAY-chayn-yee) is the best of Budapest's many bath experiences and worth ▲▲▲. Although it's increasingly discovered

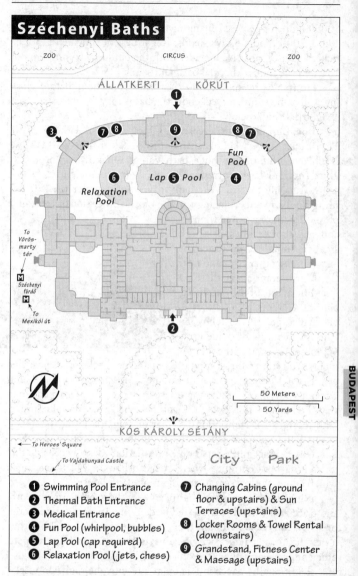

Széchenyi Baths

ZOO   CIRCUS   ZOO

ÁLLATKERTI   KÖRÚT

1

3   **7** **8**   **9**   **8** **7**

Fun Pool

6   *Lap* **5** *Pool*   **4**

Relaxation Pool

To Vörös-marty tér

Ⓜ Széchenyi fürdő

Ⓜ To Mexikói út

2

50 Meters

50 Yards

BUDAPEST

KÓS KÁROLY SÉTÁNY

← To Heroes' Square

↙ To Vajdahunyad Castle

City   Park

1 Swimming Pool Entrance

2 Thermal Bath Entrance

3 Medical Entrance

4 Fun Pool (whirlpool, bubbles)

5 Lap Pool (cap required)

6 Relaxation Pool (jets, chess)

7 Changing Cabins (ground floor & upstairs) & Sun Terraces (upstairs)

8 Locker Rooms & Towel Rental (downstairs)

9 Grandstand, Fitness Center & Massage (upstairs)

by tourists, you'll still see plenty of Hungarians here. Magyars of all shapes and sizes stuff themselves into tiny swimsuits and strut their stuff. Bankers and homemakers float blissfully in the warm water. Intellectuals and roly-poly elder statesmen stand in chest-high water around chessboards and ponder their next moves. This is Budapest at its best.

Cost: 5,500 Ft for locker (in gender-segregated locker room),

500 Ft more for personal changing cabin, cheaper if you arrive after 19:00, 200 Ft more on weekends. Regardless of which entrance or ticket you use, the price includes both the outdoor swimming pool area and the indoor thermal bath and sauna.

Hours: Daily 6:00-22:00, last entry one hour before closing. On some summer weekends, the baths may be open later (see "Night Bathing," below).

Location and Entrances: In City Park at Állatkerti körút 11, district XIV, M1: Széchenyi fürdő (tel. 1/363-3210, www.szechenyibath.hu). The huge bath complex has three entrances. The **"thermal bath entrance"** is the grand main entry, facing south (roughly toward Vajdahunyad Castle). I prefer the **"swimming pool entrance,"** facing the zoo on the other side of the complex—it's more user-friendly and has shorter lines. A third, smaller **"medical entrance"** is between the other two (and near the Metró station). If there's a long line at one of the entrances, check the others.

Massage: In the lobby, an English menu lists a wide array of massages and other treatments. You can set up an appointment and pay at the office near the towel-rental desk (expect a 30-minute wait for your appointment when it's busy). Remember that these massages are more medicinal than hedonistic. But inside the complex are some more luxurious (and more expensive) options: a Thai massage parlor at the upper level of the complex (above the swimming pool entrance—just follow the signs) and a separate "information" desk just inside the swimming pool entrance where you can book a "VIP" massage, which comes with access to an adjoining palm house.

Night Bathing: The baths are a joy in the evening, when both the price and the crowds are reduced. In cool weather, even rain or snow, the pools maintain their hot temperatures—making this a delightful after-hours activity. Busy sightseers can be extremely efficient by closing down the museums, then heading to the baths.

Additionally, Széchenyi is open late into the night on weekends for a "sparty" event, where the bath complex basically becomes one big hot-water dance club (around 16,000 Ft, tickets sell out so book online in advance, mid-Feb-early Dec Sat 22:30-late, www.szechenyispabaths.com/sparties).

Entering the Baths: These instructions assume that you're using the swimming pool entrance. First, in the grand lobby, pay the cashier, then touch your wristband to the turnstile and enter. Pause to get oriented: Straight ahead is a row of private changing cabins. If you go **up the stairs,** you'll find more changing cabins, the Thai massage area, gender-segregated "solarium" sun terraces, a well-equipped fitness center, and a grandstand overlooking the main pool. It's worth

heading upstairs just to snap some photos of the outdoor complex before you change. If you go **down the stairs,** you'll find the counter where you can rent a towel or swimsuit. From here, a long hallway lined with hairdryers and mirrors leads to locker rooms at each end (remember, men are *férfi* and women are *női*).

When ready, report to the area that you paid for: If you paid for a **cabin,** head to the cabins on the main floor, look for an electronic panel on the wall, and hold your wristband against this panel for a few seconds—you'll automatically be assigned a number for a cabin. If you paid for a **locker,** you can head down to the locker room and choose one, then use your wristband to lock it.

Taking the Waters: The bath complex has two parts, outside and inside.

For most visitors, the best part is the swimming pool area **outside.** Orient yourself to the three pools (facing the main, domed building): The pool to the left is for **fun** (cooler water—30°C/86°F, warmer in winter, lots of jets and bubbles, lively and often crowded, includes circular current pool). The pool

on the right is for **relaxation** (warmer water—38°C/100°F, mellow atmosphere, a few massage jets, chess). The **main (lap) pool** in the center is all business (cooler water—28°C/82°F in summer, 26°C/79°F in winter, people doing laps, swim cap required). You get extra credit for joining the gang in a chess match. Stairs to saunas (with cold plunge pools, cold showers, and even an ice maker) are below the doors to the indoor thermal bath complex.

Inside the main building is the thermal bath section, a series of indoor pools; each of these is designed for a specific medical treatment. You'll notice each pool is labeled with the temperature (ranging from 28°C/82°F to 36°C/97°F to 38°C/100°F; you'll also find steam rooms with an 18°C/64°F cold plunge pool nearby). The pools also have varying types and amounts of healthy minerals—some of which can make the water quite green and/or stinky.

Hungarians who use Széchenyi Baths medicinally are prescribed a specific regimen for moving from pool to pool. But if all of this smelly water is lost on you (as it is on many foreigners), it's totally fine to focus on the fun outdoor pools. (I've had many great visits to Széchenyi Baths without ever going inside.)

Leaving the Bath: When finished, continue your sightseeing...soggy but relaxed. If you're heading to the **Metró,** the station is very close but easy to miss: It's basically a pair of nondescript stairwells with yellow railings in the middle of the park, roughly toward Heroes' Square from the thermal bath entrance (look for the low-profile, yellow *Földalatti* sign; to head for downtown, take the stairwell marked *a Vörösmarty tér felé*).

Gellért Baths (Gellért Fürdő)

The ▲▲ baths at Gellért (GEH-layrt) Hotel cost a bit more than the Széchenyi Baths, and you won't run into as many locals; this is

definitely a more upscale, tourist-oriented scene. Gellért's indoor thermal pools are Budapest's most atmospheric—with exquisite porcelain details and an air of mystery. Its outdoor zone—mostly for sunbathing—is less interesting than Széchenyi, with one exception: It has a deliriously enjoyable wave pool that'll toss you around like a queasy surfer (summer only).

Cost: 5,900 Ft for a locker, 400 Ft more for a personal changing cabin; 200 Ft extra on weekends.

Hours: Daily 6:00-20:00, last entry one hour before closing.

Location: It's on the Buda side of the green Liberty Bridge (M4: Szent Gellért tér; or take trams #47 and #49 from Deák tér in Pest, or trams #19 and #41 along the Buda embankment from Víziváros below the castle, Gellért tér stop). The entrance to the baths is under the stone dome opposite the bridge, around the right

side of the hotel (Kelenhegyi út 4, district XI, tel. 1/466-6166 ext. 165, www.gellertbath.com).

Entering the Baths: The entrance doors are flanked by ticket windows; just past those, on the right, is an information desk with English-speaking staff. Choose your ticket—locker or cabin—and consider the dizzying array of **massages** and other treatment options (sort through your options and arrange a time when you buy your ticket). Upstairs, you can also book a Thai massage.

After buying your ticket, put on your wristband, and glide through the swanky lobby. You'll use the swimming pool entrance, on your right, under the grand dome. Go down the stairs, pass through a long corridor (with underwater windows into the main swimming pool), then climb up the stairs to the cabin areas and locker rooms (men/*férfi* on the left side of the complex,

and women/*nöi* on the right). Use your wristband to find and lock your cabin (or choose your own locker), as explained earlier. If you want to rent a towel or swimsuit, look for the desk near the entrance to the changing-cabin area.

Taking the Waters: Once you've changed, you can spend your time either indoors or out. From the locker room, look for signs *to the effervescent bath-pool* (for the indoor section) or *to the swimming-pool with artificial waves* (for the outdoor section).

Inside, the central, genteel-feeling hall is home to a cool-water swimming pool (swim cap required—you can buy a cheap one) and a crowded hot-water pool (36°C/97°F). This is used for swimming laps and for periodic water-exercise classes. On sunny days, they crank open the retractable roof; for nice views down onto the pool, find the stairs up near the locker rooms. Back toward the main hall

are doors to the thermal baths (easy to miss—walk to the far end of the pool and look for signs). These were once segregated into men's and women's sections, but they're now both open to everybody. These grand old halls are probably the most atmospheric part of the bath—slathered with colorful porcelain decorations. The former men's section is both hotter and more beautifully decorated than the women's section. (Hmmm...) I'd focus on the former men's section, which has big pools at either end: 36°C (97°F) and 38°C (100°F). Notice that these temperatures perfectly flank the normal temperature of the human body, allowing you to toggle your temp at will. At the far end of the bath are a steam room (45-50°C/113-122°F) and a cold plunge pool (18°C/64°F). Back out near the changing cabins is a dry sauna (a.k.a. "dry sweating rooms," 50-70°C/122-158°F). If you paid for a massage, report to the massage room in this section at your appointed time—or just show up and see if they can take you.

Outside, you'll find several sunbathing areas and a warm thermal pool, along with an atmospheric woody sauna and a big barrel-shaped plunge pool with cold water (all hiding up the stairs on the right). But the main attraction is the big, unheated wave pool in the center (generally closed Oct-April, weather dependent). Not for the squeamish, this pool thrashes fun-loving swimmers around like driftwood. The swells in the deeper area are fun and easy to float on, but the crashing waves at the shallow end are vigorous, if not dangerous. If there are no waves, just wait around for a while (you'll hear a garbled message on the loudspeaker five minutes before the tide comes in).

Rudas Baths (Rudas Fürdő)

To get to the Turkish roots of Budapest's obsession with thermal baths, head for Rudas (ROO-dawsh). Worth ▲▲, it's the most

historic, local, and potentially intimidating of the three baths I list—but it may also be the most rewarding, as it offers the most variety.

Rudas has two main sections: the dark, historic, mysterious-feeling Turkish-style thermal bath zone; and the modern, fun wellness/"sauna world"/swimming pool section. Visiting both sections provides a nice contrast (and a well-rounded bath experience) and is worth paying extra for. However, on certain days the thermal section may be open only to men or only to women, which may make the decision for you.

Overview: Rudas' **thermal section** feels more like the classic Turkish baths of yore—with an octagonal central pool under a 500-year-old dome first built by the Ottoman Turks. These baths are not about splashy fun—there are no jets, bubbles, or whirlpools. Instead, Rudas is about history and about serious temperature modulation—stepping your body temperature up and down between very hot and very cold. The thermal section is for men only on Mon and Wed-Fri, women only on Tue, and all visitors on Sat-Sun, when men and women mingle in swimsuits under the fine old dome. On Fri-Sat nights, it becomes a modern nightclub until the wee hours.

The **wellness area**—with a handful of relaxing jet pools—is the modern, accessible yin to the thermal baths' antique yang. Both men and women (in swimsuits) have access to the wellness area every day. The main reason to visit this section is the rooftop terrace, where you can sunbathe or soak while looking out over sweeping views of the Budapest skyline. Imagine: You're up to your earlobes in hot water, looking out over commuters slogging across the city's clogged bridges...and feeling pretty happy to be on vacation. The wellness area is also attached to a "sauna world" (with a half-dozen different wet or dry hot rooms) and a swimming pool—far less elegant than Gellért's and intended only for those who want to swim laps.

Cost: "All-in" ticket includes the entire complex—5,200 Ft weekdays, 6,500 Ft weekends; **thermal baths** only—3,700 Ft weekdays, discounted Mon-Fri 9:00-12:00, 4,300 Ft weekends; **wellness/saunas/pool** only—3,500 Ft weekdays, 4,800 Ft weekends.

Hours: Thermal bath open daily 6:00-20:00, wellness section daily 8:00-22:00, last entry one hour before closing. While the wellness area is mixed gender every day, the thermal baths are open only to men Mon and Wed-Fri, only to women Tue, and to both men and women Sat-Sun. The night bathing (described later) is also mixed gender.

Location: It's in a low-profile building at the foot of Gellért Hill, just south of the white Elisabeth Bridge (Döbrentei tér 9, district I, tel. 1/375-8373, www.rudasbaths.com). Trams #19 and #41, which run along the Buda embankment, stop right out front (Rudas Gyógyfürdő stop). Those trams also work from Szent Gellért tér, as do trams #56 and #56A or bus #7. From Pest, you can ride bus #7 from Astoria or Ferenciek tere to the Rudas Gyógyfürdő stop.

Night Bathing: The baths are open—to both men and women, in swimsuits—with a dance hall ambience Fri-Sat 22:00-late (5,100 Ft).

Entering the Baths: At the ticket desk, buy your ticket, and if you want, book a massage—either a relaxing "aroma relax massage" or a rougher, exfoliating "water massage with soap" in a noisy, busy room. If you want to rent a towel or a swimsuit, you'll do so inside (find the desk in your changing area before you change, as you'll need cash).

Head inside. If you're doing the thermal bath only, you'll enter on the main floor into a corridor of wood changing cabins; press your wristband to the panel to be assigned a cabin. If you bought a wellness or "all-in" ticket, you'll go upstairs to a modern locker room, with men and women mixed (but with private cabins to change in). Choose any locker, and use your wristband to lock it.

Dress Code: In the wellness, sauna, and swimming pool areas, you'll wear your swimsuit everywhere. For the thermal bath area, if you're here on a mixed day, the dress code is swimsuits. On other days, bathers wear a flimsy loincloth called a *kötény* (issued as you enter). If you're a self-conscious, gawky tourist (it happens to the best of us), you can wear your swimsuit...although you might get some funny looks.

Taking the Waters: This complex has two completely different areas with completely different protocols: the thermal bath section and the wellness/sauna world/swimming pool section. With the "all-in" ticket, you can float freely between them (using your wristband to enter the turnstiles separating them).

Thermal Bath: Rudas' thermal bath transports you half a millennium back in time. The central chamber, under an original 35-foot-high Turkish dome supported by eight pillars, is the historic core of the baths. This area is all about modulating your body temperature—pushing your body to its limit with heat, then dousing off quickly with a bucket of cold water, then heating up again, and so on. Pools of different temperatures are designed to let you do this as gradually or quickly as you like.

The main, octagonal pool in the center is surrounded by four smaller pools, each labeled with its temperature: 28°C (82°F), 30°C (86°F), 33°C (91°F), and 42°C (108°F). Conveniently, the largest, central pool—at 36°C (97°F)—is not too hot, not too cold... juuuust right.

Along one wall are entrances to the wet sauna (*nedves gőzkamra*, to the left), with 50°C (122°F) scented steam; and the dry sauna (*hőlégkamra*, to the right), with three progressively hotter rooms ranging from 45°C (113° F) to 72°C (161°F). Near the entrance to each one is a shower or—if you don't want to beat around the bush—a bucket of frigid water (if you're overheated, pull the rope for immediate relief...and a jolt).

Surrounding this central chamber are hallways with other areas: resting rooms, tanning beds (*szolarium*, costs extra), massage rooms, a cold plunge pool, and a scale to see how much sweat you've lost.

Float on your back for a while in the main octagonal pool, pondering the faintly glittering translucent tiles embedded in the dome. You'll notice that the voices echoing around that dome are mostly Hungarian—there are very few tourists here.

To move between the thermal bath and wellness sections, you'll cross through the lobby, past a snack bar, and use your wristband to go through the turnstile.

Wellness/Sauna/Pool: First you'll walk along the swimming pool (for laps, swim cap required)—either at pool level or upstairs along an outdoor sun terrace. Once you're in the far building, upstairs is the sauna world, where you can move between a variety of steam rooms and dry saunas—Finnish sauna, aroma sauna, even a salt sauna.

At the far end is the wellness area. The first room, with a huge window looking out over the busy embankment road, has three pools of different temperatures (32°C/90°F, 36°C/97°F, and a sweltering 42°C/108°F), all with powerful massage jets. In the cold plunge pool (12-14°C/54-57°F), notice the ice maker that continually drops in a cube or two, every few seconds. Thirsty? Get a drink at the stately ram's-head tiled fountains that line the walls.

But the real highlight of the wellness area is upstairs: At the end of the room, find the staircase and head on up, passing the restaurant on your way to the rooftop terrace. While other Budapest baths envelop you in opulent architecture, this is the only one that envelops you in Budapest itself. Whether soaking in rays on the sun deck or taking a dip in the 36°C/97°F thermal pool, you're surrounded by the bustle of the city. Scanning the horizon, you'll see a workaday burg going about its business...oblivious to the swimsuit-clad barnacle clinging to the base of Gellért Hill. Your solitude is broken only by the periodic rumble of trams trundling past on the road below you.

Leaving the Bath: After changing, return your rental towel and swimsuit to the attendant and get your receipt; present this at the front desk (along with your original towel receipt) to get your deposit back. Then drop your wristband through the little slot at the turnstile, head out the door, and stumble along the Danube...as relaxed as you'll ever be.

Aaaaahhh.

Entertainment in Budapest

Budapest is a great place to catch a good—and inexpensive—musical performance. In fact, music lovers from Vienna often make the three-hour trip here just to take in a fine opera in a luxurious setting at a bargain price. Options range from a performance at one of the world's great opera houses to light, touristy Hungarian folk concerts. The tourist concerts are the simplest option—you'll see fliers everywhere—but if you appreciate great music, do some homework to find real quality.

Locals dress up for the more "serious" concerts and opera, but many tourists wear casual clothes—as long as you don't show up in shorts, sneakers, or flip-flops, you'll be fine.

The following **helpful websites** offer current advice on cultural events and nightlife in Budapest: www.wherebudapest.hu (gen-

eral), www.funzine.hu (general, with a younger bent), www.servus.
hu (culture, also available in print), www.est.hu (general), www.
muzsikalendarium.hu (classical music), www.welovebudapest.com
(general), and www.xpatloop.com. At many places you can buy
tickets directly, or for many Budapest events, tickets are available
at www.jegymester.hu and www.kulturinfo.hu.

What's on can vary by **season.** Some of the best nightclubs
and bars are partly or entirely outdoors, so they're far more enjoyable in the summer. Meanwhile, the Hungarian State Opera, Puppet Theater, and other indoor cultural events tend to take a summer
break from late June into early September (though that's prime time
for outdoor music and Hungária Koncert's touristy shows).

For a list of some local **festivals,** which often include excellent
live music, see "Holidays & Festivals" in the appendix.

A Night at the Opera

Take in an opera by one of the best companies in Europe, in one
of Europe's loveliest opera houses, for bargain prices. The Hungarian State Opera performs almost
nightly (except late June through
early September), both at the
main **Opera House** (Andrássy
út 22, district VI, M1: Opera,
see page 600) and in the **Erkel
Színház theater** (not nearly as
impressive—described under
"Other Venues," later). If you
want classical opulence, choose
a performance in the Opera

House, which is scheduled to reopen in time for the 2019-2020
season. Most performances are in the original language with Hungarian and English supertitles.

Ticket prices range from 1,500 to 20,000 Ft, but the best
music deal in Europe may be the 600-Ft, obstructed-view tickets
(easy to get, as they rarely run out—even when other tickets are
sold out). If you buy one of these $2 opera tickets, you can choose
whether to sit and see nothing, or stand and crane your neck to see
about half the stage. Either way, you'll hear every note along with
the big spenders.

To get tickets, book online (www.opera.hu or www.jegy.hu),
print your ticket, and waltz right in. Or you can book by phone
with a credit card (tel. 1/353-0170, phone answered daily 10:00-
20:00), then pick up your ticket at the Opera House before the
performance. Maybe best of all, just drop by in person and see
what's available during your visit. There are often a few tickets for
sale at the door, even if it's supposedly "sold out" (box office open

Mon-Sat from 11:00 until show time—generally 19:00, or until 17:00 if there's no performance; Sun open three hours before the performance—generally 16:00-19:00, or 10:00-13:00 if there's a matinee). If you're desperate to attend a specific performance and it looks sold out online, don't give up: Try calling or stopping by the Opera House, or ask your hotelier. There's almost always a way to get a ticket.

Tourist Concerts by Hungária Koncert

Hungária Koncert offers a wide range of made-for-tourists performances of traditional music. Most of these take place in the **Duna Palota** ("Danube Palace")—formerly the Budapest Ritz, three long blocks north of Vörösmarty tér in Pest (behind Széchenyi tér and the Gresham Palace at Zrínyi utca 5, district V, M1: Vörösmarty tér). A few performances may take place at the gorgeous **Pesti Vigadó** concert hall, right along the river in central Pest (see "Other Venues," next), or at the **Budai Vigadó** concert hall, on the Buda embankment near Batthyány tér.

While highbrow classical music buffs will want a more serious concert, these shows are crowd-pleasers. The most popular options are **Hungarian Folklore** music-and-dance shows by various interchangeable troupes (7,200-10,900 Ft, May-Oct Sun-Fri at 20:00, once weekly through much of the winter, at Duna Palota or Budai Vigadó) and the **Budapest Gala Concert,** mixing classical "greatest hits" with some folkloric music, ballet, and opera (10,200-12,600 Ft, May-Oct Sat at 20:00, usually at Duna Palota but occasionally at Pesti Vigadó). Or you can take in an **organ concert** at St. István's Basilica (see "Other Venues," below).

For any performance, book direct (RS%—10 percent off when you book directly in person, by phone, or by email; on their website, you can book the "student rate"; discount may not be honored if you buy your tickets through your hotel). The main office is in the Duna Palota at Zrínyi utca 5 (daily 9:00-22:00, winter until 20:00, tel. 1/317-2754 or 1/317-1377, www.budapestxplore.com, frontoffice@hungariagroup.com).

Other Venues

Budapest has many other grand spaces for enjoying a performance. You can find details for each of these on their websites.

The **Franz Liszt Academy of Music** (Liszt Ferenc Zeneművészeti Egyetem, a.k.a. Zeneakadémia), on Franz Liszt Square, hosts high-quality professional concerts every night. Re-

BUDAPEST

stored to its stunning late-19th-century splendor, this venue rivals even the Opera House for opulence—if attending a concert, make sure it's in the Grand Hall, or Nagyterem (just off of Andrássy út at Liszt Ferenc tér 8, M1: Oktogon, www.zeneakademia.hu). They also do one-hour guided tours of the theater in English, daily at 13:30 (3,500 Ft, includes brief concert by a student).

The **former Academy of Music** (Régi Zeneakadémia)—just up Andrássy út near the House of Terror—houses the Franz Liszt Museum and hosts performances on Saturday mornings at 11:00 (Vörösmarty utca 35, www.lfze.hu).

The **Pesti Vigadó** ("Pest Concert Hall"), gorgeously restored and sitting proudly on the Pest embankment, is another fine place for a concert in elegant surroundings (Vigadó tér 1, www.vigado. hu).

The city's two finest churches—both with sumptuous interiors—host tourist-oriented concerts. As these are operated by different companies, you'll have to do a little homework to understand all of your options. Most of the shows in **St. István's Basilica** are organ concerts—including one by Hungária Koncert that usually mixes Bach and Mozart with Liszt or Bartók—along with some by classical ensembles (www.organconcert.hu or www.concertsinbudapest.com). Up on Castle Hill, **Matthias Church** hosts a variety of touristy shows, from organ recitals to string orchestras (www.matyas-templom.hu).

The **National Dance Theater** (Nemzeti Táncszínház) puts on performances ranging from ballet to folk to contemporary at various venues around town, including the Palace of Arts (at the Millennium City Center—see below), the MOM Cultural Center (near the Great Synagogue, at Csörsz utca 18), and the Royal Garden Pavilion in the Várkert Bázár complex, along the Buda riverbank just below the Royal Palace (www.dancetheatre.hu).

The **Millennium City Center** complex, sitting on the Pest riverbank near the Rákóczi Bridge south of downtown (district IX, ride tram #2 south along the Pest embankment to the Millenniumi Kulturális Központ stop), is a state-of-the-art facility with multiple venues. The **Palace of Arts** (Művészetek Palotája) features art installations as well as musical performances in two venues: the 1,700-seat Béla Bartók National Concert Hall and the 460-seat Festival Theater (www.mupa.hu). The **National Theater** (Nemzeti Színház) presents mostly Hungarian-language drama and lectures (www.nemzetiszinhaz.hu).

Nightlife in Budapest

In addition to strolling the floodlit promenades and taking an after-hours dip at a thermal bath (Széchenyi and Rudas are both partly open late—see "Experiences in Budapest," earlier), here are some ideas for after-hours fun.

Yuppie Drinking Zones

The plaza in front of **St. István's Basilica** is Budapest's most fashionable locale for a glass of wine. Of the many upscale restaurants and bars in this area, DiVino—a bar with contemporary decor and a wide range of Hungarian wines by the glass—is a good choice (see "Eating in Budapest," later).

Franz Liszt Square (Liszt Ferenc tér), a leafy and inviting zone just off Andrássy út, is lined with mostly tourist-oriented bars. The pedestrianized **Ráday utca,** near Kálvin tér just north of the Great Market Hall, has a similar scene.

For something a bit more genteel—evocative of this city's late-19th-century Golden Age—locals pass their evenings sipping wine or nibbling dessert at a **café** (see "Budapest's Café Culture" on page 669).

Ruin Pubs

These lively pubs are filled with ramshackle secondhand furniture, a bohemian-junkyard vibe—and plenty of drinkers (both locals and tourists) having the time of their lives. Think of it as pretending you're a squatter for a few hours, before returning to the comfort of your hotel.

Each ruin pub *(rom-kocsma)* is different—from mellow hangouts to hopping dance clubs—so survey several to find your favorite. Most of the clientele is in their 20s or 30s, but hip oldsters feel perfectly welcome. While some ruin pubs are edgy and high-energy, others are more fit for a hammock. To seek out your ideal ruin pub, know the terminology. A ruin pub may bill itself as a *mulató* (club, usually higher-energy) or a *kávézó* (coffeehouse, usually mellower). In good weather, the best part of a ruin pub is outdoors. Many have a *kert* ("garden"), filling deteriorating buildings' courtyards with strings of lights, hammocks, mismatched chandeliers, parachute-quilt awnings, lush houseplants, and artful graffiti. Others have a *tető* ("rooftop"), where you can get some fresh air and—often—views over the floodlit city. In winter or bad weather, find one with a cozy interior. The bigger ruin pubs

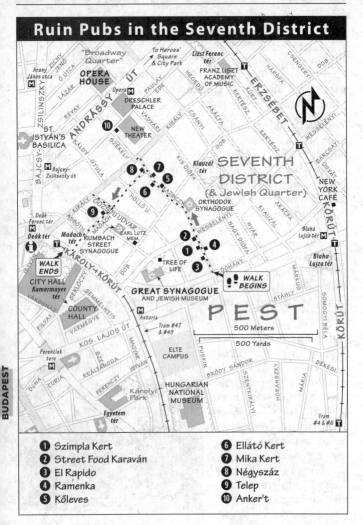

Ruin Pubs in the Seventh District

1 Szimpla Kert
2 Street Food Karaván
3 El Rapido
4 Ramenka
5 Kőleves

6 Ellátó Kert
7 Mika Kert
8 Négyszáz
9 Telep
10 Anker't

often have a burly bouncer stationed outside—but curious travelers are more than welcome. For more info, including additional listings, see www.ruinpubs.com.

Ruin-Pub Crawl in the Seventh District: Budapest's Seventh District—the historic Jewish Quarter, behind the Great Synagogue—has emerged as the city's prime nightlife zone for both locals and visitors. The neighborhood teems with clubs, bars, and creative little hole-in-the-wall eateries. Why are so many of these funky bars concentrated in the Jewish Quarter? Because it's conveniently central, yet remained largely deserted and dilapidated after the communists took over—keeping rents very low and fostering just the right rickety-chic vibe for ruin pub purveyors.

This little pub crawl connects my four favorite ruin pubs, all within a few short blocks on Kazinczy street: Szimpla, Kőleves, Ellátó, and Mika. I'd head for a nice dinner in the Seventh District (see recommendations in "Eating in Budapest," later), then check out this scene to see what appeals. If you only have time and interest for one, head straight to the first and best, Szimpla. With a little more time and a spirit of adventure, check out the others as well.

This area can be very lively any night of the week (especially in good weather), but it's best Thursday through Saturday. During the peak of summer (July-Aug), most Budapesters are out of town on holiday, making this scene a bit more touristy.

The first stop, Szimpla, is situated in the middle of this district, a couple of blocks behind the Great Synagogue, between the busy streets Wesselényi and Dohány. Just look for the street with a hubbub of nightlife and cheap eateries.

Szimpla Kert ("Simple Garden") sprawls through an old building that ought to be condemned, and spills out into an equally shoddy courtyard. Surrounding the garden is a warren of tiny rooms—each one different. It's on the route of the tourist pub-crawls, so it's gotten pretty touristy. Still, it's an amazing scene. There's live music in a soundproof concert room, and a selection of decent food upstairs (Szimpla Kitchen has the most serious menu). For a more sophisticated corner, drop by the Saloon (air-conditioned, upstairs above the front door); there's a craft beer bar and Fussball room next to the Saloon. As you enter, pick up the Szimpla map/program to get a sense of its community mission (Mon-Fri 12:00-late, Sat-Sun 9:00-late, Kazinczy utca 14, www.szimpla.hu). This space hosts Hungarian Folk Dances on Monday evenings, and a farmers market on Sunday mornings (9:00-14:00). **Note:** The building that Szimpla occupies has reportedly been sold to an investor. It's possible that it may relocate—but as the neighborhood's big trendsetter, there's very little chance it'd go away entirely. If it's not here, ask around or check their website.

Szimpla anchors a street of imitators and hangers-on, though none of them qualify as "ruin pubs." However, this is a good place to find street food. Next door to Szimpla is the handy **Street Food Karaván** food truck pod (see "Eating in Budapest," later); nearby you'll find tacos (El Rapido, at #11), ramen noodles (Ramenka, at #9), and lots more.

BUDAPEST

Let's continue with the crawl: With Szimpla at your back, turn left and walk along Kazinczy utca. You'll cross Wesselényi utca, then pass the Orthodox Synagogue (on your right). Crossing Dob street, partway down the next block on your right (on #41) is the garden *(kert)* for **Kőleves** ("Stone Soup"). The ruin pub garden has lazy hammocks and a nice, mellow vibe; it feels a bit more mature, without the stag-party chaos of some. They have basic food in the garden, and the attached restaurant has good sit-down meals (see "Eating in Budapest," later).

Continue along Kazinczy utca. A bit farther, on the left at #48, is **Ellátó Kert** ("Supplier")—a mostly outdoor ruin pub with mismatched furniture under tents, and with Latino flair and food. Since it's hidden farther down the alley, it gets fewer tourist drop-ins, and feels more purely local.

Nearly across the street (at #47) is another good ruin pub garden, **Mika Kert,** with more of a beer-garden feel.

From here, nightlife sprawls in all directions. While not quite "ruin pubs," if you're enjoying yourself, follow this little extension to some additional memorable spots: Carry on along Kazinczy. A few steps past Mika Kert, on the left, make your way down the **unnamed alley** (marked by Piritós), and plunge into the cacophony of a bewildering variety of outdoor bars, cafés, and nightspots. The best of these is probably **Négyszáz** ("400"), flanking the alley (officially at Kazinczy 52).

Continuing straight ahead to the end of the lane, you enter right into the middle of the long series of courtyards called **Gozsdu Udvar.** Stretching in both directions, Gozsdu Udvar is jammed with lively bars, cafés, and restaurants. Exploring here is a fun way to finish your ruin-pub evening.

Note that several additional ruin pubs (and similar nightspots) are close by (5-10 minutes walking). Peruse the list below and go explore.

More Ruin Pubs: Telep ("Site") is a tumble-down secondhand bar incongruously located in a residential and office-block neighborhood just around the corner from the heart of the ruin-pub scene (steps from Gozsdu Udvar). There's an art gallery upstairs, and often live music (Madách Imre utca 8, just off Rumbach utca, http://telepgaleria.tumblr.com).

Anker't, a young, brash, and slightly snooty offshoot of a popular nightclub (Anker), has a minimalist charm. It's conveniently located a short block off Andrássy út—look for the |A| sign (across the street from the Opera House at Paulay Ede utca 33).

Summer Terraces (Tető)

In addition to *kert* ("garden"), a key term for enjoying Budapest in the summer is *tető* ("roof"). Rooftop terraces offer laid-back scenery

high above the congested city. Most roof terraces are open only in the summer (typically May-Sept), in good weather, and start serving drinks and light food around midafternoon. Several offer live music. While this is an emerging scene, here are a few places worth checking out:

360 Bar is on the roof of the old Párisi Nagy Áruház (Andrássy út 39, www.360bar.hu).

High Note Sky Bar has vivid yellow sofas and point-blank views of St. István's. Don't miss the glassed-in passage that leads to spiral stairs up to the two towers—both of which offer even higher, better, unobstructed views (atop the Aria Hotel at Hercegprímás utca 5, www.ariahotelbudapest.com).

Top Rum Sky & Bar in Pest's Town Center overlooks University Square. This one is mostly enclosed (though the roof can roll back), and comes with a younger but still upscale atmosphere, including furry chairs (atop Rum Hotel at Királyi Pál utca 4, www.hotelrumbudapest.com).

Danube Riverbank Bars at the Chain Bridge

Two bars with very different characters flank the Chain Bridge on the Pest side, offering views of the landmark bridge and the castle. This is a fine spot at twilight—when the castle is floodlit, the bridge's lights twinkle on, and the sky is a hazy purple.

The more upscale-feeling option is **Raqpart,** with a modern vibe (in front of the Hotel InterContinental on Jane Haining rakpart, www.raqpart.hu). On the same side of the Danube just north of the bridge, **Pontoon** feels more rustic and downscale...almost like a ruin pub, with cheap plastic furniture spilling out under the trees onto the embankment (Antall József rakpart 1).

Local Craft Beer and Hungarian Wine

Craft Beer: Budapest has an increasing number of pubs specializing in both Hungarian and international microbrews. If you're a beer pilgrim, consider one of these places. **Keg Sörművház,** a long block up from the Gellért Baths (and Szent Gellért tér tram and Metró stop), is a nondescript cellar with 32 craft beers on tap, flashing on the electronic menu board (Orlay utca 1). **Jonás,** at the

BUDAPEST

far end of the "Whale" building (Bálna)—get it?—is another good option for trying craft beers on tap. It's less about the beer and more about the setting—with lots of outdoor tables arrayed along the Danube (Fővám tér 11).

Wine: If you prefer grapes to hops, there are several great spots to sample Hungarian wine. For perhaps the best option—with a wide range of choices available by the glass, and lively outdoor seating on the lovely Szent István tér—check out **DiVino Wine Bar** (see "Eating in Budapest," later). For top-end wines by one particularly renowned vintner, check out the **St. Andrea Wine & Gourmet Bar,** near the Nyugati/Western train station (Bajcsy-Zsilinszky út 78).

Shopping in Budapest

While it's not quite a shopper's mecca, Budapest does offer some enjoyable opportunities to hunt for that perfect Hungarian souvenir.

For a look at local life and a chance to buy some mementos, Budapest's single best shopping venue is the **Great Market Hall** (described on page 592). In addition to all the colorful produce downstairs, the upstairs gallery is full of fiercely competitive souvenir vendors. There's also a **folk-art market on Castle Hill** (near the bus stop at Dísz tér), but it's generally more touristy and a little more expensive. And, while **Váci utca** has been Budapest's main shopping thoroughfare for generations, today it features the city's highest prices and worst values.

For something a bit less touristy, drop by the **Bálna ("Whale") Cultural Center,** which sits along the Danube just behind the Great Market Hall. You'll see some souvenir stands similar to what's upstairs in the Great Market Hall, as well as a few one-off designers. While it may be potluck for shoppers, it's worth exploring—and the architecture is interesting.

As a big, cosmopolitan capital, Budapest has its share of international fashion boutiques. Most of these are along or near **Deák utca** (called "Fashion Street," connecting Vörösmarty tér and Deák tér), or along the first stretch of **Andrássy út.** A few more big-ticket shops are along and near **Váci utca,** with an intriguing cluster along the cross-street **Irányi utca** (just south of Ferenciek tere, near the river in the Town Center). A block over, at Nyáry Pál utca 7, **Eventuell Gallery** displays and sells the works of local designers (www.eventuell.hu).

To see how Hungarian urbanites renovate their flats, don't miss the home-improvement shops that line **Király utca,** which runs parallel to Andrássy út (two short blocks south). For a taste of the good old days—which somehow just feels right, here in nostalgic Budapest—wander up the city's **"antique row,"** Falk Miksa utca, just north of the Parliament.

Budapesters do most of their shopping in big, American-style **shopping malls**—three of which are downtown (most shops generally open Mon-Sat 10:00-21:00, Sun until 18:00):

• **WestEnd City Center,** next door to Nyugati/Western train station (Váci út 1, district VI, M3: Nyugati pu., tel. 1/374-6573, www.westend.hu)

• **Mammut** ("Mammoth"), two separate malls a few steps from Buda's Széll Kálmán tér (Lövőház utca 2, district II, M2: Széll Kálmán tér, tel. 1/345-8020, www.mammut.hu)

• **Arena Plaza,** near Keleti/Eastern train station (Kerepesi út 9, district XIV, M2: Keleti pu., tel. 1/880-7000, www.arenaplaza.hu)

Souvenir Ideas

The most popular souvenir is that quintessential Hungarian spice, **paprika.** Sold in metal cans, linen bags, or porcelain vases—and often accompanied by a tiny wooden scoop—it's a nice way to spice up your cooking with memories of your trip. (But remember that only sealed containers will make it through customs on your way back home.) For more, see "Paprika Primer" on page 542.

Special drinks are a fun souvenir, though they're tricky to bring home (you'll have to wrap them very carefully and put them in your checked luggage). Good choices include the unique Hungarian spirit **Unicum** or a bottle of Hungarian **wine** (such as the famous Tokaji Aszú). For more on these drinks, see page 543.

Another popular item is a hand-embroidered **linen tablecloth.** The colors are often red and green—the national colors of Hungary—but white-on-white designs are also available (and classy). If the thread is thick and the stitching is very even, it was probably done by machine, and obviously is less valuable.

Other handicrafts to look for include **chess sets** (most from Transylvania) and **nesting dolls.** While these dolls have more to do with Russia than with Hungary, you'll see just about every modern combination available: from classic peasant-girl *matryoshkas,* to Russian heads of state, to infamous terrorists, to American presidents. Tacky...but fun.

Fans of **communist kitsch** can look for ironic T-shirts that poke fun at that bygone era. The best selection is at the Memento Park gift shop, which also sells communist memorabilia and CDs of commie anthems.

For a wearable souvenir, **Tisza shoes** (Tisza Cipő) are retro and newly hip. The company dates from communist times, but went bust when Western brands became widely available. Recently, the brand was rescued by an investor with a renewed dedication to quality. They make both athletic and work shoes, as well as bags, shirts, and accessories. While you'll find Tisza products sold around the country, their flagship store is along the Small Boulevard near the Great Synagogue (at Károly körút 1, www.tiszacipo.hu).

Hipster Design and Vintage

Budapest is becoming a hipster mecca, and that means fun and idiosyncratic design, home decor, and vintage shops are popping up all around town. The fast-evolving scene makes it tricky to recommend a specific shop, but many intriguing boutiques have emerged in the **Seventh District/"Ruin Pub" zone.** Scout the possibilities on Király (with an emphasis on home decor), Dob, Rumbach, Dohány, Wesselényi, Kazinczy, and neighboring streets. **Printa,** a print shop and coffeehouse, is one reliable place to get a taste of the neighborhood's vendors. **Szimpla**—the original ruin pub—hosts a colorful farmers market each Sunday (9:00-14:00, Kazinczy utca 14, www.szimpla.hu).

Very nearby—just across Andrássy út from the Seventh District—you'll also find a smattering of intriguing shops along **Hajós utca,** behind the Opera House.

Check to see if you're in town for the **Wamp Design Fair.** One or two Sundays each month, dozens of local artists and designers gather to show off their products (free entry, 11:00-19:00, schedule at www.wamp.hu). In summer, this takes place in the city-center Elisabeth Square, while off-season it moves to an indoor venue at Millenáris Park (on the Buda side, near M2: Széll Kálmán tér).

Sleeping in Budapest

Before choosing a hotel, consider the pros and cons of the neighborhood. Most travelers find staying in Pest more convenient than sleeping in Buda. Most sights worth seeing are in Pest, which also has a much higher concentration of Metró and tram stops, making it a snap to get around. Pest feels more lively and local than stodgy, touristy Buda, but it's also much more urban. If you don't enjoy big cities, sleep in Buda instead.

In Budapest, most hotels quote rates in euros (for the convenience of international guests), and I've ranked them the same way. However, most places prefer to be paid in forints. If paying with credit card and given a choice of currencies, choose forints to avoid excessive conversion fees. The majority of hotels don't include the 4 percent tourist tax in their rates.

For some travelers, short-term, Airbnb-type rentals can be a good alternative; search for places in my recommended hotel neighborhoods. For proximity to sights and restaurants, aim for something within Pest's Great Boulevard (though staying outside

Sleep Code

Hotels in this book are categorized according to the average price of a standard double room with breakfast in high season.

$$$$	**Splurge:** Most rooms over €170 (53,000 Ft)
$$$	**Pricier:** €130-170 (40,500-53,000 Ft)
$$	**Moderate:** €90-130 (28,000-40,500 Ft)
$	**Budget:** €50-90 (15,500-28,000 Ft)
¢	**Backpacker:** Under €50 (15,500 Ft)
RS%	**Rick Steves discount**

Unless otherwise noted, credit cards are accepted, English is spoken, and free Wi-Fi is available. Comparison-shop by checking prices at several hotels (on each hotel's own website, on a booking site, or by email). For the best deal, *book directly with the hotel.* Ask for a discount if paying in cash; if the listing includes **RS%,** request a Rick Steves discount.

of that zone is cheaper). Within this core, the Seventh District/ Jewish Quarter has great restaurants and nightlife, but can be very noisy. Leopold Town—between the Parliament and Chain Bridge—is quiet and central, but with fewer restaurants. The Town Center (Belváros) is convenient, but areas near the Váci utca walking street feel more touristy and can suffer from some noise. Andrássy út (and neighboring streets)—particularly the near side of the Oktogon—is a fine and fun zone, but be aware that apartments facing the boulevard can come with street noise. For a more sedate, less urban environment, look on the Buda side; around the base of Castle Hill (Víziváros, facing the river, is convenient and scenic).

I rank accommodations from **$** budget to **$$$$** splurge. To get the best deal, contact my family-run accommodations directly by phone or email. For more information on rates and deals, making reservations, finding a short-term rental, and more, see the "Sleeping" section in the Practicalities chapter.

PEST

I've arranged my listings by neighborhood, clustered around the most important sightseeing sectors.

Near Andrássy Út

Andrássy Boulevard is handy, local-feeling, and endlessly entertaining. With its ample restaurants, upscale-residential vibe, and easy connection to downtown (via the M1/yellow line), it's the neighborhood where I prefer to sleep. The first three places listed are comparably priced, professional, and ideally located, close to the Opera House.

BUDAPEST

$$$ K+K Hotel Opera, wonderfully situated beside the Opera House, has 200 classy rooms and helpful, professional service. The rates are variable, but you can often land a great value (aircon, elevator, pay parking garage, Révay utca 24, district VI, M1: Opera, tel. 1/269-0222, www.kkhotels.com, reservations.opera@kkhotels.com).

$$$ Hotel Moments has 99 Art Deco rooms, a pristine atrium with iron railings, professional service, and a good location at the downtown end of Andrássy út, making this a fine choice at the higher end of this price range. Because it's surrounded by busy streets, light sleepers may be bothered by passing traffic (air-con, elevator, free coffee bar, Andrássy út 8, district VI, M1: Bajcsy-Zsilinszky út, tel. 1/611-7000, www.hotelmomentsbudapest.hu, reservation@hotelmoments.hu).

$$$ Casati Budapest Hotel is a solid value, and conveniently located a block off Andrássy út (across the boulevard from the Opera House, then down a side street). This classy, Swiss-run hotel has 25 rooms in four different styles, ranging from "classic" to "cool" (all the same price—review your options online and choose your favorite). Many rooms surround a peaceful courtyard—in this potentially noisy neighborhood, it's worth requesting one of these (air-con, elevator, free sauna and fitness room, Paulay Ede utca 31, district VI, M1: Opera, tel. 1/343-1198, www.casatibudapesthotel.hu, info@casatibudapesthotel.com).

$$ Kapital Inn is an upscale boutique B&B tucked behind the House of Terror. Its six rooms are perfectly stylish—there's not a pillow out of place. Albert, who lived in Boston, gives his B&B a sense of real hospitality. You'll enjoy the public spaces, from the restful, momentum-killing terrace to the giant kitchen, where Albert serves breakfast at a huge shared counter (cheaper room with shared bath, air-con, free communal minibar, pay laundry service, up several flights of stairs with no elevator, Aradi utca 30, district VI, M1: Vörösmarty utca, mobile +3630-915-2029, www.kapitalinn.com, kapitalinn@kapitalinn.com).

$$ Butterfly Home Penthouse B&B—run with care by András (OHN-drash) and Timea—has three rooms near the Oktogon (air-con, elevator, Teréz körút 1, 4th floor, suite #2, buzzer #44, district VI, M1: Oktogon, mobile +3630-964-7287, www.butterflyhome.hu, info@butterflyhome.hu). They also run **$ Budapest Bed and Breakfast,** with five cheaper, simple, yet well-equipped rooms farther from the center—in the quiet diplomatic quarter halfway between the Oktogon and City Park (air-con, a long block off Andrássy út at Benczúr utca 3, district VI, M1: Kodály körönd, mobile +3630-964-7287, info@butterflyhome.hu). And they rent rooms in the Town Center, near the Great Market Hall (see Butterfly Home Danube B&B, later).

Andrássy Út Hotels & Restaurants

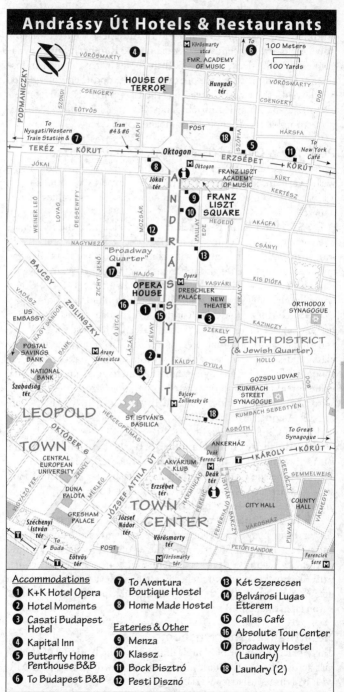

Accommodations

1. K+K Hotel Opera
2. Hotel Moments
3. Casati Budapest Hotel
4. Kapital Inn
5. Butterfly Home Penthouse B&B
6. To Budapest B&B
7. To Aventura Boutique Hostel
8. Home Made Hostel

Eateries & Other

9. Menza
10. Klassz
11. Bock Bisztró
12. Pesti Disznó
13. Két Szerecsen
14. Belvárosi Lugas Étterem
15. Callas Café
16. Absolute Tour Center
17. Broadway Hostel (Laundry)
18. Laundry (2)

In the Seventh District/Jewish Quarter: A short walk from Andrássy út, **$$ ROOMbach Hotel Budapest Center**—tucked down a gloomy but central street facing the Rumbach Street Synagogue—has 99 sleek, basic, smallish rooms with a stylish industrial-mod design. It feels modern and solid, and the triple-glazed windows do their best to keep out the ruin-pub noise (air-con, elevator, pay parking, Rumbach Sebestyén utca 14, tel. 1/413-0253, www.roombach.com, hotel@roombach.com).

Pest Town Center (Belváros), near Váci Utca

Most hotels on the very central and convenient Váci utca come with overly inflated prices. But these less-expensive options—just a block or two off Váci utca—offer some of the best values in Budapest.

$$$ Hotel Rum is a sleek retreat overlooking the rejuvenated University Square, in the heart of Pest's Town Center. Its 38 industrial-mod rooms come with concrete floors, subway tile, and ample style, and the top-floor bar has great views (air-con, elevator, Királyi Pál utca 4, district V, M3/M4: Kálvin tér, tel. 1/424-9060, www.hotelrumbudapest.com, hello@hotelrumbudapest.com).

$$ Gerlóczy Café & Rooms, which also serves good coffee and meals in its recommended café, is the best spot in central Budapest for affordable elegance. The 19 rooms, set around a classy old spiral-staircase atrium with a stained-glass ceiling, are thoughtfully and stylishly appointed. This gem is an exceptional value (breakfast extra, air-con, elevator, some street noise, just off Városház utca at Gerlóczy utca 1, district V, M3: Ferenciek tere or M2: Astoria or M1/M2/M3: Deák tér, tel. 1/501-4000, www.gerloczy.hu, info@gerloczy.hu).

$$ Butterfly Home Danube B&B, run by András (from the Butterfly Home Penthouse B&B, listed earlier), has eight rooms and Danube views (air-con, elevator, Fővám tér 2-3, 2nd floor, suite #2, district V, M4: Fővám tér, mobile +3630-964-7287, www.butterflyhome.hu, info@butterflyhome.hu).

$ Katona Apartments, with five simple units just around the corner from busy Ferenciek tere, is conscientiously run by János and Virág. It's a family-friendly budget option in the very center of the city, facing a drab—but appealingly quiet—central courtyard (no breakfast but kitchenette, air-con, elevator, Petőfi Sándor utca 6, mobile +3670-221-1797, www.katonaapartments.hu, info@katonaapartments.hu).

Near the National Museum

These places are within a couple of blocks of the National Museum, just across the Small Boulevard from the Town Center, near M3/M4: Kálvin tér (district VIII).

$$ Brody House, a hipster hangout with sprawling public spaces, began as an art gallery that provided a place for its guests to crash, and has evolved into a comfortable, full-service B&B. With a trendy, scuffed, ruin-pub vibe, it's classy yet ramshackle. It fills three spacious floors of a townhouse with eight rooms and three apartments that all ooze a funky, idiosyncratic style. Each room is named for an artist who once used it as a studio (breakfast extra, air-con in most rooms, two stories up with no elevator, Bródy Sándor utca 10, tel. 1/266-1211, www.brody.land/brody-house, bookings@brody.land).

$ Budapest Rooms is a great budget option, where the Boda family rents five simple but surprisingly stylish, nicely appointed rooms in a dull residential zone (family room, one room has private bathroom across the hall, Szentkirályi 15, tel. 1/630-4743, mobile +3620-569-9513, www.budapestrooms.eu, info@budapestrooms.eu).

Leopold Town, near the Chain Bridge

The Four Seasons is the city's most prestigious address; the Starlight is a nicely located business-class option that is worth booking if you can get a discounted rate. Both are a short stroll from the delightful St. István tér/Zrínyi utca restaurant zone. For locations of these places, see the map on page 663.

$$$$ Four Seasons Gresham Palace is unquestionably Budapest's top hotel. Stay here only if money is truly no object. You'll sleep in what is arguably Budapest's finest Art Nouveau building. Damaged in World War II, the Gresham Palace sat in disrepair for decades. Today it sparkles from head to toe, and every detail in its lavish public spaces and 179 rooms is perfectly in place. Even if you're not sleeping here, dip into the lobby to soak in the elegance (air-con, elevator, top-floor spa, Széchenyi tér 5, district V, between M1: Vörösmarty tér and M2: Kossuth tér, tel. 1/268-6000, www.fourseasons.com/budapest, budapest.reservations@fourseasons.com). For more on the building's history, see page 588.

$$ Starlight Suiten has 54 spacious, good-value suites—each with a living room, bedroom, and kitchenette—on a sleepy, sterile street directly behind the Gresham Palace (air-con, elevator, free fitness room and sauna, Mérleg utca 6, district V, M1: Vörösmarty tér, tel. 1/484-3700, www.starlighthotels.com, reservation.starlight@cpihotels.com).

Apartments near Leopold Town: $ GuestBed Budapest has a few apartments scattered around town (two in a mellow residential zone north of Leopold Town, near the Margaret Bridge and the Great Boulevard, and another near the Opera House—all well-described on their website). The apartments all come with full kitch-

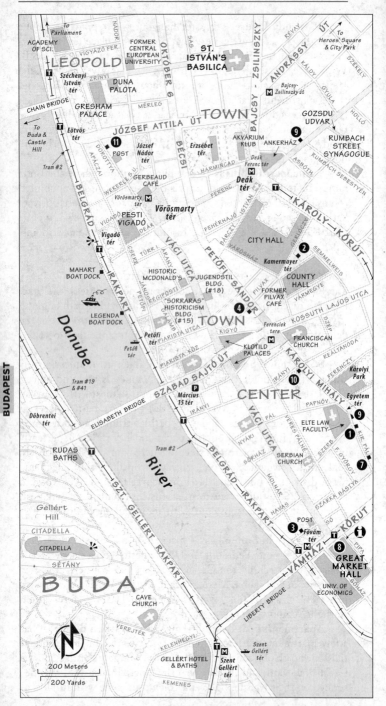

BUDAPEST

To Parliament

ACADEMY OF SCI.

LEOPOLD

VIGYÁZÓ FER.

Széchenyi István tér

ZRÍNYI

DUNA PALOTA

FORMER CENTRAL EUROPEAN UNIVERSITY

OKTÓBER 6

SAS

ST. ISTVÁN'S BASILICA

BAJCSY - ZSILINSZKY

RÉVAY

ANDRÁSSY   ÚT

To Heroes' Square & City Park

KÁLDY

SZEKELY

CHAIN BRIDGE

GRESHAM PALACE

MÉRLEG

JÓZSEF ATTILA ÚT

BÉCSI

TOWN

Bajcsy-Zsilinszky út

GYULA

HOLLÓ

GOZSDU UDVAR

RUMBACH STREET SYNAGOGUE

To Buda & Castle Hill

Tram #2

Eötvös tér

11 POST

APÁCZAI

DOROTTYA

WEKERLE U.

József Nádor tér

GERBEAUD CAFÉ

Vörösmarty tér

Erzsébet tér

AKVÁRIUM KLUB

ANKERHÁZ 9

Deák Ferenc tér

HÁRMINCAD

FERENC

Deák tér

T

KÁROLY - KÖRÚT

RUMBACH SEBESTYÉN

ASBÓTH

PESTI VIGADÓ

VIGADÓ

DEÁK

Vörösmarty tér

FEHÉRHAJÓ ISTVÁN

BARCZY

CITY HALL

GERLÓCZY

SEMMELWEIS

Vigadó tér

CSERE

TÜRR I.

ARANY

VÁCI UTCA

Kamermayer tér

COUNTY HALL

2

MAHART BOAT DOCK

HISTORIC MCDONALD'S

JÁNOS

RÉGIPOSTI

YAKOSHAZ

PETŐFI SÁNDOR

FORMER PILVAX CAFÉ

VÁRMEGYE

LEGENDA BOAT DOCK

JUGENDSTIL BLDG. (#18)

"SORRARAS" HISTORICISM BLDG. (#15)

PILVAX

KOSSUTH LAJOS UTCA

SZEP

Danube

Petőfi tér

Petőfi tér

PIARISTA UTCA

TOWN

KIGYÓ

4

Ferenciek tere

M

FRANCISCAN CHURCH

REÁLTANODA

FERENCZY

Károlyi Park

Tram #19 & #41

PIARISTA KÖZ

KLOTILD PALACES

KÁROLYI MIHÁLY

Károlyi tér

Egyetem tér

Döbrentei tér

ELISABETH BRIDGE

SZABAD SAJTÓ ÚT

Március 15 tér

P

IRÁNYI

CENTER

10

VÁCI UTCA

PAPNÖV.

9

ELTE LAW FACULTY

1

KIR. PÁL

RUDAS BATHS

Tram #2

IRÁNYI

BELGRÁD - RAKPART

PÁL

NYÁRI

VERES PÁLNÉ

SERBIAN CHURCH

SZERB

E. GYÖRGY

7

River

BÖRHÁZ

MOLNÁR

HAVAS

SZARKA BÁSTYA

SZT. GELLÉRT RAKPART

POST

3

Fővám tér

SÓ

VÁMHÁZ - KÖRÚT

i

Gellért Hill

CITADELLA

CITADELLA

SÉTÁNY

BUDA

CAVE CHURCH

VEREJTÉK

T

M

8

GREAT MARKET HALL

PIPA

UNIV. OF ECONOMICS

SZÓHÁZ

LIBERTY BRIDGE

N

200 Meters

200 Yards

KELENHEGYI

GELLÉRT HOTEL & BATHS

KEMENES

T

M

Szent Gellért tér

Szent Gellért tér

Pest Town Center Hotels & Restaurants

<u>Accommodations</u>
1. Hotel Rum
2. Gerlóczy Café & Rooms
3. Butterfly Home Danube B&B
4. Katona Apartments
5. Brody House
6. Budapest Rooms

<u>Eateries & Other</u>
7. Borssó Bistro
8. Great Market Hall
9. Hummus Bar (2)
10. Centrál Kávéház
11. Pharmacy

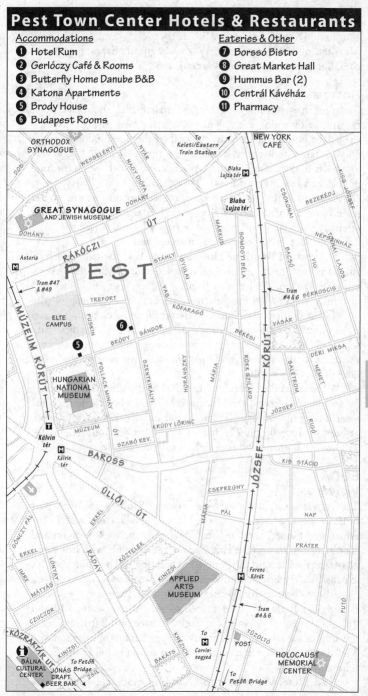

BUDAPEST

ens, and you'll enjoy the welcoming and conscientious owners, János and József (Katona József utca 39, district XIII, tram #4/#6: Jászai Mari tér, mobile +3670-258-5194, www.guestbudapestapartment. com, budapestrentapartment@gmail.com).

Hostels

Budapest has seemingly dozens of apartments that have been taken over by young entrepreneurs, offering basic, rough-around-the-edges hostel charm. You'll buzz in at the door and climb up a creaky, dank, and smelly staircase to a funky little enclave of fellow backpackers. Most of these places have just three rooms (one double and two small dorms). As each fills a niche (party, artsy, communist-themed, etc.), it's hard to recommend just one—read reviews on a hostel site (such as www.hostelworld.com) and find one that suits your philosophy. For hostel locations, see the "Andrássy Út Hotels & Restaurants" map, earlier.

¢ **Aventura Boutique Hostel** is a low-key, colorful, and stylish place in a dreary urban neighborhood near the Nyugati/Western train station. Well-run by friendly Ágnes, it's both homey and tastefully mod, with imaginatively decorated rooms (across the busy Great Boulevard ring road and a very long block from Nyugati train station at 12 Visegrádi utca, district XIII, M3: Nyugati pu., tel. 1/239-0782, www.aventurahostel.com, info@aventurahostel. com). They also rent several apartments—two nearby, the other near St. István's Basilica.

¢ **Home Made Hostel** is a fun-and-funky slumbermill artfully littered with secondhand furniture. With 20 beds in four rooms located near the Oktogon, it's managed and decorated with a sense of humor (Teréz körút 22, district VI, M1: Oktogon, tel. 1/302-2103, www.homemadehostel.com, info@homemadehostel.com).

BUDA
Víziváros

The Víziváros neighborhood—or "Water Town"—is the lively part of Buda squeezed between Castle Hill and the Danube, where fishermen and tanners used to live. Víziváros is the most pleasant and central area to stay on the Buda side of the Danube, with fine views across the river toward the Parliament building and bustling Pest. It's expensive and a little less convenient than Pest, but feels less urban.

The following hotels are in district I, between the Chain Bridge and Buda's busy Margit körút ring road. Trams #19 and #41 zip along the embankment in either direction. Batthyány tér, a few minutes' walk away, is a handy center with lots of restaurants, a Metró stop (M2/red line), and the HÉV train to Óbuda and Szentendre.

$$$ **Hotel Victoria,** with 27 stylish, spotless, business-class

rooms—each with a grand river view and attention to detail—is a class act. This tall, narrow place (three rooms on each of nine floors) is run with pride and attention to detail by on-the-ball manager Zoltán and his friendly staff (air-con, elevator, free sauna, free afternoon tea for guests 16:00-17:00, reserve ahead for pay parking garage, Bem rakpart 11, tel. 1/457-8080, www.victoria.hu, victoria@victoria.hu). The painstakingly restored 19th-century Hubay Palace behind the hotel (entrance next to reception) is used for concerts and other events. It feels like a museum, with inlaid floors, stained-glass windows, and stuccoed walls and ceilings.

$$$ At Art'otel, every detail—from the breakfast dishes to the carpets to the good-luck blackbird perched in each room—was designed by American artist Donald Sultan. This stylish hotel has 165 rooms spread between two attached buildings: the new section fronting the Danube and, just behind it, a restored older house with views of the castle (breakfast extra, air-con, elevator, free sauna and mini exercise room, Bem rakpart 16, tel. 1/487-9487, www.artotels.com, budapest@artotels.com).

$ Bellevue B&B hides in a quiet residential area on the Víziváros hillside, just below the Fisherman's Bastion staircase. This gem is owned by retired economists Judit (YOO-deet) and Lajos (LIE-yosh) Szuhay, who lived in Canada for four years; most days, you'll meet their right-hand man, Bálint. The breakfast room and some of the six straightforward, comfortable rooms have views across the Danube to the Parliament and Pest. Judit, Lajos, and Bálint love to chat, and pride themselves on offering genuine hospitality and a warm welcome—let them know what time you're arriving (cash only, air-con; M2: Batthyány tér plus a 10-minute uphill walk, or bus #16 from Deák, Széchenyi, or Clark Ádám squares to Dónati utca plus a 2-minute walk uphill, then downhill—they'll email you detailed directions; Szabó Ilonka utca 15/B, mobile +3630-964-7287, www.bellevuebudapest.com, judit@bellevuebudapest.com).

Castle Hill

Romantics may enjoy calling Castle Hill home (district I). These places couldn't be closer to the Castle Hill sights, but they're in a tourist zone—dead at night, and less convenient to Pest than other listings.

$$ St. George Residence, just a couple of short blocks from Matthias Church, is historical and classy. They rent 24 elegant rooms—each one different, all with kitchenettes—around a restful garden courtyard (air-con, Fortuna utca 4, tel. 1/393-5700, www.stgeorgehotel.hu, info@stgeorgehotel.hu).

$$ Burg Hotel, with 26 rooms on Holy Trinity Square (Szentháromság tér), is efficient: concrete, spacious, and comfy, if

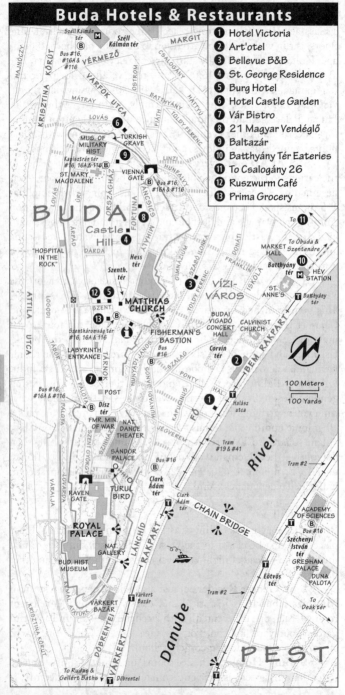

Buda Hotels & Restaurants

1 Hotel Victoria
2 Art'otel
3 Bellevue B&B
4 St. George Residence
5 Burg Hotel
6 Hotel Castle Garden
7 Vár Bistro
8 21 Magyar Vendéglő
9 Baltazár
10 Batthyány Tér Eateries
11 To Csalogány 26
12 Ruszwurm Café
13 Prima Grocery

a bit worn, with a professional staff. If you simply *must* stay in a modern hotel across the street from Matthias Church, this is it (RS%, request view room for no extra charge, family rooms, air-con, no elevator, top-floor rooms are extremely long, Szenthárom-ság tér 7, tel. 1/212-0269, www.burghotelbudapest.hu, info@ burghotelbudapest.hu).

$$ Hotel Castle Garden rents 39 businesslike rooms above an Italian restaurant in a tranquil, parklike neighborhood just outside the castle's Vienna Gate (north end). As it's roughly on the way between the castle and Széll Kálmán tér, it's relatively handy, though still less convenient than the Víziváros listings (air-con, elevator, pay parking garage, Lovas út 41, M2: Széll Kálmán tér; exit the castle through the Vienna Gate and turn left along the wall, or hike up from Széll Kálmán tér and turn right along the castle wall; tel. 1/224-7420, www.castlegarden.hu, hotel@castlegarden.hu).

Eating in Budapest

Budapest may be one of Europe's most underrated culinary destinations. Hungarian cuisine is excellent—rich, spicy, smooth, and delicious. And Budapest specializes in trendy restaurants that mix Hungarian flavors with international flair, making the food here even more interesting and fun to sample. Best of all, the prices are reasonable, especially if you venture off the main tourist trail.

Thanks to Budapest's fast-evolving culinary scene, there's no shortage of places to dine. It pays to research what's brand-new and hot; I've focused my listings on places that have been around long enough to be reliable.

International restaurants provide a break from Hungarian fare (in the unlikely event you need one). Budapest has abundant vegetarian, Italian, Indian, Chinese, and other non-Hungarian eateries; I've listed a few favorites.

EATING TIPS

I rank eateries from $ budget to $$$$ splurge. For a rundown of Hungarian cuisine and beverages, see page 540.

Tipping: Most restaurants in Budapest automatically add a service charge to the bill (look for "service," "tip," *felszolgálási díj*, or *szervízdíj*); if it's been included, an additional tip is not necessary. Otherwise, round up about 10 percent.

Dining Hours: Most Hungarians dine between 19:00 and 21:00, peaking around 20:00; trendy zones such as St. István Square and Franz Liszt Square, which attract an after-work crowd, are lively earlier in the evening.

Lunch Specials: Many Budapest restaurants—even some high-end places—offer affordable lunch specials, called *napimenü*,

BUDAPEST

Restaurant Code

Eateries in this book are categorized according to the average cost of a typical main course. Drinks, desserts, and splurge items can raise the price considerably.

$$$$ **Splurge:** Most main courses over 4,500 Ft
$$$ **Pricier:** 3,000-4,500 Ft
$$ **Moderate:** 2,000-3,000 Ft
$ **Budget:** Under 2,000 Ft

In Hungary, takeout food or a cafeteria-type place is **$;** an unpretentious sit-down eatery is **$$;** an upmarket but still casual restaurant is **$$$;** and a swanky splurge is **$$$$.**

on weekdays. As these are designed for local office workers on their lunch breaks rather than for tourists, they're often not advertised in English—but if you see the magic word *napimenü*, ask about it.

PEST

I've listed these options by neighborhood, emphasizing the areas with the best and most interesting options, for easy reference with your sightseeing.

Seventh District (Ruin-Pub Zone and Jewish Quarter)

Along with the rise of "ruin pubs" (see "Nightlife in Budapest," earlier), the Seventh District has seen the arrival of a world of great restaurants. While a few of these feature Jewish food (in a nod to this area's Jewish heritage), others are more eclectic, catering to a younger clientele.

$$$ Mazel Tov, one of Budapest's trendiest eateries (reserve ahead), fills a dilapidated old building at the edge of the ruin-pub zone. Stepping across the tattered threshold, you emerge into a vine-strewn, bare-brick courtyard where twinkling lights are strung over the hardworking open kitchen. With a wink to this district's Jewish origins, they serve creative cocktails and Israeli/Middle Eastern dishes like kebabs, shawarma, falafel, tabbouleh, and *shakshuka* (tomato-poached eggs). The joyful atmosphere captures Budapest's thriving foodie energy (Mon-Fri 12:00-late, Sat-Sun 10:00-even later, food until 23:00, Akácfa utca 47, district VII, between M1: Opera and M2: Blaha Lujza tér, mobile +3670-626-4280, www.mazeltov.hu).

$$$ KönyvBár & Restaurant, just around the corner from Mazel Tov, is refined, mellow, and creative. The small dining room feels like a sleek, minimalist library, and the menu has a fun literary theme (*könyv* means "book"). As it's small and all indoors, it can

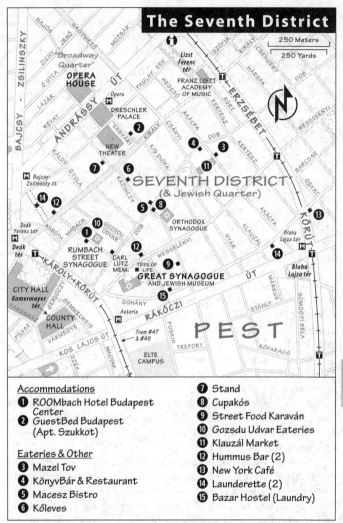

The Seventh District

250 Meters
250 Yards

Accommodations
1 ROOMbach Hotel Budapest Center
2 GuestBed Budapest (Apt. Szukkot)

Eateries & Other
3 Mazel Tov
4 KönyvBár & Restaurant
5 Macesz Bistro
6 Kőleves

7 Stand
8 Cupakós
9 Street Food Karaván
10 Gozsdu Udvar Eateries
11 Klauzál Market
12 Hummus Bar (2)
13 New York Café
14 Launderette (2)
15 Bazar Hostel (Laundry)

be warm. Bibliophiles should reserve ahead for an appealing dining experience (Mon-Sat 12:00-24:00, closed Sun, Dob utca 45, district VII, between M1: Opera and M2: Blaha Lujza tér, mobile +3620-922-7027, www.konyvbar.hu).

$$$ Macesz Bistro is a grandma's-dining-room-cozy corner restaurant serving traditional Jewish recipes with modern ingredients and technique. They also offer a seasonal menu of modern Israeli food—hummus, tabbouleh, and so on—making it easier for everyone to find something they'll like (daily 12:00-16:00 & 18:00-23:00, Dob utca 26, district VII, M1: Opera, tel. 1/787-6164).

$$ Kőleves ("Stone Soup"), filling an old kosher sausage factory, feels upscale and put-together without being stuffy. The eclectic, international menu includes several Jewish dishes. This is steps away from Macesz Bistro (see earlier), and worth trying if that place is full (daily 8:00-24:00, Kazinczy utca 41, district VII, M1: Opera, mobile +3620-213-5999). Their adjacent garden courtyard (one of several ruin pubs on this street) serves cheap pub grub.

$$$$ Stand, operated by celebrity chefs Szabina Szulló and Tamás Széll (who run the high-end lunch eatery in the Hold Street Market—described later), is the refined choice in this neighborhood. Open since 2018, it's making a play to become one of Budapest's top restaurants, with a fixed-price menu of well-executed modern Hungarian and international dishes and impeccable service in a clean, contemporary setting with an open kitchen (Mon 18:30-21:00, Tue-Sat 12:00-13:00 & 18:30-21:00, closed Sun, these are last seating times for dinner, Székely Mihály ucta 2, mobile +3630-785-9139, www.standrestaurant.hu).

$$ Cupakós has won awards for its street-food inspired menu of hearty dishes. Its motto is "Meat, meat, meat." (Vegetarians—skip it.) With a casual, industrial-mod interior of concrete and subway tile, it's a filling and affordable choice in this increasingly upscale dining area (daily 11:30-24:00, Dob 31, mobile +3670-908-4404).

Food Trucks: Just a couple of doors down from Szimpla (the oldest and best of the ruin pubs—see page 641), the **$ Street Food Karaván** fills a gravel lot with an array of creative food trucks and picnic tables. Options include burgers, burritos, sausages, paneer "burgers," soup in a bread bowl, pan-Asian dishes, and for dessert, *kürtőskalács*—delicious chimney cake (daily 11:30-late, Kazinczy utca 18, district VII, M1: Opera).

Gozsdu Udvar: This passage—which laces together a series of courtyards as it runs under apartment blocks through the busy Seventh District—is jammed with bars and restaurants, and fun for a drink, snack, meal, or just people-watching. It's a thriving and youthful mix that sprawls for blocks, with options including fish *(Stég)*, craft beers *(Léhütö)*, all-day breakfast joints, homemade pasta bars, Italian, karaoke rooms for rent...and even Hungarian cuisine.

Market Hall with Cheap Eats: At the northern edge of the ruin-pub zone is the **$ Klauzál Market,** a neighborhood market hall built in 1897. With soaring steel girders over pristinely restored food stalls and a handy Spar supermarket, it's a fine place to browse for a picnic or grab some street food (most vendors open until about 17:00; supermarket open Mon-Sat 6:30-21:00, Sun 7:00-18:00; Klauzál tér 6, runs through the block between Klauzál utca and Akácfa utca, district VII, between M1: Opera and M2: Blaha Lujza tér).

Near Andrássy Út

For locations, see the "Andrássy Út Hotels & Restaurants" map on page 649. Note that the Seventh District eateries (in the previous section) are also nearby.

$$$ Menza (the old communist word for "School Cafeteria"), the only restaurant seriously worth considering on touristy Franz

Liszt Square, wins the "Best Design" award. Recycling 1970s-era furniture and an orange-brown-gray color scheme, it's a postmodern parody of an old communist café—half kitschy-retro, half contemporary-stylish. With tasty and well-priced updated Hungarian and international cuisine, embroidered leather-bound menus, brisk but efficient service, and indoor or outdoor seating, it's a memorable spot (daily 11:00-23:00, halfway up Andrássy út at Liszt Ferenc tér 2, district VII, M1: Oktogon, tel. 1/413-1482, www.menza.co.hu).

$$$ Klassz, right on Andrássy út, is a bistro with a similarly postmodern "eclectic-mod" aesthetic, both in its decor and its food. They serve a short menu of reasonably priced, if hit-or-miss, international/nouvelle cuisine with Hungarian flair (daily 11:30-22:30, Andrássy út 41, district VI, between M1: Opera and M1: Oktogon, no reservations possible).

$$$$ Bock Bisztró, run by a prominent vintner from Villány, offers traditional Hungarian staples presented with modern flourish—almost "deconstructed," but still recognizable. It has a wine-bar ambience, with cork-filled tables. Pricey and well-regarded, with a list of 250 wines (including dozens by the glass), it's a good opportunity to sample food and wine from around the country. The service can be stuffy, but the food lives up to its reputation. Reservations are essential (daily 12:00-16:00 & 18:00-24:00, in the Corinthia Grand Royal Hotel, a couple of blocks west of the Oktogon on the Great Boulevard, Erzsébet körút 43, district VII, M1: Oktogon, right by Király utca stop on trams #4 and #6, tel. 1/321-0340, www.bockbisztropest.hu).

$$$ Pesti Disznó ("Pest Pig"), set right in the "Broadway Quarter" along the liveliest stretch of theaters in town, celebrates the prized Hungarian hairy pig called *mangalica*. The menu ranges from well-executed classics to international fare to creative fusion dishes—like a *mangalica* burger. While the interior, with tall tables surrounding the open kitchen, is fine, I'd rather sit out under the red-and-white striped awnings facing the bright lights of Budapest's theater scene (daily 11:00-24:00, Nagymező 19, district VI, M1: Oktogon, tel. 1/951-4061, www.pestidiszno.hu).

$$$ Két Szerecsen ("Two Saracens"), named for a historic coffee shop at this location that a trader filled with exotic goods, stays true to that eclectic spirit by featuring a wide variety of international cuisines—from Mediterranean to Asian. It has good indoor and outdoor seating, relatively small portions, and a menu that offers something for everyone (daily 9:00-24:00, a block off Andrássy út at Nagymező utca 14, district VI, M1: Opera, tel. 1/343-1984).

Near St. István's Basilica

The streets in front of St. István's Basilica are jammed with upscale, dressy, yuppie-oriented eateries (district V, M1: Bajcsy-Zsilinszky út). Several options line Zrínyi utca (which stretches straight down to the Danube from the basilica's front door) and its cross streets. The following choices are worth seeking out. For locations, see the "Leopold Town Restaurants & Hotels" map.

$$$ Café Kör ("Circle") is a reliable mainstay in this otherwise fast-evolving zone. This stylish but unsnooty eatery serves up mostly Hungarian and some international fare in a tasteful, tight, one-room interior and at a few sidewalk tables. It prides itself on being friendly and providing a good value. Because it's beloved by Budapest foodies, reservations are smart and essential on weekends (Mon-Sat 10:00-22:00, closed Sun, small portions available, good salads, daily specials, cash only, Sas utca 17, tel. 1/311-0053).

$$$$ Borkonyha ("Winekitchen"), with a Michelin star, serves up top-quality modern Hungarian cuisine ("Hungarian dishes—but less paprika, less fat"). And, as the name implies, they're evangelical about high-quality Hungarian wines—with about 45 types sold by the glass. The menu—especially the adventurous chalkboard specials—ventures into "nose-to-tail" cooking, using ingredients you won't find everywhere. The decor is sophisticated black, white, and gold—a dressy place where wine snobs feel at home—and they also have sidewalk seating out front. Reservations are essential (Mon-Sat 12:00-16:00 & 18:00-24:00, closed Sun, Sas utca 3, tel. 1/266-0835, www.borkonyha.hu).

$$$$ Mák Bistro is pricey but unpretentious, with a loyal following (reservations are smart). It feels like a well-kept secret, tucked down a forgotten side street parallel to the bustling Zrínyi utca pedestrian drag. Inside, it has a lively brasserie ambience under white-painted brick vaults. The short, carefully selected seasonal menu is based on what's fresh. The good-value lunch specials are an affordable way to sample the fine cuisine (Tue-Sat 12:00-15:00

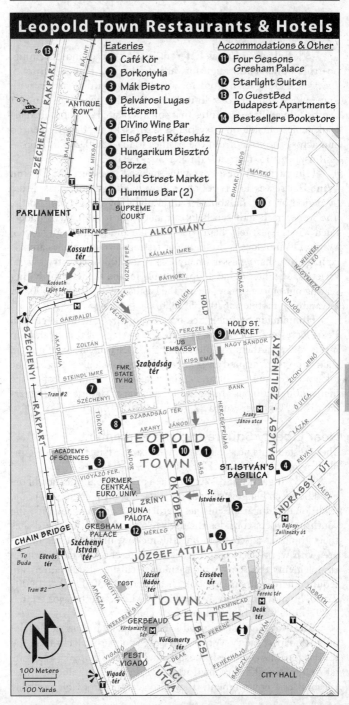

Leopold Town Restaurants & Hotels

Eateries
1. Café Kör
2. Borkonyha
3. Mák Bistro
4. Belvárosi Lugas Étterem
5. DiVino Wine Bar
6. Első Pesti Rétesház
7. Hungarikum Bisztró
8. Börze
9. Hold Street Market
10. Hummus Bar (2)

Accommodations & Other
11. Four Seasons Gresham Palace
12. Starlight Suiten
13. To GuestBed Budapest Apartments
14. Bestsellers Bookstore

BUDAPEST

& 18:00-23:00, closed Sun-Mon, Vigyázó Ferenc 4, mobile +3630-723-9383, www.mak.hu).

$$ Belvárosi Lugas Étterem is your cheap-and-charming, no-frills option for straightforward, traditional Hungarian food. *Lugas* is a Hungarian word for a welcoming garden strewn with grape vines, and the cozy dining room—with a dozen tables under overhanging vines—captures that spirit. Or sit at one of their sidewalk tables outside on busy Bajcsy-Zsilinszky út, directly behind and across the street from the basilica (daily 12:00-23:30, Bajcsy-Zsilinszky út 15, district VI, tel. 1/302-5393).

Hungarian Wines: For a wine-focused adventure, **$$ DiVino Wine Bar** serves 130 types of exclusively Hungarian wines, listed by region on the chalkboard—all available by the glass or bottle. The well-versed staff can help introduce you to Hungary's underrated wines—just tell them what you like and let them guide you. While DiVino doesn't do flights or tastings per se, couples are encouraged to share glasses (many less than 1,000 Ft) to try several varieties. The interior has a hip atmosphere, and there's also inviting seating out on the square, facing the basilica (daily 16:00-24:00, St. István tér 3, mobile +3670-935-3980).

Homemade Strudel: See how strudel *(rétes)* is made at **Első Pesti Rétesház,** a folkloric favorite among fans of this treat. Step inside to watch them roll out the long, paper-thin sheets of dough, then wrap them around a variety of fillings. Get a piece to go at the takeaway counter, or sit and enjoy your *rétes* with a cup of coffee (daily 9:00-23:00, also has a full food menu of traditional Hungarian dishes, Október 6 utca 22, tel. 1/428-0134).

Near Liberty Square and the Parliament

These restaurants near Liberty Square can be found on the "Leopold Town Restaurants & Hotels" map, earlier.

$$ Hungarikum Bisztró, tucked in an unassuming neighborhood between big government ministries, is my pick for authentic, traditional Hungarian cuisine. Rather than gouging tourists, the youthful owners consider themselves ambassadors for the dishes their grandma raised them on. The mellow, unpretentious interior—with warm service and red-and-white-checked tablecloths—complements the strictly old-fashioned cuisine. Reservations are required here—be sure to book ahead (daily 11:30-14:30 & 18:00-22:00, Steindl Imre utca 13, district V, M2: Kossuth Lajos tér, tel. 1/797-7177, www.hungarikumbisztro.hu).

$$$ Börze, tucked just off Liberty Square, is a classic "locals-only" Budapest eatery. While it sits just a couple of blocks from the tourist zone, its clientele is mostly office workers enjoying Hungarian/international dishes in an attractive, bright, brass-and-subway-tile brasserie environment. They also feature affordable weekday lunch specials (daily 7:30-24:00, Nádor utca 23, tel. 1/426-5460, www.borzeetterem.hu).

Hold Street Market (Belvárósi Piac)

The Great Market Hall was one of several neighborhood markets—with similar Industrial Age decor—built around 1896. And while that most famous example is exclusively for tourists, the market hall on Hold Street, a short walk from the Parliament and one block off Liberty Square, is what you wish the Great Market Hall could be: a truly local, affordable-yet-high-end food hall catering to neighborhood shoppers and office workers seeking an efficient, affordable, but above all *good* lunch. Eating here, you'll be surrounded by Budapesters (and by a handful of savvy foodie travelers who've done their homework). There are few more satisfying places in the city to go looking for lunch (Mon 6:30-17:00, Tue-Fri until 18:00, Sat until 16:00, closed Sun). The ground floor has mostly market vendors—meat, veggies, spices, and so on—while cheap, efficient eateries ring the upstairs. Anchoring the whole space—in the middle of the main floor—is Stand 25.

$$$$ Stand 25 is *the* choice for a quality lunch in central Budapest. Celebrity chefs Szabina Szulló and Tamás Széll created this outpost for showing off their mastery of Hungarian and international fare—a delightful fusion that combines the best of both, to wonderful effect. While it's mostly a lunch spot (choose two or three courses), they're also open for dinner on weekends. Reservations—for lunch or dinner—are recommended (Mon 8:00-17:00, Tue-Thu until 18:00, Fri-Sat until 22:00, closed Sun, three-quarters of the way down the market hall's main floor on the right, mobile +3630-961-3262).

$-$$ Upstairs Food Stalls: Find a wonderful variety of food stalls upstairs. You'll see a basic, grubby cafeteria; a branch of a local sausage chain; a stand selling Thai-style *khao man gai* (poached chicken in garlicky sauce); and lots more. Here are a few to check out before deciding: **Buja Disznó(k)** serves up wooden platters with massive schnitzels. **Lakatos Műhely** is the place for gourmet sausage. **Moszkvatér**—named for the since-rechristened "Moscow Square"—serves Russian food. **Kandalló Market** does gourmet burgers. And perhaps best of all for those who want to stay traditional, **A Séf Utcaja** dishes up hearty Hungarian classics, but with modern presentation.

BUDAPEST

Pest's Town Center (Belváros), near Váci Utca

When you ask natives about good places to eat on Váci utca, they just roll their eyes. But wander a few blocks off the tourist route, and you'll discover a few alternatives with fair prices and better food. For locations, see the "Pest Town Center Hotels & Restaurants" map on page 653.

$$$ Gerlóczy Café, tucked on a peaceful little square next to the giant City Hall, features attentive service and a concise, tasty menu of French, Hungarian, and international cuisine. The clientele is a mix of tourists and upscale-urban Budapesters, including local politicians and actors from nearby theaters. With a take-your-time ambience that's almost Parisian—and with live piano music on weekends after 19:00—this is a classy, par-

ticularly inviting spot (good breakfasts, weekday lunch specials, good-value fixed-price dinners, daily 8:00-23:00, 2 blocks from Váci utca, just off Városház utca at Gerlóczy utca 1, district V, M3: Ferenciek tere, tel. 1/501-4000).

$$$$ Borssó Bistro, near University Square (Egyetem tér), is a trendy splurge offering small portions of delicately assembled modern French cuisine with a bit of Hungarian flair. The cozy two-story interior's ambience, like the cuisine, is an elegant yet accessible blend of old and new. They also have outdoor tables and occasional live music. Reservations are important (Tue-Sun 12:00-23:00, Mon from 18:00, Király Pál utca 14, district V, M3/M4: Kálvin tér, tel. 1/789-0975, www.borsso.hu).

Great Market Hall: At the far south end of Váci utca, you can eat a quick lunch on the upper floor of the Great Market Hall (Nagyvásárcsarnok). Unfortunately, eateries here cater almost entirely to tourists; for a truly authentic market hall meal, try the far better choices at the Hold Street Market (described earlier). But if you're nearby and hungry, here are some options inside the Great Market Hall: **$$ Fakanál Étterem**—the glassed-in, sit-down cafeteria above the main entrance—is touristy, but offers good seating (Mon-Fri 10:00-17:00, Sat until 14:00, closed Sun; live music most days 12:00-15:00). The **$ sloppy, stand-up stalls** along the right side of the building

are cheaper, but quality can vary. A favorite is the heavy fry bread called *lángos* (like a savory elephant ear). Get the basic one—slathered with sour cream, cheese, and (if you dare) garlic—for about 1,000 Ft; order carefully, or they could add piles of toppings to triple or quadruple your bill. Another fun option is to use the market to assemble a **picnic,** visiting the produce and butcher stands that line the main floor; get whatever else you need at the Aldi supermarket in the basement (market hall open Mon 6:00-17:00, Tue-Fri until 18:00, Sat until 15:00, closed Sun; supermarket open longer hours, Fővám körút 1, district IX, M4: Fővám tér).

BUDA

Eateries on Castle Hill are generally overpriced and touristy—as with Váci utca, locals never eat here. The Víziváros ("Water Town") neighborhood, between the castle and the river, is a bit better. Even if you sleep in Buda, try to dine in Pest—that's where you'll find the city's best restaurants. All of the restaurants listed here (except Szent Jupát) are in district I. For locations, see the "Buda Hotels & Restaurants" map on page 656.

Castle Hill

For a quick bite, visit the handy, affordable **Prima grocery store** (Mon-Sat 7:00-20:00, Sun 9:00-18:00, on Tárnok utca near Szentháromság tér).

For coffee and cakes, try the historic **Ruszwurm** (described later, under "Budapest's Café Culture"). If you'd rather have a meal—and don't want to head down to Víziváros—try the following choices:

$ Vár Bistro is a convenient, affordable cafeteria that makes for an easy and quick way to grab a meal between sightseeing. The food is uninspired but filling, and it has delightful (if crowded) outdoor seating overlooking a pretty park. They also have a counter in front with basic sandwiches and cakes (daily 8:00-20:00, Dísz tér 8, mobile +3630-237-0039).

$$$ 21 Magyar Vendéglő ("21 Hungarian Kitchen") features traditional Hungarian fare that's updated for the 21st century (hence the name). While the mod interior is pleasant, it's also fun to sit out on pretty Fortuna utca (near the north end of the hill). Most restaurants on Castle Hill are overpriced, and this is no exception—but the quality is good. This is a rare castle-zone eatery that really takes pride in its food rather than being a crank-'em-out tourism machine (daily 11:00-24:00, Fortuna utca 21, tel. 1/202-2113).

$$$ Baltazár, near the ruins of St. Mary Magdalene Church (a few short blocks from the main sights), is trying to inject some youthful liveliness into the staid, sleepy north end of Castle Hill.

It's a fun choice, with bright, brash decor, pleasant outdoor seating, and a wood-fired charcoal grill that churns out smoky dishes (daily 7:30-24:00, Országház utca 31, tel. 1/300-7050). In the summer, you may see their inviting beer garden just up the street, under the church tower.

Batthyány Tér and Nearby

This bustling square—the transportation hub for Víziváros (on the M2 line)—is overlooked by a modernized, late-19th-century market hall (today housing a big Spar supermarket and various shops). Several worthwhile, affordable eateries—nothing fancy, just practical—cluster around this square. Survey your options before settling in.

$ Nagyi Palacsintázója ("Granny's Pancakes")—just to the right of the market hall entrance—serves up cheap sweet and savory crêpes *(palacsinta)* to a local crowd (open daily 24 hours, individual crêpes are small—order a combo for a filling meal, ask for English menu, Batthyány tér 5).

As you face the market hall, go up the street that runs along its left side (Markovits Iván utca) to reach more good eateries: At the end of the block on the right is **$ Édeni Végan,** a self-service, point-and-shoot vegetarian cafeteria (daily 8:00-20:00, tel. 1/375-7575). And tucked behind the market hall is **$ Bratwursthäusle/Kolbászda,** a fun little beer hall/beer garden with Bavarian specialties and blue-and-white checkerboard decor to match. Sit outside, or in the woody interior (daily 11:00-23:00, Gyorskocsi utca 6, tel. 1/225-3674).

Fine Dining near Batthyány Tér: The stylish, splurgy **$$$$ Csalogány 26** is a few short blocks from Batthyány tér in an otherwise dull urban neighborhood. Its modern international cuisine, served in a classy contemporary dining room, has earned its raves as one of the best eateries in this part of town—reserve ahead (Tue-Sat 12:00-15:00 & 19:00-22:00, closed Sun-Mon, Csalogány utca 26, tel. 1/201-7892, www.csalogany26.hu).

SNACKS AND LIGHT MEALS

When you're in the mood for something halfway between a restaurant and a picnic meal, look for takeout food stands, bakeries (with sandwiches to go), grocers willing to make you a sandwich, and simple eateries for fast and easy sit-down restaurant food.

Lángos is a popular snack—a savory deep-fried flatbread (similar to an elephant ear or Native American fry bread). Sold at stands on the street and upstairs in the Great Market Hall (see earlier), the most typical versions are spread with cheese and sour cream, and sometimes topped with garlic.

$ Hummus Bar, while not authentically Hungarian, is a popular expat-run chain that offers cheap Middle Eastern vegetarian meals (tasty falafel, sandwiches, and combination plates, eat in or to go) to grateful backpackers and young locals. They have multiple locations, including in the Town Center on University Square (Egyetem tér, at Kecskeméti utca 1, district V, M3/M4: Kálvin tér); in Leopold Town (Alkotmány utca 20, district V, M2: Kossuth tér); between Liberty Square and St. István Square (Október 6 utca 19); and two in the Seventh District (one at Király 8, and the other at the corner of Síp and Wesselényi). All are open roughly the same hours (Mon-Fri 10:00-22:00, Sat-Sun from 12:00).

Kürtőskalács is the best sweet street food in Budapest. This "chimney cake" pastry is twisted around a spindle, rolled in sugar, and then slowly baked on a rotisserie until it's coated in a sweet, caramelized crust. They roll it in toppings (cinnamon, coconut, chocolate) and hand it over hot. Watch for vendors at the start of Andrássy út, in front of the Nyugati/Western train station, along Váci utca near March 15 Square, in the Seventh District's food-truck zone, and elsewhere around town.

BUDAPEST'S CAFÉ CULTURE

In the late 19th century, a vibrant café culture boomed here in Budapest, just as it did in Vienna and Paris. The *kávéház* ("coffee-house") was a local institution. By 1900, Budapest had more than 600 cafés. In this crowded and fast-growing cityscape, a neighborhood café allowed urbanites to escape their tiny flats (or get a jolt of caffeine to power them through a 12-hour workday). Local people, many of whom had moved to the city from the countryside, didn't want to pay to heat their homes during the day. So instead, for the price of a cup of coffee, they could come to a café to enjoy warmth, companionship, and loaner newspapers.

Realizing that these neighborhood living rooms were breeding grounds for dissidents, the communists closed the cafés or converted them into *eszpresszós* (with uncomfortable stools instead of easy chairs) or *bisztrós* (stand-up fast-food joints with no chairs at all). But after 1989, nostalgia brought back the *kávéház* culture—both as a place to get coffee and food, and as a social institution. While some serve only coffee and cakes, most serve light meals, and some offer full meals (as noted later).

While meals at some of these grand cafés are pricey, a budget alternative is to nurse an afternoon coffee and cake in opulent surroundings. Hungary has a proud tradition of cakes and pastries, which make liberal use of sweet cheese curds *(turós)* and poppy seeds *(mákszem)*. Here are a few Hungarian favorites to look for: The classic *Dobos torta* is a sponge-cake-and-buttercream concoction with alternating layers of chocolate and vanilla, all topped with caramelized sugar. *Rákóczi turós* is a dense cake of sweet cheese curds with jam on top. *Somlói galuska* is three delectable balls of moist sponge cake—often in different flavors (walnut, chocolate, etc.)—soaked in rum, mixed with whipped cream, and drizzled with chocolate. *Krémes* is custard sandwiched between delicate wafers. And *flódni*, which originated in the Jewish community, is earthy and filling, with layers of apple, walnuts, and poppy seeds.

On the Great Boulevard

$$$$ New York Café makes the others listed here look like Starbucks. Originally built in 1894 by a big American insurance com-

pany (who believed that having the most extravagant café imaginable for their clients would inspire confidence), this fanciful, over-the-top explosion of Neo-Baroque and Neo-Renaissance epitomizes the "mix and match, but plenty of everything" Historicist style of the day. In the early 20th century, artists, writers, and musicians came here to sip overpriced coffee and bask in opulence. In the early 21st century, it's overrun by gawking, selfie-taking tourists...but still visually magnificent. There's often a line behind a fancy cord waiting for a table. While non-customers aren't allowed in, you're welcome to steal a peek from this entrance area. The food is drastically overpriced—but consider investing in a coffee and cake, just for the experience. Be sure to read the fun history in the menu (daily 8:00-24:00, inside the Boscolo Hotel at Erzsébet körút 9, district VII, tel. 1/886-6167). Take the M2/red Metró line to Blaha Lujza tér, and exit toward *Erzsébet körút* and walk a block. You can also take tram #4 or #6 from the Oktogon (at Andrássy út) around the Great Boulevard to the Wesselényi utca stop. For location, see the map on page 653.

Two Blocks Up from Váci Utca

For the locations of these places, see the map on page 653.

$$$ Gerlóczy Café, listed as a restaurant in Pest's Town Center, earlier, nicely recaptures Budapest's early-1900s ambience, with loaner newspapers on racks and a management that encourages loitering.

$$$ Centrál Kávéház is another venerable favorite. While I'd skip the food, it has an enjoyable and atmospheric two-story interior and is great for a drink (daily 8:00-23:00, Károlyi Mihály utca 9, district V, M3: Ferenciek tere, tel. 1/266-2110).

On Andrássy út, near the Opera House

$$$$ Callas features ideal outdoor seating facing the Opera House, and one of the finest Art Nouveau interiors in town, with gorgeous Jugendstil chandeliers. While their full meals are pricey, this is a wonderful spot in a prime Andrássy út location for a coffee break, a tasty dessert, or breakfast (Mon-Sat 10:00-24:00, Sun until 20:00, Andrássy út 20—see the map on page 649, district VI, M1: Opera, tel. 1/354-0954).

In Buda, atop Castle Hill

$$ Ruszwurm lays claim to being Budapest's oldest café (since 1827). Tiny but classy, with old-style Biedermeier furnishings and fine sidewalk seating, it upholds its venerable reputation with pride. Its dead-central location—a block in front of Matthias Church in the heart of the castle district—means that it has become a popular tourist spot (though it remains dear to locals' hearts). Look for gussied-up locals chatting here after the Sunday morning Mass at the church (daily 10:00-19:00, Szentháromság utca 7—see the map on page 656, district I, tel. 1/375-5284).

Budapest Connections

BY TRAIN

Hungary's train network is run by MÁV (Magyar Államvasutak). From centrally located Budapest, train lines branch out across Hungary, like spokes on a wheel. Most connections between outlying cities aren't direct—you often end up having to go back through Budapest. While Hungary's trains are generally good, some are old and fairly slow; major routes use faster, newer, and slightly more expensive InterCity trains (marked with an "IC" or a boxed "R" on schedules). To ride an InterCity train, you must pay extra for a required reservation (which is printed on a separate ticket).

If traveling to international destinations such as Bratislava or Vienna, other trains are faster and more direct than the InterCity. Between Budapest and Bratislava, EuroCity (EC) trains are fastest and most direct. If traveling from Budapest to Vienna, Austrian RailJet (RJ) trains are fastest and direct, and don't require seat assignments (but advance-purchase discounts lock you into a specific departure).

Warning: Trains can be very crowded on weekends, when it's smart to book a reservation for any train trip.

For timetables, the first place to check is Germany's excellent all-Europe site, www.bahn.com. You can also check Hungary's own timetable website at http://elvira.mav-start.hu. For general rail information in Hungary, call 0640-494-949 (from outside Hungary, dial +36-1-444-4499).

Remember that Budapest has three major train stations (*pályaudvar*, abbreviated *pu.*): Keleti ("Eastern") station, Nyugati ("Western") station, and Déli ("Southern") station.

Buying Train Tickets: For domestic tickets, it's easiest to book **online** on the Hungarian Railways website: www.mavcsoport.hu. While low-tech, the site is in English and accepts American credit cards. You can send an e-ticket to your phone (you may have to create a login to do this); then on the train, just flash your e-ticket to the conductor, who may ask to see your ID.

International connections must be issued on **paper tickets,** which means you'll have to go to a train station. Do as the locals do and use the ubiquitous MÁV ticket machines in the station. They have English instructions and take American credit cards. If you can't get one to work, look for a staffed ticket desk—marked *pénztár* or *jegypénztár*. Sometimes international tickets are sold only at a special window (marked *nemzetközi*).

Other key words: *Vágány* is track, *induló vonatok* is departures, and *érkező vonatok* is arrivals.

From Budapest by Train to: Eger (every 2 hours direct, 2 hours, more with transfer in Füzesabony, usually from Keleti/Eastern station), **Pécs** (every 2 hours direct, 3 hours; a few more connections possible with transfer at suburban Kelenföld station), **Sopron** (every 2 hours direct, 2.5 hours, more with transfer at Kelenföld), **Visegrád** (trains arrive at Nagymaros-Visegrád station, across the river—take shuttle boat to Visegrád; 1-2/hour, 45 minutes, from Nyugati/Western station), **Esztergom** (hourly, 1 hour, usually from Nyugati/Western station; but Esztergom's train station is far from the basilica, making the bus—described later—a better option), **Kecskemét** (hourly, 1.5 hours), **Szeged** (hourly, 2.5 hours).

Bratislava (*Pozsony* in Hungarian, every 2 hours direct, 2.5 hours; more with changes), **Vienna** (*Bécs* in Hungarian, every 2 hours direct on express Railjet, 2.5 hours; more with changes), **Prague** (5/day direct, 6.5 hours; plus 1 night train/day, 9.5 hours), **Kraków** (1/day, 9 hours, change in Bohumin, longer connections with more changes; 1 direct night train/day, 11 hours), **Zagreb** (2/day direct, 5.5 hours), **Ljubljana** (1/day direct, 8.5 hours; additional options with changes, 9 hours; plus 1 direct night train/day, 10 hours), **Cluj-Napoca** (hub for Transylvania in Romania, 2/day direct, 7.5 hours), **Munich** (every 2 hours direct on express RailJet, 7 hours; 1 direct night train/day, 9.5 hours).

By HÉV: Budapest has its own suburban rail network, called HÉV. For tourists, this is mostly useful for reaching **Szentendre** (from M2: Batthyány tér) and **Gödöllő** (from M2: Örs vezér tere).

BY BUS

Buses can be relatively inexpensive, but are typically slower and less convenient than trains. The only bus you're likely to take is the one to Eger (2/hour, 2 hours), which leaves from the Stadionok bus station (at the M2/Metró red line stop of the same name). You can search bus schedules at the (Hungarian-only) website www. menetrendek.hu.

BY PLANE

For information about Budapest's Liszt Ferenc Airport, see "Arrival in Budapest—By Plane" on page 559.

ROUTE TIPS FOR DRIVERS

For pointers on driving into (and parking in) Budapest, see "Arrival in Budapest—By Car" on page 560. Remember, to use Hungary's expressways, you'll need to buy a toll sticker (see page 1122). To get out of town, here are some pointers:

To Eger and Other Points East: Head out of the city center on Andrássy út, circling behind Heroes' Square to access Kós Károly sétány through the middle of City Park. You'll pass Széchenyi Baths on the left, then (exiting the park) go over the Hungária körút ring road, before getting on M-3. This expressway zips you conveniently to Eger (exit #114 for Füzesabony; go north on road 33, then follow road 3, then road 25 into Eger).

To Bratislava, Vienna, and Other Points West: From central Pest, head over the Danube on the white, modern Elisabeth Bridge (Erzsébet híd). Once in Buda, the road becomes Hegyalja út; simply follow *Bécs-Wien* signs to get on M-1.

BUDAPEST

Day Trips from Budapest

On a visit of a few days, Budapest will keep even the most avid sightseer busy. And after Budapest, Eger, covered in a chapter of its own, is one of the best Hungarian towns. But for a longer stay, a few outlying sights are worth considering. I've listed them here roughly in order of proximity to downtown Budapest.

▲▲Memento Park (a.k.a. Statue Park)

When regimes fall, so do their monuments...literally. Just think of all the statues of Stalin and Lenin that crashed to the ground in late 1989, when people throughout Eastern Europe couldn't wait to get

rid of those reminders of their oppressors. But some clever entrepreneur hoarded Budapest's, collecting them in a park in the countryside just southwest of the city—where tourists flock to get a taste of the communist era. Though it can be time-consuming to visit, this collection is worth ▲▲▲ for those fascinated by Hungary's commie past.

You'll see the great figures of the Soviet Bloc—both international (Lenin, Marx, and Engels) and Hungarian (local bigwig Béla Kun)—as well as gigantic, stoic figures representing Soviet ideals. This stiff dose of Socialist Realist art, while time-consuming to reach, is rewarding for those curious for a taste of history that most Hungarians would rather forget.

Cost and Hours: 1,500 Ft, daily 10:00-sunset, tel. 1/424-7500, www.mementopark.hu.

Getting There: It's in the countryside six miles southwest of the city center, at the corner of Balatoni út and Szabadka út, in district XXII.

The park runs a convenient **direct bus** from Deák tér in downtown Budapest (where three Metró lines converge; bus stop is near the Ritz-Carlton, facing the leafy Erzsébet tér). The trip takes 2.5 hours total, including a 1.5-hour visit to the park (4,900-Ft ticket

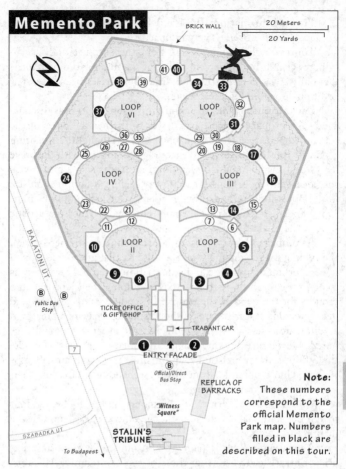

Memento Park

BRICK WALL

20 Meters
20 Yards

LOOP VI
LOOP V
LOOP IV
LOOP III
LOOP II
LOOP I

Ⓑ Public Bus Stop
Ⓑ

TICKET OFFICE & GIFT SHOP →

Ⓟ

← TRABANT CAR

❶ ❷
ENTRY FACADE

Ⓑ
Official/Direct Bus Stop

REPLICA OF BARRACKS

"Witness Square"

STALIN'S TRIBUNE →

To Budapest ↓

BALATONI ÚT

SZABADKA ÚT

7

Note: These numbers correspond to the official Memento Park map. Numbers filled in black are described on this tour.

BUDAPEST

includes round-trip and park entry, 20 percent discount if you book online at park website, runs daily at 11:00).

The **public transport** option requires a transfer: Ride the Metró's M4/green line to its end at Kelenföld. Follow signs to *Őrmező* and *Péterhegyi út* (exit B). Emerging in this bus-stop zone, consult the electronic board for the next departure time; a map directs you to your stop. You want bus #101B or #101E, which zip to Memento Park in about 10 minutes (every 10-20 minutes, Mon-Fri only). Bus #150 takes longer (about 20 minutes), but it's the only option on weekends (2-4/hour, runs daily). If you're taking bus #150, you can download a free "bonus tour" from the park website, which explains some of the landmarks you'll pass en route. On any bus, be sure the driver knows where you want to get off.

Visitor Information: The 1,500-Ft English guidebook, *In the Shadow of Stalin's Boots,* is very informative.

Tours: English tours depart from the entrance and last 50 minutes (1,200 Ft, 20 percent discount if you book online; April-Oct daily at 11:45—shortly after direct bus arrives from Deák tér, additional tours in high season).

Background: Under the communists, creativity was discouraged. The primary purpose of art was to further the goals of the state, with creative expression only an afterthought. Promoting **Socialist Realist** art served to encourage complicity with the brave new world the communists were forging. It was also a break with the "decadent" bourgeois art that came before it (Impressionism, Post-Impressionism, and other modern -isms). From 1949 until 1956, Socialist Realism was legally enforced as the sole artistic style of the Soviet Bloc.

As propaganda was an essential weapon in the Soviet arsenal, the regime made ample use of Socialist Realist art. Aside from a few important figureheads, individuals didn't matter. Everyone was a cog in the machine—strong, stoic, and doing their jobs well and proudly for the good of the people. Individual characteristics and distinguishing features were unimportant; people were represented as automatons serving their nation. Artistic merit was virtually ignored. Most figures are trapped in stiff, unnatural poses that ignore the 3,000 years of artistic evolution since the Egyptians. Sculptures and buildings alike from this era were designed to evoke feelings of power and permanence.

➜ Self-Guided Tour: The numbers in the following tour match the statue labels in the park, the official park map, and the map in this chapter.

As you approach the park, you encounter the imposing red-brick Entry Facade featuring three of the Communist All-Stars: ❶ **Vladimir Lenin,** a leader of Russia's Bolshevik Revolution; and ❷ **Karl Marx** and **Friedrich Engels,** the German philosophers whose *Communist Manifesto* first articulated the principles behind communism in 1848. (These three figures weren't offensive enough to be destroyed, but very few statues survive anywhere of the biggest "star" of all, the hated Josef Stalin.) Like the rest of the park, the gate's design is highly conceptual: It looks impressive and monumental...but, like the rotted-out pomp of communism, there's nothing behind it. It's a glossy stage-set with no substance. If you try to go through the main, central part of the gate, you'll run into an always-locked door. Instead, as with the communist system, you have to find another way around (in this case, the side gate to the left).

Inside the gate, buy your ticket and head into the park. Survey the layout and note that the main road takes you confidently toward...a dead end (the brick wall). Once again, as with life under the communists, you'll have to deviate from this main axis to actually accomplish anything. Even so, notice that the six walkways branching off the main road all loop you right back to where you started—representing the endless futility of communism.

• *Work your way counterclockwise around the park.*

Liberation Monuments (Loop I): Dominating this loop is a ❸ **giant soldier** holding the Soviet flag. This statue once stood at the base of the Liberation Monument that still overlooks the Danube from Gellért Hill. Typical of Socialist Realist art, the soldier has a clenched fist (symbolizing strength) and a face that is inspired by his egalitarian ideology.

To the left of this soldier, see the ❹ **two comrades** stiffly shaking hands: the Hungarian worker thrilled to meet the Soviet

soldier—protector of the proletariat.

Beyond them is a ❺ **long wall,** with a triumphant worker breaking through the left end—too busy doing his job to be very excited. Just another brick in the wall.

• *Cross "main street" to a group of statues commemorating the key communist holiday of...*

April 4, 1945 (Loop II): On this date, the Soviets forced the final Nazi soldier out of Hungary. The tall panel nearest the entrance shows a Hungarian woman and a Soviet woman setting free the ❽ **doves of peace.** According to the inscription, "Our freedom and peace is founded upon the enduring Hungarian-Soviet friendship." (With friends like these...)

The ❾ **woman holding the palm leaf** is reminiscent of the Liberation Monument back on the Danube—which, after all, celebrates the same glorious day. Check out the size of that palm leaf: Seems like she's overcompensating...

At the back of the loop, the ❿ **Hungarian worker and Soviet soldier** (who appear to be doing calisthenics) are absurdly rigid even though they're trying to be dynamic. (Even the statues couldn't muster genuine enthusiasm for communist ideals.)

• *Cross over and head up to the next loop to pay homage to...*

Heroes of the Workers' Movement (Loop III): Look for the ⓮ bust of the Bul-

garian communist leader **Georgi Dimitrov** (ruled 1946-1949)—
one of communist Hungary's many Soviet Bloc comrades. At the
back of this loop are ⑯ three blocky portraits. The middle figure is
the granddaddy of Hungarian communism: **Béla Kun.** To the left
is one of the park's best-loved, most-photographed, and most artistic statues: ⑰ **Vladimir Lenin,** in his famous "hailing a cab" pose.
• *Cross over—passing the giant red star made of flowers—to meet...*

More Communist Heroes (Loop IV): This group is dominated by a ㉔ dramatic, unusually emotive sculpture by a genuine

artist, **Imre Varga.** Designed
to commemorate the 100th anniversary of Béla Kun's birth,
this clever statue accomplishes
seemingly contradictory feats.
On the one hand, it reinforces
the communist message: Under
the able leadership of Béla Kun
(safely overlooking the fray from
above), the crusty, bourgeois old regime of the Habsburg Empire
(on the left, with the umbrellas and fancy clothes) was converted
into the workers' fighting force of the Red Army (on the right, with
the bayonets). And yet, those silvery civilians in back seem more
appealing than the lunging soldiers in front. And notice the lamp-
post next to Kun: In Hungarian literature, a lamppost is a metaphor for the gallows. This reminds viewers that Kun—in spite of
his groundbreaking and heroic work for the communist movement
in Hungary—was ultimately executed by communists in the Soviet
Union during Stalin's purges of the late 1930s.
• *Zig and head up again, for a lesson in...*

Communist Concepts (Loop V): Look for a rusty pair of
㉛ **workers' hands** holding a sphere (which was once adorned with
a red star). This represented the hard-won ideals of communism,

carefully protected by the hands—
but also held out for others to appreciate.

Dominating this group is a
㉝ **communist worker** charging
into the future, clutching the Soviet flag. Budapesters of the time
had a different interpretation: a
thermal bath attendant running
after a customer who'd forgotten
his towel. This is a favorite spot for
goofy posed photos.

To the left is a monument to
the communist version of the Boy

Scouts: the elementary-school-age ❸❹ **Little Drummers** and the older **Pioneers.** While these organizations existed before the communists, they were slowly infiltrated and turned into propaganda machines by the regime. These kids—with their jaunty red and blue neckerchiefs—were sent to camp to be properly raised as good little communists; today, many of them have forgotten the brainwashing but still have fond memories of the socializing.

• *Now zag once more to learn about...*

More Communist Concepts (Loop VI): The ❸❼ long, **white wall** at the back of this section tells quite a story (from left to right): The bullet holes lead up to a jumbled, frightful clutter (reminiscent of Pablo Picasso's *Guernica*) representing World War II. Then comes the bright light of the Soviet system, and by the end everyone's properly regimented—striking *Charlie's Angels* poses—and

looking boldly to the future (and enjoying a bountiful crop, to boot).

Next is a ❸❽ **fallen hero** with arm outstretched, about to collapse to the ground—mortally wounded, yet victorious. This monument to "the Martyrs of the Counter-Revolution" also commemorates those who died attempting to put down the 1956 Uprising.

• *Now continue down the main drag to, um, a...*

Dead End: The main path dead-ends at the wall, symbolizing life's frustrations under communism. Here stand statues of two Soviet officers who negotiated with the Nazis to end the WWII siege of Budapest. ❹⓿ **Captain Miklós Steinmetz** (on left)

was shot under mysterious circumstances as he returned from the successful summit. Both became heroes for the communist cause. Were they killed by wayward Nazi soldiers, as the Soviets explained—or by their own Red Army, to create a pair of convenient martyrs?

When you return to the entry gate, peruse the fun parade of communist kitsch at the **gift shop.** The stirring music may just move you to pick up the CD of *Communism's Greatest Hits,* and maybe a model of a Trabant (the classic two-stroke commiemobile). A real **Trabant** is often parked just inside the gate.

• *Now head out across the parking lot to find...*

Stalin's Tribune: This section of the complex is a re-creation of the giant grandstand that once stood along "Parade Street." Hungarian and Soviet leaders stood here, at the feet of a giant Stalin statue, to survey military and civilian processions. But during the 1956 Uprising, protesters cut Stalin off at the knees...leaving only the boots. (The entire tribune was later dismantled, and Stalin disappeared without a trace.) If you circle around behind the tribune, you'll find stairs up top for a view over the park.

• *Flanking the lot in front of the tribune are replicas of...*

Barracks: These are reminiscent of the ramshackle barracks where political prisoners lived in communist-era work camps (sometimes called gulags). These hold special exhibits, often including a good explanation of "Stalin's Boots" (with a plaster replica, and photos of the original tribune) and the events of 1956. Sit down for the creepy film, *The Life of an Agent*—a loop of four training films (10-15 minutes each) that were actually used to teach novice spies about secret-police methods and policies.

• *Our tour is over. Now, inspired by the bold propaganda of your Hungarian comrades, march proudly into the dawn of a new day.*

Óbuda

"Old Buda," just north of Buda, is the oldest part of Budapest, with roots going back to Celtic and Roman times. It has various sights that cluster around the Szentlélek tér stop of the HÉV suburban train line (catch the HÉV from the Batthyány tér Metró stop in Buda). The most interesting museum displays works by Hungarian sculptor Imre Varga, who worked from the 1950s through the 1990s, and created many popular sculptures in Budapest and throughout Hungary. You'll also find a museum filled with eye-popping, colorful paintings by Victor Vasarely, the founder of Op Art. If you ride the HÉV farther north to the Aquincum stop, you'll reach an archaeological museum at the remains of the 2,000-year-old Roman town of Aquincum and its amphitheater. All of these sights are closed on Mondays.

Gödöllő Royal Palace

Holding court in an unassuming town on the outskirts of Budapest, this pink Baroque palace was once the residence of Habsburg Emperor Franz Josef and his wife, Empress Elisabeth—better known to her beloved Hungarian subjects as Sisi (see page 881). While the Habsburg sights in Vienna and near Prague are better, this is the best place in Hungary to learn about its former monarchs.

Cost and Hours: 2,600 Ft for permanent exhibit (main palace apartments); Mon-Thu 9:00-17:00, Fri-Sun 10:00-18:00, last entry one hour before closing; Nov-March open only by guided tour at :30

past each hour Mon-Fri 10:30-14:30 (palace closes at 16:00), Sat-Sun 10:00-17:00; tel. 28/410-124, www.kiralyikastely.hu.

Getting There: Take the M2/red Metró line to Örs vezér tere, then catch the HÉV suburban train to Gödöllő—figure about one hour each way from downtown Budapest.

The Danube Bend

This string of three river towns north of Budapest offers a convenient day-trip getaway for urbanites who want to commune with nature. While I find "the Bend" less than thrilling, it's undeniably convenient to reach from the capital by train or boat; these destinations make for handy stopovers if you're driving between Budapest and Bratislava or Vienna.

Szentendre is a colorful, "Balkans in miniature" artist colony. With a tidy main square, a few engaging art galleries, and several Orthodox churches built by the Serbs and Greeks who settled the town, it offers a relaxing escape from the city. This is the easiest pleasant small town to reach from Budapest—which means it's also deluged by tourists. To reach Szentendre, hop on the HÉV suburban train at Budapest's Batthyány tér Metró (the same one that goes to Óbuda, described earlier).

Visegrád offers a small riverside museum at the scant remains of a Renaissance palace built by King Matthias Corvinus, and a dramatic hilltop castle with fine views over the Bend. While you can get here by boat or by train (to the Nagymaros-Visegrád station, then boat across the river), it's not worth the trip unless you're driving.

Esztergom Basilica is Hungary's biggest and most important church, built on the site where István, Hungary's first Christian king, was crowned in AD 1000. Packed with history, it looms grandly above the Danube (free, daily 8:00-18:00, May-Aug until 19:00, Nov-March until 16:00, www.bazilika-esztergom.hu). The easiest way to reach it is by bus from Budapest's Újpest-Városkapu bus station (at the Metró stop of the same name); trains and other buses from Budapest take you to the far end of town, an inconvenient 45-minute walk to the basilica.

BUDAPEST

EGER

Eger (EH-gehr) is a county-seat town in northern Hungary, with about 60,000 people and a thriving teacher-training college. While you've probably never heard of Eger, among Hungarians, the town has various claims to fame. Its powerful bishops have graced it with gorgeous churches. It has some of the best and most beloved spas in this hot-water-crazy country (including some worth-a-detour options in the nearby countryside). And, perhaps most of all, Eger makes Hungarians proud as the town that, against all odds, successfully held off the Ottoman advance into Europe in 1552. This stirring history makes Eger a field trip mecca for Hungarian schoolkids. If the town is known internationally for anything, it's for the surrounding wine region (its best-known red wine is Bull's Blood, or Egri Bikavér).

And yet, refreshingly, enchanting Eger remains mostly off the tourist trail. Egerites go about their daily routines amidst lovely Baroque buildings, watched over by one of Hungary's most important castles. Everything in Eger is painted with vibrant colors, and even the communist apartment blocks seem quaint. The sights are few but fun, the ambience is great, and strolling is a must. It all comes together to make Eger an ideal taste of small-town Hungary.

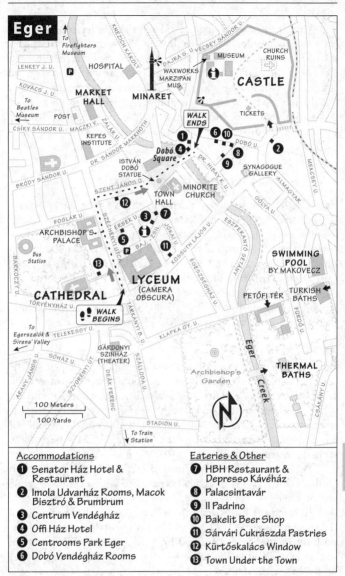

Accommodations

1. Senator Ház Hotel & Restaurant
2. Imola Udvarház Rooms, Macok Bisztró & Brumbrum
3. Centrum Vendégház
4. Offi Ház Hotel
5. Centrooms Park Eger
6. Dobó Vendégház Rooms

Eateries & Other

7. HBH Restaurant & Depresso Kávéház
8. Palacsintavár
9. Il Padrino
10. Bakelit Beer Shop
11. Sárvári Cukrászda Pastries
12. Kürtőskalács Window
13. Town Under the Town

PLANNING YOUR TIME

Mellow Eger is a fine side trip from Budapest. It's a doable round-trip in a single day (about two hours by train, car, or bus each way), but it's much more satisfying and relaxing to spend the night.

Get oriented with my self-guided town walk, including visits to the cathedral and the Lyceum's fine old library and thrillingly low-tech camera obscura. Have a memorable lunch on the square, and—if you enjoy organ music—take in the midday concert in the cathedral (May-Oct only). Then hike up to the castle for views over town. In the late afternoon, unwind at a thermal bath—either in Eger or in the countryside. Round out your day with dinner on the square or a visit to Eger's touristy wine caves in the Sirens' Valley.

In July and August (when Hungarians prefer to go to Lake Balaton), Eger is busy with international visitors; in September and October, around the wine harvest, most of the tourists are Hungarians.

Orientation to Eger

Eger Castle sits at the top of the town, hovering over Dobó Square (Dobó István tér). Two blocks west of Dobó Square—away from the castle—is the main pedestrian drag, Széchenyi utca, where you'll find the Lyceum and the cathedral. A few blocks south from the castle (along the small creek) is Eger's thermal baths complex.

Tourist Information: Staff at Eger's TI (TourInform) are eager to answer your questions (Mon-Fri 9:00-18:00, Sat-Sun until 13:00; off-season Mon-Fri 9:00-17:00, Sat until 13:00, closed Sun; Bajcsy-Zsilinszky utca 9, tel. 36/517-715, www.visiteger.com).

ARRIVAL IN EGER

By Train: Eger's tiny train station is a 20-minute walk south of the center. The baggage-deposit desk is out along the platform by track 1, between the WCs (daily 7:00-19:00; if you can't find attendant, ask at ticket desk). An ATM is at the Spar grocery store just up the street (turn left out of station, walk about 100 yards, and look for red-and-white supermarket on your right; the ATM is next to the main door, around front).

Taxis generally wait out front to take new arrivals into town (1,000-1,200 Ft). Try to take a taxi marked with a company name and number.

To catch the **bus** toward the center, go a block straight out of the station. Buses #11, #12, and #14 cut about 10 minutes off the walk into town (tickets are 350 Ft from driver or 255 Ft at train station newsstand facing track 1—ask for *helyijárat buszjegy*). Get off the bus when you reach the big yellow cathedral.

To **walk** all the way, leave the station straight ahead, walk one block, take the hard right turn with the road, and then continue straight (along busy Deák Ferenc utca) about 10 minutes until you run into the cathedral.

By Car: In this small town, most hotels will provide parking or help you find a lot. For a short visit, head for the pay parking garage near the market hall (just north of the main square), or park in the pay lot near the thermal bath complex and swimming pool on Petőfi Sándor tér (a 10-minute walk south of the main square).

GETTING AROUND EGER

Everything of interest in Eger is within walking distance. But a taxi can be helpful to reach outlying sights, including the Sirens' Valley wine caves and the thermal baths in the countryside (taxi meter starts at 450 Ft, then around 380 Ft/km; try City Taxi, tel. 36/555-555, toll-free tel. 0680-622-622).

HELPFUL HINTS

Blue Monday: Note that the castle museums, the Lyceum's library, and the Kepes Institute are closed on Mondays. But you can still visit the cathedral (and enjoy its organ concert), swim in the thermal bath, explore the market, see the castle grounds, and enjoy the local wine.

Market: Eger has a humble, old-fashioned Market Hall (Piaccsarnok), which offers a taste of local life. This ramshackle hall is a totally untouristy scene, with rough plastic tubs piled high with an abundance of fresh local produce (opens daily at 6:00; while open weekday afternoons, it's best in the mornings).

Nightlife: Things quiet down pretty early in this sedate town. Youthful student bars and hangouts cluster along the main "walking street," Széchenyi utca (especially Fri and Sat nights). Older travelers feel more at home on Little Dobó Square, with schmaltzy live music until 21:00 or 22:00 in summer; wine bars nearby may stay open later.

Eger Town Walk

Charming Eger is a delight to stroll. This walk begins near two of the city's main landmarks—in an area more local than touristy—then heads to its delightful main square, before winding up to its castle. It includes pretty much anything you'd want to see in town and takes less than an hour, not including sightseeing stops (at the Lyceum and castle).

• *We'll begin on the parklike square called Eszterházy tér, at the southern edge of the town center—between the cathedral (with two yellow rectangular towers and a dome) and the Lyceum (with a tall tower capped by an oxidized copper bulb). To get here from the main square, angle up Bajcsy-Zsilinszky utca, passing a fine Art Nouveau facade and the TI.*

Eszterházy Tér

This square is named for Bishop Károly Eszterházy (1725-1799), who helped put Eger on the map during his 40 years in power. Eszterházy had serious clout, which he wielded to transform Eger from a provincial town into a beautiful small city—with lovely architecture that far exceeded its lowly position.

Face the blocky building at the bottom of the square—the **Lyceum,** or teacher-training college. Eszterházy wanted a university in Eger, but Habsburg empress Maria Theresa refused to allow it. And so, instead, Eszterházy built the most impressive teacher-training college on the planet—and stocked it with the best books and astronomical equipment that money could buy. The Lyceum still trains local teachers (enrollment: about 2,000). Tourists also roam the halls of the Lyceum; they come to visit its classic old library and its astronomy museum (which has a fascinating camera obscura), both tucked away in the big, confusing building. For details, see "Sights in Eger," later.

Now turn 180 degrees and face the cathedral, up the grand staircase at the opposite end of the square. (We'll go inside soon.) The palace that sprawls to the right is the residence of the archbishop. And on the right side of the steps is the entrance to the **Town Under the Town** (Város a Város Alatt), a 45-minute guided tour of the archbishop's former wine cellar network (1,500 Ft, generally departs at the top of each hour—schedule posted at door, 5-person minimum, you'll get a little English sprinkled in with the Hungarian; daily 9:00-18:00, Oct-March until 17:00—these are last tour times, tel. 20/961-4019, www.varosavarosalatt.hu).

Head up the grand staircase. You'll pass saints István and László—Hungary's first two Christian kings—and then the apostles Peter and Paul.

• *At the top of the stairs, gape up at...*

Eger Cathedral

The second-biggest church in Hungary (after Esztergom's—see page 681) is worth ▲▲. The cathedral was built in the 1830s by an Austrian archbishop who had previously served in Venice and who thought Eger could use a little more class. The colonnaded Neoclassical facade, painted a pretty Habsburg yellow, boasts some fine Italian sculpture.

Cost and Hours: 300-Ft donation requested, Mon-Sat 9:00-11:00 & 12:00-18:00, Sun 13:30-18:00, Pyrker János tér 1.

Organ Concerts: The cathedral organ booms out a glorious 30-minute concert daily in summer—800 Ft, May-Oct Mon-Sat at 11:30, Sun at 12:45.

Visiting the Cathedral: As you head inside, look near the back-left corner for the statue of **Szent Rita,** a local favorite (that's the 15th-century saint Rita of Cascia, from Italy). The votive plaques that say *köszönöm* and *hálából* are offering "thanks" and "gratitude" for prayers answered.

Across from Rita is a statue honoring St. Maksymilian Kolbe (1894-1941), a Polish priest who was executed at Auschwitz; around the corner from him (in the corridor) is another 20th-century martyr, the Hungarian cardinal József Mindszenty (1892-1975), who ran afoul of the communist authorities and lived in the US embassy in Budapest until he escaped to the US.

Now walk down the nave, to the first collection box. Then, turning back to face the door, look up at the ornate **ceiling fresco:** On the left, it shows Hungarians in traditional dress; and on the

right, the country's most important historical figures. At the bottom, you see this cathedral, celestially connected with St. Peter's in Rome (opposite). This symbol of devotion to the Vatican was a brave statement when it was painted in 1950. The communists were closing churches in other small Hungarian towns, but the Eger archbishop had enough clout to keep this one open.

Continue to the transept, stopping directly underneath the main dome. The **stained-glass windows** decorating the north and south transepts were donated to the cathedral by a rich Austrian couple to commemorate the 1,000th anniversary of Hungary's conversion to Christianity—notice the dates: 1000 (when St. István converted the Magyars to Christianity), and 2000.

Turning to leave, notice the enormous **organ**—Hungary's second-largest—above the door (try to catch an organ concert—see details earlier).

• *Head back out of the church and down the stairs. When you reach the Lyceum, turn left and walk down...*

Széchenyi Utca

This is Eger's main walking street, lined with colorful townhouses, cafés, and eateries. You'll find that the businesses are mostly oriented to locals (especially students), with a few touristy spots mixed in.

One block down the street, on the left, step through the gate into the grand garden courtyard of the **Archbishop's Palace.** In the peaceful garden, observe the statue on the left, honoring St. István (see page 690), and on the right, a statue for St. Erzsébet (Elisabeth)—notice the roses in her apron, a nod to the most famous story about her. You can pay to enter the palace itself, with fine old halls described by the dryly informative audioguide (included in the entry fee). As you walk through the bishop's apartments, you'll see vestments, a model of the cathedral, chalices, rare books, a picture gallery, and a balcony looking down into the bishop's private chapel. However, it's pretty dull, and other sights in Eger are more interesting (1,800 Ft, Tue-Sun 10:00-18:00, cheaper and open until 16:00 Oct-March, closed Mon year-round).

Back out on Széchenyi utca, continue one more block, then turn right down Szent János utca (at the McDonald's). Enjoy Eger's pedestrianized core for one long block—noticing that these streets, too, are populated almost entirely by Egerites, despite being just a few steps off the main square. Near the end of the street, on the right at #10, look for the *kürtőskalács* window, selling that heavenly scented Hungarian sweet street food.

• *You'll pop out at...*

Dobó Square (Dobó István Tér)

Dobó Square—worth ▲▲—is the heart of Eger. Ringed by pretty Baroque buildings and watched over by Eger's historic castle, this square is one of the most pleasant spots in Hungary.

Looking to the left, you'll spot a huge *EGER* sign—mark-

ing a second, adjoining square along the town creek. If you walk past the sign and keep going just a couple of minutes, you'll run into the rustic town market (described earlier, under "Helpful Hints"). Between here and the *EGER* sign is a handy Spar supermarket, with an ATM by the door.

Dominating the main square are the twin towers of the exqui-

sitely photogenic **Minorite Church**—often said to be the most beautiful Baroque church in Hungary. The shabby interior is less interesting but has some appealing details. Go inside (free, daily 9:30-17:30). Notice that each of the hand-carved wooden pews has a different motif. Pay close attention to the side altars that flank the nave: The first set (left and right) are 3-D illustrations, painted to replicate the wood altars that burned in a fire; the next set are real. And looking up at the faded ceiling frescoes, you'll see (in the sec-

István Dobó and the Siege of Eger

In the 16th century, Ottoman invaders swept into Hungary. They easily defeated a Hungarian army—in just two hours—at the Battle of Mohács in 1526.

When Buda and Pest fell to the Ottomans in 1541, Eger became the last line of defense. István Dobó and his second-in-command, István Mekcsey, were put in charge of Eger's forces. They prepared the castle for a siege and waited.

On September 11, 1552—after a summer spent conquering more than 30 other Hungarian fortresses on their march northward—40,000 Ottomans arrived in Eger. Only about 2,000 Egerites (soldiers, their wives, and their children) remained to protect their town. The Ottomans expected an easy victory, but the siege dragged on for 39 days. Eger's soldiers fought valiantly, and the women of Eger also joined the fray, pouring hot tar down on the Ottomans. Gergely Bornemissza, sent to reinforce the people of Eger, startled the Ottomans with all manner of clever and deadly explosives. His "fire wheel"—a barrel of gunpowder studded with smaller jars of explosives—would be lit and rolled downhill to wreak havoc until the final, deadly explosion. Ultimately, the Ottomans left in shame, Eger was saved, and Dobó was a national hero.

The unfortunate epilogue: The Ottomans came back in 1596 and succeeded in conquering an Eger Castle guarded by unmotivated mercenaries. The Ottomans controlled the region for close to a century.

In 1897, a castle archaeologist named Géza Gárdonyi moved from Budapest to Eger, where tales of the siege captured his imagination. Gárdonyi wrote a book about István Dobó and the 1552 Siege of Eger called *Egri Csillagok* ("Stars of Eger," translated into English as *Eclipse of the Crescent Moon,* available at local bookstores and souvenir stands). The book—a favorite of many Hungarians—is taught in schools, keeping the legend of Eger's heroes alive today.

EGER

ond one from the entrance) the church's patron: St. Anthony of Padua, who's preaching God's word to the fishes after the townspeople refused to hear him.

The green, arcaded building to the right of the Minorite Church is the **Town Hall,** next to an old-fashioned **pharmacy.**

Walk to the dynamic statue in the middle of the square, which depicts **István Dobó** (EESHT-vahn DOH-boh). The square's namesake and Eger's greatest hero, Dobó defended the city—and all of Hungary—from an Ottoman invasion in 1552 (see his story in the sidebar). Next to Dobó is his co-commander, István Mekcsey. And right at their side is one of the brave women of Eger—depicted here throwing a pot down onto the attackers.

Behind the statue of Dobó is a bridge over the stream that bisects the city. Just before you reach that bridge, look to the left and you'll see the northernmost Ottoman **minaret** in Europe—once part of a mosque, it's now a tourist attraction.

At the bridge, pause and look down at the little **creek** below street level. Notice the finely manicured trail that runs along the creek, beckoning to strollers and cyclists. If you follow this creek to the right, in less than 10 minutes you'll reach Eger's excellent thermal-bathing complex (described later, under "Experiences in Eger"). Like much of Hungary, this part of Eger sits on deposits of natural thermal water...can you detect a faint whiff of sulfur?

Across the bridge is the charming **Little Dobó Square** (Kis-Dobó tér), the most atmospheric place in Eger for an al fresco drink or meal. The wine bar on the square offers tastings, and you'll find more options just up the street.

• *Our brief orientation walk is over. The town's most prominent sight—the castle—is just overhead, hovering over Little Dobó Square. To reach it, bear right at the top of the square, then turn right on Dobó utca. Follow this pleasant street—lined with an ever-changing array of gift shops, wine bars and wine shops, eateries, and other tourist-oriented businesses—a few short blocks. Soon you'll reach a little park (with a lute-playing figure on a bench); the ramp up to the castle is just beyond this, on the left.*

Sights in Eger

▲EGER CASTLE (EGRI VÁR)

The great St. István—Hungary's first Christian king—founded a church on this hill a thousand years ago. The church was destroyed by Tatars in the 13th century, and this fortress was built to repel another attack. Most importantly, this castle is Hungary's Alamo, where István Dobó defended Eger from the Ottomans in 1552—as depicted in the relief just outside the entry gate. These days, it's usually crawling with field-tripping schoolchildren from all over the country. (Every Hungarian sixth grader reads *Eclipse of the Crescent Moon*, which thrillingly recounts

the heroic siege of Eger.) For those of us who didn't grow up hearing the legend of István Dobó, the complex is hard to appreciate, and English information is sparse. Most visitors find that the most rewarding plan is simply to stroll up, wander the grounds, play "king of the castle" along the ramparts, and enjoy the sweeping views over Eger's rooftops. I'd skip the "casements tour," which costs extra and is in Hungarian only.

Cost and Hours: 1,700 Ft, 850-Ft "walking ticket" gets you into the castle grounds after the museums have closed—a good option; waxworks costs 500 Ft extra; castle grounds open daily 8:00-22:00, Nov-March until 21:00; exhibits open Tue-Sun 10:00-18:00, off-season until 16:00, closed Mon year-round; tel. 36/312-744, www.egrivar.hu. The entrance ramp to the castle is at the end of Dobó István utca, a short walk from Little Dobó Square.

Visiting the Castle: Buy your ticket at the lower gate, then hike up the entry ramp and through the inner gate into the main courtyard—with grassy fields, souvenir stands, and easy access to the ramparts.

Get your bearings by walking up to the round turret with the tall Hungarian flag, to the left as you enter, and take a visual tour over the rooftops of Eger. (If you've completed my Eger Town Walk, this is a fun recap.)

Looking left, spot what looks like a church tower with the feathers of an arrow vertically embedded in the top, next to a big, wooden, bulbous building. This is the Aladár Bitskey Pool, designed by the great Organic architect Imre Makovecz. It anchors Eger's delightful thermal bath area—well worth considering for a break from sightseeing.

Panning 90 degrees to the right, look down over Eger's charming main square, with the twin towers of the Minorite Church. Just beyond, see the round dome and two rectangular towers of the cathedral, and the boxy Baroque tower with a copper bulb on top—that's the Lyceum, with its prized camera obscura. Széchenyi utca—the main walking street—stretches from these two buildings to the right, to the twin yellow church spires.

Looking farther right, try to spot Eger's minaret (which may be hidden behind the turret)—the northernmost Ottoman minaret still standing in Europe. And all around you are the wooded Bükk Hills, which hide an important wine-growing region.

Now head into the castle proper. Face straight ahead from where you entered. The **round tower** on your left usually holds good temporary exhibitions, down deep inside. And off on the right, just inside the wall, you may see an **archery** exhibit where you can pay to test your skill shooting old-fashioned bows and crossbows.

Now walk straight ahead, through the corridor with the little information window, and emerge into a pink, Gothic-style court-

EGER

yard. Immediately to your left, notice the entrance to the **dungeon.** While the "casements" you may see advertised are not worth paying extra (or spending 45 minutes listening to Hungarian commentary), hiking down into this dungeon—covered by your castle ticket—is a similar experience. The long building on the left, next to the dungeon entrance, has the **$$$ 1552 Restaurant,** serving up big plates of hearty traditional food; upstairs are temporary exhibits.

Straight ahead, upstairs in the building with the Gothic arches, is the castle's **museum** (with English descriptions). You'll see some architectural decorations, swords and suits of armor, and models of the castle through history—including one illustrating the Ottoman siege of Eger. Also inside are some paintings and a screen showing a classic movie that dramatized the siege, adding to its legend. The most interesting exhibit is a small side room with objects the Ottomans left behind: weapons, everyday items (pots, bowls), a carpet, and some turban-shaped gravestones.

Head through the little gap between the two buildings of the courtyard to find the **waxworks,** or "Panoptikum." Run separately from the castle sights, this costs 500 Ft extra. And, while it's kind of silly, it's fun for kids or kids at heart. Think of it as a very low-tech, walk-through *Ottomans of the Caribbean.* You'll see a handful of eerily realistic heroes and villains from the siege of Eger (including István Dobó himself, and the leader of the Ottomans sitting in his colorful tent). Notice the exaggerated Central Asian features of the Egerites—a reminder that the Magyars were more Asian than European. A visit to the waxworks also lets you scramble through a segment of the  tunnels that run inside the castle walls (a plus, since it's not really worth it to wait around through the similar, Hungarian-language casements tour).

From here, you can explore the **grounds,** including the remains of a once-grand cathedral and a smaller rotunda dating from the days of St. István (10th or 11th century; at the far-right corner as you enter).

SIGHTS IN THE LYCEUM (LÍCEUM)

Eger's teacher-training college fills a historic old building that—among all the students, classrooms, and professors' offices—houses two sights worth a look: a glorious Baroque library, with shelves of historic books and a frescoed ceiling; and the "Magic Tower," with

some scientific exhibits and a working camera obscura (Eszterházy tér 1). While both are inside the same building, they are treated as separate sights. For more on the history of this building, see my Eger Town Walk, earlier.

Cost and Hours: Library and Magic Tower cost 1,000 Ft each. Library open Tue-Sun 9:30-15:30, closed Mon and generally closed off-season (since there's no heating). Magic Tower open daily 9:30-17:30; closed Mon in spring and fall; shorter hours (likely weekend mornings only) or closed altogether in winter; www.varazstorony.hu.

▲▲Baroque Library

First, visit the Lyceum's old-fashioned Baroque library one floor up: From the main entry hall, cut through the middle of the courtyard, go up the stairs to the next floor, and look for Room 223, marked *Biblioteca Eszterhazyana* (it's on the right side of the complex as you face it from the entrance). This library houses 60,000 books (here and in the two adjoining rooms, with several stacked two deep), all cataloged carefully. This is no easy task, since they're in over 30 languages—from Thai to Tagalog—and are shelved according to size, rather than topic. Only one percent of the books are in Hungarian—but half of them are in

Latin. The shelves are adorned with golden seals depicting some of the great minds of science, philosophy, and religion. Marvel at the gorgeous ceiling fresco, dating from 1778. To thank the patron of this museum, say *köszönöm* to the guy in the second row up, to the right of the podium (above the entry door, second from left, not wearing a hat)—that's Bishop Károly Eszterházy, who founded the Lyceum and for whom the library is named. A portrait of him often stands on an easel at ground level. And the display cases ringing the room show off treasures from the collection—they are changed every year, to avoid exposing any books to sunlight for too long.

▲Magic Tower (Varázstorony)

Turn right as you leave the library to find the staircase that leads up the misnamed "Magic Tower," which is really all about science (*Varázstorony*, follow signs several flights up). First you'll reach the **Astronomical Museum.** Some dusty old stargazing instruments occupy one room, as well as a meridian line in the floor (a dot of sunlight dances along this line each day around noon). Across the hall is a fun, interactive **magic room,** where you can try out scientific experiments—such as using air pressure to make a ball levitate or sending a mini "hot-air balloon" up to the ceiling.

A few more flights up is the Lyceum's treasured **camera obscura**—one of just two originals surviving in Europe (the other is in Edinburgh). You'll enter a dark room and gather around a big, bowl-like canvas, where the guide will fly you around the streets of Eger (presentations about 2/hour, maybe more when busy). Fun as it is today, this camera must have astonished viewers when it was built in 1776—well before anyone had seen "moving pictures." It's a bit of a huff to get up here (nine flights of stairs, 302 steps)—but the camera obscura, and the actual view of Eger from the outdoor terrace just outside, are worth it.

Experiences in Eger

AQUA EGER

Swimming and water sports are as important to Egerites as good wine. They're proud that many of Hungary's Olympic medalists in aquatic events have come from the surrounding county. The men's water polo team took the gold for Hungary at three Olympiads in a row (2000-2008), Katinka Hosszú shattered records at the Rio games in 2016, and speed swimmer László Cseh spent much of his career winning silver medals just behind Michael Phelps. The town's Aladár Bitskey swimming pool—arguably the most striking building in this part of Hungary—is practically a temple to water sports.

Eger also has several appealing thermal bath complexes: one right in town, and two more a few miles away (near the village of Egerszalók). Budapest offers classier bath experiences, but the Eger options are modern, fully accessible, and far less crowded with American tourists—making them, for some travelers, an all-around better experience. Before you go, be sure to read the thermal bath tips on page 624.

Baths and Pools in Eger

All of these are managed by the same organization (www.egertermal.hu). Bring your swimsuit and (if you have them) flipflops; you can rent a towel if you need to.

Getting There: Eger's bathing complex is a pleasant walk (less than 10 minutes) from the center of town. From the bridge on Dobó Square, follow the creek four blocks south (look for signs to *Strand*). When you reach Petőfi tér, you're in the aquatic area. The swimming pool is on your left (look for the unique steeple), and the thermal bathing complex is straight ahead; to reach the main entrance, continue straight into the park, then look for the entrance on your left, over a bridge, marked by a big dome. The Turkish bath entrance is around the other side of the complex.

Aladár Bitskey Swimming Pool (Bitskey Aladár Uszoda)

This striking swimming pool was designed by Imre Makovecz, the father of Hungary's Organic architectural style (see sidebar). Some Eger taxpayers resented the pool's big price tag, but it left the city with an iconic building befitting its love of water sports. The building is worth a peek—and you can swim in it, too.

Cost and Hours: 1,050 Ft, Mon-Fri 6:00-21:00, Sat-Sun 7:30-18:00, Frank Tivadar utca, tel. 36/511-810.

▲Eger Thermal Bath (Eger Termálfürdő)

For a refreshing break from the sightseeing grind, consider a splash at the spa. This is a wonderful opportunity to try a Hungarian bath: fun, accessible, and frequented mostly by locals. Note that there are two adjoining sections: the sprawling indoor/outdoor thermal bath section and the smaller Turkish bath. Each has its own ticket, but it's possible to move between them. If you're going to be at the bath complex for less than 2.5 hours, it's cheaper to enter through the Turkish bath section (see details later).

Cost and Hours: 1,900 Ft (cheaper Mon-Fri after 16:00); if you want to add on Turkish bath after buying the thermal bath ticket, it's an additional 1,300 Ft; complex open June-Aug daily 8:00-20:00, Sept-May daily 9:00-19:00, these are closing times—must be out of the pool 30 minutes earlier; Petőfi tér 2, main entrance is through Archbishop's Garden (Érsekkert), tel. 36/510-558.

Taking the Waters: Eger's bath complex uses a similar wristband system to the one in Budapest. After paying, you are issued a wristband that you'll use to access your locker. Change, stow your stuff, then head out and have fun. The complex is huge, with a wide array of different pools, each one labeled with its depth and

EGER

temperature. The best part is the double-domed, indoor-outdoor adventure bath, right at the main entrance (a very comfortable 34°C/93°F). Its cascades, jets, bubbles, geysers, and powerful current pool will make you feel like a kid again. The adjoining pool is warmer (36-38°C/97-100°F) and the most popular area to hang out—Egerites sit peacefully, ignore the slight stink, and feel their arthritis ebb away. Sprawling in both directions are additional pools—for kids, for swimming laps, and for hanging out. The waterslides at the right end (with your back to the main dome) are open only in summer, while the Turkish bath is in a smaller domed building at the opposite end, to the left.

▲Turkish Bath (Török Fürdő)

Eger recently refurbished its Turkish-style bath, tucked in one corner of the thermal bath complex. The Turk-ish bath is small but elegant. The underside of the central dome—over a 30°C/86°F pool—glitters with golden tile. Surrounding that are hotter mineral pools (34-36°C/93-97°F), as well as a sauna, steam bath, and aroma bath. This area connects to the thermal bath complex through a turnstile, and uses the same wristband system (Turkish bath entrance is around the left side, as you approach the bath complex from the center).

Cost and Hours: The 2,200-Ft Turkish bath is a great deal—it covers you for up to 2.5 hours in both the Turkish bath and the thermal bath area. (If you buy your bath ticket at the main entrance, then want to enter the Turkish bath, you'll be charged an extra entry fee—a poor value.) The Turkish bath is also open later: daily until 21:00 (Mon-Tue from 16:30, Wed-Thu from 15:00, Fri from 13:00, Sat-Sun from 9:00; exit the pools 30 minutes before closing; tel. 36/510-522). If you visit late in the day, a good strategy is to enter and change at the Turkish bath (entrance at Fürdő utca 3), head over to the thermal complex first, then move back into the Turkish bath when the rest is closed.

Baths near Eger, in Egerszalók

Two more thermal baths—Salt Hill and Demjén Cascade—sit in the countryside outside Eger, flanking a rocky hill between the vil-

Hungary's Organic Architecture

Hungary's postcommunist generation has embraced a unique, eye-catching style of architecture, called Organic, which was developed and championed by Imre Makovecz (1935-2011).

In his youth, Makovecz pursued a flowing style that was quite intentionally at odds with the rigid right angles of communist architecture. He was inspired by the Art Nouveau of a bygone and "decadent" Golden Age, and by pioneering architects from other countries (including American Frank Lloyd Wright, who employed a more angular style but a similar aesthetic of fitting his works to their surroundings).

After being blacklisted by the regime for his stubborn adherence to his architectural vision—and for his nationalistic politics—Makovecz ramped up his pursuit of something new. Makovecz made do with sticks, rocks, and other foraged building materials. He was also inspired by Transylvanian village architecture: whitewashed walls with large, overhanging mansard roofs (resembling a big mushroom).

After the fall of the regime, Makovecz swiftly became Hungary's premier architect. He believed that a building should be a product of its environment, rather than a cookie-cutter copy. Organic buildings use indigenous materials (especially wood) and take on unusual forms—often inspired by animals or plants—that blend in with the landscape. These buildings look like they're rising up out of the ground, rather than plopped down on top of it. Makovecz preferred to work in small communities such as Eger (see photo on page 695) instead of working for large corporations. Makovecz wanted his creations—from churches, thermal baths, and campgrounds to cultural centers, restaurants, and bus stations—to represent the civic pride of the local community. For more on Makovecz, visit www.makovecz.hu.

EGER

lages of Egerszalók and Demjén. While these baths lack the old-fashioned class of the Budapest options, they more than compensate with soggy fun. Here's a fun and very hedonistic afternoon plan: Take the bus or taxi to the spa, taxi back to Eger's Sirens' Valley for some wine-cave hopping, then taxi back to your Eger hotel.

Getting There: Both baths are about a mile outside the village of Egerszalók, which is itself about three miles from Eger. **Drivers** leave Eger to the south, toward *Kerecsend*/Route 25; at the roundabout on the outskirts of town, turn right toward *Egerszalók* and *Demjén*. A few minutes later, watch (on the left) for the easy-to-miss turnoff to Saliris Resort (park along the road for 450 Ft)—or, for Demjén Cascade, carry on past this, turn left at the T intersection, and head into Demjén village.

Without a car, you can take a public **bus** from Eger's bus station to the baths (take bus going toward Demjén; for Salt Hill, get off at the *Egerszalók Gyógyfürdő* stop—tell the bus driver "EH-gehr-saw-lohk FEWR-dur"—just after leaving the town of Egerszalók; for Demjén Cascade, get off at the entrance to Demjén village; bus runs 9/day Mon-Sat, fewer on Sun, 20-minute trip, 500 Ft). Check the return bus information carefully (especially on weekends, when frequency plummets). Or you can take a **taxi** from Eger (about 4,000 Ft; tel. 36/555-555 for a return taxi from Egerszalók).

Nearby Wineries: The village of Egerszalók has several fine wineries, including the excellent **St. Andrea**—fun to combine with your bath visit (for details, see the "Wineries near the Baths in Egerszalók" section, later).

▲▲Salt Hill Thermal Spa (at the Saliris Resort)

For decades, Egerites would come to this "salt hill" (a natural terraced formation caused by min-
eral-rich spring water running
down the hillside) in the middle
of nowhere and cram together to
baste in pools of hot water. Then
the developers arrived. Today,
the gigantic Saliris Resort hotel
and spa complex, built near
those original formations, offers
a world of hot-water fun tucked

into a scenic valley. With 12 indoor pools and five outdoor ones—
many cleverly overlapping one another on several levels—these baths are worth the trip outside Eger.

Cost and Hours: 5,800 Ft all day, 3,400 Ft for up to 3 hours, 2,200 Ft if you enter after 17:00, all ticket prices are 1,000 Ft extra on busy "special days"; 2,000 Ft extra for sauna world; towel rental, massage, and other treatments are also available; open June-Aug daily 10:00-20:00, pools close at 19:00, tel. 36/688-500, http://salirisresort.hu/en.

Visiting the Bath: This complex uses the same system as at Eger's thermal baths: Press your wristband against a computer screen to be assigned a locker, change in the private cabin, then have fun.

From the locker room, a blue carpet leads you out to the pools. Take some time to explore the sprawling complex. The two main pools—warm (32-34°C/90-93°F) and hot (35-39°C/95-102°F)—extend both inside and outside and cascade over several levels. Outside, down on the lower level, is a vast kiddie pool.

Tucked around the right side of the building (as you face the complex) is the "sauna world," with five different types of saunas, some quieter soaking pools, and a clothing-optional outdoor area with wood cabin-type huts that contain Finnish and Russian saunas (touch your wristband to the turnstile to pay extra for access to this area).

▲Demjén Cascade Thermal Spa

Just over the hill from Salt Hill Thermal Spa, Demjén Baths was recently converted into a high-end resort. The original "thermal valley" *(termál völgy)* part of the complex—pretty but unpretentious, with nicely rustic wooden buildings and pools—is reasonably priced and open extremely long hours, making it popular with locals. Jets, fountains, and other "adventure bath"-type features are rare, and the goal here is simply stewing in pools of warm water. A separate "aquapark" section adds waterslides and a diving pool, for an extra charge. But the big draw for thermal-bathing enthusiasts is the newer "cave bath" *(barlangfürdő)*—a subterranean complex of pools, channels, waterslides, hidden grottoes, eerie mood lighting, and a sci-fi/fantasy theme. While the Salt Hill spa described earlier is still a more enjoyable all-around experience, those intrigued by the novelty of an underground thermal playland might prefer to check out Demjén.

Cost and Hours: Thermal spa—1,900 Ft, daily 9:00-2:00 in the morning; aquapark—1,900 Ft extra, open in good weather only, closes at 20:00; cave bath—5,000 Ft, 500 Ft more on weekends, 500 Ft less if you stay 3 hours or less, ticket also includes thermal spa, Mon-Thu 10:00-21:00, Fri 10:00-22:00, Sat 9:00-22:00, Sun 9:00-21:00; mobile +3630-853-7419, www.demjencascade.hu.

EGER WINE

Eger is at the heart of one of Hungary's best-known wine regions, internationally famous for its **Bull's Blood** (Egri Bikavér). You'll likely hear various stories as to how Bull's Blood got its name during the Ottoman siege of Eger. My favorite version: The Ottomans were amazed at the ferocity displayed by the Egerites and wondered what they were drinking that boiled their blood and stained their

EGER

beards so red...it must be potent stuff. Local merchants, knowing that the Ottomans were Muslim and couldn't drink alcohol, told them it was bull's blood. The merchants made a buck, and the name stuck.

Creative as these stories are, they're all bunk—the term dates only from 1851. Egri Bikavér is a blend (everyone has their own recipe), so you generally won't find it at small producers. Cabernet sauvignon, merlot, *kékfrankos,* and *kékoportó* are the most commonly used grapes.

But Bull's Blood is just the beginning of what the Eger wine region offers. Although Eger is better known for its reds, 42 of the 62 regional varieties are white. (For details, see the "Hungarian Wines" sidebar on page 544.)

Tasting Local Wine: While it would be enjoyable to drive around the Hungarian countryside visiting a few wineries (and I've recommended one great choice, St. Andrea), the most accessible way to get a quick taste of local wine is at a wine shop in town. Several cluster on Little Dobó Square (Kis-Dobó tér) and just uphill, along Dobó István utca. As specific shops tend to come and go, I'd simply stroll this area looking for signs advertising tastings or small glasses of wine, and find a clerk who speaks enough English to help you navigate your choices.

Sirens' Valley (Szépasszony-völgy)

When the Ottoman invaders first occupied Eger, some residents moved into the valley next door, living in caves dug into the hillside. Eventually the Ottomans were driven out, the Egerites moved back to town, and the caves became wine cellars. (Most Eger families who can afford it have at least a modest vineyard in the countryside.) There are more than 300 such caves in the valley to the southwest of Eger, several of which are open for visitors.

The best selection of these caves (about 50) is in the Sirens' Valley (sometimes also translated as "Valley of the Beautiful Women"—or, on local directional signs, the less poetic "Nice Woman Valley"). While the valley can feel vacant and dead (even sometimes in the summer), if you visit when it's busy it can be a fun scene—locals showing off their latest vintage, with picnic tables and tipsy tourists spilling out into the street. At some places, you'll be offered free samples; others have a menu for tastes or glasses of wine. While you're not expected to buy a bottle, it's a nice gesture to buy one if you've spent a while at one cave (and it's usually very cheap). Most caves offer something light to eat with the wine, and the area also has full-service restaurants. Some of the caves are fancy and finished, staffed by multilingual waiters in period costume. Others feel like a dank basement, with grandpa leaning

EGER

on his moped out front and a monolingual granny pouring the wine inside.

This experience is a strange mix of touristy and local, but not entirely accessible to non-Hungarian-speakers—it works best with a bunch of friends and an easygoing, sociable attitude. Hopping from cave to musky cave can make for an enjoyable evening, but be sure to wander around a bit to survey the options before you dive in (cellars generally open 10:00-21:00 in summer, best June-Aug in the late afternoon and early evening, plus good-weather weekends in the shoulder season; it's sleepy and not worth a visit off-season, when only a handful of cellars remain open for shorter hours).

Getting to the Sirens' Valley: The valley is on the southwest outskirts of Eger. Figure no more than 1,300 Ft for a **taxi** between your hotel and the caves.

Wineries near the Baths in Egerszalók

The village of Egerszalók, near the Salt Hill and Demjén Cascade thermal baths, has a variety of fun wineries. The most interesting, and well worth a visit for wine lovers, is **St. Andrea.** This slick, modern, Napa Valley-esque facility offers cellar tours and tastings of their excellent wines, which show up on fine restaurant menus across Hungary. They're evangelical both about their spirituality (hence the name) and their wine, and enjoy explaining everything in English. They focus on blends that highlight the unique proper-ties of this region, and produce some good, pungent whites with volcanic qualities. While it may be possible to simply drop in for a tasting, it's better to call ahead and let them know you're coming (3,900 Ft/person for 6 tastings, or 8,000 Ft/person for premium wines, bottles from 2,500 Ft, Mon-Sat 10:00-18:00, closed Sun, Ady Endre út 88 in Egerszalók, tel. 36/474-018, www.standrea.hu, kostolas@standrea.hu). They also have a top-end wine bar in Bu-dapest (see page 644). It's most practical with a car (or by taxi), but you can also walk there from the bus stop in Egerszalók's town cen-ter (about a half-mile; head down Ady Endre út, toward the baths).

Sleeping in Eger

Eger is a good overnight stop. I've focused my listings on quaint, well-located hotels. There's no real "luxury" in this town—just big-ger, tour-oriented places on the outskirts. Elevators are rare—ex-pect to climb one or two flights of stairs to reach your room. Most of these hotels are in pedestrian zones, so get detailed driving and parking instructions from your hotel; many offer free or cheap parking, but it's often a block or two away. Most hotels quote their rates in euros but prefer to be paid in forints.

$ Senator Ház Hotel is one of my favorite small, family-run hotels in Eastern Europe. Though the 11 rooms are a bit worn, this place is cozy and well run by András and Csöpi Cseh and their right-hand man, Peter. It feels trapped in a nostalgic time warp, with oodles of character, all the right quirks, and a picture-perfect location just under the castle on Little Dobó Square (RS%, air-con, free parking a block away, Dobó István tér 11, tel. 36/411-711, www.senatorhaz.hu, info@senatorhaz.hu). The Cseh family also runs **$ Pátria Vendégház**—with two doubles and two luxurious apartments around a courtyard nearby.

$ Imola Udvarház rents 15 rooms and apartments—some with kitchen, living room, bedroom, and bathroom—all decorated in modern Ikea style. They're roomy, tastefully decorated, and well maintained, with a great location near the castle entrance, and the free on-site parking garage makes this a good choice for drivers (air-con, Tírodi Sebestyén tér 4, tel. 36/516-180, www.imolaudvarhaz.hu, info@imolaudvarhaz.hu).

$ Centrum Vendégház, at the bottom of the main square, has eight simple rooms and apartments around a courtyard. It's basic but comfortable, with parquet floors and traditional furnishings, and well run by László and Timea. Check in at the little grocery store on the ground floor (breakfast extra, Bajcsy-Zsilinszky 17, mobile +3630-591-3131, www.cve.hu, info@centrum-vendeghaz-eger.hu).

$ Offi Ház Hotel shares Little Dobó Square with Senator Ház (listed above). Its five rooms are classy and romantic but dated and a bit tight, with slanted ceilings. Communication can be tricky (German helps), but the location is superb (air-con, Dobó István tér 5, tel. 36/518-210, www.offihaz.hu, offihaz@upcmail.hu, Offenbächer family).

$ Centrooms Park Eger, an annex for the larger Hotel Park at the edge of town, is impersonal but indeed central, with 21 spartan but sleepable rooms right in the middle of town (breakfast extra and served at main hotel—better to just eat at a café on the square, air-con, Érsek utca 4, tel. 36/522-255, www.centroomseger.hu, info@centroomseger.hu).

¢ Dobó Vendégház, run by warm Marianna Kleszo, has seven basic but colorful rooms just off Dobó Square. Marianna speaks nothing but Hungarian but gets simple reservation emails translated by a friend (cash only, air-con in some upstairs rooms, free parking, Dobó utca 19, tel. 36/421-407, www.dobovendeghaz.hu, info@dobovendeghaz.hu).

Eating in Eger

$$ HBH Restaurant (named for the Hofbräuhaus beer on tap) offers traditional Hungarian dishes, either in a brick-and-wood dining room or—better—at fine outdoor tables at the bottom of the main square (on weekends, reserve a view table in advance). While the service can be curt, the lengthy, well-described menu and good wine list make this a fine choice for a classic Hungarian meal (daily 11:30-23:00, at the bottom of Dobó Square at Bajcsy-Zsilinszky utca 19, tel. 36/515-516, www.hbh-eger.hu).

$$$ Macok Bisztró, near the base of the ramp up to the castle, is the best choice in town for modern, upscale cuisine (and a more sophisticated dining experience). It has a classy interior, inviting tables filling a patio, a mix of Hungarian and international dishes, and an extensive wine list (Mon-Sat 10:00-22:00, Sun until 15:00, Tinódi Sebestyén tér 4, tel. 36/516-180, www.imolaudvarhaz.hu).

$$ Brumbrum is the cheaper, more casual side-restaurant of Macok. They offer tasty, unpretentious, street food-inspired plates of Hungarian and international fare, a variety of wines, and craft beer, all in an industrial-mod setting with subway tile and raw plywood (Tue-Sun 10:00-23:00, closed Mon, same contact information as above).

$$ Palacsintavár ("Pancake Castle"), near the ramp leading up to the castle, isn't your hometown IHOP. They serve up inventive, artfully presented crêpe-wrapped main courses to a mostly student clientele. The spacious interior is decorated with old cigarette boxes, rock music plays on the soundtrack, and the outdoor tables are appealing (Tue-Sun 12:00-23:00, closed Mon, Dobó utca 9, tel. 36/413-980, www.palacsintavar.hu).

$$ Restaurant Senator Ház, on Little Dobó Square, offers the best setting for al fresco dining in town, with good Hungarian and international food. Sure, you're paying a bit extra for the setting—but it's worth it for the postcard-perfect outdoor seating, from which you can survey the Little Dobó Square action (open daily 10:00-22:00, cheesy live music on summer evenings). Neighboring restaurants (such as Offi Ház) offer the same ambience.

$$ Depresso Kávéház brings a touch of modern hipness to Eger's stately main square. Despite its downer name, this young, fresh café features a wide variety of coffee drinks, wine, breakfasts, and a short menu of light meals (sandwiches, quiches, etc.). It owns a great location on the square—with fine outdoor tables facing the castle—and also has a bright, open interior (Mon-Thu 9:00-20:00, Fri-Sat until 21:00, Sun until 18:00, Érsek utca 14, mobile +3630-886-6742, www.depresso.hu).

$ Il Padrino is a popular place for simple, cheap, tasty pizzas. It's tucked down a non-touristy street a block over from the main

EGER

square, with a kitschy interior and breezy outdoor tables (daily 11:00-22:00, Fazola Henrik utca 1, mobile +3620-547-9959, www.padrinopizza.hu).

Wine and Beer: To sample either of these, begin on Little Dobó Square and head up Dobó István utca. You'll pass a few **wine bars** featuring local wines, plus **Bakelit,** a craft beer shop selling a dizzying array of Hungarian and international craft beers (daily 10:00-22:00, Dobó utca 17, www.bakelitbeer.com).

Student Eats on Széchenyi Utca: To browse for an affordable, forgettable meal, go for a walk on Eger's main walking street, which begins at the cathedral. You'll find a row of lowbrow student eateries serving a variety of pizza, gyros, and burgers, plus lots of bakeries and bars with food. A few tourist-oriented places are mixed in. Don't come here for high cuisine—but it's handy and cheap, and most places have fine outdoor seating; on weekends, the street is enlivened with dueling live music.

Dessert: *Cukrászdák* (pastry shops) line the streets of Eger. For a more local scene, find the tiny **Sárvári Cukrászda,** a block behind the Lyceum. Their pastries are good, but Egerites line up here for homemade gelato (Mon-Fri 7:00-18:00, Sat-Sun from 18:00, Kossuth utca 1, between Jókai utca and Fellner utca). You'll spot several ice-cream parlors in this town, where every other pedestrian seems to be licking a cone. Another good option is the *kürtőskalács* **window** on Szent János utca, where you can step up and grab a piping-hot chimney cake that's slow-cooked on a rotisserie, then rolled in toppings (daily 9:00-19:30, Szent János utca 10).

Eger Connections

BY TRAIN

The only major destination you'll get to directly from Eger's train station is **Budapest** (every 2 hours direct to Budapest's Keleti/Eastern Station, 2 hours; more frequent and faster with a change in Füzesabony—see below). For other destinations, you'll connect through Füzesabony or Budapest.

Eger is connected to the nearby junction town of **Füzesabony** (FEW-zesh-aw-bone) by frequent trains (13/day, 17 minutes). In Füzesabony, you can transfer to Budapest on either a slower milk-run train or a speedier InterCity train (a little pricier, as it requires a supplement, but gets you to Budapest in just under 2 hours total).

BY BUS

Eger's bus station is right in town, a five-minute uphill walk behind Eger's cathedral and the Archbishop's Palace: Go behind the cathedral and through the park, and look for the modern, green, circular building. Blue electronic boards in the center of the station show upcoming departures.

From Eger to Budapest: The direct Eger-Budapest bus service is about the same price as the train and can be a bit faster (2/hour, tickets generally available just before departure). Express buses depart Eger at :15 after each hour and make the trip in one hour and 50 minutes; slower regular buses leave at :45 after each hour and take 20 minutes longer. While Eger's bus station is closer to the town center than its train station, this bus takes you to a less central point in Budapest (near Budapest's Stadionok bus station, on the M2/red Metró line).

To the Thermal Baths near Egerszalók: Buses from the same station also connect Eger to the thermal baths near Egerszalók (Salt Hill and Demjén Cascade; see "Getting There" on page 697). However, buses marked for *Egerszalók* do not actually go to the spa; instead, you need a bus going *beyond* Egerszalók, marked for *Demjén*.

SLOVENIA

Slovenija

SLOVENIA

Tiny, overlooked Slovenia is one of Europe's most unexpectedly charming destinations. At the intersection of the Slavic, German, and Italian worlds, Slovenia is an exciting mix of the best of each culture. Though it's just a quick trip away from the tourist throngs in Croatia, Venice, Munich, Salzburg, and Vienna, Slovenia has stayed off the tourist track—making it a handy detour for in-the-know Back Door travelers. Be warned: Everyone I've met who has visited Slovenia wishes they'd allotted more time for this endearing, underrated land.

Today, it seems strange to think that Slovenia was ever part of Yugoslavia. Both in the personality of its people and in its landscape, Slovenia feels more like Austria. Slovenes are more industrious, organized, and punctual than their fellow former Yugoslavs...yet still friendly, relaxed, and Mediterranean. Locals like the balance. Visitors expecting minefields and rusting Yugo factories are pleasantly surprised to find Slovenia's rolling countryside dotted instead with quaint alpine villages and the spires of miniature Baroque churches, with snowcapped peaks in the distance.

Only half as big as Switzerland, Slovenia is remarkably diverse for its size. Travelers can hike on alpine trails in the morning and explore some of the world's best caves in the afternoon, before relaxing with a glass of local wine and a seafood dinner while watching the sun set on the Adriatic.

Though not unaffected by the Great Recession, Slovenia enjoys a prosperity unusual for a formerly communist country. The Austro-Hungarian Empire left it with a strong work ethic and an impressive industrial infrastructure, which the Yugoslav government expanded. By 1980, 60 percent of all Yugoslav industry was in little Slovenia (which had only 8 percent of Yugoslavia's popula-

tion and 8 percent of its territory). Of the 13 new nations that have joined the European Union since 2004, Slovenia was the only one rich enough to enter as a net donor (with a higher per-capita income than the average), and the first one to join the euro currency zone (it adopted the euro in January 2007). Thanks to its longstanding ties to the West and its can-do spirit, Slovenia already feels more "Western" than any other destination in this book.

The country has a funny way of making people fall in love with it. Slovenes are laid-back, easygoing, stylish, and fun. They won't win any world wars (they're too well-adjusted to even try)... but they're exactly the type of people you'd love to chat with over a cup of coffee.

The Slovenian language is as mellow as the people. While Slovenes use Serb, German, and English curses in abundance, the worst they can say in their native tongue is, "May you be kicked by a hen." For "Darn it!" they say, "Three hundred hairy bears!" In bad traffic, they might mutter, "The street is white!" (If you want to get a local hopping mad—normally a difficult feat—all you have to do is mistake their beloved homeland for Slovakia.)

Coming from such a small country, locals are proud of the few things that are distinctly Slovenian, such as the roofed hayrack. Because of the frequent rainfall in the mountainous northwest, the hayracks are covered by a roof that allows the hay to dry thoroughly. The most traditional kind is the *toplar,* consisting of two hayracks connected by one big roof. It looks like a skinny barn with open, fenced sides. Hay hangs on the sides to dry; firewood, carts, tractors, and other farm implements sit on the ground inside; and dried hay is stored in the loft above. But these wooden *toplarji* are firetraps, and a stray bolt of lightning can burn one down in a flash. So in recent years, more farmers have been moving to single hayracks *(enojni)*; these are still roofed, but have posts made of concrete rather than

wood. You'll find postcards and miniature wooden models of both kinds of hayracks (a fun souvenir).

Another uniquely Slovenian memento is a creatively decorated front panel from a beehive *(panjske končnice)*. Slovenia has a strong beekeeping tradition, and beekeepers believe that painting the

fronts of the hives makes it easier for bees to find their way home. Replicas of these panels are available at gift shops all over the country. (For more on the panels and Slovenia's beekeeping heritage, see page 808.)

Slovenia is also the land of polka. Slovenes claim that polka music was invented here, and singer/accordionist Slavko Avsenik—from the village of Begunje near Bled—cranked out popular oompah songs that made him a superstar in Germany and other alpine lands. You'll see the Avsenik ensemble (now led by Slavko's grandson) and other oompah bands on Slovenian TV, where hokey Lawrence Welk-style shows remain an institution.

To really stretch your euros, try one of Slovenia's more than 400 farmhouse B&Bs, called "tourist farms" *(turistične kmetije)*—similar to *agriturismi* in Italy. These are actual working farms (often organic) that sell meals and/or rent rooms to tourists to help make ends meet. You can use a tourist farm as a home base to explore the entire country—remember, the farthest reaches of Slovenia are only a day trip away. A comfortable, hotelesque double with a private bathroom—plus a traditional Slovenian dinner and a hearty breakfast—costs as little as €50.

Most visitors to Slovenia are, in my experience, completely charmed by the place. With all it has going for it, it's hard to believe that Slovenia is not already overrun with tourists. Somehow, this little country continues to glide beneath the radar. Exploring its mountain trails, savoring its colorful capital, and meeting its friendly locals, you'll feel like you're in on a secret.

HELPFUL HINTS

Telephones: For tips on dialing to, from, and within Slovenia, see the Practicalities chapter.

Toll Sticker: To drive on Slovenia's expressways *(avtocesta)*, you'll need to display a toll sticker *(vinjeta,* veen-YEH-tah; €15/week, €30/month). If renting your car in Slovenia, it probably comes with a sticker (but make sure); if you're driving in from elsewhere, such as Austria or Hungary, you can buy one at a gas station, post office, or some newsstands (watch for *vinjeta* signs at gas stations as you approach the border). *Be warned:* This rule is taken very seriously. If you're found driving on expressways without the sticker, you'll immediately be fined €150.

SLOVENIAN HISTORY

Slovenia has a long and unexciting history as part of various larger empires. After Illyrian, Celtic, and Roman settlements came and went, this region became populated by Slavs—the ancestors of today's Slovenes—in the late sixth century. But Charlemagne's Franks conquered the tiny land in the eighth century, and, ever since, Slovenia has been a backwater of the Germanic world—first as a holding of the Holy Roman Empire and later, the Habsburg Empire. But even as the capital, Ljubljana, was populated by Austrians (who called the city Laibach), the Slovenian language and cultural traditions survived in the countryside.

Through the Middle Ages, much of Slovenia was ruled by the Counts of Celje (highly placed vassals of the Habsburgs). In this era before modern nations—when shifting allegiances and strategic marriages dictated the dynamics of power—the Counts of Celje rose to a position of significant influence in Central and Eastern Europe. Celje daughters intermarried with some of the most powerful dynasties in the region: the Polish Piasts, the Hungarian Anjous, and the Czech Přemysls. Before long, the Counts of Celje had emerged as the Habsburgs' main rivals. In the 15th century, Count Ulrich II of Celje married into Serbia's ruling family and managed to wrest control of Hungary's massive holdings. Had he not been assassinated in 1456, this obscure Slovenian line—rather than an obscure Austrian one—may have emerged as the dominant power in the eastern half of Europe. (Instead, the Habsburgs consolidated their vanquished foe's fiefdoms into their ever-growing empire.) In homage, the three yellow stars of the Counts of Celje's seal still adorn Slovenia's coat of arms.

Soon after, with Slovenia firmly entrenched in the Counter-

SLOVENIA

Slovenia Almanac

Official Name: Republika Slovenija, or simply Slovenija.

Snapshot History: After being dominated by Germans for centuries, Slovenian culture proudly emerged in the 19th century. In the aftermath of World War I, Slovenia merged with its neighbors to become Yugoslavia, then broke away and achieved independence for the first time in 1991.

Population: Slovenia's two million people (a count similar to Nevada's) are 83 percent ethnic Slovenes who speak Slovene, plus a smattering of Serbs, Croats, and Muslim Bosniaks. Almost 60 percent of the country is Catholic.

Latitude and Longitude: 46° N and 14° E (latitude similar to Lyon, France; Montreal, Canada; or Bismarck, North Dakota).

Area: At 7,800 square miles, it's about the size of New Jersey, but with one-fourth the population.

Geography: Tiny Slovenia has four extremely different terrains and climates: the warm Mediterranean coastline (just 29 miles long—about one inch per inhabitant); the snowcapped, forested alpine mountains in the northwest (including 9,400-foot Mount Triglav); the moderate-climate, central limestone plateau that includes Ljubljana and the cave-filled Karst region; and to the east, a corner of the Great Hungarian Plain (the Prekmurje region, near Maribor and Ptuj). If you look at a map of Slovenia and squint your eyes a bit, it looks like a chicken running toward the east.

Biggest Cities: Nearly one in five Slovenes live in the two biggest cities: Ljubljana (the capital, pop. 270,000) and Maribor (in the east, pop. 158,000). Half the population lives in rural villages.

Economy: Slovenia has a gross domestic product of $67 billion and a per-capita GDP of around $32,000. Slovenia's economy is based largely on manufactured metal products (trucks and machinery), which are traded with a diverse group of partners.

Currency: Slovenia uses the euro: €1 = about $1.20.

Government: The country is led by a prime minister, who heads the leading vote-getting party in legislative elections. The prime minister governs along with a figurehead president. Slovenia's relatively peaceful secession is credited largely to former president Milan Kučan, who remains a popular figure. The National Assembly consists of about 90 elected legislators; there's also a second house of parliament, which has much less power. Despite the country's small size, it is divided into some 200 municipalities—creating a lot of bureaucracy that locals enjoy complaining about.

Flag: Three horizontal bands of white (top), blue, and red. A shield in the upper left shows Mount Triglav, with a wavy-line sea below and three stars above.

The Average Slovene: The average Slovene skis in this largely alpine country, and is an avid fan of team handball (yes, handball). He or she lives in a 250-square-foot apartment, watches 16 hours of TV a week (much of it in English with Slovene subtitles), and enjoys a drink-and-a-half of alcohol every day.

Notable Slovenes: A pair of prominent Ohio politicians from the Cleveland area—perennial presidential candidate **Dennis Kucinich** and former senator **George Voinovich**—are each half-Slovene. (In 1910, Cleveland had the biggest Slovenian population of any city in the world—just ahead of Trieste and Ljubljana.) Classical musicians might know composers **Giuseppe Tartini** and **Hugo Wolf.** Even if you haven't heard of architect **Jože Plečnik** yet, you'll hear his name a hundred times while you're in Slovenia—especially in Ljubljana (see page 755). And perhaps most famous of all is US First Lady **Melania Trump** (born Melanija Knavs in the Slovenian city of Novo Mesto).

Sporty Slovenes: If you follow alpine sports or team handball, you'll surely know some world-class athletes from Slovenia. NBA fans might recognize basketball players **Goran Dragić, Primož Brezec,** and **Bostjan Nachbar,** as well as some other less famous players. Slovenian hockey player **Anže Kopitar** plays in the NHL, and skier **Tina Maze** won two gold medals at the 2014 Winter Olympics. The athletic Slovenes—perhaps trying to compensate for the minuscule size of their country—have accomplished astonishing feats: **Davo Karničar** has skied down from the "seven summits" (the highest points in each of the seven continents—that means the peaks of Everest, Kilimanjaro, McKinley, and so on). **Benka Pulko** became the first person ever to drive a motorcycle around the world—that is, all seven continents, including Antarctica, which is also the longest solo motorcycle journey by a woman (total trip: 111,856 miles in 2,000 days; for more, see www.benkapulko.com). **Dušan Mravlje** ran across all the continents. And ultramarathon swimmer **Martin Strel** has swum nearly the entire length of several major rivers, including the Danube (of which he swam 1,866 miles), the Mississippi (2,359 miles), the Yangtze (2,487 miles), and the Amazon (3,273 miles; for more, see www.martinstrel.com).

Reformation holdings of the Habsburg Empire, the local Reformer Primož Trubar (1508-1586) strove both to put the Word of God into the people's hands, and to legitimize Slovene as a written language. This Slovenian answer to Martin Luther secretly translated the Bible into Slovene in Reformation-friendly Germany, then smuggled copies back into his homeland.

Over the next several centuries, much of Slovenia was wracked by Habsburg-Ottoman wars, as the Ottomans attempted to push north through this territory to reach Vienna. Slovenia also found itself caught in the crossfire between Austria and Venice. Seemingly exhausted by all of this warfare—and by their own sporadic, halfhearted, and unsuccessful uprisings against Habsburg rule—Slovenia languished as a sleepy backwater.

When the port city of Trieste (in Slovenian territory) was granted free status in 1718, it boosted the economy of Slovenian lands. The Enlightenment spurred a renewed interest in the Slovenian culture and language, which further flourished when Napoleon named Ljubljana the capital of his "Illyrian Provinces"—Slovenia's own mini-empire, stretching from Austria's Tirol to Croatia's Dalmatian Coast. During this brief period (1809-1813), the long-suppressed Slovene language was used for the first time in schools and the government. This kicked off a full-throated national revival movement—asserting the worthiness of the Slovenian language and culture compared to the dominant Germanic worldview of the time. Inspired by the patriotic poetry of France Prešeren (1800-1849), Slovenian pride surged.

The last century saw the most interesting chapter of Slovenian history. Some of World War I's fiercest fighting occurred at the Soča (Isonzo) Front in northwest Slovenia—witnessed by young Ernest Hemingway, who drove an ambulance there. During World War II, Slovenia was divided among Nazi allies Austria, Italy, and Hungary—and an estimated 20,000 to 25,000 Slovenes perished in Nazi- and Italian-operated concentration camps.

As Yugoslavia entered its Golden Age under war hero Marshal Tito, Slovenia's prime location where Yugoslavia meets Western Europe (a short drive from Austria or Italy)—and the diligent national character of the Slovenian people—made it a prime candidate for industrialization.

After Tito's death in 1980, the various Yugoslav republics struggled to redefine their role in the union. While many factions reverted to age-old, pre-Tito nationalistic fervor, the Slovenes grew increasingly focused on their own future...and began to press for real reforms of the communist system. Slovenia had always been Yugoslavia's smallest, northernmost, most prosperous republic. Slovenes realized that Yugoslavia needed Slovenia much more than Slovenia needed Yugoslavia.

In 1988, the iconoclastic Slovenian magazine *Mladina* pushed the boundaries of Yugoslavia's nominally "free" press, publishing articles critical of the Yugoslav People's Army. Four young reporters (including Janez Janša, who would later become Slovenia's prime minister) were tried, convicted, and imprisoned, spurring outrage among Slovenes. A few months later, the Slovenian delegation defiantly walked out of the Yugoslav League of Communists Congress.

The first-ever free elections in Slovenia on April 8, 1990, ended communist rule and swept reformer Milan Kučan into the presidency. Kučan pursued a Swiss-style confederated relationship with his fellow Yugoslav republics, but met with resistance from his counterparts who were more focused on their own ethnic self-interests. Later that year, in a nationwide referendum, 88 percent of Slovenes voted for independence from Yugoslavia.

And so, concerned about the nationalistic politics of Serbian strongman Slobodan Milošević and seeking the opportunity for true democracy and capitalism, Slovenia seceded. Because more than 90 percent of the people here were ethnic Slovenes—and because Slovenia was careful to respect the rights of its minority populations—the break with Yugoslavia was simple and virtually uncontested. Its war for independence lasted just 10 days and claimed only a few dozen lives. (For more details, see "Understanding Yugoslavia" on page 1075.)

In May 2004 Slovenia became the first of the former Yugoslav republics to join the European Union. The Slovenes have been practical about this move, realizing it's essential for their survival as a tiny nation in a modern world. But there are trade-offs, and "Euroskeptics" are down on EU bureaucracy. As borders disappear, Slovenes are experiencing more crime. Traditional farms are grappling with strict EU standards. Slovenian businesses are having difficulty competing with big German and other Western European firms. Before EU membership, only Slovenes could own Slovenian land, but now wealthy foreigners are buying property, driving up the cost of real estate. Still, overall, most Slovenes feel that EU membership was the right choice.

After independence, Slovenia impressed its European neighbors with its powerhouse economy and steady growth. However, the global financial crisis revealed that some of the affluence was deceptive: Many of Slovenia's biggest companies had been running up huge debts. As all of Europe's bubble burst in 2008, those corporate debts were assumed by Slovenia's big banks—devastating the economy and sparking financial worries.

In recent years, Slovenes have grown weary of a string of corrupt and incompetent politicians. Janez Janša, who became prime minister for the second time in 2011, was swept out of office amid a wave of protests and eventually sentenced to a prison term for corruption. His successor, Alenka Bratušek, resigned after just a year in office. One popular figure—at least in Ljubljana—is the visionary mayor Zoran Janković, who has reshaped the capital during his tenure, see page 740.

In the fall of 2015, Slovenia became the focal point of a Europe-wide debate when a flood of refugees from Syria and other nations showed up at its border. Like its neighbors Croatia and Hungary, Slovenia grappled with the challenge of caring for the new arrivals even as it facilitated their passage to wealthy northern European countries. News reports suggested that Slovenia responded to this humanitarian crisis with pragmatic compassion.

While many of the refugees expressed relief at what a friendly and competent place Slovenia was, those of us who already love the country were hardly shocked. The Slovenes are adjusting to the 21st century with their characteristic sense of humor and easygoing attitude, just as they've done throughout their history.

SLOVENIAN FOOD

Slovenes brag that their cuisine melds the best of Italian and German cooking—but they also embrace other international influences, especially French. Slovenian cuisine features many pan-Balkan elements: The savory phyllo-dough pastry *burek* is the favorite fast food here, and when Slovenes host a backyard barbecue, they grill up *čevapčići* and *ražnjići*, topped off with the eggplant-and-red-bell-pepper condiment *ajvar*. Slovenia en-  joys Italian-style dishes, with a pizza or pasta restaurant on seemingly every corner. Hungarian food simmers in the northeast corner of the country (where many Magyars reside). And in much of the country, particularly near the mountains, traditional Slovenian food has a distinctly Germanic vibe—including the "four S's": sausages, schnitzels, strudels, and sauerkraut.

Traditional Slovenian meals come with a hearty helping of groats—a grainy mush made with buckwheat, barley, or corn. Buckwheat, which thrives in this climate, often appears on Slovenian menus. You'll also see plenty of *štruklji*, a dumpling-like savory layer cake that can be stuffed with cheese, meat, or vegetables. *Repa* is turnip prepared like sauerkraut. Among the hearty soups in Slovenia is *jota*—a staple for Karst peasants, made from *repa*, beans, vegetables, and often sausage.

The cuisine of Slovenia's Karst region (the arid limestone plain

Pršut

In Slovenia, Croatia, and Montenegro, *pršut* (purr-SHOOT) is one of the essential food groups. This air-cured ham (like Ital-

ian prosciutto) is soaked in salt and some-times also smoked. Then it hangs in open-ended barns for up to a year and a half, to be dried and seasoned by the howling Bora wind. Each region produces a slightly dif-ferent *pršut*. In Dalmatia, a layer of fat keeps the ham moist; in Istria, the fat is trimmed, and the *pršut* is drier.

Since Slovenia joined the European Union, strict new standards have swept the land. Separate rooms must be used for the slaughter, preparation, and curing of the ham. While this seems fair enough for large producers, small family farms that want to produce just enough *pršut* for their own use—and maybe sell one or two ham hocks to neighbors—find they have to invest thou-sands of euros to be compliant.

south of Ljubljana) is notable. The small farms and wineries of this region have been inspired by Italy's Slow Food movement—their owners believe that cuisine is meant to be gradually appreci-ated, not rushed. The Karst's tasty air-dried ham *(pršut)*, available throughout the country, is worth seeking out (see sidebar). Istria (the peninsula just to the south of the Karst, in southern Slove-nia and Croatia) produces truffles that, locals boast, are as good as those from Italy's Piedmont region. And in the hills just north-west of the Karst, the Goriška Brda wine region—surrounded on three sides by Italy—is becoming a magnet for in-the-know food-ies seeking top-quality wines and affordable high cuisine.

Voda is water, and *kava* is cof-fee. Radenska, in the bottle with the three little hearts, is Slovenia's best-known brand of mineral water—good enough that the word *Radens-ka* is synonymous with bottled water all over Slovenia and throughout the former Yugoslavia. It's not common to ask for (or receive) tap water, but you can try requesting *voda iz pipe*.

Adventurous teetotalers should forgo the Coke and sample Cockta,

Slovenian Wines

Slovenia produces excellent *vino* (wine), abutting well-re-spected wine-growing neighbors Italy and Hungary. In fact, Slovenia's winemaking tradition originated with its pre-Roman Illyrian and Celtic inhabitants, meaning that wine has been grown much longer here than in most other European coun-tries. Wine standards plummeted with Yugoslav-era collec-tivization, but in recent years ambitious vintner families have brought quality back to Slovenian Wines.

Slovenia's three main wine-growing regions are Primor-ska, Posavje, and Podravje. The best-known is the **Primor-ska** region, in the western hills. With a Mediterranean climate (hence its name: "by the sea"), Primorska is best known for its reds. Primorska's Goriška Brda ("Hillsides of Gorica") shares the terroir of Italy's Friuli/Venezia Giulia region (and its much-vaunted, DOC-classified Collio Goriziano wines). This area pro-duces some of Slovenia's most respected wines, made mostly with grapes such as merlot and cabernet sauvignon. Goriška Brda also produces a good white using the *rebula* grape (*ri-bolla gialla* in Italian). A bit farther south (and still within Pri-morska), the Karst grows lots of *refošk (refosco)* grapes, which thrive in iron-rich red soil *(terra rossa).* The top product is the full-bodied, "big" *teran*—infused with a high lactic acid content that supposedly gives the wine healing properties. Nearby coastal areas (around Koper) also grow *refošk,* along with the white *malvazija* grape that's also widely used in Croatian Istria.

To the northeast, near Hungary, is the **Podravje** region (the Drava River Valley), dominated by white grapes—especially *laški riesling* (known internationally as Welsh riesling) and *renski ries-ling* (what we'd call simply riesling). In Ptuj or Maribor, local menus list wines produced on the steeper right bank of the Drava River (Haloze) and the left bank (Slovenske Gorice, "Slovenian Hills").

A bit to the south of Podravje is the **Posavje** region (the Lower Sava River Valley, bordering Croatia). This area produc-es both white and red wines; it's known mostly for the light, russet-colored *cviček* wine (a blend of red and white grapes).

With any type of Slovenian wine, *vrhunsko* (premium) is a mark of quality, while *kakovostno* is a notch down, and *namizno* is a table wine. Other key terms are *suho* (dry), *sladko* (sweet), and *pol-* (half).

a Slovenian cola with an unusual flavor (which supposedly comes from berry, lemon, orange, and 11 herbs). Originally called "Cock-ta-Cockta," the drink was introduced during the communist pe-riod, as an alternative to the difficult-to-get Coca-Cola. This local variation developed a loyal following...until the Iron Curtain fell, and the real Coke became readily available. Cockta sales plummeted. But in recent years—prodded by the slogan "The Taste of Your Youth"—nostalgic Slovenes are drinking Cockta once more.

The premier Slovenian brand of *pivo* (beer) is Union (OO-nee-ohn), but you'll also see a lot of Laško (LASH-koh), whose mascot is the Zlatorog (or "Golden Horn," a mythical chamois-like animal). For the full story on Slovenian wines, see the sidebar.

Regardless of what you're drinking, to toast, say, *"Na ZD-ROW-yeh!"*—if you can't remember it, think of "Nice driving!"

Slovenia's national dessert is *potica,* a rolled pastry with walnuts and sometimes also raisins. While traditionally eaten at Christmas, it's available year-round. Slovenes eat it from the hard outer crust in, saving the nutty center for last. And locals brag that Ljubljana has the finest gelato outside of Italy—which, after all, is just an hour down the road. And I agree.

SLOVENIAN LANGUAGE

Slovene is surprisingly different from the languages spoken in the other former Yugoslav republics. While Serbian and Croatian are mutually intelligible, Slovene is gibberish to Serbs and Croats. Most Slovenes, on the other hand, know Serbo-Croatian because, a generation ago, everybody in Yugoslavia had to learn it.

Linguists have identified some 46 official dialects of Slovene, and there are probably another 100 or so unofficial ones. Locals can instantly tell which city—or sometimes even which remote mountain valley—someone comes from by their accent.

The tiny country of Slovenia borders Italy and Austria, with important historical and linguistic ties to both. For self-preservation, Slovenes have always been forced to function in many different languages. All of these factors make them excellent linguists. Most young Slovenes speak flawless English effortlessly—then admit that they've never set foot in the United States or Britain, but love watching American movies and TV shows (which are always subtitled, never dubbed).

In Slovene, *c* is pronounced "ts" (as in "cats"). The letter *j* is pronounced as "y"—making "Ljubljana" easier to say than it looks (lyoob-lyee-AH-nah). Slovene only has one diacritical mark: the *strešica,* or "little roof." This makes *č* sound like "ch," *š* sound like "sh," and *ž* sound like "zh" (as in "measure"). The letter *v* is pronounced like "u"—so the Slovenian word *avto* sounds like "auto," and the mountain Triglav is pronounced "TREE-glau" (rhymes with "cow").

The only trick: As in English, which syllable gets the emphasis is unpredictable.

Learn some key Slovenian phrases (see the Slovenian survival phrases on page 721). You'll make more friends and your trip will go more smoothly.

Slovenian Survival Phrases

In the phonetics, ī sounds like the long i in "light," and bolded syllables are stressed. The vowel "eh" sometimes sounds closer to "ay" (depending on the speaker).

English	Slovenian	Pronunciation
Hello. (formal)	Dober dan.	**doh**-behr dahn
Hi. / Bye. (informal)	Živjo.	**zheev**-yoh
Do you speak English?	Ali govorite angleško?	ah-lee goh-voh-**ree**-teh ahn-**glehsh**-koh
Yes. / No.	Ja. / Ne.	yah / neh
I (don't) understand.	(Ne) razumem.	(neh) rah-**zoo**-mehm
Please. / You're welcome.	Prosim.	**proh**-seem
Thank you (very much).	Hvala (lepa).	**hvah**-lah (**leh**-pah)
Excuse me. / I'm sorry.	Oprostite.	oh-proh-**stee**-teh
problem	problem	proh-**blehm**
No problem.	Ni problema.	nee proh-**bleh**-mah
Good.	Dobro.	**doh**-broh
Goodbye.	Na svidenje.	nah **svee**-dehn-yeh
one / two	ena / dve	**eh**-nah / dveh
three / four	tri / štiri	tree / **shtee**-ree
five / six	pet / šest	peht / shehst
seven / eight	sedem / osem	**seh**-dehm / **oh**-sehm
nine / ten	devet / deset	deh-**veht** / deh-**seht**
hundred / thousand	sto / tisoč	stoh / **tee**-sohch
How much?	Koliko?	**koh**-lee-koh
local currency	euro	**ee**-oo-roh
Write it?	Napišite?	nah-**peesh**-ee-teh
Is it free?	Ali je brezplačno?	**ah**-lee yeh brehz-**plahch**-noh
Is it included?	Ali je vključeno?	**ah**-lee yeh vuk-**lyoo**-cheh-noh
Where can I find / buy...?	Kje lahko najdem / kupim...?	kyeh **lah**-koh **nī**-dehm / **koo**-peem
I'd / We'd like...	Želel / Želeli bi...	zheh-**lehl** / zheh-**leh**-lee bee
...a room.	...sobo.	**soh**-boh
...a ticket to ___.	...vozovnico do ___.	voh-**zohv**-neet-soh doh ___
Is it possible?	Ali je možno?	**ah**-lee yeh **mohzh**-noh
Where is...?	Kje je...?	kyeh yeh
...the train station	...železniška postaja	zheh-**lehz**-neesh-kah pohs-**tī**-yah
...the bus station	...avtobusna postaja	**ow**-toh-boos-nah pohs-**tī**-yah
...the tourist information office	...turistično informacijski center	too-**rees**-teech-noh een-for-maht-**see**-skee **tsehn**-tehr
...the toilet	...vece (WC)	**veht**-seh
men / women	moški / ženski	**mohsh**-kee / **zhehn**-skee
left / right / straight	levo / desno / naravnost	**leh**-voh / **dehs**-noh / nah-**rahv**-nohst
At what time...?	Ob kateri uri...?	ohb kah-**teh**-ree **oo**-ree
...does this open / close	...se odpre / zapre	seh ohd-**preh** / zah-**preh**
(Just) a moment.	(Samo) trenutek.	(sah-**moh**) treh-**noo**-tehk
now / soon / later	zdaj / kmalu / pozneje	zuh-**dī** / kuh-**mah**-loo / pohz-**neh**-yeh
today / tomorrow	danes / jutri	**dah**-nehs / **yoo**-tree

In a Slovenian Restaurant

English	Slovenian	Pronunciation
I'd like to reserve...	Rezerviral bi...	reh-zehr-**vee**-rahl bee
We'd like to reserve...	Rezervirali bi...	reh-zehr-**vee**-rah-lee bee
...a table for one / two.	...mizo za enega / dva.	**mee**-zoh zah **eh**-neh-gah / dvah
Is this table free?	Ali je ta miza prosta?	**ah**-lee yeh tah **mee**-zah proh-stah
Can I help you?	Izvolite?	eez-**voh**-lee-teh
The menu (in English), please.	Jedilni list (v angleščini), prosim.	yeh-**deel**-nee leest (vuh ahn-**glehsh**-chee-nee) **proh**-seem
service (not) included	postrežba (ni) vključena	post-**rehzh**-bah (nee) vuk-**lyoo**-cheh-nah
cover charge	pogrinjek	poh-**green**-yehk
"to go"	za s sabo	zah **sah**-boh
with / without	z / brez	zuh / brehz
and / or	in / ali	een / **ah**-lee
fixed-price meal (of the day)	(dnevni) meni	(duh-**new**-nee) meh-**nee**
specialty of the house	specialiteta hiše	speht-see-ah-lee-**teh**-tah **hee**-sheh
half portion	polovična porcija	poh-loh-**veech**-nah **port**-see-yah
daily special	dnevna ponudba	duh-**new**-nah poh-**nood**-bah
fixed-price meal for tourists	turistični meni	too-**rees**-teech-nee meh-**nee**
appetizers	predjedi	prehd-yeh-**dee**
bread	kruh	krooh
cheese	sir	seer
sandwich	sendvič	**send**-veech
soup	juha	**yoo**-hah
salad	solata	soh-**lah**-tah
meat / poultry	meso / perutnina	meh-**soh** / peh-root-**nee**-nah
fish / seafood	riba / morska hrana	**ree**-bah / **mor**-skah **hrah**-nah
fruit	sadje	**sahd**-yeh
vegetables	zelenjava	zeh-lehn-**yah**-vah
dessert	sladica	slah-**deet**-sah
(tap) water	voda (iz pipe)	**voh**-dah (eez **pee**-peh)
mineral water	mineralna voda	mee-neh-**rahl**-nah **voh**-dah
milk	mleko	**mleh**-koh
(orange) juice	(pomarančni) sok	(poh-mah-**rahnch**-nee) sohk
coffee	kava	**kah**-vah
tea	čaj	chī
wine	vino	**vee**-noh
red / white	rdeče / belo	ahr-**deh**-cheh / **beh**-loh
sweet / dry / semi-dry	sladko / suho / polsuho	**slahd**-koh / **soo**-hoh / **pohl**-soo-hoh
glass / bottle	kozarec / steklenica	koh-**zah**-rehts / stehk-leh-**neet**-sah
beer	pivo	**pee**-voh
Cheers!	Na zdravje!	nah **zdrow**-yeh
More. / Another.	Še. / Še eno.	sheh / sheh **eh**-noh
The same.	Isto.	**ees**-toh
Bill, please.	Račun, prosim.	rah-**choon** proh-**seem**
tip	napitnina	nah-peet-**nee**-nah
Delicious!	Odlično!	ohd-**leech**-noh

LJUBLJANA

Ljubljana (lyoob-lyee-AH-nah) is irresistible. With a lazy Old Town clustered around a castle-topped hill, Slovenia's capital is often likened to Salzburg. It's an apt comparison—but only if you inject a healthy dose of breezy Adriatic culture, add a Slavic accent, and replace favorite son Mozart with local architect Jože Plečnik.

Ljubljana feels smaller than its population of 270,000. With several clusters of good museums that try hard—but have only so much to say—it does its best to please sightseers. But ultimately, this town is all about ambience. The idyllic, cobbled core of Ljubljana is slathered with one-of-a-kind architecture. Festivals fill the summer, and people enjoy a Sunday stroll any day of the week. Fashion boutiques and al fresco cafés jockey for control of the Old Town, while the leafy riverside promenade crawls with stylishly dressed students sipping *kava* and polishing their near-perfect English. Laid-back Ljubljana is the kind of place where graffiti and crumbling buildings seem elegantly atmospheric instead of shoddy. But more and more of those buildings have been getting a facelift recently, as a spunky mayor has been spiffing up the place and creating gleaming traffic-free zones left and right—making what was already an exceptionally livable city a pedestrians' paradise.

Batted around by history, Ljubljana has seen cultural influences from all sides—most notably Prague, Vienna, and Venice. This has left the city a happy hodgepodge of cultures. Being the midpoint between the Slavic, Germanic, and Italian worlds gives Ljubljana a special spice.

The Story of Ljubljana

In ancient times, Ljubljana was on the trade route connecting the Mediterranean (just 60 miles away) to the Black Sea. (Toss a bottle off the bridge here, and it can float to the Danube and, eventually, all the way to Russia.) Legend has it that Jason and his Argonauts founded Ljubljana when they stopped here for the winter on their way home with the Golden Fleece. Some stories say Jason slayed a dragon here, while according to others, it was St. George; either way, the dragon remains the city mascot to this day.

Some of the area's earliest known inhabitants during the Neolithic and Bronze ages lived in rustic houses on tall wooden piles in the marshy lands surrounding today's city center. They poled around the shallow lagoons in dugout canoes. Sometimes called "crannog dwellers" (after similar homes in the Scottish Highlands), these earliest Ljubljanans left behind precious few artifacts, save for half of a wooden wheel and axle that's 5,200 years old.

The area was later populated by the Illyrians and Celts, and was eventually Romanized (and called Emona) before being over-run by Huns, only to be resettled by Slavs—the ancestors of to-day's Slovenes.

In 1335, Ljubljana fell under the Habsburg emperors, who called it Laibach and steered its development for the next six centuries. Slovenian language and culture were considered back-wards, as most of Laibach's inhabitants spoke German and lived essentially Austrian lifestyles. This Austrian vibe persists today, thanks to abundant Austrian Baroque and Viennese Art Nouveau architecture.

Napoleon put Ljubljana on the map when he named it the capital of his Illyrian Provinces, a realm that stretched from the Danube to Dubrovnik, and from Austria to Albania (for just four short years, 1809-1813). For the first time, the Slovene language

PLANNING YOUR TIME

Ljubljana deserves at least a full day. Rather than checking off a list of museums, spend most of your time strolling the pleasant town center, exploring the many interesting squares and architectural gems, browsing the produce market, shopping at the boutiques, and sipping coffee at sidewalk cafés along the river.

Here's the best plan for a low-impact sightseeing day: Begin on Prešeren Square, the heart of the city. Cross the Triple Bridge and wander through the riverside produce market before joining the town walking tour at 10:00 (at 11:00 in Oct-March). Then wander south along the Ljubljanica River and through the Krakovo gardens to tour the Jože Plečnik House (closed Mon). In the after-noon, commit some quality time to people-watching at a riverside

was taught in schools, awakening a newfound pride in Slovenian cultural heritage. People still fondly recall this very brief era, which was the only time Ljubljana rose to prominence on the world stage. (Despite spending more than 600 years as part of the Habsburg Empire, Ljubljana has no "Habsburg Square"...but it does have a "French Revolution Square.")

In the mid-19th century, the railway connecting Vienna to the Adriatic (Trieste) was built through town—and Ljubljana boomed. An earthquake rocked the city in 1895, damaging many buildings. Locals cleverly exaggerated the impact (propping up buildings that were structurally sound, and even tearing down unwanted old houses that had been unharmed) in preparation for the visit of Emperor Franz Josef—who, just as they hoped, took pity on the city and invested generously in its reconstruction. Ljubljana was made over in the Art Nouveau style. A generation later, architect Jože Plečnik bathed the city in his distinctive, artsy-but-sensible, classical-meets-modern style.

In World War II, Slovenia was occupied first by the Italians, then by the Nazis. Ljubljana had a thriving resistance movement that the Nazis couldn't suppress—so they simply fenced off the entire city and made it a giant prison for three years, allowing in only basic food shipments. But the Slovenes—who knew their land far better than their oppressors did—continued to slip in and out of town undetected, allowing them to agitate through the end of the war.

In 1991, Ljubljana became the capital of one of Europe's youngest nations. Today the city is filled with university students, making it feel very youthful. Ljubljana is on the cutting edge when it comes to architecture, public art, fashion, and trendy pubs—a tendency embodied by its larger-than-life mayor, Zoran Janković. And yet, Ljubljana's scintillating avant-garde culture has soft edges—hip, but also nonthreatening and user-friendly.

café, window-shop at some colorful boutiques (perhaps following my self-guided shopping stroll in the Old Town), or do more sightseeing (good options include the City Museum of Ljubljana, near several Jože Plečnik landmarks downtown; the Serbian Orthodox Church and Tivoli Park, with the Contemporary History Museum, west of downtown; or the Slovenian Ethnographic Museum and other sights in Metelkova, north of downtown).

Ljubljana is sleepy on Sundays (many shops are closed and the produce market is quiet, but museums are generally open, a modest flea market stretches along the riverfront, and the TI's walking tour still runs). The city is also relatively quiet in August, when the students are on break and many locals head to beach resorts. They say that in August, even homeless people go to the coast.

Orientation to Ljubljana

Ljubljana's central zone is compact, and with a little wandering, you'll quickly get the hang of it. The Ljubljanica River—lined with cafés, restaurants, and a buzzing outdoor market—bisects the city, making a 90-degree turn around the base of a castle-topped hill. Most sights are either along or just a short walk from the river. Visitors enjoy the distinctive bridges that span the Ljubljanica, including the landmark Triple Bridge (Tromostovje) and pillared Cobblers' Bridge (Čevljarski Most)—both designed by Jože Plečnik. Between these two is a plain bridge (with great views) called Brv (roughly, "simple footbridge"). The center of Ljubljana is Prešeren Square, watched over by a big statue of Slovenia's national poet, France Prešeren.

I've organized the sights in this chapter based on which side of the river they're on: the east (castle) side of the river, which is where Ljubljana began and has more medieval charm; and the west (Prešeren Square) side of the river, which has a more Baroque/Art Nouveau feel and most of the urban sprawl. At the northern edge of the tourist's Ljubljana is the train station and Metelkova museum and nightlife zone; at the southern edge are the garden district of Krakovo and the Jože Plečnik House; and at the western edge is Tivoli Park.

Ljubljana's Two Big Ps: You'll hear the following two easy-to-confuse names constantly during your visit. Mind your Ps, and your visit to Ljubljana becomes more meaningful: **Jože Plečnik** (YOH-zheh PLAYCH-neek, 1872-1957) is the architect who shaped Ljubljana, designing virtually all the city's most important landmarks. **France Prešeren** (FRAHN-tseh preh-SHAY-rehn, 1800-1849) is Slovenia's greatest poet and the namesake of Ljubljana's main square.

TOURIST INFORMATION

Ljubljana's helpful, businesslike TI has a useful website (www. visitljubljana.com) and two branches: at the **Triple Bridge,** across from Prešeren Square (daily 8:00-21:00, Oct-May until 19:00, Stritarjeva 1, tel. 01/306-1215); and at the upper corner of the **market** (with bikes to rent and information about the rest of Slovenia; daily 8:00-21:00; Oct-May Mon-Fri 8:00-19:00, Sat-Sun 9:00-17:00; Krekov trg 10, tel. 01/306-4575). At either TI, pick up a pile of free resources, including the big city map, the *Tourist Guide,* and the monthly events guide.

The **Ljubljana Tourist Card,** which includes access to public transportation and covers entry to many city museums as well as the TIs' walking tours and boat trips, could save busy sightseers some money (€27/24 hours, €34/48 hours, €39/72 hours).

ARRIVAL IN LJUBLJANA

By Train: Ljubljana's modern, user-friendly train station (Železniška Postaja) is at the northern edge of the city center. Emerging from the passage up to track 1a, turn right and walk under the long canopy to find the yellow arrivals hall. Everything is well-signed in English, including the handy train-information office (with useful handouts outlining journeys to several domestic and international destinations), lockers, and—near the front of the station—a big ticket office with an ATM. Arrivals are *prihodi,* departures are *odhodi,* and track is *tir.*

You can **walk** to any of my recommended hotels within about 20 minutes (often less). To reach Prešeren Square at the city's center, exit the station to the right and walk a long block along the busy Trg Osvobodilne Fronte (or "Trg O.F." for short, with the bus station in the middle). After passing the bus stalls, turn left across Trg O.F. and go down Miklošičeva (look for the building with the round, red-brick columns). This takes you past some of Ljubljana's most appealing architecture to Prešeren Square.

Avoid unscrupulous **taxis** waiting to spring on unsuspecting tourists at the station—call one that charges fair rates instead (around €4-5 to any of my recommended hotels). Taking just a few more minutes to wait for your cab could easily save you €10 or more. See "Getting Around Ljubljana—By Taxi," later, for recommended taxi companies.

By Bus: Ljubljana's bus station (Autobusna Postaja) is a low-profile building (with ticket windows, a bakery, and newsstands) in the middle of Trg O.F., right in front of the train station. To get into the city center, see "By Train," above.

By Car: Ljubljana is not car-friendly; much of the central zone along the river is entirely traffic-free. Even several blocks of the main thoroughfare, Slovenska cesta—north of Congress Square, between Šubičeva ulica and Gosposvetska cesta—are closed to all traffic except buses. To reach the southern part of the city when entering downtown from the north, you need to circumnavigate the core by looping east along Resljeva cesta, over the Dragon Bridge by the market, and through the tunnel beneath the castle; from here, Karlovška cesta cuts back west over the river to the southern stretch of Slovenska cesta.

Ask your hotel about parking—most have some available, usu-

LJUBLJANA

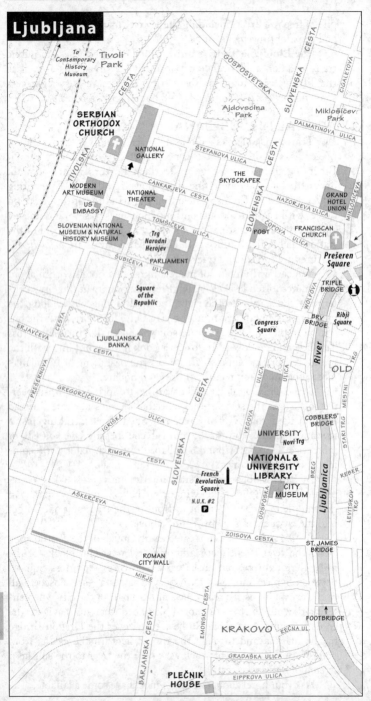

Ljubljana

To Contemporary History Museum

Tivoli Park

SERBIAN ORTHODOX CHURCH

NATIONAL GALLERY

GOSPOSVETSKA

Ajdovščina Park

Miklošičev Park

DALMATINOVA ULICA

ŠTEFANOVA ULICA

THE SKYSCRAPER

MODERN ART MUSEUM

NATIONAL THEATER

CANKARJEVA CESTA

NAZORJEVA ULICA

GRAND HOTEL UNION

US EMBASSY

SLOVENIAN NATIONAL MUSEUM & NATURAL HISTORY MUSEUM

TOMŠIČEVA ULICA

Trg Narodni Herojev

ČOPOVA ULICA

POST

FRANCISCAN CHURCH

Prešeren Square

SUBIČEVA ULICA

PARLIAMENT

TRIPLE BRIDGE

WOLFOVA

ERJAVČEVA CESTA

Square of the Republic

Congress Square

BRV BRIDGE

Ribji Square

River

OLD

LJUBLJANSKA BANKA

PREŠERNOVA

GREGORČIČEVA

IGRIŠKA ULICA

RIMSKA CESTA

SLOVENSKA CESTA

VEGOVA

ULICA

COBBLERS BRIDGE

UNIVERSITY
Novi Trg

STARI TRG

MESTNI

NATIONAL & UNIVERSITY LIBRARY

French Revolution Square

GOSPOSKA

REBER

BREG

Ljubljanica

LEVSTIKOV TRG

AŠKERČEVA

N.U.K. #2

CITY MUSEUM

ST. JAMES BRIDGE

ZOISOVA CESTA

ROMAN CITY WALL

MIRJE

EMONSKA CESTA

FOOTBRIDGE

BARJANSKA CESTA

KRAKOVO

KEČNA UL.

GRADAŠKA ULICA

PLEČNIK HOUSE

EIPPROVA ULICA

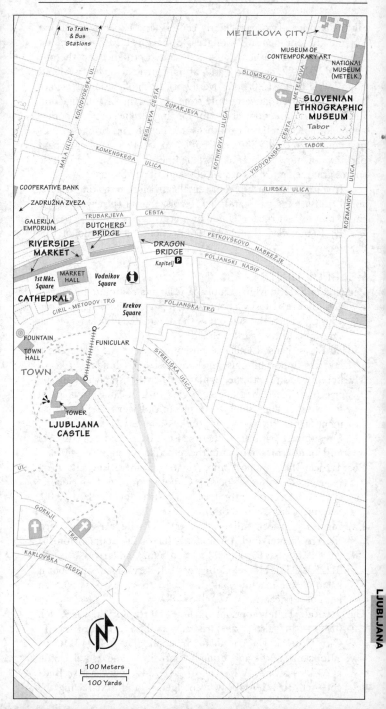

ally for a price. Two particularly central (and expensive) parking lots are the one beneath **Congress Square** (€1.20/hour for first 3 hours, then €2.40/hour, or €1.80/hour overnight) and the one called **N.U.K. #2,** near the National and University Library (€1.20/hour 7:00-19:00, €1.80/hour overnight). Both of these lots are accessible on Slovenska cesta only from the south—if coming from the north, see directions above for looping around town. Another handy lot is **Kapitelj,** just southeast of the Dragon Bridge (€1.90/first hour, then €2.40/hour, or €1.50/hour 18:00-6:00). Legal, paid parking downtown is marked by blue lines (look for meters); these spaces are free Saturdays after 13:00 and all day Sunday.

If you need to gas up your rental car before returning it here, you'll find a huge gas station on Tivolska cesta (just west of the train station, near the big Union brewery).

By Plane: See "Ljubljana Connections" at the end of this chapter.

HELPFUL HINTS

Pedestrian Safety: Many Ljubljana residents commute by bike—and they're not shy about whizzing past pedestrians. Keep your eyes open and stay out of the designated bike lanes on the sidewalks (often marked in red).

Closed Days: Most Ljubljana museums (except the castle and a few less-important museums) are closed on Mondays.

Markets: In addition to the regular **market** that sprawls along the riverfront (described under "Sights in Ljubljana"), a colorful **flea market** hops along the Ljubljanica River's Breg embankment (across the river from the castle) every Sun 8:00-14:00. On summer Saturdays, there's also a lively and colorful **arts and handicrafts market** in the same place (Sat 8:00-14:00).

Post Office: The main post office *(pošta)* is in a beautiful yellow Art Nouveau building a block up Čopova from Prešeren Square, at the intersection with Slovenska cesta (Mon-Fri 8:00-19:00, Sat until 12:00, closed Sun).

Laundry: For pricey full service, try **Tekstilexpress,** between the city center and Tivoli Park (takes 24 hours, Mon-Fri 7:00-19:00, Sat 9:00-13:00, closed Sun, Cankarjeva 10B, tel. 01/252-7354). **Hostel Celica** has self-service laundry—but it has only one machine, and hostel guests have priority (cheap but not very central at Metelkova 8).

Car Rental: Handy options include **Hertz** (Trdinova 9, tel. 01/434-0147, also at the airport, www.hertz.si), **Europcar** (in City Hotel at Dalmatinova 15, mobile 059-077-040, www.europcar.si), **Avis** and **Budget** (both in Grand Hotel Union at Miklošičeva 3; Avis—tel. 01/241-7340, www.avis.si; Budget—tel. 01/421-7340, www.budget.si), and **Sixt** (facing the main platform at the train station, tel. 01/234-4650, www. sixt.si).

Best Views: The Skyscraper's observation deck offers the best views in town (see page 751). Views from the castle are nearly as good. At street level, my favorite views are from the bridge called Brv (between the Triple and Cobblers' bridges), especially at night. On sunny days, the colorful architecture on and near Prešeren Square pops, and you'll snap photos like crazy along the river promenade.

GETTING AROUND LJUBLJANA

By Bus: Virtually all of Ljubljana's sights are easily accessible by foot. And using the buses is a bit of a headache: First, you have to buy a plastic Urbana card for €2, which you then load with credit to pay for rides (you can't pay the driver). A ride costs €1.20 (valid for up to 90 minutes, card shareable by up to three people). Buy the card at the TI, where you can return it to reclaim your €2 at the end of your trip. Transit info: www.lpp.si.

By Taxi: Always call for a cab, or you'll get ripped off. Because cabbies can legally charge whatever they want, even if they use the meter you'll still pay way too much. Legitimate taxis usually start at about €1.50, and then charge €1 per kilometer. But many unscrupulous cabbies legally charge far more, and tack on bogus additional "surcharges." If you call a reputable taxi company, Ljubljana is a fantastic taxi town with very affordable rates—a ride within the city center (such as from the station to a hotel) should run less than €5. Good companies include **Metro Taxi** (tel. 080-1190, mobile 041-240-200), **Laguna** (tel. 01/511-2314), and **Intertours** (tel. 080-311-311, mobile 031-311-311). Don't be intimidated—dispatchers speak English, and your hotel, restaurant, or the TI can call a cab for you.

By Bike: Ljubljana is a cyclist's delight, with lots of well-marked bike lanes. It's easiest to rent bikes at the market square TI (€2/2 hours, €8/day; see "Tourist Information," earlier). Like many European cities, Ljubljana has a subsidized borrow-a-bike program (called BicikeLJ) with 30 locations around the city center. Once you register online with a credit card (€1 fee for a weekly subscription), rides are free or very cheap (free for the first hour, €1 for the second, €2 for the third, and so on). If you're planning on doing lots of biking, it's worth the hassle to sign up (http://en.bicikelj.si).

By Shuttle Bus: After Ljubljana pedestrianized much of its downtown core a few years back, the natives began to squawk about the hassle of getting around without a car. To mollify critics, the city subsidizes a network of green electric carts, called **Kavalir,** which anyone (even tourists) can flag down or call to take them anywhere within the pedestrian zone...for free. Just wave one down and tell them where you want to go (or phone them—April-Oct call 031-666-331 or 031-666-332; Nov-March call 031-666-299).

Tours in Ljubljana

To help you appreciate Ljubljana, taking a walking tour—either through the TI or by hiring your own local guide—is worth ▲▲.

Walking Tour

The TI organizes excellent two-hour guided town walks of Ljubljana in English, led by knowledgeable guides. In summer, the walk also includes either a funicular ride up to the castle or a 30-minute boat ride on the river. From April through September, there are three tours daily at 10:00, 14:00, and 17:00. From October through March, the walking tour goes daily at 11:00 (€13, meet at Town Hall around corner from Triple Bridge TI). They also offer a variety of other tours, including a food tour, a beer tour, a wine tour, a Town Hall tour, and so on—get details at the TI.

Local Guides

Having an expert show you around his or her hometown for two hours for €70 has to be the best value in town. **Marijan Krišković,** who leads tours for me throughout Europe, is an outstanding guide (mobile 040-222-739, kriskovic@yahoo.com). **Barbara Jakopič,** thoughtful and extremely knowledgeable, also leads my tours (mobile 040-530-870, b_lucky2@yahoo.com). **Minka Kahrič,** who's traveled to the North Pole, also leads tours closer to home—including walks around Ljubljana and excursions into the countryside (€70/2-hour walking tour; driving: €100/up to 4 hours, €140/up to 8 hours; mobile 041-805-962, polarnimedo@yahoo.com). You can also book a guide through the TI (arrange at least 24 hours in advance).

Boat Cruise

A boat trip on the Ljubljanica River is more romantic than informative. You have two options for your one-hour cruise (weather permitting): with English commentary from a live guide (€10, 2/day in summer, departs from near the Triple Bridge—about one block along the embankment away from the market, get details from TI), or unguided (€8, may have audioguides, 2-3/hour in summer 10:00-20:00, operated by various companies and from various docks—they'll approach you as you walk past).

Excursions from Ljubljana

Many worthwhile sights near Ljubljana are tricky to reach by public transportation. To hit several efficiently in one day, join an excursion. Three relatively well-established outfits are **Roundabout** (their one-day "Karst and Coast Mystery" tour takes you to Pred-

Ljubljana at a Glance

▲▲▲**People-Watching** Ljubljana's single best activity is sitting at an outdoor café along the river and watching the vivacious, stylish, fun-loving Slovenes strut their stuff.

▲▲**Riverside Market** Lively market area in the Old Town with produce, clothing, and souvenirs. **Hours:** Best in the morning, especially Sat; market hall open Mon-Fri 7:00-16:00, Sat until 14:00, closed Sun. See page 737.

▲▲**Serbian Orthodox Church of Sts. Cyril and Methodius** Beautifully decorated house of worship giving insight into the Orthodox faith. **Hours:** Daily 8:00-19:00. See page 748.

▲▲**National and University Library** Jože Plečnik's pièce de résistance, with an intriguing facade, piles of books, and a bright reading room. **Hours:** Main staircase open Mon-Fri 8:00-20:00, Sat 9:00-18:00, closed Sun; student reading room open to the public mid-July-mid-Aug daily 11:00-18:00, rest of year Sat 14:30-18:00. See page 753.

▲▲**Jože Plečnik House** Final digs of the famed hometown architect who shaped so much of Ljubljana, explained by an enthusiastic guide. **Hours:** Tue-Sun 10:00-18:00, English tours begin at the top of each hour, last tour departs at 17:00, closed Mon. See page 754.

▲▲**Slovenian Ethnographic Museum** Engaging, well-presented collection celebrating Slovenian culture. **Hours:** Tue-Sun 10:00-18:00, closed Mon. See page 757.

▲**Cathedral** Italian Baroque interior and bronze doors with intricate, highly symbolic designs. **Hours:** Open long hours daily but closed 12:00-15:00. See page 739.

▲**Ljubljana Castle** Tower with good views and so-so 3-D film. **Hours:** Grounds—daily 9:00-23:00, shorter hours Oct-May; castle—daily 9:00-21:00, shorter hours Oct-May. See page 742.

▲**Contemporary History Museum** Baroque mansion in Tivoli Park, with exhibit highlighting Slovenia's last 100 years. **Hours:** Tue-Sun 10:00-18:00, closed Mon. See page 749.

▲**City Museum of Ljubljana** Modern, high-tech exhibit covering the city's history. **Hours:** Tue-Sun 10:00-18:00, Thu until 21:00, closed Mon. See page 751.

jama Castle, Škocjan Caves, Lipica, and Piran for €49 plus admission to the caves and an optional wine tasting; www.roundabout.si; their "off the beaten track" tours delve deeper into local culture), **Slovenia Explorer** (their ambitious "Slovenia in 1 Day" trip visits Lake Bled, Postojna Caves, and Predjama Castle for €119; www.slovenia-explorer.com), and **Nature Adventures** (focused on active trips including rafting, paragliding, skydiving, and horseback riding; www.adventures-nature.com). For multiday trips around the country, check out the **Loopyslovenia** hop-on, hop-off bus service (www.loopyslovenia.com).

Prešeren Square Spin Tour

The heart of Ljubljana is the people-friendly, traffic-free Prešeren Square (Prešernov trg, rated ▲▲), which is described in this self-guided spin tour.

The city's meeting point is the large **statue of France Prešeren,** Slovenia's greatest poet, whose works include the lyrics to the Slo-

venian national anthem (and whose silhouette adorns Slovenia's €2 coin). The statue shows Prešeren, an important catalyst of 19th-century Slovenian nationalism, being inspired from above by a Muse. This statue provoked a scandal and outraged the bishop when it went up a century ago—a naked woman sharing the square with a church! To ensure that nobody could be confused about the woman's intentions, she's conspicuously depicted with typical Muse accessories: a laurel branch and a cloak. Even so, for the first few years citizens covered the scandalous statue with a tarp each night. And the model who posed for the Muse was so disgraced that no one in Slovenia would hire her—so she emigrated to South America and never returned.

Stand at the base of the statue to get oriented. The bridge crossing the Ljubljanica River is one of Ljubljana's top landmarks, Jože Plečnik's **Triple Bridge** (Tromostovje). The middle (widest) part of this bridge already existed, but Plečnik added the two side spans to more efficiently funnel the six streets of traffic on this side of the bridge to the one street on the other side. The

bridge's Venetian vibe is intentional: Plečnik recognized that Ljubljana, located midway between Venice and then-capital Vienna, is itself a bridge between the Italian and Germanic worlds. Across the bridge are the TI, WCs, ATMs, market and cathedral (to the left), and the Town Hall (straight ahead).

Now turn 90 degrees to the right, and look down the first street after the riverbank. Find the pale-orange woman in the picture frame on the second floor of the first yellow house. This is **Julija,** the unrequited love of Prešeren's life. Tour guides spin romantic tales about how the couple met. But the truth is far less exciting: He was a teacher in her father's house when he was in his 30s and she was 4. Later in life, she inspired him from afar—as she does now, from across the square—but they never got together. She may have been his muse, but when it came to marriage, she opted for wealth and status.

When Ljubljana was hit by an earthquake in 1895, locals took the opportunity (using an ample rebuilding fund from the Austro-Hungarian Empire) to remake their city in style. Today Ljubljana—especially the streets around this square—is an architecture-lover's paradise. The **Hauptmann House,** to the right of Julija, was the only building on the square to survive  the quake. A few years later, the owner redecorated it in the then-trendy Viennese Art Nouveau style you see today, using bright colors (since his family sold dyes). All that remains of the original structure is the little Baroque balcony above the entrance.

Just to the right of the Hauptmann House is a car-sized **model** of the city center—helpful for orientation. The street next to it (with the McDonald's) is **Čopova,** once the route of Ljubljana's Sunday promenade. A century ago, locals would put on their Sunday best and stroll from here to Tivoli Park, listening to musicians and dropping into cafés along the way. Plečnik called it the "lifeline of the city," connecting the green lungs of the park to this urban center. Through the 20th century, this route became less pedestrian-friendly, as Slovenska cesta and railroad tracks were both laid across it. But more recently—with the closure of Slovenska to all traffic except buses—Čopova is enjoying something of a Renaissance.

Continue looking to the right, past the big, pink landmark Franciscan Church of St. Mary. Next door, the characteristic glass awning marks **Galerija Emporium**—the first big post-quake department store, today government-protected. At the top of the building is Mercury, God of commerce, watching over the square that has been Ljubljana's commercial heart since the city began. (If you look carefully, you can see the mustachioed face of the building's owner hiding in the folds of cloth by Mercury's

left foot.) Since this area was across the river from medieval Ljubljana (beyond the town's limits...and the long arm of its tax collector), it was the best place to buy and sell goods. Today this sumptuously restored building houses a top-end fashion mall, making it the heart of Ljubljana's boutique culture. Step inside for a glimpse at the grand staircase.

The street between Galerija Emporium and the pink church is **Miklošičeva cesta,** which connects Prešeren Square to the train station. When Ljubljana was rebuilding after the 1895 earthquake, town architects and designers envisioned this street as a showcase of its new, Vienna-inspired Art Nouveau image.

Up Miklošičeva cesta and on the left is the prominent **Grand Hotel Union,** with a stately domed spire on the corner. When these buildings were designed, Prague was the cultural capital of the Slavic world. The new look of Ljubljana paid homage to "the golden city of a hundred spires" (and copied Prague's romantic image). The city even had a law for several years that new corner buildings had to have these spires. Even the trees you'll see around town were part of the vision. When the architect Plečnik designed the Ljubljanica River embankments a generation later, he planted tall, pointy poplar trees and squat, rounded willows—imitating the spires and domes of Prague.

Detour a block up Miklošičeva cesta to see two more architectural gems of that era (across from the Grand Hotel Union): First is a Secessionist building— marked **Zadružna Zveza**—with classic red, blue, and white colors (for the Slovenian flag). Next is the noisy, pink, zigzagged **Cooperative Bank.** The bank was designed by Ivan Vurnik, an ambitious Slovenian architect who wanted to invent a distinctive national style after World War I, when the Habsburg Em-

pire broke up and Eastern Europe's nations were proudly emerging for the first time.

Prešeren Square is the perfect springboard to explore the rest of Ljubljana. Now that you're oriented, visit some of the areas listed next.

Sights in Ljubljana

Ljubljana is bursting with well-presented, we-try-harder museums celebrating Slovenian history and culture. These include the Slovenian History Exhibition at the castle, the City Museum of Ljubljana, and the Contemporary History Museum in Tivoli Park. As these are similar and largely overlapping, if you get museumed out easily, just pick the one that's handiest to your sightseeing plan.

THE MARKET AND OLD TOWN

The castle (east) side of the river is the city's most colorful and historic quarter, packed with Old World ambience.

▲▲Riverside Market (Tržnice)

In Ljubljana's thriving Old Town market, big-city Slovenes enjoy buying directly from the producer. Prices go down as the day gets late and as the week goes on. The market, worth an amble anytime, is best on Saturday mornings, when the townspeople take their time wandering the stalls. In this tiny capital of a tiny country, you may even see the president searching for the perfect melon.

◐ Self-Guided Walk: Begin your walk through the market at the Triple Bridge (and TI). The riverside **colonnade,** which echoes the long-gone medieval city wall, was designed by (who else?) Jože Plečnik. This first stretch—nearest the Triple Bridge—is good for souvenirs: wood-carvings, replica painted frontboards from beehives, honey products (including honey brandy), and lots of colorful candles (bubbly Marta will gladly paint a special message on your candle for no extra charge). For lots more shopping tips—here and nearby—see "Shopping in Ljubljana," later.

Farther in, the market is almost all local, and the colonnade is populated by butchers, bakers, fishermen, and lazy cafés. Peek down at the actual river and see how the architect wanted the town and river to connect. The lower arcade (which you can access directly from the Triple Bridge or by going down the spiral staircase by the beehive panels) is a people zone, with public WCs, inviting cafés, and a stinky fish market *(ribarnica)* offering a wide variety. The recommended restaurant just below, **Ribca,** serves fun fishy plates, beer, and coffee with great riverside seating.

Across from the stairs that lead down into the fish market, about where the souvenir stands end, you reach the first small market square. On your right, notice the 10-foot-tall concrete **cone.** Plečnik wanted to make Ljubljana the "Athens of the North" and imagined a huge cone-shaped national acropolis—a complex for government, museums, and culture. This ambitious plan didn't make it off the drawing board, but part of Plečnik's Greek idea came true: this marketplace, based on an ancient Greek agora. Plečnik's cone still captures the Slovenes' imaginations...and adorns Slovenia's €0.10 coin.

At the top of this square, you'll find the 18th-century **cathedral** standing on the site of a 13th-century Romanesque church (check out its finely decorated doors—and, if they're open, go inside; for a complete description, see later).

The building at the end of the first market square is the seminary palace. In the basement is a **market hall** *(pokrita tržnica)*, with vendors selling cheeses, meats, baked goods, dried fruits, nuts, and other goodies (Mon-Fri 7:00-16:00, Sat until 14:00, closed Sun). This place is worth a graze—walk all the way through. Most merchants are happy to give you a free sample (point to what you want, and say *probat, prosim*—"a taste, please").

Leaving the market hall at the opposite end, turn left to reach the modern **Butchers' Bridge.** Jože Plečnik designed a huge roofed bridge to be built here, but—like so many of his designs—the plans were scuttled. Decades later, aware of Plečnik's newfound touristic currency, some town politicians dusted off the old plans and proposed building the bridge. The project stalled for years until the arrival of Mayor Zoran Janković, who swiftly constructed this modern version of the bridge. While it looks nothing like Plečnik's original plans, the bridge kept the old name and has been embraced by the community (there's a handy public WC down below on the lower level). The sculptures on the bridge, by local artist Jakov Brdar, were originally intended to be temporary—but people loved them, so they stayed. (The wild-eyed, wild-bearded Brdar often hangs out near the bridge, asking passersby how they like his creations.) Notice the mournful pose of the Adam and Eve statues (being evicted from the Garden of Eden) at the market end of the bridge. And don't miss the bizarre smaller sculptures along the railing—such as the ones that look like mischievous lizards breaking out of their eggs. Almost as soon as it was built, the bridge's railings were covered with padlocks—part of the recent Europe-wide craze for young couples to commemorate their love by locking a padlock to a bridge railing. But all those locks put too much strain on the railing—they are regularly cut off, soon to be replaced by new ones.

Sprawling up from the bridge is the **main market square,** packed with produce and clothing stands. (The colorful flower market hides behind the market hall.) The vendors in the row nearest the colonnade sell fruit from all over, but the ones located deeper in the market sell only locally grown produce. These producers go out of their way to be old-fashioned—a few of them

still follow the tradition of pushing their veggies on wooden carts (called *cizas*) to the market from their garden patches in the suburbs. Once at the market, they simply display their goods on top of their cart, turning it into a sales kiosk. Tell the vendor what you want—it's considered rude for customers to touch the fruits and vegetables before they're bought. Over time, shoppers develop friendships with their favorite producers. On busy days, you'll see a long line at one stand, while the other merchants stand bored. Your choice is simple: Get in line, or eat subpar produce.

Near the market hall, look for the little **scales** in the wooden kiosks marked *Kontrolna Tehtnica*—allowing buyers to immediately check whether the producer cheated them (not a common problem, but just in case). The Habsburg days left locals with the old German saying, "Trust is good; control is better." Nearby, look for the innovative "Nonstop Mlekomat" stand, a vending machine that lets you buy a plastic bottle, then fill it with a liter of raw, unskimmed, farm-fresh milk for €1.

At the far end of the market—close to the Dragon Bridge—you may see a few **food trucks** selling roasted chicken and deep-fried seafood.

Two more sights are immersed in the market action (both described next); the cathedral sits at the top of the market area, near the Triple Bridge, while the Dragon Bridge spans the river just beyond the end of the market colonnade.

▲Cathedral (Stolnica)

Ljubljana's cathedral is dedicated to St. Nicholas, protector against floods and patron saint of the fishermen and boatmen who have long come to sell their catch at the market. While the interior is worth a peek, the intricately decorated doors—created for Pope John Paul II's visit here in 1996—are even more interesting.

Mayor Zoran Janković

The latest chapter in Ljubljana's story has been written by its mayor, Zoran Janković. Sort of the Michael Bloomberg of Slovenia, this successful businessman transformed himself into a broadly supported mayor who is unafraid to pursue an ambitious civic agenda.

As chairman of the huge Mercator supermarket chain, Janković was famous for prowling around the front lines of his stores, micromanaging all day-to-day business. After corporate political shuffling forced him out, Janković turned his attention to the municipal realm—and, in 2006, was elected mayor of Ljubljana in a landslide.

The people of this city had grown accustomed to well-intentioned but ineffectual leaders who would propose and then cancel ambitious projects. But Janković's no-nonsense follow-through finally made things happen. Project after project materialized, on time and under budget: the funicular to the castle, several new bridges (including the Butchers' Bridge at the market), the creation of quaintly cobbled traffic-free zones throughout almost the entire town center, the rejuvenation of miles of riverfront embankment for pedestrians, and closing a several-block stretch of one of Ljubljana's most heavily used downtown streets (Slovenska cesta) to all car traffic. The sweeping changes have had their critics, among them elderly people who can no longer easily drive to their homes in the now-traffic-free center. Janković has attempted to assuage them with free shuttle buses. Ultimately, most Ljubljanans are thrilled with the transformation of their city—he was reelected in landslides in 2012 and 2018. Janković embodies the ideal of how a progressive electorate can trust a capable leader to wisely invest public funds in urban-beautification projects that benefit the common good.

Cost and Hours: Free, open long hours daily but closed 12:00-15:00.

Visiting the Cathedral: Begin outside, at the top of the small market square. Go under the high arch and take a close look at the cathedral's remarkable **main door.** Buried deeply in the fecund soil of the nation's ancient and pagan history, the linden tree of life sprouts with the story of the Slovenes. The ceramic pots represent the original Roman settlement here. Just to the left, above the tree, are the Byzantine missionaries Cyril and Methodius, who came here to convert the Slavs to Christianity in the ninth century. Just above, Crusaders and Ottomans do battle. Near the top, see the Slovenes going into the cave—entering the dark 20th century (World War I, World War II, and communism). At the top is Pope John Paul II (the first Slavic pontiff, who also oversaw the fall of communism). Below him are two men who are on track to becoming Slovenia's first saints; the one on the right is Frederic Baraga, a 19th-century bishop who became a missionary in Michigan and codified Chippewa grammar (notice the Native American relief on the book he's holding). In the upper right-hand corner is a sun, which has been shining since Slovenia gained its independence in 1991. Around back of the cathedral is a similar door, carved with images of the six 20th-century bishops of Ljubljana.

The cathedral's **interior** is stunning Italian Baroque. The transept is surrounded by sculptures of four bishops of Roman Ljubljana (when it was called Emona, or Aemon). Left of the main altar, notice the distinctive chair. This was designed by the very religious Jože Plečnik, whose brother was a priest here. Look up over the nave to enjoy the recently restored, gorgeous ceiling fresco.

▲Dragon Bridge (Zmajski Most)

The dragon has been the symbol of Ljubljana for centuries, ever since Jason (of Argonauts and Golden Fleece fame) supposedly slew one in a nearby swamp. This

is one of the few notable bits of Ljubljana architecture *not* by Plečnik (but by Jurij Zaninović, a fellow student of Vienna architect Otto Wagner). While the dragon is the star of this very photogenic Art Nouveau bridge, the bridge itself was officially dedicated to the 40th anniversary of Habsburg Emperor Franz

Josef's reign (see the dates on the side: 1848-1888). Tapping into the emp's vanity got new projects funded—vital as the city rebuilt after the 1895 earthquake. But the Franz Josef name never stuck; those dragons are just too darn memorable.

From near the Dragon Bridge, it's an easy funicular ride or steep hike up to Ljubljana Castle (described later). Or you can head back through the market to reach the Town Square and Old Town (see next), where I've narrated a self-guided shopping tour.

▲Town Square (Mestni Trg) and the Old Town

Ljubljana's Town Square, just across the Triple Bridge and up the street from Prešeren Square, is home to the **Town Hall** (Rotovž), highlighted by its clock tower and pillared loggia. Step inside the Renaissance courtyard to see paintings, artifacts, and a map of late 17th-century Ljubljana. Studying this map, notice how the river, hill, and wall worked together to fortify the town. Courtyards like this (but humbler) are hidden throughout the city. As rent in these old places is cheap, many such courtyards host funky and characteristic little businesses. Be sure to get off the main drag and poke into Ljubljana's nooks and crannies.

In the square between the Town Hall and the cathedral is a recent replica of the **Fountain of Three Carniolan Rivers,** inspired in style and theme by Rome's many fountains. The figures with vases represent this region's three main rivers: Ljubljanica, Sava, and Krka. This is one of many works in town by Francesco Robba, an Italian who came to Ljubljana for a job, fell in love with a Slovene, and stayed here the rest of his life—decorating  the city's churches with beautiful Baroque altars. (Robba's original fountain is at the National Gallery, described later.)

Now turn with the Town Hall on your left. You're staring down the single street that constitutes Ljubljana's Old Town. In the early 19th century, Ljubljana consisted mainly of this solitary main drag, running along the base of Castle Hill (plus a small "New Town" across the river). Stretching south from here are two other "squares"—Stari trg (Old Square) and Gornji trg (Upper Square)—which have long since grown together into one big, atmospheric promenade lined with quaint boutiques, great restaurants, and cafés. Virtually every house along this drag has a story to tell of a famous resident or infamous incident. As you walk, keep your eyes open for Ljubljana's mascot dragon—it's everywhere.

For a self-guided shopping stroll that runs the length of this delightful street—and highlights several fine shops en route—see "Shopping in Ljubljana," later.

▲Ljubljana Castle (Ljubljanski Grad)

The castle above town offers enjoyable views of Ljubljana and the surrounding countryside. There has probably been a settlement on this site since prehistoric times, though the first true fortress here was Roman. The 12th-century version was gradually added on to over the centuries, until it fell into disrepair in the 17th century.

Today's castle—rebuilt in the 1940s and renovated in the 1970s—is a hollow-feeling replica, lacking any sense of real history. However, in recent years they've filled this shell with some worthwhile attractions and respectable restaurants. It also offers a fine view, looking out over Ljubljana's rooftops and to the Alps on the horizon. The

castle is home to the Ljubljana Festival, with concerts throughout the summer (tel. 01/306-4293, www.ljubljanafestival.si).

Cost and Hours: The grounds are free to visit and open daily 9:00-23:00, shorter hours Oct-May. To enter the sights, you'll pay €7.50 (or €10 with the round-trip funicular) for the history exhibition, film, castle tower, and puppetry museum. The attractions are open daily 9:00-21:00, shorter hours Oct-May, tel. 01/232-9994, www.ljubljanskigrad.si.

Tours: For €2 extra, you can add either an audioguide or a guided tour—choose between the "Time Machine" tour (by guides dressed as historical figures) or the "Behind Bars" tour (with a medieval crime-and-punishment theme; tours depart from castle information center May-June 2/day, July-Sept 4/day, Oct-April 2/day Sat-Sun only).

Getting to the Castle: A slick **funicular** whisks visitors to the top in a jiff (€2.20 one-way, €4 round-trip, also included in combo-tickets described earlier, runs every 10 minutes, 1-minute ride, runs during castle opening times noted above, catch it at Krekov trg—across the street from the market square TI). From the top, you'll find free WCs and a few easy flights of stairs up into the heart of the castle complex (or take the elevator). There are also two handy **trails** to the castle. The steeper-but-faster route begins near the Dragon Bridge: Find Študentovska lane, just past the statue of Vodnik in the market. This lane dead-ends at a gravel path, which you'll follow up to a fork. Turn left to zigzag up the steepest and fastest route, which deposits you just below the castle wall; from here, turn left again and curl around the wall to reach the main drawbridge. Slower but a bit less steep is Reber, just off Stari trg, a few blocks south of the Town Hall: Walk up to the top of Reber, and, at the dead end, turn right and start climbing up the stairs. From here on out, keep bearing left, then go right when you're just under the castle (follow *Grad* signs).

Visiting the Castle: The castle's information office is on the courtyard above the top of the funicular (where you came up the stairs). Across the way are the well-stocked Rustika gift shop and three eateries (see "Eating in Ljubljana," later). The upper floors house two wedding halls—Ljubljana's most popular places to get married (free for locals).

Most of the sights worth seeing at the castle are in the opposite wing, clustered around the base of the tallest tower. As you face the tower, the entrance to the history exhibit is to the left, while the "Virtual Castle" film and tower climb itself are to the right. The Museum of Puppetry is near the information office.

The **Slovenian History Exhibition** offers a concise but engaging overview of this little country's story. As you enter, ask to borrow the free audioguide, then head downstairs and work your way up. Dark display cases light up when you approach, revealing artifacts, video clips, and touchscreens with more information. A unique feature of the museum is that you're invited to touch replicas of important historic items (in many cases, the originals are in other Ljubljana museums). Don't miss the top floor of the exhibit (go up the glassed-in staircase), which is the most interesting—covering the tumultuous 20th century. You'll learn about topics ranging from the battlefields of World War I, to the creation of the first Yugoslavia, to the fascist occupation and harrowing Italian-run concentration camps of World War II, to the cult of personality around Partisan war hero-turned-Yugoslav president Tito, to Slovenia's bid for independence.

Entering the door to the right of the tower, you'll first find the small **penitentiary** exhibit, recalling the post-Napoleonic era, when the castle was converted to a prison. It saw the most action during World War I, when it housed political prisoners (including the beloved Slovenian writer Ivan Cankar) and POWs. Modest exhibits inside actual former cells describe the history and list the names of past inmates.

If you head downstairs from the entrance, you'll find a Gothic **chapel** with Baroque paintings of St. George (Ljubljana's patron saint, the dragon-slayer) and coats of arms of the various aristocratic families that have called this castle home.

Heading up the stairs, you'll find the informative, entertaining, and nicely animated **"Virtual Castle" film,** in which Ljubljana's mascot dragon describes this hill's layers of history (12 minutes, plays all day on the half-hour; often in English, but otherwise borrow English headset).

Finally, climb the 92 spiral steps up to the **castle tower,** with one of the best views in town.

Don't miss the oddly fascinating **Museum of Puppetry** (ride up the elevator inside the gift shop near the castle information office). This traces the history of puppetry as an art form, which flourished in the Modernist milieu of early-20th-century Ljubljana. You'll step into a surreal world of marionettes, shadow puppets, and other creations. This is not a goofy attraction for kids; in fact, some of the puppets are quite grotesque and disturbing. You'll see marionettes of Adolf Hitler and Partisan troops, watch grainy footage of famous puppet masters (including Milan Klemenčič, who pioneered the form here in 1910), then climb up to the mezzanine and put on a show of your own.

The castle also often has **temporary exhibits**—look for signs or ask at the information desk.

Eating: You can combine your visit to the castle with a meal at the recommended **$$$$ Gostilna na Gradu,** with the best traditional Slovenian food in town, or the top-end **$$$$ Strelec** (both described later, under "Eating in Ljubljana"). **$ Gradska Kavana** ("Castle Café") serves only drinks and cakes.

THE MUSEUM ZONE AND TIVOLI PARK

The Prešeren Square (west) side of the river is the heart of modern Ljubljana, and home to several prominent squares and fine museums. These sights are listed roughly in order from Prešeren Square and can be linked to make an interesting walk. (See the "Ljubljana" map earlier in this chapter for the route.)

• *Leave Prešeren Square in the direction the poet is looking, bear to your left (up Wolfova, by the relief of Julija), and walk a block to...*

Congress Square (Kongresni Trg)

This grassy, tree-lined square hosts big events. It's ringed by some of Ljubljana's most important buildings: the university headquarters, the Baroque Ursuline Church of the Holy Trinity, a classical mansion called the Kazina, and the Philharmonic Hall. The green belt at the heart of the square, called Park Zvezda ("Star Park") for its radiating paths, is fronted by several inviting cafés and restaurants; the recommended **Zvezda Kavarna** is a top spot for its local cakes and ice cream.

At the top end of the square, by the entry to a pedestrian underpass, a Roman sarcophagus sits under a gilded statue of a **Roman citizen**—a replica of a Roman tomb sculpture from 1,700 years ago, when this town was called Emona. The busy street above you has been the site of the main trading route through town since ancient Roman times. Information boards tell you more.

Take a few steps into the underpass, and look left to find the easy-to-miss **Chopin Passage** (Chopinov Prehod), which displays exposed parts of the original Roman-era road and a model of Emona in ancient times.

• *Continue the rest of the way through the underpass beneath Slovenska cesta, then walk straight through the gap in the Maxi shopping mall into the...*

LJUBLJANA

▲Square of the Republic (Trg Republike)

This unusual plaza is ringed by an odd collection of buildings. While hardly quaint, the Square of the Republic gives you a good taste of a modern corner of Ljubljana. And it's historic—this is where Slovenia declared its independence in 1991.

The **twin office towers** (with the world's biggest digital watch, flashing the date, time, and temperature) were designed by Plečnik's protégé, Edvard Ravnikar. As harrowing as these structures seem, imagine if the builders had followed the original plans—the towers would be twice as tall as they are now and connected by a bridge, representing the gateway to Ljubljana. These buildings were originally designed as the Slovenian parliament, but they were scaled back when Tito didn't approve (since it would have made Slovenia's parliament bigger than the Yugoslav parliament in Belgrade). Instead, the **Slovenian Parliament** is across the square, in the low-profile office building with the sculpted entryway. The carvings are in the Socialist Realist style, celebrating the noble Slovenian people conforming to communist ideals for the good of the entire society. Completing the square are a huge conference center (Cankarjev Dom, the white building behind the skyscrapers), a shopping mall, and some public art.

• *Just a block north, across the street and through the grassy park (Trg Narodni Herojev), you'll find the...*

Slovenian National Museum (Narodni Muzej Slovenije) and Slovenian Museum of Natural History (Prirodoslovni Muzej Slovenije)

These two museums share a single historic building facing a park behind the Parliament. They're both average but worth considering if you have a special interest or if it's a rainy day.

The **National Museum** focuses on archaeological finds (their Metelkova branch—described later—features applied arts). On the ground floor are temporary exhibits and a lapidarium with carved-stone Roman monuments and exhibits on Egyptian mummies. Upstairs and to the right are more exhibits of the National Museum, with archaeological findings including the museum's two prized possessions: a fragment of a 45,000-year-old Neanderthal flute fashioned from a cave bear's femur—supposedly the world's oldest musical instrument; and the "figural situla," a beautifully decorated hammered-bronze bucket from the fifth century BC. Embossed with scenes of everyday Iron Age life, this object has been a gold mine of information for archaeologists.

Upstairs and to the left is the **Natural History** exhibit, featuring the flora and fauna of Slovenia. You'll see partial skeletons of a mammoth and a cave bear, plenty of stuffed reptiles, fish, and birds, and an exhibit on "human fish" (*Proteus anguinus*—long, skinny, pale-pink, sightless salamanders unique to caves in this part of Europe).

Cost and Hours: €6 for National Museum, €4 for Natural History Museum, or €8.50 for both, some English descriptions, both open daily 10:00-18:00—except June-Sept Thu-Sat, when the National Museum is open 8:00-22:00, Prešernova 20, tel. 01/241-4400, www.nms.si and www.pms-lj.si.

• *At the far end of the building is a glassed-in annex displaying Roman stone monuments (free). Turning left around the museum building and walking one block, you'll see the...*

US Embassy

This pretty yellow chalet (with brown trim and a red roof, at Prešernova cesta 31) wins my vote for quaintest embassy building in the world. Resist the urge to snap a photo...those guards are all business.

• *Just up Prešernova cesta from the embassy are two decent but skippable art museums.*

▲National Gallery (Narodna Galerija)

This fine museum presents a good, chronological exhibit of works by Slovenian and European artists, as well as temporary exhibits. While Slovenia doesn't have a particularly renowned artistic tradition, this well-presented collection nicely paints a picture of the nation's story and culture.

Cost and Hours: €7, more for special exhibits, permanent collection free first Sun of the month, open Tue-Sun 10:00-18:00, Thu until 20:00, closed Mon; two entrances: one at Cankarjeva 20 facing the National Museum, and another at the big glass box between two older buildings at Prešernova 24; tel. 01/241-5418, www.ng-slo.si.

Visiting the Museum: You'll begin with a walk through medieval church art (carvings, altar paintings, and tapestries), then head upstairs to works from the 17th through 19th centuries. Spend some time with Marko Pernhart's Romantic views of the Slovenian countryside, including stunning panoramas of the Julian Alps (ringing the top of the stairwell). Then you'll cross the modern skybridge (peeking down to see the original Fountain of Three Carniolan Rivers, from the Old Town's central square) to the 19th and 20th centuries. Pause in Room 18 to enjoy evocative portraits—bursting with personality—by Ivana Kobilca (1861-1926),

LJUBLJANA

a Slovenian painter working on the cusp of Impressionism. Art lovers enjoy her serene and lifelike *Summer* (1889-90), in which a young woman (Kobilca's self-portrait) plays with kids and flowers. Farther along, in Room 20, are pointillist works by Ivan Grohar (1867-1911), who painted Slovenian landscapes with a dash of Van Gogh and a dab of Seurat. On your way out, stop by the small room near the Cankarjeva entrance with small, faded, abstracted works by another beloved Slovenian artist, Zoran Mušič (1909-2005).

Museum of Modern Art (Moderna Galerija Ljubljana)

This museum has a permanent collection of modern and contemporary Slovenian artists, as well as temporary exhibits by both homegrown and international artists. To explore the "Continuities and Ruptures" permanent collection (aptly named for a place with such a fractured, up-and-down recent history), borrow the English floor plan and take a chronological spin through the 20th century. Unusual for a "modern" art museum is the room with Partisan art, with stiff, improvised, communist-style posters from the days when Tito and his crew were just a ragtag militia movement.

Cost and Hours: €5, ask about combo-ticket with contemporary branch at Metelkova—see page 758, Tue-Sun 10:00-18:00, Thu until 20:00 in July-Aug, closed Mon, Tomšičeva 14, tel. 01/241-6800, www.mg-lj.si.

• *By the busy road near the art museums, look for the distinctive Neo-Byzantine design (tall domes with narrow slits) of the...*

▲▲Serbian Orthodox Church of Sts. Cyril and Methodius

Ljubljana's most striking church interior isn't Catholic, but Orthodox. This church was built in 1936, soon after the Slovenes joined a political union with the Serbs.
Wealthy Slovenia attracted its poorer neighbors from the south—so it built this church for that community. Since 1991, the Serb population has continued to grow, as people from the struggling corners of the former Yugoslavia flock to prosperous Slovenia. Its gorgeous interior— which feels closer to Moscow than to Rome—offers visitors a taste of this important faith.

Cost and Hours: Free, daily 8:00-19:00; divine liturgy Sun at 9:00, other days services at 8:30 and 18:00; Prešernova cesta 35, www.spc-ljubljana.si.

Visiting the Church: Step inside for the best glimpse of the Orthodox faith this side of Dubrovnik. The church is colorfully decorated without a hint of the 21st century, mirroring a very con-servative religion. Many of the church's colorful frescoes are cop-ies of famous frescoes that decorate medieval Serbian Orthodox monasteries throughout the Balkans. On the balcony (at the back of the nave), you'll see Cyrillic script that explains the history of the church. Notice that there are no pews, because worshippers stand throughout the service. On the left, find the little room with tubs of water, where the faithful light tall, skinny beeswax candles (pur-chased at the little window in the back corner). The painted screen, or iconostasis, is believed to separate our material world from the spiritual realm behind it. Ponder the fact that several centuries ago, before the Catholic Church began to adapt to a changing world, all Christians worshipped this way. For more on the Orthodox faith, see the sidebar on page 1034.

• *On the other side of the busy street is...*

Tivoli Park (Park Tivoli)

This huge park, just west of the center, is where Slovenes relax on summer weekends. The easiest access is through the underpass from Cankarjeva cesta (be-tween the Serbian Orthodox Church and the Museum of Modern Art). As you emerge, the Neoclassical pillars lead-ing down the promenade clue you in that this part of the park was designed by Jože Plečnik. Along this "main boulevard" of the park, vari-ous changing photographic exhibitions are displayed.

• *Aside from taking a leisurely stroll, the best thing to do in the park is visit the...*

▲Contemporary History Museum (Muzej Novejše Zgodovine)

In a Baroque mansion (Cekinov Grad) in Tivoli Park, a well-done exhibit called "Slovenians in the 20th Century" traces the country's most eventful hundred years—from World War I, through the Yu-goslav period, to independence in 1991 and EU membership today. Out front is a yellow Zastava car, which were ubiquitous during the Yugoslav years. Inside, the ground floor displays temporary exhib-its, and upstairs you'll find several rooms using models, dioramas, light-and-sound effects, and English explanations to creatively tell the story of one of Europe's youngest nations. While it's a little dif-ficult to fully appreciate, the creativity and the spunky spirit of the place are truly enjoyable.

LJUBLJANA

Cost and Hours: €4.50, permanent exhibit free first Sun of the month, Tue–Sun 10:00-18:00, closed Mon, guidebook-€5, in Tivoli Park at Celovška cesta 23, tel. 01/300-9610, www.muzej-nz.si.

Getting There: The museum is a 20-minute walk from the center, best combined with a wander through Tivoli Park. The fastest approach: As you emerge from the Cankarjeva cesta underpass into the park, climb up the stairs, then turn right and go straight ahead for five minutes. You'll continue straight up the ramp, then turn left after the tennis courts and look for the big pink-and-white mansion on the hill.

Visiting the Museum: The exhibit begins at the dawn of the 20th century, during Slovenia's waning days as part of the Austro-Hungarian Empire. Spiral stairs lead up to more exhibits about World War I. Back on the main floor, you'll walk through a simulated trench from the Soča Front, then learn about the creation of the post-World War I Kingdom of Serbs, Croats, and Slovenes (or, as this exhibit pointedly puts it, "Kingdom of Slovenes, Croats, and Serbs"). During this time, some of what had historically been Slovenian became part of Italy.

Your footfalls echo loudly as you enter the room describing Slovenia's WWII experience. You'll learn how during that war, Slovenia was divided between neighboring fascist powers Germany, Italy, and Hungary. Each one tried (but failed) to exert linguistic and cultural control over the people, hoping to eradicate the Slovenian national identity. Video screens show subtitled interviews with people who lived through those war years.

Passing through the ballroom, you reach the "Slovenia 1946-1960" exhibit, outlining both the good (modernization) and the bad (prison camps and secret police) of the early Tito years. Despite his ruthless early rule, Tito remains popular here; under his stern bust, page through the photo album of Tito's visits to Slovenia. Find the display of the country's former currencies. Examining the Yugoslav dinar, notice that the figureheads on that communist currency were generic, idealized workers, farmers, and other members of the proletariat...except for a few notable individuals (including Tito). Meanwhile, Slovenia's short-lived post-Yugoslav currency, the *tolar* (1991-2006, R.I.P.), featured artists and scientists rather than heads of state and generals.

The most evocative room (1991-2008) has artifacts from the Slovenes' brave declaration of independence from a hostile Yugoslavia in 1991. The well-organized Slovenes had only to weather a 10-day skirmish to gain their freedom. It's chilling to think that at one point bombers were en route to level this gorgeous city. The planes were called back at the last minute, by a Yugoslav People's Army officer with allegiances to Slovenia.

• *As you exit, the giant, modern, blocky, light-blue building across the busy road is the* **Pivovarna Union**—*the brewery for Ljubljana's favorite industrial-produced beer, with a brewpub and the option of a brewery tour (www.union-experience.si).*

On your way back to the center, you could stop by...

▲The Skyscraper (Nebotičnik)

This 1933 building was the first skyscraper in Slovenia, for a time the tallest building in Central Europe, and one of the earliest European buildings that was clearly influenced by American architecture. Art Deco inside and out, it's a thrill for architecture fans and anyone who enjoys a great view—the top floor, which hosts a restaurant, café, and observation deck, offers the best panorama of Ljubljana's skyline. Zip up in the elevator just to take a peek, or stay for a drink or meal.

There are three levels: The best is floor #12, with a **$ café** where you can sit outside (or, in bad weather, head up the spiral stairs to the glassed-in terrace) and enjoy a drink or a light meal with unobstructed views over the city and castle. One floor below (#11) is the indoor club/lounge, with a similar menu. And on the next floor down (#10) is the **$$ restaurant**, with a full menu and less-impressive views. Good-value lunch deals are available in either place. I'd skip the restaurant and the club, and just grab a drink or snack up on the terrace.

Cost and Hours: Free to ride the elevator up for a peek, but you should buy at least a drink if you want to stick around; terrace and club open daily 9:00-very late; restaurant open Mon-Sat 12:00-16:00 & 18:00-22:00, closed Sun; 2 blocks from Prešeren Square at Štefanova 1, tel. 040-601-787, www.neboticnik.si.

• *A few blocks south, near several Jože Plečnik sights (see next section) at the river end of French Revolution Square, you'll find the...*

▲City Museum of Ljubljana (Mestni Muzej Ljubljana)

This thoughtfully presented, kid-friendly museum, located in the recently restored Auersperg Palace, offers a high-tech, in-depth look at the story of this city. Though everything is well-described in English (and touchscreens provide even more information), a student on the museum's staff might be able to show you around if it's not too busy—ask. (Note that the museum may be closed for renovation during your visit; exhibit locations may differ from what's described.)

Cost and Hours: €6, €4 if no temporary exhibits, Tue-Sun 10:00-18:00, Thu until 21:00, closed Mon, Gosposka 15, tel. 01/241-2510, www.mgml.si.

Visiting the Museum: In the cellar are Roman ruins (including remains of the original Roman road and sewer system, found right here) and layers of medieval artifacts. A model of the modern city—sitting upon footprints of the Roman (red) and medieval (blue) settlements—illustrates Ljubljana's many layers of history. If it's not traveling to other museums (as it usually is), you may see the world's oldest wooden wheel on an axle, dating from around 3200 BC and discovered in the Ljubljana marshlands. Upstairs are the mayor's room (with a few exhibits) and the ever-evolving exhibit about the past and present of Ljubljana. You may see an actual Fiat Zastava 750 car, the classic "Fičko" car that everyone owned—or wanted to own—in communist Yugoslavia (sort of a proto-Yugo). Rounding out the collection is a range of temporary exhibits.

Nearby: Your ticket includes admission to two archaeological sites nearby (summer only)—pick up a map at the front desk.

• *If visiting the museum, don't miss the nearby National and University Library and French Revolution Square—both described in the next section.*

JOŽE PLEČNIK'S ARCHITECTURE

Jože Plečnik is to Ljubljana what Antoni Gaudí is to Barcelona: a homegrown, amazingly prolific genius who shaped his town with a unique and beautiful vision. And Plečnik's mark on Ljubljana, much like Gaudí's on Barcelona, has a way of turning people who couldn't care less about architecture into fans. There's plenty to see. In addition to the Triple Bridge, the riverside market, and the sights listed here, Plečnik designed the embankments along the Ljubljanica and Gradaščica rivers in the Trnovo neighborhood; the rebuilt Roman wall along Mirje street, south of the center; the Church of St. Francis, with its classicist bell tower; St. Michael's Church on the Marsh; Orel Stadium; Žale Cemetery; and many more buildings throughout Slovenia.

Some of the best Plečnik sights are near the river, just south of Congress and Prešeren squares. I've linked them into a short self-guided walk (shown on the "Ljubljana" map earlier in this chapter).

• *From Prešeren Square, stroll south along the river. After the plain bridge called Brv, you'll come to the...*

▲Cobblers' Bridge (Čevljarski Most)

Named for the actual cobblers who set up shop along the river in olden times, the bridge encapsulates Plečnik's style perhaps better than any other structure: simple, clean lines adorned with classical columns. Ideal for people-watching (with the castle hovering scenically overhead), this is one of Ljubljana's most appealing spots.

• *Continue past Cobblers' Bridge*

on the right side of the river, past the fountain. After about a block, turn right up the parked-up street called Novi trg. At the top of this street, on the left, is a red-brick building embedded with gray granite blocks in an irregular checkerboard pattern. This is the...

▲▲National and University Library
(Narodna in Univerzitetna Knjižnica, or NUK)

Widely regarded as Plečnik's masterpiece, this building is a bit underwhelming...until an understanding of its symbolism brings it to life.

Cost and Hours: The staircase is free to enter and open Mon-Fri 8:00-20:00, Sat 9:00-18:00, closed Sun. The quiet main reading room is open to visitors (for €2) only during very brief windows: Most of the year, you can enter on Saturday afternoons (14:30-18:00), but hours are longer during the student break in the summer (mid-July-mid-Aug daily 11:00-18:00).

Visiting the Library: Begin by standing outside and surveying the **exterior.** On the surface, the red-and-gray color scheme evokes the red soil and chunks of granite of the Karst region, south of Ljubljana. But on a deeper level, the library's design conveys the theme of overcoming obstacles to attain knowledge. In the facade, the blocks of irregular size and shape represent a complex numerological pattern that suggests barriers on the path to enlightenment. The sculpture on the river side is Moses—known for leading his people through 40 years of hardship to the Promised Land. On the right side of the building, find the horse-head doorknobs—representing the winged horse Pegasus (grab hold, and he'll whisk you away to new levels of enlightenment).

Step **inside.** The main staircase is dark and gloomy—modeled after an Egyptian tomb. But at the top, through the door marked *Velika Čitalnica*, is the bright, airy main reading room: the ultimate goal, a place of learning. The top-floor windows are shaped roughly like open books. Sadly, most of the time you can't actually enter the reading room; if it's not open you'll just have to look at postcards in the shop, and imagine young Ljubljan-

ans hunched studiously over their books, surrounded by Plečnik's bookshelves, railings, and high windows.

Aside from being a great work of architecture, the building also houses the most important library in Slovenia, with more than two million books (about one per Slovene). The library is supposed to receive a copy of each new book printed in the country. In a freaky bit of bad luck, this was the only building in town damaged in World War II, when a plane crashed into it. But the people didn't want to see their books go up in flames—so hundreds of locals formed a human chain, risking life and limb to save the books from the burning building.

• *Directly behind the library is a mellow square with an obelisk in the middle. This is...*

French Revolution Square (Trg Francoske Revolucije)

Plečnik designed the **obelisk** in the middle of the square to commemorate Napoleon's short-lived decision to make Ljubljana the capital of his Illyrian Provinces. It's rare to find anything honoring Napoleon outside of Paris, but he was good to Ljubljana. Under his rule, Slovenian culture flourished, the Slovene language became widely recognized and respected for the first time, schools were established, and roads and infrastructure were improved. The monument contains ashes of the unknown French soldiers who died in 1813, when the region went from French to Austrian control.

The Teutonic Knights of the Cross established the nearby **monastery** (Križanke, ivy-capped wall and gate, free entry) in 1230. The adaptation of these monastery buildings into the Ljubljana Summer Theatre was Plečnik's last major work (1950-1956).

• *From here, it's a scenic 10-minute walk to the next sight. From the obelisk, walk down Emonska toward the twin-spired church. You'll pass (on the left) the delightful Krakovo district—a patch of green countryside in downtown Ljubljana. Many of the veggies you see in the riverside market come from these carefully tended gardens. When you reach the Gradaščica stream, head over the bridge (also designed by Plečnik) and go around the left side of the church to find the house.*

▲▲Jože Plečnik House (Plečnikova Zbirka)

One of Ljubljana's most interesting sights is the house of the ar-

chitect who redesigned much of the city. Today the house is decorated exactly as it was the day Plečnik died, containing much of his equipment, models, and plans. The house can be toured only with a guide, whose enthusiasm brings the place to life. There are very few barriers,

Jože Plečnik (1872-1957)

No other single architect has shaped one city as Jože Plečnik (YOH-zheh PLAYCH-neek) shaped Ljubljana. From libraries, cemeteries, and stadiums to riverside embankments and market halls, Plečnik left his mark everywhere.

Plečnik was born in Ljubljana to a cabinet maker. He dabbled as a self-trained architect, catching the eye of the great Secessionist architect Otto Wagner—who invited him to study in Vienna. Plečnik's first commissions, around the turn of the 20th century in Vienna, were pretty standard Art Nouveau. Then Tomáš Masaryk, president of the new nation of Czechoslovakia, decided that Prague Castle could use a new look by a Slavic architect. In 1921, Masaryk chose Jože Plečnik, who sprinkled the castle grounds with his distinctive touches. By now, Plečnik had perfected his simple, eye-pleasing style, which mixes modern and classical influences, with ample columns and pyramids—at once austere and playful.

By the time Plečnik finished in Prague, he had made a name for himself. His prime years were spent creating for the Kingdom of Yugoslavia (before the ideology-driven era of Tito).

Plečnik returned home to Ljubljana and set to work redesigning the city, both as an architect and as an urban planner. He lived in a humble house (now a recommended museum) behind the Trnovo Church. On his daily walk to work, he pondered ways to make the city even more livable. As you wander through town, notice how thoughtfully he incorporated people, nature, the Slovenian heritage, town vistas, and symbolism into his works—it's feng shui on a grand urban scale.

For all of Plečnik's ideas that became reality, even more did not. After World War II, the very religious Plečnik fell out of favor with the communist government. (It's fun to imagine how this city might look if Plečnik had always gotten his way.) After his death in 1957, Plečnik was virtually forgotten by Slovenes and scholars alike.

But a 1986 exposition about Plečnik at Paris' Pompidou Center jump-started interest in the architect. Within a few years, Plečnik was back in vogue. Today, scholars laud him as a genius who was ahead of his time...while locals and tourists enjoy the elegant simplicity of his works.

so you are in direct contact with the world of the architect. Still furnished with unique, Plečnik-designed furniture, one-of-a-kind inventions, and favorite souvenirs from his travels, the house paints an unusually intimate portrait of an artist. It's a ▲▲▲ pilgrimage for those who get caught up in Ljubljana's idiosyncratic sense of style.

Cost and Hours: €6, or €4 for just the modest museum, Tue-Sun 10:00-18:00—last tour departs at 17:00, closed Mon, 45-minute English tours begin at the top of each hour, Karunova 4, tel. 01/280-1604, www.mgml.si.

Getting Tickets: Tours are limited to seven people and can sell out, especially on summer weekends. Since you can only buy tickets in person (no reservations possible), it's smart to show up 15-20 minutes early at busy times.

Getting There: It's directly behind the twin steeples of the Trnovo Church. The 15-minute stroll from the center—the same one Plečnik took to work each day—is nearly as enjoyable as the house itself. You can either walk south along the river, then turn right onto Gradaška and stroll along the stream to the church; or, from French Revolution Square, head south on Emonska. If taking Emonska, you'll pass through the garden district of Krakovo, where pea patches and characteristic Old World buildings gracefully cohabitate. On the way to or from the museum, it's enjoyable to get a meal in Krakovo (two great restaurants—Pri Škofu and Manna—are described later, under "Eating in Ljubljana").

Background: Ljubljana's favorite son lived here from 1921 until his death in 1957. He added on to an existing house, building a circular bedroom for himself and filling the place with bric-a-brac he designed, as well as artifacts, photos, and gifts from around the world that inspired him as he shaped Ljubljana. Living a simple, almost monastic lifestyle, Plečnik knew what he liked, and these tastes are mirrored in his home.

Visiting the House: While waiting for your tour to begin, explore the modest but engaging **museum,** offering biographical details about Plečnik along with his personal effects (such as notebooks, tools, and eyeglasses). In one room, a model of Ljubljana locates the many structures he designed all around the city. You'll also see descriptions and photos of his greatest works, and large wooden models of two of his biggest "unrealized plans" that never made it off the drawing board: the cone-shaped "Cathedral of Freedom" and the roofed Butchers' Bridge at the market. One room features his redesign of Prague Castle, including a small model of his gardens and walkways. You can try sitting on chairs that Plečnik designed, and watch a video loop of short films about the architect.

The **tour** takes you through the actual rooms where Plečnik lived: kitchen, circular bedroom, sitting room, studio, and green-house. As you tour the place, be patient. Listen to its stories. Appreciate the subtle details. Notice how reverently your guide (and other Slovenes) speaks of this man. Contrast the humbleness of Plečnik's home with the dynamic impact he had on the cityscape of Ljubljana and the cultural heritage of Slovenia. Wandering Plečnik's hallways, it's hard not to be tickled by this man's sheer creativity and by the unique world he forged for himself to live in. As a visitor to his home, you're in good company. He invited only his closest friends here—except during World War II, when Ljubljana was occupied by Nazis and the university was closed, and Plečnik allowed his students to work with him here.

IN METELKOVA

Three museums face each other on a slick modern plaza next to the park called Tabor, about a 15-minute walk northeast of Prešeren Square in the dull but up-and-coming district of Metelkova. Nearby, you can explore the funky squatters' colony of Metelkova City (with Ljubljana's famous prison-turned-youth hostel).

▲▲Slovenian Ethnographic Museum (Slovenski Etnografski Muzej)

Housed in a state-of-the-art facility, this delightful museum is Ljubljana's most underrated attraction. With both permanent and temporary exhibits, the museum strives to explain what it is to be Slovene, with well-presented and well-described cultural artifacts from around the country. If you've caught the Slovenian folk culture itch, this is the place to scratch it.

Cost and Hours: €4.50, free first Sun of month, Tue-Sun 10:00-18:00, closed Mon, great café, Metelkova 2, tel. 01/300-8745, www.etno-muzej.si.

Visiting the Museum: The ground and first floors have good temporary exhibits, while upstairs you'll find two permanent exhibits.

The best exhibit, filling the third floor, is called **"Between Nature and Culture."** As you exit the elevator, turn left and find the shrunken head, which comes with a refreshingly frank exhibit that acknowledges the shortsighted tendency for museum curators—including at this museum—to emphasize things that are foreign or different. Continue through "Reflections of Distant Worlds" (non-European cultures) to reach the core of the collection, which focuses on Slovenia. A good but slow-moving film visits the country's four major regions. Another exhibit ponders how people half a world away—in Slovenia and in North America—simultaneously invented a similar solution (snowshoes) for a common problem. One display deconstructs Slovenian clichés (including this coun-

LJUBLJANA

try's odd fascination with its traditional hayracks). The arrangement of the collection emphasizes the evolution of an increasingly complicated civilization, from basic farming tools to ceramics to modern technology. You'll see exhibits on traditional Slovenian beekeeping, blacksmithing, weaving, shoemaking, costumes and customs, pottery, furniture, and religious objects. The children's "Ethnoalphabet" area features an A-to-Ž array of engaging, hands-on activities.

The other permanent exhibit, on the second floor (from the elevator, turn left to find the entrance), is called **"I, We, and Others."** A bit too conceptual for its own good, this heady exhibit ponders the notion of belonging. Designed for Slovenes more than foreigners (with very limited posted English information—borrow the free English audioguide from the ticket desk before heading up), it explores various aspects of how people define who they are, from individual and family to community and nation. Videos and sounds enhance the exhibits, and the curators neatly juxtapose well-known icons from different cultures (such as various national parliament buildings) in thought-provoking ways. While it's easy to get lost amid the navel-gazing, there is something particularly poignant about this topic here in the identity-obsessed Balkans.

Slovenian National Museum-Metelkova (Narodni Muzej Slovenije)

Next door to the Ethnographic Museum is this facility, where items (mostly applied arts) from the Slovenian National Museum that were formerly tucked away in storage are now displayed on two floors. The very pretty historical bric-a-brac is neatly presented without much context—it's just an excuse to get a bunch of interesting stuff out into public view. Each room has a different collection: furniture, pottery and ceramics, church vestments, weapons and armor, and more. The painting gallery is nicely organized by century and style. The museum also features temporary exhibits. Everything's labeled in English, and a guide can show you around, if they're not too busy.

Cost and Hours: €6, Tue-Sun 10:00-18:00, closed Mon, Maistrova 1, tel. 01/230-7032.

Museum of Contemporary Art-Metelkova (Muzej Sodobne Umetnosti Metelkova, MSUM)

This cutting-edge branch of the Museum of Modern Art opened in 2012 to showcase changing exhibitions of present-day, mostly Slovenian and Eastern European artists. The modern space is at once sleek and playful, making this museum worth a visit for art lovers who appreciate works from the 1960s to the present.

Cost and Hours: €5, ask about combo-ticket with Museum of

Modern Art, Tue-Sun 10:00-18:00, closed Mon, Maistrova 3, tel. 01/241-6825, www.mg-lj.si.

Metelkova City (Metelkova Mesto)

The heart of Slovenia's counterculture, this former military installation is now a funky, graffiti-slathered squatter's colony, billed as an "autonomous cultural center." Built by the Habsburgs in the 1880s, the complex—with barracks, warehouses, and a prison—was used by a laundry list of later occupiers, from Italian fascists to Nazis to the Yugoslav People's Army. After Yugoslavia pulled its troops out of Slovenia (following the Ten-Day War), the cluster of buildings sat derelict and abandoned. In 1993, transient artists moved in and set up galleries, theaters, bars, and nightclubs. While controversial at first, Meltelkova City has gradually become accepted by most Ljubljanans, and the city (which owns the property) not only tolerates but actively encourages this hotbed of youthful artistic expression. While edgy, this place is fascinating to explore—it's sleepy by day and lively by night (www.metelkovamesto.org).

Anchoring the area is **Hostel Celica,** one of Europe's most notable youth hostels, which fills a former prison building. Twenty artists were invited to decorate cells that have been turned into accommodations, and the ground floor features vibrant public spaces, a good and affordable restaurant (a nice place for a lunch or a light dinner), and a shoes-off "Oriental café." The message: Thoughtful art and architecture can transcend an ugly history. You can drop by to see the building anytime, and ask to borrow a flashlight to explore the dank and gloomy basement solitary confinement cells, with a small but interesting exhibition on the history of the building (and the various prisoners who have called it home—including Janez Janša, who did time here during communism and later became Slovenia's prime minister). But if you're interested in this place, make a point to visit at 14:00 for a free guided tour of the complex (tours run daily; you can also try calling to arrange a tour at other times, tel. 01/230-9700, www.hostelcelica.com).

Shopping in Ljubljana

Ljubljana, with its easygoing ambience and countless boutiques, is made to order for whiling away an afternoon shopping. It's also a fun place to stock up on souvenirs. Popular items include wood carvings and models (especially of the characteristic hayracks that dot the countryside), different flavors of schnapps (the kind with a whole pear inside—cultivated to actually grow right into the bottle—is a particularly classy gift), honey mead brandy (*medica*— sweet and smooth), bars of soap wrapped in wool (good for exfoliating), and those adorable painted panels from beehives (described on page 808). Rounding out the list of traditional Slovenian items are wrought-iron products from Kropa, crystal from Rogaska, lace from Idrija, and salt from Piran.

There are two convenient areas in the city center that offer abundant shopping opportunities: at **Ciril-Metodov trg and near the market;** and, beginning a few steps away, the **Old Town** pedestrian lane that cuts through the downtown core. I've described options in both places later. (A third street worth exploring—with a bit more funky student style—is the graffiti-slathered **Trubarjeva cesta,** a block up from the river and easy to find from Prešeren Square.)

AT CIRIL-METODOV TRG AND NEAR THE MARKET

The most atmospheric trinket-shopping is in the first stretch of the **market colonnade,** along the riverfront next to the Triple Bridge. See the "Ljubljana Hotels & Restaurants" map for locations.

If you're looking for serious handicrafts rather than trinkets, drop by the **Rustika** gallery, just over the Triple Bridge (on the castle side). In addition to beehive panels, they also have lace, painted chests and boxes, and other tasteful local-style mementos (daily 9:00-21:00, Stritarjeva 9, mobile 031-459-509). There's another Rustika location up at the castle courtyard. A somewhat more downscale souvenir shop with a wide variety is **Dom Trgovina,** across from the TI on the main market square (Mon-Sat 9:00-21:00, Sun from 10:00, Ciril-Metodov trg 5).

Kraševka sells high-quality artisanal products (mostly foods) from the Karst region, and also acts as a sort of information office for that area (Mon-Fri 9:00-19:00, Sat until 15:00, closed Sun, Vodnikov trg 4, tel. 01/232-1445).

Trgovina Ika, a small artisan boutique with its own hip and idiosyncratic sense of style, is a delightful place to browse for truly authentic Slovenian stuff that goes beyond souvenirs. Its unique items by local designers—jewelry, hats, scarves, shoes, and so on—are modern and fashionable (Mon-Fri 10:00-19:30, Sat 9:00-18:00, Sun 10:00-14:00, Ciril-Metodov trg 13, tel. 01/123-21743).

IN THE OLD TOWN

Ljubljana's main Old Town street—which changes names from Mestni trg to Stari trg, then Gornji trg—is also lined with several characteristic shops, selling a few of the unique gift items produced in this proud little country. Here's a lightly narrated tour of this inviting street, from start to finish. Unless otherwise noted, all of these shops are open long hours on weekdays (often until 20:00); most close a bit earlier on Saturdays (around 17:00), and close in the early afternoon on Sundays (usually by 13:00 or 14:00).

◑ Self-Guided Shopping Stroll: Begin in front of the Town Hall. Before you start the walk, take the opportunity to browse the shops along Ciril-Metodov Trg, noted above (all of which are within a five-minute walk of here). When you're ready, head down the street.

First, on the left at Mestni trg 7, **Honey House** sells products harvested by beekeeper Luka. For tips on browsing your honey options, see page 808. Next door at #8, **Piranske Soline** sells products from the giant salt pans that sit just south of Piran on Slovenia's tiny coastline. You can pick up some locally harvested sea salt, or peruse their salt-based beauty products (bath salts, body milk, and other exfoliants, www.soline.si). Just beyond, **La Chocolate** is the first of two artisanal *čokoladnice* (chocolate shops) along this strip (www.lachocolate.si).

Farther along, on the right (at #17), **Galerija Idrijske Čipke** shows off handmade lace from the town of Idrija (www.idrija-lace.com). Next door, **Dobrote Dolenjske** sells a variety of flavored schnapps and some handicrafts from the Dolenje region in the southeast (www.dobrote-dolenjske.si).

Continuing past various clothes boutiques, look for (on the left, at #11) another chocolate shop, **Čokoladnica Cukrček**. A bit pricier than La Chocolate, this shop is best known for its foil-wrapped "Prešeren Balls" chocolates—a clever and civic-minded takeoff on Salzburg's "Mozart Balls," replacing the composer with Slovenia's greatest poet (www.cukrcek.si). Down the adjacent passage is the stylish **Formadoma** design shop, specializing in housewares (closed Sun, www.formadoma.eu). At #12 is **Devur,** a small hole-in-the-wall with handcrafted wooden items.

Continue along the street (which here changes names from Mestni trg to Stari trg), passing more clothes shops. On the left, at Stari trg 3, **Cha** tea shop sells over 100 varieties of tea, plus porcelain teapots and cups from all over. It's attached to the recommended **Čajna Hiša teahouse.**

A few steps down on the left (at #5), **Cafetino** is the best place in town for coffee. They have more than 20 types available—espresso or Turkish-style, plus beans to take home.

Next door, follow the passage to reach **Za Popen't Pivoteka,** a "bottle shop" selling 200 kinds of beer in individual bottles. While they stock a few Slovenian beers, they focus on international microbrews—including several American brands. The name is a play on words, loosely meaning "foamy goodness" (www.zapopent.si).

Now you'll wade through a stretch of enticing restaurants with wonderful outdoor tables (for my recommendations here, see the Old Town listings in "Eating in Ljubljana"). Notice Julija and Romeo, facing each other wistfully across the street.

After the little "restaurant row," the lineup of shops resumes.

LJUBLJANA

Sleep Code

Hotels are classified based on the average price of a standard double room with breakfast in spring and fall. Prices may go up in summer, and down in winter.

$$$$	**Splurge:** Most rooms over €150
$$$	**Pricier:** €110-150
$$	**Moderate:** €80-110
$	**Budget:** €50-80
¢	**Backpacker:** Under €50
RS%	**Rick Steves discount**

Unless otherwise noted, credit cards are accepted, hotel staff speak basic English, and free Wi-Fi is available. Comparison-shop by checking prices at several hotels (on each hotel's own website, on a booking site, or by email). For the best deal, *book directly with the hotel.* Ask for a discount if paying in cash; if the listing includes **RS%,** request a Rick Steves discount.

On the left at Stari trg 11, look for **Wool Art Knitwear,** with unique (and very well-insulated) Serbian-style clothing.

From here, you'll pass a few more funky shops, as well as some rare books and antique shops. On the right at #26, don't miss **Woodway,** with locally made wooden jewelry, sunglasses, and phone cases, and cork handbags and wallets from Portugal (www. woodway.si).

The cobbled charm culminates at the square called **Gornji trg.** Look uphill and notice the village charms of some of the oldest buildings in town: four medieval houses with rooflines slanted at the ends, different from the others on this street.

Sleeping in Ljubljana

Ljubljana has good accommodations in all price ranges. I've focused my listings in or within easy walking distance of the city center. To get the best value, book ahead. The most expensive hotels raise their prices even more during conventions (Sept-Oct, and sometimes also June).

$$$$ Lesar Hotel Angel, on a cobbled square in the Old Town, feels plush and high-end. Its 12 rooms have crisp white decor, and the private garden is inviting (air-con, lots of stairs with no elevator, pay parking, Gornji trg 7, tel. 01/425-5089, www. angelhotel.si, info@angelhotel.si, warm Jovan).

$$$$ Vander Urbani Resort is a unique concept: Nestled central as can be just off the in-love-with-life riverfront embankment, it really does feel like an intensely hip resort in the city center—right down to the minuscule rooftop swimming pool and sundeck. The resort prides itself on the cutting-edge urban design of its 20 rooms, and tries to use Slovenian and organic products wherever possible (air-con, elevator, café, restaurant, champagne bar, Krojaška ulica 6, tel. 01/200-9000, www.vanderhotel.com, info@vanderhotel.com).

$$$$ Cubo Hotel is a jolt of trendy minimalism on Ljubljana's hotel scene. Its 26 large rooms are the best place in town for sleek, urban elegance. Choose between streetside rooms, which enjoy castle views but get some traffic noise, or quieter courtyard rooms (air-con, elevator, Slovenska cesta 15, tel. 01/425-6000, www.hotelcubo.com, reception@hotelcubo.com).

$$$ Adora Hotel, tucked behind a church at the edge of the cobbled Old Town zone, has 10 rooms with a restrained rustic style. They also rent two apartments in the passage that runs over the busy street, which can be noisy (air-con, elevator, free loaner bikes, pay parking, Rožna ulica 7, mobile 082-057-240, www.adorahotel.si, info@adorahotel.si).

$$ Meščanka ("City Woman") rents seven cozy, well-equipped rooms and apartments in a fantastic location right along the bustling riverfront promenade. The decor is mod, funky, and colorful, and the good windows work hard to provide silence (no breakfast, air-con, reception open 10:00-12:00 & 14:00-19:00—let them know if you're coming outside that time, Ključavničarska 4, mobile 051-880-044, www.mescanka.si, info@mescanka.si, Saša).

$$ Hotel Mrak has 34 comfortable rooms in a pleasant neighborhood near French Revolution Square. This trusty old place is my sentimental favorite in Ljubljana (RS%, air-con, elevator, restaurant with terrace under an old vine, pay parking, Rimska 4, tel. 01/421-9650, www.hotelmrak.si, info@hotelmrak.si, Koharič family).

$$ Slamič B&B has 17 modern rooms with hardwood floors, tasteful decor, and absentee management. Over an appealing upscale café in a nondescript but central neighborhood, this is a fine spot for affordable elegance (air-con, free parking, reception open Mon-Sat 7:30-22:00, Sun 9:00-14:00—call ahead if coming outside these times, Kersnikova 1, tel. 01/433-8233, www.slamic.si, info@slamic.si).

$$ Hotel Emonec (eh-MOH-nets), with some of the most centrally located cheap beds in Ljubljana, hides just off Wolfova lane between Prešeren and Congress squares. Its 54 rooms—in three buildings across a courtyard from each other—feel like a cookie-cutter chain hotel, with tight bathrooms and a shoestring staff. But the price and ideal location make it worth considering (family rooms, air-con in some rooms, pay parking garage, self-service laundry, Wolfova 12, tel. 01/200-1520, www.hotel-emonec.com, hotelemonec@siol.net).

LJUBLJANA

Ljubljana Hotels & Restaurants

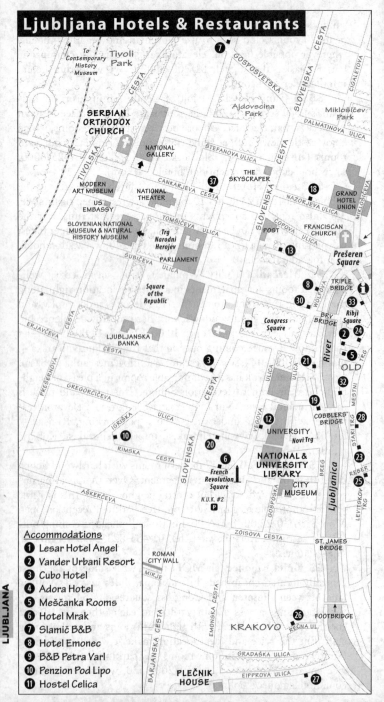

Accommodations
1. Lesar Hotel Angel
2. Vander Urbani Resort
3. Cubo Hotel
4. Adora Hotel
5. Meščanka Rooms
6. Hotel Mrak
7. Slamič B&B
8. Hotel Emonec
9. B&B Petra Varl
10. Penzion Pod Lipo
11. Hostel Celica

LJUBLJANA

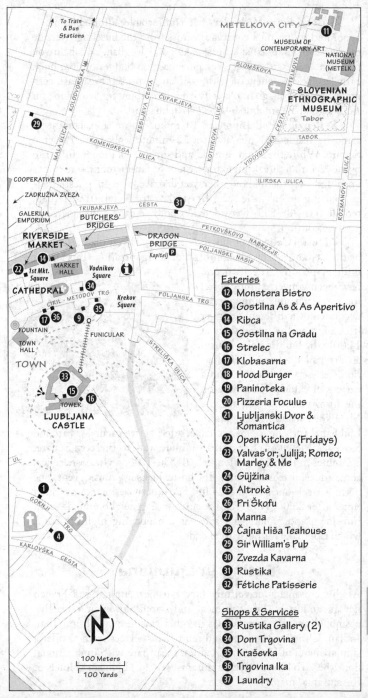

To Train & Bus Stations

METELKOVA CITY ⑪

MUSEUM OF CONTEMPORARY ART

NATIONAL MUSEUM (METELK.)

SLOVENIAN ETHNOGRAPHIC MUSEUM
Tabor

SLOMŠKOVA

KOLODVORSKA UL.

RESLJEVA CESTA

ČUFARJEVA

KOTNIKOVA ULICA

METELKOVA

VIDOVDANSKA CESTA

TABOR

ULICA

ROZMANOVA

KOMENSKEGA ULICA

MAJA ULICA

⑲

COOPERATIVE BANK

ZADRUŽNA ZVEZA

GALERIJA EMPORIUM

ILIRSKA ULICA

TRUBARJEVA CESTA

BUTCHERS' BRIDGE

③①

RIVERSIDE MARKET

FETKOVŠKOVO NABREŽJE

DRAGON BRIDGE

POLJANSKI NASIP

Kapitelj ℗

㉒ 1st Mkt. Square

MARKET HALL

Vodnikov Square

CATHEDRAL

⑭

㉞

CIRIL - METODOV TRG

Krekov Square

POLJANSKA TRG

⑰ ㊱ ⑨ ㉟

FOUNTAIN

TOWN HALL

FUNICULAR

STRELIŠKA ULICA

TOWN

㉝

⑮

TOWER ⑯

LJUBLJANA CASTLE

①

GORNJI TRG

④

KARLOVŠKA CESTA

UL.

N

100 Meters
100 Yards

Eateries

⑫ Monstera Bistro
⑬ Gostilna As & As Aperitivo
⑭ Ribca
⑮ Gostilna na Gradu
⑯ Strelec
⑰ Klobasarna
⑱ Hood Burger
⑲ Paninoteka
⑳ Pizzeria Foculus
㉑ Ljubljanski Dvor & Romantica
㉒ Open Kitchen (Fridays)
㉓ Valvas'or; Julija; Romeo; Marley & Me
㉔ Güjžina
㉕ Altrokè
㉖ Pri Škofu
㉗ Manna
㉘ Čajna Hiša Teahouse
㉙ Sir William's Pub
㉚ Zvezda Kavarna
㉛ Rustika
㉜ Fétiche Patisserie

Shops & Services

㉝ Rustika Gallery (2)
㉞ Dom Trgovina
㉟ Kraševka
㊱ Trgovina Ika
㊲ Laundry

LJUBLJANA

$ B&B Petra Varl offers five comfortable, affordable, nicely appointed rooms on a courtyard across from the bustling riverside market. Petra, an artist who speaks good English, will help you feel at home. As this place is Ljubljana's top budget option, book early (includes kitchenette with basic do-it-yourself breakfast, cash preferred, air-con, go into courtyard at Vodnikov trg 5 and look for *B&B* sign at 5A, mobile 041-389-470, bb@varl.si).

$ Penzion Pod Lipo has 10 rooms above a restaurant in a mostly residential area about a 12-minute walk from Prešeren Square. While the rooms are old and simple, it's thoughtfully run by jolly Marjan (breakfast extra, cash only, family room, sometimes unstaffed—let them know when you'll arrive, air-con, guest kitchen, putting green on terrace, Borstnikov trg 3, tel. 01/251-1683, mobile 031-809-893, www.penzion-podlipo.com, info@penzion-podlipo.com).

¢ Hostel Celica, a proud, innovative, and lively place, is owned by the city and run by a nonprofit student organization. This former military prison's 20 cells *(celica)* have been converted into hostel rooms—each one unique and decorated by a different designer (free tours of the hostel daily at 14:00). The building also houses an art gallery, tourist information, self-service laundry, and a variety of eateries. For more on the history of this site, see the Metelkova section in "Sights in  Ljubljana" (private rooms available, offers active excursions around Slovenia, Metelkova 8, a dull 15-minute walk to Prešeren Square, 8 minutes to the train station, tel. 01/230-9700, www.hostelcelica.com, info@hostelcelica.com). The hostel hosts live music events one night a week until around 24:00, but otherwise maintains "quiet time" after 23:00. However, the surrounding neighborhood—a bit run-down and remote, but safe—is a happening nightlife zone, which can make for noisy weekends.

Eating in Ljubljana

At this crossroads of cultures (and cuisines), Italian and French flavors are just as "local" as meat-and-starch Slovenian food. This cosmopolitan city also dabbles in other cuisines; you'll find Thai, Indian, Chinese, Mexican, and more. Most places seem to offer a similar menu of Slovenian/Mediterranean fare with international flourishes. To locate these restaurants, see the "Ljubljana Hotels & Restaurants" map.

Lunch Deals: To stretch your budget, have your main meal at lunch, when most of Ljubljana's top eateries serve a high-quality three-course meal (starter, main, dessert) at a very affordable price—usually around €10, not including drinks. You won't have much choice (they may only have one or two options each day), but the quality is high and the value is outstanding. Some places offer these deals only on weekdays. After a big lunch, you can have a light dinner—picnic, *burek*, pizza, sandwich...or just gelato. I've noted "lunch special" where applicable.

IN THE CITY CENTER

$$$$ Monstera Bistro is a magnet for foodies seeking top-quality, seasonal, international fare in a tight, cozy dining room. Owner Bine Volčič, who prides himself on sustainability (minimizing waste by finding creative uses for every possible ingredient), is distinguishing himself as one of Slovenia's top chefs. The bistro is open most days for a more affordable lunch (Mon-Sat 11:30-16:00), and weekends only for a pricier, fixed-price dinner (Thu-Sat 19:00-23:00). Either way, the prices are reasonable for the quality, and it's essential to reserve at least a week ahead (Gosposka 9, tel. 040/431-123, www.monsterabistro.si).

$$$$ Gostilna As ("Ace"), tucked into a courtyard just off Prešeren Square, is a venerable mainstay that pleases fish lovers. It's dressy, pricey, and pretentious (the service is deliberate, and waiters ignore the menu and recommend what's fresh). It's loosely based on the Slow Food model: Servings are small, and you're expected to take your time and order two or three courses—which can add up. The dining room is old-fashioned and a bit stuffy, but in good weather, their rooftop terrace is gorgeous (mostly fish and Italian dishes, daily 12:00-24:00, reservations smart, Čopova 5A, or enter courtyard with *As* sign near relief of Julija on Wolfova, tel. 01/425-8822, www.gostilnaas.si). For cheaper food and drinks from the same kitchen, eat at the attached **$$$ As Aperitivo**, a much livelier, more casual spot. You'll sit in the leafy courtyard or the winter garden, with big windows that stay open in the summer (salads, sandwiches, pastas, and main courses, food served daily 12:00-24:00, longer hours for drinks, good gelato counter inside). The courtyard also has a couple of other fun eateries—and, in the summer, live music.

LJUBLJANA

Restaurant Price Code

I've assigned each eatery a price category, based on the average cost of a typical main course. Drinks, desserts, and splurge items (steak and seafood) can raise the price considerably.

$$$$	**Splurge:**	Most main courses over €14
$$$	**Pricier:**	€10-14
$$	**Moderate:**	€6-10
$	**Budget:**	Under €6

In Slovenia, a takeout spot is **$**; a basic sit-down eatery is **$$**; a casual but more upscale restaurant is **$$$**; and a swanky splurge is **$$$$**.

$ Ribca ("Fish") hides under the first stretch of market colonnade near the Triple Bridge. This is your best bet for a relatively quick and cheap riverside lunch. Choose between the two straightforward menus: grilled fillets or fried small fish. They also serve (gulp!) fish-topped pizzas. With the fragrant fish market right next door, you know it's fresh. If you just want to enjoy sitting along the river below the bustling market, this is also a fine spot for a coffee or beer (Mon-Sat 8:00-21:00, Sun 11:30-18:00, tel. 01/425-1544).

Traditional Slovenian Food: Because Slovenes head into the countryside when they want traditional fare, Ljubljana isn't the best place to find authentic Slovenian grub. But if you'd like to try some, your best budget bet may be **$ Klobasarna,** listed below. For a more formal sit-down meal, head for **$$$$ Gostilna na Gradu,** in the castle courtyard high above town—if you don't mind going up to the castle to get it (the handy funicular costs €4 round-trip). Run by a team of well-respected chefs (including Ana Roš of the world-famous Hiša Franko—see "The Julian Alps" chapter), it serves up a seasonal menu of traditional flavors with modern flair, at fairly high prices. Choose between the dull vaulted interior, the glassed-in arcade, or the outdoor tables. Reservations are recommended before you make the trip up here (Mon-Sat 10:00-24:00—food served until 22:00, Sun 9:00-18:00—food served until 17:00, Grajska Planota 1, mobile 031-301-777, www.nagradu.si).

With Pretense at the Castle: In addition to the more traditional Gostilna na Gradu (listed above), the castle is home to the top-end **$$$$ Strelec** restaurant—a heavily themed, quite pretentious option with a big-name chef, elaborately described menu items, and a growing reputation. Reserve ahead (Mon-Sat 12:00-22:00, closed Sun, tel. 031/687-648, www.kaval-group.si).

Fast and Cheap: $ Klobasarna is a budget foodie option specializing in *kranjska klobasa*—traditional Carniolan sausage, from the Slovenian uplands. The menu is simple—one wiener or two, extra for *jota* (hearty turnip stew)—and delicious. They also serve the Slovenian dumplings called *štruklji* (Mon-Sat 10:00-23:00, Sun until 15:00, Ciril-Metodov trg 15, mobile 051-605-017). **$ Hood Burger,** part of a locally beloved chain, is Slovenia's answer to In-N-Out. The owners pride themselves on using locally sourced ingredients ("100 percent Slovenian beef!"), and cultivate a personal relationship with their producers. The result is tasty, authentic burgers (daily 11:00-24:00, handiest location is just off Prešeren Square at Nazorjeva 4). **$ Paninoteka,** with wonderful outdoor seating overlooking Cobblers' Bridge and fine interior seating, has affordable and tasty sandwiches; their full menu is good, but more expensive (daily 9:00-22:00, Jurčičev trg 3, mobile 040-349-329).

Pizzerias: $ Pizzeria Foculus, tucked in a boring alleyway a few blocks up from the river, has a loyal local following, a happening atmosphere, an inviting interior, a few outdoor tables, and Ljubljana's best pizza (over 50 types, daily 11:00-24:00, just off French Revolution Square across the street from Plečnik's National and University Library at Gregorčičeva 3, tel. 01/251-5643). **$ Ljubljanski Dvor** enjoys the most convenient and scenic location of any pizzeria in town. On a sunny summer day, the outdoor riverside terrace is unbeatable; I'd skip the dull interior and the pricier pasta restaurant higher up (Mon-Sat 10:00-24:00, Sun from 12:00, 50 yards from Cobblers' Bridge at Dvorni trg 1, tel. 01/251-6555). Ljubljanski Dvor also has a handy **$ takeout window** (go around back to the walk-up window on Congress Square). Enjoy a cheap slice at one of their outdoor tables facing Congress Square, or get it to go and munch it along the river.

Friday Street Food: On good-weather Fridays from spring through fall, Ljubljana's outdoor market hosts the **Open Kitchen** (Odprta Kuhna)—a sprawling al fresco food court where the country's best chefs gather to showcase their creations. For the people of Ljubljana, this is both a culinary event and a social one. Foodies make this a priority (mid-March-mid-Oct Fri 10:00-21:00, until 23:00 in summer, in the heart of the outdoor market zone—in front of the cathedral—at Pogačarjev trg, www.odprtakuhna.si).

IN THE OLD TOWN

The main drag through the Old Town (which starts at the Town Hall and changes names as it goes: Mestni trg, then Stari trg, then Gornji trg) is lined with inviting eateries. Tables clutter the cobbled pedestrian street. If you're at a loss for where to eat in town, stroll here to survey your options, then pick your favorite menu and ambience. As many restaurants along here are uniformly good, no one place really has the edge.

Several popular options cluster in one particularly atmospheric stretch; all except Romeo offer a similar menu of Mediterranean-

Slovenian cuisine and wonderful outdoor seating: **$$$$ Valvas'or,** the upscale option, has a dressy dining room and a posh gold color scheme (weekday lunch deal, Mon-Sat 12:00-23:00, closed Sun, Stari trg 7, tel. 01/425-0455). **$$$ Julija** features homey country-Slovenian decor inside (lunch deals, daily 12:00-22:00, Stari trg 9, tel. 01/425-6463). **$ Romeo,** across the street, is a lowbrow bar serving unexceptional Mexican food...but the name sure is clever (get it? "Romeo and Julija"). And **$$ Marley & Me** comes with a warm welcome from Matej (weekday lunch specials, daily 11:00-23:00, Stari trg 9, tel. 08/380-6610). I've also enjoyed a great salad lunch at the nearby **$ Čajna Hiša** teahouse (described later, under "Drinks and Treats.") Additional options are just a few steps away:

$$$ Gújžina highlights food and wine from the Hungarian-influenced region of Slovenia called Prekmurje. The tight but cozy dining room offers a menu of rich, flavorful dishes (including *bograč*—a spicy, goulash-like stew served in its own kettle—and the roasted dumplings called *dödöle*) and a chance to sample the products of one of Slovenia's top wine-growing regions. This is a fine place to try *gibanica* poppyseed layer cake—originating in Prekmurje, and beloved throughout Slovenia (daily 8:00-24:00, Mestni trg 19, mobile 083-806-446).

$$$ Altrokè highlights cuisine from Istria—the region shared by southern Slovenia and northern Croatia. That means Adriatic seafood, *pršut,* and lots of truffles, served in a cozy stone-walled dining room right along the Old Town's main drag (daily 12:00-23:00, Stari trg 19, mobile 082-055-282).

IN KRAKOVO

The Krakovo district—just south of the city center, where garden patches nearly outnumber simple homes—is a pleasant area to wander. It's also home to two tasty restaurants. If the nearby Jože Plečnik House is open during your visit, you could combine your visit there with a meal at one of these options.

$$$ Pri Škofu ("By the Bishop") is a laid-back, leafy place with appealing outdoor seating, a nondescript modern interior, and a focus on freshness, serving international cuisine with a Slovenian flair. This hidden gem is deliciously memorable; reserve ahead (creative soups, lunch specials, homemade desserts, Tue-Fri 10:00-23:00, Sat-Sun from 12:00, closed Mon, Rečna 8, tel. 01/426-4508).

$$$$ Manna, with artfully presented, seasonal Slovenian-Mediterranean fusion cuisine, sits along the pleasant Gradaščica canal. The interior is pure Secession—the Gustav Klimt-era, early-20th-century, gold-accented Viennese style that was so influential in Ljubljana. I prefer the more artistic, café-like downstairs to the stuffy upstairs dining room, but the seating out front is hard to beat

on a nice day. This is another fine splurge that you can enjoy affordably through their lunch special (Mon-Sat 12:00-24:00, Sun until
21:00, Eipprova 1A, tel. 05/992-2308).

DRINKS AND TREATS

Riverfront Cafés: Enjoying a coffee, beer, or ice-cream cone along
the Ljubljanica River embankment (between the Triple and Cob-
blers' bridges) is Ljubljana's
single best experience—
worth ▲▲▲. Tables spill
into the street, and some
of the best-dressed, best-
looking students on the
planet happily fill them
day and night. (A com-
mon question from first-
time visitors to Ljubljana:
"Doesn't anybody here have a job?") This is some of the top people-
watching in Europe. Just explore and find the spot with the breezy
ambience you like best. When ordering, the easiest choice is a *bela
kava* (white coffee)—a caffe latte.

Teahouse: If coffee's not your cup of tea, go a block inland to
the teahouse **$ Čajna Hiša.** They serve about 50 types of tea, light
food (including great salads and sandwiches), and desserts (Mon-
Fri 8:00-22:00, Sat until 15:00, closed Sun, on the atmospheric
main drag in the Old Town a few steps from Cobblers' Bridge at
Stari trg 3, tel. 01/421-2444). They also have an attached tea shop,
Cha (described on page 761).

Beer: Sir William's Pub is where beer aficionados go to get a
taste of Slovenia's burgeoning craft beer scene. It has a few outdoor
tables and a classic British pub interior, and a thoughtfully curated
menu of both domestic and international microbrews on tap and by
the bottle (no food, Mon-Fri 8:00-24:00, Sat from 10:00, Sun from
17:00, Tavčarjeva ulica 8A, mobile 059-944-825). The city also has
a few well-stocked bottle shops, including **Za Popen't Pivoteka**
(Stari trg 5, tel. 01/256-5916).

Cakes: Zvezda Kavarna, a trendy, central place at the bottom of Congress Square, is a local favorite for cakes, pastries, and
ice cream. A nostalgic favorite here—once popular in communist
times, and recently reintroduced to great acclaim—is the *emona
kocka* (Emona cube), a layer cake with nuts, cake, and chocolate
(Mon-Sat 7:00-23:00, Sun 10:00-20:00, a block from Prešeren
Square at Wolfova 14, tel. 01/421-9090). Their **deli,** one door toward Prešeren Square, has takeaway coffee and smoothies, a wide
variety of cakes to go, and some of the most decadent ice cream in
town (same hours).

LJUBLJANA

Chocolates and Ice Cream: Local chain **Rustika** sells tasty homemade chocolates, cookies (including one kind with four types of chocolate), and a wide variety of unusual and delicious artisanal ice cream flavors. The menu changes from day to day, but highlights can include balsamic vinegar with vanilla or strawberry, very dark chocolate, Kanada (with maple syrup and walnuts), and Greek yogurt with honey and nuts. The handiest location is about an eight-minute walk from Prešeren Square, and comes with a delightful stroll along colorful Trubarjeva cesta (ice cream available summer only, Mon-Fri 8:00-19:00, Sat 9:00-13:00, closed Sun, Trubarjeva cesta 44, mobile 059-935-730). Don't confuse this sweet shop with the Rustika gift shop.

More Ice Cream: Ljubljana is known for its Italian gelato-style ice cream. You'll see fine options all along the Ljubljanica River embankment, but many places serve ice cream only in summer. **Romantica,** just up the steps from the river, is the foodies' choice, with creative and delicious artisanal flavors (just uphill from Ljubljanksi Dvor pizzeria at Dvorni trg 1). **Fétiche Patisserie,** along the riverfront café embankment, is another good choice, with some unusual, pungent, Asian-themed flavors.

Ljubljana Connections

As Slovenia's transportation hub, Ljubljana is well-connected to both domestic and international destinations. When checking schedules, be aware of city name variations: In Slovene, Vienna is "Dunaj," Budapest is "Budimpešta," and Venice is "Benétke."

Local Alternative: When considering bus and train connections, don't overlook the very handy **GoOpti** shared transfer service, which is often more convenient and not much more expensive. Locals swear by this service for airport transfers and reaching otherwise tricky-to-connect places like Venice and Istria (described later).

BY TRAIN

From Ljubljana by Train to: Lesce-Bled (roughly hourly, 40-60 minutes—but bus is better because it goes right to Bled town center), **Postojna** (nearly hourly, 1 hour), **Divača** (close to Škocjan Caves and Lipica, nearly hourly, 1.75 hours), **Sežana** (close to Lipica, nearly hourly, 2 hours), **Piran** (direct bus is better—see next; otherwise allow 4 hours, train to Koper, 4/day, 2.5 hours; then bus to Piran, 7/day, 30 minutes), **Maribor** (hourly, 2-3 hours, most with a transfer in Zidani Most), **Ptuj** (2/day direct, 2.5 hours, more with transfer in Pragersko or Maribor), **Zagreb** (4/day direct, 2.5 hours), **Rijeka** (1/day direct, 3 hours), **Split** (1/day, 12 hours, transfer in Zagreb), **Vienna** (that's **Dunaj** in Slovene, 1/day direct, 6 hours;

otherwise 4/day with transfer in Villach or Maribor, 6.5 hours), **Budapest** (that's **Budimpešta** in Slovene; 1/day direct, 8.5 hours, other connections possible with 1-2 changes but complicated, no convenient night train), **Venice** (called **Benétke** in Slovene; fastest by bus or GoOpti—see later; otherwise 2/day with a transfer in Trieste, 5.5 hours), **Salzburg** (2/day direct, 4.5 hours, an additional 2/day possible with transfer in Villach), **Munich** (2/day direct, 6.5 hours, including 1 night train; also possible 2/day with transfer in Villach). Train info: Toll tel. 01/291-3332, www.slo-zeleznice.si.

BY BUS

The bus station is a low-profile building in front of the train station. Buses depart from the numbered stalls in the middle of the street. For any bus, you have to buy tickets at the bus station ticket windows or at the automated e-kart kiosk (pay with credit card or cash), not from the driver. For bus information, pick up one of the blue phones inside the station to be connected to a helpful English-speaking operator. Bus info: www.ap-ljubljana.si, www.getbybus.com, or www.flixbus.com.

By Bus to: Bled (Mon-Sat hourly—usually at the top of each hour, fewer on Sun, 1.25 hours), **Postojna** (at least hourly, 1 hour), **Divača** (close to Škocjan Caves and Lipica, about every 2-3 hours, 1.5 hours), **Piran** (5/day Mon-Fri, 2/day Sat, 4/day Sun, 2.5 hours, more with change in Portorož), over the **Vršič Pass** to **Bovec** (2/day July-Aug at 6:30 and 15:00, June and Sept Sat-Sun only at 6:30, 4.5 hours to Bovec, none Oct-May), **Kobarid** (1/day in July-Aug over Vršič Pass, 5 hours; otherwise faster but less scenic via Idrija, 3.5 hours), **Rijeka** (2/day, fewer off-season, 2.5 hours), **Zagreb** (10/day, less on weekends, 2.5 hours). To reach Croatia's Istria—specifically **Rovinj**—the bus is your best option (usually at least 2/day direct, 4-5 hours).

Flixbus offers frequent, direct, long-distance buses to cities including **Venice** (4 hours), **Zagreb** (2.5 hours), **Vienna** (5.5 hours), **Munich** (5.5 hours), and **Budapest** (6.5 hours)—often faster and cheaper than by train. And Nomago also offers bus connections to **Venice,** its **Marco Polo Airport,** and **Treviso Airport**—opening up alternatives to Slovenia's lone airport (www.nomago.si).

BY SHARED SHUTTLE SERVICE

If bus and train schedules don't quite serve your needs, **GoOpti**—a company with an innovative business model for shared minibus transfers—can be a convenient and inexpensive alternative. First, go to www.goopti.com and select your destination, date, and preferred time of arrival or departure. Then, 24 hours before departure, you'll get an update of the specific pickup time, based on the needs of other passengers. Prices can flex dramatically, but it's quite affordable (for example, an advance nonrefundable purchase from Ljubljana could be €15 to Piran, or €20 to Venice or Zagreb; for the best price, book two months ahead). They also offer airport transfers to or from downtown Ljubljana for less than €10. For a few euros extra, they can pick you up at your hotel rather than the train or bus station; to lock in a specific time, you can pay extra for a "VIP" transfer.

GoOpti reaches destinations throughout Slovenia (including Ljubljana, the airport, Lake Bled, towns in the Karst such as Postojna and Sežana, and Piran and other Slovenian coastal destinations), but it's also handy for farther-flung international destinations—such as Venice or its airport, Trieste, various Austrian cities (Vienna, Salzburg, Klagenfurt, etc.), and Croatian cities such as Zagreb and Pula.

BY PLANE

Slovenia's only **airport** (airport code: LJU) is 14 miles north of Ljubljana, about halfway to Bled. Confusingly, the airport goes by three names: Ljubljana Airport (the international version); Brnik (for the town that it's near); and Jože Pučnik Airport (a politician for whom it was controversially renamed in 2007). Most flights are operated by Slovenia's national airline, Adria Airways (www. adria-airways.com), but additional flights are run by EasyJet (www. easyjet.com), Wizz Air (www.wizzair.com), and various national carriers (Air France, Turkish Airlines, and so on). The airport is small and manageable. Morning flights tend to cluster around the same time frame (between 6:45 and 7:30); as the airport doesn't open until 5:00, there's no need to show up before then. If you need to kill time here, follow signs (around to the left as you exit the terminal) to *Razgledna Terasa* and *Terasa Avionček* and ride the elevator up to the rooftop terrace with a café, where you can sip a coffee while you watch planes land and take off. Airport info: tel. 04/206-1000, www.lju-airport.si.

Getting Between Downtown Ljubljana and the Airport: Locals swear by the **GoOpti** service described earlier, which is the ideal mix of price (typically less than €10) and convenience; book a day or more ahead on their website. Otherwise, two kinds of buses connect the airport with Ljubljana's bus station: **public bus #28** (labeled *Ljubljana-Brnik,* to the right as you exit the airport; Mon-Fri hourly until 20:00, only 7/day Sat-Sun, 45 minutes, €4.10), and a **minibus** (to the left as you exit the airport, scheduled to depart after various arriving flights—look for schedule posted near bus stop). Two different companies run the minibus transfers, which take about 30 minutes and cost €9 to downtown: Markun (mobile 041-792-865, www.prevozi-markun.com) and Marko Nowotny (mobile 040-771-771, www.mnj.si). I'd take whichever one is departing first. Most expensive is a **taxi;** the fair rate is around €30, but to avoid rip-off cabbies, it's best to call for a taxi (or, if you're at the airport, ask the information desk to call one for you).

To Lake Bled: For tips on going from the airport directly to Lake Bled, see "Lake Bled Connections" in the next chapter.

Airport Alternatives: Ljubljana's airport—the only one in the country—charges high taxes and fees, and has limited connections to some European destinations. To save money (or to avoid a layover), many Slovenes fly in and out of relatively nearby airports in neighboring countries: **Zagreb** (2-hour drive from Ljubljana); **Venice** (3-hour drive from Ljubljana); **Treviso** (2.5-hour drive from Ljubljana); **Trieste** (2-hour drive from Ljubljana); and **Klagenfurt/Kärnten** (especially for those going to Lake Bled, from which it's a 2-hour drive). To get between these airports and your Slovenian destination, GoOpti, described earlier, is typically cheaper than a taxi and more convenient than a bus or train connection.

LAKE BLED

Lake Bled—Slovenia's leading mountain resort—comes complete with a sweeping alpine panorama, a fairy-tale island, a cliff-hanging medieval castle, a lazy lakeside promenade, and the country's most sought-after desserts. And the charms of its glorious mountain vistas and traditional folk life only crescendo as you explore the surrounding areas. Taken together, there are few more enjoyable places to simply be on vacation.

Since the Habsburg days, Lake Bled (locals pronounce it like "blade") has been *the* place where Slovenes wow visiting diplomats. In the late 19th century, local aristocrats surrounded the humble lakefront village with classy villas. Tito also had one of his vacation homes here (today's Hotel Vila Bled), where he entertained illustrious guests. But above all, Lake Bled feels like a place that Slovenes enjoy alongside their visitors.

Lake Bled has plenty of ways to idle away an afternoon. While the lake's main town, also called Bled, is more functional than quaint, it offers postcard views of the lake and handy access to the region. Hike up to Bled Castle for intoxicating vistas. Ride a traditional *pletna* boat out to the island, climb up to the church, ring the bell, and make a wish. Wander or bike the dreamy path around the lake. Sit on a dock, dip your feet in the water, and watch the lake's resident swans. Then dive into some of Bled's famous cakes while you take in the view of Triglav, Slovenia's favorite mountain. Bled quiets down at night—there's no nightlife beyond a handful of pubs—giving hikers and other holiday makers a chance to recharge.

Bled is also a great jumping-off point for a car trip through the Julian Alps (see next chapter), and a wide variety of other worthwhile side-trips are right at its doorstep. These include the less-developed lake named Bohinj, even deeper in the mountains; a spectacular (yet easy) hike in the nearby mountain gorge of Vintgar; the pleasant Old Town of Radovljica, with its fascinating little beekeeping museum; and the ironworking town of Kropa, boasting a museum that attracts the kind of people who wonder how things work.

PLANNING YOUR TIME

Bled and its neighboring mountains deserve at least two days. With one day, spend it in and around Bled (or, spend a quick morning in Bled and an afternoon day-tripping). With a second day and a car, drive through the Julian Alps using the self-guided tour in the next chapter. The circular route takes you up and over the stunning Vršič Pass, then down the scenic and historic Soča River Valley. Without a car, skip the second day, or spend it doing nearby day trips: Bus or bike to Radovljica and its bee museum, hike to Vintgar Gorge, or visit Lake Bohinj (all described under "Near Lake Bled," at the end of this chapter).

Orientation to Lake Bled

The town of Bled is on the east end of 1.5-mile-long Lake Bled. The lakefront is lined with soothing parks and chunky resort hotels. A 3.5-mile path meanders around the lake. As no motorized boats are allowed, Lake Bled is particularly peaceful.

The tourists' center of Bled has two parts, which melt into each other: a ragtag village and a cluster of giant hotels. The main thoroughfare, called **Ljubljanska cesta,** leads out of Bled town toward Ljubljana and most other destinations. Just up from the lakefront is the modern **commercial center** (Trgovski Center Bled), with a supermarket, ATM, shops, and a smattering of lively cafés. Nicknamed "Gaddafi," the commercial center was designed for a city in Libya, but the deal fell through—so the frugal Slovenes built it here instead.

Bled's less-touristy Old Town, under the castle, has a web of tight streets and big but humble old houses surrounding the pointy spire of St. Martin's Church. Here you'll find the bus station, some good restaurants, a few hostels, and more locals than tourists.

The mountains poking above the ridge at the far end of the

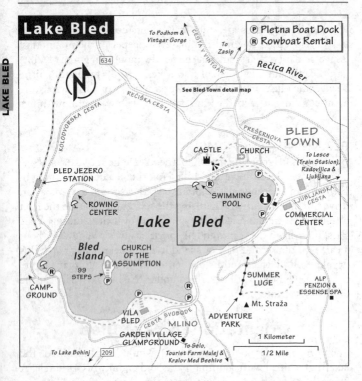

lake are the Julian Alps, crowned by the three peaks of Mount Triglav. The big mountain behind the town of Bled is Stol ("Chair"), part of the Karavanke range that defines the Austrian border.

TOURIST INFORMATION

Bled's most central TI is in the long, lakefront casino building across the street from the big, white Hotel Park (as you face the lake, the TI is hiding around the front at the far left end, overlooking the lake). Pick up the map with the lake on one side and the whole region on the other and the free Bled information booklet, with up-to-date details on local attractions and transportation options. Get advice on hikes and day trips, confirm transit schedules, and if you're doing any serious hiking, spring for a good regional map. They also have free Wi-Fi and rent cars (July-Aug Mon-Sat 8:00-21:00, Sun 9:00-17:00; May-June and Sept-Oct Mon-Sat 8:00-19:00, Sun 9:00-17:00; Nov-April Mon-Sat 8:00-18:00, Sun 9:00-16:00; Cesta Svobode 10, tel. 04/574-1122, www.bled.si).

The TI's other branch is harder to reach for nondrivers—on the main road out of town—but it conveniently shares an office with the **Triglav National Park Information Center,** which offers lots of helpful advice for those heading into the mountains. The center, with free parking, is called "Triglavska Roža" (bike rentals, maps and guidebooks for sale, daily 8:00-18:00, off-season until 16:00, Ljubljanska cesta 27, tel. 04/578-0205, www.tnp.si).

ARRIVAL IN BLED

By Train: Two train stations have the name "Bled." The **Bled Jezero** ("Bled Lake") station is across the lake from Bled town and is used only by infrequent, slow, tourist-oriented trains into the mountains. You're much more likely to use the **Lesce-Bled** station in the nearby village of Lesce (pronounced lest-SEH). The Lesce-Bled station is on the main line and has far better connections to Ljubljana and international destinations. So if you're buying a train ticket or checking schedules, request "Lesce-Bled" rather than just "Bled." (This is so important, I'll remind you again later.)

The small **Lesce-Bled station** is in Lesce, about 2.5 miles from Bled. From the station in Lesce, you can take the bus into Bled town (2/hour, 10 minutes, catch it across the street from the train station); or pay about €14 for a taxi into town. If taking the train out of Lesce-Bled, you can buy tickets at this station or on the train—nobody in Bled town sells tickets.

By Bus: Bled's main bus station is just up from the lake in the Old Town. To reach the lake, walk straight downhill on Cesta Svobode. Note that many buses also stop on the way into town, along Ljubljanska cesta, which is handier for walking to many of my recommended accommodations (for details, see "Sleeping in Bled," later)—be sure to ask your driver.

By Car: Coming from Ljubljana, you'll wind your way into Bled on Ljubljanska cesta, which rumbles through the middle of town before swinging left at the lake. Parking is tricky; if you're sleeping in town, ask your hotel. But if you're here for a quick visit (2-hour limit), you can try to find a spot in the short-term parking lot just above the commercial center (free for 1 hour, €2/2 hours), or along the lake (€2/hour). To stretch your visit, head for the underground lot between Hotel Krim and the ice rink (€2/hour, 4-hour limit). If you're staying even longer, park at the lot by the Triglav National Park Information Center and TI, next to the Mercator supermarket on the road into town (described earlier; free for a quick stop or €10/24 hours). Also see "Route Tips for Drivers" under "Lake Bled Connections," later.

By Plane: For details on getting from Ljubljana's airport to Bled, see "Lake Bled Connections," later.

HELPFUL HINTS

Money: Bled town's handiest ATMs are at **SKB Banka** (upstairs in round building at commercial center), **Gorenjska Banka** (at far end of Hotel Park), and **NLB** (on the main road into town, at Pension Union).

Laundry: Call **Anže Štalc** to arrange drop-off, and pick it up cleaned and folded 24 hours later (extra charge for same-day express service, mobile 041-575-522). There's also a **Speed Queen** self-service launderette near the top of town (daily 7:00-21:00, Prešernova cesta 50, mobile 041-366-323).

Car Rental: The Julian Alps are ideal by car. Several companies have branches in Bled, including **Europcar** (mobile 031-382-055), **Budget** (mobile 041-578-0320), **Hertz** (tel. 04/201-6999), and the local **Avantcar** (mobile 041-400-980); as the offices tend to move around, inquire in Bled about the current locations.

Massage and Spa Treatments: If you're here to relax, consider a visit to the **Essense** wellness center at the recommended Alp Penzion. This modern, classy facility—hiding in the country-side about a 20-minute walk or 5-minute taxi ride above the lake—offers a wide range of spa treatments, including pedi-cures and Thai massage. A standard 50-minute massage will run you about €45; €10 more buys you access to three saunas and a garden hot tub (call first to arrange, Cankarjeva cesta 20A, mobile 040-996-666, www.essense.si, info@essense.si). You'll also find wellness centers with massage, saunas, and whirlpools at a few of the big hotels (all open to nonguests). The biggest is the **Živa** spa at Golf Hotel, with a swimming pool, lakeview hot tubs, and massages; Park Hotel's **Thai Center** spa also does good massages (information for both at www.sava-hotels-resorts.com). There are also spas at **Hotel Astoria** and the recommended **Hotel Lovec**.

GETTING AROUND LAKE BLED (LITERALLY)

By Bike: You can rent a mountain bike at the TI (€3.50/hour, €6/3 hours, €8/half-day, €11/day). The TI also has electric bikes, which give you a much-appreciated boost (€5/1 hour, €10/4 hours, €15/8 hours). While walking around the lake is slo-mo bliss, biking it lets you fast-forward between the views of your choice. If you go clock-wise, you'll have to use the busy lakefront road for the first stretch. But after the village of Mlino, traffic thins out. The best views are from the lakefront gravel path; just above this runs an easy, mostly level, paved road, where the views can be more obstructed by trees. Bikes are technically forbidden along the gravel path, but if it's not too crowded with walkers, you can try to pedal there discreetly. If there are too many people, you can walk alongside your bike for the prettiest patches—or just take lots of breaks to enjoy the views.

Biking is also a great way to reach Vintgar Gorge—about three mostly level miles one-way, perfect for combining a countryside pedal with a walk immersed in nature. The separated bike path to the nearby town of Radovljica (and its bee museum) is about four level miles one-way (get details at the TI). And for an even more ambitious trip, ask about the long-distance bike path that's planned all the way from Bled to Kranjska Gora, at the base of the Vršič Pass (part of this trail—deep in the mountains—is already complete). For other ideas, ask for the TI's excellent biking map, with various bike trips clearly marked and described.

By Horse and Buggy: Buggies called *fijakers* are the romantic, expensive, and easy way to get around the lake. Hire one along the lakefront between Hotel Park and the castle (see the "Bled Town" map for location; around the lake—€50, one-way up to castle—€50, round-trip to castle with 30-minute wait time—€60, mobile 041-710-970, www.fijaker-bled.si).

By Tourist Train: A little train makes a circuit around the lake every 40 minutes in summer (€5, daily 9:00-21:00, shorter hours off-season, weather-dependent, mobile 051-337-478).

By Tourist Bus: In the summer, a handy shuttle bus for tourists starts from the main bus station, then goes up to the castle and on to the Vintgar Gorge entrance (€1/ride, 6/day in July-Aug, confirm schedule at TI or bus station or check www.alpetour.si).

A different summertime bus is designed to reach villages to the east that are otherwise poorly served by public transportation, including Kropa (ironwork museum) and the musical village of Begunje, along with some larger towns such as Radovljica. The bus runs only two days a week, with a different route each day (€5/day, July-Aug only, ask for schedule at TIs or hotel receptions).

By Taxi: Your hotel can call a taxi for you. Or contact **Bled Tours,** run by Sandi and Cvetka, and their team of English-speaking drivers (€15 to the castle or Vintgar Gorge including admission, €50 to Ljubljana airport, €120 to Klagenfurt airport in Austria, office in Hotel Krim, Ljubljanska cesta 7, mobile 031-321-122, www.bledtours.si, info@bledtours.si).

By Boat: For information on renting your own boat, see "Boating" under "Sights at Lake Bled," later. For details on riding the characteristic *pletna* boats, see "The Island," later.

By Private Plane: If you have perfect weather, there's no more thrilling way to experience Slovenia's high-mountain scenery than from a small propeller plane soaring over the peaks. Private flights depart from a grass airstrip near the village of Lesce, a 10-minute drive or taxi ride from Bled. It's expensive...but unforgettable (€95 for 15-minute hop over Lake Bled only, €160 for 30-minute flight that also buzzes Lake Bohinj, €225 for deluxe 45-minute version around the summit of Triglav, price covers up to 3 passengers, arrange at least a day in advance, tel. 04/532-0100, www.alc-lesce.si, info@alc-lesce.si).

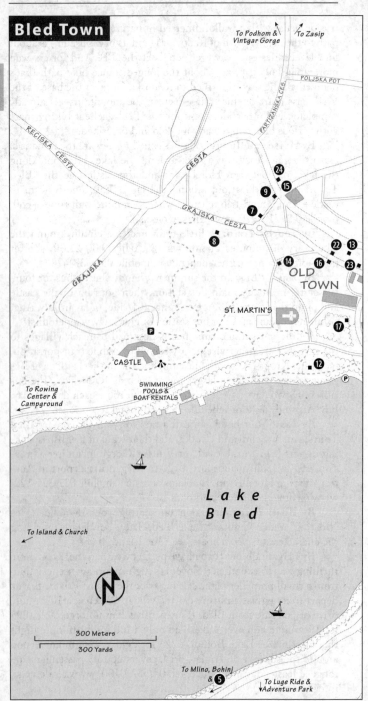

LAKE BLED

Bled Town

To Podhom &
Vintgar Gorge

To Zasip

POLJSKA POT

PARTIZANSKA CES.

RECISKA CESTA

CESTA

GRAJSKA CESTA

24

9   15

7

8

GRAJSKA

22   13

14   16   23

OLD
TOWN

ST. MARTIN'S

17

CASTLE

12

P

To Rowing
Center &
Campground

SWIMMING
POOLS &
BOAT RENTALS

P

Lake
Bled

To Island & Church

N

300 Meters

300 Yards

To Mlino, Bohinj
& 5

To Luge Ride &
Adventure Park

LAKE BLED

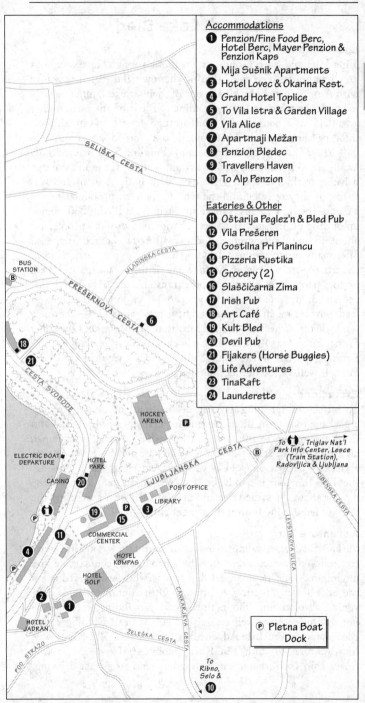

<u>Accommodations</u>
① Penzion/Fine Food Berc,
   Hotel Berc, Mayer Penzion &
   Penzion Kaps
② Mija Sušnik Apartments
③ Hotel Lovec & Okarina Rest.
④ Grand Hotel Toplice
⑤ To Vila Istra & Garden Village
⑥ Vila Alice
⑦ Apartmaji Mežan
⑧ Penzion Bledec
⑨ Travellers Haven
⑩ To Alp Penzion

<u>Eateries & Other</u>
⑪ Oštarija Peglez'n & Bled Pub
⑫ Vila Prešeren
⑬ Gostilna Pri Planincu
⑭ Pizzeria Rustika
⑮ Grocery (2)
⑯ Slaščičarna Zima
⑰ Irish Pub
⑱ Art Café
⑲ Kult Bled
⑳ Devil Pub
㉑ Fijakers (Horse Buggies)
㉒ Life Adventures
㉓ TinaRaft
㉔ Launderette

SELIŠKA CESTA

BUS
STATION
Ⓑ

PREŠERNOVA CESTA

MLADINSKA CESTA

⑥

⑱
㉑

CESTA SVOBODE

HOCKEY
ARENA
Ⓟ

ELECTRIC BOAT
DEPARTURE

HOTEL
PARK

LJUBLJANSKA CESTA
Ⓑ

To 🚶 Triglav Nat'l
Park Info Center, Lesce
(Train Station),
Radovljica & Ljubljana

RIBENSKA CESTA

CASINO
⑳

POST OFFICE

Ⓟ

🚻

⑲

Ⓟ
⑮

LIBRARY
③

Ⓟ

⑪

COMMERCIAL
CENTER

HOTEL
KOMPAS

LEVŠTIKOVA ULICA

④

Ⓟ

HOTEL
GOLF

②

①

HOTEL
JADRAN

POD STRAŽO

ŽELEŠKA CESTA

CANKARJEVA CESTA

To
Ribno,
Selo &

⑩

Ⓟ Pletna Boat
   Dock

Tours at Lake Bled

Local Guides

Tina Hiti and **Sašo Golub,** an energetic young couple, are both excellent guides who enjoy sharing the town and region they love with American visitors. Hiring one of them can add immeasurably to your enjoyment and understanding of Bled and the surrounding area (€45 for 2-hour tour of Bled, arrange several days in advance, info@pg-slovenia.com, Tina's mobile 040-166-554, Sašo's mobile 040-524-774, www.pg-slovenia.com). Tina and Sašo are especially handy for side-tripping into the countryside if you don't want to drive yourself. I've spent great days with both of them and was thankful they were behind the wheel. Their most popular trip is a day in the Julian Alps (€190 round-trip from Bled, €230 to pick up or drop off in Ljubljana, extra charge for 5 or more people, ask about adding a picnic lunch for a small extra charge). They also offer many other options, including all-day shore excursions from the cruise port in Koper (€300 for a day visiting Ljubljana and Bled, up to 3 people), food tours, airport transfers, and trips in the Slovenian countryside to research your roots. As Tina and Sašo both lead tours for me in Europe—and have two young kids—they may send you off with a well-trained substitute. Tina's father **Gorazd,** a former Yugoslav Olympian in ice hockey, brings the older generation's perspective to the trip; **Ervin** provides a younger view; and **Petra** is well-versed in mountain herbs.

Excursions

To hit several far-flung day-trip destinations in one go, consider a package tour from Bled. Destinations range from Ljubljana and the Karst region to the Austrian Lakes to Venice. For example, an all-day Julian Alps trip to the Vršič Pass and Soča Valley runs about €40 per person (sold by various agencies around town—ask the TI). This tour is handy, but two people can rent a car for the day for about the same price and do it at their own pace using the self-guided driving tour in the next chapter.

Adventure Trips

Various Bled-based companies specialize in taking tourists on active, outdoorsy excursions into the surrounding countryside and mountains. One popular, all-day trip is white-water rafting on the Soča River (around €90/person). Other options include canyoning, river tubing, mountain biking, paragliding, rock climbing, and more. Two well-established companies have offices near Bled's bus station: **Life Adventures** (mobile 040-508-853, www. lifeadventures.si) and **TinaRaft** (mobile 041-646-255, www. tinaraft.si). Note that these companies tend to attract a young, sometimes rowdy crowd that enjoys lubricating their adventures with alcohol.

Sights at Lake Bled

Bled doesn't have many sights, but there are plenty of rewarding and pleasant activities.

▲▲▲Walk Around the Lake

Strolling the 3.5-mile lake perimeter is enjoyable, peaceful, and scenic. At a leisurely pace, it takes about an hour and a half...not counting stops to snap photos of the ever-changing view. On the way, you'll pass some great villas, mostly from the early 19th century. The most significant one was a former residence of Marshal Tito—today the Hotel Vila Bled—where the dictator entertained international big shots, from Indira Gandhi to Nikita Khrushchev to Kim Il-Sung to Raúl Castro (you'll pass the base of the stairs on the lakeside path; its café terrace is open for visitors, but there's not much to see). For the more adventurous, hiking paths lead up into the hills surrounding the lake  (ask TI for details and maps; or hike to—and through—Vintgar Gorge, described on page 802).

▲▲The Island (Blejski Otok)

Bled's little island—capped by a super-cute church—nudges the lake's quaintness level over the top. Locals call it simply "The Island" *(Otok).* While it's pretty to look at from afar, it's also fun to visit.

The island has long been a sacred site with a romantic twist. On summer Saturdays, a steady procession of brides and grooms, cheered on by their entourages, heads for the island. Ninety-nine steps lead from the island's dock up to the Church of the Assumption on top. It's tradition for the groom to carry—or try to carry—his bride up these steps. About four out of five are successful (proving themselves "fit for marriage"). During the communist era, the church was closed and weddings were outlawed here. But the tradition reemerged—

illegally—even before the regime ended, with a clandestine ceremony in 1989.

Cost and Hours: Free to visit island, church—€6, ticket includes tower climb, daily 9:00-19:00, April and Oct until 18:00, Nov-March until 16:00.

Getting There: The most romantic route to the island is to cruise on one of the distinctive *pletna* boats (€14/person round-trip, trip takes 20-25 minutes each way, includes 30-minute stay on the island—allow about an hour and a half for the full experience; might have to wait for more passengers to fill the boat; boats generally run from dawn, last boat leaves one hour before church closes; replaced by enclosed electric boats in winter—unless the lake freezes, in which case you can rent ice skates; mobile 031-316-575). Look for *pletna* boats at various spots around the lake. If you're in town, the handiest options are directly below Hotel Park, or in front of Grand Hotel Toplice. Farther around the lake, you can also catch a *pletna* in the village of Mlino; at the bottom of the grand staircase leading up to Vila Bled (it's a shorter trip from here, but the same cost); and at the campground. For more on these characteristic little vessels, see the "*Pletna* Boats" sidebar. Note that *pletna* boatmen stick close to the 30-minute waiting time on the island—which can go very fast. Another option—cheaper but far less romantic—is to take an **electric boat** (€11 round-trip, departs about hourly from the lakefront below Hotel Park). You could also **rent your own boat** and row to the island (see "Boating" listing, later). It's even possible to **swim,** especially from the end of the lake nearest the island (see "Swimming" listing, later), but you're not allowed into the church in your swimsuit. Guess you'll just have to go in naked.

Visiting the Island: At the top of the stairs, the **Potičnica café** sells *potica*, the Slovenian nut-roll cake that's traditional at Christmastime but delicious any day of the year. The attached **souvenir shop** is the best in Bled, well-stocked with a variety of high-quality Slovenian gifts, trinkets, and keepsakes. Upstairs in the same building is an easy-to-miss **art gallery,** which displays changing exhibits.

The island's main attraction is the **church.** An eighth-century Slavic pagan temple dedicated to the goddess of love and fertility once stood here; the current Baroque version (with Venetian flair—the bell tower is separate from the main church) is the fifth to occupy this spot. Go inside and find the rope for the church bell, hanging in the middle of the aisle just before the altar. A local superstition claims that if you can get this bell to ring three times with one big pull of the rope, your dreams will come true. Worth a try—but be careful if you're slight of build, as the rope can take you for a ride.

If you're waiting for a herd of tourists to ring out their wishes, pass the time looking around the area in front of the altar. When the church was being renovated in the 1970s, workers dug up several medieval graves (you can see one through the glass under the bell rope). They also discovered Gothic frescoes on either side of the altar, including, above the door on the right, an unusual ecclesiastical theme: the *bris* (Jewish circumcision ritual) of Christ.

Your ticket also includes the **bell tower.** At 91 steps, it's a shorter climb than the one up from the boat dock. Up top, you'll find a restored pendulum mechanism from 1890 and fine lake views that are marred by a mesh covering that makes it impossible to snap a clear picture.

To descend by a different route, walk down the trail behind the church (around the right side), then follow the path around the island's perimeter back to where your *pletna* boat awaits.

▲▲Bled Castle (Blejski Grad)

Bled's cliff-hanging castle, dating in one form or another from 1,000 years ago, was the seat of the Austrian bishops of Brixen, who controlled Bled in the Middle Ages. Today it's a fine tourist attraction with a little history and lots of big views. The various sights at the castle—a decent history museum, a frescoed chapel, an old-fashioned printing press, and a wine cellar—are more cute than interesting, but the real reason to come up here is to bask in the sweeping panoramas over Lake Bled and the surrounding mountainscapes.

Cost and Hours: €11, daily 8:00-20:00, July-Aug until 21:00, Nov-April 9:00-18:00, printing press and wine cellar close one hour earlier; tel. 04/572-9782, www.blejski-grad.si.

Getting There: To really earn those views, you can **hike** up the steep hill (20-30 minutes). The handiest trails are behind big St. Martin's Church: Walk past the front door of the church with the lake at your back, and look left after the first set of houses for the *Grad* signs marking the steepest route (follow the wooden stakes all the way up the steep switchback steps); or, for a longer but less steep route, continue past the church on the same street about five minutes, bearing uphill (left) at the fork, and find the *Grad 1* sign just

Pletna Boats

The *pletna* is an important symbol of Lake Bled. In addition to providing a pleasant way to reach the island, these boats also carry on a tradition dating back for generations. In the 17th century, Habsburg Empress Maria Theresa granted the villagers from Mlino—the little town along the lakefront just beyond Bled—special permission to ferry visitors to the island. (This provided a much-needed source of income for Mlino residents, who had very limited access to farmland.) They built their *pletna*s by hand, using a special design passed down from father to son for centuries—like the equally iconic gondolas of Venice. Eventually, this imperial decree and family tradition evolved into a modern union of *pletna* oarsmen, which continues to this day.

Today *pletna* boats are still hand-built according to that same centuries-old design. There's no keel, so the skilled oarsmen work hard to steer the flat-bottomed boat with each stroke—boats piloted by an inexperienced oarsman can slide around on very windy days. There are 21 official *pletna*s on Lake Bled, all belonging to the same union. The gondoliers dump all their earnings into one fund, give a cut to the tourist board, and divide the rest evenly amongst themselves. Occasionally a new family tries to break into the cartel, underselling his competitors with a "black market" boat that looks the same as the official ones. While some see this as a violation of a centuries-old tradition, others view it as good old capitalism. Either way, competition is fierce.

after the Penzion Bledec hostel on the left. Once you're on this second trail, don't take the sharp-left uphill turn at the fork (instead, continue straight up, around the back of the hill). If you'd rather skip the hike, you can take the summer **tourist bus** (July-Aug only, see "Getting Around Lake Bled," earlier), your **rental car** (€3 for parking up to 2 hours), a **taxi** (around €12), or—if you're wealthy and romantic—a **horse and buggy** (€50, €10 extra for driver to wait

30 minutes and bring you back down). However, all these options take you only to the parking lot, from which it's still a steep and slippery-when-wet five-minute hike up to the castle itself.

Eating: The **$$$$ restaurant** at the castle is pricey, but worth the splurge for the views and excellent, rotating menu featuring regional cuisine. Come for dinner while it's still light out and savor the setting. The sleek, woody interior is often jammed with tour groups; in good weather, I'd rather dine on the outside terrace. Call far ahead to book a view table—they fill up quickly. If you have a reservation to dine here, it's free to enter the castle grounds (daily in summer 11:00-22:00, shorter hours off-season, tel. 04/620-3444, www.jezersek.si). Paupers can grab an overpriced sandwich at the simple **$ café** by the round tower, or bring their own **picnic** to munch along the wall with million-dollar views over Lake Bled (buy sandwiches at the Mercator grocery store in the commercial center before you ascend—see page 799).

Summer Performance: From late June through mid-September, the castle hosts a weekly, kid-pleasing, knights' tournament-themed show called "Sir Lambergar's Adventure" (likely Tue at 17:00, details on castle website).

Visiting the Castle: After buying your ticket, go through the gate and huff the rest of the way up to the outer courtyard. We'll tour the castle clockwise, starting from here. As the castle is continually being spruced up, some details may be different than described.

Turning left at the entrance, you'll pass WCs, then the door to Mojster Janez's working replica of a **printing press** *(grajska tiskarna/manufaktura)* from Gutenberg's time. You can buy your own custom-made souvenir certificate using this very old technology. While this may seem like a tourist gimmick, there's actually some interesting history here. As in many lands, the printing press was a critical tool in the evolution of Slovenia's culture. Look above the press for a life-size mannequin of Primož Trubar (1508-1586), a Slovenian cross between Martin Luther and Johannes Gutenberg. In Trubar's time, Slovene was considered a crude peasants' language—not just unworthy of print, but actually illegal to print. So this Reformer went to Germany and, in 1550—using presses like this one—wrote and printed the first two books in the Slovene language: *Abecedarium* (an alphabet primer to teach illiterate Slovenes how to read) and *Catechismus* (a simplified version of the New Testament). Trubar smuggled his printed books back to Slovenia (hidden in barrels of playing cards) and, en route to Ljubljana, was briefly given refuge in this castle. (Trubar is still much-revered today, appearing on the Slovenian €1 coin.) Up the stairs is an exhibition in English about early printing methods and the importance of moveable type for advancing the Protestant Reformation, whose goal was to get the Word of God more easily into the hands of everyday people. You'll also see one of those first Trubar books—notice it was printed in Tübingen, Germany, an early enclave of the Reformation. There's also a small painting gallery showcasing local artists.

Just past the printing press is the castle's oldest tower, from the 11th century, which is filled with a **"Beehouse"** selling various honey products under a hive-like dome. Nearby is a **café terrace** offering pricey drinks and basic sandwiches with grand views.

Continue past the café and begin climbing the stairs up to grander and grander **views** over the lake. Reaching the terrace at the very top, you'll find the best vistas; the restaurant; a tiny chapel with 3-D frescoes that make it seem much bigger than it is (next to the museum entrance); a small shop selling iron items that are still forged the traditional way; and the well-presented castle **museum,** which strains to make the story of Bled, the castle, and the surrounding region of Carniola interesting. The ground floor has exhibits about geology, prehistoric artifacts, ironworking, and the seasonal life cycle of the region, while the upstairs has a cool 3-D model of the surrounding mountains, smaller models illustrating the growth of the castle structure, information about early inhabitants, and exhibits on the development of tourism at Lake Bled (including its many fine vacation villas). While video screens and some English information are helpful, there's only so much to say.

When you're done up here, head down the stairs between the museum and restaurant (passing WCs). Coming back down into the lower courtyard, turn left down the ramp to find the **wine cellar,** where you can bottle and cork your own souvenir bottle of wine (you're paying for the experience more than the wine). Slovenian wines are well-explained by attendants who dress as monks, since winemaking was a monastic responsibility in the Middle Ages.

Before leaving the castle, climb the stairs up to the wooden **defensive gallery** for the best views in town of the mountains east of Bled. The biggest one is called Stol ("Chair"). In the foreground, you can see the steeple marking the town of Podhom; just to the left, the folds in the hills hide the dramatic Vintgar Gorge (described later).

Boating

Bled is the rowing center of Slovenia. Town officials even lengthened the lake a bit so it would perfectly fit the standard two-kilometer laps, with 100 meters more for the turn (on maps, you can see the little divot taken out of the far end). Bled hosted its fourth world championship in August 2011. The town has produced many Olympic medalists, who've won gold in Sydney, silver in Athens, and bronze in London. Notice that local crew team members, whom you'll likely see running or rowing, are characters—with a tradition of wild and colorful haircuts. This dedication to rowing adds to Bled's tranquility, since no motorized boats are allowed on the lake.

If you want to get into the action, you'll find **rental rowboats** at various points around the lake (€10-20/hour). Look for them at Pension Pletna in the lakeside village of Mlino (a scenic 15-minute walk around the lake from Bled); at the swimming pool under the castle (the closest but priciest option); under Grand Hotel Toplice; and in the modern building just before the campground on the far end of the lake.

Swimming

Lake Bled has several suitable spots for a swim. The swimming pool complex under the castle uses lake water and routinely earns the "blue flag," meaning the water is top-quality. There's also a waterslide and an inviting cluster of sunning beds (€7 to swim all day, less for afternoon only, daily 8:00-19:00, closed Oct-mid-June and in bad weather, tel. 04/578-0528).

Lake Bled's main beach is at the campground at the far end of the lake, though you can also swim near the village of Mlino. If you swim to the island, remember that you can't enter the church in your swimsuit.

Luge Ride (Poletno Sankanje)

Bled's "summer toboggan" luge ride, atop Mount Straža overlooking the lake, allows you to scream down a steep, curvy metal rail track on a little plastic sled. This is a really scary one—speedy, with lots of tight turns, and with great views over the lake—but it's quite pricey. A chairlift takes you to the top of the track, where you'll sit on your sled, take a deep breath, and remind yourself: Pull back on the stick to slow down, push forward on the stick to go faster. You'll drop 480 feet in altitude on the 570-yard-long track, speeding up to about 25 miles per hour as you race toward the lake.

Cost and Hours: €8/ride, cheaper for multiple rides, chairlift only—€4, weather-dependent—if it rains, you can't go. In summer, it's open daily (July-Aug 10:00-20:00, June 11:00-19:00, shoulder season generally 11:00-18:00, closed mid-Oct-early April).

Getting There: The base of the chairlift is on the hillside just south of town, beyond Grand Hotel Toplice and just behind the Hostel Vila Viktorija.

Adventure Park (Pustolovski Park)

Next to the luge at the top of Mount Straža, this park has a series of five high-ropes courses designed for everyone age five and up. You'll get rigged up in a safety harness and go through a training course, then be set loose on your choice of courses (with help from spotters on the ground); plan on spending about two hours to do all of them. It's a steep hike up the hill, or you can pay €4 to ride the chairlift for the luge ride (or pay €8 to ride the chairlift up and luge back down).

Cost and Hours: €20 for adults, €16 for kids 7-14, €10 for kids under 7, similar hours to luge ride—described earlier, last entry two hours before closing, mobile 031-761-661, www.pustolovski-park-bled.si.

▲Kralov Med Beehive Demonstration

Tucked in Selo village, a long walk or short drive from Bled, this fascinating countryside sight is worth ▲▲▲ (or zzz) for fans of the apicultural arts. (First, read up on beekeeping on page 808.) Local beekeepers Blaž and Danijela Ambrožič have built an apiary (freestanding house of beehives) and teach visitors all about this very Slovenian form of agriculture. First you'll see the painted panels, with bees buzzing in and out. Their prized possession is a gigantic Winnie-the-Pooh-style hive that they transplanted from a tree trunk. They'll demonstrate how you can hold your hand within inches of the buzzing hive without getting stung, thanks to the peaceful nature of the indigenous Carniolan bee. Inside, you can watch through a big (and safe) window as they pull out the honeycomb frames from the hive and work with the bees. You'll see the centrifuge-like device they use to safely extract honey from the comb. In another hut is an "api-therapy" room, where a specially designed bunk lets you watch and listen to the mesmerizing bees without any danger of being stung. You can also sample (and buy) different types of honey and pollen, along with other bee-related gifts. Outside is a perennial garden that demonstrates when various plants blossom, providing much-needed pollen for the bees.

Cost and Hours: €5, call or email a day ahead to arrange a time, demonstrations usually last an hour or more and may even run for just two people, apiary and parking are next to the house at Selo pri Bledu 42—once parked there, call Danijela at 041-227-407 or Blaž at 041-657-120 and they'll come meet you, www.kralov-med.si, blazambrozic@gmail.com.

Getting There: Blaž's beehives are in the village of Selo, a five-minute drive or taxi ride or 30-minute walk from Bled town. Head out of town along the lake (past Grand Hotel Toplice), then turn left (inland) at the Mercator grocery store in the village of Mlino. In the next village, Selo, look for the two colorful beehive apiaries below the main road, just above the recommended Tourist Farm Mulej.

Nightlife in Bled

BLED PUB CRAWL

Bled is quiet after hours. However, the town does have a few fun bars that are lively with a young crowd (all open nightly until late). Since many young people in Bled are students at the local tourism school, they're likely to speak English...and eager to practice with a native speaker. Try a Smile, a Corona-type Slovenian lager. *Šnops* (schnapps) is a local specialty—popular flavors are plum *(slivovka)*, honey *(medica)*, blueberry *(borovničevec)*, and pear *(hruškovec)*.

Kick things off with the fun-loving local gang at **Gostilna Pri Planincu** near the bus station (described later, under "Eating in Bled"). Then head down Cesta Svobode toward the lake; just below Hotel Jelovica, you'll find the rollicking **Irish Pub** (a.k.a. "The Pub"), with Guinness and indoor or outdoor seating. For the hippest scene in town, duck across the street and wander a few more steps down toward the lake to find the **Art Café,** with a mellow interior reminiscent of a Van Gogh painting. Around the lake near the commercial center, **Bled Pub** (a.k.a. "The Cocktail Bar" or "Troha"—for the family that owns it) is a trendy late-night spot where bartenders sling a dizzying array of mixed drinks to an appreciative, youthful crowd (between the commercial center and the lake, above the recommended Oštarija Peglez'n restaurant). If you're still standing, several other bars and cafés percolate in the commercial center, including **Kult Bled,** facing the main road at the base of the round tower. Slathered with iconic film images and neon colors, it attracts a thirtysomething crowd and occasionally hosts live music. **Devil** is open even later (on the lower level of Hotel Park, facing the lake).

Sleeping in Bled

Bled has more hotel beds per capita than anywhere in Slovenia—and most of them are in big convention hotels. I prefer staying in smaller, more characteristic, pension-type accommodations on the town's fringe—most of them an easy walk from the lake. These quaint little family-run places book up early; reserve well ahead. For even cheaper beds, consider one of the many *sobe* (rooms in private homes) scattered around the lake; look for signs in the neighborhood just above Prešernova cesta.

Sleep Code

Hotels are classified based on the average price of a standard double room with breakfast in spring and fall. Prices may go up in summer, and down in winter.

$$$$	**Splurge:** Most rooms over €150
$$$	**Pricier:** €110-150
$$	**Moderate:** €80-110
$	**Budget:** €50-80
¢	**Backpacker:** Under €50
RS%	**Rick Steves discount**

Unless otherwise noted, credit cards are accepted, hotel staff speak basic English, and free Wi-Fi is available. Comparison-shop by checking prices at several hotels (on each hotel's own website, on a booking site, or by email). For the best deal, *book directly with the hotel*. Ask for a discount if paying in cash; if the listing includes **RS%,** request a Rick Steves discount.

ABOVE THE LAKE

These friendly, cozy, characteristic accommodations are Bled's best values. The only catch is that they're perched on a hilltop a 5- to 10-minute climb up from the lake (easier than it sounds). There are two ways to find these from the town center: Walk around the lake to Grand Hotel Toplice, then go up the stairs around the right side of the Hotel Jadran (on the hill across the street from Grand Hotel Toplice). Or, from the main road into town (Ljubljanska cesta), take the small service road just above the commercial center (in front of Hotel Lovec), and loop up around the big Kompas and Golf hotels. If arriving by bus, ask nicely if your driver will let you disembark along Ljubljanska cesta (just above the traffic light) to avoid the long walk from the bus station. From this bus stop, you can walk down Ljubljanska cesta and take the road just above the post office, which leads up to this area.

$$$ Penzion Berc (pronounced "berts") is the classiest option in this area, with 10 sharp, comfortable, woody rooms—all with balconies—filling a tidy chalet. It's well-run by Miha, who offers thoughtful touches like free loaner electric bikes and minifridges stocked with free drinks, and also runs the excellent Fine Food Berc restaurant and arranges excursions (air-con, Želeška cesta 15, tel. 04/574-1838, www.penzion-berc.si, penzion@berc-sp.si).

$$ Hotel Berc, across the street and run by Miha's brother Luka, has 15 great rooms with many of the same amenities, such as balconies and loaner bikes (air-con, Pod Stražo 13, tel. 04/576-5658, www.berc-sp.si, hotel@berc-sp.si).

$$ Mayer Penzion, next door and thoughtfully run by the Trseglav family (relatives of the Berc brothers), comes with 13

great-value rooms, a helpful staff, a tasty restaurant
for guests only, and beautifully handcrafted Slo-
venian woodwork (cash
only, family rooms, el-
evator, Želeška cesta 7, tel.
04/576-5740, www.mayer-
sp.si, penzion@mayer-sp.

si). They also rent a cute, newly restored two-story Slovenian farm
cottage in the garden.

$$ Penzion Kaps, owned by Peter (whose father, Anton, is a
great craftsman), has 13 comfortable rooms with balconies, mod-
ern bathrooms, and classic old wood carvings in a Shangri-La kind
of place. The inviting breakfast room clusters around a giant ce-
ramic stove (cash only, air-con, free loaner bikes, Želeška cesta 22,
mobile 059-117-746, www.penzion-kaps.si, info@penzion-kaps.si).

$ Friendly **Mija Sušnik** rents out two comfortable two-
bedroom apartments. Modern, tidy, and equipped with kitchens,
these are a good budget choice for families (cash only, no breakfast,
laundry service, free parking, Želeška cesta 3, tel. 04/574-1731,
susnik@bled-holiday.com). It's just toward the lake from the bigger
pensions, with a big crucifix out front. Her sister Ivanka also rents
apartments, but they're farther from the lake.

ON OR NEAR THE LAKE

You'll pay a premium to be closer to the lake—but it's hard to argue
with the convenience.

$$$$ Hotel Lovec (LOH-vets), a Best Western Premier, sits
in a convenient (but non-lakefront) location just above the com-
mercial center. Gorgeously appointed inside and out, and run by
a helpful staff, it's professional yet welcoming and cheery. Its 60
plush rooms come with all the comforts and a respected restaurant
(family rooms, great breakfast, air-con, elevator, indoor pool, free
parking, Ljubljanska cesta 6, tel. 04/620-4100, www.lovechotel.
com, reservations@kompas-lovec.com).

$$$$ Grand Hotel Toplice (TOHP-leet-seh) is the grande
dame of Bled, with 87 high-ceilinged rooms, parquet floors, a gen-
teel lakeview café/lounge, posh decor, all the amenities, and a long
list of high-profile guests—from Madeleine Albright to Jordan's
King Hussein to Slovene-by-marriage Donald Trump (ask to see
their "wall of fame"...or is it "shame"?). Once elegant, this place is
a bit faded these days, but it's still a classic. Rooms in the back are
cheaper, but have no lake views and overlook a noisy street—try to
get one as high up as possible (air-con, elevator, free parking, Cesta
Svobode 12, tel. 04/579-1000, www.hotel-toplice.com, ghtoplice@

LAKE BLED

hotelibled.com). The hotel's name—*toplice*—means "spa"; guests are free to use the hotel's swanky, natural-spring-fed indoor swimming pool (a chilly 72 degrees Fahrenheit).

$$$ Vila Istra is housed in a prominent and gorgeously restored Art Nouveau villa from 1887. The remarkably spacious rooms include one double and five sprawling suites. Room furnishings gild the lily a bit, but respect the history of the building. It's a scenic 15-minute walk outside of the town center, almost to the village of Mlino (air-con, Cesta Svobode 35, mobile 059-080-808, www.vila-istra.info, booking@bled.net).

NEAR THE OLD TOWN

$$$ Vila Alice, a beautifully appointed option along the main road through the sleepy upper part of town, offers seven rooms in a classy villa with elegant public spaces, a private garden, and a sauna (air-con, free parking, convenient for drivers at Prešernova cesta 26, mobile 059-958-780, www.vila-alice.com, info@vila-alice.com).

¢ Apartmaji Mežan, run by welcoming Janez and Saša, has four family-friendly apartments in a modern home buried in the middle of town, just uphill from the church. As it's next to an old barn, it's technically a tourist farm (cash only, no breakfast, Riklijeva 6, mobile 041-210-290 or 041-516-688, www.apartmaji-mezan.si, sasa.mezan@gmail.com).

¢ Penzion Bledec (BLED-ets), a family-run, official IYHF hostel, is just below the castle at the top of the Old Town. Each of the 12 rooms has its own bathroom. They have dorms, private rooms, and great family rooms (breakfast extra, full-service laundry for guests, restaurant, Grajska 17, tel. 04/574-5250, www.bledec.si, info@bledec.si).

¢ Travellers Haven is a low-key hostel run with a smile by Mirjam. The 31 beds fill eight rooms in a nicely renovated hundred-year-old villa in the Old Town. The lodgings are well-maintained and the hangout areas are inviting, though the tight bathrooms offer little privacy (reception open 8:00-13:00 & 16:00-23:00, laundry machines, rental bikes, Riklijeva cesta 1, mobile 041-396-545, travellers-haven@t-2.net).

OUTSIDE TOWN

The following listings are a bit farther out: Alp Penzion is a 20-minute walk from the lakefront, but still doable for nondrivers, while the tourist farm and "glampground" are best for drivers.

$$$$ Garden Village is pricey...but very cool. Alternately billed as a "glampground" and a "green resort," this splurge combines the closeness to nature of camping with the amenities of a hip resort. From the main lodge, restaurant, and rustic pond/pool, the complex tumbles down a ravine toward a gushing river, connected by slippery plank walks. You can choose between the tree house (with a loft and netted hammock area up top for kids); the glamping tents, with canvas walls and nestled in an abundant produce garden; or the simpler pier tents on stilts over the river. All of these include breakfast, Wi-Fi, and other amenities, but additional charges for cleaning and shorter stays can really add up (on the road toward Lake Bohinj, turn off on the left just before Vila Bled, Cesta Gorenjskega odreda 16, tel. 08/389-9220, www.gardenvillagebled. com, reservations@gardenvillagebled.com).

$$ Tourist Farm Mulej, possible for hardy walkers but much better for drivers, is a new but traditional farmhouse in a tranquil valley about a half-mile from the lake (1.5 miles from Bled town). Damjana and Jože, who run this working farm (with 70 milk cows... and their smells), also rent out eight modern rooms and four apartments—all with balconies—and serve breakfasts and dinners made with food they produce. Be sure to see the udderly fascinating, fully automated cow-milking machine called Lely, who's practically a member of the family (cash only, family rooms, air-con, free loaner bikes, horseback riding free for experienced guests, Selo pri Bledu 42a, tel. 04/574-4617 or 04/022-4888, www.mulej-bled.com, info. mulej@gmail.com). It's in the farm village of Selo—drive along the lakeside road south from Bled, then turn off in Mlino toward Selo, and look for the signs (to the right) once in the village.

$ Alp Penzion makes the most of a peaceful countryside setting amid hayfields, within a 20-minute, partly uphill walk of the lake (better for drivers or for those who don't mind the walk). With 12 rooms (some with balconies), this kid-friendly place is enthusiastically run by the Sršen family, who offer lots of fun extras, including a summer barbecue grill/outdoor pub (family rooms, dinner possible in summer—ask when you book, air-con, free loaner bikes, Cankarjeva cesta 20A, tel. 04/574-1614, www.alp-penzion. com, bled@alp-penzion.com). Just next door is the relaxing Essense spa (described earlier, under "Helpful Hints").

Eating in Bled

Bled has several good restaurants, but most everything is quite similar. (For variety, wait for Ljubljana.) As there's a finite number of restaurants in town, places can fill up at dinnertime—it's always best to book ahead. In addition to the places recommended here, consider the high-quality (and expensive) restaurant up at the castle, described on page 789.

$$$$ Fine Food Berc—just up the hill from the lakefront, at the recommended Penzion Berc—is a dreamy splurge restaurant. You'll dine at white-tablecloth tables positioned just so on the lush lawn, or in the country-cozy interior. The menu is tempt-

Restaurant Price Code

I've assigned each eatery a price category, based on the average cost of a typical main course. Drinks, desserts, and splurge items (steak and seafood) can raise the price considerably.

$$$$	**Splurge:** Most main courses over €14
$$$	**Pricier:** €10-14
$$	**Moderate:** €6-10
$	**Budget:** Under €6

In Slovenia, a takeout spot is **$**; a basic sit-down eatery is **$$**; a casual but more upscale restaurant is **$$$**; and a swanky splurge is **$$$$**.

ing and high-end, a mix of traditional Slovenian and international dishes (daily 17:00-23:00, closed Nov-March, Želeška cesta 15, tel. 04/574-1838).

$$$$ Okarina serves a diverse array of cuisines, all of them well-executed: international fare, traditional Slovenian specialties (with an emphasis on game), and Indian (Himalayan) dishes. Creative cooking, fine presentation, friendly service, and an atmosphere as tastefully eclectic as the food make this place a great splurge (Mon-Fri 12:00-15:00 & 18:00-23:00, Sat-Sun 12:00-23:00, closed Nov-mid-April, next to recommended Hotel Lovec at Ljubljanska cesta 8, tel. 04/574-1458, www.okarina.com).

$$ Oštarija Peglez'n ("The Old Iron"), conveniently located on the main road between the commercial center and the lake, cooks up tasty Slovenian and Mediterranean meals, with an emphasis on fish and fun family-style shareable plates. Choose between the delightful Slovenian cottage interior or the shady streetside terrace (daily 12:00-23:00, Cesta Svobode 19A, tel. 04/574-4218).

$$$ Vila Prešeren is a handy lakeside choice, featuring mod decor, good international cuisine (as well as some traditional Slovenian dishes), and tables on a giant terrace reaching down to the lakefront. In good weather, this is a great spot to linger on the terrace over a meal, a drink, or a classic Lake Bled dessert; if it's raining, skip it (daily 7:00-23:00, Veslaška promenada 14, tel. 04/575-2510).

$$ Gostilna Pri Planincu ("By the Mountaineers") is a homey, informal bar coated with license plates and packed with fun-loving and sometimes rowdy natives. A big, dull dining area sprawls behind the small, local-feeling pub, and there's outdoor seating out front and on the side patio. The menu features huge portions of stick-to-your-ribs Slovenian pub grub, plus Balkan grilled-meat specialties. Look for their huge, home-style traditional daily specials. Service is playfully opinionated and not always efficient—

Bled Desserts

While you're in Bled, be sure to enjoy the town's specialty, a cream cake called **kremna rezina** (KRAYM-nah ray-ZEE-nah; often referred to by its German-derived name, **kremšnita,** KRAYM-shnee-tah). It's a layer of cream and a thick layer of vanilla custard artfully sandwiched between sheets of delicate, crispy crust. Heavenly. Slovenes travel from all over the country to sample this famous dessert. You may also see some newfangled strawberry and chocolate *kremšnita* variations, but purists swear by the original.

Slightly less renowned—but just as tasty—is **grmada** (gur-MAH-dah, "bon-fire"). This dessert was developed by Hotel Jelovica as a way to get rid of their day-old leftovers. They take yesterday's cake, add rum, milk, custard, and raisins, and top it off with whipped cream and chocolate syrup.

There's also *prekmurska gibanica*—or just **gibanica** (gee-bah-NEET-seh) for short. Originating in the Hungarian corner of the country, *gibanica* is an earthy pastry filled with poppy seeds, walnuts, apples, and cheese, and drizzled with rum.

Yet another dessert is the very traditional **potica** (poh-TEET-seh), a walnut roll that's usually eaten at Christmastime. While it's rare to find this in bakeries, the café on the island in the lake sells several varieties.

Desserts are typically enjoyed with a lake-and-mountains view—the best spots are the terrace at Vila Prešeren, the Panorama restaurant by Grand Hotel Toplice, and the terrace across from Hotel Park (figure around €5 for cake and coffee at any of these places). For a more local but non-lakeview setting, consider the recommended Slaščičarna Zima (only slightly cheaper).

don't come here if you're in a rush (daily 9:00-23:00, Grajska cesta 8, tel. 04/574-1613, www.pri-planincu.com). Upstairs is a timbered **$ pizzeria** dishing up wood-fired pies (opens at 11:00). The playful cartoon mural along the outside of the restaurant shows different types of mountaineers (from left to right): thief, normal, mooch ("gopher"), climber, and naked (...well, almost).

$ Pizzeria Rustika, in the Old Town, offers wood-fired pizzas and salads. Its upstairs terrace is relaxing on a balmy evening (daily 12:00-23:00, Riklijeva cesta 13, tel. 04/576-8900).

Supermarket: The **$ Mercator** grocery store, in the commercial center, has the makings for a bang-up picnic. They sell sandwiches to go for about €3, or will make you one to order (point to what you want). This is a great option for hikers and budget travelers (Mon-Fri 7:30-20:00, Sat until 18:00, Sun 8:00-15:00). There's another location closer to the Old Town and castle (Mon-Sat 7:00-21:00, Sun 8:00-17:00).

Dessert: While tourists generally gulp down their cream cakes on a hotel restaurant's lakefront terrace, residents favor the desserts at **Slaščičarna Zima** (a.k.a. the "Brown Bear," for the bear on the sign). It's nicely untouristy, but lacks the atmosphere of the lakeside spots (daily 7:30-21:00, near bus station at Grajska cesta 3, tel. 04/574-1616).

Splurge Restaurant Near Bled

$$$$ Vila Podvin, in the village of Mošnje (about a 15-minute drive from Lake Bled, just past Radovljica), has gained a big culinary reputation in recent years. The talented celebrity chef, Uroš Štefelin (who has been featured on some popular Slovenian cooking shows), prides himself on melding traditional Slovenian recipes with modern techniques and flavors. The dressy but inviting interior and fine garden are equally enjoyable places to dine. Their lunch special—available until 15:00—is a nice way to affordably sample their menu. Reservations are smart (Tue-Sat 12:00-22:00, Sun until 17:00, closed Mon, Mošnje 1, tel. 08/384-3470, www.vilapodvin.si). They also rent very sharp rooms and offer cooking classes (explained on their website).

Lake Bled Connections

The most convenient train connections to Bled leave from the Lesce-Bled station, about 2.5 miles away (see details under "Arrival in Bled," earlier). Remember, when buying a train ticket to Lake Bled, make it clear that you want to go to the **Lesce-Bled station** (not the Bled Jezero station, which is poorly connected to the main line). No one in the town of Bled sells train tickets; buy them at the station just before your train departs (open Mon-Fri 5:30-21:00, Sat 7:00-15:00, Sun 14:30-19:30). If the ticket window there is closed, buy your ticket on board from the conductor (who will likely waive the surcharge).

Note that if you're going to **Ljubljana,** it's better to take the bus (which leaves from Bled town itself) rather than the train (which leaves from the Lesce-Bled train station).

From Lesce-Bled by Train to: Ljubljana (roughly hourly, 40-60 minutes), **Salzburg** (3/day, 4 hours, some change in Villach, Austria), **Munich** (3/day, 5.5 hours, some change in Villach), **Vienna** (that's **Dunaj** in Slovene, 3/day, 5.25-6 hours, transfer in Villach), **Venice** (2/day with transfer in Villach, 5 hours; instead consider a GoOpti minibus—described under "Ljubljana Connections" at the end of the previous chapter), **Zagreb** (4/day direct, 3-3.5 hours).

By Bus to: Ljubljana (Mon-Sat hourly—usually at :30 past the hour, fewer on Sun, 1.25 hours), **Radovljica** (Mon-Fri 2-3/ hour, Sat hourly, Sun almost hourly, 15 minutes), **Lesce-Bled train station** (2-3/hour, 10 minutes), **Lake Bohinj** (hourly, 40 minutes to Bohinj Jezero stop, 50 minutes to Bohinj Vogel or Bohinj Zlato-rog stop, 1/day in summer continues all the way to Savica Waterfall trailhead), **Vintgar Gorge** (direct tourist bus July-Aug, otherwise take a public bus to Podhom or Spodnje Gorje and walk 15 min-utes, or pay for a shuttle bus transfer from Bled; for details, see "Vintgar Gorge," later. Confirm times at the TI or by using the schedules posted at the Bled bus station. Buy tickets on the bus).

By Plane: Ljubljana Airport (airport code: LJU) is between Lake Bled and Ljubljana, about a 45-minute drive from Bled. The best compromise of cost and speed is to book a shared minivan transfer with GoOpti, which usually runs around €12 (see "Lju-bljana Connections" at the end of the previous chapter). A taxi costs around €45 (set price up front—since it's outside of town, they don't use the meter; try to use a Bled-based taxi, because a Lju-bljana-based taxi will likely be more expensive). The Zup Prevozi shuttle bus costs €13, but it runs only a few times each day (gen-erally coordinated to meet EasyJet flights—see schedule at www.zup-prevozi.eu). For details on the Ljubljana airport, see "Ljubljana Connections" at the end of the previous chapter.

Route Tips for Drivers: Bled is less than an hour north of Ljubljana on the slick A-2 expressway. The exit is marked for *Lesce*, but you'll also see signs for *Bled*, which will lead you directly to the lake (where the road becomes Ljubljanska cesta).

To reach **Radovljica** (bee museum) or **Lesce** (train station), drive out of Bled on Ljubljanska cesta toward the expressway. Watch for the turnoff to *Lesce* on the right. They're on the same road: Lesce first (to reach train station, divert right when enter-ing town), then Radovljica. (Signs to *Radovljica* will divert you out to the main road that parallels the expressway, then back down into Radovljica; instead, you could follow signs to Lesce, and drive through that town for the more direct route.)

Near Lake Bled

The countryside around Bled offers several day trips that can be done easily without a car (bus connection information is described in each section). The three trips listed here are the best (one small-town/museum experience, two hiking/back-to-nature options). They're more convenient than can't-miss, but each is worthwhile on a longer visit, and all give a good taste of the Julian Alps. For a self-guided driving tour through farther-flung (and even more striking) parts of the Julian Alps, see the next chapter.

Vintgar Gorge

For those seeking an easy yet spectacular walk, Vintgar (VEENT-gar), worth ▲▲, is one of my favorite low-impact hikes in Slovenia or Croatia. Just north of Bled, the River Radovna has carved this mile-long, picturesque gorge into the mountainside. Boardwalks and bridges put you right in the middle of the magic in this "poor man's Plitvice." Shaded and relatively cool, this is a refreshing place for a walk on a hot day.

The gorge—easily reachable from Bled by bus or foot—works well for those who are itching for a hike but don't have a car. From the entrance, allow about 1.5 hours for a round-trip hike, including time for photos (and there will be photos). On sunny days, the gorge can be crowded (and less idyllic) after about 11:00—if you anticipate crowds, get an early start.

Cost and Hours: €5 to enter gorge, open daily 8:00-19:00 or until dusk, June-Aug maybe until 20:00, closed Nov-March, tel. 04/572-5266.

Getting to Vintgar Gorge: The gorge is 2.5 miles north of Bled. To reach the gorge entrance, you can walk (takes at least one hour one-way), pedal a rental bike (about 30 minutes, easiest with an electric bike), take a bus (15-minute ride plus 15-minute walk, or 30-minute ride on summer tourist bus), or drive (less than 10 minutes).

Walkers and **cyclists** leave Bled on the road between the castle and St. Martin's Church and take the uphill (left) road at the fork. Just after the little yellow chapel, turn right on the road with the big tree, then immediately left at the Mercator grocery store. When the road swings left, continue straight onto Partizanska (marked for *Podhom* and a walking sign for *Vintgar;* ignore the bus sign for

Near Lake Bled

109 To Kranjska Gora
To Italy
206
202
Mojstrana
Vršič Pass
SLOVENIA
Mount Triglav
JULIAN ALPS
Savica Waterfall
HOTEL ZLATOROG & STARE PENSION
Lake Bohinj
Bohinjska Bistrica
Ribčev Laz
WWI CEMETERY
(Lift)
Polje
Vogel Mtn.
Car Train to Most na Soči
Podbrdo

To Villach and Klagenfurt Airport
(TUNNEL)
85
AUSTRIA
KARAVANKE MTNS
Jesenice
A2
Stol Mtn.
VINTGAR GORGE
Podhom
Bled Town
Spodnje Gorje
Krnica
BLED JEZERO STATION
Mlino
Selo
Lake Bled
LESCE-BLED STATION
Begunje
Radovljica
Mošnje
To Airport & Ljubljana
Sava River
Kropa
To Ljubljana
209
Sava Bohinjka R.

5 Kilometers
5 Miles
·········· Lake Boats

Vintgar pointing left). At the fork just after the little bridge, go left for Podhom, then simply follow signs for *Vintgar*.

In summer (July-Aug), the easy **tourist bus** takes you right to the gorge entrance (only runs in the morning; see "Getting Around Lake Bled," earlier). It's possible that, on weekday mornings in spring and fall, a direct **public bus** will connect Bled to the gorge entrance (ask locally); otherwise, you can take the public bus either to Podhom (Mon-Fri hourly, none Sat-Sun, 15 minutes) or Spodnje Gorje (take bus in direction of Krnica, hourly, 15 minutes); from either of these bus stops, it's a 15-minute walk to the gorge (follow signs for *Vintgar*). Various companies in town also offer a €10 round-trip **shuttle bus** service to the gorge; look for signs around Bled, or ask your hotel or a travel agency.

Drivers follow signs to *Podhom*, then *Vintgar* (see walking/cycling instructions), and park for free right at the gorge entrance.

Gorge Hike: After buying your ticket, you'll hit the boardwalk trail (sometimes a bit slippery) and crisscross over the most dramatic and narrow stretch, tiptoeing over several waterfalls and marveling at the clarity of the water. Then the gorge—and the trail—flattens out and passes under a high stone footbridge and over a scenic dam. Finally, at the end of the gorge, you'll reach a footbridge over a plunging waterfall (next to a snack stand and WCs). For more views, continue on five minutes downhill (following the *Pod Slap* signs), then circle over the river again to reach a knoll where you can peer up at the waterfall and bridge you just crossed.

When finished, you can simply go back the way you came, or take a prettier return to Bled (described next).

Scenic Hike Back to Bled: If you still have energy once you reach the end of the gorge, consider this longer hike back with panoramic views. Behind the snack stand deep in the gorge, find the trail marked *Pod Katarina*. You'll go uphill for 25 strenuous minutes (following the red-and-white circles and arrows) before cresting the hill and enjoying beautiful views over Bled town and the region. Continue straight down the road 15 minutes to the typical, narrow old village of Zasip, then walk (about 30 minutes) or take the bus back to Bled.

Radovljica

The town of Radovljica (rah-DOH-vleet-suh, "Radol'ca" for short), perched on a plateau above the Sava River, has the charming Old Town that Bled lacks (refreshingly, it also lacks much of Bled's summer crowds). The traffic-free core of the town, once hemmed in by a stout wall (still faintly visible in some areas), is jammed with historic buildings that surround the long, skinny main square called Linhartov trg. While Radovljica's Old Town is

a pleasant place to stroll or nurse a coffee, you can see it all in a few minutes. The main reason to visit here is to tour its small but strangely fascinating beekeeping museum—despite having only a few rooms, it still ranks as one of Europe's biggest on the apiarian arts. Skip the town on Mondays, when the museum is closed (and be aware that the museum has shorter hours off-season).

Tourist Information: The enthusiastic TI loves to help visitors appreciate the town (daily 9:00-19:00; Oct-April Mon-Fri 9:00-16:00, Sat-Sun until 18:00; Linhartov trg 1, tel. 04/531-5112, www.radolca.si).

GETTING TO RADOVLJICA

Buses to Radovljica generally leave Bled at least every half-hour (fewer on weekends, buy ticket from driver, trip takes about 15 minutes). To reach the town center and the bee museum from the bus station, leave the station going straight ahead, cross the bus parking lot and the next street, then turn left down the far street (following brown sign for *Staro Mesto*). In five minutes, you'll reach the start of the pedestrianized Linhartov trg (with the TI—on the right—and the start of my "Old Town Stroll").

Drivers leave Bled on Ljubljanska cesta and follow the directions under "Route Tips for Drivers" under "Lake Bled Connections," earlier. The road dead-ends at Radovljica's pedestrian zone, where you'll find a parking lot (by the rustic garage), the TI, and the start of my "Old Town Stroll."

A handy **bike** path scenically and peacefully connects Bled with Radovljica (about 4 miles, get details at TI).

Sights in Radovljica

Old Town Stroll

Whether arriving by bus or by car, you'll enter the Old Town next to the TI. If you curl around below the main road (that is, the downhill road by the TI), you'll find the scant remains of the city's original **moat**—the only surviving one in Slovenia.

On the left, just as you enter the Old Town, you'll see **Vinoteka Sodček,** a wine bar and shop that offers a handy opportunity to learn about and sample Slovenian wines. Their €15 tasting includes five wines, plus cheese and *pršut* (air-dried ham)—it's best to call ahead to arrange this. You can also buy bottles of wine here for €10-15. Owner Aleš and his well-trained staff know their stuff; this is an easygoing, low-pressure place for learning and stocking up (Mon-Sat 9:00-22:00, closed Sun, Linhartov trg 8, tel. 04/531-5071).

Continuing into the Old Town, after a half-block you'll pass a fun little **secondhand shop** on the right—crammed with everything from beat-up modern appliances to genuine Slovenian antiques.

Beyond that, the street opens up into **Linhartov trg,** a charming square fronted by historic buildings. On the left, look for the *Keramika* sign marking the **Magušarjeva Hiša,** a fine old Gothic house where potter Urban Magušar lives, has a studio and exhibition space, and teaches pottery classes—if you're curious, step into the courtyard and ask him if you can see the house (Trubarjeva 1, mobile 041-734-808).

Just beyond, the **Vidičeva Hiša** café serves great ice cream and cakes. Farther along is the traditional, recommended **Lectar** restaurant, with a "living museum" in the basement where you can watch bakers making traditional gingerbread ornaments (€2 entry).

Across the street is a monument with a student holding a big medallion image of **Josipina Hočevar,** a Radovljica native who later helped fund the town's water system (see the old well nearby) and a school and many important buildings in Krško, near Zagreb.

Next to that is the **Šivičeva Hiša,** an atmospheric late-Gothic house that's open to the public (closed Mon). If you go a block down any street to the right, you'll come to a fine valley **viewpoint** emphasizing Radovljica's dramatic position on a long promontory.

Dominating the main part of the square is the big, yellow **town "castle"** (actually a mansion); upstairs you'll find the **Apicultural Museum** (described next), the Linhart Museum, and the Baroque Hall.

Beyond the mansion (and connected to it by a gallery) is **St. Peter's Church;** to its right is its rectory, where you can dip into the pretty courtyard.

Circle all the way around the church, then go through the gate to the edge of the ravine. Burrowed into the hillside is a **WWII-era bunker** left behind by the Nazis. Peeking into the window of the bunker, you'll see it's been turned into a chapel dedicated to Edith Stein, a 20th-century Polish Jew who became a Carmelite nun but was arrested by the Nazis and executed at Auschwitz. She was later made a saint by Pope John Paul II (notice the menorah and Star of David inside the chapel, on the right). While she has no official ties to Radovljica, locals are inspired by Edith's example.

▲▲Apicultural Museum (Čebelarski Muzej)

This museum celebrates Slovenia's long and very proud beekeeping heritage. While the exhibits about the history of beekeeping are oddly fascinating, the highlight is the extensive collection of colorfully painted frontboard panels (used on the front of hives)—one of Slovenia's most cherished folk arts. Replicas of these panels are sold in souvenir shops nationwide, but these are the real deal.

Cost and Hours: €3, good English descriptions, €1.60 English guidebook is a nice souvenir; Tue-Sun 10:00-18:00, closed Mon, shorter hours Nov-April, Jan-Feb closed Sat-Mon; clean and easy WCs, upstairs at Linhartov trg 1, tel. 04/532-0520, www. mro.si.

Visiting the Museum: Everything is well-described in English, but this commentary will help you locate the highlights.

The **first room** of the museum traces the history of beekeeping, from the time when bees were kept in hollowed-out trees to the present day. The bust celebrates beekeeper extraordinaire Anton Janša. On the nearby wall, you'll see excerpts from his first-ever textbook on beekeeping, as well as documents from other VIBs (very important beekeepers).

In the **second room** are old-fashioned tools. When a new queen bee is born, the old queen takes half the hive's bees to a new location. Experienced beekeepers used the long, skinny instrument (a beehive stethoscope) to figure out when the swarm was working up a steady buzz, indicating they were ready to fly the coop. Then, once the bees had moved to a nearby tree, the beekeeper used the big spoons to retrieve the queen—surrounded by an angry ball of her subjects—from her new home before she could get settled in. The beekeeper transferred the furious gang into a man-made hive designed for easier, more sanitary collection of honey. You can also see the tools beekeepers used to create smoke, which makes bees less aggressive. Even today, some of Slovenia's old-fashioned beekeepers simply light up a cigarette and blow smoke on any bees that get ornery. The life-size model of a man carrying a box on his back illustrates how dedicated beekeepers would trudge uphill with their hives to help them reach higher and higher blossoms as the summer wore on. You'll also see a variety of old beehives (and a press used to squeeze every last drop of honey out of that comb), as well as photos of apiaries—large, freestanding buildings that house multiple hives. The map on the wall shows how the Carniolan bee—favored by beekeepers for its relatively mellow personality and fast growth in springtime—has been exported far and wide throughout the world, thanks to its adaptability to new climates.

The **third room** features the museum's highlight: whimsically painted beehive frontboards (called *panjske končnice*). Beekeepers, believing these paintings would help the bees find their way home,

developed a tradition of decorating their hives with religious, historical, and satirical folk themes. It was also a creative way to mark their own hives. The oldest panel dates from 1758, but the practice really took off in the 19th century. Take your time perusing these delightful illustrations. The depiction of a hunter's funeral shows all the animals happy...except his dog. In another panel, animals shave the hunter—evoking an old Slovenian saying about "shaving the fool." Panels also reveal professional stereotypes of the time: One popular panel shows two farmers fighting over a cow, while a lawyer milks it. Another features a giant snail running over very slow-moving tailors (who were considered extremely lethargic in sewing new clothes). Historical panels include a bloody beheading during a local battle and several scenes of troublesome Turks.

Slovenian Beekeeping

Slovenian farmer Anton Janša (1734-1773) is considered the father of modern beekeeping. Habsburg Empress Maria Theresa brought him to Vienna to become Europe's first official teacher of this art. Even today, beekeeping is considered a crucial part of Slovenian culture. The area around Lake Bled (Carniola) has about 6,000 inhabitants, including 65 beekeepers who manage 5,000 hives—the most bees per capita of any place in Europe.

Slovenian hives always face southeast, to enjoy sun in the morning and shade in the afternoon. Each individual hive is painted in bright colors, often depicting creative folk scenes, which help both the bees and the beekeepers distinguish the hives. Replicas of those characteristic beehive panels are available at shops in Bled and Ljubljana, and make for appealing souvenirs.

The taste of honey can differ tremendously from hive to hive and is determined by the specific flowers and blossoms from which a hive's bees gathered pollen. In general, honeys made from mixed flowers and linden blossoms have the sweetest, mildest flavor; those made from chestnut or pine trees can have a bitter aftertaste.

Besides honey, beekeepers also make money by raising new queen bees. Each hive has one, and they can't be bred—one of the larvae is simply fed special "royal jelly" that encourages her to become a leader. In the springtime, when bees are born, the beekeeper keeps a close eye on the hive to figure out whether there are any potential queens. If he finds one, he'll move the old queen—who brings half the hive with her—to a new home (before she can find one on her own).

Slovenes still reserve an importance and affection for bees that's rare in modern times. For example, the Slovene language has two different words for "to give birth" and "to die": One they use exclusively for humans and bees, and a different one for all other animals. If a beekeeper dies, it's believed that the new beekeeper must formally "introduce" himself to the hive by going there and explaining to the bees what has happened; otherwise, they become confused and agitated, and often die themselves.

To learn more about Slovenian beekeeping, visit the insightful Apicultural Museum in Radovljica. For an even more vivid, practical experience, call Blaž at Kralov Med near Bled for a demonstration (see page 792). At either place, you'll get a sense for just how proud Slovenes are of their bees.

There's everything from portraits of Habsburg emperors, to a "true crime" sequence of a man murdering his family as they sleep, to proto-"Lockhorns" cartoons of marital strife, to awkward depictions of foreign lands (based on likely incomplete or faulty descriptions of the day), to 18th-century erotica (one with a woman showing some leg and another with a flip-up, peek-a-boo panel). A few panels blur the line between humorous and misogynistic: Look for the devil sharpening a woman's tongue on a wheel; the mill where old women are put in and young women are pulled out; or the man carrying a cross—and his wife—on his back. (Equal-opportunity offenders, beekeepers also painted scenes of drunk men being yanked out of bars and away from card games by their wives.) The life-size wooden statues were used to "guard" the beehives—and designed to look like fearsome Ottoman and Napoleonic soldiers.

The **fourth room** examines the biology of bees. In the summer only, look for the actual, functioning beehive. Try to find the queen—she's usually marked with a dot on her back. The surround-sound hive nearby lets you step inside to hear the noise of a buzzing queen. You'll also see bee-related products, including wax items, ornaments, and pastries. Another exhibit shows how bees—so respected here in Slovenia, and around the world—are a popular decorative motif, adorning everything from coins to buildings (in many cultures, diligent bees, who store their honey, are symbolic of banks).

The **fifth room** features a modern beekeeper's house, special exhibits, and a good but dry, detailed 14-minute film about the Carniolan bee. Just beyond is another room of antique beekeeping equipment.

Back at the entrance, the ticket desk sells a few choice souvenirs, including hand-painted replicas of frontboards, honey brandy, candles, ornaments, and other bee products.

Nearby: Sharing a ticket desk with the bee museum, the skippable **Linhart Museum** celebrates one of Slovenia's leading Enlightenment thinkers: Radovljica-born Anton Linhart, the 18th-century politician and historian who wrote some of the first plays in the Slovenian language, setting the stage for France Prešeren (€5 combo-ticket with Apicultural Museum, same hours).

Eating in Radovljica

Several Radovljica restaurants near the bee museum have view terraces overlooking the surrounding mountains and valleys.

$$$ Lectar offers pricey, hearty Slovenian fare in a rural-feeling setting with a user-friendly, super-traditional menu. Its several heavily decorated rooms are often filled with tour groups, but in good weather, don't miss the terrace out back. Come here if you want to linger over rustic Slovenian specialties. The restaurant is known for its heart-shaped gingerbread cookies (called *lect*), inscribed with messages of love. In the cellar is a "living museum" where you can pay €2 to watch costumed bakers make and decorate these hearts according to the traditional recipe (daily 12:00-22:00, family-friendly, Linhartov trg 2, tel. 04/537-4800).

$$ Gostilna Avguštin, across the street, is the simpler local alternative for a nice variety of unpretentious, stick-to-your-ribs Slovenian fare, including hearty pastas, meal-sized salads, and vegetarian options. Their terrace in back enjoys an even better view than Lectar's (daily 11:00-24:00, Linhartov trg 15, tel. 04/531-4163).

Lake Bohinj

The pristine alpine Lake Bohinj (BOH-heen), 16 miles southwest of Bled, enjoys a quieter scene and (in clear weather) even better vistas of Triglav and the sur-

rounding mountains. This is a real back-to-nature experience, with just a smattering of hotels and campgrounds, rather than the well-oiled resort machine of Bled. Some people adore Bohinj; others are bored by it. While spectacular in clear, sunny weather, it's disappointing in the clouds (and, because of its position deep in the mountains, it can be socked-in here even when it's clear in Bled). But if the weather is great and you're finding Bled too touristy to allow you to really enjoy nature, go to Bohinj.

GETTING TO LAKE BOHINJ

From Bled, hourly **buses** head for Bohinj, stopping at three destinations: Bohinj Jezero (the village of Ribčev Laz, 40 minutes), then Bohinj Vogel (a 10-minute walk from the base of the Vogel Mountain cable car, 50 minutes), and finally a few hundred yards more to Bohinj Zlatorog (Hotel Zlatorog and the one-hour hike to the Savica Waterfall trailhead, 50 minutes). In summer (July-Aug), one daily bus continues all the way to the Savica Waterfall trailhead (see details under "Savica Waterfall," later). Off-season, there are fewer buses—confirm times before you depart.

Drivers leave Bled going south along the lakefront road, Cesta Svobode; in the village of Mlino, you'll peel off from the lake and follow signs to *Boh Bistrica* (a midsize town near Lake Bohinj). Once in the town of Bohinjska Bistrica, turn right, following *Boh*

Jezero signs. The road takes you to the village of Ribčev Laz and along the lakefront road with all the attractions—the drive from Bled to the lake takes about 30 minutes. You can follow this road all the way to the Vogel cable-car parking lot; at the Vogel turnoff, you can continue straight ahead to reach the Savica Waterfall trailhead, or turn right and cross the bridge to curl around the far end of the lake and see the pristine river that feeds the lake (which flows out of the pool at the base of the Savica Waterfall).

Sights at Lake Bohinj

A visit to Bohinj has three main options: a village (offering boat trips on the lake), a cable car (and nearby cemetery), and a waterfall hike. I've listed them as you'll reach them along the main road from Bled, which runs along the south side of the lake. If you plan to do everything (boat trip, cable car, waterfall hike), ask at the TI in Ribčev Laz about a combo-ticket to save some money. The lake's website is helpful: www.bohinj.si.

Ribčev Laz Village

Coming from Bled, your first views of Bohinj will be from the little village called Ribčev Laz (loosely translated as "Good Fishin'

Hole") at the southeast corner of the lake. Here you'll find a TI, a handful of hotels and ice-cream stands, and the Bohinj Jezero bus stop.

On the way into town, on a small hill to the right, is a **monument** to the four Bohinj-area mountaineers who first summited Mount Triglav on August 26, 1778.

The town's main landmark is its picturesque lakefront church, **St. John the Baptist** (to your right as you face the lake, past the stone bridge; not open to visitors).

A five-minute stroll down the main lakefront road is a dock where you can catch an electric **tourist boat** to make a silent circuit around the lake (€10.50 round-trip, €9 one-way, 5/day April–mid-Nov). The boat stops at the far end of the lake, at Camp Zlatorog—a 10-minute walk from the Vogel cable car (see next page).

Across from the Ribčev Laz dock is a fun concrete 3-D model of Triglav. Finally, a few more steps down the road, just beyond a boat rental dock, is a statue of **Zlatorog,** the "Golden Horn"—a mythical chamois-like creature native to the Julian Alps.

▲Vogel Mountain Cable Car

For a mountain perch without the sweat, take the cable car up to the top of Vogel Mountain, offering impressive panoramic views of Mount Triglav and the Julian Alps. On a clear day, this is the best mountain panorama you can get without wings (the light is best in the morning).

Cost and Hours: €15 round-trip, daily 8:00-18:00, runs every 30 minutes in summer and continuously in winter, closed Nov, www.vogel.si.

Getting There: To reach the cable-car station, drivers follow signs to *Vogel* (to the left off the main lakefront road, marked *1915* and *1917*); by bus, get off at the Bohinj Vogel stop (request this stop from driver) and hike about 10 minutes up the steep road on the left (away from the lake).

Visiting the Summit: After you arrive at the top, savor the views from the metal platform where you exit the cable car...just don't look down. Walking up through the cable-car station (past the Viharnik snack bar, with basic food and far-from-basic views), you'll pop out at the summit, a ski-in-winter, hike-in-summer area with a pasture filled with grazing cows and smaller chairlifts to various recreation areas.

The first chairlift is designed for skiers and doesn't run in summer, but if you hike down into the little valley, you can take the second chairlift up the adjacent summit (Orlove Glave) for views into another valley on the other side. Then, from Orlove Glave, you can hike or ride the chairlift back to where you started. With plenty of time and very strong knees, you could even hike from Orlove Glave all the way back down to Lake Bohinj.

If you need a break near the cable-car station, the alpine hut Merjasec ("Wild Boar") offers tasty strudel and a wide variety of local brandies (including the notorious "Boar's Blood"—a concoction of several flavors guaranteed to get you snorting).

World War I Cemetery

Back down below the cable car, on the main road just beyond the Bohinj Vogel bus stop, look for the metal gate on the left marking the final resting place for some WWI Soča Front soldiers (see sidebar on page 838). While no fighting occurred here (it was mostly on the other side of these mountains), injured soldiers were brought to a nearby hospital, and those who didn't recover ended up here. Notice that many of the names are not Slovenian, but Hungarian, Polish, Czech, and so on—a reminder that the entire multiethnic

LAKE BLED

Austro-Hungarian Empire was involved in the fighting. If you're walking down from the cable-car station, the cemetery makes for a poignant detour on your way to the main road (look for it through the trees).

Savica Waterfall (Slap Savica)

Up the valley beyond the end of the lake is Bohinj's final treat, a waterfall called Slap Savica (sah-VEET-seh). Hardy hikers enjoy

following the moderate-to-strenuous uphill trail (including 553 stairs) to see the cascade, which dumps into a remarkably pure pool of aquamarine snowmelt.

Cost and Hours: €3, daily in summer from 8:00 until dusk, allow up to 1.5 hours for the round-trip hike.

Getting There: Drivers follow the lakefront road to where it ends, right at the trailhead. Without a car, getting to the trailhead is a hassle. Boats on the lake, as well as most public buses from Bled, take you only as far as the Bohinj Zlatorog stop—still a one-hour hike from the trailhead. However, in summer (July-Aug), one bus a day goes from Bled all the way to the Savica trailhead (likely departing Bled at 10:00, returning at 12:20). Otherwise, you can change to a local bus in the Bohinj area to reach the falls. Frankly, if the connections don't fit your itinerary, it's not worth the fuss.

Sleeping at Lake Bohinj

If you'd like to get away from it all and settle in at Bohinj, consider **$$ Stare Pension** (STAH-reh). Well-run by mild-mannered Jože, it has 10 older, rustic but well-maintained rooms (five with balconies) in a pristine setting at the far end of the lake (Ukanc 128, mobile 040-558-669, www.impel-bohinj.si, info@impel-bohinj.si). They also rent an eight-person villa for longer stays (info@rent-villa-slovenia.com).

THE JULIAN ALPS

Vršič Pass • Soča River Valley • Bovec • Kobarid

The countryside around Lake Bled is plenty spectacular. But to top off your Slovenian mountain experience, head for the hills. The northwestern corner of Slovenia—within yodeling distance of Austria and Italy—is crowned by the Julian Alps. Here, mountain culture has a Slavic accent.

The Slovenian mountainsides are laced with hiking paths, blanketed in deep forests, and speckled with ski resorts and vacation chalets. Beyond every ridge is a peaceful alpine village nestled around a quaint Baroque steeple. And in the center of it all is Mount Triglav—ol' "Three Heads"—Slovenia's national symbol and, at 9,396 feet, its tallest mountain.

The single best day in the Julian Alps is spent driving up and over the 50 hairpin turns of breathtaking Vršič Pass (vur-SHEECH) and back down via the Soča (SOH-chah) River Valley, lined with offbeat nooks and Hemingway-haunted crannies. As you curl between the cut-glass peaks, you'll enjoy stunning high-mountain scenery, whitewater rivers with superb fishing, rustic rest stops, thought-provoking WWI sights, and charming hamlets.

A pair of Soča Valley towns watches over the region. Centrally situated Bovec is all about good times (it's the whitewater-adventure sports hub), while Kobarid has Old World charm and better restaurants, and attends to more serious matters (WWI history). Though neither is a destination in itself, both Bovec and Kobarid are pleasant, functional, and convenient home bases for lingering in this gloriously beautiful region.

PLANNING YOUR TIME

Most visitors do this area as a surgical strike on a full-day side-trip from Lake Bled or Ljubljana—and even that fleeting glimpse is very satisfying. But there's plenty here to make it worth slowing down and spending a night (or possibly more). If you'd like to take advantage of the Soča Valley's hiking trails, evocative WWI historical sites, and many adventure sports (especially river rafting on the Soča), give yourself multiple nights.

GETTING AROUND THE JULIAN ALPS

The Julian Alps are best by **car.** Even if you're doing the rest of your trip by train, consider renting a car here for maximum mountain day-trip flexibility. I've included a self-guided driving tour that incorporates the best of the Julian Alps: Vršič Pass (usually open May-Oct) and the Soča Valley.

If you're without your own wheels, hiring a **local guide with a car** can be a great value, maximizing not only what you see, but what you learn. Or you can choose a cheaper but less personalized day-trip **excursion** from Bled. (Both options are explained under "Tours at Lake Bled" in the previous chapter.)

In the summer, a **public bus** more or less follows the driving-tour route, described next, over the Vršič Pass (departs Ljubljana daily July-Aug at 6:30 and 15:00, June and Sept Sat-Sun only at 6:30, 4.25 hours to Bovec, afternoon bus also continues to Kobarid in 5 hours total, no buses in winter). Additional Vršič Pass buses leave from Kranjska Gora at the foot of the mountains, which is also connected by bus to Ljubljana and Bled. (Yet another option is to take a direct bus from Ljubljana to Bovec that uses the somewhat less scenic southerly route via Idrija—but then you'd miss going over Vršič Pass.) To confirm schedules, see www.ap-ljubljana.si.

If you lack the time or transport to reach the Vršič Pass and Soča Valley, you could stay closer to Bled, and get a taste of the Julian Alps with a more convenient day trip to the Vintgar Gorge or Lake Bohinj (easy and frequent bus connections; see "Near Lake Bled" in the previous chapter).

Julian Alps Driving Tour

This all-day, self-guided driving tour—rated ▲▲▲—takes you over the highest mountain pass in Slovenia, with stunning scenery and a few quirky sights along the way. From waterfalls to hiking trails, WWI history to queasy suspension bridges, this trip has something for everyone.

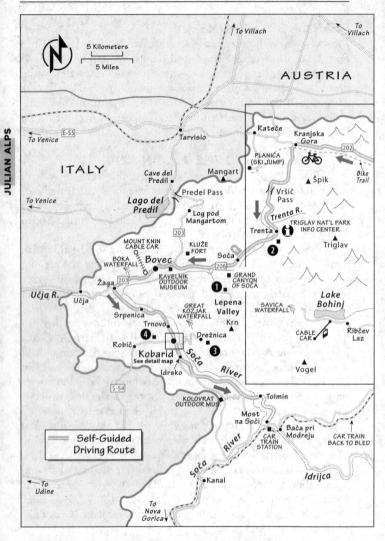

ORIENTATION TO THE JULIAN ALPS

Most of the Julian Alps are encompassed by Triglav National Park (Triglavski Narodni Park). This drive is divided into two parts: the Vršič Pass and the Soča River Valley. While not for stick-shift novices, all but the most timid drivers will agree that the scenery is worth the many hairpin turns. Frequent pullouts offer plenty of opportunities to relax, stretch your legs, and enjoy the vistas.

Planning Your Time: This drive can be done in a day, but consider spending the night along the way for a more leisurely pace. You can start and end in Bled or Ljubljana. You can return to your

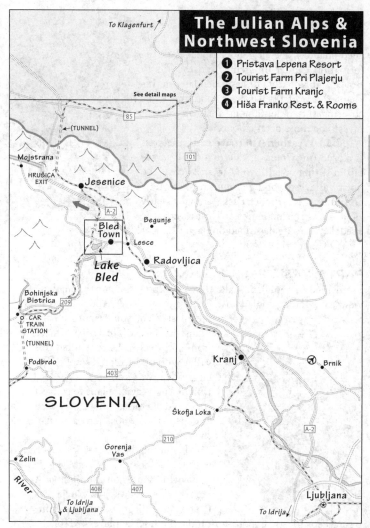

The Julian Alps & Northwest Slovenia

① Pristava Lepena Resort
② Tourist Farm Pri Plajerju
③ Tourist Farm Kranjc
④ Hiša Franko Rest. & Rooms

starting point, or do this trip one-way as a very scenic detour between these two destinations.

Length of This Tour: These rough estimates do not include stops: Bled to the top of Vršič Pass—1 hour; Vršič Pass to Trenta (start of Soča Valley)—30 minutes; Trenta to Bovec—30 minutes; Bovec to Kobarid—30 minutes; Kobarid to Ljubljana or Bled—2 hours (remember, it's an hour between Ljubljana and Bled). In other words, if you started and ended in Bled and drove the entire route without stopping, you'd make it home in less than five hours...but you'd miss so much. It takes at least a full day to do the region justice.

Tourist Information: The best sources of information are the Bled TI (see the Lake Bled chapter), the Triglav National Park Information Center in Trenta, and the TIs in Bovec and Kobarid (all described later in this chapter). Local TIs hand out good, free maps covering this mountainous area, or you can invest in a more detailed one.

Bad-Weather Alternative: If the pass is closed (in winter, or due to a freak snowfall in spring or fall), you can still access the Soča Valley by looping around through Italy and taking the Predel Pass—a route nearly as scenic as this main option. Just reverse the Predel Pass route described on page 828.

OK...let's ride.

PART 1: VRŠIČ PASS

From Bled or Ljubljana, take the A-2 expressway north, enjoying views of Mount Triglav on the left as you drive. About 10 min-

utes past Bled, you'll approach the industrial city of **Jesenice,** whose iron- and steelworks once filled this valley with multicolored smoke. The city, which was known as the "Detroit of Yugoslavia," plans to convert these old factories (most of which closed in the 1980s) into a sort of theme park.

Just after the giant smokestack with the billboards, the little gaggle of colorful houses on the right (just next to the freeway) is **Kurja Vas** ("Chicken Village"). This unassuming place is locally famous for producing hockey players: 18 of the 20 players on the 1971 Yugoslav hockey team—which went to the World Championships—were from this tiny hamlet.

As you zip past Jesenice, keep your eye out for the exit marked *Jesenice-zahod, Trbiž/Tarvisio, Kr. Gora,* and *Hrušica* (it's after the gas station, just before the tunnel to Austria). When you exit, turn left toward *Kranjska Gora* and *Trbiž/Tarvisio* (yellow sign).

Just after the exit, the big blue building surrounded by tall lights was the former border station (the overpass you'll go under leads into Austria). Locals have fond memories of visiting Austria during the Yugoslav days, when they smuggled back forbidden Western goods. Some items weren't available at home (VCRs,

Coca-Cola, designer clothes), while other goods were simply better in Austria (chocolate, coffee, dishwasher soap).

Slovenes brag that their country—"with 56 percent of the land covered in forest"—is Europe's second-greenest. As you drive toward Kranjska Gora, take in all this greenery...and the characteristic Slovenian hayracks (recognized as part of the national heritage and now preserved). The Vrata Valley (on the left) is a popular starting point for climbing Mount Triglav. Paralleling the road on the left is a "rails-to-trails" bike path—converted from an old railway bed—that loops from here through Italy and Austria, allowing bikers to connect three countries in one day. On the right, watch for the statue of Jakob Aljaž, who actually bought Triglav—back when such a thing was possible (he's pointing at his purchase). Ten minutes later, in Gozd Martuljek, you'll cross a bridge and enjoy a great head-on view of Špik Mountain.

Kranjska Gora is a leading winter resort and popular with Croatian skiers. As every Slovene and Croatian wants a ski bungalow here, it has some of the highest property values in the country. A well-traveled bicycle path gorgeously connects Kranjska Gora to Mojstrana in one direction, and in the other to Planica, the last stop before the Italian border.

Entering Kranjska Gora, you'll see a turnoff to the left marked for *Bovec* and *Vršič*, which leads up to the pass. But winter sports fanatics (or anyone, on a clear day) may first want to take a 15-minute detour to see the biggest ski jump in the world, a few miles ahead at **Planica:** Stay straight through Kranjska Gora, then turn left at signs for *Planica*. You'll drive in along a row of eight dizzyingly high ski jumps to the modern, wood-clad Nordic Center (pay parking), with 360-degree views of alpine scenery. Every few years, tens of thousands of sports fans flock to this little valley to watch the ski-flying world championships. This is where a local boy was the first human to fly more than 100 meters on skis. Today's competitors routinely set new world records (currently 784 feet—that's 17 seconds in the air) on the outrageously steep ski-flying jump directly across from the Nordic Center. Thrill seekers who'd like to get a small taste of that experience can invest €25 (or €40 for a tandem run) in the adrenaline-pumping zipline that runs parallel to the jump. For something lower-impact, explore the Nordic Center, which has an information desk, WCs in the basement, a café with a sunny terrace, a small alpine-sports museum (overpriced and skippable for nonenthusiasts), and a wind-tunnel skydiving simulator (free entry to Nordic Center, daily 9:00-16:00, www.planica.si). In the lower stairwell, peek through the window into the parking garage—where, in summer, they pump in artificial snow for cross-country ski practice.

Before leaving Planica, ponder this: From this spot, you're a

JULIAN ALPS

Mount Triglav

Mount Triglav ("Three Heads") stands watch over the Julian Alps, and all of Slovenia. Slovenes say that its three peaks are the guardians of the water, air, and earth. This mountain defines Slovenes, even adorning the nation's flag: You'll often see the national seal, with three peaks (the two squiggly lines under it represent the Adriatic). Or take a look at Slovenia's €0.50 coin.

From the town of Bled, you'll see Triglav peeking up over the ridge on a clear day. (You'll get an even better view from nearby Lake Bohinj.)

It's said that you're not a true Slovene until you've climbed Triglav. One native took these words very seriously and climbed the mountain 853 times...in one year. Climbing to the summit—at 9,396 feet—is an attainable goal for any hiker in decent shape. If you're here for a while and want to become an honorary Slovene, befriend a local and ask if he or she will take you to the top.

If mountain climbing isn't your style, relax at an outdoor café with a piece of cream cake and a view of Triglav. It won't make you a Slovene...but it's close enough on a quick visit.

few minutes' walk from both Italy and Austria. This region spanning three nations lobbied unsuccessfully under the name Senza Confini (Italian for "without borders") to host the 2006 Winter Olympics. This philosophy is in tune with the European Union's vision for a Europe of regions, rather than nations.

Back in Kranjska Gora, follow the signs for *Vršič*. Before long, you'll officially enter **Triglav National Park** and come to the first of this road's 50 hairpin turns (24 up, then 26 down)—each one numbered and labeled with the altitude in meters. Notice that the turns are cobbled to provide better traction. If the drive seems daunting, remember that 50-seat tour buses routinely conquer this pass...if they can do it, so can you. Better yet, imagine—and watch for—the bicyclists who regularly pedal to the top. The best can do it in less than 30 minutes—faster than driving.

After switchback #8, with the cute waterfall, park your car on the right and hike up the stairs on the left to the little **Russian Orthodox chapel.** This road was built during World War I by at least 10,000 Russian POWs of the Austro-Hungarian Empire to supply the Soča Front. The POWs lived and worked in terrible conditions,

and several hundred died of illness and exposure. On March 8, 1916, an avalanche thundered down the mountains, killing hundreds more workers. This chapel was built where the final casualty was found. Take a minute to pay your respects to the men who built the road you're enjoying today.

Back on the road, after #17, look up as high as you can on the cliff face to see sunlight streaming through a **"window"** in the rock. This natural formation, a popular destination for intrepid hikers, is big enough for the Statue of Liberty to crawl through.

After #22, at the pullout for Erjavčeva Koča restaurant, you may see tour-bus groups making a fuss about the mountain vista. They're looking for a ghostly face in the cliff wall, supposedly belonging to the mythical figure **Ajda.** This village girl was cursed by the townspeople after correctly predicting the death of the Zlatorog (Golden Horn), a magical, beloved, chamois-like animal. Her tiny image is just above the tree line, a little to the right—try to get someone to point her out to you (you can see her best if you stand at the signpost near the road). The picnic tables here are one of the best places along this drive for a do-it-yourself feast.

After #24, you reach the **summit** (5,285 feet). Consider getting out of the car to enjoy the views (in peak season, you'll pay an

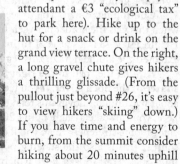

attendant a €3 "ecological tax" to park here). Hike up to the hut for a snack or drink on the grand view terrace. On the right, a long gravel chute gives hikers a thrilling glissade. (From the pullout just beyond #26, it's easy to view hikers "skiing" down.) If you have time and energy to burn, from the summit consider hiking about 20 minutes uphill to the Poštarski Dom ("Fifth Hut," with good food). Along the way, you'll see the ruins of a cable-car line, which ran supplies between here and the valley floor during World War I. You'll also enjoy some of the best possible views of the Ajda face.

As you begin the descent, keep an eye out for old WWI debris. A lonely guard tunnel stands after #28, followed by a tunnel

Hemingway in the Julian Alps

It was against the scenic backdrop of the Slovenian Alps that a young man from Oak Park, Illinois, first came to Europe—the continent with which he would forever be identified. After graduating from high school in 1917 and working briefly as a newspaper reporter, young Ernest Hemingway wanted to join the war effort in Europe. Bad vision kept him out of the army, but he craved combat experience—so he joined the Red Cross Ambulance Corps instead.

After a short detour through Paris, Hemingway was sent to the Italian Front. On his first day, he was given the job of retrieving human remains—gruesomely disfigured body parts—after the explosion of a munitions factory. Later he came to the Lower Piave Valley, not far from the Soča Front. In July 1918, his ambulance was hit by a mortar shell. Despite his injuries, he saved an Italian soldier who was also wounded. According to legend, Hemingway packed his own wound with cigarette butts to stop the flow of blood.

Sent to Milan to recuperate, Hemingway fell in love with a nurse, but she later left him for an Italian military officer. A decade later, Hemingway wrote about Kobarid (using its Italian name, Caporetto), the war, and his case of youthful heartbreak in *A Farewell to Arms*.

marked *1916* (on the left) that was part of the road's original path. A bit later, watch for the turnoff at the right, at a little gravel parking lot with a picnic table. From the platform viewpoint, you can see mountain valleys formed in two different ways: To the left, the jagged V-shaped Soča Valley, carved by a raging river; and on the right, the gentle U-shaped Trenta Valley, gouged by a glacier.

Continuing down, you'll see abandoned checkpoints from when this was the border between Italy and the Austro-Hungarian Empire. At #48 is a statue of **Julius Kugy,** an Italian botanist who explored the alpine flora of this region.

At #49, the road to the right (marked *Izvir Soče*) leads to the **source of the Soča River.** If you feel like stretching your legs, drive about five minutes down this road to a restaurant parking lot. From here, you can take a challenging 20-minute uphill hike (which includes some stretches where you'll cling to guide wires) to the Soča source. This is also the starting point for the well-explained, 12-mile Soča Trail (Soška Pot), which leads all the way to the town of Bovec.

Nearing the end of the switchbacks, follow signs for *Bovec.* Crossing the Soča River, you begin the second half of this trip.

PART 2: SOČA RIVER VALLEY

During World War I, the terrain between here and the Adriatic made up the Soča (Isonzo) Front. As you follow the Soča River south, down what's nicknamed the "Valley of the Cemeteries," the scenic mountainsides tell the tale of this terrible warfare. Imagine a young Ernest Hemingway driving his ambulance through these same hills (see sidebar).

But it's not all so gloomy. There are plenty of other diversions—interesting villages and churches, waterfalls and suspension bridges, and more. Perhaps most impressive is the remarkable clarity and milky-blue color of the Soča itself, which Slovenes proudly call their "emerald river."

After switchback #49, you'll cross a bridge, then pass a church and a botanical garden of alpine plants (Alpinum Juliana, summer only). Across the street from the garden (on the right) is the parking lot for the Mlinarica Gorge. While the gorge is interesting, the bridge leading to it was damaged in a severe storm and hasn't yet been rebuilt—so it's best left to hardy hikers.

At long last—well after you think you're done with the pass—you finally reach the last Vršič switchback (#50), which sends you into the village of **Trenta.** As you get to the cluster of buildings in Trenta's "downtown," look on the left for the **Triglav National Park Information Center,** which also serves as a regional TI (daily July-Aug 9:00-19:00, May-June and Sept-Oct 10:00-18:00, Dec-April 10:00-14:00, closed Nov, tel. 05/388-9330, www.tnp.si). The €5 museum here provides a look (with English explanations) at the park's flora, fauna, traditional culture, and mountaineering history. An AV show celebrates the region's forests, and a poetic 15-minute slideshow explains the wonders and fragility of the park (included in museum entry, ask for English version as you enter).

After Trenta, you'll pass through a tunnel; then, on the left, look for a classic **suspension footbridge.** Pull over to walk out for

a bounce, enjoying the river's crystal-clear water and the spectacular mountain panorama. Or you can take your pick among many such bridges for the next several miles; the best is coming up soon (I'll point it out).

About five miles beyond Trenta, in the town of Soča, is the **Church of St. Joseph** (with reddish-brown steeple, tucked behind the big tree on the right). Step inside to see some fascinating art. During World War II, an artist hiding out in the mountains filled this church with patriotic symbolism. The interior is bathed in Yugoslav red, white, and blue—a brave statement made when such nationalistic sentiments were dangerous. On the ceiling is St. Michael (clad in Yugoslav colors) with Yugoslavia's three WWII enemies at his feet: the eagle (Germany), the wolf (Italy), and the serpent (Japan). The tops of the walls along the nave are lined with Slavic saints. Finally, look carefully at the Stations of the Cross and find the faces of hated Yugoslav enemies: a lederhosen-clad Hitler (pulling a rope to lift up the cross; fourth from altar on left) and Mussolini (seated, as Herod; first from altar on right).

Behind the church, above the lovingly tended town graveyard, the stylized cross on the hill marks a **WWI cemetery**—the final resting place of some 1,400 Austro-Hungarian soldiers who were killed in action. Notice one small corner of the main cemetery (just before the WWI section) that's marked with a red star and labeled *Padli Borci Nov* (Our Fallen Fighters). These are the graves of local partisans who—two generations later—

fought alongside Tito to force out the Nazis (notice the death dates: 1943, 1944, 1945).

For another good example of how the Soča River cuts like God's band saw into the land, stop about two minutes past the church at the small gravel lot (on the left) marked *Velika Korita Soče* (**Grand Canyon of Soča**). While the entire Soča Valley is dramatic, this half-mile stretch, 30 to 50 feet deep, is considered the most impressive. Venture out onto the suspension bridge over the gorge...and bounce if you dare. If the water's high, notice the many side streams pouring into the churning river in a series of mini waterfalls. For more views, cross over the bridge and hike down along the treacherously uneven and narrow, rocky path downstream to another bridge.

Just beyond the suspension bridge is the turnoff (on the left) to the Lepena Valley, home of the recommended Pristava Lepena ranch, with accommodations and Lipizzaner horses (see "Sleeping in Bovec," later). If you head up this valley, you'll find a big gravel pullout on the right (marked *Velika Korita*) that lets you cross another springy bridge over a particularly wide stretch of the river. This is a popular place for those who enjoy hiking up alongside the "Grand Canyon" we passed earlier (about 5 miles round-trip, uneven terrain).

Soon after the Lepena Valley turnoff, watch on the left for the large **barn** (marked *Žičnica Golobar*). Pull over here if you'd like a close look at one of the stations for a primitive, industrial cable-car line, which was used mostly for logging.

Roughly five miles after the town of Soča, you exit the national park, pass a WWI graveyard (on the left), and come to a fork in the road. The main route leads to the left, through Bovec. But first, take a two-mile detour to the right (marked *Trbiž/Tarvisio* and *Predel/Kluže*), where the WWI **Kluže Fort** keeps a close watch over the narrowest part of a valley leading to Italy (free to enter

main courtyard, €3 to tour exhibit about local history and nature; July-Aug daily 9:00-20:00; June and Sept daily 9:00-17:00, Sat until 18:00; May and Oct open Sat-Sun only 10:00-17:00; closed Nov-April; www. kluze.net). In the 15th century, the Italians had a fort here to defend against the Ottomans. Five hundred years later, during World War I, Austrians used it to keep Italians out of their territory. Notice the ladder rungs fixed to the cliff face across the road from the fort—allowing soldiers to quickly get up to the mountaintop.

Back on the main road, immediately after the Kluže turnoff, watch for the gravel pullout on the left with the little wooden hut (look for the green sign with old photos). To see some original **WWI-era fortifications,** pull over here and hike on the gravel path 10 minutes through the woods to reach the Ravelnik Outdoor Museum. Here you can see trenches dug into the dirt and rocks, abandoned pillboxes, rusty sheds, and other features of an evocative wartime landscape. While not entirely typical of Soča Front embattlements—which were mostly high on the mountaintops—Ravelnik offers a more accessible taste of those times. (For a more authentic, mountaintop outdoor museum, drive 30 minutes beyond Kobarid and up to Kolovrat—described on page 841.)

Continue following the main road to **Bovec,** which saw some of the most vicious fighting of the Soča Front. The town was hit hard by earthquakes in 1994, 1998, and 2004, but today it's been rebuilt and remains the adventure-sports capital of the Soča River Valley, famous for its whitewater activities. (The Soča's water, which comes from high-mountain runoff, never goes above 68 degrees Fahrenheit.) For good lunch stops in Bovec, turn right at the roundabout as you first reach the town; you'll pass Martinov Hram's inviting restaurant terrace on the right, and soon after, the Letni Vrt pizzeria and Thirsty River brewery (for details on these, see "Eating in Bovec," later). But if you're not eating or spending the night in Bovec, you could skip the town entirely and not miss much (continue along the main road to bypass the town center).

About three miles past Bovec, as you cross the bridge (with the yellow *Boka* sign), look high up on the rock wall in the gorge to your right to spot the **Boka waterfall,** which carves a deep gouge into the cliff as it tumbles into the valley. (Hardy hikers can climb up for a better view of this fall—the trailhead is just after the bridge on the right—but it's an extremely strenuous hike.)

Head south along the river, with water somehow both perfectly clear and spectacularly turquoise. When you pass the intersection at the humble village of **Žaga,** you're just four miles from Italy. Continuing south, you'll pass a pullout (just before Srpenica) that is a popular put-in point for kayaking trips along the river. Keep an eye out for happy kayakers.

Soon you'll see signs for **Kobarid,** home to a sleepy main square and some fascinating WWI sights. Don't blink or you'll miss the Kobarid turnoff on the right—it lets you skirt into town past the highly recommended Kobarid Museum, which tells the tale of the WWI-era Soča Front. Farther along, you'll reach the tidy main square. Driving up to the Italian mausoleum hovering over the town is a must. (These sights are described later, under "Sights in Kobarid.")

Leaving Kobarid, continue south along the Soča to **Tolmin.** (For a steep, scenic detour to some poignant WWI sites, you can head up to the Kolovrat Outdoor Museum—described on page 841.) Before you reach Tolmin, decide on your preferred route back to civilization...

FINISHING THE DRIVE

While you could go back over the pass the way you came, there are various ways to make your trip a loop by circling through some more varied scenery. Which way you go depends on your final destination: Ljubljana or Bled.

To Ljubljana (or Southern Slovenia/Croatia)

From Tolmin, you have two possible driving routes to the capital. Either option brings you back to the A-1 expressway south of Ljubljana, and will get you to the city in about two hours (though the second route has fewer miles).

Nova Gorica Route: The option you'll encounter first (turnoff to the right before Tolmin) is the smoother, longer route southwest to Nova Gorica. Along this road, you'll pass a hydroelectric dam and go under a 1906 rail viaduct that once connected this area to the port of Trieste. In the charming town of Kanal, you'll cross over the Soča on a picturesque bridge that's faintly reminiscent of Mostar's (as in that city, young people stage a competition that involves jumping off this bridge into the raging river below). Farther along, the striking Solkan Bridge (another link in the Trieste rail line) is the longest single-span stone arch bridge in the world. Soon after, you arrive in Nova Gorica. This fairly dull city is divided in half by the Italian border (the Italian side is called "Gorizia"). Because Italians aren't allowed to gamble in their hometowns, Nova Gorica is packed with casinos that cater to them. In fact, it's home to Europe's biggest casino. Rocks spell out "TITO" on a hillside above town—a strange relic of an earlier age. From Nova Gorica, you can hop on the H-4 expressway, which links easily to the main A-1 expressway. Also notice that the road from Nova Gorica to Ljubljana takes you through the heart of the Karst region—famous for its wineries and caves.

Idrija Route: For a more off-the-beaten-path, ruggedly scenic approach, continue through Tolmin, then head southeast through the hills back toward Ljubljana. Along the way, you could stop for a bite and some sightseeing at the town of Idrija (EE-dree-yah), known to all Slovenes for three things: its tourable mercury mine, fine delicate lace, and tasty *žlikrofi* (like ravioli). Back at the expressway (at Logatec), head north to Ljubljana.

To Bled

To reach Bled, you could follow either of the Ljubljana-bound routes outlined earlier, then carry on northward for another hour to Bled (allow about 3 hours total). But the following options are more direct.

Car Train: The fastest option is to load your car onto a "Car Train" (Autovlak) that cuts directly through the mountains. The train departs at 18:35 from Most na Soči (just south of Tolmin, along the Idrija route described above) and arrives at Bohinjska Bistrica, near Lake Bohinj, at 19:07 (€14 for the car; afternoon departures—14:45 and 18:35—run late April-late Sept only, also departs year-round at 7:35 and 10:34—confirm schedule at the Bled TI before making the trip). No reservations are necessary, but arrive at the train station about 30 minutes before the scheduled departure to allow time to load the car. Note: This is a very old train that can be quite jerky and bumpy. You'll stay inside your car the entire time. If you're claustrophobic, prone to motion sickness, or both, consider giving this train a miss.

To get to the car train, drive through Tolmin, then Most na Soči (turning left for *Ljubljana*). About a mile from Most na Soči, watch on the right for the big bridge over the river, marked for *Čepovan* and *železniška postaja* (train station). Crossing the bridge, turn right to find the train station; once there, go around the far-left side of the long station building and drive up the ramp to wait your turn to load. You'll buy your ticket, load on your car, pull your hand brake, turn off the engine, and put the car in gear. Then you'll stay in the car and enjoy the scenery. Taking off, you'll cross a scenic viaduct, then twist through the mountains, going through multiple tunnels including a final 10-minute passage from Podbrdo beneath the mountains to Bohinjska Bistrica, where you'll unload your car. From there, it's less than a half-hour drive back to Bled, or a 10-minute drive (in the opposite direction) to Lake Bohinj.

Through Italy via Predel Pass: Although this route requires some backtracking, it also includes a fun detour through Italy—and some different scenery. From Kobarid, drive back the way you came (through Bovec), then turn off for the Kluže Fort, marked for *Predel* and Italy. In a few miles, after passing the fort, the road curves up through two small villages (first Log pod Mangartom, then Strmec na Predelu directly above it). Continue past the ruined fortress and cross the Italian border (there's generally no need to stop). Then curl down a few hairpin turns past the end of tranquil, scenic Lake Predel, and continue straight through the industrial city of Cave del Predil (overhead are the five rounded peaks of the Cinque Punte formation) and along the valley road, following signs for Slovenia. Approaching Tarvisio, turn right (continuing to follow signs for *Kranjska Gora* and Slovenia); from here, it's about a half-hour (10 miles) back across the Slovenian border to Kranjska Gora. This is where you first began your ascent of the Vršič Pass—just retrace your steps back to Bled.

Other Driving Routes: The fastest route (about 2 hours) essentially follows the car train route, but goes over rather than through the mountains. This route is partially on a twisty, rough, very poor-quality road (go through Tolmin, turn off at Bača pri Modreju to Podbrdo, then from Petrovo Brdo take a very curvy road through the mountains into Bohinjska Bistrica and on to Bled). For timid drivers, it's more sane and not too much longer to start out on the Idrija route toward Ljubljana (described earlier), but turn off in Želin (before Idrija) toward Skofja Loka and Kranj, then continue on to Bled.

Bovec

The biggest town in the area, Bovec (BOH-vets) has a happening main square and all the tourist amenities. It's best known as a hub for whitewater adventure sports. While not exactly quaint, Bovec is pleasant enough to qualify as a good lunch stop or overnight home base. If nothing else, it's a nice jolt of civilization wedged between the skyscraping alpine cliffs.

Orientation to Bovec

TOURIST INFORMATION

The helpful TI is on the main square (June-Aug Mon-Fri 8:00-20:00, Sat 9:00-20:00, Sun 9:00-17:00; May and Sept Mon-Fri 8:30-17:30, Sat 9:00-18:00, Sun 9:00-13:00; shorter hours off-season and closed Sat-Sun; Trg Golobarskih Žrtev 8, tel. 05/384-1919, www.bovec.si).

JULIAN ALPS

ARRIVAL IN BOVEC

The main road skirts Bovec, but you can turn off (watch for signs on the right) to go through the heart of town, then rejoin the main road farther along. The turnoff road goes right past the main square, Trg Golobarskih Žrtev, with the TI, various tour companies, and eateries. You'll find a big parking lot behind the Mercator supermarket (on the left just before the main square; park here for up to one hour free with a clock on your dashboard—but check locally) and a few parking spaces on or near the square itself.

Activities near Bovec

As the de facto capital of Slovenia's "Adrenaline Valley," Bovec offers many opportunities to enjoy the nature all around it. For great mountain views of the surrounding terrain, simply hike five minutes up (or drive) to the church at the top of town.

Adventure Sports

The Soča Valley offers abundant opportunities to get out on the rushing, crystal-clear waters of the river. The main options are rafting, kayaking, and hydrospeeding (a masochistic variation on boogie boarding—lying face-down on a short surfboard and shooting headfirst toward the rapids). The official season is March 15 until October 31, but from an adrenaline perspective, these activities are best in spring—when the water is highest. The river is tamer in summer, and by fall, water levels are even lower.

When conditions are ideal, most **rafting** companies put in near the Boka waterfall (just downriver from Bovec), and pick up at the village of Trnovo ob Soči. (When water levels are low, companies put in near Sprenica instead.) Most rafting trips last about

JULIAN ALPS

2.5-3 hours, with about 1.5 hours actually on the river and extra time to swim.

Kayaking is available at various points along the river, with a dramatic range in level of difficulty; the TI's free *Water-Adventure-Sport* map outlines your options and notes areas that are unsafe. To get a glimpse of kayakers, hang out at Napoleon Bridge, just outside Kobarid.

The most popular place for **canyoning**—a risky activity that involves wading and rappelling in rushing rivers—is in Canyon Sušec, about halfway between Bovec and Kobarid.

Other popular activities include skydiving and paragliding; biking (including electric mountain bikes); ziplines (there's a course above Bovec and another high in the Učja Valley); and even—gasp!—golf (Bovec has a 9-hole course, www.golfbovec.si). All of these activities come with some degree of risk (except, perhaps, golf); use common sense and investigate the safety record of any company that offers trips. The Bovec TI is a good source of information, and an ever-changing roster of local adventure travel companies runs a variety of tours. Well-established outfits include Bovec Šport Centar (www.bovec-sc.si) and Soča Rafting (www.socarafting.si), but it's also a good idea to consult recent online reviews (such as on TripAdvisor).

Sightseeing Flights
Aero Taxi runs scenic sightseeing flights from Bovec's little airport (€90/20-minute "introductory" flight for up to 3 people, longer itineraries available, mobile 041-262-726, www.janezlet.si).

Fly Fishing
The Soča River is a popular spot for fishing, predominantly for the endemic marble trout. Only fly fishing is allowed; some areas are catch-and-release, and all areas require a permit. **Bovec Fly Fishing** offers information, fly-fishing gear, and tours (mobile 031-227-744, www.bovecfishing.com).

Knin Cable Car
A cable car slo-o-owly trundles visitors 7,200 feet above sea level to near the summit of Mount Knin, which overlooks Bovec and a scenic swath of the Soča Valley. On a clear day, you can see all the way to the Adriatic. Up top, you can walk around an irregular limestone landscape (but watch your step—there are some extremely deep hidden crevasses) and pay extra to try out a fixed-anchor (a.k.a. *via ferrata*) climbing course.

Sleep Code

Hotels are classified based on the average price of a standard double room with breakfast in spring and fall. Prices may go up in summer, and down in winter.

$$$$	**Splurge:**	Most rooms over €150
$$$	**Pricier:**	€110-150
$$	**Moderate:**	€80-110
$	**Budget:**	€50-80
¢	**Backpacker:**	Under €50
RS%	**Rick Steves discount**	

Unless otherwise noted, credit cards are accepted, hotel staff speak basic English, and free Wi-Fi is available. Comparison-shop by checking prices at several hotels (on each hotel's own website, on a booking site, or by email). For the best deal, *book directly with the hotel.* Ask for a discount if paying in cash; if the listing includes **RS%,** request a Rick Steves discount.

Cost and Hours: €17 round-trip, 40 minutes each way, hours sporadic and weather-dependent but typically June-mid-Sept daily 7:00-15:00, Sat-Sun only in shoulder season, bottom station is just outside Bovec near the road to Kobarid, www.kanin.si.

Sleeping in Bovec

Dobra Vila and Hotel Sanje ob Soči are situated near the turnoff from the main road into central Bovec (about a 10-minute walk into town). Martinov Hram and Stari Kovač are closer to the main square, in the town center.

$$$ Dobra Vila, run with class by Juri, has 11 boldly stylish yet classic rooms and a generous rear terrace. You'll stay in a gorgeously restored former telephone office that feels like an enticing whisper of ages past (air-con, Mala vas 112, tel. 05/389-6400, www.dobra-vila-bovec.si, welcome@dobra-vila-bovec.si). They also have the most elegant restaurant in town (see "Eating in Bovec," later).

$$ Hotel Sanje ob Soči means "Dreams by the Soča"—which describes both what you'll do here and the vision that entrepreneurial owners Boštjan and Valentina have for their sleek, modern, spa-like lodgings. The 10 rooms and nine apartments fill a pine-clad, Scandinavian-feeling shell on the edge of Bovec. The rooms—all with terraces, and each one named for the mountain that dominates its view—are fairly simple and Ikea-furnished (breakfast extra, air-con, children's play area, Mala vas 105a, tel. 05/389-6000, mobile 031-331-690, www.sanjeobsoci.com, bostjan@sanjeobsoci.com).

$ Martinov Hram has 12 nice, modern rooms over a popular restaurant a few steps from Bovec's main square. While the rooms are an afterthought to the busy restaurant (reception at the bar), they're comfortable (rooms on sunny side have air-con, Trg Golobarskih Žrtev 27, tel. 05/388-6214, www.martinov-hram.si, sara.berginc@gmail.com).

$ Stari Kovač B&B is your basic budget option, with eight apartments in an old-feeling guesthouse a steep block downhill from the main square (breakfast extra, cash only, Rupa 3, tel. 05/388-6699, mobile 041-646-427, www.starikovac.com, info@starikovac.com).

NEAR BOVEC

$$$$ Pristava Lepena is a relaxing oasis hiding out in the Lepena Valley just north of Bovec. This place is its own little village, with a series of rustic-looking but comfy cabins, a restaurant, exercise room, kids' play area, tennis court, outdoor swimming pool, sauna/whirlpool, and resident Lipizzaner horses and mountain goats. The 13 cozy rooms have wood-burning stoves and all the amenities (closed in winter, multinight stays preferred, lunch and dinner available for extra charge; just south of the village of Soča, exit the main road at the sign for *Lepena*, and follow the white horses to Lepena 2; tel. 05/388-9900, www.pristava-lepena.com, info@pristavalepena.com).

$ Tourist Farm Pri Plajerju is on a picturesque plateau at the edge of Trenta (at the bottom of the Vršič Pass road). Run by the Pretner family (gregarious Marko is a park ranger, shy Stanka is "the boss"), this organic farm raises sheep and rents five apartments in three buildings separate from the main house. The Soča Valley doesn't have many tourist farms, and this is one of your best options. But its location deeper in the mountains makes it a bit less convenient for side-tripping—it's 30 minutes to Bovec and an hour to Kobarid (breakfast and dinner extra; watch for signs to the left after coming over the pass and going through Trenta, Trenta 16a; tel. 05/388-9209, mobile 041-600-590, www.eko-plajer.com, info@eko-plajer.com).

Eating in Bovec

$$$ Martinov Hram, run by the Berginc family (sisters Sara and Suzi), has an inviting outdoor terrace under a grape trellis. Inside, the nicely traditional decor pairs well with regional specialties with a focus on lamb, delicious pancakes, and homemade bread (Tue-Sun 10:00-23:00, closed Mon; on the main road through Bovec, just before the main square on the right at Trg Golobarskih Žrtev 27; tel. 05/388-6214).

$$ Letni Vrt is big, with an outdoor terrace facing Bovec's

Restaurant Price Code

I've assigned each eatery a price category, based on the average cost of a typical main course. Drinks, desserts, and splurge items (steak and seafood) can raise the price considerably.

$$$$	**Splurge:** Most main courses over €14
$$$	**Pricier:** €10-14
$$	**Moderate:** €6-10
$	**Budget:** Under €6

In Slovenia, a takeout spot is **$**; a basic sit-down eatery is **$$**; a casual but more upscale restaurant is **$$$**; and a swanky splurge is **$$$$**.

main intersection, and sprawling indoor dining rooms—including a nice winter garden that's inviting on cold days. The menu is almost comically lengthy—I'd stick with the good and affordable pizzas (Wed-Mon 11:00-23:00, closed Tue and Nov-Dec, in off-season may be open only Fri-Sun, Trg Golobarskih Žrtev 1, tel. 05/389-6383).

$$$$ Dobra Vila, also a recommended hotel, is the only place in town for an elegant, upscale meal of well-presented international cuisine with local flair. It's smart to book ahead (fixed-price meals only, daily 19:00-22:00, see contact information earlier).

Brewpub and Alpine Street Food: Thirsty River is an inviting microbrew tasting room with a wonderful location right on Bovec's main square. The basic interior is rustic and cozy, but in good weather, the outdoor tables will kill your momentum (as will the excellent beers; daily 15:00-23:00). They don't serve food, but across the street in summer you can look for a little **$ wooden shed,** where Bojan and daughter Anja serve up delicious, filling portions of hearty mountain foods, with lots of mushrooms and melted cheese (June-Sept daily 11:00-20:00, closed off-season, www.gobenabovskem.si).

Bovec Connections

From Bovec by Bus to: Kobarid (6/day Mon-Fri, 2-3/day Sat-Sun, 30 minutes), **Ljubljana** (direct over scenic Vršič Pass: 2/day July-Aug, 1/day Sat-Sun only June and Sept, none off-season, 4.25 hours; some additional buses may go over Vršič Pass to Kranjska Gora, where you can change to other destinations; otherwise less scenic via Idrija).

Kobarid

Kobarid (KOH-bah-reed) feels older and a bit more appealing
than its big brother Bovec. This humble
settlement was immortalized by Ernest
Hemingway, who drove an ambulance in
these mountains during World War I. He
described Kobarid as "a little white town
with a campanile in a valley. It was a clean
little town and there was a fine fountain
in the square." Sounds about right. Even
though Kobarid loves to tout its Hemingway connection, historians believe that
Papa did not actually visit Kobarid until
he came back after the war to research his
book.

Aside from its brush with literary
greatness, Kobarid is known as a hub of information about the Soča
Front (with an excellent WWI museum, a hilltop Italian mausoleum, and walks that connect to surrounding sites). You won't find
the fountain Hemingway wrote about—it's since been covered up
by houses. You will find a modern statue of Simon Gregorčič (overlooking the main intersection), the beloved Slovenian priest-poet
who came from and wrote about the Soča Valley.

Orientation to Kobarid

The main road, Gregorčičeva, cuts right through the heart of little
Kobarid, bisecting its main square (Trg Svobode). The Kobarid
Museum is along this road, on the left before the square.

TOURIST INFORMATION
The TI has good information on the entire area, plus free Wi-Fi
(July-Aug 9:00-20:00; May-June and Sept 9:00-13:00 & 14:00-
19:00—from 15:00 Sat-Sun; in off-season shorter hours and closed
Sun; on the main square at Trg Svobode 16—follow the white
footprints behind the statue of Gregorčič, tel. 05/380-0490, www.
dolina-soce.com).

ARRIVAL IN KOBARID
Driving into town from Bovec, watch carefully on the right for the
poorly marked first turnoff into Kobarid (if you miss the turnoff,
just carry on a bit longer, then turn right later to reach the main
square). Turning into town, you could make a sharp left turn to
reach the cheese factory (marked by the big modern tower), or con-

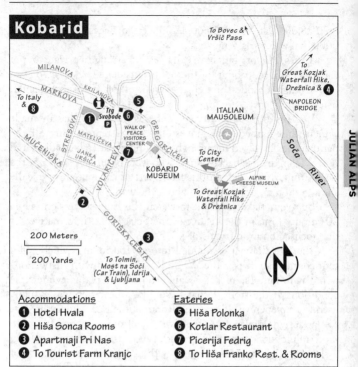

Kobarid

MILANOVA

MARKOVA

KRILANOVA

To Italy & **8**

STRESOVA

MATELIČEVA

JANKA URŠIČA

VOLARIČEVA

MUČENIŠKA

GORIŠKA CESTA

Trg Svobode **1** **i** P

WALK OF PEACE VISITORS CENTER

6

GREGORČIČEVA

5

7

KOBARID MUSEUM

2

3

To Tolmin, Most na Soči (Car Train), Idrija & Ljubljana

To Bovec & Vršič Pass

ITALIAN MAUSOLEUM

To City Center

ALPINE CHEESE MUSEUM

To Great Kozjak Waterfall Hike & Drežnica

To Great Kozjak Waterfall Hike, Drežnica & **4**

NAPOLEON BRIDGE

Soča River

200 Meters

200 Yards

N

<u>Accommodations</u>
1 Hotel Hvala
2 Hiša Sonca Rooms
3 Apartmaji Pri Nas
4 To Tourist Farm Kranjc

<u>Eateries</u>
5 Hiša Polonka
6 Kotlar Restaurant
7 Picerija Fedrig
8 To Hiša Franko Rest. & Rooms

tinue straight ahead to pass the Kobarid Museum, then the main square. You'll find pay parking on the main square, from which it's an easy five-minute stroll back to the museum.

Sights in Kobarid

▲▲Kobarid Museum (Kobariški Muzej)

This modest but world-class museum—worth ▲▲▲ for history
buffs—offers a haunting look at
the tragedy of the Soča Front. The
tasteful exhibits, with fine English
descriptions and a pacifist tone, take
an even-handed approach to the
fighting—without getting hung up
on identifying the "good guys" and
the "bad guys." The museum's focus
is not on the guns and heroes, but
on the big picture of the front and
the stories of the common people
who fought and died here.

Cost and Hours: €6, daily

9:00-18:00, Oct-March 10:00-17:00, Gregorčičeva 10, tel. 05/389-0000, www.kobariski-muzej.si.

Tours: History buffs can call ahead to arrange a private tour of the collection (€20/hour) or the sights outside (€25/hour). You can also arrange a guide through the Walk of Peace Visitors Center, listed later.

Visiting the Museum: The entry is lined with hastily made cement and barbed-wire gravestones, flags representing all the nationalities involved in the fighting, and pictures of soldiers and nurses from diverse backgrounds who were brought together at the Soča Front. The rooms in this front part of the museum typically show good temporary exhibits about the war.

Buy your ticket and ask to watch the English version of the 20-minute film on the history of the Soča Front (informative but dry, focused on military history).

The first floor up is divided into several rooms, which you'll tour counterclockwise. The White Room—filled with rusty crampons, wire-cutters, pickaxes, and shovels—explains wintertime conditions at the front. What looks like a bear trap was actually used to trap enemy soldiers. The Room of the Rear shows the day-to-day activities away from the front line, from supplying troops to more mundane activities (milking cows, washing clothes, getting a shave, lifting weights, playing with a dog). Peruse the case of personal effects that troops carried to the front line. The somber and heartbreaking Black Room commemorates the more than one million casualties of the Soča Front. Horrific images of war injuries juxtaposed with medals earned prompts the question, was it worth it? Nearby is a display case of artificial limbs. The little altar was purchased by schoolchildren, who sent it to the front to offer the troops some solace. The door—etched with personal messages from troops—was relocated here from a military prison near Kobarid.

Through the door marked *The Krn Range Room* (also on the first floor up), pass the small model of the mountaintop war zone and find your way to the Kobarid Rooms, which trace the history of this region from antiquity to today. High on the wall, look for the timelines explaining the area's turbulent past. In the second room, a timeline shows wave after wave of invaders (including Ottomans, Habsburgs, and Napoleon). In the next room, above a display case with military uniforms, another timeline shows the many flags that flew over Kobarid's main square during the 20th century alone.

On the top floor, you'll see a giant model of the surrounding mountains, painstakingly tracing the successful Austrian-German *Blitzkrieg* attack during the Battle of Kobarid. Crawl into the small cave and press the button to hear a patriotic song about a soldier, who reads a letter he's written to his family.

▲▲Italian Mausoleum (Kostnica)

The 55 miles between Kobarid and the Adriatic are dotted with more than 75 cemeteries, reminders of the countless casualties on the Soča Front. One of the most dramatic is this mausoleum, overlooking Kobarid. The access road, across Kobarid's main square from the side of the church, is marked by stone gate towers with the word *Kostnica*—one tower is topped with a cross and the other with a star for the Italian army.

Take the road up Gradič Hill—passing Stations of the Cross—to the mausoleum. Built in 1938 (when this was still part of Italy) around the existing Church of St. Anthony, this octagonal pyramid holds the remains of 7,014 Italian soldiers. The stark, cold Neoclassical architecture is pure Mussolini. Names are listed alphabetically, along with mass graves for more than 1,700 unknown soldiers *(militi ignoti)*.

Walk behind the church and enjoy the **view.** Scan the WWI battlements high on the mountain's rock face. Incredibly, troops fought on these treacherous ridges; civilians in the valleys only heard the distant battles. Looking up and down the valley, notice the "signal churches" evenly spaced on hilltops, each barely within view of the next—an ancient method for quickly spreading messages or warnings across long distances.

If the **church** is open, go inside and look above the door to see a brave soldier standing over the body of a fallen comrade, fending off enemies with nothing but rocks.

When Mussolini came to dedicate the mausoleum, local revolutionaries plotted an assassination attempt that they believed couldn't fail. A young man planned to suicide-bomb Mussolini as the leader came back into town from this hilltop. But as Mussolini's car drove past, the would-be assassin looked at his fellow townspeople around him, realized the innocent blood he would also spill, and had a last-minute change of heart. Mussolini's trip was uneventful, and fascism continued to thrive in Italy.

Alpine Cheese Museum

This humble exhibit, at the big Planika ("Edelweiss") dairy at the edge of town, examines the history of cheesemaking in this area since ancient times.

Cost and Hours: €2.70; Mon-Sat 10:00-12:00 & 16:00-18:00, closed Sun except Aug 10:00-12:00; Oct shorter hours; closed Nov-

The Soča (Isonzo) Front

The valley in Slovenia's northwest corner—called Soča in Slovene and Isonzo in Italian—saw some of World War I's fiercest fighting. While the Western Front gets more press, this eastern border between the Central Powers and the Allies was just as significant. In a series of 12 battles involving 22 different nationalities along a 60-mile-long front, 300,000 soldiers died, 700,000 were wounded, and 100,000 were declared MIA. In addition, tens of thousands of civilians died. A young Ernest Hemingway, who drove an ambulance for the Italian army in nearby fighting, would later write the novel *A Farewell to Arms* about the battles here (see the "Hemingway in the Julian Alps" sidebar, earlier).

On April 26, 1915, Italy joined the Allies. A month later, it declared war on the Austro-Hungarian Empire (which included Slovenia). Italy unexpectedly invaded the Soča Valley, quickly taking the tiny town of Kobarid, which it planned to use as a home base for attacks deeper into Austro-Hungarian territory. For the next 29 months, Italy launched 10 more offensives against the Austro-Hungarian army, which was encamped on higher ground on the mountaintops. None of the Italian offensives was successful, even though the Italians outnumbered their opponents three to one. This was unimaginably difficult warfare—Italy had to

attack uphill, waging war high in the mountains, in the harshest of conditions. Trenches had to be carved into rock instead of mud. The fighting coincided with the most brutal winter in a century; many unprepared conscripts—brought here from faraway lands and unaccustomed to the harsh winter conditions atop the Alps—froze to death. Some 60,000 soldiers were killed by avalanches.

Visitors take a look at this tight valley, hemmed in by seemingly impassible mountains, and wonder: Why would people fight

April; Gregorčičeva 32, tel. 05/384-1013, www.mlekarna-planika. si/muzej. To get here, turn right into Kobarid, then take the sharp left turn that leads you down beneath the underpass to the cheese factory (marked by the tall modern tower).

Great Kozjak Waterfall (Veliki Kozjak) Hike

If you have time to kill in Kobarid and want to go for a sturdy hike, consider trekking to the Great Kozjak Waterfall—a dramatic cascade that flows through an extremely narrow gorge and plunges 50

so fiercely over such inhospitable terrain? At the time, Slovenia was the natural route from Italy to the Austro-Hungarian capitals at Vienna and Budapest. The Italians believed that if they could hold this valley and push over the mountains, Vienna—and victory—would be theirs. Once committed, they couldn't turn back, and the war devolved into one of attrition—who would fall first?

In the fall of 1917, Austro-Hungarian Emperor Karl appealed to his ally Germany, and the Germans agreed to assemble an army for a new attack to retake Kobarid and the Soča Valley. In an incredible logistical accomplishment, they spent just six weeks building and supplying this new army by transporting troops and equipment high across the mountaintops under cover of darkness...above the heads of their oblivious Italian foes dozing in the valley below.

On October 24, Austria-Hungary and Germany launched an attack that sent 600,000 soldiers down into the town of Kobarid. This crucial twelfth battle of the Soča Front, better known as the Battle of Kobarid, was the turning point—and saw the introduction of battlefield innovations that are commonplace in the military today. German field commanders were empowered to act independently on the battlefield, reacting immediately to developments rather than waiting for approval. For the first time ever, the Austrian-German army used elements of a new surprise-attack *Blitzkrieg* technique. (German officer Erwin Rommel made great strides in the fighting here, later becoming Hitler's "Desert Fox" in North Africa.)

The attack caught the Italian forces off-guard and quickly broke through three lines of defense. Within three days, the Italians were forced to retreat. The Austrians called their victory the "Miracle at Kobarid." But Italy felt differently. The Italians see the battle of Caporetto (the Italian name for Kobarid) as their Alamo. To this day, when an Italian finds himself in a mess, he might say, "At least it's not a Caporetto."

A year later, Italy came back—this time with the aid of British, French, and US forces—and easily retook this area. On November 4, 1918, Austria-Hungary conceded defeat. After more than a million casualties, the fighting at Soča was finally over.

feet into a beautiful pool. Local signs clock the hike at 30 minutes from the town center, but plan on closer to 45 minutes each way. The trailhead is at the Bovec end of Kobarid: As you approach the town from Bovec, turn right into the town, then take an immediate and sharp left to go back under the main road, passing the cheese factory and following signs for *Kamp Koren*. Wind down to cross the Napoleon Bridge over the Soča, then turn left and head up the hill (you'll pass Kamp Koren). You can park in the big pay lot across the street from the camp. Walk along the gravel path down into the ravine, passing views of a smaller waterfall. Go right at the fork, continue into the gorge, and take the high, narrow bridge over the stream (which has no railing—a little nerve-racking for those afraid of heights). Finally, follow the boardwalk as it curls around a cliff for great views of the falls. A different, longer trail follows the Soča River Valley, eventually looping up and around to Kozjak.

WWI Sights near Kobarid

For those fascinated by this region's WWI history, there's much to see beyond the excellent museum and mausoleum in Kobarid. Several outdoor museums in the area let you get close to the places where the fighting actually occurred. Some are reachable by car, while others require a challenging mountain hike. Along the main road, you can see a stirring WWI cemetery behind the town church in Soča, or hike through scant fortifications at the Ravelnik Outdoor Museum just outside Bovec (both described on the self-guided driving tour, earlier). For those interested in seeing more, consider these options.

▲Walk of Peace (Pot Miru)

This walking route—which extends more than 140 miles from these mountains all the way to the Adriatic—is designed to link museums, cemeteries, churches, and other sites related to the warfare of the Soča Front. But it also celebrates and introduces visitors to all aspects of the region's culture and natural sites. To learn more about shorter hikes along its route, and the many outdoor museums and cemeteries in this region, visit the **Walk of Peace Foundation Visitors Center,** across the street from the Kobarid Museum. They hand out good, free maps and booklets, and sell a fine guidebook to WWI sights in the area. Tour their engaging, state-of-the-art exhibition, with additional temporary exhibits upstairs (free, July-Aug Mon-Fri 9:00-13:00 & 14:00-19:00, Sat-Sun 10:00-13:00 & 14:00-19:00, shorter hours spring and fall, and closed Nov-March—but you can try knocking on weekdays, Gregorčičeva 8, tel. 05/389-0167, www.potmiru.si). They can arrange **guides** to join you for part of the walk (€25/hour). Contact them at least one day ahead to check their schedule and/or arrange a tour.

Kobarid Historical Walk

This shorter walk to WWI sights around Kobarid is well explained by the free brochure available at the TI, museum, and information center (3 miles, mostly uphill, allow 3-5 hours; or you can just do a shorter, easier stretch along the river, 1-2 hours).

▲Kolovrat Outdoor Museum

For drivers (especially those headed to points south) who want to get a vivid, high-altitude look at what life was like along the Soča Front, this is perhaps the area's most worthwhile outdoor museum. It's located high on a ridge—straddling Slovenia and Italy—about 30 minutes from Kobarid, a manageable detour on the way to the Karst, Goriška Brda, Venice, or Croatia.

Getting There: Leave Kobarid on the main road toward Tolmin. Just a mile out of town, in the village of Idrsko, turn right toward *Livek* and twist up, up, up the hillside. At the far end of the village of Livek, watch for brown *Kolovrat* signs to the left. Following this road, you'll drive along a mountain spine for about five miles, watching for the small parking area and information boards for Kolovrat. When you're ready to leave the museum, carry on along the same road, then turn left at the fork to wind back down into Tolmin.

Visiting the Museum: This area—an Italian-built mountaintop fortification—is free and always open. The gentle pasture sprawling away from the

parking area is scattered with half-ruined concrete bunkers; if you walk through this area and keep going, you'll be in Italy in five minutes. But the most interesting area is along the hilltop above, where trenches carved into the rock have been excavated and restored. You can clamber around inside a fortified labyrinth sculpted into the mountaintop and reinforced with wood and sandbags. Peer out through strategically placed viewpoint slits, and imagine the impossibly difficult life of the soldiers stationed along the Soča Front.

Sleeping in Kobarid

My first listing is right on the main square. The other two hide on side streets about a block off the main road through town, between the museum and the main square (about a three-minute walk to either).

$$ Hotel Hvala is the only real hotel in town. Run by the Hvala family, its 32 contemporary rooms are faded but central; the cheaper "mansard" rooms are on the top floor. The mural on the wall in the elevator shaft tells the story of the Soča Valley as you go up toward the top floor (elevator, Trg Svobode 1, tel. 05/389-9300, www.hotelhvala.si, info@hotelhvala.si).

JULIAN ALPS

$ **Hiša Sonca** ("House of the Sun"), in a cheery, yellow family home along the main road, has two comfortable rooms and one big apartment that sleeps up to eight. My favorite place in Kobarid is well-run by Natalija, who offers a common kitchen and a shared hot tub. She also has another apartment a block closer to the town center (breakfast extra, cash only, 2 blocks from main square at Mučeniška 1, mobile 031-664-253, www.apartmakobarid.com, hisasonca@gmail.com).

$ **Apartmaji Pri Nas** ("Our Place") has six stylish apartments in a pleasant suburban home along the main road that skirts the town center of Kobarid (no breakfast but kitchens in each unit, air-con, Goriška cesta 5, mobile 031-377-585, www.pri-nas.si, prinas.kobarid@gmail.com).

In the Mountains High Above Kobarid: One of my favorite Soča Valley accommodations hides in a tiny village a twisty 10-minute drive up from Kobarid's main square. $ **Tourist Farm Kranjc** is a remote but scenic, well-run working sheep farm with eight comfortable rooms, organic meals prepared with homegrown produce, and a huge view terrace. While this farm—which feels traditional, but has modern style—is a bit less convenient to the sights, it's ideal if you want to huddle high in the mountains (dinner extra, air-con, also ask about their "glamping" cots with private bathroom, Koseč 7, tel. 05/384-8562, mobile 041-946-088, www.turizem-kranjc.si, info@turizem-kranjc.si, Urška and the Kranjc family). It's in the village of Koseč. From Kobarid, leave town by crossing the Napoleon Bridge (toward Kamp Koren and Great Kozjak Waterfall). Just after that bridge, turn left and twist up to Drežnica, where you'll turn right to reach Koseč; once in the village, look for signs directing you up the steep road to the left.

Eating in and near Kobarid

While Kobarid has a handful of good eateries, foodies make a pilgrimage for Hiša Franko—just outside town.

$$ **Hiša Polonka** ("Blue House"), a side project of the people who run the esteemed Hiša Franko (see next page), is my favorite lunch stop in town. Conveniently located on the road between Kobarid's main square and the museum, this is the place for well-prepared traditional, local fare (including microbrews) at reasonable prices. The vibe is pubby and casual; the service is relaxed (Thu-Tue 13:00-23:00, Wed open for drinks only 16:00-23:00, Gregorčičeva 1, tel. 05/995-8194).

$$$ **Kotlar Restaurant,** on the main square, has a classy interior that sprawls around the prow of a faux sailboat. The emphasis is on seafood and locally sourced meats (Thu-Mon 12:00-15:00 &

18:00-22:00, closed Tue-Wed, Trg Svobode 11, tel. 05/389-1110, www.kotlar.si).

$ Picerija Fedrig serves up good pizzas (Mon 18:00-21:30, Wed-Sun 12:00-21:30, closed Tue, shorter hours off-season, a block south of the main square at Volaričeva 11, tel. 05/389-0115).

Near Kobarid: $$$$ Hiša Franko, less than a five-minute drive outside of Kobarid, is becoming internationally known as one of Slovenia's finest restaurants. Chef Ana Roš (profiled on *Chef's Table* and named World's Best Female Chef 2017) has a deep respect for locally sourced ingredients and Slovenian alpine culinary tradition. But she's also experimental, injecting international touches into her cooking. The place is welcoming and unpretentious—you'll want to book far ahead here for modern Slovenian cuisine at its very best (fixed-price meals only, Tue-Fri 19:00-23:00, Sat-Sun 12:00-15:00 & 19:00-23:00, closed Mon, closed Tue off-season, closed entirely Jan-March). They also rent 13 rooms—choose between **$$$** modern rooms in the main building or **$$** simpler ones in the adjacent yellow house (Staro Selo 1, tel. 05/389-4120, www.hisafranko.com, info@hisafranko.com). To reach Hiša Franko, leave Kobarid following signs for *Italija* and *Robič,* and look for the restaurant's sign on the right.

Kobarid Connections

From Kobarid by Bus to: Bovec (6/day Mon-Fri, 2-3/day Sat-Sun, 30 minutes), **Ljubljana** (1/day in July-Aug over Vršič Pass, 5 hours; otherwise faster but less scenic via Idrija, 3.5 hours—or, longer but more scenically, with a change in Kranjska Gora).

AUSTRIA

Österreich

VIENNA

Wien

Vienna is the capital of Austria, the cradle of classical music, the home of the rich Habsburg heritage, and one of the world's most livable cities. The city center is skyscraper-free, pedestrian-friendly, dotted with quiet parks, and traversed by electric trams. Many buildings still reflect 18th- and 19th-century elegance, when the city was at the forefront of the arts and sciences. Compared with most modern European urban centers, the pace of life is slow.

For much of its 2,500-year history, Vienna (*Wien* in German—pronounced "veen") was on the frontier of civilized Europe. Located on the south bank of the Danube, it was threatened by Germanic barbarians (in Roman times), marauding Magyars (today's Hungarians, 10th century), Mongol hordes (13th century), Ottoman Turks (the sieges of 1529 and 1683), and encroachment by the Soviet Union after World War II.

The Habsburg dynasty ruled their great empire from Vienna, setting the stage for its position as an enduring cultural capital. Among the Habsburgs, Holy Roman Empress Maria Theresa in the late 1700s was famous for having 16 children and cleverly marrying many of them into royal families around Europe to expand the family's reach.

Vienna reached its peak in the 19th century, when it was on par with London and Paris in size and importance. Emerging as a cultural powerhouse, it was home to groundbreaking composers (Beethoven, Mozart,

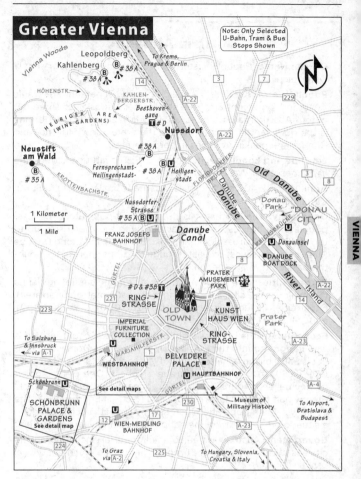

VIENNA

Brahms, Strauss), scientists (Doppler, Boltzmann), philosophers (Freud, Husserl, Schlick, Gödel, Steiner), architects (Wagner, Loos), and painters (Klimt, Schiele, Kokoschka). By the turn of the 20th century, Vienna was one of the world's most populous cities and sat on the cusp between stuffy Old World monarchism and subversive modern trends.

After the turmoil of two world wars and the loss of Austria's empire, Vienna has settled down into a somewhat sleepy, pleasant place where culture is still king. Classical music is everywhere. People nurse a pastry and coffee over the daily paper at small cafés. It's a city of world-class museums, big and small. Anyone with an interest in painting, music, architecture, beautiful objects, or Sacher torte with whipped cream will feel right at home.

From a practical standpoint, Vienna serves as a prime gateway

VIENNA

Austria Almanac

Official Name: Republik Österreich ("Eastern Realm"), or simply Österreich.

Population: Of Austria's 8.7 million people, 91 percent are ethnic Austrians; 4 percent are from the former Yugoslavia. Three out of four Austrians are Catholic; about one in 20 is Muslim. German is the dominant language (though there are a few Slovene- and Hungarian-speaking villages in border areas).

Latitude and Longitude: 47°N and 13°E. The latitude is the same as Minnesota or Washington state.

Area: With 32,400 square miles, Austria is similar in size to South Carolina.

Geography: The northeast is flat and well-populated; the less-populated southwest is mountainous, with the Alps rising up to the 12,450-foot Grossglockner peak. The 1,770-mile-long Danube River meanders west-to-east through the upper part of the country, passing through Vienna.

Biggest Cities: One in five Austrians lives in the capital of Vienna (1.8 million in the city; 2.6 million in the greater metropolitan area). Other cities include Graz (population 280,000), Linz (203,000), and Salzburg (152,000).

Economy: Austria borders eight other European countries and is well-integrated into the EU economy. The Gross Domestic Product is $390 billion (similar to that of Massachusetts). Its per-capita GDP of $44,700 is among Europe's highest. One of its biggest moneymakers is tourism. Austria produces wood, paper products (nearly half the land is forested)...and Red Bull Energy Drink. The country's aging population increasingly collects social security—a situation that will strain the national budget in years to come.

Government: Austria has been officially neutral since 1955, and its citizens take a dim view of European unity. Like much of Europe,

city. Its central location is convenient to most major Eastern European destinations. Actually farther east than Prague, Ljubljana, and Zagreb, and just upstream on the Danube from Budapest and Bratislava, Vienna is an ideal launchpad for a journey into the East.

PLANNING YOUR TIME

For a big city, Vienna is pleasant and laid-back. Packed with sights, it's worth two days and two nights on even the speediest trip.

If you're visiting Vienna as part of a longer European trip, you could sleep on the train on your way in and out—Berlin, Kraków, Venice, Rome, and Frankfurt are each a handy night-train journey away.

Palace Choices: The Hofburg and Schönbrunn are both

Austria has seen right-leaning parties make substantial gains in recent elections—particularly the nationalist Freedom Party. The federal president, Alexander Van der Bellen, is a member of the Green Party; the current chancellor, Sebastian Kurz of the center-right Austrian People's Party, has formed a coalition with the Freedom Party.

Flag: Three horizontal bands of red, white, and red.

Cuisine: Austrian treats include Wiener schnitzel (breaded veal cutlet), *Knödel* (dumplings), *Apfelstrudel* (apple strudel), *Kaiserschmarrn* (fluffy pieces of caramelized crêpe served with fruit or nuts), and fancy desserts like the Sacher torte, Vienna's famous chocolate cake.

Language: Austria's official language is German. It's customary to greet people in the breakfast room and those you pass on the streets or meet in shops. The Austrian version of "Hi" is a cheerful *"Grüss Gott."* You'll get the correct pronunciation after the first volley—listen and copy. For German survival phrases, see the charts at the end of this chapter.

Gemütlichkeit: The Austrians are not Germans—and they cherish their distinct cultural and historical traditions. Austria is mellow and relaxed compared to Deutschland. *Gemütlichkeit* is the word most often used to describe this special Austrian cozy-and-easy approach to life. On the other hand, Austria feels relatively stiff and formal compared to most of Eastern Europe (except maybe Hungary).

The Average Austrian: A typical Austrian is 43 years old, has 1.4 children, and will live to be 81. He or she inhabits a 900-square-foot home, and spends leisure time with a circle of a few close friends. Chances are good that someone in that circle is a smoker—Austrians are among the highest consumers of cigarettes in Europe.

world-class palaces, but seeing both is redundant if your time or money is limited. If you're rushed and can fit in only one palace, make it the Hofburg. It comes with the popular Sisi Museum, is adjacent to perhaps Europe's best collection of crown jewels, and is right in the town center, making for an easy visit. With more time, a visit to Schönbrunn—set outside town amid a grand and regal garden—is also a great experience.

Vienna in One to Four Days

Below is a suggested itinerary for how to spend your daytime sightseeing hours. The best options for **evenings** are taking in a concert, opera, or other musical event; enjoying a leisurely dinner (and people-watching) in the stately old town; heading out to the

Heuriger wine pubs in the foothills of the Vienna Woods; or touring the Haus der Musik interactive music museum (open nightly until 22:00). Plan your evenings based on the schedule of musical events. If you've downloaded my audio tours (see "Rick Steves Audio Europe" sidebar on page 12), the Vienna City Walk works wonderfully in the evening. Whenever you need a break, linger in a classic Viennese café.

Day 1

9:00   Circle the Ringstrasse by tram (following my self-guided tram tour).

10:30   Drop by the TI for planning and ticket needs.

11:00   Tour the Vienna State Opera (schedule varies, confirm at TI).

14:00   Follow my Vienna City Walk, including visits to the Kaisergruft and St. Stephen's Cathedral (nave closes at 16:30, or 17:30 July-Aug).

18:00   Dinner and romantic stroll in the old center.

Day 2

9:00   Browse the colorful Naschmarkt.

11:00   Tour the Kunsthistorisches Museum.

14:00   Tour the Hofburg Palace Imperial Apartments and Treasury.

Day 3

8:00   Tour Schönbrunn Palace to enjoy the imperial apartments and grounds (reserve in advance).

14:00   Visit Belvedere Palace, with its fine Viennese art and great city views.

Day 4

10:00   Enjoy (depending on your interest) the engaging Karlsplatz sights (Karlskirche, the Secession) or the Natural History Museum.

14:00   Do some shopping along Mariahilfer Strasse, or rent a bike and head out to the modern Donau City "downtown" sector, Danube Island (for fun people-watching), and Prater Park (with its amusement park).

Orientation to Vienna

Vienna sits between the Vienna Woods (Wienerwald) and the Danube River (Donau). To the southeast is industrial sprawl. The Alps, which arc across Europe from Marseille, end at Vienna's wooded hills, providing a popular playground for walking and sipping new wine. This greenery's momentum carries on into the city. More than half of Vienna is parkland, filled with ponds, gardens, trees, and statue-maker memories of Austria's glory days.

Think of the city map as a target with concentric circles: The bull's-eye is St. Stephen's Cathedral, the towering spired church south of the Danube. Surrounding that is the old town, bound tightly by the circular road known as the Ringstrasse, marking what used to be the city wall. The Gürtel, a broader, later ring road, contains the rest of downtown. Outside the Gürtel lies the uninteresting sprawl of modern Vienna.

Much of Vienna's sightseeing—and most of my recommended restaurants—are located in the old town, inside the Ringstrasse. Walking across this circular area takes about 30 minutes. St. Stephen's Cathedral sits in the center, at the intersection of the two main (pedestrian-only) streets: Kärntner Strasse and the Graben.

Several sights sit along, or just beyond, the Ringstrasse: To the southwest are the Hofburg and related Habsburg sights, as well as the Kunsthistorisches Museum; to the south is a cluster of intriguing sights near Karlsplatz; to the southeast is Belvedere Palace. A branch of the Danube River borders the Ring to the north.

As a tourist, concern yourself only with this compact old center. When you do, sprawling Vienna becomes easily manageable.

TOURIST INFORMATION

Vienna's main TI is a block behind the Vienna State Opera at Albertinaplatz (daily 9:00-19:00, includes theater box office, tel. 01/211-140, www.vienna.info). It's a rare example of a TI in Europe that is really a service (possible because tourists pay for it with a hotel tax). There are also TIs at the airport (daily 7:00-22:00) and the train station (daily 9:00-19:00). You'll get the same price here for theater tickets as you would at the venues or from the goofy sales people on the street—the advantage here is that they have all the options, you can review them with a knowledgeable sales person, and you can study the various venues. They also sell discount train and intercity bus tickets.

Look for the monthly program of concerts (called *Wien-Programm*), the annual city guide (called *Vienna Journal*), and two good brochures: *Walks in Vienna* and *Architecture from Art Nouveau to the Present*. Ask about their program of guided walks (€16 each), and consider buying a Vienna Pass, which includes entry to many sights and lets you skip some lines (see "Sights in Vienna," later).

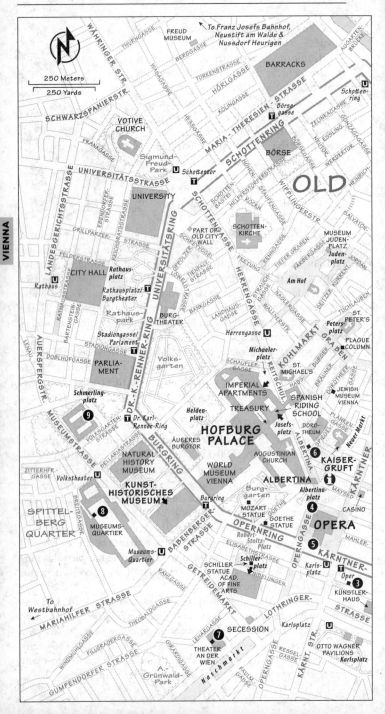

N

250 Meters
250 Yards

To Franz Josefs Bahnhof,
Neustift am Walde &
Nussdorf Heurigen

FREUD
MUSEUM

BARRACKS

WÄHRINGER STR.

THURNGASSE

BERGGASSE

TÜRKENSTRASSE

HÖRLGASSE

KOLINGASSE

MARIA-THERESIEN STRASSE

Börse-
gasse

Schotten-
ring

SCHWARZSPANIERSTR.

VOTIVE
CHURCH

FRANKGASSE

Sigmund-
Freud-
Park

SCHOTTENRING

BÖRSE

HÖHEN-
STAUFENGASSE

WIPFLINGERSTR.

OLD

UNIVERSITÄTSSTRASSE

Schottentor

SCHOTTENGASSE

SCHOTTEN-
BASTEI

HELFERSTORFERSTRASSE

STAUFENGASSE

SALVATOR-

HEINRICH-

UNIVERSITY

PART OF
OLD CITY
WALL

SCHOTTEN-
KIRCHE

MUSEUM
JUDEN-
PLATZ

Juden-
platz

EBENDORFER-
STRASSE

GRILLPARZER-

REICHSRATSTRASSE

FELDERSTRASSE

FREYUNG

RENNGASSE

TIEFER GRABEN

FARBERGASSE

JORDAN

CITY HALL

Rathaus-
platz

Rathausplatz/
Burgtheater

Am Hof

SEITZERGASSE

KURRENT.

Rathaus

Rathaus-
park

LÖWELSTRASSE

HERRENGASSE

NAGLERGASSE

TÜCHLAUBEN

ST.
PETER'S

LANDESGERICHTSSTRASSE

BARTENSTEIN-
GASSE

Burg-
theater

Herrengasse

Peters-
platz

PLAGUE
COLUMN

Stadiongasse/
Parlament

Volks-
garten

Michaeler-
platz

SCHAUFLER-
GASSE

ST.
MICHAEL'S

KOHLMARKT

GRABEN

DOBLHOFGASSE

PARLIA-
MENT

IMPERIAL
APARTMENTS

SPANISH
RIDING
SCHOOL

JEWISH
MUSEUM
VIENNA

AUERSPERGSTR.

Schmerling-
platz

9

Dr. Karl-
Renner-Ring

Helden-
platz

TREASURY

Josefs-
platz

DORO-
THEUM

Neuer Markt

ÄUSSERES
BURGTOR

HOFBURG
PALACE

6

KAISER-
GRUFT

MUSEUMSTRASSE

ZITTERHFR-
GASSE

NATURAL
HISTORY
MUSEUM

WORLD
MUSEUM
VIENNA

AUGUSTINIAN
CHURCH

ALBERTINA

Albertina-
platz

KÄRNTNER-

Volkstheater

KUNST-
HISTORISCHES
MUSEUM

Burg-
garten

4

CASINO

SPITTEL-
BERG
QUARTER

8

MUSEUMS-
QUARTIER

Burgring

MOZART
STATUE

GOETHE
STATUE

OPERNRING

OPERA

MAHLER-

Museums-
Quartier

BABENBERGER
STRASSE

Robert-
Stoltz-
Platz

5

KÄRNTNER-

BREITEGASSE

ELISABETHSTR.

Schiller-
platz

Karls-
platz

Oper

3

To
Westbahnhof

RAHLGASSE

SCHILLER
STATUE

ACAD.
OF FINE
ARTS

NIBELUNGEN.

KÜNSTLER-
HAUS

MARIAHILFER STRASSE

THEOBALDGASSE

GETREIDEMARKT

LOTHRINGER-

STRASSE

FILLGRADERGASSE

WINDMÜHLGASSE

LEHARGASSE

SECESSION

7

Karlsplatz

Karlsplatz

U

OTTO WAGNER
PAVILIONS

GUMPENDORFER STRASSE

GIRARDIGASSE

THEATER
AN DER
WIEN

Naschmarkt

PAULN.
GASSE

A.-
Grünwald-
Park

RESSEL-
GASSE

OPERNGASSE

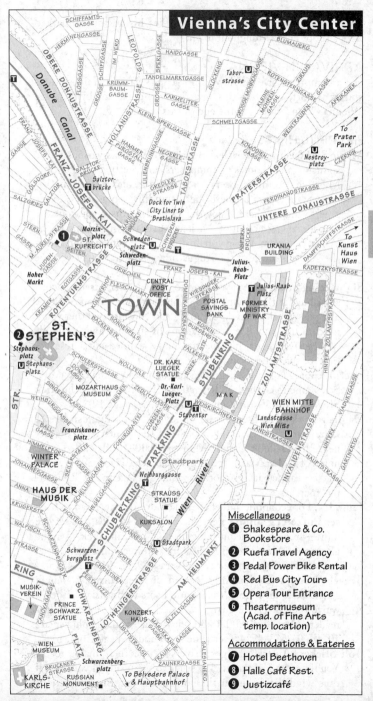

Vienna's City Center

VIENNA

Danube Canal

OBERE DONAUSTRASSE

FRANZ-JOSEFS-KAI

SCHIFFAMTS-GASSE
HERMINENGASSE
GROSSE SCHIFFGASSE
IM WERD
LEOPOLDS
HAIDGASSE
SPERLGASSE
BLUMAUERG.

To Prater Park

KRUMM-BAUM-GASSE
KARMELITER-GASSE
TANDELMARKTGASSE
GLOCKENG.
Tabor-strasse
ROTENSTERNGASSE
ZIRKUSG.
AFRIKANER-
CZERNIN

HOLLANDSTRASSE
HAMMER-PURGSTALL
LILIENBRUNNGASSE
NEGERLE-GASSE
TABORSTRASSE
SCHMELZGASSE
KOMÖDIEN-GASSE
Nestroy-platz

FRANZ-JOSEFS-KAI
GÖLSDORF-
SALZGRIES
SALZTOR-
Salztor-brücke
GREDLER-STRASSE
FERDINANDSTRASSE

Dock for Twin City Liner to Bratislava

UNTERE DONAUSTRASSE

STERN-GASSE
M.-AUREL-STRASSE
Morzin-platz
ST.-RUPRECHT'S
SEITEN-
Schweden-platz
Schweden-platz
URANIA BUILDING

To Kunst Haus Wien

Hoher Markt
UDEN-
ROTGASSE
ROTENTURMSTRASSE
KOLLNERHOF
FLEISCHMARKT
GRIECHEN-
FRANZ-JOSEFS-KAI
WIESINGER-STRASSE
Julius-Raab-Platz
Julius-Raab-Platz

CENTRAL POST OFFICE
POSTAL SAVINGS BANK
FORMER MINISTRY OF WAR

KRAMER-
KÄRNTNERHOF
SONNENFELS-
BÄCKERSTR.
DOMINIKANERBASTEI
BIBERSTR.
FALKESTR.

TOWN

ST. STEPHEN'S

Stephans-platz
Stephans-platz
DOM-
SCHULERSTRASSE
WOLLZEILE
DR. KARL LUEGER STATUE

STR.
SINGERSTRASSE
MOZARTHAUS MUSEUM
RIEMER-
ZEDLITZGASSE
Dr.-Karl-Lueger-Platz
WEISSKIRCHNERSTR.
STUBENRING
MAK

WEIHBURGGASSE
Franziskaner-platz
Stubentor
WIEN MITTE BAHNHOF
Landstrasse Wien Mitte

BALL-GASSE
COBLEN-GASSE
COBURGBASTEI
PARKRING

HIMMELPFORT-
WINTER PALACE
JOHANNESGASSE
SEILERSTÄTTE
SCHELLINGGASSE
LANDSTRASSER
INVALIDENSTRASSE

ANNA-
KRUGERSTR.
HAUS DER MUSIK
WALFISCH-
SCHWARZENBERGSTR.
FICHTEGASSE
HEGELGASSE
Stadtpark
Weihburggasse
STRAUSS STATUE
Wien River
Stadtpark

STRASSE
SCHUBERTRING
JOHANNESGASSE
KURSALON

Schwarzen-bergplatz
FICHTE-
CHRISTINEN-
PESTALOZZI-
AM HEUMARKT

RING
MUSIK-VEREIN
PRINCE SCHWARZ. STATUE
KONZERT-HAUS
LOTHRINGERSTRASSE
MARXER-
LISZTSTRASSE
ZAUNERGASSE

WIEN MUSEUM
BRUCKNER-STRASSE
SCHWARZENBERG PLATZ
Schwarzenberg-platz
RUSSIAN MONUMENT
OLZELTGASSE
TRAUNGASSE
SALESIANERG.

KARLS-KIRCHE
To Belvedere Palace & Hauptbahnhof

Miscellaneous
1 Shakespeare & Co. Bookstore
2 Ruefa Travel Agency
3 Pedal Power Bike Rental
4 Red Bus City Tours
5 Opera Tour Entrance
6 Theatermuseum (Acad. of Fine Arts temp. location)

Accommodations & Eateries
7 Hotel Beethoven
8 Halle Café Rest.
9 Justizcafé

The *Vienna from A to Z* booklet identifies historic spots marked with a set of flags throughout town.

ARRIVAL IN VIENNA
For a comprehensive rundown on Vienna's various train stations and its airport, as well as tips on arriving or departing by boat, see "Vienna Connections," at the end of this chapter.

HELPFUL HINTS
Music Sightseeing Priorities: Be wary of Vienna's various music sights. Many "homes of composers" are pretty disappointing. My advice to music lovers is to take in a concert, tour the Vienna State Opera or snare cheap standing-room tickets to see a performance there, enjoy the Haus der Musik, or scour the wonderful Collection of Ancient Musical Instruments in the World Museum Vienna. If in town on a Sunday, don't miss the glorious music at the Augustinian Church Mass (see page 887).

Sightseeing Strategies: If you plan to do a lot of sightseeing, consider buying the Vienna Pass or one of several combo-tickets. The pass is pricey, so do the math and consider whether you'll need to use public transportation. In summer and on good-weather weekends, it's smart to make a timed-entry reservation for the Schönbrunn Palace.

Useful App: ∩ For free self-guided audio tours (Vienna City Walk, St. Stephen's Cathedral, Ringstrasse Tram Tour), get the **Rick Steves Audio Europe** app (for details, see page 12).

English Bookstore: Stop by the woody and cool **Shakespeare & Co.,** in the historic and atmospheric Ruprechtsviertel district near the Danube Canal (Mon-Sat 9:00-21:00, closed Sun, north of Hoher Markt at Sterngasse 2, tel. 01/535-5053, www.shakespeare.co.at). For location, see the "Vienna's City Center" map.

Laundry: For economic and efficient laundry service, head to **Kaiser Putzerei Laundry** near the opera house. It's full-service only—drop off in the morning, pay per kilo, and pick up in the afternoon (Mon-Fri 7:30-18:00, next to recommended Hotel zur Wiener Staatsoper at Krugerstrasse 9, tel. 01/512-4356).

Travel Agency: Conveniently located on Stephansplatz, **Ruefa** sells tickets for flights, trains, and boats to Bratislava. They'll waive the €8 service charge for train and boat tickets for my readers (Mon-Fri 9:00-18:30, closed Sat-Sun, Stephansplatz 10, tel. 01/513-4524, Gertrude and Sandra speak English).

Toll Sticker: Austria charges drivers to use their major roads. You'll need a *Vignette* sticker stuck to the inside of your rental car's windshield (buy at the border crossing, big gas stations near borders, or a rental-car agency; www.asfinag.at). The cost is €9 for 10 days, or €26 for two months. Not having one earns you a stiff fine. Place it on your windshield exactly as shown on the back of the sticker, and keep the lower tear-off portion—it's your receipt.

GETTING AROUND VIENNA
By Public Transportation

Take full advantage of Vienna's efficient transit system, operated by **Wiener Linien,** which includes trams, buses, U-Bahn (subway), and S-Bahn (faster suburban) trains. It's fast, clean, and easy to navigate.

I generally stick to the tram to zip around the Ring (trams #1, #2, #71, #D, and #O) and take the U-Bahn to outlying sights, ho-

tels, and Vienna's train stations (see the "Vienna's Public Transportation" map). There are five color-coded U-Bahn lines: U-1 red, U-2 purple, U-3 orange, U-4 green, and U-6 brown. If you see a bus number that starts with *N* (such as #N38), it's a night bus, which operates after other public transit stops running. Transit info: tel. 01/790-9100, www.wienerlinien.at.

Tickets and Passes: Trams, buses, and the U-Bahn and S-Bahn all use the same tickets. Except on days spent entirely within the Ring, buying a single- or multiday pass is usually a good investment (and pays off if you take at least four trips). Many people find that once they have a pass, they end up using the system more.

Buy tickets from vending machines (easy and in English), ticket offices in stations, or at tobacco shops. Most trams have ticket machines (single tickets only), but some only take coins, so it's best to purchase tickets ahead of time. You cannot purchase tickets on buses.

You have lots of choices:
- Single tickets (€2.40, €2.60 on tram, good for one journey with necessary transfers)
- 24-hour transit pass (€8)
- 48-hour transit pass (€14.10)
- 72-hour transit pass (€17.10)
- 7-day transit pass (*Wochenkarte*, €17.10—the catch is that the pass runs from Monday to Monday, so you may get less than seven days of use)
- 8-day "Climate Ticket" (*Acht-Tage-Klimakarte*, €40.80, can be shared—for example, four people for two days each).

Vienna's Public Transportation

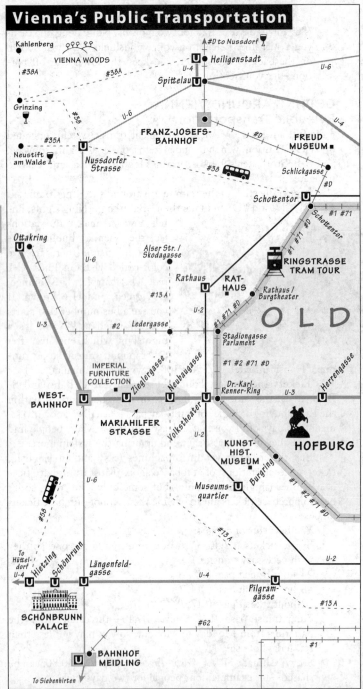

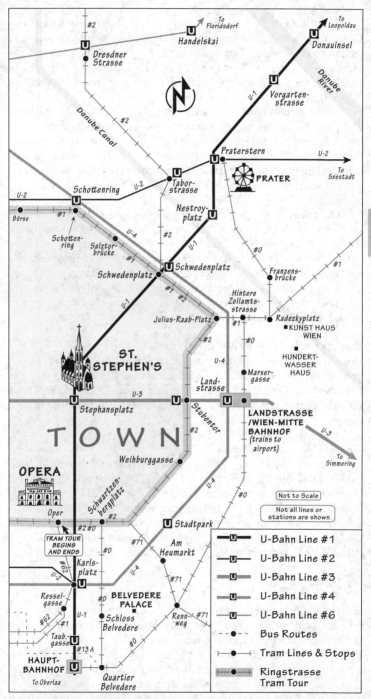

VIENNA

Transit Tips: To get your bearings on buses, trams, the U-Bahn, and the S-Bahn, know the end-of-the-line stop in the direction you're heading. For example, if you're in the city center at Stephansplatz and you want to take the U-Bahn to the main train station (Hauptbahnhof), you'd take U-1 going in the direction "Oberlaa."

Stamp your ticket at the barriers in U-Bahn and S-Bahn stations, and in the machines on trams and buses (stamp multiple-use passes only the first time you board). When purchasing tickets from vending machines, you can choose to have them validated before being printed. There are no formal checks, but you may see random stops; cheaters pay a stiff fine (about €100), plus the cost of the ticket.

On trams, stop announcements are voice-only and easy to miss—carry a map. Rookies miss stops because they fail to open the door. Push buttons, pull latches—do whatever it takes.

Before you exit a U-Bahn station, study the wall-mounted street map and choose the right exit to save lots of walking.

Cute little electric buses wind through the tangled old center (from Schottentor to Stubentor). Bus #1A is best for a joyride—hop on and see where it takes you.

By Taxi, Uber, or Private Driver

Vienna's comfortable, civilized, and easy-to-flag-down **taxis** start at €3.80 (higher rates at night). You'll pay about €10 to go from the opera house to the Hauptbahnhof. Pay only what's on the meter—the only legitimate surcharges are for calling a cab (€3) or for riding to the airport (€13).

If you like Uber, the ride service (and your app) works in Vienna just like it does at home.

Consider the luxury of having your own **car and driver.** Johann (a.k.a. John) Lichtl is a gentle, honest, English-speaking cabbie who can take up to four passengers in his car (€25/hour for 2 hours or more, €27 to or from airport, mobile 0676-670-6750). Consider a custom-tailored city driving tour (2 hours), a day trip to the Danube Valley (€160), or a visit to the Mauthausen Memorial with a little Danube sightseeing en route (€240).

By Bike

With more than 600 miles of bike lanes (and a powerful Green Party), Vienna is a great city on two wheels. Consider using a rental bike for the duration of your visit (Pedal Power is the best option, see listing later in this section); you'll go anywhere in town faster than a taxi can take you. Biking (carefully) through Vienna's many traffic-free spaces is no problem. Bikes ride the U-Bahn for free (but aren't allowed during weekday rush hours).

The bike path along the Ring is wonderfully entertaining—you'll enjoy the shady parklike ambience of the boulevard while rolling by many of the city's top sights.

Besides the Ring, your best sightseeing by bike is along the Danube Canal, across Danube Island, and out to the modern Donau City business district. These routes are easy to follow on the free tourist city map available from the TI (some routes can also be downloaded from the TI website). Red-colored pavement is the usual marking for bike lanes, but some bike lanes are marked just with white lines.

Borrowing a Free/Cheap Bike: Citybike Wien lets you borrow bikes from public racks all over town (toll tel. 0810-500-500, www.citybikewien.at).

The three-speed bikes are heavy and clunky (with solid tires to discourage thieves)—and come with a basket, built-in lock, and ads on the side—but they're perfect for a short, practical joyride in the center (such as around the Ringstrasse).

The system is easy to use. Bikes are locked into more than 100 stalls scattered through the city center. To borrow one, register your credit card at the terminal at any rack, create a password (save it for future rentals), then unlock a bike (you can also register online at www.citybikewien.at). First-time registration is €1 (only one bike per credit card—couples must use two different cards). Since the bikes are designed for short-term use, it costs more per hour the longer you keep it (first hour—free, second hour—€1, third hour—€2, €4/hour after that). When you're done, drop off your bike at any stall (being sure it's solidly locked back in the rack).

Renting a Higher-Quality Bike: To ride beyond the town center—or for a better set of wheels—rent from **Pedal Power** (€6/hour, €19/4 hours, €30/24 hours, RS%—10 percent with this book, daily May-Sept 9:00-18:00, shorter hours April and Oct, rental office near the opera house, a block beyond the Ring, at Bösendorferstrasse 5, see the "Vienna's City Center" map, earlier, tel. 01/729-7234, www.pedalpower.at). For €16 extra they'll deliver a bike to your hotel and pick it up when you're done. They also organize bike tours (described later).

VIENNA

Tours in Vienna

🎧 To sightsee on your own, download my free audio tours that illuminate some of Vienna's top sights and neighborhoods, including my Vienna City Walk and tours of St. Stephen's Cathedral and the Ringstrasse. The city walk and tram tour of the Ringstrasse start at the opera house and work nicely in the evening as well as during the day. The cathedral tour can be spliced into the city walk for efficiency. Once downloaded, you can listen to these offline.

ON FOOT

TI's "Walks in Vienna" Program

The TI's "Walks in Vienna" brochure lists more than a dozen walks given in English, all for €16. Their basic 1.5-hour "Vienna at First Glance" introductory walk is offered daily throughout the summer (leaves at 14:00 from in front of the main TI, just behind the opera house, in English and German, just show up, tel. 01/774-8901, www.wienguide.at).

Good Vienna Tours

This company (one of several offering such walks) offers a "pay what you like" 2.5-hour, English-only walk through the city center. While my Vienna City Walk is much more succinct, this can be an entertaining ramble with a local telling stories of the city. (Unlike other countries offering "free" walks, Austria requires that such guides be trained and licensed.) Just show up (pay what you think it's worth at the end—no coins, paper only, daily departures at 10:00 and 14:00, also at 17:00 July-Aug, maximum 35 people, meet at fountain at tip of Albertina across from TI, mobile 0664/554-4315, www.goodviennatours.eu).

ON WHEELS

Consider a tour by bus, bike, or even horse-and-buggy.

Red Bus Panorama City Tours

This one-hour, big-bus tour loops around the city, hitting the highlights with recorded narration. Along with the Ringstrasse, it also zips through Prater Park, over the Danube for a glimpse of the city's Danube Island playground, and into the Donau City skyscraper zone (€17, buses leave from Albertinaplatz, buy ticket from salesperson at the curb, opposite the TI behind the opera house; daily at 11:30, 14:30, and 17:30; tel. 01/512-4030, www.redbuscitytours.at).

Hop-On, Hop-Off Bus Tours

Two companies (Big Bus—red, Vienna Sightseeing—yellow) offer a complicated and busy program of hop-on, hop-off bus tours.

Both offer 24-, 48-, and 72-hour tickets, including a circular bus route (with departures every 10-15 minutes) and options to add river cruises and walking tours. Prices start at around €30 for 24 hours. You'll see booths at major stops (including the opera house for Vienna Sightseeing and Albertinaplatz for Big Bus) with flyers and staff that lay out all the options. While the ride can be scenic, gets you from sight to sight conveniently, and offers a stress-free overview, the recorded narration is almost worthless and cluttered with instructions, warnings, and cross-promotions. If you're adept at public transit, a good walker, and can read this guidebook, these hop-on, hop-off tours are not a good value.

Ringstrasse Tram Tour

One of Europe's great streets, the Ringstrasse is lined with many of the city's top sights. Take a tram ride around the ring with my free audio tour (see page 12), which gives you a fun orientation and a ridiculously quick glimpse of some major sights as you glide by. Neither tram #1 nor #2 makes the entire loop around the Ring, but you can see it all by transferring between them (at the Schwedenplatz stop). You can use a single transit ticket to cover the whole route, including the transfer (though you can't interrupt your trip, except to transfer). For more on riding Vienna's trams, see earlier, under "Getting Around Vienna."

The Vienna Ring Tram, a yellow, made-for-tourists streetcar, is an easier though pricier option, running clockwise along the entire Ringstrasse (€9 for 30-minute loop, 2/hour 10:00-17:30, recorded narration, www.wienerlinien.at). The 25-minute tour starts every half-hour at Schwedenplatz. At each stop, you'll see a sign for this tram tour (look for *VRT Ring-Rund Sightseeing*). The schedule notes the next departure time.

Pedal Power

Tours cover the central district in three hours and go twice daily from May to September (€36/tour includes bike, €20 extra to keep bike for the day, RS%—10 percent discount with this book, English tours depart at 10:00 just beyond the Ring near the opera house at Bösendorferstrasse 5, tel. 01/729-7234, www.pedalpower. at). They also rent bikes (see "Getting Around Vienna," earlier).

Horse-and-Buggy Tour

These traditional 19th-century horse-and-buggies, called *Fiaker*, take rich romantics on clip-clop tours lasting 20

Vienna at a Glance

▲▲▲Hofburg Imperial Apartments Lavish main residence of the Habsburgs. **Hours:** Daily 9:00-17:30, July-Aug until 18:00. See page 878.

▲▲▲Hofburg Treasury The Habsburgs' collection of jewels, crowns, and other valuables—the best on the Continent. **Hours:** Wed-Mon 9:00-17:30, closed Tue. See page 883.

▲▲▲St. Stephen's Cathedral Enormous, historic Gothic cathedral in the center of Vienna. **Hours:** Foyer and north aisle—daily 6:00-22:00; main nave—Mon-Sat 9:00-11:30 & 13:00-16:30, Sun 13:00-16:30, July-Aug until 17:30. See page 892.

▲▲▲Vienna State Opera Dazzling, world-famous opera house. **Hours:** By guided tour only, July-Aug generally Mon-Sat at top of hour 10:00-15:00; fewer tours Sept-June and Sun. See page 895.

▲▲▲Kunsthistorisches Museum World-class exhibit of the Habsburgs' art collection, including works by Raphael, Titian, Caravaggio, Rembrandt, and Bruegel. **Hours:** Daily 10:00-18:00, Thu until 21:00, closed Mon Sept-May. See page 899.

▲▲▲Schönbrunn Palace Spectacular summer residence of the Habsburgs, rivaling the grandeur of Versailles. **Hours:** Daily 8:00-17:30, July-Aug until 18:30, Nov-March until 17:00. See page 911.

▲▲World Museum Vienna Four museums in one: Uncrowded collection of armor, musical instruments, ancient Greek statues, and ethnographic treasures in the elegant halls of a Habsburg palace. **Hours:** Thu-Tue 10:00-18:00, Fri until 21:00, closed Wed. See page 885.

▲▲Albertina Museum Habsburg residence with state apartments, world-class collection of graphic arts and modernist classics, and first-rate special exhibits. **Hours:** Daily 10:00-18:00, Wed and Fri until 21:00. See page 888.

▲▲Kaisergruft Crypt for the Habsburg royalty. **Hours:** Daily 10:00-18:00. See page 889.

▲▲Haus der Musik Modern museum with interactive exhibits on Vienna's favorite pastime. **Hours:** Daily 10:00-22:00. See page 896.

▲▲Natural History Museum Big, beautiful catalog of the natural world, featuring the ancient *Venus of Willendorf*. **Hours:** Thu-Mon 9:00-18:30, Wed until 21:00, closed Tue. See page 903.

▲▲**Belvedere Palace** Elegant palace of Prince Eugene of Savoy, with a collection of 19th- and 20th-century Austrian art (including Klimt). **Hours:** Daily 10:00-18:00, Fri until 21:00. See page 907.

▲**Spanish Riding School** Prancing white Lipizzaner stallions. **Hours:** Performances nearly year-round (except Jan and mid-June–mid-Aug), usually Sat-Sun at 11:00, plus training sessions generally Tue-Fri 10:00-12:00 (except July–mid-Aug). See page 886.

▲**St. Michael's Church Crypt** Final resting place of about 100 wealthy 18th-century Viennese. **Hours:** By tour Mon-Sat at 11:00 and 13:00, Nov-Easter Thu-Sat only, no tours Sun. See page 891.

▲**St. Peter's Church** Beautiful Baroque church in the old center. **Hours:** Mon-Fri 7:00-20:00, Sat-Sun 9:00-21:00. See page 897.

▲**Karlskirche** Baroque church offering the unique chance to ride an elevator up into the dome. **Hours:** Mon-Sat 9:00-18:00, Sun 12:00-19:00. See page 904.

▲**Academy of Fine Arts Painting Gallery** Small but exciting collection by 15th- to 18th-century masters, temporarily housed at the Theatermuseum. **Hours:** Wed-Mon 10:00-18:00, closed Tue. See page 904.

▲**The Secession** Art Nouveau exterior and Klimt paintings in situ. **Hours:** Tue-Sun 10:00-18:00, closed Mon. See page 905.

▲**Naschmarkt** Sprawling, lively outdoor market. **Hours:** Mon-Fri 6:00-19:30, Sat until 18:00, closed Sun, closes earlier in winter. See page 905.

▲**Museum of Military History** Huge collection of artifacts tracing the military history of the Habsburg Empire. **Hours:** Daily 9:00-17:00. See page 909.

▲**Kunst Haus Wien Museum** Modern art museum dedicated to zany local artist Hundertwasser. **Hours:** Daily 10:00-18:00. See page 909.

▲**Imperial Furniture Collection** Eclectic collection of Habsburg furniture. **Hours:** Tue-Sun 10:00-18:00, closed Mon. See page 911.

VIENNA

minutes (Old Town—€55), 40 minutes (Old Town and the Ring—€80), or one hour (all the above, but more thorough—€110). Before the advent of cars, one-horse versions of these served as Vienna's taxis. You can share the ride and cost with up to four people (some may allow five). Because it's a kind of guided tour, talk to a few drivers before choosing a carriage, and pick someone who's fun and speaks English (tel. 01/401-060).

LOCAL GUIDES

Vienna becomes particularly vivid and meaningful with the help of a private guide. I've enjoyed working with these guides; any of them can set you up with another good guide if they are already booked.

Quality Conventional Guides: Lisa Zeiler is a good story-teller with years of guiding experience (€160/2-3 hours, mobile 0699-1203-7550, lisa.zeiler@gmx.at). **Adrienn Bartek-Rhomberg** offers themed walks in the city as well as Schönbrunn Palace tours (€160/3 hours, €300/full day on foot, €280 "Panorama City Tour"—a 4-hour minibus and walking tour for up to six people, mobile 0650-826-6965, www.experience-vienna.at, office@experience-vienna.at).

Philosopher Guides: Wolfgang Höfler, a generalist with a knack for having psychoanalytical fun with history, enjoys the big changes of the 19th and 20th centuries. He'll take you around on foot or by bike (€160/2 hours, €50 for each additional hour, bike tours—€160/3 hours, mobile 0676-304-4940, www.vienna-aktivtours.com, office@vienna-aktivtours.com). **Gerhard Strassgschwandtner,** who runs the Third Man Museum (see page 921), is passionate about history in all its marvelous complexity (€160/2 hours, mobile 0676-475-7818, www.special-vienna.com, gerhard@special-vienna.com).

Vienna City Walk

This self-guided walk connects the top three sights in Vienna's old center: the Vienna State Opera, St. Stephen's Cathedral, and Hofburg Palace. These and many of the other sights you'll see along this walk are covered in more detail later in this chapter (see "Sights in Vienna," later).

Allow one hour for the walk alone, and more time if you plan to stop at any major sights along the way. This walk works just as well in the evening as it does during the day, as long as you don't plan on touring some of the sights you'll pass.

Tours: ∩ Download my free Vienna City Walk audio tour. For efficiency, splice my St. Stephen's Cathedral audio tour into this walk.

• *Begin at the square outside Vienna's landmark opera house, home of the*

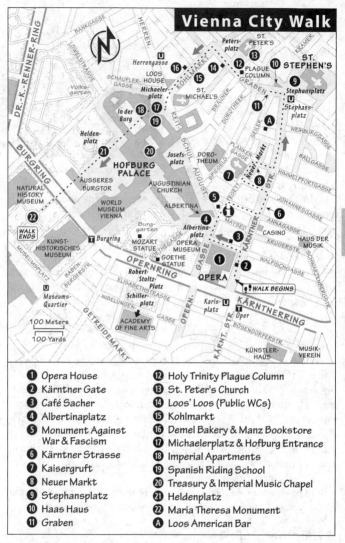

Vienna City Walk

1. Opera House
2. Kärntner Gate
3. Café Sacher
4. Albertinaplatz
5. Monument Against War & Fascism
6. Kärntner Strasse
7. Kaisergruft
8. Neuer Markt
9. Stephansplatz
10. Haas Haus
11. Graben
12. Holy Trinity Plague Column
13. St. Peter's Church
14. Loos' Loos (Public WCs)
15. Kohlmarkt
16. Demel Bakery & Manz Bookstore
17. Michaelerplatz & Hofburg Entrance
18. Imperial Apartments
19. Spanish Riding School
20. Treasury & Imperial Music Chapel
21. Heldenplatz
22. Maria Theresa Monument
A. Loos American Bar

Vienna State Opera. (The entrance faces the Ringstrasse; we're starting at the busy pedestrian square that's to the right of the entrance as you're facing it.)

❶ Opera House

If Vienna is the world capital of classical music, this building is its throne room, one of the planet's premier houses of music. It's typical of Vienna's 19th-century buildings in that it features a revival style—Neo-Renaissance—with arched windows, half-columns, and the sloping, copper mansard roof typical of French Renaissance *châteaux*.

Since the structure was built in 1869, almost all of the opera world's luminaries have passed through here. Its former musical directors include Gustav Mahler, Herbert von Karajan, and Richard Strauss. Luciano

Pavarotti, Maria Callas, Placido Domingo, and many other greats have sung from its stage.

In the pavement along the side of the opera house (and all along Kärntner Strasse, the bustling shopping street we'll visit shortly), you'll find star plaques forming a Hollywood-style walk of fame. These represent the stars of classical music—famous composers, singers, musicians, and conductors.

Looking up at the opera, notice the giant outdoor screen onto which some live performances are projected (as noted in the posted schedules and on the screen itself).

If you're a fan, take a guided tour of the opera. Or consider springing for an evening performance (standing-room tickets are surprisingly cheap; see "Entertainment in Vienna," later). Regular opera tickets are sold at various points near here: The closest ticket office is the small one just below the screen, while the main one is on the other side of the building, across the street on Operngasse. For information about other entertainment options during your visit, check in at the Wien Ticket kiosk in the booth on this square.

The opera house marks a busy intersection in Vienna, where Kärntner Strasse meets the Ring. The Karlsplatz U-Bahn station in front of the opera is an underground shopping mall with fast food, newsstands, and lots of pickpockets.

• *With your back to the Ringstrasse and the opera house on your left, face the busy pedestrian boulevard that leads into the center of town.*

❼ Kärntner Gate

Even though the center of town sits on an irregular medieval street plan, you'll notice the parallel rows of more modern, uniform buildings in front of you. These were built where the city wall once stood. The opera's lower stage is where the old moat used to be— outside the walls. This was a main gate, through which a road led to the Kärnten (Carinthia) region of southern Austria.

Notice the pedestrian signals and how they feature both gay and straight couples. Vienna's Green Party is part of the city's current ruling coalition and they like to remind the world that, while Austria's national government is more conservative (reflecting the fears and concerns of rural and small-town voters), urban Vienna celebrates diversity.

• *Walk behind the opera and across the street toward the dark-red awning to find the famous...*

❸ Café Sacher

This is the home of the world's classiest chocolate cake, the Sacher torte: two layers of cake separated by apricot jam and covered in dark-chocolate icing, usually served with whipped cream. It was

invented in a fit of improvisation in 1832 by Franz Sacher, dessert chef to Prince Metternich (the mastermind diplomat who redrew the map of post-Napoleonic Europe). The cake became world famous when the inventor's son served it next door at his hotel (you may have noticed the fancy doormen). Pop in for a peek at 19th-century elegance. Many locals complain that the cakes here have gone downhill, and many tourists are surprised by how dry they are—you really need that dollop of *Schlagobers*. Still, coffee and a slice of cake here can be €8 well invested

for the history alone (daily 8:00-24:00). While the café itself is grotesquely touristy, the adjacent Sacher Stube has ambience and natives to spare (same prices, daily 10:00-24:00). For maximum elegance, sit inside.

• *Continue past Hotel Sacher. At the end of the street is a small, triangular, cobbled square adorned with memorial sculptures.*

❹ Albertinaplatz

Overlooking the square, the tan-and-white Neoclassical building marks the tip of the Hofburg Palace—the sprawling complex of buildings that was long the seat of Habsburg power (we'll end this

walk at the palace's center). The balustraded terrace up top was originally part of Vienna's defensive rampart. Later, it was the balcony of Empress Maria Theresa's daughter Maria Christina, who lived at this end of the palace. Today, her home houses

the **Albertina Museum,** topped by a sleek, controversial titanium canopy (called the "diving board" by critics). The museum's plush,

19th-century state rooms are the only Neoclassical (post-Rococo) palace rooms anywhere in the Habsburg realm.

High above (just left of the "diving board"), a statue of Archduke Albrecht looks down on the city. A symbol of Habsburg oppression, he brutally suppressed popular uprisings in Vienna and Italy in the mid-1800s.

At street level is a grand fountain of Danubius, the Danube River God, flanked by six little Gods. Each represents a major tributary that feeds the Danube as it flows through Austria.

The hotdog stand to the left of Danubius (with the bunny on the rooftop, a reminder that the famous Albrecht Dürer watercolor *Hare* is in the adjacent Albertina) is known for its quality local sausages. This is the operagoers' hangout...they gather here in their fine ballgowns and tuxedos enjoying some of the best of Vienna's beloved wurst.

Albertinaplatz itself is filled with sculptures that make up the powerful, thought-provoking ❺ **Monument Against War and Fascism,** which commemorates the dark years when Austria came under Nazi rule (1938-1945).

The memorial has four parts. The split white monument, *The Gates of Violence,* remembers victims of all wars and violence. Standing directly in front of it, you're at the gates of a concentration camp. Then, as you explore the statues, you step into a montage of wartime images: clubs and WWI gas masks, a dying woman birthing a future soldier, victims of cruel medical experimentation, and chained slave laborers sitting on a pedestal of granite cut from the infamous quarry at Mauthausen concentration camp (located not far from Vienna). The hunched-over figure on the ground behind is a Jew forced to scrub anti-Nazi graffiti off a street with a brush. Of Vienna's 200,000 Jews, more than 65,000 died in Nazi concentration camps. The sculpture with its head buried in the stone is Orpheus entering the underworld, meant to remind Austrians (and the rest of us) of the victims of Nazism...and the consequences of not keeping our governments on track. Behind that, the 1945 declaration that established Austria's second republic—and enshrined human rights—is cut into the stone.

Viewing this monument gains even more emotional impact when you realize what happened on this spot: During a WWII bombing attack, several hundred people were buried alive when the cellar they were using as shelter was demolished.

Austria was led into World War II by Germany, which annexed the country in 1938 with disturbingly little resistance, saying Austrians were wannabe Germans anyway. But Austrians are not Germans (this makes for an interesting topic of conversation with Austrians you may meet). They're quick to proudly tell you that Austria was founded in the 10th century, whereas Germany wasn't born until 1870. For seven years just before and during World War II (1938-1945), there was no Austria. In 1955, after 10 years of joint occupation by the victorious Allies, Austria regained total independence on the condition that it would be forever neutral (and never join NATO or the Warsaw Pact). To this day, Austria is outside of NATO (and Germany).

Behind the monument is **Café Tirolerhof,** a classic Viennese café. Refreshingly air-conditioned, it's full of things that time has passed by: chandeliers, marble tables, upholstered booths, waiters in tuxes, and newspapers. For more on Vienna's cafés, see page 940.

This square is where many of the city's walking tours and bus tours start. You may see Red Bus City Tour buses, big private tour buses, and color-coded umbrellas advertising "free" walking tours. The Vienna TI (with a handy ticket desk for concerts) also overlooks the square.

• *From the café, turn right on Führichsgasse. Walk one block until you hit...*

❻ Kärntner Strasse

This grand, traffic-free street is the people-watching delight of this in-love-with-life city. Today's Kärntner Strasse (KAYRNT-ner SHTRAH-seh) is mostly a crass commercial pedestrian mall—its famed elegant shops long gone, and today full of shoppers and street musicians. But locals know it's the same road Crusaders marched down as they headed off from St. Stephen's Cathedral for the Holy Land in the 12th century.

Where Führichsgasse meets Kärntner Strasse, note the old Grundemann Esterházy Palace—now a **Casino** (across the street and to your right, at #41)—once venerable, now tacky, it exemplifies the worst of the street's evolution. Turn left to head up Kärntner Strasse, going away from the opera house. As you walk along, be sure to look up, above the modern storefronts, for glimpses of the street's former glory.

Local shops can't compete with the international chains, considering the high rent here. But one venerable shop that has survived is near the end of the block, on the left at #26: **J & L Lobmeyr Crystal** ("Founded in 1823") still has its impressive brown storefront with gold trim, statues, and the Habsburg double eagle. In the market for some $400 napkin rings? Lobmeyr's your place.

Inside, breathe in the classic Old World ambience as you climb up to the glass museum (free entry, closed Sun).

• *At the end of the block, turn left on Marco d'Aviano Gasse (passing the fragrant flower stall) to make a short detour to the square called Neuer Markt. Straight ahead is an orange-ish church with a triangular roof and cross, the Capuchin Church. In its basement is the...*

❼ Kaisergruft

Under the church sits the Imperial Crypt, filled with what's left of Austria's emperors, empresses, and other Habsburg royalty. For centuries, Vienna was the heart of a vast empire ruled by the Habsburg family, and here is where they lie buried in their fancy pewter coffins. You'll find all the Habsburg greats, including Maria Theresa, her son Josef II (Mozart's patron), Franz Josef, and Empress Sisi. Before moving on, consider paying your respects here.

• *Stretching north from the Kaisergruft is the square called...*

❽ Neuer Markt

A block farther down, in the center of Neuer Markt, the **four rivers fountain** shows Lady Providence surrounded by figures symbolizing the rivers that flow into the Danube. The sexy statues offended Empress Maria Theresa, who actually organized "Chastity Commissions" to defend her capital city's moral standards. The modern buildings around you were built after World War II.

• *Lady Providence's one bare breast points back to Kärntner Strasse (50 yards away), where you'll turn left. Continuing down Kärntner Strasse, you'll find lots of shops filled with merchandise proven to entice tourists. Pass the U-Bahn station (which has WCs) where the street spills into Vienna's main square...*

❾ Stephansplatz

The cathedral's frilly spire looms overhead, worshippers and tourists pour inside the church, and shoppers buzz around the outside. You're at the center of Vienna.

The Gothic **St. Stephen's Cathedral** (c. 1300-1450) is known for its 450-foot south tower, its colorful, patterned roof, and its place in Viennese history. When it was built, it was a huge church for what was then a tiny town, and it helped put the fledgling city on the map. At this point, you may want to take a break from the walk to tour the church (for details, see page 892).

Where Kärntner Strasse hits Stephansplatz, the grand, soot-covered building with red columns is the **Equitable Building** (filled with lawyers, bankers, and insurance brokers). It's a fine example of Neoclassicism from the turn of the 20th century—look up and imagine how slick Vienna must have felt in 1900.

Facing St. Stephen's is the sleek concrete-and-glass ❿ **Haas Haus,** a postmodern building by noted Austrian architect Hans Hollein (finished in 1990). The curved facade is supposed to echo the Roman fortress of Vindobona (its ruins were found near here). Although the Viennese initially protested about having this stark modern tower right next to their beloved cathedral, since then, it's become a fixture of Vienna's main square. Notice how the smooth, rounded glass reflects St. Stephen's pointy architecture, providing a great photo opportunity—especially at twilight.

• *Exit the square with your back to the cathedral. Walk past the Haas Haus, and bear right down the street called the...*

⓫ Graben

This was once a *Graben*, or ditch—originally the moat for the Roman military camp. Back during Vienna's 19th-century heyday, more than 200,000 people were packed into the city's inner center (inside the Ringstrasse), walking on dirt streets. Today this area houses 20,000. The Graben was a busy street with three lanes of traffic until the 1970s, when the city inaugurated its new subway system and the street was turned into one of Europe's first pedestrian-only zones. Take a moment to enjoy a slow 360-degree spin tour. Absorb the scene—you're standing in an area surrounded by history, postwar rebuilding, grand architecture, fine cafés, and people enjoying life...for me, quintessential Europe.

Stroll down the Graben. Eventually, you reach Dorotheergasse, on your left, which leads (after two more long blocks) to the **Dorotheum** auction house. Consider poking your nose in here later for some fancy window shopping. Also along this street are two recommended eateries: the sandwich shop Trześniewski—one of my favorite places for lunch—and the classic Café Hawelka.

In the middle of the Graben pedestrian zone is the extravagantly blobby ❷ **Holy Trinity plague column** *(Pestsäule)*. The 60-foot pillar of clouds sprouts angels and cherubs, with the wonderfully gilded Father, Son, and Holy Ghost at the top (all protected by an anti-pigeon net).

In 1679, Vienna was hit by a massive epidemic of bubonic plague. Around 75,000 Viennese died—about a third of the city. Emperor Leopold I dropped to his knees (something emperors never did in public) and begged God to save the city. (Find Leopold about a quarter of the way up the monument, just above the brown banner. Hint: The typical inbreeding of royal families left him with a gaping underbite.) His prayer was heard by Lady Faith (the statue below Leopold, carrying a cross). With the help of a heartless little cupid, she tosses an old naked woman—symbolizing the plague—into the abyss and saves the city. In gratitude, Leopold vowed to erect this monument, which became a model for cities throughout the empire that were ravaged by the same plague. (The three golden banners represent the core of that empire: Austria, Hungary, and Bohemia.)

• *Thirty yards past the plague monument, look down the short street to the right, which frames a Baroque church with a stately green dome.*

❸ St. Peter's Church

Leopold I ordered this church to be built as a thank-you for surviving the 1679 plague. The church stands on the site of a much older church that may have been Vienna's first (or second) Christian church. Inside, St. Peter's shows Vienna at its Baroque best. Note that the church offers free organ concerts (daily at 15:00, advertised at the entry).

• *Continue west on the Graben, where you'll immediately find some stairs leading underground to...*

❹ Loos' Loos

In about 1900, a local chemical maker needed a publicity stunt to prove that his chemicals really got things clean. He purchased two wine cellars under the Graben and had them turned into classy

WCs in the Modernist style (designed by turn-of-the-20th-century architect Adolf Loos), complete with chandeliers and finely crafted mahogany. While the chandeliers are gone, the restrooms remain a relatively appealing place to do your business. (In the men's room, the 1883 urinals survive but are enjoying a peaceful retirement behind protective glass.) Locals and tourists happily pay €0.50 for a quick visit.

• *The Graben dead-ends at the aristocratic supermarket Julius Meinl am Graben. From here, you could turn right into Vienna's "golden corner," with the city's finest shops. But we'll turn left. In the distance is the big green-and-gold dome of the Hofburg, where we'll head soon. The street leading up to the Hofburg is...*

⓯ Kohlmarkt

This is Vienna's most elegant and unaffordable shopping street, lined with Cartier, Armani, Gucci, Tiffany, and the emperor's palace at the end. Strolling Kohlmarkt, daydream about the edible window displays at ⓰ **Demel,** the ultimate Viennese chocolate shop (#14, daily 9:00-19:00). Step into the shop, where even the decor is sugary. The room is filled with Art Nouveau boxes

of Empress Sisi's choco-dreams come true: *Kandierte Veilchen* (candied violet petals), *Katzenzungen* (cats' tongues), and so on. The cakes here are moist (compared with the dry Sacher tortes). The enticing window displays change monthly, reflecting current happenings in Vienna.

Wander inside. There's an impressive cancan of Vienna's most beloved cakes—displayed to tempt visitors (point to the cake you want). Farther in, you can see the bakery in action. Sit inside, with a view of the cakemaking, or outside, with the street action (upstairs is less crowded). Shops like this boast "K.u.K."—signifying that during the Habsburgs' heyday, it was patronized by the *König und Kaiser* (king and emperor—same guy). If you happen to be looking through Demel's window at exactly 19:01, just after closing, you can witness one of the great tragedies of modern Europe: the daily dumping of its unsold cakes.

Next to Demel, the **Manz Bookstore** has a Loos-designed facade.

• *Kohlmarkt ends at the square called...*

VIENNA

⓱ Michaelerplatz

This square is dominated by the **Hofburg Palace.** Study the grand Neo-Baroque facade, dating from about 1900. The four heroic giants illustrate Hercules wrestling with his great challenges (Emperor Franz Josef, who commissioned the gate, felt he could relate). The facade's Hercules statues remind mere mortals to stay in their place.

In the center of this square, a scant bit of **Roman Vienna** lies exposed just beneath street level.

Spin Tour: Do a slow, clockwise pan to get your bearings, starting (over your left shoulder as you face the Hofburg) with **St. Michael's Church,** which offers fascinating tours of its crypt. To the right of that is the fancy **Loden-Plankl shop,** with traditional Austrian formalwear, including dirndls. Farther to the right, across Augustinerstrasse, is the wing of the palace that houses the **Spanish Riding School** and its famous white Lipizzaner stallions. Farther down this street lies **Josefsplatz,** with the Augustinian Church, and the Dorotheum auction house. At the end of the street are Albertinaplatz and the opera house (where we started this walk).

Continue your spin: Two buildings over from the Hofburg (to the right), the modern **Loos House** (now a bank) has a facade featuring a perfectly geometrical grid of square columns and windows. Compared to the Neo-Baroque facade of the Hofburg, the stern Modernism of the Loos House appears to be from an entirely different age. And yet, both of these—as well as the Eiffel Tower and Mad Ludwig's fairy-tale Neuschwanstein Castle—were built in the same generation, roughly around 1900. In many ways, this jarring juxtaposition exemplifies the architectural turmoil of the turn of the 20th century, and represents the passing of the torch from Europe's age of divine monarchs to the modern era.

• *Let's take a look at where Austria's glorious history began—at the...*

Hofburg Imperial Palace

This is the complex of palaces where the Habsburg emperors lived out their lives (except in summer, when they resided at Schönbrunn Palace). Enter the Hofburg through the gate, where you immediately find yourself beneath a big rotunda (the netting is there to keep birds from perching). The doorway on the right is the entrance to the ⓲ **Imperial Apartments,** where the Habsburg emperors resided in chandeliered elegance. Today you can tour its lavish rooms, as

well as a museum about Empress Sisi, and a porcelain and silver collection. To the left is the ticket office for the ⓐ **Spanish Riding School.**

Continuing on, you emerge from the rotunda into the main courtyard of the Hofburg, called **In der Burg.** The Caesar-like statue is of Habsburg Emperor Franz II (1768-1835), grandson of Maria Theresa, grandfather of Franz Josef, and father-in-law of Napoleon. Behind him is a tower with three kinds of clocks (the yellow disc shows the phase of the moon tonight). To the right of Franz are the Imperial Apartments, and to the left are the offices of Austria's mostly ceremonial president (the more powerful chancellor lives in a building just behind this courtyard).

Franz Josef faces the oldest part of the palace. The colorful red, black, and gold gateway (behind you), which used to have a drawbridge, leads over the moat and into the 13th-century Swiss Court (Schweizerhof), named for the Swiss mercenary guards once stationed there. Study the gate. Imagine the drawbridge and the chain. Notice the Habsburg coat of arms with the imperial eagle above and the Renaissance painting on the ceiling of the passageway.

As you enter the Gothic courtyard, you're passing into the historic core of the palace, the site of the first fortress, and, historically, the place of last refuge. Here you'll find the ⓐ **Treasury** (Schatzkammer) and the **Imperial Music Chapel** (Hofmusikkapelle), where the Boys' Choir sings Mass. Ever since Joseph Haydn and Franz Schubert were choirboys here, visitors have gathered like groupies on Sundays to hear the famed choir sing.

Returning to the bigger In der Burg courtyard, face Franz and turn left, passing through the **tunnel,** with a few tourist shops and restaurants, to spill out into spacious ⓐ **Heldenplatz** (Heroes' Square). On the left is the impressive curved facade of the **World Museum Vienna** (formerly the New Palace). This vast wing was built in the early 1900s to be the new Habsburg living quarters (and was meant to have a matching building facing it). But in 1914, the heir to the throne, Archduke Franz Ferdinand—while waiting politely for his long-lived uncle, Emperor Franz Josef, to die—was assassinated in Sarajevo. The archduke's death sparked World War I and the eventual end of eight centuries of Habsburg rule.

Spin Tour: Make a slow 360-degree turn, and imagine this huge square filled with people.

In 1938, 300,000 Viennese gathered here, entirely filling vast Heroes' Square, to welcome Adolf Hitler and celebrate their annexation with Germany—the *"Anschluss."* The Nazi tyrant stood on the balcony of the then New Palace and declared, "Before the face of German history, I declare my former homeland now a part of the

Third Reich. One of the pearls of the Third Reich will be Vienna."
He never said "Austria," a word that was now forbidden.

When pondering why the Austrians—eyes teary with joy and
vigorously waving their Nazi flags—so willingly accepted Hitler's rule, it's important to remember that Austria was already a
fascist nation. Austrian Chancellor Engelbert Dollfuss, though
pro-Catholic, pro-Habsburg, and anti-Hitler, was a fascist dictator who silenced any left-wing opposition. Also, memories of the
grand Habsburg Empire were still fresh in the collective psyche.
The once vast and mighty empire of 50 million at its 19th-century
peak came out of World War I a tiny landlocked land of six million
that now suffered terrible unemployment. The opportunistic Hitler
promised jobs along with a return to greatness—and the Austrian
people gobbled it up.

Standing here, it's fascinating to consider Austrian aspira-
tions for grandeur. In fact, the Habsburgs envisioned an ancient
Rome-inspired Imperial Forum stretching from here across the
Ringstrasse.

• *Walk on through the Greek-columned passageway (the Äusseres Burgtor), cross the Ringstrasse, and stand between the giant Kunsthistorisches
and Natural History Museums, built in the 1880s to house the private
art and scientific collections of the empire and to celebrate its culture and
power. A huge statue of perhaps the greatest of the Habsburgs, Maria
Theresa, stands in the center of it all.*

❷ Maria Theresa Monument

Vienna's biggest monument shows the empress (the empire's only
female ruler) holding a scroll from her father granting the right of
a woman to inherit his throne. The statues and reliefs surrounding
her speak volumes about her reign: Her four top generals sit on
horseback while her four top advisers stand. Behind them, reliefs
celebrate cultural leaders of her day, including little Wolfie Mozart with mentor "Papa" Joseph Haydn (with his hand on Mozart's
shoulder, facing the Natural History Museum). The moral of this
propaganda: that a strong military and a wise ruler are prerequisites
for a thriving culture—attributes that characterized the 40-year
rule of the woman who was perhaps Austria's greatest monarch.

• *Our walk is finished. You're in the heart of Viennese sightseeing. Surrounding this square are some of the city's top museums. And the Hofburg
Palace itself contains many of Vienna's best sights and museums. From
the opera to the Hofburg, from chocolate to churches, from St. Stephen's to
Sacher tortes—Vienna waits for you.*

Sights in Vienna

Vienna has a dizzying number of sights and museums, which cover the city's rich culture and vivid history through everything from paintings to music to furniture to prancing horses. Just perusing the list on your TI-issued Vienna city map can be overwhelming. To get you started, I've selected the sights that are most essential, rewarding, and user-friendly, and arranged them by neighborhood for handy sightseeing.

SIGHTSEEING PASSES AND COMBO-TICKETS

Avid sightseers should consider a pass or combo-ticket, but do the math first. Add up the cost of all the sights you think you'll see, then consider whether you'd like to use the hop-on, hop-off bus to get around (included with the Vienna Pass). If you prefer to walk or take public transportation, you may be better off with one or more of the combo-tickets described below.

Note that those under 19 get in free to state-run museums and sights.

Passes: The **Vienna Pass** includes free entry to the city's top 60 sights and unlimited access to Vienna Sightseeing's hop-on, hop-off tour buses (€59/1 day, €89/2 days, €119/3 days; purchase at TIs and several other locations around town—check at www.viennapass.com). It also lets you skip lines at some sights, but not at the Schönbrunn Palace where lines are the most frustrating. You have to be really busy to make this pass pay for itself.

The much-promoted **Vienna Card** (www.wienkarte.at) is not worth the mental overhead for most travelers.

Combo-Tickets: The €34 **Sisi Ticket** covers the Hofburg Imperial Apartments (with its Sisi Museum and Silver Collection—must be seen the same day), Schönbrunn Palace's Grand Tour, and the Imperial Furniture Collection. At Schönbrunn, the ticket lets you enter the palace immediately, without a reserved entry time. Buy your Sisi Ticket in advance online (www.schoenbrunn.at) or at the Imperial Furniture Collection where lines are shortest.

If you're seeing the **Hofburg Treasury** (royal regalia and crown jewels) and the **Kunsthistorisches** (world-class art collection), the €20 combo-ticket is well worth it.

The **Haus der Musik** (mod museum with interactive exhibits) has a combo deal with **Mozarthaus Vienna** (exhibits and artifacts about the great composer) for €18—saving a few euros for music lovers (though the Mozarthaus will likely disappoint all but the most die-hard Mozart fans).

HOFBURG PALACE AND RELATED SIGHTS

The imposing Imperial Palace, with 640 years of architecture, art, and history, demands your attention. This first Habsburg residence grew with the family empire from the 13th century until 1913, when the last "new wing" opened. The winter residence of the Habsburg rulers until 1918, the Hofburg is still home to the Austrian president's office, 5,000 government workers, and several important museums.

Don't get confused by the Hofburg's myriad courtyards and many museums. Focus on three sights: the Imperial Apartments, the Treasury, and the museums at World Museum Vienna. With more time, consider the Hofburg's many other sights, covering various facets of the imperial lifestyle.

Eating at the Hofburg: Down the tunnel between the In der Burg courtyard and Heldenplatz is the tiny but handy **$ Hofburg Stüberl** sandwich bar—ideal for a cool, quiet sit and a drink or snack (open daily). The recommended **Soho Kantine,** off the Burggarten near the butterfly house, is also a cheap and practical option (see "Eating in Vienna," later).

▲▲▲Hofburg Imperial Apartments (Kaiserappartements)

These lavish, Versailles-type, "wish-I-were-God" royal rooms are the downtown version of the suburban Schönbrunn Palace. Palace visits are a one-way romp through three sections: a porcelain and silver collection, a museum dedicated to the enigmatic and troubled Empress Sisi, and the luxurious apartments themselves.

The Imperial Apartments are a mix of Old World luxury and modern 19th-century conveniences. Here, Emperor Franz Josef I lived and worked along with his wife Elisabeth, known as Sisi. The Sisi Museum traces the development of her legend, analyzing her fabulous but tragic life as a 19th-century Princess Diana. You'll read bits of her poetic writing, see exact copies of her now-lost jewelry, and learn about her escapes, dieting mania, and chocolate bills.

Cost and Hours: €15, includes well-done audioguide, covered by Sisi Ticket; daily 9:00-17:30, July-Aug until 18:00, last entry one hour before closing; €3 guided tours daily at 14:00; enter from under rotunda just off Michaelerplatz, through Michaelertor gate; tel. 01/533-7570, www.hofburg-wien.at.

Overview: Your ticket grants you admission to three separate exhibits, which you'll visit on a one-way route. The first floor holds a collection of precious porcelain and silver knickknacks *(Silberkammer).* You then go upstairs to the Sisi Museum, which has displays about her life. This leads into the 20 or so rooms of the Imperial Apartments *(Kaiserappartements),* starting in Franz Josef's rooms, then heading into the dozen rooms where his wife Sisi lived.

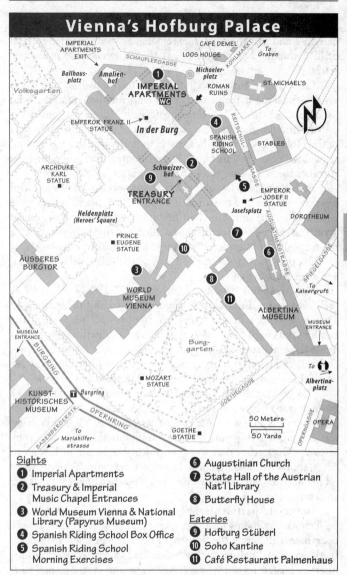

Vienna's Hofburg Palace

IMPERIAL APARTMENTS EXIT

CAFÉ DEMEL
LOOS HOUSE

SCHAUFLERGASSE

To Graben

Ballhaus-platz

Amalien-hof

Volksgarten

①

Michaeler-platz

IMPERIAL APARTMENTS
WC

ROMAN RUINS

ST. MICHAEL'S

EMPEROR FRANZ II STATUE

In der Burg

④

SPANISH RIDING SCHOOL

STABLES

ARCHDUKE KARL STATUE

Schweizer-hof

②

⑨

⑤

EMPEROR JOSEF II STATUE

TREASURY ENTRANCE

Josefsplatz

DOROTHEUM

Heldenplatz (Heroes' Square)

PRINCE EUGENE STATUE

⑩

⑦

AUSSERES BURGTOR

③

⑥

To Kaisergruft

WORLD MUSEUM VIENNA

⑧

⑪

ALBERTINA MUSEUM

MUSEUM ENTRANCE

Burg-garten

MUSEUM ENTRANCE

BURGRING

■ MOZART STATUE

To Albertina-platz

KUNST-HISTORISCHES MUSEUM

T Burgring

OPERNRING

GOETHE STATUE ■

50 Meters
50 Yards

OPERA

To Mariahilfer-strasse

VIENNA

N

RENZSCHUL-GASSE

AUGUSTINERSTRASSE

SPIEGELGASSE

OPERNGASSE

GOETHEGASSE

BABENBERGERSTR.

Sights
① Imperial Apartments
② Treasury & Imperial Music Chapel Entrances
③ World Museum Vienna & National Library (Papyrus Museum)
④ Spanish Riding School Box Office
⑤ Spanish Riding School Morning Exercises
⑥ Augustinian Church
⑦ State Hall of the Austrian Nat'l Library
⑧ Butterfly House

Eateries
⑨ Hofburg Stüberl
⑩ Soho Kantine
⑪ Café Restaurant Palmenhaus

If you listen to the entire audioguide, allow 40 minutes for the porcelain and silver collection, 30 minutes for the Sisi Museum, and 40 minutes for the apartments.

Visiting the Imperial Apartments: Your visit (and the excellent audioguide) starts on the ground floor.

Imperial Porcelain and Silver Collection: Browse the collection to gawk at the opulence and to take in some colorful Habsburg trivia. (Who'da thunk that the court had an official way to fold a napkin—and that the technique remains a closely guarded secret?) Still, I wouldn't bog down here, as there's much more to see upstairs.

Once you're through all those rooms of dishes, climb the stairs—the same staircase used by the emperors and empresses who lived here. At the top is a timeline of Sisi's life. Swipe your ticket to pass through the turnstile, and enter the room with the model of the Hofburg. Circle to the far side to find where you're standing right now, near the Hofburg's largest dome. That dome tops the entrance to the Hofburg from Michaelerplatz.

A world within a world, the Hofburg was a kind of forbidden city accessible only to the ruling elite until 1891. Stand at the center and imagine the unfinished bit filled in, and ponder the imperial greatness of the palace complex. To the left of the dome (as you face the facade) is the steeple of the Augustinian Church. It was there, in 1854, that Franz Josef married 16-year-old Elisabeth of Bavaria, and their story began.

Sisi Museum: Empress Elisabeth (1837-1898)—a.k.a. "Sisi" (SEE-see)—was Franz Josef's mysterious, beautiful, and narcissistic wife. This museum traces her fabulous but tragic life. The exhibit starts with Sisi's sad end, showing her **death mask,** photos of her **funeral procession** (by the Hercules statues facing Michaelerplatz), and an **engraving** of a grieving Franz Josef. It was at her death that the obscure, private empress' legend began to grow.

Sisi was nearly 5'8" (a head taller than her husband), had a 20-inch waist (she wore very tight corsets), and weighed only about 100 pounds. (Her waistline eventually grew...to 21 inches. That was at age 50, after giving birth to four children.) A statue, a copy of one of 30 statues that were erected in her honor in European cities, shows her holding one of her trademark fans. It doesn't show off her magnificent hair, however, which reached down as far as her ankles in her youth.

Imperial Apartments: These were the private apartments and public meeting rooms for the emperor and empress. **Franz Josef's apartments** illustrate the lifestyle of the last legendary Habsburg. In these rooms, he met with advisors and welcomed foreign dignitaries; hosted lavish, white-gloved balls and stuffy formal dinners; and raised his children. He slept (alone) on his austere bed while his beloved wife Sisi retreated to her own rooms. He suffered through the execution of his brother, the suicide of his son and heir, the murder of his wife, and the assassination of his nephew, Archduke Ferdinand, which sparked World War I and spelled the end of the Habsburg monarchy.

Among the rooms you'll see is the **audience room** where Franz Josef received commoners from around the empire. Imagine you've

Sisi (1837-1898)

Empress Elisabeth—Franz Josef's beautiful wife—was the 19th-century equivalent of Princess Diana. Born on Christmas Eve and known as "Sisi" since childhood, she became an instant celebrity when she married Franz Josef at 16.

The daughter of a Bavarian duke, Sisi enjoyed an idyllic girlhood riding horses in the forests near Munich. But after marrying, she became obsessed with preserving her reputation as a beautiful empress, maintaining her Barbie-doll figure and tending to her fairy-tale, ankle-length hair. In the 1860s, she was considered one of the most beautiful women in the world. After turning 30, she refused to allow photographs or portraits, and was generally seen in public with a delicate fan covering her face (and bad teeth).

Complex and influential, Sisi was adored by Franz Josef, whom she respected. Although Franz Josef was supposed to have married Sisi's sister Helene (in an arranged diplomatic marriage), he fell in love with Sisi instead. It was one of the Habsburgs' few marriages for love.

Sisi's personal tragedy was the death of her son Rudolf, the crown prince, in an apparent suicide. Disliking Vienna and the confines of the court and eager for time out of the spotlight, Sisi traveled more and more frequently.

As the years passed, the restless Sisi and her hardworking husband became estranged. In 1898, while visiting Geneva, Switzerland, she was murdered by an Italian anarchist.

VIENNA

traveled for days to have your say before the emperor. You're wearing your new fancy suit—Franz Josef required that men coming before him wear a tailcoat, women a black gown with a train. He'd stand at the **lectern** (far left) as the visiting commoners had their say (but for no more than two-and-a-half minutes). On the lectern is a partial **list** of 56 appointments he had on January 3, 1910 (three columns: family name, meeting topic, and *Anmerkung*—the emperor's "action log").

Franz Josef's **study** evokes how seriously the emperor took his responsibilities as the top official of a vast empire. Famously energetic, Franz Josef lived a spartan life dedicated to duty; in his **bedroom,** notice his no-frills **iron bed.** He typically rose before dawn and started his day in prayer, kneeling at the **prayer stool** against the far wall. While he had a typical emperor's share of mistresses, his dresser was always well-stocked with **photos** of Sisi.

In **Sisi's bedroom,** refurbished in the Neo-Rococo style in

Emperor Franz Josef (1830-1916)

Franz Josef I—who ruled for 68 years (1848-1916)—was the embodiment of the Habsburg Empire as it finished its six-century-long ride. Born in 1830, Franz Josef had a stern upbringing that instilled in him a powerful sense of duty and—like so many men of power— a love of all things military.

His uncle, Ferdinand I, suffered from profound epilepsy, which prevented him from being an effective ruler. As the revolutions of 1848 rattled royal families throughout Europe, the Habsburgs forced Ferdinand to abdicate and put 18-year-old Franz Josef on the throne. He spent the first part of his long reign understandably paranoid, as social discontent continued to simmer.

Franz Josef was very conservative. But worse, he wrongly believed that he was a talented military tactician, leading Austria into catastrophic battles against Italy (which was fighting for its unification and independence) in the 1860s.

Wearing his uniform to the end, Franz Josef never saw what a dinosaur his monarchy was becoming. He had no interest in democracy and pointedly never set foot in Austria's parliament building. His passion for low-grade paperwork earned him the nickname "Joe Bureaucrat." Mired in these petty details, he missed the big picture. In 1914, he helped start a Great War that ultimately ended the age of monarchs. The year 1918 marked the end of Europe's big royal families: Hohenzollerns (Prussia), Romanovs (Russia), and Habsburgs (Austria).

1854, there's a red carpet, covered with oriental rugs. The room always had lots of fresh flowers. Sisi not only slept here, but also lived here—the bed was rolled in and out daily—until her death in 1898. The **desk** is where she sat and wrote her letters and sad poems. In her **dressing/exercise room,** servants worked three hours a day on Sisi's famous hair. She'd exercise on the **wooden structure** and on the **rings** suspended from the doorway to the left. Afterward, she'd get a massage on the red-covered **bed.**

In the small salon, notice the portrait of **Crown Prince Rudolf,** Franz Josef's and Sisi's only son. On the morning of January 30, 1889, the 30-year-old Rudolf and a beautiful baroness were found shot dead in an apparent murder-suicide in his hunting lodge in Mayerling. The scandal shocked the empire and tainted the Habsburgs; Sisi retreated further into her fantasy world, and Franz Josef carried on stoically with a broken heart.

The tour ends in the dining room. It's dinnertime, and Franz Josef has called his extended family together. The settings are modest...just silver. Gold was saved for formal state dinners. Next to each name card was a menu listing the chef responsible for each dish. (Talk about pressure.) Franz Josef enforced strict protocol at mealtime: No one could speak without being spoken to by the emperor, and no one could eat after he was done. While the rest of Europe was growing democracy and expanding personal freedoms, the Habsburgs preserved their ossified worldview to the bitter end.

In 1918, World War I ended, Austria was created as a modern nation-state, the Habsburgs were tossed out...and Hofburg Palace was destined to become the museum you've just toured.

VIENNA

▲▲▲Hofburg Treasury
(Kaiserliche Schatzkammer Wien)

One of the world's most stunning collections of royal regalia, the Hofburg Treasury shows off sparkling crowns, jewels, gowns, and assorted Habsburg bling in 21 darkened rooms. The treasures, well explained by an audioguide, include the crown of the Holy Roman Emperor, Charlemagne's saber, a unicorn horn, and more precious gems than you can shake a scepter at.

Cost and Hours: €12, €20 combo-ticket with Kunsthistorisches; Wed-Mon 9:00-17:30, closed Tue; audioguide-€5 or €7/2 people, €3 guided tours daily at 16:00; from the Hofburg's central courtyard pass through the black, red, and gold gate, then follow *Schatzkammer* signs to the Schweizerhof; tel. 01/525-240, www.kaiserliche-schatzkammer.at.

Visiting the Treasury: The Habsburgs saw themselves as the successors to the ancient Roman emperors, and they wanted crowns and royal regalia to match the pomp of the ancients. They used these precious objects for coronation ceremonies, official ribbon-cutting events, and their own personal pleasure. You'll see the prestigious crowns and accoutrements of the rulers of the Holy Roman Empire (a medieval alliance of Germanic kingdoms so named because it wanted to be considered the continuation of the Roman Empire). Here's a rundown of the highlights (the audioguide is much more complete).

Room 2: The personal **crown of Rudolf II** (1602) occupies the

center of the room along with its accompanying scepter and orb; a bust of Rudolf II (1552-1612) sits nearby. The crown's design symbolically merges a bishop's miter ("Holy"), the arch across the top of a Roman emperor's helmet ("Roman"), and the typical medieval king's crown ("Emperor").

Two centuries later (1806), this crown and scepter became the official regalia of Austria's rulers, as seen in the large **portrait of Franz I** (the open-legged guy behind you). Napoleon Bonaparte had just conquered Austria and dissolved the Holy Roman Empire. Franz (r. 1792-1835) was allowed to remain in power, but he had to downgrade his title from "Franz II, Holy Roman Emperor" to "Franz I, Emperor of Austria."

Rooms 3 and 4: These rooms contain some of the **coronation vestments and regalia** needed for the new Austrian (not Holy Roman) Emperor. There was a different one for each of the emperor's subsidiary titles, for example, King of Hungary or King of Lombardy. So many crowns and kingdoms in the Habsburgs' vast empire!

Room 5: Ponder the **Cradle of the King of Rome,** once occupied by Napoleon's son, who was born in 1811 and made King of Rome. While pledging allegiance to democracy, he in fact crowned himself Emperor of France and hobnobbed with Europe's royalty. When his wife Josephine could not bear him a male heir, Napoleon divorced her and married into the Habsburg family.

Room 6: For Divine Right kings, even child-rearing was a sacred ritual that needed elaborate regalia for public ceremonies. The 23-pound **gold basin and pitcher** were used to baptize noble children, who were dressed in the **baptismal dresses** displayed nearby.

Room 7: These **jewels** are the true "treasures," a cabinet of wonders used by Habsburgs to impress their relatives (or to hock when funds got low).

Religious Rooms: Several rooms display **religious objects**—crucifixes, chalices, mini-altarpieces, reliquaries, and bishops' vestments. Like the medieval kings who preceded them, Habsburg rulers mixed the institutions of church and state, so these precious religious accoutrements were also part of their display of secular power.

Regalia of the Holy Roman Empire: The next few rooms (10-12) contain some of the oldest and most venerated objects in the Treasury—the robes, crowns, and sacred objects of the Holy Roman Emperor.

The big red-silk and gold-thread **coronation mantle,** nearly 900 years old, was worn by Holy Roman Emperors when they received their crown. The collection's highlight is the 10th-century **crown of the Holy Roman Emperor.** It was probably made for Otto I (c. 960), the first king to call himself Holy Roman Emperor. The Imperial Crown swirls with symbolism "proving" that the emperor was both holy and Roman: The cross on top says the HRE ruled as Christ's representative on earth, and the jeweled arch over the top is reminiscent of the parade helmet of ancient Romans. The jewels themselves allude to the wearer's kinghood in the here and now. Imagine the impression this priceless, glittering crown must have made on the emperor's medieval subjects.

Nearby is the 11th-century **Imperial Cross** that preceded the emperor in ceremonies. Encrusted with jewels, it had a hollow compartment (its core is wood) that carried substantial chunks thought to be from *the* cross on which Jesus was crucified and *the* Holy Lance used to pierce his side (both pieces are displayed in the same glass case). Holy Roman Emperors actually carried the lance into battle in the 10th century. Look behind the cross to see how it was a box that could be clipped open and shut, used for holding holy relics. You can see bits of the "true cross" anywhere, but this is a prime piece—with the actual nail hole.

Another case has additional objects used in the coronation ceremony: The **orb** (orbs were modeled on late-Roman ceremonial objects, then topped with the cross) and **scepter** (the one with the oak leaves), along with the sword, were carried ahead of the emperor in the procession. In earlier times, these objects were thought to have belonged to Charlemagne himself, the greatest ruler of medieval Europe, but in fact they're mostly from 300 to 400 years later (c. 1200).

Now picture all this regalia used together. The **Josef II painting** shows the coronation of Maria Theresa's son as Holy Roman Emperor in 1764. Set in a church in Frankfurt (filled with the bigwigs—literally—of the day), Josef is wearing the same crown and royal garb that you've just seen.

More Hofburg Sights
▲▲World Museum Vienna (Welt Museum Wien)
The World Museum Vienna houses four separate collections—an armory (with a killer collection of medieval weapons), historical musical instruments, classical statuary from ancient Ephesus, and an impressive ethnographic museum. They're all part of one grand "World Museum": They have the same entry times, and are covered in one ticket. An added bonus of the World Museum is a chance to wander among the royal Habsburg halls, stairways, and painted ceilings virtually alone. You can enjoy the Hall of Columns (central courtyard, c. 1910)—the hub of the complex—for free.

Cost and Hours: €12, Thu-Tue 10:00-18:00, Fri until 21:00, closed Wed; tel. 01/534-30-5052, www.weltmuseumwien.at.

▲Spanish Riding School (Spanische Hofreitschule)

This stately 300-year-old Baroque hall at the Hofburg Palace is the home of the renowned Lipizzaner stallions. The magnificent building was an impressive expanse in its day. Built without central pillars, it offers clear views of the prancing horses under lavish chandeliers, with a grand painting of Emperor Charles VI on horseback at the head of the hall.

Lipizzaner stallions are known for their noble gait and Baroque profile. These regal horses have changed shape with the tenor of the times: They were bred strong and stout during wars, and frilly and slender in more cultured eras. But they're always born black, fade to gray, and turn a distinctive white in adulthood.

Seeing the Horses and Buying Tickets: The school offers three ways to see the horses—performances, morning exercises, and guided tours of the stables (check the events list on the school's **website** at www.srs.at; enter your dates under "Event Search"). You can purchase tickets online or at the **box office** (opens at 9:00, located inside the Hofburg—go through the main Hofburg entryway from Michaelerplatz, then turn left into the first passage, tel. 01/533-9031). Photos are not allowed at any events, nor are children under age 3.

To **see the horses for free,** just walk by the stables at any time of day when the horses are in town. From the covered passageway along Reitschulgasse, there's a big window from where you can usually see the horses poking their heads out of their stalls.

Performances: The Lipizzaner stallions put on great 80-minute performances featuring choreographed moves to jaunty recorded Viennese classical music. The pricey seats book up months in advance, but standing room is usually available the same day. With just a few rows of seats and close-up standing-room spots, there's not a bad view in the house (seats about €50-160, standing room about €25, prices vary depending on the show; Feb-mid-June and mid-Aug-Dec usually Sat-Sun at 11:00, no shows Jan and mid-June-mid-Aug).

Morning Exercises: For a less expensive, more casual experience, morning exercises with music take place on weekday mornings in the same hall and are open to the public. Don't have high expectations, as the horses often do little more than trot and warm up. Tourists line up early at Josefsplatz (the large courtyard between Michaelerplatz and Albertinaplatz), at the door marked *Spanische Hofreitschule*. But there's no need to show up when the doors open at 10:00, since tickets never really "sell out" (€15, available at the door in high season—otherwise buy at visitors center on

Michaelerplatz, family discounts, generally Tue-Fri 10:00-12:00, occasionally also on Mon, no exercises July-mid-Aug).

Guided Tours: One-hour guided tours in English are given almost every afternoon year-round. You'll see the Winter Riding School with its grand Baroque architecture, the Summer Riding School in a shady courtyard, and the stables (€18; tours usually daily at 13:00, 14:00, 15:00, and 16:00; reserve ahead by emailing office@srs.at or calling the box office).

▲Augustinian Church (Augustinerkirche)

Built into the Hofburg, this is the Gothic and Neo-Gothic church where the Habsburgs got married. Today, the royal hearts are in the church vault.

Cost and Hours: Church—free, open long hours daily; vault—€2.50, open to the public only after Sunday Mass at about 12:45; at Augustinerstrasse 3, facing Josefsplatz.

Visiting the Church: Process as if a bride or groom up the main aisle. In the front (above the altar on the right), notice the windows, from which royals witnessed the Mass in private. Don't miss the exquisite, pyramid-shaped memorial (by the Italian sculptor Antonio Canova) to Maria Theresa's favorite daughter, Maria Christina. The hearts of 54 Habsburg nobles are in urns in a vault off the church's Loreto Chapel (on the right beyond the Maria Christina memorial).

The church's 11:00 Sunday Mass is a hit with music lovers. It's both a Mass and a concert, often with an orchestra accompanying the choir (acoustics are best in front). Pay by contributing to the offering plate and buying a CD afterward. Check posters by the entry or www.hochamt.at to see what's on—typically you'll hear one of Mozart's or Haydn's many short Masses.

State Hall (Prunksaal) of the Austrian National Library

The National Library's State Hall (Prunksaal) is a postcard-perfect Baroque library (entered from Josefplatz, next to the Augustinian

Church, see "Vienna's Hofburg Palace" map, earlier). In this former imperial library, with a statue of Charles VI in the center, you'll find yourself whispering. The setting takes you back to 1730 and gives you the sense that, in imperial times, knowledge of the world was for the elite—and with that knowledge, the elite had power. The glorious paintings (with impressive 3-D) celebrate high culture and the library's patron, Charles VI. More than 200,000 old books line the walls, but patrons go elsewhere to read them—the hall is just for show these days. Special exhibits fill glass cases down the nave-like main aisle with literary treasures, all well described in English.

Cost and Hours: €8, daily 10:00-18:00, Thu until 21:00, closed Mon Oct-May, tel. 01/53410, www.onb.ac.at.

Butterfly House (Schmetterlinghaus) in the Palace Garden (Burggarten)

The Burggarten greenbelt, once the backyard of the Hofburg and now a people's park, welcomes visitors to loiter on the grass. The iron-and-glass pavilion (c. 1910 with playful Art Nouveau touches) now houses the recommended Café Restaurant Palmenhaus and a small, fluttery butterfly exhibit.

Cost and Hours: €7, daily 10:00-16:45, Sat-Sun until 18:15, Nov-March daily until 15:45, tel. 01/533-8570, www.schmetterlinghaus.at.

▲▲Albertina Museum

This impressive museum has three highlights: the imposing state rooms of the former palace, noteworthy collections of classic modernist paintings and European graphic arts (sketches, etching, watercolors—especially Dürer), and excellent temporary exhibits.

The building, at the southern tip of the Hofburg complex (near the opera), was the residence of Maria Theresa's favorite daughter, Maria Christina, who was allowed to marry for love rather than political strategy. Her many sisters were jealous. (Marie-Antoinette had to marry the French king...and lost her head over it.) Maria Christina's husband, Albert of Saxony, was a great collector of original drawings and prints, which he amassed to cover all the important art movements from the late Middle Ages until the early 19th century (including prized works by Dürer, Rembrandt, and Rubens). As it's Albert and Christina's gallery, it's charmingly called the "Alber-tina."

Cost and Hours: €13, daily 10:00-18:00, Wed and Fri until 21:00, helpful audioguide-€4, overlooking Albertinaplatz across from the TI and opera, tel. 01/534-830, www.albertina.at.

Visiting the Museum: After the turnstile, on the entry level you'll likely see photography exhibits. Climbing the stairs you reach the main attractions (clearly labeled)—the state rooms *(Prunkräume)* on your left on level 1, and the Batliner Collection on your right on level 2. Excellent special exhibitions (generally featuring modern art and included in your ticket) are shown on level 2 and in the basement galleries.

State Rooms (*Prunkräume*, level 1): Wander freely under chandeliers and across parquet floors through a handful of rooms of 18th-century imperial splendor, unconstrained by velvet ropes.

The exhibit spaces (never crowded, well described in English, and air-conditioned) are nearly as impressive as those at Schönbrunn Palace. Many rooms are often closed for special functions, but even a few rooms give a good look at imperial Classicism—this is the only post-Rococo palace in the Habsburg realm.

Batliner Collection (level 2): This manageable collection sweeps you quickly through modern art history, featuring minor works by major artists (such as Monet, Degas, Klimt, Matisse, Kirchner, Nolde, and Bacon). Though the collection is permanent, what's on display rotates through about 100 works selected from the 300 in the archives.

Church Crypts near the Hofburg

Two churches near the Hofburg offer starkly different looks at dearly departed Viennese: the Habsburg coffins in the Kaisergruft and the commoners' graves in St. Michael's Church.

▲▲Kaisergruft (Imperial Crypt)

Visiting the imperial remains of the Habsburg family is not as easy as you might imagine. As bodies needed to lie in state to prove to nobility that they were actually dead (in an age of "seeing is believing") the newly dead were gutted like a fish, with all the quick-to-go-bad parts removed (hearts and innards). These original organ donors left their bodies—about 150 in all—in the unassuming Kaisergruft, their hearts in the Augustinian Church (viewable Sun after Mass), and their entrails in the crypt below St. Stephen's Cathedral.

Cost and Hours: €7.50, daily 10:00-18:00, free map includes Habsburg family tree and a chart locating each coffin, crypt is in the Capuchin Church at Tegetthoffstrasse 2 at Neuer Markt; tel. 01/512-685-388.

Visiting the Kaisergruft: Descend into a crypt full of gray metal tombs. Start up the path, through tombs ranging from simple caskets to increasingly big monuments with elaborate metalwork ornamentation. You soon reach the massive pewter tomb of **Maria Theresa** under the dome, enjoying natural light. The only female Habsburg monarch, she had to be granted special dispensation to rule. Her 40-year reign was enlightened and progressive. She and her husband, **Franz I,** recline Etruscan-style atop their fancy coffin, gazing into each other's eyes as a cherub crowns them with glory. They were famously in love (though Franz was less than faithful), and their numerous children were married off to Europe's royal houses. Maria Theresa outlived her husband by 15 years, which she spent in mourning. Old and fat, she installed a special lift to transport herself down into the Kaisergruft to visit her dear, departed Franz. At the four corners of the tomb are the Habsburgs'

Empress Maria Theresa (1717-1780) and Her Son, Emperor Josef II (1741-1790)

Maria Theresa was the only woman to officially rule the Habsburg Empire in that family's 640-year reign. She was a strong and effective empress (r. 1740-1780), but Austrians are also quick to remember Maria The-

resa as the mother of 16 children (10 survived into adulthood). Ponder the fact that the most powerful woman in Europe either was pregnant or had a newborn for most of her reign. Maria Theresa ruled after the Austrian defeat of the Ottomans, when Europe recognized Austria as a great power. (Her rival, the Prussian king, said, "When at last the Habsburgs get a great man, it's a woman.")

Maria Theresa's reign marked the end of the feudal system and the beginning of the era of the grand state. The first of the modern rulers of the Age of Enlightenment, she was a great social reformer. During her reign, she avoided wars and expanded her empire by skillfully marrying her children into the right families. For instance, after daughter Marie-Antoinette's marriage into the French Bourbon family (to Louis XVI), a country that had been an enemy became an ally. (Unfortunately for Marie-Antoinette, Maria Theresa's timing was off.)

To stay in power during an era of revolution, Maria Theresa had to be in tune with her age. She taxed the Church and the nobility, provided six years of obligatory education to all children, and granted free health care to all in her realm. Maria Theresa also welcomed the boy genius Mozart into her court.

The empress' legacy lived on in her son, Josef II, who ruled as emperor for a decade (1780-1790). He was an even more avid reformer, building on his mother's accomplishments. An enlightened monarch, Josef mothballed the too-extravagant Schönbrunn Palace, secularized the monasteries, established religious tolerance within his realm, freed the serfs, made possible the founding of Austria's first general hospital, and promoted relatively enlightened treatment of the mentally ill. Josef was a model of practicality (for example, he banned slow-to-decompose coffins and allowed no more than six candles at funerals)—and very unpopular with other royals. But his policies succeeded in preempting the revolutionary anger of the age, largely enabling Austria to avoid the anti-monarchist turmoil that shook so much of the rest of Europe.

four crowns: the Holy Roman Empire, Hungary, Bohemia, and Lombardy. At his parents' feet lies **Josef II**, the patron of Mozart and Beethoven. Compare the Rococo splendor of Maria Theresa's tomb with the simple coffin of Josef, who was known for his down-to-earth ruling style during the Age of Enlightenment.

Head on through the next room—created in 1960—featuring Napoleon's wife, Marie Louise, and a plaque to Franz Ferdinand (assassinated in 1914 in Sarajevo), then head down three steps to a room il-  lustrating the Habsburgs' fading 19th-century glory. There's the appropriately austere military tomb of the long-reigning **Franz Josef** (ruled 1848 to 1916, see sidebar on page 882). Alongside is his wife, **Elisabeth**—a.k.a. Sisi (see page 881)—who always wins the "Most Flowers" award. Their son was Crown Prince **Rudolf**. Rudolf and his teenage mistress supposedly committed suicide together in 1889 at Mayerling hunting lodge...or was it murder?

VIENNA

In the final room (with humbler copper tombs), you reach the final Habsburgs. **Karl I** (see his bust, not a tomb), the last of the Habsburg rulers, was deposed in 1918. His sons Crown Prince **Otto** and Archduke **Karl Ludwig** are entombed near their mother, **Zita**.

Today there are about 700 living Habsburg royals, mostly living in exile. When they die, they will be buried in their countries of exile, not here.

▲St. Michael's Church Crypt (Michaelerkirche)

St. Michael's Church, which faces the Hofburg on Michaelerplatz, offers a striking contrast to the imperial crypt. Regular tours take visitors underground to see a typical church crypt, filled with the rotting wooden coffins of well-to-do commoners.

Cost and Hours: €7 for 45-minute tour, Mon-Sat at 11:00 and 13:00, no tours Sun, Nov-Easter Thu-Sat only, tours in German and English, wait at church entrance at the sign advertising the tour and pay the guide directly, mobile 0650-533-8003, www.michaelerkirche.at.

Visiting the Crypt: Climbing below the church, you'll see about a hundred 18th-century coffins and stand on three feet of debris, surrounded by niches filled with stacked lumber from decayed coffins and countless bones. You'll meet a 1769 mummy in lederhosen and a wig, along with a woman who is clutching a cross and has flowers painted on her high heels. You'll learn about death in those times, including how the wealthy—not wanting to end up in standard shallow graves—instead paid to be laid to rest below the church, and how, in 1780, Emperor Josef II ended the practice of cemetery burials in cities but allowed the rich to become the stinking rich in crypts under churches.

MORE SIGHTS WITHIN THE RING
▲▲▲St. Stephen's Cathedral (Stephansdom)
This massive Gothic church with the skyscraping spire sits at the center of Vienna. Its highlights are the impressive exterior, the view

from the top of the south tower, a carved pulpit, and a handful of quirky sights associated with Mozart and the Habsburg rulers.

Cost and Hours: Church foyer and north aisle—free, daily 6:00-22:00; main nave—€6 includes audioguide and guided tour (daily at 10:30); open Mon-Sat 9:00-11:30 & 13:00-16:30, Sun 13:00-16:30, July-Aug until 17:30; south and north towers, catacombs, and treasury have varying costs and hours—see below; English mass each Sat at 19:00, tel. 01/515-523-526, www.stephanskirche.at.

Tours: The tours in English are entertaining (free with €6 entry, daily at 10:30, check information board inside entry to confirm schedule). Otherwise the included audioguide is helpful.

🎧 Download my free St. Stephen's Cathedral audio tour.

Treasury: Consider riding the elevator (just inside the cathedral's entry) to the treasury, with precious relics, dazzling church art, a portrait of Rudolf IV (considered the earliest German portrait), and wonderful views down on the nave (€6, daily 9:00-16:30, July-Aug until 17:30).

Catacombs: The catacombs are open to the public only by guided tour (€6, daily 10:00-11:30 & 13:30-16:30, tours generally depart on the half-hour and are in German and English together). Meet the guide at the stairs in the left/north transept—you'll pay at the end. You'll see a crypt for bishops and archbishops, and Crock-Pots of Habsburg guts filling dusty shelves.

Towers: The iconic **south tower** rewards a tough climb up a claustrophobic, 343-step staircase with dizzying views through windows near the top. You can reach it via the entrance outside the church, around the right as you face the west facade (€5, daily 9:00-17:30).

The shorter **north tower** holds the famous "Pummerin" bell, and you ascend via elevator (no stairs). But it's much lower, not as exciting, and has lesser views (€6, daily 9:00-18:30 & 19:00-21:30, entrance inside the church on the left/north side of the nave; you can access this elevator without buying a ticket for the main nave).

○ **Self-Guided Tour:** Before we go inside, let's look at the church's impressive exterior.

Cathedral Exterior: As you face the church's main entry, go to the right across the little square. From here, you can absorb the sheer magnitude of this massive church, with its skyscraping spire. The church we see today is the third one on this spot. A tall, black, glassy info post describes the Virgil Chapel that stood here 800 years ago. Its dank shell survives today below your feet, viewable from the nearby U-Bahn station. Today's church dates mainly from 1300 to 1450, when builders expanded on an earlier structure and added two huge towers at the end of each transept.

The impressive 450-foot **south tower**—capped with a golden orb and cross—took 65 years to build and was finished in 1433. The tower is a rarity among medieval churches in that it was completed before the Gothic style—and the age of faith—petered out.

The cathedral was heavily damaged at the end of World War II. (Near where you are standing, at the base of the tower, there may be **old photos** showing the destruction.) In 1945, Vienna was caught in the chaos between the occupying Nazis and the approaching Soviets. Allied bombs sparked fires in nearby buildings, and the embers leapt to the cathedral rooftop. The original timbered Gothic roof burned, the cathedral's huge bell crashed to the ground, and the fire raged for two days. Civic pride prompted a financial outpouring, and the roof was rebuilt to its original splendor by 1952—doubly impressive considering the bombed-out state of the impoverished country at that time.

• *Now stand at the back of the square, across from the main entrance.*

Main Entrance: The Romanesque-style main entrance includes bits of the oldest part of the church (which stood here in the 1200s). Right behind you is the site of Vindobona, a Roman garrison town. Before the Romans converted to Christianity, there was a pagan temple here, and this entrance pays homage to that ancient heritage. Roman-era statues are embedded inside the facade, and the two **octagonal towers** flanking the main doorway are dubbed the "heathen towers" because they're built with a few recycled Roman stones (flipped over to hide the pagan inscriptions and expose the smooth sides).

• *Enter the church.*

Cathedral Interior: Find a spot to peer through the gate down the immense nave—more than a football field long and nine stories tall. It's lined with clusters of slender pillars that soar upward to

VIENNA

support the ribbed crisscross arches of the ceiling. Stylistically, the nave is Gothic with a Baroque overlay. It's a spacious, glorious venue that's often used for high-profile concerts (there's a ticket office outside the church, to the right as you face the main doorway).

Over the main doorway is the choir loft, with the 10,000-pipe **organ,** a 1960 replacement for the famous one destroyed during World War II. This organ is one of Europe's biggest, but it's currently broken and sits unused...too large to remove. Architects aren't sure whether it serves a structural purpose and adds support to the actual building.

Along the left wall is the **gift shop.** Step in to marvel at the 14th-century statuary decorating its wall—some of the finest carvings in the church. To the left of the gift shop is the gated entrance to the **Chapel of Prince Eugene of Savoy.** Prince Eugene (1663-1736), a teenage seminary student from France, arrived in Vienna in 1683 as the city was about to be overrun by the Ottoman Turks. He volunteered for the army and helped save the city, launching a brilliant career as a military man for the Habsburgs. His specialty was conquering the Ottomans. He was well-rewarded and eventually owned six palaces in and around Vienna including the Belvedere. When he died, the grateful Austrians buried him here, under this chapel, marked by a tomb hatch in the floor.

• *Nearby is the entrance to the* ***main nave.*** *Buy a ticket and start down the nave toward the altar. At the second pillar on the left is the...*

Pulpit: This Gothic sandstone pulpit (c. 1500) is a masterpiece carved from three separate blocks (see if you can find the seams). A spiral stairway winds up to the lectern, surrounded and supported

by the four "Latin Church Fathers," who translated the Bible into Latin in the 4th century (making it more widely accessible to the faithful) and whose writings influenced early Catholic dogma.

The pulpit is as crammed with religious meaning as it is with beautifully realistic carvings. The top of the stairway's railing swarms with lizards and toads—symbols of corrupt teaching. The "Dog of the Lord" stands at the top, making sure none of those toads pollutes the sermon. Below the toads, wheels with three parts (the Trinity) roll up, while wheels with four spokes (the four seasons and four cardinal directions, symbolizing mortal life on earth) roll down.

Find the guy peeking out from under the stairs. This may be a self-portrait of the sculptor. In medieval times, art was done for the glory of God, and artists worked anonymously. But this pulpit was carved as humanist Renaissance ideals were creeping in from Italy—and individual artists were becoming famous. So the artist included what may be a rare self-portrait bust in his work. He leans out from a window, sculptor's compass in hand, to observe the world and his work.

• *Continue up the nave. Halfway up, turn right and enter the south transept. Go all the way to the doors, then look left to find the...*

Mozart Plaque: Wolfgang Amadeus Mozart (1756-1791) spent most of his adult life in Vienna. He attended Mass and was married in St. Stephen's, and two of his children were baptized here. He set up house in a lavish apartment a block east of the church (now the lackluster Mozarthaus museum). Mozart lived at the heart of Viennese society—among musicians, actors, and aristocrats. He played in a string quartet with Joseph Haydn. Mozart may have heard Haydn playing the pipe organ right here.

After his early success, Mozart fell on hard times. When he died at 35, his remains were dumped into a mass grave outside town. But he was honored with a funeral service here in St. Stephen's.

• *Now head to the chapel at the front-right corner of the church.*

Tomb of Frederick III: This imposing, red-marble tomb is like a big king-size-bed coffin with an effigy of Frederick lying on top (not visible—but there's a photo of the effigy on the left). The top of the tomb is decorated with his coats of arms, representing the many territories he ruled over. Frederick III (1415-1493) is considered the "father" of Vienna for turning the small village into a royal city with a cosmopolitan feel.

• *Walk to the middle of the church.*

High Altar: The tall, ornate, black marble altar (1641, by Tobias and Johann Pock) is topped with a statue of Mary that barely fits under the towering vaults of the ceiling. It frames a large painting of the stoning of St. Stephen, painted on copper. Stephen (at the bottom), having refused to stop professing his faith, is pelted with rocks by angry pagans. As he kneels, ready to die, he gazes up to see a vision of Christ, the cross, and the angels of heaven.

▲▲▲Vienna State Opera (Wiener Staatsoper)

The opera house, facing the Ring and near the TI, is a central point for any visitor. Vienna remains one of the world's great cities for classical music, and this building still belts out some of the finest opera, both classic and cutting-edge. While the critical reception of the building 130 years ago led the architect to commit suicide, and though it's been rebuilt since its destruction by WWII bombs, it's still a sumptuous place. The interior has a chandeliered lobby and carpeted staircases perfect for making the scene. The theater itself features five wraparound balconies, gold-and-red decor, and a bracelet-like chandelier. The only way to see the interior (besides attending a performance) is with a guided 45-minute tour.

Cost and Hours: €9, tours generally at the top of each hour 10:00-15:00 but schedule varies due to rehearsals and performances; more tours July-Aug (when there are no performances), fewer tours Sept-June and Sun year-round; no reservations taken, and they don't sell out—just show up at the tour entrance (southwest corner of building) 20 minutes ahead; current month's tour schedule posted online, at the door, or in the opera's *Prolog* magazine; tel. 01/514-442-606, www.wiener-staatsoper.at.

▲▲Haus der Musik

Vienna's "House of Music" is a fun and interactive experience that celebrates this hometown forte. The museum, spread over several floors and well-described in English, is unique for its effective use of touch-screen computers and headphones to explore the physics of sound. One floor is dedicated to the heavyweight Viennese composers (Mozart, Beethoven, and company) who virtually created classical music as we know it. Really experiencing the place takes time. It's open late and is so interactive, relaxing, and fun that it can be considered an activity more than a sight—an evening of joy for music lovers.

Cost and Hours: €13, half-price after 20:00, €18 combo-ticket with Mozarthaus, daily 10:00-22:00, two blocks from the opera house at Seilerstätte 30, tel. 01/513-4850, www.hausdermusik.com. Your ticket includes a free app for added info as you visit.

Visiting the Museum: It's a one-way system, just follow the arrows on the floor. The first floor highlights the Vienna Philharmonic Orchestra, known the world over for their New Year's Eve concerts. (In a mini concert hall, a one-hour video—on a loop—lets you enjoy the event.) See Toscanini's baton, Mahler's cap, and well-used scores. Throw the dice to randomly "compose" a piece of music.

The second floor explores the physics of sound—wander through the "sonosphere" and marvel at the amazing acoustics. Interactive exhibits explore the nature of sound and music; I could actually hear what I thought only a piano tuner could discern. You can twist, dissect, and bend sounds to make your own musical language, merging your voice with a duck's quack or a city's traffic roar.

The third floor celebrates the famous hometown boys: Haydn, Mozart, Beethoven, Schubert, Strauss (father and son), Mahler, Schönberg, Webern, and Berg. (With the app, you can enjoy appropriate music in each room as you stroll.) Before leaving, pick up a virtual baton to conduct the Vienna Philharmonic.

▲Dorotheum Auction House (Palais Dorotheum)

For an aristocrat's flea market, drop by Austria's answer to Sotheby's. The ground floor has shops, an info desk with a schedule of upcoming auctions (Sept-June only), and a few auction items. Some pieces are available for immediate sale (marked *VKP*, for *Verkaufpreis*—"sales price"), while others are up for auction (marked *DIFF. RUF*).

The first floor (above the mezzanine) has antique furniture and fancy knickknacks; the second floor has a showy antique gallery with fixed prices.. Wandering through here, you feel like you're touring a museum with exhibits you can buy.

Cost and Hours: Free, Mon-Fri 10:00-18:00, Sat 9:00-17:00, closed Sun, classy little café on second floor, between the Graben pedestrian street and Hofburg at Dorotheergasse 17, tel. 01/51560, www.dorotheum.com.

▲St. Peter's Church (Peterskirche)

Baroque Vienna is at its best in this architectural gem, tucked away a few steps from the Graben. Admire the rose-and-gold, oval-shaped Baroque interior, topped with a ceiling fresco of Mary kneeling to be crowned by Jesus and the Father, while the dove of the Holy Spirit floats way up in the lantern. The church's sumptuous elements—especially the organ, altar painting, pulpit, and coat of arms (in the base of the dome) of church founder Leopold I—make St. Peter's one of the city's most beautiful and ornate churches.

Cost and Hours: Free, Mon-Fri 7:00-20:00, Sat-Sun 9:00-21:00; free organ concerts Mon-Fri at 15:00, Sat-Sun at 20:00; just off the Graben between the Plague Monument and Kohlmarkt, tel. 01/533-6433, www.peterskirche.at.

Mozarthaus Vienna Museum

In September 1784, 27-year-old Wolfgang Amadeus Mozart moved into this spacious apartment with his wife, Constanze, and their week-old son Karl. For the next three years, this was the epi-center of Viennese high life. It was here that Mozart wrote *Marriage of Figaro* and *Don Giovanni* and established himself as the toast of Vienna. Today, the actual apartments are pretty boring (mostly bare rooms), but the museum does flesh out Mozart's Vienna years with paintings, videos, and a few period pieces.

Cost and Hours: €11, includes audioguide, €18 combo-ticket with Haus der Musik, daily 10:00-19:00, a block behind the cathedral, go through arcade at #5a and walk 50 yards to Domgasse 5, tel. 01/512-1791, www.mozarthausvienna.at.

Jewish Museum Vienna (Jüdisches Museum Wien)

The museum operates two buildings a 10-minute walk apart. The **Jewish Museum Dorotheergasse** (near the Hofburg) fills a four-story downtown building with exhibits, a bookstore, and a small, reasonably priced café serving Middle Eastern fare. The main part of the exhibit is on the second floor, covering the history of Vienna's Jews up to World War II; a ground-floor exhibit carries the story forward to the present day.

The smaller, less interesting **Museum Judenplatz** (near Am Hof) was built around the scant remains of the medieval synagogue that served Vienna's 1,500 Jewish residents up until their massacre in 1420. Its main exhibit is an underground hall where you see the synagogue's foundations. The classy square above the ruins, called Judenplatz, is now dominated by a blocky **memorial** to the 65,000 Viennese Jews killed by the Nazis.

Cost and Hours: €12 ticket includes both museums; Dorotheergasse location, at #11—Sun-Fri 10:00-18:00, closed Sat, videoguide-€4; Judenplatz location, at #8—Sun-Thu 10:00-18:00, Fri until 17:00, closed Sat; tel. 01/535-0431, www.jmw.at.

Austrian Postal Savings Bank (Österreichische Postsparkasse)

Built between 1904 and 1912, the Postal Savings Bank was one of the key buildings in the development of modern architecture. Today it's a pilgrimage site for architects from all over the world (for whom it's a ▲▲▲ sight), though its future is in doubt (it may have been turned into lofts by the time you visit). If it's open, hard-core Jugendstil fans may want to visit the pleasant, small museum inside, which tells the building's story through plans, photos, and news reports, and preserves the original bank-teller counters.

Cost and Hours: Free, foyer and atrium open Mon-Fri 7:00-17:30, closed Sat-Sun; museum open Mon-Fri from 10:00, closed

Sat-Sun; just inside the Ringstrasse at Georg-Coch-Platz 2, tel. 059-9053-3825, www.ottowagner.com.

MUSEUM DISTRICT

In the 19th century, the Habsburgs planned to link their palace and museum buildings with a series of arches across the Ringstrasse. Although that dream was never fully realized, the awe-inspiring museums still face off across Maria-Theresien-Platz, with a monument to Maria Theresa at its center.

▲▲▲Kunsthistorisches Museum

The Kunsthistorwhateveritis Museum—let's just say "Kunst" (koonst)—houses the family collection of Austria's luxury-loving Habsburg rulers. Their joie de vivre is reflected in this collection— some of the most beautiful, sexy, and fun art from two centuries (c. 1450-1650). At their peak of power in the 1500s, the Habsburgs ruled Austria, Germany, northern Italy, the Netherlands, and Spain—and you'll see a wide variety of art from all these places and beyond.

While there's little Viennese art here, you will find world-class European masterpieces galore (including canvases by Raphael, Caravaggio, Velázquez, Rubens, Vermeer, Rembrandt, and a particularly exquisite roomful of Bruegels), all well displayed on one glorious floor, plus a fine display of Egyptian, classical, and applied arts.

Cost and Hours: €15, €20 combo-ticket with Hofburg Treasury; daily 10:00-18:00, Thu until 21:00, closed Mon Sept-May; audioguide-€5, on the Ringstrasse at Maria-Theresien-Platz, U: Volkstheater/Museumsplatz, tel. 01/525-240, www.khm.at.

Visiting the Museum: Of the museum's many exhibits, we'll tour only the Painting Gallery (Gemäldegalerie) on the first floor. Italian-Spanish-French art is on one half of the floor, and Northern European art on the other. The museum seems to constantly move paintings from room to room, so be flexible (and pick up the current floorplan brochure in the lobby).

Titian, *Danae* and *Ecce Homo:* In the long career of Titian the Venetian (it rhymes), he painted portraits, Christian Madonnas, and sexy Venuses with equal ease. Here, Titian captured Danae—a luscious nude reclining in bed—as she's about to be seduced. Zeus, the king of the Gods, descends as a shower of gold to consort with her—you can almost see the human form of Zeus

within the cloud. Danae is enraptured, opening her legs to receive him, while her servant tries to catch the heavenly spurt with
a golden dish. How could ultra-conservative Catholic emperors
have tolerated such a downright pagan and erotic painting? Apparently, without a problem.

In the large canvas *Ecce Homo*, a crowd mills about, when suddenly there's a commotion. They nudge each other and start to point. Follow their gaze diagonally up the stairs to a battered figure entering way up in the corner. "Ecce Homo!" says Pilate. "Behold the man." And he presents Jesus to the mob.

Raphael, *Madonna of the Meadow:* Young Raphael epito-
mized the spirit of the High Renaissance, combining symmetry,
grace, beauty, and emotion. This Madonna is a mountain of moth-
erly love—Mary's head is the summit and her flowing robe is the
base—enfolding Baby Jesus and John the Baptist. The geometric
perfection, serene landscape, and Mary's adoring face make this a
masterpiece of sheer grace—but then you get smacked by an ironic
fist: The cross the little tykes play with foreshadows their gruesome
deaths.

Correggio and Parmigianino: The Kunst displays excellent
small canvases in the smaller side rooms. For example, in a room
near Raphael, you may find Correggio's Jupiter and Io, showing
Zeus seducing another female, this time disguised as a cloud.
Parmigianino's *Self-Portrait in a Convex Mirror* depicts the artist
gazing into a convex mirror and perfectly reproducing the curved
reflection on a convex piece of wood. Amazing.

Arcimboldo, *Portraits of the Seasons:* These four cleverly deceptive portraits by the Habsburg court painter depict the four seasons (and elements) as people. For example, take *Summer*—a.k.a.
"Fruit Face." With a pickle nose, pear chin, and corn-husk ears,
this guy literally is what he eats. Its grotesque weirdness makes it
typical of Mannerist art.

**Caravaggio, *Madonna of the Rosary and David with the Head
of Goliath:*** Caravaggio shocked the art world with brutally honest reality. Compared with Raphael's super-sweet *Madonna of the
Meadow*, Caravaggio's *Madonna of the Rosary* (the biggest canvas in
the room) looks perfectly ordinary, and the saints kneeling around
her have dirty feet.

In *David with the Head of Goliath*, Caravaggio turns a third-
degree-interrogation light on a familiar Bible story. David shoves
the dripping head of the slain giant right in our noses. This David

is not a heroic Renaissance man like Michelangelo's famous statue, but a homeless teen that Caravaggio paid to portray God's servant. And the severed head of Goliath is none other than Caravaggio himself, an in-your-face self-portrait.

Velázquez, Habsburg Family Portraits: When the Habsburgs ruled both Austria and Spain, cousins kept in touch through portraits of themselves and their kids. Diego Velázquez was the greatest of Spain's "photojournalist" painters—heavily influenced by Caravaggio's realism, capturing his subjects without passing judgment, flattering, or glorifying them.

For example, watch little Margarita Habsburg grow up in three different portraits on the same wall, from age two to age nine. Margarita was destined from birth to marry her Austrian cousin, the future Emperor Leopold I. Pictures like these, sent from Spain every few years, let her pen pal/fiancé get to know her.

Also see a portrait of Margarita's little brother, *Philip Prosper,* wearing a dress. Sadly, Philip was a sickly boy who would only live two years longer. The amulets he's wearing were intended to fend off illness. His hand rests limply on the back of the chair—above an adorable puppy who seems to be asking, "But who will play with me?"

Canaletto: Before leaving this wing, find paintings of the Habsburg summer palace, Schloss Schönbrunn, by Canaletto, one of which also shows the Viennese skyline in the distance. Then cross under the dome and through the café, and walk into the part of the museum dedicated to Northern European art, through Saal XV and into XIV and XIII for the big-canvas, bright-colored world of Baroque.

Peter Paul Rubens: In Rubens' *Self-Portrait,* admire the darling of Catholic-dominated Flanders (northern Belgium) in his prime: famous, wealthy, well-traveled, the friend of kings and princes, an artist, diplomat, man about town, and—obviously—confident. Rubens' work runs the gamut, from realistic portraits to lounging nudes, Greek myths to altarpieces, from pious devotion to violent sex. But, can we be sure it's Baroque? Ah yes, I'm sure you'll find a pudgy, winged baby somewhere, hovering in the heavens.

How could Rubens paint all of these enormous canvases in one lifetime? He had help. He ran a busy studio with about 60 artists. Rubens generally painted a small model "cartoon" (you can see several here) from which his team of artists would paint the big canvas. He'd then amp up their work with what he called "the fury of the brush" and it was shipped out...another Rubens masterpiece. For example, the giant canvas *The Miracles of St. Ignatius of Loyola* was painted partly by assistants, guided by Rubens' sketches.

Jan Vermeer: In his small canvases, the Dutch painter Jan Vermeer quiets the world down to where we can hear our own heartbeat, letting us appreciate the beauty in common things.

The curtain opens and we see *The Art of Painting,* a behind-the-scenes look at Vermeer at work. He's painting a model dressed in blue, starting with her laurel-leaf headdress. The studio is its own little dollhouse world framed by a chair in the foreground and the wall in back. Then Vermeer fills this space with the few gems he wants us to focus on—the chandelier, the map, the painter's costume. Everything is lit by a crystal-clear light, letting us see these everyday items with fresh eyes.

Rembrandt van Rijn: Rembrandt became wealthy by painting portraits of Holland's upwardly mobile businessmen, but his greatest subject was himself. In the *Large Self-Portrait* we see the hands-on-hips, defiant, open-stance determination of a man who will do what he wants, and if people don't like it, tough.

In typical Rembrandt style, most of the canvas is a dark, smudgy brown, with only the side of his face glowing from the darkness. (Remember Caravaggio? Rembrandt did.) Unfortunately, the year this was painted, Rembrandt's fortunes changed.

Looking at the *Small Self-Portrait* from 1657, consider Rembrandt's last years. His wife died, his children died young, and commissions for paintings dried up as his style veered from the popular style of the day. He had to auction off paintings to pay his debts, and he died a poor man.

Pieter Bruegel the Elder: The undisputed master of the slice-of-life village scene was Pieter Bruegel the Elder (c. 1525-1569)—think of him as the Norman Rockwell of the 16th century. He celebrated their simple life, but he also skewered their weaknesses—not to single them out as hicks, but as universal examples of human folly. About a quarter of all known Bruegel paintings are gathered in this exciting room.

The Peasant Wedding, Bruegel's most famous work, is less about the wedding than the food. It's a farmers' feeding frenzy, as the barnful of wedding guests scrambles to get their share of free eats. Two men bring in the next course, a tray of fresh porridge. Everyone's going at it, including a kid in an oversized red cap who licks the bowl with his fingers. In the middle of it all, look who's been completely forgotten—the demure bride sitting in front of the blue-green cloth. According to Flemish tradition, the bride was not allowed to speak or eat at the party, and the groom was not in attendance at all.

▲▲Natural History Museum (Naturhistorisches Museum)

The twin building facing the Kunsthistorisches Museum still serves the exact purpose for which it was built: to show off the Habsburgs' vast collection of plant, animal, and min-

eral specimens and artifacts. It's grown to become an exceptionally well-organized and enjoyable catalogue of the natural world, with 20 million objects, including moon rocks, dinosaur stuff, and the fist-sized *Venus of Willendorf* (at 25,000 years old, the world's oldest sex symbol). Even though the museum has kept its old-school charm, nearly everything on display is presented and described well enough to engage any visitor, from kids to scientifically inclined grown-ups.

Cost and Hours: €10, Thu-Mon 9:00-18:30, Wed until 21:00, closed Tue; €5 audioguide ("Top 100") isn't necessary, but can help you hit the highlights; on the Ringstrasse at Maria-Theresien-Platz, U: Volkstheater/Museumsplatz, tel. 01/521-770, www.nhm-wien.ac.at.

MuseumsQuartier

The vast grounds of the former imperial stables now corral a cutting-edge cultural center for contemporary arts and design. Among several impressive museums, the best are the Leopold Museum, specializing in 20th-century Austrian modernists (Schiele, Klimt, and Kokoschka, among others), and the Museum of Modern Art, Austria's leading gallery for international modern and contemporary art. For many, the MuseumsQuartier is most enjoyable as a spot to gather in the evening for a light, fun meal, cocktails, and people-watching.

Cost and Hours: Leopold Museum—€13, open daily 10:00-18:00, Thu until 21:00, closed Tue Sept-May, audioguide-€4 or €7/2 people, tel. 01/525-700, www.leopoldmuseum.org; Museum of Modern Art—€12, €8 Thu after 18:00, open Mon 14:00-19:00, Tue-Sun 10:00-19:00, Thu until 21:00, good audioguide-€3.50, tel. 01/52500, www.mumok.at. The main entrance/visitors center is at Museumsplatz 1 (ask about combo-tickets here if visiting more

than just the Leopold and Modern Art museums; U: Volkstheater/
Museumsplatz, tel. 01/525-5881, www.mqw.at).

KARLSPLATZ AND NEARBY

These sights cluster around Karlsplatz, just southeast of the Ringstrasse (U: Karlsplatz). If you're walking from central Vienna, use
the U-Bahn station's passageway (at the opera house) to avoid
crossing busy boulevards.

Karlsplatz

This picnic-friendly square, with its Henry Moore sculpture in
the pond, is the front yard of Vienna's Technical University. The
massive, domed Karlskirche and its twin spiral columns dominate
the square. The small green, white, and gold pavilions that line
the street across the square from the church are from the late-
19th-century municipal train system *(Stadtbahn)*. With curvy iron
frames, decorative marble slabs, and painted gold trim, these are
pioneering works in the Jugendstil style, designed by the Modernist architect **Otto Wagner,** who influenced Klimt and the Secessionists. One of the pavilions has a sweet little exhibit on Wagner
that illustrates the Art Nouveau lifestyle around 1900 (€5, Tue-Sun
10:00-18:00, closed Mon and Nov-March, near the Ringstrasse,
tel. 01/5058-7478-5177, www.wienmuseum.at).

▲Karlskirche (St. Charles Church)

This "votive church" was proposed by Emperor Charles VI and
dedicated to his patron saint, St. Charles Borromeo, in 1713 when
an epidemic spared Vienna. The church offers some over-the-top
Baroque designs, with a unique combination of columns (showing scenes from Borromeo's life, à la Trajan's Column in Rome),
a classic pediment, an elliptical dome, and a terrific close-up look
at its frescoes, thanks to a construction elevator that's open to the
public. The dome's colorful 13,500-square-foot fresco—painted in
the 1730s by Johann Michael Rottmayr—shows Signor Borromeo
(in red-and-white bishop's robes) gazing up into heaven, spreading
his arms wide, and pleading with Christ to spare Vienna from the
plague. Skip the dome if you're even slightly afraid of heights.

   Cost and Hours: €8, Mon-Sat 9:00-18:00, Sun 12:00-19:00,
dome elevator runs until 17:30, pick up the free info booklet, www.
karlskirche.at. There are often classical music concerts performed
here on period instruments (usually Thu-Sat, www.concert-vienna.
info).

▲Academy of Fine Arts Painting Gallery
(Akademie der Bildenden Künste Gemäldegalerie)

Vienna's art academy has a small but impressive collection of paintings, most of which is being temporarily housed at the nearby

Theatermuseum while the academy is undergoing a multiyear renovation. The highlights—a triptych by the master of medieval surrealism, Hieronymus Bosch, and works by Guardi, Titian, Rubens, Van Dyck, and other great masters—can be seen at the temporary location.

Cost and Hours: Temporary exhibit at Theatermuseum—€12, Wed-Mon 10:00-18:00, closed Tue; audioguide-€2, in the Palais Lobokowitz at Lobkowitzplatz 2, tel. 01/588-162-201, www.akbild.ac.at; Academy of Fine Arts—closed until at least 2020, when open it's three blocks from the opera house at Schillerplatz 3.

▲The Secession

This little building was created by the Vienna Secession movement, a group of nonconformist artists led by Gustav Klimt, Otto Wagner, and friends.

Having turned their backs on the stuffy official art academy, the Secessionists used the building to display their radical art. The stylized trees carved into the exterior walls and the building's bushy "golden cabbage" rooftop are symbolic of a cycle of renewal. Today, the Secession continues to showcase contemporary cutting-edge art, and it preserves Gustav Klimt's famous *Beethoven Frieze*. A masterpiece of Viennese Art Nouveau, this 105-foot-long fresco was the multimedia centerpiece of a 1902 exhibition honoring Ludwig van Beethoven.

Cost and Hours: €9.50 includes special exhibits, Tue-Sun 10:00-18:00, closed Mon, audioguide-€3, Friedrichstrasse 12, tel. 01/587-5307, www.secession.at.

▲Naschmarkt

In 1898, the city decided to cover up its Vienna River. The long, wide square they created was filled with a lively produce market that still bustles most days. It's long been known as *the* place to get exotic faraway foods. In fact, locals say, "From here start the Balkans."

Hours and Location: Mon-Fri 6:00-19:30, Sat until 18:00, closed Sun, closes earlier in winter; restaurants open until 23:00; between Linke Wienzeile and Rechte Wienzeile, U: Karlsplatz.

Visiting the Naschmarkt: The stalls of the Naschmarkt (roughly, "Nibble Market") stretch along Wienzeile street, just a short stroll south of the opera house. This "Belly of Vienna" comes with two parallel lanes—one lined with fun and reasonable eateries, and the other featuring the town's top-end produce and gourmet goodies. This is where top chefs like to get their ingredients. At the gourmet vinegar stall, you can sample the vinegar as you would perfume—with a drop on your wrist (see photo). Farther from the center, the Naschmarkt becomes likably seedy, less expensive, and surrounded by sausage stands, Turkish *döner kebab* stalls, cafés, and theaters. At the market's far

end is a line of buildings with fine Art Nouveau facades. Each Saturday, the Naschmarkt is infested by a huge flea market (sets up west of the Kettenbrückengasse U-Bahn station).

▲Wien Museum Karlsplatz

This underappreciated city history museum walks you through the story of Vienna with well-presented artifacts and good English descriptions. It will likely be closed by the time you visit for a modern facelift and expansion project (Karlsplatz 8, tel. 01/505-8747, www.wienmuseum.at).

▲Mariahilfer Strasse Stroll

While there are more stately and elegant streets in the central district, the best opportunity to simply feel the pulse of workaday Viennese life is a little farther out, along Mariahilfer Strasse. The street has recently gone mostly pedestrian-only, and is fast becoming an attraction in itself. An easy plan is to ride the U-3 to the Zieglergasse stop, then stroll and browse your way downhill to the MuseumsQuartier U-Bahn station.

If you're interested in how Austria handles its people's appetite for **marijuana,** search out three interesting stops along this corridor: Bushplanet Headshop (at Esterhazygasse 32, near the Neubaugasse U-Bahn stop), Hemp Embassy Museum (next to Bushplanet Headshop—basically a display of big, sparkling marijuana plants), and Bushplanet Growshop (set back in a courtyard off Mariahilfer Strasse at #115, both Bushplanet locations open Mon-Fri 10:00-19:00, Sat until 18:00, closed Sun, www.bushplanet.at; see map on page 929).

To add some fine-art culture to your stroll, drop in at the nearby **Imperial Furniture Collection,** where you'll see everything from Habsburg thrones to commodes (see listing later in this chapter).

For a fine and free city view (along with reasonable eating), escalate to the top floor of the honeycombed Gerngross shopping center and find the **Brandauer** restaurant (at Mariahilfer Strasse #42).

Just off Mariahilfer Strasse #24 (near Capistrangasse) is a passageway (sometimes closed) leading to a chilling bit of WWII history: a Nazi **flak tower** built in 1944. Mighty towers like this, which housed antiaircraft guns and doubled as bomb shelters, survive in Hamburg, Berlin, and Vienna (where six still stand). This bomb shelter is connected by tunnel to today's Austrian government and still serves as a bunker of last resort.

SIGHTS BEYOND THE RING

The following museums and sights are located outside the Ring-strasse but inside the Gürtel, or outer ring road (see the "Greater Vienna" map on page 847).

South of the Ring
▲▲Belvedere Palace (Schloss Belvedere)

This is the elegant palace of Prince Eugene of Savoy (1663-1736), the still much-appreciated conqueror of the Ottomans. Today you

can tour Eugene's lavish palace, see sweeping views of the gardens and the Vienna skyline, and enjoy world-class art starring Gustav Klimt, French Impressionism, and a grab bag of other 19th- and early-20th-century artists. While Vienna's other art collections show off works by masters from around Europe, this has the city's best collection of homegrown artists.

The palace complex includes the Upper Palace (world-class art collection), smaller Lower Palace (historical rooms and temporary exhibits), the 21er Haus (modern pavilion mostly filled with contemporary art), and pleasantly beautiful Baroque-style gardens (free and fun to explore). For most visitors, only the Upper Palace is worth the entrance fee.

Cost and Hours: €15 for Upper Belvedere Palace only, €22 for Klimt Ticket covering Upper and Lower Palaces (and special exhibits), gardens free; daily 10:00-18:00, Fri until 21:00, grounds open until dusk; audioguide-€4 or €7/2 people; good English descriptions; entrance at Prinz-Eugen-Strasse 27, tel. 01/7955-7134, www.belvedere.at.

Eating at the Belvedere: There's a charming little sit-down

VIENNA

café on the ground floor of the Upper Palace; in summer you can dine outdoors in the garden.

Getting There: The palace is a 15-minute walk south of the Ring. To get there from the center, catch tram #D at the opera house (direction: Hauptbahnhof). Get off at the Schloss Belvedere stop (just below the Upper Palace gate), cross the street, walk uphill one block, go through the gate (on left), and look immediately to the right for the small building with the ticket office.

Visiting the Belvedere: The two grand buildings of the Belvedere Palace are separated by a fine garden that slopes down from the Upper to Lower Palace. For our purposes, the **Upper Palace** is what matters. There are two grand floors, set around impressive middle halls.

From the entrance, climb the staircase to the first floor and enter a grand red-and-gold, chandeliered **Marble Hall.** This was Prince Eugene's party room. *Belvedere* means "beautiful view," and the view from the Marble Hall is the most iconic of the city (it's notably captured in Canaletto's painting displayed at the Kunsthistorisches Museum). Look over the Baroque gardens, the Lower Palace, and the city.

Then head into the **east wing.** Sumptuous paintings by **Gustav Klimt** and his contemporaries (including Monet) fill the rooms in the east wing. To Klimt, all art was erotic art. He painted during the turn of the 20th century, when Vienna was a splendid laboratory of hedonism. Even fully clothed, his women have a bewitching eroticism in a world full of pollen and pistils.

At the far end of the east wing you'll find what is perhaps Klimt's best-known painting, *The Kiss*, where two lovers are wrapped up in the colorful gold-and-jeweled cloak of bliss. Klimt's woman is no longer dominating, but submissive, abandoning herself to her man in a fertile field and a vast universe. In a glow emanating from a radiance of desire, the body she presses against is a self-portrait of the artist himself.

While Klimt's works are seductive and otherworldly, **Egon Schiele**'s tend to be darker and more introspective. One of Schiele's most recognizable works, *The Embrace*, shows a couple engaged in an erotically charged, rippling moment of passion. Striking a darker tone is *The Family*. This melancholy painting from 1918 is Schiele's last major painting—he and his pregnant wife died in the influenza epidemic that swept through Europe after World War I.

The **rest of the Upper Palace** collection goes through the whole range of 19th- and 20th-century art: Historicism, Romanticism, Impressionism, Realism, tired tourism, Expressionism, Art Nouveau, and early Modernism. In the west wing of the first floor is the Belvedere's collection of Austrian Baroque art, including a fascinating corner room of grotesquely grimacing heads by **Franz Xaver Messerschmidt** (1736-1783), a quirky 18th-century Habsburg court sculptor who left the imperial life to follow his own, somewhat deranged muse. After his promising career was cut short by mental illness, Messerschmidt relocated to Bratislava and spent the rest of his days sculpting a series of eerily lifelike "character heads" *(Kopfstücke)* whose unusual faces are contorted by extreme emotions.

▲Museum of Military History (Heeresgeschichtliches Museum)

A big part of Habsburg history is military. And this huge place, built about 1860 as an arsenal by Franz Josef, tells the story well with a thoughtful motto (apparently learned from the school of hard knocks): "Wars belong in museums." This vast museum holds a rich collection of artifacts and historic treasures. The interesting 20th-century section includes exhibits devoted to Sarajevo in 1914, Chancellor Dollfuss and the pre-Hitler Austrian Fascist party, the Anschluss, and World War II.

Cost and Hours: €6, includes good audioguide, free first Sun of the month; daily 9:00-17:00, small café on site, on Arsenalstrasse, tel. 01/795-610, www.hgm.at. It's a five-minute walk from the Quartier Belvedere tram/S-Bahn stop behind the Belvedere Palace (see the "Greater Vienna" map on page 847).

East of the Ring
Museum of Applied Arts (Museum für Angewandte Kunst, a.k.a. MAK)

Facing the old town from across the Ring, the MAK, as it's called, is a design museum best known for its collection of furniture and decorative art from Vienna's artistic Golden Age, which is showcased in the permanent Vienna 1900 exhibit. The museum's unique gift shop also makes for a fun diversion.

Cost and Hours: €12, €5 Tue after 18:00; open Tue 10:00-22:00, Wed-Sun until 18:00, closed Mon; multimedia guide-€2, classy restaurant with pleasant garden seating, Stubenring 5—take U-Bahn or tram #2 to Stubentor, tel. 01/711-360, www.mak.at.

▲Kunst Haus Wien Museum and Hundertwasserhaus

This "make yourself at home" museum and nearby apartment complex are a hit with lovers of modern art, mixing the work and philosophy of local painter/environ-mentalist Friedensreich Hundertwasser (1928-2000), a.k.a. "100H$_2$O."

The museum provides by far the best look at Hundertwasser, but for an actual lived-in apartment complex by the green master, walk 10 minutes to the one-with-nature Hundertwasserhaus (at Löwen-gasse and Kegelgasse). This complex of 50 apartments, subsidized by the government to provide affordable housing, was built in the 1980s as a breath of architectural fresh air in a city of boring, blocky apartment complexes. While not open to visitors, it's worth seeing for its fun and colorful patchwork exterior.

Cost and Hours: €11 for museum, €12 combo-ticket includes special exhibitions, open daily 10:00-18:00, audioguide-€3, tel. 01/712-0491, www.kunsthauswien.com.

Getting There: It's located at Untere Weissgerberstrasse 13, near the Radetzkyplatz stop on trams #O and #1 (signs point the way). Take the U-Bahn to Landstrasse and either walk 10 minutes downhill (north) along Untere Viaduktgasse (a block east of the station), or transfer to tram #O (direction: Praterstern) and ride three stops to Radetzkyplatz.

▲Prater Park (Wiener Prater)

Since the 1780s, when the reformist Emperor Josef II gave his hunting grounds to the people of Vienna as a public park, this place has been Vienna's playground. For the tourist, the "Prater" is the sugary-smelling, tired, and sprawling amusement park (Wurstel-prater). For locals, the "Prater" is the vast, adjacent green park with its three-mile-long, tree-lined main boulevard (Hauptallee). The park still tempts visitors with its huge 220-foot-tall, famous, and lazy Ferris wheel *(Riesenrad),* fun roller coasters, bumper cars, Lil-liputian railroad, and endless eateries. Especially if you're traveling with kids, this is a fun place to share the evening with thousands of Viennese and tourists.

Cost and Hours: Park is free and always open; amusement park—rides cost €2-8 and run May-Oct roughly 10:00-22:00, but often later in good weather in summer, fewer rides open in off-season; U: Praterstern, www.prater.at.

North of the Ring
Sigmund Freud Museum

Freud enthusiasts (and detractors) enjoy seeing the apartment and home office of the man who fundamentally changed our understanding of the human psyche. Dr. Sigmund Freud (1856-1939), a graduate of Vienna University, established his practice here in 1891. For the next 47 years, he received troubled patients who hoped to find peace by telling him their dreams, life traumas, and secret urges. It was here that he wrote his influential works, including the landmark *Interpretation of Dreams* (1899). The museum is narrowly focused on Freud's life. If you're looking for a critical appraisal of whether he was a cocaine-addicted charlatan or a sincere doctor groping toward an understanding of human nature, you won't find it here.

The museum may be under renovation when you visit; if it is, a temporary exhibit will be set up nearby (at Berggasse 15) with a few artifacts on display at a reduced entrance fee.

Cost and Hours: €12, includes app, daily 10:00-18:00, tiny bookshop, half-block from the Schlickgasse stop on tram #D, Berggasse 19, tel. 01/319-1596, www.freud-museum.at.

West of the Ring
▲Imperial Furniture Collection (Hofmobiliendepot)
Bizarre, sensuous, eccentric, or precious, this underappreciated collection (on four fascinating floors) is your peek at the Habsburgs' furniture—from the empress's wheelchair ("to increase her fertility she was put on a rich diet and became corpulent") to the emperor's spittoon—all thoughtfully described in English. Evocative paintings help bring the furniture to life.

The Habsburgs had many palaces, but only the Hofburg was permanently furnished. The rest were done on the fly—set up and taken down by a gang of royal roadies called the "Depot of Court Movables" (Hofmobiliendepot). When the monarchy was dissolved in 1918, the state of Austria took possession of the Hofmobiliendepot's inventory—165,000 items. Now this royal storehouse is open to the public in a fine and sprawling museum.

Cost and Hours: €9.50, includes audioguide, covered by Sisi Ticket, Tue-Sun 10:00-18:00, closed Mon, Mariahilfer Strasse 88, main entrance around the corner at Andreasgasse 7, U: Zieglergasse, tel. 01/5243-3570, www.hofmobiliendepot.at.

Tip: To avoid lines at the Schönbrunn Palace and the Hofburg Imperial Apartments, buy your Sisi Ticket here first or purchase in advance online (www.schoenbrunn.at).

SIGHTS ON VIENNA'S OUTSKIRTS
▲▲▲Schönbrunn Palace (Schloss Schönbrunn)
The Habsburgs' former summer residence, just a 10-minute subway ride from downtown Vienna, is second only to Versailles among Europe's grand palaces. Originally built in the 16th century as a small hunting lodge near a beautiful spring *(schön-brunn)*, the resi-

dence grew over the next 300 years into the palace you see today. The highlight of the vast complex's many sights is a tour of the Imperial Apartments where the Habsburg nobles lived (including Maria Theresa and her 16 children, and Franz Josef and Sisi). You can also stroll the palace gardens, visit the world's oldest zoo, and view royal transport from the 19th century at the Imperial Carriage Museum.

Cost: Visits to the palace are by timed-entry tours (book in advance, see below). The Imperial Apartments offer two tour options: The best is the 40-room **Grand Tour** (€20, 50 minutes, includes audioguide, covered by Sisi Ticket), which includes both the rooms of Franz Josef and Sisi, as well as the (more impressive) Rococo rooms of Maria Theresa. The **Imperial Tour** (€16, 35 minutes, includes audioguide) covers only the less-interesting first 22 rooms. For €3 more you can do the Grand Tour with a real guide, but since these live tours are offered only a few times a day, I wouldn't bother.

If venturing beyond the apartments, consider the **Classic Pass** combo-ticket (€24, available April-Oct only), which includes the Grand Tour, as well as the Gloriette viewing terrace, maze, orangery, and privy garden.

Hours: Imperial Apartments open daily 8:00-17:30, July-Aug until 18:30, Nov-March until 17:00; gardens generally open 6:30-20:00 but varies with season. The palace is busiest from 9:00 to 12:00, and crowds start to subside after 14:00.

Information: Tel. 01/8111-3239, www.schoenbrunn.at.

Advance Tickets Recommended: In summer and on good-weather weekends, definitely make a reservation. Otherwise you'll likely have to stand in line at the ticket desk, and then you'll probably have to wait again for your assigned entry time—which could be hours later. To get right in, book your entry time in advance online. Those with a Sisi Ticket can enter without a reserved entry time (buy your Sisi Ticket online or at the Imperial Furniture Museum—see page 877 for details).

If you don't have a reservation, come early or late in the day. You can save some time in line by using one of the ticket machines. If you have time to kill before your entry time, spend it exploring the gardens or Imperial Carriage Museum.

Getting There: Schönbrunn is an easy 10-minute subway ride from downtown Vienna. Take U-4 (which conveniently leaves from Karlsplatz) to Schönbrunn (direction: Hütteldorf) and follow signs for *Schloss Schönbrunn*. Exit bearing right, then cross the busy

Schönbrunn Palace

Fasangarten

GUDENTWEG

MAXING-STRASSE

GLORIETTE

Tirolergarten

KLEINE GLORIETTE

Botanical Garden

NEPTUNE FOUNTAIN

ZOO

OBELISK

ZOO ENTRANCE

WC

"ROMAN RUINS"

Japanese Garden

MAIN ZOO ENTRANCE

SCHÖNER BRUNNEN

MAZE

PALM HOUSE

DESERT EXPERIENCE HOUSE

GRÜNBERGSTRASSE

GARDENS

WC

WC

WC

Am Platz

WC

CAFÉ

CHILDREN'S MUSEUM

Privy Garden

PALACE

Sisi Gardens

ORANGERY GARDEN

PALACE ENTRANCE

IMPERIAL CARRIAGE MUSEUM

SCHLOSS-STRASSE

U Hietzing

SCHÖNBRUNNER

U Schönbrunn

Wien

VISITORS CENTER (TICKETS)

River

HADIKGASSE

200 Meters

200 Yards

LINKE WIENZEILE

To ↙ City Center

VIENNA

road and continue to the right, to the far, far end of the long yellow building. There you'll find the visitors center, where tickets are sold.

Planning Your Time: Allow at least three hours (including transit time) for your excursion to Schönbrunn Palace. The palace itself is sprawling and can be mobbed. After viewing the Imperial Apartments, wander the gardens (most of which are free). With more time and energy, pick and choose among the other sightseeing options and buy tickets as you go.

▲▲▲Imperial Apartments

In the 1500s, the Habsburgs built a small hunting lodge near a beautiful spring, and for the next three centuries, they made it their summer getaway from stuffy Vienna. The palace's exterior (late 1600s) is Baroque, but the interior was finished under Maria Theresa (mid-1700s) in let-them-eat-cake Rococo.

Visiting the Apartments: Your tour of the apartments, accompanied by an audioguide, follows a clearly signed one-way route. Think of the following minitour as a series of bread crumbs, leading you along while the audioguide fills in the details.

Begin in the **guards' room,** where jauntily dressed mannequins of Franz Josef's bodyguards introduce you to his luxurious world. Continue through the Billiard Room to the **Walnut Room.** Wow. Rococo-style wood paneling and gilding decorate this room where Franz Josef—a hardworking modern monarch—received official visitors. Nearby is the **study**—Franz Josef (see his mustachioed portrait) worked at this desk, sometimes joined by his beautiful, brown-haired wife Sisi (see her portrait). In the **bedchamber,** where he died barely more than a century ago, a praying stool, iron bed, and little toilet all attest to Franz Josef's spartan lifestyle (though the paintings here remind us of the grand scale of his palace).

Empress Sisi's Study and Dressing Room: See her portrait in a black dress, as well as (a reconstruction of) the spiral staircase that once led down to her apartments. The long-haired mannequin and makeup jars in the dressing room indicate how obsessive Sisi was about her looks.

Franz Josef's and Sisi's Bedroom: The huge wood-carved double bed suggests marital bliss, but the bed is not authentic—and as for the bliss, history suggests otherwise. Nearby is **Sisi's salon.** Though this was Sisi's reception room, the pastel paintings show her husband's distinguished ancestors—the many children of Maria Theresa (including Marie-Antoinette, immediately to the left as you enter).

Follow along to the **dining room.** The whole family ate here at the huge table; today it's set with dinnerware owned by Maria Theresa and Sisi. Next is the **children's room,** with portraits of Maria Theresa (on the easel) and some of her 11 (similar-looking) daughters.

Hall of Mirrors: In this room, six-year-old Mozart performed for Maria Theresa and her family (1762). He amazed them by playing without being able to see the keys, he jumped playfully into the empress' lap, and he even asked six-year-old Marie-Antoinette to marry him.

Great Gallery: Imagine the parties they had here: waltzers spinning across the floor, lit by chandeliers reflecting off the mirrors, beneath stunning ceiling frescoes, while enjoying views of the gardens and the Gloriette monument (described later). When WWII bombs rained on Vienna, the palace was largely spared. It took only one direct hit—crashing through this ballroom—but, thankfully, that bomb was a dud.

More Fancy Rooms: It was in the **Blue Chinese Salon,** in 1918, that the last Habsburg emperor made the decision to relinquish power, marking the end of more than six centuries of Habsburg rule. Up next, the black-lacquer **Vieux-Laque Room** was remodeled by Maria Theresa as a memorial to her beloved husband who died unexpectedly. Continue to the **Napoleon Room.** When Napoleon conquered Austria, he took over Schönbrunn and made this his bedroom. He dumped Josephine and took a Habsburg princess as his bride, and they had a son (cutely pictured holding a wreath of flowers).

Rich Bedchamber: This darkened room has what may have been Maria Theresa's wedding bed, where she and her husband Franz produced 16 children. Then comes their **study,** with a fitting end to this palace tour—a painting showing the happy couple who left their mark all over Schönbrunn.

▲▲Palace Gardens

The large, manicured grounds fill the palace's backyard, dominated

by a hill-topping monument called the Gloriette. Unlike the gardens of Versailles, meant to shut out the real world, Schönbrunn's park was opened to the public in 1779 while the monarchy was in full swing. It was part of Maria Theresa's reform policy, making the garden a celebration of the evolution of civilization from autocracy into real democracy.

Today it's a delightful, sprawling place to wander—especially on a sunny day. You can spend hours here, enjoying the views and the people-watching. And most of the park is free, as it has been for more than two centuries (open daily sunrise to dusk, entrance on either side of the palace). Note that a number of specialty features in the gardens charge admission but are included in the Schönbrunn passes described earlier (under "Cost").

If the weather is good, huff up the zigzag path above the Neptune Fountain to the **Gloriette,** a purely decorative monument celebrating an obscure Austrian military victory. To gain access to the view terraces, you can pay for a pricey drink in the café or shell out for an admission ticket (€4.50)—but views are about as good from the lawn just in front of the monument.

Getting Around the Gardens: A tourist train makes the rounds all day, connecting Schönbrunn's many attractions (€8, 2/hour in peak season, none Nov-mid-March, one-hour circuit).

Schönbrunn Zoo (Tiergarten Schönbrunn)

The world's oldest zoo, next door to the palace grounds, was built in 1752 by Maria Theresa's husband for the entertainment and education of the court. He later opened it up to the public—provided that they wore proper attire. Today, it's a modern A (anteater) to Z (zebra) menagerie that's especially appealing to families.

Cost and Hours: Adults—€20, kids—€10, daily 9:00-18:30, closes earlier off-season, www.zoovienna.at.

▲Imperial Carriage Museum (Kaiserliche Wagenburg)

The Schönbrunn coach museum is a 19th-century traffic jam of 50 impressive royal carriages and sleighs. It's overpriced (but worth it if you have time to kill before your palace reservation). Highlights include silly sedan chairs, the death-black hearse carriage (used for Franz Josef in 1916, and most recently for Empress Zita in 1989), and an extravagantly gilded imperial carriage pulled by eight Cinderella horses.

Cost and Hours: €9.50, daily 9:00-17:00, Dec-April until 16:00, audioguide-€2, 200 yards from palace, walk through right arch as you face palace, tel. 01/525-243-470, www.kaiserliche-wagenburg.at.

Entertainment in Vienna

Vienna—the birthplace of what we call classical music—still thrives as Europe's music capital. On any given evening, you'll have your choice of opera, Strauss waltzes, Mozart chamber concerts, and lighthearted musicals. The Vienna Boys' Choir lives up to its worldwide reputation.

Besides music, you can spend an evening enjoying art, watching a classic film, or sipping Viennese wine in a village wine garden. Save some energy for Vienna after dark.

MUSIC

In Vienna, it's music *con brio* from September through June, reaching a symphonic climax during the Vienna Festival each May and June. Sadly, in summer (generally July and August), the Boys' Choir, opera, and many other serious music companies are—like you—on vacation. But it's OK: Vienna hums year-round with live classical music and tickets to touristy, crowd-pleasing shows are always available.

For music lovers, Vienna is also an opportunity to make pilgrimages to the homes (now mostly small museums) of favorite composers. If you're a fan of Schubert, Brahms, Haydn, Beethoven, or Mozart, there's a sight for you. But I find these homes inconveniently located and generally underwhelming. The centrally located Haus der Musik (see listing under "Sights in Vienna," earlier) is my favorite setting for celebrating the great musicians and composers who called Vienna home.

Venues: Vienna remains the music capital of Europe, with 10,000 seats in various venues around town mostly booked with classical performances. The best-known entertainment venues are the Staatsoper (State Opera House), the Volksoper (for musicals and operettas), the Theater an der Wien (opera and other performances), the Wiener Musikverein (home of the Vienna Philharmonic Orchestra), and the Wiener Konzerthaus (various events). Schedules for these venues are listed in the monthly *Wien-Programm* (available at TI). You can also check event listings at www.viennaconcerts.com.

Buying Tickets: Most tickets run from €45 to €60 (plus a stiff booking fee when purchased in advance by phone or online, or through a box office like the one at the TI). A few venues charge as little as €30; look around if you're not set on any particular concert. While it's easy to book tickets online long in advance, spontaneity is also workable, as there are invariably people selling their extra tickets at face value or less outside the door before concert time. If you call a concert hall directly, they can advise you on the availability of (cheaper) tickets at the door. Vienna takes care of its starving artists (and tourists) by offering cheap standing-room tickets to top-notch music and opera (generally an hour before each performance).

Vienna Boys' Choir (Wiener Sängerknaben)

The boys sing (from a high balcony, heard but not seen) at the 9:15 Sunday Mass from mid-September through June in the Hofburg's **Imperial Music Chapel** (Hofmusikkapelle). The entrance is at Schweizerhof; you can get there from In der Burg square or go through the tunnel from Josefsplatz.

Reserved seats must be booked in advance (€10-36; reserve by sending an email to office@hofmusikkapelle.gv.at; call 01/533-9927 for information only—they can't book tickets at this number; www.hofmusikkapelle.gv.at).

Much easier, standing room inside is free and open to the first 60 who line up. Even better, rather than line up early, you can simply swing by and stand in the narthex just outside, where you can hear the boys and see the Mass on a TV monitor.

The Boys' Choir also performs at the **MuTh** concert hall on Fridays at 17:30 in September and October (€40-90, Am Augartenspitz 1 in Augarten park, U: Taborstrasse, tel. 01/347-8080, www.muth.at, tickets@muth.at).

They're talented kids, but, for my taste, not worth all the commotion. Remember, many churches have great music during Sunday Mass. Just 200 yards from the Hofburg's Boys' Choir chapel, the Augustinian Church has a glorious 11:00 service each Sunday (which generally features its wonderful organ, a choir, and a small orchestra; see listing on page 887).

Opera
Vienna State Opera (Wiener Staatsoper)

The Vienna State Opera puts on 300 performances a year (in July and August the singers are on summer break). Since there are dif-

ferent operas nearly nightly, you'll see big trucks out back and constant action backstage—all the sets need to be switched each day. The excellent "electronic libretto" translation screens help make the experience worthwhile for opera newbies.

Opera Tickets: Main-floor seats go for €120-240; bargain hunters get limited-view seats for €13-30. You can book tickets in advance online (www.wiener-staatsoper.at). In person, head to one of the opera's two box offices: on the west side of the building (across Operngasse and facing the opera house), or the smaller one just under the big screen on the east side of the opera (facing Kärntner Strasse; both offices open Mon-Fri 9:00 until two hours before each performance, Sat 9:00-12:00, closed Sun).

Standing-Room Tickets: Unless Placido Domingo is in town, it's easy to get one of 567 standing-room tickets (*Stehplätze*, €3 up top or €4 downstairs, can purchase one ticket/person). While the front doors open one hour before the show starts, a side door (middle of building, on the Operngasse side) opens 80 minutes before curtain time, giving those in the know an early grab at standing-room tickets. Just walk straight in, then head right until you see the ticket booth marked *Stehplätze*. If fewer than 567 people are in line, there's no need to line up early. If you're one of the first 160 in line, try for the €4 "Parterre" section and you'll end up dead-center at stage level, directly under the Emperor's Box. Otherwise, you can choose between the third floor *(Balkon)*, or the fourth floor *(Galerie)*. Dress is casual (but do your best) at the standing-room bar. Locals save their spot along the rail by tying a scarf to it. Once you've saved your spot with your scarf, you can then walk around and explore the amazing building.

Rick's Crude Tip: For me, three hours is a lot of opera. But just to see and hear Vienna's opera in action for a half-hour is a treat. And if you go, you'll get the added entertainment of seeing Vienna all dressed up. I'd buy a standing-room ticket and plan to just watch the first part of the show. Before cutting out, have a glass of champagne at the opera's most glamorous bar (on the first floor, center front).

"**Live Opera on the Square**": Demonstrating its commitment to bringing opera to the masses, each spring and fall the Vienna State Opera projects several performances live on a huge screen on its building, puts out chairs for the public to enjoy...and it's all free. (These projected performances are noted as *Oper Live am Platz* in the official opera schedule—posted all around the opera building; they are also listed in the *Wien-Programm* brochure and at www.wiener-staatsoper.at.

Vienna Volksoper

For less-serious operettas and musicals, try Vienna's other opera house, located along the Gürtel, west of the city center (see *Wien-Programm* brochure or ask at TI for schedule, Währinger Strasse 78, tel. 01/5144-43670, www.volksoper.at).

Theater an der Wien

Considered the oldest theater in Vienna, this venue was designed in 1801 for Mozart operas—intimate, with just a thousand seats. It treats Vienna's music lovers to a different opera every month (except summer)—generally Mozart with a contemporary setting and modern interpretation (facing the Naschmarkt at Linke Wienzeile 6, tel. 01/58885, www.theater-wien.at).

Touristy Mozart and Strauss Concerts

Powdered-wig, costumed orchestra performances of the greatest hits of Mozart and Strauss are given almost nightly in grand traditional settings (€30-60). These are casual, easygoing concerts with lots of tour groups attending. While there's not a Viennese person in the audience, the tourists generally enjoy the evening.

To sort through your options, check with the ticket office in the TI (same price as on the street, but with all venues to choose from). Savvy locals suggest getting the cheapest tickets, as no one seems to care if cheapskates move up to fill unsold pricier seats.

Mozarthaus Concert Venue

Of the many fine venues in Vienna, the Sala Terrena at Mozarthaus might be my favorite. Intimate chamber-music concerts with musicians in historic costume take place in a small room richly decorated in Venetian Renaissance style (€49-59, Thu-Fri and Sun at 19:30, Sat at 18:00, near St. Stephen's Cathedral at Singerstrasse 7, tel. 01/911-9077, www.mozarthaus.at). Don't confuse this with the Mozarthaus Vienna Museum on Domgasse, which also holds concerts.

Strauss and Mozart Concerts in the Kursalon

For years, Strauss and Mozart concerts have been held in the Kursalon, the hall where the "Waltz King" himself directed wild-

ly popular concerts 100 years ago (€45-69, concerts generally nightly at 20:15, Johannesgasse 33 at corner of Parkring, tram #2: Weihburggasse or U: Stadtpark, tel. 01/512-5790 to check on availability—generally no problem to reserve—or buy online at www.soundofvienna.at). Shows last two hours and are a mix of ballet, waltzes, and a 15-piece orchestra. It's touristy but the performance is playful, visually fun, fine quality for most, and with a tried-and-tested, crowd-pleasing format.

NIGHTLIFE

Vienna is a great place to just be out and about on a balmy evening. While tourists are attracted to the historic central district and its charming, floodlit corners, locals go elsewhere. Depending on your mood and taste, you can join them. Survey and then enjoy lively scenes with bars, cafés, trendy restaurants, and theaters in these areas: **Donaukanal** (the Danube Canal, especially popular in the summer for its imported beaches); **Naschmarkt** (after the produce stalls close up, the bars and eateries bring new life to the place through the evening); **MuseumsQuartier** (surrounded by far-out museums and a young scene of bars with local students filling the courtyard); and **City Hall** (on the parklike Rathausplatz, where in summer free concerts and a food circus of eateries attract huge local crowds—described next).

Open-Air Music-Film Series and Food Circus

A convivial, free-to-everyone people scene erupts each evening in summer (July-Aug) on Rathausplatz, the welcoming park in front of City Hall (right on the Ringstrasse). Thousands of people keep a food circus of

simple stalls busy. There's not a plastic cup anywhere, just real plates and glasses—Vienna wants the quality of eating to be as high as the music that's about to begin. And most stalls are outposts of local restaurants—including some of Vienna's most esteemed—making this a fun and easy way to sample some of the city's most interesting options. About 2,000 spots on comfy benches face a 60-foot-wide screen up against the City Hall's Neo-Gothic facade. When darkness falls, an announcer explains the program, and then the music starts. The program is different every night so check the website—mostly films of opera and classical concerts, but with some jazz and R&B, too (www.filmfestival-rathausplatz.at, programs generally last about 2 hours, starting when it's dark—between 21:30 in July and 20:30 in Aug).

Balls and Waltzing

Renowned for its ball scene, Vienna boasts hundreds of balls each year, where the classic dance is the waltz. The height of ball season falls generally between December and February, when Viennese and visitors of all ages dress up and swirl to music ranging from waltzes to jazz to contemporary beats. Balls are put on by the Vienna Philharmonic, Vienna Boys' Choir, Vienna State Opera, and others (search for events at www.events.wien.info). The glamorous **Hofburg Silvesterball** takes place on New Year's Eve at the Hofburg Palace, featuring big-name orchestras, bands, and opera singers, a sumptuous dinner, and champagne toast (www.hofburgsilvesterball.com).

English Cinema

Several great theaters offer three or four screens of English movies nightly (€6-9). **Burg Kino,** a block from the opera house, facing the Ring (see next), tapes its weekly schedule to the door—box office opens 30 minutes before each showing. **English Cinema Haydn** is near my recommended hotels on Mariahilfer Strasse (Mariahilfer Strasse 57, tel. 01/587-2262, www.haydnkino.at), and **Artis International Cinema** is right in the town center a few minutes from the cathedral (Schultergasse 5, tel. 01/535-6570).

The Third Man at Burg Kino

This movie is set in 1949 Vienna—when it was divided, like Berlin, between the four victorious Allies. Reliving the cinematic tale of a divided city about to fall under Soviet rule and rife with smuggling is an enjoyable two-hour experience while in Vienna (€7-9, in English; about 3 showings weekly—usually Sun afternoon, Fri evening, and Tue early evening; Opernring 19, tel. 01/587-8406, www.burgkino.at).

Third Man fans will love the quirky **Third Man Museum** (Dritte Mann Museum), a lovingly curated collection of artifacts about the film, its popularity around the world, and postwar Vienna (€10, RS%—€2 discount with this book, Sat only 14:00-18:00, also some guided tours on summer Wed at 14:00—confirm on website, tour lasts 80 minutes; U: Kettenbrückengasse, a long block south of the Naschmarkt at Pressgasse 25, tel. 01/586-4872, www.3mpc.net).

Sleeping in Vienna

Accommodations in Vienna are plentiful and relatively cheap—a €100 double here might go for €150 in Munich and €200 in Milan. Within the Ring, you'll need to shell out over €100 for a double room with bath. But around Mariahilfer Strasse, two people can stay comfortably (though with no frills) for €75. Expect rates to spike for conventions (most frequent Sept-Oct), and to drop in November and from January to March. For some travelers, short-term, Airbnb-type rentals can be a good alternative; search for places in my recommended hotel neighborhoods.

Many of the hotels I've listed here share buildings with other businesses or residences which can mean lots of stairs or (hopefully) an elevator. Viennese elevators and stairwells can be confusing: In most of Europe, 0 is the ground floor, and 1 is the first floor up (our "second floor"). But in Vienna, thanks to a Habsburg-legacy quirk, older buildings have at least one extra "mezzanine" floor (labeled on elevators as P, H, M, and/or A) between the ground floor and the "first" floor, so floor 1 can actually be what we'd call the second, third, or even fourth floor.

Though the government has not yet enforced legislation to ban smoking in restaurants and bars, most hotels in Vienna are now completely nonsmoking.

For more information on rates and deals, making reservations, finding a short-term rental, and more, see the "Sleeping" section in the Practicalities chapter.

WITHIN THE RING, IN THE OLD CITY CENTER

You'll pay extra to sleep in the atmospheric old center, but if you can afford it, staying here gives you the classiest Vienna experience and enables you to walk to most sights. You won't need a car, but if you are coming with one, plan ahead and ask your hotel where to park.

$$$$ Hotel am Stephansplatz is an impersonal four-star business hotel with 56 rooms. It's plush but not over-the-top, and reasonably priced for its sleek comfort and central location facing the cathedral. Every detail is modern and high-quality, and breakfast is superb, with a view of the city waking up around the cathedral (air-con, elevator, gym and sauna, Stephansplatz 9, U: Stepha-

Sleep Code

Hotels are classified based on the average price of a standard double room with breakfast in high season.

$$$$	**Splurge:** Most rooms over €170
$$$	**Pricier:** €130-170
$$	**Moderate:** €90-130
$	**Budget:** €50-90
¢	**Backpacker:** Under €50
RS%	**Rick Steves discount**

Unless otherwise noted, credit cards are accepted, hotel staff speak basic English, and free Wi-Fi is available. Comparison-shop by checking prices at several hotels (on each hotel's own website, on a booking site, or by email). For the best deal, *book directly with the hotel.* Ask for a discount if paying in cash; if the listing includes **RS%,** request a Rick Steves discount.

nsplatz, tel. 01/534-050, www.hotelamstephansplatz.at, office@hotelamstephansplatz.at).

$$$ Aviano Boutique Hotel is a friendly, family-run place and is the best value among my pricier listings. It has 17 rooms, all comfortable and some beautiful, with flowery carpets and other Baroque frills. It's on the third and fourth floors of a typical city-center building, but feels peaceful (breakfast extra, fans, elevator, between Neuer Markt and Kärntner Strasse at Marco d'Avianogasse 1, U: Karlsplatz or Stephansplatz, tel. 01/512-8330, www.avianoboutiquehotel.com, office@avianoboutiquehotel.at, Frau Kavka).

$$$ Hotel Pertschy, circling an old courtyard, is big and elegantly creaky. Its 56 huge rooms have chandeliers and Baroque touches. Those on the courtyard are quietest (fans, elevator, Habsburgergasse 5, U: Stephansplatz, tel. 01/534-490, www.pertschy.com, info@pertschy.com).

$$$ Hotel zur Wiener Staatsoper is quiet, with a more traditional elegance than many of my other listings. Its 22 tidy rooms come with high ceilings, chandeliers, and fancy carpets on parquet floors (fans on request, elevator, a block from the opera house at Krugerstrasse 11; U: Karlsplatz; tel. 01/513-1274, www.hotel-staatsoper.at, info@hotel-staatsoper.at, manager Ursula).

$$$ Pension Nossek offers 32 rooms with a great location on the pedestrian-only Graben...but the rooms, though decorated with lace and flowers, are worn and threadbare (air-con, elevator, Graben 17, U: Stephansplatz, tel. 01/5337-0410, www.pension-nossek.at, reservation@pension-nossek.at).

$$$ Pension A und A, with nine rooms, offers a modern break from crusty old Vienna. This place, conveniently located just

Hotels in Central Vienna

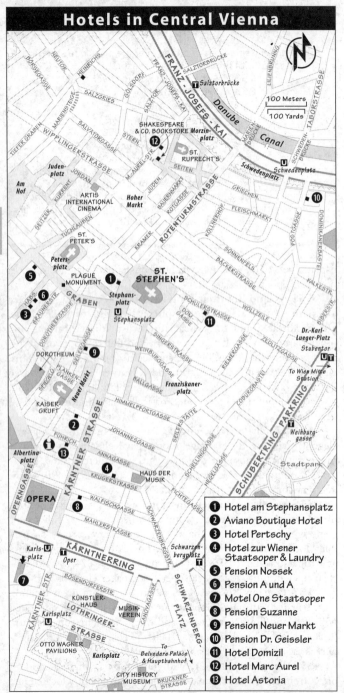

1 Hotel am Stephansplatz
2 Aviano Boutique Hotel
3 Hotel Pertschy
4 Hotel zur Wiener Staatsoper & Laundry
5 Pension Nossek
6 Pension A und A
7 Motel One Staatsoper
8 Pension Suzanne
9 Pension Neuer Markt
10 Pension Dr. Geissler
11 Hotel Domizil
12 Hotel Marc Aurel
13 Hotel Astoria

off the Graben, has a nice entryway and period elevator—but open the door and you'll find white minimalist hallways and contemporary style in the rooms (air-con, Habsburgergasse 3, U: Stephansplatz, tel. 01/890-5128, www.aunda.at, office@aunda.at).

$$ Motel One Staatsoper, part of a German chain of "budget design hotels," features sleek, smallish, modern rooms outfitted with quality materials but no frills, a 24-hour reception, funky lounge spaces, and refreshingly straightforward pricing; it's perfect for budget travelers looking for something nicer. This location—right between the opera house and Karlsplatz—has 400 rooms, including some larger options, in a smartly renovated building that's kept its Old World charm (no triples but you can slip in a child under 6 for free, breakfast extra, air-con, elevator, Elisabethstrasse 5, U: Karlsplatz, tel. 01/585-0505, www.motel-one.com, wien-staatsoper@motel-one.com).

$$ Pension Suzanne, as Baroque and doily as you'll find in this price range, is located a few yards from the opera house. It's small and without a real lobby, but run with the class of a bigger hotel. The 26 rooms are packed with properly Viennese antique furnishings (RS%, spacious apartment for up to 6 available, fans on request, elevator, Walfischgasse 4; U: Karlsplatz; tel. 01/513-2507, www.pension-suzanne.at, info@pension-suzanne.at, manager Michael).

$$ Pension Neuer Markt is perfectly central, with 37 comfy but faded pink rooms, and worn hallways with a cruise-ship ambience (in hot weather request a quiet courtyard-side room when you reserve, fans, elevator, Seilergasse 9, U: Stephansplatz, tel. 01/512-2316, www.hotelpension.at, neuermarkt@hotelpension.at).

$$ Pension Dr. Geissler, has 23 small plain-but-comfortable rooms on the eighth floor of a modern, nondescript apartment building just off Schwedenplatz, about 10 blocks northeast of St. Stephen's, near the Bratislava ferry terminal (elevator, Postgasse 14, U: Schwedenplatz—Postgasse is to the left as you face Hotel Capricorno, tel. 01/533-2803, www.hotelpension.at, dr.geissler@hotelpension.at).

NEAR NASCHMARKT

$$$ Hotel Beethoven is a smartly decorated boutique property with 47 colorful rooms and lots of attention to detail. Its comfy communal spaces and access to coffee and tea throughout the day keep it feeling like home. The location, near the Naschmarkt and overlooking the Theater an der Wien, puts you close to the action but away from the crowds and late-night noise (air-con, elevator, Sunday classical concerts, Papagenogasse 6, U: Karlsplatz, see "Vienna's City Center" map on page 853, tel. 01/587-44820, www.hotel-beethoven.at, info@hotelbeethoven.at).

ON OR NEAR MARIAHILFER STRASSE

Lively, pedestrianized Mariahilfer Strasse connects the Westbahnhof and the city center. The U-3 subway line runs underneath the street on its way between the Westbahnhof and St. Stephen's Cathedral, and most of these listings are within a five-minute walk of a U-Bahn stop. This vibrant, inexpensive area is filled with stores, cafés, and even a small shopping mall. Its smaller hotels and pensions are often immigrant-run, often by well-established Hungarian families. As you'd expect, the far end of Mariahilfer Strasse (around and past the Westbahnhof) is rougher around the edges, while the section near downtown is more gentrified.

Closer to Downtown

$$$ NH Collection Wien Zentrum, part of a Spanish chain, is a stern, stylish-but-passionless business hotel on Mariahilfer Strasse. It rents 73 rooms, including a few "suites" that are ideal for families (breakfast extra, air-con, elevator, Mariahilfer Strasse 78, U: Zieglergasse, tel. 01/524-5600, www.nh-hotels.com, nhcollectionwienzentrum@nh-hotels.com).

$$ Hotel Pension Corvinus is proudly run by a hard working Hungarian family: parents Miklós and Judith and sons Anthony and Zoltán. Its 15 comfortable rooms are bright and spacious with nice extra touches (discount if you pay cash, ask about family rooms and apartments with kitchens, air-con, elevator, Mariahilfer Strasse 57, U: Neubaugasse, tel. 01/587-7239, www.corvinus.at, hotel@corvinus.at).

$$ Hotel Kugel is run with style by hands-on owners Johannes and Christina Roller. Its 25 unique rooms, some with canopy beds, are a great value and decorated with a feminine touch (family rooms, fans, some tram noise, Siebensterngasse 43, at corner with Neubaugasse, U: Neubaugasse, tel. 01/523-3355, www.hotelkugel.at, office@hotelkugel.at).

$$ Hotel Pension Mariahilf's 12 rooms are bright, well-priced, and good-sized (if a bit outmoded), with high ceilings. Just steps from the U-Bahn, it's especially convenient (breakfast extra, served in supermarket across the street Mon-Sat and in lobby Sun, fans, elevator, Mariahilfer Strasse 49, U: Neubaugasse, tel. 01/586-1781, www.mariahilf-hotel.at, info@mariahilf-hotel.at, friendly Babak).

$$ K&T Boardinghouse rents five modern, spacious rooms on the first floor of a quiet building a block off Mariahilfer Strasse (cash only but reserve with credit card or PayPal, 2-night minimum, no breakfast, pay air-con, Chwallagasse 2, U: Neubaugasse, mobile 0676-553-6063, www.ktboardinghouse.at, kt2@chello.at, Tina). From Mariahilfer Strasse, turn left at Café Ritter and walk down Schadekgasse one short block; tiny Chwallagasse is the first right.

$ Pension Kraml is a charming, 17-room place tucked away on a small street between Mariahilfer Strasse and the Naschmarkt. It's run by hardworking Stephan and feels classic, with breakfast served in the perfectly preserved family restaurant (no longer open to nonguests) that his grandmother ran in the 1950s. The rooms, which surround a pleasantly leafy courtyard, are big and quiet, with a homey, Old World ambience (family apartment available, fans, no elevator, Brauergasse 5, midway between U: Zieglergasse and Pilgramgasse, tel. 01/587-8588, www.pensionkraml.at, pension.kraml@chello.at).

$ Pension Hargita rents 28 bright and attractive rooms. While the pension is directly on bustling Mariahilfer Strasse, its windows block noise well. Don't let the dingy sign out front put you off—this spick-and-span, well-located place is a good value (breakfast extra, fans, lots of stairs and no elevator, bike parking, corner of Mariahilfer Strasse at Andreasgasse 1, right at U: Zieglergasse, tel. 01/526-1928, www.hargita.at, office@hargita.at).

Near the Westbahnhof

$$ Motel One Westbahnhof, a more affordable outpost of the chain described earlier, has 441 rooms, lots of modern flair, and a vibrant lobby with plenty of inviting spaces to unwind (no triples but you can slip in a child under 6 for free, breakfast extra, air-con, attached to the Westbahnhof at Europaplatz 3, tel. 01/359-350, www.motel-one.com, wein-westbahnhof@motel-one.com).

$$ Hotel Ibis Wien Mariahilf, an impersonal high-rise hotel with American charm, is ideal for anyone tired of quaint old Europe. Its 341 cookie-cutter rooms are bright, comfortable, and modern, with all the conveniences (breakfast extra, air-con, elevator; exit Westbahnhof to the right and walk 400 yards, Mariahilfer Gürtel 22, U: Westbahnhof; tel. 01/59998, www.accorhotels.com, h0796@accor.com).

DORMS AND HOSTELS

These budget-minded options cluster near Mariahilfer Strasse and the Westbahnhof. For the first three, use the Westbahnhof U-Bahn stop.

¢ Hostel Ruthensteiner is your smallest and coziest option, with 100 beds in 4- to 8-bed dorms and lots of little touches (private rooms available, breakfast extra, laundry, comfy common areas with piano and guitars, bike rental; Robert-Hamerling-Gasse 24; tel. 01/893-4202, www.hostelruthensteiner.com, info@hostelruthensteiner.com). From the Westbahnhof, follow Maria-

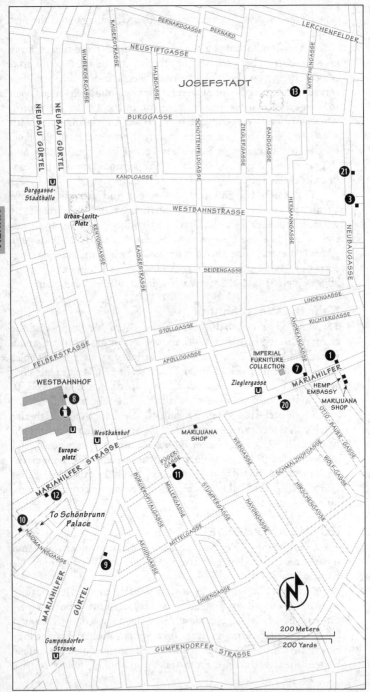

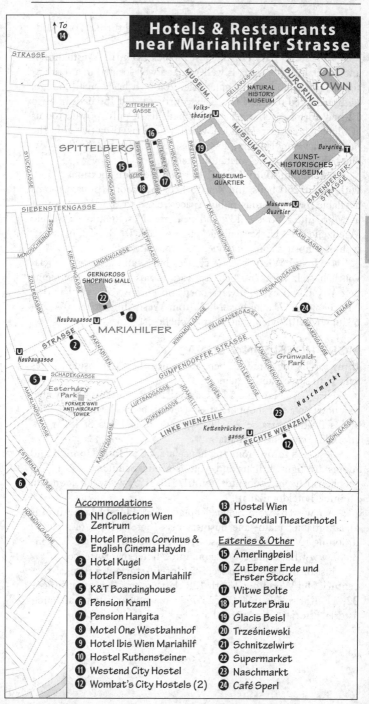

Hotels & Restaurants near Mariahilfer Strasse

STRASSE

To 14

MUSEUM.

BELLARIASTR.

BURGRING

OLD TOWN

NATURAL HISTORY MUSEUM

ZITTERHFR.-GASSE

Volkstheater U

MUSEUMSPLATZ

Burgring T

KUNST-HISTORISCHES MUSEUM

SPITTELBERG

16
15
18 17
19

SCHOTTENFELDGASSE
SIGMUNDSGASSE
GUTENBERGGASSE
KIRCHENGASSE
SPITTELBERGGASSE
BREITEGASSE

MUSEUMS-QUARTIER

Museums U Quartier

BABENBERGER-STRASSE

STUCKGASSE

SIEBENSTERNGASSE

KARL-SCHWEIGHOFER

RAHLGASSE

MONDSCHEINGASSE

KIRCHENGASSE

STIFTGASSE

LINDENGASSE

THEOBALDGASSE

ZOLLERGASSE

GERNGROSS SHOPPING MALL

22

24

Neubaugasse U

4

MARIAHILFER

WINDMÜHLGASSE
FILLGRADERGASSE

LEHARG.

GIRARDIGASSE

2

STRASSE

BARNABITEN

U Neubaugasse

GUMPENDORFER STRASSE

KÖSTLERGASSE
STEGEN
LANGGRUBENGASSE

A. Grünwald-Park

5 SCHADEKGASSE

Esterházy Park
FORMER WWII ANTI-AIRCRAFT TOWER

LUFTBADGASSE
JOANELLI
PÜRKGASSE
GFRÖRNGASSE

LINKE WIENZEILE

Naschmarkt

23

AMERLINGSTRASSE

KAUNITZGASSE

Kettenbrücken-gasse U

RECHTE WIENZEILE

MÜHLGASSE

6

ESTERHÁZYGASSE

HOFMÜHLGASSE

12

Accommodations
1 NH Collection Wien Zentrum
2 Hotel Pension Corvinus & English Cinema Haydn
3 Hotel Kugel
4 Hotel Pension Mariahilf
5 K&T Boardinghouse
6 Pension Kraml
7 Pension Hargita
8 Motel One Westbahnhof
9 Hotel Ibis Wien Mariahilf
10 Hostel Ruthensteiner
11 Westend City Hostel
12 Wombat's City Hostels (2)

13 Hostel Wien
14 To Cordial Theaterhotel

Eateries & Other
15 Amerlingbeisl
16 Zu Ebener Erde und Erster Stock
17 Witwe Bolte
18 Plutzer Bräu
19 Glacis Beisl
20 Trześniewski
21 Schnitzelwirt
22 Supermarket
23 Naschmarkt
24 Café Sperl

VIENNA

hilfer Strasse away from the center to #149, and turn left on Haid-mannsgasse. Go one block, then turn right.

¢ **Westend City Hostel,** just a block from the Westbahnhof and Mariahilfer Strasse, is well-run and well-located in a residential neighborhood, so it's quiet after 20:00. It has a small lounge, high-ceilinged rooms, a tiny back courtyard, and 180 beds in 4- to 12-bed dorms, each with its own bath (cash only, private rooms available, breakfast included when you book directly with the hostel, elevator, laundry, Fügergasse 3, tel. 01/597-6729, www.viennahostel.at, info@westendhostel.at).

¢ **Wombat's City Hostel** has two well-run locations—both with about 250 beds and 4 to 6 beds per room (private rooms available, bar, generous public spaces; close to the Westbahnhof at Mariahilfer Strasse 137 and near the Naschmarkt at Rechte Wienzeile 35—U: Kettenbrückengasse; tel. 01/897-2336, www.wombats-hostels.com, bookvienna@wombats.eu).

¢ **Hostel Wien** is your classic, huge, and well-run official youth hostel, with 260 beds (private rooms available, nonmembers pay €3.50 extra, always open, no curfew, coin-op laundry, Myrthengasse 7, take bus #48A from Westbahnhof, tel. 01/523-6316, www.1070vienna.at, hostel@chello.at).

MORE HOTELS IN VIENNA

If my top listings are full, here are some others to consider. Rates vary with season and demand.

Near City Hall, the **$$$ Cordial Theaterhotel** is a shiny gem of a hotel on a fun shopping street (several blocks beyond the Ring at Josefstädter Strasse 22, U: Rathaus, tel. 01/405-3648, www.cordial.at, chwien@cordial.at).

A stone's throw from Stephansplatz, **$$$ Hotel Domizil**'s 40 rooms are light, bright, and neat as a pin (Schulerstrasse 14, U: Stephansplatz or Stubentor, tel. 01/513-3199, www.hoteldomizil.at, info@hoteldomizil.at).

A few steps from Schwedenplatz, **$$$ Hotel Marc Aurel** is an affordable, plain-Jane business-class hotel with rare air-conditioning (Marc Aurel Strasse 8, U: Schwedenplatz, tel. 01/533-3640, www.hotel-marcaurel.com, info@hotel-marcaurel.com).

Just off Kärntner Strasse, **$$ Hotel Astoria** is a turn-of-the-century Old World hotel with 128 classy rooms (Kärntner Strasse 32, U: Karlsplatz, tel. 01/515-771, www.austria-trend.at/hotel-astoria, astoria@austria-trend.at).

Eating in Vienna

The Viennese appreciate the fine points of life, and right up there with waltzing is eating. The city has many atmospheric restaurants. As you ponder the Hungarian and Bohemian influence on many menus, remember that Vienna's diverse empire may be no more, but its flavors linger. In addition to restaurants, this section covers two Viennese institutions: the city's café culture and its *Heuriger* wine pubs. For a fun foodie guide to Vienna, see ViennaWuerstelstand. com.

EATING TIPS

Austrian Specialties: Traditional Austrian dishes tend to be meat-heavy (although fish is very popular and generally good in this landlocked country). The classic Austrian dish—and a stand-by on menus—is Wiener schnitzel (a veal cutlet that's been pounded flat, breaded, and fried). Pork schnitzel, which is cheaper, is also common. Austrian *Gulasch,* a meat stew, is a favorite comfort food. Sausage *(Wurst)* is also a staple.

Best of the Wurst: Sausage *(Wurst)* is a staple here. Most restaurants offer it (often as the cheapest thing on the menu), but it's more commonly eaten at a takeout stand *(Würstelstand).*

Sausages can be boiled or grilled. The generic term *Bratwurst* simply means "grilled sausage." *Brühwurst* is boiled. Generally, the darker the weenie, the spicier it is.

At sausage stands, *wurst* usually comes in or with a roll (*Semmel*—not your typical hot-dog bun). You might be given the choice of a slice of bread *(Brot),* a pretzel *(Breze),* or in restaurants, potato salad. Sauces and sides include *Senf* (mustard; ask for *süss*—sweet, or *scharf*—spicy), ketchup or curry-ketchup (*Currysauce*—curry-infused ketchup), *Kraut* (sauerkraut), and sometimes horseradish (called *Kren* in Austria and southern Germany).

Smoking in Restaurants: Although legislation has mandated a complete smoking ban in restaurants and bars, a new right-wing government has kept the ban at bay. In the meantime, some restaurants have nonsmoking sections, but expect secondhand smoke wherever you sit. Fortunately for nonsmokers, many eateries offer plenty of outdoor seating.

Cafés, Coffee, and Pastries: Vienna is known for its classic cafés—perfect places to sip some coffee and read a newspaper. A café is also a great place to try one of Vienna's famous desserts, as the city is the birthplace of the Sacher torte and a bevy of other cakes and pastry treats. See "Vienna's Café Culture," later in this section.

Heurigen: Make sure to check out a wine-garden restaurant (or *Heuriger;* the plural is *Heurigen*), nestled in the foothills of the

VIENNA

Restaurant Price Code

I've assigned each eatery a price category, based on the average cost of a typical main course. Drinks, desserts, and splurge items (steak and seafood) can raise the price considerably.

$$$$	**Splurge:** Most main courses over €20
$$$	**Pricier:** €15-20
$$	**Moderate:** €10-15
$	**Budget:** Under €10

In Austria, a *wurst* stand or other takeout spot is **$**; a beer hall, *Biergarten,* or basic sit-down eatery is **$$**; a casual but more upscale restaurant is **$$$**; and a swanky splurge is **$$$$**.

Vienna Woods. At most *Heurigen,* you'll try the latest vintage wine, pick from an assortment of prepared foods, and listen to live music. For more on these, and a list of recommended places, see "Vienna's Wine Gardens," later in this section.

Viennese Drinks: *Gemischter Satz* is a wine that's uniquely Viennese. A blend of grapes grown and harvested together in the same vineyard, it was long considered a cheap table wine. Now it's more respected and worth trying. For a nonalcoholic and refreshing local drink, I like *Apfelsaft gespritzt* (called *Apfelschorle* in Germany), which is apple juice mixed with soda. For a refreshing light-beer drink, go for *Radler* (half beer, half 7Up).

FINE DINING IN THE CENTER

The heart of the city offers plenty of options for a relaxing and expensive dining experience; here are some of my favorites. Reservations are always wise in the evening.

$$$ Lugeck serves the classics with a modern flair to a local "business casual" crowd with professional service but no pretense. Their slogan: "Genuine classics are always in fashion." Choose between a big, fresh, Art Deco interior, or tables on a quiet little square under a towering statue of Gutenberg. It's just a block from the recommended Zanoni & Zanoni gelato place—handy if you want a different scene for your dessert course (daily 11:30-23:00, Lugeck 4, tel. 01/512-5060, www.lugeck.com).

$$$ Artner Restaurant am Franziskanerplatz is a classy place with a smart clientele (it's a favorite of Austrian politicians). Diners enjoy the cozy interior as well as the outside seating on a quaint square. They offer a meaty and inviting modern international menu with nicely presented dishes, including gourmet hamburgers and great steaks (lunch specials, Mon-Sat 12:00-24:00, closed Sun, Franziskanerplatz 5, tel. 01/503-5034, www.artner.co.at).

$$ Zum Schwarzen Kameel Bistro ("The Black Camel")

has a posh, gourmet Viennese **$$$$** restaurant in the back with a thriving and more casual wine bar fronting the street. The delightfully Art Nouveau wine bar, filled with a professional local crowd enjoying small plates from the fancy restaurant kitchen, is *the* place for horseradish and thin-sliced ham (*Beinschinken mit Kren; Achtung*—the horseradish is *hot*). The kitchen is the same one they use for the fine restaurant. Eat well by ordering high on the menu; eat cheaply by sticking with the tiny open-face finger sandwiches (€1.50 each, self-serve from counter, with little pastries to assemble, too). Stand, grab a stool, find a table on the street, or sit anywhere you can (prices are the same)—it's customary to share tables. Fine Austrian wines are sold by the *Achtel* (eighth-liter glass) and listed on the board (daily 12:00-23:00, Bognergasse 5, tel. 01/533-8125).

$$$ Zum Weissen Rauchfangkehrer (The White Chimney Sweep), with a charming woody interior and live piano nightly, is popular for its rustic elegance and traditional cuisine (near the cathedral at Weihburggasse 4, tel. 01/512-3471).

$$$ Café Restaurant Palmenhaus overlooks the Hofburg Palace Garden. Tucked away in a green and peaceful corner two blocks behind the opera house, this is a world apart. If you want to eat modern Austrian cuisine surrounded by palm trees, this is the place. And, since it's at the edge of a huge park, it's great for families. It's an elegant, dressy, and expensive place at night, but there are moderately priced daily specials for lunch (12:00-15:00). They specialize in fresh fish with generous vegetables—options are listed on the chalkboard (daily 12:00-24:00, Jan-Feb closed Mon-Tue; extensive wine list, indoors in greenhouse or outdoors, Burggarten 1, tel. 01/533-1033).

CASUAL EATERIES AND TRADITIONAL STANDBYS
Near St. Stephen's Cathedral

Each of these eateries is within about a five-minute walk of the cathedral (U: Stephansplatz).

$ Gigerl Stadtheuriger offers a fun, near-*Heuriger* wine cellar experience without leaving the city center. You can sit and order from the menu (*Gulasch,* schnitzel, and so on) or go to the self-service counter for mostly cold cuts—just point to what looks good. As in other *Heurigen,* food is designed to go well with the wine. It's sold by the piece or weight; 100 grams *(10 dag)* is about a quarter-pound (cheese and cold meats cost about €5 per 100 grams, salads are about €2 per 100 grams; price sheet posted on wall to right of buffet line). They also have entrées, spinach strudel, quiche, *Apfelstrudel,* and, of course, casks of new and local wines. Servers take your wine order (daily 15:00-24:00, indoor/outdoor seating; behind

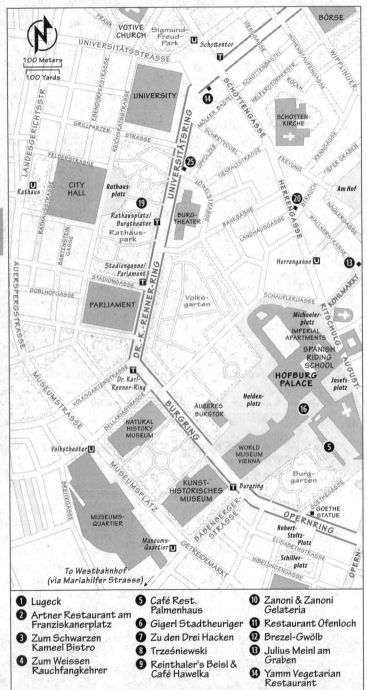

1. Lugeck
2. Artner Restaurant am Franziskanerplatz
3. Zum Schwarzen Kameel Bistro
4. Zum Weissen Rauchfangkehrer
5. Café Rest. Palmenhaus
6. Gigerl Stadtheuriger
7. Zu den Drei Hacken
8. Trześniewski
9. Reinthaler's Beisl & Café Hawelka
10. Zanoni & Zanoni Gelateria
11. Restaurant Ofenloch
12. Brezel-Gwölb
13. Julius Meinl am Graben
14. Yamm Vegetarian Restaurant

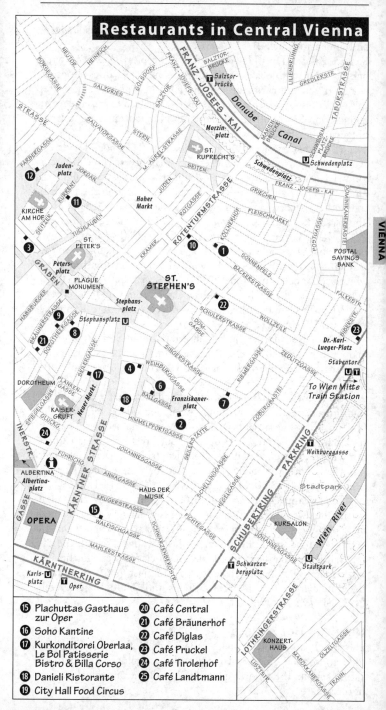

Restaurants in Central Vienna

VIENNA

15 Plachuttas Gasthaus zur Oper
16 Soho Kantine
17 Kurkonditorei Oberlaa, Le Bol Patisserie Bistro & Billa Corso
18 Danieli Ristorante
19 City Hall Food Circus

20 Café Central
21 Café Bräunerhof
22 Café Diglas
23 Café Pruckel
24 Café Tirolerhof
25 Café Landtmann

cathedral, a block off Kärntner Strasse, just off Rauhensteingasse on Blumenstock, tel. 01/513-4431).

$$ Zu den Drei Hacken, a fun and typical *Weinstube* (wine pub), is a hit with locals for its old-fashioned specialties. In other words, if you're a carnivore looking for a nose-to-tail adventure, this is it. These are finely prepared dishes that used to be standard at home (Mon-Sat 11:00-23:00, closed Sun, indoor/outdoor seating, Singerstrasse 28, tel. 01/512-5895).

$$ Trześniewski is an institution—justly famous for its elegant open-face finger sandwiches and small beers. Three different sandwiches and a *kleines Bier (Pfiff)* make a fun, fast, and light €5 lunch. Point to whichever delights look tasty (or grab the English translation sheet and take time to study your 22 sandwich options). The classic favorites are *Geflügelleber* (chicken liver), *Matjes mit Zwiebel* (herring with onions), and *Speck mit Ei* (bacon and eggs). Pay for your sandwiches and a drink. Take your drink tokens to the lady on the right. Sit on the bench and scoot over to a tiny table when a spot opens up (Mon-Fri 8:30-19:30, Sat 9:00-17:00, closed Sun; 50 yards off the Graben, nearly across from Café Hawelka—see "Vienna's Café Culture," later in this chapter; Dorotheergasse 2, tel. 01/512-3291).

They have another branch at Mariahilfer Strasse 95 (near many recommended hotels—see the "Hotels and Restaurants on or near Mariahilfer Strasse" map, Mon-Fri 8:30-19:00, Sat 9:00-18:00, closed Sun, U: Zieglergasse).

$$ Reinthaler's Beisl is another time warp that serves simple, traditional fare all day. It's handy for its location (a block off the Graben, across the street from Trześniewski) and because it's a rare restaurant in the center that's open on Sunday. Its fun, classic interior winds way back, and it also has a few tables on the quiet street (use the handwritten daily menu rather than the printed English one, daily 11:00-23:00, Dorotheergasse 4, tel. 01/513-1249).

Ice Cream: *Gelateria* **Zanoni & Zanoni,** run by an Italian family for several generations, is a fun, high-energy spot mobbed by happy Viennese hungry for their €2 two-scoop cones from an extravagant ice-cream lover's menu. Just two blocks from the cathedral, with a big terrace of tables, it's a classic scene for licking and people-watching—or take it to-go and just grab a spot under the Gutenberg statue a block away (daily until 24:00, Lugeck 7, tel. 01/512-7979).

Near Am Hof Square

The streets around the square called Am Hof (U: Herrengasse) hide atmospheric medieval lanes with both indoor and outdoor eating action. The following eateries are all within a block or two of the square.

$$$ Restaurant Ofenloch serves good, traditional Viennese cuisine with formal service, both indoors and out. This delightfully intimate 300-year-old eatery has a refined yet relaxed ambience (Mon-Sat 11:00-23:00, closed Sun, Kurrentgasse 8, tel. 01/533-8844).

$$ Brezel-Gwölb, a Tolkienesque nook with tight indoor tables and outdoor dining on a quiet little square, serves simple Viennese classics in an unforgettable atmosphere. With its dark and candlelit interior and secretive-feeling outdoor seating, it's ideal for a romantic late-night glass of wine (three-course weekday lunch specials—including vegetarian option, daily 11:30-24:00; leave Am Hof on Drahtgasse, then take first left to Ledererhof 9; tel. 01/533-8811).

Gourmet Supermarket: Located right on the Graben, **Julius Meinl am Graben,** with two floors of temptations, has been famous since 1862 as a top-end delicatessen with all the gourmet fancies. Assemble a meal from the picnic fixings on the shelves. There's also a café, with light meals and great outdoor seating; a stuffy and pricey restaurant upstairs; and a takeout counter with good benches out front for people-watching while you munch (shop open Mon-Fri 8:00-19:30, Sat 9:00-18:00, closed Sun; restaurant open Mon-Sat until 24:00, closed Sun; Am Graben 19, tel. 01/532-3334).

Near the University

$$ Yamm Vegetarian Restaurant (German for "yummy") is a stylish, youthful, self-service hit with foodies for its quality vegetarian fare. Pick up a payment card and plate, serve yourself, then weigh and pay (there's plenty of friendly help). A typical plate runs about €15. They serve breakfast and have takeout options (seating inside and out, smoothies, vegan cakes, daily 8:00-22:00, Sun until 15:00, on the Ring, 100 yards from the recommended Café Landtmann, Universitätsring 10, tel. 01/532-0544).

Near the Opera

These eateries are within easy walking distance of the opera house (U: Karlsplatz).

$$$ Plachuttas Gasthaus zur Oper, a proudly Austrian place a block from the opera, has a contemporary, classy interior and inviting seating on the street. It's big, high-energy, and specializes in the local classics like *Tafelspitz* (boiled beef) and Wiener schnitzel—they actually hand out a little souvenir recipe titled "the art of the perfect Wiener schnitzel" (daily 11:00-24:00, Walfischgasse 5, tel. 01/512-2251).

$ Soho Kantine is a cave-like, government-subsidized cantina, serving the National Library staff but open to all, and offering unexciting, institutional, bargain lunches in the Hofburg. Pay for your meal—your choice of meat or vegetarian—and a drink at the bar, take your token to the kitchen, and then sit down and eat with the locals. Wednesday is schnitzel day and Friday is fish day. Facing the Burggarten's butterfly house, turn left and go 40 yards—it's hiding in a forlorn little square, through a plain door that's not signed (Mon-Fri 11:30-15:00, closed Sat-Sun and mid-July-Aug, Burggarten, mobile 0676-309-5161, Reni).

$$ Kurkonditorei Oberlaa may not have the royal and plush fame of Demel (see page 873), but this is where Viennese connoisseurs serious about the quality of their pastries go to get fat. With outdoor seating on Neuer Markt, it's particularly nice on a summer day. Upstairs has more temptations and good seating (three-course weekday lunch specials, great selection of cakes, daily 8:00-20:00, Neuer Markt 16, tel. 01/5132-9360).

$$ Le Bol Patisserie Bistro (next to Oberlaa) satisfies your need for something French. The staff speaks to you in French, serving fine salads, baguette sandwiches, and fresh croissants on a small terrace or inside the cozy bistro (Mon-Sat 8:00-23:00, Sun from 9:00, Neuer Markt 14, mobile 0699-1030-1899).

$$$ Danieli Ristorante is your best classy Italian value in the Old Town. White-tablecloth dressy, but not stuffy, it has reasonable prices. Dine in their elegant, air-conditioned back room or on the street (daily 11:30-23:00, 30 yards off Kärntner Strasse opposite Neuer Markt at Himmelpfortgasse 3, tel. 01/513-7913).

Supermarket: A top-end version of the Billa supermarket chain, **Billa Corso** has three floors of food and sells hot, gourmet, ready-made meals (by weight). You're welcome to sit and enjoy whatever you've purchased inside (air-con) or out on the square. They also have a great deli selection of salads, soups, and picnic items (Mon-Fri 8:00-20:00, Sat until 19:00, Sun 10:00-18:00, Neuer Markt 17, on the corner where Seilergasse hits Neuer Markt, tel. 01/961-2133).

Spittelberg

This charming cobbled grid of traffic-free lanes is a favorite dining neighborhood for the Viennese. It's handy, set between the MuseumsQuartier and Mariahilfer Strasse (U: Volkstheater/Museumsplatz). Tables tumble down sidewalks and into breezy courtyards; the charming buildings here date mostly from the early 1800s, before the Mariahilfer Strasse neighborhood was built. It's only worth a special trip on a balmy summer evening, as it's dead in bad weather. Stroll Spittelberggasse, Schrankgasse, and Gutenberggasse, then pick your favorite. Don't miss the vine-strewn wine garden at Schrankgasse 1. To locate these restaurants, see the "Hotels & Restaurants near Mariahilfer Strasse" map.

$ Amerlingbeisl is a charming, local place with a casual at-

mosphere both on the cobbled street and in its vine-covered courtyard. It's a great value, serving a mix of traditional Austrian and
international dishes (check the board with daily specials—some
vegetarian, Mon-Fri 11:30-24:00, Sat-Sun from 9:00, shorter
hours in winter, Stiftgasse 8, tel. 01/526-1660).

$$$ Zu Ebener Erde und Erster Stock (loosely translated as
"Downstairs, Upstairs") is a popular little restaurant with a mostly
traditional Austrian menu that includes their signature *Tafelspitz*
(boiled beef). Filling a cute 1750 building, it's true to its name,
with two dining rooms: casual and woody downstairs (tradition-
ally for the poor) and a fancy Biedermeier-style dining room with
red-velvet chairs and violet tablecloths upstairs (where the wealthy
convened). There are also a few al fresco tables along the quiet side
street. Reservations are smart (seasonal specials, Mon-Fri 12:00-
22:00, last seating at 20:30, closed Sat-Sun, Burggasse 13, tel.
01/523-6254, www.zu-ebener-erde-und-erster-stock.at).

$$$ Witwe Bolte is classy. The interior is tight, but its tiny
square has a wonderful leafy ambience (daily 11:45-23:00, in Ju-
ly-Aug opens at 17:30 Mon-Fri, Gutenberggasse 13, tel. 01/523-
1450).

$$ Plutzer Bräu, next door to Amerlingbeisl, feels a bit more
commercial. It's a big, sprawling, impersonal brewpub serving for-
gettable pub grub: ribs, burgers, traditional dishes, and Czech beer
(daily 10:00-24:00, Schrankgasse 4, tel. 01/526-1215).

$$ Glacis Beisl, at the top edge of the MuseumsQuartier just
before Spittelberg, is popular with locals. A gravelly wine garden
tucked next to a city for-
tification, its outdoor tables and breezy ambience
are particularly appeal-
ing on a balmy evening
(weekday lunch specials,
reservations smart, daily
11:00-24:00, Breitegasse
4, tel. 01/526-5660, www.
glacisbeisl.at).

Mariahilfer Strasse and the Naschmarkt

Mariahilfer Strasse (see the "Hotels & Restaurants near Mariahilfer Strasse" map) is filled with reasonable cafés serving all types of
cuisine.

$$ Trześniewski's sandwich bar is *the* place for a quick yet
traditional bite. Consider the branch at Mariahilfer Strasse 95 (see
the Trześniewski listing earlier in this chapter for ordering tips), or
its imitators (one is at #91).

$ Schnitzelwirt is an old classic with a 1950s patina and a mixed local and tourist clientele. In this working-class place, no one finishes their schnitzel (notice the self-serve butcher paper and plastic bags for leftovers). Walking to the back, you pass the kitchen piled high with breaded cutlets waiting for the deep fryer. The schnitzels are served with a starch or salad; if you order the smallest portion, you may want to add a side dish. They also serve Austrian standards including *Szegediner Gulasch* (Mon-Sat 11:00-21:30, closed Sun, Neubaugasse 52, U: Neubaugasse, tel. 01/523-3771).

Supermarket: Look for the big **Merkur** in the basement of the Gerngross shopping mall at Mariahilfer Strasse 42 (Mon-Fri until 20:00, Sat until 18:00, closed Sun, U: Neubaugasse).

Naschmarkt: For a picnic or a trendy dinner, try the Naschmarkt, Vienna's sprawling produce market. This thriving Old World scene comes with plenty of fresh produce, cheap local-style eateries, cafés, kebab and sausage stands, and the best-value sushi in town (market open Mon-Fri 6:00-19:30, Sat until 18:00, closed Sun, closes earlier in winter; restaurants open later; U: Karlsplatz, follow *Karlsplatz* signs out of the station). Pic-

nickers can buy supplies at the market and eat on nearby Karlsplatz (plenty of chairs facing the Karlskirche) or pop into the nearby Burggarten, behind the famous Mozart statue.

In recent years, the Naschmarkt has become fashionable for dinner (or cocktails), with an amazing variety of local and ethnic eateries to choose from. Prices are great, the produce is certainly fresh, and the dinners are as local as can be. The best plan: Stroll through the entire market to survey the options, and then pick the place that appeals. For more on the Naschmarkt, see page 905.

VIENNA'S CAFÉ CULTURE

In Vienna, the living room is down the street at the neighborhood coffeehouse. This tradition is just another example of the Viennese expertise in good living. Each of Vienna's many long-established (and sometimes even legendary) coffeehouses has its individual character (and characters). These classic cafés can be a bit tired, with a shabby patina and famously grumpy waiters who treat you like an uninvited guest invading their living room. Yet these spaces somehow also feel welcoming, offering newspapers, pastries, sofas, quick and light workers' lunches, elegant ambience, and "take all the time you want" charm for the price of a cup of coffee. Rather than read the news on your mobile device, relax with a cup of coffee and read an actual newspaper, Vienna-style, in a café.

Café Tips: Once you claim a table or sofa in a café, make a trip to the glass display case to see the pastries of the day. The menu has all the standard offerings, but won't list the specials.

It's standard practice for your coffee to be served on a little silver tray, with a glass of tap water and perhaps a piece of chocolate on the side.

Coffee-Ordering Lingo: As in Italy and France, coffee drinks in Austria are espresso-based. *Kaffee* means coffee and *Milch* is milk; *Obers* is cream, while *Schlagobers* is whipped cream. Here are some Austrian coffee terms: Use them elsewhere, and you'll probably get a funny look (some are unique just to Vienna).

Schwarzer or *Mokka:* Straight, black espresso; order it *kleiner* (small) or *grosser* (big)

Verlängeter ("lengthened"): Espresso with water, like an Americano

Brauner: With a little milk

Schale Gold ("golden cup"): With a little cream (Vienna)

Melange: Like a cappuccino

Franziskaner: A *Melange* with whipped cream rather than foamed milk, often topped with chocolate flakes

Kapuziner: Strong coffee with a dollop of sweetened cream

Verkehrt ("incorrect") or *Milchkaffee:* Two-thirds milk and one-third coffee (Vienna)

Einspänner ("buggy"): With lots and lots of whipped cream, served in a glass with a handle. (It was the drink of horse-and-buggy drivers, who only had one hand free.)

Fiaker ("horse-and-buggy driver"): Black, served with a *sliwowitz* (plum schnapps) or rum (Vienna)

(Wiener) Eiskaffee: Coffee with ice cream

Maria Theresia: Coffee with orange liqueur

Cafés in the Old Center

These are some of my favorite Viennese cafés located inside the Ring (see the "Restaurants in Central Vienna" map, earlier).

$$ Café Central is overrun with tourists. Still, it remains a classic place: lavish under Neo-Gothic columns, celebrated by 19th-century Austrian writers, and featuring live piano entertainment—schmaltzy tunes on a fine, Vienna-made Bösendorfer each evening from 17:00 to 22:00 (daily 7:30-22:00, Sun from 10:00, corner of Herrengasse and Strauchgasse, U: Herrengasse, tel. 01/533-3764).

$ Café Bräunerhof, between the Hofburg and the Graben, offers traditional ambience with few tourists and live music on weekends (Sat-Sun 15:00-18:00), along with cheap lunches on weekdays (Mon-Fri 8:00-19:30, Sat 8:00-18:00, Sun 10:00-18:00, no hot food after 15:00, Stallburggasse 2, U: Stephansplatz, tel. 01/512-3893).

$ Café Hawelka has a dark, "brooding Trotsky" atmosphere, paintings by struggling artists who couldn't pay for coffee, a saloon-wood flavor, chalkboard menu, smoked velvet couches, an international selection of newspapers, and a phone that rings for regulars. Frau Hawelka died just a couple weeks after Pope John Paul II did. Locals suspect the pontiff wanted her much-loved *Buchteln* (marmalade-filled doughnuts) in heaven. The café, which doesn't serve hot food, remains family-run (daily 8:00-24:00, just off the Graben at Dorotheergasse 6, U: Stephansplatz, tel. 01/512-8230).

Other Classics in the Old Center: All of these places are open long hours daily: **$$ Café Diglas** (good lunches, piano nightly, 2 blocks behind St. Stephen's Cathedral at Wollzeile 10); **$ Café Pruckel** (at Dr.-Karl-Lueger-Platz, across from Stadtpark at Stubenring 24); **$ Café Tirolerhof** (2 blocks from the opera house, behind the TI on Tegetthoffstrasse, at Führichgasse 8); and **$ Café Landtmann** (directly across from the City Hall on the Ringstrasse at Universitätsring 4). The Landtmann is unique, as it's the only grand café built along the Ring with all the other grand buildings.

Near the Naschmarkt

$$ Café Sperl dates from 1880 and is still furnished identically to the day it opened—from the coat tree to the chairs (Mon-Sat 7:00-22:00, Sun 11:00-20:00 except closed in July-Aug, near the Naschmarkt at Gumpendorfer Strasse 11, U: MuseumsQuartier, tel. 01/586-4158; see the "Hotels & Restaurants on Mariahilfer Strasse" map).

WEIN IN WIEN: VIENNA'S WINE GARDENS

The *Heuriger* (HOY-rih-gur) is unique to Vienna, dating back to the 1780s, when Emperor Josef II decreed that vintners needed no special license to serve their own wines and juices to the public in their own homes. Many families grabbed this opportunity and opened *Heurigen* (HOY-rih-gehn)—wine-garden restaurants.

A tradition was born. Today, *Heurigen* are licensed, but do their best to maintain the old-village atmosphere, serving each fall's vintage until November 11 of the following year, when a new vintage year begins. To go with your wine, a *Heuriger* serves a variety of prepared foods that you choose from a deli counter. This is the most intimidating part of the *Heuriger* experience for tourists, but it's easily conquered—see the sidebar for tips. Some *Heurigen* compromise by offering a regular menu that you can order from. At many establishments, strolling musicians entertain—and ask for tips.

Hours: Most *Heurigen* open up in the afternoon (generally between 14:00 and 16:00) and close late (about 24:00), though some may stop serving food earlier (around 21:00). Some *Heurigen* may close in winter, during the grape-picking season, or just for vacation, so call or check websites if you have a specific place in mind.

Getting There: I've listed two good *Heuriger* neighborhoods on the northern outskirts of town (see the "Greater Vienna" map at the beginning of this chapter). To get here from downtown Vienna, it's best to use public transit (cheap, 30 minutes, runs late in the evening, find specific directions under each section). You can also take a 15-minute taxi ride (about €20 from the Ring).

Choosing a Place: With more than 1,700 acres of vineyards within Vienna's city limits, there are countless *Heuriger* taverns.

Each neighborhood I've described is a square or hub with two or three recommended spots and many other wine gardens worth considering. Wander around, then choose the *Heuriger* with the best atmosphere. Or ask a local—every Viennese will be only too glad to tell you about their favorite. (And for a near-*Heuriger* experience without leaving downtown Vienna, drop by Gigerl Stadtheuriger, described earlier in this chapter, which has the same deli-counter system as a *Heuriger*, but not the semirural atmosphere.)

Neustift am Walde

This district is farthest from the city but is still easy to reach by public transit. It feels a little less touristy than other places and is the only area I list where you'll actually see the vineyards.

Getting There: Take the U-6 subway to Nussdorfer Strasse, then ride bus #35A (direction: Salmannsdorf, roughly 18 minutes, leaves from stop across the street from north side of the U-Bahn station). For Weinhof Zimmerman, get off at the Agnesgasse stop; for the other two, use the Neustift am Walde stop.

$$ Weinhof Zimmermann, a 10-minute uphill walk from the bus stop, is my favorite. It's a sprawling farmhouse where the green tables on patios echo the terraced fields all around. While

The *Heuriger* Experience

To understand how a traditional *Heuriger* works, think of a full-service deli counter at an American supermarket, with a seating section nearby. Choose from the array of prepared items and hot dishes, pay at the buffet counter, and find a table. Then order (and pay for) your wine or other drinks from the waiter who will appear at your table. (That said, many of the *Heurigen* I've listed have regular menus and table service as well.)

A quarter-liter (*Viertel,* FEER-tehl, 8 oz) glass of new wine costs about €2-3. *Most* (mohst) is lightly alcoholic grape juice—wine in its earliest stages, and usually available only in autumn. Once it gets a little more oomph, it's called *Sturm* (shtoorm), also strictly a fall drink—sometimes only during the narrow *"Sturmzeit"* window (late Sept-mid-Oct). Teetotalers can order *Traubenmost* (TROW-behn-mohst), grape juice.

Food is generally sold by weight, often in *"10 dag"* units (that's 100 grams, or about a quarter-pound). The buffet has several sections: The core of your meal is a warm dish, generally meat (such as ham, roast beef, roast chicken, roulade, or meat-loaf) carved off a big hunk. There are also warm sides *(Beilagen),* such as casseroles and sauerkraut, and a wide variety of cold salads and spreads. Rounding out the menu are bread and cheese (they'll slice it off for you).

Many *Heuriger* staff speak English, and pointing also works. Here's a menu decoder of items to look for...or to avoid:

dining, you'll feel like you're actually right in the vineyard. The idyllic setting comes with rabbits in petting cages, great food, fine hillside vistas, and a coziness unmatched by the other *Heurigen* mentioned here (opens at 15:00, closed Mon, tel. 01/440-1207). From the Agnesgasse stop, hike a block uphill and turn left on Mitterwurzergasse to #20.

$$ Das Schreiberhaus Heurigen-Restaurant is a popular, family-owned place right at the bus stop. Its creaky, old-time dining rooms are papered with celebrity photos. There are 600 spaces inside and another 600 outside, music nightly after 19:00 unless it's slow, and a cobbled backyard that climbs in steps up to the vineyards. Alone among my listings, this place offers a cheap all-you-can-eat lunch buffet on weekdays until 14:00 (opens at 12:00, Rathstrasse 54, tel. 01/440-3844).

Backhühner: Roasted chicken
Blutwurst or **Blunzn:** Blood sausage
Bohnen: Big white beans
Bratlfett: Gelatinous jelly made from fat drippings
Erdapfel: Potato
Fleckerl: Noodles
Fleischlaberln: Fried ground-meat patties
Kernöl: Vegetable oil
Knoblauch: Garlic
Knödl: Dumpling
Kornspitz: Whole-meal bread roll
Krapfen: Doughnut
Kren: Horseradish
Kummelbraten: Crispy roast pork with caraway
Lauch: Leek
Leberkäse: Finely ground corned beef, pork, bacon, and onions
   that's baked as a loaf
Liptauer: Spicy cheese spread
Presskopf: Jellied brains and innards
Roastbeef: Roast beef
Schinken: Ham
Schinkenfleckerln: Ham and noodle casserole
Schmalz: Spread made from rendered pig or goose fat
Spanferkel: Suckling pig
Speck: Fatty bacon
Specklinsen: Lentils with bacon
Stelze: Grilled knuckle of pork
Sulz: Gelatinous brick of meaty goo
Waldbauernflade: Rustic bread
Zwiebel: Onion

VIENNA

   $$ Fuhrgassl Huber, which brags it's the biggest *Heuriger* in
Vienna, can accommodate 1,000 people inside and just as many
outside. You can lose yourself in its sprawling backyard, with
vineyards streaking up the hill from terraced tables. Musicians
stroll most nights after 19:00 (opens at 14:00, a few steps past Das
Schreiberhaus at Neustift am Walde 68, tel. 01/440-1405, family
Huber).

Nussdorf
An untouristy district, characteristic and popular with the Vien-
nese, Nussdorf has plenty of *Heuriger* ambience. This area feels
very real, with a working-class vibe, streets lined with local shops,
and characteristic *Heurigen* that feel a little bit rougher around the
edges.

Getting There: Take tram #D from the Ringstrasse (stops include the Opera, Hofburg/Kunsthistorisches Museum, and City Hall) to its endpoint, the Beethovengang stop (despite what it says on the front of the tram, the Nussdorf stop isn't the end—stay on for one more stop). Exit the tram, cross the tracks, go uphill 40 yards, and look for Schübel-Auer and Kierlinger on your right.

$ Schübel-Auer Heuriger is my favorite here, with a peaceful leafy garden and a rustic interior. The buffet is big and user-friendly—most dishes are labeled and the patient staff speaks English (opens at 16:00, closed Sun-Mon and mid-Oct-mid-March, Kahlenberger Strasse 22, tel. 01/370-2222).

$ Heuriger Kierlinger, next door, is also good, with a particularly rollicking, woody room around its buffet and a courtyard shaded with chestnut trees (opens at 15:30, closed most of August and periodically in off-season, Kahlenberger Strasse 20, tel. 01/370-2264).

Vienna Connections

BY TRAIN

Vienna has an impressive new Hauptbahnhof (main train station), and is consolidating most—but not all—train departures there. Be sure to confirm which station your train uses. From Vienna's two biggest stations, the handiest connection to the center is the U-Bahn (subway). For some stations, there's also a handy tram connection (see the "Vienna's Public Transportation" map earlier in this chapter.)

For schedules, check Germany's excellent all-Europe timetable at www.bahn.com. The Austrian federal railway's timetable at www.oebb.at includes prices, but it's not as user-friendly as the German site—and it doesn't always remind you about discounts or special passes. For general train information in Austria, call 051-717 (to get an operator, dial 2, then 2).

Wien Hauptbahnhof

Vienna's huge central station (just a few U-Bahn stops south of downtown) has 12 pass-through tracks, shopping, and all the services you may need—including baggage lockers, a TI desk (daily 9:00-19:00), *Reisezentrum* (long hours daily), food court (some outlets open very late), restaurants (including outposts of the recommended Oberlaa pastry shop and Akakiko Sushi), ATMs, grocery stores (some open daily until late), drugstores, bookstores, mobile-phone shops, a car-rental desk (Europcar), bike-rental shop, and a post office. Most shops are open Mon-Fri until 21:00, Sat until 18:00, and (unlike in the city center) many are open on Sunday.

Getting to the City Center: To reach the city center, including all my recommended hotels in the center, ride the U-1 for two to four stops (direction: Leopoldau) to Karlsplatz, Stephansplatz, or Schwedenplatz—from the main hall follow the red *U1* signs; ticket machines are near the escalators. You can also take tram #D (which runs along the Ring) from outside the main entrance. To reach Mariahilfer Strasse, ride U-1 three stops to Stephansplatz, then change to U-3 (direction: Ottaring), or hop on bus #13A. Tram #O runs from the station to Landstrasse and the Wien-Mitte station (for airport trains).

The private **Westbahn** train (www.westbahn.at), which connects Vienna and Salzburg, also leaves from here and offers an alternative to the state-run ÖBB trains. For purchase on short notice, Westbahn's regular fares are half those of ÖBB, with the option to buy your ticket on board at no extra charge.

When timing any train trip out of Vienna, keep in mind that the U-Bahn stop is a bit of a walk from the main train platforms— allow at least 10 minutes to get from the U-Bahn stop to your train.

Westbahnhof

This station (at the west end of Mariahilfer Strasse, on the U-3 and U-6 lines) has a bright, user-friendly mall of services, shops, and eateries (including the recommended Trześniewski—near track 9—with cheap-and-elegant finger sandwiches). You'll find a ticket office (daily 6:00-20:00), travel agencies, grocery stores, ATMs, a post office, and baggage lockers (on the ground floor by the WC). The private **Westbahn** railroad (www.westbahn.at) also serves this station.

Getting to the City Center: Follow orange signs to the U-3 (direction: Simmering). If your hotel is along Mariahilfer Strasse, your stop is on this line, but it may be simpler to walk.

Franz-Josefs-Bahnhof

This small station in the northern part of the city serves **Krems** and other points on the **north bank of the Danube.** Connections from Český Krumlov in the Czech Republic sometimes arrive here, too.

Getting to the City Center: There's no U-Bahn stop at the station, but convenient tram #D connects it to the city center. Also note that trains coming into town from this direction stop at the Spittelau station (on the U-4 and U-6 lines), one stop before they end at the Franz-Josefs-Bahnhof; consider hopping off your train at Spittelau for a handy connection to other points in Vienna. (Similarly, if you're headed out of town and you're not near the tram #D route, take the U-Bahn to Spittelau and catch your train there.)

Wien-Mitte Bahnhof

This smaller station, just east of the Ring, is the terminus for S-

Bahn and CAT trains to the airport and sits below a busy shopping mall. Be aware that its U-Bahn station is called **"Landstrasse."** From here, take the U-3 to hotels near Stephansplatz or Mariahilfer Strasse, and the U-4 to hotels that are closer to the airport. It's also connected directly to the Hauptbahnhof by tram #O.

Train Connections

Before leaving your hotel, confirm which station your train leaves from.

From Vienna by Train to: Bratislava (2/hour, 1 hour, alternating between Bratislava's main station and Petržalka station, or try going by bus or boat; described in the Bratislava chapter), **Salzburg** (3/hour, 3 hours), **Hallstatt** (at least hourly, 4 hours, last connection leaves around 15:00, change in Attnang-Puchheim), **Budapest** (nearly hourly direct, 2.5 hours, more with transfers; cheaper by bus: hourly, 3 hours, www.flixbus.com), **Prague** (7/day direct, 4 hours; more with change), **Český Krumlov** (5/day with 2 changes, 5 hours), **Munich** (7/day direct, 4 hours; otherwise about hourly, 4.5 hours, transfer in Salzburg), **Zürich** (5/day direct, 8 hours; nearly hourly with 1-2 changes, 9 hours; night train, 9 hours), **Ljubljana** (1/day direct, 6 hours; 4/day with change in Villach, 6.5 hours), **Zagreb** (4/day, 7-9 hours, 1 direct, others with 1-3 changes), **Kraków** (3/day, 6-7 hours with 1-2 changes; night train, 8 hours), **Warsaw** (3/day, including 2 direct, 7 hours; night train, 10 hours), **Rome** (4/day, 12.5 hours, 1-3 changes; night train, 14 hours), **Venice** (2/day direct, 8 hours; 3/day with changes, 8-10 hours; night train, 11 hours), **Frankfurt** (5/day direct, 6.5 hours; night train, 9 hours).

BY BUS

The main bus station is located just east of the ring at the U-3 Erdberg stop. **Flixbus** offers dirt-cheap rates to **Salzburg, Budapest, Prague, Bratislava,** and points beyond (www.flixbus.com).

BY PLANE
Vienna International Airport

The airport, 12 miles from the center, is easy to reach from downtown (airport code: VIE, airport tel. 01/700-722-233, www.viennaairport.com). The arrivals hall has an array of services: TI, shops, ATMs, eateries, and a handy supermarket. Ramps lead down to the lower-level train station.

Getting Between the Airport and Central Vienna

By Train: Trains connect the airport with the Wien-Mitte Bahnhof, on the east side of the Ring (described earlier). Choose between two ways of getting to Wien-Mitte: the regular S-7 S-Bahn train (€4.20, 24 minutes), and the express CAT train (€12, 16 minutes). Both run twice an hour on the same tracks. The airport tries to steer tourists into taking the CAT train, but it's hard to justify spending almost €8 to save eight minutes of time. I'd take the S-7, unless the CAT is departing first and you're in a big hurry. Trains from downtown start running about 5:00, while the last train from the airport leaves about 23:30.

The **S-Bahn** works just fine and is plenty fast. From the arrivals hall, go down either of the big ramps, follow the red ÖBB signs, then buy a regular two-zone public transport ticket from the multilingual red ticket machines. It's easiest to just type in your final destination and let the machine do the work. The €4.20 price includes any transfers to other trams, city buses, or S- and U-Bahn lines (see www.wienerlinien.at). Trains to downtown are marked "Floridsdorf." If you'll be using public transportation in Vienna a lot, consider buying a transit pass from the machines instead of a single ticket (see "Getting Around Vienna," near the beginning of this chapter). As these passes are only valid in Vienna's central zone, you'll need to also buy a €2.40 single ticket to cover the stretch between the airport and the limits of the inner zone.

To take the fast **CAT** (which stands for City Airport Train), follow the green signage down the ramp to your right as you come out into the arrivals hall and buy a ticket from the green machines (one-way—€12, or €14.40 to also cover the connecting link from Wien-Mitte to your final destination by public transit; round-trip ticket valid 30 days—€21, 4 tickets—€42; usually departs both airport and downtown around :08 and :38 past the hour, www.cityairporttrain.com).

By Bus: Convenient express airport buses operated by ÖBB go to various points in Vienna: Morzinplatz/Schwedenplatz U-Bahn station (for city-center hotels, 20 minutes), Westbahnhof (for Mariahilfer Strasse hotels, 45 minutes), and Wien-Meidling Bahnhof (30 minutes). Double check your destination as you board (€8, round-trip—€13, 2/hour, buy ticket from driver, tel. 051-717 for info, www.viennaairportlines.at).

By Taxi: The 30-minute ride into town costs a fixed €36 from the several companies with desks in the arrivals hall. You can also take a taxi from the taxi rank outside; you'll pay the metered rate (plus a trivial baggage surcharge), which should come out about the same. Save by riding the cheap train/bus downtown, then taking a taxi to your destination.

Connecting the Airport and Other Cities

Direct buses serve **Bratislava** and its airport (roughly hourly, 1 hour, buses leave from platforms 7, 8, and 9; two companies: **Flixbus,** www.flixbus.com, and **Slovak Lines/Postbus,** www.slovaklines.

sk; **Budapest** (almost hourly, 3 hours, www.flixbus.com); **Prague** (4/day, 7 hours, www.studentagency.eu, also stops in **Brno**).

Bratislava Airport
The airport in nearby Bratislava, Slovakia—a hub for some low-cost flights—is an hour away from Vienna (see the Bratislava chapter).

BY BOAT
High-speed boats connect Vienna to the nearby Slovakian capital of Bratislava. While it's generally cheaper and faster to take the train (€16 round-trip with ÖBB Bratislava-Ticket)—and the boat is less scenic and romantic than you might imagine—some travelers enjoy the Danube riverboat experience.

The **Twin City Liner** runs 3-5 times daily from the terminal at Vienna's Schwedenplatz, where Vienna's town center hits the canal (€30-35 one-way, 1.5 hours; U: Schwedenplatz, late March-Oct only, can fill up—reservations smart, Austrian tel. 01/904-8880, www.twincityliner.com). Their main competitor, **LOD,** is a bit cheaper, but runs only twice a day at most and is less convenient—since it uses Vienna's Reichsbrücke dock on the main river, farther from the city center (€25 one-way, €44 round-trip, 1.5 hours; Handelskai 265, U: Vorgartenstrasse, tel. from Austria 00-421-2-5293-2226, www.lod.sk).

German Survival Phrases for Austria

When using the phonetics, pronounce ī sounds like the long i in "light." Bolded syllables are stressed.

English	German	Pronunciation
Good day.	Grüss Gott.	**grews** gote
Do you speak English?	Sprechen Sie Englisch?	**shprehkh**-ehn zee **ehgn**-lish
Yes. / No.	Ja. / Nein.	yah / nīn
I (don't) understand.	Ich verstehe (nicht).	ikh fehr-**shtay**-heh (nikht)
Please.	Bitte.	**bit**-teh
Thank you.	Danke.	**dahng**-keh
I'm sorry.	Es tut mir leid.	ehs toot meer līt
Excuse me.	Entschuldigung.	ehnt-**shool**-dig-oong
(No) problem.	(Kein) Problem.	(kīn) proh-**blaym**
(Very) good.	(Sehr) gut.	(zehr) goot
Goodbye.	Auf Wiedersehen.	owf **vee**-der-zayn
one / two	eins / zwei	īns / tsvī
three / four	drei / vier	drī / feer
five / six	fünf / sechs	fewnf / zehkhs
seven / eight	sieben / acht	**zee**-behn / ahkht
nine / ten	neun / zehn	noyn / tsayn
How much is it?	Wieviel kostet das?	**vee**-feel **kohs**-teht dahs
Write it?	Schreiben?	**shrī**-behn
Is it free?	Ist es umsonst?	ist ehs oom-**zohnst**
Included?	Inklusive?	in-kloo-**zee**-veh
Where can I buy / find...?	Wo kann ich kaufen / finden...?	voh kahn ikh **kow**-fehn / **fin**-dehn
I'd like / We'd like...	Ich hätte gern / Wir hätten gern...	ikh **heh**-teh gehrn / veer **heh**-tehn gehrn
...a room.	...ein Zimmer.	īn **tsim**-mer
...a ticket to ___.	...eine Fahrkarte nach ___.	ī-neh **far**-kar-teh nahkh
Is it possible?	Ist es möglich?	ist ehs **mur**-glikh
Where is...?	Wo ist...?	voh ist
...the train station	...der Bahnhof	dehr **bahn**-hohf
...the bus station	...der Busbahnhof	dehr **boos**-bahn-hohf
...the tourist information office	...das Touristen-informations-büro	dahs too-**ris**-tehn-in-for-maht-see-**ohns**-**bew**-roh
...the toilet	...die Toilette	dee toh-**leh**-teh
men	Herren	**hehr**-rehn
women	Damen	**dah**-mehn
left / right	links / rechts	links / rehkhts
straight	geradeaus	geh-**rah**-deh-ows
What time does this open / close?	Um wieviel Uhr wird hier geöffnet / geschlossen?	oom **vee**-feel oor veerd heer geh-**urf**-neht / geh-**shloh**-sehn
At what time?	Um wieviel Uhr?	oom **vee**-feel oor
Just a moment.	Moment.	moh-**mehnt**
now / soon / later	jetzt / bald / später	yehtst / bahld / **shpay**-ter
today / tomorrow	heute / morgen	**hoy**-teh / **mor**-gehn

In a German/Austrian Restaurant

English	German	Pronunciation
I'd like / We'd like...	Ich hätte gern / Wir hätten gern...	ikh **heh**-teh gehrn / veer **heh**-tehn gehrn
...a reservation for...	...eine Reservierung für...	ī-neh reh-zer-**feer**-oong fewr
...a table for one / two.	...einen Tisch für eine Person / zwei Personen.	ī-nehn tish fewr ī-neh pehr- zohn / tsvī pehr-zohnehn
Non-smoking.	Nichtraucher.	**nikht**-rowkh-er
Is this seat free?	Ist hier frei?	ist heer frī
Menu (in English), please.	Speisekarte (auf Englisch), bitte.	**shpī**-zeh-kar-teh (owf **ehng**-lish) **bit**-teh
service (not) included	Trinkgeld (nicht) inklusive	**trink**-gehlt (nikht) in-kloo-**zee**-veh
cover charge	Eintritt	**īn**-trit
to go	zum Mitnehmen	tsoom **mit**-nay-mehn
with / without	mit / ohne	mit / **oh**-neh
and / or	und / oder	oont / **oh**-der
menu (of the day)	(Tages-) Karte	(**tah**-gehs-) **kar**-teh
set meal for tourists	Touristenmenü	too-**ris**-tehn-meh-new
specialty of the house	Spezialität des Hauses	shpayt-see-ah-lee-**tayt** dehs **how**-zehs
appetizers	Vorspeise	**for**-shpī-zeh
bread / cheese	Brot / Käse	broht / **kay**-zeh
sandwich	Sandwich	**zahnd**-vich
soup	Suppe	**zup**-peh
salad	Salat	zah-**laht**
meat	Fleisch	flīsh
poultry	Geflügel	geh-**flew**-gehl
fish	Fisch	fish
seafood	Meeresfrüchte	**meh**-rehs-**frewkh**-teh
fruit	Obst	ohpst
vegetables	Gemüse	geh-**mew**-zeh
dessert	Nachspeise	**nahkh**-shpī-zeh
mineral water	Mineralwasser	min-eh-**rahl**-vah-ser
tap water	Leitungswasser	**lī**-toongs-vah-ser
milk	Milch	milkh
(orange) juice	(Orangen-) Saft	(oh-**rahn**-zhehn-) zahft
coffee / tea	Kaffee / Tee	kah-**fay** / tay
wine	Wein	vīn
red / white	rot / weiß	roht / vīs
glass / bottle	Glas / Flasche	glahs / **flah**-sheh
beer	Bier	beer
Cheers!	Prost!	prohst
More. / Another.	Mehr. / Noch eins.	mehr / nohkh īns
The same.	Das gleiche.	dahs **glīkh**-eh
Bill, please.	Rechnung, bitte.	**rehkh**-noong **bit**-teh
tip	Trinkgeld	**trink**-gehlt
Delicious!	Lecker!	**lehk**-er

For more user-friendly German phrases, check out *Rick Steves' German Phrase Book and Dictionary* or *Rick Steves' French, Italian & German Phrase Book*.

SLOVAKIA

Slovensko

BRATISLAVA

The Slovak capital, Bratislava, is an unexpected charmer. Its old town bursts with colorfully restored facades, lively outdoor cafés, and swanky boutiques. The ramshackle industrial quarter to the east is rapidly being redeveloped into a forest of skyscrapers. The hilltop castle gleams from a recent facelift. And even the glum communist-era suburb of Petržalka has undergone a Technicolor makeover. Bratislava and Vienna have forged a new twin-city alliance for trade and commerce, making this truly the nexus of Central Europe.

It's easy to get the feeling that workaday Bratislavans—who strike some visitors as gruff—are being pulled to the cutting edge of the 21st century kicking and screaming. But many Slovaks embrace the changes and fancy themselves as the yang to Vienna's yin: If Vienna is a staid, elderly aristocrat sipping coffee, then Bratislava is a vivacious young professional jet-setting around Europe. Bratislava at night is a lively place; thanks in part to tens of thousands of university students, its youthful center thrives.

Bratislava's location—on the Danube (and the tourist circuit) smack-dab between Budapest and Vienna—makes it a convenient "on the way" destination. I admit that Bratislava used to leave me cold. But changes over the last 10-15 years have transformed it into a delightful destination. And its energy is inspiring.

PLANNING YOUR TIME

A few hours are plenty to get the gist of Bratislava. Head straight to the old town and follow my self-guided walk, finishing with one or more of the city's fine viewpoints: Ascend to the "UFO" observation deck atop the funky bridge, ride the elevator up to the

Sky Bar for a peek (and maybe a drink), or hike up to the castle for the views. With more time, stroll along the Danube riverbank to the thriving, modern Eurovea development. If you spend the evening in Bratislava, you'll find it lively with students, busy cafés, and nightlife.

Note that museums and galleries are closed on Monday.

Day-Tripping Tip: Bratislava can be done as a long side-trip from Budapest (or a short one from Vienna), but it's most convenient as a stopover to break up the journey between Budapest and Vienna. Pay careful attention to train schedules, as connections alternate between Bratislava's two train stations: Hlavná Stanica (serving all trains to/from Prague and Budapest and half of all trains to/from Vienna) and Petržalka (remaining trains to/from Vienna). If checking your bag at the station, be sure that your return or onward connection will depart from there.

Orientation to Bratislava

Bratislava, with 430,000 residents, is Slovakia's capital and biggest city. It has a compact, colorful old town *(staré mesto)*, with the castle on the hill above. Most of the old town is traffic-free. This small area is surrounded by a vast construction zone, rotting residential districts desperately in need of beautification, and a sprawling communist-built suburb that is seeing new life (Petržalka, across the river).

TOURIST INFORMATION

The helpful TI is at Klobučnícka 2, on Primate's Square behind the Old Town Hall (daily 9:00-19:00, Nov-April until 18:00, tel. 02/16186, www.visitbratislava.com). They also have a branch at the main train station (Hlavná Stanica; daily 9:30-18:00).

Bratislava City Card: The TI sells this card (€15/1 day, €18/2 days), which includes free transit and free or discounted admission to local sights. It's worthwhile only if you're doing the included old town walking tour (€14 without the card—see "Tours in Bratislava," later).

ARRIVAL IN BRATISLAVA

For information on Bratislava's trains, buses, riverboats, and airport, see "Bratislava Connections" at the end of this chapter.

HELPFUL HINTS

Taxis: Taxis come in handy here, but are poorly regulated—they can charge whatever rates they want. Any ride in the city center *should* be around €5. However, cabbies waiting at the train station and tourist spots (such as the castle) are accustomed to

Slovakia Almanac

Official Name: Slovenská Republika, though locals call it Slovensko. The nation is the eastern half of the former Czechoslovakia (split peaceably in 1993).

Population: 5.5 million people. The majority are native Slovaks who are Roman Catholic and speak Slovak. But one in ten has Hungarian roots ("stranded" here when Hungary lost this land after WWI), and many—likely between 2 and 8 percent—are Roma (Gypsy). Slovakia has struggled to incorporate both of these large and often-mistreated minority groups.

Latitude and Longitude: 48°N and 19°E (similar latitude to Paris or Vancouver, BC).

Area: 19,000 square miles (the size of Massachusetts and New Hampshire put together).

Geography: The northeastern half of Slovakia features the beautiful rolling hills and spiky, jagged peaks of the Carpathian Mountains. The southwestern half is quite flat—a continuation of the Great Hungarian Plain. The climate is generally cool and cloudy.

Biggest Cities: Only two cities have more than 100,000 inhabitants: Bratislava in the west (the capital, 430,000) and Košice in the east (240,000).

Economy: The Gross Domestic Product is about $96 billion, and the GDP per capita is about $31,000.

Currency: Slovakia uses the euro (€1 = about $1.20). You'll find ATMs at the train stations and airport.

Government: Slovakia's mostly figurehead president, Andrej Kiska, heads a government that isn't dominated by any single political party. Slovakia also has a 150-seat National Council (like a parliament), the leader of which is the prime minister, Peter Pellegrini.

quoting an inflated, flat price—usually more like €10 or €15. To improve your odds, look for a taxi with a logo and telephone number prominently on the door, and insist that they use the meter. Locals call taxis rather than hailing them on the street—you can ask a hotelier or restaurant staffer to call one for you.

Supermarket: Centrally located, **Billa** is big and handy. Find it across from the Philharmonic, on Mostová street (Mon-Sat 7:00-21:00, Sun from 8:00).

Local Guidebook: For in-depth suggestions on Bratislava sightseeing, dining, and more, look for the eye-pleasing *Bratislava Active* guidebook (around €10, sold at every postcard rack).

Toll Sticker: Slovakia requires cars on its expressways to display a toll sticker (vignette—a.k.a. *úhrada*, €10/10 days, https://

Flag: Horizontal bands of white, blue, and red with a shield bearing a "patriarchal cross" (with two crossbars instead of one) atop three humps. The three humps represent three historic mountain

ranges of Slovakia: Mátra (now in northern Hungary, near Eger), Fatra, and Tatra. The double-barred cross represents St. Stephen (István) of Hungary, commemorating the many centuries that Slovakia was part of Hungary.

Language: The official language is Slovak, which is closely related to Czech and Polish—although many Bratislavans also speak English. The local word used informally for both "hi" and "bye" is easy to remember: *ahoj* (pronounced "AH-hoy," like a pirate). "Please" is *prosím* (PROH-seem), "thank you" is *ďakujem* (DYAH-koo-yehm), "good" is *dobrý* (DOH-bree), and "Cheers!" is *Na zdravie!* (nah ZDRAH-vyeh).

Slovaks You May Recognize: Andy Warhol (American Pop artist who gained more than his 15 minutes of fame, born to Slovak immigrants), Martina Hingis (Swiss tennis player born in Slovakia), film director Ivan Reitman (*Ghostbusters, Stripes;* born in Slovakia to Jewish Holocaust survivors), actor Paul Newman (whose mother was born in Slovakia), Tomáš Garrigue Masaryk (founder of Czechoslovakia, whose father was Slovak), Alexander Dubček (leader of the 1968 Prague Spring uprising), and Štefan Banič (emigrated to America and invented the parachute).

BRATISLAVA

eznamka.sk/en). If your car doesn't have one, buy one at a gas station when you cross the border. You don't need one if you'll be dipping into the country on minor roads—only for major highways.

Tours in Bratislava

Walking Tours

The TI offers a one-hour old town walking tour in English every day in summer at 14:00 (€14, free with Bratislava City Card). For €28, two people can book the same hour-long tour with the same guides as a private tour at whatever time is convenient. The TI can arrange this for you with a few hours' notice (see "Tourist Informa-

BRATISLAVA

Welcome to Slovakia

Sitting quietly in the very center of Central Europe, wedged between bigger and stronger nations (Hungary, Austria, the Czech Republic, and Poland), Slovakia was brutally disfigured by the communists, then overshadowed by the Czechs. But in recent years, this fledgling republic has found its wings. While the east of Slovakia is still catching up, locals brag that the region around Bratislava has the hottest economy and highest income per capita of any region in the former communist region of Europe.

Recent economic reforms have caused two very different Slovakias to emerge: the modern, industrialized, flat, affluent west, centered on the capital of Bratislava; and the remote, poorer, mountainous, "backward" east, with high unemployment and traditional lifestyles.

Slovakia has spent most of its history as someone else's backyard. For centuries, it was ruled from Budapest and known as "Upper Hungary." At other times, it was an important chunk of the Habsburg Empire, ruled from neighboring Vienna. But most outsiders think first of another era: the 75 years that Slovakia was joined with the Czech Republic as the country of "Czechoslovakia." From its start in the aftermath of World War I, this union of Czechs and Slovaks was troubled; some Slovaks chafed at being ruled from Prague, while many Czechs resented the financial burden of their poorer neighbors to the east.

After gaining their freedom during 1989's peaceful Velvet

tion," earlier in this chapter). This can be a great way to become friends with the city.

Local Guide

MS Agency, run by **Martin Sloboda,** offers quality guides (€130/3 hours, €160/4 hours, mobile 0905-627-265, www.bratislava-guide.sk, sloboda@msagency.sk). Martin, a can-do entrepreneur and tireless Bratislava booster (and author of the great *Bratislava Active* guidebook described earlier) helped me put this chapter together. He's part of the ambitious young generation that came of age as communism fell—and whose energy and leadership are reshaping the city.

Revolution, the Czechs and Slovaks began to think of the future. The Slovaks wanted to rename the country Czecho-Slovakia (with that all-important hyphen signifying an equal partnership), and to give themselves more autonomy. The Czechs balked, relations gradually deteriorated, and Slovak nationalist candidate Vladimír Mečiar fared surprisingly well in the 1992 elections. Taking it as a sign that the two peoples wanted to part ways, politicians pushed through (in just three months) the peaceful separation of the now-independent Czech and Slovak Republics. The "Velvet Divorce" became official on January 1, 1993.

At first the Slovaks struggled. Communist rule had been particularly unkind to them, and their economy was in shambles. Visionary leaders set forth bold solutions, including a flat tax (19 percent), followed by EU membership in 2004 and adoption of the euro currency in 2009. Before long, major international corporations began to notice the same thing the Soviets had: This is a great place to build stuff, thanks to its strategic location (300 million consumers live within a day's drive), low labor costs, and a well-trained workforce. Today multiple foreign automakers have plants here, and Slovakia produces one million cars a year, making it the world's biggest car producer per capita.

Bratislava's success story is impressive. The capital region enjoys almost full employment, and seems poised to lead Slovakia into a bright future.

Bratislava Old Town Walk

This self-guided orientation walk circles delightfully traffic-free old Bratislava (figure 1.5 hours, not including sightseeing stops).
• *Start on the bridge about 50 yards uphill from the green copper spire of the watchtower, St. Michael's Gate (it looks like a church spire, at the top of the old town)—with the tram tracks of the ring road just beyond.*

St. Michaels Bridge
You're standing below a watchtower marking St. Michael's Gate (Michalská Brána), part of the town's medieval wall. It's capped with the Archangel Michael busy killing a dragon.

The Hungarian king gave Pressburg (as Bratislava was called back then) city status in 1291. This meant the city had permis-

BRATISLAVA

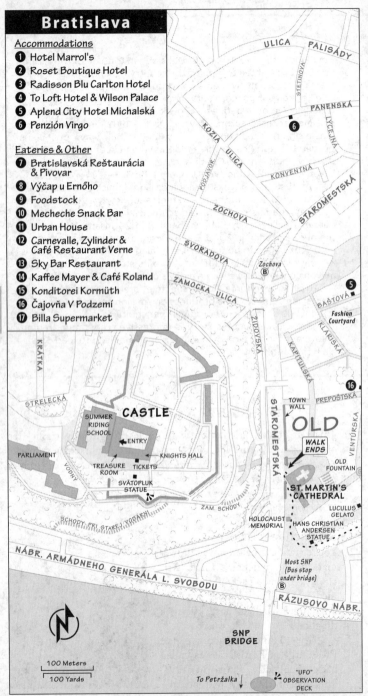

Bratislava

Accommodations
1. Hotel Marrol's
2. Roset Boutique Hotel
3. Radisson Blu Carlton Hotel
4. To Loft Hotel & Wilson Palace
5. Aplend City Hotel Michalská
6. Penzión Virgo

Eateries & Other
7. Bratislavská Reštaurácia & Pivovar
8. Výčap u Ernőho
9. Foodstock
10. Mecheche Snack Bar
11. Urban House
12. Carnevalle, Zylinder & Café Restaurant Verne
13. Sky Bar Restaurant
14. Kaffee Mayer & Café Roland
15. Konditorei Kormüth
16. Čajovňa V Podzemí
17. Billa Supermarket

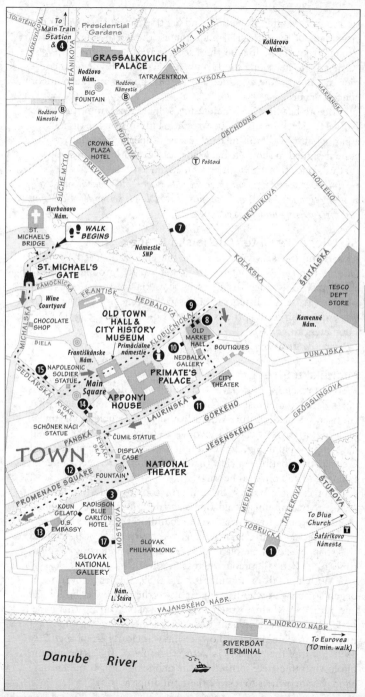

sion to fortify, offer protection, and tax trade. Bratislava was at the crossroads of two medieval trade routes (the north-south "Amber Route" from the Baltics to the Mediterranean, and the east-west "Oriental Route" along the Danube). You're standing over the former dry moat, now a garden of the city library and an outdoor concert venue.

Before heading into the old town, look away from the tower. Notice the sleek-in-the-1920s Art Deco building on the right. Now a bar, when it was built in 1929 it was a supermodern department store designed to show off Bata shoes (a Czechoslovakian company that was once the largest shoe company in the world).

• *Stroll over the bridge and enter the old center. You're outside the wall, walking through a barbican—shaped like an "L" for better defense. Pause just after passing under the gate.*

St. Michael's Gate (Michalská Brána)

This is the last surviving tower of the city wall. Just below the gate, notice the "kilometer zero" plaque in the ground, marking the point from which distances in Slovakia are measured. But I wouldn't trust the distances...unless we're somehow on the equator: According to this, the North and South Poles are both 4,667 kilometers away.

• *Before you stretches...*

Michalská Street

Pretty as it is now, Bratislava's old center was a decrepit ghost town during the communist era. The communist regime believed that Bratislavans of the future would live in large, efficient apartment buildings. They saw the old town as a useless relic of the bad old days of poor plumbing, cramped living spaces, social injustice, and German domination—a view that left no room to respect, or maintain, the town's physical heritage.

For example, notice the uniform cobbles underfoot. In the 1950s, the communists sold Bratislava's original medieval cobbles to cute German towns that were rebuilding themselves in a way that preserved their elegant Old World character. Locals avoided this stripped-down, desolate corner of the city, preferring to spend time in the Petržalka suburb across the river.

With the fall of communism in 1989, the new government began sorting out who had the rights to the old town's buildings, and returning them to their original owners. During this time, little repair or development took place (since there was no point investing in a building until ownership was clearly established). By 1998, most of the property issues were resolved. The city made the old town traffic-free, spruced up the public buildings, and encouraged private owners to restore their buildings as well.

Two decades later, the result is this delightful street, lined with inviting cafés and restaurants. Poke around to experience Bratislava's charm. Courtyards and passageways—most of them open to the public—burrow through the city's buildings. Half a block down on the left, the courtyard at #12 was once home to vintners; their former cellars are now coffee shops, massage parlors, crafts boutiques, and cigar shops. More dead-end passages with characteristic shops are across the street, at #7 and #5.

The **Cukráreň na Korze** chocolate shop (on the left, at #6) is highly regarded among locals for its delicious hot chocolate and creamy truffles. Above the shop's entrance, the **cannonball** embedded in the wall recalls Napoleon's two sieges of Bratislava (the 1809 siege was 42 days long), which caused massive suffering—even worse than during World War II (the French consumed all of the wine stocks). This is just one of several cannonballs around town. Keep an eye out for more of these reminders of one of Bratislava's darkest times.

• *Two blocks down from St. Michael's Gate, where the street changes to Ventúrska (at the signpost and big rock in the street), turn left along Sedlárska street.*

Peek into **Konditorei Kormüth** *(a few doors down on the right, at #8). Mr. Kormüth dedicated many years and lots of money to creating a 17th-century setting for his café. For €10, you can enjoy a coffee and slice of cake in this unforgettable setting while reading his story on the menu.*

Farther on, you reach the historic...

Main Square (Hlavné Námestie)

This modest square, the centerpiece of Bratislava's old town, feels too petite for a national capital. Its style is a mishmash—every building around it seems to date from a different architectural period.

The **fountain,** the most beautiful and historic in town, is a history lesson just waiting to happen. It celebrates the 1563 coronation of Maximillian II—the first Habsburg emperor to also be crowned "King of Hungary." Back then, Slovakia was part of Hungary, which was ruled from Austria. (Got that?) As a mark of respect to the locals, Austrian emperors were crowned a second time, as Hungarian kings. (The German phrase for this arrangement—*König und Kaiser,* "king and emperor," often abbreviated *"K+K"*—remains a mark of quality to this day.) I suppose if your choice as a Hungarian was to be ruled by the Ottomans or by an Austrian Habsburg, the answer was easy.

This arrangement also helps explain why Vienna and Bratislava—the present-day capitals of Austria and Slovakia—are the closest of any two capitals in Europe (you can actually see the lights of one from the other). This closeness wasn't an accident—it was for security. Long before "Slovakia" existed, Bratislava (then called Pozsony) was the capital of "rump" Hungary—what was left of Hungary after most of its territory, including the capital Buda, was conquered by the Ottomans. Bratislava was as far from the Ottoman Turks as possible, while still being in Hungary, and very well fortified. The castle crowning the hill high above the old town was the royal residence and protector of the crown jewels during this time. (For more on the complicated tricultural mix of the city—Austrian/German, Hungarian, and Slavic/Slovak—see the "City of Three Cultures" sidebar, later in this chapter.)

Standing in the middle of the main square, do a quick clockwise spin tour. (You'll need to circle around the fountain to see everything.) Begin with the bold yellow tower of the **Old Town Hall** (Stará Radnica), which dominates the square. It's Gothic at the core, but with a Baroque facade. Near the bottom of the tower, to the left of the pointed window, there's another Napoleonic cannonball embedded in the facade.

Down the street to the right of the Old Town Hall is the **Apponyi House,** the mansion of an 18th-century aristocrat that also holds the Slovak National Collection of Wine (described under "Sights in Bratislava").

Turn farther right and note the venerable cafés. The classic choice is **Kaffee Mayer,** with dark awnings and outdoor seating facing the fountain. They've been selling coffee and cakes to a genteel clientele since 1873. You can enjoy your pick-me-up in the swanky old interior or out on the square.

At the corner in front of Kaffee Mayer (you may have to walk closer to see it) is a beloved statue. The jovial chap doffing his top hat is **Schöner Náci,** who lived in Bratislava until the 1960s. This eccentric old man, a poor carpet cleaner, would dress up in his one black suit and top hat, and go strolling through the city, offering gifts to the women he fancied. (He'd often whisper *"schön"*—German for "pretty," which is how he got his nickname.) Schöner Náci now gets to spend eternity greeting visitors outside his favorite café.

Across the street, the Art Nouveau **Café Roland** is known for its 1904 Klimt-style mosaics and historic photos of the city known as Pressburg (Austrian times) or Pozsony (Hungarian times). The building was once a bank. Step inside. These days the barista stands where a different kind of bean counter once did, guarding a vault that now holds coffee.

Now walk toward the Old Town Hall. Up the little side-square to the left is a jumble of cute **mini kiosks**—sporting old-time cityscape engravings on their roofs—selling local handicrafts and knickknacks. In December, the square transforms into the city's popular and atmospheric Christmas market.

Step through the passageway leading to the Old Town Hall's gorgeously restored courtyard, with its Renaissance arcades. (The entrance to the excellent **City History Museum**—described later—is inside the courtyard.)

Continue all the way through the courtyard into **Primate's Square** (Primaciálne Námestie). The pink mansion on the right is the **Primate's Palace**—the new town hall in the old archbishop's residence—with a fine interior decorated with English tapestries (described later). At the far end of this square is the **TI**.

Continue straight ahead (with the TI on your right) down the street called Klobučnícka—**"Hatters Street."** In the Middle Ages, craftsmen gathered according to their trade, and streets were named for the craft found there. If you needed a hat, you knew where to find one.

• *Continue two blocks straight ahead to a square on your right, fronted by a fine two-story Neoclassical market hall.*

Old Market Hall (Stará Tržnica)

Built in 1910, this busy community center today hosts concerts and a Saturday market. The market hall square is a lively gathering place, too; see details on its monthly food-truck festivals under "Eating in Bratislava," later.

On the right side of the square is a stark 12-story building—the tallest in town before WWII. If it looks barren, that was the point. It's from the Bauhaus school—the rage among German architects between the world wars. The battle cry for these harbingers of modernity: "form follows function," "less is more," and "luxury does not require ornamentation." Today its ground floor is home to a dingy bingo parlor (visitors welcome).

The bombs of World War II mostly spared the old town but pulverized a nearby oil refinery and dynamite plant—targeted by Allies because they were a key part of the occupying Nazi war economy. But a few bombs went awry and hit the area just uphill from here, which accounts for all the post-1945 buildings. The concrete jungle beyond the tram tracks is modernist architecture of the 1960s communist era.

• *Find a door just to the left of the Old Market Hall facade marked* Centrál Pasáž *(press buzzer if closed). It leads through a 1920s Art Deco shopping gallery (cutting edge a century ago) to a busy pedestrian boulevard.*

BRATISLAVA

Laurinská Street—Bratislava's Fashion Drag

This street is lined with fun-to-browse boutiques. In the little nook where the street bends (just to the left) are three popular, very Slovak shops: **Slowatch,** with casual clothes and bags; **Slávica,** a high-end design shop with jewelry and accessories; and **Kompot,** selling a fun variety of unique, Slovak-themed T-shirts. This is a good spot to browse for a quality, non-kitschy souvenir.

Across the street from where you entered Laurinská is the chillingly blocky facade of the communist-era **City Theater** (Mestské Divadlo). On the upper floor are Socialist Realist stained-glass windows—hard to see during the day, but illuminated at night, like a communist night light. We'll see the much fancier National Theater in a moment.

Turn right on Laurinská and stroll like a local for three long blocks—people-watching and window-shopping at more high-end shops. Soon you reach the Bratislava city seal in the cobbles (a three-towered castle with a gate half-open).

• *Just beyond that, on the left, look out or you might stumble over a bronze fellow peeking out of a manhole.*

Čumil ("the Peeper")

Čumil was the first—and is still the favorite—of the many whimsical statues that dot Bratislava's old town (such as Schöner Náci, whom we met earlier). Most date

from the late 1990s, when city leaders wanted to entice locals back into the newly prettied-up and fun-loving center. There's no story behind this one—the artist simply wanted to create a playful icon and let the townspeople make up their own tales. Čumil has survived being driven over by a truck—twice—and he's still grinning.

• *Turn left at the man in the manhole and follow Rybárska to reach the long, skinny square called...*

Promenade Square (Hviezdoslavovo Námestie)

At the near end of this square is Bratislava's impressive opera house, the silver-topped **Slovak National Theater** (Slovenské Národné Divadlo). When the theater opened in the 1880s, half the shows were in German and half in Hungarian. Today, the official language is Slovak. Across the way, the opulent, beige, Neo-Baroque building is home to the Slovak Philharmonic (Slovenská Filharmónia).

Right in front of the opera house, look down into the round, glass **display case** to see the foundation of the one-time Fishermen's Gate into the city. Water surrounds the base of the gate: This entire square was once a tributary of the Danube, and the Raddison Blu Carlton Hotel (long the VIP hotel in town) across the way was once a series of inns on different islands. The buildings along the old town side of the square mark

where the city wall once stood. Now the square is a lively zone on balmy evenings, with several fine restaurants offering al fresco tables jammed with happy diners.

Turn right and stroll down the long square. Underfoot is a gigantic, cobbled version of Bratislava's city seal. After passing a statue of the square's namesake (Pavol Országh Hviezdoslav, a beloved Slovak poet), look for an ugly fence and barriers on the left. As usual, the US Embassy is the most heavily fortified building in the capital.

Just past the embassy is the low-profile entrance to the **Sky Bar,** an affordable rooftop restaurant with excellent views (ride the elevator to the seventh floor). The glass-roofed pavilion in the center of the square is a popular venue for summer concerts. Behind it, on the old-town side of the square, is **Luculus,** where people are likely lined up outside for ice cream. (For ice cream without a lineup, you can backtrack to **Koun Gelato**—just before the US Embassy and immediately to the right of the Carlton Hotel.) On the right near the end of the park, a statue of Hans Christian Andersen is a reminder that the Danish storyteller enjoyed his visit to Bratislava, too.

• *Reaching the end of the square, you run into the barrier for a busy highway. Turn right and walk one block to find the big, black marble slab facing a modern monument.*

Holocaust Memorial

This was the site of Bratislava's original synagogue. You can see an etching of the building in the big slab. At the base of the memorial sculpture, look for the word "Remember" carved into the granite in Hebrew and Slovak, commemorating the 90,000 Slovak Jews who were deported to Nazi death camps. The fact that the town's main synagogue and main church (described next) were located side by side illustrates the tolerance that characterized Bratislava before

BRATISLAVA

City of Three Cultures:
Pressburg, Pozsony, Bratislava

Historically more of an Austrian and Hungarian city than a Slovak one, Bratislava has always been a Central European melting pot.

Over the years, notable visitors from Hans Christian Andersen to Casanova have sung the praises of this bustling burg on the Danube.

For most of its history, Bratislava was part of the Austrian Empire and known as Pressburg, with a primarily German-speaking population. (Only the surrounding rural areas were Slovak.) The Hungarians used Pozsony (as they called it) as their capital during the century-and-a-half that Buda and Pest were occupied by Ottoman invaders.

By its turn-of-the-20th-century glory days, the city was a rich intersection of cultures—about 40 percent German, 40 percent Hungarian, and 20 percent Slovak. Shop clerks greeted customers in all three languages. It was said that the mornings belonged to the Slovaks (farmers who came into the city to sell their wares at market), the afternoons to the Hungarians (diplomats and office workers filling the cafés), and the evenings to the Austrians (wine producers who ran convivial neighborhood wine pubs where all three groups would gather). In those wine pubs, the vintner would listen to which language his customers used, then bring them a glass with the serving size expected in their home country: 0.3 liters for Hungarians, 0.25 liters for Austrians, and 0.2 liters for Slovaks (a distinction that still exists today). Jews (one-tenth of the population), and Roma (then called Gypsies) rounded out the city's ethnic brew.

Hitler. Ponder the modern statue: The open doors of an evacuated home with shadows of people who once lived there, all crowned with bullet holes and the Star of David. It evokes the fate of the more than 80,000 Slovak Jews who died in the Holocaust.

Hike up the stairs to the adjacent church. At the top of the stairs, pause to appreciate the view. Looking toward the river, you can't miss the huge **SNP Bridge** (Most SNP), the communists' pride and joy. The "SNP" is shorthand for the 1944 Slovak National Uprising against the Nazis, a common focus of communist remembrance. As with most Soviet-era landmarks in former communist countries, locals aren't crazy about this structure—not only for the questionable Starship Enterprise design, but also because

When the new nation of Czechoslovakia was formed from the rubble of World War I, the city shed its German and Hungarian names, and took the newly created Slavic name of Bratislava. The Slovak population was on the rise, but the city remained tricultural.

World War II changed all of that. With the dissolution of Czechoslovakia, Slovakia became an "independent" country under the thumb of the Nazis—who all but wiped out the Jewish population. At the end of the war, Czechoslovakia reunited under the USSR, and expelled the city's ethnic Germans and Hungarians in retribution for the misdeeds of Hitler and Horthy (Hungary's wartime leader).

Bratislava's urban heritage suffered terribly under the communists. The historic city's multilayered charm and delicate cultural fabric were ripped apart, then shrouded in gray. The communists were prouder of their ultramodern SNP Bridge than of the city's historic Jewish quarter—which they razed to make way for the bridge. Now the bridge and its highway slice through the center of the old town, and heavy traffic rattles the stained-glass windows of St. Martin's Cathedral. The city's Germanic heritage was also deliberately obscured.

But Bratislava's most recent chapter is one of great success. Since the fall of communism, the city has gone from gloomy victim to thriving economic center and social hub. With a healthy free market economy, it now has the chance to re-create itself as Slovakia's national capital. And its advantageous position on the Danube, a short commute from Vienna, is prompting its redevelopment as one of Europe's up-and-coming cities. Once again, the streets of Bratislava are filled with German- and Hungarian-speakers...tourists and business travelers from nearby Vienna and Budapest.

of the oppressive regime it represented. However, the restaurant and observation deck up top have been renovated into a posh eatery called (appropriately enough) "UFO." You can visit it for the views, a drink, or a full meal. (For details, see the listing, later.)

While the bridge was a groundbreaking design in 1972, the freeway that runs across it messed up the city. If the highway thundering a few feet in front of this historic church's door were any closer, the off-ramp would go through the nave. In the next decade, the plan is to move the highway into a tunnel that will emerge at the bridge—returning peace to this corner of Bratislava.

• *Now turn your attention to the church towering overhead.*

St. Martin's Cathedral (Dóm Sv. Martina)

Nineteen Hungarian kings and queens were crowned in this church—more than anywhere else in Hungary. A replica of the Hungarian crown still tops the steeple.

There's relatively little to see inside the cathedral—but if it's open, duck in (Mon-Sat 9:00-11:30 & 13:00-18:00, Sun 13:30-16:30). In the fairly gloomy interior you'll find some fine carved-wood altarpieces (a Slovak specialty).

Just beyond the church is a stretch of the 15th-century **town wall.** The church was actually built into the wall, which explains its unusual north-side entry. In fact, look up to notice the fortified watchtower (with a WC drop on its left—and a security camera hanging out its hole) built into the corner of the church just above you.

• *Our walk is over. From here, you could either hike up to the* **castle** *(backtracking to the Holocaust Memorial, take the underpass beneath the highway, go up the stairs*

on the right marked by the Hrad/Castle *sign, then turn left up the stepped lane marked* Zámocké Schody*), hike over the SNP Bridge (pedestrian walkway on lower level) to ride the elevator up the* **UFO viewing platform,** *or head for the river and stroll downstream to the thriving and futuristic new Bratislava—***Eurovea** *(all of these are described under "Sights in Bratislava," later).*

Or, you could carry on as described below to end up back where you started...

Back To St. Michael's Gate

Continue the rest of the way around the church and take the grand stony staircase back down to busy Panská street. Turn left and follow Panská to the corner with Ventúrska. The **old fountain** here marks the actual cross point of the two great medieval trade routes (north-south from the Baltics to the Mediterranean, and east-west along the Danube). Head left, uphill (or north toward the Baltics, if you're an amber merchant) toward St. Michael's Gate.

Over the next few blocks, you may see the names of great **composers** on plaques marking historical buildings. Franz Liszt performed in Bratislava at age nine for local aristocrats and was discovered and sent to Vienna. Beethoven composed his *Moonlight Sonata* here. Mozart performed here at age six. Haydn conducted the orchestra here, and in the 20th century Béla Bartók called Bratislava home.

If you feel like a cup of tea along the way—or you're nervous about a nuclear attack—at #9 on the left (a long block after the fountain), climb through the thick iron door and down into Čajovňa V Podzemí ("The Underground Tea Room," daily 14:00-22:00 except Tue and Thu from 11:00), which fills an old bomb shelter with pillows, incense, and herby frills. A couple more blocks takes you back to where you started this walk.

Sights in Bratislava

Although Bratislava's museums are underwhelming—and you could easily have a great day here without visiting any—a few right in the old town are worth considering.

ON OR NEAR THE OLD TOWN'S MAIN SQUARE
▲Primate's Palace (Primaciálny Palác)
This tastefully restored French-Neoclassical mansion (formerly the residence of the archbishop, or "primate") dates from 1781. The religious counterpart of the castle, it filled in for Esztergom—the Hungarian religious capital—after that city was taken by the Ottomans in 1543. Even after the Ottoman defeat in the 1680s, this remained the winter residence of Hungary's archbishops. In the courtyard gurgles a  fountain with St. George slaying a three-headed dragon; the exhibits are upstairs.

Cost and Hours: €3, Tue-Sun 10:00-17:00, closed Mon, Primaciálne Námestie 1, tel. 02/5935-6394, www.bratislava.sk.

Visiting the Museum: The palace, which now serves as the town hall, offers one fine floor of exhibits. Follow signs up the grand staircase to the ticket counter, then proceed up one more flight to the entrance lobby. From here, the Hall of Mirrors is on your left; straight ahead leads to a series of state apartments decorated with precious tapestries (on the right); and at the far end is a long picture gallery leading to the chapel.

Portraits hang in the lobby of the German-speaking royals

who ruled Hungary, which ruled the Slovaks, who lived in this part of the vast Habsburg empire...history here is like a set of Russian stacking dolls. You'll see not one, but two portraits of Habsburg Empress Maria Theresa—young and old—as well as her father, Charles VI, and her son, Josef II. While Hungary was under Ottoman occupation, these Habsburg emperors came to Bratislava to also be crowned "kings of Hungary."

Hall of Mirrors: This is perhaps the most historic room in the city. In 1805, the "Peace of Pressburg" treaty was signed here—sorting out logistics after Napoleon beat the Austrians and Russians at the Battle of Austerlitz. This victory marked the peak of Napoleon's power. Today, the hall is used for concerts, city council meetings, and other important events. On the wall in the antechamber is a list of Bratislava's mayors since the 1280s.

State Rooms and Tapestries: This series of large public rooms, originally designed to impress, is now an art gallery. Distributed through several of these rooms is the museum's pride, and for many its highlight: a series of six English tapestries, illustrating the ancient Greek myth of the tragic love between Hero and Leander.

The tapestries were woven in England by Flemish weavers for the court of King Charles I (in the 1630s). They were kept in London's Hampton Court Palace until Charles was deposed and beheaded in 1649. Cromwell sold them to France to help fund his civil war, but after 1650, they disappeared...for centuries. In 1903, restorers broke through a false wall in this mansion and discovered the six tapestries, neatly folded and perfectly preserved. Nobody knows how they got here (perhaps they were squirreled away during the Napoleonic invasion, and whoever hid them didn't survive). The archbishop—who had just sold the palace to the city—cried foul and tried to claim the tapestries (valued at triple the sales price of the entire palace)...but the city said, "A deal's a deal."

Picture Gallery and Chapel: After traipsing through the grand rooms, go to the end of the main corridor and turn left down the hallway. This leads through the smaller rooms of the archbishop's private quarters, which are now a picture gallery decorated with minor Dutch, Flemish, German, and Italian paintings. At the end of this hall, a bay window looks down into the archbishop's own private chapel. When the archbishop became too ill to walk down to Mass, this window was built so he could take part in the service in his pajamas.

▲City History Museum (Mestské Múzeum)

Delving thoughtfully into Bratislava's past, this museum is rich in artifacts and well described in English and by the included audioguide. The core of the museum offers a sprawling, chronological look at local history through the 1920s, on two floors. The first floor features ecclesiastical art, including wood-carved statues. Upstairs, you'll have a chance to climb up into the Old Town Hall's tower, offering so-so views over the square, cathedral, and castle. Then you'll see more exhibits in rooms once used by the town council—courthouse, council hall, chapel, and so on. This is a fascinating look at Habsburg rule and slice-of-life Bratislava in the early 20th century. Look for the model of "Pressburg" during the age of Maria Theresa. Farther along, trilingual street signs are a reminder that historically, this was a city of three cultures and three languages (Slovak, German, Hungarian). The finale is down in the cellar: a graphic torture exhibit in the "law and order" zone, with replicas of torture equipment from the 16th through 18th centuries. At the far end of the exhibit, crouch down the passage to see three dreary and depressing cells...enough to make anybody behave.

Cost and Hours: €5, includes excellent audioguide, €6 combo-ticket with Apponyi House; open Tue-Fri 10:00-17:00, Sat-Sun 11:00-18:00, closed Mon; in the Old Town Hall—enter through courtyard, tel. 02/259-100-811, www.muzeum.bratislava.sk.

Apponyi House (Apponyiho Palác)

This nicely restored mansion of a Hungarian aristocrat is meaningless without the included audioguide (dull but informative). The museum has two parts. The cellar and ground floor feature an interesting exhibit on the vineyards of the nearby "Small Carpathian" hills, with historic presses and barrels, and a replica of an old-time wine-pub table. (If this exhibit interests you, consider a stop at the Slovak National Collection of Wine, also at Apponyi House and listed next). Upstairs are two floors of urban apartments from old Bratislava, called the Museum of Period Rooms. The first floor up shows off the 18th-century Rococo-style rooms of the nobility—fine but not ostentatious, with ceramic stoves. The second floor up (with lower ceilings and simpler decor) illustrates 19th-century bourgeois/middle-class lifestyles, including period clothing and some Empire-style furniture.

Cost and Hours: €4, includes audioguide, €6 combo-ticket with City History Museum, Tue-Fri 10:00-17:00, Sat-Sun 11:00-18:00, closed Mon, Radničná 1, tel. 02/5920-5135, www.muzeum.bratislava.sk.

Slovak National Collection of Wine

Run by the union of Slovak vintners, this room at the Apponyi House showcases the region's wines, 80 percent of which are white. Filling a 16th-century, brick-vaulted wine cellar, it features 100 Slovak wines that are open and eager to be tasted. Pick up the degustation list and track down what you like. An English-speaking sommelier is at your service.

Cost and Hours: Small tastings with explanations are an option, but for €23 you can taste up to 72 wines in 100 minutes... do this at the end of your sightseeing day (Tue-Fri 10:00-18:00, Sat from 11:00, closed Sun-Mon, Radničná 1, tel. 02/4552-9967, www.salonvin.sk).

▲Nedbalka Gallery of Slovak Modern Art

This sleek and modern gallery is owned by a local tech millionaire and run as a private nonprofit. Ride the elevator to the top floor and work chronologically through the permanent collection of 20th-century Slovak art in four delightful floors. The ground floor is dedicated to temporary exhibits. You'll notice glass is big in Slovakia (Chihuly is a Czech name, and Dale is well known and celebrated here). Admission includes a tablet multimedia guide and a nice coffee in the café.

Cost and Hours: €5, Tue-Sun 13:00-19:00, closed Mon, next to the Old Market Hall at Nedbalova 17, tel. 02/5441-0287, www.nedbalka.sk.

BEYOND THE OLD TOWN
Bratislava Castle and Museum (Bratislavský Hrad a Múzeum)

The imposing Bratislava Castle, crowning Bratislava's hill, is the city's most prominent landmark. Big and iconic as it is, it's frankly

dull up close—and the exhibits inside are not too exciting. Still, it's almost obligatory to head up here simply for the grand views over Bratislava and the Danube...though, if the weather's bad, you'd be forgiven for skipping it.

Cost and Hours: Castle grounds—free, museum—€10; Tue-Sun 10:00-18:00, Nov-March 9:00-17:00, closed Mon year-round, last entry one hour before closing; tel. 02/2048-3110, www.snm.sk.

Getting There: For the best walking route to the castle, see the end of the "Bratislava Old Town Walk," earlier in this chapter.

Background: When Habsburg Empress Maria Theresa took a liking to Bratislava in the 18th century, she transformed the castle from a military fortress to a royal residence suitable for holding court. She added a summer riding school (the U-shaped complex next to the castle), an enclosed winter riding school out back, and lots more. Maria Theresa's favorite daughter, Maria Christina, lived here with her husband, Albert, when they were newlyweds. Locals nicknamed the place "little Schönbrunn," in reference to the Habsburgs' summer palace on the outskirts of Vienna.

The palace became a fortress-garrison during the Napoleonic Wars, then burned to the ground in an 1811 fire started by careless soldiers, and was left as a ruin for 150 years. An extensive rebuild, based on the original plans discovered in the Habsburg archives in 2008, has breathed new life into the castle (which is surrounded by a delightful public park).

Visiting the Castle: The best part of a visit here is the **grand view balcony** in front, overlooking the Danube, the Petržalka suburb across the river (marked by the SNP Bridge—described next), and—just below and upstream—the nondescript, boxy, white office building that houses the Slovak parliament. The castle is surrounded by gardens that are enjoyable on a nice day.

The dynamic statue in front of the castle's main entrance—with a knight waving his sword, rearing up on horseback—honors **Svätopluk** (846-894), the warrior-king who ruled over Great Moravia. His reign was the Slovaks' historical high-water mark, when its territory included parts of the present-day Czech Republic, Austria, Germany, Poland, Bulgaria, Romania, Serbia, Croatia, and Slovenia. Unfortunately, this dominance was short-lived; in the early 10th century, soon after Svätopluk's death, his kingdom was invaded by Magyars and folded into what became the Kingdom of Hungary—which Slovak lands would remain a part of for a thousand years. "Slovakia" has existed as a sovereign nation only since 1993; before that, you have to go all the way back to Svätopluk.

The castle **interior** features some modest exhibits and an opportunity to climb its tallest tower. It's overpriced and skippable, though the exhibits are gradually expanding—those with an interest in Slovak history might find it interesting. Inside, you'll pass through a modest exhibit about the restoration of the castle, then make your way up the grand, red-carpeted staircase to several floors of exhibits. On the third floor is a café (tucked amid a fun exhibit of nostalgic advertisements) and the "History of Slovakia" exhibit, which begins with the prehistoric Celts, tracks the arrival of the Slavs, and ends with the fall of Great Moravia after Svätopluk's time. Also on this floor, you can climb 87 steep, vertigo-inducing stairs to the top of the Crown Tower—the tallest part of the castle—for views over the city and the Danube basin (though the views from up top are not that much better than from down below).

▲▲SNP Bridge and UFO

Bratislava's flying-saucer-capped bridge, completed in 1972 in heavy-handed communist style, has been reclaimed by capitalists.

The saucer-shaped structure called the UFO (at the Petržalka end of the bridge) is now a spruced-up café/restaurant and observation deck, allowing sweeping 360-degree views of Bratislava from about 300 feet above the Danube.

Cost and Hours: €7.50, for €2.50 more you can return for the view after dark, open daily 10:00-23:00, elevator free if you have a meal reservation or order food at the pricey restaurant, restaurant opens at 12:00, tel. 02/6252-0300, www.redmonkeygroup.com.

Getting There: Walk across the bridge from the old town (walkways cross the bridge on a level below the road; the elevator entrance is a few steps down from the downstream-side walkway).

Visiting the UFO: The **"elevator"** that takes you up is actually a funicular—you may notice you're moving at an angle. At the top, walk up the stairs to the observation deck, passing photos of the bridge's construction.

Begin by viewing the **castle** and **old town.** The area to the right of the old town, between and beyond the skyscrapers, is a

massive construction zone where the new Bratislava is taking shape.

The huge TV tower caps a forested hill beyond the old town. Below and to the left of it, the pointy monument is **Slavín,** where more than 6,800 Soviet soldiers who fought to liberate Bratislava from the Nazis are buried. Under communist rule, a nearby church was forced to take down its steeple so as not to draw attention away from the huge Soviet soldier on top of the monument.

Now turn 180 degrees and cross the platform to face **Petržalka,** a planned communist suburb that sprouted here in the 1970s. The site was once occupied by a village, and the various districts of modern Petržalka still carry their original names (which now seem ironic): "Meadows" *(Háje)*, "Woods" *(Lúky)*, and "Courtyards" *(Dvory)*. The ambitious communist planners envisioned a city laced with Venetian-style canals to help drain the marshy land, but the plans were abandoned after the harsh crackdown on the 1968 Prague Spring uprising. Without the incentives of private owner- ship, all they succeeded in creating was a grim and decaying sea of miserable concrete apartment *paneláky* ("panel buildings," so-called because they're made of huge prefab panels).

Today, one in six Bratislavans lives in Petržalka, and things are looking better. Like Dorothy opening the door to Oz, the for- merly drab buildings have been splashed with bright new colors, and the interiors have been modernized. Far from being a slum, Petržalka is now a popular neighborhood for Bratislavan yuppies who can't yet afford to build their dream houses.

Petržalka is also a big suburban-style shopping zone (note the supermall down below). But there's still some history here. The **park** called Sad Janka Kráľa (originally, in German, Aupark)—just downriver from the bridge—was technically the first public park in Europe in the 1770s and is still a popular place for locals to relax and court.

Scanning the **horizon** beyond Petržalka, two things stick out: on the left, the old communist oil refinery (which has been fully updated and is now state-of-the-art); and on the right, a forest of modern windmills. These are just over the border, in Austria...and Bratislava is sure to grow in that direction quickly. Austria is about three miles that way, and Hungary is about six miles farther to the left.

Before you leave, consider a drink at the café. If nothing else, be sure to use the memorable WCs.

Blue Church of St. Elisabeth (Kostol Svätej Alžbety)

Just east of the old town—through a nicely manicured new park— is a fine little neighborhood of cheery, colorful Art Nouveau buildings. The main landmark here is the gentle-blue, fancifully decorated Church of St. Elisabeth—also called simply the "Little

Blue Church." It's straight out of a fairy tale, with rounded edges, pretty flourishes, and vivid colors. Designed by the great Hungarian Secessionist architect Ödön Lechner, and completed in 1913, it's worth the short walk from the old town for architecture fans. While the interior is open limited hours to the public, you can often peek through the glass doors to see the similarly soft and pretty interior (Bezručova 2).

▲Eurovea and the New Bratislava

Just downstream from the old town is the modern Eurovea complex, with four layers, each a quarter-mile long: a riverside park, luxury condos, a thriving modern shopping mall, and an office park. While it's essentially a big riverfront shopping mall, those looking for a peek at the "new Bratislava" find it worth the lovely, short riverfront stroll from the old town...which is also a chance to check out all of the moored riverboats.

Eurovea's central public space is a fountain- and statue-filled people zone between the Danube and Bratislava's new National Theater. Directly in front of the theater, the pavement is pulled back to show original Roman paving stones that were excavated here (a reminder of the city's long history as a trade crossroads). At the river end of the square, under the lion-topped pillar, a statue features General Milan Rastislav Štefánik, who represented Slovakia in a 1918 meeting in Pittsburgh and signed the "Pittsburgh Agreement"—creating the combined state of Česko-Slovensko. He's holding a bronze copy of the document as he looks out at the Danube.

The riverfront strip of Eurovea is the embryo of a huge vision for a new Bratislava. Dozens of skyscrapers are being built at once, as the city's old industrial zone (destroyed in World War II, and now destined to be the city's future tech-industry home) is one big construction site.

Exploring the old town gives you a taste of where this country has been. But wandering this riverside park, enjoying a drink in one of its chic outdoor lounges, and then browsing the thriving mall, you'll enjoy a glimpse of where Slovakia is heading.

Sleeping in Bratislava

Because Bratislava is more business city than tourist city, you'll find weekends are a little less expensive.

$$$ Hotel Marrol's, on a quiet urban street, is the town's most enticing splurge. Although the immediate neighborhood isn't interesting, it's just a five-minute walk from the old town, the public spaces are plush and generous, and its 53 rooms are luxurious and tastefully appointed Old World country-style. While pricey, rates drop on weekends (air-con, elevator, gorgeous lounge, Tobrucká 4, tel. 02/5778-4600, www.hotelmarrols.sk, rec@hotelmarrols.sk).

$$$ Roset Boutique Hotel, facing the ring road's tram tracks at the eastern edge of the old town (with some street noise), feels classy and upmarket. Its 28 rooms are spacious and plush (air-con, elevator, Štúrova 10, tel. 02/3217-1819, www.rosethotel.sk, reservations@rosethotel.sk).

$$$ Radisson Blu Carlton Hotel has been hosting VIPs for decades, with 170 rooms and all the big corporate trappings and expected services. It's beautifully located, facing the National Theater and Promenade Square (air-con, elevator, Hviezdoslavovo Námestie 3, tel. 02/5939-0000, www.radissonblu.com/hotel-bratislava, reservation.bratislava@radissonblu.com).

$$ Loft Hotel is an appealing midrange choice, tucked along the highway between the main train station and the old town (ask for a quieter back room facing the garden). It's professional, stylish, and trendy—with comfy leather couches in the lobby, an onsite brewpub, and a staff that prides itself on its service. Of the 121 rooms, the "standard" rooms are fine but forgettable; consider paying a bit more for a cushier, retro-industrial "superior" room (air-con, elevator, pay parking garage, Štefánikova 4, tel. 02/5751-1000, www.lofthotel.sk, reservation@lofthotel.sk). They also have 10 more expensive, high-end rooms in the attached **Wilson Palace,** in the original building facing the main road.

$ Aplend City Hotel Michalská is a tight little hotel with a peaceful back garden tucked just inside St. Michael's Gate in the old town. The 14 rooms are comfortable, and the location—on a picturesque lane—is ideal (air-con, elevator, Baštová 4, tel. 903/998-111, www.aplendcity.com/en/hotel-michalska, michalska@aplendcity.com).

$ Penzión Virgo, on a quiet residential street an eight-minute walk from the old town, rents 12 boutique-ish rooms (breakfast extra, reserve ahead for inexpensive parking, Panenská 14, tel. 02/2092-1400, mobile 0948-350-878, www.penzionvirgo.sk, reception@penzionvirgo.sk).

Eating in Bratislava

Slovak cooking involves some Hungarian and Austrian influences, but it's closer to Czech cuisine—lots of starches and gravy, and plenty of pork, cabbage, potatoes, and dumplings. Keep an eye out for Slovakia's intensely filling national dish, *bryndzové halušky* (small potato dumplings with sheep's cheese and bits of bacon). For a fun drink and snack that locals love, try a Vinea grape soda and a sweet, crescent-shaped *Pressburger* bagel in any bar or café.

Like the Czechs, the Slovaks produce excellent beer (*pivo*, PEE-voh). The dominant brand is Zlatý Bažant ("Golden Pheasant"). Bratislava's beer halls are good places to sample Slovak beers—whether macrobrews or microbrews—and to get a hearty, affordable meal of stick-to-your-ribs pub grub. The Bratislava region also produces wines, similar to the ones that Vienna is known for. But, as nearly all is consumed locally, most outsiders don't think of Slovakia as wine country.

Bratislava is packed with inviting new eateries. In addition to heavy Slovak staples, you'll find trendy new bars and bistros, and a smattering of non-European offerings. The best plan may be to stroll the old town and keep your eyes open for the setting and cuisine that appeals to you most. Or consider the areas listed below. All are within a short walk and offer a better, more interesting dining experience than the grotesquely touristy eateries that line Michalská street and other busy streets in the old town.

Traditional Beer Hall on Námestie SNP

A couple of blocks north of the old town (and named for the Slovak National Uprising), the right side of this square is dominated by the following operation.

$$ Bratislavská is a sprawling complex of eateries. The main location (door on the right) is the Bratislavská Reštaurácia. Walk through a maze of old-timey rooms, then up a flight of stairs to a huge dining hall that smells hoppy and feels happy (with the waitstaff sporting "Bar-tislava" and "Bra-tislava" T-shirts). The menu features classic Slovak dishes, and the portions are hearty and cheap. For a more intimate setting, the door to the left leads to the tight, woody Kláštorný Pivovar ("Monastery Brewery"), with a cozier ambience and the same menu. They also have tables outside on the square (daily 12:00-23:00, Námestie SNP 8, mobile 0917-927-673).

Near the Old Market Hall

While there's often nothing actually inside the Old Market Hall (which fills a city block at the eastern edge of the old town—a 5-minute walk from the main square), it's surrounded by intriguing and trendy options. Once a month, the square in front features a

"Street Food Park" with a wide variety of food trucks (worth planning around—check schedule at www.staratrznica.sk). At other times, walk around the block to survey your options (listed in order, from the front door).

$ Výčap u Ernőho is a popular, no-frills beer hall with a row of taps up front featuring a changing selection of quality beers. If you'd like to enjoy Slovak beers with local hipsters instead of the sloppy beer-hall tourist crowd, do it here (no food, Tue-Sat 12:00-24:00, Sun from 16:00, Mon from 15:00, Námestie SNP 25, mobile 0948-360-153).

$ Foodstock is an enticing, hip, and healthy vegetarian place that advertises "good mood food." It got its start as a food truck, and now serves up a brief menu of delicious, Asian-inspired dishes and all-you-can-drink homemade iced teas in a patchouli-scented space (daily 10:00-22:00, Klobučnícka 6, mobile 0905-456-654).

$$ Mecheche Snack Bar serves tiny, fancy sandwiches as if channeling a Barcelona tapas bar (Tue-Sat 17:00-24:00, closed Sun-Mon, Nedbalova 12, mobile 0948-853-444).

$$ Urban House, behind the Old Market Hall on fashionable Laurinská street, is California-trendy with a sprawling, industrial-mod, woody-bookstore ambience, great outdoor tables, and an appealing menu. The food (burgers, pizza, and so on) is nothing special, but the scene is fun (daily 9:00-24:00, Laurinská 14, mobile 0904-001-021).

Restaurants on Promenade Square (Hviezdoslavovo Námestie)

This square is lined with restaurants, nearly all with open-feeling interior seating and mellow tables out on the square under the trees—ideal for enjoying the promenade of strollers. There's no traffic, just the sound of fountains and the breeze. A strip of three places, side-by-side, makes for easy comparison-shopping; for a view, head up to Sky Bar.

$$$ Carnevalle is a hit for its steak. Their greeting? "Nice to meat you!" Their indoors feels outdoors—a spacious, glassed-in dining hall—and their tables on the square are inviting. The tasty dishes are nicely presented by a professional waitstaff (daily 11:00-24:00, at #20, mobile 0903-123-164).

$$ Zylinder ("Top Hat") re-creates a circa-1900 atmosphere to serve classy bourgeoise cuisine that leans closer to Austrian than traditional Slovak—think sausages and schnitzels (daily 11:00-22:00, at #19, mobile 0903-123-134).

$ Café Restaurant Verne, university-owned and unburdened by the high rent of its neighbors, feels like the dive bar of the strip—with mismatched antique tables spilling out onto the cobbles. It has a cozy, lowbrow, and mellow student vibe with stick-to-your-rib plates (pasta, goulash, salads) and drinks. You get what you pay for, but the price is right (Mon-Fri 8:00-24:00, Sat-Sun from 10:00, at #18).

Rooftop View: $$$ Sky Bar Restaurant, just past the fenced-in US Embassy, features a Thai-meets-Mediterranean menu on its seventh-floor open-roof terrace. It's a pretentious place, with local big shots dropping by and stuffy service. But the food's good and so are the views. It's smart to reserve a view table in advance to dine here—or just drop by for a pricey vodka cocktail (daily 12:00-late, Hviezdoslavovo Námestie 7, mobile 0948-109-400, www.skybar. sk).

Eurovea

This modern development facing the Danube River (a short walk downstream from the old town) has huge outdoor terraces rollicking with happy eaters. A variety of upscale and high-energy **$$-$$$ restaurants** lines the swanky riverfront residential and shopping-mall complex. Options include international—French, Italian, Brazilian—as well as branches of the Czech beer-hall chain **Kolkovna** and the British pan-Asian restaurant **Wagamama.** Or head to the **$ food court** in the shopping mall, where you'll eat cheap. While the restaurants here are nothing special, it's a fun excuse for a stroll along the Danube promenade, and to get a peek at the emerging "new Bratislava" zone beyond the old-town cobbles.

Bratislava Connections

BY TRAIN

Bratislava has two major train stations: the main station, walkable to some accommodations and the old town (Hlavná Stanica, abbreviated "Bratislava hl. st." on schedules); and Petržalka station, in a suburb across the river and linked to town by bus. When checking schedules, pay attention to which station your train uses. Frequent bus #93 connects the two stations in about 10 minutes. For public transit info and maps, see http://imhd.sk.

Hlavná Stanica (Main Train Station)

This decrepit station is about a half-mile north of the old town. A left-luggage desk is to your right as you exit the tracks (*úschovňa batožín;* confirm open hours for pickup). There are also a few lockers along track 1; more are to the left from the main hall (after the vending machines and through the door). The station also has a TI window, and there's an ATM in the main hall. A nicer, more modern waiting area is down the hallway to the left (with the tracks at your back).

Getting Downtown: It's a short bus ride or a boring 15-minute walk to the town center. (**Taxis** stand by, but with rip-off prices—they'll try to charge €15 rather than the legitimate €5 drop charge for the short ride. You can try insisting on the meter, but since they're basically unregulated, it likely won't help.)

Bus #93 leaves every five minutes from the right-hand curb 50 yards in front of the station; it stops at Grassalkovich Palace, Zochova (nearest the old town), and Most SNP (the bus station under the SNP Bridge, by the river). Buy a 15-minute *základný lístok/basic* ticket from the machine for €0.70, and stamp it as you get on the bus.

To **walk** downtown, exit out the station's front door and follow the covered walkway past the bus stops. After the road bends right, take the pedestrian overpass, then head straight downhill on the busy main drag, Štefánikova. You'll pass the presidential gardens, then Grassalkovich Palace, Slovakia's "White House." The old town—marked by the green steeple of St. Michael's Gate (the start of my self-guided walk)—is a long block ahead of you.

Petržalka Train Station (ŽST Petržalka)
Half of the trains from Vienna arrive at this quiet, modern little train station, across the river in the modernized suburb of Petržalka. The main hall has an ATM and luggage lockers (by the door to the tracks).

Getting Downtown: Two different buses head to the old town from opposite sides of the station. For either bus, buy a 15-minute *základný lístok/basic* ticket from the machine for €0.70, and stamp it as you board. The stop closest to the old town is Zochova. **Bus #80** stops closest to the station but makes more stops on the way to town: From the main hall, exit, cross the street, and turn left to find the stop (direction: Kollárova nám). **Bus #93** is more direct but a longer walk from the station: Take the long tunnel under the tracks, exit on the other side, and follow the crosswalk straight across the busy highway to find the stop (direction: Hlavná Stanica).

From Bratislava by Train to: Budapest (6/day direct, 2.5 hours), **Vienna** (2/hour, 1 hour; departures alternate between the two stations—half from main station usually leaving hourly at :38, half from Petržalka usually leaving hourly at :15), **Sopron** (nearly hourly direct from Petržalka, 2.5 hours on RegionalExpress/ REX), **Prague** (5/day direct, 4 hours). To reach other Hungarian destinations (including **Eger** and **Pécs**), it's generally easiest to change in Budapest.

BY BUS
Two companies run handy buses that connect Bratislava, **Vienna**, and the **airports** in each city: Flixbus (www.flixbus.com) and Slo-

vak Lines/Postbus (tel. 0810-222-3336, www.slovaklines.sk) get you to Vienna for just €5-8. You can book ahead online, or (if arriving at the airport) just take whichever connection is leaving first.

BY BOAT

Riverboats connect Bratislava to Vienna. Conveniently, these boats dock right along the Danube in front of Bratislava's old town. While they are more expensive, less frequent, and slower than the train, some travelers enjoy getting out on the Danube. (Sail with your passport, as you'll be crossing a border.)

The **Twin City Liner** runs modern catamarans between a dock at the edge of Bratislava's old town, along Fajnorovo nábrežie, and Vienna's Schwedenplatz (where Vienna's town center hits the canal; €30-35 each way, 3-5/day, late March-Oct only, 1.5 hours; reservations smart, Austrian tel. 00-43-1-904-8880, www.twincityliner.com).

The competing Slovak **LOD** line connects the cities a little more cheaply (on older Russian hydrofoils), but runs just twice a day and uses Vienna's less-convenient Reichsbrücke dock on the main river, farther from the city center (€25 one-way, €44 round-trip, 1.5 hours, tel. 02/5293-2226, www.lod.sk).

BY PLANE

While Bratislava has a small airport (used mostly by discount airlines), the Vienna Airport is so close it's considered the local airport.

Bratislava Airport (Letisko Bratislava)

This airport (airport code: BTS, www.bts.aero) is six miles northeast of downtown Bratislava. Budget airline Ryanair has many flights here. Some airlines market it as "Vienna-Bratislava," thanks to its proximity to both capitals. It's compact and manageable, with all the usual amenities.

From the Airport to Downtown Bratislava: The airport has easy **public bus** connections to Bratislava's main train station (Hlavná Stanica, €1.20 one-hour ticket, bus #61, 3-4/hour, 30 minutes). A **taxi** from the airport into central Bratislava should cost about €20.

To Budapest: Take the bus or taxi to Bratislava's main train station, then hop a train to Budapest.

To Vienna: You can take the **Flixbus** to the Erdberg stop on Vienna's U-3 subway line (€8, runs every 1-2 hours, 1 hour, www.flixbus.com) or the **Slovak Lines/Postbus** bus to Vienna's Hauptbahnhof (€10, 1-2/hour, 2 hours, www.slovaklines.sk). A **taxi** from Bratislava Airport directly to Vienna costs €60-90 (depending on whether you use a cheaper Slovak or more expensive Austrian cab).

Vienna International Airport

This airport, 12 miles from downtown Vienna and 30 miles from downtown Bratislava, is well connected to both capitals (airport code: VIE, airport tel. 01/700-722-233, www.viennaairport.com). For a full description of this airport, see page 948. If you're heading straight to Bratislava, there's no need to go into Vienna from here. The easiest option is to take the Flixbus or Slovak Lines/Postbus bus described earlier. Check schedules on the airport website (under "Arrival & Parking") or ask the airport TI which bus is leaving first, then head straight out the door and hop on. After about 45 minutes, the bus stops in downtown Bratislava, then heads to the Bratislava airport.

MORE EASTERN
EUROPE

MORE EASTERN EUROPE

The preceding chapters cover what I consider to be, for most travelers, the core of Eastern Europe. But in a sense, "Eastern Europe" is like the Louisiana Purchase...you can delve in as far as you like. That's where this section comes in.

The next five chapters offer a brief, practical introduction to countries that lie just beyond the core of this book. Because this is designed to get you started—with candid advice about where to go, and what you might do in each place—I've included only the most basic advice for logistics such as transportation, accommodations, and restaurants. These chapters are intended only as a first step—not the final word. In each one, I offer a quick overview, a rundown of practical country facts, some itinerary-planning advice, a few tips on the local cuisine and language, and a concise rundown of the best destinations (focusing on the attractions that are most deserving of your valuable time).

In the following pages, you'll find an overview of these destinations:

Croatia: Eastern Europe's Riviera is a natural add-on for travelers going to Slovenia—it's just down the road. For a quick taste of Croatia, you can dip into the northern Istrian Peninsula (which borders Slovenia) and enjoy one of Croatia's top seaside towns, Rovinj. Those taking the train between Budapest and Ljubljana will pass through Croatia's underrated capital, Zagreb, which is worth at least a few hours' exploration (or even a night or two). And if you have plenty of time, you can head south—via the waterfall wonderland of Plitvice Lakes National Park—to the Dalmatian Coast: Dubrovnik, Split, and the islands of Hvar and Korčula.

Bosnia-Herzegovina: Croatia wraps around this inviting country, with a dramatic landscape and a vibrant culture. I've focused on two top destinations: The small city of Mostar is an easy

More Eastern Europe at a Glance

Croatia Gorgeous coastline, islands, natural wonders (Plitvice Lakes), dreamy seaside towns (Dubrovnik, Rovinj, and Korčula), and great cities (Zagreb and Split).

Bosnia-Herzegovina A gregarious and gorgeous land with complex history, a rich Muslim tradition, and fascinating cities small (Mostar) and large (Sarajevo).

Montenegro Ruggedly beautiful landscape—from beaches to peaks—just south of Croatia.

Bulgaria Culturally rich land with ancient artifacts, scintillating cities (Plovdiv, Sofia), charming historic towns (Veliko Tarnovo), great food, and kind people.

Romania Big, complex country with a thriving capital (Bucharest), Transylvanian castles and towns, vibrant folk culture (in Maramureș), and vividly painted monasteries (in Bucovina).

side-trip from Croatia's Dalmatian Coast, and offers an accessible and intriguing first look at Bosnia. With more time, it's rewarding to venture farther to the even more engaging capital, Sarajevo.

Montenegro: Just south of Croatia, Montenegro's glorious Bay of Kotor—with stunning scenery and characteristic seaside towns—is an easy side-trip for those based in Dubrovnik. With more time, you could head up into the hills to see the historic capital, Cetinje.

Bulgaria: A cultural detour that's well worth taking, Bulgaria involves a long overland journey (through the rugged Balkan Peninsula) or a quick flight from the core Eastern European countries. From the mellow and user-friendly capital, Sofia, you can head for the fun and fascinating second city, Plovdiv; the dramatically set historic capital, Veliko Tarnovo; and a variety of countryside sights: remote and majestic Rila Monastery, the ancient artifacts and fragrant rose fields of the Thracian Plain, and mountain-capping monuments such as the bizarre communist-era conference hall called Buzludzha.

Romania: Romania is a big, crazy, fascinating, time-consuming destination—but for many, it's worth the effort. Romania borders Hungary, and parts are accessible on a long train ride or drive from Budapest. But given the long distances, it may be easier to fly into Bucharest (the capital) and continue from there. Bucharest deserves a quick look, but the main concentration of famous sights are a few hours north—in Transylvania. Choose a home-base town or two (the best options are Brașov—near castles; Sighișoara—near fortified churches; and Sibiu—best all-around town)...and then explore. If you're captivated by traditional folk life, you could take the long drive even farther north, to the rustic corner called Maramureș. And with even more time, consider swinging through the northeastern region of Bucovina, famous for its vividly painted monasteries.

Additional Information: For some of these countries—Croatia, Bosnia-Herzegovina, and Montenegro—you can find my complete coverage in a separate book: *Rick Steves Croatia & Slovenia*. For the others—Bulgaria and Romania—I haven't produced a full-length book, but plenty of other guidebooks and online resources are available to fill in the gaps and advance your planning. Also, in Bulgaria and Romania, local guides are particularly affordable and worth hiring to make your trip-planning easier—I've recommended my favorites in each country.

CROATIA

Hrvatska

Sunny beaches, succulent seafood, and a taste of *la dolce vita*...in Eastern Europe?

With thousands of miles of inviting seafront, Croatia's coastline is Eastern Europe's Riviera. Holiday-makers love its pebbly beaches, predictably balmy summer weather, and dramatic mountains. Croatia is also historic. From ruined Roman arenas and Byzantine mosaics to Venetian bell towers, Habsburg villas, and even communist concrete, past rulers have left their mark. And for thoughtful travelers, a trip to Croatia comes with an opportunity to better understand Europe's most violent conflict since World War II: the breakup of Yugoslavia (see page 1075). All in all, Croatia offers something to everyone—there's good reason that it's one of Europe's hottest emerging destinations.

Where to Go: Croatia has more than 3,600 miles of coastline and more than a thousand islands. To be selective, zoom in on these three areas:

The **Dalmatian Coast,** a dramatic limestone coastline, features a bustling big city with the best ancient ruins in the country (Split); several alluring islands (most notably Korčula and Hvar); and Croatia's showcase city: romantic, walled Dubrovnik.

Istria, a wedge-shaped peninsula in northern Croatia, has rolling hills, wineries, truffles, charming hill towns, ancient ruins (in Pula), and the finest coastal town between Venice and Dubrovnik: Rovinj.

The **Croatian interior** boasts the country's surprisingly appealing capital, Zagreb, which lies near Hungary and Austria. And two hours south, deep in the countryside, is one of Europe's top natural wonders, Plitvice Lakes National Park.

For a quick visit of just a few days, focus either on the Dalmatian Coast (and possibly add in some Bosnia and Montenegro—covered in the next two chapters) or on the sights in the north (Istria and the interior). With more time—a week or more—you can hit the highlights of all three regions.

Seasonality: Croatia is the most seasonal destination in this book. July and August are the peak of peak—everything is jammed up with European vacationers, and prices are high. Late May, June, September, and early October are the best times to visit...it's cooler (but still warm) and less crowded. But off-season (after about mid-October, or before early May), while big cities like Dubrovnik and Split remain open for business, smaller towns close up tight.

Accommodations: Especially in the coastal towns, hotels tend to be big, overpriced resorts. Instead, carefully consider private accommodations: a *soba* (room) or *apartman* (apartment).

Croatia Practicalities

Money: Croatia uses the kuna: $1 = about 7 kuna (kn, or HRK). One kuna is broken down into 100 lipa.

Geography and People: The country is 22,000 square miles, similar to West Virginia. Of the 4.5 million people, 90 percent are ethnic Croats (Catholic) and 4.5 percent are Serbs (Orthodox). Its biggest cities are the capital, Zagreb (pop. 790,000) and Split (pop. 178,000). The country's GDP is $80 billion ($18,000 GDP per capita).

Snapshot History: After losing their independence to Hungary in 1102, the Croats watched as most of their coastline became Venetian and their interior was conquered by Ottomans. Croatia was "rescued" by the Habsburgs, but after World War I it became part of Yugoslavia—a decision many Croats regretted until they finally gained independence in 1991 through a bitter war with their Serb neighbors. Today, Croatia is proudly independent.

Famous Croatians: Roman Emperor Diocletian, explorer Marco Polo, Nikoka Tesla (a Croatia-born Serb), and several Croatian-Americans, including Roger Maris, John Malkovich, John Kasich, and Dennis Kucinich.

Emergencies: Dial 92 for police; dial 112 for medical or other emergencies.

Consular Services in Zagreb: The US Embassy is at Ulica Thomasa Jeffersona 2 (tel. 01/661-2300, after-hours tel. 01/661-2400, https://hr.usembassy.gov). The Canadian Embassy is at Prilaz Đure Deželića 4 (tel. 01/488-1200, www.croatia.gc.ca). Call ahead for passport services.

Telephone Country Code: +385, then drop the initial 0 of the phone number.

Tourist Information: https://croatia.hr

CROATIA

These offer double the cultural intimacy for a fraction the price of a big hotel—and many are quite comfortable and hotelesque, with modern amenities and all of the independence you like. For the best prices, book directly (I've listed websites or email addresses for my favorites).

Getting Around: Croatia's trains are of limited usefulness, but their bus network is strong (for schedules, see www.getbybus.com or www.autobusni-kolodvor.com). Coastal destinations (including the islands) are well-connected by bus and by ferry—either big, lumbering car ferries (mostly operated by Jadrolinija, www.jadrolinija.hr) or speedy catamarans (handy ones on the Dalmatian Coast include www.jadrolinija.hr, www.krilo.hr, and www.gv-line.hr). Croatia is also easy for drivers, with excellent roads including a slick network of expressways (with tolls).

Croatian Cuisine: Like Italian fare, Croatian cooking includes lots of pasta, pizza, seafood, and *pršut* (prosciutto). Fill the tank at a pizzeria, but every so often splurge on a seafood feast. Try octopus salad or "black risotto" (a rice dish with cuttlefish simmered in its own ink). Ice-cream stands are abundant. In the interior, meat is popular (especially prepared with a *peka*—simmered for hours under a metal baking lid covered in hot coals). While the cuisine scene in most of the famous coastal destinations is uninspired, Istria—with its proximity to Italy and its own abundant truffles—is a step above. Croatia also produces excellent wines (*bijelo* is white, *crno* is red).

Croatian Language: Most Croatians speak excellent English, so the language barrier is minimal. But just in case, here are a few helpful Croatian phrases: "Hello" is *Dobar dan* (formal) or *Bok* (informal); "please" is *molim;* "thank you" is *hvala;* and "Goodbye" is *Do viđenija*.

Top Croatian Destinations

The following sections are designed to get you started planning a trip to Croatia. For in-depth coverage—including self-guided walks and museum tours, detailed hotel and restaurant listings, and lots of practical advice—consider my *Rick Steves Croatia & Slovenia* guidebook.

THE DALMATIAN COAST
Of Croatia's long coastline, the southern third—stretching 200 miles from Zadar to Dubrovnik—contains many of the country's most popular destinations.

▲▲▲Dubrovnik
Dubrovnik is a living fairy tale that shouldn't be missed. It feels like a small town today, but 500 years ago, Dubrovnik was an independent city-state and major

maritime power, with the third-biggest navy in the Mediterranean. Still jutting confidently into the sea and ringed by thick medieval walls, Dubrovnik deserves its nickname: the Pearl of the Adriatic. Within the ramparts, the traffic-free Old Town is a fun jumble of steep alleys, low-impact museums, al fresco cafés, and kid-friendly squares. For tourist information, see www.tzdubrovnik.hr.

Visiting Dubrovnik: Though it's a sprawling city of 50,000 people, most visitors focus on its compact Old Town. Simply strolling the ▲▲▲ **Stradun** (main drag) is a highlight. Several churches, museums, and other attractions hide within the City Walls. All of them are skippable, but it's worth dipping into the fine ▲ **Cathedral** (with its quirky treasury collection); the restful cloisters of the ▲ **Franciscan and Dominican monasteries** (each with a modest museum); and the ▲ **Rector's Palace** (the historical residence of the rulers of this independent city-state). The Old Town also has a historical synagogue, a finely decorated Serbian Orthodox church and icon collection, good ethnographic and maritime museums, an aquarium, and a poignant exhibition of wartime photography.

Dubrovnik's single-best attraction is strolling the scenic mile-and-a-quarter around the top of the remarkably well-preserved ▲▲▲ **City Walls.** As you meander along this lofty perch—with a sea of orange roofs on one side and the azure sea on the other—you'll get your bearings, peer into secluded gardens, and snap pictures like mad of the ever-changing views. Walk the walls early or late—the ticket line gets long with cruise-ship passengers at midday.

For an even higher viewpoint, ride the ▲▲▲ **cable car** from just above the City Walls up to the summit of Mount Srđ. There you'll enjoy sweeping views down over the red rooftops of Dubrovnik, and out to offshore islands that recede into the sunset (www.dubrovnikcablecar.com).

The city can get very crowded midday, so it can be nice to escape to a nearby **beach** (several scenic spots line the road outside the Ploče Gate, southeast of the Old Town). Or head to the **Old Port**—at the mouth of the Old Town—where local captains offer sightseeing cruises. Popular destinations include little Lokrum Island (just offshore, great hiking and uncrowded beaches) and the Elaphite Islands (a trio of larger islands, each with small villages and beaches).

Sleeping in Dubrovnik: $$ Dubrovnik Gardens, an excellent value, is located in a private little garden inside the Old Town (Roberto and Marija, www.dubrovnikgardens.com). For private rooms on a sleepy, skinny, stepped lane inside the Old Town, try **$$ Villa Ragusa** (run by Pero, www.villaragusadubrovnik.com) or **$$ Apartments Paviša** (run by a different Pero, www.apartmentspavisa.com); if they're full, their neighbors often have rooms. Other good rooms around town include the simple but cheery **$ Plaza Apartments** (Lidija, lidydu@yahoo.com) and the upscale and trendy **$$$$ Fresh Sheets Kathedral B&B** (Jon and Sanja, www.freshsheetskathedral.com).

Eating in Dubrovnik: Avoid the overpriced tourist traps on the main drag and on the glitzy "restaurant row," Prijeko street. One exception is **Nishta,** a well-run vegetarian eatery with an eclectic international menu (on Prijeko street, www.nishtarestaurant.com). For traditional Dalmatian food done well, try classy **Dalmatino** (Miha Pracata 6, www.dalmatino-dubrovnik.com) or **Kopun,** on a gravelly square facing a church (Poljana Ruđera Boškovića 7, www.restaurantkopun.com). To sample local wines (paired with light local dishes), don't miss **D'Vino Wine Bar** (Palmotićeva 4a, www.dvino.net). And for the most scenic setting in town, get a drink at one of two bars called **Cold Drinks "Buža"**—that means "hole in the wall"—which is literally what you'll have to climb through to reach these delightful perches, clinging like barnacles to the seaward side of the City Walls (ask locals for help to find the entrances).

Private Drivers: Many travelers splurge on hiring their own private driver for side-trips to destinations described in the next two chapters: Bosnia's Mostar and Montenegro's Bay of Kotor (figure around €250 for a full-day trip). Good options include **Pepo Klaić** (www.dubrovnikshoretrip.com) and **Petar Vlašić** (www.dubrovnikrivieratours.com).

▲▲Split

Split (pronounced as it's spelled) is Croatia's second city, bustling with 178,000 people. If you've been hopping along the coast, landing in urban Split feels like a return to civilization. While most Dalmatian coastal towns seem made for tourists, Split is real and vibrant—a shipbuilding city with ugly sprawl surrounding an atmospheric Old Town, which teems with Croatians living life to the fullest. As this is a transportation hub for the coast,  you'll likely pass through at some point. It's well worth spending a night (or more) to fully experience this underrated city. For tourist information, see www.visitsplit.com.

Though Split throbs to a modern, youthful beat, its history goes way back—all the way to the Roman Empire. And today, Split has some of the best Roman ruins this side of Italy. In the fourth century AD, the Roman Emperor Diocletian (245-313) wanted to retire in his native Dalmatia, so he built a huge palace here. Eventually, the palace was abandoned. Then locals, fleeing seventh-century Slavic invaders, moved in and made themselves at home, and a medieval town sprouted from the rubble of the old palace. This—combined with Venetian influence starting in the 15th century—has left Split a fascinating study in the layers of history.

Visiting Split: The city's top experience is exploring the ruins of ▲▲▲ **Diocletian's Palace,** which are integrated into the townscape of the Old Town. The Old Town's streets were literally the hallways of the palaces; you can see where later settlers grafted windows and doors onto the original structure. And those windows and doors are still in use today.

Begin by exploring **Diocletian's Cellars,** the cavelike foundation that Roman engineers built to support the massive palace. Then

head up to the **Peristyle**—once the palace's grand entryway, it's now the Old Town's main square. Café cushions line the steps (buy a drink if you want to rest on one), and up the stairs is a majestic entry vestibule where a cappella singers perform traditional Dalmatian *klapa* music.

Towering over the Peristyle is the **Cathedral of St. Domnius,** which began life as Diocletian's mausoleum. Inside, you can see what was supposed to be the final resting place of the emperor, who was notorious for torturing Christians. In a bit of poetic justice, today his mausoleum is a cathedral honoring those martyrs... and Diocletian is nowhere to be found.

Another wonderful experience is sauntering along Split's main pedestrian promenade, called **the Riva.** Filling the broad strip between the Old Town (Diocletian's Palace) and the busy modern port, it's the perfect place to people-watch, lick an ice-cream cone, or nurse a coffee. Best around sunset—when it seems the whole town is out strolling—this mellow scene also sprawls up Marmontova street from the harbor.

Most of Split's museums (covering city history, archaeology, ethnography, and an old synagogue) are skippable. But one is a must: the ▲▲ **Meštrović Gallery,** displaying the works of local sculptor Ivan Meštrović (1883-1962). After a successful career in interwar Yugoslavia, Meštrović built a mansion and studio overlooking the Adriatic Sea on the outskirts of Split. Today that mansion—an easy bus or taxi ride from the Old Town—displays his expressive sculptures, which were greatly admired by his contemporary, Auguste Rodin. Meštrović's works still grace parks and squares all over Croatia (and in Chicago, where the artist fled after World War II).

Split is also a great city for relaxing. It has several distinctive and inviting squares; a green park peninsula, called **Marjan,** with hiking trails and beaches; and a lively, user-friendly nightlife scene.

Sleeping in Split: Just outside of the Old Town are some small, well-run guesthouses, including **$$ Villa Ana** (www.villaana-split. hr) and **$$ Villa Matejuška** (www.villamatejuska.hr). Within the Old Town—which can be noisy at night, especially on weekends—you can splurge at **$$$$ Marmont Hotel** (www.marmonthotel. com) or the cozy luxury B&B called **$$$$ Palača Judita** (www. juditapalace.com), or sleep more affordably at **$$ Kaleta Apartments** (www.kaletaapartments.com) or **$ Sobe "Base"** (www.base-rooms.com).

Eating in Split: You'll eat well inside the Old Town at the hole-in-the-wall **Villa Spiza** (Petra Kružića 3), the high-end bistro **Bokeria** (Domaldova 8), or the fish-oriented **Trattoria Bajamont** (Bajamontijeva 3). More options are just a short walk west of the Old Town, in the Varoš neighborhood: cozy **Konoba Fetivi** (Tomića Stine 4) or the bustling **Šperun Restaurant** (Šperun 3).

▲▲Dalmatian Islands: Korčula and Hvar

Croatia is famous for its islands, and some of the most popular are in Dalmatia. Many travelers argue that *their* favorite island is the very best island, but I'll let you in on a little secret: They're all equally good. While each has its claim to fame, the Croatian islands are essentially variations on a theme: a warm stone Old Town with a Venetian bell tower, a tidy boat-speckled harbor, ample seafood restaurants, a few refurbished resort hotels on the edge of town, and *sobe* and *apartman* signs by every other doorbell. My two favorites are relatively well-connected to each other and to the mainland: ritzy Hvar and mellow, dramatically situated Korčula.

Hvar: Hvar's hip cachet, upscale-ritzy "Croatian Riviera" buzz, and easy proximity to Split (one hour by express catamaran) have quickly turned this tidy Dalmatian fishing village into one of the most popular destinations in Croatia (www.tzhvar.hr). With a charming old town, a ruined fortress overhead, luxury yachts bobbing the harbor, and arguably the best nightlife in Croatia, Hvar is an enjoyable place to be on vacation. You can tour its churches, or visit the Benedictine convent where nuns make delicate lace from natural plant fibers. Or, to get out of town, enjoy one of the island's beaches, go for a hike, or take a boat ride to the offshore Pakleni Islands.

Good rooms in and near Hvar town include **$ Apartments Nona** (ivanka.hvar@gmail.com) and **$ Ivana and Paško Ukić** (ivanaukic@net.hr)—both of which are buried in the steep lanes above the town center. Just a 10-minute walk west of the Old Town is **$ Apartments Mare** (Marica and Gianni, www.apartments-mare-hvar.com). For a centrally located splurge hotel, try **$$$$ Villa Nora** (www.villanora.eu) or **$$$$ Hotel Park** (www.hotelparkhvar.com).

For meals, consider **Konoba Menego,** serving Croatian classics tapas-style (in the steep lanes above the main square, www.menego.hr); **Alviž,** with simple but delicious meals near the bus station (Hanibala Lucića 1); **Dalmatino,** with high-end cooking at reasonable prices just off the main square (Sveti Marak 1, www.dalmatino-hvar.com); or, for a splurge, **Gariful Restaurant,** with seafood along the harbor embankment (www.hvar-gariful.hr).

Korčula: The island town of Korčula (KOHR-choo-lah)—a bit closer to Dubrovnik, with workable connections—boasts an atmospheric Old Town, a smattering of little museums, and a dramatic, fjord-like mountain backdrop. Humbler and sleepier than its glitzy big sister Hvar, Korčula has an appealing backwater charm (www.visitkorcula.eu). The peninsular Old Town pokes out into the Adriatic, with a fish-skeleton street plan, a variety of museums (including the supposed former home of Marco Polo, whom Korčulans claim was born here), and a variety of pizza, pasta, and seafood restaurants. Twice weekly in summer, Lazy Korčula snaps to life when locals perform a medieval folk dance called the *Moreška*.

My favorite private rooms are **$$ M&J Central Suites** (mjcentralsuites@yahoo.com), **$ Old Town Apartments** (Branko and Ulrike, branko.r@onlinehome.de), and **$ Royal Apartments** (Zvonko and Marija, www.korcularoyalapartments.com). The best hotel option is **$$$$ Hotel Korsal** (www.hotel-korsal.com).

Several great restaurants—including **Aterina**—are on the square called Trg Korčulanskih Klesara i Kipara. For a scenic setting, browse the eateries along the seawall, from the basic **Pizzeria Tedeschi** to Asian-fusion **Silk** to the splurgy **Filippi.**

ISTRIA

Idyllic Istria, the wedge-shaped peninsula at Croatia's northwest corner, reveals itself to you gradually and seductively: Pungent truffles, Roman ruins, striking hill towns, quaint coastal villages, carefully cultivated food and wine, and breezy Italian culture all compete for your attention. The highlight is the gorgeous seaside town of Rovinj, but with more time (and a car), Istria has much to offer. Everything mentioned here is within a one-hour drive of Rovinj.

▲▲▲Rovinj

Among Croatian coastal towns, Rovinj (roh-VEEN) is particularly romantic (www.tzgrovinj.hr). Its streets are delightfully twisty, its ancient houses are characteristically crumbling, and its harbor—lively with real-life fishermen—is as salty as they come. Like a little Venice on a hill, Rovinj is the atmospheric setting of your Croatian seaside dreams.

Visiting Rovinj: Rovinj's main attraction is simply its gorgeous ▲▲▲ **Old Town**—rising dramatically from the Adriatic as though being pulled up to  heaven by its grand bell tower. Enjoy stunning views from the town parking lot, then walk into town, pausing at the lively open-air market. Once inside the Old Town, you're swallowed up by a creaky and colorful townscape.

Narrow, stepped lanes climb up the hill to the ▲ **Church of St. Euphemia,** where you can learn about the local patron saint and climb rickety stairs up to the top of the bell tower. Rovinj has a few low-impact museums, including the ▲ **House of the Batana Boat,** celebrating a unique local fishing boat and the culture that goes along with it (www.batana.org). Rovinj has some rocky beaches, with sandy ones a short bike or boat ride away.

Sleeping in Rovinj: This town is a delightful home base for exploring Istria. The Old Town holds several appealing private rooms and guesthouses, including **$$$ Villa Markiz** (Milica and Andrej, stylish apartments, www.markizrovinj.com), **$$$ Casa Garzotto** (with rustic rooms and apartments scattered around the Old Town, www.casa-garzotto.com), **$ Hey Rovinj** (fresh, creative, and youthful, at the top of town, booking@heyrovinj.com), and **$$ Villa Cissa** (tasteful apartments rented by engaging Veljko, www.villacissa.com).

Eating in Rovinj: Restaurants line up along Rovinj's "restaurant row" facing the harbor; good options include classy **Scuba,** rustic **Veli Jože,** romantic **Santa Croce,** and—at the end of the strip—the scenic splurge **La Puntuleina.** In the mainland part of town, you'll find good food and good value at **Bookeria** (with a literary theme and Croatian/international dishes, Trg Pignaton) and **Maestral** (affordable seafood and pizzas with views across Rovinj's harbor, Obala V. Nazora).

Rovinj also has delightful nightlife. Istrian wines are excellent, and Rovinj has two handy wine bars where you can learn more: **Bacchus Wine Bar,** just outside the Old Town gate at Carera 5 (Paolo), and **Piassa Granda,** on a charming little square right in the heart of the Old Town (Veli trg 1). For a memorable setting, keep an eye on the water as you stroll "restaurant row" to find **Valentino Cocktail Bar,** where you can nurse an overpriced drink "on the rocks"—literally—as the sun sets and fish come close to investigate the underwater lights.

▲▲Istrian Hill Towns

Istria's interior is dotted with sleepy, picturesque hill towns, speckled with wineries and olive-oil farms, embedded with precious truffles, and grooved by meandering rural roads. Spend a half-day (or more) joyriding from town to town, stopping at some countryside wineries and making time for a truffle feast.

Visiting the Istrian Hill Towns: The most appealing hill town is **Motovun,** overlooking vineyards and truffle-filled oak forests. Hike up its shop-lined main street to the cute little square with a pretty church, a big hotel (the recommended Hotel Kaštel, www.hotel-kastel-motovun.hr), and views over the countryside. Behind the hotel is a sweet little museum of town history.  Motovun is also a foodie destination, with a pair of excellent restaurants for an Istrian meal: the trendy but unpretentious **Mondo Konoba** (just below the Old Town's lower gate), and the more traditional **Konoba pod Voltom** (inside the Old Town's upper gate).

Other fine hill towns include **Grožnjan** (a time warp on a bluff—flatter and easier to drive to than Motovun), **Buje** (more workaday), and **Završje** (almost deserted and very atmospheric).

Most towns have a restaurant specializing in truffle dishes, but Istria's gastronomic epicenter is **Livade,** in the valley below Motovun. This is home to the local Zigante truffle company, with a big shop and upscale restaurant.

Wine lovers enjoy stopping for tastings at countryside wineries, which are scattered across the region. Near Momjan (northwest of Motovun), good choices are the traditional **Kabola** (www.kabola.hr) and the sophisticated **Kozlović** (www.kozlovic.hr).

▲Pula

At Istria's southern tip, Pula is a big, industrial port city. But its urban core holds priceless ancient Roman ruins that rival Split's. Park near the remarkably well-preserved amphitheater, which is worth touring. Then walk into the town center. On the main square (formerly the ancient forum) is a largely-intact ancient temple; a Roman floor mosaic hides behind some nearby shops.

THE CROATIAN INTERIOR

Most travelers to Croatia focus exclusively on the coast. That's a shame, because they miss the country's interior—with two of its best destinations: the capital city and a stunning natural wonder.

▲▲Zagreb

You can't get a complete picture of modern Croatia without a visit here—away from the touristy resorts, in the lively and livable city

that is home to one out of every six Croatians (pop. 790,000). In Zagreb, you'll find historic neighborhoods, a thriving café culture, my favorite urban people-watching in Croatia, an Old World streetscape, and virtually no tourists. The city is also the country's best destination for museum-going, and has Croatia's best foodie scene—both of which are in short supply along the coast.

Visiting Zagreb: Zagreb's main square, **Jelačić Square** (Trg bana Jelačića) is a hive of activity. Shoppers, commuters, and trams zip in and out of the square. The surrounding downtown zone is a delight to explore, with galleries, boutiques, and gourmet coffee shops.

Near Jelačić Square, a short funicular climbs up to Zagreb's old town, called Gradec. Its centerpiece is St. Mark's Square, where governmental buildings (including the parliament and president's residence) face the colorfully tiled roof of the Church of St. Mark.

Two of Croatia's top museums are within a block of St.

Mark's Square. The small but riveting ▲▲▲ **Croatian Museum of Naive Art** displays lovingly detailed works by self-taught peasant artists—dating from the early 20th century, when art-world insiders sought to prove that artistic ability was an inborn talent (www.hmnu. org). And nearby, the innovative ▲▲ **Museum of Broken Relationships** collects true stories of failed couples from around the world, tells their story in their own words, and displays the tale alongside an actual item that embodies the relationship (https:// brokenships.com). The Gradec area also has a fine city history museum and an atelier and collection of works of the great Croatian sculptor, Ivan Meštrović.

The adjacent, formerly walled district of Kaptol is home to Zagreb's ▲▲ **Cathedral**—containing various monuments celebrating the city's tumultuous history and Croatia's proud Catholic heritage.

Between Gradec and Kaptol is Zagreb's colorful (and largely untouristy) indoor-outdoor public **market,** a fun place to browse for a picnic. Nearby is the trendy café street called **Tkalčićeva,** with lots of lively al fresco eateries and the best people-watching in town.

Sleeping in Zagreb: Good, central choices include the cozy-yet-modern **$$$ Jägerhorn Hotel** (www.hotel-jagerhorn. hr) or the big, well-located **$$$$ Hotel Dubrovnik** (www. hotel-dubrovnik.hr). Smaller B&B-type options include **$ Sobe Zagreb 17** (www.sobezagreb17.com) or **$$ 4 City Windows** (www.4citywindows.com).

Eating in Zagreb: It's fun to browse the restaurants along the bustling, traffic-free Tkalčićeva street, including the big, sloppy **Pivnica Mali Medo** (a Czech-style beer hall, at #36) or **La Štruk,** specializing in the local ravioli, *štrukli* (Skalinska 5). In Gradec, **Trilogija** feels upscale but still affordable and unpretentious (Kamenita 5, www.trilogija.com). And for foodie places in the downtown zone around Jelačić Square, check out **Lari & Penati** (Petrinjska 42A), **Bistro Fotić** (Ljudevita Gaja 25, www.

CROATIA

bistrofotic.com), and **Mundoaka** (international street food, Petrinjska 2).

▲▲▲Plitvice Lakes National Park

Plitvice (PLEET-veet-seh) is one of Europe's most spectacular natural wonders. Imagine Niagara Falls diced and sprinkled over a heavily forested Grand Canyon. There's nothing like this lush valley of 16 terraced lakes, separated by natural travertine dams and laced together by waterfalls, boat rides, and miles of pleasant plank walks (www.np-plitvicka-jezera.hr).

Visiting Plitvice: Deep in the countryside about two hours south of Zagreb (roughly on the way to Split), Plitvice is worth a little extra effort to reach. It's easiest for drivers, but many public buses from Zagreb or Split also stop here (bus stop along main road—ask locals or the driver to be clear on where to get off or on, best connections are provided by the summer-only Prijevoz Knežević express bus).

Once at the park, you can see the highlights in just a few hours' walk. It's easy (on well-tended paths and boardwalks), but can get crowded—in busy times, get an early start. (It works well to arrive in the evening, sleep near the park, hit the trails first thing the next morning, then move on to your next destination after lunch.) The lakes are divided into two sections, upper and lower. I prefer to buy my park ticket at Entrance 1 and do the Lower Lakes first. You'll hike steeply down to the trail, then walk gradually uphill—past glorious cascades and pools of strangely colorful water—to the largest lake. From there, an electric boat shuttles you silently across to the Upper Lakes, which is yet another wonderland of boardwalks, waterfalls, and tranquil ponds. From the far end, you can ride a shuttle bus back to your starting point.

Sleeping and Eating at Plitvice: Most visitors stay at the national park lodges, which are functional but comfortable, and come with industrial-strength dining rooms. The best choices are **$$ Hotel Plitvice** and the slightly pricier **$$$ Hotel Jezero** (book either through www.np-plitvicka-jezera.hr). For a more personal experience, drivers should stay at a family-run inn outside the park. My favorite, just a couple of minutes south of Plitvice, is the friendly **$$ Plitvice Mirić Inn** (www.plitvice-croatia.com). Others cluster near the road about 10 minutes' drive north of Plitvice, including the homey, picturesque **$$ Villa**

Plitvička Sedra (www.restoran-sedra.hr) and the big, roadside **$$$$ Hotel Degenija** (www.hotel-degenija.com). Each of these also has its own restaurant—ideal for dinner. For lunch near the trails, a few humble eateries—ranging from basic grocery stores selling sandwiches to sit-down places—cluster near the national park entrances and near the boat dock at the top of the Lower Lakes. But the food at these official national park eateries is nothing special; consider packing a picnic instead.

BOSNIA-HERZEGOVINA

Bosna i Hercegovina

The 1990s weren't kind to Bosnia-Herzegovina: War. Destruction. Genocide. But apart from the tragic way it separated from Yugoslavia, the country has long been—and remains—a remarkable place, with ruggedly beautiful terrain, a unique mix of cultures and faiths, kind and welcoming people who pride themselves on their hospitality, and some of the most captivating sightseeing in southeastern Europe. A visit here offers a fascinating opportunity to sample the cultures of three major faiths within a relatively small area: In the same day, you can inhale incense in a mystical-feeling Serbian Orthodox church, hear the subtle clicking of rosary beads in a Roman Catholic cathedral, and listen to the Muslim call to prayer echo across a skyline of prickly minarets.

Where to Go: The highlights of Bosnia are just a short drive from Croatia's Dalmatian Coast. Many side-trip from Dubrovnik or Split to **Mostar,** which is the country's most accessible and tourist-friendly town. But for a more authentic and complete Bosnian experience, it's worth going a few hours farther to reach **Sarajevo**— the gorgeously set capital, with its fascinating history (both old and recent) and lively contemporary life. Three or four days is enough time to visit both great cities, with quick stops in some other towns and attractions in between, giving you an insightful first look at Bosnia.

Getting Around: Trains are slow and old (www.zfbh.ba); locals prefer to go by bus. Most buses are operated by the Bosniak-run companies (www.autoprevoz-bus.ba and www.centrotrans.

Bosnia-Herzegovina

Serbs
Croats

CROATIA

SERBIA

Bihać • Novi Grad • Banja Luka • Doboj • Brčko • Bijelina

BOSNIA-HERZEGOVINA

Bosna R.

Zvornik •

Zavidovići

Drvar • Jajce • Travnik • Zenica • Srebrenica

Vrbas R.

DINARIC ALPS

Bugojno • Visoko • Sarajevo ⊛

Višegrad •

Ivan Planina ▲

Livno • Jablanica • Konjic • Goražde • Foča

Neretva R.

Drina R.

Široki Brijeg •

Mostar • Blagaj

Međugorje •

Počitelj •

Bileća •

MONTE-NEGRO

Trebinje •

100 Kilometers

100 Miles

Adriatic Sea

Dubrovnik

Podgorica ⊛

com), while other connections are Croat-operated (www.globtour. com)—check the options before you book. Bosnia is also a fine country for driving: The roads are surprisingly good (though there are few freeways), and traffic is light. Given the mountainous terrain, affordable flights can save time; for example, Croatia Airlines often flies from Sarajevo to Zagreb for around $100 (www. croatiaairlines.com).

Bosnian Cuisine: The local food resembles what you may think of as "Greek" or "Turkish" food—with lots of tomatoes, peppers, soft cheeses, and grilled meats. The top street food is *burek*—

a savory phyllo-dough pastry filled with meat, cheese, or spinach. Another Bosnian classic is *ćevapčići* (or *ćevapi*), a mix of minced meat (usually lamb and beef) formed into a sausage-link shape, then grilled. It's served with other grilled meats, chopped raw onions, a soft and spreadable cheese called *kajmak*,

Bosnia Practicalities

Money: Bosnia uses the Convertible Mark (Konvertibilna Marka, abbreviated KM locally, BAM internationally). The official exchange rate is $1 = about 1.60 KM. Euros and Croatian kunas are widely accepted in Mostar, but less so in Sarajevo.

People: The official population is about 3.9 million. A citizen of Bosnia-Herzegovina, regardless of ethnicity, is called a "Bosnian." But the population is divided into three major ethnic groups: Muslims, called "Bosniaks" (about half of the population); Eastern Orthodox Christians, called "Serbs" (about a third); and Roman Catholics, called "Croats" (about 15 percent).

Geography: Bosnia and Herzegovina are two distinct regions that share the same mountainous country. Bosnia constitutes the majority of the country (in the north, with the capital, Sarajevo—pop. 310,000), while Herzegovina is the southern tip (Mostar is its biggest city and de facto capital, with 130,000 people). It's fine to call the entire country "Bosnia" for short. The Dayton Peace Accords that ended the conflict here in 1995 gerrymandered the nation into two major, semi-autonomous zones: the Federation of Bosnia and Herzegovina (shared by Bosniaks and Croats, roughly in the western and central parts of the country) and the Republika Srpska (dominated by Serbs, generally to the north and east). For the most part, each of the three native ethnic groups stay in "their" part of this divided country, but tourists can move freely among them. While the Dayton Accords brought peace, the nation is still politically splintered and economically struggling—the per capita GDP is just over $10,000.

Snapshot History: Bosnia's history was dominated first by the Illyrians, then by the Romans, and eventually by the Slavs. But in the late 15th century, it became part of the Ottoman Empire for 400 years (during which many Bosnians adopted Islam—their descendants remain Muslims today). Bosnia was briefly part of the Austro-Hungarian Empire beginning in 1878, then Yugoslavia after World War I, until it declared independence in the spring of 1992. The bloody three-way war that ensued came to an end in 1995. (For details, see "Understanding Yugoslavia" on page 1075.)

Emergencies: Dial 112.

Consular Services in Sarajevo: The US Embassy is at Ulica Robert C. Frasure 1 (tel. 033/704-000, http://ba.usembassy.gov). The nearest Canadian Embassy is in Budapest, Hungary (see page 1083).

Telephone Country Code: +387, then drop the initial 0 of the phone number.

Tourist Information: www.bhtourism.ba

BOSNIA-HERZEGOVINA

the pita-like *lepinje* bread, and the powerful red pepper and egg-plant spread called *ajvar*. Bosnian desserts are gooey with honey: baklava or the shredded-wheat-style *kadaif*. And Bosnian coffee *(bosanska kafa)*—a hearty unfiltered brew simmered in a copper kettle and served in a little ceramic cup—is as much a slow-down-and-smell-the-tulips social ritual as it is a drink.

Bosnian Language: English is widely spoken, especially in tourist areas. Bosnian is very close to Croatian (in fact, until a generation ago they were considered one language); key phrases include these pleasantries: "Hello" is *Dobar dan* (formal) or *Zdravo* (informal); "please" is *molim;* "thank you" is *hvala;* and "goodbye" is *Do viđenija*. Bosniaks and Croats use basically the same Roman alphabet we do, while Serbs use the Cyrillic alphabet. You'll see both alphabets on currency, official documents, and road signs, but the Roman alphabet predominates in the destinations covered here.

Top Bosnian Destinations

The following sections are designed to get you started planning a trip to Bosnia. For in-depth coverage—including self-guided walks and museum tours, detailed hotel and restaurant listings, and lots of practical advice—pick up my *Rick Steves Croatia & Slovenia* guidebook.

▲▲▲Sarajevo

Though once torn by the wars of the 1990s, the Bosnian capital of Sarajevo—picturesequely situated in a mountain valley blan-keted with cute Monopoly houses—is a comfortable and safe place to visit (www.sarajevo-tourism. com). It's a city of power-ful experiences: Step into historic houses of worship from each of this region's four major faiths—Mus-lim, Catholic, Orthodox

Christian, and Jewish—and notice the similarities. Visit the street corner where World War I began. Climb up into the hills to the Olympic stadium that commanded the world's attention in 1984, or ascend even higher for sweeping views over the capital. Make friends with a gregarious Sarajevan—it's easy to do—and ask him the best way to prepare and drink Bosnian coffee. Ponder the scars of war, hunch over to squeeze through the tunnel that was the be-sieged Sarajevans' one lifeline to the world, and listen to a local relate personal stories from the harrowing time of the siege. Shop your way through the copper-laden canyons of the Turkish-style bazaar, bartering down the price of a hand-hammered Bosnian coffee set. Relax in a hidden caravansary, take a slow drag on a *šiša* (water pipe spewing sweet plumes of fruity smoke), and sample some honey-dripping pastry treats. Go ahead—it's OK to enjoy Sarajevo.

Visiting Sarajevo: Sarajevo is brought to life with the help of a good local guide; **Amir Telibečirović** is excellent and affordable (teleamir@gmail.com).

Begin in the Ottoman-flavored Old Town, called the **Baščaršija**—with cobbles, bazaars, minarets, and hardworking coppersmiths. In this area, ogle Sarajevo's iconic fountain (called Sebilj), do some window-shopping, and consider dropping into the good ▲ **City History Museum,** filling a former covered market. After hours, don't miss the atmospheric courtyard (behind the TI) called Trgovke—filled with gregarious locals, thumping Balkan music, and the sweet smoke of water pipes.

A few blocks to the west begins a totally different-feeling part of town, with Habsburg-style architecture from the late 19th

and early 20th centuries (the short-lived period when Bosnia was part of Austria-Hungary). The main drag, **Ferhadija,** feels worlds—rather than steps—away from the Baščaršija. During this Habsburg era, Sarajevo was the site of one of the most famous and important events in modern history: the assassination of the Habsburg heir, Franz Ferdinand, in 1914. You can see the riverside corner where the archduke and his wife were shot, visit the adjacent museum, or walk five minutes along the river to see the finest piece of architecture from this period, the Neo-Moorish City Hall, which Franz Ferdinand visited on that fateful day.

In this central zone of Sarajevo, various historic houses of worship sit a few steps apart. Stop in at Sarajevo's big, showpiece ▲▲ **Gazi Husrev-Bey Mosque** and associated buildings; the atmospheric ▲ **Old Serbian Orthodox Church,** with a museum of icons; the Neo-Gothic **Catholic Cathedral;** and the city's ▲▲ **Old Synagogue and Bosnian Jewish Museum.** (For more Jewish her-

itage, the sometimes-closed National Museum displays the priceless Jewish prayer book called the Sarajevo Haggadah.)

Sarajevo offers many powerful lessons in the grotesque genocide of the Yugoslav Wars. In the early 1990s, this multiethnic city—surrounded by the snipers of Bosnian Serb leaders Radovan Karadžić and Ratko Mladić—withstood the longest siege in modern military history (more than 1,300 days). Many locals are willing to share their harrowing stories from that time—being relentlessly shelled and shot at, day in and day out, for three and a half years. All around the city, watch for blast craters in the pavement that have been filled with red resin; these memorials, called "Sarajevo roses," have been preserved to commemorate that difficult time.

For sites relating to the siege, visit the still-busy **Markale Market,** the site of a notorious bombing that killed dozens of innocent shoppers. The emotionally wrenching **Memorial to the Children of Sarajevo** pays respects to the more than 1,600 children who were among the estimated 10,000 Sarajevans killed during the siege. A few blocks away, you can freely walk through the  skyscraper zone called Marijin Dvor, which was then known as **"Sniper Alley"**—where gunmen on the hillsides above would rain bullets down on civilians trying to live their lives in peace. Nearby, the ▲ **Historical Museum of Bosnia-Herzegovina** collects everyday items and "Sarajevo inventions" that allowed the Sarajevans to survive the siege. And in the town center, the ▲▲ **Srebrenica Exhibition** collects photography and video testimony about the brutal ethnic cleansing campaign that systematically murdered at least 8,000 residents of a small Bosnian town.

Perhaps the most powerful sight relating to the Siege of Sarajevo is the ▲▲ **Sarajevo War Tunnel Museum.** Here you can actually walk a few steps through the claustrophobic supply tunnel that ran a half-mile underneath the airport runway during the siege. This was the only safe way for besieged Sarajevans to escape to the outside world and bring home supplies to their loved ones (a taxi ride from downtown, www.tunelspasa.ba).

Sleeping in Sarajevo: Friendly, well-run guesthouses in or near the Old Town include **$ Halvat Guest House** (www.halvat. com.ba), **$ Ada Hotel** (www.adahotel.ba), and **$ Hotel Old Town** (www.hoteloldtown.ba). For a higher-end choice, **$$$ Isa Begov Hamam Hotel** fills part of an Ottoman-style bathhouse (www. isabegovhotel.com).

Eating in Sarajevo: There are plenty of options for traditional Bosnian fare in the Old Town. My favorite *burek*s (savory phyllo pastry) are at **Buregdžinica Sač** (just off the main square, in the alley called Bravadžiluk Mali). Good choices for *ćevapčići* are **Mrkva** (Bravadžiluk 15) and **Petica** (Oprkanj 2). For a satisfying sit-down meal, try **Apetit** (tiny and with no printed menu—the server explains your options, Josipa Štadlera 6, www.apetit.ba) or **To Be ~~Or Not~~ To Be** (a classic buried in the Old Town, Čizmedžiluk 5). And for a scenic meal—with sweeping views over Sarajevo's valley—head up into the hills to the pricier (but still affordable) **Kibe Mahala** (Vrbanjuša 164, easiest to reach by taxi, www.kibemahala.ba).

▲▲Mostar

For those side-tripping into Bosnia from the Dalmatian Coast, Mostar is ideal: It's a convenient and very accessible microcosm of traditional Bosnian culture.

Mostar straddles the banks of the gorgeous Neretva River, with tributaries and waterfalls that carve their way through the rocky landscape. The sightseeing—mosques, old Turkish-style houses, and the city's spine-tingling Old Bridge—is engaging. And for those interested in recent history, the locals—who saw their city torn apart by the Yugoslav Wars of the 1990s, and have worked hard to rebuild—are often eager to share their stories. If you're curious about Bosnia and only have a day to spend here, Mostar is the place.

Visiting Mostar: Almost everything of interest is within about a 15-minute walk in the town center. A local guide helps bring both the history and the powerful recent stories to life. I recommend **Alma Elezović** (aelezovic@gmail.com); her husband, Ermin, can be hired to drive you around Bosnia, or even to pick you up in Croatia.

The city's centerpiece and icon is its **Old Bridge,** commissioned in 1557 by the Ottoman Sultan Süleyman the Magnificent. Dramatically arched and flanked by two boxy towers, the bridge is stirring. In 1993, as the various factions of the city fought amongst themselves, Serb artillery on the mountaintop above fired on the Bosniak-held bridge. It was destroyed and fell into the river. In 2004, the bridge was rebuilt and remains a symbol of reconciliation. And today, as they have for generations, local young men hustle for tips from tourists before they swan-dive from the bridge 75 feet down into the icy-cold Neretva below.

The area around the bridge has a few small historical and photo exhibitions about the war, and a cobbled bazaar (called Coppersmiths' Street) where locals sell trinkets to tourists.

While it continues to repair itself, Mostar also has several poignant reminders of the war. You'll still see a few bombed-out husks of buildings, tucked between rebuilt ones. And scattered around Mostar are poignant "new" cemeteries—former parks now filled with turban-shaped headstones, each one marked 1993 or 1994. When the Serb forces laid siege to the Muslims in Mostar's Old Town, bodies had to be buried in small parks in the city center, in the dark of night, for fear of snipers. Today, the city of Mostar remains effectively divided, between the Muslim community (around the Old Bridge, where most tourists go) and the Croat community (the modern sprawl to the west).

For those interested in Islam, Mostar offers the opportunity to visit various mosques. ▲ **Koski Mehmet-Pasha Mosque,** over-

looking the Old Bridge, is the most representative and welcomes tourists. And you can step into a historical ▲ **Ottoman-style house,** to see how Mostarians lived under the rule of the sultans and pashas (the Bišćević House or the Muslibegović House—both just above the river not far from the bridge—are equally good). Across the river is the towering concrete steeple of the **Church of Sts. Peter and Paul**—built after the war by local Croats, seemingly to one-up the minarets all over town.

Sleeping in Mostar: Guesthouses here are a great value. I like the **$$ Muslibegović House** (a historical monument that also welcomes guests into its traditional rooms with modern comforts, www.muslibegovichouse.com), **$ Shangri La Mansion** (on the hill above the Old Bridge, www.shangrila.com.ba), **$ Villa Anri** (modern comfort near the Old Bridge, villa.anri@gmail.com), and **$ Hotel Kriva Ćuprija** (with lots of rooms tucked deep in the river valley near the Old Bridge—plus more in a modern annex, www.motel-mostar.ba).

Eating in Mostar: It seems all Mostar restaurants have the same tourist-oriented menu of Bosnian classics: grilled-meat *ćevapčići*, flaky *burek* pastries, and so on. Most visitors prioritize the view over the food, settling in at one of the places clinging to the lush cliffs overlooking the river, with stunning views of the Old Bridge. For slightly better food (but less exciting views), **Restoran Hindin Han** has somewhat more refined food and a nice setting on a smaller canyon (Jusovina 10), and **Irma-Tima,** on the main drag near the Old Bridge, has great grilled meats (Onešćukova).

▲Sights near Mostar

Drivers exploring the area near Mostar can choose from several tempting stopovers.

Just outside of Mostar, the historical capital of **Blagaj** has an old dervish monastery *(tekija)* that sits at the bottom of a dramatic cliff face, where the Buna River bubbles up from underground.

On the main road between Mostar and the Dalmatian Coast, it's hard to resist stopping at **Počitelj**—dramatically set on chalky mountains, with a ruined castle and a proud mosque and minaret.

Also between Mostar and the coast—on a less-traveled route—is a powerful site of pilgrimage for Catholics: **Međugorje,** where six local teens claimed to have seen miraculous visions of the Virgin Mary in 1981. While there's little to see beyond a modern church, believers (and the curious) find something spiritually powerful here.

MONTENEGRO

Crna Gora

Small and rugged, Montenegro gets overlooked. It's tucked in a rocky and complicated part of the world between Croatia, Serbia, and Albania. And yet, it sits just a temptingly short drive away from the region's top destination, Dubrovnik. Today's Montenegro is a strange mix of big-money international investment (Russian-owned luxury resort hotels, the exclusive Porto Montenegro yacht harbor) and challenging local poverty (which is

evident as you pass through ragtag cities and humble towns). But nothing can mar Montenegro's natural beauty: Devote a day (or more) to making this easy side-trip, and you'll discover a land of stunning mountains, bays, and forests.

Where to Go: Most people see Montenegro as a quick side-trip from Dubrovnik—which, for those on a tight timeframe, is a smart plan. The main highlight is the **Bay of Kotor,** with scenery that only improves on Croatia's Dalmatian Coast; some fine seaside towns (including tiny Perast and atmospheric Kotor); and the chance to ride out to a church-topped island in the middle of the bay, wrapped in 360 degrees of stunning scenery. With more time, beach bums can head for the **Budva Riviera;** celebrity-seekers can daydream about past glories at the striking hotel-peninsula of **Sveti Stefan;** and romantics can corkscrew up into the mountains to sample the Balkans' best smoked ham at **Njeguši** and visit the country's remote original capital at **Cetinje.**

Getting Around: Most visitors simply drive in for the day

Montenegro Practicalities

Money: Though it's not a member of the European Union, Montenegro officially uses the euro as its currency: €1 = about $1.20.

Geography and People: Montenegro (5,415 square miles, slightly smaller than Connecticut) is home to about 650,000 people. Of these, the vast majority are Eastern Orthodox Christians (45 percent Montenegrins, 29 percent Serbs), with minority groups of Muslims (including Bosniaks and Albanians, about 11 percent total) and Catholics (1 percent). The country is characterized by a rocky terrain that rises straight up from the Adriatic and almost immediately becomes a steep mountain range. Montenegro has 182 miles of coastline, about a third of which constitutes the Bay of Kotor. The only real city is the capital, Podgorica (190,000 people). Montenegro is a relatively poor country (per capita GDP is $16,500) that relies heavily on international investment.

Snapshot History: Named "Black Mountain" for the thickly forested hills that sailors saw when approaching this land, Montenegro was first inhabited by the ancient Illyrians (the mysterious distant ancestors of today's Albanians), who were later conquered by the Romans. Slavic migrants established a sovereign state here in the 10th century, and in the 14th century, the area flourished under the powerful Serbian emperor Dušan the Mighty. But soon, with the rising threat of the Ottomans, the Montenegrin coastline became part of the Republic of Venice for about 450 years (15th-19th centuries). In the 20th century, Montenegro joined Yugoslavia (and was often overshadowed by its "big brother," Serbia)—until it declared independence from Serbia, peacefully, in a landmark vote on June 3, 2006.

Emergencies: Dial 112.

Consular Services in Podgorica: The US Embassy is at Žona Džeksona 2 (tel. 020/410-500, me.usembassy.gov); Canadians use the embassy in Belgrade, Serbia (tel. +381-11-306-3000).

Telephone Country Code: +382, then drop the initial 0 of the phone number.

Tourist Information: www.visit-montenegro.com or www.montenegro.travel

from Dubrovnik—using their own rental car, hiring a Dubrovnik-based private driver (listed in the "Dubrovnik" section on page 998), or joining a package tour. Montenegro is also relatively well-served by buses (for connections to and from Kotor, see www.autobuskastanicakotor.me). It's also a popular and easy cruise port—ships put in right across the street from Kotor's Old Town.

Montenegrin Cuisine: Along the Bay of Kotor, the cuisine is

similar to Croatia's—that means seafood, pasta, and pizza. *Njeguški pršut* is the rich, salty, smoky prosciutto from the village of Njeguši (described later) that goes well with the local cow's cheese—smoked, of course. Montenegro also produces some surprisingly good wines (Plantaže Podgorica is the biggest company): A good red is the dry, medium-bodied *vranac* (related to zinfandel), and for white, you'll see the dry, fruity *krstač* (similar to Riesling).

Montenegrin Language: Montenegrin is closely related to both Croatian and Bosnian. "Hello" is *Dobar dan* (formal) or *Zdravo* (informal); "please" is *molim;* "thank you" is *hvala;* and "Goodbye" is *Do viđenija.* You'll see both "our" Roman alphabet and the Cyrillic alphabet used, more or less equally; for a crash course in Cyrillic, see page 1027.

Top Montenegrin Destinations

The following sections are designed to get you started planning a trip to Montenegro. For in-depth coverage—including a self-guided driving tour, detailed hotel and restaurant listings, and lots of practical advice—pick up my *Rick Steves Croatia & Slovenia* guidebook.

▲▲Bay of Kotor Driving Loop

For a look at the untamed Adriatic, take a spin on the winding road around Montenegro's steep and secluded Bay of Kotor. The area's main town, also called Kotor, has been protected from centuries of would-be invaders by its position at the deepest point of the fjord—and by its imposing town wall, which scrambles in a zigzag line up the mountain behind it. Wander the enjoyably seedy streets of Kotor, drop into some Orthodox churches, and sip a coffee at an al fresco café.

Visiting the Bay of Kotor: Most people do a loop around the Bay of Kotor in one day from Dubrovnik. Here's the basic plan:

From Dubrovnik, head south on the main coastal road (signs to *Ćilipi*), past Cavtat and the airport; in about 40 minutes, you'll reach the **border** at Debeli Brijeg (where you'll need to show your passport and your rental car's proof-of-insurance "green card"). To avoid lines at the border, get an early start—on busy summer weekends, consider leaving Dubrovnik by 7:30 to beat the tour buses. (There's also a less crowded alternate border crossing called Konfin—ask locals for directions.)

Once across the border, you'll head through the big, dreary city of **Herceg Novi,** then curve around the headland at the **Verige Strait**—the quarter-mile-wide entrance to the huge, fjord-like bay (underlining Kotor's strategic importance). From here, you'll curl along the bay's waters—through crescendoing scenery and tiny towns—until you reach the village of ▲ **Perast.** Park, stretch your legs, and explore this tiny, well-preserved town (with a big waterfront main square and a half-built cathedral).

From Perast, pay a few euros per person to be shuttled out across the bay for a closer look at a pair of islands: **St. George** (Sv. Đorđe) and ▲▲ **Our Lady of the Rocks** (Gospa od Škrpjela). It's said that two local fishermen saw a light emanating from a reef deep below the surface near the isle of St. George. Discovering an icon of Mary, they were inspired to build a second island

on that holy spot. So, for two centuries, locals dropped rocks and even sank old ships there—eventually creating the island of Our Lady of the Rocks. You can stroll the island and dip into the church, filled with votives honoring the miraculous icon that was found here.

Back in Perast, get back on the road and carry on around the bay about another 30 minutes until you reach the town of **Kotor;** with more time, you can continue farther to the **Budva Riviera,** or head up into the mountains and **Cetinje** (all described later).

To return to Dubrovnik, just head back the way you came. Or, for a shortcut (and to see different scenery), you can continue around the bay past Kotor, then continue all the way around to Lepetani, where a frequent and easy ferry *(trajekt)* travels a few minutes across the bay to Kamenari—near Herceg Novi and a short drive from the Croatian border.

▲▲Kotor

Butted up against a steep cliff, cradled by a calm sea, naturally sheltered by its deep-in-the-fjord position, and watched over by an imposing network of fortifications, the town of Kotor is as impressive as it is well protected. Though it has enjoyed a long and illustrious history, today's Kotor is a time-capsule retreat for travelers seeking an unspoiled Adriatic town (www.tokotor. me). For a good local guide, contact **Stefan Đukanović** (www. miroandsons.com, djukan@t-com.me).

Visiting Kotor: You can see the entire compact Old Town in a short stroll. Pass through the Main Town Gate (with a TI kiosk) and into the **Square of Arms,** fronted by a grand old palace and the town's bell tower. From here, get lost in the twisty lanes.

Make your way to the ▲ **Cathedral of St. Tryphon,** with its mismatched towers, fine interior, and quirky treasury collection (featuring an icon that, like Montenegro itself, seems to merge Eastern and Western Christian traditions). Just off the cathe-

dral square, you can dip into the **Maritime Museum of Montenegro,** with modest exhibits on the bay's history and seafaring traditions (www. museummaritimum.com).

A few lanes over, ▲ **St. Luke's Square** has

two Eastern Orthodox Churches—one big, one little. Either offers a fascinating look at the Eastern Orthodox faith (see page 1034).

Kotor's main attraction—for those who are fit enough to tackle it—is climbing the ▲▲ **city walls** that climb up the sheer cliff face behind town in a dizzying zigzag line. (If there's a more elaborate city wall in Europe, I haven't seen it.) This involves climbing 1,355 steps (an elevation gain of more than 700 feet)—don't overestimate your endurance or underestimate the heat. Find the ticket desk and trailhead at the back-left corner of the Old Town (near St. Mary's Church, through the

alley with the two arches over it). Then get climbing, following a clockwise route that ascends to the Church of Our Lady of Health (the halfway mark), then all the way up to the Fortress of St. John. Allow at least an hour and a half round-trip, wear good shoes (uneven and rocky footing), and bring plenty of water and sun protection.

Sleeping in Kotor: I'd rather bunk in Dubrovnik—Kotor is pricey and can be noisy after dark. But if you need a bed, consider the stony-chic **$$$ Hotel Villa Duomo** (www.villaduomo.com), the businesslike and super-central **$$$ Hotel Vardar** (www.hotelvardar.com), or the affordable **$ D&Sons Apartments** (www.dandsons.com).

Eating in Kotor: City Restaurant has solid, basic food and outdoor tables next to the cathedral. **Cesarica** offers unpretentious seafood in a casual, stony interior buried deep in the Old Town (Stari Grad 375). And for a wine tasting or to browse bottles to take home, drop by **The Old Winery** (Stara Vinarija, at Stari Grad 483).

Budva Riviera

A 15-mile stretch of coarse-sand and fine-pebble beaches run along the coastline about 30 minutes south of Kotor. This "Budva Riviera" is unappealingly built up with a mix of cheap and luxury resort hotels. But the seafront is inviting, and the main town, **Budva,** has a charming Old Town crammed with souvenir shops and holiday-making Serbs and Russians. Two churches (Catholic and Orthodox) face each other near the town's imposing (but empty) citadel.

The main draw along the Budva Riviera is the famous hotel island of ▲ **Sveti Stefan**—which hovers like a mirage just off-

shore, about a 20-min-
ute drive south of Budva.
Once an actual, living
town (connected to the
mainland only by a nar-
row, natural causeway),
Sveti Stefan was convert-
ed into a luxury hotel in
the 1950s. Its promise of

privacy attracted celebrities, rock stars, royalty, and dignitaries—
from Sophia Loren to Kirk Douglas to Sly Stallone. More recently, it was again renovated into a super-exclusive, €1,000-plus-
a-night Aman Resort (www.aman.com). Only paying guests
(no exceptions) can actually enter the island, but anyone is free
to gaze over it from the road above, or to rent a pricey chair on
the beaches that flank its causeway (there are a few free beach
areas—ask the guard for pointers).

Montenegrin Interior

While the coastline gets all the buzz, the true heart of Montenegro beats behind the sheer wall of mountains rising up from
that seafront. From near Kotor, an almost comically twisty road
spirals up, up, up to the village of **Njeguši**—famous among
Montenegrins for two reasons: as the hometown of the House
of Petrović-Njegoš, the dynasty that ruled Montenegro for much
of its history (1696-1918); and as the birthplace of Montenegrins'
favorite food, the smoke-
cured ham called *Njeguški
pršut* (sold by various restaurants in town).

    From here, the road
winds across a startling-
ly desolate landscape
to **Cetinje**—the now-
humble historic capital
of Montenegro. Stuck
in an economic rut, Cetinje tickles romantic historians but has
few tangible sights. On its main square is a collection of small
museums, and nearby—marking the birthplace of the town—is
the local monastery, dedicated to a charismatic local priest who
famously carried a cross in one hand and a sword in the other, established the first set of laws among Montenegrins, and inspired
his people to defend Christian Montenegro against the Muslim
Ottomans.
    Even higher up from Cetinje, a winding road heads up to

the mountaintop monument called **Lovćen,** which is capped by an elaborate mausoleum—designed by the great 20th-century Croatian sculptor Ivan Meštrović, and devoted to King Petar II Petrović-Njegoš. From here, you can ogle the grandiose statues of a long-forgotten dynasty and, in the turn of a head, see a significant percentage of Montenegro.

BULGARIA

България / Bălgariya

Endearing, surprising Bulgaria is a rewarding and all-too-often-overlooked destination. With a prime location at the intersection of civilizations—going all the way back to antiquity—it has an unusually rich cultural heritage.

Despite (or perhaps because of) the country's tumultuous history, the Bulgarian people are sweet and soulful—eager to share their homeland's many underappreciated gems. Travelers who venture here enjoy thriving cities, remarkable ancient sites, a flavorful cuisine, a ruggedly beautiful landscape, and powerful memories. If more travelers realized how impressive (and how affordable) Bulgaria is, it'd be jammed. But they don't...so it isn't. You'll feel like you're in on Eastern Europe's best-kept secret.

Where to Go: I've arranged this chapter's destinations in a counterclockwise loop that focuses on the highlights. On a short visit, the culturally rich "second city" of **Plovdiv** is the single most rewarding choice. With more time, the church-and-museum-packed modern capital of **Sofia** and the historic capital of **Veliko Tarnovo**—with its dramatic setting and chatty craftspeople—each deserve a day. With even more time, make a pilgrimage to the stunningly set **Rila Monastery** (worth the effort) and linger a bit at the **Thracian Plain** (ancient tombs) and **Shipka Pass** (modern monuments)—both between Plovdiv and Veliko Tarnovo. And if you have time to spare and want to hit the beach, consider adding the **Black Sea Coast.**

Getting Around: Trains (www.bdz.bg/en) and **buses** (www.

bgrazpisanie.com) connect the country well—if slowly—and make sense for those linking up the cities. But if you want to explore the countryside, **driving** is (outside of congested Sofia) relatively easy in Bulgaria. Major roads are in good repair (though back roads can be somewhat deteriorated), traffic is fairly light, and drivers are generally courteous. To use expressways, you'll need a toll sticker (most cars rented here come with one).

Bulgarian Cuisine: Bulgaria boasts one of the tastiest and most interesting cuisines of Eastern Europe. Similar to Greek or Turkish food, Bulgarian cooking includes plenty of red peppers and tomatoes, hearty grilled meats, crumbly cheeses, and lots and lots of herbs and spices. (The pungent, powdered savory spice mix called *chubritsa*—used in just about everything—is a great culinary souvenir. The bright-red, tomatoes-peppers-and-egg-

plant condiment *lyutenitsa* also packs a punch.) When in Bulgaria, I begin each meal with a *shopska* salad: chopped tomatoes, cucumbers, onions, parsley, and sometimes red peppers, all with a generous topping of feta-like cheese called *sirene*. Yogurt *(kiselo mlyako)* is big in Bulgaria. One of the tastiest ways to try it is in the refreshing cucumber-and-yogurt cold soup *tarator*—sprinkled with nuts, dill, and olive oil. For the main dish, you'll see lots of grilled meats; staples include *kyufte* (meatballs) and *kebapche* (kebabs). Another beloved dish is *sarmia*—stuffed grape or cabbage leaves. And the

Bulgaria Practicalities

Money: The currency is the Bulgarian lev/лев (plural leva/лева), which is divided into 100 stotinki/стотинки. $1 = about 1.75 leva.

Geography and People: Bulgaria is 43,000 square miles, roughly the size of Tennessee, with just over 7 million people. About 85 percent are ethnic Bulgarians, with large minorities of Muslims (9 percent, mostly of Turkish ancestry) and Roma (an estimated 5 percent). It's fairly mountainous and bounded by the Danube to the north and the Black Sea to the east, but most of the population lives in cities in its central plain (including the capital, Sofia, pop. 1.2 million; Plovdiv, pop. 340,000; and Varna, pop. 335,000). Bulgaria is one of the European Union's poorest countries, with a per capita GDP of $21,700.

Snapshot History: At the intersection of the Greek, Turkish, and Slavic worlds, Bulgaria has more than its share of history. The Thracians had a rich and robust culture here during antiquity. After the fall of Rome, the Slavs (sixth century) and the Bulgars (seventh century) created the First Bulgarian Kingdom (9th-10th centuries)—which reached its peak during the reign of Simeon the Great (r. 893-927). After a period of decline, the Asen dynasty oversaw a medieval Golden Age (12th-14th centuries), when the Second Bulgarian Kingdom stretched from the Black Sea to the Adriatic. But then the Ottomans invaded, absorbing Bulgaria into their empire for 482 years. In 1877-1878, a Bulgarian-Russian army secured independence, giving rise to modern Bulgaria...and a series of devastating Balkan Wars with neighbors, which led directly into defeat in World War I. Since then, Bulgaria has taken a more peaceful tack, becoming part of the Soviet Bloc from 1945 to 1989, and now a fully modern, capitalistic, and democratic member of the European Union.

Famous Bulgarians: Spartacus (leader of a slave revolt) was born in ancient Thrace, and Cyril and Methodius—the missionary brothers who invented the Cyrillic alphabet and introduced Christianity to the Slavs in the ninth century—were born in Thessaloniki (then part of Bulgaria). In modern times, famous Bulgarians include opera singer Boris Christoff, "monument-wrapping" artist Christo, and actress Nina Dobrev.

Emergencies: Dial 112. You can also dial 150 for an ambulance, 160 for fire, or 166 for police.

Consular Services in Sofia: The US Embassy is at ulitsa Kozyak 16 (tel. 02-937-5100, http://bg.usembassy.gov). Canadians use the embassy in Bucharest, Romania (see page 1085).

Telephone Country Code: +359, then drop the initial 0 of the phone number.

Tourist Information: www.bulgariatravel.org

main Bulgarian street food is *banitsa*—a savory, cheesy phyllo-dough pastry (like a *burek* or a Greek *kopeta*) that's also popular at breakfast. And for dessert, Bulgarian sweets resemble Turkish ones: phyllo- and honey-based (baklava, *kadaif*) and halva (with sesame or sunflower-seed tahini). Bulgaria produces some decent wines that are worth trying...but not writing home about.

Bulgarian Language: Bulgarian is a Slavic language, closely related to Russian, Croatian, Bosnian, and Serbian. Bulgaria officially uses the Cyrillic alphabet—intimidating at first, but easy to sound out, once you've done a little studying (see sidebar). Many Bulgarians—particularly those in the tourist trade—speak some English. In this chapter, I've listed both the Cyrillic and "our" Roman spellings for key place names. Some key phrases: "Hello" is *Zdravejte*/Здравейте (formal) or just *Zdravei*/Здравей (informal); "Please" is *Molya te*/Моля те; "Thank you" is *Blagodarya*/Благодаря; and "Goodbye" is *Dovizhdane*/Довиждане.

Local Guide: In Bulgaria, hiring your own guide is a great investment. Stefan Bozadzhiev and the gang at **Lyuba Tours** offer everything from architectural walks of Sofia to fully guided, in-depth private tours around Bulgaria (www.lyubatours.com). Thanks to Stefan and Lyuba Tours for their help with the information in this chapter.

Top Bulgarian Destinations

The following sections are designed to get you started planning a trip to Bulgaria.

▲▲Sofia (София)

Bulgaria's capital, Sofia (locals say SOH-fee-yuh, not soh-FEE-ya) is delightfully livable. Its 1.2 million inhabitants enjoy an airy street plan, fine architecture, lush parks, snow-capped mountains on the horizon, and a relaxed pace of life (www.visitsofia.bg).

Visiting Sofia: Most of the sights mentioned here are in the easily walkable town center; a slick two-line Metro system and extensive tram network make longer jumps easy.

Sofia's ▲▲▲ **Alexander Nevsky Cathedral** is one of the largest Orthodox churches in Christendom—and the only national church I can think of that's named for an important saint of a different country: Russia. (The Bulgarians feel a Slavic kinship with Russia, who helped liberate them from nearly five centuries of Ottoman rule. The church is

Learning the Cyrillic Alphabet

If you're going to Bulgaria—even if just on a short visit—you'll have a much richer, smoother experience if you take the time to learn the Cyrillic alphabet. Once you know the basics, you can (slowly) sound out signs, and some of those very long, confusing words will become familiar.

The table shows the Cyrillic alphabet (both capital and lowercase), and in the second column, the Roman equivalent. Notice that the letters fall—very roughly—into four categories: Some letters are basically the same sound as in English, such as A, E, K, M, O, and T. Others are easy if you know the Greek alphabet: Г—gamma (g), Д—delta (d), П—pi (p), and Ф—phi (f). Some are unique to Cyrillic; most of these are "fricative" sounds, like ts, sh, ch, sht, or kh (Ж, З, Ц, Ч, Ш, Щ, Х). And the fourth category seem designed to trip you up: "false friends" that have a different sound than the Roman letter they resemble, such as В, С, Н, Р, Х, and У. It can be helpful to remember that the "backward" Roman consonants are actually vowels (И, Й, Я).

Cyrillic	Roman	Cyrillic	Roman
Аа	a	Пп	p
Бб	b	Рр	r
Вв	v	Сс	s
Гг	g	Тт	t
Дд	d	Уу	u
Ее	e	Фф	f
Жж	zh	Хх	kh
Зз	z	Цц	ts
Ии	i	Чч	ch
Йй	y	Шш	sh
Кк	k	Щщ	sht
Лл	l	Ъъ	uh
Мм	m	ьь	y
Нн	n	Юю	yu
Оо	o	Яя	ya

dedicated to Russian soldiers lost in that fight.) Built at about the same time as the Eiffel Tower, it's newer than it looks—with a steel frame clad in limestone veneer, and invisible buttresses that hold up its cascading gold and copper domes. The church is a pan-national creation: designed by Russian architects and decorated with Venetian mosaics, Slovenian oak doors, and Bohemian crystal chandeliers.

Inside, you're immersed in a rich aroma of incense and beeswax candle smoke. Shoulder-level candelabras represent prayers for the living; knee-level ones are for the deceased (buy candles in the entryway). Every available surface is slathered with gold-mosaic icons—depicting 247 saints and 25 scenes from the life of Jesus. In front of the marble iconostasis are two marble thrones: One for the czar, and the other for the patriarch (head of the Bulgarian Orthodox Church). Per tradition, the czar's throne is bigger—demonstrating the Orthodox belief that a divinely ordained monarch has supremacy over the head of the church (the opposite of Catholic tradition). And yet, the czar's throne faces the pulpit, where an eagle (symbol of the Church) hovers in judgment over a lion (symbol of the czar)—a none-too-subtle reminder that the final reckoning comes later. On the smaller iconostasis to the left of the main altar, a cheeky Czech artist infused his saints with personality rare in Orthodox church art. Mary looks like a real mom, tenderly kissing the arm of her Baby Jesus—who's not a serene cherub, but a fidgety toddler.

Across the street is Sofia's most historic church, and its namesake: the ▲ **Church of Sveta Sofia** ("Holy Wisdom"), with an austere brick basilica floor plan. The core of the church was built by the Byzantine Emperor Justinian in the sixth century. Underfoot sprawl lovingly excavated mosaic floors (now a museum). Outside, the **Tomb of the Unknown Soldier** is guarded by a stone lion—the national symbol—who looks not proud or fierce, but sad...suggesting the Bulgarians' generally pacifistic attitude after a grueling 20th century.

From this area, enjoy the parks, squares, and streets of Sofia's mellow downtown. Sofia even has an actual **yellow brick road.** When Austria's Emperor Franz Josef visited Sofia in 1907, he had to trudge through muddy streets. When he was invited back, he donated these bricks—made from a vivid-yellow limestone—to pave Sofia's streets.

A few blocks to the west (just follow the yellow brick road), you'll run into **Independence Square** (Ploshtad Nezavisimost)—ringed by an ensemble of severe communist-style governmental buildings called the Largo. The former Communist Party House—with its bold spire—faces a 65-foot-tall pillar that was once occupied by Vladimir Lenin. Today that pillar is topped by a statue of **Sveta Sofia** (Holy Wisdom). Near the

pillar, head down into the Metro underpass to see Roman ruins dating back two millennia. Archaeologists are constantly finding, excavating, and displaying fragments of the Roman town of

"Serdica"—a reminder that an ancient world sprawls beneath the feet of modern commuters.

Just to the right of the former communist HQ is a little square fronted by the president's residence (featuring an extremely modest changing of the guard out front) and—housed in a huge former mosque—the ▲ **National Archaeological Museum,** with an exquisite collection of golden jewelry from ancient Thrace (www.naim.bg).

One block north of the Sveta Sofia monument is the **central market hall,** a great place to pick up a snack or some picnic fix-

ings. Tucked just behind the market is Europe's third-largest **synagogue,** designed by an Austrian architect in the early 20th century (www.sofiasynagogue.com). Bulgaria was one of the only countries in Nazi territory that refused to turn its Jewish population over to Hitler. All 49,000 Bulgarian Jews survived the Holocaust.

Across the busy street from the market is the elegant, early-20th-century **Central Mineral Baths** complex, now renovated and gleaming (and home to the city history museum). Sofia prides itself on its natural springs, which attracted the first settlers here in ancient times. Poke through the park on the left (near the tram stop) to find a bunch of perpetually-flowing public taps, where locals fill up big jugs of warm, mineral-tasting, supposedly very healthy spring water.

From this area, the pedestrianized, shop-and-restaurant-lined **Vitosha Boulevard** runs to the south. This lively people

zone is where the people of Sofia promenade, nurse a coffee, and catch up with their friends. It leads to the communist-era **National Palace of Culture** and a surrounding park—with Sofians enjoying their city while ignoring the boldly socialist-style architecture. At the northern end of the park, notice the partly dismantled monument. All over Bulgaria, controversy swirls around rusting communist monuments like this one—how long should they stand before being torn down?

Those interested in the communist period can track down

some other intriguing artifacts. Just to the northeast, in Knyazhes-ka Park, stands the **Monument of the Soviet Army,** honoring the Soviets who helped liberate Bulgaria in World War II. One panel on the side of the main plinth is regularly (and creatively) defaced with pointed political graffiti.

To see more statues that once intimidated the cityscape, head about three miles southeast of the center to the ▲ **Museum of Socialist Art.** You'll see—preaching their message to each other in an empty field—the Lenin that once topped the pillar in the center of town; Georgi Dimitrov, the "Bulgarian Lenin"; the red star that capped the Communist Party HQ; and several stoic soldiers and workers.

Two more important sights are in the Boyana district, in the foothills of the Mount Vitosha, about five miles southwest of the center. The humble brick ▲▲ **Boyana Church** contains a treasure trove of stunning 13th-century frescoes, combining a strong Orthodox faith with very early-Renaissance Western European styles (think Giotto). The Boyana frescoes are unique in their early use of basic perspective, fluid motion, natural rather than stiff poses, subjects with real human emotions and personalities, and the skillful use of bold colors to suggest three dimensions—you can practically see bodies moving around under the subjects' clothes (www.boyanachurch.org). Nearby, housed in a particularly boxy old communist-era palace, is the ▲ **National Historical Museum,** with a fine collection of fragments from the full span of Bulgarian history (www.historymuseum.org).

Sleeping in Sofia: Two good options in the walkable town center are the professional, upscale **$$$ Crystal Palace Boutique Hotel** (www.crystalpalace-sofia.com), and the simpler **$$ Arte Hotel** (www.artehotelbg.com).

Eating in Sofia: It's easy to simply stroll Vitosha Boulevard, which is lined with tempting options. Along here I've eaten well at **Shtastliveca** (Щастливеца, long menu of traditional Bulgarian dishes in a kitschy mod-traditional setting, at #27, www.shtastliveca.com). A pocket of fun, trendier eateries is just west of Vistosha near Karnigradska and Solunska streets. And for a youthful, fast-changing foodie scene, explore the streets just east of the City Garden (behind the National Theatre). In this area, **Raketa Rakia Bar** is a trendy, communist-kitsch-themed nightspot with Bulgarian cuisine and more than 100 types of *rakia* (Balkan fire-water; at Yanko Sakazov 17). Nearby, the **Club of the Architects** is the spot for a genteel dinner of international fare in a big yellow mansion, or (better yet) in its serene garden (Krakra 11).

BULGARIA

▲▲▲Rila Monastery (Rilski Manastir/Рилски Манастир)

Bulgaria's spiritual heart and soul reside about 80 miles south of the capital, deep in the Rila (REE-lah) Mountains. Here you'll

find Rila Monastery—a fortress on the outside, spiritual sanctuary inside. The monastery was founded in the 930s by Bulgaria's patron saint, St. John of Rila (or Ivan Rilski, as Bulgarians call him), who came here seeking a hermetic way of life. During the Dark Ages, monks at Rila kept the faint embers of

Bulgarian Orthodox thought glowing. Later, during a period of Ottoman occupation—when conversion to Islam was strongly encouraged—remote monasteries like Rila became lifeboats for the Bulgarian faith, language, literature, and cultural artifacts. Today, Rila is a place of pilgrimage for Bulgarians, who consider it their faith's single most important site. And tourists are amazed by its pristine setting (tucked between mountains and forests), the reverent spirituality that fills its stony courtyard, and the vivid art that decorates its church.

Visiting Rila Monastery: The monastery is best for drivers, who can reach it in about two hours from Sofia (mostly on the slick A-3 expressway). It's also possible to reach by public bus, or—better—on a dedicated shuttle bus (also stops at Boyana Church—described earlier, reserve ahead, www.rilamonasterybus.com).

Stepping from the parking lot through the hulking outer wall, you emerge into a serene courtyard facing a red-and-white-striped church and a mountain backdrop. The stout **Hrelyo Tower** is the oldest part of the complex, from the 1330s; this was the place of last refuge in case of attack.

The complex's centerpiece church was built in the 1830s, after a fire. The walls and ceilings of its **porch** are slathered with sumptuous, colorful frescoes—all crammed with details and symbolism. You'll see biblical stories, angels, devils, saints, and sinners. One elaborate scene shows the 40 days of trials your soul goes through after death, as a guardian angel accompanies the soul—

represented by a small child—through a gauntlet of temptations.

The **church interior** is gloomy and atmospheric—air heavy

with candle soot and incense. Next to each important icon hangs a small towel, used to wipe off smeared lipstick from reverent kisses. The right transept holds the heart of Czar Boris III, who capably led his country through World War II. Boris preserved Bulgarian sovereignty by politically allying with Nazi Germany. And yet, the czar defied orders to send Bulgaria's Jewish population to concentration camps, and refused to formally declare war on Bulgaria's biggest historic ally, the Soviet Union. Because Hitler needed access to Bulgaria's Black Sea ports—and lacked the resources to invade—he put up with it...until the summer of 1943, when Boris died mysteriously after a private audience with Hitler in Berlin. Many suspect a slow-acting poison, and Boris remains revered by the Bulgarian people.

Behind the church, find the **museum** holding treasures that devoted Bulgarians have donated or created to honor their most hallowed site. The highlight is the Rafail Cross, with 23 panels (each smaller than a deck of cards) depicting 36 Bible scenes populated by 650 toothpick-sized figures, all on a cross about the size of a hubcap. The monk who carved it over the course of 12 years literally went blind in the process—yet another remarkable act of devotion in this place that specializes in it.

Sleeping and Eating at Rila Monastery: While Rila is an active monastery (with resident monks), some of the **$ cells** have been converted into rustic accommodations for pilgrims and tourists (www.rilamonastery.pmg-blg.com). Just outside the north entrance to the monastery (opposite the parking lot) is a popular window selling fresh doughnuts, and a good sit-down restaurant. Additional hotels and restaurants line the road between the monastery and the expressway.

▲▲▲Plovdiv (Пловдив)

If you visit only one city in Bulgaria, make it Plovdiv (PLOHV-div). The country's "second city" (with about 340,000 people), Plovdiv has it all: excellent sightseeing, a charming Old Town, and a bustling New Town (www.visitplovdiv.com). It's fascinating to explore and easy to enjoy. And people have enjoyed it for a very long time: Plovdiv claims to be one of the oldest continually inhabited cities in the world. The ancient Greeks dubbed it Philippopolis (for the father of Alexander the Great), and the Romans called it Trimontium (for the "three hills" it was built upon). Today you'll see a ruined acropolis, a well-preserved ancient theater, gorgeous 19th-century homes filled with the art of local painters, Bulgaria's most thriving pedestrian boulevard, and a hipster zone with creative restaurants and even more creative graffiti.

Visiting Plovdiv: Plovdiv has two parallel worlds, just steps apart and equally worth exploring: The Old Town (draped over a hill) and the New Town (filling the flat valley below). The city is compact—you can easily see everything on foot.

The **Old Town** blankets the slopes of some of the many hills that make up Plovdiv. Its rustic streets—with ankle-wrecking river-stone cobbles—are lined with dozens of homes in the eye-pleasing **Bulgarian National Revival style.** In the mid-19th century, when the ruling Ottoman Empire was in decline, the Bulgarians sought to celebrate their  culture with this unique style: wooden-beam construction with upper floors that bulge outward, tastefully painted in vivid colors.

Today, many of these buildings house museums, including the ▲ **Hindliyan House**—dating from 1840 and decorated to the taste of its merchant owner. It still feels lived-in, with opulent sitting rooms, a starburst-painted ceiling, a Turkish-style *hamam*, a rose water fountain, and "souvenir" wall paintings showing off some of the merchant's far-flung business travels, from Stockholm to Venice.

Another house contains an art gallery celebrating a little-known but supremely talented Bulgarian painter. ▲▲▲ **Zlatyu**  **Boyadzhiev** (1903-1976) was already a well-established artist when his health took a terrible turn. In 1951, he suffered a stroke that rendered his right hand useless. Boldly embarking on a second act, Boyadzhiev's left hand began painting scenes that looked nothing like the ones his right hand had produced. Over the next 25 years, he reveled in bright colors with a childlike exuberance, slapping thick, Van Gogh-like brushstrokes onto the canvas. Boyadzhiev's best works feature timeless slices of peasant life: People praying not in temples, but under trees. Locals sitting around a public fountain sipping glasses of wine. Peasant women clustered around a fire, knitting as they eke out warmth. A fattened pig being slaughtered for Christmas; above the victim, each weathered face could tell a story.

Boyadzhiev also had a subversive streak. In *Public Prayer*, scrawny villagers come together to pray for good fortune; everyone is skinny...except the fat priest. In *The Orphanage*, a motley collection of disabled beggars (and their disabled pets) huddle behind

Eastern Orthodox Church

Bulgaria is one of many Eastern European countries that is predominantly Eastern Orthodox Christian. (Others include entire nations—Russia, Serbia, and Greece—or a significant percentage of the population, as in Bosnia, Montenegro, and Slovenia.)

As you explore an Orthodox church, keep in mind that these churches carry on the earliest traditions of the Christian faith. Orthodox and Catholic Christianity came from the same roots, so the oldest surviving early-Christian churches (such as the stave churches of Norway) have many of the same features as today's Orthodox churches.

Notice that there are no pews. Worshippers stand through the service, as a sign of respect (though some older parishioners sit on the seats along the walls). Women stand on the left side, men on the right (equal distance from the altar—to represent that all are equal before God). The Orthodox Church uses essentially the same Bible as Catholics, but it's written in the Cyrillic alphabet, which you'll see displayed around any Orthodox church. Following Old Testament Judeo-Christian tradition, the Bible is kept on the altar behind the iconostasis, the big screen in the middle of the room covered with curtains and icons (golden paintings of saints), which separates the material world from the spiritual one. At certain times during the service, the curtains or doors are opened so the congregation can see the Holy Book.

Unlike the decorations in many Catholic churches, Orthodox icons are not intended to be lifelike. Packed with intricate symbolism, and cast against a shimmering golden background, they're meant to remind viewers of the metaphysical nature of Jesus and the saints rather than of their physical form, which is considered irrelevant. You'll almost never see a statue, which is thought to overemphasize the physical world...and, to Orthodox people, feels a little too close to violating the commandment, "Thou shalt not worship graven images." Orthodox services generally involve chanting (a dialogue that goes back and forth between the priest and the congregation), and the church is filled with the evocative aroma of incense.

The incense, chanting, icons, and standing up are all intended to heighten the experience of worship. While many Catholic and Protestant services tend to be more of a theoretical and rote consideration of religious issues (come on—don't tell me you've never dozed through the sermon), Orthodox services are about creating a religious experience. Each of these elements does its part to help the worshipper transcend the physical world and join in communion with the spiritual one.

their larger-than-life chieftain. Boyadzhiev was also captivated by the Karakachani, a nomadic tribe that herded their wooly sheep throughout the Balkans until the communists ended their way of life in the 1950s. Boyadzhiev worked under the communist regime, but managed to buck the predominant Socialist Realism style. Because he glorified peasant life without threatening any of the communists' sacred cows, Boyadzhiev was allowed to carry on. This makes Boyadzhiev the rare artist who thrived under communism... and also had real talent.

The Old Town hillside also has some ancient sites. Up at the very top of town, the scant remains of the **acropolis** offer grand views over the modern skyline. And partway down the hill is a remark-ably intact ▲▲ **ancient theater.** This 5,000-seat theater—built by Emperor Trajan—wasn't discovered until the 1960s. Now excavated, the theater's wall  is mostly intact, the stony seats are still etched with their original numbers, and the acoustics remain perfect. Plays are performed here regularly.

Just below the theater, an underpass below the busy main thoroughfare leads to the **New Town.** The twisty streets straight  ahead constitute the district called **Kapana** ("The Mouse-trap"). Not long ago, this was a dreary, deserted, and dangerous quarter. But a recent initiative to pedestrianize and cobble the streets has turned the area into a hipster paradise. The streets are lined with bars, cafés, and creative galleries (look for PLO-VEdiv, with prints that put a whimsical pop-culture spin on old communist icons). This zone also has more than its share of creative, government-subsidized graffiti. Local authorities figure that street artists will tag buildings anyway—so they might as well focus all that creativity, and pay them to do it.

A couple of blocks south, you'll pop out at the ▲ **Dzhumaya Mosque.** Dating from the 1360s, this mosque is one of the few that remain of the dozens that filled the streets of Plovdiv during Ottoman times. Renovated in 2006, today the evocative mosque is an active house of worship serving Plovdiv's substantial Muslim population. Outside of prayer times, visitors are invited to step inside.

Directly in front of the mosque, they've excavated the seats at the end of a long and skinny ▲▲ **stadium** built in the first century AD. You can walk down to see the seats, or just enjoy a drink at the café. On some evenings, outdoor movies and other events fill this space.

From here, the ancient racecourse runs (unseen) beneath Plovidv's **main walking street** (officially named Knyaz Alexander I Street). Lined with cafés and busy shoppers, this drag is a delightful place to simply stroll. Partway down, at the grand staircase, look for the big blocky footprint in the middle of the street—marking what was the far end of the stadium. Those stairs lead up behind the burgundy-colored National Theatre; along its back wall is more city-sponsored graffiti (facing a rocky cliff with graffiti of Bulgarian VIPs).

Back on the main drag, continue heading south, past the American fast-food chain Макдоналдс. Soon after, the street opens up into an inviting fountain square. Just beyond is the giant, blocky, communist-era post office, anchoring the vast Central Square (Ploshtad Tsentralen)—which still has intimidating echoes of communist times, from the elite communist-era Hotel Trimontium (now a more run-of-the-mill Ramada) to the conceptual sculpture-fountain. Sprawling on your right is the gorgeous Tsar Simeon Garden, a well-used public park with footpaths, fountains, playgrounds, and the people of Plovdiv enjoying their city.

Sleeping in Plovdiv: In the Old Town, **$$ Hebros Hotel** fills a cozy old Bulgarian National Revival mansion with characteristic rooms and a great restaurant (www.hebros-hotel.com). The smaller **$$ Hotel Renaissance,** between the Old and New Towns, is also a good choice (www.atrenaissancesq.com). At the other end of town, **$$$ Hotel Trimontium**—once the top-of-the-top communist-era hotel—is now a comfortable Ramada with easy access to the New Town's main drag (www.wyndhamhotels.com).

Eating in Plovdiv: The Kapana ("Mousetrap") district has several trendy bars and cafes, and the excellent **Pavaj** (Паваж) restaurant, which updates Bulgarian classics and international dishes with a hipster/foodie aesthetic (Zlatarska 7). The recommended **Hotel Hebros** restaurant has an upscale (but still affordable) vibe, with well-executed upscale Bulgarian dishes in a classy dining room or a leafy patio (www.hebros-hotel.com). On or near the New Town's main walking drag, consider the **Vino Culture** wine bar (Otets Paisiy 5); the tacky but popular **Happy** chain (basically the Applebees of Bulgaria, Vasil Levski 2, www.happy.bg); the more upscale-feeling **Hemingway** (Gurko 10, www.hemingway.bg); or the kitschy-touristy-traditional **Dayana** (Даяна, three branches—most central at Knyaz Al. Dondukov-Korsakov 4, www.dayanabg.com).

Nearby: About a half-hour south of Plovdiv, in the Rhodope Mountain foothills, is **Bachkovo Monastery** (Бачковски манастир). It plays second

fiddle to Rila—with a less romantic location and less dramatic frescoes—but for those based in Plovdiv, it's far easier to reach. Come here for an accessible look at a soulful Bulgarian Orthodox monastery. The two-story ossuary has some particularly fine frescoes from the 11th through 14th centuries.

▲Thracian Plain (Тракийска Низина)

Defined by Bulgaria's two major mountain ranges, the Thracian Plain was a busy funnel of trade throughout ancient times. This was the home of the Thracians (explained in the sidebar), who left behind tombs filled with ancient treasure.

Kazanlak (Казанлък, KAH-zahn-luk), with around 50,000 people, is the main town of the Thracian Plain. The workaday town—with a broad main square and a low-rise, communist-concrete aesthetic—is mainly of interest for sights relating to the Thracian tombs (www.muzei-kazanlak.org).

In the town of Kazanlak itself, the **Kazanlak replica tomb** demonstrates how even in the afterlife, the deceased would be

surrounded by colorful slices of Thracian life. You'll squeeze through a narrow passage, then crouch under a dome painted with vivid scenes: The eternal banquet of the Thracian who's buried here, flanked by servants, musicians, and horses.

Three more interesting tombs are within about a 10-minute drive of Kazanlak. At **Shushmanets** (Шушманец, SHOOSH-mah-nets), you can see how a single, stout column supported a heavy load. You'll also see a block with a well-worn hole, illustrating how the double stone doors could swing open and closed on a pivot. Nearby, **Ostrusha** (Оструша, OS-troo-sha)

The Thracians and Their Tombs

Four centuries before Christ—when Socrates and Plato were doing their thing in Athens (about 300 miles to the south)—today's Bulgaria was known as Thrace, with a sophisticated civilization all its own. Famous Thracian figures include Spartacus (the charismatic leader of a Roman slave rebellion), Orpheus (a mythical musician and poet, likely based on an actual Thracian prince), and several emperors (including Justinian the Great). Thracians traded with other civilizations near and far. They had a reputation as redheads and fearsome fighters. And they had a remarkable skill for crafting jewelry as exquisite as anything you'll see today.

Thracians buried their royalty in distinctive, igloo-shaped tombs that were covered in earth. Dozens of these tombs (called *tumuli*) are scattered across the Thracian Plain, along with hundreds of decoy mounds designed to fool grave robbers. Buried deep under those piles of earth, the tombs were impressive feats of fourth-century-BC engineering. The dead were buried with troves of golden treasure, now displayed in museums throughout Bulgaria (including the museum in Kazanlak and Sofia's National Archaeological Museum and National Historical Museum).

Fans of ancient sites enjoy visiting a few of the tombs near Kazanlak, the region's main town (described in this chapter). True aficionados make a pilgrimage to the even bigger and more impressively decorated tomb at Sveshtari, in northeastern Bulgaria (about 4 hours from Kazanlak, or 2.5 hours from Veliko Tarnovo). Either way, you'll be impressed by the sophisticated engineering and delicate artistry of people who lived two and a half millennia ago.

began as a temple. The entire block-like structure was carved out of one gigantic chunk of rock. That's 60 tons—triple the size of the blocks used for the Egyptian pyramids—transported here from the mountains 12 miles away. And then they had to carve it without cracking it. On the ceiling inside survives a fresco of a ghostly, enigmatic face—showing how Thracians were usually depicted as redheads. And **Kosmatka** (Косматка, kos-MAT-kah)—the tomb of Seuthes III—lets you peek into a multichambered tomb similar to the Kazanlak replica.

For a look at some of the breathtaking items found inside those tombs, back in Kazanlak,

visit the ▲ **Iskra-Kazanlak Historical Museum.** The museum includes a room of Thracian artifacts: an intimidating helmet, with an attachable wreath of gilded leaves; a double-handled golden wine cup, or kylix; a solid-gold clamshell case; and some finely detailed jewelry. Red-and-black Greek vases were likely obtained in exchange for Thracian copper ore and gold.

Kazanlak is also the capital of Bulgaria's **rose-oil** industry. (This area is known as the "Valley of the Roses.") Each May and June, hardworking laborers rise early to pick the delicate roses that have bloomed overnight, then take them to a distillery where they can be converted to fragrant oil. (It looks—and smells—like they're making very rosy moonshine.) Shops around town—and all over Bulgaria—sell the final product. It all culminates in Kazanlak's Rose Festival, usually in early June.

Sleeping in Kazanlak: The accommodations here are nothing special; **$ Hotel Palas** is central, just a short walk from the main square (www.hotel-palas.com).

▲▲Balkan Mountains and Shipka Pass

Between the Thracian Plain and Veliko Tarnovo run the Balkan Mountains (which gave their name to this entire peninsula). Crossing over this range, you'll pass several worthwhile sights. For a visual orientation, scan the mountainous horizon from the valley near Kazanlak and try to pick out three big landmarks: the flying-saucer shaped Buzludzha monument; the blocky Shipka Pass monument; and—down below that—the glimmering golden domes of Shipka Church.

▲▲ **Buzludzha** (Бузлуджа, BOOZ-lood-zhah)—an abandoned monument to the Bulgarian Communist Party—is easily

worth ▲▲▲ for those captivated by Bulgaria's communist heritage. This gigantic conference hall was built in the 1980s, in the waning days of communist rule. With the end of the Cold War and the arrival of capitalism, Buzludzha was abandoned. Today, you can drive, up, up into the mountains and stand

before this decaying souvenir of a failed system. The lyrics of the international communist anthem are literally falling off the walls. And the Coke-aping "Enjoy Communism" graffiti makes it clear who won the Cold War. You can try to find a way inside the structure (while it's officially closed, some intrepid visitors shimmy through gaps to get inside; this is—I cannot stress enough—at your own risk). The interior is an eerie, crumbling world of vandalized propaganda, muddy asbestos, a roof that's barely held up by its hammer and sickle, and disintegrating mosaics—once so proud, and now just a humble artifact of a fallen empire. The monument is a twisty, 20-minute (each way) drive from the valley. To find the road up, look for the turnoff along the main road between Kazanlak and Shipka, marked by the stoic communist-era statue standing by a pillar.

The sumptuous ▲▲ **Shipka Church** sits on a hillside above the simple town of Shipka. The church—completed in 1902 by

some of the leading Russian architects of the day—is exuberant "Muscovite-style"...over-the-top Baroque-meets-Byzantine. It's dedicated to the Russian and Bulgarian troops (now buried in the crypt) who fought fiercely to defeat the Ottomans in 1877 (see next). Stepping inside, you enter a world of glittering icons, a rich haze of incense, and hundreds of tall, skinny candles. The 175-foot-tall steeple, flanked by bulbous golden onion domes that shimmer in the sunshine, holds a giant bell cast from discarded artillery cartridges after the battle.

Higher up on the road to Veliko Tarnovo, you'll pass a turnoff for **Shipka Pass** (Shipchenski Prohod/Шипченски Проход). It's worth a quick detour to the monument marking the summit. A long staircase leads up to the boxy tower that honors the pivotal 1877 battle—fought right here—in which elite Russian forces came to help homegrown Bulgarian troops put an end to the nearly five centuries of Ottoman rule. This was a key turning point in Bulgarian history, and led directly to the creation of a modern, fully independent Bulgarian state. It also gave Bulgarians a soft spot for their big ally, Russia (unlike in most of Eastern Europe, where Russia is seen as an unwanted bully). This is partly why, a century later, Bulgaria was the most docile of the Soviet satellite states.

Descending from Shipka Pass on the north (Veliko Tarnovo) slope, you'll coast into the town of Palauzovo. Here you can turn off for a 30-minute drive to ▲ **Tryavna** (Трявна, tree-AHV-nah), a touristy village with an abundance of traditional Bulgarian National Revival-style homes. Stout stone foundations support whitewashed walls and heavy slate roofs, and each door seems to lead to a souvenir shop. While you can also see a version of this style in Plovdiv and in Veliko Tarnovo, Tryavna is a pleasant stretch-your-legs small-town option. From here, you can simply continue north (via Tsareva Livada) to rejoin the main Veliko Tarnovo road.

If you skip the Tryavna turnoff, you'll pass through the big, gritty city of **Gabrovo** (Габрово). Filling an isolated valley with heavy industry, Gabrovo is the butt of many jokes for its people's thrifty ways. But these days, Gabrovo has the last laugh as the home of a museum called the House of Humor and Satire (you'll pass right by it on the main road, www.humorhouse.bg).

▲▲Veliko Tarnovo (Велико Търново)

One of Europe's most dramatically set cities, Veliko Tarnovo (VEH-lee-koh TAR-noh-voh) bunny-hops through a misty gorge

at a sharp bend of the Yantra River. The town's hillsides are blanketed with both tradition-al homes and dreary concrete housing blocks. In this town that's more vertical than hori-zontal, going for a walk around the block feels like climbing a ladder. Tarnovo was the capi-tal of the Second Bulgarian Kingdom, which was the medieval high-water mark of Bulgarian civilization. Today—with 70,000 inhabitants, and a prestigious university with around 18,000 students—it's called *Veliko* (Great) Tarnovo to honor its illustrious past. Aside from its stunning set-ting and rich history, Veliko Tarnovo offers the chance to meet some craftspeople, scramble around a ruined castle, and side-trip to some worthwhile sights (www.velikoturnovo.info).

Visiting Veliko Tarnovo: Perched on the rim of a gorge, Ve-liko Tarnovo is shaped like a natural amphitheater. And center stage—dominating a little peninsula defined by the tight river bend—is a giant sword thrusting skyward, ringed by fearsome horseback warriors. This monument commemorates the **Asen clan,** who ruled over the Second Bul-garian Kingdom (13th-14th century). According to legend, these brothers planted their sword on this spot and said, "Here shall be Bulgaria." While Bulgarian history can be obscure to outsiders, the Second Bulgarian King-dom really was a big deal—an era when the Asen dynasty dominated the Bal-

kan Peninsula from Ukraine to Greece. Their decline ushered in the Ottoman rule that would dominate Bulgarian history for nearly five centuries. You can circle all the way around town to find the bridge that goes out to the monument (and the art gallery just behind it); the best views from afar are along the charming, cobbled Gurko Street (near Hotel Gurko).

Veliko Tarnovo's town center lines up along **Stambolov Street,** which follows the curve of the river a few very steep blocks uphill. Branching off from this main drag is the town's most appealing lane, Rakovski Street—which I think of as ▲▲ **"Craftspeople Street."** Along this cobbled street are several talented artisans who enjoy inviting visitors to watch them create traditional crafts. Do some window-shopping, and

drop in on any shop that grabs your attention: Silversmith Todor Kushlev creates intricate filigree jewelry by hand—or, in the case of his blowtorch—by mouth. Nina and her son create pottery with patterns dating back centuries. Miglena operates an old-fashioned loom. Rumi carves wooden items. Rashko painstakingly paints icons. And Greti carefully pours a thin stream of dough on a spinning griddle to create delicate shredded wheat-like strands for the honey-soaked treat, *kadaif*. (She doesn't sell the *kadaif*, mind you—just the strands. B.Y.O. honey.)

Farther south, Stambolov Street passes above what many consider to be the first parliament of Bulgaria—today the **Revival and Assembly Museum.** With the 1877-1878 expulsion of the Ottoman Empire (with Russian help), Bulgaria was free to create a modern nation. The National Assembly convened right here for the first time in 1879 and ratified a constitution. Today you can see the original assembly hall and peruse a fine museum with vivid photographs documenting the Bulgarian National Revival movement and the creation of the modern Bulgarian state (www.museumvt.com). The building itself was designed by Kolyu Ficheto (1800-1881)—Bulgaria's leading 19th-century architect—who is honored by a statue out front. On a little crest just above, the striking, green-domed **Cathedral of the Nativity of the Virgin** (Rozhdestvo Bogorodichno, also designed by Ficheto) has a terrace with a great view over the gorge and castle.

Just over the ridge, the ruins of ▲ **Tsarevets Fortress** mark the site of the heavily fortified Asen headquarters. While little survives, tourists enjoy nocking imaginary arrows from the bastions, taking in the views, and tiptoeing up to the so-called "Execution Rock"—where no ax or gallows were needed...just a firm shove into a deep gorge. The (reconstructed) church at the summit has unusual modern decorations. These were commissioned by Lyudmila Zhivkova (1942-1981)—the communist-era President of Art and Culture (and daughter of the Bulgarian dictator)—who, after surviving a car wreck and getting into yoga, used her influence to try to merge communist ideology with counterculture art and New Age philosophy. (She was being groomed as her father's heir apparent, and it would have been fascinating to see what direction she'd have steered the country...if she hadn't died—mysteriously, some say—of a brain tumor at age 38.) An elevator zips sightseers up to the steeple's crenelated top for the best high-altitude views in town.

Sleeping and Eating in Veliko Tarnovo: Friendly **$$ Hotel Gurko** enjoys an atmospheric Old Town setting (www.hotel-gurko.com). They also have a decent restaurant, but I prefer to hike (essentially straight uphill) to **Shtastliveca** (Щастливеца); ask for (or reserve) a table on the little cliff-hanging terrace with breathtaking canyon views (Stambolov 79, www.shtastliveca.com).

▲Arbanasi (Арбанаси)

The village of Arbanasi (ahr-bah-NAH-see), which overlooks Veliko Tarnovo from an adjacent ridge (about a 15-minute drive away), is a handy side-trip. The main attraction here is the ▲▲ **Church of the Nativity,** with magnificent frescoes in a dark, claustrophobic, wonderfully historic-feeling space. Typical of modest 16th- and 17th-century Orthodox church architecture (under Ottoman

rule), it feels like a hay barn inside. The L-shaped gallery curves into the nave—and all of it is covered in still-vivid frescoes. Nearby, the **Konstantsalieva House** re-creates life here during Ottoman times. Also in Arbanasi, perched overlooking Veliko Tarnovo is the **Arbanasi Palace Hotel**—the former residence of communist dictator Todor Zhivkov, who ruled Bulgaria for 35 years (the longest of any socialist dictator in Europe). While definitely faded, the hotel still enjoys the same grand views over Veliko Tarnovo that lured Zhivkov here—and you can sleep in his presidential suite.

Black Sea Coast (Chernomorie/Черноморие)

With more time, consider venturing to the eastern edge of Bulgaria: the Black Sea Coast, a popular budget beach destination for in-the-know Brits and Europeans. While I'm more drawn to Bulgaria's cultural treasures (and beaches are better in Croatia or Greece), the Black Sea Coast has its fans, and helps round out your Bulgaria experience.

The main coastal city is **Varna** (Варна, VAR-nah, pop. 335,000). Varna has a skyscraper core; long, sandy, resort-lined

BULGARIA

beaches; the lush and sprawling Primorski ("Seaside") Park; ancient ruins, including a second-century Roman bathhouse; beautiful churches; and the excellent Varna Archaeological Museum, displaying the oldest jewelry in the world (from the fifth millennium BC), discovered in a local necropolis (visit.varna.bg).

The small-town alternative is **Nesebar** (Несебър, neh-SAY-bar, pop. 15,000), connected to the rest of Bulgaria by a narrow isthmus watched over by an iconic windmill (www.visitnessebar.org). This little town has an unusually rich cultural heritage, with artifacts from ancient Greek, Roman, Byzantine, Ottoman, and Bulgarian National Revival times. Nesebar is known for its many fine, partly ruined, striped-brick, Byzantine-style churches. It's also an enjoyable place to simply let your pulse slow, hit the beach, go for a boat ride, and get to know some real, working fishermen. And, for a little more activity, Nesebar adjoins the hard-partying, aptly-named **Sunny Beach** (Slanchev Bryag/Слънчев бряг) resort—as popular now as when it was purpose-built in communist times.

ROMANIA

România

Still haunted by legends of Vlad the Impaler and Nicolae Ceaușescu, Romania is complex—with an epic history, a multifaceted ethnic mix, and an unusually rich cultural heritage. It may not be the easiest place to travel, but for adventurous souls, it's exceptionally rewarding. It's a land that layers gritty cities, charming cobbled towns, glorious castles, ragtag countryside, cut-glass peaks, playing chicken with horse carts, and connecting with kindhearted people living in a crazy world...sometimes all in the same day. Love it or hate it (and often both at once), Romania presents a powerful and memorable travel experience.

Where to Go: Romania is a vast and varied country. To focus your visit, break it into four chunks: Wallachia (Bucharest); Transylvania (cute towns and castles); Maramureș (traditional folk life); and Bucovina (painted monasteries).

Wallachia consists of Romania's flatlands, wrapped around the Carpathian Mountains and stretching from Transylvania to the Danube (and Bulgaria). From a traveler's perspective, the only place here worth visiting is **Bucharest.** The exquisite **Peleș Castle** is also (just barely) in Wallachia, but feels closer to Transylvania.

Transylvania is Romania's heartland and where most visitors focus their time. You could spend many days here, sampling great cities, evocative castles and fortified churches, and a mountainous landscape. For home-base towns, big but charming **Brașov** works

well for venturing into the mountains and touring castles (including **Bran, Râșnov,** and **Peleș**). Little, well-preserved **Sighișoara** is the most charming town and handy for touring fortified churches (such as the ones in **Biertan** and **Viscri**). **Sibiu** is Romania's most livable city, with a thriving historical core; it's relatively close to the dramatic **Corvin Castle.** And sprawling **Cluj-Napoca,** Transylvania's biggest city and de facto capital, has bustling squares, inviting parks, and busy nightlife.

Maramureș—in the far-north of the country, squeezed just inside the Ukrainian border—is time-consuming to reach. But it's definitely worth the effort for those interested in **traditional lifestyles** (and the gorgeous **Merry Cemetery**). Make a home base in the countryside near **Sighetu Marmației** and explore.

Bucovina, another traditional region to the east of Transylvania, is famous for its glorious **painted monasteries** (mostly near the town of Gura Humorului).

When planning your itinerary, don't underestimate the long distances (or the slow traffic—see next). To avoid spending all of your time on the road, be selective. With just a few days, focus on Transylvania, dividing your time between two home-base towns (Brașov and Sighișoara are handiest). With more time, add Maramureș and/or Bucharest. Bucovina's painted monasteries are beautiful, but the region has little else to see, and it's a time-consuming detour—include Bucovina only if you have ample time. For an even longer visit, the Dobrogea region (with the lush Danube Delta and the city of Constanța)—not covered in this book—is the most logical add-on.

Getting Around: Bucharest and other big cities are relatively well-connected by the slow **train** network (www.cfrcalatori.ro) or by **bus** (www.autogari.ro). But visitors wanting to scour the countryside—which is Romania's most appealing draw—are better off **driving.** Roads are in decent condition, but progress is slow; there are virtually no expressways, country roads are generally two-lane, and city bypasses are rare—you'll usually have to drive right through the town center. On the other hand, drivers get a front-row seat for Romania's weird and wonderful ways—it's a fascinating place to just watch life unfold.

Romanian Cuisine: Romanian cooking is heavy peasant fare. Meals begin with a wooden platter of rustic mountain cheeses, greasy pork (including *jumări*—little strips of pork fat), and raw onions. Next is a simple but tasty soup *(supă)*; a variety of "sour soups" called *ciorbă* are available (and typically delicious). Then comes the main course: pork, chicken, or fish. One popular protein is *mici* (MEE-chee)—minced-meat grilled sausages (like *ćevapčići* in the former Yugoslavia). Polenta *(mămăligă)*—often drizzled with sour cream—is the standard side, and *sarmale* (cabbage roll) is the national dish. A filling dessert is *papanași*—baseball-sized fried doughnuts smothered in jam and sour cream. Romanian wines and beers are nothing special, but try the fruity, 100-proof Romanian moonshine, *palinka* (a.k.a. *țuică*)...carefully. They say that when you drink *palinka,* "Your brain is OK, but your body is not OK."

Romanian Language: Romanian is a Romance language. If you speak French, Spanish, or Italian, you'll find that you may understand Romanian...a little. For example, "Good evening" is *Bună seara.* The character *ș* sounds like "sh," and *ț* is "ts." Some key survival phrases: "Hello" is *Bună ziua* (formal) or *Alo* (informal); "Please" is *Vă rog;* "Thank you" is *Mulțumesc* (or simply *Mersi*); and "Goodbye" is *La revedere.*

Local Guides: Hiring your own guide here is an exceptional investment. Prices are affordable, the guides I've recommended are top-notch, and Romania is much easier to take with a little local help. I've personally worked with each of the following guides, and highly recommend their services. While I've listed each one's area of specialty, most of them work throughout the country—consider hiring one to be with you for several stops (or even your entire trip): **Daniel Gheorghiță** at Covinnus Travel (throughout Romania, www.covinnus.com, office@covinnus.com), **Dan Nica** (Bucharest and beyond, www.tourguidesromania.com, dsnica@gmail.com), **Ana Adamoae** (Bucharest and Transylvania, www.guidedtoursbucharest.wordpress.com, aadamoae@gmail.com), **Ciprian "Chip" Slemco** at Hello Bucovina (Bucovina and throughout Romania—and beyond, www.hellobucovina.com, contact@hellobucovina.com), and **Teo Ivanciuc** (just Maramureș, www.maramurestour.com, teofilivanciuc@yahoo.com).

Romania Practicalities

Money: Romanians use the leu ("lion," plural *lei*): $1 = about 4 lei. One leu is broken down into 100 bani.

Geography and People: Romania is 92,000 square miles, about the size of Oregon or the United Kingdom. Of its 22 million people, the majority consider themselves ethnic Romanians (83 percent), with large minorities of Hungarians (just over 6 percent) and Roma (an estimated 3-4 percent); many Romanians are a mix of these, along with strong German and Russian/Ukrainian influences. The Carpathian Mountains take a big bite out of the middle of Romania, defining its biggest and most famous region, Transylvania (and several cultural fault lines). The capital and biggest city is Bucharest, with around 2 million people; other large cities, each with around 300,000 people, are Cluj-Napoca, Iași, Timișoara, and Brașov. Although a member of the EU since 2007, Romania still struggles economically (per capita GDP is $24,500).

Snapshot History: Romania's pagan Dacian tribes were taken over by soldiers of the Roman Empire, most of whom later returned to Rome—but left behind their DNA and their language (which evolved into today's Romanian). In the late ninth century came the Hungarians, who would rule the core of the region (Transylvania) for nearly a millennium. In the 12th century, seeking help to settle and defend the land, the ruling Hungarian dukes invited German (or "Saxon") merchants to establish towns and villages, and trade here. Meanwhile, powerful eastern neighbors—Russia and the Ottoman Empire—frequently invaded and occupied other parts of the Romanian lands. In the late 19th century, Romania finally threw off its foreign rulers and imported royalty from Germany (King Carol I) to help lead them into the modern age. But after World War II, Romania became part of the communist bloc, and had arguably one of the worst communist periods in Europe (under megalomaniacal strongman Nicolae Ceaușescu—see page 1051). In 1989, Ceaușescu was executed, and Romania began a new chapter: capitalistic, democratic, and fully independent.

Famous Romanians: Gymnast Nadia Comăneci (and coaches Béla and Márta Károlyi, of Hungarian ancestry), author Elie Wiesel (born to a Jewish family in Maramureș), composer George Enescu, and public radio commentator Andrei Codrescu.

Emergencies: Dial 112.

Consular Services in Bucharest: The US Embassy is at Bulevardul Dr. Liviu Librescu 4 (tel. 021-200-3300); the Canadian Embassy is at StradaTuberozelor 1 (tel. 021-307-5000).

Telephone Country Code: +40, then drop the initial 0 of the phone number.

Tourist Information: www.romaniatourism.com

Top Romanian Destinations

WALLACHIA
▲Bucharest (Bucureşti)

Romania's capital, Bucharest—with about two million people—is a muscular and gritty tangle of buildings. It can be hard to like at

first glance, but with a thoughtful look, it reveals its charms. Between the dreary apartment blocks hides an impressive architectural heritage. Once called the "Little Paris of the East," Bucharest flourished in the late 19th century, when independent Romania was born. Later it was brutally disfigured by the communist dictator Ceauşescu, who left behind a starkly Socialist-style residential zone and the city's main landmark (the Palace of the Parliament). But today's Bucharest is working hard to move forward. In recent years, they've rejuvenated the once-derelict Old Town—transforming it into one of the liveliest nightlife zones in Eastern Europe. Taken together, Bucharest is a fascinating place to grapple with for a day or two.

Visiting Bucharest: For a glimpse at Bucharest's genteel past, go for a stroll along ▲▲ **Victory Avenue** (Calea Victoriei)—with

grand belle époque architecture that has recently been scrubbed of its communist-era grime. Pause by the horseback statue of King Carol I (1839-1914), across the street from the Royal Palace. In the 1860s, Romania became a modern state for the first time. With no royal family to call their own, the Romanians went shopping for a king who could connect their country to the European mainstream. They found one in Germany, where a prince looking for a throne agreed to become King Carol I of Romania. King Carol embraced his new homeland: He learned the language and adopted the culture while bringing Western reforms and securing true independence for Romania. Under King Carol, Bucharest blossomed. He imported French architects to give Bucharest the romantic allure visitors still enjoy along Victory Avenue. Just up the street is the **Athenaeum** concert hall, one of the finest examples of Bucharest's Golden Age of architecture.

ROMANIA

Nearby, **Revolution Square** (Piața Revoluției) is marked by a stark monument honoring the more than 1,000 Romanians who died to bring freedom to their country in 1989. It stands in front of the former Communist Party Headquarters, where dictator Nicolae Ceaușescu would deliver speeches from the little balcony. On December 21, 1989—as revolution swept Romania—Ceaușescu had to abandon his podium midspeech when the crowd turned on him. (For the rest of the story, see the sidebar.)

Just a few blocks south sits Bucharest's ▲▲ **Old Town.** From communist times through the early 2000s, this area was deserted, dilapidated, and dangerous. But now it's being systematically rejuvenated. Grand, glittering belle époque buildings (including several bank headquarters) have been scrubbed and polished. Formerly abandoned shopping galleries are newly inviting. Historical monuments—like the delightful Hanul Manuc, an early-19th-century caravansary—have been painstakingly restored. And an al fresco dining and drinking scene enlivens the traffic-free streets. The lanes of the Old Town are a revelation after dark (especially on weekends), when the entire neighborhood feels like one big, sprawling cocktail party.

Also scattered around the Old Town are a few modest but colorfully decorated Romanian Orthodox churches. Observing passersby in front of any church, you'll notice that—while religion was discouraged in communist times—these days, faith is an increasingly important part of everyday life. One of the best examples is the tiny ▲ **Biserica Stavropoleos convent,** unassumingly tucked between trendy restaurants and ritzy offices. Still  tended by cloaked nuns, it feels like a transplanted time warp. A colorful *Last Judgment* painting fills the entranceway, and the little garden courtyard offers visitors a peaceful respite from the busy city.

Thriving as it is today, Bucharest's Old Town was lucky to survive the communist period. In the early 1980s, after an inspiring visit to North Korea, Nicolae Ceaușescu ripped out 80 percent of the historical center—30,000 houses, schools, and churches—to create the **Civic Center** (Centrul Civic) district, with wide boulevards, stone-faced apartment blocks, gurgling fountains, and a Pyongyang aesthetic. (Urban planners managed to save a few churches by secretly relocating them inside city blocks, where you can still find them today.) This area, just across the neglected little

Nicolae Ceaușescu (1918-1989)

From uneducated peasant roots, Nicolae Ceaușescu (chow-SHESS-koo) rose through the communist ranks to take power in 1965. During his 24 years in power, Ceaușescu's brittle mental health and ballooning ego made him arguably Europe's most damaging communist dictator aside from Joseph Stalin. Early on, his aggressive deals with foreign leaders mortgaged Romania's future. (He turned his back on the Warsaw Pact and favored partnering with non-aligned countries in Asia and Africa—which made him paranoid about the likelihood of a Soviet invasion.) And later, Ceaușescu grew obsessed with paying off the country's debt just as he was becoming addicted to grandiose projects without budgets.

In the 1970s and 1980s, Ceaușescu erected massive factories and refineries, dammed the Danube, rerouted rivers for irrigation, and built an impossibly twisty road over the country's steepest mountains (see page 1055). And in his capital, Ceaușescu razed more than three-quarters of the historical quarter to build a new "Civic Center" district, capped by a palace fit for a megalomaniac.

Meanwhile, Ceaușescu exported vital resources even as his own people were starving. Expired frozen fish was all you could buy in grocery stores, and many Romanians resorted to subsistence farming and raised their own pigs to survive the harsh winters. As a cost-saving measure, power was routinely cut off at night, and hot and cold water were intermittent. To stem a dwindling population, Ceaușescu outlawed abortion and divorce, and extended elite status to mothers of multiple children. (Tens of thousands of unwanted children were later abandoned, creating a surge in US adoptions of Romanian orphans during the 1990s.) Ceaușescu also employed ruthless Stalinesque tactics to keep dissent at a minimum—through his huge, KGB-style secret police force, the Securitate.

All of this created a powerful anti-Ceaușescu sentiment. In the late fall of 1989, with winds of change sweeping across the Eastern Bloc, revolution reached Romania. As Ceaușescu delivered a speech, furious protesters filled the square. Ceaușescu ordered the police to open fire, while he fled to a dramatic rooftop helicopter rescue. But Ceaușescu and his wife were soon arrested, given a brief televised trial, and shot on Christmas Day 1989. To reassure the Romanians that their hated ruler was gone for good, the Ceaușescus' bodies were shown on national television. In all of Eastern Europe, Romania was the only country where the transition from communism to democracy came with a violent revolution—and the only one that ended in an execution.

Even now, Romanians are scarred from the Ceaușescu years. His legacy—economical, psychological, and physical—looms large. Looking back on Ceaușescu's excesses, Romanians say, "We can't even paint everything Ceaușescu built."

river from the Old Town, is worth a stroll to better understand the scale of Ceaușescu's ambition, not to mention his ego.

In the core of the Civic Center, rows of fountains lead from Unity Square (Piața Unirii) to the massive ▲▲▲ **Palace of Parliament**—

the largest building in Europe (four million square feet, with more than a thousand rooms). Ceaușescu built this monstrosity as a symbol of his power. Today it houses the Romanian parliament, three skippable museums, and an international conference center—and is still about 70 percent vacant space.

Guided tours lead gawking visitors around its cavernous, empty, and dimly lit halls (if they turned on all the lights, the palace would consume as much electricity as a small city). On the one-hour tour (bring your passport, www.cic.cdep.ro/en), visitors see the grand entry hall; the theater, with its gargantuan five-ton crystal chandelier; and the ballroom, big enough to host a football match and with a glass ceiling that, it's rumored, could slide open to allow a helicopter to land. You'll also step out onto the balcony that Ceaușescu designed specifically for delivering speeches, while looking down a boulevard grand enough to echo his self-importance. (To be sure it met his expectations, builders erected full-scale cardboard models of facades along the entire street for his personal sign-off.)

Throughout the tour, ogle the details: The wall-to-wall carpets had to be delivered in pieces and sewn together on-site. The curtains are stitched with silver-and-gold threads. Garage-sized

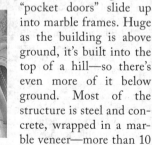

"pocket doors" slide up into marble frames. Huge as the building is above ground, it's built into the top of a hill—so there's even more of it below ground. Most of the structure is steel and concrete, wrapped in a marble veneer—more than 10 million square feet of it. The building sinks a quarter-inch each year under its sheer weight. They say underground tunnels go all the way to the airport—an emergency escape route for the paranoid Ceaușescu.

The dictator threw resources at his pet project like a crazed pharaoh. For six years, 700 architects and 20,000 laborers worked

on it 24/7. Hundreds of workers died. Total cost: around three billion dollars. And even then, a third of the interior was never completed. Ceaușescu was executed halfway through its construction,
and overnight, the "Presidential Palace" became the "Palace of the
People"—and those people were stuck with it. Nobody could possibly afford to buy the building, and finishing it was cheaper than
tearing it down. When it finally opened in 1994, the Romanian
people—whose food had been rationed for years to help pay for
the palace—were both wonderstruck and repulsed when they wan-
dered its opulent halls.

Next door, others are carrying on Ceaușescu's legacy of outsize
projects. Just to the southwest, work crews are erecting the world's
largest Orthodox church: The **Romanian People's Salvation Cathedral,** with a capacity of 6,000 worshippers, was consecrated in
2018 (though it's still not complete).

While Bucharest has plenty of fine museums, on a short visit
I find it more interesting to simply explore the zones described
above and tour the parliament. But to dig deeper into the story of
Romania, consider the **National Museum of Romanian History**
(right in the Old Town, www.mnir.ro) and the **National Museum
of the Romanian Peasant** (folk-life artifacts on Victory Square/
Piața Victoriei, www.muzeultaranuluiroman.ro; this is redundant
if you're heading to Maramureș).

Sleeping in Bucharest: The small, welcoming **$$ Rembrandt
Hotel** is well-located at the edge of the bustling Old Town dining
and nightlife zone (www.rembrandt.ro). Also central is the more
upscale, suite-oriented **$$$ Hotel Cișmigiu** (www.hotelcismigiu.
ro).

Eating in Bucharest: The Old Town has ample dining options; for a memorable meal of Romanian classics, consider the
classic upmarket-beer-hall vibe of **Caru' cu Bere** (www.carucubere.
ro); the atmospheric caravansary setting of **Hanul' lui Manuc**
(www.hanulluimanuc.ro); or the touristy and traditional **Crama
Domnească** (www.cramadomneasca.net).

▲▲▲Peleș Castle

Peleș (PEH-lesh) Castle, on a wooded hillside above the lovely
mountain resort town of Sinaia, is Romania's answer to Bavaria's
Neuschwanstein: a fanciful, over-the-top, Romantic interpretation
of a Gothic hunting palace, prickly with spires but far too pretty
to repel an actual siege. Designed to impress, Peleș ranks among
Europe's best Romantic Age palaces.

Background: Peleș was built in the 1880s by King Carol I,
who had moved here from Germany. Carol was desperate to keep
up with his rivals back home (such as "Mad" King Ludwig of Bavaria). And so, in a mountainous and forested landscape that re-

minded him of Germany, Carol imported German architects to create the ultimate palace. Here at Peleş, King Carol and Queen Elizabeth felt free from the stifling climate of German royalty: They slept together in the same bed, dressed in Romanian peasant costume, and decorated the place with Transylvanian folk themes. But Carol didn't abandon his German efficiency. Au-

diences took place standing at his upright desk and lasted about five minutes. His queen, Elizabeth (look for her portrait in traditional Romanian costume), used her Germanic know-how to both celebrate and elevate her adopted culture. Inspired by Transylvanian fairy tales, Elizabeth even wrote some of her own. It's no wonder that many contemporary Romanians still have great affection for their onetime-imported royalty.

Visiting Peleş Castle: You can get inside only with a guided tour (www.peles.ro). The interior is a rich world of sumptuous detail: cozy wood-paneled elegance, glittering Bohemian crystal chandeliers, whimsical paintings, colorful stoves, gilded stucco, Meissen porcelain, secret passages, and elaborate knickknacks (watch for the teak elephant table—a gift from the maharajah of India). Tours begin in the Hall of Honor—with its red carpets, grand staircase, venerable portraits, and inlaid-wood pictures of German castles (suggesting the king's sense of one-upsmanship). One particularly grandiose apartment—built for Emperor Franz Josef, who never actually slept here—has leather-tooled walls and a cozy breakfast room in the turret. In the Music Room, Queen Elizabeth hosted concerts and literary gatherings—and had scenes from her fairy tales painted on the walls. Meanwhile, the king's impressive armory collection (Europe's largest at the time) was designed both to intimidate and to stoke conversation. The private music halls and theaters were the site of many exclusive performances. And the library shows off the royal couple's passion for education. But remember: This was a Romantic Age, faux-medieval castle, built in the 1880s, so it also had all the modern conveniences: bathrooms with running water, forced-air heating, elevators, a central vacuum cleaner system, and even its own power plant.

If one castle isn't enough, you can also visit a second palace nearby, built by the next king (Carol's nephew)—a half-timbered mini-Peleş called **Pelişor Castle.**

▲▲Transfăgărășan Road

The most challenging road connecting Bucharest to Transylvania—and, quite possibly, between any two points in Europe—is the Transfăgărășan (trans-fah-gah-rah-SHAHN) Road. It twists and turns and bends back on itself several times as it crosses the cut-glass peaks of the Făgăraș Mountains, summiting at 6,670 feet.

This improbable road is another artifact of Nicolae Ceaușescu's rule. Following the 1968 Soviet invasion of Czechoslovakia to put down the Prague Spring uprising, a paranoid Ceaușescu wanted an escape route from Romania's flat capital to its easier-to-defend mountains. According to the story, Ceaușescu simply put his finger on a map and said, "Build it here." And they did. After incalculable costs and 40 workers' lives lost, Ceaușescu's dream was complete.

Today, the 56-mile-long Transfăgărășan Road has little practical value, but it's a popular scenic drive for tourists...as long as you're very comfortable with mountain driving. (Note that the road is only open when all snow has melted—typically late June through late October.) Consider the Transfăgărășan as a time-consuming but super-scenic alternate route for connecting Transylvania (it's off E-68, between Brașov and Sibiu) to Bucharest (via Pitești, where you can hop on the freeway).

At the southern (Bucharest) end of the pass, you'll pass **Poenari Castle.** Unlike the "Dracula Castle" at Bran (described later), Poenari has a real connection to Vlad Țepeș, who actually spent time here. (It's quite different than Bran, with a less striking interior; unless you have time and calories to burn, it's not worth the 1,400 stairs to reach the entrance.)

TRANSYLVANIA
▲Brașov

Brașov (BRAH-shohv, pop. 295,000), about a three-hour drive north of Bucharest, is scenically tucked against Carpathian foothills. Brașov was one of the original seven towns founded by Saxon settlers (see sidebar). It thrived then. It thrived during the Ceaușescu years, when it was aggressively developed into an industrial powerhouse. And it thrives today, with a rejuvenated old town center that's a popular

ROMANIA

Transylvanian History

Transylvania's castle-capped hills and fortress-like churches are a testament to a hard-fought past. With a stout tower standing guard over every village, it's clear this region has frequently been a crossroads of history.

From the late ninth century until the end of World War I, Transylvania was part of Hungary. The Hungarian dukes who ruled this remote region called it Erdély (which, like "transylvania," means "beyond the forest"). Seeking help to settle the rugged land, and to defend it against potential invasions from Tatars and Ottomans, the Hungarians invited merchants from today's Luxembourg, Belgium, and northwestern Germany to establish towns and trade here. Those settlers—called "Saxons"—founded seven fortified towns, including Brașov, Sighișoara, and Sibiu. (The German name for Transylvania is Siebenbürgen—"Seven Towns.") Meanwhile, German settlers in the countryside, who were outside of town walls and vulnerable to attack, beefed up their churches.

And so, for much of its history, Transylvania was divided along these societal strata: Hungarian rulers, German merchants, and Romanian peasants. But in modern times, things began to change. During a late-19th-century wave of emigration, many Saxons relocated to Germany. Then Hungary came up on the losing side of World War I, making Transylvania part of Romania. In the waning days of World War II, many Saxons fled the advancing Soviet Army, and under communism, the Romanian government literally sold its few remaining Saxons back to Germany.

And then there are the Roma (whom Romanians—eager to avoid any "Roma" vs. "Romanian" confusion—usually call Gypsies; see page 199). Today, Romania has one of Europe's largest Roma populations: officially 620,000 people, but—considering the difficulty of conducting a census of people who live off the grid—likely far more. The classic Roma stereotype is of desperately poor people living in shacks on the edge of town. You'll see plenty of that in Romania, but that's only part of the story. Most Roma live side-by-side with their Romanian neighbors, more or less integrated into mainstream society.

In today's Transylvania, the German minority is less than 1 percent. The Hungarian minority (about 6 percent of the population)—called Székelys—are scattered around Romania, but are concentrated in Hungarian-speaking enclaves in the central part of the country (east of Târgu Mureş). Travelers who can recognize each language are aware they're in a Balkan melting pot. Today, most Transylvanian towns are home to a mix of Romanians, Roma, Hungarians, and sometimes a few Germans—fitting for a region with such a rich and complex history.

springboard for the mountains: hiking in the summer, skiing in the winter, and castle-hopping anytime. Enjoyable but low-impact on its own, Brașov is an ideal home base for a Transylvanian "castle day"—with a car and an early start, you can easily side-trip to Peleș, Bran, and Râșnov in a single day.

Visiting Brașov: While Brașov's main appeal is its convenient location, its gorgeous main square and pedestrianized core are a big bonus. The town is a fine mix of tourism and real, contemporary Romanian life. Its main square, **Piața Sfatului**—and the lively walking streets that flow away from it—are a delightful people zone.

Brașov's centerpiece is the **Black Church** (Biserica Neagră). The biggest Gothic church between Vienna and Istanbul, it got its nickname when it was charred by a 1689 fire. Inside, each bank of pews is lovingly decorated with the seal of the guild that financed it—suggesting the importance of trades and crafts in medieval Transylvania. The goldsmiths and other wealthy guilds sat near the front; poorer guilds, like the tailors and weavers, had the cheap seats in back. The mid-nave pews are reversible—with backs that can be flipped to face either the pulpit or the grand pipe organ. And the most extensive Turkish carpet collection outside of Turkey fills the nave. These were donated by European traders, pilgrims, and crusaders who passed through this crossroads town on their way home from the Holy Land.

For a low-impact hike, head north across the little river and walk a few minutes up into the hills, where you can visit the **Black Tower** and the **White Tower**—part of the stout network of fortifications that protected the city in its medieval heyday. From the White Tower, you enjoy sweeping views over the tidy town center, the cable car that trundles to the adjacent mountaintop, and the big, white, Hollywood-like letters that spell out B-R-A-Ș-O-V.

Beyond the delightful urban core, Brașov features row after row of uniform concrete apartment blocks. But, revealing the city's

relative affluence, many are now refurbished and colorfully repainted. The sprawl is for good reason: Soon after the Iron Curtain slammed shut, Brașov was rechristened Orașul Stalin— "Stalintown." Ceaușescu built an extensive network of auto and armaments factories here, imported and retrained peasants from the wilds of Moldavia to staff them, and erected forests of concrete apartment blocks to house them. (For a time, Brașov was Romania's second-biggest city.) Trees with white bark were strategically planted on the hillside above to spell out the name S-T-A-L-I-N. And newlyweds felt compelled to have their picture taken with a big statue of "Father" Stalin in the park.

Sleeping in Brașov: Several cozy guesthouses are in the town center, including **$$ Hotel Bella Muzica** (www.bellamuzica.ro) and the simpler **$ Casa Albert** (www.casa-albert.ro). For a glitzy option near the train station (in the modern sprawl—a long walk or short drive from the Old Town), **$$$ Hotel Kronwell** is a big, slick design hotel with all the comforts (www.kronwell.com).

Eating in Brașov: You'll find plenty of options in the pedestrianized town center. **La Ceaun** ("The Cauldron") is good for traditional Romanian fare (www.laceaun.com), while the Italian-oriented **Prato** feels dressier but is still affordable (www.prato.ro). Both have appealing outdoor tables.

▲▲Castles near Brașov

You can link up all three of these castles in one busy day from Brașov. Or consider stopping off at Peleș on your way between Bucharest and Brașov, letting you linger and enjoy some time in Brașov itself.

The single best castle in the area (technically in Wallachia, just over the hills from Brașov) is **▲▲▲ Peleș Castle,** described earlier.

The mega-touristy **▲▲ Bran Castle** perches evocatively on a bluff overlooking a busy valley road (www.bran-castle.com). De-

spite the tacky vampire-themed kitsch that clutters the pathway up, Bran has virtually no real connection to Dracula or to Vlad the Impaler...but it sure is striking. Fanciful legends aside, Bran is a good example of an authentic medieval fortress, dating from the 14th century. In the 1920s, Romania's royal family converted Bran into a rustic country retreat. And that, rather than vampires, is what you'll learn about in the whitewashed interior. As you follow the one-way route through the castle, exhibits introduce you to Romania's King Ferdinand I (the nephew of King Carol I) and his wife, Princess Marie (the granddaughter of Britain's Queen Victoria). Bran is also simply a fun kid-in-the-castle experience: Exploring the MC Escher floor plan, you'll discover a humble armory, a secret passage, and a fairy-tale courtyard.

▲ **Râșnov Castle** (RUZH-nohv) is your ruined-fortress-on-a-mountaintop experience. From the humble village of Râșnov (with its own Hollywood-like sign on the hills), you'll curl around

Dracula: Behind the Cape

Transylvania's tourist industry loves to milk its connection to

Dracula. In reality, Dracula was the invention of a British novelist who never set foot in Transylvania, but was inspired, in part, by a real historical figure called Vlad the Impaler. Confused? To help you sort out fact from legend, here are the basics:

Vlad III (1431–1477) was a 15th-century prince of Wallachia who was taken captive by his Ottoman rivals. Some say he rotted in a prison, while others believe he apprenticed at the sultan's court in Constantinople. Either way, after six years the authorities believed him "rehabilitated" and returned him to his homeland—with the expectation that he would serve

as their obedient puppet ruler of Wallachia.

Instead, Vlad quickly turned on his former captors, and joined the Hungarian fight to push back the Ottoman advance into Europe. According to later (and likely exaggerated) accounts, Vlad's methods for dealing with his enemies were brutal: Slowly and sadistically, he'd drive stakes into the bodies of his victims as they screamed in agony. Then he'd display their mutilated corpses along busy roads as a warning to would-be foes. Vlad dispatched tens of thousands of victims this way, earning him a vivid nickname: Vlad Țepeș—"the Impaler." He was also known by another name: Dracula, stemming from his father's membership in the chivalric "Order of the Dragon" (*Dracul* in Romanian).

While feared by the Transylvanian nobles, Vlad the Impaler was beloved by the peasants, who cheered his heroic defense of their homeland. And after his death, his legend only grew in a Europe terrified of the ever-looming threat of Ottoman invasion.

By the late 1800s, the English novelist Bram Stoker (1847-1912)—like many before and after him—found his imagination captivated by the sadism of Vlad the Impaler. Stoker was also inspired by completely separate Transylvanian folk tales of the undead. Stoker merged the two storylines and, in 1897, published the Victorian Gothic novel *Dracula*. Stoker never traveled to Romania to research his book; the vampire called Dracula, and his evocative Transylvanian settings, all came purely from Stoker's imagination.

All of this means that—from a sightseer's perspective—there are no actual sights in Romania relating to "Dracula," and only tenuous ties to Vlad the Impaler. Vlad may have lived for a brief time in Sighișoara. But it's likely that he never even set foot in the most famous "Dracula" sight, Bran Castle (at most, he spent a night or two there). Of course, the locals will never set you straight...all that Dracula lore is just too lucrative.

the back of the hill, park, buy
your ticket, then hike or ride a
shuttle bus to the castle on top.
Once inside the stout walls,
a few houses and turrets still
stand, which—along with the
foundations of others—give you
a sense of the safety these castles
provided during difficult times.
Râșnov also enjoys grand views
down over the valley.

▲▲Sighișoara

Sighișoara (sih-gih-SHO-rah, pop. 28,000) is Romania's showpiece jewel-box town—the Transylvanian version of Rothenburg

ob der Tauber or Český Krumlov.
Sighișoara is the best-preserved of the
original seven Saxon towns—it feels
like a time warp. Sleep here if cuddly
cobbles are your goal. Sighișoara is also
a good home base for seeing the fortified churches, or as a stopover between
Brașov and Maramureș.

Visiting Sighișoara: The entire fortified hilltop of Sighișoara—
perched on a little plateau halfway up a
wooded hill—forms the town's mighty
Citadel. (Many tourists who come to
Sighișoara ask, "So where's the castle?"

They don't realize they're already in it.) This walled area was both a
home to craftsmen and a place of last refuge in case of invasions or
raids—which were frequent. Nine of Sighișoara's 15 pointy-topped
watchtowers still survive—each one named for the guild that defended it.

Sighișoara's icon is its **Clock Tower**—marked with symbols
that proudly trumpet its special privileges. Inside, visitors spiral up
and up on creaky wooden stairs, and peek out over the shoulders of
the figures that change with the day of the week. At each landing
are modest exhibits: a model of the town at its peak, and a display
of the products of each of the main guilds that put this place on
the map.

If you need a Dracula photo op, you'll find a statue of **Vlad
Țepeș** (who may have lived here briefly) on the square called Piața
Muzeului, just above the Monastery Church; nearby, a garden terrace features views over the rooftops of Sighișoara's workaday modern town.

From Sighişoara's town center, a covered staircase—called the **"Stairs of the Students"**—leads 175 steps up to the hilltop. After every sixth step is a landing—a reminder to rest on the seventh day.

At the top, a school, a church, and a cemetery honor those original Saxon pioneers. German names fill the graveyard. And inside the **church** is a collection of artifacts from smaller German churches around the region—most now all but abandoned. You can see how, when austere Lutheranism reached Transylvania, frugal village churches kept their old Catholic altars, but removed the showiest statues. Dowry chests were found squirrelled away in the attic of a village church, untouched for centuries. The tomb of a furrier recalls a time when it was cheaper to wear heavy cloaks on Sunday morning than to heat this huge space.

Sleeping in Sighişoara: Several quaint hotels and pensions line the cobbled streets of the Citadel. The biggest outfit is **$$ Hotel Sighişoara** and its annex, the upscale **$$$ Fronius Residence** (for both: www.sighisoarahotels.ro). Or try the simpler **$ Pension am Schneiderturm** (www.schneiderturm.ro).

Eating in Sighişoara: In this touristy town, don't go looking for a memorable meal—just pick the setting you enjoy best. I've eaten well at **Casa cu Cerb** (www.casacucerb.ro) and at the recommended **Hotel Sighişoara**.

▲▲Fortified Saxon Churches

Some of Romania's best castles aren't castles at all—they're churches. While big towns like Sighişoara and Braşov were well protected, smaller Saxon settlements were vulnerable—especially after a devastating Tatar invasion in the 13th century. So what did the industrious settlers do? They fortified their churches.

Dozens of fortified German churches—mostly built in the 13th and 14th centuries—are scattered across Transylvania. From the outside, they look like medieval fortresses: beefy bastions, stout lookout towers, narrow slits for raining arrows on enemies, distinctly Transylvanian trapezoidal turrets (to shed the heavy snowfall), and wrap-around defensive galleries. While most Germans have long since left Romania, their heritage lives on here: The signs, the services, and the hymnals in the pews are all still in German. And periodically, some of these churches hold Lutheran services.

Visiting Fortified Churches: As you explore Transylvania—

especially the area between Brașov and Sighișoara—you'll drive past several of these fortified churches (a particularly fine example is in Saschiz). But a few are worth going a bit out of your way to see.

Close to Brașov, **Prejmer** (PREHZH-mehr) has a particularly well-preserved, half-timbered-and-whitewashed courtyard, showing how townspeople could flock into the protection of the church in times of crisis. Each cell was reserved for one family—notice that each rustic door is labeled. You can even see the little one-room "schoolhouse" tucked into the wall. (Nearby, **Hărman** has another well-preserved example.)

Between Sighișoara and Sibiu, **Biertan** (BEER-tahn) has one of the newest fortified churches (early 16th century)—illus-

trating the architecture style at its most evolved. Looking out from the top, you can see the surviving three concentric walls (of the original five) that protect the church. But stepping inside, you could be in any village church in medieval Germany. The original 16th-century stone pulpit still stands. And, like the Black Church in Brașov, each bank of pews is marked with the seal of a local guild. On the door to the left of the altar, the locksmiths' guild showed off with an elaborate locking mechanism. In the church courtyard is a "divorce chamber," where a quarrelling couple would be forced to share one bed, one pot, and one plate—for however long it took to resolve their differences. (From 1500 to 1800, only one divorce was recorded.)

The whitewashed and ramshackle church of **Viscri** (VEE-scree, from the German Weiss Kirch—white church), hidden deep in the hills between Brașov and Sighișoara, is one of the old-est (c. 1100). Most of the pews don't have backs. That's because of the starched dresses and long headdresses of traditional village women, who wanted to avoid creases. The pews with backs were for the only families who were from elsewhere: the

preacher's and the teacher's. The very humble dirt-street town of Viscri—where locals selling colorful woolens to tourists seems to be the only economy—is fun to explore. One of the houses belongs to (believe it or not) Prince Charles, who loves the anonymity this off-the-grid corner of Europe provides. Locals claim that Prince Charles and Prince Harry retreated here to hide from the press in the days following the 2011 royal wedding of William and Kate.

▲▲Sibiu

Charming Sibiu (SEE-bee-yoo) may be Romania's most livable city. Sibiu began life as Hermannstadt, the biggest and most important of the original seven Saxon towns. And today, while only about one in a hundred residents has German ancestry, Sibiu's tidy townscape still feels very Germanic. (In 2000, Sibiu elected Klaus Iohannis to be the first German mayor in Romania since World War II; beloved and hugely successful locally, he went on to be elected Romania's president in 2014.) While not quite as practical a home base as Brașov or Sighișoara (it's farther from Transylvania's main sights), Sibiu is more appealing in its own right. It's just the right size to be interesting yet still manageable (pop. 150,000), and the creaky, cobbled, atmospheric, and mostly traffic-free city center is a delightful place to simply hang out.

Visiting Sibiu: The atmospheric Upper Town core consists of three interlocking squares, each with a different personality:

The aptly named **Grand Square** (Piața Mare) dominates an inviting and wide-open expanse fronted by stately municipal buildings (climb the Council Tower for sweeping views over town). **Small Square** (Piața Mică) is quaint, lined with al fresco cafés and a double-decker street plan that offers fine views from the "Liar's Bridge." And **Huet Square** (Piața Huet) is dominated by the gigantic German Protestant church—a reminder of Sibiu's strong Saxon pedigree.

From Grand Square, a pedestrian street called **Strada Nicolae Bălcescu** bursts with life as it proceeds several blocks south through the city center. Where the traffic-free zone ends, turn left and follow Strada Cetății along a tranquil park that delineates the former moat—passing three stout fortified brick **towers** that stand as bold reminders of Sibiu's militaristic past.

Beyond simply strolling its tidy core, Sibiu has some low-impact sightseeing options. Its giant, Neo-Byzantine-style ▲ **Holy Trinity Cathedral** is one of the country's most impressive Romanian Orthodox churches. The ▲ **Brukenthal Museum** collects a wealth of both Romanian and European artwork (www.brukenthalmuseum.ro). And ASTRA, a Romanian literature and culture society, operates several museums of its own, including one

ROMANIA

of the country's best ▲ **open-air folk museums** on the outskirts of town (www.muzeulastra.ro).

Sleeping in Sibiu: There are plenty of guesthouses to choose from. I slept well at **$$ Huet Residence** (www.huet-residence.ro).

▲▲Corvin Castle (Castelul Corvinilor; a.k.a. Hunyadi/ Hunedoara Castle)

Corvin Castle may be the most visually striking reminder that Transylvania was part of Hungary for most of its history. This is the home castle of János Hunyadi, the hero of the 15th-century fight against the Ottomans, and his son, Mátyás Corvinus, who became the only Hungarian king in more than 600 years of foreign rule (see page 615). With a certain "Hogwarts Gothic" quality, Corvin is also one of the most picturesque castles in a country where picturesque castles are a forté. When Budapest was building a faux-"Transylvanian" castle in their City Park in 1896, they modeled it after this one (see page 608). The evocative but mostly-empty castle sits unceremoniously along a gritty road on the outskirts of Hunedoara—about an hour and a half drive west of Sibiu (www.castelulcorvinilor.ro). While striking, it's worth the long detour only if you're a connoisseur of Transylvanian castles, Hungarian history, or both (or if you're driving from central Transylvania to Timișoara or Hungary).

Nearby: The area around Hunedoara has one of Romania's highest concentrations of **"Gypsy palaces"**: over-the-top-osten-

tatious mansions built just outside city limits by powerful members of the Roma community. Striking and controversial (and rumored to be funded through illegal activity), these are worth a fascinating drive-by to appreciate one more facet of the Romanian Roma experience. Be discreet about stopping or taking photos—the people living here often don't appreciate unwanted attention. Several "Gypsy palaces" line up along road 687, at the south end of Hunedoara, on the way to Călan (beginning just east of Corvin Castle).

Cluj-Napoca

Cluj-Napoca—or simply Cluj (kloozh) for short—is Transylvania's de facto capital (pop. 324,000) and a major center of culture, universities, and business. While the compact historical core has its charm, the busy sprawl of Cluj feels like an urban jungle—making it challenging to appreciate on a quick visit. For that reason, Cluj ranks lower on my list of "must-visit" Transylvanian cities. But if you go, you'll find a congested historic core that's worth a stroll.

Visiting Cluj: The city's landmarks reflect its multiethnic heritage—like Transylvania itself, it's a mix of Romanian, Hungarian, and German. Towering high above Unity Square (Piața Unirii) is the Gothic steeple of ▲ **St. Michael's Church,** built by Hungarian Catholics in the 15th century. Nearby stands a bulky statue of the Hungarian king **Mátyás Corvinus**—honoring Cluj's

substantial Hungarian-speaking minority (about 15 percent of the population). But just a couple of blocks to the east—as if to one-up the Hungarians—stands the skinny, slotted dome of the ▲ **Dormition of the Theotokos Romanian Orthodox Cathedral,** and out front, a statue of Avram Iancu, a proud Romanian who fought *against* Hungarian influence in Transylvania. Just to the northwest, between the Old Town and the river, is Cluj's lively and inviting **Central Park,** with beautifully-restored pavilions and the city's cutting-edge soccer stadium. After hours, youthful Cluj is busy with nightlife. The university zone to the west—called Hașdeu—is edgy. Mellower and more inviting is the **Museum Square** (Piața Muzeului) pedestrian zone, tucked in the heart of the Old Town.

MARAMUREȘ

Maramureș (mah-rah-MOO-rehsh) is Europe's most traditional corner. Here you'll find time-warp locals farming fields, getting

around by horse cart, and living agrarian—almost biblical—lifestyles, seemingly oblivious to the modern world just over the hills. This is the place in Romania to savor being far off the beaten track: Slow down, go for a lazy drive, pull over at anything that catches your eye, and marvel at the simplicity of it all. While it takes some effort to reach, Maramureș is well worth the effort for those who want to see a real, living open-air folk museum.

Orientation: To the north of sprawling Transylvania, the tourist's Maramureș is small: a skinny sliver of land between the Gutâi Mountains and the Ukrainian border. From Transylvania, it's a long drive up to the main city of Maramureș—dreary Baia

ROMANIA

Mare, with Europe's third-tallest smokestack looming overhead—and even then, you're still more than an hour away, over a twisty mountain pass. The best corner of Maramureș clusters around the town of Sighetu Marmației.

Local Guide: Particularly here in Maramureș, a good local guide is an essential investment to get the most of out of your time (and to make it worth the long drive here). Knowledgeable **Teo Ivanciuc** excels at putting you in touch with traditional lifestyles, and giving them meaning (www.maramurestour.com, teofilivanciuc@yahoo.com).

Sleeping in Maramureș: Expect rustic but cozy accommodations. While Sighetu Marmației has some big hotels, for the full Maramureș experience, stay in the countryside. Local guide **$ Teo Ivanciuc,** listed above, rents rooms (www.amizadil.com)—or can refer you to other locals who do. For a bigger but still-traditional option, try **$$ Hotel Grădina Morii,** on the outskirts of Sighetu Marmației (www.hotelgradinamorii.ro).

Sighetu Marmației

With close to 40,000 inhabitants, "Sighet" (SEE-geht, as locals call it) is the area's main town. Many locals don't even call it Sighet—they just call it "the town." With a scruffy main square (which hosts a daily farmers market) and dreary apartment blocks, Sighet is not particularly attractive—but you can't avoid passing through several times on your visit to Maramureș.

Sighet was the birthplace of the Holocaust survivor, author, and Nobel Peace Prize laureate **Elie Wiesel** (whose novel *Night* is a definitive work of Holocaust literature). His birthplace—near a synagogue that the Nazis burned down in 1944 (now rebuilt)—is today a modest museum, with informational signs and a few artifacts. Wiesel lived in Sighet until he was taken away to Auschwitz at age 16.

Thanks to its remote location—closer to Budapest than to Bucharest—communist-era Sighet became a sort of "Siberia of Romania." It was the site of the Securitate's main prison, where dissenters, intellectuals, clergy, journalists, and political opponents of the regime were sent to rot, far from mainstream society. Many died. Today, the prison houses the ▲▲ **Memorial for the Victims of Communism,** with a modern, powerful, well-presented exhibit detailing the communist period in Romania (www.memorialsighet.ro).

Sighet also has a good **Village Museum** (with wooden houses) and an **Ethnographic Museum,** but you don't really need them—Maramureș itself is the best sight.

▲▲▲Maramureş Joyriding

Maramureş is a rolling, pastoral landscape speckled with haystacks. Go for an aimless drive and just take it all in. Thanks to its rug-

ged landscape and its great distance from Bucharest, Maramureş avoided communist farm collectivization—so people still tend their small family plots by hand. Horse carts outnumber cars. Men in overalls and funny little straw hats pile hay onto their wooden wagons. Women wear big, puffy skirts just above the knee, babushkas on their heads, and baskets laden with heavy goods on their backs. While not ignorant of the modern world, Maramureş feels like Europe's Amish Country, where centuries-old ways endure. It's not for the benefit of tourists—it's just their way of life.

Locals are very open and welcoming to curious travelers. This is an ideal place to be an amateur anthropologist...simply observe the way people live. (While you can do this on your own, it's easier and more rewarding with a local guide.)

Wander through any village and peek into family compounds. Each one is marked with a huge, ceremonial wooden gateway—

just big enough for a hay-loaded horse cart to trot through. (These gateways show off the Romanian knack for flaunting whatever wealth you have... even if it's not much. Another status symbol is hanging colorful pots from tree branches.) The gates are carved with a whole iconography of local symbols: starburst (pagan sun worship), wolf teeth (protection), bull horns (masculinity), leaves (nature), and—most importantly—the "rope of life" motif, a helix-like design suggesting the continuity of life from generation to generation. Inside each courtyard, you'll usually see—in addition to the main house—a humble barn with a paddock, a garden patch, and an old-fashioned, hand-pulled well.

You'll be surprised how often you'll be invited inside. Many Maramureş residents are eager to show curious visitors their humble homes. Every house has a "show room," where people collect their nicest belongings: colorful piles of blankets, pillows, and so on (often from the dowry of the woman of the house). This room is reserved exclusively for guests, while the family spends most of their time in much humbler surroundings.

It's fine to simply wander around the area and see what you may stumble upon, but here are some areas you could focus on:

The little **Cosău River Valley**—especially the stretch between Călineşti and Budeşti (each with a wooden church)—is a picturesque throwback. The rushing river powers all manner of medieval industry. You'll see carpet laundries, where wooden canals channel water into a naturally-powered spin cycle. People use the flowing water to operate brandy stills, making their own plum firewater *(horinca)*. Grist mills grind grains into both polenta and animal feed. And tucked deep inside family compounds, people spin wool into yarn and use creaky old looms to weave it into a loose fabric. That fabric is then taken to a fulling mill, where water-powered wooden hammers pound and pound and pound, mashing it into a dense, heavy material that's used in the traditional winter costume. (Gheorghe Opris, in the village of Sârbi, operates a mill that does all of these things; you can try dropping by, but as he speaks no English, it's better to visit with a local guide.)

For a scenic drive, take the **high road** between Călineşti and Văleni, offering high-altitude views over the rolling farm fields of Maramureş—and, if you're lucky, hardworking farmers making haystacks.

From Văleni, you can coast down into **Bârsana,** which has the busy wood workshop of Toader Bârsan. Out in the courtyard, young lumberjacks artfully carve new wooden gates that look old. Toader himself sits on the stoop, hand-carving trinkets and wearing his distinctive little Maramureş straw hat. He loves to explain how he once met Hillary Clinton. (The wooden Bârsana monastery complex—described later—is at the edge of this town.)

Horse Market: Ocna Şugatag, a larger, functional town sitting on a plateau, is fairly dull—except on Thursday mornings, when the weekly livestock market makes it feel like a 17th-century car show. The people-watching is marvelous.

▲▲▲Merry Cemetery (Cimitirul Vesel)

A 30-minute drive west of Sighet is one of Romania's top cultural treasures: the Merry Cemetery. In 1935, woodcarver Stan Ioan Pătraş—inspired by a long-forgotten local tradition for colorful grave markers—began filling the Săpânţa village cemetery with a forest of technicolor memorials. Today there are more than 1,300—each one

with a pointy roof to protect from the rain, a painting of the departed doing something they loved (or in the moment of death), and a whimsical poem. It's all painted a cheery blue to match the heavens where the souls are headed. The Merry Cemetery is a poignant celebration of each individual's life, a chronicle of village history, and an irreverent raspberry in the face of death.

Although the cemetery is dubbed "merry," many of the poems are downright morose. Tales of young lives cut short by tragic accidents, warriors mowed down in the prime of life, or people who simply never found happiness are a reminder that death, and life, are sometimes nothing to be cheerful about.

Even if you can't read the poems, the images speak volumes: Weaver. Loved bikes. Television repairman. Soldier. Hit by a car. Struck by lightning. Nagging mother-in-law.

Tucked behind the church, you can find the grave of the artist who started it all, Stan Ioan Pătraş, who died in 1977. His apprentices carry on the work today.

Nearby: Across the highway (and a half-mile back toward Sighet), **Săpânţa Peri Monastery Church** towers 250 feet tall. Completed in 2003, the church demonstrates that in Maramureş, wood remains as popular as it ever was. Inside, the technical mastery of Maramureş woodworkers is on display: chunky but precisely-cut dovetailing keeps massive walls firmly in place, and the artistic shinglework cascades tidily from peak to eaves.

▲▲Wooden Churches

In Maramureş, surrounded by thickly forested mountains, wood is king. And some of the finest wooden churches in Europe are right here. These centuries-old structures resemble Norwegian stave churches, but with less flair. They are graceful wooden pagodas with eye-pleasing lines angling up to the heavens. Inside, faded "wood frescoes" look like silly-puttied Sunday comics pages, stretched out and plastered against the wall—illustrating a medieval interpretation of Christianity. Dozens of these churches are scattered around the region, but most are generally closed to the public (local guides can usually get the key). Some of the churches are modern, including the **Săpânța Peri** monastery church (near the Merry Cemetery, described previously) and a striking ensemble of wooden ecclesiastical buildings at the **Bârsana** monastery complex (about a 30-minute drive southeast of Sighet).

BUCOVINA

Within the large, eastern Romanian region of Moldavia sits the smaller sub-region called Bucovina (BOO-koh-vee-nah)—known for its traditional folk life, its rolling Carpathian foothills, and, most of all, its glorious painted monasteries. Unfortunately, Bucovina presents a time-consuming detour for travelers connecting the core of Transylvania with the folk-culture treasures of Maramureș. And if you're very tight on time, Bucovina is skippable—since there's relatively little to see in this region beyond the monasteries. But if you can make the time, the monasteries are worth the trip.

Local Tours: If you make a special trip to Bucovina, invest in a tour to connect the painted monasteries (and other cultural sights) and bring them to life. **Hello Bucovina,** well-run by Ciprian "Chip" Slemco, offers a range of well-designed tours, from a quick spin to the monasteries to multiday routes connecting Bucovina, the rest of Moldavia, and neighboring countries (www.hellobucovina.com).

▲▲Painted Monasteries of Bucovina

Remote and feisty Bucovina sits on the cusp of cultures. It's just outside the Carpathian Mountains, squeezed between two would-be oppressors: The Hungarians of Transylvania to the west, and the Ottomans to the east. So maybe it's no surprise that this stubbornly traditional region chose to cling fast to its faith in the rough-and-tumble 15th and 16th centuries, erecting dozens of fortified and vividly decorated monasteries. And today, many

of the churches still survive—their outside walls slathered in colorful Byzantine-style fresco murals of saints and Bible stories.

Background: The tradition of painted monasteries began

during the reign of Prince Stephen the Great of Moldavia (1433-1504)—a contemporary of Vlad the Impaler of Wallachia, King Mátyás Corvinus of Hungary, and Sultan Mehmet the Conqueror of the Ottoman Empire. It was a frightening time, as big egos struggled for control of the Romanian lands—but Stephen the Great stubbornly asserted his Romanian Orthodox faith. According to legend, to celebrate his many military victories, Stephen would climb a mountain, shoot arrows into the rolling hills, and build a monastery where each arrow fell. Stephen's son, Petru Rareș (1487-1546), was inspired by Renaissance frescoes on a visit to Florence, and decided to decorate the monasteries with a similar technique. Their Moldavian subjects were very poor, very religious, and eager to do God's work for low wages. And most people were illiterate, making the vivid illustrations a powerful educational tool. Of the dozens of monasteries built by Stephen the Great, nine still survive.

While each church has its own unique flourishes, all of them are wrapped in glorious, exceptionally well-preserved frescoes. You'll see row after row of saintly icons, local religious figures, ancient philosophers, Bible stories, lush visions of heaven, terrifying depictions of hell, and epic historical scenes. Each church has its own distinctive coloring (for example, "Voroneț blue").

Each church has a giant *Last Judgment* **mural** on its western wall. These are packed with symbolism that's worth disentangling. (While this works best at Voroneț, the basic composition is standard across churches.) Striping the mural are five horizontal tiers (top to bottom):

1. At the top sits God, flanked by 12 signs of the zodiac—merging Christian and pagan beliefs, driving home the eternal nature of God, and evoking the 12 Apostles.

2. Floating in a celestial bubble is Jesus—in his "furious vengeance" mode. He's flanked by Mary, John the Baptist, and pews with 12 seated Apostles (with other saintly figures in the cheap seats behind them). From Jesus flows a river of flames that spreads out toward the lower-right corner...and the open mouth of a hideous, multiheaded Beelzebub.

3. A dove (the Holy Spirit) sits on the Throne of Judgment, flanked by Adam and Eve—who committed the original sin, and are now eyewitnesses to how it all turns out. To the right—cut off from the holiness by Jesus' river of flames—are condemned pagans

(depicted as the Moldavians' historical enemies: Jews, Ottomans, Tatars, and Armenians). At the front of this pack, Moses gestures frantically with the Ten Commandments, hoping for some last-minute conversions. Meanwhile, to the left of the river of flames stand smug clumps of righteous believers: prophets, bishops, theologians, and so on.

4. Below the Holy Spirit, the hand of God holds the scales of judgment. Drama ensues, as angels and devils pile good and bad deeds on the scale in a struggle for the man's soul. On the right, hideous beasts prowl a barren landscape where souls emerge from tombs—hoping to be rescued by the angels. Below them, a female figure lovingly cradles a ship—representing salvation even for those lost at sea. Meanwhile, on the left end of this tier is a saintly legion, halos aglow.

5. Finally, along the bottom level, we see (from left to right) the saved, kicking back in the garden of paradise (look for Mary, the archangels Gabriel and Michael, Abraham, Isaac, Jacob, the face of Moses' burning bush, and the cross-toting thief who repented as he was crucified next to Jesus); the righteous waiting to enter heaven, led by St. Peter—about to use his key to open that golden door; and King David playing a traditional Moldavian instrument (one of many subtle references to local culture) in a mountainous terrain, flanked by the deaths of a righteous man (saved by angels) and a sinner (skewered by devils).

Elsewhere on the church, you'll typically see a *Tree of Jesse,* tracing Jesus' family tree from Mary all the way back to Jesse and King David. Another standard Orthodox theme is the *Deesis,* with Christ Pantocrator ("Ruler of All") enthroned in heaven and surrounded by saints. And many churches illustrate the Christian defense of Constantinople (today's Istanbul) during the Persian siege of 626. The "Persians" are dressed in Turkish  clothes...a not-so-subtle reminder that these monasteries were built as bastions of Christendom against the rising tide of Islam.

You'll also see lots of unofficial decoration. Bucovina's painted monasteries were a popular destination in the Romantic Age of the late 19th century, when Bucovina was part of the Habsburg Empire. Mostly German-speaking tourists scratched their own initials into the colorful plaster—century-old-graffiti that's still readable.

Assuming there are no services going on, you can enter the church itself. People enter at the porch—traditionally, the unbaptized could go no farther. Inside, each church is divided into three

sections, representing the holy trinity. First comes the pro-nous (pro-nave—sometimes outside on smaller churches), where regular people worshipped. Then comes the nous (nave), with benches for VIPs and a fresco of the donor who built the church. Finally there's the altar area, with the iconostasis. Each section is richly decorated with golden icons and colorful frescoes.

You may see a priest or nun walking around the courtyard, knocking on a piece of wood with a mallet. This means it's time for worship—and for tourists to leave the church interior.

Visiting the Painted Monasteries: The best painted monasteries are near the town of Gura Humorului (pop. 12,000). On a quick, targeted visit, you can simply visit Voroneț (the best one overall) and Humor—each about a 10-minute drive from Gura Humorului (in opposite directions). With more time, do a loop through the hills north of Gura Humorului to also see Moldovița and Sucevița. I've listed these in the order of an all-day loop.

Voroneț Monastery (voh-roh-NETS, from 1487) is the most striking and most famous—sometimes called the "Sistine Chapel of the East." Its vivid frescoes—with their distinctive "Voroneț blue" hue—are sumptuous and richly detailed. Voroneț also has the finest *Last Judgment* fresco. You could stare at it for hours, picking out details (for starters, see "Background," earlier). If

you see only one painted monastery, make it this one.

Moldovița Monastery (MOHL-doh-veet-sah, from 1532) is less crowded, filling a serene courtyard, and has art nearly as impressive as Voroneț's. Moldovița has a particularly evocative fresco showing the siege of Constantinople; a fine *Tree of Jesse* mural; and the most evident examples of "graffiti" scratched into the plaster by 19th-century tourists (especially under the porch).

Between Moldovița and Sucevița, you'll twist up and over a dramatic mountain pass with great views.

Sucevița Monastery (SOO-cheh-veet-sah) was the final painted monastery built (1581), with the best-preserved fortifications and the biggest, richest interior. Even more than the others, from the outside it feels more like a fortress than a monastery. The frescoes include a particularly exquisite *Ladder to Paradise* (or *Jacob's Ladder*): The angled ladder (where each rung represents a holy virtue required to reach heaven) slices the composition in half, with a heavenly host of angels at the top and, below, grotesque beasts torturing sinners who missed a rung. If you're in shape, hike up the steep hill behind for a fine view down over the monastery, the valley, and the wooded hills.

Just west of Sucevița, and on the way to Humor, you'll pass through the workaday town of Marginea—famous for its many black pottery workshops.

Humor Monastery (a.k.a. Humorului, hoo-moo-ROO-lee, from 1530) is sleepier and lower-impact, with a lone fortified tower that stands taller than the church itself. Its *Last Judgment* fresco curls up under the roofline of the porch, protected from the elements.

Sleeping near the Painted Monasteries: The handiest home base is the functional crossroads town of Gura Humorului, which has several big hotels and smaller guesthouses. To sleep in the countryside, try **$ Casa Bunicilor,** a rustic but comfortable retreat a few minutes' drive out of town, near the Humor Monastery (www.casabunicilor.com).

Nearby: Suceava (soo-cheh-AH-vah, pop. 90,000), Bucovina's largest city, is about 25 miles to the east. It's workable as a home base, but its sparse sights (an empty-feeling old fortress and a mediocre open-air folk museum) and its distance from the monasteries make it less appealing than Gura Humorului.

UNDERSTANDING YUGOSLAVIA

If you're struggling to understand the complicated breakup of Yugoslavia, read this admittedly oversimplified, as-impartial-as-possible history to get you started. (For a more complete version, see www.ricksteves.com/yugo.)

The Balkan Peninsula—between the Adriatic and the Black Sea, basically running from Hungary to Greece—has always been a crossroads of cultures, divided by a series of cultural, ethnic, and religious fault lines. The most important religious influences were **Western Christianity** (i.e., Roman Catholicism, introduced by Charlemagne and later championed by the Austrian Habsburgs), **Eastern Orthodox Christianity** (from the Byzantine Empire), and **Islam** (from the Ottomans).

Two major historical factors made the Balkans what they are today: The first was the **split of the Roman Empire** in the fourth century AD, dividing the Balkans down the middle into Roman Catholic (west) and Byzantine Orthodox (east)—roughly along today's Bosnian-Serbian border. The second was the **invasion of the Ottomans** (from today's Turkey) in the 14th century, which kicked off five centuries of Islamic influence in Bosnia-Herzegovina and Serbia, further dividing the Balkans into Christian (north) and Muslim (south).

Because of these and other events, several distinct ethnic identities emerged. The major ethnicities of Yugoslavia are all considered "South Slavs." They're all descended from the same ancestors and speak closely-related languages, but are distinguished by their religious practices. Roman Catholic **Croats** and **Slovenes** are found mostly west of the Dinaric Mountains (Croats along the Adriatic coast and Slovenes farther north, in the Alps); Orthodox Christian **Serbs** live mostly east of the Dinaric range; and Muslim **Bosniaks** (whose ancestors converted to Islam under the

Ottomans) live mostly in the Dinaric Mountains. The region also has several smaller ethnic groups: the Slavic **Montenegrins** and **Macedonians,** plus **Hungarians** (concentrated in the north) and **Albanians** (concentrated in Kosovo and the south). The groups overlapped a lot—which is exactly why the breakup of Yugoslavia was so contentious.

The lands of Yugoslavia were shuttled between various kingdoms and empires for much of their history, but by the late 19th century, most of the area was part of the Austro-Hungarian Empire. When that empire split apart at the end of World War I, the various mostly-Slavic groups in the region formed a new country: Yugoslavia ("Land of the South Slavs"). The union was almost immediately contentious, as various groups—especially Serbs and Croats—struggled to take control. By the dawn of World War II, it was already clear that Yugoslavia was a troubled proposition.

The seeds of the 1990s interethnic conflict were planted in World War II. Yugoslavia was invaded by Nazi Germany, then chopped up into puppet states for the Axis Powers. Some groups took advantage of changing circumstances in wartime Yugoslavia to exact revenge on their former compatriots. In occupied Croatia, the puppet Ustaše party imprisoned and executed large numbers of Serbs. In the eastern mountains, a Serbian royalist paramilitary group called the Četniks were every bit as brutal against Croats and Bosniaks. A third group—the homegrown Partisan Army—fought against Nazis, Ustaše, and Četniks to secure freedom for Yugoslavia. Unlike the other "Eastern European" countries, Yugoslavia was not liberated by the Soviet Union. This unique status allowed it to determine its own path after the war.

After the short but rocky Yugoslav union between the World Wars, it seemed that no one could hold the southern Slavs together in a single nation. But one man could, and did: Partisan war hero Josip Broz, who is better known by his code name, Tito. With a Slovene for a mother, a Croat for a father, a Serb for a wife, and a home in Belgrade, Tito was a true Yugoslav. Tito had a compelling vision that this fractured union of the South Slavs could function (see the sidebar).

Tito's new incarnation of Yugoslavia aimed for a more equitable division of powers. It was made up of six republics, each dominated by one ethnic group: **Croatia, Slovenia, Serbia, Bosnia-Herzegovina, Montenegro,** and **Macedonia.** Within Serbia, Tito set up two autonomous provinces, each one an enclave for an ethnicity that was a minority in greater Yugoslavia: Albanians in **Kosovo** (to the south) and Hungarians in **Vojvodina** (to the north). By allowing these two provinces some degree of independence, Tito hoped they would balance the political clout of Serbia, preventing a single republic from dominating the union.

While each republic had a measure of self-rule, the union was carefully overseen by President-for-Life Tito. Tito respected—and even celebrated—the diversity of his union, but he placed Yugoslav unity above all. He said that the borders between the republics should be "like white lines in a marble column."

Tito's Yugoslavia was communist, but it wasn't Soviet communism. He refused to formally join either the Warsaw Pact or NATO, and ingeniously played the East and the West against each other. Economically, Tito's vision was for a "third way," somewhere between communism and capitalism. While large industries were collectivized, small businesses were also permitted. Though Yugoslavs could not become really rich, through hard work it was possible to attain modest wealth to buy a snazzy car, a vacation home, Western imports, and other niceties. Yugoslavia was also the most free and open of the communist states. Tourists (from both East and West) flocked here for vacation, and Yugoslavs could travel to far more places abroad than could residents of the Eastern Bloc.

Tito died in 1980, and before long, the fragile union he had

Tito (1892-1980)

The Republic of Yugoslavia was the vision of a single man, who made it reality. Josip Broz—better known as Marshal Tito—presided over the most peaceful and prosperous era in this region's long and troubled history. Three decades after his death, Tito is beloved by many of his former subjects...and yet, he was a communist dictator who dealt brutally with his political enemies. This love-him-and-hate-him autocrat is one of the most complex figures in the history of this very complicated land.

Josip Broz was born in 1892 to a Slovenian mother and a Cro-atian father in the northern part of today's Croatia (then part of the Austro-Hungarian Empire). After growing up in the rural countryside, he was trained as a metalworker. He was drafted into the Austro-Hungarian army, went to fight on the Eastern Front during World War I, and was captured and sent to Russia as a prisoner of war. Freed by Bolsheviks, Broz fell in with the Communist Revolution...and never looked back.

At war's end, Broz returned home to the newly independent Yugoslavia, where he worked alongside the Soviets to build a national Communist Party. As a clandestine communist operative, he adopted the code name he kept for the rest of his life: Tito. Some believe this was a Spanish name he picked up while participating in that country's civil war, while others half-joke that the name came from Tito's authoritarian style: *"Ti, to!"* means "You, do this!" But one thing's clear: In this land where a person's name instantly identifies his ethnicity, "Tito" is ethnically neutral.

When the Nazis occupied Yugoslavia, Tito raised and commanded a homegrown, communist Partisan Army. Through guerilla tactics, Tito's clever maneuvering, and sheer determination, the Partisans liberated their country. And because they did so mostly without support from the USSR, Yugoslavia was able to set its own postwar course.

The war hero Tito quickly became the "president for life" of postwar Yugoslavia. But even as he introduced communism to his country, he retained some elements of a free-market economy—firmly declining to become a satellite of Moscow. He also pioneered the worldwide Non-Aligned Movement, joining with nations in Africa, the Middle East, Asia, and Latin America in refusing to ally with the US or USSR. Stubborn but suitably cautious, Tito expertly walked a tightrope between East and West.

There was a dark side to Tito. In the early years of his regime, Tito resorted to brutal, Stalin-esque tactics to assert his control. Immediately following World War II, the Partisan Army massacred tens of thousands of soldiers who had supported the Nazis. Then Tito systematically arrested, tried, tortured, or executed those who did not accept his new regime. Survivors whose lives were ruined during this reign of terror will never forgive Tito for what he did.

But once he gained full control, Tito moved away from strong-arm tactics and into a warm-and-fuzzy era of Yugoslav brotherhood. Tito believed that the disparate peoples of Yugoslavia could live in harmony. For example, every Yugoslav male had to serve in the People's Army, and Tito made sure that each unit was a microcosm of the complete Yugoslavia—with equal representation from each ethnic group. Yugoslavs from diverse backgrounds were required to work together and socialize—as a result, they became friends. He also worked toward economic diversification: Yugoslav tanks, some of the best in the world, were made of parts assembled in five different republics.

Tito's reign is a case study in the power of the cult of personality. Rocks on hillsides throughout Yugoslavia were rearranged to spell "TITO," and his portrait hung over every family's dinner table. Each of the six republics renamed one of its cities for their dictator. The main street and square in virtually every town were renamed for Tito. Each year, young people would embark on a months-long, Olympics-style relay, from each corner of Yugoslavia, to present a ceremonial baton to Tito on his official birthday (May 25). Tito also had vacation villas in all of Yugoslavia's most beautiful areas, including Lake Bled, the Brijuni Islands, and the Montenegrin coast. People sang patriotic anthems to their Druža (Comrade) Tito: "Comrade Tito, we pledge an oath to you."

Tito died in 1980 in a Slovenian hospital. His body went on a grand tour of the Yugoslav capitals: Ljubljana, Zagreb, Sarajevo, and Belgrade, where he was buried before hundreds of thousands of mourners, including more heads of state than at any other funeral in history. At his request, his tomb was placed in the greenhouse where he enjoyed spending time.

The genuine outpouring of grief at Tito's death might seem unusual for a man who was, on paper, an authoritarian communist dictator. But even today, many former Yugoslavs—especially Slovenes and Bosniaks—believe that his iron-fisted government was a necessary evil that kept the country strong and united. The eventual balance Tito struck between communism and capitalism, and between the competing interests of his ethnically diverse nation, led to this region's most stable and prosperous era. In a recent poll in Slovenia, Tito had a higher approval rating than any present-day politician, and 80 percent of Slovenes said they had a positive impression of him.

And yet, the Yugoslavs' respect for their former leader was not enough to keep them together. Tito's death began a long, slow chain reaction that led to the end of Yugoslavia. As the decades pass, the old joke seems more and more appropriate: Yugoslavia had eight distinct peoples in six republics, with five languages, three religions (Orthodox Christian, Catholic, and Muslim), and two alphabets (Roman and Cyrillic), but only one Yugoslav—Tito.

held together started to unravel. The breakup began in the late 1980s in the autonomous province of Kosovo, with squabbles between the Serb minority and the ethnic-Albanian majority. Serbian politician Slobodan Milošević traveled to Kosovo to rouse his Serb comrades, which alarmed some of the other republics. When Milošević-led Serbia annexed Kosovo soon after, and negotiations among the Yugoslav republics broke down, Croatia and Slovenia decided it was time to declare independence (both on June 25, 1991). Small, relatively homogenous Slovenia weathered a brief 10-day skirmish (see page 717), while Croatia—which had a large Serb minority—was pulled into a gruesome war lasting several years. Bosnia-Herzegovina declared its independence a few months later. But, because that republic was by far Yugoslavia's most ethnically diverse (with large populations of Muslim Bosniaks, Serbs, and Croats), its separation was hotly contested—plunging Bosnia into a horrifying four years of guerrilla warfare, medieval-style sieges, systematic rape, and ethnic cleansing.

Peace accords in 1995 brought an end to most of the hostilities throughout Yugoslavia, establishing the borders of Croatia and Bosnia that still exist today. Over the next several years, Slobodan Milošević and others accused of war crimes were arrested and tried by an international tribunal at The Hague, Netherlands (though Milošević died behind bars before a verdict was handed down). Later, additional parts of the former Yugoslavia split off, leaving behind seven independent nations where once was one: Croatia, Slovenia, Bosnia-Herzegovina, Montenegro, Serbia, Macedonia, and Kosovo.

Peace has reigned in these countries for more than two decades. The physical scars of war have mostly been repaired. And, considering that hospitality has been a forte of this region since long before the age of Yugoslavia, outside visitors feel welcome and safe—and are impressed at the candor of the people they meet, who are often willing to share their own wartime experiences. But, understandably, the psychological scars will take the longest to heal. Tensions still persist between formerly warring groups.

Thoughtful visitors to the former Yugoslavia grapple with trying to understand what happened here just a generation ago. Many find it hard to get an impartial take on the current situation, or even on historical "facts." A very wise Bosniak once told me, "Listen to all three sides—Muslim, Serb, and Croat. Then decide for yourself what you think." A Serb told me a similar local saying: "You have to look at the apple from all sides."

PRACTICALITIES

This chapter covers the practical skills of European travel: how to get tourist information, pay for things, sightsee efficiently, find good-value accommodations, eat affordably but well, use technology wisely, and get between destinations smoothly. For more information on these topics, see www.ricksteves.com/travel-tips.

Tourist Information

National tourist offices are a wealth of information (see websites on the next page). Before your trip, get the free general information packet and request any specifics you may want (such as regional and city maps and festival schedules).

In Eastern Europe, a good first stop in every town is generally the tourist information office (abbreviated **TI** in this book). You'll find local TIs are usually well-organized and always have an English-speaking staff. While many TIs in Eastern Europe are still primarily government-run—and therefore have the sole priority of helping you have a better trip—others are in cahoots with local, private tour operators, which tends to color their advice. I find TIs a great place to flip through brochures, pick up a free map, and ask basic questions. But I supplement what I learn there with advice from my hotel, other local contacts, and online sources. TIs also offer information on public transit (including bus and train schedules), walking tours, special events, and nightlife. Some TIs have information on the entire country or at least the region, so try to pick up maps and printed information for destinations you'll be visiting later in your trip.

Czech Tourist Office: www.czechtourism.com
Polish Tourist Office: www.poland.travel
Hungarian Tourist Office: https://hellohungary.com
Slovenian Tourist Office: www.slovenia.info
Austrian Tourist Office: www.austria.info
Slovakian Tourist Office: www.slovakia.travel

Travel Tips

PRACTICALITIES

Emergency and Medical Help: In all of the countries in this book, dial 112 for any emergency service—ambulance, police, or fire—from a mobile phone or landline. Operators, who in most countries speak English, will deal with your request or route you to the right emergency service. If you get sick, do as the locals do and go to a pharmacist for advice. Or ask at your hotel for help—they'll know the nearest medical and emergency services.

Theft or Loss: To replace a passport, you'll need to go in person to the appropriate embassy or consulate (see next). If your credit and debit cards disappear, cancel and replace them (see "Damage Control for Lost Cards," later in this chapter). File a police report, either on the spot or within a day or two; you'll need it to submit an insurance claim for lost or stolen rail passes or travel gear, and it can help with replacing your passport or credit and debit cards. For more information, see www.ricksteves.com/help.

US Embassies and Consulates: For additional information, visit the US State Department's website, travel.state.gov.

Austria—Boltzmanngasse 16, Vienna, tel. 01/313-390; consular services at Parkring 12a, Vienna, passport services available Mon-Fri 8:00-11:30, tel. 01/313-397-535, http://at.usembassy.gov.

Czech Republic—Tržiště 15, Prague, emergency passport services available Mon-Fri 8:00-11:30 (by appointment only), tel. 257-022-000, http://cz.usembassy.gov.

Hungary—Szabadság tér 12, Budapest, passport services available Mon-Thu 8:00-12:00 & 13:00-16:00, Fri 8:00-12:00, tel. 1/475-4400, https://hu.usembassy.gov/.

Poland—Aleje Ujazdowskie 29, Warsaw, appointments required for routine services, tel. 022-504-2000, http://pl.usembassy.gov; also a US Consulate in Kraków at ulica Stolarska 9, appointments required for routine services, tel. 012-424-5100, https://pl.usembassy.gov/embassy-consulate/krakow.

Slovakia—Hviezdoslavovo námestie 4, Bratislava, passport services available Mon-Fri 8:00-11:45 & 14:00-15:15, tel. 02/5443-0861, https://sk.usembassy.gov/.

Slovenia—Prešernova 31, Ljubljana, passport services available Mon-Fri 9:00-11:30 & 12:00-14:00, tel. 01/200-5500, https://si.usembassy.gov/.

Canadian Embassies and Consulates: For after-hours emergencies, Canadian citizens can call collect to the Foreign Services Office in Ottawa at 613/996-8885.

Austria—Laurenzerberg 2, Vienna, passport services available Mon-Fri 8:30-12:30 & 13:30-15:30, tel. 01/531-383-000, www.austria.gc.ca.

Czech Republic—Ve Struhách 95/2, Prague, passport services Mon-Thu 9:00-12:00, Fri and afternoons by appointment, tel. 272-101-800, www.czechrepublic.gc.ca.

Hungary—Ganz utca 12-14, Budapest, passport services available Mon-Thu 8:30-12:30 & 13:00-16:30, Fri 8:00-13:30, tel. 1/392-3360, www.hungary.gc.ca; also provides services for Bosnia-Herzegovina and Slovenia.

Poland—Ulica Jana Matejki 1-5, Warsaw, passport services available Mon-Fri 8:30-16:30, tel. 022-584-3100, www.poland.gc.ca.

Slovakia—Mostová 2, Bratislava, passport services available Mon-Fri 8:30-12:30 & 13:30-16:30, tel. 02/5920-4031.

Slovenia (consulate office)—Linhartova cesta 49a, Ljubljana; passport services available Mon, Wed, and Fri 8:00-12:00; tel. 01/252-4444, some services provided through Canadian Embassy in Budapest, Hungary (listed above).

Borders: All of the core countries in this book have officially joined the open-borders Schengen Agreement. That means that there are no border checks between any of these countries, or between them and Western European countries such as Germany, Austria, and Italy. You'll usually zip through the border without stopping, though in a few cases, you may need to stop briefly to flash a passport.

Non-Schengen countries (including Bosnia-Herzegovina, Montenegro, Bulgaria, Romania, and Croatia) still have traditional border checkpoints—you'll have to stop upon entering or exiting these countries. But whether traveling by car, train, or bus, you'll find that border crossings are generally a nonevent: Flash your passport, maybe wait a few minutes, and move on. Drivers may be asked to show proof of car insurance ("green card"), so be sure you have it when you pick up your rental car.

Even as border checkpoints fade, when you cross any interna-

PRACTICALITIES

tional border, you must still change currencies (in most cases) and postage stamps.

Time Zones: Most of the countries listed in this book are generally six/nine hours ahead of the East/West Coasts of the US. (Bulgaria and Romania are one hour ahead of the rest of these countries—that's seven/ten hours ahead of the East/West Coasts.) The exceptions are the beginning and end of Daylight Saving Time: Europe "springs forward" the last Sunday in March (two weeks after most of North America), and "falls back" the last Sunday in October (one week before North America). For a handy time converter, use the world clock app on your mobile phone or download one (see www.timeanddate.com/worldclock).

Weekends: Saturdays are virtually weekdays, but with earlier closing hours and no rush hour (though transportation connections can be less frequent than on weekdays). Sundays have the same pros and cons as they do for travelers in the US (special events, limited hours, banks and many shops generally closed, limited public-transportation options, no rush hour).

Watt's Up? Europe's electrical system is 220 volts, instead of North America's 110 volts. Most newer electronics (such as laptops, battery chargers, and hair dryers) convert automatically, so you won't need a converter, but you will need an adapter plug with two round prongs, sold inexpensively at travel stores in the US. Avoid bringing older appliances that don't automatically convert voltage; instead, buy a cheap replacement in Europe.

Discounts: Discounts for sights are generally not listed in this book. However, seniors (age 60 and over), youths under 18, and students and teachers with proper identification cards (www.isic.org) can get discounts at many sights—always ask. Some discounts are available only to European citizens.

Online Translation Tip: Google's Chrome browser instantly translates websites; Translate.google.com is also handy. The Google Translate app converts spoken or typed English into most European languages (and vice versa) and can also translate text it "reads" with your phone's camera.

Money

Here's my basic strategy for using money in Europe:
- Upon arrival, head for a cash machine (ATM) at the airport and withdraw some local currency, using a debit card with low international transaction fees.
- Pay for most purchases with your choice of cash or a credit card. You'll save money by minimizing your credit and debit card exchange fees. The trend is for bigger expenses to be paid

by credit card, but cash is still the standby for small purchases and tips.
• Keep your cards and cash safe in a money belt.

PLASTIC VERSUS CASH

Although credit cards are widely accepted in Europe, cash is sometimes the only way to pay for cheap food, taxis, tips, and local guides. Some businesses (especially smaller ones, such as B&Bs and mom-and-pop cafés and shops) may charge you extra for using a credit card—or might not accept credit cards at all. Having cash on hand helps you out of a jam if your card randomly doesn't work.

I use my credit card to book and pay for hotel reservations, to buy advance tickets for events or sights, and to cover most other expenses. It can also be smart to use plastic near the end of your trip, to avoid another visit to the ATM.

EXCHANGE RATES

Most of the countries in this book still use their traditional currencies. To date, only Slovenia, Austria, and Slovakia officially use the euro currency—and the others are unlikely to adopt it anytime soon. But even in countries that don't officially use the euro, many businesses (especially hotels) quote prices in euros anyway. (Even if they do, they typically prefer payment in the local currency.)

Here are the rough exchange rates for each country. I've also suggested a strategy for roughly converting prices into US dollars. Note that in some cases, I've favored easier-to-remember equations even if they offer less-precise conversions. For a more precise conversion, use the online tool at www.oanda.com/currency/converter.

1 euro (€) = about $1.20 (used in Slovenia, Austria, and Slovakia, and unofficially elsewhere). To convert prices in euros to dollars, add about 20 percent: €20 = about $24, €50 = about $60. Just like the dollar, one euro (€) is broken down into 100 cents. Coins range from €0.01 to €2, and bills from €5 to €200.

20 Czech crowns (*koruna*, Kč) = about $1. To roughly convert prices in crowns to dollars, divide by 2 and drop the last digit. So that tasty lunch for 160 Kč is about $8.

4 Polish złoty (zł, or PLN) = about $1. To calculate prices in dollars, divide by four: 80 zł = about $20.

275 Hungarian forints (Ft, or HUF) = about $1. To very roughly figure dollars, divide by three and drop the last two digits: 1,000 Ft = about $3 (actually $3.60).

So, that 20-zł Polish woodcarving is about $5, the 5,000-Ft Hungarian dinner is about $17, and the 2,000-Kč taxi ride through Prague is...uh-oh.

WHAT TO BRING

I pack the following and keep it all safe in my money belt.

Debit Card: Use this at ATMs to withdraw local cash.

Credit Card: Handy for bigger purchases (at hotels, shops, restaurants, travel agencies, car-rental agencies, and so on), payment machines, and ordering online.

Backup Card: Some travelers carry a third card (debit or credit; ideally from a different bank), in case one gets lost, demagnetized, eaten by a temperamental machine, or simply doesn't work.

A Stash of Cash: I always carry $100-200 (or €100-200) as a cash backup. A stash of cash comes in handy for emergencies, such as if your ATM card stops working.

What NOT to Bring: Resist the urge to buy local currencies before your trip or you'll pay the price in bad stateside exchange rates. Wait until you arrive to withdraw money. I've yet to see a European airport or major train station that didn't have plenty of ATMs.

BEFORE YOU GO

Use this pre-trip checklist.

Know your cards. Debit cards from any major US bank will work in any standard European bank's ATM (ideally, use a debit card with a Visa or MasterCard logo). As for credit cards, Visa and MasterCard are universal, American Express is less common, and Discover is unknown in Europe.

Know your PIN. Make sure you know the numeric, four-digit PIN for all of your cards, both debit and credit. Request it if you don't have one and allow time to receive the information by mail.

All credit and debit cards now have chips that authenticate and secure transactions. Europeans insert their chip cards into the payment machine slot, then enter a PIN. American cards should work in most transactions without a PIN—but may not work at self-service machines at train stations, tollbooths, gas pumps, or parking lots. I've been inconvenienced a few times by self-service payment machines in Europe that wouldn't accept my card, but it's never caused me serious trouble.

If you're concerned, a few banks offer a chip-and-PIN card that works in almost all payment machines, including those from Andrews Federal Credit Union (www.andrewsfcu.org) and the State Department Federal Credit Union (www.sdfcu.org).

Report your travel dates. Let your bank know that you'll be using your debit and credit cards in Europe, and when and where you're headed.

Adjust your ATM withdrawal limit. Find out how much you can take out daily and ask for a higher daily withdrawal limit if you want to get more cash at once. Note that European ATMs will withdraw funds only from checking accounts; you're unlikely to have access to your savings account.

Ask about fees. For any purchase or withdrawal made with a card, you may be charged a currency conversion fee (1-3 percent) and/or a Visa or MasterCard international transaction fee (1 percent). If you're getting a bad deal, consider getting a new debit or credit card. Reputable no-fee cards include those from Capital One, as well as Charles Schwab debit cards. Most credit unions and some airline loyalty cards have low-to-no international transaction fees.

IN EUROPE
Using Cash Machines
European cash machines have English-language instructions and work just like they do at home—except they spit out local currency instead of dollars, calculated at the day's standard bank-to-bank rate.

In most places, ATMs are easy to locate. When possible, withdraw cash from a bank-run ATM located just outside that bank. Ideally use it during the bank's opening hours so if your card is munched by the machine, you can go inside for help.

If your debit card doesn't work, try a lower amount—your request may have exceeded your withdrawal limit or the ATM's limit. If you still have a problem, try a different ATM or come back later—your bank's network may be temporarily down.

Avoid "independent" ATMs, such as Travelex, Euronet, Moneybox, Cardpoint, and Cashzone. These have high fees, can be less secure than a bank ATM, and may try to trick users with "dynamic currency conversion" (see later).

Exchanging Cash
In general, avoid exchanging money in Europe; it's a big rip-off. But because the countries in this region have different currencies, you may wind up with leftover cash. Coins can't be exchanged once you leave the country, so spend them before you cross the border. Bills are easy to convert to the "new" country's currency, but remember that regular banks have the best rates for the conversion. Post offices and train stations usually change money if you can't get to a bank.

Using Credit Cards
US cards no longer require a signature for verification, but don't be surprised if a European card reader generates a receipt for you to sign. Some card readers will accept your card as is; others may prompt you to enter your PIN (so it's important to know the code

PRACTICALITIES

EU Enlargement and the "New Europe"

The European Union (EU) began as a political and economic alliance of mostly Western European nations, with Germany, France, and Italy at the helm. But since 2004, 11 formerly communist "Eastern European" countries—including most of the ones in this book—have joined the EU, shifting the geographical and political center of Europe from Brussels to Prague. This enlargement of the EU has been a fitful process, both for the existing members and for the new ones.

Many Eastern Europeans, concerned that EU bureaucracy could threaten their prized traditions, have a "Euroskeptic" take on things. One Polish farmer grumbled that he has to get "passports" for each of his cows. EU hygiene standards are incompatible with slow-simmering national specialties. (My Czech friend complained, "The EU has made many of our best dishes illegal.") And many are simply exhausted after generations of outside meddling. A wise Czech grandmother pointed out that in her lifetime, her country had been ruled from Vienna (Habsburgs), Berlin (Nazis), and Moscow (communists). She said, "Now that we're finally ruled from Prague, why would we want to turn our power over to Brussels?"

Longstanding EU members have had their own doubts. Wealthy nations have spent vast fortunes to improve the floundering economies of poorer member countries (such as Portugal, Greece, and Ireland), and are reluctant to take on more "charity cases." Some Westerners fret about the influx of cheap labor from the East (see "The Polish Plumber Syndrome," later in this chapter). Others worry that their political clout will be diluted. And in the fall of 2015, refugees fleeing war in Syria flooded through Eastern Europe as they attempted to reach safety and jobs in the West. Eastern European countries—pressured by their big EU allies—had to weigh their open-borders commitments against their EU interests.

On the other hand, the advantages of the EU are evident everywhere. New expressways, airports, train stations, public spaces, and museums throughout Eastern Europe were paid for, at least partly, by EU funds. Countries that have adopted the euro currency (including Slovenia and Slovakia) find they match up pretty well, economically, with their Western European counterparts. And, just as intended, Western companies are enjoying easier access to the affordable resources and labor of Eastern Europe.

As what's been called the "New Europe" takes shape, players on both sides will continue to define their roles and seek compromise. But so far, despite the challenges, the general consensus in the East is that joining the EU was the right move.

for each of your cards). If a cashier is present, you should have no problems.

At self-service payment machines (transit-ticket kiosks, parking, etc.), results are mixed, as US cards may not work in unattended transactions. If your card won't work, look for a cashier who can process your card manually—or pay in cash.

Drivers Beware: Be aware of potential problems using a US credit card to fill up at an unattended gas station, enter a parking garage, or exit a toll road. Carry cash and be prepared to move on to the next gas station if necessary. When approaching a toll plaza, use the "cash" lane.

Dynamic Currency Conversion

If merchants offer to convert your purchase price into dollars (called dynamic currency conversion, or DCC), refuse this "service." You'll pay extra for the expensive convenience of seeing your charge in dollars. If an ATM offers to "lock in" or "guarantee" your conversion rate, choose "proceed without conversion." Other prompts might state, "You can be charged in dollars: Press YES for dollars, NO for euros." Always choose the local currency.

Security Tips

Pickpockets target tourists. Keep your cash, credit cards, and passport secure in your money belt, and carry only a day's spending money in your front pocket or wallet.

Before inserting your card into an ATM, inspect the front. If anything looks crooked, loose, or damaged, it could be a sign of a card-skimming device. When entering your PIN, carefully block other people's view of the keypad.

Don't use a debit card for purchases. Because a debit card pulls funds directly from your bank account, potential charges incurred by a thief will stay on your account while the fraudulent use is investigated by your bank.

While traveling, to access your accounts online, be sure to use a secure connection (see the "Tips on Internet Security" sidebar, later).

Damage Control for Lost Cards

If you lose your credit or debit card, report the loss immediately to the respective global customer-assistance centers. Call these 24-hour US numbers collect: Visa (tel. 303/967-1096), MasterCard (tel. 636/722-7111), and American Express (tel. 336/393-1111).

To make a collect call from any phone, use these numbers: Austria tel. 800-200-288; Czech Republic tel. 00-800-222-55288; Hungary tel. 06-800-011-11; Poland tel. 00-800-111-1111; Slovakia tel. 0800-000-101; Slovenia tel. 1180. Press zero or stay on the line for an English-speaking operator. European toll-free numbers can also be found at the websites for Visa and MasterCard.

You'll need to provide the primary cardholder's identification-verification details (such as birth date, mother's maiden name, or Social Security number). You can generally receive a temporary card within two or three business days in Europe (see www.ricksteves.com/help for more).

If you report your loss within two days, you typically won't be responsible for any unauthorized transactions on your account, although many banks charge a liability fee of $50.

TIPPING

Tipping in Europe isn't as automatic or as generous as in the US. For special service, tips are appreciated, but not expected. As in the US, the proper amount depends on your resources, tipping philosophy, and the circumstances, but some general guidelines apply.

Restaurants: At sit-down eateries, tip a small amount by rounding up the bill 5-10 percent. In a few cities (like Prague and Budapest), a service charge may be automatically added to your bill. For details on tipping in restaurants, see page 1105.

Taxis: For a typical ride, round up your fare a bit (for instance, if the fare is €42, pay €45). If the cabbie hauls your bags and zips you to the airport to help you catch your flight, you might want to toss in a little more. But if you feel like you're being driven in circles or otherwise ripped off, skip the tip.

Services: In general, if someone in the tourism or service industry does a super job for you, a small tip (the equivalent of a euro or two) is appropriate...but not required. If you're not sure whether (or how much) to tip, ask a local for advice.

GETTING A VAT REFUND

Wrapped into the purchase price of your Eastern European souvenirs is a Value-Added Tax (VAT) that varies per country—see the sidebar for specific rates. You're entitled to get most of that tax back if you make a purchase of more than a set amount at a store that participates in the VAT refund scheme. Typically, you must ring up the minimum at a single retailer—you can't add up your purchases from various shops to reach the required amount. (If the store ships the goods to your US home, VAT is not assessed on your purchase.)

Getting your refund is straightforward...and worthwhile if you spend a significant amount on souvenirs.

Get the paperwork. Have the merchant completely fill out the necessary refund document. You'll have to present your passport. Get the paperwork done before you leave the store to ensure you'll have everything you need (including your original sales receipt).

Get your stamp at the border or airport. Process your VAT

VAT Rates

To be eligible to get a VAT refund, you usually need to spend the listed minimum at a single store.

Country of Purchase	VAT Standard Rate*	Minimum in Local Currency	Approx. Minimum in US $
Austria	20%	€75.01	$85
Czech Republic	21%	2,001 Kč	$100
Hungary	27%	54,001 Ft	$189
Poland	23%	200 zł	$53
Slovakia	20%	€175.01	$200
Slovenia	22%	€50.01	$55

*VAT rates fluctuate based on many factors, including what kind of item you are buying. Your refund will likely be less than the rate listed above, especially if it's subject to processing fees.

document with the customs agent who deals with VAT refunds at your last stop in the country in which you made your purchase (or, if you bought it in the European Union, at your last stop in the EU). Arrive an additional hour before you need to check in to allow time to find the customs office—and wait. Some customs desks are positioned before airport security; confirm the location before going through security.

It's best to keep your purchases in your carry-on. If they're not allowed as carry-on (such as knives), pack them in your checked bags and alert the check-in agent. You'll be sent (with your tagged bag) to a customs desk outside security; someone will examine your bag, stamp your paperwork, and put your bag on the belt. You're not supposed to use your purchased goods before you leave. If you show up at customs wearing your chic Czech shirt, officials might look the other way—or deny you a refund.

Collect your refund. You can claim your VAT refund from refund companies, such as Global Blue or Premier Tax Free, with offices at major airports, ports, or border crossings (either before or after security, probably strategically located near a duty-free shop). These services (which extract a 4 percent fee) can refund your money in cash immediately or credit your card (within two billing cycles). Otherwise you'll need to mail the stamped refund documents to the address given by the shop where you made your purchase.

CUSTOMS FOR AMERICAN SHOPPERS

You can take home $800 worth of items per person duty-free, once every 31 days. Many processed and packaged foods are allowed, including vacuum-packed cheeses, dried herbs, jams, baked goods, candy, chocolate, oil, vinegar, mustard, and honey. Fresh fruits and vegetables and most meats are not allowed, with exceptions for some canned items. As for alcohol, you can bring in one liter duty-free (it can be packed securely in your checked luggage, along with any other liquid-containing items).

To bring alcohol (or liquid-packed foods) in your carry-on bag on your flight home, buy it at a duty-free shop at the airport. You'll increase your odds of getting it onto a connecting flight if it's packaged in a "STEB"—a secure, tamper-evident bag. But stay away from liquids in opaque, ceramic, or metallic containers, which usually cannot be successfully screened (STEB or no STEB).

For details on allowable goods, customs rules, and duty rates, visit http://help.cbp.gov.

Sightseeing

Eastern Europe's best attractions are modern museums that chronicle the communist regime and celebrate its demise (such as Budapest's House of Terror and Memento Park, and Gdańsk's European Solidarity Center). But many museums here are dusty, old-fashioned collections of art or historical artifacts. While these don't quite rank with the Louvre or the Prado, they can be surprisingly engaging if you take the time to learn more. With the right attitude, it's an exciting opportunity to be introduced to talented artists and important historical figures who are relatively unknown outside of their home countries. Generally, you'll follow a confusing, one-way tour route through a maze of rooms with squeaky parquet floors, trailed by grumpy attendants who listlessly point you in the right direction. While some museums label exhibits in English, most don't post full explanations; you'll have to buy a book or borrow laminated translations. In some cases, neither option is available.

Sightseeing can be hard work. Use these tips to make your visits to Eastern Europe's finest sights meaningful, fun, efficient, and painless.

MAPS AND NAVIGATION TOOLS

A good map is essential for efficient navigation while sightseeing. The maps in this book are concise and simple, designed to help you locate recommended destinations, sights, and local TIs, where you can pick up more in-depth maps.

You can also use a mapping app on your mobile device. Be

aware that pulling up maps or looking up turn-by-turn walking directions on the fly requires an internet connection: To use this feature, it's smart to get an international data plan. With Google Maps or City Maps 2Go, it's possible to download a map while online, then go offline and navigate without incurring data-roaming charges, though you can't search for an address or get real-time walking directions. A handful of other apps—including Apple Maps, OffMaps, and Navfree—also allow you to use maps offline.

PLAN AHEAD

Set up an itinerary that allows you to fit in all your must-see sights. For a one-stop look at opening hours, see the "At a Glance" sidebars for major cities (Prague, Kraków, Warsaw, Budapest, Ljubljana, and Vienna). Most sights keep stable hours, but you can easily confirm the latest by checking with the TI or by visiting museum websites.

Don't put off visiting a must-see sight—you never know when a place will close unexpectedly for a holiday, strike, or restoration. Given how precious your vacation time is, I recommend getting reservations for any must-see sight that offers them (see page 9). Many museums are closed or have reduced hours at least a few days a year, especially on holidays such as Christmas, New Year's, and Labor Day (May 1). A list of holidays is in the appendix; check online for possible museum closures during your trip. In summer, some sights may stay open late; in the off-season, hours may be shorter.

Going at the right time helps avoid crowds. This book offers tips on the best times to see specific sights. Try visiting popular sights very early or very late. Evening visits (when possible) are usually peaceful, with fewer crowds.

If you plan to hire a local guide, reserve ahead by email. Popular guides can get booked up.

Study up. To get the most out of the sight descriptions in this book, read them before you visit. Note: To avoid redundancy, many cultural or historical details are explained for one sight in this book and not repeated for another; to get the full picture, read the entire chapter for each destination you'll visit.

AT SIGHTS

Here's what you can typically expect:

Entering: Be warned that you may not be allowed to enter if you arrive less than 30 to 60 minutes before closing time. And guards start ushering people out well before the actual closing time, so don't save the best for last.

Some sights have a security check. Allow extra time for these lines. Many sights require you to check daypacks and coats. (If

The Polish Plumber Syndrome

You'll enjoy a taste of Eastern European culture on your next trip...to London or Dublin. When eight Eastern European countries joined the European Union in 2004, Great Britain and Ireland were required to welcome their new comrades to work without a visa. This sparked a wave of immigration into the British Isles. Many Poles, Czechs, and Estonians ended up in the hospitality industry, and tourists to Britain and Ireland began to encounter desk clerks who didn't quite speak fluent English.

The transplants enjoyed more money and an irreplaceable cross-cultural experience. But their home countries went through an alarming "brain drain," as many of their brightest westward-thinking young people sought opportunities elsewhere. But as the global financial crisis tightened the job market, immigration became less appealing to expat workers, as well as to the countries hosting them. Quite a few transplants lost their jobs and returned home to the East. And a general sentiment against immigrants (focused both on Eastern Europeans and those from farther away) partly propelled the 2016 "Brexit" vote. Britain's planned departure from the EU poses serious questions about the status (societally, if not legally) of the many Eastern Europeans who have put down roots in the UK.

The EU has compelled other Western European countries to open their borders—and rarely without controversy. One popular symbol—invented by a right-wing French politician—was an invading "Polish plumber" who'd put French plumbers out of a job. The Polish tourist board countered by putting up clever ads in France featuring an alluring Polish hunk stroking a pipe wrench, saying, "I'm staying in Poland... come visit me!"

European Gen Xers have been dubbed the "Erasmus Generation"—after the Erasmus Student Network, an EU organization that fosters study-abroad opportunities within Europe. For Europeans in their 40s and under, who have grown up accustomed to freely traveling to, working in, and attending universities in other countries, it seems more natural to identify as "Europeans" than as Spaniards, Slovenes, or Swedes. Multilingualism, international résumés, and cross-cultural marriages are the norm—just one more step in the Europe-wide process of integration.

But as the UK wrestles with how to disentangle itself from the EU, the conversation has turned from integration to nationalism, and how much European togetherness is *too much* togetherness. It will be interesting to see whether the idealistic vision of "European first" survives.

you'd rather not check your daypack, try carrying it tucked under your arm like a purse as you enter.)

Photography: If the museum's photo policy isn't clearly posted, ask a guard. Generally, taking photos without a flash or tripod is allowed. Some sights ban selfie sticks; others ban photos altogether.

Temporary Exhibits: Museums may show special exhibits in addition to their permanent collection. Some exhibits are included in the entry price, while others come at an extra cost (which you may have to pay even if you don't want to see the exhibit).

Expect Changes: Artwork can be on tour, on loan, out sick, or shifted at the whim of the curator. Pick up a floor plan as you enter, and ask museum staff if you can't find a particular item.

Audioguides and Apps: Many sights rent audioguides, which generally offer dull recorded descriptions in English. Audioguides often have a standard output jack, so if you bring your own earbuds you can often enjoy better sound. To save money, bring a Y-jack and share one audioguide with your travel partner. Museums and sights often offer free apps that you can download to your mobile device (check their websites). And, I've produced free, downloadable audio tours for my Prague City Walk, Vienna City Walk, Vienna's St. Stephen's Cathedral, and Vienna's Ringstrasse Tram Tour; look for the 🎧 in this book. For more on my audio tours, see page 12.

Services: Important sights usually have a reasonably-priced on-site café or cafeteria (handy places to rejuvenate during a long visit). The WCs at sights are free and generally clean.

Before Leaving: At the gift shop, scan the postcard rack or thumb through a guidebook to be sure that you haven't overlooked something that you'd like to see. Every sight or museum offers more than what is covered in this book. Use the information in this book as an introduction—not the final word.

Sleeping

Extensive and opinionated listings of good-value rooms are a major feature of this book's Sleeping sections. Rather than list accommodations scattered throughout a town, I choose hotels in my favorite neighborhoods that are convenient to your sightseeing.

My recommendations run the gamut, from dorm beds to fancy rooms with all the comforts. I like places that are clean, central, relatively quiet at night, reasonably priced, friendly, small enough to have a hands-on owner or manager, and run with a respect for local traditions. I'm more impressed by a handy location and fun-loving philosophy than flat-screen TVs and a fancy gym. Most of my recommendations fall short of perfection. But if I can find a place with most of these features, it's a keeper.

Book your accommodations as soon as your itinerary is set, especially if you want to stay at one of my top listings or if you'll be traveling during busy times. For certain popular destinations, I've also noted times of year when accommodations are likely to book up fast. Also see the appendix for a list of major holidays and festivals in Eastern Europe.

Some people make reservations as they travel, calling ahead a few days to a week before their arrival. It's best to call hotels at about 9:00 or 10:00, when the receptionist knows which rooms will be available. If you encounter a language barrier, ask the fluent receptionist at your current hotel to call for you. Some apps—such as HotelTonight—specialize in last-minute rooms, often at business-class hotels in big cities.

RATES AND DEALS

I've categorized my recommended accommodations based on price, indicated with a dollar-sign rating (see sidebar). The price ranges suggest an estimated cost for a one-night stay in a standard double room with a private toilet and shower in high season, and assume you're booking directly with the hotel (not through a booking site, which extracts a commission). Room prices can fluctuate significantly with demand and amenities (size, views, room class, and so on), but relative price categories remain constant. Taxes, which can vary from place to place, are generally insignificant (a dollar or two per person, per night).

Room rates are especially volatile at larger hotels that use "dynamic pricing" to set rates. Prices can skyrocket during festivals and conventions, while business hotels can have deep discounts on weekends when demand plummets. Of the many hotels I recommend, it's difficult to say which will be the best value on a given day—until you do your homework.

Some accommodations quote their rates in euros, while others use the local currency.

Booking Direct: Once your dates are set, compare prices at several hotels. You can do this by checking Hotels.com, Booking.com, and hotel websites. To get the best deal, contact family-run hotels directly by phone or email. When you go direct, the owner avoids the commission paid to booking sites, thereby leaving enough wiggle room to offer you a discount, a nicer room, or a free breakfast (if it's not already included). If you prefer to book online or are considering a hotel chain, it's to your advantage to use the hotel's website.

Getting a Discount: Some hotels extend a discount to those who pay cash or stay longer than three nights. And some accommodations offer a special discount for Rick Steves readers, indicated in this guidebook by the abbreviation **"RS%."** Discounts

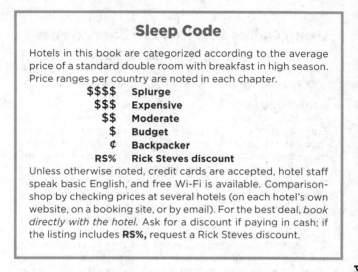

Sleep Code

Hotels in this book are categorized according to the average price of a standard double room with breakfast in high season. Price ranges per country are noted in each chapter.

$$$$	Splurge
$$$	Expensive
$$	Moderate
$	Budget
¢	Backpacker
RS%	Rick Steves discount

Unless otherwise noted, credit cards are accepted, hotel staff speak basic English, and free Wi-Fi is available. Comparison-shop by checking prices at several hotels (on each hotel's own website, on a booking site, or by email). For the best deal, *book directly with the hotel.* Ask for a discount if paying in cash; if the listing includes **RS%,** request a Rick Steves discount.

vary: Ask for details when you reserve. Generally, to qualify for this discount, you must book direct (not through a booking site), mention this book when you reserve, show this book upon arrival, and sometimes pay cash or stay a certain number of nights. In some cases, you may need to enter a discount code (which I've provided in the listing) in the booking form on the hotel's website. Rick Steves discounts apply to readers with either print or digital books. Understandably, discounts do not apply to promotional rates.

TYPES OF ACCOMMODATIONS
Hotels

In Eastern Europe, you can choose from a delightful variety of stylish and charming hotels and guesthouses. And rates are reasonable;

you can find a central, straightforward-but-comfortable double for $100 just about anywhere. Plan on spending $90-130 per double in big cities, and $60-90 in smaller towns. You can uncover some bargains, but I think it's worth paying a little more for comfort and a good location.

Some hotels can add an extra bed (for a small charge) to turn a double into a triple; some offer larger rooms for four or more people (I call these "family rooms" in the listings). In general, a triple room is cheaper than the cost of a double and a single. Three or four people can economize by requesting one big room.

Using Online Services to Your Advantage

From booking services to user reviews, online businesses are playing a greater role in travelers' planning than ever before. Take advantage of their pluses—and be wise to their downsides.

Booking Sites

Hotel booking websites, including Priceline's Booking.com and Expedia's Hotels.com, offer one-stop shopping for hotels. While convenient for travelers, they present a real problem for small, independent, family-run hotels. Without a presence on these sites, these hotels become almost invisible. But to be listed, a hotel must pay a sizeable commission...and promise that its own website won't undercut the price on the booking-service site.

Here's the work-around: Use the big sites to research what's out there, then book directly with the hotel by email or phone, in which case hotel owners are free to give you whatever price they like. Ask for a room without the commission mark-up (or ask for a free breakfast if not included, or a free upgrade). If you do book online, be sure to use the hotel's website. The price will likely be the same as via a booking site, but your money goes to the hotel, not agency commissions.

As a savvy consumer, remember: When you book with an online booking service, you're adding a middleman who takes roughly 20 percent. To support small, family-run hotels whose world is more difficult than ever, book direct.

Short-Term Rental Sites

Rental juggernaut Airbnb (along with other short-term rental sites) allows travelers to rent rooms and apartments directly from locals, often providing more value than a cookie-cutter hotel. Airbnb fans appreciate feeling part of a real neighborhood and getting into a daily routine as "temporary Europeans." Depending on the host, Airbnb can provide an opportunity to get to know a

Arrival and Check-In: Hotels and B&Bs are sometimes located on the higher floors of a multipurpose building with a secured door. In that case, look for your hotel's name on the buttons by the main entrance. When you ring the bell, you'll be buzzed in.

Hotel elevators are becoming more common, though some older buildings still lack them. You may have to climb a flight of stairs to reach the elevator (if so, you can ask at the front desk for help carrying your bags up). Elevators are typically very small—pack light, or you may need to send your bags up without you.

The EU requires that hotels collect your name, nationality, and ID number. When you check in, the receptionist will normally ask for your passport and may keep it for anywhere from a couple of minutes to a couple of hours. (If not comfortable leaving your

local person, while keeping the money spent on your accommodations in the community.

Critics view Airbnb as a threat to "traditional Europe," saying it creates unfair, unqualified competition for established guesthouse owners. In some places, the lucrative Airbnb market has forced traditional guesthouses out of business and is driving property values out of range for locals. Some cities have cracked down, requiring owners to occupy rental properties part of the year (and staging disruptive "inspections" that inconvenience guests).

As a lover of Europe, I share the worry of those who see residents nudged aside by tourists. But as an advocate for travelers, I appreciate the value and cultural intimacy Airbnb provides.

User Reviews

User-generated review sites and apps such as Yelp and TripAdvisor can give you a consensus of opinions about everything from hotels and restaurants to sights and nightlife. If you scan reviews of a restaurant or hotel and see several complaints about noise or a rotten location, you've gained insight that can help in your decision-making.

But as a guidebook writer, my sense is that there is a big difference between the uncurated information on a review site and the vetted listings in a guidebook. A user-generated review is based on the limited experience of one person, who stayed at just one hotel in a given city and ate at a few restaurants there. A guidebook is the work of a trained researcher who forms a well-developed basis for comparison by visiting many restaurants and hotels year after year.

Both types of information have their place, and in many ways, they're complementary. If something is well reviewed in a guidebook and also gets good online reviews, it's likely a winner.

passport at the desk for a long time, ask when you can pick it up. Or if you packed a color photocopy of your passport, you can generally show that rather than your original.)

If you're arriving in the morning, your room probably won't be ready. Check your bag safely at the hotel and dive right into sightseeing.

In Your Room: Most hotel rooms have a TV, telephone, and free Wi-Fi (although in old buildings with thick walls, the Wi-Fi signal might be available only in the lobby). Simpler places rarely have a room phone.

More pillows and blankets are usually in the closet or available on request. Towels and linens aren't always replaced every day, so hang your towel up to dry.

Breakfast and Meals: Breakfast, almost always served buffet-style, usually includes rolls, cold cuts, cheese, cereal, yogurt, fruit, coffee, milk, and juice; some places also provide eggs.

Checking Out: While it's customary to pay for your room upon departure, it can be a good idea to settle your bill the day before, when you're not in a hurry and while the manager's in.

Hotelier Help: Hoteliers can be a good source of advice. Most know their city well, and can assist you with everything from public transit and airport connections to finding a good restaurant, the nearest launderette, or a late-night pharmacy.

Hotel Hassles: Even at the best places, mechanical breakdowns occur: Sinks leak, hot water turns cold, toilets may gurgle or smell, the Wi-Fi goes out, or the air-conditioning dies when you need it most. Report your concerns clearly and calmly at the front desk.

If you find that night noise is a problem (if, for instance, your room is over a nightclub), ask for a quieter room in the back or on an upper floor. To guard against theft in your room, keep valuables out of sight. Some rooms come with a safe, and other hotels have safes at the front desk. I've never bothered using one and in a lifetime of travel, I've never had anything stolen from my room.

For more complicated problems, don't expect instant results. Above all, keep a positive attitude. Remember, you're on vacation. If your hotel is a disappointment, spend more time out enjoying the place you came to see.

Rooms in Private Homes

Private accommodations offer travelers a characteristic and money-saving alternative for a fraction of the price of a hotel. Rooms in private homes are called *sobe* in Slovenia and Croatia; the German word *Zimmer* works there, too, and throughout Eastern Europe. These places are inexpensive, at least as comfortable as a cheap hotel, and a good way to get some local insight. The boss changes the sheets, so people staying several nights are most desirable—and those who stay less than three nights are often charged a lot more (typically 20-50 percent; this surcharge is often waived outside of peak season). Renting a room in someone's home is a good option for those traveling alone, as you're more likely to find true single rooms—with just one single bed, and a price to match. While you can't expect your host to also be your tour guide, some may be interested in getting to know the travelers who come through their home.

Short-Term Rentals

A short-term rental—whether an apartment, house, or room in a local's home—is an increasingly popular alternative, especially if you plan to settle in one location for several nights. For stays longer than a few days, you can usually find a rental that's comparable to—and cheaper than—a hotel room with similar amenities. Plus, you'll get a behind-the-scenes peek into how locals live.

Many places require a minimum stay and have strict cancellation policies. And you're generally on your own: There's no hotel reception desk, breakfast, or daily cleaning service.

Finding Accommodations: Aggregator websites such as Airbnb, FlipKey, Booking.com, and the HomeAway family of sites (HomeAway, VRBO, and VacationRentals) let you browse properties and correspond directly with European property owners or managers. If you prefer to work from a curated list of accommodations, consider using a rental agency such as Interhomeusa.com or Rentavilla.com. Agency-represented apartments typically cost more, but this method often offers more help and safeguards than booking direct.

Before you commit, be clear on the location. I like to virtually "explore" the neighborhood using the Street View feature on Google Maps. Also consider the proximity to public transportation and how well-connected the property is with the rest of the city. Ask about amenities (elevator, air-conditioning, laundry, Wi-Fi, parking, etc.). Reviews from previous guests can help identify trouble spots.

Think about the kind of experience you want: Just a key and an affordable bed...or a chance to get to know a local? There are typically two kinds of hosts: those who want minimal interaction with their guests, and hosts who are friendly and may want to interact with you. Read the promotional text and online reviews to help shape your decision.

Confirming and Paying: Many places require you to pay the entire balance before your trip. It's easiest and safest to pay through the site where you found the listing. Be wary of owners who want to take your transaction offline; this gives you no recourse if things go awry. Never agree to wire money (a key indicator of a fraudulent transaction).

Apartments or Houses: If you're staying somewhere for four or more nights, it's worth considering an apartment or rental house (shorter stays aren't worth the hassle of arranging key pickup, buying groceries, etc.). Apartment or house rentals can be especially cost-effective for groups and families. European apartments, like hotel rooms, tend to be small by US standards. But they often come with laundry machines and small, equipped kitchens, making it easier and cheaper to dine in.

Other Options: Swapping homes with a local works for people with an appealing place to offer (don't assume where you live is not interesting to Europeans). A good place to start is HomeExchange.

PRACTICALITIES

PRACTICALITIES

Making Hotel Reservations

Given the erratic accommodations values in Eastern Europe (and the quality of the places I've found for this book), I recommend that you reserve your rooms as soon as you've pinned down your travel dates. For busy national holidays, it's wise to reserve far in advance (see page 1127).

Requesting a Reservation: For family-run hotels, it's generally cheaper to book your room directly via email or a phone call. For business-class hotels, or if you'd rather book online, reserve directly through the hotel's official website (not a booking website). For complicated requests, send an email. Almost all of my recommended hotels take reservations in English.

Here's what the hotelier wants to know:

- Type(s) of rooms you want and size of your party
- Number of nights you'll stay
- Your arrival and departure dates, written European-style as day/month/year (18/06/20 or 18 June 2020)
- Special requests (en suite bathroom, cheapest room, twin beds vs. double bed, quiet room)
- Applicable discounts (such as a Rick Steves reader discount, cash discount, or promotional rate)

Confirming a Reservation: Most places will request a credit-card number to hold your room. If you're using an online reservation form, look for the *https* or a lock icon at the top of your browser. If you book direct, you can email, call, or fax this information.

Canceling a Reservation: If you must cancel, it's courteous—and smart—to do so with as much notice as possible, especially for

com. To sleep for free, Couchsurfing.com is a vagabond's alternative to Airbnb. It lists millions of outgoing members who host fellow "surfers" in their homes.

Hostels

A hostel provides cheap beds in dorms where you sleep alongside strangers for about $20-30 per night. Travelers of any age are welcome if they don't mind dorm-style accommodations and meeting other travelers. Most hostels offer kitchen facilities, guest computers, Wi-Fi, and a self-service laundry. Hostels almost always provide bedding, but the towel's up to you (though you can usually rent one for a small fee). Family and private rooms are often available.

Independent hostels tend to be easygoing, colorful, and informal (no membership required; www.hostelworld.com). You may pay slightly less by booking directly with the hostel. **Official hostels** are part of Hostelling International (HI) and share an online

From:	rick@ricksteves.com
Sent:	Today
To:	info@hotelcentral.com
Subject:	Reservation request for 19-22 July

Dear Hotel Central,

I would like to stay at your hotel. Please let me know if you have a room available and the price for:
• 2 people
• Double bed and en suite bathroom in a quiet room
• Arriving 19 July, departing 22 July (3 nights)

Thank you!
Rick Steves

smaller family-run places. Cancellation policies can be strict; read the fine print before you book. Many discount deals require pre-payment, with no cancellation refunds.

Reconfirming a Reservation: Always call or email to reconfirm your room reservation a few days in advance. For B&Bs or very small hotels, I call again on my day of arrival to tell my host what time to expect me (especially important if arriving late—after 17:00).

Phoning: For tips on how to call hotels overseas, see the "How to Dial" sidebar.

booking site (www.hihostels.com). HI hostels typically require that you be a member or else pay a bit more per night.

Eating

Eastern Europe offers good food for relatively little money—especially if you steer clear of the easy-to-avoid tourist-trap restaurants. This is affordable sightseeing for your palate.

Slavic cuisine has a reputation for being heavy and hearty, with lots of pork, potatoes, and cabbage. And, to be fair, some of that reputation is well-earned. But the food here is also delicious, and there's a lot more diversity from country to country than you might expect. For example, Hungarian cuisine is rich and spicy (think paprika), while Slovenia has a knack for Mediterranean cooking (seafood, pastas), and Polish food is more "northern" (with lots of dill, berries, and cream—like Russian cuisine). Tune in to the regional and national specialties and customs (see each country's introduction in this book for details).

For a change of pace, seek out vegetarian, Italian, Indian, sushi, and similar places, which are especially good in big cities such as Prague, Budapest, or Kraków (I've listed a few tasty options).

For listings in this guidebook, I look for restaurants that are convenient to your hotel and sightseeing. When restaurant-hunting, choose a spot filled with locals, not the place with the big neon signs boasting, "We Speak English and Accept Credit Cards." Venturing even a block or two off the main drag leads to higher-quality food for a better price.

Locals eat better at lower-rent locales. Most restaurants tack a menu onto their door for browsers and have an English menu inside. If the place isn't full, you can usually just seat yourself (get a waiter's attention to be sure your preferred table is OK)—the American-style "hostess," with a carefully managed waiting list, isn't common here. Once seated, feel free to take your time. In fact, it might be difficult to dine in a hurry. Only a rude waiter will rush you. Good service is relaxed (slow to an American).

When you're in the mood for something halfway between a restaurant and a picnic meal, look for takeout food stands, bakeries (with sandwiches and savory pastries to go), shops selling pizza by the slice, or simple little eateries offering fast and easy sit-down restaurant food. In Poland, don't miss the enticingly cheap "milk bar" cafeterias (see page 222). Many grocery stores sell sandwiches, and others might be willing to make one for you from what's in the deli case.

The Czech Republic is beer country, with Europe's best and cheapest brew. Poland also has fine beer, but the national drink is *wódka*. Hungary and Slovenia are known for their wines. Each country has its own distinctive liqueur, most of them a variation on *slivovice* (SLEE-voh-veet-seh)—a plum brandy so highly valued that it's the de facto currency of the Carpathian Mountains (often used for bartering with farmers and other mountain folk). Menus list drink size by the tenth of a liter, or deciliter (dl). Nondrinkers will find all the standard types of Coke and Pepsi, along with some fun-to-sample local alternatives (such as Slovenia's Cockta, described on page 717).

Restaurant Price Code

Eateries in this book are categorized according to the average cost of a typical main course. Drinks, desserts, and splurge items can raise the price considerably. Price ranges per country are noted in each chapter.

$$$$	Splurge
$$$	Pricier
$$	Moderate
$	Budget

In Eastern Europe, a milk bar or takeout spot is **$**; a basic sit-down eatery is **$$**; a casual but more upscale restaurant is **$$$**; and a swanky splurge is **$$$$**.

TIPPING

Tip only at restaurants that have table service. If you order your food at a counter, don't tip.

At restaurants that have a waitstaff, round up the bill 5-10 percent after a good meal. My rule of thumb is to estimate about 10 percent, then round slightly to reach a convenient total (for a 370-Kč meal, I pay 400 Kč—an 8-percent tip). Anywhere in Eastern Europe, a tip of over 10 percent is overly generous, verging on extravagant.

At most restaurants in Budapest, and at tourist-oriented ones in Prague, a service fee of around 10-12 percent is automatically added to the bill. Check your bill carefully; if this appears, then there's no need to tip any extra. If you're not sure whether your bill includes the tip, just ask.

RESTAURANT PRICING

I've categorized my recommended eateries based on the average price of a typical main course, indicated with a dollar-sign rating (see sidebar). Obviously, expensive specialties, fine wine, appetizers, and dessert can significantly increase your final bill.

The categories also indicate the personality of a place: **Budget** eateries include street food, takeaway, order-at-the-counter shops, basic cafeterias, and bakeries selling sandwiches. **Moderate** eateries are nice (but not fancy) sit-down restaurants, ideal for a straightforward, fill-the-tank meal. Most of my listings fall in this category—great for getting a good taste of the local cuisine on a budget.

Pricier eateries are a notch up, with more attention paid to the setting, presentation, and (often inventive) cuisine. **Splurge** eateries are dress-up-for-a-special-occasion-swanky—typically with an

Hurdling the Language Barrier

Many visitors are pleasantly surprised to find that the language barrier in Eastern Europe is no bigger than in Western Europe. In fact, I find it much easier to communicate in Hungary or Slovenia than in Italy or Spain. Why? Because these countries are small and not politically powerful, their residents realize that it's unreasonable to expect visitors to learn Hungarian (with only 12 million speakers worldwide) or Slovene (2 million). It's essential to find a common language with the rest of the world—so they learn English early and well. (I've had surprisingly eloquent conversations with Slovenian grade-schoolers.)

Of course, not everyone speaks English. But in these situations, it's relatively easy to get your point across. I've often bought a train ticket simply by writing out the name of my destination (preferably with the local spelling—for example, "Praha" instead of "Prague"); the time I want to travel (using the 24-hour clock); and, if I'm not traveling on the same day I'm buying the ticket, I include the date I want to leave (day first, then the month as a Roman numeral, then the year). Here's an example of what I'd show a ticket-seller at a train station: "Warszawa, 17:30, 15.VII.18."

Eastern Europeans, realizing that their language intimidates Americans, often invent easier nicknames for themselves—so Šárka goes by "Sara," András becomes "Andrew," and Jaroslav tells you, "Call me Jerry."

The people in most of this book's destinations (except Hungary, Austria, and Romania) speak Slavic languages. These languages are closely related to one another and to Russian, and are, to varying degrees, mutually intelligible (though many spellings change—for example, Czech *hrad*, or "castle," becomes Slovene *grad*). Slavic languages have simple vocabularies but are highly inflected—that is, the meaning of a sentence depends on complicated endings that are tacked onto the ends of the words (as in Latin).

Slavic words are notorious for their seemingly unpronounceable, long strings of consonants. Slavic pronunciation can be tricky. In fact, when the Christian missionaries Cyril and Methodius came to Eastern Europe a millennium ago, they invented a whole new alphabet to represent these strange Slavic sounds. A modified version of that alphabet—called Cyrillic—is still used today in the eastern Slavic countries (such as Serbia and Russia).

Fortunately, nearly all of the destinations covered in this

PRACTICALITIES

book use the same Roman alphabet we do, but they add lots of different diacritics—little markings below and above some letters—to represent a wide range of sounds (for example, č, ą, ó, đ, ł). I explain each of these in this book's various country introductions. (The Cyrillic alphabet is used throughout Bulgaria, and in parts of Bosnia and Montenegro—but even in these places, many signs are still in "our" alphabet. For a primer on Cyrillic, see the Bulgaria chapter.)

Hungarian is another story altogether—it's completely unrelated to Slavic languages, German, or English. For more on the Magyar tongue, see the end of the Hungary chapter.

It's easy to throw up your arms in defeat and assume you'll never pronounce these words. But unlike English, Eastern European languages are entirely phonetic—you can always sound words out with confidence, once you learn a few basic rules. My advice: Take the time to wrestle with each language, and you'll be amazed how quickly you get comfortable.

German is spoken in Vienna. As part of the same language family as English, German sounds more familiar to American ears than the Slavic languages. Throughout Eastern Europe, speaking German can come in handy, especially if you're interacting with somebody over age 50 (while few people under communism learned English, German ranked right up there with Russian as a popular second language). A few words of Italian can come in handy in Slovenia and Croatia.

There are certain universal English words all Eastern Europeans know: hello, please, thank you, super, pardon, stop, menu, problem, and no problem. Another handy word that people throughout the region will understand is *Servus* (SEHR-voos)— the old-fashioned greeting from the days of the Austro-Hungarian Empire. If you draw a blank on how to say hello in the local language, just offer a cheery *"Servus!"*

Get an ear for the local language (see the language section in each of this book's country introductions), learn the key phrases (find survival phrases for each language in the country chapters), and travel with a phrase book. Consider Lonely Planet's good *Eastern Europe Phrasebook,* which covers all the languages spoken in the destinations in this book (except German—consider the *Rick Steves German Phrase Book,* available at www.ricksteves. com).

Don't be afraid to interact with locals. Eastern Europeans can initially seem shy or even brusque—a holdover from the closed communist society—but often a simple smile is the only icebreaker you need to make a new friend. You'll find that doors open a little more quickly when you know a few words of the language. Give it your best shot, and the natives will appreciate your efforts.

elegant setting, polished service, intricate cuisine, and an expansive (and expensive) wine list.

Staying Connected

One of the most common questions I hear from travelers is, "How can I stay connected in Europe?" The short answer is: more easily and cheaply than you might think.

The simplest solution is to bring your own device—mobile phone, tablet, or laptop—and use it just as you would at home (following the tips below, such as getting an international service plan or connecting to free Wi-Fi whenever possible). Another option is to buy a European SIM card for your US mobile phone. Or you can use European landlines and computers to connect. Each of these options is described next; more details are at www.ricksteves.com/phoning. For a very practical one-hour talk covering tech issues for travelers, see www.ricksteves.com/mobile-travel-skills.

USING A MOBILE PHONE IN EUROPE

Here are some budget tips and options.

Sign up for an international plan. To stay connected at a lower cost, sign up for an international service plan through your carrier. Most providers offer a simple bundle that includes calling, messaging, and data. Your normal plan may already include international coverage (T-Mobile's does).

Before your trip, call your provider or check online to confirm that your phone will work in Europe, and research your provider's international rates. Activate the plan a day or two before you leave, then remember to cancel it when your trip's over.

Use free Wi-Fi whenever possible. Unless you have an unlimited-data plan, you're best off saving most of your online tasks for Wi-Fi. You can access the internet, send texts, and even make voice calls over Wi-Fi.

Most accommodations in Europe offer free Wi-Fi, but some—especially expensive hotels—charge a fee. Many cafés (including Starbucks and McDonald's) have free hotspots for customers; look for signs offering it and ask for the Wi-Fi password when you buy something. You'll also often find Wi-Fi at TIs, city squares, major museums, public-transit hubs, airports, and aboard trains and buses.

Minimize the use of your cellular network. Even with an international data plan, wait until you're on Wi-Fi to Skype, download apps, stream videos, or do other megabyte-greedy tasks. Using a navigation app such as Google Maps over a cellular network can take lots of data, so do this sparingly or use it offline.

Limit automatic updates. By default, your device constantly

Tips on Internet Security

Make sure that your device is running the latest versions of its operating system, security software, and apps. Next, ensure that your device and key programs (like email) are password- or passcode-protected. On the road, use only secure, password-protected Wi-Fi hotspots. Ask the hotel or café staff for the specific name of their Wi-Fi network, and make sure you log on to that exact one.

If you must access your financial info online, use a banking app rather than accessing your account via a browser. A cellular connection is more secure than Wi-Fi. Avoid logging in to any personal finance sites on a public computer.

Never share your credit-card number (or any other sensitive information) online unless you know that the site is secure. A secure site displays a little padlock icon, and the URL begins with *https* (instead of the usual *http*).

checks for a data connection and updates apps. It's smart to disable these features so your apps will only update when you're on Wi-Fi. Also change your device's email settings from "auto-retrieve" to "manual" (or from "push" to "fetch").

When you need to get online but can't find Wi-Fi, simply turn on your cellular network just long enough for the task at hand. When you're done, avoid further charges by manually turning off data roaming or cellular data (either works) in your device's Settings menu. Another way to make sure you're not accidentally using data roaming is to put your device in "airplane" mode (which also disables phone calls and texts), and then turn your Wi-Fi back on as needed.

Use Wi-Fi calling and messaging apps. Services such as Skype, WhatsApp, and FaceTime are great for making free or low-cost calls or sending texts over Wi-Fi. With an app installed on your phone, tablet, or laptop, you can log on to a Wi-Fi network and contact friends or family members who use the same service. If you buy credit in advance, with some of these services you can call or send a text anywhere for just pennies per minute.

Some apps, such as Apple's iMessage, will use the cellular network if Wi-Fi isn't available: To avoid this possibility, turn off the "Send as SMS" feature.

USING A EUROPEAN SIM CARD

With a European SIM card, you get a European mobile number and access to cheaper rates than you'll get through your US carrier. This option works best for those who want to make a lot of local calls, need a local phone number, or want faster connection speeds

PRACTICALITIES

How to Dial

International Calls

Whether phoning from a US landline or mobile phone, or from a number in another European country, here's how to make an international call. I've used one of my recommended Dubrovnik hotels as an example (tel. 385-20/453-834).

Initial Zero: Drop the initial zero from international phone numbers—except when calling Italy.

Mobile Tip: If using a mobile phone, the "+" can replace the international access code (for a "+", press and hold "0").

US/Canada to Europe

Dial 011 (US/Canada international access code), country code (385 for Croatia), and phone number.

▶ To call the Dubrovnik hotel from home, dial 011-385-20/453-834.

Country to Country Within Europe

Dial 00 (Europe international access code), country code, and phone number.

▶ To call the Dubrovnik hotel from Slovakia, dial 00-385-20/453-834.

Europe to the US/Canada

Dial 00, country code (1 for US/Canada), and phone number.

▶ To call from Europe to my office in Edmonds, Washington, dial 00-1-425-771-8303.

Domestic Calls

In Eastern Europe, to call within the same country, except Hungary (such as from one Croatian landline or mobile phone to another), simply dial the phone number, including the initial 0 if there is one.

▶ To call a recommended Dubrovnik hotel from within Dubrovnik, dial 20/453-834.

Calls within Hungary

Calling in Hungary works slightly differently than elsewhere in Europe (examples below with one of my Eger hotels— tel. 36/411-711.

Landline Within the Same Hungarian City: Dial direct, with no area code.

▶ To call the Eger hotel from within Eger, dial 411-711.

Landline Long-Distance Call Within Hungary: Add the prefix 06, followed by the area code (36 for Eger).

▶ To call the Eger hotel from Budapest, dial 06-36/411-711.

than their US carrier provides. It's simple: You buy a SIM card in Europe to replace the SIM card in your "unlocked" US phone or tablet (check with your carrier about unlocking it) or buy a basic cell phone in Europe.

SIM cards are sold at department-store electronics counters, some newsstands, and vending machines. If you need help setting

Hungarian Mobile Phones: Hungarian mobile phone numbers begin with +3620, +3630, +3631, or +3670. Use this prefix when calling from a mobile phone to another mobile phone. If you call these numbers from a landline within Hungary (such as from your hotel room phone), you'll need to replace the +36 with 06.

▶ To call a local guide with the number +3620-926-0557, dial exactly that from your US phone or Hungarian mobile phone—but from a Hungarian land line, dial 06-20-926-0557.

More Dialing Tips

Toll-Free Calls: International rates apply to US toll-free numbers dialed from any country in Eastern Europe—they're not free.

More Phoning Help: See www.howtocallabroad.com.

European Country Codes		Ireland & N. Ireland	353 / 44
Austria	43	Italy	39
Belgium	32	Latvia	371
Bosnia-Herzegovina	387	Montenegro	382
Croatia	385	Morocco	212
Czech Republic	420	Netherlands	31
Denmark	45	Norway	47
Estonia	372	Poland	48
Finland	358	Portugal	351
France	33	Russia	7
Germany	49	Slovakia	421
Gibraltar	350	Slovenia	386
Great Britain	44	Spain	34
Greece	30	Sweden	46
Hungary	36	Switzerland	41
Iceland	354	Turkey	90

PRACTICALITIES

it up, buy one at a mobile-phone shop (you may need to show your passport). Costing about $5-10, SIM cards usually include prepaid calling credit, with no contract and no commitment. Expect to pay $20-40 more for a SIM card with a gigabyte of data.

There are no roaming charges for EU citizens using a domestic SIM card in other EU countries. Theoretically, providers don't have to offer Americans this "roam-like-at-home" pricing, but most do. To be sure, buy your SIM card at a mobile-phone shop and ask if non-EU citizens also have roam-like-at-home pricing.

When you run out of credit, you can top your SIM card up at newsstands, tobacco shops, mobile-phone stores, or many other businesses (look for your SIM card's logo in the window), or possibly online.

WITHOUT A MOBILE PHONE

It's possible to travel in Europe without a mobile device. You can make calls from your hotel and check email or browse websites using public computers.

Most **hotels** charge a fee for placing calls—ask for rates before you dial. You can use a prepaid international phone card (usually available at newsstands, tobacco shops, and train stations) to call out from your hotel. Dial the toll-free access number, enter the card's PIN code, then dial the number.

You'll only see **public pay phones** in a few post offices and train stations. Most don't take coins but instead require insertable phone cards, which you can buy at a newsstand, convenience store, or post office. Except for emergencies, they're not worth the hassle.

Some hotels have **public computers** in their lobbies for guests to use; otherwise you may find them at public libraries (ask your hotelier or the TI for the nearest location). On a European keyboard, use the "Alt Gr" key to the right of the space bar to insert the extra symbol that appears on some keys. If you can't locate a special character (such as @), simply copy and paste it from a web page.

MAIL

You can mail one package per day to yourself worth up to $200 duty-free from Europe to the US (mark it "personal purchases"). If you're sending a gift to someone, mark it "unsolicited gift." For details, visit www.cbp.gov, select "Travel," and search for "Know Before You Go." The Eastern European postal services work fine, but for quick transatlantic delivery (in either direction), consider services such as DHL (www.dhl.com).

Transportation

In Eastern Europe, I travel mostly by public transportation. For long distances between big cities (such as Prague to Kraków, Warsaw to Budapest, or Vienna to Ljubljana), I prefer to take a cheap flight or a night train. For shorter distances (like Gdańsk to Warsaw or Budapest to Bratislava), I take a daytime train or bus. In areas with lots of exciting day-trip possibilities, such as the Czech countryside (castles) or Slovenia's Julian Alps (mountain scenery), I rent a car for a day or two. Or you can hire a local driver to take you around—freeing you up to enjoy the scenery...and the company (in this book, I recommend several drivers and tour guides with cars). If you're tackling an ambitious itinerary spanning several countries, think carefully before renting a car for your entire trip. Distances are long, and the international drop-off fees can be prohibitively expensive (details later).

When deciding between flights, car rental, and train or bus trips, be aware of the potential downside of each option: A car is an expensive headache in any major city; with trains and buses you're at the mercy of a timetable; and flying entails a trek to and from a usually distant airport.

For more detailed information on transportation throughout Europe, see www.ricksteves.com/transportation.

TRAINS

Trains are generally punctual and cover cities well, but frustrating schedules make a few out-of-the-way destinations difficult—or impossible—to reach (usually the bus will get you there instead; see "Buses," later).

Schedules: Pick up train schedules from stations as you go, or print them out from an online source. To study ahead on the web, check www.bahn.com, Germany's excellent all-Europe timetable. Individual countries also have their own train timetable websites:

- **Czech Republic:** www.idos.cz
- **Poland:** www.rozklad-pkp.pl
- **Hungary:** www.mavcsoport.hu
- **Slovenia:** www.slo-zeleznice.si
- **Austria:** www.oebb.at
- **Slovakia:** www.cp.sk

Tickets: You can usually buy tickets in advance online, and download an eticket to your phone (saving a trip to the station). Otherwise, buy tickets at the train station. Try using the ticket machines, which typically have English instructions and take American credit cards.

Some tickets may not be available through the machines, in which case you'll buy tickets from a staffed ticket window. In many big-city train stations, it can be tricky to find the correct line (you'll see separate ticket windows for domestic trips, international journeys, immediate departures, and other concerns). Before getting in line, confirm with fellow travelers that you've chosen the right one. Many ticket-sellers speak limited English—be prepared to write out your destination and time. Bigger stations (such as in Warsaw and Ljubljana) have train-ticket offices where you can take a number to wait for an English-speaking clerk to sort through your options; I've listed these in this book. Especially if you have a com-

PRACTICALITIES

Public Transportation in Eastern Europe

To Nynäshamn (Sweden)

To Aarhus & Copenhagen
To Rødby & Copenhagen (Denmark)
To Ystad (Sweden)
To Ystad & Copenhagen
To Karlskrona (Sweden)

Baltic Sea

LITH.

KALININGRAD (RUSSIA)

Gdynia
Sopot Gdańsk

To Vilnius via Grodno (Belarus)

Lübeck Puttgarten
Hamburg
Swinoujście
Tczew
Malbork

To Amsterdam
Szczecin

Toruń

To Brest & Moscow

Frankfurt an der Oder
Poznań

To Amsterdam Berlin
Warsaw

GERMANY
Forst
POLAND

Leipzig Görlitz
Zgor. Wrocław Częstochowa

Dresden Opole Oświęcim (Auschwitz)

To Frankfurt Schona Lichkov. Katowice Kraków

Karlovy Vary CZECH. REP. Zeb. Medyka

Cheb Prague Ostrava Krynica To L'viv

Plzeň Brno Žil. Zak.

Furth Český České Bud. Telč Levoča Plaveč UKR.

Nürnberg Krumlov Sum. Břeclav Spišska Košice

To Frankfurt Passau Gmünd SLOVAKIA

Munich Linz Melk Bratislava Eger Cana

Salzburg Vienna Miskolc

Innsbruck Hegy. Füzesabony

To Zürich Graz Győr Budapest

AUSTRIA Sopron

Klagen-furt Siófok Curtici

Villach Spiel. HUNGARY

Tarvisio Jes. Mar. To Bucharest

ITALY Bled Hodos Pécs

To Milan Verona SLOVENIA Kop.

Ljubljana Subotica

Venice Trieste Zagreb ROMANIA

Koper Rijeka CROATIA

Piran Šid

Rovinj Zadar Plitvice Belgrade

Bologna Pula BOSNIA-HERZ. SERBIA

ITALY Split Sarajevo Niš BULG.

Adriatic Sea Mostar Kalotina

Florence Hvar Cap. To Sofia & Istanbul

Ancona Korčula M Pres.

Rome Dubrovnik O KOS MACE-DONIA

N Kotor N Skopje

To Naples Not to Scale Bar T To Athens

Bari A L B.

- - - - Bus Route .... Ferry Route

———— Railway —o— Border Station

plicated request (such as reserving a night-train berth a few days ahead), these offices can save you some frustration. If the station is unstaffed, you can buy tickets on board—but find the conductor before they find you.

While most short-haul journeys do not require a reservation, you are required to reserve for some high-speed trains (including premium trains in Poland, such as the Warsaw-Kraków express). Schedules will indicate when a seat assignment is required on EuroCity or InterCity long-distance trains. It's also smart to reserve a sleeping berth if you're taking a night train.

Night Trains: To cover the long distances between the major destinations in this book, consider using night trains. Each night on the train saves a day for sightseeing. However, Eastern European night trains aren't as new, plush, or comfy as those in Western Europe (such as Austria's slick Nightjet). Expect a bumpy, noisy ride and gross WCs. In general, if a higher degree of comfort is important to you, look for an affordable flight (see "Flights," later), hire a driver to take you door-to-door (perhaps with some sightseeing stops en route), or take a day train. Thefts on night trains do occur, so lock the door of your compartment and secure your belongings (to make it difficult—or at least noisy—for thieves to rip you off). When sleeping on a night train, I wear my money belt.

Rail Passes: Since point-to-point train tickets are cheap throughout Eastern Europe, a rail pass isn't likely to save you much money. The main reason to buy a rail pass in this region is to avoid the hassle of buying tickets as you go. If a rail pass happens to match the countries you plan to visit, it can be a smart choice.

One handy option may be the European East Pass, covering the Czech Republic, Hungary, Slovakia, and Austria. The more expensive Eurail Global Pass covers most of Europe, including all the countries in this book. Each country except Slovakia, Bosnia, and Montenegro has its own individual Eurail pass, valid only within that country. There's also a Balkan Pass priced more logically for the eight countries it covers. Various preselected two- and three-country options are also available.

For more detailed advice on figuring out the smartest rail pass options for your train trip, and for point-to-point ticket-cost maps, visit RickSteves.com/rail.

BUSES

Increasingly, private bus companies are offering stiff competition to the established rail lines, with cheaper and sometimes faster connections between major cities, especially on international routes. The dominant outfit in Eastern Europe is the German-owned Flixbus (www.flixbus.com), which offers easy online booking and generally comfortable buses with air-conditioning and Wi-Fi. For a few key routes, the national rail company operates a bus instead of a train (such as the Kraków-Berlin connection). Other companies seem to come and go regularly, so search online to find the latest options (GetByBus.com is a good place to start, but is not comprehensive for locations in this book).

There are areas within Eastern Europe where buses are simply better than trains. For example in Slovenia, Ljubljana and Lake Bled are connected by both train and bus—but the bus station is right in the town center of Bled, while the train station is a few miles away. And a few destinations are accessible only by bus. When in doubt, ask at the local TI for advice.

TAXIS AND RIDE-BOOKING SERVICES

In Eastern Europe, legitimate taxis are a good value. In many cities, two people can travel short distances by cab for little more than the cost of bus or subway tickets. However, corruption is rampant and difficult to tame. Be sure you're using a well-established company. In countries where taxis are well regulated, it's easy to spot legit cabs (for example, in Budapest they have yellow license plates). In other countries, taxis can charge whatever they want—and hopping in the first one you see in front of a train station or major sight and paying what's on the meter is a great way to get overcharged. Locals always call for a cab from a reputable company (I've listed phone numbers throughout this book)—and get a fair fare. You can ask your hotel, the restaurant where you're dining, or even TIs inside train stations to call you a legitimate taxi.

For those who like ride-booking services such as Uber, their apps work in some parts of Europe just like they do in the US: Request a car on your mobile phone (connected to Wi-Fi or data), and the fare is automatically charged to your credit card. Uber operates in some countries (for example, Poland), but is prohibited by local regulations in others (such as Hungary). When you arrive, open your Uber app to see if it's available. This can be a great way to sidestep the headache of finding a legitimate taxi—and, aside from "surge" pricing at very busy times, it's usually much cheaper than even well-regulated taxi fares.

RENTING A CAR

It's cheaper to arrange most car rentals from the US, so research and compare rates before you go. Most of the major US rental agencies (including Avis, Budget, Enterprise, Hertz, and Thrifty) have offices throughout Europe. Also consider the two major Europe-based agencies, Europcar and Sixt. Consolidators such as Auto Europe/Kemwel (www.autoeurope.com—or the sometimes cheaper www.autoeurope.eu) compare rates at several companies to get you the best deal.

Wherever you book, always read the fine print. Ask about add-on charges—such as one-way drop-off fees, airport surcharges, or mandatory insurance policies—that aren't included in the "total price."

Rental Costs and Considerations

Figure on paying roughly $250 for a one-week rental for a basic compact car. Allow extra for supplemental insurance, fuel, tolls, and parking. To save money on fuel, request a diesel car.

Manual vs. Automatic: Almost all rental cars in Europe are manual by default—and cars with a stick shift are generally cheaper. If you need an automatic, request one in advance. When selecting a car, don't be tempted by a larger model, as it won't be as maneuverable on narrow, winding roads or when squeezing into tight parking lots.

Age Restrictions: Some rental companies impose minimum and maximum age limits. Young drivers (25 and under) and seniors (69 and up) should check the rental policies and rules section of car rental websites. If you're considered too young or too old, look into leasing (covered later), which has less stringent age restrictions.

Choosing Pickup/Drop-off Locations: Always check the hours of the locations you choose: Many rental offices close from midday Saturday until Monday morning and, in smaller towns, at lunchtime. When selecting an office, plug the address into a mapping website to confirm the location. A downtown site is generally cheaper—and might seem more convenient than the airport. But pedestrianized and one-way streets can make navigation tricky when returning a car at a big-city office or urban train station. Wherever you select, get precise details on the location and allow ample time to find it.

Have the Right License: If you're renting a car in Eastern Europe, bring your driver's license. In Austria, Bosnia-Herzegovina, Hungary, Poland, and Slovenia you're also technically required to have an International Driving Permit—an official translation of your license (sold at AAA offices for about $20 plus the cost of two passport-type photos; see www.aaa.com). While that's the letter of the law, I generally rent cars without having this permit. How this is enforced varies from country to country: Get advice from your car-rental company.

Crossing Borders in a Rental Car: It's typically not a problem to cross borders between Schengen countries—but if venturing beyond this open-borders area (for example, into Croatia or Romania), there may be restrictions. Always tell your car-rental company exactly which countries you'll be entering. Some companies levy extra insurance fees for trips taken in certain countries with certain cars (such as BMWs, Mercedes, and convertibles). Double-check

Driving in Eastern Europe

N · Not to Scale

GERMANY

To Gdańsk
110m · 2h

Toruń — 135m · 3h — Warsaw

Berlin

180m · 3h — Poznań — 190m · 3.5h

120m
2.25h

265m · 4.5h

210m · 3.5h — 140m · 2.5h

POLAND

185m · 3.5h

390m · 7h

Dresden

Częstochowa — 90m · 2h

65m
1.5h

290m · 5.5h — 65m 1.75h

40m · 1.25h — Kraków

Terezín — 40m 1h — Auschwitz

100m · 2.75h

Prague — 40m 1.25h — 80m · 2h

25m · .75h — Kutná Hora

CZECH REPUBLIC

Zakopane — 115m · 3.5h

Karlštejn Castle

130m · 2h — 175m · 3.5h

45m 1.5h

Poprad

100m · 2.25h — 210m · 3.5h

200m · 4h — SLOVAKIA

Brno — 200m — 80m 2h

Český Krumlov — 135m · 3.25h

80m 1.5h — 3.5h

240m 5.5h

240m 4h

Munich

140m · 2.5h — Vienna — 40m 1h — Bratislava

Eger

80m · 2h

90m 1.5h

200m · 3.5h — 125m · 2h — To Maramureș 210m · 6h

Salzburg

235m · 4h — 150m · 2.5h

Budapest — To Cluj-Napoca 290m · 6.5h

150m
2.5h

290m · 5h — 520m · 10h — To Bucharest

AUSTRIA

Pécs — 145m · 2.5h — HUNGARY

Bled

30m 1h — 90m · 2h — 150m · 3.5h — SERBIA

60m 1.5h — Ljubljana

SLOVENIA

140m · 3.5h — Zagreb — CROATIA

ITALY

75m 2h — 100m · 2h — 260m · 4h — 260m · 6h

100m · 1.75h

Trieste

50m · 1.5h — 85m · 2h

Venice — Rovinj — Rijeka — 90m · 2.5h

30m · .75h — 55m 1.5h — 140m · 3.5h — Plitvice — BOSNIA-HERZEGOVINA

Pula

85m 1.75h — Sarajevo — To Sofia

90m 2.5h — 380m · 9h

Adriatic Sea — Zadar — 100m · 2h — Mostar

65m 2h — 110m · 2.5h

Split — 105m · 2.5h — Ston — MONT.

.5h — 35m 1h — 60m 2h

Korčula — 3-4h — Dubrovnik — Kotor

Note: Your times may vary based on traffic, construction, and road conditions.

m = miles
h = hours
--- = car ferry

with your rental agent that you have all the documentation you need before you drive off; at border checkpoints, it's likely you'll be asked to present proof of insurance (called a "green card"). Note that picking up a car in one country and dropping it off in another can be quite expensive—see "International Drop-Off Fees," below.

Picking Up Your Car: Before driving off in your rental car, check it thoroughly and make sure any damage is noted on your rental agreement. Rental agencies in Europe tend to charge for even minor damage, so be sure to mark everything. Find out how your car's gearshift, lights, turn signals, wipers, radio, and fuel cap function, and know what kind of fuel the car takes (diesel vs. unleaded). When you return the car, make sure the agent verifies its condition with you. Some drivers take pictures of the returned vehicle as proof of its condition.

International Drop-Off Fees

If you're planning a multicountry itinerary by car, be aware of often-astronomical international drop-off fees. There's typically no extra charge for picking up and dropping off a car in different towns within the same country—but you'll pay through the nose to drop off across the border. (For example, you can generally pick up a car in Kraków, drive it six hours to Gdańsk, and turn it in there for no charge—but if you drive the same car from Vienna just an hour to Bratislava and drop it off, it can cost you hundreds of extra dollars.)

For some itineraries, you may just have to live with the extra expense. But in most cases, you can plan your itinerary smartly to avoid it. Some people plan a circular itinerary (for example, Prague-Kraków-Budapest-Bratislava-Vienna-Prague) to ensure they can drop the car off where they picked it up. Others connect the longer distances on their itinerary with trains or flights, then rent a car strategically for a day or two in places where it's warranted (such as the Czech or Slovenian countrysides). This is a particularly smart plan when you remember that in most big cities, a car is an expensive and worthless burden (i.e., fighting urban traffic and paying for pricey secure parking).

Car Insurance Options

When you rent a car in Europe, the price typically includes liability insurance, which covers harm to other cars or motorists—but not the rental car itself. To limit your financial risk in case of damage to the rental, choose one of these options: Buy a Collision Damage Waiver (CDW) with a low or zero deductible from the car-rental company (roughly 30-40 percent extra), get coverage through your credit card (free, but more complicated), or get collision insurance as part of a larger travel-insurance policy.

Basic **CDW** costs $15-30 a day, and typically comes with a

$1,000-2,000 deductible, reducing but not eliminating your financial responsibility. When you reserve or pick up the car, you'll be offered the chance to "buy down" the deductible to zero (for an additional $10-30/day; this is sometimes called "super CDW" or "zero-deductible coverage").

If you opt for **credit-card coverage,** you must decline all coverage offered by the car-rental company—which means they can place a hold on your card for up to the full value of the car. In case of damage, it can be time-consuming to resolve the charges. Before relying on this option, quiz your card company about how it works.

If you're already purchasing a **travel-insurance policy** for your trip, adding collision coverage can be an economical option. For example, Travel Guard (www.travelguard.com) sells affordable renter's collision insurance as an add-on to its other policies; it's valid everywhere in Europe except the Republic of Ireland, and some Italian car-rental companies refuse to honor it, as it doesn't cover you in case of theft.

For more on car-rental insurance, see www.ricksteves.com/cdw.

Leasing

For trips of three weeks or more, consider leasing (which automatically includes zero-deductible collision and theft insurance). By technically buying and then selling back the car, you save money on taxes and insurance. Leasing provides you a brand-new car with unlimited mileage and a 24-hour emergency assistance program. You can lease for as little as 21 days to as long as five and a half months. Car leases must be arranged from the US. One of several companies offering affordable lease packages is Auto Europe. Note that leases aren't generally available in Eastern Europe—you'll have to pick up and drop off the car elsewhere in Europe (such as Germany or Italy).

Navigation Options

If you'll be navigating using your phone or a GPS unit from home, remember to bring a car charger and device mount.

Your Mobile Phone: The mapping app on your phone works just as well for navigation in Europe. But driving all day can burn through a lot of very expensive mobile data. The economical workaround is to use map apps that work offline. By downloading maps in advance (from Google Maps, Apple Maps, HereWeGo, or Navmii) you can still have turn-by-turn voice directions and maps that recalibrate even though they're offline. (Though if you're offline, you won't get traffic updates.)

For this to work, you must download your maps before you go offline—and it's smart to select large regions. Then turn off your data connection. Call up the map, enter your destination, and you're on your way. Even if you have unlimited data, this option is great for navigating in areas with poor connectivity.

GPS Devices: If you want the convenience of a dedicated GPS unit, consider renting one with your car ($10-30/day). These units offer real-time turn-by-turn directions and traffic without the data requirements of an app. The unit may come loaded only with maps for its home country; if you need additional maps, ask. Also make sure your device's language is set to English before you drive off.

A less expensive option is to bring a GPS device from home. Be sure to buy and install the European maps you'll need before your trip.

Maps and Atlases: Even when navigating primarily with a mobile app or GPS, I always make it a point to have a paper map. It's invaluable for getting the big picture, understanding alternate routes, and filling in when my phone runs out of juice. The free maps you get from your car-rental company usually don't have enough detail. It's smart to buy a better map before you go, or pick one up at a European gas station, bookshop, newsstand, or tourist shop.

Driving

Road Rules: Be aware of typical European road rules; for example, many countries—including most of the ones in this book—require headlights to be turned on at all times, and nearly all forbid handheld mobile-phone use. In Europe, you're not allowed to turn right on a red light, unless a sign or signal specifically authorizes it, and on expressways it's illegal to pass drivers on the right. Ask your car-rental company about these rules, or check the "International Travel" section of the US State Department

website (travel.state.gov, search for your country in the "Country Information" box, then click on "Travel and Transportation").

Fuel: Gas is expensive—often about $6-8 per gallon. Diesel cars are more common in Europe than back home, so be sure you know what type of fuel your car takes before you fill up. Fuel pumps are color-coded for unleaded (green) or diesel (black).

Road Conditions: Eastern Europe is nearing the end of an impressive binge of superhighway construction. It's not unusual to discover that a much faster road has been built between major destinations since your five-year-old map was published. (This is another good reason to travel with the most up-to-date maps possible, and study them before each drive.) Over the last several years, superhighways have opened between Dresden and Prague (A-17) and between Warsaw and Berlin (A-2).

Occasionally backcountry roads are the only option. These can be bumpy and slow, but they're almost always paved (or, at least, they once were). In Poland, where the network of new expressways is far from complete, locals travel long distances on two-lane country roads. Since each lane is about a lane and a half wide, passing is commonplace. Slower drivers should keep to the far-right of their lane, and not be surprised when  faster cars zip past them. Especially in Croatia and Slovenia, keep a close eye out for bikers—you'll see scads of them on mountain roads, struggling to earn a thrilling downhill run.

Tolls: In many countries, driving on highways requires a toll sticker (generally available at the border, post offices, gas stations, and sometimes car-rental agencies). You'll need a sticker in the **Czech Republic** (*dálniční známka*, 310 Kč/10 days, 440 Kč/1 month, www.sfdi.cz); **Slovakia** (*úhrada*, €10/10 days, €14/month, www.dialnicnenalepky.sk); **Hungary** (*autópálya matrica*, 3,500 Ft/10 days, 4,780 Ft/month, www.motorway.hu); **Slovenia** (*vinjeta*, €15/week, €30/month, www.dars.si); and **Austria** (*Vignette*, €9.50/10 days, €26/2 months, www.asfinag.at). Fines for not having a toll sticker can be stiff. Your rental car may already come with the necessary sticker—ask. In **Poland,** you'll take a toll ticket as you enter the expressway, then pay when you get off, based on how far you've traveled.

Parking: Parking is a costly headache in big cities. You'll pay about $10-25 a day to park safely. Rental-car theft can be a problem in cities (especially Prague), so ask at your hotel for advice.

FLIGHTS

To compare flight costs and times, begin with a travel search engine: Kayak.com is the top site for flights to and within Europe, easy-to-use Google.com/Flights has price alerts, and Skyscanner.com includes many inexpensive flights within Europe.

Flights to Europe: Start looking for international flights about four to six months before your trip, especially for peak-season travel. Depending on your itinerary, it can be efficient and no more expensive to fly into one city and out of another. If your flight requires a connection in Europe, see my hints on navigating Europe's top hub airports at www.ricksteves.com/hub-airports.

Flights Within Europe: Flying between European cities has become surprisingly affordable. Before buying a long-distance train or bus ticket, first check the cost of a flight on one of Europe's airlines, whether a major carrier or a no-frills outfit. Two well-established budget airlines are based in Eastern Europe: **Wizz Air** (www.wizzair.com, with a hub in Budapest) and **Smart Wings** (www.smartwings.net, based in Prague). Well-known cheapo airlines that fly to Eastern European destinations include **Easy-Jet** (www.easyjet.com), **Ryanair** (www.ryanair.com), **Air Berlin** (www.airberlin.com), and **Norwegian Air** (www.norwegian.no).

Many national carriers also charge reasonable fares for short-distance trips. For example, check out Poland's LOT Airlines

(www.lot.com). On recent trips, I've flown affordably on LOT between Kraków and Ljubljana, and between Kraków and Budapest, avoiding lengthy overland journeys.

Be aware of the potential drawbacks of flying with a discount airline: nonrefundable and nonchangeable tickets, minimal customer service, time-consuming treks to secondary airports, and stingy baggage allowances (also an issue on major airlines). To avoid unpleasant surprises, read the small print about the costs for "extras" such as reserving a seat, checking a bag, or checking in and printing a boarding pass.

Flying to the US and Canada: Because security is extra tight for flights to the US, be sure to give yourself plenty of time at the airport. It's also important to charge your electronic devices before you board because security checks may require you to turn them on (see www.tsa.gov for the latest rules).

PRACTICALITIES

Resources from Rick Steves

Begin Your Trip at RickSteves.com

My mobile-friendly **website** is *the* place to explore Europe in preparation for your trip. You'll find thousands of fun articles, videos, and radio interviews; a wealth of money-saving tips for planning your dream trip; travel news dispatches; a video library of my travel talks; my travel blog; my latest guidebook updates (www.ricksteves. com/update); and my free Rick Steves Audio Europe app. You can also follow me on Facebook and Twitter.

Our **Travel Forum** is a well-groomed collection of message boards where our travel-savvy community answers questions and shares their personal travel experiences—and our well-traveled staff chimes in when they can be helpful (www.ricksteves.com/forums).

Our **online Travel Store** offers bags and accessories that I've designed to help you travel smarter and lighter. These include my popular carry-on bags (which I live out of four months a year), money belts, totes, toiletries kits, adapters, guidebooks, and planning maps (www.ricksteves.com/shop).

Our website can also help you find the perfect **rail pass** for your itinerary and your budget, with easy, one-stop shopping for rail passes, seat reservations, and point-to-point tickets (www.ricksteves.com/rail).

Rick Steves' Tours, Guidebooks, TV Shows, and More

Small Group Tours: Want to travel with greater efficiency and less stress? We offer more than 40 itineraries reaching the best destinations in this book...and beyond. Each year about 30,000 travelers join us on about 1,000 Rick Steves bus tours. You'll enjoy great guides and a fun bunch of travel partners (with small groups of 24 to 28 travelers). You'll find European adventures to fit every vacation length. For all the details, and to get our tour catalog, visit www.ricksteves.com or call us at 425/608-4217.

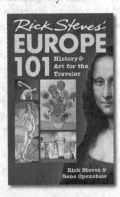

Books: *Rick Steves Eastern Europe* is one of many books in my series on European travel, which includes country and city guidebooks, Snapshots (excerpted chapters from bigger guides), Pocket Guides (full-color little books on big cities), "Best Of" guidebooks (condensed, full-color country guides), and my budget-travel skills handbook, *Rick Steves Europe Through the Back Door.*

A more complete list of my titles—including phrase books, cruising guides, and more—appears near the end of this book.

TV Shows and Travel Talks: My public television series, *Rick Steves' Europe,* covers Europe from top to bottom with over 100 half-hour episodes—and we're working on new shows every year (watch full episodes online for free). Or, to raise your travel I.Q., check out the video versions of our popular classes (covering most European countries as well as travel skills, packing smart, cruising, tech for travelers, European art, and travel as a political act—www.ricksteves.com/travel-talks).

Radio: My weekly public radio show, *Travel with Rick Steves,* features interviews with travel experts from around the world. It airs on 400 public radio stations across the US, or you can hear it as a podcast. A complete archive of programs is available at www.ricksteves.com/radio.

Audio Tours on My Free App: I've produced dozens of free, self-guided audio tours of top sights in Europe. For those tours and other audio content, get my free Rick Steves Audio Europe app, an extensive online library organized by destination. For more on my app, see page 12.

PRACTICALITIES

APPENDIX

Holidays and Festivals

This list includes selected festivals in this region, plus national holidays observed throughout Eastern Europe. Many sights and banks close on national holidays—keep this in mind when planning your itinerary. Catholic holidays are celebrated in Poland, Slovakia, and Slovenia (and to a lesser extent in Hungary and the Czech Republic). Before planning a trip around a festival, verify its dates with the festival's website or tourist information website.

Jan 1	New Year's Day
Jan 6	Epiphany, Catholic countries
Jan 19	Anniversary of Jan Palach's death, Prague (flowers in Wenceslas Square)
Feb 8	National Day of Culture, Slovenia (celebrates Slovenian culture and national poet France Prešeren)
March	One World International Human Rights Film Festival, Prague (www.oneworld.cz)
March 15	National Day, Hungary (celebrates 1848 Revolution)
Late March	Ski Jumping World Cup Finals, Planica, Slovenia (3 days, www.planica.si)

April	Easter weekend (Good Friday-Easter Monday): April 19-22, 2019; April 10-April 13, 2020
April	Budapest Spring Festival (2 weeks; opera, ballet, classical music; www.btf.hu)
April 27	National Resistance Day, Slovenia
April 30	Witches' Night, Czech Republic (similar to Halloween, with bonfires)
April-June	Ramadan: May 5-June 4, 2019; April 23-May 23, 2020 (Muslim holy month)
May	Ascension: May 30, 2019; May 21, 2020 (Catholic countries)
May 1	Labor Day
May 3	Constitution Day, Poland (celebrates Europe's first constitution)
May 8	Liberation Day, Czech Republic and Slovakia
May-June	Pentecost and Whitmonday: June 9-10, 2019; May 31-June 1, 2020 (Catholic countries)
May-June	Vienna Festival of Arts and Music (www.festwochen.at)
Early May	Prague International Marathon (www.runczech.com)
Mid-May-early June	"Prague Spring" Music Festival (www.festival.cz)
Late May-mid-June	Jewish Art Days, Budapest (2 weeks, www.zsidomuveszetinapok.hu)
June	Corpus Christi: June 20, 2019; June 11, 2020 (Catholic countries)
June	Five-Petalled Rose Celebration, Český Krumlov, Czech Republic (medieval festival, music, theater, dance, knights' tournament)
June-July	Prague Proms, Prague (music festival, www.pragueproms.cz)
June 25	National Day, Slovenia
Late June	Wianki Midsummer Festival, Kraków, Poland (wreaths on rafts in Vistula River, fireworks, music)
Late June	Jewish Culture Festival, Kraków, Poland (www.jewishfestival.pl)
Late June	Midsummer Eve celebrations, Austria
July 5	Sts. Cyril and Methodius Day, Czech Republic and Slovakia
July 6	Jan Hus Day, Czech Republic

Early July–Sept	Ljubljana Festival, Slovenia (www.ljubljanafestival.si)
Mid-July–mid-Aug	International Music Festival, Český Krumlov, Czech Republic (www.festivalkrumlov.cz)
Late July	Formula 1 races, Budapest (www.hungaroinfo.com/formel1)
Late July–mid-Aug	St. Dominic's Fair, Gdańsk, Poland (3 weeks of market stalls, music, and general revelry)
Aug	Sziget Festival, Budapest (rock and pop music, www.sziget.hu)
Aug 15	Assumption of Mary, Catholic countries
Aug 20	St. István's Day, Hungary (also known as Constitution Day; fireworks, celebrations)
Aug 29	National Uprising Day, Slovakia (commemorates uprising against Nazis)
Sept	Dvořák's Prague Music Festival, Prague (www.dvorakovapraha.cz)
Sept–Oct	Jewish High Holy Days (Rosh Hashanah: Sept 29–Oct 1, 2019, Sept 18-20, 2020; Yom Kippur: Oct 8-9, 2019, Sept 27-28, 2020; Jewish sites may close)
Sept 1	Constitution Day, Slovakia
Sept 28	St. Wenceslas Day, Czech Republic (celebrates national patron saint and Czech statehood)
Mid-Oct–early Nov	International Jazz Festival, Prague (www.agharta.cz)
Mid-Oct	Café Budapest Festival (contemporary arts, www.cafebudapestfest.hu)
Oct 23	Republic Day, Hungary (remembrances of 1956 Uprising)
Oct 26	National Day, Austria
Oct 28	Independence Day, Czech Republic
Oct 31	Reformation Day, Slovenia
Nov 1	All Saints' Day/Remembrance Day, Catholic countries (religious festival, some closures)
Nov 11	Independence Day, Poland; St. Martin's Day (official first day of wine season), Austria and Slovenia
Nov 17	Velvet Revolution Anniversary, Czech Republic and Slovakia
Dec 5	St. Nicholas Eve, Prague (St. Nick gives gifts to children in town square)
Dec 24-25	Christmas Eve and Christmas Day

APPENDIX

| Dec 26 | Boxing Day/St. Stephen's Day; Independence and Unity Day, Slovenia |
| Dec 31 | St. Sylvester's Day, Prague and Vienna (fireworks) |

Books and Films

To learn about Eastern Europe past and present, check out a few of these books and films.

Nonfiction

Lonnie Johnson's *Central Europe: Enemies, Neighbors, Friends* is the best historical overview of the countries in this book. Timothy Garton Ash has written several good "eyewitness account" books analyzing the fall of communism in Eastern Europe, including *History of the Present* and *The Magic Lantern*. Michael Meyer's *The Year that Changed the World* intimately chronicles the exciting events of 1989, culminating in the fall of the Berlin Wall. Anne Applebaum's *Iron Curtain: The Crushing of Eastern Europe 1944-1956* is a readable account of how the Soviets exerted their influence on the nations they had just liberated from the Nazis; her *Gulag: A History* delves into one particularly odious mechanism they used to intimidate their subjects. Tina Rosenberg's dense but thought-provoking *The Haunted Land* asks how those who actively supported communism in Eastern Europe should be treated in the postcommunist age. And Benjamin Curtis' *The Habsburgs: The History of a Dynasty* is an illuminating portrait of the Austrian imperial family that shaped so much of Eastern European history.

Patrick Leigh Fermor's *Between the Woods and the Water* is the vivid memoir of a young man who traveled by foot and on horseback across the Balkan Peninsula (including Hungary) in 1933. Rebecca West's classic, bricklike *Black Lamb and Grey Falcon* is the definitive travelogue of the Yugoslav lands (written during a journey between the two World Wars).

James Michener's *The Bridge at Andau* tells the story of the 1956 Uprising in Budapest, and the Hungarians who fled following its crushing defeat.

For a more recent take, Croatian journalist Slavenka Drakulić has written a quartet of insightful essay collections from a woman's perspective: *Café Europa: Life After Communism; The Balkan Express; How We Survived Communism and Even Laughed;* and *A Guided Tour Through the Museum of Communism*. Drakulić's *They Would Never Hurt a Fly* profiles Yugoslav war criminals.

Dominika Dery's memoir, *The Twelve Little Cakes*, traces her experience growing up in communist Czechoslovakia in the 1970s.

For a thorough explanation of how and why Yugoslavia broke

apart, read *Yugoslavia: Death of a Nation* (by Laura Silber and Allan Little).

For information on Eastern European Roma (Gypsies), consider the textbook-style *We Are the Romani People* by Ian Hancock, and the more literary *Bury Me Standing* by Isabel Fonseca.

Fiction

The most prominent works of Eastern European fiction have come from the Czechs. These include *I Served the King of England* (Bohumil Hrabal), *The Unbearable Lightness of Being* (Milan Kundera), and *The Good Soldier Švejk* (Jaroslav Hašek). Czech existentialist writer Franz Kafka wrote many well-known novels, including *The Trial* and *The Metamorphosis*. Bruce Chatwin's *Utz* is set in communist Prague.

James Michener's *Poland* is a hefty look into the history of the Poles. *Zlateh the Goat* (Isaac Bashevis Singer) includes seven folktales of Jewish Eastern Europe. Joseph Roth's *The Radetzky March* details the decline of an aristocratic Slovenian family in the Austro-Hungarian Empire.

Imre Kertész, a Hungarian-Jewish Auschwitz survivor who won the Nobel Prize for Literature in 2002, is best known for his semiautobiographical novel *Fatelessness (Sorstalanság)*, which chronicles the experience of a young concentration-camp prisoner. Márai Sándor's reflective *Embers* paints a rich picture of cobblestoned, gaslit Vienna just before the empire's glory began to fade.

Arthur Phillips' confusingly titled 2002 novel *Prague* tells the story of American expats negotiating young-adult life in postcommunist Budapest, where they often feel one-upped by their compatriots doing the same in the Czech capital (hence the title).

Films

Each of these countries has produced fine films. Below are a few highlights.

Czech Republic

The Czech film industry is one of the strongest in Eastern Europe; even under communism, its films were seen and honored worldwide. Before he directed *One Flew Over the Cuckoo's Nest* and *Amadeus*, Miloš Forman directed *Loves of a Blonde* (1965), about the relationship between a rural Czech woman and a jazz pianist from Prague; and *The Firemen's Ball* (1967), a satirical look at small-town Czechoslovakia under communism. Another Czech New Wave film, *Intimate Lighting* (1965), finds two musicians reuniting in the 1960s.

In *Alice* (1988), Czech artist Jan Švankmajer adapts Lewis Carroll's *Alice's Adventures in Wonderland* in stop-motion animation combined with live action. The comedy *Czech Dream* (2004) features two film students who document the opening of a fake hypermarket in a hilarious, disturbing commentary on consumerism.

Two films directed by Jiří Menzel cover everyday life during World War II. The Oscar-winning *Closely Watched Trains* (1966) follows a young Czech man working at a German-occupied train station. *I Served the King of England* (2006), an adaptation of Bohumil Hrabal's novel, finds a man reminiscing about his past as an ambitious waiter who suffers the consequences of World War II.

Other great Czech films about World War II include *Divided We Fall* (2000), where a Czech couple hides a Jewish friend during Nazi occupation; *Protektor* (2009), whose main character must reconcile his job at a Nazi-propaganda radio station and his relationship with his Jewish wife; and *All My Loved Ones* (1999), the story of a Jewish family whose son is sent to England in the "Kindertransports" organized by Nicholas Winton (the British humanitarian who saved almost 700 Czech Jewish children).

Recent Czech films also cover life under communism and the Velvet Revolution. *The Elementary School* (1991), set in the late 1940s, looks at a rowdy classroom in suburban Prague that faces reform under the strict guidance of a war-hero teacher. The mystery *In the Shadow* (2012) tracks a burglary in 1950s Czechoslovakia that sets off a political investigation of Jewish immigrants. *Larks on a String* (1990) covers bourgeois Czechs who are forced into communist labor camps and struggle to maintain their humanity. The TV miniseries *Burning Bush* (2013) details the communist occupation of Czechoslovakia and the Prague Spring, focusing on Jan Palach, the Czech student who set himself on fire and died in protest against the Soviet occupation. In the Oscar-winning *Kolya* (1996), a concert cellist in Soviet-controlled Czechoslovakia must care for an abandoned Russian boy just before the Velvet Revolution breaks out.

The Czechs also have a wonderful animation tradition that successfully competes with Walt Disney in Eastern Europe and China. The most popular character is Krtek (or Krteček, "Little Mole"), who gets in and out of trouble. You'll see plush black-and-white Krtek figures everywhere. Křemílek and Vochomůrka are brothers who live in the woods, Maxipes Fík is a clever dog, and the duo Pat and Mat are builders who can't seem to get anything right.

Poland

Several Polish films have won Oscars and major awards at Cannes. In *Katyń* (2007), acclaimed, Oscar-winning director Andrzej Wajda re-creates the Soviet Army's massacre of around 22,000 Polish officers, enlisted men, and civilians during World War II.

Some of Wajda's earlier works include *Ashes and Diamonds* (1958), *The Promised Land* (1979), and the two-part series *Man of Marble* (1977) and *Man of Iron* (1981).

Polish filmmaker Krzysztof Kieslowski made several master-pieces, including *The Decalogue* (1989), consisting of 10 short films inspired by the Ten Commandments. Kieslowski also filmed the multilingual Three Colors Trilogy: *Red* (1994), *White* (1994), and *Blue* (1993).

Among other recent films, one Polish favorite is *Karol: A Man Who Became Pope* (2005), a Polish-Italian biopic made in English about the humble beginnings of St. John Paul II. Another fascinating religious tale is *Ida* (2014), the story of a young novitiate nun in 1960s Poland, who—just before taking her vows—discovers a terrible family secret.

A trip to the poignant Holocaust sites of Poland—Auschwitz, Kazimierz (in Kraków), and Warsaw's former ghetto area—is made immeasurably richer if you watch *Schindler's List* and *The Pianist* before you go (see "Hollywood Meets Eastern Europe," later).

Hungary

The surreal dark comedy *Kontroll* (2003) is about ticket inspectors on the Budapest Metró whose lives are turned upside down by a serial killer lurking in the shadows. *Fateless*, the 2005 adaptation of Imre Kertész's Nobel Prize-winning novel about a young man in a concentration camp, was scripted by Kertész himself. *The Witness* (a.k.a. *Without a Trace*, 1969), a cult classic about a simple man who mysteriously wins the favor of communist bigwigs, is a biting satire of the darkest days of Soviet rule. *Time Stands Still* (1981), a hit at the 1982 Cannes Film Festival, tells the story of young Hungarians in the 1960s. *Children of Glory* (2006) dramatizes the true story of the Hungarian water polo team that defiantly trounced the Soviets at the Olympics just after the 1956 Uprising.

Slovenia (and Other Former Yugoslav Countries)

To grasp the wars that shook this region in the early 1990s, there's no better film than the Slovene-produced *No Man's Land*, which won the 2002 Oscar for Best Foreign Film. Angelina Jolie wrote and directed (but did not appear in) 2011's wrenching, difficult-to-watch *In the Land of Blood and Honey*, a love story set against the grotesque backdrop of the war in Bosnia.

On a lighter note, a classic from Tito-era Yugoslavia, *The Battle of Neretva* (1969), imported Hollywood talent in the form of Yul Brynner and Orson Welles to tell the story of a pivotal and inspiring battle in the fight against the Nazis. More recent Croatian films worth watching include *Border Post* (2006), about various Yugoslav soldiers working together just before the war broke out; and *When Father Was Away on Business* (1985), about a prisoner on

APPENDIX

the Tito-era gulag island of Goli Otok, near Rab. Other local movies include *Armin* (2007), *How the War Started on My Island* (1996), *Underground* (1995), and *Tito and Me* (1992).

Documentaries

Documentaries about this region are also worth looking for. The BBC produced a remarkable, definitive six-hour documentary series called *The Death of Yugoslavia,* featuring interviews with all of the key players (it's difficult to find on DVD, but try searching for "Death of Yugoslavia" on YouTube; the book *Yugoslavia: Death of a Nation,* noted earlier, was a companion piece to this film). The BBC also produced a harrowing documentary about the infamous Bosnian massacre, *Srebrenica: A Cry from the Grave* (also available on YouTube). The 1998 Oscar-winning documentary *The Last Days* recounts the fate of Jews when the Nazis took over Hungary in 1944.

Hollywood Meets Eastern Europe

Several award-winning films have covered key moments in Eastern European history. *Schindler's List* (1993), Steven Spielberg's Best Picture-winner, tells the story of a compassionate German businessman in Kraków who saved his Jewish workers during the Holocaust. Roman Polanski's *The Pianist* (2002) is a biopic about the struggle for survival of Władysław Szpilman (played by Adrien Brody, in an Oscar-winning role), a Jewish concert pianist in Holocaust-era Warsaw.

The Unbearable Lightness of Being (1988), starring a young Daniel Day-Lewis, adapts the Milan Kundera novel about a love triangle set against the backdrop of the Prague Spring uprising. And *Sunshine* (1999, starring Ralph Fiennes, directed by István Szabó) somewhat melodramatically traces three generations of an aristocratic Jewish family in Budapest, from the Golden Age, through the Holocaust, to the Cold War.

Two acclaimed German movies offer excellent insight into the surreal and paranoid days of the Soviet Bloc. The Oscar-winning *Lives of Others* (2006) chronicles the constant surveillance that the communist regime employed to keep potential dissidents in line. For a funny and nostalgic look at postcommunist Europe's fitful transition to capitalism, *Good Bye Lenin!* (2003) can't be beat. Another insightful look at this period of communist paranoia is Steven Spielberg's 2015 *Bridge of Spies,* which follows Tom Hanks into 1960s Berlin—just as the Berlin Wall is going up—to walk the diplomatic tightrope of a prisoner swap with the Soviets.

Eastern European filmmakers have always been very active in Hollywood. "Crossover" directors—who started out making films in their own countries and then turned out English-language Oscar winners—include Michael Curtiz (from Hungary; *Casablanca, White Christmas*), Miloš Forman (from Czechoslovakia; *One Flew*

Over the Cuckoo's Nest, Amadeus), and Roman Polanski (from Poland; *Chinatown, The Pianist*). Other great Eastern European filmmakers include Steven Spielberg's favorite cinematographer, Janusz Kamiński, from Poland (*Schindler's List, Saving Private Ryan, Lincoln,* and most other Spielberg films).

You may recognize Eastern Europe backdrops in many blockbuster Hollywood movies—particularly Prague, whose low costs and well-trained filmmaking workforce appeal to studios. In many cases, Prague stands in for another European city. Films shot at least partly in Prague include everything from *Amadeus* to *Mission: Impossible;* from *The Chronicles of Narnia* to *Wanted;* from *The Bourne Identity* to the *Hostel* films; and from *Hannibal* to *Shanghai Knights.* Elsewhere in the Czech Republic, they've filmed the James Bond reboot *Casino Royale* and *The Illusionist.* Many American studios have taken advantage of Hungary's low prices to film would-be blockbusters in Budapest, including *Spy, A Good Day to Die Hard,* and *Mission: Impossible—Ghost Protocol.* More often, Budapest stands in for other cities—for example, as Buenos Aires in the 1996 film *Evita,* and as various European locales in Stephen Spielberg's 2005 film *Munich.*

Conversions and Climate

Numbers and Stumblers

- Europeans write a few of their numbers differently than we do. 1 = 1, 4 = 4, 7 = 7.
- In Europe, dates appear as day/month/year, so Christmas 2020 is 25/12/20. In Hungary, dates are written as year/month/day, so Christmas 2020 is 2020/12/25 (or dots can be used instead: 2020.12.25).
- Commas are decimal points and decimals are commas. A dollar and a half is $1,50, one thousand is 1.000, and there are 5.280 feet in a mile.
- Hungarians usually list their surname first (for example, Bartók Béla instead of Béla Bartók).
- When counting with fingers, start with your thumb. If you hold up your first finger to request one item, you'll probably get two.
- What Americans call the second floor of a building is the first floor in Europe.
- On escalators and moving sidewalks, Europeans keep the left "lane" open for passing. Keep to the right.

Metric Conversions

A **kilogram** equals 1,000 grams (about 2.2 pounds). One hundred

grams (a common unit at markets) is about a quarter-pound. One **liter** is about a quart, or almost four to a gallon.

A **kilometer** is six-tenths of a mile. To convert kilometers to miles, cut the kilometers in half and add back 10 percent of the original (120 km: 60 + 12 = 72 miles). One **meter** is 39 inches—just over a yard.

1 foot = 0.3 meter	1 square yard = 0.8 square meter
1 yard = 0.9 meter	1 square mile = 2.6 square kilometers
1 mile = 1.6 kilometers	1 ounce = 28 grams
1 centimeter = 0.4 inch	1 quart = 0.95 liter
1 meter = 39.4 inches	1 kilogram = 2.2 pounds
1 kilometer = 0.62 mile	32°F = 0°C

Clothing Sizes

When shopping for clothing, use these US-to-European comparisons as general guidelines (but note that no conversion is perfect).

Women: For pants and dresses, add 30-32 (US 10 = European 40-42) For blouses and sweaters, add 8 for most of Europe (US 32 = European 40). For shoes, add 30-31 (US 7 = European 37-38).

Men: For shirts, multiply by 2 and add about 8 (US 15 = European 38). For jackets and suits, add 10. For shoes, add 32-34.

Children: Clothing is sized by height—in centimeters (2.5 inches = 1 cm), so a US size 8 roughly equates to 132-140. For shoes up to size 13, add 16-18, and for sizes 1 and up, add 30-32.

Eastern Europe's Climate

First line is the average daily high; second line, average daily low; third line, average number of rainy days. For more detailed weather statistics for destinations in this book (as well as the rest of the world), check www.wunderground.com.

J	F	M	A	M	J	J	A	S	O	N	D

AUSTRIA • Vienna

J	F	M	A	M	J	J	A	S	O	N	D
34°	38°	47°	58°	67°	73°	76°	75°	68°	56°	45°	37°
25°	28°	30°	42°	50°	56°	60°	59°	53°	44°	37°	30°
15	14	13	13	13	14	13	13	10	13	14	15

CZECH REPUBLIC • Prague

J	F	M	A	M	J	J	A	S	O	N	D
31°	34°	44°	54°	64°	70°	73°	72°	65°	53°	42°	34°
23°	24°	30°	38°	46°	52°	55°	55°	49°	41°	33°	27°
13	11	10	11	13	12	13	12	10	13	12	13

HUNGARY • Budapest

J	F	M	A	M	J	J	A	S	O	N	D
34°	39°	50°	62°	71°	78°	82°	81°	74°	61°	47°	39°
25°	28°	35°	44°	52°	58°	62°	60°	53°	44°	38°	30°
13	12	11	11	13	13	10	9	7	10	14	13

APPENDIX

J	F	M	A	M	J	J	A	S	O	N	D

POLAND • Kraków

32°	34°	45°	55°	67°	72°	76°	73°	66°	56°	44°	37°
22°	22°	30°	38°	48°	54°	58°	56°	49°	42°	33°	28°
16	15	12	15	12	15	16	15	12	14	15	16

SLOVENIA • Ljubljana

36°	41°	50°	60°	68°	75°	80°	78°	71°	59°	47°	39°
25°	25°	32°	40°	48°	54°	57°	57°	51°	43°	36°	30°
7	7	7	9	10	9	6	6	6	7	9	9

Fahrenheit and Celsius Conversion

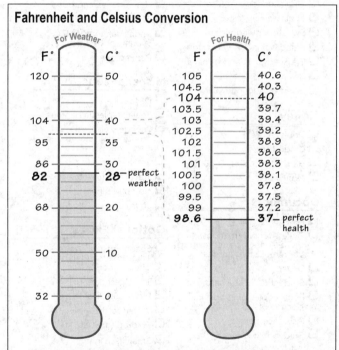

Europe takes its temperature using the Celsius scale, while we opt for Fahrenheit. For a rough conversion from Celsius to Fahrenheit, double the number and add 30. For weather, remember that 28°C is 82°F—perfect. For health, 37°C is just right. At a launderette, 30°C is cold, 40°C is warm (usually the default setting), 60°C is hot, and 95°C is boiling. Your air-conditioner should be set at about 20°C.

Packing Checklist

Whether you're traveling for five days or five weeks, you won't need more than this. Pack light to enjoy the sweet freedom of true mobility.

Clothing

- ☐ 5 shirts: long- & short-sleeve
- ☐ 2 pairs pants (or skirts/capris)
- ☐ 1 pair shorts
- ☐ 5 pairs underwear & socks
- ☐ 1 pair walking shoes
- ☐ Sweater or warm layer
- ☐ Rainproof jacket with hood
- ☐ Tie, scarf, belt, and/or hat
- ☐ Swimsuit
- ☐ Sleepwear/loungewear

Money

- ☐ Debit card(s)
- ☐ Credit card(s)
- ☐ Hard cash (US $100-200)
- ☐ Money belt

Documents

- ☐ Passport
- ☐ Tickets & confirmations: flights, hotels, trains, rail pass, car rental, sight entries
- ☐ Driver's license
- ☐ Student ID, hostel card, etc.
- ☐ Photocopies of important documents
- ☐ Insurance details
- ☐ Guidebooks & maps

Toiletries Kit

- ☐ Basics: soap, shampoo, toothbrush, toothpaste, floss, deodorant, sunscreen, brush/comb, etc.
- ☐ Medicines & vitamins
- ☐ First-aid kit
- ☐ Glasses/contacts/sunglasses
- ☐ Sewing kit
- ☐ Packet of tissues (for WC)
- ☐ Earplugs

Electronics

- ☐ Mobile phone
- ☐ Camera & related gear
- ☐ Tablet/ebook reader/laptop
- ☐ Headphones/earbuds
- ☐ Chargers & batteries
- ☐ Phone car charger & mount (or GPS device)
- ☐ Plug adapters

Miscellaneous

- ☐ Daypack
- ☐ Sealable plastic baggies
- ☐ Laundry supplies: soap, laundry bag, clothesline, spot remover
- ☐ Small umbrella
- ☐ Travel alarm/watch
- ☐ Notepad & pen
- ☐ Journal

Optional Extras

- ☐ Second pair of shoes (flip-flops, sandals, tennis shoes, boots)
- ☐ Travel hairdryer
- ☐ Picnic supplies
- ☐ Water bottle
- ☐ Fold-up tote bag
- ☐ Small flashlight
- ☐ Mini binoculars
- ☐ Small towel or washcloth
- ☐ Inflatable pillow/neck rest
- ☐ Tiny lock
- ☐ Address list (to mail postcards)
- ☐ Extra passport photos

Pronouncing Eastern European Place Names

Remember that in all of these languages, j is pronounced as "y," and c is pronounced "ts." Diacritical markings over most consonants (such as č, š, ś, or ž) have the same effect as putting an h after it in English; for example, č is "ch," š or ś is "sh," ž is "zh."

Name	Pronounced
Auschwitz (Concentration Camp, Poland)	OWSH-vits
Birkenau (Concentration Camp, Poland)	BEER-keh-now
Bled (Slovenia)	bled (as it's spelled); locals say "blayd"
Bohinj (Slovenia)	BOH-heen
Bovec (Slovenia)	BOH-vets
Bratislava (Slovakia)	brah-tee-SLAH-vah
Budapest (Hungary)	BOO-dah-pest in English, BOO-daw-pesht in Hungarian
Český Krumlov (Czech Republic)	CHESS-key KROOM-loff
Eger (Hungary)	EH-gehr
Gdańsk (Poland)	guh-DAYNSK
Gdynia (Poland)	guh-DIN-yah
Kazimierz (Poland)	kah-ZHEE-mezh
Kobarid (Slovenia)	KOH-bah-reed
Konopiště (Castle, Czech Republic)	KOH-noh-peesh-tyeh
Kraków (Poland)	KRACK-cow in English, KROCK-oof in Polish
Kutná Hora (Czech Republic)	KOOT-nah HO-rah
Ljubljana (Slovenia)	lyoob-lyee-AH-nah
Oświęcim (Poland)	ohsh-VEENCH-im
Praha (Czech name for Prague, Czech Republic)	PRAH-hah
Radovljica (Slovenia)	rah-DOH-vleet-suh
Soča (River Valley, Slovenia)	SOH-chah
Sopot (Poland)	SOH-poht
Terezín (Concentration Camp, Czech Republic)	TEH-reh-zeen
Vintgar (Gorge, Slovenia)	VEENT-gar
Vršič (Pass, Slovenia)	vur-SHEECH
Warszawa (Polish name for Warsaw, Poland)	vah-SHAH-vah
Wieliczka (Salt Mine, Poland)	veel-EECH-kah
Wien (German name for Vienna, Austria)	veen

INDEX

INDEX

MAP INDEX

Start your trip at

Our website enhances this book and turns

Explore Europe

At ricksteves.com you can browse through thousands of articles, videos, photos and radio interviews, plus find a wealth of money-saving travel tips for planning your dream trip. And with our mobile-friendly website, you can easily access all this great travel information anywhere you go.

TV Shows

Preview the places you'll visit by watching entire half-hour episodes of Rick Steves' Europe (choose from all 100 shows) on-demand, for free.

ricksteves.com

your travel dreams into affordable reality

Radio Interviews

Enjoy ready access to Rick's vast library of radio interviews covering travel

tips and cultural insights that relate specifically to your Europe travel plans.

Travel Forums

Learn, ask, share! Our online community of savvy travelers is a great resource for first-time travelers to Europe, as well as seasoned pros. You'll find forums on each country, plus travel tips and restaurant/hotel reviews. You can even ask one of our well-traveled staff to chime in with an opinion.

Travel News

Subscribe to our free Travel News e-newsletter, and get monthly updates from Rick on what's happening in Europe.